ASHE Reader on
COLLEGE STUDENT
DEVELOPMENT THEORY

ASHE Reader Series

Edited by Maureen E. Wilson & Lisa E. Wolf-Wendel

PEARSON

Custom
Publishing

Cover Art: *The Awakening*, by Robin MacDonald-Foley

Printed in the United States of America

10 9 8 7 6 5 4 3 2 1

ISBN 0-536-85970-1

2004220157

EH/SL

Please visit our web site at *www.pearsoncustom.com*

PEARSON CUSTOM PUBLISHING
75 Arlington Street, Suite 300, Boston, MA 02116
A Pearson Education Company

COPYRIGHT ACKNOWLEDGMENTS

"From Passive Acceptance to Active Commitment: A Model of Feminist Identity Development for Women," by N.E. Downing and K.L. Roush, reprinted from *Counseling Psychologist* 13, (1985), by permission of Sage Periodicals Press.

"Transgenderism and College Students: Issues of Gender Identity and Its Role on Our Campuses," by K.A. Carter, reprinted from *Toward Acceptance: Sexual Orientation Issues on Campus*, edited by V.A. Wall and N.J. Evans, (2000), by permission of the American College Personnel Association.

"Identity Development and Sexual Orientation: Toward a Model of Lesbian, Gay and Bisexual Development," by A.R. D'Augelli, reprinted from *Human Diversity*, edited by E.J. Trickett, R.J. Watts, and D. Birman), (1994), by Jossey-Bass Publishers, Inc.

"Lesbian, Gay, and Bisexual Identity and Student Development Theory," by R.E. Fassinger, reprinted from *Working with Lesbian, Gay, Bisexual, and Transgender College Students: A Handbook for Faculty and Administrators*, (1998), by permission of the Greenwood Publishing Group.

"Revisioning Sexual Minority Identity Formation: A New Model of Lesbian Identity and Its Implications for Counseling and Research," by S.R. McCarn, and R.E. Fassinger, reprinted from *The Counseling Psychologist* 24, (1996), by Sage Periodicals Press.

"A Conceptual Framework for Understanding Race, Class, Gender, and Sexuality," by L. Weber, reprinted from *Psychology of Women Quarterly* 22, (1998), by Blackwell Publishing, Ltd.

"A Conceptual Model of Multiple Dimensions of Identity," by S.R. Jones, and M.K. McEwen, reprinted from the *Journal of College Student Development* 41, (2000), by permission of the American College Personnel Association.

"The Complexities of Diversity: Exploring Multiple Oppressions," by A.L. Reynolds, and R.L. Pope, reprinted from the *Journal of Counseling and Development* 70, (1991), by permission of the American College Personnel Association.

"Different Worlds in the Same Classroom: Students' Evolution in Their Vision of Knowledge and Their Expectations of Teachers," by W.G. Perry, reprinted from *On Teaching and Learning: The Journal of the Harvard Danforth Center* 1, (1985), by the Derek Bok Center for Teaching and Learning.

"Sharing in the Costs of Growth," by W.G. Perry, Jr., reprinted from *Encouraging Development in College Students*, edited by C.A. Parker, (1978), by permission of the University of Minnesota Press.

"Reflective Judgment: Theory and Research on the Development of Epistemic Assumptions through Adulthood," by P.M. King, and K.S. Kitchener, reprinted from *Educational Psychologist* 39, (2004), by permission of Lawrence Erlbaum Associates, Inc.

"Revisiting Women's Ways of Knowing," by B.M. Clinchy, reprinted from *Personal Epistemology: The Psychology of Beliefs about Knowledge and Knowing*, edited by B.K. Hofer and P.R. Pintrich, (2002), by Lawrence Erlbaum Associates, Inc.

"Connected and Separate Knowing: Toward a Marriage of Two Minds," by B.M. Clinchy, reprinted from *Knowledge, Difference, and Power: Essays Inspired by Women's Ways of Knowing*, edited by N. Goldgerger, J. Tarule, B. Clinchy, and M. Belenky, (1996), by the Perseus Books Group.

"Moral Stages and Moralization: The Cognitive-Developmental Approach," by Lawrence Kohlberg, reprinted from *The Psychology of Moral Development: Essays on Moral Development*, Volume 2, (1984), by HarperCollins Publishers, Inc.

"Two Moral Orientations," by C. Gilligan and J. Attanucci, reprinted from *Mapping the Moral Domain*, edited by C. Gilligan, J.V. Ward, and J.M. Taylor, (1988), by Harvard University Press.

"Letter to Readers," by C. Gilligan, reprinted from *In a Different Voice: Psychological Theory and Women's Development*, (1993), by permission of Harvard University Press.

CONTENTS

Acknowledgements

We would like to thank Len Foster, Washington State University, ASHE Reader Series Editor, for his support and assistance. Many thanks to Christopher Cimino, Managing Editor and Erik Herman, Associate Editor at Pearson Custom Publishing for their assistance in the development and publication of the Reader. We are grateful to our friends and colleagues who served on the advisory board and so ably assisted us in the difficult selection process for the Reader:

Marcia B. Baxter Magolda, Miami University

Lamont Flowers, University of Florida

Florence Guido-DiBrito, University of Northern Colorado

Mary Howard-Hamilton, Indiana University

Susan R. Jones, Ohio State University

Patricia M. King, University of Michigan

Patrick Love, New York University

Marylu K. McEwen, University of Maryland

Anna Ortiz, California State University, Long Beach

Raechele L. Pope, University at Buffalo

Kristen Renn, Michigan State University

C. Carney Strange, Bowling Green State University

Dafina L. Stewart, Ohio University

Vasti Torres, Indiana University

EDITED BY

Maureen E. Wilson
Bowling Green State University

Lisa E. Wolf-Wendel
University of Kansas

A NOTE TO THE READER

We anticipate that this edition of the *ASHE Reader on Student Development Theory* will be in print for about three years, at which time a revised edition is expected. Your assistance in shaping the contents (e.g., what is particularly useful, what should be added) will be appreciated.

Please send your suggestions, comments, and recommendations for the *ASHE Reader* to the editors:

Maureen E. Wilson
Higher Education and Student Affairs
330 Education Building
Bowling Green State University
Bowling Green, OH 43403
mewilso@bgsu.edu

Lisa E. Wolf-Wendel
Higher Education
432 JRP
1122 West Campus Road
University of Kansas
Lawrence, KS 66045
lwolf@ku.edu

Suggestions about other topics that might be addressed by the *ASHE Reader Series*, or other comments about the series, should be sent to:

Len Foster
Educational Leadership and Counseling Psychology
Washington State University
College of Education
356 Cleveland
Pullman, WA 99164
Email: lenf@wsu.edu

INTRODUCTION

Background of the Reader

Courses in college student development theory examine ways in which students and other adults make meaning of their experiences and how faculty and administrators can promote their learning, growth, and development. The Council for the Advancement of Standards in Higher Education includes student development theory as one of five required areas of study for master's level graduate programs for student affairs professionals. These theories examine a wide range of development in students including psychosocial, intellectual, moral, and spiritual development. Newer theories of identity development address more diverse groups of students and consider how multiple dimensions of identity interplay to influence development.

Student development theory is a foundation upon which the profession of student affairs administration rests. Many of the policy and practice decisions made by professionals in the field are based on the belief that students learn, develop, and grow in certain predictable ways and that it is the responsibility of colleges and universities to create environments that facilitate that development. Graduate programs in student affairs and higher education have the responsibility of educating their students about these theories and their application. The students in higher education and the developmental issues they confront are more diverse and complex than ever. The growing body of literature on student development reflects these changes, but comes from a variety of disciplinary areas and is therefore not readily accessible by faculty who teach these subjects, by graduate students, or by professionals in the field. This Reader compiles some of the best work on student development theory.

Among the challenges in creating this ASHE Reader was agreeing on an organizing framework. Traditional presentations of theory typically address families of theories such as psychosocial and identity, cognitive-structural, and typology. A shortcoming of that schema is that it can fail to recognize the complexity of development. In other words, psychosocial development can be influenced by cognitive structures and vice versa. Racial and ethnic identity development happens in tandem with the development of gender, spiritual, and sexual orientation identity. Many of the pieces included in this Reader consider development from more holistic and integrated perspectives. Indeed, the first section of this reader focuses on holistic models.

Another challenge, of course, was deciding which pieces to include and which to exclude. Working with the advisory board, we selected key pieces that represented the different types of theories. We included some early works that laid a foundation from which later theories were developed. We also selected newer works that critique or augment the traditional theories. It is important to note that due to space limitations we were unable to include every topic that might have been included in this Reader. For example, we made the difficult decision to exclude readings on typology theories. While we recognized the usefulness and importance of such theories, we decided to exclude them because they are not technically student development theories and devoted that space to other theories. Further, given the shifting patterns of enrollment with regard to age of students, we contemplated the necessity of adding a section devoted to lifespan development. Due to space limitations, however, we opted to add a few key pieces addressing the developmental concerns of older students within existing sections rather than create a separate section. In terms of selecting among individual pieces addressing similar themes within sections, we typically chose the more recent article and/or included pieces that were more difficult to find. For those interested, the list of additional references at the back of the Reader provides citations for more excellent resources, many of which present empirical studies based on a variety of theories.

Purpose of the Reader

This Reader is intended to serve as a resource of primary source literature on college student development theory and as a text for courses on student development theory. Graduate students and other users are introduced to key student development theories by reading original works of the theorists, developing an awareness of the context in which development occurs, and examining applications of theory to practice. The Reader will also be useful in on-going professional development efforts for student affairs practitioners who lack formal study of student development theory or who wish to become familiar with more recent work on the topic. Those who work with college students and want to create programs and services to promote their learning, growth, and development will find a wealth of resources here to aid in those efforts.

Overview of the Reader

Unit 1: Introduction to the Study of Student Development Theory

The first unit of the Reader provides an overview of student development theory, particularly as a field of study. The three chapters in the unit provide an overview of the nature and uses of theory within a student affairs context, discuss the evolution of the concept of student development, present a framework of propositions as an agenda for scholars and practitioners in the field, and examine the adequacy of the theoretical knowledge base.

Unit 2: Holistic Versions of Student Development

The two sections in Unit 2 present holistic aspects of development. Contemporary theorists are moving toward looking at development from a holistic or integrated perspective, rather than as separate dimensions. We introduce the theory section of the Reader with these holistic models because they provide an overarching framework through which to understand the more specific dimensions of development that follow.

In Section 2, Integrated Developmental Models, Kegan's orders of consciousness and the mental demands of adolescence are reviewed. Kegan advocates the notion of integrated development and serves as the basis for subsequent work in this area. The journey into adulthood and self-authorship are overviewed via Baxter Magolda's longitudinal study of development. A developmental model of intercultural maturity is also presented. Finally questions regarding the infusion of recent social critiques into the methods of higher education research are examined.

In Section 3, Spiritual and Faith Development, a model of the journey toward mature adult faith is presented. Although some argue that spiritual and faith development are subsets of moral development (Unit 4, Section 10), our Advisory Board strongly encouraged us to think about these models as more integrative, suggesting that spiritual and faith development integrates intellectual, psychosocial, and identity development. We begin the section with a chapter by Sharon Parks, whose work is deemed to be crucial for setting the context through which scholars and practitioners can understand the development of faith among college students. In the second piece, it is argued that spirituality has been ignored in theory and in student affairs and that this should change. The role of faith in the development of an integrated identity is considered in the third chapter in this section.

Unit 3: Intrapersonal/Interpersonal Dimensions of Development

Intrapersonal dimensions of development address how individuals actively construct their sense of self. Interpersonal dimensions of development relate to the sense of self in relation to others. The five sections in this unit address both intrapersonal and interpersonal dimensions of development.

Section 4 focuses on psychosocial theories addressing personal and interpersonal aspects of development. Following Chickering and Reisser's well known seven vectors of development, women's identity development is explored through the work of Josselson. The remaining three pieces in the section address psychosocial development for students of color, examining the relevance of various psychosocial theories to historically underrepresented groups of students.

The next three sections of the unit examine the dynamics of race and ethnicity, gender, and sexual orientation on development. In Section 5, Dynamics of Race and Ethnicity in Development, pieces address racial identity terminology, models of racial oppression and sociorace, the psychology of Nigrescence, identity development of biracial individuals, Asian American identity development, ethnic identity development, ethnic identity development of Latino college students, and identity development of Indigenous Americans who are lesbian, gay, or bisexual.

Section 6, Dynamics of Gender in Development, has four chapters. The first examines relational theory as a context for understanding women's development. The social construction of college men's identity and a model of feminist identity development for women are the topics of the next two pieces. The development of transgendered people is addressed in the fourth chapter in this section.

A model of lesbian, gay and bisexual identity development and LGB issues in student development theory are two chapters in Section 7, Dynamics of Sexual Orientation in Development. The third piece considers a new model of lesbian identity and its implications for counseling and research.

Finally, as development results from the complex interplay of many factors and characteristics, Section 8 is Multiple Dimensions of Development. The three chapters address a conceptual framework for understanding race, class, gender, and sexuality; a conceptual model of multiple dimensions of identity; and an exploration of multiple oppressions.

Unit 4: Cognitive Dimensions of Development

Cognitive theories examine how we come to know and believe. Section 9 contains theories of intellectual development beginning with William Perry's foundational work. The Reflective Judgment Model is presented as is the work on Women's Ways of Knowing, including separate and connected knowing.

Section 10 addresses moral development in light of research by Kohlberg, Gilligan, and Attanucci. Insights from the Defining Issues Test are addressed in the final chapter of the section.

Unit 5: Theory to Practice

An important aspect of student development theory is applying it to practice. Section 11, Utilizing Theory, presents exemplars of theory-based practice. The Learning Partnerships Model is a framework for promoting self-authorship. King and Baxter Magolda advance an integrated perspective on learning and personal development. The use of student development theory to guide institutional policy and the dilemmas of translating theory to practice are considered in the next two chapters. Meaning-making in the learning and teaching process and deconstructing Whiteness as part of a multicultural educational framework are the final two chapters of the text.

UNIT I

INTRODUCTION TO THE STUDY OF STUDENT DEVELOPMENT THEORY

Section 1

STUDENT DEVELOPMENT THEORY: AN OVERVIEW

CHAPTER 1

THE NATURE AND USES OF THEORY

MARYLU K. MCEWEN

As an academic advisor to students who have not yet made a decision about their major, it is difficult for you to understand some of the differences among your advisees—why, for example, many of your first-year student advisees, regardless of their background and abilities, seem almost preoccupied with whether they can handle college-level work.

You regularly conduct diversity training with groups of student leaders. You have noticed that some students are open and excited about the training and others seem highly resistant, and you are confused by their different reactions.

As a residence hall director, you supervise resident assistants and undergraduate students in four different buildings. In two units the students seem to possess a true sense of community; in another there are difficulties with discipline, vandalism, and hate speech; in the fourth unit the students seem passive and indifferent. You can't make sense of why this would be the case.

You observe that the administrative division and the academic affairs division in the college where you work always seem to conduct their business differently. When someone from the administrative division wants to meet with you, he or she has always involved, and received permission, from his or her supervisor. But when a faculty member or an assistant academic dean meets with you, it is unusual for either the department chair or the dean to know about it. On the other hand, you usually inform your supervisor but rarely ask for permission. You wonder how and why all these units within the same college function so differently.

The differences in the above situations are most likely neither just chance nor random occurrences, and they may be understood through various theories and theoretical perspectives. Theories about how college students develop can help to understand the first two examples. Theories about how people and environments interact and models of the design of environments for educational purposes provide clues about the differences among the four residence hall units. Organizational theory offers perspectives on how different organizations function and what kinds of outcomes might be expected in different situations. More important, however, theory not only helps us to understand what we experience and observe but provides a foundation for practice in student affairs. The use of theory is one way of assisting student affairs professionals to be expert scholar-practitioners.

The six purposes of this chapter are to consider the following: (1) why student affairs professionals need theory; (2) families of theory that inform practice in student affairs; (3) purposes and development of theory and the role of theory in student affairs; (4) theory as social construction; (5) contemporary challenges to theory; and, (6) how one makes individual choices about which theories to use, including the importance of looking at oneself in learning, selecting, and applying theories.

Note: I wish to acknowledge the generous assistance of Ralph Komives in the computer design of Figures 1 and 2.

Why Student Affairs Professionals Need Theory

Student affairs professionals should use theory for many reasons. First and perhaps most important, a theoretical basis for knowledge, expertise, and practice serves as a foundation for a profession, which student affairs is and has been for almost a century. Second, knowing and understanding theory provides a medium of communication and understanding among student affairs professionals. Third, theory can serve as a "common language" within a "community of scholars" (Knefelkamp, 1982).

A student affairs professional needs theory because it is difficult for one person to hold simultaneously in his or her understanding all the aspects of a particular phenomenon he or she is interested in—for instance, all the characteristics of a student's identify or all the components of a particular environment. Ivey (1986) has suggested that "there is more going on in development than meets the eye of consciousness, and development is too complex for us to be aware of it all" (p. 312). Each one of us has our own informal theories about people, environments, students, human development, and how to work with students, although these theories or perspectives may not always be a conscious or clear part of our awareness. Thus people turn to theory—both formal and informal—to make the many complex facets of experience manageable, understandable, meaningful and consistent rather than random.

Since the primary goals of student affairs professionals are to facilitate students' development, to understand and design educationally purposeful environments, and to be experts about organizations and how they function, it is our responsibility, both professionally and ethically, to know and understand the individuals, groups, and institutions with whom we work. One important way to do this is through theory. Student affairs professionals are primarily theory users, consumers, and interpreters rather than formal theorists (although they are informal theory developers).

Theories, models, and perspectives used in student affairs come from familiar sources such as the disciplines of human development, developmental psychology, organizational behavior, counseling psychology, and social psychology. Researchers who have studied the development and success of college students and the charac-teristics of organizations of higher education are other sources. Theories and perspectives also evolve out of our own and others' observations and experiences and from literature and stories. Student affairs professionals can acquire a comprehensive understanding of theory about student and human development, higher education, and organizations in an interdisciplinary fashion, drawing from the literature not only in psychology and education but also in ethnic studies, women's studies, sociology, history, literature, anthropology, philosophy, business, and management, as well as from oral and written stories and from one's own observations.

Families of Theories in Student Affairs

Rich sets of theories and models about students have evolved since the mid-1960s. These theories concern how students develop during college, how they learn, what elements come together to contribute to students' success, and how the dynamics of college environments relate to educational purposes. In Part Three, six authors discuss these perspectives about students and how higher education organizations and environments are constructed and function. The model in Figure 1 portrays the families of theories that inform practice in student affairs and the hypothesized relationships among the theory families. Figure 2 is an elaboration of developmental theories, representing the relationships among the subsets of developmental theories and how developmental theories come together in developmental synthesis. Brief descriptions of the families of theories are provided below, followed by a narrative portrayal of the dynamic relationships among the theory families and a rationale for the organization of the theory sets. Names and foci of specific theories associated with each family and subcategory of theories are identified in Exhibit 1.

Developmental Theories

Development, growth, and change are often used synonymously and interchangeably. Sanford (1967), however, contrasts these three terms, suggesting that they have different meanings. In a general sense, development is about becoming a more complex individual (with, for example, a more complex identity, more complex cognition, or more complex values). A more precise defi-

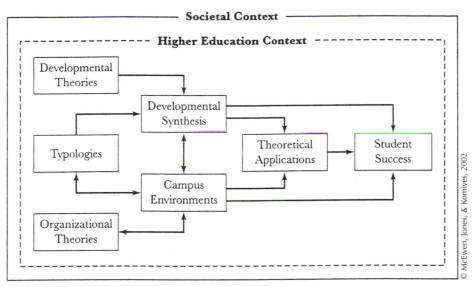

Figure 1 Working model of relationships among families of theories in student affairs.

nition is that development represents the "organization of increasing complexity" (Sanford, 1967, p. 47), or an increasing differentiation *and* integration of the self (Sanford, 1962, p. 257). Thus, development involves change, and it may include growth; but more specifically, it represents a qualitative enhancement of the self in terms of the self's complexity and integration.

Positive values are usually attached to the word *development*; for example, highly developed is better than less developed, and greater development represents increased maturity.

Knefelkamp, Widick, and Parker (1978) identified four essential components of theoretical knowledge about student development for student affairs professionals: "Who the college (*text continues on page 13*)

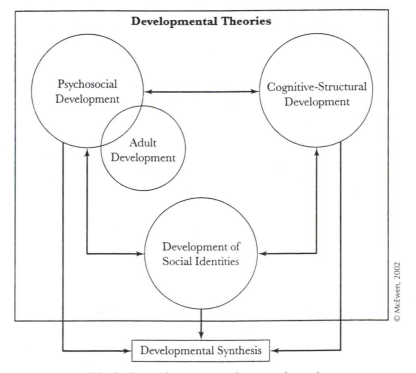

Figure 2 Model of relationships among theories about the development of college students.

EXHIBIT 1   Theories About College Students, Environments, and Organizations.

Theory Family	Subcategory	Focus of Theory	Specific Theories
Psychosocial Development	General psychosocial development	Foundational theory	Erikson
		Challenge and support	Sanford
		Vectors of development	Chickering
		Young adults and alienated students	Keniston
		Patterns of continuity versus crisis in personality change	King
		Crisis and commitment	Marcia
		Women's development	Josselson
	Career development	Life-span development and self-concept implementation	Super
	Adult development	Life stage	Erikson; Gould; Levinson; Vaillant
		Life events	Fiske; Schlossberg, Waters, & Goodman; Sugarman; Whitbourne
		Life course	Neugarten; Bengston; Elder; Hughes & Graham
Cognitive-Structural Development	General cognitive-structural development	Foundational theory	Piaget
		Perry scheme	Perry
		Women's ways of knowing	Belenky, Clinchy, Goldberger, & Tarule
		Reflective judgment	King & Kitchener
		Epistemological reflection	Baxter Magolda
		Conceptual systems and training environments	Harvey, Hunt, & Schroder

(continued)

EXHIBIT 1 Theories About College Students, Environments, and Organizations. *(continued)*

Theory Family	Subcategory	Focus of Theory	Specific Theories
	Moral development	Justice and rights	Kohlberg
		Care and responsibility	Gilligan
		Moral reasoning	Rest, Narvaez, Bebeau, & Thoma
	Faith development	Faith	Fowler
		Spirituality	Parks
		Black womanist ethics	Cannon
		Mujerista theology	Isasi-Díaz
Development of Social Identities	Contextual analysis		Weber
	Racial identity	Black racial identity	Cross; Helms; Jackson
		White racial identity	Helms; Hardiman
		Asian American racial identity	Kim; Sodowsky, Kwan, & Pannu
		Native American racial identity	Horse
		Latino racial identity	Bernal & Knight; Casas & Pytluk; Ferdman & Gallegos
		People of Color racial identity	Helms
		Biracial identity	Poston; Kich; Kerwin & Ponterotto
		Multiracial identity	Root; Wijeyesinghe
	Ethnic identity	Crisis and commitment	Phinney
		Ethnic identity	Ruiz
		Bicultural orientation	Torres
	Sexual identity	Gay and lesbian identity	Cass; Fassinger; D'Augelli
		Bisexual identity	Klein
		Heterosexual identity	Mueller; Worthington, Savoy, Dillon, & Vernaglia
		General sexual identity	Klein, Sepekoff, & Wolf; Sullivan

EXHIBIT 1   Theories About College Students, Environments, and Organizations.   *(continued)*

Theory Family	Subcategory	Focus of Theory	Specific Theories
	Gender identity	Feminist identity	Downing & Roush
		Womanist identity	Ossana, Helms, & Leonard
		Gender role	O'Neil
	Minority identity		Atkinson, Morten, & Sue
	Social class and background		
	Religious identity		
	Abilities and disabilities		
	Multiple identities	Multiple oppressions	Reynolds & Pope
		Multiple identities	Jones & McEwen
Developmental Synthesis		Maturity	Douglas Heath
		Self-evolution	Kegan
Typologies	Personality	Intercultural maturity	King & Baxter Magolda
		Temperament and development	Roy Heath
		Psychological type	Myers-Briggs
		Vocational personality types	Holland
	Learning	Learning style	Kolb
		Field dependence and independence	Witkin
		Multiple intelligences	Gardner
		Surface and deep approaches	Marton & Säljö
		Self-regulated learning	

(continued)

EXHIBIT 1 Theories About College Students, Environments, and Organizations.   (*continued*)

Theory Family	Subcategory	Focus of Theory	Specific Theories
Organizational Theories	Conventional approaches	Rational-bureaucratic	Weber
		Collegial	Austin & Gamson
		Political	Baldridge
	Postconventional views	Organized anarchy	Cohen & March
		Cultural phenomenon	Kuh & Whitt; Schein; Tierney
		Learning organization	Morgan; Senge
		Multicultural organizational development	Jackson & Holvino; Manning & Coleman-Boatwright; Pope; Tierney; Grieger; Talbot
	Organizational redesign		Eckel, Hill, Green, & Mallon; Kezar & Eckel; Peterson, Dill, Mets, & Associates; Tierney
Campus Environments	Physical components		Barker; Dober; Gaines; Moffatt; Michelson; Sommer; Stern
	Human aggregates	Subcultures	Astin; Clark & Trow; Holland; Kolb; Myers
		Person-environment interactions	Holland
	Organized environments	Organizational structures and dynamics	Hage & Aiken
	Constructed environments	Environmental press	Pace & Stern; Moos
		Campus culture	Chaffee & Tierney; Horowitz; Kuh; Kuh & Whitt; Moffatt; Schein

EXHIBIT 1 Theories About College Students, Environments, and Organizations.   *(continued)*

Theory Family	Subcategory	Focus of Theory	Specific Theories
	Design for educational success	Inclusion and safety, involvement, community	Strange & Banning
	Environmental impact		Moos; Strange & Banning
Theoretical Applications	Involvement		Astin
	Mattering and marginality		Schlossberg
	Transition theory		Schlossberg
Student Success	Student departure	Economic	Becker
		Organizational	Berger & Braxton
		Psychological	Individual level—Bean & Eaton; student development theories
			Environmental level—Moos; Baird
		Sociological	Cultural capital—Bourdieu
			Student culture—Kuh & Love
			Interactionalist theory—Tinto
	Nontraditional student attrition		Bean & Metzner
	Modified model of student persistence		Berger & Milem

Source: McEwen, 2002.

student is in developmental terms; how development occurs; how the college environment can influence student development; and toward what ends development in college should be directed" (p. x). They suggested, "knowledge in these four areas would give specific and concrete meaning to the task of encouraging student development" (p. x).

Psychosocial development theories are concerned with the *content* of development (Evans, Forney, & Guido-DiBrito, 1998), that is, "*what* students will be concerned about" (Knefelkamp et al., 1978, p. xii). The major issues that students think about and what they are preoccupied with, and how those major issues and preoccupations evolve over time, are at the core of psychosocial development theory. Although these theories generally focus on the individual (the "psychological" part of psychosocial), the environment (the "social" part) also plays a critical role. Included within psychosocial development are *adult development* and *career development theories*.

Cognitive-structural development theories address "how students will think about those [psychosocial] issues and what shifts in reasoning will occur" (Knefelkamp et al., 1978, p. xii), *not* what they think about. These theories propose cognitive structures, which might be thought of as filters or lenses, of increasing complexity through which one takes in information, perceives experiences, and constructs meanings. Cognitive-structural development theories also include those theories specific to moral development and faith development.

Social identity development theories address the ways in which individuals construct their various social identities, namely, race, ethnicity, gender, and sexual orientation, and the intersection of these multiple identities. Social class, ability and disability, and religion are three other identity dimensions considered within this family. Many of the identity development theories are concerned *both* with *what* students think about their specific social identity and *how* they think about it. Models of multiple identities, because they focus primarily on social identities, are also part of this family of theories.

Developmental synthesis models consider students' development holistically—that is, their psychosocial and cognitive development in interaction with one another. Social identity development, although not incorporated within the few existing models, may be included in future development of integrative models.

Other Theories and Models About College Students

Typology models consider certain persistent characteristics or behaviors of individuals that remain relatively stable over time. Typology models do not describe development, although some of the models' creators have discussed a developmental component underlying the typologies. Many of these models consider learning styles or personality styles. Some of the early typology models (Clark & Trow, 1966; Holland, 1966; Newcomb, Joenig, Flacks, & Warwick, 1967) concerned person-environment interaction and student subcultures.

Theoretical applications consider ways in which students' development and their environments come together to affect their college experiences. Theories include those of student involvement (Astin, 1984), mattering and marginality (Schlossberg, 1989), and transition (Schlossberg, Waters, & Goodman, 1995).

Student success theories address what happens to students as they enter and matriculate through colleges and universities. Models and theories concern student departure, attrition, and persistence.

Theories of Organizations and Campus Environments

Organizational theories concern the behavior of individuals and groups within complex organizations. *Theories about campus environments* address the dimensions and dynamics of environments and the design and redesign of environments for educational purposes.

Relationships Among Theory Families

Relationships among theory families are presented graphically in Figures 1 and 2. Let's first address the large grouping of developmental theories in Figure 2. Psychosocial and adult development theories are one major subset, represented by two intersecting circles. Although some theories of adult development (life stage) are part of psychosocial development, others (such as life events and life course) extend beyond the constructs of psychosocial development theories. Social identity development and psychosocial development are also closely intertwined and influence one another (indicated by bidirectional arrows). Bidirectional arrows illustrate the cognitive-structural aspect of many social identity theories and the interaction between psychosocial development and cognitive-structural development. Psychosocial, adult, social identity, and cognitive-structural development theories all contribute theoretically to development synthesis; this is represented in Figure 1 by the arrows from each of these groupings to developmental synthesis.

Let's now return to Figure 1. Theories about students and higher education environments and organizations should be considered within environmental, historical, and sociocultural contexts, represented in Figure 1 by the two large rectangles. The larger outer rectangle represents the societal context, primarily in the United States but also in the larger global society. The inner rectangle represents the context of a particular institution of higher education; the dashed line of the inner rectangle suggests that higher education institutions do not exist separately from the larger society. All theories must be considered within these two contexts.

The three sets of theories on the left in Figure 1, namely, the development of college students, typologies about college students, and theories about the organizations of colleges and universities, are hypothesized to occur simultaneously. Developmental theories and typologies take place concurrently and in interaction with one another to form developmental synthesis, suggested by the unidirectional arrows. Similarly, typologies about students and organizations interact to create campus environments and are also influenced by campus environments, indicated by the bidirectional arrows. The relationship of organizational theories to student development theories is hypothesized to be indirect, and thus there is no arrow connecting the two groupings.

Developmental synthesis and campus environments contribute directly to student success and also indirectly through theoretical applications, that is, students' transitions, to how they feel they matter or how marginalized they feel, and their involvement. Campus environments contribute to students' development (developmental synthesis), and, in turn, students' development can influence campus environments (bidirectional arrow).

It should be noted that college students enter institutions of higher education with certain characteristics, such as race and gender, and previous experiences, for example, academic, social, and family experiences. Who students are and what experiences they have had, then, become part of and shape their development in college.

In addition, although Figure 1 represents student success as the ultimate outcome, student success (or lack thereof) also affects students' development and how higher education organizations and environments are structured. Thus, the model in Figure 1 suggests dynamic relationships among the theory families and also a feedback mechanism of student success to students' development and higher education organizations and environments.

Rationale for Theory Families

The psychosocial development, cognitive-structural development, developmental synthesis, and typology theory families are congruent with Knefelkamp et al.'s (1978) organization of theories in student development and with others' (Evans et al., 1998; Rodgers, 1980) use of similar categories. Families of career development, adult development, student success, organizational theories, and theoretical applications are included because of their importance to student affairs professionals' knowledge and understanding of students.

The family of social identity development theories is the one not consistently considered as a separate family. For example, Evans et al. (1998) placed identity development theories as a subset of psychosocial development. Evans et al.'s approach is clearly appropriate, because identity is considered a psychosocial construct and because the central developmental task of Erikson's (1968) life-span development theory is the development of identity. I have chosen, however, to place identity development theories as a separate family for three reasons. First, because social identity development is important and encompasses a vast and diverse array of models, a separate category seems necessary. Second, many of the identity development models involve *how* one thinks about one's specific social identity as well as *what* the conceptualization of that identity is; thus, cognitive-structural development is a part of social identity development. Third, and most important, is the political stance in highlighting this group of theories, which have evolved from the oppressed status of certain groups in the United States. These theories then are not so much about a personal or global identity (Deaux, 1993) but an identity that occurs because of sociopolitical environments and conditions.

Theory Definition, Purpose, Evolution, and Role in Student Affairs

What are theories? Why do we need them? How do they come about? What use will theory be in the practice of student affairs? This section addresses these important questions.

Definition and Description

Theory can be thought of as a description of the interrelationships among concepts and constructs. These interrelationships are often represented by a particular set of hypotheses—about human development, about organizations, about the dynamics of environments—developed by an individual or a group of individuals. Some hypotheses are empirical in nature, evolving from the collection and examination of quantitative or qualitative data. Others are rational in nature, based not on formal data but rather on ideas and relationships that attempt to explain a particular phenomenon. Thomas (2001) defined theory as "a proposal about (a) which components or variables are important for understanding such a phenomenon as human development and (b) how those components interact to account for why the phenomenon turns out as it does" (p. 1). Thomas identified model, explanatory scheme, and paradigm as synonyms, but he noted, "some authors assign separate meanings to each of those terms" (p. 1).

Theory frequently serves to simplify the complex—to connect what appears to be random and to organize what appears to be chaotic. Theory is inherently reductionistic; it helps one reduce or organize many difficult-to-manage pieces or dimensions into fewer, simpler parts and an integrated, organized whole. One aspect of theory usually not described or discussed is that theory—whether empirical or rational—is developed through the lenses, or perspectives, of those who create or describe it. Thus theory is not objective, as frequently claimed, but evolves from the subjectivity of the theorist or researchers. L. L. Knefelkamp (personal communication, October 16, 1980) has suggested that all theory is autobiographical—that is, theory represents the knowledge, experience, and worldviews of the theorists who construct it. King (1994) echoes this idea in stating that "we produce ourselves as theorists and remember ourselves at the center(s) of theory building" (p. 29). For example, even if they have completed exhaustive research, scholars developing a theory about human behavior in organizations might observe in their data (and thus reflect in their theory) only those dimensions that reflect their own experience in organizations. Their theory becomes, in essence, an autobiographical account of their own organizational experiences. Thus it is important to be aware of the subjectivity and context of any theory.

Purposes and Elements of Theory

Theory is a framework through which interpretations and understandings are constructed. Theory is used to describe human behavior (Knefelkamp et al., 1978, p. xiii), to explain, to predict, and to generate new knowledge and research. Moore and Upcraft (1990) offer a fifth purpose, based on Harmon's work, that theory provides the tools to "influence outcomes" (p. 3). A sixth use of theory—often not cited—is to assess practice. Presenting the uses of theory in a slightly different way, theory should help us to develop a more comprehensive and precise understanding of students, institutions, and related processes and dynamics, such that we can "inform our practice" and thus "transform it" (Hall, as cited in Apple, 1993, p. 25).

These purposes or uses of theory can be applied to student affairs. For example, different theories may help us do the following: (a) *describe* first-year college students in terms of their concerns and their behavior, (b) *explain or understand* the differences in behavior between students who live in coeducational versus single-sex residence halls, (c) *predict* how staff in an office may act when a supervisor with a collaborative style is replaced by one with an autocratic style, (d) *generate* new research and theory about first-generation college students, (e) *influence* the development of students in an honors program by designing the program in certain ways, and (f) *assess* an institution's practices for creating a positive multicultural environment.

Formal criteria exist for evaluating theories. Patterson (1980) has summarized the following eight criteria for use in considering the adequacy of a theory: it should be (1) important, not trivial; (2) precise and understadable; (3) comprehensive; (4) simple and parsimonious but still comprehensive; (5) able to be operationalized; (6) empirically valid or verifiable; (7) able to generate new research, new knowledge, and new thinking and ideas; and (8) useful to practitioners. It is quite likely that many theories that seem valid and useful do not meet all of these criteria; nevertheless, the criteria provide appropriate goals for further theory development and refinement. For example, a theory may be comprehensive but not parsimonious, or a theory may be precise, understandable, and useful but difficult to put into operation

Each family of theories usually contains certain elements. For example, among developmental theories, most include stages with corresponding developmental tasks. Each stage represents a predominant developmental issue or a certain quality or complexity of thinking. Whether and how one addresses the developmental task or issue relates to two conditions for development: a readiness within the person and stimuli to challenge the individual, to upset an existing psychological equilibrium within the person (Sanford, 1962, 1967). Further, stages occur in a prescribed order evolving from more simple to increasingly complex. Each successive stage builds on the preceding stages and how well one negotiates, or does not negotiate, the preceding stages. And, although theories about the development of college students address the development of individuals, all the theories incorporate to some degree the role of the environment, an often overlooked aspect of these theories.

Differences also exist within major families. Among psychosocial theories, as order is prescribed but is considered to be variable. In contrast, the order is invariant in cognitive-structural development theories, that is, one *must* progress through the stages in the order prescribed. Within social identity development theories, and similar to cognitive-structural development theories, Helms (1992, 1995) suggests that, as one develops, the individual has access to, and in fact is likely to draw upon, stages or statuses through which one has already passed. For Black racial identity development, Parham (1989) suggests that persons can recycle through the developmental tasks represented within the various stages or statuses. Perry (1981) and Kegan (1982) write about a similar phenomenon in considering development as a helix, in that persons can revisit issues similar to those of earlier stages but in more complex ways.

How Theories Evolve

Scholars present their theories and models through scholarly literature and professional conferences. If a theory meets the criteria of a good theory, then it serves to generate new research and new ideas, which in turn inform new theories. When research disputes theory, theory is either revised or new theory is created. Practice also informs theory, as well as scholarly and public critiques. Theory generates new theory.

Theory development also takes place because of shifts in paradigms. Kuh, Whitt, and Shedd (1987) define a paradigm as a set of "assumptions and beliefs about fundamental laws or relationships that explain how the world works" (p. 2). A dominant paradigm represents the prevailing, overriding set of assumptions about the nature of a given subject (such as human development). Kuh et al. explain, "when paradigms shift, understandings are markedly altered" (p. 2). They elegantly describe the "silent revolution" (p. 1) that takes place when a dominant paradigm gives way to an emergent paradigm, the accompanying theoretical shifts in related disciplines, and the implications of paradigm shifts for student affairs. Conventional views or beliefs about, for example, the goal-directed nature of organizations or the highly individualistic nature of human beings are replaced within the emergent paradigm by alternate perspectives describing the relational and contextual aspects of organizations or individuals. With different or changing beliefs and assumptions now at the core of people's understanding of reality, new theories are developed.

Theory generation and development is a constantly evolving, dynamic process. Some theories may stand the tests of time, practice, and research and continue to exist in a minimally changed state. Some theories encounter few challenges from scholars and practitioners; others face many challenges. In general, however, the evolution of a theory follows an identifiable cycle: a new theory leads to research and new forms of practice, which in turn inform the existing theory, which is then modified or changed. Sometimes a theory is changed by a theorist; other times an alternate theory is proposed by others. Examples of theory evolution are Chickering's psychosocial development theory (Chickering & Reisser, 1993), moral development theories, and Helms's (1995) People of Color racial identity development theory.

Chickering's theory of the psychosocial development of college students (1969) was modified in work by Chickering and Reisser in 1993. The modifications were based both on new understandings from the original theorists (Thomas & Chickering, 1984) and on research by others. Kohlberg's (1975) theory of moral development also evolved based on his own work and that of colleagues. However, Gilligan (1982), formerly a student of Kohlberg (Larrabee, 1993), found that a gender-related perspective of care seemed to have been left out of Kohlberg's theory and developed her own perspective on moral development. Kohlberg's and Gilligan's theories of moral development now exist side by side, one theory having provided a partial springboard for the development of the other. These two theories also represent different paradigms; Kohlberg's was the conventional paradigm, Gilligan's the emergent one. Helms (1995) created a theory of People of Color racial identity development from the confluence of her adaptation of Cross's model of Black racial identity development and Atkinson, Morten, and Sue's minority identity development.

Theory in Student Affairs

Theory, some formal, some informal, has no doubt existed in student affairs from the beginning. Some of the early textbooks on student affairs provide evidence of the use of traditional psychological theories and, to some degree, theories on management, organizations, and administration.

Research specific to college students and their development can be traced to the 1950s and early 1960s, first to Nevitt Sanford and his colleagues at Vassar College (Canon, 1988) and then to the publication of Sanford's classic, *The American College* (1962). The 1960s and early 1970s were a time of much writing and research about college students, primarily by the psychologists Heath (1964), Heath (1968), Keniston (1971), King (1973), Chickering (1969), and Perry (1970), in addition to Sanford. The student affairs profession embraced these theorists and their research. Brown's (1972) call for student development to become central to the profession was enthusiastically answered, and student development theory became a foundation of the student affairs profession in the mid to late 1970s. Parker, Knefelkamp, and Widick, at the Uni-versity of Minnesota, brought the multiple theoretical and research bases of student development theory together, providing an organized schema of theories for understanding student development and practicing student affairs (Knefelkamp et al., 1978).

Other theories about students are also important to student affairs. Models of person-environment interaction (Walsh, 1973) emerged in the 1960s. Models such as wellness (Hettler, 1980), student involvement (Astin, 1984), and mattering and marginality (Schlossberg, 1989) were added to the rich theoretical foundations of student affairs in the 1980s.

Knefelkamp (1982) has suggested that student development theory provides a common language for both student affairs professionals and faculty in higher education. Contemporary attention to student learning (American College Personnel Association, 1996) and holistic student development emphasizes the continuing value of student development theory for student affairs. Thus, the value and centrality given to theory by the student affairs profession is primarily due to the importance of student development theory to the field, although environmental and organizational theory are also influential.

Theory as Social Construction

Although theories have always been viewed as providing varying perspectives on certain constructs and relationships, within the past decade increasing attention has been given to the contextual basis for theories. That is, theories are developed and considered within certain sociological, historical, and political contexts. Further, these contexts change both with the passage of time and with changing ideas and issues within U.S. and world societies.

Earlier in this chapter, shifts in paradigms, from a dominant, conventional paradigm to an emergent one, were identified as one of many reasons about why and how new theory is developed. Part of the dominant, conventional paradigm, the mode of inquiry that has traditionally been used in both education and psychology is logical positivism, also known as the natural scientific method, which has provided important and significant contributions to the theory and research base of student affairs. It is this mode of inquiry that has produced most of our knowledge to date about the development of college students, how individuals and environments interact, and how organizations function.

Focus on the emergent paradigm in considering the relational and contextual aspects of organizations or individuals has led to closer examination of the logical positivistic mode of inquiry. According to Borg and Gall (1989), some scholars have been rethinking many of the assumptions of logical positivism; much of this reexamination was stimulated by Thomas Kuhn's (1962) book *The Structure of Scientific Revolutions.* Critics of logical positivism have also raised important questions about whether theory and research under the dominant, conventional paradigm can truly be objective and value-free. For example, Isasi-Diaz (1993) suggests that "what is called objectivity [e.g., theory] . . . is the subjectivity of those who have the power to impose it as objectivity" (p. 6).

A contemporary and important perspective is that theories are socially constructed and that objects of theories and constructs incorporated within theories are also socially constructed. This perspective comes from the idea that knowledge is never neutral and "that social scientists are participants [rather than impartial researchers] in the socio-historical development of human action and understanding" (Comstock, 1982, p. 377). Further, Comstock suggests the value of understanding "society as humanly constructed and, in turn, human nature as a collective self-construction" (p. 377).

Many constructs, such as race or sexual orientation, have meaning only when they are viewed or considered within social, political, and historical contexts. For instance, it is not the biological meaning of race that we draw on; rather, it is how this society at this point in history conceives of race. In the United States, *race* refers to skin color, language, cultural traditions, patterns of communication, and values and beliefs. It is surrounded by the context of the civil rights movement and the shared history of specific groups of people. *Race*, therefore, is not an objective term meaning what genetically constitutes different groups of people; rather, it is a subjective term that has been socially constructed.

The objects of theories, including identity, learning, environments, and organizations, are themselves socially constructed. Individuals, organizations, and environments, including students and organizations of higher education, do not exist or develop in a vacuum. Individual live in social settings, each with historical and political elements. Individuals have their unique family histories, and different cohorts of individuals have varying sociopolitical and historical experiences. The identity that one creates for oneself comes out of one's lived experience. Organizations and environments are composed of people and created by people; organizations and environments also have different heritages and various sociopolitical and historical elements. Even what I, as the author of this chapter, write about here is socially constructed. This chapter is constructed at a certain point in history, and it is influenced by what I know and how I see the world.

Just as concepts and objects of theories are socially constructed, so too are theories. Theories are composed of concepts and interrelationships—concepts that are socially constructed and interrelationships formed from the social constructions of theorists. Theories are therefore extensions of social constructions, informed by the data from which they are developed. Important dimensions of the social construction of theory include who the theorist is, on whom the theory is based, for whom the theory is designed, and in what socio-historical context the theory has been developed. Thus theories are not value-free, they are not objective, and they are not "pure" representations of human development. Sue, Ivey, and Pedersen (1996) suggest, "each [theory] has its own interpretation of reality" (p. 7).

A significant problem with many theories is that the theorists have not put forth their concepts, assumptions, and hypotheses *as* socially constructed. In other words, theorists have not usually stated who they are in terms of socially constructed characteristics, backgrounds, values, and other factors that may influence the development and presentation of their theory. Further, in theories of human development, the basis for the theory—for example, the participants, the nature of the research, where the research was conducted—is often minimally provided, if at all. Not having adequate information about either the theorist or the basis for the theory means that the theory may be applied too broadly or that concepts and hypotheses may be readily accepted without question. Chickering's (1969; Chickering & Reisser, 1993) work can be used to illustrate this issue. To understand and apply Chickering's work, it is important to know that he developed the seven vectors from research conducted at

Goddard College between 1959 and 1965 and that he identified the hypotheses related to the key environmental influences from research at thirteen small colleges between 1964 and 1969 (Thomas & Chickering, 1984). The revision of his work (Chickering & Reisser, 1993) incorporated recent research findings of others, but is not based on additional research conducted by Chickering. Illustrative comments within the 1993 edition came from students over a three-year period of time who took classes or workshops taught by Linda Reisser. Too freqeuntly, for example, student affairs professionals can identify Chickering's theory of seven vectors without being aware of the foundation of the vectors nor understanding the complexity of the theory.

Examining the ways in which a theory is socially constructed means making the invisible social constructions visible, the hidden purposes explicit, and the camouflaged populations for whom the theory is intended known and acknowledged. This challenge also means revealing the social constructions of the concepts included in the theory. Further, it is necessary for us to examine ourselves to make known what lenses and filters we are using to understand, portray, and apply theory.

In understanding the social construction of theories, it may be necessary to undo, or unravel, some of the theory. Sampson (1989) indicates that deconstruction usually becomes "the analysis of language and symbolic practices as the key to be deciphered. Each seriously challenges the Western understanding of the person-society relationship, in particular the centriality and the sovereignty of the individual" (p. 6). The difficulty, Sampson says, is "that the tools used to deconstruct this tradition come from that very tradition" (p. 7). Sampson suggests that the difficulty in deconstructing theory involves using tools that are familiar to try to unravel a theory that is familiar and commonly known (p. 7). So the question is whether, through lenses created out of Western thought and understanding, we can undo and unveil those very structures—the language, symbolism, constructs, and theories—that are at the very heat of the Western tradition. Sampson offers a particularly important caution: that to deconstruct a theory means "to undo, not to destroy" (p. 7). hooks (1994) echoes Sampson's caution in critiquing the sexism in Paulo Freire's work, when she says that "critical interrogation [of a theory] is not the same as dismissal" (p. 49).

Also a part of understanding theory as social construction and emerging from a literature known as critical theory is to identify the dimensions of power and oppression implicit in theory, dimensions that are frequently not addressed. Fine (1992) points out characteristics such as gender, race, and class are usually studied as differences; the power dimensions between or within genders, races, or social classes are usually not addressed. When power is not addressed, then women, people of color, and other oppressed groups appear in the research as "less than," as not meeting the "standards" or norms of the dominant group, as a special case. Fine cautions us against our vulnerability "to the possibilities of *gender essentialism and racial/ethnic/class erasure*" (p. 15). (Essentialism means treating a particular characteristic such as gender or race as having an inherent "biological inequality." [Frankenberg, 1993, p. 14.]) Taking an activist stance toward feminist researches, Fine (1992) offers advice that we in student affairs would do well to heed: If we "do not take critical, activist, and open stances on our work, then we collude in reproducing social silences through the social sciences" (p. 206). In other words, Fine is suggesting that not to engage in critical inquiry is to perpetuate the errors, omissions, and overgeneralizations residing within the theories that we use in student affairs.

Hill Collins (1991) talks about what theories should be: "Theory and intellectual creativity are not the province of a select few but instead emanate from a range of people" (p. xiii). She also points out that "oppressed groups are frequently placed in the situation of being listened to only if we frame our ideas in the language that is familiar to and comfortable for a dominant group" (p. xiii). Addressing power from the consideration of privilege, Hill Collins encourages us to be cognizant of theory's role "in sustaining hierarchies of privilege" (p. xii).

In summary, to consider theory as social construction means taking a social constructivist view of both the central concepts of the theory and the ways in which the theory has been created. It implies that we need to engage in a "peeling away of the layers" of the theory to uncover and discover its hidden and unstated bases and intentions. How power and oppression function within a theory, its development, and its applications also should be examined. By engaging in self-reflection and critical analysis, we in student affairs can develop deeper and clearer understandings of the theories available to us and of how and why we select certain theories to aid us in practice.

Contemporary Challenges to Theory

It can be easy to accept theory without question and use it in practice without challenge. Yet one of the important components of knowing and using theory is to evaluate it, both within practice and in relationship to new literature and new research. There are also, however, other considerations in using theory.

Sampson (1989) identified six challenges to psychological theory that can be applied to theories used in student affairs: (1) cross-cultural investigation, which points out that a Western worldview is frequently assumed in theory and looks for perspectives that are not part of the dominant literature; (2) feminist reconceptualizations, which challenge patriarchal views and offer alternative perspectives; (3) social constructionism, which proposes that concepts and theories are "social and historical constructions, not naturally occurring objects" (p. 2); (4) systems theory, in which persons and constructs are viewed in relation to an overall whole rather than as separate individual entities; (5) critical theory, which "claims that through self-reflection it reveals the distortions and malformations of social life" (Gibson, 1986, p. 36); and (6) deconstructionism, which challenges "all notions that involve the primacy of the subject (or author)"— or theorist—in order "to undo, not to destroy" (Sampson, 1989, pp. 2, 7). These challenges, although different, are overlapping and not mutually exclusive. Understanding theory as social construction is also closely related to Sampson's challenges.

These challenges suggest six ways in which student affairs professionals need to consider and examine theory. First, theory must be examined in terms of its implicit worldview and those worldviews or cross-cultural perspectives that are absent. In many theories of human behavior, for example, individualism is valued, but how one relates to others (such as seeing oneself as part of a family) is ignored or negated. Second, underlying assumptions about gender (and other individual conditions), patriarchy, dominance,

and power should be identified. Theories that embrace personal independence and devalue social interdependence reflect a male orientation. Third, how a theory has been socially constructed—under what social conditions, at what point in history, by whom, and with whom—should be considered. For instance, knowing that many theories and models about college students were developed in the 1950s and 1960s— usually by male psychologists and based on research with male students at private, elite colleges—has a significant impact on one's understanding of how student development has traditionally been conceptualized.

A fourth consideration is whether or not a theory regards the person as part of a whole or as a separate, discrete entity, seemingly without an external context and impervious to the influence of others. Excellent examples are early retention models about underrepresented student groups, in which deficits in the students were identified, but the institutional systems they were recruited into were not considered. Critical theory, a fifth challenge, reminds us to engage people as active participants in theory and research rather than solely as subjects. For instance, studying the involvement of commuter students might mean not only collecting traditional data about their participation but also examining, with their participation, what it means to be involved and creating a dialogue with them about the tentative findings. The sixth challenge is to consider how a theory can be deconstructed (without destroying it). One way to deconstruct a theory of human behavior is to "peel away" the layers of the central constructs and relationships within it. For instance, to deconstruct a theory of identity development, we might first look at how the construct of identity is conceptualized, whose perspectives are reflected in such conceptualizations, what basis exists for the theory, and alternative ways to construct the theory, given that theory base.

King (1994) talks about theory as a political object. She raises a number of questions about theory: What political and personal beliefs are incorporated within a theory? How do formal, generic theories mask or hide informal, specialized ones? On the other hand, what "specialized" theories are really broad and comprehensive? King (1994) adds a question raised by Hill Collins: "When is it important *not* to display under the sign 'theory' and for what reasons?" (p. 29). In considering environmental theories, for example, King might ask the following questions: What is implicit in a theory about what an environment should be? (That is, what is a "positive" environment?) Do formal, generic environmental theories gloss over important information about the college classroom setting or student participation in the campus community? Does a particular environmental theory presented as broad and comprehensive more accurately represent a specialized environment, such as student organizations, than some purportedly specialized theories? And drawing from Hill Collins's (1991) question, what kinds of environments are not addressed by environmental theories, and why not? For example, theories about the culture or environment of a university president's office may not have been created, in part to keep hidden the intimate and innermost workings that may go on in such an office. Or, using an example from Hill Collins (1991), persons who study something such as "cultures of resistance" may choose not to describe their work as "theory." Some researchers or scholars may see theory as antagonistic or contradictory to the liberation or emancipation implied in "culture of resistance" (p. 18).

Choosing Which Theories to Use

A value both explicit and implicit in student affairs is that student affairs professionals should guide and inform their professional practice with appropriate theories. As you will see in the chapters that follow, there are multiple theories for the many phenomena and constructs relevant to student affairs. An important question, often overwhelming, is how do you select which theory or theories to guide your practice? Before choosing theories, however, you should consider the importance and value of looking at yourself.

The Importance of Looking at Self

Knowing and examining oneself is especially important in relation to learning, critiquing, and using theories about student and human development. It is also pertinent to understanding and using other theories, such as organizational and environmental theory. Who each of us is, including the experiences and history we carry within us, creates the filters and frameworks through which we interpret others' experiences and perspectives (including those of organizations) and the theories we use in our work.

Thus each of us must begin by examining who we are and what we believe—our identity and our perspectives or informal theories on human nature, how people change, and the nature and functioning of organizations. For example, we should look at how we see race and how we view sexual orientation, whether we behave in ageist or sexist ways, and if we have anti-Semitic attitudes. We should also examine what we think about organizations and whether we are likely to be more attuned to the structure and processes of an organization or to the individuals and groups within it. Most important, each student affairs professional must see and understand himself or herself as a person with multiple characteristics (a certain race, gender, sexual orientation, ethnicity, social class, place of origin, and so on), which are part of his or her identity.

Examples exist in the literature about how theory is closely connected to one's sense of self. Helms's 1992 book *A Race Is a Nice Thing to Have* implies that White persons' understanding of theories and literature about people of color is inextricably linked with their sense of self as White. Research has shown that encountering a disability in another person elicits feelings about the self, about one's own helplessness, needs, and dependencies (Asch & Fine, 1988), thus hampering one's ability to see beyond the disability and understand the other person as an individual. In speaking about multiculturalism, Taylor (1992) described this effect succinctly: It "is *not* a commitment to learning about *them*; instead, it is a commitment to learning about myself—and ultimately, us" (p. 1).

Student affairs professionals need to ask questions of themselves, such as Who am I, as an able-bodied, middle-class, educated White woman? or a second-generation bisexual Asian man? or an African American woman? or a person with any other combination of characteristics? Such self-reflection will help you discover and understand those frameworks you use in both the consideration and the application of theory. Thoughtful, insightful, and continuing introspection about oneself is a necessary part of a student affairs professional's journey of learning, understanding, and using theory—about organizations, environments and their interactions with students, and, especially, college students and their development.

Selecting Appropriate Theories

Many perspectives exist about the selection and use of theory. One perspective offers a "purist" approach—that for a particular phenomenon, such as understanding organizational change or students' cognitive development, one should select and use a *single* theory. Proponents of this perspective believe a "true" theory can stand alone—that is, it provides assumptions, defines relationships, and describes how those relationships occur under given conditions. Further, using more than one theory may violate the assumptions of individual theories and thus may invalidate the relationships and beliefs prescribed within any theory.

A second perspective is to adopt an "eclectic" model. Eclectic use of theory means a professional draws on the useful and relevant aspects of multiple theories and combines those aspects into a meaningful whole. Some people believe this permits them to use the best parts of many theories, thus making the combined usage stronger than any one theory. Opponents of such a perspective argue that various assumptions of the individual theories may not be honored or may even be violated. It is also possible that there is little if any consistency, for any one individual, from one usage to another, and little consistency from one individual to another. Thus there is no common language or framework within which professionals can discuss or deal with the phenomena of common interest.

In spite of the challenges to eclectic theory, many persons do not believe that any one theory is comprehensive enough to adequately describe any given phenomenon. And, practically speaking, there are few individuals who adopt one theory exclusive of all others in a similar family or grouping of theories. Thus, what guidelines can a student affairs professional use in selecting theories? I offer the following guidelines.

Select a theory or theories that you understand and that make sense to you. For instance, if a certain theory resonates for you and seems to appropriately describe a certain phenomenon, then you are more likely to internalize that theory, understand it more deeply, and apply it in your practice. On the other hand, if a theory isn't very clear to you or doesn't "come alive," then you may find it more difficult to apply in your practice.

Knowing yourself will help you decide which theories to choose and which ones to "put back on the shelf." For theories that seem to fit you and your understanding of the world, ask yourself what it is about them that fits. Is it because they describe your own experiences? If so, whose experiences do they not describe?

Because theories "operate from both explicit and implicit assumptions that guide their formulations" (Sue et al., 1996, p. 1), Sue et al. recommend an "assumption audit" as a part of using theory. An assumption audit therefore would identify those assumptions both explicit and implicit within a theory. Some implicit assumptions about student development undergird many of the theories and student affairs professionals' application and use of such theories, but they are frequently not articulated. Two assumptions are that development of students is good, and thus that greater developmental complexity is desirable, and that a goal of student affairs professionals is to promote the development of students. A third assumption with some of the student success models, sometimes explicit and sometimes implicit, is that involvement and engagement in the academic community is valued.

As noted earlier, theories are reductionistic—they describe some relationships and concepts but not others. So, what theory or theories do you draw on for *each* phenomenon of interest? In thinking about a student, you may be interested in understanding his or her psychosocial and cognitive development as well as his or her racial identity development. How, then, do you combine a theory or theories for each of these areas with one another? Or, you may want to draw on several theories to describe a single phenomenon. In either case, think about how the theories fit together. Do the assumptions of each theory fit with one another, or do some conflict? If they conflict, how do you understand the conflict, and on what basis could you decide the incongruence is not pertinent? What parts of each theory do you draw upon? What, then, is your own modified version of this melding of certain theories? Be thoughtful, be intentional, and, as Evans says, be intelligent about using theory. Be explicit about the theories you use.

Conclusion

The theories available to use in student affairs come from many different sources, and they serve multiple and varied purposes. Theories are evolving, both in their own development and in how we use them in student affairs. Yet we must remember that theories are not pure; they are not perfect; they were not created and do not exist in a vacuum. Sampson's (1989) six challenges about theory and knowing and taking into account our own personal filters and values are important complements to the selection and use of theory. Critical science offers a method by which we can examine how a theory has been socially constructed and how it may need to be deconstructed. Finally, as a student affairs professional, it is necessary that one be thoughtful, intentional, and systematic in selecting which theory or theories to draw upon. It is also important to know why one has selected a theory, to know its strengths and limitations, and to be conscious of how selecting and applying a given theory relates to who you are as a person and as a student affairs professional.

References

American College Personnel Association. (1996). The student learning imperative: Implications for student affairs. *Journal of College Student Development, 37*, 118–122.

Apple, M. W. (1993). Constructing the "other": Rightist reconstructions of common sense. In. C. McCarthy & W. Crichlow (Eds.), *Race, identity, and representation in education* (pp. 24–39). New York: Routledge & Kegan Paul.

Asch, A., & Fine, M. (1988). Introduction: Beyond pedestals. In M. Fine & A. Asch (Eds.), *Women with disabilities: Essays in psychology, culture, and politics* (pp. 1–37). Philadelphia: Temple University Press.

Astin, A. W. (1984). Student involvement: A developmental theory for higher education. *Journal of College Student Personnel, 25*, 297–308.

Borg, W. R., & Gall, M. D. (1989). *Educational research: An introduction* (5th ed.). White Plains, NY: Longman.

Brown, R. D. (1972). *Student development in tomorrow's higher education: A return to the academy* (Student Personnel Monograph No. 16). Washington, DC: American College Personnel Association.

Cannon, K. G. (1988). *Black womanist ethics.* Atlanta, GA: Scholars Press.

Canon, H. J. (1988). Nevitt Sanford: Gentle prophet, Jeffersonian rebel. *Journal of Counseling and Development, 65*, 451–457.

Chickering, A. W. (1969). *Education and identity.* San Francisco: Jossey-Bass.

Chickering, A. W., & Reisser, L. (1993). *Education and identity* (2nd ed.). San Francisco: Jossey-Bass.

Clark, B. R., & Trow, M. (1966). The organizational context. In T. M. Newcomb & E. K. Wilson (Eds.), *College peer groups: Problems and prospects for research* (pp. 17–70). Chicago: Aldine.

Comstock, D. E. (1982). A method for critical research. In E. Bredo & W. Feinberg (Eds.), *Knowledge values in social and educational research* (pp. 370–390). Philadelphia: Temple University Press.

Deaux, K. (1993). Reconstructing social identity. *Personality and Social Psychology Bulletin, 19*, 4–12.

Erikson, E. H. (1968). *Identity: Youth and crisis.* New York: Norton.

Evans, N. J., Forney, D. S., & Guido-DiBrito, F. (1998). *Student development in college: Theory, research, and practice.* San Francisco: Jossey-Bass.

Fine, M. (1992). *Disruptive voices: The possibilities of feminist research.* Ann Arbor: University of Michigan Press.

Frankenberg, R. (1993). *The social construction of whiteness: White women, race matters.* Minneapolis: University of Minnesota Press.

Gibson, R. (1986). *Critical theory and education.* London: Hodder & Stoughton.

Gilligan, C. (1982). *In a different voice: Psychological theory and women's development.* Cambridge, MA: Harvard University Press.

Heath, D. H. (1968). *Growing up in college.* San Francisco: Jossey-Bass.

Heath, D. H. (1980). Wanted: A comprehensive model of healthy development. *Personnel and Guidance Journal, 38*, 391–398.

Heath, R. (1964). *The reasonable adventurer.* Pittsburgh, PA: University of Pittsburgh Press.

Helms, J. E. (1992). *A race is a nice thing to have: A guide to being a White person, or understanding the White persons in your life.* Topeka, KS: Content Communications.

Helms, J. E. (1995). An update of Helms's White and People of Color racial identity models. In J. G. Ponterotto, J. M. Gasas, L. A. Suzuki, & C. M. Alexander (Eds.), *Handbook of multicultural counseling* (pp. 181–198). Thousand Oaks, CA: Sage.

Hettler, B. (1980). Wellness promotion on a university campus. *Journal of Health Promotion and Maintenance, 3*(1), 77–95.

Hill Collins, P. (1991). *Black feminist thought: Knowledge, consciousness, and the politics of empowerment.* New York: Routledge, Chapman & Hall.

Holland, J. L. (1966). *The psychology of vocational choice: A theory of personality types and model environments.* Waltham, MA: Blaisdell.

Hooks, B. (1994). *Teaching to transgress: Education as the practice of freedom.* New York: Routledge.

Isasi-Diaz, A. M. (1993, March). *Educating for a new world order.* Presented at the conference of the National Association for Women in Education, Seattle, WA.

Isasi-Diaz, A. M. (1996). *Mujerista theology: A theology for the twenty-first century.* Maryknoll, NY: Orbis.

Ivey, A. E. (1986). *Developmental therapy: Theory into practice.* San Francisco: Jossey-Bass.

Kegan, R. (1982). *The evolving self: Problem and process in human developemnt.* Cambridge, MA: Harvard University Press.

Keniston, K. (1971). *Youth and dissent.* New York: Harcourt, Brace, Jovanovich.

King, K. (1994). *Theory in its feminist travels: Conversations in U.S. women's movements.* Bloomington: Indiana University Press.

King, P. M., & Baxter Magolda, M. (2001, November). *The development of intercultural maturity: Examining how facets of development are interrelated.* Paper presented at the conference of the Association for the Study of Higher Education, Richmond, VA.

King, S. H. (1973). *Five lives at Harvard: Personality change during college.* Cambridge, MA: Harvard University Press.

Knefelkamp, L. L. (1982). Faculty and student development in the '80s: Renewing the community of scholars. In H. F. Owens, C. H. Witten, & W. R. Bailey (Eds.), *College student personnel administration: An anthology* (pp. 373–391). Springfield, IL: Thomas.

Knefelkamp, L. L., Widick, C., & Parker, C. A. (1978). Editors' notes: Why bother with theory? In L. Knefelkamp, C. Widick, & C. A. Parker (Eds.), *Applying new developmental findings* (New Directions for Student Services No. 4, pp. vii–xvi). San Francisco: Jossey-Bass.

Kohlberg, L. (1975). The cognitive-developmental approach to moral education. *Phi Delta Kappan, 56,* 670–677.

Kuh, G. D., Whitt, E. J., & Shedd, J. D. (1987). *Student affairs work, 2001: A paradigmatic odyssey.* Washington, DC: American College Personnel Association.

Kuhn, T. S. (1962). *The structure of scientific revolutions.* Chicago: University of Chicago Press.

Larrabee, M. J. (1993). Gender and moral development: A challenge for feminist theory. In M. J. Larrabee (Ed.), *An ethic of care: Feminist and interdisciplinary perspectives* (pp. 3–16). New York: Routledge & Keran Paul.

Moore, L. V., & Upcraft, M. L. (1990). Theory in student affairs: Evolving perspectives. In L. V. Moore (Ed.), *Evolving theoretical perspectives on students* (New Directions for Student Services No. 51, pp. 3–23). San Francisco: Jossey-Bass.

Newcomb, T. M., Joenig, K. E., Flacks, R., & Warwick, D. P. (1967). *Persistence and change: Bennington College and its students after 25 years.* New York: Wiley.

Parham, T. A. (1989). Cycles of psychological Nigrescence. *Counseling Psychologist, 17,* 187–226.

Patterson, C. H. (1980). *Theories of counseling and psychotherapy* (3rd ed.). New York: Harper & Row.

Perry, W. G., Jr. (1970). *Forms of intellectual and ethical development in the college years: A scheme.* New York: Holt, Rinehart and Winston.

Perry, W. G., Jr. (1981). Cognitive and ethical growth: The making of meaning. In A. W. Chickering & Associates, *The modern American college.* San Francisco: Jossey-Bass.

Rodgers, R. F. (1980). Theories underlying student development. In D. G. Creamer (Ed.), *Student development in higher education: Theories, practices & future directions.* Washington, DC: American College Personnel Association.

Sampson, E. E. (1989). The deconstruction of the self. In J. Shotter & K. J. Gergen (Eds.), *Texts of identity* (pp. 1–19). Newbury Park, CA: Sage.

Sanford, N. (1962). *The American college.* New York: Wiley.

Sanford, N. (1967). *Where colleges fail: A study of the student as a person.* San Francisco: Jossey-Bass.

Schlossberg, N. K. (1989). Marginality and mattering: Key issues in building community. In D. C. Roberts (Ed.), *Designing campus activities to foster a sense of community* (New Directions for Student Services No. 48, pp. 5–15). San Francisco: Jossey-Bass.

Schlossberg, N. K., Waters, E. B., & Goodman, J. (1995). *Counseling adults in transition* (2nd ed.). New York: Springer.

Sue, D. W., Ivey, A. E., & Pedersen, P. B. (1996). *A theory of multicultural counseling & therapy.* Pacific Grove, CA: Brooks/Cole.

Taylor, K. (1992, March 31). *Remarks.* Presented at the awards luncheon of the annual conference of the National Association of Student Personnel Administrators, Cincinnati, OH.

Thomas, R., & Chickering, A. W. (1984). Education and identity revisited. *Journal of College Student Personnel, 25,* 392–399.

Thomas, R. M. (2001). *Recent theories of human development.* Thousand Oaks, CA: Sage.

Walsh, W. B. (1973). *Theories of person-environment interaction: Implications for the college student.* Iowa City, IA: American College Testing Program.

CHAPTER 2

STUDENT DEVELOPMENT: THE EVOLUTION AND STATUS OF AN ESSENTIAL IDEA

CARNEY STRANGE

This article illustrates the evolution of the concept of student development in the higher education and student affairs literature. The current status of this concept is presented in a framework of 14 propositions as an agenda for scholars and practitioners in the field.

From the early Colonial colleges to the current era of the multiversity, American higher education has concerned itself with the development of individual students for positions of societal leadership and influence. In the "age of the college" (Hofstadter, 1955), a period from the first institutions in America until just prior to the Civil War, preparation of the "gentleman scholar" was compelled by a vision of character development emphasizing command of the classics and refinement of civilized graces. With the inception of modern behavioral sciences in the subsequent "age of the university" (Metzger, 1955), a vision of human development emerged that focused on complex, measurable traits and systems of thought, emotions, motivations, and capacities, presumed to culminate in an integrated state of maturity. The human personality was seen as a function of numerous underlying dimensions that manifested themselves in a variety of observable behaviors and actions. This view was given further credence in the growth of the occupational aptitude assessment movement following the First World War as concepts of human personality traits were applied to the selection and training of personnel in industry and the vocational advisement of students on the college campus. It is this latter vision of development, grounded in the study of human psychology and sociology, that has persisted into the last decade of the Twentieth Century. Over the last 50 years in particular, this vision has been proffered in the academy by professionals in student affairs under the rubric of "student development."

What are the philosophical and educational roots of this vision? What are the implications of its knowledge base for the design and practice of education, both in and out of the classroom, in our American system of higher learning? These questions are addressed in a sequence of five articles. First, I identify what I believe to be some of the foundations of student development in the form of a very brief historical outline of two principal educational movements of the Twentieth Century; I then summarize the current status and meaning of the extant student development knowledge base in the form of propositional statements emanating from a collective of exemplary models and theories in the literature. Second, Patricia King addresses the adequacy and relevance of this knowledge base as a theoretical framework for understanding students and their interactions with our higher education systems. Third, Patrick Terenzini examines the implications of this knowledge base for shaping a future research agenda in American higher education. Fourth, Michael Coomes explores the meaning of these propositions for how campus administrators conceive and implement educational policies. Fifth, Lee Upcraft addresses the dilemmas and challenges of transferring these propositions to the design and conduct of student affairs practice in higher education.

A Recent Historical Overview

Although rooted in the fundamental tenets of Neohumanism (emphasizing the primary importance of human interests, values, and dignity), Instrumentalism (emphasizing the value of ideas in human experience and progress), and Rationalism (emphasizing self-evident propositional forms of knowledge), student development, as constructed by current scholars, has been fueled particularly by several key philosophical and educational movements of the Twentieth Century. From the Progressive Education Movement of the 1920s (Mayhew, 1977) came an emphasis on student self-direction, the importance of experiential learning techniques, the role of educators as resource guides rather than task masters, the importance of establishing comprehensive evaluative records, and the need for education to work closely with other societal institutions to effect the total development of students. It was within this context that the American Council on Education commissioned the Student Personnel Point of View (American Council on Education, 1937), advocating attention to holistic learning and individual differences in responding to college student needs. Reflecting this same orientation, campus educators and professional association leaders began to call attention to the implications of these tenets for campus personnel practices and for student learners. For example, Jack E. Walters, Director of Personnel in the School of Engineering at Purdue University, and President of the American College Personnel Association from 1930 to 1933, authored monographs entitled *Student Development: How to Make the Most of College Life* (Walters, 1931) and *Individualizing Education by Means of Applied Personnel Procedures* (Walters, 1935), extolling further the importance of holistic development and student responsibility in the educational process. These same themes were underscored once again, following the Second World War, as requisites for global democratic reform in *The Student Personnel Point of View, 1949* (American Council on Education, 1949).

Postulates of the Nontraditional Education Movement of the 1960s (Mayhew, 1977) continued to further shape this student development framework in higher education. Emphasizing the importance of student interests and needs in the design of curriculum and learning, the merits of self-direction, and the relevance of real-life experiences for learning and development, this movement challenged higher education to examine further the nature of student differences and the relationship of these differences to the outcomes of college attendance. Scholars such as Sanford (1962), in *The American College*, focused attention on the connection between formal education and the transition between late adolescence and young adulthood. Researchers such as Trent and Medsker (1968), in *Beyond High School*, and Feldman and Newcomb (1969) in *The Impact of College on Students*, began to methodically address questions about how the college experience influences personality development and student attitudes and beliefs. Observers of college student growth, such as Heath (1968), Perry (1970), Kohlberg (1969), and Chickering (1969), building upon previous analyses of identity and youth (e.g., Erikson, 1963; Keniston, 1965; White, 1958), published seminal models charting patterns of human development during the college years. In the latter part of the decade, professional organizations such as the American College Personnel Association (ACPA) and the National Association of Student Personnel Administrators (NASPA) embraced the concept of student development and reflected this new focus in a variety of professional venues. Student development emerged in their journals, as it did for the first time in 1966 in the *NASPA Journal* (Trent, 1966); in their professional organization agendas, as it first did in 1968 with the initiation of Phase I of ACPA's Tomorrow's Higher Education (T.H.E.) Project; and in their professional conferences, as it first did in 1968 in a collaborative meeting between NASPA and the Berkeley Center for Research and Development in Higher Education. The goal of student development in higher education also caught the attention of national foundations and councils during this period. The Hazen Foundation, for example, issued a report calling for a reaffirmation of the developmental teaching mission of postsecondary education (The Committee on the Student in Higher Education, 1968), and the Commission on Professional Development of the Council of Student Personnel Associations in

Higher Education (COSPA) began the process of describing student development services in higher education, authoring a paper which was subsequently distributed and published as the "COSPA Statement" (Commission on Professional Development of COSPA, 1975).

The decade of the 1970s was equally powerful in advancing higher education's attention to the development of students. Bowen (1977), in a comprehensive summary of developmental outcomes, argued the many benefits of college attendance to individuals and society alike. Brown (1972), Parker (1978), and Cross (1976) also played significant roles during this time in bringing student development to the forefront of the student affairs agenda in higher education. Under the aegis of the T.H.E. Project, Brown (1972) authored his *Student Development in Tomorrow's Higher Education: A Return to the Academy*, a monograph invoking student development as a unifying mission of higher education. Parker (1978) brought a number of key student development educators together for purposes of addressing relationships between theories of human development and educational practice, publishing *Encouraging Development in College Students*. During this same period, others such as Banning (1978) and Morrill, Hurst, and Oetting (1980) began conducting studies and writing on the consequences of campus environments for various dimensions of student growth and development. Also during this decade Cross (1971, 1976) emerged as a leader in alerting higher education to the developmental needs and concerns of nontraditional students in *Beyond the Open Door* and *Accent on Learning*. In response to Cross' caution, and to new sensitivities highlighted by the work of theorists like Gould (1978) and Levinson and Associates (1978), higher education began to take notice of the importance of incorporating models of life-span development in understanding college students.

From the early 1980s to the present the "science" of student development, although some have challenged such a description (see Bloland, Stamatakos, & Rogers, 1994), continued to evolve and mature with the emergence of a full range of psychosocial, cognitive developmental, typological, and person-environment interaction models (Rodgers, 1980). The connections between personal development and formal education were further enhanced with the appearance of works like: Chickering and Associates' (1981) *Modern American College*, which explored the relevance of the developmental model for the teaching mission in a variety of disciplines; Cross' (1981) *Adults as Learners*, which further iterated a model for understanding needs of returning adult students in higher education; Pascarella and Terenzini's (1991) *How College Affects Students*, which summarized, in the legacy of Feldman and Newcomb (1969), 20 years of research on the outcomes of college attendance; and Kuh et al.'s (1991) *Involving Colleges*, which examined the role of student experiences outside the classroom in attaining stated or espoused educational missions. Advocates such as Knefelkamp (1981, 1984, 1986), a frequent keynote speaker at various professional conferences during this period, continued to focus the attention of the higher education community on the preeminence of the student development mission. Researchers such as Winston, Miller, and Prince (1979) focused on developing instruments to measure the outcomes of student development (e.g., The Student Development Task Inventory); and scholars like Pace (1984) continued work on assessing the nature and impact of institutional environments with The College Student Experiences Questionnaire.

The student development movement, though, was not without its critics during this period, with scholars such as Gilligan (1982), Josselson (1987), and Belenky, Clinchy, Goldberger, and Tarule (1986) identifying perceived biases of extant developmental models, especially as they pertained to patterns of women's growth and development. Others like Moore (1990) and Evans and Wall (1991) also directed attention to questions about the applicability of the student development knowledge base to increasingly diverse student populations, emphasizing the need to reconceptualize knowledge of various campus subpopulations and minority groups. More recently Bloland, Stamatakos, and Rogers (1994) have formulated a comprehensive ideological critique of student development with prescriptions for a realignment of the field with the educational mission of institutions and a refocusing on the facilitation of learning.

Current Status

Although the goal of human development has long served as a foundation for liberal learning in higher education (see Kuh, Shedd, & Whitt, 1987; Newman, 1973), the history of student development as outlined here has been a relatively brief one in the scheme of American postsecondary education. In that brief period, however, it has posited a body of literature that is both complex and rich in ideas about college students and their educational environments. The current status of this knowledge base is presented here as a framework of theoretical propositions and concepts addressing the growth and development of individual college students, the features and impacts of educational environments, and the dynamics of person-environment interaction. From the perspective of Lewin's (1936) differential interactionist paradigm [B = f(P, E)], this knowledge base emphasizes the importance of both the person and the environment in understanding human behavior. Knefelkamp, Widick, and Parker (1978) edited one of the first summaries of this emerging student development knowledge base and challenged the student affairs profession with the goal of establishing developmental communities in higher education. Accordingly, they argued that such a goal requires a theoretical knowledge base capable of describing four areas:

1. Who the college student is in developmental terms. We need to know what changes occur and what those changes look like.

2. How development occurs. We need to have a grasp of the psychological and social processes which cause development.

3. How the college environment can influence student development. We need to know what factors in the particular environment of a college or university can either encourage or inhibit growth.

4. Toward what ends development in college should be directed. (Parker, Widick, & Knefelkamp, 1978, p. x)

"Knowledge in these four areas," the authors further claimed "would allow us to establish feasible developmental goals; to design interventions that take into account 'where students are'; and to draw on the processes underlying developmental change." They concluded that "making student development theory work involves identifying how and to what extent a theory describes the nature of young adult/adult development and explains the process of developmental change in a higher education context" (p. x).

Within the framework of these four questions, the student development knowledge base has continued to evolve and mature over the past 20 years, yielding a number of propositions about college students and their campus environments. As "propositions," these are constructed as tentative, and sometimes conflicting, distillations of thought emerging in the literature on college student development and are presented here for purposes of challenging practitioners and scholars to examine their relevance for what they practice and for how they come to inquire about and understand the college experience. What "truths" guide and define these propositions? What is their meaning and value to the design of educational policy and the conduct of educational practice?

The Student in Developmental Terms

Within the context of Parker, Widick, and Knefelkamp's (1978) first question ("Who is the college student in developmental terms?"), four propositions are identified, each illustrated by exemplary theorists, and followed by a brief discussion of their potential implications for higher education:

Proposition 1: Students differ in age-related developmental tasks that offer important agendas for "teachable moments" in their lives. This proposition underscores the importance of aspects of students' psychosocial lifespan and their definition as age-related developmental challenges that culminate into age-appropriate states of maturity or resolution at each chronological phase. The works of Chickering (1969), Chickering and Reisser (1993), Neugarten (1968), Erikson (1950, 1959), and Levinson and Associates (1978) address human development from this perspective; and their concepts are important for understanding the needs of traditional as well as nontraditional students. A key implication of this perspective is that, when learning tasks are relevant (or closely related) to developmental choices embedded in students' current life phase, a highly motivating experience, which Havighurst (1972) identified as a "teachable moment," occurs. For example, a course in ethics and philosophy may be an especially powerful experience for a student who is formulating a personalized set of values for the first time ("Developing Integrity," as Chickering labels the task), or participating in an interpersonal skills workshop in a residence hall may be a highly relevant learning experience for a student engaged in a new significant relationship.

Another implication from this psychosocial-developmental-task perspective emanates from its conception of the progression of human life through repeated structural phases of stability and transition (Levinson & Associates, 1978). During periods of stability closure is sought, firm choices are made, and life proceeds in response to a framework of significant commitments, usually related to various occupational and relational aspects of the life span. In contrast, during periods of transition, questions are paramount; and previous life structures must be dissolved, evaluated, and considered for inclusion in (or exclusion from) the next life structure. The import of this is that educators need to understand and make connections (and encourage students to do so) between what they are learning and the psychosocial developmental tasks they are addressing in their lives. Furthermore, during periods of stability, education must serve to enhance commitments rather than challenge them; and at points of transition, education best serves to frame important questions rather than to insist on firm conclusions.

Proposition 2: Students differ in how they construct and interpret their experiences, and such differences offer important guides for structuring the education process. This proposition underscores the importance of cognitive structures, or patterns of meaning-making, that students bring to their educational experiences. Theoretical models that exemplify this perspective include Perry (1970), Kohlberg (1969), Gilligan (1982), and King and Kitchener (1994). According to these models, individuals progress through a sequence of hierarchical stages or positions, each characterized by greater complexity and qualitatively different assumptions about how the world functions with respect to a particular domain. Early simplistic assumptions are gradually replaced by more advanced assumptions, as individuals seek new meanings for the events and experiences in their lives. For example, Kohlberg's model (1969) addresses the domain of moral reasoning, describing how individuals resolve issues of fairness and justice, with reference to the consequences of their actions, their membership in society, and the principles, norms, and rules that define systems of social order. Thus, an individual exhibiting characteristics of earlier stages of moral reasoning tends to interpret issues of justice egoistically, with concerns for the potential gains or losses to self that might result from a particular course of action. In contrast, a person constructing meaning from more advanced stages might understand justice

as a matter of fidelity to self-chosen principles that underlie systems of social order and that are codified in the form of laws delineating participants' contracted rights and responsibilities.

In the domain of intellectual reasoning, the work of King and Kitchener (1994) shares a similar set of assumptions about the course of human development. According to their model of reflective judgment, individuals progress through increasingly complex forms (or stages) of reasoning as they advance in their ability to resolve problems of an "ill-structured" nature, with reference to experts in the field, to the compelling quality of available evidence, and to established rules of inquiry. Thus, a person holding assumptions characteristic of early stages of reasoning might argue that the "truth value" of one point of view is established unquestionably by concurrence of an authority, or simply because one "believes it to be so," acknowledging that all points of view are equally valid since "no one knows for sure." At more advanced stages, though, a person acknowledges the difference between facts, opinions, and interpretations, reflecting a complex understanding of inquiry as an inherently fallible process of critical review over a long period of time, involving many sources of input from many individuals, and yielding solutions only approximate in their truth value.

Whether referring to the cognitive structures delineated by Kohlberg (1969) or those identified by King and Kitchener (1994), understanding such differences is important for educators in responding to students effectively. For instance, assuming that growth along a dimension of cognitive-intellectual development similar to that described in King and Kitchener is an appropriate goal of education, it is important to remember that students in the earlier stages benefit more from learning tasks that emphasize diverse viewpoints and employ experiential modes, supported by a high degree of structure and a personal atmosphere (Widick & Simpson, 1978). At more advanced stages, students thrive on tasks that are abstract, ambiguous, and self-directed in nature, when also supported by a high degree of personalism. Dimensions, like those described in Kohlberg, that emphasize social roles and responsibilities as well as the systems of rules established to define and maintain those roles and responsibilities, serve to challenge students appropriately at the early stages of development. Emphasis on principles that underlie such systems is more appropriate at the more advanced stages.

Proposition 3: Students differ in the styles with which they approach and resolve challenges of learning, growth and development, and such differences are important for understanding how and why students function in characteristic manners. This third proposition underscores the importance of concurrent stylistic differences among students and how such differences reveal themselves in consistent patterns with which students approach a variety of tasks. Theoretical models that exemplify this proposition describe styles or patterns of behaviors with respect to a variety of dimensions in students' lives, such as their career interests (Holland, 1973), their personalities (Myers, 1980), their learning orientations (Kolb, 1983), or their preferred style for processing information (Witkin, 1976). These approaches recognize that as individuals mature they develop consistent patterns in how they interpret and resolve various learning challenges. In that respect, they become somewhat predictable as others recognize their "usual way of doing things." For example, from the widely recognized work of Carl Jung, as modified by Isabel Myers and Katherine Briggs, readers have learned how various "Myers-Briggs types" exhibit preferred ways of using "their minds, specifically the way they perceive and the way they make judgments" (Myers, 1980, p. 1). Some perceive primarily through the senses, whereas others rely upon intuition; some use a logical process of thinking to arrive at judgments, whereas others judge out of their appreciation and feelings for the event or situation. According to the model, either kind of perception can team up with either kind of judgment. Furthermore, depending on individuals' relative interest in their outer world (extraversion) or inner world (introversion), as well as their preference for a perceptive versus a judging attitude, a variety of 16 combinations emerge reflecting "different kind[s] of personality, characterized by [differing] interests, values, needs, habits of mind, and surface traits" (Myers, 1980, p. 4). In a similar vein, Holland (1973) identified six vocational interest types (Realistic, Investigative, Artistic, Social, Enterprising, and Conventional), each with a different pattern of values, interests, expectations, and skills suited to the challenges of different occupational work environments. For example, "social types" enjoy working with people, prefer "activities that entail

the manipulation of others to inform, train, develop, cure, or enlighten" (p. 16), and use their social competencies to solve problems. In contrast, "realistic types" prefer "activities that entail the explicit, ordered, or systematic manipulation of objects, tools, machines, [or] animals" (p. 14), and oftentimes lack ability in human relations. Kolb (1983) described various learning orientation preferences individuals acquire as they exhibit differing cognitive processes. Thus, "accommodative learners" rely primarily on concrete experience and active experimentation as their preferred processes, in contrast to "assimilative learners" who prefer reflective observation and abstract conceptualization. In a final example, Witkin (1976) identified a continuum of two contrasting cognitive styles, each with its own preferred mode of learning: "field dependence," with a capacity and preference for wholistic approaches to problem solving; and "field independence," with an orientation and attraction toward analytic reasoning.

An important implication of these perspectives on human differences is that students develop relatively stable and consistent styles of behavior and performance that need to be taken into account when designing educational practice. Cognitive and personal styles function much like software systems in computers; in order to "run them" effectively, knowledge of the software system is paramount. Strategies incompatible with the software system in use simply will not work. In designing educational experiences compatible with students' identified styles, educators should allow students to exercise their strengths and preferred modes of functioning. On the other hand, as Cross (1976) warned, educators may not be serving students well by feeding them a steady diet of their own predilections. Rather, given the challenges of a complex and changing world, perhaps they should focus on strategies that encourage students to "stretch" and develop their nonpreferred strategies as well. Achieving flexibility in that respect may be the most important and desirable outcome of learning.

Proposition 4: Students differ in the resolution of tasks of individuation according to their gender, culture, ethnicity, and sexual orientation; such differences offer important contexts for understanding the challenges students face in their search for personal identity. This fourth proposition has emerged out of recent critiques that have identified various sources of perceived bias and limitation attributed to many current student development models. The works of Josselson (1987) and Gilligan (1982) have drawn attention to the claim that women's perspectives and issues have not been sufficiently accounted for in the constructs and models of human development. Within such a critique, current models of growth and development are challenged as products of male conception, treating concerns and issues important to women's lives as aberrations, delays, or evidence of lack of development. For example, models of psychosocial development have been criticized for their failure to acknowledge adequately the importance of family in charting the life cycles of women; models of intellectual or moral reasoning have also been challenged for falling short in acknowledging the role of intuitive processes or the importance of relational aspects to women in arriving at various judgments and conclusions. Atkinson, Morten, and Sue (1983), among others, have examined the applicability of current models of growth and development to the experiences of cultural ethnic minorities. They concluded that, as a consequence of minority status, various racial ethnic groups experience unique, as well as common, patterns of identity development (e.g., conformity, dissonance, immersion, and introspection) as they progress toward a state of synergy with the dominant culture. Development of a healthy self-concept is inescapably involved with the development of a positive cultural identity. Cass (1979, 1984) leveled similar criticism, arguing that, because of a heterosexual bias in the dominant culture, gay men and lesbians focus on substantially different developmental issues in their resolution of identity. Much like cultural ethnic minorities, gay, lesbian, and bisexual persons are portrayed as progressing through discrete stages of development toward an advanced level of identity synthesis within the dominant culture.

In light of this proposition, educators must consider more carefully the consequences of majority-minority dynamics and interactions as a critical context for understanding the growth and development of students. Concepts and assumptions of "normalcy" and "average" are inevitably products of dominant culture and values. Individuals who do not share those values or participate in that culture are challenged often by a press toward conformity in two divergent cultures: one (a subculture) that acknowledges and supports their identities as members of a minority, and another that challenges their identities for their failure to match commonly held expectations and norms. Rejection of the subculture removes an important source of support; rejection of the dominant culture results in barriers to achievement. In effect, for these individuals, success often entails a dual existence, capable of sustaining both the minority and dominant culture. Consequently, issues and tasks of development may be accompanied by additional degrees of stress and difficulty.

In summary, the "college student in developmental terms" is a person who is engaged in a variety of age-related developmental tasks; who constructs meaning from and approaches the challenges of learning in characteristic patterns or styles; and who must resolve issues of individuation within a dynamic cultural context of gender, ethnicity, and sexual orientation. Individual differences in these aspects are to be expected and accommodated if the full potential of an educational experience is to be realized.

The Nature of Development

In response to Parker, Widick, and Knefelkamp's (1978) second question ("How does development occur?'), five propositions emerge:

Proposition 5: Development occurs as individuals reach points of readiness and respond to timely and appropriate learning experiences. This view of growth and change underlies many of the psychosocial models of human development (e.g., Erikson, 1950, 1959). According to this "epigenetic perspective," the human organism essentially "unfolds" over time as developmental issues and choices ascend and recede at predictable points in the life-span. These points of time or "phases," each with a respective list of "age-appropriate tasks," evolve as individuals interact with important others in their psychosocial environments (e.g., family, school, workplace). For example, in American culture, establishing independent living arrangements, going away to college, starting a full-time job, and selecting a mate are typical developmental tasks associated with the transition from late adolescence to young adulthood (for most, between ages 18 and 22). Others' expectations relative to these tasks, as well as self-expectations, serve as both brakes and prods on behavior (Neugarten, 1968), at times admonishing individuals with a sense of urgency ("Isn't it about time you settle down and get a job?") and at other times warning that a person may not be quite ready yet for whatever appears on the horizon (e.g., retirement, independence, or a commitment of marriage). All of this suggests that timing is a critical factor in understanding the outcome of any educational opportunity. Simply put, people are most receptive to learning when they are ready developmentally to address the learning task at hand. For example, the experience of learning about self-interests, skills, and values is most powerful for a person when the task of becoming an independent, self-reliant adult is imminent. Conversely, learning associated with a task already completed, or one not yet encountered, such as identifying an entry-level job objective, does little to stimulate interest, motivation, or desire to pursue it further.

An implication of this proposition is that educational interventions are not likely to have a significant impact if they are untimely (i.e., too early or too late). In such cases, waiting for the right time to capitalize on a "teachable moment," or forfeiting an opportunity altogether by being too late, are perhaps the most appropriate strategies. Readiness to learn, develop, and grow is a function of timing.

Proposition 6: Development occurs as individuals respond to novel situations and tasks that challenge their current level or capacity. This proposition underscores the importance of challenge and response in the process of human development (Sanford, 1966). Quite different from the epigenetic view in the previous proposition, this "homeostatic" understanding of growth suggests that human beings intentionally seek and maintain a sense of stability, where preferences, choices, and tasks are extensions of the familiar and comfortable; in other words, individuals prefer and enjoy most doing what they already know how to do. When given the choice, they will choose what is compatible with and familiar to their current structures of understanding and competence. New situations threaten current stability, and due to the inevitable discomfort accompanying such experiences, they are usually resisted or avoided. A consequence of this perspective is the assumption that change and development of people entails exposure to the unfamiliar, in Sanford's (1966) words, situations "to which they cannot adapt with the use of devices already present" (p. 44), experiences that "upset the existing equilibrium, produce instability, [and] set in motion

activity leading to stabilization on a higher level" (p. 37). This view of change has been underscored more recently under the guise of "system theory" and "chaos theory," where unpredicted new levels of self-organization emerge from creative fluctuations in the free exchange of energy between an organism and its environment (Caple, 1987a, 1987b). Accordingly, disequilibrium rather than stability offers the most fertile condition for growth and development. One important implication of such views is that growth and change are inherently unsettling and perhaps even disturbing processes. Resistance, discomfort, and stress are to be expected as new challenges are introduced. A steady diet of the familiar, although satisfying and comforting, is rarely growth-producing.

Proposition 7: Development occurs as individuals evaluate a learning task to be sufficiently challenging to warrant change and sufficiently supportive to risk an unknown result. This proposition further articulates the essential processes of growth and development, underscoring the notion of developmental dissonance. Building upon Festinger's (1957) concepts of cognitive dissonance, Sanford's (1966) notions of challenge and support, and Rodger's (1991) integration of these perspectives in the context of person-environment interactions, this proposition suggests that, for development to occur, learning experiences must contain elements that are both unsettling as well as reassuring to individuals engaged in them. There is a potential range of dissonance, both supportive and challenging, that encourages a person to risk something new and, therefore, to develop a response at a higher level, employing skills, abilities, or ways of making meaning she or he never before exhibited. This range of opportunity has been labeled "developmental or optimal dissonance" (Rodgers, 1980, p. 41). The extent to which learning opportunities are developmentally dissonant is a matter of personal construction that, in turn, is usually a function of developmental level. For example, drawing from illustrations of developmental instruction in Widick and Simpson (1978), students, on the one hand, who hold "dualistic" assumptions about knowledge are challenged by multiple, conflicting perspectives moderated (i.e., supported) by higher degrees of structure in the learning environment. On the other hand, students who hold "relativistic" assumptions are challenged by learning environments requiring intellectual commitments moderated by lower degrees of structure. Failure to accurately gauge and provide appropriate levels of either dimension (challenge or support), according to this proposition, results in reinforcement of the individual's current assumptions and ways of making meaning (assimilation). To further illustrate, from the same example, high structure, in the absence of multiple perspectives, simply confirms the expectations of certainty held by the "dualist;" and low structure, in the absence of a challenge to make commitments of some sort, allows the "relativist" to exploit the freedom of multiple perspectives. In both cases, the individual simply reinterprets the learning environment in the context of assumptions already held and, thus, fails to change. Challenging and supportive elements are simultaneously required for change and development to occur.

Proposition 8: Development proceeds through qualitative and cyclical changes of increasing complexity. The nature of this proposition derives from both the cognitive-structural and psychosocial perspectives on human development. "Development" might be distinguished from "change" as more complex in nature and involving the achievement of qualitatively different and presumably more adequate degrees of integration. These degrees of integration are most often understood in the context of a hierachical sequence, where each step or level represents an inherently more complex structure and therefore reflects a greater degree of maturity. For example, from a cognitive-structural perspective (e.g., Kohlberg, 1969), how individuals resolve questions of fairness and justice proceeds from early levels of integration, involving the simplest reflections on power and fear of the consequences of an action (a "punishment and obedience orientation," in the parlance of Kohlberg's model), to more advanced levels with consideration for the interplay of self and society, adjudicated by a principled system of mutual rights and responsibilities (a perspective of "social cooperation"). This latter form of justification represents a qualitatively different and more advanced level of integration in that it is more complex, taking into consideration a greater number of concerns and issues than earlier forms. From Rest (1979) it is learned that these changes occur across levels simultaneously, as preferences for earlier forms of meaning recede

gradually and new forms ascend. Thus, evidence of "development" is apparent in new and integrated structures, higher consciousness and greater autonomy (Caple, 1987a, 1987b; Kuh, Whitt, & Shedd, 1987) involving multiple complex changes.

Chickering (1969) described the path of human development as a revolving course through cycles of differentiation and integration. Phases of "differentiation," where things previously seen as unitary are challenged by questions and insights of new subtleties and distinctions, yield to phases of "integration," when things previously seen as different are now seen as unitary. What may have appeared to an individual as an adequate resolution (or integration) of a particular issue at one time in his or her life may appear to that same individual at another point in time as simplistic and inadequate. For example, achieving autonomy (Chickering's third vector of development) for the first time may require leaving home, establishing a sense of independence, and making new friends in an unfamiliar place. At another point in the life cycle, that same issue of autonomy may express itself more complexly in purchasing a home or venturing into a new career or business with responsibility for support of a family or other dependents. In this case, the issue of autonomy remains essentially the same; however, its manifestations are different and more complex as development and maturity proceed. And so it is with other issues of human development, such as developing competence, managing emotions, establishing identity, freeing interpersonal relationships, and establishing purpose and integrity (Chickering & Reisser, 1993). This view of development underscores the importance of recurring, yet more complex, themes and issues throughout the lifespan. "Settling an issue" is only a temporary, situational resolution at one point in time, likely to be followed by subsequent resolutions of different quality and greater complexity.

Proposition 9: Development occurs as an interactive and dynamic process between persons and their environments. This proposition is grounded in Lewin's (1936) differential interactionist paradigm of human behavior. Two assumptions are important in this proposition. First, human development cannot be understood adequately by reference to individual human differences alone. Rather, it must be examined within the context of environmental differences as well. Second, it is assumed that although environments influence the characteristics of individuals, at the same time, individuals influence the nature and characteristics of their environments. Human development results from this dynamic process of mutual shaping and influence, an assumption that is central to the emergent view of student development (Kuh, Whitt, & Shedd, 1987). For example, the patterned stylistic differences discussed in Proposition 3 (e.g., Myers-Briggs Types or Holland Types) illustrate how various environments might exact differing responses from individuals, depending upon their characteristics, as well as how individuals of differing characteristics might influence the environment in different ways. A Holland "Realistic" type will likely respond to a quiet, introverted environment with a certain degree of comfort, because such an environment may reinforce that individual's preference for time alone dedicated to more introspective activities. That person's response will tend to reinforce the quiet, introverted characteristics of the setting. A "Social" type, on the other hand, due to individual preferences for more extroverted, people-oriented activities, may express displeasure with such an environment and proceed to organize it to encourage more social activities that have potential for reinforcing his or her outgoing nature. Thus, both individuals are influenced by the totality of their environment, and each, in turn, continues to shape various aspects of that environment.

In summary, development takes place at recurring points of personal readiness, when conditions of sufficient novelty and familiarity engage individuals to construct new forms of differing quality and greater complexity. This process is dynamic and a result of the interactive mutual shaping of persons and environments.

Influence of Campus Environments

In response to Parker, Widick, and Knefelkamp's (1978) third question ("How does the college environment influence student development?"), four propositions are articulated, each addressing respectively one of four different aspects influencing the nature and characteristics of a campus environment: (a) its natural and synthetic physical features; (b) the people who inhabit the environment; (c) the manner in which it is organized; and (d) the meaning that members of the campus environment attach to these aspects (i.e., the physical features, the inhabitants, and the organizational structures).

Proposition 10: Educational environments restrict and enable individuals by the form and function of their natural and synthetic physical characteristics. This proposition emerges from a wealth of material across a variety of fields. Concepts from diverse disciplines such as art and architecture (e.g., Dober, 1992; Gaines, 1991; Sommer, 1969), ecological psychology (e.g., Barker, 1968), and cultural anthropology (e.g., Moffatt, 1989) have contributed to an understanding of the college campus as a "place apart" (Stem, 1986), whose physical features interact with and influence a range of behaviors, attitudes, and outcomes relative to its educational mission. The knowledge base supporting this proposition underscores the importance of natural features, such as location, terrain, and climate; and synthetic features, such as architectural design, space, amenities, and distance. These features combine, through varying conditions of light, density, noise, temperature, air quality, and accessibility, to create a powerful influence on students' attraction to, satisfaction, and stability within a particular setting. From an intercampus perspective, for example, the natural wooded setting providing the environmental backdrop for a University of the Redlands may influence students to behave in ways very different (e.g., whether or not to walk about alone or in groups) from those at a University of Chicago, ensconced in the middle of a large urban metropolis. From an intracampus perspective, there's a different "feel" to the design and spatial arrangement of a 15-story, high-rise hall with 1200 residents, in comparison to a much smaller "house" arrangement where 15 students occupy a single floor structure. Likewise, a small, flexible seminar room presents a much different atmosphere than a tiered, theater-style lecture hall. Such features of the physical environment set broad limits on the phenomena that can occur in any given setting, making some behaviors more or less likely to occur (Michelson, 1970).

When considered in light of campus social systems (e.g., student groups, departments, living units, classes), this proposition gives rise to issues of facilities usage and control, human interaction, territoriality, privacy and personal space, community, isolation, noise, access, identity, and comfort. These issues, in turn, depending upon how they may or may not be resolved, are important for the quality of students' campus experiences and can serve as prohibitive or positive forces for development in students' lives (Strange, 1983).

Proposition 11: Educational environments exert a conforming influence through the collective, dominant characteristics of those who inhabit them. This proposition draws from many of the same models and theories discussed in Proposition 3 (e.g., Holland, 1973; Myers, 1980). Recognizing that individuals differ in the characteristic ways they approach a variety of tasks, Proposition 11 examines such differences from a human aggregate (or group) focus, asserting that environments are transmitted collectively through their inhabitants. The dominant features of any particular environment, therefore, are simply a reflection of the dominant characteristics of the people within that environment (Astin, 1962, 1968; Astin & Holland, 1961). Using descriptors from Holland's (1973) model, for example, "social" environments are characterized by a predominant number of social types, and "conventional" aggregates of individuals create characteristically "conventional" environments.

According to Holland (1973), human aggregates may be conceived of as highly "differentiated" (i.e., they are comprised of individuals primarily of one given type or characteristic such as enterprising) or "undifferentiated" (i.e., composed of individuals of many different types) and "consistent" (i.e., sharing a high degree of type similarity such as artistic and social) or "inconsistent" (i.e., having fewer similarities such as conventional and investigative). Highly differentiated and consistent aggregates are homogeneous in character and therefore exhibit a high degree of focus. The dynamics of human aggregates attract, satisfy, and retain individuals who are most similar in type to the dominant characteristics of those individuals comprising the aggregate. In other words, artistic individuals are attracted to, satisfied within, and retained more readily by artistic human aggregates. Conversely, individuals who are dissimilar to the dominant type are more likely to be repelled by, dissatisfied within, and rejected by a particular aggregate. Consequently, since human aggregates are more attractive to individuals congruent with the existing dominant type, they reinforce and accentuate their own characteristics over time. Individuals within the aggregate, in turn, are encouraged and rewarded for exhibiting those dominant characteristics and are discouraged from exhibiting dissimilar or incongruent characteristics. One implication of these dynamics is that, if attraction, satisfaction, and stability are to be maximized, congruence of persons and environments (human aggregates) must be achieved; and homogeneous aggregates are the most effective arrangement for facilitating such ends. The importance of this "person-environment fit" is reflected in a variety of policies and practices on most college campuses, where admissions and recruitment personnel search for the "right kind of student;" fraternity, sorority, and student organizations look for new members who will "fit in;" and academic and career advisors explore department majors or job placements that are most "compatible" with students' interests, values, and skills.

Proposition 12: Educational environments, as purposeful and goal directed settings, enable or restrict behavior by how they are organized. All educational environments, whether classrooms, academic departments, student groups, residence halls, or entire campuses, share characteristics of organized systems. In each of these settings, certain goals or outcomes are established (explicitly or implicitly) by participants and constituents; and these goals shape decisions about the use of various resources and strategies. To facilitate such decisions, it is common practice to "get organized" for purposes of establishing plans, rules, and guidelines of group functioning; for allocating resources; and for identifying those who will share authority and responsibility for making various substantive or procedural decisions (Etzioni, 1964). Thus, faculty develop syllabi to outline course goals and assignments; departments define procedural guidelines and degree requirements; student groups plan for and implement programs; residence life staff create structures for encouraging student participation and leadership; and campus administrators establish rules for effective and efficient use of limited resources.

How such systems are organized can be thought of as primarily "dynamic" in character, or "static" (Hage & Aiken, 1970). Dynamic environments respond to change; static environments tend to resist change. Although all organized systems contain elements of both, whether a system exhibits an overall dynamic or static pattern is a function of various organizational structures, such as the degree of centralization (how power is distributed) or formalization (the number and specificity of enforced rules) in a system. A highly formalized (i.e., having many rules) and centralized organization (i.e., power is highly concentrated in only a few participants) establishes a static pattern where the status quo is preserved, and innovation and opportunities for meaningful involvement of participants are discouraged or restricted. Dynamic organizations, maintained by lower degrees of centralization and formalization, exhibit characteristics of "self-organizing systems" as they evolve toward nonequilibrium (Caple, 1987b, p. 101), encouraging substantive involvement, responsibility, and creativity on the part of members. Providing such opportunities in organized educational environments offers an important key for stimulating students' growth and development (Astin, 1985; Strange, 1981, 1983).

Proposition 13: The effects of educational environments are a function of how members perceive and evaluate them. The notion that environments exert their influence through participants' perceptions forms the basis of this proposition. Environmental features are actively constructed or interpreted by members; thus, one person may evaluate a setting as "friendly," "warm," and "unrestricted," whereas another person may evaluate that same environment as "distant," "cool," and "confining." The importance of this distinction is that such perceptions are thought to be predictive of how individuals might likely respond to a given environment. Negative perceptions and interpretations are likely to contribute to dissatisfaction, instability, and the desire to leave a particular environment; positive perceptions are usually predictive of satisfaction, stability, and the desire to remain in an environment.

The constructs implicit in this proposition emerged from some of the earliest systematic studies of college students (e.g., Murray, 1938; Pace & Stem, 1958), where environments were understood in terms of "presses," inferred from consensual self-reports of participants' activities, which, in turn, encourage certain behaviors (e.g., studying quietly) or discourage others (e.g., playing loud music). Such "presses" are constructed by those within as well as those outside of the environment. The extent to which the dominant press of an environment corresponds to an individual's "need" (e.g., to study quietly) is presumed to be predictive of attraction to that environment, if outside, and satisfaction and sta-

bility, if within. When environmental press is congruent with individual need, growth is encouraged; a need-press mismatch is more likely to be growth inhibiting.

Within a similar but more recent line of inquiry, Moos (1979) constructed a model of social climates, or environmental personalities, which exert their influence on participants through relationship dimensions, personal growth and development dimensions, and system maintenance and change dimensions. The nature and quality of these dimensions become important as participants evaluate their expectations of environments, their perceptions of ideal environments, and their actual experiences with environments. Thus, individuals may expect a high level of relationship dimensions (e.g., emotional support and involvement of participants) in a particular environment, but find the reality discrepant with their expectations or ideals; in such cases, they are more likely to leave the environment. When environmental expectations, ideals, and realities are congruent, satisfaction and persistence in the environment is much more likely.

Last, this line of inquiry has been enriched with a focus on elements of organizational and institutional culture (Chaffee & Tierney, 1988; Kuh, 1993; Kuh & Whitt, 1988). From this perspective, campus cultures are social constructions (that is, they are invented, discovered, or developed) reflected in various cultural artifacts, including traditions, stories, ceremonies, history, myths, heroines and heroes, interactions among members, policies and practices, symbols, and mission and philosophy. The importance of these cultural artifacts is taught to new members as a means of integrating them into the environment and assisting them in interpreting and understanding the meaning of events and actions. Failure to understand or embrace key elements of campus culture may jeopardize participants' satisfaction or stability in that setting. Like the other two models discussed in the context of this proposition, need-press and social climate, models of institutional culture underscore the importance of examining environments from the perspective and meaning of the members of those environments. Participants' perceptions and constructions are an important source of information for designing responsive educational environments, and educators must be particularly sensitive to any discrepancies between their views of institutional environments and those of students.

In summary, these four propositions suggest that the college environment positively influences student development through physical features that are enabling; aggregate characteristics that are attractive, satisfying, and reinforcing; and organizational structures that are open and dynamic. However, the nature of the effects of these campus environment features is a function of the meanings attached to them and sustained by participant members.

The Goals of Education

In response to the fourth question posed by Parker, Widick, and Knefelkamp (1978) ("Toward what ends should development in college be directed?"), a final proposition is considered, emphasizing the axiological (value) dimensions of education.

Proposition 14: Educational systems are embedded in various contexts of select values and assumptions that shape their expectations, processes, and outcomes. Education by its very nature is both a purveyor and process of culture. In that sense, all educational systems embrace certain values and assumptions (to the exclusion of others) thought to be important in a particular culture, and, on that basis, establish goals (explicit or implicit) for purposes of directing educational programs and interventions. Educational success is gauged then by how well those goals (or goals that emerge in the process) are achieved. American higher education, and its orientation toward student development discussed here, is certainly not an exception to this phenomenon of cultural embedment. For example, the preoccupation with individual rights and practicality of results dominant in American culture lends itself to a higher education system that places increasing value on consumer rights and expectations; and that frequently underscores education as a means to an end-more specifically, to a job or career.

In American culture, definitions of growth and maturity, key constructs in any student development model, are also embedded in a premium placed on independence and autonomy as signs of having reached an advanced level of development. This stands in sharp contrast to Eastern cultures, for example, where individual goals and achievement are usually superseded by group or community needs as the more desirable value. In a similar fashion, the emphasis on maintenance of harmony in Eastern societies may preempt the exercise of candor and directness (Garner, 1989), qualities that might be more appreciated in American society. Such differences map contrasting directions of what it means to be an educated person and the manner in which the knowledge and skills associated with such a state are assessed.

Cultural values also establish parameters for the means and methods of education. For example, Lipset (1989) and Skolnik (1990) distinguished cultural differences between Canada and the United States, noting that the United States is a product of revolution whereas Canada emerged from a process of counterrevolution. Consequently, the United States "devolved a political culture characterized by antistatism, individualism, populism, and egalitarianism," in contrast to Canada, which has developed as a "more class-conscious, elitist, law-abiding, statist, collectivity-oriented, and particularistic [society]" (Skolnik, 1990, p. 82). Thus, Canadian universities tend to be more elitist in their orientation, with less attention being given to how residential communities or cocurricular activities on campus can serve in the education of students. The character of the U. S. system is more egalitarian, at least in its espoused values, and, consistent with its more holistic view of students, is much more likely to include on-campus residential experiences and cocurricular activities as important components of campus culture.

The importance of this proposition is that educators must be more observant of the values and assumptions that form the context of their policies and practices. Especially as they attempt to encourage a more global, multicultural perspective among students, educators must also increase their sensitivity to a wider range of assumptions and values about the "educated person" and the means by which such a goal can be achieved. Heightened awareness in that respect can yield a greater range of options for students. The student development models addressed in these propositions represent a limited context of values and assumptions, primarily embedded in Western rationalism and American pragmatism. There are other legitimate contexts that warrant thoughtful consideration as well.

Summary and Conclusion

I have argued previously (Strange, 1983; Strange & King, 1990) that what distinguishes professionals at work is their ability to bring reasoned explanations, grounded in evidence, to the phenomena about which they claim expertise. These explanations, in turn, become the basis for implementing action, in the form of various policies, practices, and interventions; and they serve as a framework for evaluating the effectiveness of such action. Student affairs professionals bring to the academy an espoused expertise on students' development, and their explanations are derived from theories about how students learn, grow, and mature during the college experience. Over the past several decades, considerable insight into these phenomena has been gained, the core of which I have attempted to capture here in propositional form under the rubric of student development.

Is this knowledge base sufficient for a comprehensive explanation of how students develop? What might be the points of contradiction and redundancy here, and are there gaps where further conceptual work is warranted? What researchable questions are suggested by these propositions? Is there adequate evidence to support these claims? What is the import of these claims for what is required of students as reflected in accepted educational policies and codes? Are the expectations of educators appropriate and sufficient in light of these propositions? What is the meaning of this student development framework for how professionals on campus go about their work? Do these claims about student growth and development, and about campus environments, support the continuance of current programs and practices? Do they call into question others that may have been long accepted without challenge? These are illustrative of questions that map an agenda to be pursued if a new level of understanding of the power of higher education to effect change in students' lives is to be realized. I have provided the foil here; now I turn to my colleagues for further insight. There is much yet to be mined.

Note

The author acknowledges with appreciation reviews and comments on drafts of this manuscript by Robert Brown, George Kuh, and Louis Stamatakos. Earlier versions of this paper were presented at the annual meetings of the American College Personnel Association, Kansas City, March, 1993 and the Association for the Study of Higher Education, Pittsburgh, November, 1993.

References

American Council on Education. (1937). *The student personnel point of view* (American Council on Education Studies, Series 1, Vol. 1, No. 3). Washington, DC: Author.

American Council on Education, Committee on Student Personnel Work. (E. G. Williamson, Chair). (1949). *The student personnel point of view* (rev. ed.) (American Council on Education Studies, Series 6, No. 13). Washington, DC: Author.

Astin, A. W. (1962). An empirical characterization of higher educational institutions. *Journal of Educational Psychology, 53,* 224–235.

Astin, A. W. (1968). *The college environment.* Washington, DC: American Council on Education.

Astin, A. W. (1985). *Achieving educational excellence: A critical assessment of priorities and practices in higher education.* San Francisco: Jossey-Bass.

Astin, A. W., & Holland, J. L. (1961). The environmental assessment technique: A way to measure college environments. *Journal of Educational Psychology, 52,* 308–316.

Atkinson, D., Morten, G., & Sue, D. (1983). *Counseling American minorities: A cross-cultural perspective* (2nd ed.). Dubuque, IA: Brown.

Banning, J. H. (Ed.). (1978). *Campus ecology: A perspective for student affairs* (National Association of Student Personnel Administrators Monograph). Cincinnati, OH: National Association of Student Personnel Administrators.

Barker, R. G. (1968). *Ecological psychology: Concepts and methods for studying the environment of human behavior.* Stanford, CA: Stanford University Press.

Belenky, M. F., Clinchy, B. M., Goldberger, N. R., & Tarule, J. M. (1986). *Women's ways of knowing: The development of self, voice, and mind.* New York: Basic Books.

Bloland, P. A., Stamatakos, L. C., & Rogers, R. R. (1994). *Reform in student affairs: A critique of student development.* Greensboro, NC: ERIC Counseling and Student Services Clearinghouse.

Bowen, H. R. (1977). *Investment in learning: The individual and social value of American higher education.* San Francisco: Jossey-Bass.

Brown, R. D. (1972). *Student development in tomorrow's higher education: A return to the academy.* Washington, DC: American College Personnel Association.

Caple, R. B. (1987a). The change process in developmental theory: A self-organization paradigm, part 1. *Journal of College Student Personnel, 28*, 4–11.

Caple, R. B. (1987b). The change process in developmental theory: A self-organization paradigm, part 1. *Journal of College Student Personnel, 28*, 100–104.

Cass, V. C. (1979). Homosexual identity formation: A theoretical model. *Journal of Homosexuality, 4*, 219–235.

Cass, V. C. (1984). Homosexual identity formation: Testing a theoretical model. *Journal of Sex Research, 20*, 143–167.

Chaffee, E. E., & Tierney, W. G. (1988). *Collegiate culture and leadership strategies.* New York: American Council on Education/Macmillan.

Chickering, A. W. (1969). *Education and identity.* San Francisco: Jossey-Bass.

Chickering, A. W., & Associates. (1981). *Modern American college.* San Francisco: Jossey-Bass.

Chickering, A. W., & Reisser, L. (1993). *Education and identity* (2nd ed.). San Francisco: Jossey-Bass.

Commission on Professional Development of COSPA. (1975). Student development services in post secondary education. *Journal of College Student Personnel, 16*, 524–528.

Cross, K. P. (1971). *Beyond the open door: New students to higher education.* San Francisco: Jossey-Bass.

Cross, K. P. (1976). *Accent on learning: Improving instruction and reshaping the curriculum.* San Francisco: Jossey-Bass.

Cross, K. P. (1981). *Adults as learners.* San Francisco: Jossey-Bass.

Dober, R. P. (1992). *Campus design.* New York: Wiley.

Erikson, E. H. (1950). Growth and crisis of the healthy personality. In M.J.E. Senn (Ed.), *Symposium on the healthy personality,* Supplement II (pp. 91–146). New York: Josiah Macy, Jr., Foundation.

Erikson, E. H. (1959). *Identity and the life cycle* (Psychological Issues Monograph 1). New York: International Universities Press.

Erikson, E. H. (1963). *Childhood and society.* New York: Norton.

Etzioni, A. (1964). *Modern organizations.* Englewood Cliffs, NJ: Prentice-Hall.

Evans, N. J., & Wall, V. A. (1991). *Beyond tolerance: Gays, lesbians and bisexuals on campus.* Alexandria, VA: American College Personnel Association.

Feldman, K. A., & Newcomb, T. M. (1969). *The impact of college on students. Volume 1: An analysis of four decades of research.* San Francisco: Jossey-Bass.

Festinger, L. (1957). *A theory of cognitive dissonance.* New York: Row, Peterson.

Gaines, T. A. (1991). *The campus as a work of art.* New York: Preager.

Garner, B. (1989). Southeast Asian culture and classroom culture. *Journal of College Teaching, 37,* 127–130.

Gilligan, C. (1982). *In a different voice: Psychological theory and women's development.* Cambridge, MA: Harvard University Press.

Gould, R. (1978). *Transformations: Growth and change in adult life.* New York: Simon & Schuster.

Hage, J., & Aiken, M. (1970). *Social change in complex organizations.* New York: Random House.

Havighurst, R. J. (1972). *Developmental tasks and education* (3rd ed.). New York: McKay.

Heath, D. H. (1968). *Growing up in college.* San Francisco: Jossey-Bass.

Heilweil, M. (1973). The influence of dormitory architecture on residence behavior. *Environment and Behavior, 5,* 377–412.

Hofstadter, R. (1955). *Academic freedom in the age of the college.* New York: Columbia University Press.

Holland, J. L. (1973). *Making vocational choices: A theory of careers.* Englewood Cliffs, NJ: Prentice Hall.

Josselson, R. (1987). *Finding herself: Pathways to identity development in women.* San Francisco: Jossey-Bass.

Keniston, K. (1965). Social change and youth in America. In E. H. Erikson (Ed.), *The challenge of youth* (pp. 191–222). New York: Doubleday.

King, P. M., & Kitchener, K. S. (1994). *Developing reflective judgment: Understanding and promoting intellectual growth and critical thinking in adolescents and adults.* San Francisco: Jossey-Bass.

Knefelkamp, L. L. (1981, March). *Future promises.* Keynote speech presented at the annual meeting of the American College Personnel Association, Cincinnati, OH.

Knefelkamp, L. L. (1984, April). *Renewal of intellect.* Keynote speech presented at the annual meeting of the American College Personnel Association, Baltimore, MD.

Knefelkamp, L. L. (1986, April). *Generativity.* Keynote speech presented at the annual meeting of the American College Personnel Association, New Orleans, LA.

Knefelkamp, L. L., Widick, C., & Parker, C. A. (Eds.). (1978). *Applying new developmental findings* (New directions in student services, no. 4). San Francisco: Jossey-Bass.

Kohlberg, L. (1969). Stage and sequence: The cognitive developmental approach to socialization. In D. Goslin (Ed.), *Handbook of socialization theory and research* (pp. 347–480). Chicago: Rand McNally.

Kolb, D. (1983). *Experiential learning: Experience as the source of learning and development.* Englewood Cliffs, NJ: Prentice-Hall.

Kuh, G. D. (Ed.). (1993). *Cultural perspectives in student affairs work.* Washington, DC: American College Personnel Association.

Kuh, G. D., Schuh, J. H., Whitt, E. J., Andreas, R. E., Lyons, J. W., Strange, C. C., Krehbiel, L. E., & MacKay, K. A. (1991). *Involving colleges: Encouraging student learning and personal development through out of-class experiences.* San Francisco: Jossey-Bass.

Kuh, G. D., Shedd, J. D., & Whitt, E. J. (1987). Student affairs and liberal education: Unrecognized (and unappreciated) common law partners. *Journal of College Student Personnel, 28,* 252–60.

Kuh, G. D., & Whitt, E. J. (1988). *The invisible tapestry: Cultures in American colleges and universities* (ASHE-ERIC Higher Education Report Series, No. 1). Washington, DC: Association for the Study of Higher Education.

Kuh, G. D., Whitt, E. J., & Shedd, J. D. (1987). *Student affairs work, 2001: A paradigmatic odyssey.* Alexandria, VA: American College Personnel Association.

Levinson, D. J., & Associates. (1978). *Seasons of a man's life.* New York: Ballantine.

Lewin, K. (1936). *Principles of topological psychology.* New York: McGraw-Hill.

Lipset, S. M. (1989). *Continental divide: The values and institutions of the United States and Canada.* Toronto: C. D. Howe Institute.

Mayhew, L. B. (1977). *The legacy of the seventies.* San Francisco: Jossey-Bass.

Metzger, W. P. (1955). *Academic freedom in the age of the university.* New York: Columbia University Press.

Michelson, W. (1970). *Man and his urban environment: A sociological approach.* Reading, MA: Addison-Wesley.

Moffatt, M. (1989). *Coming of age in New Jersey: College and American culture.* New Brunswick, NJ: Rutgers University Press.

Moore, L. V. (Ed.). (1990). Evolving theoretical perspectives on students. *New Directions for Student Services, No. 51.* San Francisco: Jossey-Bass.

Moos, R. H. (1979). *Evaluating educational environments.* San Francisco: Jossey-Bass.

Morrill, W., Hurst, J., & Oetting, E. (1980). *Dimensions of intervention for student development.* New York: Wiley.

Murray, H. (1938). *Exploration in personality.* New York: Oxford University Press.

Myers, I. B. (1980). *Gifts differing.* Palo Alto, CA: Consulting Psychologists Press.

Neugarten, B. L. (1968). Adult personality: Toward a psychology of the life cycle. In B. L. Neugarten (Ed.), *Middle age and aging* (pp. 137–147). Chicago: University of Chicago Press.

Newman, J. H. (1973). *The idea of a university.* Westminster, MD: Christian Classics.

Pace, C. R. (1984). *Measuring the quality of college student experiences: An account of the development and use of The College Student Experiences Questionnaire.* Los Angeles: University of California Higher Education Research Institute.

Pace, C. R., & Stern, G. G. (1958). An approach to the measurement of psychological characteristics of college environments. *Journal of Educational Psychology, 49,* 269–277.

Parker, C. A. (Ed.). (1978). *Encouraging development in college students.* Minneapolis: University of Minnesota Press.

Parker, C., Widick, C., & Knefelkamp, L. (Eds.). (1978). Editors' notes: Why bother with theory. In L. L. Knefelkamp, C. Widick, & C. A. Parker (Eds.), *Applying new developmental findings* (New directions in student services, no. 4). San Francisco: Jossey-Bass.

Pascarella, E. T., & Terenzini, P. T. (1991). *How college affects students.* San Francisco: Jossey-Bass.

Perry, W. G. (1970). *Forms of intellectual and ethical development in the college years: A scheme.* New York: Holt, Rinehart, & Winston.

Rest, J. R. (1979). *Development in judging moral issues.* Minneapolis: University of Minnesota Press.

Rodgers, R. F. (1980). Theories underlying student development. In D. G. Creamer (Ed.), *Student development in higher education: Theories, practices & future directions* (ACPA Media Publication Number 27). Alexandria, VA: ACPA Media.

Rodgers, R. F. (1991). Using theory in practice in student affairs. In T. K. Miller, R. B. Winston, Jr., & Associates (Eds.), *Administration and leadership in student affairs: Actualizing student development in higher education* (pp. 203–251). Muncie, IN: Accelerated Development.

Sanford, N. (Ed.). (1962). *The American college: A psychological and social interpretation of the higher learning.* New York: Wiley.

Sanford, N. (1966). *Self and society: Social change and individual development.* New York: Atherton Press.

Skolnik, M. L. (1990). Lipset's *Continental Divide* and the ideological basis for differences in higher education between Canada and United States. *Canadian Journal of Higher Education, XX-2,* 81–93.

Sommer, R. (1969). *Personal space.* Englewood Cliffs, NJ: Prentice-Hall.

Stern, R. A. (1986). *Pride of place: Building the American dream.* New York: Houghton Mifflin.

Strange, C. (1981). Organizational barriers to student development. *National Association of Student Personnel Administrators Journal, 19,* 12–20.

Strange, C. (1983). Human development theory and administrative practice in student affairs: Ships passing in the daylight? *National Association of Student Personnel Administrators Journal, 21,* 2–8.

Strange, C., & King, P. (1990). The professional practice of student development. In D. Creamer & Associates (Eds.), *College student development: Theory and practice for the 1990's* (pp. 9–24; ACPA Media Publication No. 49). Alexandria, VA: American College Personnel Association,

The Committee on the Student in Higher Education. (1968). *The student in higher education.* New Haven, CT: The Hazen Foundation.

Trent, J. W. (1966). Encouragement of student development. *NASPA Journal, 4,* 35–45.

Trent, J. W., & Medsker, L. L. (1968). *Beyond high school.* San Francisco: Jossey-Bass.

Walters, J. E. (1931). *Student development: How to make the most of college life.* New York: Pitman.

Walters, J. E. (1935). *Individualizing education by means of applied personnel procedures.* New York: Wiley.

White, R. W. (1958). *Lives in progress.* New York: Dryden Press.

Widick, C., & Simpson, D. (1978). Developmental concepts in college instruction. In C. A. Parker (Ed.), *Encouraging development in college students* (pp. 27–59). Minneapolis: University of Minnesota Press.

Winston, R. B., Jr., Miller, T. K., & Prince, J. S. (1979). *Student Development Task Inventory* (2nd ed.). Athens, GA: Student Development Associates.

Witkin, H. A. (1976). Cognitive style in academic performance and in teacher-student relations. In S. Messick & Associates (Eds.), *Individuality in learning* (pp. 38–89). San Francisco: Jossey-Bass.

CHAPTER 3

THEORIES OF COLLEGE STUDENT DEVELOPMENT: SEQUENCES AND CONSEQUENCES

PATRICIA M. KING

This article evaluates the concept of student development from the perspective of the adequacy of its theoretical knowledge base and with reference to the 14 specific propositions about student development identified by Strange (1994).

This series of articles discusses the major tenets of student development outlined by Strange in this issue of the Journal of College Student Development as 14 propositions. The following four articles include critiques of the theoretical knowledge base (the current article), research on student development (by Terenzini), as well as the implications of the major tenets of student development for policy and practice (articles by Coomes and Upcraft, respectively). These articles are designed to stimulate the thinking, understanding, and refinement of the concept of student development, an idea that has been variously described as powerful (Parker, 1978), as essential (Strange, 1994), and as a concept that offers a unifying educational purpose (Chickering, 1981), but also as "a slippery term" (Bloland, Stamatakos, & Rogers, 1994, p. vii) that reflects "an eclectic melange of concepts without theory" (Bloland, Stamatakos, & Rogers, 1994, p. 35).

How can one concept be at once essential and of questionable merit? Concepts that are not only interpreted but defined differently are certainly candidates for such a wide range of descriptions. But as Flavell (1977) has noted, the process of defining and refining concepts is seldom clean and straightforward:

> The really interesting concepts of this world have the nasty habit of avoiding our most determined attempts to pin them down, to make them say something definite and make them stick to it. Their meanings perversely remain multiple, ambiguous, imprecise, and above all unstable and open—open to argument and disagreement, to sometimes drastic reformulation and redefinition, and to the introduction of new and often unsettling concept instances and examples. It is perhaps not a bad thing that our prize concepts have this kind of complexity and instability (some might call it richness and creativity). In any event, they do seem to have these properties, and therefore we would be wise not to expend too much of our time and energy trying to fix them in formal definition. (p. 1)

The concept of student development is one of these really interesting concepts: it is complex and rich, has multiple meanings, is open to argument and disagreement, and connotes a variety of ideas and images to those who use (or avoid) the term. For example, as Miller and Winston (1991) have noted, the term student development is used interchangeably to refer to the process of growth and change, the outcome of this process, intervention strategies designed to promote development, and student services administrative offices. Use of the term in these ways also varies across professional preparation programs. Some taxonomies of student development theories differentiate person-environment interaction theories from cognitive developmental theories, even though the latter are explicitly grounded in a Piagetian interactionist paradigm. Further, there is no one set of theories or theoretical assumptions that constitute the student development knowledge base. In light of such inconsistencies, it is not surprising that the term is used to mean so many things.

However, even when referring only to descriptions of the process of growth and change in young adults (the aspect most commonly addressed by theories of student development), there is still room for disagreement and misunderstanding. This is in part because the concept is multifaceted and the sophistication of the theory and research is variable across facets. Heeding Flavell's (1977) advice, it is better to think of student development using images that connote the complexity and richness of the concept. For example, it may be helpful to think of a student's growth and development as a kaleidoscope or mosaic of changing skills, attitudes, beliefs, and understandings, acknowledging that each student represents a slightly different set of shapes, colors, and textures that constitute his or her own personal kaleidoscope, each with its own specific set of developmental attributes. With new experiences, these attributes shift (whether slightly or dramatically), and the picture in the individual's kaleidoscope changes accordingly. A more narrow or precise approach may not do justice to the richness of this "really interesting" concept.

The purpose of this article is to evaluate the concept of student development from the perspective of the adequacy of its theoretical knowledge base. In this article the four major questions posed by Parker, Widick, and Knefelkamp (1978) will be used as an organizing framework (they serve as the major headings); the 14 specific propositions about student development identified by Strange (1994) are referenced within each major question. Departing from the order of this framework, however, I will address the last question first, since it has the strongest implications for student learning and development and for how a person answers the other three questions.

Toward What Ends Should Development in College Be Directed?

What should graduates of our colleges and universities understand and be able to do? Several excellent summaries of collegiate goals for students are available (Association of American Colleges, 1985, 1991; Bok, 1986; Bowen, 1980; Newman, 1852/1973; Rosovsky, 1990). Such lists are typically grounded in the needs of American society at the time they were written or reflect the values and priorities of the author(s). Although some attributes of an educated person are clearly applicable across generations (such as the attributes of education identified by Cardinal Newman in 1852), current societal and international needs require the attention of people who bring different kinds of knowledge and skills. Schneider and Green (1993) raised the following questions about the kinds of skills necessary to address the complex problems of the 21st Century:

- What should an educated person know to function as a contributing member of our democratic, diverse, technologically advanced society?

- What must the college graduate know to participate in the global community in the fast-approaching twenty-first century?

- What intellectual capacities are required for full participation in both our national life and the global community?

- What values are required for this participation?

- What kinds of learning will help students develop the needed knowledge, intellectual capacities, and values?

- How can we impart to graduates the ability to continue their learning across the life span? (p. 1)

To answer these questions requires a forward-looking, "wide lens" view of the future of colleges and universities. Implementing curricula, programs, and services that assist students to develop these skills and knowledge will require broader, more comprehensive models of student development than currently exist. These are attributes educators (faculty and student affairs staff alike) need to at least know about, and preferably personally demonstrate to students if they are to help fulfill this educational mission. Accordingly, they should be able to identify which attributes of an educated person their classes, programs, and services are designed to enhance.

Boyer's (1987) critique of the American collegiate experience offers another helpful resource for understanding the purposes of the collegiate curriculum, broadly defined, and for answering the "Toward what ends . . . ?" question. He noted two common types of goals associated with attending college: individual goals (developing skills, preparing for careers) and community goals (becoming an effective citizen of a democracy). The focus of many student development theories and of many higher education mission statements is on individual development. Many colleges, their faculty, and staff rather effectively communicate expectations regarding independence, self-reliance, self-motivation, autonomy, personal responsibility, and other individual traits. Much theoretical attention has also been given to the development of these attributes.

Much less attention has been given to the community-related goals (for example, how subgroups on campus form and dissolve, how individuals learn to take responsibility within communities, how peer pressure is created, how students learn when and how to resist it). Many students seem more interested in and adept at learning how to "work the system so it works for me" than at creating and using social and institutional systems for the common good. However, the increase among entering freshmen interested in promoting racial understanding and in influencing social values is a refreshing antidote to this trend (Dey, Astin, & Korn, 1991).

Colleges appear to be less effective in communicating the more community-oriented goals of interdependence and altruism, creating just and caring communities, showing compassion and respect for all students (or the negative effects of selfish or self-serving behavior), being productive, responsible, honest, and compassionate members of many communities, teaching that being a part of a community requires some degree of involvement and positive participation, and demonstrating that making individual sacrifices is sometimes necessary for the good of the community. Power, Higgins, and Kohlberg (1989) offer a fine summary of research and other resources on moral communities and moral education for educators interested in this important topic.

Educational goals for college students and models of student development need to go beyond the development of individually-oriented knowledge and skills to the development of abilities that directly affect how students contribute to the communities of which they are a part—from families, friends, organizations, and colleges, to towns, nations, and international communities. The need for colleges to focus their attention on communities may be a result of the Eurocentric foundation of the dominant culture in the United States and the changing demographic characteristics of college students. As Jones (1990) has pointed out, the Eurocentric perspective is the only major U.S. cultural perspective that focuses on individual values rather than collateral values; in the latter, "people are seen as individuals and also as members of many groups and subgroups; they are independent and dependent at the same time" (p. 64). This collateral perspective is found among Asian/Pacific Americans, American Indians, African Americans, and Hispanic Americans, whose cultural experiences and values offer many insights for fostering community values on college campuses, as well as for preparing students to live and work effectively in a multicultural society.

Determining educational goals for today's students requires deciding what it means to be an educated person at the end of the 20th Century. Of course, the definition of an educated person differs across contexts and institutional missions and the values of a given institution, as noted in Proposition 14. These assumptions, whether held explicitly or implicitly, affect the choice of what knowledge, skills, and attitudes to foster in promoting student learning and development, and of how to do so. They also affect the choice of which desired college outcomes to assess. In other words, the way a college or university answers this major question conveys the educational values it purports to engender and encourage.

Who Is the College Student in Developmental Terms?

Despite the importance of understanding the developmental characteristics of college students, it should first be acknowledged that the term "the college student" is simply an editorial convenience: there is no such entity as the college student, which suggests a degree of uniformity that simply does not exist. A more precise approach to determining which characteristics of developing human beings merit attention for descriptive purposes would be to ask: "What are the developmental characteristics of college students, and do they differ for relevant student subgroups?"

A brief note about the nature of developmental change is in order before proceeding further. Developmental changes, such as those many student development theories attempt to describe, are typically changes that are assumed to serve an adaptive function: they enable the individual to demonstrate not just different skills, but more adequate skills; they reflect not just a different perspective, but a more mature perspective. Developmental changes are characterized by greater complexity, seen through differentiation (e.g., being able to recognize several components within a problem or a perspective) and integration (seeing how those pieces fit back together again in a way that results in greater meaning or a more complete picture).

Just as increasing differentiation and integration reflects students' increasing maturity and complexity, these attributes also reflect the evolution of the student development knowledge base. An example of increasing differentiation may be seen in the available descriptions of identity development. In the early 1970s, Erikson's (1968) concept of identity development and his developmental stages were differentiated from two related ideas, self-concept and self-esteem. More than 20 years later, there are separate models for specific aspects of identity: sexual identity (Cass, 1979, 1984), cultural/ethnic identity (Helms, 1990; Nagasawa & Espinosa, 1992; Parham & Helms, 1981; Sue, 1981), women's identity (Baker-Miller, 1986; Gilligan, 1989; Josselson, 1987; Schaef, 1981), and even ethical identity (Noddings, 1984).

A second example of increasing differentiation in the student development knowledge base may be found in the domain of moral development. In the early 1970s, the major approaches to the study of morality were behaviorist, Freudian, and cognitive-developmental. Now there is a new model of the major aspects of morality that subsumes these prior theoretical approaches, Rest's (1983, 1984) Four-Component Model of the psychology of morality, which helps account for previously discrepant or contradictory findings. (This model will be discussed further below.)

An increasing integration of the knowledge base may also be seen in the heightened awareness and understanding of ways various aspects of development interact with each other (Kitchener, 1982). For example, several studies have shown that progress or advancement in one area, such as intellectual development, may facilitate development in another area, such as moral or identity development (Glatfelter, 1982; King & Kitchener, 1994; King, Kitchener, Wood, & Davison, 1989; Kitchener, King, Davison, Parker, & Wood, 1984; Polkosnik & Winston, 1989; Wood, 1993). As Rest (1983) noted, the successful resolution of thorny ethical issues requires moral sensitivity, complex reasoning skills, the willingness to select moral values over other competing values, and the ego strength to ask the tough questions and "do the right thing." Creativity in framing an ethical response that fits the given context is also often required (Welfel, 1990). Clearly, there is a need for greater understanding about these interrelationships and for new theoretical models (a point noted by Brown & Barr, 1990).

One of the great contributions of the student development literature is that it addresses issues of individual differences in students (Propositions 1, 2, 3, and 4). Although there is nothing new about this idea for student affairs professionals (it served as a central tenet of the 1937 Student Personnel Point of View, American Council on Education, 1937), the importance of this sensitivity cannot be overstated. Respecting individual differences is a central educational value (Proposition 14), and many assumptions about development are grounded in the acknowledgment of and appreciation for individual differences.

In this regard, the knowledge base on college students has also become increasingly differentiated, as exemplified by the increasing attention during the past decade to issues of race and gender when describing, measuring, and attempting to enhance students' development. But just as the appreciation of individual differences is important (e.g., *differences within* subgroups), so is the appreciation of similarities between individuals (e.g., *similarities across* subgroups). For example, even though men and women are stereotypically categorized as using "thinking" and "feeling" orientations, respectively, about 40% of men who have taken the Myers-Briggs Typology Inventory (Myers &

McCaulley, 1987) use a "feeling" orientation, and a comparable percentage of women use a "thinking" orientation. In other words, although sensitivity to gender differences is important, it is just as important not to overgeneralize. In this example, gender by itself is not a good predictor of Myers-Briggs type.

Consider, too, the question of gender differences in moral development, which has received a great deal of attention in the last 20 years and has provided fertile soil for the growth of new conceptual, methodological, and empirical insights. For example, gender differences are common (Brabeck, 1983) in the aspect of moral development called "moral sensitivity," which includes recognizing the moral dimension in a problem and showing empathy for another (Rest, 1983, 1984). By contrast, in the aspect of moral development called "moral reasoning" (the aspect described in Kohlberg's [1989] theory of moral development), gender differences are minimal: one-half of one percent of the variance in moral judgment is attributable to gender. The effect of education is 250 times more powerful than this (Rest, 1986). Are there gender differences in morality? With more differentiated theoretical models, it is now clear that the answer to this question depends on the aspect of morality being considered. With this clearer picture of the various components of morality, it is incumbent upon educators and researchers to qualify their responses and generalizations accordingly. Doing so will acknowledge similarities among the differences and may dissuade generalizations of widespread differences where they only exist in part.

By the same token, many student development theories have been criticized as "potentially ethnocentric, sexist, and culturally biased in origin" (Garland & Grace, 1993, p. 85). As constructivist theorists from Baldwin (1902) and Piaget (1937) to von Glaserfeld (1984) and Guba and Lincoln (1990) have noted, humans actively create their own particular reality. (For an introduction to the constructivist developmental approach, see Hayes, 1994.) So in this sense, some degree of "bias" (or how a particular theorist creates meaning from experience and forms a perspective) is to be expected. However, "bias" understood as inappropriate generalizations from one subgroup to another is more problematic. Theories or models that are developed from or normed on one population may or may not provide adequate descriptors for other populations. Making this determination requires informed reflection. The presumption of theoretical inadequacy is just as "biased" as the presumption of theoretical generalizability. Although researchers and practitioners alike are wise to recognize the potential for inappropriate generalizations (and there are good reasons to be cautious), they also are wise to recognize the potential for similarities across subgroups and to take note of appropriate points of overlap.

Although it is helpful to identify differences in subgroups (especially ethnic/cultural subgroups that have not received adequate attention in the college student literature), it is also important to move beyond the obvious and visible categories of race, gender, and age in understanding differences. Educators and researchers alike should think about student differences using less visible categories (e.g., learning styles and preferences, skills mastered, experiences with a handicapping condition, motivation for education, etc.). I worry that our collective emphasis on subgroup differences has served to downplay the many common human characteristics that can serve to pull together people from different cultures. For example, people of many different backgrounds share basic needs: the need to be loved; to matter to someone (Schlossberg, Lynch, & Chickering, 1989); to feed, protect, and educate their children; and to celebrate important family or cultural events. Providing aid to victims of natural disasters around the world and developing an AIDS vaccine are examples of responses to people's common vulnerabilities and illustrate the need to work together cooperatively toward a common end.

Recent international events show the negative side of people's common characteristics: territoriality, the resolution of ethnic conflict through violence, and the debilitating effects of alcohol and drug abuse that are not limited to the people of one nation, one cultural group, one race, or one gender. These are things people have in common, and that require a collective effort.

As educators and researchers attempt to better answer the question, "What are the developmental characteristics of college students?" I suggest the following:

- be as explicit about students' common characteristics as their differences;

- recognize the limitations of personal experiences when trying to understand others' experiences;

- look at a broad cross-section of many different types of students (not just the common student subgroups); and

- in doing so, do not rely solely on the familiar and visible categories of differences (gender, race, age), nor solely on theories that are limited to traditional-age college students.

As Garland and Grace (1993) have noted, "Students mirror a changing society through the characteristics they bring to campus" (p. 34). In other words, "the college student" changes as society changes. This insight provides yet another reason to continue to ask whether a given theory of student development is appropriate for a given group of students and to develop models that are sensitive to the relevant differences between student groups (e.g., how one interacts with the dominant culture and how this affects a student's transition to college).

How Does Development Occur?

How does development toward greater maturity, content mastery, and skill acquisition and refinement take place? In discussing factors that affect cognitive development, Flavell (1977) raised a series of questions that are quite relevant for understanding how student development occurs:

What factors or variables play what roles in influencing the nature, rates of growth, and ultimate adult level of various forms of knowledge and cognitive ability? Possible variables here include: hereditary and maturational factors; diverse forms of social and nonsocial experience; developmental principles, processes, or mechanisms, such as differentiation, coordination, integration, and equilibrium. . . . Experience is obviously very important in the child's cognitive evolution, but how shall we conceptualize experience and its developmental effects? . . . More generally, how shall we think about the "processes" of cognitive growth, those events taking place in the child's mind which cause his mind to exhibit developmental changes? . . . In sum, how and to what extent can we explain the various changes we may have diagnosed? (p. 231)

The question of how development occurs is of particular interest to educators, since understanding the process of development provides a way of understanding the steps or issues that may be involved in helping students achieve a given desired educational outcome. For guidelines promoting development, assumptions about the nature of development (such as those identified in Propositions 5 to 9) are just as important (if not more so) than descriptions of students in development terms (Propositions 1 to 4).

Sanford's dual insights about the process of development, that development proceeds through cycles of differentiation and integration (1962) and through a balancing of challenge and support (1967), continue to be powerful concepts for educators. Concepts such as readiness and time on task ("involvement" in more current vernacular) also continue to be helpful "process variables." But there are other recent theoretical advances that are still unknown or quite new to many in student affairs.

For example, it is still common at student affairs conferences to hear the phrase "being in a stage" in reference to a student's developmental status on one of several known cognitive developmental stage theories or models. Efforts to determine what stage a student is "in" implies what is called a "simple stage" model of development where an individual is presumed to move through a sequence of stages in a rather lock-step fashion, one stage at a time, with no overlap between stages except during times of transition between two adjacent stages (Rest, 1979). While development was portrayed this way in the early work of some major stage theorists (e.g., Flavell, 1971; Kohlberg, 1969), research in the last 25 years has failed to document such strict developmental progressions in either cognitive or moral development (Fischer, 1983; Fischer & Bullock, 1981; King & Kitchener, 1994; Rest, 1979, 1986).

Student affairs professionals have been understandably skeptical of such portrayals of development, since they fail to match the observable everyday vicissitudes of development and call into question the appropriateness of any developmental progression that suggests a stage-like sequence. Researchers, too, have observed discontinuities in development. For example, an individual's response may vary due to task demands (e.g., level of difficulty or whether a recognition or production task is used) or situational variables (e.g., distractions, fatigue, emotional distress, emotionally-laden circumstances), which can affect how thoughtfully or thoroughly she or he responds in a given situation. "Complex stage" models of development, by contrast, take intraindividual variability into account. As Rest (1979) noted, these models portray "a messier and complicated picture of development" (p. 65). When Wood (in press) graphed the data on response variability from 15 studies using the Reflective Judgment Interview, the resulting graph (see King & Kitchener, 1994, Figure 6.2, p. 139) bore a striking resemblance to Rest's hypothesized representation of complex stage models. A stage-like pattern of development is still quite apparent, but without the restrictive assumptions of simple stage theory.

A second related theoretical advance is Fischer's (1980) proposition that individuals operate within a range of developmental stages, from functional or typical level to optimal level, the highest level of performance of which an individual is capable. Individuals tend to operate at their optimal levels under supportive conditions, where there is the opportunity to practice a response and receive feedback about one's performance (Kitchener & Fischer, 1990; Kitchener, Lynch, Fischer, & Wood, 1993). These theoretical advances about the nature of development are relevant for educators who encourage students to think and act at their optimal levels of development and who intentionally strive to provide supportive conditions for development.

Educators who aspire to effectively enhance the learning experiences for college students need better theoretical resources to help them understand the process of development. As Garland and Grace (1993) have noted, "The failure of theories of student development to clearly detail the process by which growth actually takes place has limited their practical utility. . . . Many theories often neglect or only superficially address the process by which students actually undergo such growth" (p. 84). In light of such criticism, it is important to recognize that theory construction is an evolving process, the first step of which is often limited to a description of the aspect of development that is of interest. Typically, it is not until later in the theory development process (after instrument refinement and validation studies) that steps are taken to investigate the "mechanisms" of development. Clearly, there is a need for focused research attention on questions of the process as well as the content of student development.

How Can the College Environment Influence Student Development?

As this question implies, development occurs in a context, not in a vacuum. College student development occurs in the context of collegiate environments (broadly defined). The term environment is sometimes used so loosely that it becomes virtually meaningless. However, as Propositions 10 to 13 (and their theory bases) show, the term can be defined in more specific ways that provide helpful frameworks practitioners can use to describe, create, and enhance specific educational contexts. As this set of propositions shows, structuring collegiate environments requires an understanding of the contexts for development and how a given context can be beneficial or detrimental to students' learning and development. Doing so also requires clarity of educational goals and a willingness to take a stand about what is important for students to learn (Proposition 14).

Educators have long attempted to create educationally purposeful environments, or optimal contexts for learning. However, educational contexts too often tolerate racism, violence, harassment, sexism, and homophobia (Palmer, 1993). Such contexts are antithetical to the educational values espoused by most colleges and universities; they also serve to actively discourage large groups of students from achieving the desired educational outcomes.

Another environmental factor that serves to impede or retard student development is the anti-intellectual bias that pervades some segments of society and even higher education. When serious students are ostracized as "nerds" or when female students continue to feel that they must choose between being smart and being liked, they are experiencing an anti-intellectual climate. Further, when issues of race, gender, "political correctness," or even choice of research methodology are associated with such tension, rancor, and name-calling that people are reluctant to engage in the discussion, an anti-intellectual climate is created or sustained. Campuses that do not convey to students that they are welcome, that their opinions matter, that many in the college hold high expectations for their achievement, and that respect for other persons is paramount, are campuses where a student's perceptions about the campus may well impede his or her success ("I am an outsider here" or "If I say what I really believe here, I'll be ostracized"). To fulfill the promise of student development in higher education, educators need to look carefully at the many environments on campus that contribute to students' learning and development, *and* at those that discourage students from taking best advantage of their educational opportunities.

The current knowledge base about environments provides educators with a powerful tool for understanding and identifying ways to improve students' experiences in higher education by focusing on specific aspects of a campus environment. However, as Cross (1981) has noted, theory without practice is empty. Theoretical concepts about campus environments, however elegant, will not realize their potential until they are applied, which entails assessment and evaluation. Just as "the college student" changes from cohort to cohort, campus environments are also in flux. Keeping a finger on "the pulse of the campus" requires constant assessment and evaluation, both formal and informal. For this purpose, some campuses and student affairs divisions rely on offices of institutional research and evaluation. Others rely on staff members who have the expertise to conduct studies and interpret the results to decision-makers. Still others rely solely on informal conversations with students. All can yield information about how students perceive their university experiences and what really matters to them. For most student affairs practitioners, listening to students is part of their jobs every day. Those who rely solely on informal assessment, however, need to be cautious not to limit their conversations to selected students (e.g., student leaders) or students who are easier to contact (e.g., those who eat in residence hall dining rooms). Effective practice requires timely, accurate information based on relevant and applicable concepts about students and collegiate environments. Just as Cross's adage reminds student development theorists that practice should be used to inform theory, the other half of her adage, that practice without theory is blind, should remind practitioners of the value of understanding campus environments.

Theories of campus environments can help practitioners understand and address a wide array of issues, such as entering students' expectations of their campus experiences (especially when those expectations are not met, Proposition 13), or why year after year, some residence hall floors are known as "the zoo" and some sororities have long histories of eating disorders (Proposition 11). They can also help explain why innovative ideas are so hard to implement in some administrative offices (Proposition 12), to how student unions or libraries could be renovated so they will be more comfortable, appealing places for students to spend their time (Proposition 10).

Summary

The theoretical propositions identified by Strange (1994) provide frameworks, not recipes, for promoting student development. As such, they use a "broad brush" to paint a series of pictures of campus environments and to summarize several major concepts for understanding student development. The strength of these 14 propositions is their simplicity: each offers a distinct conceptual filter for focusing on a specific aspect of college students' educational experiences. At the same time, this simplicity can also be seen as a weakness: no proposition is specific enough to serve as a guide-for practice. As such, their value is tangible only when approached as a general framework, a scaffolding upon which many more details will be identified and then put in place. Those who assume that useful student development theories include clear and unambiguous instructions for practice will probably be disappointed by this list. By contrast, those who assume that people and educational systems are too complex and unpredictable for simple instructions will probably find comfort in the lack of prescription in this framework.

As Schoen (1983) has suggested, reflective practitioners develop the thoughtful habit of consciously and habitually asking questions such as, "Why are we doing this?" and "Should we continue doing so this way?" Toward this end, the four major questions posed by Parker, Widick, and Knefelkamp (1978) provide an organizing framework not only for a student development knowledge base, but for engaging in reflective practice. Student affairs practitioners can use these questions to evaluate their practice from four major perspectives: the intended outcomes of education, the developmental needs of today's students, the nature of developmental processes, and the ways different environments affect learning and development. Within these four perspectives, educators can also use Strange's (1994) 14 propositions about student development to ask 14 specific questions as they engage in daily decision-making. For example: "How are these students interpreting their learning and social experiences?" (from Proposition 2). "How are the dominant characteristics of this group of students influencing their behaviors?" (from Proposition 11); and "What are the educational values being conveyed here ?" (from Proposition 14).

Is the student development knowledge base obsolete? I don't think so. To reject all models of development because there are weaknesses in some and omissions overall would be like throwing the proverbial baby "out with the bath water." Is there merit in the knowledge base for today's college students? Yes! Are some of the theories and their research more applicable to students of the past than for today's students? Probably. Are there gaps in this knowledge base? Of course. It is important for theorists, researchers, and practitioners alike to listen to the skeptics as these questions are asked, as they provide good sources of information and new insights about existing descriptions of student development and uses of student development theories. Taken as a whole, this knowledge base, evolving as it is, provides a rich set of frameworks for understanding students and how to enhance their collegiate experiences.

Although the student development knowledge base has grown dramatically in the last two decades (Pascarella & Terenzini, 1991), there are still many gaps, perspectives are still limited (Terenzini, 1994), and assessment techniques leave much to be desired. But taken as a whole, a substantive, theoretical framework exists for refining research, assessment and educational programs for and about college students, as both Coomes (1994) and Upcraft (1994) illustrate. Further, this knowledge base has much to offer to both faculty and student affairs professionals, and to both those who emphasize student learning and those who emphasize student development. The educational values that inform the first question raised here, "Toward what ends should development in college be directed?" grounds the discussion in the educational mission of colleges and universities, which subsumes both academic and student affairs missions in terms of desired outcomes for students. An institution's educational goals provide a common ground between campus professionals in many roles and need not be a divisive point among student affairs practitioners who aspire to promote both learning and development.

For the weaknesses noted above to be addressed, student affairs professionals and researchers must decide if they are committed to improving the student development knowledge base. The alternative, relying solely on informal theories (perspectives grounded only in personal experiences) or on dated theories and research, suggests an unwillingness to continue to learn and to be informed by others' perspectives, an alternative that is inconsistent with the educational philosophy of most institutions of higher learning. By contrast, the propositions listed here offer a provocative set of concepts for expanding the theoretical knowledge base of student development to better understand college students and college outcomes, guide assessment efforts, and inform and improve educational practice.

References

American Council on Education, Committee on Student Personnel Work. (1937). *The student personnel point of view.* Washington, DC: American Council on Education.

Association of American Colleges. (1985). *Integrity in the curriculum: A report to the academic community* (Project on Redefining the Meaning and Purpose of Baccalaureate Degrees). Washington, DC: Author.

Association of American Colleges. (1991). *The challenge of connecting learning* (Project on liberal learning, study-in-depth, and the arts and science major). Washington, DC: Author.

Baker-Miller, J. (1986). *Toward a new psychology of women* (2nd ed.) Boston: Beacon.

Baldwin, J. M. (1902). *Social and ethical interpretations in mental development.* New York: Macmillan. (Original work published in 1897).

Bloland, P. A., Stamatakos, L. C., & Rogers, R. R. (1994). *Reform in student affairs: A critique of student development.* Greensboro, NC: ERIC Counseling and Student Services Clearinghouse.

Bok, D. (1986). *Higher learning.* Cambridge, MA: Harvard University Press.

Bowen, H. (1980). *Investment in learning: The individual and social value of American higher education.* San Francisco: Jossey-Bass.

Boyer, E. (1987). *College: The undergraduate experience in America.* New York: Harper & Row.

Brabeck, M. (1983). Moral judgment: Theory and research on differences between males and females: *Developmental Review, 3,* 274-291.

Brown, R. D., & Barr, M. (1990): Student development: Yesterday, today, and tomorrow. In L. V, Moore (Ed.), Evolving theoretical perspectives on students (pp. 83-92; New Directions for Student Services, No. 51). San Francisco: Jossey-Bass.

Cass, V. C. (1979). Homosexual identity formation: A theoretical model. *Journal of Homosexuality, 4,* 219-235.

Cass, V. C. (1984). Homosexual identity formation: Testing a theoretical model. *Journal of Sex Research, 20,* 143-167.

Chickering, A. (1981). Introduction. In A. Chickering and Associates, *The modern American college* (pp. 1-11). San Francisco: Jossey-Bass.

Coomes, M. D. (1994). Using student development to guide institutional policy. *Journal of College Student Development, 35,* 428-437.

Cross, P. K. (1981). Adults as learners. San Francisco: Jossey-Bass.

Dey, E. L., Astin, A. W., & Korn, W. S. (1991). *The American freshman: Twenty-five year trends, 1966-1990.* Los Angeles: Higher Education Research Institute, UCLA.

Erikson, E. H. (1968). *Identity: Youth and crisis.* New York: Norton.

Fischer, K. (1980). A theory of cognitive development: The control and construction of hierarchies of skills. *Psychological Review, 87,* 477-531.

Fischer, K. (1983). Illuminating the processes of moral development. *Monographs of the Society for Research in Child Development, 48* (1-2, Serial No. 200).

Fischer, K., & Bullock, D. (1981). Patterns of data: Sequence, synchrony, and constraint in cognitive development. In K. W. Fischer (Ed.), *Cognitive development.* (pp. 69-78; New Directions for Child Development, No. 12). San Francisco: Jossey-Bass.

Flavell, J. (1971). Stage related properties of cognitive development. *Cognitive Psychology, 2,* 421-453.

Flavell, J. (1977). *Cognitive development.* Englewood Cliffs, NJ: Prentice-Hall.

Garland, P. H., & Grace, T. W. (1993). *New perspectives for student affairs professionals: Evolving realities, responsibilities and roles* (ASHE-ERIC Higher Education Report No. 7). Washington, DC: The George Washington University, School of Education and Human Development.

Gilligan, C. (1989). *Mapping the moral domain.* Cambridge, MA: Harvard University Press.

Glatfelter, M. (1982). Identity development, intellectual development, and their relationship in reentry women students. *Dissertation Abstracts International, 43,* 3543A.

Guba, E. G., & Lincoln, Y. S. (1990). Can there be a human science? Constructivism as an alternative. *Person-Centered Review, 5,* 130-154.

Hayes, R. L. (1994). Counseling in the postmodern world: Origins and implications of a constructivist developmental approach. *Counseling and Human Development, 26*(6), 1-12.

Helms, J. (1990). A model of White racial identity development. In J. Helms (Ed.), Black and white racial identity: *Theory, research and practice* (pp. 49-80). New York: Greenwood Press.

Jones, W. T. (1990). Perspectives on ethnicity. In L. V. Moore, (Ed.), *Evolving theoretical perspectives on students* (pp. 59-72; New Directions for Student Services, No. 51). San Francisco: Jossey-Bass.

Josselson, R. (1987). *Finding herself: Pathways to identity development in women.* San Francisco: Jossey-Bass.

King, P. M., & Kitchener, K. S. (1994). *Developing reflective judgment: Understanding and promoting intellectual growth and critical thinking in adolescents and adults.* San Francisco: Jossey-Bass.

King, P. M., Kitchener, K. S., Wood, P. K., & Davison, M. L. (1989). Relationships across developmental domains: A longitudinal study of intellectual, moral and ego development. In M. L. Commons, J. D. Sinnott, F. A. Richards, & C. Armon (Eds.), *Adult development, Vol. I: Comparisons and applications of developmental models* (pp. 57-72). New York: Praeger.

Kitchener, K. S. (1982). Human development and the college campus: Sequences and tasks. In G. R. Hanson (Ed.), *Measuring student development* (pp. 17-45). New Directions for Student Services, No. 20. San Francisco: Jossey-Bass.

Kitchener, K. S., & Fischer, K. W. (1990). A skill approach to the development of reflective thinking. In D. Kuhn (Ed.), *Contributions to human development: Developmental perspectives on teaching and learning,* (Vol. 21), pp. 48-62. Basel, Switzerland: Karger.

Kitchener, K. S., King, P. M., Davison, M. L., Parker, C. A., & Wood, P. K. (1984). A longitudinal study of moral and ego development in young adults. *Journal of Youth and Adolescence, 13,* 197-211.

Kitchener, K. S., Lynch, C. L., Fischer, K. W., & Wood, P. K. (1993). Developmental range of reflective judgment: The effect of contextual support and practice on developmental stage. *Developmental Psychology 29,* 893-906.

Kohlberg, L. (1969). Stage and sequence: The cognitive-developmental approach to socialization. In D. A. Goslin (Ed.), *Handbook of socialization theory and research* (pp. 347-480). Skokie, IL: Rand McNally.

Kohlberg, L. (1989). *Essays on moral development (vol. 1): The philosophy of moral development.* New York: Harper & Row.

Miller, T. K., &Winston, R. B., Jr. (1991). Human development and higher education. In T. K. Miller, & R. B. Winston, Jr. (Eds.), *Administration and leadership in student affairs* (pp. 3-35). Muncie, IN: Accelerated Development.

Myers, I. B., & McCaulley, M. H. (1987). *Manual: A guide to the development and use of the Myers-Briggs Type Indicator.* Palo Alto, CA: Consulting Psychologists Press.

Nagasawa, R., & Espinosa, D. J. (1992). Education achievement and the adaptive strategy of Asian American college students: Facts, theory, and hypotheses. *Journal of College Student Development, 33,* 137-142.

Newman, J. H. (1973). *The idea of a university.* Westminster, MD: Christian Classics. (Originally published in 1852.)

Noddings, N. (1984). *Caring: A feminine approach to ethics and moral education.* Berkeley and Los Angeles: University of California Press.

Palmer, C. (1993). *Violent crimes and other forms of victimization in residence halls.* Asheville, NC: College Administration Publications.

Parham, T. A., & Helms, J. E. (1981). The influence of Black students' racial identity attitudes on preferences for counselor's race. *Journal of Counseling Psychology, 28,* 250-257.

Parker, C. A. (Ed.). (1978). *Encouraging development in college students,* Minneapolis: University of Minnesota Press.

Parker, C. A., Widick, C., & Knefelkamp, L. L. (Eds.). (1978). *Applying new developmental findings* (New Directions for Student Services, No. 4). San Francisco: Jossey-Bass.

Pascarella, E. T., & Terenzini, P. T. (1991). *How college affects students: Findings and insights from twenty years of research.* San Francisco: Jossey-Bass.

Piaget, J. (1937). *Construction du Réel chez l'enfant [The construction of reality in the child].* Neuchatel: Delachaux et Niestle.

Polkosnik, M. D., & Winston, R. B., Jr. (1989). Relationships between students' intellectual and psychological development: An exploratory investigation. *Journal of College Student Development, 30,* 10-19.

Power, F. C., Higgins, A., & Kohlberg, L. (1989). *Lawrence Kohlberg's approach to moral education.* New York: Columbia University Press.

Rest, J. R. (1979). *Development in judging moral issues.* Minneapolis: University of Minnesota Press.

Rest, J. R. (1983). Morality. In J. H. Flavell & E. M. Markman (Eds.), *Cognitive development, (Vol. III, 4th edition), Handbook of Child Psychology* (pp. 556-629). New York: Wiley.

Rest, J. R. (1984). The major components of morality. In W. M. Kurtines & J. L. Gewirtz (Eds.), *Morality, moral behavior; and moral development* (pp. 24-38). New York: John Wiley.

Rest, J. R. (1986). *Moral development: Advances in research and theory.* New York: Praeger.

Rest, J. R. (with M. Bebeau & J. Volker). (1986). An overview of the psychology of morality. In J. R. Rest (1979), *Moral development: Advances in research and theory* (pp. 1-27). New York: Praeger.

Rosovsky, H. (1990). *The university: An owner's manual.* New York: Norton.

Sanford, N. (1962). Developmental status of the entering freshman. In N. Sanford (Ed.), *The American college: A psychological and social interpretation of the higher learning* (pp. 253-282). New York: Wiley.

Sanford, N. (1967). *Where colleges fail.* San Francisco: Jossey-Bass.

Schaef, A. W. (1981). *Women's reality.* Minneapolis, MN: Winston Press.

Schlossberg, N. K., Lynch, A. Q., & Chickering, A. W. (1989). *Improving higher education environments for adults: Responsive programs and services from entry to departure.* San Francisco: Jossey-Bass. Schneider, C. G., & Green, W. S. (1993). Editors' Notes. In C. G. Schneider, & W. S. Green (Eds.), *Strengthening the college major* (pp. 1-9; New Directions for Higher Education, No. 84). San Francisco: Jossey-Bass.

Schoen, D. A. (1983). *The reflective practitioner: How professionals think in action.* Basic Books.

Strange, C. C. (1994). Student Development: The evolution history and status of an essential idea. *Journal Of College Student Development, 35,* 399-412.

Sue, D. W. (1981). *Counseling the culturally different.* New York: Wiley-Interscience.

Terenzini, P. T. (1994). Good news and bad news: The implications of Strange's propositions for research. *Journal of College Student Development, 35,* 422-427.

Upcraft, M. L. (1994). The dilemmas of translating theory to practice. *Journal of College Student Personnel, 35,* 438-443.

von Glaserfeld, E. (1984). An introduction to radical constructivism. In P. Watzlawick (Ed.), *The invented reality: How do we know what we believe we know: Contributions to constructivism* (pp. 17-40). New York: Norton.

Welfel, E. R. (1990). Ethical practice in college student affairs. In D. Creamer &Associates (Eds.), *College student development: Theory and practice for the 1990s* (pp. 195-216). Alexandria, VA: ACPA Media.

Wood, P. K. (in press). Context and development of reflective thinking: A secondary analysis of the structure of individual differences. In J. Smart (Ed.), *Higher education: Handbook of theory and research.* New York: Agathon Press.

UNIT II

Holistic Versions of Student Development

Section 2

INTEGRATED DEVELOPMENTAL MODELS

CHAPTER 4

KEGAN'S ORDERS OF CONSCIOUSNESS

PATRICK G. LOVE AND VICTORIA L. GUTHRIE

Kegan's orders of consciousness are useful in developing a holistic understanding of college students' ways of knowing that incorporates their thinking, feeling, and social relating.

Robert Kegan first introduced his theory of meaning making and the evolution of consciousness in *The Evolving Self: Problem and Process in Human Development* (1982). His subsequent book, *In Over Our Heads: The Mental Demands of Modern Life* (1994), extended his original theory and framed it in the context of the mental demands that the "curriculum" of modern life makes on adults. Here Kegan used the theory as an analytical tool to examine contemporary culture and illustrated his constructs using examples from multiple arenas of life (partnering, parenting, working, dealing with difference, learning).

A psychologist with a background in the humanities, Kegan acknowledged the inspiration of Erik Erikson and particularly Jean Piaget on his own thinking and his constructive-developmental theory. He also worked closely with and learned from both Lawrence Kohlberg and William Perry at Harvard. He classifies his theory as a "neo-Piagetian" approach that focuses on the person as an "ever progressive motion engaged in giving itself a new form" (Kegan, 1982, p. 8). Kegan (1982, p. vii) describes himself as a teacher, therapist, and researcher who seeks to engage others through his work in "an exploration of just how much can be understood about a person by understanding his or her meaning system."

According to Kegan (1982), meaning making is a physical activity (grasping, seeing), a social activity (it requires another), and a survival activity (in doing it, we live). It is an intrinsically cognitive activity, but it is no less affective. His 1982 work describes the individual's personal evolution of meaning as a balancing and rebalancing of subject and object, or self and other. *The Evolving Self* describes six different levels of sense making that occur throughout the life span. The basic premise of *In Over Our Heads* is that there exists a "mismatch" between the culture's complex "curriculum" and our mental capacity to deal with the demands of adult living. If educators purport to prepare students for the demands of life after college, this "mismatch" must concern them and shape the educational agenda for college students.

Although Kegan's work seldom specifically addresses college student development, it is valuable in understanding this development in the wider context of the life span. Moreover, unlike the other cognitive theories examined in this volume, his theory addresses cognitive, social, and emotional development together as elements of a system of meaning formation. Though the language, terminology, and graphic representation Kegan uses to describe the framework of his theory change from his 1982 work to his 1994 work, the underlying theoretical constructs remain the same. The explanation below uses his more recent description and language while attempting to capture the fullness of the theory as described in both sources. In 1982, Kegan described his theory as "empirically grounded speculation" (p. ix) based on his years as a therapist and teacher. The 1994 extension is further grounded in cross-sectional studies and longitudinal research conducted by Kegan and colleagues using the

Subject-Object Interview (Lahey and others, 1988), which they developed at Harvard after Kegan's original work was published.

The Subject-Object Distinction

Central to comprehending Kegan's theory is an understanding of the subject-object distinction. In simplest terms, we *are* subject and we *have* object. Subject is that which we cannot see because it comprises us. We therefore cannot be responsible for or in control of it, nor can we reflect on it. The root *ject* in *object* refers to the motion or activity of throwing. *Object* can be understood to refer to that which meaning making has made separate and distinct from us. Kegan (1994, p. 32) offers the following definitions:

> "Subject" refers to those elements of our knowing or organizing that we are identified with, tied to, fused with, or embedded in.
>
> "Object" refers to those elements of our knowing or organizing that we can reflect on, handle, look at, be responsible for, relate to each other, take control of, internalize, assimilate, or otherwise act upon.

An example is a preteen who is able to assert her independence from her parents and advocate forcefully for her needs (newly acquired abilities because her separateness and impulses, which earlier in her life were inseparable from her sense of self, are now *object*). However, she is yet unable to consider the needs and feelings of others in her decision making and actions (because her needs, interests, and wishes are still *subject*).

Kegan's Five Orders of Consciousness

Kegan's theory centers around five "orders of consciousness," which are principles of mental organization that affect thinking, feeling, and relating to self and others. Kegan uses the term *order* to indicate a dimensional quality (that is, a level) rather than a strict sequence (such as the term *stage* suggests). Each successive principle transcends the last in that the new way of knowing incorporates the meaning-making abilities of the last and the individual becomes able to reflect on these abilities. In addition to its cognitive properties, each order has both *intra*personal (self-concept) and *inter*personal (relationship) dimensions.

Two of these orders, the first and fifth, are not directly applicable to the experiences of undergraduate college students. Children make the transition from first- to second-order thinking between the ages of five and ten, long before college. Regarding the other end of the continuum, Kegan (1994, p. 352) indicates that "it is rare to see people moving beyond the fourth order, but when they do, it is never before their forties." Therefore, this summary will touch only briefly on the first and fifth orders.

The potential to affect college students' development intentionally is most powerful in the transitions between orders of consciousness. In fact, Kegan's concept of the person as continually evolving makes directing our attention to the transitions, rather than to the temporary balance represented by each "order," much more theoretically consistent. The following analysis therefore pays particular attention to the two transitional periods student affairs educators are most likely to encounter: from the second to the third order and from the third to the fourth order.

Fundamental Assumptions. Five important assumptions underlie Kegan's theory. First, the orders of consciousness not only refer to how one thinks but more generally to how one constructs experience, which includes thinking, feeling, and relating to others. Second, Kegan's orders concern the *organization* of one's thinking, feeling, and social relating rather than the *content*. Third, each order of consciousness is constituted by a different subject-object relationship. Kegan's fourth assumption is that the orders of consciousness are related to each other. One does not simply replace the other; rather, each successive principle subsumes the prior principle. Thus, the new order is higher, more complex, and more inclusive. Finally, what is taken as subject and object is not fixed: what was subject at one order becomes object at the next order. Therefore, there is a developing ability to relate to or see that in which we were formerly enmeshed. Figure 1 summarizes elements of the orders of consciousness and portrays the movement of subject toward becoming object in the next order of consciousness.

First Order of Consciousness. At the first order of consciousness, young children (from birth to age seven or eight) do not have the capacity for abstract thought. Rather, physical objects principally represent the child's momentary perceptions of them. Meaning is made from a very egocentric, fantasy-filled position. The world is not concrete, and there is no realization that others have separate minds, separate intentions, and separate vantage points.

Order	Subject	Object	Focus	Thinking
First: Single point, immediate	Fantasy, impulse, perception	Movement and sensation	Particulars	Concrete
Second: Durable categories	Self-concept, needs, preferences	Fantasy, impulse, perception	Structures, categories	Relating concrete concepts
Third: Cross-categorical thinking	Abstractions, mutuality, subjectivity	Self-concept, needs, preferences	Abstract thinking, relationships	Abstract
Fourth: Cross-categorical constructing	Ideology, multiple roles, self-authorship	Abstractions, mutuality, subjectivity	Constructing, self-authoring	Relating abstract concepts
Fifth: Transsystem	Oppositeness, interpenetration of self and others, interindividuation	Ideology, multiple roles, self-authorship	Multipleness	Systems

Figure 1 Summary of Orders of Consciousness

At this order, children are able to recognize objects separate from self, but those objects are subject to the children's perception of them. Thus, from the children's perspective, if their perception of an object changes, the object itself changes. Children come to *have* reflexes rather than *be* them, and the self is that which coordinates the reflexes through perceptions and impulses. Impulse control is not possible because children are subject to their impulses, and nonexpression raises the threat of risking "who I am."

Second Order of Consciousness. From late childhood until sometime in adolescence or early adulthood, individuals make meaning by learning to construct "durable categories"—lasting classifications in which physical objects, people, and desires come to have properties of their own that characterize them as distinct from "me." In the transition from first- to second-order consciousness, momentary impulses and immediate perceptions move from being the subject to being the object of experiencing. The new subject becomes the durable category.

In the construction of durable categories, physical objects, people, and desires change from being seen solely from the individual's momentary perceptions of them. The ability develops to classify them according to their properties using ongoing rules that are not dependent on individual perceptions. For example, a child comes to recognize that some animals fall into the category "dog" whereas others do not fit into this category because of properties such as fins, trunks, or wings. Children now recognize that they are individuals with characteristics, and this creates a self-concept. In addition, other people become "property-bearing selves distinct from me" (Kegan, 1994, p. 23). For example, distinctions between family, friends, and strangers become possible: some are friendly and fun; others are uncomfortable and stiff when they are around kids.

Desires change from being principally about moment-to-moment impulses or wishes to being about ongoing needs or preferences. For instance, individuals begin to classify themselves as people who like to read, enjoy playing sports, or hate vegetables. A shift from a fantasy orientation to a reality orientation occurs in which individuals begin to develop self-sufficiency and take on the social role of a child. A capacity develops to "take the role" of another and to see that others have a perspective of their own.

Individuals are still concerned primarily with the pursuit and satisfaction of their own interests, are not yet able to own membership in a wider community than the one defined by self-interest, and are not yet able to think abstractly. At the second order, individuals' actions are determined in the context of their own point of view or needs. However, a primary determinant of how they feel is how others will react to their actions.

Transition from the Second to the Third Order. Between ages twelve and twenty, the gradual transformation of mind from the second to the third order takes place. Though likely to occur during adolescence, this transition may also take place as young adults enter college or, less likely, during the collegiate experience. Society's mental demands most likely have already resulted in this transition for adult learners.

Kegan notes that many adolescents are unable to meet the expectations the adult culture holds of them. Thus, student affairs educators should consider whether the expectations held of beginning college students are appropriate for their developmental level. If thinking abstractly and seeing oneself as a member of a community are required, students in the midst of this transition may need some real support and guidance as they develop this type of thinking.

If individuals do not yet construct the particular way of knowing demanded of them, "the difficulty might be more a matter of not understanding the rules of the game than one of an unwillingness to play" (Kegan, 1994, p. 38). Student affairs professionals must help students understand the "rules of the game" (such as behavioral expectations and responsibilities) so that they are able to meet the expectations society and college have of them. For example, if the expectation is that students be able to take other people's feelings into account even when considering themselves, this might be insisting on "rules of a game" that students still at the second order of consciousness are not yet able to comprehend.

Those working with students can help them see how their point of view relates to that of others or accept when their particular preferences or needs must be subordinated to those of others. These issues arise in the familiar conflicts between roommates in residence halls (for example, when one student is unable to understand how the constant presence of her boyfriend in the room infringes on her roommate's privacy) or when individual rights must be limited to accommodate the best interests of a larger whole (such as when a student living in a residence hall is asked to turn down his stereo in consideration of others' need to study). Opportunities to learn about themselves in a reflective manner when values, broad beliefs, and social roles are considered can assist students in making this transition.

Third Order of Consciousness. In this order of consciousness, one is able to "think abstractly, identify a complex internal psychological life, orient to the welfare of a human relationship, construct values and ideals self-consciously... and subordinate one's own interests" (Kegan, 1994, p. 75). The primary capacity of this order is the ability to experience the self in relation to a given category rather than as the category itself. For example, individuals might start to reflect on the *type* of friends they are. Individuals also begin to consider not just what will happen to them or to their wants but what will happen to the bonds or relationships in their life. As a result, individuals become able to subordinate some of their own interests to a shared interest instead of only being able to get their own needs met.

At this order, in addition to the ability to construct one's own point of view, the recognition emerges that others are constructing their own point of view as well. Individuals can further subordinate their own point of view to the relationship between their point of view and that of others. This requires movement from "I am my point of view" to "I have a point of view." Prosocial expectations, such as being a good citizen, require this type of cross-categorical knowing. For example, a college student may start to consider the effect a choice to stay out all night may have on the roommate who worries that something may have happened and to consider how that might affect their relationship.

Cross-categorical thinking also makes possible experiencing emotions as inner psychological states. This requires integrating the simpler, categorical self into a more complex context that *relates to* the self. For example, rather than simply experiencing depression (emotion as subject— I am depressed), individuals might recognize themselves as being in a state of depression as opposed to a normal state of being (emotion as object—I am experiencing depression). It is also at the third order of consciousness that values, ideals, and broad beliefs can be constructed. The

previous, more concrete way of thinking allowed individuals only to consider themselves as honest or dishonest people rather than as people who value honesty and strive to live up to that ideal (whether or not it is always attained).

Transition from the Third to the Fourth Order. Kegan asserts that this is the principal transformation of consciousness in adulthood. It basically involves attaining self-authorship: the ability to "write" one's own life. Educational settings can provide a conducive context for it to occur. At the third order of consciousness, the system by which individuals make meaning still rests outside the self, in realities shared with others. Kegan speaks of this as being both "the triumph and limit of the third order" (Kegan, 1994, p. 126). In gaining the ability to become part of a community or society, individuals triumph. However, they are still limited by being unable to stand apart from this co-construction to reflect and act on it.

The transition to the fourth order is sometimes signaled when a student feels life has suddenly come to a halt or when a student loses concentration, energy, and purpose. Students may describe themselves as having become lazy or even angry as they struggle to extricate self from others' expectations (which have become excessive or seem to conflict) and to determine "Who is in charge around here, anyway?" The precipitating event for this shift can be the loss of an important relationship, whether self-initiated or through rejection or betrayal, because at the third order, students *are* their relationships (subject) rather than *having* them (object).

Students begin to develop an independent selfhood with an ideology of their own and will often insist on being taken seriously as an adult and equal. The source of judgment and expectation comes to reside within the self rather than being confused with others. For example, guilt might be experienced as a result of a violation of one's own internal standard, irrespective of others' expectations. Going away to college "can provide a new evolutionary medium that recognizes and cultures the moves toward self-authorship" (Kegan, 1982, p. 186).

Being caught between one way of meaning making and another can be very disruptive and painful. This is particularly true in the transition of the structure of "relationship" from subject to object, during which students may experience loss and loneliness, as well as a feeling of self-ishness. Educators can offer students several types of support in this transition: recognition of students as independent individuals in their own right; an opportunity for publicly recognized personal achievement; a chance to participate in a group based on an aspect of their self-authored identity; and guidance regarding entry into the world of work.

Fourth Order of Consciousness. Kegan labels the fourth order of consciousness "cross-categorical constructing" (as opposed to third-order "cross-categorical thinking"), highlighting the individual's new ability to construct generalizations across abstractions. An internally consistent organization (identity) comes into being that uses a formal system to relate concrete and context-bound particulars, as well as abstractions. However, "one-half to two-thirds of the adult population appear not to have fully reached the fourth order of consciousness" (Kegan, 1994, p. 191).

This order represents a step beyond the third-order capacity to generalize across concrete particulars and form cross-categorical structures, such as values. Individuals who reach this order develop the capacity to stand outside of their values and form a deeper internal set of convictions that form a context for and regulate behavior. These values *about* values provide a means for choosing among values when they conflict. Rather than being regulated by and held to the standard of a value, ideal, or belief, an individual at the fourth order would have to be able to "subordinate a perfectly respectable ideal (like 'openness and honesty') to a bigger theory or ideology that can regulate the ideal" (Kegan, 1994, pp. 89–90). An example is when a student weighs a larger principle, such as "doing no harm," against how much honesty is called for when she suspects her best friend's partner of being unfaithful.

The making of an ideology involves an ability "to subordinate, regulate, and indeed create (rather than be created by) our values and ideals—the ability to take values and ideals as the object rather than the subject of our knowing" (Kegan, 1994, p. 91). This capacity is referred to as *self-authorship* and incorporates the ideas of self-regulation, identity, autonomy, and individuation, as opposed to relying on others to frame the problems or determine whether things are going acceptably well.

The capacity for self-authorship is a qualitatively more complex system for organizing experience than the mental operations of previous orders, which create values, beliefs, generalizations, abstractions, interpersonal loyalty, and intrapersonal states of mind. It is an internal identity that can coordinate, integrate, or act on them. It also fosters a sense of identity that is "more enduring than earlier co-constructed versions because the internal self is the source of belief rather than the social surround that was the source of the belief in the third order" (Baxter Magolda, forthcoming, pp. 2–3).

Interpersonally, this ability translates into the capacity to stand outside a relationship and make judgments about its demands without feeling the relationship itself has thereby been fundamentally violated. An "I" is brought into being that *has,* rather than *is,* its relationships. In moving beyond another's expectations or claims, an individual utilizing fourth-order consciousness can create a larger mental context that involves a "relationship to the relationship" (Kegan, 1994, p. 92). An example is when individuals realize they have become too dependent on a relationship with a partner as the source of their personal happiness. Realizing this dependence, one can look at ways to become less reliant on the relationship as a source of satisfaction and fulfillment, without changing or ending the relationship itself.

Self-authorship is an outcome reflected in many universities' mission statements and a goal for many divisions of student affairs: to foster the student's development as a self-directed learner, an individual who acts on the world for the betterment of society (rather than is acted on), and an engaged citizen with a strong sense of values and a clear identity that is internally defined. Kegan argues persuasively that in order to be effective as partners, as parents, in work, and in leading, individuals must be capable of self-authorship.

Fifth Order of Consciousness. Fifth-order thinking is relatively rare and never appears before individuals reach their forties (Kegan, 1994). An individual's identity system moves from subject to object and brings into being a new interindividual way of organizing reality that emphasizes a refusal to see oneself or the other as a single system or form. This order is built on a realization of the human tendency to pretend toward completeness while actually being incomplete. It is only in relationship that we are who we are.

This is a "somewhat controversial" claim as it "flies in the face of cherished notions of maturity" (Kegan, 1982, p. 228) by suggesting that a highly differentiated psychological autonomy may not be the fullest picture of maturity. Rather, it suggests a notion of development beyond the autonomy of establishing one's identity and points to a level of development that relies on the individual being able to experience a sharing or intimacy with others.

At this order individuals begin to use a perspective of "multipleness." Relationships become "a context for a sharing and an interacting . . . in which the *many* forms or systems that *each self is* are helped to emerge" (Kegan, 1994, p. 313). Individuals hold suspect their sense of their own and each other's wholeness; they reject false assumptions of distinctness or completeness. The self-as-system is seen as incomplete—only a partial construction of all that the self is. It is the process of creating self through relationships that is imperative.

The shift to this way of meaning making can be accompanied by an experience of losing one's balance or a sense that one's personal organization is threatened or about to collapse. A sense of boundaries being violated may be felt. Fears also may develop about losing one's control and sense of being distinct.

One of the central features of this new way of thinking is an orientation toward contradiction and paradox. Rather than feeling a need to choose between the two poles in a paradox, an individual recognizes the contradiction and orients toward the relationship between the poles. Therefore, contradictions do not threaten the system or necessarily need to be reconciled.

In an attempt to illustrate and clarify this complex concept, Kegan gives the example of a cylinder, which can be seen as a glass tube that has two openings. On the other hand, using a fifth-order perspective, "we could conclude that what the cylinder really is, is two openings connected by a glass tube. We could see the glass tube as the connector or relater of the two ends" (Kegan, 1994, p. 313). This is the view of relationships from the fifth order, which focuses on the bond or link between the parts. For example, individuals at the fifth order of consciousness might view their own leadership style as providing a context in which all constituencies

involved, the leader included, can together create a vision, mission, or purpose that can collectively be upheld.

Creating Bridges to More Complex Orders

Kegan's focus has been to develop and illustrate his theory within the general context of the demands of adult life. Therefore, a degree of translation and extension is necessary to obtain specific implications for working with college students outside the classroom. Key concepts and strategies with substantial promise for applicability to student affairs practice include coaching, holding environments, and bridge building.

Student affairs practitioners need to be effective in creating environments where challenge and support are blended to foster students' growth. Kegan asserts that society in general is far better at providing challenges than supporting individuals' growth. The college environment also may be providing more than adequate challenge. Nonetheless, as Kegan (1994) maintains, it is not necessarily a bad thing to be "in over our heads," provided there is effective support available. Today's college students are living in a time of profound change and facing enormous pressure—economically, politically, socially, and psychologically (Levine and Cureton, 1998). Perhaps in the challenging environment of today's college campus, students' overwhelming need is for support.

Kegan suggests the concept of "sympathetic coaching" to provide the needed support. Sympathetic coaches have a concern for the developmental process within a successful program or popular activity. They provide "welcoming acknowledgment to exactly who the person is right now as he or she is" (Kegan, 1994, p. 43) while an individual is gradually outgrowing a way of knowing the world.

Confirmation for the students' current way of meaning making is not the only function of sympathetic coaches; they must also "nurture the seeds of its productive undoing" (Kegan, 1994, p. 45) by providing contradiction that supports the *transformation* of knowing. Student affairs professionals must recognize and respect where the students are, thus gaining their interest and involvement in the intervention, yet provide glimpses of and attractive opportunities to try out aspects of the next higher order. For example, students using the second order of consciousness might initially be enticed to participate in community service by emphasizing opportunities for increased personal competence and personal reward. Once individuals are "hooked," they may begin to change their way of meaning making with regard to the service activities. They may start to recognize that in order to gain their desired outcomes, they need to become members in a community of interest greater than themselves and to subordinate their own welfare to that of others. Eventually they may even feel a loyalty to or identification with the individuals being served. Engaging others in service by appealing to personal gains and rewards may be a technique professionals use in facilitating community service programming. Yet, how many truly acknowledge or welcome the students who approach in this manner? And how often is this seen as an opportunity to promote development of consciousness?

Kegan identifies two primary ways that educators fail to provide support: by neglecting to build a bridge out of and beyond the old world and by expecting individuals to take up immediate residence in the new world. Although educators should never be critical of where students are, they must do more than acknowledge and support students where they are. Kegan suggests that educators should "fashion a bridge that is more respectfully anchored on both sides of the chasm, instead of assuming that such a bridge already exists and wondering why the other has not long ago walked over it" (Kegan, 1994, p. 332).

Kegan's theory addresses the environment of development more explicitly than any of the other cognitive theories examined in this volume. He asserts that sympathetic coaches can be developmentally supportive through their role as part of the psychosocial environment in which individuals develop. The term *holding environment* specifically recognizes one of the primary functions of the environment—its function to hold securely by confirming and supporting as opposed to keeping or confining.

Peers are also important elements of holding environments, being part of the old way of knowing and also part of the new. For example, relationships with peers can facilitate movement from the second to the third order of consciousness by providing an opportunity to "get inside" a view separate from one's own. Even if the other's point of view is perceived as being basically the same as one's own, slight differences inevitably emerge. As individuals try to restore a sense of their identity between the two views, a completely different order of consciousness can emerge. Peer relationships also provide opportunities for transition to the fourth order as individuals begin to consider their relationship to these relationships.

Kegan's theory underscores the value of creating programs that are highly acknowledging of, and sensible to, students' current ways of meaning making while at the same time promoting the development of the next higher order of consciousness. The programs must artfully recognize and welcome the individual's current order of consciousness while "quite deliberately creat[ing] the circumstances for its productive undoing" (Kegan, 1994, p. 46). This can be done by placing values consistent with the higher order *not* in the foreground but in the background of the program and by communicating with participants at the most fundamental level of their meaning making. For instance, a program that insists that participants work in groups, learn each other's skills and limitations as well as their own, and hold each other in mind even as they pursue their own ends facilitates third-order thinking. However, the key to interesting and engaging the students in the program (the "hook") must be aimed at their current level of meaning formation.

It is most important for educators to realize that if their interest is actually to engage, or in some way relate to, their students, they must first understand their students. Educators must hold themselves "to the rigors of addressing the person in the experience of meaning-making, rather than the meaning the person has made" (Kegan, 1994, p. 293). Baxter Magolda (forthcoming) illustrates this primary tenet of Kegan's theory in her suggestion that focusing on how the third order of mind makes meaning might lead to better understanding of common campus issues, such as abusive dating relationships, alcohol abuse, or hazing. Kegan's theory provides a powerful lens though which to view and learn about college students and support them in their developmental evolution.

CHAPTER 5

THE HIDDEN CURRICULUM OF YOUTH:
"WHADDAYA WANT FROM ME?"

ROBERT KEGAN

Peter and Lynn are wide awake at two in the morning, but they are not having a good time. They are having a teenager. Matty, their son, was due home two hours ago. He is sixteen, his curfew is midnight, and they have heard nothing from him. They are wide awake and angry, and most of all, they are worried.

But this is not going to be one of those nights that changes anyone's life. Nobody is going to die. Nothing of this night will be on the news. This is the ordinary night nobody writes about. Matty is going to come home in another half hour hoping his parents have long since gone to sleep so he can assure them tomorrow that he was in "only a little past twelve." When his hopes are dashed by the sight of his wide-awake parents, he will have an excuse about somebody's car and somebody else's mother and a third person who borrowed the first person's jacket with his car keys and left the party early, and maybe it's just because it's now nearly three in the morning, but the story will sound to Peter and Lynn so freshly made up that all its pieces barely know how to fit together.

Lynn won't be thinking about it now, but only six years ago—not a long time to her—she had been stuck by how independent Matty had become. This clingy kid who seemed to need her so much had become a little ten-year-old fellow full of purpose and plans, in business for himself, with a sign on his bedroom door: "Adults Keep Out." A part of her missed the little boy who didn't want to be left alone, but a bigger part of her was pleased for both of them by this development. But six years later, at two-thirty in the morning, it will not occur to her to say, "Matty, my son, I'm so impressed by the way you are able to take care of yourself, by how much you can do for yourself, by the way you just go wherever you want to and come home whenever you want to, by how little you seem to need your dad and me. You're really growing up, son. Your dad and I just wanted to stay up until two-thirty in the morning to tell you how proud we are!" No, what it will occur to Lynn to say is something more like *"This isn't a hotel here, buddy!* You can't just come and go as you please! You're a part of a family, you know! Your father and I have feelings, too! How do you think we feel when it's two in the morning and we haven't heard a thing from you? We're worried sick! For all we know you could be splattered all over the highway. How *would* we know? You don't call us! It's time you joined this family, buddy, and started *thinking about somebody other than just yourself!"*

Peter and Lynn want something more of Matty now than they wanted when he was ten. What even delighted them then, Matty's "independence," is a source of anger, worry, and frustration now when it shows up as a "lack of trustworthiness."

But what kind of thing is it Matty's parents want of him? One answer is that it is a behavior, a way of acting. They want him to stop doing certain things he does and start doing others. But a little thought reveals that it is more than behavior Peter and Lynn want from their son. In Lynn's exasperated words we can hear that she is also asking for a certain attitude in Matty. She doesn't just want him to do the right thing for whatever reason. Even if he did always get home at the appointed hour, but did so only because he wanted to avoid the certain consequences of his parents' terrible swift sword, his mother would not honestly be satisfied. No, she wants to feel that she and her husband can retire from the Parent Police and start relating to their growing-up son as a trustworthy, self-regulating member of a common team. She wants him to "behave," but she wants him to do so out of his feelings for members of the family of which he sees he is a part. So perhaps the "something" Matty's parents want from him is more than behavior; it is about feeling a certain way. They want him to feel differently about them, about his willingness to put his own needs ahead of his agreements, about his responsibility to his family. What at first seemed to be a claim for a certain outer behavior now appears to be about his inner feelings.

But where do these inner feelings come from? Or, to put it another way, what would have to change in order for Matty's feelings to change? The answer, I believe, is that Matty's feelings come from the way he understands what the world is all about, the way he knows who he is, *the way he cares about what his parents care about.* In order for Matty really to feel differently about coming in at two-thirty in the morning he would have to know all this differently. What Lynn and Peter and any other parent of teenagers like Matty really want is for Matty to change not just the way he behaves, not just the way he feels, but the way he knows—not just what he knows but the *way* he knows. So, odd as it sounds, and unlikely as it is that they would ever think about it this way, what Lynn and Peter most want at three in the morning, now that they know their son is alive and well, is for his mind to be different. They want him to alter his consciousness, to change his mind. (That, and for them all to get some sleep!)

As it turns out, Matty's parents are not the only ones who want him to change his mind. In fact, like every teenager in America, Matty is also under a rather constant barrage of expectations at school, in the community, and even with some of his friends to know the world in a way different from the now "too independent" way it took him nearly the first decade of his life to achieve. Sometimes we will hear these expectations proclaimed in public discourse by the schools, the Department of Labor, or the politicians. Most of the time these expectations are pre-

sent but private—particular, subtle, and unspoken in the intimate arenas of family and neighborhood.

What do we want of Matty? Well, as I say, lots of things—lots of quite different-sounding things. Some people want Matty to be employable. Now, what does this mean? When we look into it, it is always less that they want him to know specific content or skills he can bring into the workforce ("Nah, we can teach him all that when we hire him") and much more that they want him to be someone they can count on, someone who shows up on time, someone who can get along with others, someone who can develop some loyalty to the company, someone it is worth putting in the time and money to train because when he makes a commitment he will keep it.

Other people want Matty to be a good citizen, a member of a democratic society. What does this mean? Well, for most people it does not really mean they hope he will go to the polls regularly and vote at election time. It usually means they hope he won't break into their homes when they are visiting their relatives in Florida. It means that in a society with a great deal of personal freedom, they hope Matty won't abuse that freedom.

The people who actually know Matty, his family and his friends, want a similar thing for Matty, though they express it in a way that is more personal than "good citizenship." They want him to be decent and trustworthy, someone who will hold up his end of a relationship, someone who will take them into account. They want to know that if Matty has a midnight curfew and he's going to be late they can count on him to call.

The schools want all these things from Matty and more besides. They want him to be able to think well—reflectively, abstractly, critically. They want him to understand the denotative meaning but also the connotative meaning, data and inference, instance and generalization, example and definition.

In addition to all these, we have expectations about how Matty feels. Not only clinicians and therapists and school counselors, but in many instances teenagers' parents and even their friends want them to be able to identify and share an inner psychological life. We expect teenagers to identify their inner motivations, to acknowledge internal emotional conflict, to be to some extent psychologically self-reflective, and to have some capacity for insight and productive self-consciousness.

As if this isn't enough, a lot of people want Matty to have good common sense, a whole different thing from thinking well. They want him to know that he should look before he leaps, that he should consider the longer-term consequences of choices that may seem momentarily appealing but are ultimately too costly. They want him to know the difference between reasonable risk and foolish risk. They want him to have friends but not be led around by them. They want him to have a mind of his own.

And a lot of people want that mind to have values, ideals, beliefs, principles—and not just values about good conduct that will help them feel safe knowing they are sharing the street with Matty. Because they care about Matty independent of their own welfare, they want him to have, and to feel he is ready to begin having, a meaningful life. Because the adults that surround Matty differ among themselves over what constitutes a meaningful life, which particular values, beliefs, and ideals they may want him to have will differ. In the 1960s and 1970s there were adults who wanted teens to value patriotic duty and there were those who wanted them to value the questioning of, and resistance to, authority. In the 1990s there are adults who want teens to value safe sex and those who want them to value abstinence. There are adults who want teenage girls to take on the values of traditional femininity and those who want them to value retaining the pluck and energy of their childhood voices. But although these adults may differ among themselves over which ideals they think teens should form, and no doubt they are more aware of what distinguishes them from each other than what they share, what they do share is a common claim upon adolescents to form ideals to which they feel loyal, with which they are identified, and from which they can lean toward what they imagine would be a better future for themselves and the world of which they are a part.

So, we want Matty to be employable, a good citizen, a critical thinker, emotionally self-reflective, personally trustworthy, possessed of common sense and meaningful ideals. This is a lot to want. It grows out of our concern for ourselves, our concern for others who live with Matty, and our concern for Matty himself. Will he be up to all these expectations?

To answer that we have to ask the same question we asked of his parents' disappointed expectation at two in the morning. What kind of expectation did they have? I have suggested that although it looks like an expectation about how Matty should behave, it is really an expectation about more than his outer behavior, and although it looks like an expectation about his inner feelings or attitudes, it is about even more than this, because his feelings and attitudes come from how he knows. I think the same thing can be said about every one of the expectations I have just mentioned. They are all about more than how we want teenagers to behave, more than how we want them to feel, more than what we want them to know. They are all expectations about *how* we want them to know, the *way* we want them to make meaning of their experience. They are claims on adolescents' minds.

Although we don't realize it, we have some shared expectations about what the mind of a teenager should be like. Whatever definition of "adolescence" we might cull from a textbook, the one that is operating most powerfully on the human being who happens to be going through adolescence is the hidden definition derived from the culture's claims or expectations about how an adolescent should know.

The very word *adolescence* shares an intimate relationship with the word *adult:* both come from the same Latin verb, *adolescere,* which means "to grow up." The past participle of the same word is *adultus,* "having grown up," or "grown-up." The word *adolescence,* then, suggests that by looking at what a culture asks its youth to "grow up to" we can discover that culture's definition of adulthood, the implication being that the culmination of adolescence constitutes adulthood. This may have been true once, but is it true today?

How *do* we want an adolescent's mind to change? Let's back up a bit. At some point in childhood, usually by the age of seven or eight, children undergo a qualitative change in the way they organize their thinking, their feeling, and their social relating. They move beyond a fantasy-filled construction of the world in which toy dinosaurs can plausibly transform themselves into the six-foot singing Barney, and instead come to scrutinize Steven Spielberg's *Jurassic Park* for the tiniest errors he may have allowed to creep into his depiction of *Tyrannosaurus rex.* In other words, they begin to construct a concrete world that conforms for the first time to the laws of nature, and they are interested in the limits and possibilities within that world. They read *The Guinness Book of World Records* to learn about the biggest cookie ever baked and the most expensive stationery ever printed.

At the same time, they move beyond a socially egocentric construction of the world, in which they imagine that others share the same mind and views as they do, and come to recognize that people have separate minds, separate intentions, and separate vantage points. They stop engaging bewildered parents in the second half of conversations, the first half of which they have conducted in their own head ("So what did you and Richie do after *that?*" the four-year-old may ask her mother, who has no idea what her daughter is talking about). Where before their speech was a more ancillary or peripheral aspect of their social interaction, it now becomes the necessary bridge between distinct minds.

At the same time, by the age of seven or eight, most children have emerged from a moment-to-moment relationship to their desires, preferences, and abilities. Younger children are neither able to delay gratification for more than a minute nor plagued on Tuesday by an experience of failure on Monday. But by the age of ten they organize their desires as things that persist through time. Issues of self-esteem have become more salient because there is a self whose abilities are not reconstituted from one moment to the next: ("I'm bad at math" doesn't just mean "I'm not enjoying it at this moment").

Between the ages of five and ten, in other words, a child makes a host of discoveries that seem to have nothing to do with each other. Consider, for example, these three: (1) the quantity of a liquid does not change when it is poured from one glass into another, smaller glass; (2) a person who could have no way of knowing that another person would be made unhappy by his actions cannot be said to be "mean"; (3) when I tell you "I don't like spinach," or think to myself, "I'm a Catholic girl," I mean that this is not just how I feel and think now, but that these things are ongoing, these are how I am or tend to be. Now, as different as these three discoveries are (they are about one's understanding of the physical, social, and personal worlds), it is the same principle, or way of knowing, that makes all of them possible.

In each case, the discovery arises out of the same ability to see that the phenomenon being considered (thing, other, self) has its own properties, which are elements of a class or set, and that the phenomenon (thing, other, self) is itself known as this class, which, like all classes, has durable, ongoing rules creating the idea of class membership and regulating that membership.

"Liquid," for example, becomes a class that has as a member the property of *quantity*, and that property is not regulated by my perception. It may look as if there is more water in the smaller glass, but, unlike the three-year-old, who believes it has actually become more water, the ten-year-old does not regulate meaning by how something appears. "Other person" is a class that has as a member the property of *intention*, and that property is not determined by my wishes. I may be unhappy or even angry that my father unwittingly got home too late to take me to watch the little league game, but since I know his mind is separate from mine, I could not, like the three-year-old, regard him as "mean" or as "a bad daddy." "Self" is a class that has as members the properties of *preference*, *habit*, and *ability*, and—since the self is a class, something that has properties—these things are aspects of me in some ongoing way, as opposed to merely what I want to eat or do now. Hence, new ways of knowing in such disparate domains as the inanimate, the social, and the introspective may all be occasioned by a single transformation of mind. In each case, what is being demonstrated is the ability to construct a mental set, class, or category to order the things of one's experience (physical objects, other people, oneself, desires) as property-containing phenomena (see Figure 1).

This ability to create the mental organization I call "durable categories" changes physical objects from being principally about my momentary perceptions of them to being about their existence as property-bearing "classes" with ongoing rules about what elements may or may not be properties, irrespective of my perceptions. It changes other people from being principally about my wishes in relations to them to being about their existence as property-bearing selves distinct from me, with ongoing rules about which intentions or characteristics actually belong to this class, irrespective of my wishes. It changes my own desires from being principally about my present impulse to being about the class of my ongoing, time-enduring needs or preferences, which class or category may contain my moment-to-moment impulses or wishes. What I am suggesting is that the ability to construct a concrete world, independent points of view, and a property-bearing self is expressive of a single form of consciousness. A common organizing principle or "order of mind" is at work, the durable category. Now we can ask: How adequate would this order of mind be for

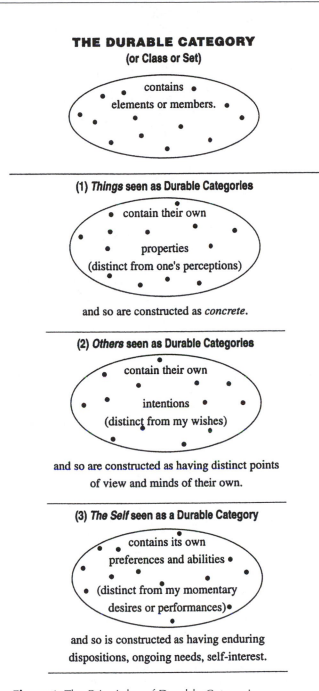

THE DURABLE CATEGORY
(or Class or Set)

contains elements or members.

(1) *Things* seen as Durable Categories

contain their own

properties
(distinct from one's perceptions)

and so are constructed as *concrete*.

(2) *Others* seen as Durable Categories

contain their own

intentions
(distinct from my wishes)

and so are constructed as having distinct points
of view and minds of their own.

(3) *The Self* seen as a Durable Category

contains its own
preferences and abilities

(distinct from my momentary
desires or performances)

and so is constructed as having enduring
dispositions, ongoing needs, self-interest.

Figure 1 The Principles of Durable Categories

Matty in meeting his parents' expectations on a Saturday night?

Whether it is a community's demand that Matty be a "good citizen" or his family's demand that he "keep us in mind," both are really aspects of a common expectation that Matty will be able to take out loyalty to or membership in a wider human community than the one defined by his own self-interest. In the private realm of personal relations we are hearing from Matty's parents a hope or an expectation that he will demonstrate

to them a trustworthiness born out of their accurate sense that he not only knows what they care about but in some way shares in what they care about, that he attends to what they care about not merely to get his own needs met or to calculate the consequences of defying them, but because these are to some extent what he cares about too. They want to believe that he will care about what they care about—for example, that everyone in the family keeps his word or that everyone in the family recognizes everyone else's need to know they are all right—even to the extent of subordinating some of his own particular interest (staying out past midnight with his friends) to that shared interest. Matty's parent, in other words, want to experience themselves in real relationship *with* their son, who is fast becoming a young man. He is looking more like a young man, talking more like a young man, and demanding the greater freedoms of a young man. Although they may not exactly know it, they believe that if they are to see him more as a man than as a child, they should be able to experience him on the other side of a relationship that no longer requires them to regulate an unsocialized, self-interested creature who needs their behavioral limits and who is constantly testing whether they will effectively keep playing and keep winning a game of control. Their expectation is that Matty's own relationship to what he knows they care about will allow them to feel themselves included in shared bonds of mutual trust and concern.

This is an expectation, clearly, that goes beyond *what* Matty will know. It is an expectation about *how* he will know what he knows. Would Matty be able to meet this expectation if he knew the world through the order of mind I call "durable categories," the order of mind that first comes into being around the age of seven or eight?

If he were knowing the world through the principle of durable categories, he could certainly understand his parents' point of view, see it as distinct from his own, provide his parents with the accurate sense that he understood their point of view, and even "take on" this point of view when it cost his own point of view nothing. He could thereby confuse them into thinking that he actually identifies with their point of view: that he not only understands their sense of its importance but shares that sense. He could do all this from a durable categories order of mind. But all this is *not* their expectation.

In order for him actually to hold their point of view in a way in which he could identify with it, he would have to give up an ultimate or absolute relationship to his own point of view. In order to subordinate his own point of view to some bigger way of knowing to which he would be loyal, in order to subordinate it to some integration or co-relation between his own and his parents' point of view, in order for his sense of himself to be based more on the preservation and operation of this correlation than on the preservation and operation of his own independent point of view—for all this to happen, Matty would have to construct his experience out of a principle that was more complex than the principle of durable categories. He would have to construct his experience out of a principle that subsumes or subordinates the principle of durable categories to a higher order principle. Instead of a principle that has elemental properties as its members, he would need a principle that had durable categories themselves as its members! (See Figure 2.) Lynn and Peter's demand, in other words, is an unrecognized claim that Matty's principle of mental organization should be of an order qualitatively more complex than categorical knowing. It is a claim that he should be able to make categorical knowing an element of a new principle, what we might call "cross-categorical" knowing.

In other words, if we know that Matty considers staying on at the party past his curfew although he is aware that his parents want him in the house by his curfew, we still really do not know how he understands the situation in which he finds himself until we see what principle of mental organization he brings to bear on these particulars. If he makes his own point of view or his own intentions, preferences, or needs the basic context in which to decide his course of action, then his decision to stay or not to stay will be governed by one set of calculations ("Will I get caught? What will happen if I get caught? Is staying at the party worth running these risks? How can I keep from getting caught? How can I keep from being punished if I am caught?") If he subordinates his own point of view to the relationship between his point of view and his parents' point of view, or if he subordinates the construction of self as a set of particular intentions, preferences, or needs to the construction of self identified in the relationship between his own collection of intentions, preferences, and needs (one category) and those of his parents (another category), then he frames the situation as something quite different, and the decision to say or not to stay will be governed by a whole different set of calculations ("Will my staying be damaging to the bond of trust between my parents and me? How *can* I stay? I'd feel so guilty; what will they think of me if I disregard our agreement?"). These questions betoken the existence of a different way of being *in* one's involvements with others, that of orienting not

THE PRINCIPLE OF THE DURABLE CATEGORY
(In the Interpersonal Domain)

A HIGHER ORDER PRINCIPLE
(Durable Categories as an *element* of a *new* principle)

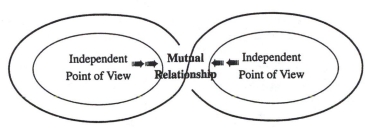

Figure 2 The Transformation from the Principle of Durable Categories to a Higher Order Principle

just to what will happen to me or to my wants but what will happen to my bond or connection or relationship. Relationships thus move from being extrinsically valuable to being intrinsically valuable. This different way of knowing is what Lynn and Peter expect of Matty.

And Lynn and Peter are not alone. As it turns out, every one of the expectations we generally hold of teenagers makes the identical demand! The expectation that Matty will be a "good citizen" as a member of a town, a school, or any social institution that has rules for good order is an expectation not only that he will understand the institution's rules and regulations, not only that he will understand the consequences of violating them, and not only that he will keep from violating them, but that he will share in the bigger purposes of social regulation and fair treatment those rules serve. The expectation is not merely that Matty will be well contained by his fear of the consequences to him of violation, that the system will work its controlling forces on him. Were that the expectation, the principle of durable categories would be enough to allow Matty to meet it. No, the expectation is that Matty will be a fellow citizen, himself a sharer in the idea and activity of preserving the societal bonds of the commonwealth. To do this, Matty

will need a way of knowing at least as complex as the cross-categorical principle.

And it is not just these more prosocial expectations that require cross-categorical knowing. All the expectations do. Wanting someone to subordinate his self-interest to the needs and value of a relationship seems like quite a different thing from wanting someone to think abstractly. But for Matty to think reflectively, inferentially, connotatively, or thematically requires that the concrete (a durable category) become an element of his principle of knowing rather than the principle of knowing itself. "Definition" is minimally a cross-categorical way of knowing because it takes the concrete example as an instance or an element of a bigger principle of knowing that includes all the concrete examples. Examples must therefore be an element or member, not the principle itself. "Inference" is a minimally cross-categorical way of knowing because it takes the category of datum or fact as an instance or element. Data must therefore be element, not principle. *Re*flective thinking requires a mental "place" to stand apart from, or outside of, a durably created idea, thought, fact, or description. The idea, thought, fact, or description is made subordinate (as figure or element) to a *super*ordinate ground or principle that is now capable of "bending back" (the literal meaning of *reflective*) its attention to focus on its own products. Each of these expectations about thinking is really an expectation for yet another expression of what it means to think abstractly. But each of these expectations for "abstractness" is identical in its organizational principle to the expectations for interpersonal trustworthiness.

The expectation that adolescents experience their emotions as inner psychological states is also a demand for the subordinating or integrating of the simpler, categorical self ("I'm mad at my sister. I like BLT sandwiches. I don't' like it when my father cooks my eggs too runny") into a more complex context that relates to the categorical self ("I'm much more confident. I used to be just super insecure, very self-conscious"). Thus, the expectation that adolescents be able to identify inner motivations, hold onto emotional conflict internally, be psychologically self-reflective, and have a capacity for insight all implicate the cross-categorical capacity to experience the self in relation to a given set or category rather than as the set or category itself.

The construction of values, ideals, and broad beliefs also requires at least a cross-categorical principle of mental organization. Knowing that people are operating from such a principle tells us nothing about what their values or ideals will be or what they will "set their hearts on." But to construct *any* kind of generalizable value or ideal they must subordinate the factual and the actual to the bigger array of the possible or the currently contrary-to-fact.

The very idea of the future as something one lives with as real in the present rather than as the-present-that-hasn't-happened-yet requires the same cross-categorical emancipation from actual/factual/present reality. The most common kind of lack of common sense we find in teenagers is often mistakenly referred to as "poor impulse control," an imprecise characterization paying too much respect to the "raging hormones" view of adolescence. The categorical order of mind is enough to handle impulse control. What we are asking here of adolescents is more complex, because it is rarely unmediated impulses that actually lead adolescents into the more foolish risks they are willing to run.

Much more often it is an embeddedness in the short-term, immediate present—a present lacking a live relation to the longer-term future.

What Lynn and Peter want of their son, what his teachers want, what his neighbors want, what his potential employers want—what we adults want to teenagers—is not just a new set of behaviors or even a new collection of disparate mental abilities. What we want is a single thing: a qualitatively new way of making sense, a change of mind as dramatic as the change a child undergoes between the ages of five and ten. The common, single organizational principle at work in every expectation we have of adolescents entails the subordination and the integration of the earlier form—durable categories—into a new form capable of simultaneously relating one durable category to another. The principle of mental organization reflected in all the expectations of adolescents is this *trans-categorical* or *cross-categorical* construction (see Figure 3).

By now it should be clear that when I refer to "mind" or "mental" or "knowing" I am not referring to thinking processes alone. I am referring to the person's meaning-constructive or meaning-organizational capacities. I am referring to the selective, interpretive, executive, construing capacities that psychologists have historically associated with the "ego" or the "self" I look at people as the active organizers of their experience. "Organisms organize," the developmental psychologist William Perry once said: "and human organisms organize *meaning.*" This kind of "knowing," this work of the mind, is not about "cognition" alone, if what we mean by cognition is thinking divorced from feeling and social relating. It is about the organizing principle we bring to our thinking and our feelings and our relating to others and our relating to parts of ourselves.

In *The Evolving Self* I looked at psychological growth as the unself-conscious development of successively more complex principles for organizing experience. Building on the work of Piaget and those who came after him, I took the idea of such principles of mental organization and extended its "breadth" (beyond thinking to affective, interpersonal, and intrapersonal realms) and its "length" (beyond childhood and adolescence to adulthood). I have already mentioned three of these principles for organizing experience (their differing capacities are summarized in Table 1).

The first and least complex of these principles is the one most commonly used by young children, the principle of *independent elements.*

DURABLE CATEGORIES
(Second Order of Consciousness)

CROSS-CATEGORICAL MEANING-MAKING
(Third Order of Consciousness)

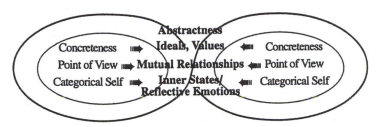

Figure 3 The Transformation from Durable Categories to Cross-Categorical Meaning-Making (and its products in the cognitive, sociocognitive, and intrapersonal-affective domains)

Their attachment to the momentary, the immediate, and the atomistic makes their thinking fantastic and illogical, their feelings impulsive and fluid, their social-relating egocentric. The second of these principles is the *durable category*, the principle children usually evolve in latency, or between the ages of seven and ten. During these years, children's capacity to organize things, others, and the self as possessors of elements or properties enables their thinking to become concrete and logical, their feelings to be made up of time-enduring needs and dispositions rather than momentary impulses, and their social-relating to grant to themselves and to others a separate mind and a distinct point of view. The third of these principles, *cross-categorical knowing*, is the one we unwittingly expect of adolescents. The capacity to subordinate durable categories to the interaction between them makes their thinking abstract, their feelings a matter of inner states and self-reflexive emotion ("self-confident," "guilty," "depressed"), and their social-relating capable of loyalty and devotion to a community of people or ideas larger than the self.

These principles share several important features. First, they are not merely principles for how one thinks but for how one constructs experience more generally, including one's thinking, feeling, and social-relating. Second, they are principles for the organization (the form or complexity) of one's thinking, feeling, and social-relating, not the content of one's thinking, feeling, or social-relating. Knowing that someone is in the grip of the second principle tells us a lot about *how* he or she thinks or feels, but it doesn't really tell us anything about *what* he or she thinks or feels.

Third, a principle of mental organization has an inner logic or, more properly speaking, an "epistemologic." The root or "deep structure" of any principle of mental organization is the subject-object relationship. "*Object*" refers to those elements of our knowing or organizing that we can reflect on, handle, look at, be responsible for, relate to each other, take control of, internalize, assimilate, or otherwise operate upon. All these expressions suggest that the element of knowing is not the whole of us; it is distinct enough from us that we can do something with it.

"*Subject*" refers to those elements of our knowing or organizing that we are identified with, tied to, fused with, or embedded in. We *have* object; we *are* subject. We cannot be responsible for, in control of, or reflect upon that which is subject. Subject is immediate; object is mediate.

TABLE 1
Three Principles of Meaning Organization

| First Principle
Roughly 2 to 6 years | Second Principle
Roughly 6 years to teens | Third Principle
Teenage years and beyond |
|---|---|---|
| **Logical-Cognitive Domain**
Can: recognize that objects exist independent of own sensing of them ("object permanence")

Cannot: distinguish own perception of an object from the actual properties of the object; construct a logical relation between cause and effect | *Can*: grant to objects their own properties irrespective of one's perceptions; that is, reason consequentially, that is, according to cause and effect; construct a narrative sequence of events; relate one point in time to another; construct fixed categories and classes into which things can be mentally placed

Cannot: reason abstractly; subordinate concrete actuality to possibility; make generalizations; discern overall patterns; form hypotheses; construct ideals | *Can*: reason abstractly, that is, reason about reasoning; think hypothetically and deductively, form negative classes (for example, the class of all not-crows); see relations as simultaneously reciprocal

Cannot: systematically produce all possible combinations of relations; systematically isolate variables to test hypotheses |
| **Social-Cognitive Domain**
Can: recognize that persons exist separate from oneself

Cannot: recognize that other persons have their own purposes independent of oneself: take another person's point of view as distinct from one's own | *Can*: construct own point of view and grant to others their distinct point of view; take the role of another person; manipulate others on behalf of own goals; make deals, plans, and strategies

Cannot: take own point of view and another's simultaneously; construct obligations and expectations to maintain mutual interpersonal relationships | *Can*: be aware of shared feelings, agreements, and expectations that take primacy over individual interests

Cannot: Construct a generalized system regulative of interpersonal relationships and relationships between relationships |

(continued)

TABLE 1 (*continued*)
Three Principles of Meaning Organization

First Principle *Roughly 2 to 6 years*	*Second Principle* *Roughly 6 years to teens*	*Third Principle* *Teenage years and beyond*
Intrapersonal-Affective Domain *Can*: distinguish between inner sensation and outside stimulation *Cannot*: distinguish one's impulses from oneself, that is, is embedded in or driven by one's impulses	*Can*: drive, regulate, or organize impulses to produce enduring dispositions, needs, goals; delay immediate gratification; identify enduring qualities of self according to outer social or behavioral manifestations (abilities—"fast runner"; preferences—"hate liver"; habits—"always oversleep") *Cannot*: internally coordinate more than one point of view or need organization; distinguish one's needs from oneself; identify enduring qualities of the self according to inner psychological manifestations (inner motivations—"feel conflicted"; self attributions—"I have low self-esteem"; biographic source—"My mother's worrying has influenced the way I parent".)	*Can*: internalize another's point of view in what becomes the co-construction of personal experience, thus creating new capacity for empathy and sharing at and internal rather that merely transactive level; coordinate more than one point of view internally, thus creating emotions experienced as internal subjective states rather than social transactions *Cannot*: organize own states or internal parts of self into systematic whole; distinguish self from one's relationship; see the self as the author (rather than merely the theater) of one's inner psychological life

Source: R. Kegan, "The Child behind the Mask," in W. H. Reid et al., eds., *Unmasking the Psychopath* (New York: W.W. Norton 1986), pp. 45–77. Copyright © 1986 by W. W. Norton and Co. Adapted by permission.

Subject is ultimate or absolute; object is relative. When the child evolves the second principle, for example, the momentary impulse or the immediate perception then moves from being the subject of her experiencing to being the object of her experiencing. Now the durable category (not impulse but ongoing preference or need; not appearance but concrete reality) becomes the new subject of her experiencing. And this new subject governs or regulates or acts on what has become object (she controls impulses; she reflects on appearance and distinguishes it from reality). If the adolescent evolves the third principle, then *durable category* moves from being the *subject* of one's experiencing to being the *object* of one's experiencing. Now cross-categorical meaning-making (not concreteness but abstraction; not the ultimacy of self-interest but its subordination to a relationship) becomes the new *subject* of experiencing, acting upon or regulating what has become object. Each principle of mental organization differs in terms of what is subject and what is object, but every principle is constituted by a subject-object relationship.

Fourth, the different principles of mental organization are intimately related to each other. They are not just different ways of knowing, each with its preferred season. One does not simply replace the other, nor is the relation merely additive or cumulative, an accretion of skills. Rather, the relation is transformative, qualitative, and incorporative. Each successive principle subsumes or encompasses the prior principle. That which was subject becomes object to the next principle. The new principle is a higher order principle (more complex, more inclusive) that makes the prior principle into an element or tool of its system. A geometric analogy for the relation between these three principles might be that of the *point,* the *line,* and the *plane:* each subsequent geometric form contains the previous one. A line is a "metapoint" in a sense; it contains an infinite number of points, but as elements subordinated to the more complex organizational principle of the line, where earlier the point was itself an organizational principle. Similarly, a plane is a "metaline," an organizational principle containing line as an element.

We can see this analogy almost literally at work by considering how people might make use of the three principles to explain a movie such as *Star Wars,* which had broad age-appeal because it was no doubt interesting to moviegoers with a variety of organizational principles.

Young children using the first principle demonstrate no sense of a story or of a logical connection between one part of the movie and another. Instead, they talk about a single point in time in the movie, or they talk about a single character with no indication that they understand his importance to the story ("I loved Chewbaka; he was so big and hairy"). Children using the second principle can subordinate point to line but not line to plane; they can string the events together to create a linear narrative of the story at a concrete level, but they do not organize an abstract theme of which this particular story is an expression. "What the movie is about" is the linear sequence of events that happened in the movie (as any exasperated parent knows who has asked this question, but was not prepared for the marathon recounting of the entire story that followed). It is only by making recourse to the third principle that the movie might be "about" the battle between good and evil or some such thematic abstraction in which the line of the story's plot is subordinated to a larger field or plane of consideration. In other words, the principles of mental organization are not only "natural epistemologies" (subject-object structures found in nature), they are developmentally related to each other: each one is included in the next.

Fifth and finally, the suggestion that a given individual may over time come to organize her experience according to a higher order principle suggests that what we take as subject and what we take as object are not necessarily fixed for us. They are not permanent. They can change. In fact, transforming our epistemologies, liberating ourselves from that in which we were embedded, making what was subject into object so that we can "have it" rather than "be had" by it—this is the most powerful way I know to conceptualize the growth of the mind. It is a way of conceptualizing the growth of the mind that is as faithful to the self-psychology of the West as to the "wisdom literature" of the East. The roshis and lamas speak to the growth of the mind in terms of our developing ability to relate to what we were formerly attached to. The experiencing that our subject-object principle enables is very close to what both East and West mean by "consciousness" and that is the way I intend the term throughout this book. In Figure 4 I represent these first three principles of mental organization as "orders of consciousness," highlighting

	SUBJECT	OBJECT	UNDERLYING STRUCTURE
			LINES OF DEVELOPMENT
			K COGNITIVE / E INTERPERSONAL / Y INTRAPERSONAL
1	PERCEPTIONS / *Fantasy*	Movement	Single Point/ Immediate/ Atomistic
	SOCIAL PERCEPTIONS		
	IMPULSES	Sensation	
2	CONCRETE / *Actuality* / Data, Cause-and-Effect	Perceptions	Durable Category
	POINT OF VIEW / Role-Concept / Simple Reciprocity (tit-for-tat)	Social Perceptions	
	ENDURING DISPOSITIONS / Needs, Preferences / Self Concept	Impulses	
3	ABSTRACTIONS / *Ideality* / Inference, Generalization / Hypothesis, Proposition / Ideals, Values	Concrete	Cross-Categorical Trans-Categorical
	MUTUALITY/INTERPERSONALISM / Role Consciousness / Mutual Reciprocity	Point of View	
	INNER STATES / Subjectivity, Self-Consciousness	Enduring Dispositions / Needs, Preferences	

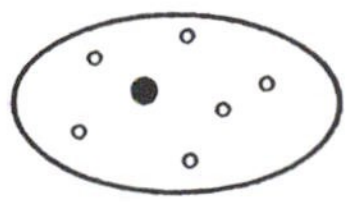

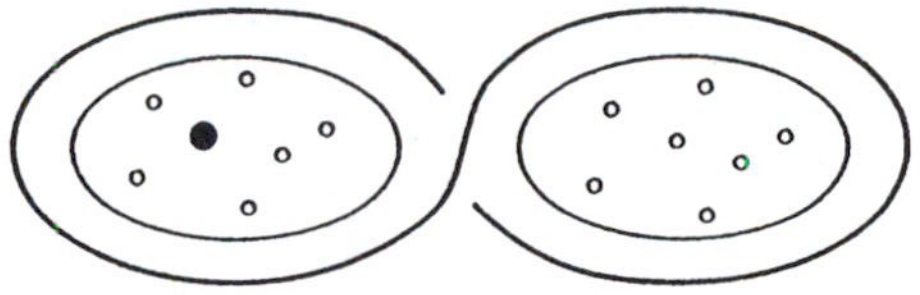

Figure 4 Three Orders of Consciousness

all five of these features. (I use the term "order" not in the sense of "sequence" but in the sense of "dimension." Each successive principle "goes meta" on the last; each is "at a whole different order" of consciousness.)

In *The Evolving Self* I explored psychological growth as the unselfconscious development of more inclusive and complex principles for organizing experience. Here I want to suggest that to the list of phenomena a culture creates and we study we should add "claims on the minds of its members." This book examines the relationship between the principles we may possess and the complexity of mind that contemporary culture unrecognizedly asks us to possess through its many claims and expectations—the mental demands of modern life. *The Evolving Self* was particularly concerned with the costs inherent in the processes of growth. This book is also concerned with a kind of psychological cost or burden, the one we must bear if the demands made of us are over our heads.

In this chapter we have seen one-half of an untold story about present-day adolescence. What gives to that which we call "adolescence" a coherence as a distinct time of life might be something more than a distinct biology or even a distinct psychology possessed by those in this age group. Surely adolescents reflect a variety of biologies and a variety of psychologies. But something that might be true across the myriad diversities within any real group of teens is the common claim upon them for a distinct level of consciousness. In spite of all our present-day difference, in the midst of the current American experience of more *pluribus* than *unum*, lacking a self-conscious commonality of value, purpose, or persuasion, divided by geography, race, gender, and social position, it appears that there may exist, nonetheless, this odd and interesting national concert, an unwitting collective agreement about what we want from the adolescent mind. This is half of the story, the real answer to the adolescent's question, "Whaddaya want from me?" The other half has to do with whether adolescents can give us what we want.

CHAPTER 6

COMPLEX LIVES

MARCIA B. BAXTER MAGOLDA

The five or six years that follow college are critical years for learning. Get out of the structured atmosphere; try your own wings; fly on your own! What is supposed to be good, what is important to me, what are my real values? For the first time I have a chance to listen to my own voice. I finally got to a point [in my mid-twenties] where I was paying a lot of attention to that. During that time I was processing all that I had been gathering for the prior years. I was finally able to see a clear path, chart a course, and now am on the course.

Gwen

If I think about the future too much it scares the living bejesus out of me.

Phillip

Gwen and Phillip are two of 39 participants in a longitudinal study of young adults' learning and development from ages 18 to 30. I open this book with their two comments because the driving questions of young adult life for the total group of participants are highlighted in these brief excerpts. Gwen's emphasis on listening to her own voice captures perhaps the most pressing issue this group faced during their twenties. Exploring one's values, processing information gathered from the external world in prior years, envisioning a path, and proceeding down that path mark the major themes of these participants' lives during their twenties. Phillip's sentiment conveys the emotion he and his peers felt during this age range.

This chapter portrays the complexity of young adulthood as a backdrop for the participants' journeys toward self-authorship. The pressing questions that occupied their twenties—"How do I know?" "Who am I?" "What relationships do I want with others?"—reveal this complexity from the participants' vantage point. The societal expectations they encountered—rapid change, ambiguity, and multiple lifestyle choices—sketch this complexity from the vantage point of contemporary society. I then use a student development lens to show the developmental complexity these expectations entail, essentially that they require self-authorship in the epistemological, intrapersonal, and interpersonal dimensions of development. Interconnections among the most complex phases of each dimension depict the complex transformation required of young adults in today's society. The role of higher education in stewarding this transformation is introduced next, followed by an overview of the participants' college journeys to provide context for their journey through their twenties. Thus the chapter closes with the participants standing at the threshold of self-authorship.

Driving Questions of the Twenties

As one might expect, the central concerns for most participants after college were career success, finding meaningful relationships, finding their way in the adult world, establishing families, and in general "being happy." Hearing variations on these concerns over time revealed a few driving questions that stood at the core of these issues. As mentioned previously these included: 'How do I know?' 'Who am I?' and 'What relationships do I want with others?' A key issue in all three questions was hearing one's own voice regarding each of these questions. The particulars of participants' experiences illustrate the essence of these questions.

How Do I Know?

Mark described the twenties as a time to articulate the questions, "What is causing my unhappiness? What would make me happy? Trying to understand that." These questions arose in Mark's life despite his success at the law school of his choice; they occurred to others despite success in their post-college careers. Heather asked herself, "What is the most important thing in my life? Is there one? Am I doing the right thing?" Dissatisfaction or lack of fulfillment in their initial career choices led to the issue of how one knows what to do. Gwen articulated the issue best by saying:

> The 'how you know' question was huge for me. Then career exploring, where are the answers? Learn to figure out what is important to you; learn to find what fits for you in work settings rather than thinking I have to work in advertising. Learning where your values are first, rather than putting things first that you don't know about.

Gwen followed the plan others had suggested for career success in her early twenties. During her twenties, however, she realized that "how *you* know" really came down to "how *I* know." She conveyed the struggle to know in weighing a marriage decision, saying:

> There are some things that just don't come with guarantees or instructions and you just have to trust your gut, take the leap of faith and muddle through with your instincts. . . . It's just one of those things where you set everything in line as best you can and then you look at it and you say, "Well, is it going to be a go?" And you go and you hope. And you just trust that what you thought was right. But again, that's totally against everything—I want a crystal ball. I want to know when and where and how and if.

Gwen wanted to know but she did not know how. As her quote at the outset of the chapter indicated, she discovered that listening to her own voice was the key to knowing.

Lindsey conveyed the changing nature of the "how you know" question throughout the years after college. Talking about changes in learning, he offered:

> A lot of these experiences are less technical than ones I talked about when I was a sophomore—then I was learning how to differentiate an algebraic equation. Ten years later you find yourself trying to quiet a baby. Eight years ago I was studying pricing theory and ramifications thereof; now I'm thinking about managing styles. I'm trying to learn to be a good daddy. It's ironic that when you have more knowledge than you have ever had, the types of things you are learning are less technical, less hard to learn. The process doesn't stop, it is just different. Also the ramifications back then if you didn't learn it, fine, try something else. Now, if you don't learn how to be a good parent, there are big ramifications. Or your career path goes to manager and you flop. The ramifications are pretty serious. Learning has become less intense, yet the ramifications become more intense. Different pressures. Different reasons for wanting to learn something; and different methods you use.

Although Lindsey did not label the difference other than technical and less technical, it seemed that he was describing the difference between learning and knowing in circumstances where there were tangible answers (i.e., the algebraic equation) and circumstances in which knowing was more subjective (i.e., quieting a baby). Encountering complexity and ambiguity in knowledge construction and learning facilitated movement toward self-authorship in how one knows (the epistemological dimension). The need to choose "how *I* know" from among the alternatives drew participants toward self-authorship.

Who Am I?

A closely related and equally pressing question was "Who am I?" Answering the "how I know" question necessitated defining who the "I" was. Al described changes in this arena during his twenties:

> In my early twenties, I was kind of out there swinging. Living for the day. Working and making good money, doing a lot of what I wanted to do. I didn't have anybody to account to or worry about. I was playing basketball, working out, and dating a lot of peo-

ple. It was a much more selfish time for me. In my mid-twenties I figured out, okay, that wasn't fulfilling. When I focused energy on selfless things, I had more fun. I developed a more mature attitude.

Part of Al's decision about who he was related to changing from computer consulting to medical school. Al reported that when you realize you are going to be working for the rest of your life, the meaning of that work takes on a new importance. Another dimension involved volunteering as a big brother and becoming involved in his church. In response to a lack of fulfillment, he listened more carefully to his own voice in guiding life choices.

Barry described a similar experience. He recounted what happens when the "honeymoon" is over:

> You start settling into a job. The first year of working, the honeymoon of wearing a suit, when you look forward to doing that in the beginning. And you're not really thinking about your future; you're thinking about the next day. You're not thinking long term, you're like, "Okay, I have a job. Now let's see how I like it." But then after the first year, you start thinking about what you want to do down the road. You start saying, "Do I want to be doing this for the next twenty years? What do I want to be doing? If it's not this, what is it and how do I get there?" And where do you want to live? Not only what do I want to do, but also where do I want to do it and whom do I want to do it with? Do I want to spend the rest of my life with this person or do I want to give up my freedom?

Like Al, when Barry realized that these are long-term decisions, he began to question who he really wanted to be. Phillip was struggling with the same questions:

> If I think about the future too much it scares the living bejesus out of me. It would be nice to think something good is coming around the corner tomorrow. I have my own place, I'm paying the rent, it is stable, that doesn't scare me. But I keep thinking, "Am I going to be staying here the rest of my life?" I don't think I will, but I haven't opened up my eyes enough to see there is a niche for what I do. Being good at music doesn't matter here—that might be different in Nashville. A person invited me to Nashville for a training session. I went, and they are doing a lot of stuff there. I enjoy country music, but it is not my main thing. I'd like to be able to do a vari-

ety of things if I got into music production. Then other things, questions in my mind about people around me. The people living in my building are twenty- and thirty-somethings; some are going to prestigious schools, driving expensive cars, hoping to become doctors of various kinds, or professionals in the city. I don't see how, with my background, I can relate to these people. I hang out with my girlfriend on her side of town— row houses, working class people. A lot of people there are not college educated, do not speak English very well—for a kid from the suburbs seeing that is a shake-up. Nothing in common there either. It doesn't seem like a natural fit. I'm not trying to be snobbish; I can adapt to my surroundings and different lifestyles. These are a lot of things I do think about—I have periods of angst and periods of calmness.

Phillip was looking for a niche—for what he wanted to do (music production) and for what kind of person he wanted to or could be. Unable to find a fit either with his building mates or his girlfriend's community, he was still exploring.

Alice's dilemma was somewhat different, although still focused on the "who am I" question. Alice was satisfied with her career, but also wanted a child. She shared the dilemma of juggling the two:

> I have always known that [having a child] is something I want; the intensity of wanting it is increasing drastically. My spouse is on the same wavelength. We both have strong family relationships and want this. [The challenge will be] juggling. Honestly, my initial thoughts were "That isn't fair that I have to balance because I am the woman; nothing will change for him. Why should I have to give up what I have worked so hard for?" Probably six months I felt that. I felt that wasn't getting anywhere; then my thinking became, "Family is priority one, so given that, how can I keep things I enjoy about professional life?" Child is number one, profession is two. How can I make number two as satisfying as possible? Being mad about [professional sacrifice] doesn't change anything . . . biologically determined. I've worked as hard as he has. We talked about it. Reality is, it affects me more. Since then it has been a matter of accepting and embracing it. Deciding that I wanted it, not feeling like it had to be. That is the biggest challenge right now. How will it play out to manage professional responsibilities while going through a preg-

nancy? We've talked about how we will do this with a kid. Something will have to change and something will work out. . . . I have always been confident [of my ability] to direct my own life.

Alice wanted to be both a career professional and a mother. Although she in some ways knew the answer to the "who am I" question, she was initially bothered by external constraints she faced and later concerned about what this identity would really look like. Participants' struggle with the "who am I" question (the intrapersonal dimension) stemmed from their discovery that self was central to knowledge construction. Clarification of their values and priorities was necessary for them to make good career and personal decisions.

What Kind of Relationships Do I Want to Construct with Others?

Once the internal sense of self materialized, it was necessary to incorporate it into relationships. Thus the flip side of the "who am I" question was "What kind of relationships do I want?" Lynn conveyed the reciprocal nature of these two questions:

I think it is a hard time relationship wise. Because you and your prospective other—you both are changing. I know as far as that goes with a lot of friends, they are divorced—got married too early. A lot of people make that mistake; happily it wasn't me. You tend to grow, a huge change time, especially the first three years out of college. Trying to find your niche in your environment—move to a new city, or start a new job, or, as in my case, to find that real job. Becoming independent, growing up. You are an adult now; you have to be accepting of all your situations that you put yourself into and sometimes that's not good. But I think that my twenties were a time of maturing and finding myself and becoming happy, becoming a positive person. I didn't just get to 30 and say, "Okay, I'm here"—it just didn't happen. It's a huge process and I think people get there at different ages and stages. I had friends who were ready at age 24; they found it, they got it, whatever *it* is-they got *it*. It took me a couple years more and that's fine. It takes everybody a certain time. Can't say you need to be here at age 25. You can't do it—too many obstacles in the way. I think inde-

pendence and maturity are something that I would say sum up my twenties. Feeling all right, okay with what's going on.

Lynn articulated that as people grow and change who they are, they sometimes find themselves having difficulty with relationships. Many participants did struggle with maintaining, and in some cases dissolving, relationships due to their own self-evolution. Others struggled with whether they were ready for various kinds of relationships. Justin explained his worry about the upcoming birth of his first child:

It scares me to death. It is a major life change; don't know if I'm ready. We planned it, now it is really going to happen. There is no going back now. I'm anxious about it, it makes me nervous. It is going to be a huge time commitment; I am afraid about the normal stuff like we won't have enough money, or I'll screw something up and not be able to take care of it, or it might screw up our marriage. I'm nervous as hell. I'm in over my head. But it is exciting too. Sometimes I feel like things just happen to you. Things just roll. You just make decisions; it's weird. Time determines a lot of things—decisions are made because of something you did or didn't do. This whole decision making process—deciding to have a baby. My spouse had a big say in that; I kept putting it off. She was 30, and she said, "We can't wait much longer." There was pressure to do that because she was afraid if we waited it would be risky. I felt pressured there; but she was right. I don't want to be that old when my kid is in high school. Felt pressured, a little resentment, but then what can you do, because she was right. That is part of my anxiety—do I really want this? Too late now. I'm sure it will be great when it happens; I hope so. It is an overwhelming experience; all these thoughts and doubts will go out window when the baby comes.

Part of Justin's fear came from not being totally sure he wanted "this"—his fear of the relationship of father and child. He was also not totally sure about a career change he was preparing for—a move from classroom teacher to principal—due to his relationship with his father. He shared his issues:

There aren't many men in elementary special education. My dad is a teamster electrician, big union man. My grandfather was a pipe fitter, uncle was an engineer, and another was a maintenance supervisor—

manly jobs. It is stupid that I care about that. [He laughed.] Wanting to be accepted by males in the family. I don't want them to think I'm a wuss. That is the biggest thing I don't like about my job; when I go to work, I like it. But I'm not doing some big industrial job. I don't want to do something because my parents want it. My dad is proud of what I do. But I've always thought in back of my head, of whether he thinks I don't have a manly job. It's a weird thing to say, but that is how I feel. Moving toward a principal position is a little more accepted. It sucks that I want to work for something that is more accepted; but that is not the only reason. I do want to make changes.

Justin did make career changes during his twenties, including going back to school to become a special education teacher and again to move toward a position as principal. He made these decisions based on an increasing sense of who he was, yet his concern about his relationships with others still affected his thinking.

Genesse, like Justin, struggled with what she wanted versus what others wanted for or from her. She found herself in a number of frustrating work environments in her twenties and often sacrificed what she wanted to meet others' expectations. Of her twenties, she said, "I try to stand up for myself more—not all the time, but more. If there is one underlying theme of my twenties, that is it." Relationship struggles (the interpersonal dimension) occurred in the context of the shift from external to internal self-definition. As Lynn noted, relationships were hard when both parties were changing. Bringing one's internal sense of self to this layer of knowledge construction altered relationships that pre-dated the external to internal shift. Standing up for oneself, however, was not a selfish matter of having one's own way; it was, rather, a matter of including oneself as a mutual partner in the relationship. Participating in mutual construction of relationships prompted interpersonal growth toward self-authorship. As Genesse noted, the process was not easy.

Complications

Finding their own voices and standing up for themselves was complicated for many participants by personal dynamics and external events.[1] Although all participants were engaged in a search for meaning around the three driving questions, some struggled under additional burdens. One participant shared the additional layer of the "who am I" question posed by exploring sexual orientation. Coming to an acceptance and celebration of this aspect of self also affected how to construct relationships with others in a society that marginalizes gay/lesbian/bisexual people. A few participants identified parts of who they were as problematic and sought therapy to reconstruct them. Sometimes these issues came from difficult family relationships or hereditary health conditions.

External events also challenged participants in their twenties. A number of participants lost a grandparent or parent during this time, putting other life issues in perspective. Two participants experienced the murder of a family member, bringing the violence of contemporary society directly into their lives. Many knew friends or family members who suffered from terminal illnesses. Being in relationships with these persons prompted questions about the meaning of life. Others shared their concern regarding parents' divorces and their role in helping both parents while reconstructing their idea of what their family was like. These experiences also made them fear the future of their own relationships. One participant also faced an abortion decision due to the high probability of serious birth defects.

Regardless of their particular circumstances, all participants faced the fact that young adult life was not without struggles. Lynn captured this when she said:

> I've faced the facts of life that it's a cruel world out there. You hear it, but it's true. It's not this nice little piece of cake, you walk out of college and there's a job on a silver platter. I've been through a year of frustration and hard work and brown-nosing and the works to know that hard work doesn't always pay off like we all hoped it would. Dealing with politics, knowing who to work with and who not to work with, who to talk to and who not to talk to, who to trust and who not to trust.

Just as Lynn learned that life is not always fair in job searching, others learned that life dealt unexpected blows or involved struggles in coming to terms with one's internal voice. The driving questions were common among participants as was the complexity of each of their experiences in resolving the questions.

Societal Expectations of Young Adults

The driving questions of the twenties articulated by this group of young adults are not surprising in the context of contemporary society's expectations for them. In fact, the ambiguity of expectations contributed to these driving questions. Levine and Cureton (1998) noted that this generation of young people live "in a time of profound changes—demographic, economic, technological, global, social" (p. 9). The U.S. economy generally declined during this period, technology expanded substantially, and organizational change that alters the nature of work emerged— all dynamics that affect the nature of work expectations for young adults. Oblinger and Verville (1998) articulated the skills they say business needs of higher education graduates—"initiative, persistence, integrity, the ability to communicate effectively, to think creatively as well as critically, and to work with others to solve problems" (p. 73). In describing these skills, Oblinger and Verville stressed the evolving nature of learning, the need for self-discipline, self-confidence, and self-direction as well as the interdependence that stems from more flexible organizational structures. Exploring more flexible visions of organizations, Zohar (1997) emphasized the need to cope with uncertainty and rapid change, the need for employees to be "cocreative partners" (p. 87) with employers, and the ability to work with multiple perspectives and supervisory styles. These expectations materialized in the work experiences of my longitudinal participants. They were often expected to work independently, to initiate their own work and problem-solving strategies, to cope with change, and to participate in the creation of their company's practice. Ambiguity was a common dynamic in their work, as was the need to work with others different from themselves. Thus the questions of how to know, self-identity, and relations with others were central to those complex work settings.

Ambiguity in social roles was also prevalent for these young adults because of changing attitudes and gender roles. Greater higher education opportunities for women were coupled with changing attitudes about women establishing career as a priority. The women in my study, like the men, had high career aspirations and intended to put their education to work both due to their interests and the economic necessity of working. Yet most wanted relationships and families as well, although the timing of acting on this desire varied considerably. Most participants' families expected them to spend the first few years out of college getting settled in their careers and establishing financial security. They perceived that their college peers expected them to develop prestigious careers and demand high salaries. By the mid-twenties many also received the societal message that it was time to marry and have children. As Leah explained it, "you graduate college, then you get married, then you have kids. It's the next step in our lives." Despite growing acceptance of multiple sexual orientations, the overall societal pressure was still for heterosexual relationships.

As you just heard in Gwen's struggle with the marriage decision and Lynn's commentary on friends making marriage mistakes, the decision to marry was difficult for most. Divorce had become a common occurrence in this country as these young adults grew up; in fact many reported that their parents had divorced during their childhood or adolescence or that their parents were divorcing now that they were out of college. Many shared hesitation with deciding to marry—either working on the decision over a number of years, breaking engagements, or hesitating even after living together for some substantial period of time. Similar to young adults portrayed in a Newsweek article on marriage (Hamilton and Wingert, 1998), they questioned whether commitments could last and did not want to find themselves in a divorce.

Decisions to have children and the resulting questions of balancing work and advanced education were also complex. As Alice recounted above, even though she wanted children she still resented giving up her professional career for which she had worked hard. Many participants shared household roles with their partners, and in two cases the fathers took care of infants and pursued advanced education while the mothers continued their careers. In most cases, however, the mother made some adjustments in her professional role to raise children. The need for dual incomes and the importance of graduate or professional education complicated these decisions. Some participants put off starting families for financial reasons; others maintained dual careers after having children out of financial necessity. Mothers who kept active professional lives often worried about the quality of their parenting whereas mothers who made raising children their primary career often wondered what others thought about them. Some tried to excel in both roles. While this led to what Granrose and Kaplan (1996) call "role overload" (p. 7) for some, others found it workable. Much of the confusion in making these decisions for both mothers and fathers stemmed from societal expectations for career success, more flexible perspectives on male and females roles, yet strong messages that remained regarding traditional roles and issues around the quality of life for children.

Social roles in the community were also a factor in these young adults' lives. Perhaps due to the increasing diversity of their generation, or the growth of crime, poverty, and homelessness, or their own experience with economic struggle, they felt responsible for contributing to their community. Some committed extensive time and resources (both financial and emotional) to long-term relationships with young adolescents through Big Brother or Big Sister programs. Others participated in programs to help individuals with financial planning, community maintenance, and assistance to individuals in need. Some took official roles in their churches or community organizations to contribute to their communities. They engaged in these activities despite heavy work schedules and family responsibilities. Their experience seems similar to reports that this generation volunteers more than any other does (Bagby, 1998). Certainly contributing to community and helping to ease America's ills is a societal message they hear regularly. Both Bagby (1998) and Loeb (1994) report extensive service initiatives led by young adults committed to improving the conditions of others in the community.

The Nature of These Expectations: The Transformation to Self-Authorship

Meeting societal expectations and making one's way into young adulthood are complex tasks. Taking on adult responsibilities, managing one's life effectively, and making informed decisions as a member of a community require something beyond learning particular skills and acquiring particular behaviors. They require, instead, the "capacity for self-authorship—the ability to collect, interpret, and analyze information and reflect on one's own beliefs in order to form judg-

ments" (Baxter Magolda, 1998, p. 143). Self-authorship is more than an acquired skill. As Robert Kegan (1994) explained, it requires complex ways of making meaning of our experience. For example, Kegan noted that as workers, adults are expected to:

> invent or own our work . . . to be self-initiating, self-correcting, self-evaluating . . . to be guided by our own visions . . . to take responsibility for what happens to us . . . to be accomplished masters of our particular work roles, jobs, or careers. (p. 153)

These expectations require self-authorship because they require the ability to construct our own visions, to make informed decisions in conjunction with coworkers, to act appropriately, and to take responsibility for those actions. As noted earlier, many longitudinal participants were asked to figure out the direction and details of their work independently and act on those responsibly. Similarly, in the private domains of parenting and partnering, Kegan sketched demands such as:

> establish rules and roles; institute a vision of family purpose . . . manage boundaries (inside and outside the family) . . . be psychologically independent from, but closely connected to, our spouses . . . set limits on children, in-laws, oneself, and extrafamily involvements. (p. 86)

Many participants shared their struggles with balancing independence and connection with partners, spouses, parents, and children. They struggled to create their nuclear families in the context of differences with parents and in-laws. These expectations, like those in public work life, call for understanding relationships in a complex way that allows adults to assess and contrast individual and family needs, determine a course of action in connection with, but not subsumed by, other family members, and take responsibility for those actions. These are not simply skills or behaviors; they emerge from how adults organize, or make meaning of, their experiences and their world.

The driving questions these young adults identified during their twenties—"How do I know?," "Who am I?," "How do I want to construct relationships with others?"—illustrate the intertwining of the multiple dimensions of self-authorship. "How I know?" represents the *epistemological* dimension of self-authorship—the evolution of assumptions about the nature, limits, and certainty of knowledge. The extent to which participants viewed knowledge as certain and the purview of authorities versus uncertain and within their ability to construct mediated the balance of external and internal forces in coming to know. The shift Gwen described from "how do *you* know?" to "how do *I* know?" conveys the emergence of the self-authored voice as the source of knowing, an internal voice from which to interpret and judge knowledge claims from the external world. This self-authored voice required an internal sense of self, the result of work on the "who am I" question. "Who am I?" represents the *intrapersonal* dimension of self-authorship—the evolution of how one thinks about one's sense of self and identity. Most participants initially adopted external expectations as their own without genuine exploration, constructing their identities primarily through external forces. The struggle in the twenties with the "who am I" question was one of finding, listening to, and constructing the internal self-authored voice as the source of self-definition and the internal compass to guide decisions about "how I know." The reciprocal question, "what kind of relationships do I want to construct?" represents the *interpersonal* dimension of self-authorship—the evolution of how one perceives and constructs one's relationships with others. As Lynn succinctly pointed out in her commentary on marrying early, relationships constructed before the internal voice emerged sometimes required reshaping after its arrival. Relationships constructed from an externally-defined identity emphasized what the other wanted whereas relationships constructed from an internally-defined identity brought what the self wanted into the forefront to be negotiated. This same negotiation occurred in weighing others' perspectives in deciding what to believe and how to view the self. This negotiation between external and internal forces (the latter emerging in the shift to internal self-definition) highlights the idea that self-authorship is not self-centered. Self-authorship could be described as "self-in-context," indicating that the self acknowledges external forces and takes them into account as appropriate, rather than "self independent of context," or having one's way regardless of others' perspectives (P. M. King, personal communication, October 2, 2000). The shift to internal self-definition allows the self, previously overshadowed by external forces, to join the external world in a mutual, interdependent partnership.

Although the driving questions emerged from an inductive analysis of the longitudinal stories, the three dimensions they represent are not a construction of this project. Extensive literature exists about each one. The longitudinal participants' experiences in their twenties, however, offer new possibilities regarding what these dimensions involve and how they interconnect. In the next section, a summary of the relevant literature provides a context for the new possibilities inherent in the longitudinal participants' stories.

The Epistemological Dimension

The epistemological dimension is grounded in the constructive-developmental framework of the Piagetian tradition. Jean Piaget (1950) described intelligence in terms of qualitatively different structures through which persons made meaning of their experience. These structures were characterized by particular assumptions about the nature, limits, and certainty of knowledge; assumptions that Kitchener (1983) labeled epistemic. The constructive developmental framework suggests that people construct sets of assumptions to account for their experience and that these evolve over time according to regular principles of stability and change (Kegan, 1982).

Perry (1970) offered the first theory of the evolution of adult epistemological structures based on his study of college men. This evolution involved a shift from accepting knowledge from authorities to making one's own decisions about knowledge claims. Perry described a period he called dualism in which younger adults regarded knowledge in the dual categories of right and wrong. Thus they looked to authorities for the truth. Discrepancies in knowledge and encountering authorities who claimed that knowledge was not dualistic ushered in a period of multiplicity, or the belief that some knowledge was uncertain. Dissonance between this view and experience led older students in Perry's study to adopt a relativistic stance. This way of knowing assumed that knowledge was uncertain and knowledge claims had to be made by judging the relevant evidence.

King and Kitchener (1994) reported a similar evolution in their Reflective Judgment Model, in which development moves from accepting knowledge from authority to making judgments based on evidence and reasonable inquiry. In the pre-reflective thinking they witnessed in late adolescence, students did not acknowledge, or in some cases even perceive, that knowledge could be uncertain. Pre-reflective thinkers relied on authorities much the way Perry's dualists did. In quasi-reflective thinking, which King and Kitchener's research suggests occurs later in college, students recognized the uncertainty inherent in knowledge claims but were not yet able to see how to use evidence in making knowledge claims. In reflective thinking, a phase more typical after college, adults assume that knowledge is relative. Upon arriving at this assumption, individuals rely on evidence and rules of inquiry (e.g., faith or scientific evidence) in a particular context to form a perspective. They later become able to compare and contrast evidence across contexts, leading to the realization that "knowing as a process requires action on the part of the knower; the spectator view of the knower that characterizes earlier thinking will no longer suffice" (King & Kitchener, 1994, p. 66). This ability to compare and contrast evidence across contexts leads to the final stage of reflective thinking in which individuals "take on the role of inquirers; they are agents involved in constructing knowledge" (p. 70). They realize that inquiry is ongoing and that conclusions are open to reevaluation based on further inquiry.

Belenky, Clinchy, Goldberger, and Tarule (1986) constructed a similar portrait of adult epistemological structures based on a study of college and adult women. Their theory involved a shift from taking in knowledge from others to constructing it oneself. In the early phases, women were either silent on the assumption that they were not capable of knowing, or received knowledge from authorities. Experiences that called these sets of assumptions into question led to subjective knowing in which women turned to their own voices. Eventually they turned to procedures to make sense out of their experience, a way of knowing similar to King and Kitchener's quasi-reflective knowing. When these procedures seemed to create a distance between the knower and the known, these women moved to constructed knowing, a concept similar to King and Kitchener's reflective thinking. Belenky et al. (1986; Clinchy, 1996) also described two forms of knowing that emerged in their procedural phase: separate and connected. The separate knower stood at arm's length from the object to be known and approached perspectives from a doubting stance in order to come to know. The connected knower entered into the object to be known, trying to see what could be believed about it. Belenky and her colleagues noted that women in their study demonstrated both patterns and that the separate pattern was more closely aligned with Perry's descriptions.

The possibility of gender-related patterns within epistemological structures was the impetus for the longitudinal project upon which this book is based. I used an inductive approach to the college phase of the study to construct a gender-inclusive model of epistemological development (Baxter Magolda, 1992). The model resulting from the college phase described the movement from absolute knowing (in which knowledge is assumed to be certain), through transitional knowing (in which some knowledge is believed to be uncertain), to independent knowing (in which knowledge is assumed to be largely uncertain). Although some evidence of contextual knowing (in which knowledge claims are made based upon relevant evidence within a context) emerged, this occurred rarely. Thus this model repeated earlier models in movement from accepting knowledge from authorities to constructing knowledge oneself. Two gender-related patterns emerged in that process—one impersonal and one relational. The impersonal pattern reflected knowing through separation or detachment, whereas the relational pattern reflected knowing through connection and getting inside the object of knowing. These patterns show some parallel to Belenky et al.'s separate and connected knowing, however they were evident in absolute, transitional and independent knowing. I concluded that they represented gender-related patterns within epistemological structures.

The Intrapersonal and Interpersonal Dimensions

The intrapersonal dimension is most often referred to as identity or self-evolution. Ruthellen Josselson wrote, "Identity is what we make of ourselves within a society that is making something of us" (1996, p. 28). Her comment reveals the difficulty of separating these two dimensions; I deal with them together here due to their close relationship. The concept of identity is most often associated with Erik Erikson (1968), who conceptualized identity as a psychosocial process involving challenges from the interaction of physical and cognitive growth with the demands of the environment. Arthur Chickering's (1969;

Chickering & Reisser, 1993) theory of college students' identity emerged from this perspective as did Ruthellen Josselson's (1987, 1996) theory of women's identity development. These theories painted identity development as an evolving process in which we continually rework our sense of ourselves and our relationships with other people as we encounter challenges in the environment that call our current conceptualizations into question. Forms of identity in the early years of college, according to Checkering, Reisser, and Josselson, were highly dependent on external forces. The college experience offered opportunities for questioning and exploration, raising the possibility of constructing an identity separate from external forces. This often resulted in new identities formed on the basis of adult's own internal voices. Thus the formation of identity is closely tied to the relationships one has with external others.

Similarly, the relationships one has with external others are mediated by one's identity development. For example, Kegan (1994) describes a phase of self-evolution (called the third order of consciousness) in late adolescence and early adulthood in which identity is consumed by our relationships with others—we *are* our relationships in this phase. In the next phase, called fourth order, we become able to stand apart from our relationships and reflect upon them. Kegan described this as having a relationship to our relationships. In the early phases of identity development when external definition is strongest, young adults are most likely consumed by their relationships. In later years after the internal voice has emerged in other dimensions, relationships are reconstructed to account for the needs of the individual and the needs of others.

Judith Jordan (1997) spoke to this latter notion using the concept of mutuality. She has defined *mutuality* as "involv[ing] commitment to engage in the development and support of both people; it involves respectfully building a relationship together that both sustains and transcends the individuals engaged in it" (p. 32). As such, mutuality requires that each person be able to "represent her or his own experience in a relationship, to act in a way which is congruent with an 'inner truth' and with the context, and to respond to and encourage authenticity in the other person" (p. 31). Mutuality neither sacrifices self nor other too much. Jordan has suggested that in this new vision autonomy takes the form

of being clear in our thoughts and actions, acting with intention, but at the same time recognizing the impact of our actions on others. The concept of mutuality constitutes interdependence.

The concepts of separation and connection emerging from study of the epistemological dimension also arose in the intrapersonal and interpersonal dimensions. Initially, identity development was conceptualized (based primarily on studies of men) as a story of increasing independence and individuation from others (Chickering, 1969; Erikson, 1968). This conceptualization called for the development of agency, or the ability to separate from others and function as an autonomous individual. Bakan (1966) initially coined the term *agency,* noting that it focuses on "the existence of an organism as an individual" (p. 15). He offered self-protection, self-assertion, and self-expansion as dynamics of agency. Thus agency is characterized by increasing individuation and separation from others to achieve control, autonomy, and independence in relationship to others. A focus on agency often leads to sacrificing others' needs in relationships to maintain autonomy. The individual freedom and achievement valued in Western, democratic societies led to a preference for agency as the guiding characteristic of maturity.

Further investigation of the identity development of women yielded another version of the story, this one based on communion, or the ability to connect with others and to function in a collaborative way (Brown and Gilligan, 1992; Chickering & Reisser, 1993; Gilligan, 1982; Straub, 1987). Bakan (1966) also coined the term *communion,* using it to refer to "the participation of the individual in some larger organism of which the individual is a part" (p. 15). Bakan described communion as "being at one with other organisms, . . . manifest in contact, openness, and union" (p. 15). Thus communion is characterized by connection to and fusion with others to achieve acceptance in relationships. This focus on connection often leads to behavior seen as dependent and self-sacrificing.

The question of how agency and communion related to maturity was most intensely discussed in the debate over Kohlberg's (1984) portrayal of the justice voice and Gilligan's (1982) portrayal of the care voice in moral development. Although many perspectives exist regarding the relationship of agency and communion, I find Kegan's (1994) notion of them as style, rather than structure, most informative. Kegan included his own work in the scholarship that, he argued, initially confused structure and style. He explained that autonomy and differentiation were initially viewed as synonymous with agency or separation. Autonomy constitutes the structural element of one's meaning making, whereas separation (or connection) constitutes the stylistic element or preference one has about meaning making. For example, one transitional knower prefers to stand apart from knowledge to assess opinions, whereas another prefers to get inside others' thoughts to assess opinions. Both share the same underlying structure of knowing, approached via different styles. The college phase data on gender-related patterns (Baxter Magolda, 1992) supports the notion that agency and communion are stylistic preferences within epistemological structures. Kegan has pointed out that the styles of connection and separation exist within the structures inherent in intrapersonal and interpersonal development as well.

Interconnections among the Three Dimensions

Perry (1970) noted that the shift from assuming that knowledge is certain to assuming that it is uncertain constituted a revolutionary restructuring in one's view of knowledge and oneself. Because knowing and valuing becomes contingent upon context, and because contexts constantly change, what one knows and values can potentially change as well. Perry believed that these realizations prompted restructuring one's identity as the one who chooses to what to devote one's energy, care, and identity. Moving through the relativity of knowledge and choice to make commitments about what to believe and stand for related more to identity than to new epistemological assumptions (King, 1978).

Belenky, Clinchy, Goldberger, and Tarule (1986) also emphasized the link between identity and ways of knowing in women's development. Their description of "constructed knowing" in which one integrates one's own experience and external information to construct a perspective became the basis of commitments to oneself, others, and one's community. Belenky and her colleagues noted that there was a paucity of this way of knowing in their college data. King and Kitchener (1994) also emphasized the role of the self as active knowledge constructor in the latter phases of Reflective Judgment.

Jane Loevinger's (1976) theory of ego development focused primarily on thinking processes that guided personal development, and she argued for integration of the dimensions involved in making meaning of experience. Robert Kegan (1982, 1994) articulated this integration clearly in his theory of the evolving self, finally bringing together the cognitive and affective realms of development in a constructive-developmental framework.

Kegan (1994) argued that people make meaning from various "orders of the mind," each characterized by a particular organizing principle that affects thinking, feeling, and relating to self and others. These principles are *how* we make meaning of our thinking, feeling, and social-relating, not the content of our meaning making. He described the core—or structure—of these organizing principles as the subject-object relationship. He defined *object* as "those elements of our knowing or organizing that we can reflect on, handle, look at, be responsible for, relate to each other, take control of, internalize, assimilate, or otherwise operate on" (p. 32). *Subject,* in contrast, "refers to those elements of our knowing or organizing that we are identified with, tied to, fused with, or embedded in" (p. 32). The difference, then, is that we cannot operate on that which is subject because we cannot stand apart from it. As Kegan stated, "We *have* object; we *are* subject" (p. 32).

Kegan (1994) emphasized that evolution of the subject-object relationship gives rise to evolution of the organizing principles we use to make meaning. Because what is subject and object for us is not permanent but rather changes as we adjust to account for new experience, dimensions of our cognitive, intrapersonal and interpersonal meaning-making that are subject in one organizing principle, or order of the mind, become object in the next. For example, in Kegan's third order of mind one's relationships with others are subject. Identity is consumed by these relationships—we *are* our relationships in the third order. In the fourth order, relationships become object as we become able to stand apart from them and reflect upon them. Thus each new principle subsumes the prior one, resulting in a more complex way of making meaning. As Kegan explained, "Liberating ourselves from that in which we were embedded, making what was subject into object so that we can 'have it' rather than be 'had by it'—this is the most powerful way I know to conceptualize the growth of the mind" (p. 34). Kegan clearly stated that his use of the word *mind* does not refer to cognition alone but rather to the capacity of individuals to construct and organize meaning in their thinking, feeling, and relating to self and others. Kegan described three orders of mind from which adults tend to make meaning: third order, in which we are subject to and consumed by the external influences of others around us; fourth order, in which our meaning-making system becomes internal and thus mediates the influences of others; and fifth order, in which our meaning-making system itself becomes an object for our reflection.

Kegan's third order coordinates knowing through external sources, identifying oneself through external expectations, and constructing relationships based on others' needs. His research described many college-age persons as being in what he calls the third order of consciousness. The third order equips students with some of the cognitive processes to engage in knowledge construction (e.g., ability to think abstractly, hypothetically, and deductively). Yet the intrapersonal dimensions of the third order embeds the student in making meaning through shared realities with others who are external to the self. As a result the interpersonal dimensions also rests on external definition. Because the system by which meaning is made rests outside the self, self-authorship is not possible in any dimension. Deciding "how I know," "who I am," and "what kind of relationships do I want to construct" takes place in the context of what external others expect.

As was the case with previous theories of development, the increasingly complex phases of Kegan's theory described the emerging role of the internally defined self in knowing, identity, and relationships. Kegan's fourth order of consciousness is characterized by self-authorship, the new coordinator of the three dimensions. In fourth order, values, beliefs, convictions, generalizations, ideals, abstractions, interpersonal loyalty, and intrapersonal states of mind emerge from being conconstructed with others external to the self. Instead, the fourth order:

> takes all of these as objects or elements of its system, rather than the system itself; it does not identify with them but views them as parts of a new whole. This new whole is an ideology, an internal identity, a *self-authorship* that can coordinate, integrate, act upon, or

invent values, beliefs, convictions, generalizations, ideals, abstractions, interpersonal loyalties, and intrapersonal states. It is no longer *authored by* them, it *authors them* and thereby achieves a personal authority. (1994, 185, italics in original)

This system brings the creation of belief "inside" the self, separate from the shared realities and coconstructions of the third order. The existence of this system that generates beliefs makes self-authorship of knowledge possible. It also makes possible identity formation that is more enduring than the earlier coconstructed versions because the internal self—rather than the social context—is the source of belief. The ability to relate to one's own intrapersonal states, rather than being made up by them, makes it possible to see oneself as the maker (rather than experiencer) of one's inner psychological life.

Mutuality, as Jordan (1997) described it, seems to require Kegan's (1994) fourth order structure and a blend of the styles of agency and communion. Mutuality is neither agency nor communion at their extremes, but rather an effective combination of individual authenticity and connection to others. Acting congruently with one's inner truth stems from the internal meaning-making system of the fourth order. Presenting one's own experience in the relationship represents agency, whereas responding to and encouraging authenticity in the other represents communion. Mutuality is a blend of agency and communion; too much of either does not constitute mutuality. Juxtaposing Kegan's and Jordan's ideas enables one to see the distinction between the structure of interpersonal maturity and the styles it requires. Contextual knowing also requires both styles as well as an internal meaning-making system that frees one to make judgments.

My longitudinal study focused on the epistemological dimension during the college years. During the post-college years, participants introduced the intrapersonal and interpersonal dimensions more readily and they moved to the foreground of our conversations. It seemed that they could not address the epistemological dimension, or the "how you know" question, without working with the other two dimensions. Stories from their twenties convey that adopting contextual assumptions about the nature of knowledge was necessary but insufficient for contextual knowing. In order to know and make decisions contextually they also needed to construct an internal self-definition that enabled them to choose what to believe and mediate their relations with the external world. The preferred styles prevalent in earlier portions of their developmental journeys also became more flexible as they moved from external to internal self-definition. Their collective stories told throughout this book extend our understanding of the three dimensions, how they interweave during the journey through the twenties, and what contexts aid in the transformation to self-authorship.

Higher Education's Role in Stewarding the Transformation

Establishing an internal belief system and a sense of self from which to join others in mutual relationships was the central challenge my participants faced in their twenties. Their career, advanced educational and personal environments demanded that they make the transformation from external definition to self-authorship. Their college education was intended to help them prepare for success and leadership roles in society. Educators hope that college graduates will experience a transformation from reliance on authority to complex ways of making meaning in which they are able to integrate multiple perspectives and make informed judgments. For example, Parks Daloz, Keen, Keen, and Daloz Parks (1996) wrote:

> The deep purpose of higher education is to steward this transformation so that students and faculty together continually move from naiveté through skepticism to commitment rather than becoming trapped in mere relativism and cynicism. This movement toward a mature capacity to hold firm convictions in a world which is both legitimately tentative and irreducibly interdependent is vitally important to the formation of citizens in a complex and changing world. (p. 223)

My longitudinal participants experienced the beginning of this transformation in college; that story is told in detail in *Knowing and Reasoning in College: Gender-Related Patterns in Students' Intellectual Development* (Baxter Magolda, 1992) and summarized later in this chapter as the backdrop for their journey through this transformation. The work, community, and personal contexts they encountered after college, however, called for them to complete the transformation

to the mature capacity to hold firm convictions—to self-authorship.

Returning to Josselson's statement that "[I]dentity is what we make of ourselves within a society that is making something of us" (1996, p. 28), my study participants' focus during college seemed to be on what society was making of them, or more precisely, what they *should* become and believe to be successful in adult life. Like Gwen, they were not aware until much later that they were not listening to their own voices. Their own voices were so entwined with societal voices that the two were one. At various points in their twenties, however, these young adults began to hear their own voices as separate from those of others, become aware of external forces they used to define themselves, and to actively construct an internally defined sense of self and belief system. Thus their focus shifted to what to make of themselves within the context of the society around them. Nearing the end of their twenties, many felt they were on a path of their own making; others were less certain about who had constructed the path.

The transformation to self-authorship was a complex task for these young adults. Much of what they learned in college called into question the values and beliefs instilled in them by their upbringing. Greater flexibility in gender roles opened new options for them, yet their families varied in the degree to which these new options were modeled or accepted. Taking risks to adopt new roles was often fraught with concern about unspoken expectations of masculinity or femininity, or with little conceptualization about how to adopt new roles yet keep old ones (e.g., career and family). Changing family structures left some at awkward crossroads—a place where choosing marriage and/or family was complicated by parents' divorce. Many of these adults learned that marriage and children were no longer a given but rather choices that entailed consequences. Their college experience conveyed a society different in most cases from the one in which they had grown up. Increasing diversity of perspectives, questions about the equity and justice in current societal arrangements, globalization, and technology all suggested that their adulthood would be different from that of their parents. Participants from working-class backgrounds were torn between pursuing success and maintaining their connections to their heritage. These dynamics yielded a tension between hopes and dreams developed in one context and how to live them out in another. The expectation and pressure for success were high, yet questions about the meaning of power and privilege complicated it. And while predictions and prescriptions for more complex social roles are plentiful, models for what they look like are few.

Despite the difficulty of this transformation in contemporary society, the need for self-authorship has never been greater. The diversity of our society and the global community requires that we be able to appreciate and work effectively with multiple perspectives. The recognition of inequity demands that we reevaluate the balance of our individual goals and our responsibility to the community. The increasing interdependence of people within our society and the world community makes addressing these issues imperative. The speed with which information and technology changes requires us to think in complex ways to keep pace. Self-authorship is necessary not only for survival in the 21st century but for the ability to offer leadership to model new forms of adult life and citizenship.

Stewarding this transformation—from naivete to commitment, from primarily external to primarily internal definition—is a complex challenge. Higher education has a responsibility to help young adults make the transition from their socialization by society to their role as members and leaders in society's future. The curriculum and cocurriculum of undergraduate, graduate, and professional educational settings are opportunities to steward this transformation. Willimon and Naylor (1995) wrote that a college education should:

> . . . provide a conceptual framework and a process to facilitate the search for meaning that attempts to integrate the spiritual, intellectual, emotional, and physiological dimensions of life, . . . encourag[ing] students . . . to formulate a *personal strategy* to address the most important quest human beings face— the need for their lives to have enduring meaning. (p. 130)

The workplace, the context in which most of my longitudinal participants experienced identity development and the search for meaning during their twenties, is also a site for stewarding this transformation. In many cases, these young adults found assistance with this transformation through connections with others in volunteer work, church, friends, and family.

Tracing their epistemological, intrapersonal, and interpersonal journey through their twenties offers insight into how contemporary society—higher education, workplaces within college contexts, and community within the college context—can be shaped to steward this crucial transformation. The stories of these young adults are particularly useful in this endeavor for two reasons. First, their growth during college has been documented, establishing a foundation for understanding their experience from the start of college. Second, by their early thirties, these adults' experiences covered a wide range of contexts including graduate and professional education in diverse fields, diverse work roles, and diverse family settings (marriage, divorce, children, and sexual orientation). The core themes of their experience as well as the rich texture of diverse experiences raise possibilities for mentoring people through the transformations of young adulthood. As concern grows over the ability of the next generation to assume leadership, the experiences of my longitudinal participants shed light on how these struggles might be approached.

Part One of the Journey: The College Years

I offer a brief synopsis of the college portion of these participants' journeys here as the context for their journey through the twenties (for an extensive report on the college phase of the study, see Baxter Magolda, 1992). They began college in 1986. One hundred and one students joined me for interviews during their first year; 80 of those interviewed all four years during college. Our annual interviews focused on their assumptions about the nature of knowledge; the role of the learner, instructor, peers, and evaluation in learning; and the nature of decision-making. Although the intrapersonal and interpersonal dimensions of development surfaced occasionally, the epistemological dimension took the foreground. This is most likely due to my framing of the study around learning as well as the learning focus of the college context. I constructed a portrait of the evolution of epistemology based on the college phase of the study.

Epistemological Reflection: Four Ways of Knowing[2]

The epistemological assumptions inherent in the four ways of knowing—absolute, transitional, independent, and contextual—are advanced here as relevant to the longitudinal participants. Because this study is constructivist in nature, I make no claim that this journey is transferable to other young adults unless their circumstances are similar to those described here.

Absolute Knowing. Discussing his view of learning as a first year student, Jim offered a perspective that captures the essence of absolute knowing:

> The factual information is cut and dry. It is either right or wrong. If you know the information, you can do well. It is easy because you just read or listen to a lecture about the ideas. Then you present it back to the teacher.

The core assumption held by absolute knowers is that knowledge exists in an absolute form, or in Jim's words, is either right or wrong. They often assume that right and wrong answers exist in all areas of knowledge and that authorities know these answers. Uncertainty does not exist in knowledge per se, although it might exist in the student's lack of knowing the answer. The roles students describe for instructors, peers, and themselves as learners all hinge on knowledge being the purview of the instructor. As learners, absolute knowers focus on obtaining the information—a task Jim describes as reading or listening to lectures. They expect instructors to communicate knowledge clearly to them to aid in their acquiring it. They do not expect peers to have legitimate knowledge, although peers can share what they have learned from authority figures. Notice that Jim does not mention peers in his comment on how to do well. Absolute knowers' views of effective evaluation of students' work reflect the instructor's mastery of knowledge as well as the instructor's ability to determine whether students have acquired knowledge. When Jim presents what he has learned back to the teacher, she will know whether he knows the right answers. Students interpret discrepancies they encounter in the learning process as variations in explanations rather than true differences in knowledge. Finally, they approach educational decisions by looking for the right answers about educational programs, majors, and career directions. Sixty-eight percent of the longitudinal participants expressed absolute knowing during their first year of college. It steadily declined to 46 percent the sophomore year, 11 percent the junior year, and only 2 percent the senior year.

Two reasoning patterns were evident in absolute knowing: receiving and mastery. The *receiving pattern* was used more often by women than men in the study. A central characteristic of the receiving pattern is its internal approach, as shown in Toni's comment:

> I like to listen—just sit and take notes from an overhead. The material is right there and if you have a problem you can ask him and he can explain it to you. You hear it, you see it, and then you write it down.

Toni, a sophomore, makes it clear that this approach involves minimal interaction with instructors. Her receiving pattern peers also emphasized the importance of comfort in the learning environment, relationships with peers, and ample opportunities to demonstrate their knowledge. They resolved knowledge discrepancies via personal interpretation.

The *mastery pattern* was used more often by men than by women in the study. Mastery pattern students preferred an active approach to learning, were critical of instructors, and expected interactions with peers and instructors that helped them master the material. The active approach to learning permeates most aspects of the learning process. For example, Tim (a first year student), offered:

> I like getting involved with the class. Just by answering questions, asking questions . . . even if you think you know everything, there's still questions you can ask. When he asks questions you can try to answer them to your best ability. Don't just let the teacher talk, but have him present questions to you.

Thus Tim believes asking and answering questions is necessary to learn; he is not content to listen and take notes as Toni is. Tim and his mastery pattern peers reported engaging each other in debates to further their learning, showing the instructor they were interested, and resolving knowledge discrepancies via research and asking authorities.

Absolute knowers shared the common belief that knowledge is certain and held by authorities. Beyond their shared set of assumptions, receiving and mastery pattern students differed in three areas: voice, identification with authority, and relationships with peers. There was really no student voice per se in absolute knowing. However, mastery pattern students attempted to express themselves while their receiving pattern counterparts remained essentially silent. Mastery pattern students seemed to imitate the voice of authority and worked hard at reproducing it in an effort to join authorities as knowers. Receiving pattern students listened carefully to the voice of authority and repeated it in an effort to show that they had acquired the knowledge.

Although all absolute knowers viewed authorities as holders of truth and knowledge, receiving pattern students exhibited minimal identification with authority figures whereas mastery pattern students exhibited considerable identification with authority. Students in the receiving pattern exhibited a detachment from authority. They described learning as a transaction largely void of interaction with authority unless clarification was needed. Despite their motivation for receiving knowledge, they did not view identification or interaction with authority as a central part of that process. Students in the mastery pattern showed the beginnings of taking their place "next to" authorities in the arena of knowledge. Their learning behaviors resembled those of the active apprentice trying to master the trade.

Relationships with peers were a third point of difference for receiving and mastery pattern students. Receiving pattern students valued peers as providers of comfort in the learning atmosphere. Knowing others in the class made it more intimate, more comfortable, and an easier setting in which to learn and ask questions. For these students peers were a source of assistance in receiving knowledge. Collaboration took the form of support and sharing notes and information. Mastery pattern students valued peers as partners in striving for and testing achievement. They assisted each other in mastering knowledge and took turns testing each other's progress. Collaboration in this form was characterized by individual autonomy.

The path from absolute to transitional knowing involves the realization that not all knowledge is certain, and that authorities are not all

knowing as a result. As the students' stories in transitional knowing reveal, mastery and receiving pattern students encounter this experience differently. Mastery pattern students' identification with authority prompts them to stay with certainty and logic as much as possible in the face of emerging uncertainty. Receiving pattern students' detachment from authority makes it easier to let go of certainty, thus endorsing uncertainty. Endorsing uncertainty leads to an increase in activity level over and above listening. Peers are important to students of both patterns but students endorsing uncertainty more readily assign legitimacy to peers' knowledge.

Transitional Knowing. Uncertainty, upon its discovery, was usually perceived to exist only in particular areas while certainty remained in other knowledge arenas. Fran's statement reflects this perspective:

> Genetics isn't an opinionated kind of subject. Genetics is "These are the experiments; that's what happens. This is what we know now." You wouldn't sit around and have a discussion in calculus . . . or chemistry. In the AIDS class, it's just open discussion, and it makes you really say what you want and think through what you want to think about.

Genetics retained its certainty for Fran, as did calculus and chemistry. On the topic of AIDS, however, uncertainty emerged. This shift in the nature of knowledge sparked changes in the roles students perceived for themselves and others. Students shifted their focus from acquiring knowledge to understanding it. This focus on understanding required that instructors use methods aimed at understanding, many of which included applying knowledge in class and to life in general. Peers took on more active roles, perhaps because understanding was described as requiring more exploration than that required for the acquisition of knowledge. Evaluation was perceived as appropriate to the extent that it measured students' understanding of the material. Uncertainty permeated decision making as well, as students struggled to figure out options for the future. Processes believed to lead to future success replaced direct reliance on authorities for educational decision making. All transitional knowers held these core assumptions. Transitional knowing assumptions were held by 32 percent of the participants during the first year. It increased to 53 percent the sophomore year and to 83 percent the junior year. Eighty percent of the seniors still used transitional knowing; it declined rapidly the first year after college to 31 percent.

Within transitional knowing some students, usually women, used an interpersonal approach whereas other students, usually men, used an impersonal approach. *Interpersonal pattern* students were involved in learning through a collection of others' ideas, expected interaction with peers to hear their views and provide exposure to new ideas, wanted a rapport with the instructor to enhance self-expression, valued evaluation that takes individual differences into account, and resolved uncertainty by personal judgment. Kris's comments capture the new expectations of peers:

> I get into discussions. Classroom discussions are better for me to learn. You have an opening lecture where you have the professor discuss. Then students can contribute—listening to other students contribute their ideas and putting in my own inputs—that makes learning better for me because it makes me think more and try to come up with more generative ideas as to what I would do in a situation. We react to the material, look at ideas and relate it to ourselves, look at what kinds of action we can take. It's a hands-on type class.

Kris clearly wants to hear the professor but only briefly; then she wants to hear her peers and express her own opinion. International pattern knowers tended to focus on those areas that were uncertain and viewed this as an opportunity to express their own views for the first time.

Impersonal pattern students wanted to be forced to think, preferred to exchange their views with instructors and peers via debate, expected to be challenged by instructors, valued evaluation that is fair and practical, and resolved uncertainty by logic and research. Scott described the result of being forced to think:

> The debate and discussion process for me is really interesting; I learn a lot more because I remember questions and I guess I learn the most when I sit and I'm actually forced to raise my hand and then I have to talk. I have to sit there and think on the spot. I learn it better than in a note-taking class that is regurgitation.

Scott has rejected the absolute knowers' approach of presenting information back to the teacher, but he does not endorse Kris's interest in peers' comments. Instead he focuses on his own thinking about the material. Impersonal pattern students also demonstrated a dual focus on certainty and uncertainty and wanted to resolve uncertainty when it existed.

Students in both patterns exhibit development of their voice in transitional knowing as compared to absolute knowing. The impersonal pattern voice remains consistent in its closeness to the voice of authority, reflecting now the process of learning rather than the answers. The interpersonal pattern voice diverges more from authority than does the impersonal pattern. The discovery of uncertainty seems to be viewed by interpersonal pattern students as an opportunity to become involved in knowing, resulting in greater activity and exercise of personal judgment. Moreover, a subtle division remains between the interpersonal pattern knower's knowledge and that of authority. Some students remarked that their learning from other students did not necessarily help them learn the material in the book. Yet the interpersonal pattern voice has gained greater distance from authority than has the impersonal pattern voice. Using relationship with authority as a point of departure toward independent knowing, interpersonal pattern students would seem to be more ready to adopt their own voice.

The interpersonal and impersonal difference in the two patterns is clear. Interpersonal pattern students care about their peers' perspectives, want to know their peers, and want instructors to care about them. Relationships are central to the learning process because knowing others promotes sharing perspectives and sharing perspectives promotes adding to one's knowledge. If instructors are uncaring, teaching (and thus learning) is ineffective. For impersonal pattern students these themes did not surface. Although no student wants to be mistreated by instructors, impersonal pattern students prefer challenge to caring. Perhaps this reflects the impersonal pattern students' focus on individual learning whereas the interpersonal pattern students focus on the relationships made possible during learning. Considering peer relationships as a point of departure toward independent knowing, we could expect that interpersonal pattern students would have little difficulty accepting peers' views as valid. For them this will be an extension of knowing in the uncertain arena. For impersonal pattern students a shift will be required to add peers (and themselves) to the ranks of authority.

Independent Knowing. The core assumption of uncertainty in independent knowing changes both the process and source of knowing substantially. The shift is evident in Laura's description of her discovery of uncertainty:

> Everything's relative; there's no truth in the world, that sort of thing. So I've decided that the only person that you can really depend on is yourself. Each individual has their own truth. No one has the right to decide, "This has to be your truth, too." As long as you feel—it feels right, then it must be right because if everybody is stuck on, "What do the other people think?" then you just waste your whole life. You just do what you feel like you have to do. That's why sometimes I felt that I had to get into business because everybody was going into business. I don't think the world rotates around the business world and money and materialism. Now I'm relaxed and I'm thinking of what I want, what's best for me and not for anybody else.

Given this newfound uncertainty, discrepancies among authorities represent the variety of views possible in an uncertain world. Authorities are no longer the only source of knowledge but instead become equal with students, who for the first time view their opinions as valid. The emergence of self-authored knowledge rivets the student's attention on thinking for oneself. Learning how to think independently involves expressing one's own views as well as hearing others. Instructors are expected to promote this type of activity in class. They are no longer responsible for providing knowledge, but rather providing the context in which to explore knowledge. Evaluation, likewise, should reward independent thinking and should not penalize the student for holding views different from the instructor or authors of texts. Peers become a legitimate source of knowledge rather than part of the process of knowing. Independent knowers emphasize being open-minded and allowing everyone to believe what they will, as illustrated by Laura's comment on how she decides what to believe: "I don't know (how I decide on my opinion). Something works inside my head and it's just there." Independent knowing was rare in the early college years (1 percent of sophomores and 3 percent of juniors). Sixteen percent used independent knowing as seniors; it rose dramatically the first year after college to 57 percent.

Gender-related patterns appeared in independent knowing as well. The *interindividual pat-tern* was used more often by women than men in the study. Interindividual pattern knowers believed that different perspectives resulted from each person bringing her or his own interpretation, or in some cases bias, to a particular knowledge claim. They simultaneously advocated listening to other interpretations or biases and espousing their own perspectives, describing how the interaction of the two helped them form their perspective. Alexus offered an example of this view during her fifth year interview. Reflecting on her senior year classes, she commented that senior year was a time "when you should be most open because you should be able to listen to what other people say and then come up with your own opinion on how you feel about a particular thing." When asked how she did that, she replied:

> I listen to their arguments for it and then I listen to other people's arguments against it. And then basically it's just my own personal view really, whether I can establish the credibility—so I guess it really stems from credibility of the person who's saying it also, as well as just the opinion on it. I listen to both sides. Really I usually throw some of my own views into it as well. So I'm influenced by other people, but in the end I think that each—like each member of the group should be influenced by each other. But then when the final vote comes in, you should go with what you believe.

Alexus clearly valued hearing others' ideas and felt people should influence each other. She simultaneously held her own view and tried to integrate it with the views of others she perceived as credible.

The *individual pattern* knowers, like their interindividual pattern counterparts, espoused thinking independently and exchanging views with others. However, their primary focus was on their thinking and they sometimes struggled to listen carefully to other voices. Fully acknowledging that everyone had their own beliefs, individual pattern knowers described the role theirs played when differences of opinion took place. Lowell shared an experience in which he and other students had different ideas:

> I'd consider myself conservative. And there was one guy in our group who was quite liberal and acknowledged it. I guess it gave me another viewpoint, another aspect to look at this. Like it or not we're all kind of ingrained

one way or another, whether it's to the liberal end or the conservative end. He looked at it in this way and I looked at it in another way. And everybody in the group had their own ways on it. It was a spectrum of—and to try to get your point across without sounding too dominating—I'm searching for words and not finding them. To try to listen to theirs, to really listen, not to just hear it and let it go through. And then to try to take that into account and reach a compromise. There was quite a bit of discussion. But I don't think the attempt was to try to change each other's mind. It was just, "Your point is all right, but you've got to look at this part, too, because this is as relevant."

Lowell's genuine attempt to hear his liberal classmate and his insistence that his conservative perspective also be taken into account stopped short of changing either perspective.

The equality of numerous views in the face of prevailing uncertainty made independent thinking possible. Equality of perspectives also changed the relationship of the knower to her or his peers and to authority. In the case of interindividual pattern knowers this prompted connection to peers and to authority. Connection to peers was evident earlier for interpersonal transitional knowers, but interindividual pattern knowers became more open to peers' views. Their exchanges became interindividual by virtue of the knower including her or his own voice. When the potential hazards to connection posed by criticism were removed by equality of views, interindividual pattern knowers connected more intensely with their peers. This connection freed them to express their voices, which appear to have existed internally prior to this point. For them, the adjustment to independent knowing came in the form of including their own voice as equal to that of peers and of authority. Interindividual pattern knowers reconnected to authority once their own voice was legitimized. Thus the interindividual pattern represents a union of one's own voice and the voices of others.

In the case of individual pattern knowers the equality of perspectives had a different effect on relationships with peers and authority. Peers' roles in knowing created a relationship that bordered on becoming a connection. Individual pattern knowers listened to peers but struggled to hear them clearly and also to keep their own voice in the forefront. The adjustment to independent knowing for individual pattern knowers came in the form of including other voices as equal to one's own. Thus their voices, expressed routinely in previous ways of knowing, were slightly threatened by the genuine consideration of others' voices. Their interest in and attempt to hold both voices in balance appeared to mark the beginning of genuine connection to others. At the same time, equality of views seemed to free individual pattern knowers from authority to pursue their own independent thinking. The individual pattern includes both self-authored knowledge and the views of others, with the balance of the scale tipped toward self-authored knowledge.

The variation in interindividual and individual knowing can also be cast in the language of communion and agency (Baken, 1966) discussed earlier in the chapter. Communion involves connection and relationship with others whereas agency involves separateness from others. Both patterns moved toward communion: interindividual pattern knowers in terms of intense openness to others' views and individual pattern knowers in terms of genuine consideration of others' views. Both patterns also moved toward agency in the emergence of self-authored knowledge and for individual pattern knowers in separation from authority in the learning process. The degree of movement toward communion or agency is best understood in light of the degree to which either was reflected in earlier ways of knowing. Receiving and interpersonal pattern knowers demonstrated communion in previous ways of knowing but agency represented a shift for them. Mastery and impersonal pattern knowers demonstrated agency in earlier ways of knowing, such that communion represented a shift for them. Thus while interindividual pattern knowers still lean toward communion and individual pattern knowers still lean toward agency, both are moving closer together than in previous ways of knowing.

Contextual Knowing. The fourth set of epistemological assumptions noticeable for a few students (1 percent of juniors and 2 percent of seniors) toward the end of college emerged more completely during the postcollege interviews. Contextual knowers looked at all aspects of a situation or issue, sought out expert advice in that particular context, and integrated their own and others' views in deciding what to think, Gwen, reflecting on her senior year, illustrates this perspective in her comment on whether to believe others' viewpoints: "I don't care if people feel this way or that way about it. But if they can support their stance and have some background and backing for that, to my thinking that is valid." Thus the student voice develops to the point of cognitive self-authorship; peers and authority both have valid knowledge if they can support their stance. The nature of contextual knowing, and the integration of the two gender-related patterns, is further explored in the remainder of this volume via the stories of participants during their twenties.

At the Threshold of Self-Authorship

The longitudinal participants stood at the threshold of self-authorship at the end of college. They recognized uncertainty in some areas and would recognize it as more prevalent soon after college. They left college with an initial awareness that they would have to make their own decisions, but without internal mechanisms to do so. I invite you to come along on the journey they shared from college graduation to age 30. Their stories offer rich descriptions of how

the three dimensions of development intertwine, how the transformation to self-authorship is facilitated or hindered, and the intensity of the struggle to achieve an internal belief system and sense of self from which to join others in mutual relationships. As was the case with the college phase of the study, the post-college phase was approached from the constructivist perspective Thus the transformation to self-authorship described by these participants is offered as a possibility rather than as a generalizable portrait of all young adults' experience in their twenties.

Notes

1. Despite using fictitious names for participants throughout the book, I share these dynamics anonymously to protect the privacy of the participants.
2. Portions of this description are reproduced with permission from Baxter Magolda, M. B. (1992). *Knowing and reasoning in college: Gender-related patterns in students' intellectual development.* San Francisco: Jossey-Bass and from Baxter Magolda, M. B. (1999). *Creating contexts for learning and self-authorship: Constructive-developmental pedagogy.* Nashville, TN: Vanderbilt University Press.

CHAPTER 7

TOWARD A DEVELOPMENTAL MODEL OF INTERCULTURAL MATURITY: AN HOLISTIC APPROACH TO COLLEGIATE EDUCATION

PATRICIA M. KING AND MARCIA B. BAXTER MAGOLDA

Introduction

A commonly cited intended learning outcome of American higher education is for students to gain awareness and understanding of other cultures (Bok, 1986; Bowen, 1980; Rosovsky, 1990) from both contemporaneous and historical perspectives, and both within and beyond our national borders. This long-endorsed outcome has recently been the topic of discussion not only among educators, but also among business leaders, who have argued that a dynamic and highly competitive global market has created a demand for workers who can demonstrate intercultural competencies that allow them to function effectively in an increasingly diverse marketplace. For example, the RAND Institute identified cultural competence as the most critical human resource need in the globalisation of American institutions (Bikson & Law, 1994). Professional organisations have also directed their efforts to issues of diversity-related issues, including intercultural awareness, global appreciation, etc. The Association of American Colleges and Universities (AACU, 1998) has taken a leading role in this effort and has linked discussions of diversity-related educational goals to the goals of liberal learning. In their Statement on Liberal Learning, they note:

> Because liberal learning aims to free us from the constraints of ignorance, sectarianism, and myopia, it prizes curiosity and seeks to expand the boundaries of human knowledge. By its nature, therefore, liberal learning is global and pluralistic. It embraces the diversity of ideas and experiences that characterise the social, natural, and intellectual world. To acknowledge such diversity in all its forms is both an intellectual commitment and a social responsibility, for nothing less will equip us to understand our world and to purpose fruitful lives.

This statement illustrates how educational efforts around issues of diversity can—indeed should—be grounded in fundamental collegiate purposes, linking the attainment of diversity knowledge and skills to broader educational goals and in ways that enable students to apply their skills in new and unforeseen contexts.

Demonstrating one's intercultural skills requires several types of expertise, including knowledge of cultures and cultural practices, complex cognitive skills for decision-making, social skills to function effectively in diverse work groups, and personal attributes that include flexibility and openness to new ideas. Although colleges are in many ways well suited to foster the development of these skills, "they are what corporations find in shortest supply among entry-level candidates" (Bikson & Law, 1994, p. 26). Similarly, students often expect faculty and student affairs staff members to be knowledgeable about and sensitive to intercultural issues, effective in teaching about diversity concepts, and in some settings, to effectively mediate cultural conflict; however, many faculty and staff report that they are unprepared to serve in these roles (Holcomb-McCoy & Myers, 1999; King & Howard-Hamilton, 2003; Talbot & Kocarek, 1997).

In times of increased global interdependence, producing interculturally competent citizens who can engage in informed, ethical decision-making when confronted with problems that involve a diversity of viewpoint is becoming an urgent priority. For example, when a group of Fortune 500 companies filed a brief in support of the University of Michigan's affirmative action policies (Kennelly, Mehrberg, & Hennink, 2000), they noted that students with an appreciation for diversity:

> are better prepared to understand, learn from and collaborate with others from a variety of racial, ethnic and cultural backgrounds; demonstrate creative problem solving by integrating differing perspectives; exhibit the skills required for good teamwork; and demonstrate more effective responsiveness to the needs of all types of consumers.

Educators on many college campuses expect students to show tolerance toward those of other cultural backgrounds and to demonstrate understanding of cultural concepts as they reflect the learning goals of their classes and co-curricular activities. However, persistent reports of racially-motivated hate crimes on college campuses strongly suggest the need to find better ways to help students achieve this desired collegiate outcome. In their discussion of the growing tension on US campuses around multicultural issues, Levine and Cureton (1998) noted that "multiculturalism remains the most unresolved issue on campus [in the US] today" (p 91).

Several scholars have proposed conceptual models to describe intercultural (or multicultural) competencies (eg, Howard-Hamilton, Richardson & Shuford, 1998; Pope and Reynolds, 1997; Storti, 1990). These models provide a useful starting point for identifying the attributes that are associated with this ability. For example, Pope & Reynolds (1997) include among their listing of multicultural skills "the ability to identify and openly discuss cultural differences and issues," to "differentiate between individual differences, cultural differences, and universal similarities," and "to use cultural knowledge and sensitivity to make more culturally sensitive and appropriate interventions" (p 271). However,

educators not only need a goal toward which to direct their efforts, but benchmarks that indicate progress toward this goal. Further, when looking at a complex phenomenon such as intercultural competence that includes emotionally- and socially-laden dimensions, they need models that take into account a wide range of factors that affect the development of students' competence. In other words, educators would be well-served by having models that indicate what is required within the individual to demonstrate the attributes that reflect intercultural competence. Existing models rely heavily on the assessment of attitudes; while these are arguably a necessary element, they are not sufficient for the production of competent behavior. Further, the assessment of existing models tends to rely on self-report methodologies, which provides an insufficient approach to measuring this outcome.

These factors have motivated us to look for alternative ways of viewing and describing the development of intercultural competence. The charges in students' intercultural skills being called for today require "genuine development," not just knowing more facts or having more awareness, but achieving a level of individual transformation that enables them to apply their knowledge and skills in a variety of contexts. That is, educators are being asked to produce graduates who see the world, themselves, and their own agency in more sophisticated and enabling ways, and who can appropriately draw upon that understanding as the need arises. While some professors have embraced the idea of education as a transforming process for a long time, for many, this will be a much broader orientation to their educational role. To achieve this ambitious goal, we believe that to be effective, teaching for intercultural competence must be approached in a manner that is holistic in nature (described below) and that acknowledges the developmental pathways students often follow as they move toward the achievement of an educational outcome.

A More Holistic Approach to Understanding Collegiate Outcomes

As noted above, intercultural competence is a complex, multi-faceted phenomenon that appears to require a wide variety of attributes; these include having an informed understanding of cultural practices, reasoning abilities that enable one to analyse complex problems and construct solutions, social skills that enable one to enhance conversations among diverse groups, and personal attributes (such as tolerance, openness, and the courage to stand up for one's beliefs) that enhance and support the application of one's knowledge and skills. As this list shows, being interculturally competent requires not just one skill but many, and not just a series of separate skills that develop independently, but skills that are interdependent and mutually reinforcing. Further, we argue that competence is not sufficient as an educational goal, but rather, that educators should direct their efforts toward promoting intercultural maturity. By "maturity," we are referring to the developmental capacity that undergirds the ways learners come to make meaning, that is, the way they approach, understand, and act on their concerns; here, our interest is how they do so in intercultural situations. We elaborate on these ideas below.

We draw our conceptualisation of maturity from the college student and adult development literatures, and in particular, from Kegan's (1994) concept of an individual's "mature capacity" to effectively address life's demands. This broader framework encompasses cognitive, identity, interpersonal development and their interconnections. Kegan argued that development in all three dimensions is required for a person to be able to use one's skills, thus providing what we refer to as an "holistic" framework. Those for whom development in one or more dimensions is not adequate for the complex life tasks they face often report being overwhelmed or "in over their heads" (a point emphasised in the title of his book). This approach is illustrated by the reaction of Christine, whose story is described by King and Baxter Magolda (1996). Christine, a white college student who had grown up in an all-white community, had a friendly interaction with an African-American student, was initially interested in seeing him again, and gave him her phone number. However, she soon learned that neither her sister nor her roommate approved of her dating a Black man and upon further reflection, Christine believed that her parents would disapprove as well. Fearing loss of approval of her family members, Christine decided this friendship was not an option for her. Although Christine's initial reaction was to be open to a friendship with someone of another race, her sense of self was too firmly grounded in the need to do what she thought others expected of her for her to accept his friendship. This story illustrates how factors such as the importance of others' approval and assumptions about how to earn this can affect a person's response in a situation with an intercultural dimension.

According to Kegan (1994), mature individuals would approach and respond differently to such situations because they exemplify what he has termed "self-authorship." He described this way of mentally "organizing" (or making meaning of) experiences as follows:

> This new whole is an ideology, an internal identify, a *self-authorship* than can coordinate, integrate, act upon, or invent values, beliefs, convictions, generalisations, ideals, abstractions, interpersonal loyalties, and interpersonal states. It is no longer *authored by* them, it *authors them* and thereby achieves a personal authority. (p 185, italics in original)

In this new internal identity, individuals act as authors of their lives (not just the stage on which their lives are played out), balancing external influences with their internal voice. Many demands placed on adults in contemporary society "require self-authorship because they require the ability to construct our own visions, to make informed decisions in conjunction with co-workers, to act appropriately, and to take responsibility for those actions" (Baxter Magolda, 2001, p 14). Self-authorship requires complex ways of making meaning of experience, drawing on one's understanding in all three dimensions of development noted above:

- cognitive, evaluating one's own views in light of existing evidence and constructing a reasonable perspective based on available evidence
- interpersonal, taking others' perspective into account rather than being consumed by them; and
- intrapersonal, possessing an internally generated belief system that regulates one's interpretations of experience and guides one's choices.

Figure 1 is a visual representation of these dimensions.

In Figure 1 these domains are presented as separate domains of development, which is consistent with much of the research examining each of these aspects of development (cognitive or intellectual development, intrapersonal or iden-

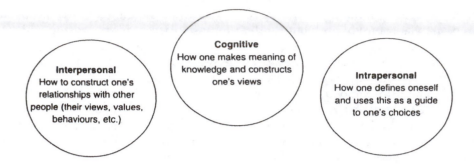

Figure 1 Domains of development

tity development, and interpersonal, eg, moral development, respectively).

By contrast, consider Figure 2, which shows two additional approaches to conceptualising these domains of development. The "separate domains" model from Figure 1 is followed by a visual depiction of a "related domains" approach, which allows for an examination of relationships between and among domains. This second approach is exemplified by King & Kitchener's (1994) longitudinal research on the relationship between intellectual and moral development, in which they presented evidence suggesting that cognitive development may be necessary but not sufficient for moral development and referred to the two models as "different but related" (p 207). They also noted structural similarities between the theories in the two domains (see Kitchener, 1982 and Kitchener & Fischer, 1990 for additional examples), which

suggested the kinds of relationships sketched in the third depiction in Figure 2, an integrated approach. This approach is bolstered by other empirical evidence indicating that the production of moral behavior requires more than complex cognitive skills. Rest (1986) identified four components that influence whether and how people behave morally: moral sensitivity (awareness of how one's actions affect other people), moral judgement (applying a moral standard, such as fairness to all parties), moral motivation (giving priority to moral over non-moral values such as loyalty or political sensitivity), and moral character (resisting distractions and overcoming frustrations to follow through on a moral plan of action). He noted that these components interact with and affect each other, and that failure to act morally can result from a deficiency in any one component:

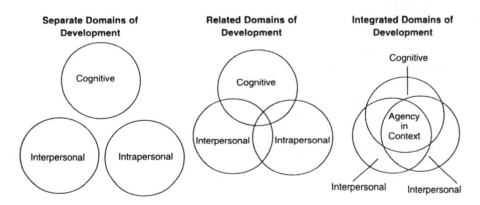

Figure 2 Separate, related and integrated perspectives on domains of development

A person who demonstrates great facility at one process is not necessarily adequate in another. We all known people who can render very sophisticated judgments but who never follow through on any course of action; we know people who have tremendous follow-through and tenacity but whose judgment is simple-minded. In short, the psychology of morality cannot be represented as a single variable or process. (p 4)

Similarity, the production of interculturally mature behavior appears to require the self-authored capacities reflected in the cognitive, intrapersonal, and interpersonal domains of development described above.

Other scholars of human development have also argued that a more holistic approach to educational research and practice is required if we are to be successful in helping students develop the array of skills that will enable them to tackle complex contemporary problems, especially those with an intercultural dimension (Baxter Magolda 1997, 1999; Jones & McEwen, 2000; Kegan, 1994; Ortiz, 2000; Storti, 1990). Looking at intercultural maturity using a more holistic perspective provides a possible explanation for the ineffectiveness of simpler, more superficial approaches to intercultural competence: perhaps, they are ineffective because they fail to consider one or more domains (cognitive, identity; interpersonal) of development. For example, omitting the cognitive component in conflict resolution risks being ineffective with students who see the world in "black and white" terms, and who are thus cognitively unable to analyse an intercultural conflict from the perspective of both parties involved. Similarly, omitting the interpersonal component risks being ineffective with students who decide how to act based on others' expectations, and whose behaviors are thus based on their perceptions of others' views, rather than on the interculturally appropriate criteria that educators may have tried to teach them. The third model depicted in Figure 2 illustrates an approach that integrates domains of development, emphasizing the overlap (interrelationships) among three domains of development.

An integrated approach to intercultural competence requires a multi-faceted definition of multicultural competence. Pope and Reynolds (1997) offered one such definition; they identified three groups of multicultural attributes: knowledge (about cultural histories, traditions,

values, and practices), skills when interacting with those from other cultures (for examples, skills that reflect one's understanding and respect), and attitudes or awareness that show an appreciation of ways people's actions can reflect their own attitudes, beliefs, values and self-awareness. Similarly, intercultural sensitivity often refers to awareness, knowledge, and appreciation of the "other" where other is identified as a person from a culture different from one's own. This range of attributes illustrates the complexity of the concept. Further, their finding that the factor analysis yielded one factor, not three (Pope & Mueller, 2000; replicated by King and Howard-Hamilton, in press) suggests that these attributes reflect one larger underlying construct rather than three separate sets of attributes.

Examining scholarship on intercultural or multicultural competencies with a holistic lens allows one to identify underlying capacities that may guide (or at least affect) a learner's ability to integrate knowledge, skills, and awareness, and to consistently act in an interculturally mature manner. We argue that the developmental ability that undergirds regarding another culture favorably is the same ability that undergirds one's ability to regard any interpersonal difference favorably. That is, the developmental complexity that allows a learner to understand and accept the general idea of "difference from self" without feeling "threat to self" enables this person to offer positive regard to the "other" across many types of difference, such as race, ethnicity, social class, gender, sexual orientation and religion, among others. While students may be able to learn about cultural differences with or without this foundation in place, they will find it difficult if not impossible to use this knowledge in an intercultural interaction without this foundation in place. In other words, less complex levels of cognitive and intrapersonal (identity) development may hinder one's ability to use one's intercultural skills.

Our understanding of the interrelationships between and among these dimensions has been informed by many years of collective experience teaching graduate students and researching college student development. In particular, Baxter Magolda's (2001) extensive interviews illuminate these relationships. The following examples were selected to illustrate two aspects of this discussion: a) adults' own descriptions of their self-authorship, and b) how the various elements of self-authorship are interrelated in their descriptions.

Example of Mature Reflection that Illustrates Self-Authorship

Evan, a participant in Baxter Magolda's (2001) longitudinal study of young adult development, described what it is like to self-author one's life:

> I told you about this feeling that I had once I became "aware." That is the best word that I can use to describe the difference between how I view my intellectual level now, versus how I felt prior to "noticing" my surroundings and my relationship with the world around me. It was like I woke up one day and things just clicked in my brain and things became clear to me for the first time. The most dramatic difference between before and after was my ability to think, and the subsequent confidence in my abilities and trust in my decisions. I have developed my own approach to solving problems, one which has proven to me to be a good one, and one which has proven to be a good teacher. When it becomes apparent to me that I have relied on this ability, I often try to remember what I did before I began to understand how my mind worked. (Baxter Magolda, 2001, p 121–122)

Evan was refining how his mind worked and simultaneously refining how he thought about himself:

> As my personality and sense of self have really begun to develop and become more refined, my ability to direct my life accordingly has became increasingly confident. As I realise who I am, and what is important to me, it becomes easier for me to establish my priorities. Identifying and arranging my priorities has helped me to develop a "road map" for reaching short and long-term goals. Don't get me wrong, I am not trying to predict the future and I by no means know exactly what I want, but I have developed a general idea and use my knowledge as a guide. (Baxter Magolda, 2001, p 122)

Refining who he was also involved refining relationships with others:

> I find that I am constantly rebalancing my identity in relationship to others. With my parents' divorce two years ago, and the purchase of my home, I am becoming a central figure in the extended family and have left behind my "youth" oriented identify. At work, my identify continues to grow almost as fast as my personal identity: Since I began

with the current crew 2 1/2 years ago, I have been titled Asset Manager, Senior Asset Manager, Assistant Vice President, and now Vice President. My identity within the group has changed very much. I owe this to my abilities in being aware of how my mind works and dealing with my personal set of realities. (Baxter Magolda, 2001, p 122-23)

Evan's comments reveal the interweaving of the epistemological, intrapersonal, and interpersonal dimensions of self-authorship. Figuring out how his mind worked answered the epistemological question of "How do I know?" Refining his sense of self answered the intrapersonal question of "Who am I?" This resolution led him to identify and arrange priorities and develop a plan for pursuing them. Evan attributed progress on these two dimensions as central to his evolution in relations with others, both in work and home life. Rebalancing his identity in relation to others answered the interpersonal question of "What kind of relationships do I want to construct?" His experience clearly illustrates the integrated model of development shown in Figure 2.

Looking at the interrelationships across dimensions of development can also illustrate the development of intercultural maturity. Lauren, another participant in Baxter Magolda's longitudinal study, worked in various business contexts during her twenties. During this time she was struggling to shift from relying on her parents for direction to making her own choices. By her mid-twenties she had acted on her own internal voice both in career and personal choices. She also reported changes in her relations with others:

> I also matured in my relationships because people my age were not plentiful, so I did make some new friends that were older. And, also, different types of friends. In high school and college, everybody I hung around with was like me. You should give everybody an opportunity to be your friend regardless of where they work or where they went to school or if they didn't go to school or if their economic background was different than yours. And I can honestly say that I didn't give the other people a chance [before]. And I don't know why. But coming here opened some doors. You just really realise that everybody's different and everybody's unique in their own way. That doesn't mean that they're less because they don't have a college degree, for example. And I'll tell you, too, I think I'm more appreciative right now

because from what I see there are so many other sides and walks of life. Everybody's situation isn't like the situation that I have. So maybe a little bit more open, I guess. (Baxter Magolda, 2001, p 288)

Lauren's experience with people different from herself in age and economic background helped her understand multiple realities. Her shift from external to internal self-definition allowed her to be open to these new realities, leading her to construct relationships with people she would have (and in fact did, as she reports below) avoided.

Example of Reasoning about Intercultural Issues Prior to Self-Authorship

In contrast to her post-college reasoning, Lauren relied on external authority to define herself during college. Her stance on differences was apparent in this story:

> One thing that living off campus showed me the most is that it's really hard sometimes to live with your friends and be good friends with them at the same time. I lived with my best friend last year, and that might have been a mistake because we fought over trivial matters. But it turned into bigger things. This year, we are in the same house but on different floors. We haven't had a fight yet. It's important to learn that they're your friends; however, you can't eat, breathe, and live twenty-four hours a day with them. (Baxter Magolda, 1992, pp 313–314)

Lauren and her best friend fought about their differences when they lived in the same room, leading Lauren to suspect it might have been a mistake to live together. Lauren's revelation the second year that it was easier to get along with friends when living on different floors or not being together so much conveys that maintaining relationships requires avoiding difference. From the vantage point of external self-definition, others' approval is crucial to maintaining relational bonds. Thus difference threatens relationships. This perspective no doubt contributed to Lauren's focus on building friendships with those who were like her during college. This stance does not reflect the ability to deal effectively with difference—a key aspect of intercultural maturity.

A Holistic Approach to Integrating Identity Development Theories

There has been a virtual explosion of literature on identity development in the last decade, especially research addressing particular dimensions of identity development, including racial (Helms, 1995; Thompson & Carter, 1997), ethnic (Phinney, 1990), and sexual orientation (Evans & D'Augelli, 1996). While these models tend to focus on culturally distinct differences, they also contain some noteworthy similarities, especially when examined from an holistic, development perspective. For example, these theories tend to describe movement from lack of awareness of one's particular identify, through a period of confusion and exploration, to a complex, internally defined perspective on how one's race, ethnicity, or sexual orientation are integrated into one's view of oneself and the world. These common developmental progressions clearly include elements from cognitive, identity, and interpersonal domains. In addition, these theories indicate that intercultural competence requires an internally defined sense of self to avoid feeling threatened by difference (Kegan, 1994). This internal sense of self also supports what is often described as a cognitive skill, acknowledging that people hold multiple perspectives on many issues, including intercultural issues (Baxter Magolda, 2000; Ortiz, 2000), and for defensible reasons (King & Shuford, 1996). In other words, there appear to be overarching theoretical perspectives that in some ways subsume or overlap with theories addressing particular dimensions of identity development.

Juxtaposing these theories with the three dimensions of development yields possibilities for an integrated model of development in general and development in intercultural maturity in particular. For example, at the early phases of development, learners accept authorities' views (epistemological dimension), define themselves through external others (intrapersonal dimension), and act in relationships to acquire approval (interpersonal dimension). In the context of racial, ethnic or sexual orientation identity development, these characteristics are consistent with the lack of awareness of one's particular identity that stems from accepting external (often dominant) perspectives. Dissonance in various aspects of identify development often stems from marginalisation by external others, which can call the validity of external authority into question. As learners struggle through the confusion that comes with realising that all knowledge is not certain and that individuals must consider establishing their own views (epistemological dimension), their reliance on external others for definition (intrapersonal) and seeking others' approval in relationships (interpersonal) is also called into question. The particulars of race, ethnicity, or sexual orientation are intertwined in this confusion and exploration. The need to explore these issues for oneself and move away from accepting authorities' views is consistent with the exploration phases of these layers of identity. In later, more complex phases of development where self-authorship on all three dimensions is achieved, an internally defined perspective on how one's race ethnicity, or sexual orientation is integrated into one's view of oneself is possible. Table 1 summarises these implications for the development of intercultural maturity of students' developmental levels.

We now offer some examples of current research on intercultural maturity that draws on multiple dimensions and illustrates interrelationships among them.

Role of the Cognitive Dimension

There is cognitive complexity in the presence of diverse worldviews, and complex thinking skills that enable students to understand and accept ambiguity and relativism are necessary. Perry's (1968), Baxter Magolda's (1992), and King and Kitchener's (1994) models all posit that earlier, more simplistic stages of cognitive development involve concrete thinking and a belief in absolute knowledge, whereas later, more complex levels reflect an ability to consider knowledge grounded in context, deriving judgments from personal experiences, evidence from other sources, and from the perspectives of others. This raises the distinct possibility that exposure to culturally different worldviews may lead to greater complexity in thinking, as suggested by King and Shuford (1996) and by Ortiz, (1995) finding that women of colour evidenced higher stages of cognitive development. Intercultural perspective taking, another cognitive task, also has application as students are able to develop the ability to consider both cognitive and affective elements that have an impact on culturally different students (Kappler, 1998; Steglitz, 1993). Further, in a study of intercultural competence in US students abroad, Moore and Ortiz (1999) found that interculturally competent students were critical thinkers who suspended judgment until the evidence was in, and who included a diverse range of knowledge in what they considered as evidence. These findings suggest that there are strong reasons to continue to explore the role of cognitive development in various aspects of intercultural maturity.

Role of the Identity and Interpersonal Dimensions

The second and third dimensions of intercultural competence involve identity development and the ability to interact effectively with others. Several, ethnic identity models have

TABLE 1
How Developmental Levels Affect Intercultural Maturity

Developmental Level	Implications for Intercultural Maturity
Early	
• Learners accept authority's views (cognitive domain)	• Learners exhibit lack of awareness of one's particular identity that stems from accepting external (especially socially-dominant) perspectives
• Learners define themselves externally through others (intrapersonal domain)	
• Learners act to acquire approval of others (interpersonal domain)	
Advanced	
• Learners exhibit self-authorship in all three dimensions	• It is now possible to construct an internally-defined perceptive on how one's race, ethnicity and/or sexual orientation is integrated into one's view of oneself.

attended to the intersection of race and ethnicity in the development of ego identify (Cross, 1991; Helms, 1995; Phinney, 1992). In these models, individuals at more complex stages of development have considered and integrated their ethnicity into a sense of self that is maintained through interactions with diverse others and in participation in majority-defined and -dominated society. In a campus community where culture is expressed, opportunities for learning are enhance by students who are successful at integrating their ethnicity into their identity (Ortiz, 1997). For example, Howard-Hamilton (2000) showed how a student's level of racial identity development could affect his or her response to and performance on class assignments that call for analysis of issues that involve racial dynamics. This example, along with the experience of Christine, reported above (King and Baxter Magolda, 1996), illustrates the central role of identity development in achieving intercultural maturity. Since cognitive development is given so much attention as an intended college outcome, research exploring the role of these other dimensions of development on intercultural maturity (or even on cognitive development itself) could provide extremely useful information to those who might not be attuned to the apparent roles of these other aspects of development. An example of this is provided by Derryberry and Thoma (2000), who looked at the relationship between college students' moral developmental and the quality of their friendships. They found that students with higher scores on moral judgment:

> viewed the diversity of college populations in a positive light, were more open to forming friendships in college, were more likely to enter into a range of activities with their college friends, and were more likely to discuss a range of topics than their peers with lower moral reasoning scores. (p 16)

In other words, the quality of one's friendships (the interpersonal domain) may mediate not only one's use of principled moral reasoning, but also one's openness to diversity experiences. These examples all show the value of a broader theoretical perspective that frames separate dimensions of developmental in a way that illustrates their interconnectedness.

In this discussion, we have contrasted three approaches to conceptualising and researching domains of development, separate domains, related domains, and integrated domains. Table 2 notes implicit theoretical assumptions underlying each approach, along with a description of research strategies used for each approach to investigate intercultural understanding. These strategies may be useful to those who are attempting to document the effectiveness and/or impact of existing campus programmes and practices, or of new initiatives designed to promote intercultural maturity.

Educational Implications

We have described a model of intercultural maturity that integrates three major domains of development (cognitive, intrapersonal and interpersonal), and have suggested that an integrative model provides a much more powerful tool for understanding and promoting development than do models that take a "separate" or "related" approach. Further, we have emphasised that the development of intercultural maturity unfolds gradually and in a manner that reflects an individual's maturity in each of the three dimensions. How are these insights reflected in educational practices? Next, we offer several resources that exemplify this approach.

In an exceptionally well-crafted article on multicultural education, Ortiz and Rhoads (2000) proposed a framework for multicultural education that illustrates the power and potential of an integrative, developmental approach. They outline a series of five elements (which they refer to as steps) that are part of an individual's journey toward what we have called intercultural maturity. These are: understanding culture; learning about other cultures; recognising and deconstructing white culture; recognising the legitimacy of other cultures; and developing a multicultural outlook. For each, they list a "cognitive goal" that reflects a more complex understanding of the element; for the first, the goal is "to develop a complex understanding of culture (culture shapes people's lives and people shape culture)" (p. 85). These goals also reflect substantive changes in the ways individuals come to understand ("make meaning") of the notion of culture and how they and others experience both their own and others' cultures. In addition, Ortiz and Rhoads chart beginning and ending ways students might frame the problems being addressed for each element, and discuss educational activities designed to facilitate students' understanding of each of the elements. They also

TABLE 2
Separate, Related and Integrated Perspectives on Domains of Development

	Separate Domains	Related Domains	Integrated Domains
Implicit Theoretical Assumptions	There are separate domains of development informed by theories that focus on one domain. Development in each domain evolves independently of development in the others, and is affected by different sets of educational factors.	There are separate domains of development informed by theories that focus on one domain. However, they may be interrelated, and the extent of these relationships can be examined empirically.	Although the separate domains are articulated as specific to a given aspect of development, the domains share a common foundation in participles of maturity. Further, these common elements and the interrelationships across models can illuminate key insights into educational outcomes.
Research Strategy for Studying Intercultural Understanding	Example domains of development separately, typically focusing on only one domain (eg, cognitive) and the factors that affect development in this domain (eg, greater cognitive complexity or improvement of perspective-taking skills among students in diversity courses).	Assess development independently across domains (eg, cognitive and identity), and note relationships found. Examine factors affecting development that may be common to both (eg, participation in campus diversity programming).	Assess development both within and across the three domains, with an eye toward interdependent aspects of development. Examine factors affecting integration of the three domains (eg, emphasising self as central to knowledge construction).

argue that an important educational goal is enthusiasm for learning in general and cultural learning in particular. Many students (especially majority White students) report being afraid to discuss diversity issues, either not feeling comfortable with the language of the topic, or afraid that their comments will be misunderstood and labeled racist; both discourage motivation for cultural learning. This model explicitly starts at a lower threshold of risk to encourage (not shut off) the conversation.

Fernandez (2002) adapted the Ortiz and Rhoads (2000) framework to examine the development of intercultural competence. She looked specifically at students' experiences with culture shock, exploring how these could be used to enhance self-authorship. For each of five developmental steps, she noted specific self-authorship goals, cognitive dissonance caused by culture shock, and the role of the guide in providing support for students trying to understand (make meaning of) their experiences. This framework provides a rich conceptual base for

diversity educators who help students navigate cultural immersion experiences to became interculturally mature.

Zúñiga (2003) has worked extensively with intergroup dialogue programmes on college campuses to promote student interaction and understanding among students from different social backgrounds. This approach "combines experiential learning and participatory methods with critical analyses of the social realities that shape relationships between social groups in our society" (p 3). Students from different social identity groups that have a history of conflict meet for sustained face-to-face facilitated conversations. Such groups include men and women; White people, biracial/multi-racial/ethnic people, and people of colour; Blacks, Latinos and Native Americans; lesbians, gay men, bisexual and heterosexual people; working, middle and upper socio-economic class; and, Christians, Muslims and Jews. The dialogues are structured to explore students' own experiences and assumptions as the basis for enabling them to understand more fully the idea of socially constructed group distinctions, and how these are played out in intergroup interactions in the US. As Zúñiga explains:

> By encouraging direct encounter and exchange about contentious issues, especially those associated with issues of social identity and social stratification, the intergroup dialogues invite students to actively explore the meanings of singular (as men or women), or intersecting social identities (as men of colour or white men, as white women or women of colour) and to examine the dynamics of privilege and oppression shaping the relationship between social groups in our society. (p 4)

The class opens by establishing the foundations for dialogue, including introductions and guidelines (eg, no personal attacks, respect confidentiality). At the second stage, the purpose is to develop a shared vocabulary around issues of social identities and social stratification, and then to introduce and explore concept such as prejudice, in/out group dynamics, discrimination, and privilege, and how each affects intergroup relationships. Not until the third stage are "hot topics" the focus of the dialogue, difficult or controversial issues such as separation/self-segregation on campus, racism on campus. Facilitators encourage students to voice their concerns and raise their questions.

> They support the process by posing questions, probing for deeper levels of thinking and feeling, and by inviting participants to fully explore the disagreements and conflicts that ensure in the conversation. The encourage collective thinking and questioning, facilitators invite participants to respond to what others are saying and to build on each other's comments and experiences. In closing each topic, participants are asked to identify questions to ponder or specific actions that can be taken to explore or address a particular issue on campus. (p 16)

The last stage is designed to prepare students for post-dialogue experiences, especially for action planning and for building alliances.

The effects of participation in these dialogues are impressive (see Hurtado, 2001 and Stephan and Stephan, 2001 for details of these studies):

> ... dialogue participation is linked with positive effects on cognitive outcomes such as knowledge about other groups and discrimination in society, stereotype and prejudice

reduction, the development of complex thinking, social awareness of self and others in systems of inequality, and increased understanding about the causes of conflict between social groups. Dialogue participation is also found to reduce anxiety about intergroup contact, and to enhance skills related to communication across differences, conflict exploration, comfort dealing with diversity, and perspective taking. Finally, participation in intergroup dialogues, as a participant or a student facilitator, seems to promote more active involvement in social justice work. (Zúñiga, in press, p18)

These outcomes are noteworthy not only for diversity education, but as indices of the kinds of broader collegiate outcomes mentioned in the AAC&U (1998) Statement of Liberal Learning noted above. In addition, the approaches summarized here (Fernandez, 2002; Ortiz and Rhoads, 2000; Zúñiga, in press) are consistent with the calls made by Baxter Magolda (2001, in press) for educators to acknowledge the central role of the self in knowledge construction, identity development, and in building relationships with others. In addition to these examples, Baxter Magolda (2003) describes three other existing progammes in both curricular and co-curricular setting that are designed in ways that foster self-authorship. In each case, students are expected and encouraged to take responsibility for their learning and their behaviors, they are expected to become more knowledgeable about themselves and the world around them, and to develop internal compasses to guide their choices and behaviors, turning to others for information and advice, but taking responsibility for their own decisions and actions. Clearly, being able to act in each of these ways requires development in all three developmental domains noted above (the cognitive, intrapersonal and interpersonal domains). Designing educational programmes that take all three of these dimensions into account allows for a more complete approach to the development of complex outcomes such as intercultural maturity.

Conclusion

In this paper we have introduced an integrated model of development that we think has great potential for better understanding the nature of intercultural maturity and why efforts to promote it have met with mixed success. We encourage other researchers who are interested in examining intercultural maturity from an integrated perspective to conduct studies that will address the questions raised in the research agenda presented above. This is an ambitious undertaking, an agenda that not only presents interesting conceptual and methodological challenges, but that has taken on an urgency in light of recent national and international events. The need to address intercultural issues personally and with more than one's intellect is not a new insight; in fact, it was captured eloquently in 1947 by Aldous Huxley:

> . . . proverbs are always platitudes until you have experienced the truth of them. The newly arrested thief knows that honesty is the best policy with an intensity of conviction which the rest of us can never experience. And to realise that it takes all sorts to make a world one must have seen a certain number of the sorts with one's own eyes. There is all the difference in the world between believing academically, with the intellect, and believing personally, intimately, with the whole living self. [Jesting Pilate, 207] [Quoted by Storti, 1990, p 53]

"Believing academically" may be a good first step in the development of intercultural maturity. We propose this integrated framework and identify educational programmes that exemplify its major components as steps toward the end of helping students to gain the maturity to believe personally and "with the whole living self."

References

Association of American Colleges and Universities (1998). Statement on Liberal Learning. Retrieved 8/20/02, www.aacu.org/about/mission

Baxter Magolda, MB (1992). *Knowing and reasoning in college: Gender-related patterns in students' intellectual development*. San Francisco: Jossey-Bass.

Baxter Magolda, M (1997). Facilitating meaningful dialogues about race. *About Campus*, 2(5), 14–18.

Baxter Magolda, M (1999). *Creating contexts for learning and self-authorship: Constructive-developmental pedagogy*. Nashville, Tennessee: Vanderbilt University Press.

Baxter Magolda, MB (2000). Teaching to promote holistic learning and development. In Baxter Magolda, MB (Ed), Teaching to promote intellectual and personal maturity: Incorporating students' worldviews and identities into the learning, process, **82**, 88–98. *New Directions for Teaching and Learning*. San Francisco: Jossey-Bass.

Baxter Magolda, MB (2001). *Journeys into adulthood: Narratives for transforming higher education to pro-mote self-understanding*. Sterling, VA: Stylus Publishing.

Baxter Magolda, MB (in press). Identity and learning: Student affairs' role in transforming, higher education. Journal of College Student Development.

Bikson, TK and Law, SA (1994). *Global Preparedness and Human Resources: College and Corporate Perspectives*. Santa Monica, CA: RAND Corporation.

Bowen, H (1980). *Investment in learning: The individual and social value of American higher education*. San Francisco: Jossey-Bass, Publishers.

Bok, DC (1986). *Higher learning*. Cambridge MA: Harvard University Press.

Cross, WEJ (1991). *Shades of Black: Diversity in African-American identities*. Philadelphia: Temple University Press.

Derryberry, P and Thoma, S (2000). The friendship effect: Its role in the development of moral thinking in students. *About Campus*, 5(2), 13–18.

Evans, NJ and DiAugelli, AR (1996). Lesbians, gay men, and bisexual people in college. In Savin-William, RC and Cohen, KM (Eds), *The lives of lesbians, gays, and bisexuals: Children to adults*, pp 201–226. For Worth, TX: Harcourt Brace.

Fernandez, E (2002). Framing incidents of culture shock: A growth process for intercultural maturity. Unpublished paper, University of Michigan. Available from the author, Center for the Study of Higher and Postsecondary Education, 2117 Education Building, 610 East University Avenue, Ann Arbor, MI 49109.

Fortune 500 corporations file brief in support of diversity in higher education. (2000, October, 16). [Online press release]. Available at: http://www.umich.edu/-urel/admissions/releases/fortune.html

Helms, JE (1995). An update of Helms' white and people of colour racial identity models. In Ponterotto, JG, Casas, JM, Suzuki, LA, and Alexander, CM (Eds), *Handbook of multicultural counselling*. Thousand Oaks, CA: Sage.

Holcomb-McCoy, CC and Myers, JE (1999). Multicultural competence and counselor training: A national survey. *Journal of Counseling and Development*, **77**, 294–302.

Howard-Hamilton, MF (2000). Creating a culturally responsive learning environment for African American students. In Baxter Magolda, MB (Ed), Teaching to promote intellectual and personal maturity: Incorporating students' worldviews and identities into the learning process. *New Directions for Testing and Learning*, **82**, 45–53. San Francisco: Jossey-Bass

Howard-Hamilton, MF, Richardson, S and Shuford, BC (1998). Promoting multicultural education: A holistic approach. *College Student Affairs Journal*, **18**(1), 5–17.

Hurtado, S (2001). Research and evaluation on intergroup dialogues. In Schoem, D and Hurtado, S (Eds), *Intergroup dialogue: Deliberative democracy in school, college, community and workplace*, pp 22–36. Ann Arbor: The University of Michigan Press.

Jones, SR and McEwen, MK (2000). A conceptual model of multiple dimensions of identity. *Journal of College Student Development*, **41**(4) 405–414.

Kappler, BJ (1998). Refining Intercultural Perspective-Taking. Unpublished doctoral dissertation, University of Minnesota, Minneapolis.

Kegan, R (1994). *In over our heads: The mental demands of modern life*. Cambridge, MA: Harvard University Press.

King, PM and Baxter Magolda, MB (1996). A developmental perspective on learning. *Journal of College Student Development*, **37**(2), 163–173.

King, PM & Howard-Hamilton, MF (in press). An assessment of multicultural competence. NASPA Journal.

King, PM, and Kitchener, KS (1994). *Developing reflective judgment*. San Francisco: Jossey-Bass.

King, PM and Shuford, BC (1996). A multicultural view is a more cognitively complex view: Cognitive development and multicultural education. *American Behavioral Scientist*, **40**(2), 153–164.

Kitchener, KS (1982). Human development and the college campus: Sequences and tasks. In Hanson, GR (Ed), Measuring student development. *New Directions for Students Services*, **20**, 17–45.

Kitchener, KS and Fischer, KW (1990). A skill approach to the development of reflective thinking. In Kuhn, D (Ed), *Contributions to human development: Development perspectives on teaching and learning*, 21 Basel, Switzerland: Karger.

Levine, A and Cureton, JS (1998). *When hope and fear collide*. San Francisco: Jossey-Bass.

Mentkowski, M and Associates (2000). *Learning that lasts: Integrating learning, development, and performance in college and beyond*. San Francisco: Jossey-Bass.

Moore, KA, and Ortiz, AM (1999). The Intercultural Competence Project: Site Visit and Focus Group Report. A Report to the Institute on the International Education of Students. Michigan State University.

Ortiz, AM (1995). Promoting Racial Understanding: A Study of Educational and Developmental Interventions. Paper presented at the annual meeting of the Association for the Study of Higher Education in Orland, FL, November 1995.

Ortiz, AM (1997). Defining Oneself in a Multicultural World: Ethnic Identity in College Students. Unpublished doctoral dissertation, University of California Los Angeles.

Ortiz, AM (2000). Expressing cultural identity in the learning community: Opportunities and challenges. In Baxter Magolda, MB (Ed), Teaching to promote intellectual and personal maturity: Incorporating students' worldviews and identities into the learning process. *New Directions for Teaching and Learning*, pp 67–79. San Francisco: Jossey-Bass.

Ortiz, AM and Rhoads, RA (2000). Deconstructing whiteness as part of a multicultural educational framework: From theory to practice. *Journal of College Student Development*, **41**(1) 81–93.

Perry, WG (1968). *Forms of Intellectual and Ethnical Development in the College Years: A Scheme*. New York: Rinehart and Winston, Inc.

Pettigrew, TF (1998). Intergroup contact theory. *Annual Review of Psychology*, **49**, 65–85.

Phinney, JS (1990). Ethnic identity in adolescents and adults: Review of research. *Psychological Bulletin*, **108** (3), 499–514.

Phinney, JS (1992). The Multigroup Ethnic Identity Measure: A New Scale for Use with Diverse Groups. *Journal of Adolescent Research*, 7(2), 156–176.

Pope, RL and Reynolds, AL (1997). Student affairs core competencies: Integrating multicultural awareness, knowledge, and skills. *Journal of College Student Development*, **38**, 266–277.

Pope, RL and Mueller, JA (2000). Development and initial validation of the Multicultural Competence in Students Affairs-Preliminary 2 Scale. *Journal of College Student Development*, **41** (6), 599–607.

Rest, JR (1986). *Moral development: Advances in research and theory*. New York: Praeger

Rosovsky, H (1990). *The university: An owner's manual*. New York: WW Norton & Company, Inc.

Stephan, W and Stephan, CW (2001). *Improving intergroup relations*. Thousand Oaks, CA: Sage.

Storti, C (1990). *The art of crossing cultures*. Yarmouth, ME: Intercultural Press.

Steglitz, I (1993). Intercultural Perspective-Taking: The Impact of Study Abroad. Unpublished doctoral dissertation, University of Minnesota, Minneapolis.

Talbot, DM, and Kocarek, C (1997). Student affairs graduate faculty members' knowledge, comfort, and behaviors regarding issues of diversity. *Journal of College Student Development*, **38**, 278–287.

Thompson, CE, and Carter RT (1997). *Racial identity theory: Applications to individual, group, and organizational interventions*. Mahway, NJ: Lawrence Erlbaum Chapter 2, 15–32.

Zúñiga, Ximena (in press). Bridging differences through intergroup dialogue. About Campus.

CHAPTER 8

HIGHER EDUCATION'S SELF-REFLEXIVE TURN: TOWARD AN INTERCULTURAL THEORY OF STUDENT DEVELOPMENT

GREG TANAKA

In December 1992, Tierney published an article in which he asked whether Tinto's (1975) theory of student social and academic integration was in effect "assimilation" in disguise. Embedded in Tierney's critique was a concern that research on college student development had been ethnocentric and that core assumptions underlying theories of cognitive and social development would need to be revised. While Tierney's inquiry echoes an earlier call from the campus ecology movement to modify student development theory in the late 1960s (e.g., Altman & Haythorn, 1967; Banning & Aulepp, 1971), it also gives rise to a more current theoretical question: Why have research methods on college student development not kept pace with the proliferation of social theory since the 1970s addressing the connection between culture, power, and knowledge?

This article seeks to (1) infuse critiques from recent social theory into survey instruments traditionally made available to higher education research and (2) offer a framework based on those critiques for a new "intercultural theory" of college student development. Thus, although it would be valuable to examine how institutions change how power operates in increasingly intercultural contexts (e.g., Darder, 1991; Tanaka, in press; Tanaka & Cruz, 1998; Tierney, 1991), the purpose of this article is specifically to promote dialogue about whether to infuse recent social critiques into the *methods* of higher education research (see e.g., Cherryholmes, 1988; Foster, 1994; Gitlin, 1994).

I. Modern Theories of Student Development Circa 1975

Tinto's original theory of "social and academic integration" (1975) had sought to explain why some students persisted and others dropped out of college. By integration, he meant the extent to which students adapted themselves to the culture of the institution. As suggested by Nora (1987) and Murguia, Padilla, and Pavel (1991), Tinto's theory can also be applied to campuses with ethnically diverse students. Similarly, A. W. Astin's (1975) ground-breaking theory of "student involvement" has had several glosses over time. Not only can students improve their success in college through greater personal involvement, but the institution can take steps to enhance a student's "talent development" (Astin, 1991). Like the theoretical work of Tinto and Astin, Pace's (1984) "quality of effort"

Special thanks to Jennifer Gong, Parker Johnson, Laila Aaen, Michael Pavel, N. Brian Hu, Dale Appelbaum, Beth Stoddard, and a journal reviewer, whose recommendations are everywhere apparent in this article.

model compares student progress in college against personal participation in "various activities related to the use of facilities and opportunities" on campus.

What all three modern constructs have in common are (1) an interest in measuring the impact of student participation in the institution and (2) a tendency *not* to examine the underlying cultures of that institution (often Western European, straight, upper middle class, and male). However, in times of fragmentation linked to rapidly changing student racial demographics and heightened awareness of difference based on race, gender, and sexual orientation, a culturally neutral perspective may overlook differential impacts from participation by diverse groups and fall short of providing the data policymakers will need to foster meaning and harmony *across groups*. Although not something modern theorists could have predicted in the 1970s, there is growing empirical evidence that current approaches are no longer adequate to explain the increasingly complex experience of contemporary college students (e.g., Bischoping & Bell, 1998, p. 191; Dey & Hurtado, 1996, p. 30; Kraemer, 1997, p. 173; Levine & Cureton, 1998, pp. 143–146; Love, 1998, pp. 303–305; Baxter Magolda, 1992, pp. 277–279, 1996, pp. 297–303; Richardson & Skinner, 1990, p. 507; Tanaka, 1996, 1997, 1999; Tanaka & Cruz, 1998; Thompson & Fretz, 1991, p. 445; Wolf-Wendel, 1998, p. 175. See also Foster, 1994, pp. 137–140, 1997; Nozaki, 2000, p. 375; Pascarella & Terenzini, 1998, p. 155; Popkewitz, 1997, pp. 25–27, 1998, p. 560).

To examine the potential for rearticulating modern theory and methods, this article submits the survey instruments used by Tinto, Astin, and Pace to five probes. In addition, it will review the models of "reference group formation" by Cross (1971), "different voice" by Gilligan (1977), and "social construction" by Tierney (1992). The probes are:

(a) *Voice:* Does the construct treat members of each cultural group not as objects but as people who have "subject position" and can author their own cultural histories? (Feminist theory, queer theory, and multiculturalism)

(b) *Power:* Does the construct include within its scope a recognition that power and knowledge are interconnected? (From poststructural critique)

(c) *Authenticity:* Is construct validity maintained by locating students in their own time and history? (From postcolonial or transnational anthropology)

(d) *Self-reflexivity:* Does the construct promote self-knowledge for the researcher by making his or her culture and social location a part of the analysis? (From postmodern theory)

(e) *Reconstitution:* Is the researcher urged to use personal story to reveal needed change in the structures and reward mechanisms of his or her own discipline and academic department? (From critical race theory)

Although there are many excellent points of departure from social theory at the turn of the century, I have selected the above five because of their potential for making an immediate impact on current research in college student development.

Data for this article come from the categories contained in *survey instruments* used by Astin, Pace, and Tinto; a sampling of *social theory* since the 1970s; and a review of *literature* by modern theorists. For example, modern surveys of student development have traditionally been very effective at measuring student progress along academic and social lines. These include the Cooperative Institutional Research Program (CIRP) developed by Astin, the College Student Experiences Questionnaire (CSEQ) developed by Pace, and Tinto's use of four preexisting surveys—the National Longitudinal Survey (NLS), High School and Beyond (HSB), the American College Testing Program Survey of Institutions (ACT), and the Survey of Retention at Higher Education Institutions.

Categories in modern surveys thus include measures of cognitive growth, social development, aesthetic creativity, critical skills, and institutional characteristics like school size, whether private or public, and faculty attitudes (see e.g., Pascarella & Terenzini, 1991, pp. 15–61). None of these designs, however, takes into account the impact of student racial demographic shifts, issues of power, or the cultural norms that may impact student development. Though others have focused with some success on categories that locate a student within a historical context of domination, marginality, or self-identity (e.g., Cross, 1971, regarding African Americans;

Gilligan, 1977, regarding women; and Tierney, 1992, regarding Native Americans), none of these measures student cognitive and social development—what the modernist techniques had done so well. The challenge is to examine the possibility of combining benefits from both approaches under one analysis.

II. A Flowering of Social Theory Since the 1970s

Although the following extracted concepts cannot do justice to recent social theory, they are offered in the spirit of initiating discussion about how to broaden research on college student development to accommodate the rapidly shifting cultural terrain on U.S. college and university campuses, where social locations of race, gender, and sexual orientation are of growing salience in the student experience. For example, the percentage of students who are of color in U.S. colleges and universities rose from 15.7% in 1976 to 27% in 1998 (National Center for Educational Statistics, 1977). In California, the percentage of students of color rose from 21.5% in 1979 to 48.5% by 1998 (California Postsecondary Education Commission; Hu & Tanaka, 2000).

A. "Voice:" Seeing People as Agents Who Can Author Their Own Cultural Histories (Feminist, Queer, and Multicultural Theory)

To address these trends, I want to advance a thesis that comes from three allied thrusts. Feminist theory was among the first to suggest the metaphor of "voice" as a means of promoting the end of one culture's dominance in academe. In lieu of a centralizing tendency of male writers to speak for women, the feminist theorist would end male characterization of women as "the other" and move the woman's voice from the margin to the center. Expanding on this, bell hooks (1984) urged that class and race oppression also be included when ending a hegemonic knowledge system. In other words, the goal should not be for one group or another (this time white feminists) to "gain social equality with ruling class white men" but rather to end dualism altogether (p. 15). Using this perspective, it would not be enough to add a question or two on gender to a survey instrument; it would be

necessary to reexamine the entire instrument for voice. Having voice means having culture. For each student this will mean having survey questions that locate his or her culture in relation to such core experiences as course content, grading, and professor/student relations.

Queer theory added to the idea of voice by calling for a "denorming" of academic practices. Researchers here are urged to "work to understand how norms came into existence, how they have been maintained and how strategies have been employed to silence different groups" (Tierney, 1997, p. 63). For Tierney, greater voice will mean more than just creating new survey questions that probe the maintenance of heterosexual norms on a campus. It will also mean that research on sexual orientation must reveal the norms contained within the research process itself. (In other words, the research function will itself need to be "denormed.") In my view, a critical denorming would not replace old norms with new ones that favor a new group but advance a new ethical framework that values particularity and does not favor any one group's voice.

Like feminist and queer theorists, multicultural writers use the metaphor of "voice" to validate the cultures of people of color. Noting, however, that multicultural gains of the 1960s have been "appropriated by dominant humanism," McCarthy (1993) now urges that constructions of knowledge be radically redefined from heterogeneous perspectives rather than merely settling for having one's voice included. Following McCarthy's critique, research instruments should make multiple, shifting social locations based on gender, race, ethnicity, class, sexual orientation, and other identifiers the *central* focus rather than merely being added on.

What these progressive thrusts have in common is a preference for broader and more complex applications of "voice" to validate many diverse cultures in education. It is important here to envision "culture" broadly to encompass shared meanings of a group of people that derive from race, ethnicity, gender, sexual orientation, class, immigrant status, physical capability, and combinations thereof (Tanaka, 1997, pp. 275–276). A student thus might see herself or himself as an African lesbian, or an economically disadvantaged European-American male, or an economically privileged Vietnamese woman who is ethnic Chinese. There is also great variation and shifting within categories, so that the act of knowing each student's social location is a search for an evolving, negotiated, multilayered cultural perspective.

In this way, "culture" is not reduced to essentialized categories, and researchers have an interest in finding better ways to study the interactions between complex social locations of individuals and their institutions. Toward the end of this article, I offer some suggestions about how this concern might be operationalized. The attempt flows from a belief that it would be self-limiting for quantitative researchers to abdicate to "qualitative research" the responsibility to research these issues at a time when they are becoming so salient. It might even enhance research to take tropes arising from qualitative studies and use them to inform a quantitative research design (see e.g., Antonio, 1998; Mau, 1993 p. 348; McDonough, Korn, & Yamasaki, 1997, pp. 297–298; Tanaka, in press).

B. The Close Relationship Between Power and Knowledge (Poststructural Analysis)

To evaluate this, I will apply to higher education research the poststructural concept that knowledge about culture is mediated by power. This thesis holds that people in power will tend to advance a rendition of knowledge and history that favors them and keeps them in power (Foucault, 1972). Whereas power is frequently used to convey a sense of political control over others or over social fields, as in Gramsci's concept of hegemony (1977, pp. 276, 325, 349), I will use power here in two different ways—as a reflection of both the systemic and discourse-based notion of power articulated by Foucault (1976, pp. 93–94, 100–102) and of the meaning that comes from feeling a fundamental interconnectedness with other human beings as advanced by Kondo (1990, pp. 9–10). Applying a discourse-based conceptualization of power helps the researcher consider that writers of history will often mask any connection between published knowledge and their own power by making claims to universal truth. The problem arises when there is increased particularity deriving from race, gender, sexual orientation, and other social identifiers at college or university campuses. A discourse-based examination of power may not fully reveal how an individual finds meaning and self-validation (or does not) in such complex social spaces. In such contexts, a second measure of power would

examine one's ability to feel a sense of meaning from connectedness with others on a campus.

What I want to suggest is that now is a good time to make "power" a formal category of analysis in higher education research by including it in survey instruments. This means examining what determines what counts as knowledge on a campus and whether that process is friendly or unfriendly to a student's multiple cultures. Instead of studying "minorities" in relation to an unexamined dominant culture, the proposal here is to study the social positions and cultures of *all* students *in relation to* other cultures on campus. In operationalizing concepts like power, privilege, and oppression, care must of course be taken to avoid reducing complex behavior to simplistic categories of analysis, but the need for caution should not be a reason to shy away from this responsibility either.

In making the power dynamics of knowledge systems less opaque, poststructural theory thus reveals how culture, power, and knowledge are intertwined whenever monological (e.g., Western, straight, and male) frames of reference attempt to speak for all cultures. But how can researchers make sense of power at a time when campuses are so embroiled in "culture wars"? For this I will turn to theory from postcolonial, or transnational, anthropology.

C. Authenticity and Questions of Validity in the Research Function (Transnational Anthropology)

The key to understanding power in higher education research, in my view, will come from acknowledging the wider historical context of transnationalism that impacts today's undergraduate experience. With recent trends in immigration, the infusion of students of color into campuses (with two-thirds of a recent entering class of color at the University of California at Berkeley) underscores the inadequacy of doing research from a one-culture view of history. In fact, a widening gap between traditional assumptions and today's student experience suggests that the research function may be askance of actual campus conditions. The westward thrust of European peoples into the United States is now recontextualized as just one of many transmigrations across oceans and continents, and diasporas triggered by Western colonialism have ironically come home to rest in the sacred space of the Eurocentric U.S. university. Here, research methods can no longer afford to be "timeless" or overlook the onrush of multiple cultural histories. What Popkewitz (1997, p. 21) had once called the "regulating effect of power"—a universalized conception of time—is starting to come unraveled.

"Authenticity," as I use the term, therefore refers to the act of locating each student in his or her own time and history—what Radhakrishnan (1996, p. 123) calls "personal authenticity." In education research, this would mean studying the historical context of power for the ethnic culture, gender, sexual orientation, and other social identifiers of each student. For example, too much information is lost in treating Asian Americans as a homogeneous, exoticized category (see Kondo, 1997, p. 195). Authenticity will instead require researchers to study the *multiple and shifting* sources of power and social location of each Asian American—in my case, an educationally and economically privileged, straight, third generation, Japanese American male—in relation to the power of other cultures on the campus (see, e.g., Love, 1998, p. 303, on authenticity for LGBT students).

A nuanced rendering of social location would thus require a researcher to avoid essentializing authenticity by treating categories as homogeneous or exotic or by leaving them unexamined (e.g., Trinh, 1989, pp. 89–94). Provision for variance would enable researchers to then move "into and out of " a rhetoric of authenticity (Pratt, 1995, p. 194). In other words, the goal of quantitative research in increasingly polycultural contexts should be to enhance the ability of a researcher to uncover *greater particularity* and at the same time avoid the tendency to oversimplify existing categories of analysis. Seeking personal authenticity can thus constitute an initial step in helping a researcher connect up (in one analysis) the rich strands of culture, power, and knowledge for each student.

In this vein, a potentially widening gap between traditional assumptions and today's student experience of diversity raises the distinct possibility that the research function may be losing its ability to reflect actual campus conditions. If closed to the growing importance of authenticity, student-based research could begin to sacrifice both its ethical goals (de Certeau, 1986, p. 200) and its construct validity—that close connection between meaning and a research operation (Cherryholmes, 1988, p. 100). An "allochronic" approach that leaves time out of the equation too easily reproduces the researcher's view of events (Fabian, 1983, pp. 52–69) and ironically undercuts that researcher's own assertion of objectivity.

But authenticity is not without its risks. One is the trap of reducing complex, shifting cultural behavior to neat "authentic" categories (Trinh, 1989, p. 94). Another can occur when a researcher thinks he can truly "know" the history and emotions of a student coming from a culture different from his own. To avoid *in*authenticity (e.g., Astin, Astin, Antonio, Astin, & Cress, 1999, pp. 14–18), researchers will need to construct questionnaires that allow students to self-report the nuances of their own cultural identities and histories in the social context of the institutions they attend. This means asking a student how much he learned about his own sense of power, agency, and ethnic identity (or sexual orientation or gender) in college, rather than whether there is "too much" or "too little" emphasis on a broad, abstract category like "race" or "multiculturalism" on a campus.

To operationalize authenticity fully, researchers will first need to be aware of any bias that might stem from their own sources of authenticity; they will need to locate themselves in their work. How does one insert oneself into the analysis?

D. Self-Reflexivity—Locating the Researcher in the Analysis (Postmodern Critique)

Although postmodern critique too often falls into the trap of celebrating the very fragmentation it examines, it does offer some useful concepts. One of the most promising is self-reflexivity (discussed in Tierney & Rhoads, 1993, p. 326, but not Bloland, 1995, or Mourad, 1997). "Selfreflexivity" would be what happens when a researcher uses what he learns about another culture to better understand all cultures, including his own (Marcus & Fischer, 1986, p. x). In effect, new knowledge about "the other" forces the researcher to reflect back on himself. Self-reflexivity can thus be the mirror by which a researcher compares his or her own place in time and history with the historical/social context of the students being studied.

In quantitative research, this means the researcher will need to construct survey instruments that make his own social markers—e.g., being male or heterosexual—a part of the analysis. For example, if current practice assigns to these identities a universal but unstated norm status to which all students must presumably adapt, reflexivity will require the researcher who wants to study a diverse student body to move away from this unexamined bias by making his own power, culture, and knowledge a part of the equation.

With reflexivity thus comes this thought: that research on student development may already be out of step with campus demographics precisely *because* the norms of its most progressive researchers have been unstated. To examine how liberal researchers might have come to occupy the very status quo they once critiqued, I will turn next to the work of critical race theory.

E. Reconstitution—Seeking Actual Change in Academic Structures and Reward Mechanisms (Critical Race Theory)

The thesis I want to explore here holds that liberal scholars now ironically extend the status quo by leaving in place the very structures and reward mechanisms they critique (Tanaka & Cruz, 1998, p. 145; Tate, 1997, p. 203). While critiquing hierarchical structures and practices, liberal researchers often enjoy the benefits of those very systems (e.g., tenure, access to elite publishing channels, high university salaries, and star professor status). With this so often the case, critical race theorists are calling for a shift in scholarship to require personal storytelling that surfaces specific areas of practice in need of change, beginning with one's home department and academic discipline. Implicit in a critical race theorist critique is a wish for ways to replace old hierarchy not with criteria for a new hierarchy (e.g., Torres, 1998) but with "a level playing field" for scholarly exchange.

A critical race theorist would thus ask: "Have criteria and practices resulted in hiring and promoting faculty of color, gays/lesbians, and women in the researcher's own department?" Or "Why is promotion and tenure even needed at all?" Or, "Are new faculty of color mentored by senior faculty—or left to fend for themselves?" "Are minority graduate students made coauthors in publications—or used to generate research about diversity for the professor's own gain?" "Is your publishing conducted under a heterogeneous process—or through journal hierarchies and review panels peopled by scholars from one homogeneous group?" Questions like these will need to be made a formal part of the analysis and incorporated into the protocol rather than left to interpretation.

In other words, higher education researchers can begin to identify specific ways to change their own departmental structures and reward mechanisms to accommodate the new demographics. In fact, critical race theory would suggest that higher education research now has a duty to do so. Campuses are already swirling from an influx of many students of color, a questioning of traditional knowledge systems, and demands to reexamine culture and power. Because of their unique positions as scholars who chart and make recommendations for higher education, these researchers arguably have an obligation to identify ways to mitigate the harsh effects of systemic upheaval on their own students by actual change in their own schools of education. Even greater potential here lies in testing new research methods that will generate models for organizational change elsewhere.

In sum, while any of the five above inquiries would bring fresh infusion of new theory into higher education research, they also go hand in hand. Tropes of voice, power, authenticity, self-reflexivity, and reconstitution overlap and borrow from each other. To reflect the increasingly heterogeneous student experience, methods will likely need to incorporate lessons and perspectives about culture, power, and knowledge from all five.

III. A Review of Modern Constructs for College Student Development

A. Social and Academic Integration (Tinto, 1975)

Vincent Tinto's (1975) theory of social and academic integration was proposed to help explain why some students persist and others drop out of college. To apply this theory he employed survey instruments developed earlier by other researchers. In the National Longitudinal Study of 1972 (NLS), questions were designed to track student progress through college in comparison to their senior year of high school. Questions in the 1972 survey dealt with personal and family background, educational and work experiences, plans, aspirations, attitudes, and opinions (U.S. Department of Education, 1977). The questions in the follow-up survey were tailored to find out the extent to which earlier student "plans and aspirations persisted over time or were eventually fulfilled," the extent to which "educational experiences prepared young people for their work," and the financial considerations "in setting low-aspiration goals and in failing to meet high-aspiration goals," and so on (U.S. Department of Education, 1977).

The original survey, consisting of 104 questions, was thus primarily directed at career goals, work experience, and other factors steering a student toward a productive life as a working member of society. None of the 104 questions inquired about the impact of multiple cultural histories or transnational racial demographic shifts on the student experience. Importantly, none of these questions examined whether the cultural history of each student was nurtured by the campus. Finally, none of these questions attempted to examine power relations within the college campus that might reproduce inequalities in race, gender, or sexual orientation. With these items left out of the protocol, scholars who now use the NLS instrument are not led to examine their own identities in relation to the data or to learn about their own social position. Nor can they generate ideas about how to change academic structures or reward mechanisms to "reconstitute" social relations and institutional practices to better accommodate different forms of diversity.

In retrospect, we now know that Tinto's original conception of integration was handicapped by the surveys—and jargon—of his time. Cultural bias seems embedded in the very name of the theory, "integration," implying assimilation to dominant norms. Thus, although Tinto's conception might allow researchers to discover how to help American Indian students adjust to a "mainstream" white college environment, it does little to expose and unseat the undemocratic play of power there. Tinto's theory of social and academic integration thus falls short on all five of the inquiries from social theory. In a more recent book, Tinto (1993) addresses Tierney's critique obliquely by suggesting that his theory can accommodate "diversity" by encompassing the needs of older students and those attending community college. In continuing to overlook racial, ethnic, and other socially constructed distinc-

tions (e.g., Tinto, 1998), Tinto's formulation is unable to provide for an examination of issues of voice, power, authenticity, and reflexivity or to make reconstitution possible.

B. Student Involvement (A. W. Astin, 1975)

Perhaps most cited of modern theories of student development, Astin's (1975) theory of "student involvement" is the basis for my own graduate training. Stating that a student who gets personally involved in college will enhance his or her chances of persistence, this theory has evolved over time and in many ways has gone the farthest in adapting modern approaches to today's student demographic diversity. Although some scholars challenge the notion that Astin's formulation constitutes a "theory," the idea of student involvement has over the years proven to be a robust, heuristic conceptualization that predicts the impact of a broad range of interacting factors on student outcomes. These characteristics would seem to satisfy Kerlinger's (1979, p. 64) definition of a theory as "a set of interrelated constructs, definitions, and propositions that presents a systematic view of phenomena by specifying relations among variables." Evans, Forney, and Guido-DiBrito (1998, pp. 16, 26–27) reach the same conclusion after applying the definitions of a theory developed by Rodgers (1980, p. 81) and Strange and King (1990, p. 17).

Adding "talent development" in the 1980s, Astin argued that an institution could be changed to meet the needs and interests of its students. It may be for this reason that Astin's national survey—the Cooperative Institutional Research Program, or CIRP— now encompasses not only social, personal, intellectual, and professional growth but also a number of inquiries about race, gender, and sexual orientation. Thus, while the 1985 CIRP Freshmen Survey had focused on issues considered important in the 1970s and 1980s—

Is it important to you to influence social values?

Is it important to you to influence the political structure?

Is it important to you to help others in difficulty?

Do you intend to join a social fraternity, sorority, or club?

Do you think abortion should be legalized?

Do you think federal military spending should be increased?

—the 1989 CIRP "Follow-up" survey instrument widened this scope considerably by including questions relating to gender and race:

Have you attended a racial/cultural awareness workshop?

Have you enrolled in an ethnic studies course?

Have your enrolled in a women's studies course?

Have you experienced a change in your acceptance of different races/cultures?

Is it important to you to promote interracial understanding?

Is it a college priority to increase the number of minorities in the faculty and administration?

Is it a college priority to increase the number of women in the faculty and administration?

Is it a college priority to create a diverse multicultural environment?

Is there a lot of racial conflict here?

Are faculty sensitive to issues of minorities?

Do many courses include the minority perspective?

Do many courses include feminist perspectives?

Do students of different ethnic backgrounds communicate?

By the measure of "voice," the CIRP instrument has arguably become a leading force in the study of student diversity.

What this instrument can do next is de-center such dominant cultural practices as Eurocentrism and maleness by making these social locations a formal part of the protocol. Future iterations could also add questions asking students about the power they feel in the classroom, in interactions with professors in the student's major, in one-on-one interactions with a faculty advisor, or in relation to course content. For example, Astin recently encouraged and joined in an article dealing with power and college student admissions (Tanaka, Bonous-Hammarth, & Astin, 1998) —signaling that power may soon find its way into specific survey questions. In 1995 the CIRP instrument contained an experimental question asking faculty whether "Western civilization and culture should be the foundation of the undergraduate curriculum." If made permanent, this question would further bring the survey into the present time experience of a college student on a diverse campus. In other words, authenticity will be even better developed under Astin's approach when all cultures of a campus, including those of dominant groups, are subjected to the same analysis.

Similarly, the 1995 CIRP instrument contained an experimental question asking students how much they had learned about their own racial or cultural identity while in college. A question like this would explore the impact of the college experience on the identities of white students as well as students of color and make possible an examination of interaction effects between institutional practices and the identity and power, on campus, of all students. Future iterations of CIRP could then assess the impact of specific attempts to reconstitute social relations, academic structures, and reward mechanisms as well as self-understanding and personal authenticity for the researcher. In addressing voice, Astin's theory of student involvement is thus better positioned to explain behavior than Tinto's theory in today's context of complex student racial demographics and other diverse interests. The next step would be to fully extend the scope of CIRP to encompass the interplay of power and social location affecting each student, the institution, and the researcher.

C. Quality of Effort (Pace, 1984)

In his College Student Experiences Questionnaire (CSEQ), Pace examined "how often, during the current school year, students engage in various activities related to the use of facilities and opportunities." He related these activities to library experiences; experiences with faculty; course learning; the student union; art, music, theater; athletic and recreation facilities; clubs and organizations; personal experiences; experience in writing; student acquaintances; science; campus residence; topics of conversation; and information in conversations. Pace then compared scores on these 14 measures against scores from 8 indices of college environment and 23 estimates of gains, namely, How often have you "used the library as a quiet place to read or study materials you brought with you?" How often have you "made an appointment to meet with a faculty member in his/her office?" How much does your college emphasize "being critical, evaluative, and analytical?" How often have you "changed your opinion as a result of the knowledge or arguments presented by others?" Using this protocol, Pace theorized that a student's success in college would in large part be determined by the "quality of effort" invested by the student in the college experience.

Pace's CSEQ questionnaire thus creatively combined measures of intellectual and professional growth and personal qualities in one instrument. Crafted at the end of the 1970s, it did not set out to examine such items as (1) the multiple voices of women, gays and lesbians, or people of color, (2) power relationships on a campus, (3) student personal authenticity in the research design, (4) self-reflexivity for the researcher, or (5) the need to reconstitute academic structures and social relations based on shifts in power and student demographics. Thus, although Pace himself found "no noticeable difference in quality of effort between any ethnic groups" on 10 of 14 activity measures (Pace, 1990, p. 90, 1991, 1992), other scholars may now wish to extend Pace's time-tested and parsimonious analysis by, for example, drawing a distinction between campuses that accommodate effort from diverse students and those that do not, and then comparing student responses from each. This could be achieved by linking existing data bases to the CSEQ or by using the CSEQ environment item dealing with diversity or by creating an "exposure to diversity" subscale from existing CSEQ items.

While Pace had been first to break down the categories in which a student might expend his or her effort, the next step would be to take "effort" to a greater level of cultural specificity by distinguishing, for example, whether the impact of time spent in "clubs and organizations" is different for a Chicana participating in an ethnic club like MEChA that nurtures the student's identity versus a campuswide activity like the student government. One way to do this would be to invite each institution to add a sheet with an identification number that lists those organizations on its campus.

Like Tinto's theory, Pace's construct can be misused by researchers if they choose not to examine the underlying cultural norms of the institution, thinking simply that the more you immerse yourself in the general activities of the campus, the more likely you are to "persist" and do well academically. But by ascribing to every campus the same "universal" quality of a culturally neutral space, that researcher would run the risk of *under*-estimating the differential effects of campus culture on students who are not members of the dominant group and a parallel risk of *over*estimating the importance of effort where students in fact think that further engagement would only harm their sense of self-worth. Research has now shown, for example, that white students attending increasingly diverse institutions will experience different levels of cultural awareness and overall satisfaction with college depending on their personal engagement with cultures different from their own (Tanaka, Bonous-Hammarth, & Astin, 1998). It would not be too great a stretch to conclude that if outcomes for white students are impacted when they attend campuses that emphasize multiculturalism, there might also be differential impacts from a campus culture on students of color, particularly if that culture is presumed superior to theirs (see, e.g., McCarthy, 1993, pp. 294–297).

Thus, although Pace's theoretical construct adds volition to student development research, his CSEQ instrument does not require a researcher to distinguish between activities that reaffirm a dominant culture and those that nurture alternative identities, experiences, desires, and histories. Absent new questions, it would be difficult to evaluate a student's ability to self-define in an institutional context of power/knowledge and see whether this affects the student's success in college.

It is important to pause here to consider whether it is even reasonable to insist that the Pace instrument examine such issues as power and voice when CSEQ-based studies have shown time and again that what matters most is what students themselves do in a given institutional context. I will note here that the original impetus for this article came from my review of 31 self-studies conducted by the University of California system in the late 1980s and early 1990s. Studies using the CSEQ (Morrell & Lare at U.C. San Diego, 1988, p. 63; Amos at U.C. Davis, 1990, p. 4), the ACT (Amos, 1988, pp. 26, 29; Arias at U.C. Riverside, 1989, p. 15; Low at U.C. Davis, 1991, p. 27), and CIRP (Henson & Shepard at UCLA, 1989) revealed differential outcomes for racial minorities at those institutions but could not uncover clear causes or solutions. Amos (1990, pp. 26–29), using the CSEQ, found that despite having the highest Quality of Effort of any ethnic group at U.C. Davis, the investment by African Americans was "not paying off in high graduation rates." Similarly, Morrell and

Lare (1988, pp. 31, 48) found that among all ethnic groups, African American students perceived the highest level of academic emphasis by U.C. San Diego but had a low level of actual education gains in comparison to other groups. No clear causes—or solutions—were identified.

With this lacuna in existing instruments, a new genre of "campus climate" studies came into being that traced the problem to a mismatch between a dominant culture on campus and the cultures of racial minorities (Aaron at U.C. Irvine, 1988, pp. 66–95; Duster at U.C. Berkeley, 1990, p. 24; and Astin, Trevino, & Wingard at UCLA, 1991, pp. 16–21), women graduate students (Mercer at U.C. Riverside, 1990, p. 21), and lesbian and gay students (Nelson & Baker at U.C. Santa Cruz, 1990, p. 16). Recommending specific changes to mentoring and housing practices (Jacobi-Gray at UCLA, 1990, p. 15), the curriculum (Maslach at U.C. Berkeley, 1991, p. 14), and departmental policy (Mercer, 1990, p. 41),these "campus climate" studies served clear notice that the causes of differential experience were indeed tangible and were not being measured by instruments like the CSEQ.

With issues of culture and power finding even greater salience today, my point is that proven instruments like the CSEQ—now administered by Kuh (Kuh & Vesper, 1997)—can be strengthened further by adding new questions to the original array that would enable researchers to examine potential causes of differential impacts arising from differences in power between the dominant cultures of a campus and the social identities of its individual students. With such questions, it might be possible to avoid having to conduct a second study of "campus climate" at every diverse campus.

In this regard, Pace's model already fares better than Tinto's framework, and this is because it is so "interactive." His construct presumes that the student will enter the college environment *as an actor*—a person who influences his success by the extent to which he puts an effort into what he does. Because it is based in part on a measure of agency, Pace's questionnaire is ideally suited to the addition of new questions that address issues of power, social location, and historical context.

In sum, the instruments employed by Tinto, Astin, and Pace share several traits. First, they arguably emphasize the systemic impact of the college on the student. In doing this, their work represents a practical advancement over the theoretical work of stage theorists like Perry and Kohlberg, who had employed individual paradigms but not sought to examine the impact of institutions on students. In pursuing institutional impacts, however, none of the modern instruments examined the differential match-ups of culture (and power) between the institution and the student. As a result, the theoretical frameworks could not account for students' ability to define their own cultural trajectory or "alter the conditions of their own existence" (Rosaldo, 1989, p. 102). Ironically, by remaining culturally neutral, the modern constructs were then not able to make the asymmetries between cultures a part of the calculus, leaving for whiteness, maleness, and heterosexuality the quality of timeless "universal" against which all students must presumably measure up.

Second, under modern approaches, the study of oppressed groups can be accommodated but does not become a means of de-centering unstated norms. This kind of research is susceptible to misuse by those who might unwittingly assign to assumptions from an earlier time a status of "objectivity" and then interpret all new data through that same lens, including data about diversity. Warning against precisely that possibility, Pascarella and Terenzini (1998, p. 155) write: "As student diversity increases, understanding the experience of college and its various impacts will undoubtedly become much more complex. Research approaches that try to isolate the influence of a few variables for all students will simply miss the point and probably provide little in the way of useful, practice-or policy-relevant evidence."

Thus, although the instruments of modern researchers have been used successfully to examine subgroups in U.S. society—and their utility remains extremely high—they are in their current iterations unable to correct for undercurrents of *social reproduction* contained potentially within their own assumptions and psychometrics. Terms like "integration," "student effort," "persistence," "impact" on the student, and "retention rates" can too easily be misused to confuse academic success with conformance to a dominant culture at an institution or overlook the power of the student to determine his or her own cultural trajectory and exert an impact on the institution. The challenge is to renew the underlying theoretical bases for these modern instruments by recontextualizing them within today's shifting, overlapping, polycultural terrain.

IV. End-of-the-Century Frameworks Directing Education Research Toward "Reconstitution," or Actual Change

A. Social Construction (Tierney, 1992)

Tierney's theory of "social construction" arguably presaged the current crisis over changing student demographics by noting how colleges and universities reproduce fixed meanings that tell a society how to treat issues of race, gender, and sexual orientation. In Tierney's view, researchers need to deconstruct (take apart) the hidden power dimensions contained in the social constructs or hierarchies that a college transmits to its students. Criticizing Tinto for "inserting minorities into a dominant cultural frame" (1992, p. 611) and for failing to account for the way social institutions "reproduce" the hierarchy that maintains the elite class on top, he urged that student development instead allow for "agency," or the ability of a student to put a spin on his or her own development.

On measures of "voice" and "power," Tierney's (1992) theory of "social construction" would therefore rate high. His ethnographic approach allows researchers to explore the play of power on a campus, and this approach can create the expectation of a new and more egalitarian social arrangement. Seeking "not merely to describe the world, but to change it" (p. 603), Tierney's research is by nature reconstitutive. His use of narrative lends itself to the study of the researcher's own positionality and, through this, to the making of recommendations about how to change reward systems and structures in academe. One limitation in Tierney's approach is that it is qualitative and does not encompass the wide range of traditional measures of student success of Astin, Pace, and Tinto. Tierney can also test his theorizing by evoking actual change at a setting to demonstrate that "agency" is indeed possible.

B. Theory of Nigrescence (Cross, 1971, 1991)

Cross's theory of "nigrescence," or black identity formation, would also rate high along the dimensions raised here, because it moves off of a Eurocentric epistemology and substitutes a

new framework for identity formation that is empowering to African Americans. In 1971 Cross advanced five stages of identity formation based on a close review of 45 original studies of black identity and his own life experiences. These are

(1) "pre-encounter," where the individual learns over the years to favor a Eurocentric cultural perspective, (2) "encounter," where an experience shatters that identity or world view, (3) "immersion/emersion," in which the individual throws off the familiar by demonizing white people and culture, (4) "internalization," where the individual moves from rage toward white people to controlled anger at oppressive systems, and (5) "internalization/commitment," where the individual translates the new sense of blackness into a plan of action (see also Tse, 1990). What is interesting here is that Cross links positive black identity formation to a rejection of whiteness. Although this is an act of severance rather than reflexivity, it does make sense in view of the tendency of whiteness to mark blackness as inferior (Morrison, 1992).

On measures of voice, power, authenticity, and reconstitution, Cross's model would therefore rate very high. The idea that black identity can form only after rejecting the dominant culture's definition, and appropriation, of blackness is a powerful notion. In addition, Cross's hint at more change to come from creating plans of action is reconstitutive. Though Cross's model may be underappreciated in some research circles, it does aggressively de-center the Eurocentric bias of traditional thinking. As a result, I now believe his work should be made a major part of any new theoretical construct that attempts to locate student development in particular historical and diasporic contexts. What is needed next, however, is a way of looking at all identities under one lens—including the evolving ones of European Americans (Tanaka, 1996, p. 309). In breaking away from hegemonic notions of identity, Cross's work fuels this article and makes possible the study of *inter*culturalism.

C. Different Voice (Gilligan, 1982)

Where Cross links black identity formation to active separation from and rejection of white culture, Gilligan's "different voice" model derives from a direct comparison between opposing thought processes. This approach is by nature reflexive. For example, noting how Kohlberg's model of moral development penalizes women for emphasizing relationships and communication as a means of resolving dilemmas, Gilligan (1982, p. 18) concludes: "Herein lies a paradox, for the very traits that traditionally have defined the 'goodness' of women, their care for and sensitivity to the needs of others, are those that mark them as deficient in moral development." Under Kohlberg's theorizing, a woman is automatically labeled "a full stage lower in maturity" than a male.

Urging that human development for women be seen in women's own terms, Gilligan critiques modern theories for being male-centered and argues persuasively that Kohlberg's model of moral development is wrong for placing high importance on the self, where women place greater value on relationships (see also Bischoping & Bell, 1998; Clinchy & Zimmerman, 1993; Baxter Magolda, 1992; Wolf-Wendel, 1998). Though based narrowly on studies of white women, Gilligan's model nonetheless passes muster under the social theory applied here. On measures of voice, power, authenticity, reflexivity, and reconstitution, the "different voice" model rates high. Like Tierney and Cross, Gilligan's emphasis on relationships adumbrates an intercultural theory of human development.

V. Toward an "Intercultural" Theory of Student Development

Interculturalism is not new (e.g., Cornwell & Stoddard, 1994; Marranca & Dasgupta, 1991; Tanaka, 1994). In contrast to multiculturalism, which promotes the cultural stories of people of color in the United States, interculturalism moves beyond the addition of new voices to focus on "the interrelations of cultures as they evolve through time" (Cornwell & Stoddard, 1994, p. 43). Applied to colleges and universities, interculturalism might thus be initially defined as "a process of learning and sharing across difference where no one culture dominates" (Tanaka, in press). What is important here is looking at the point of cultural contact. To writers in the arts, for example, "interculturalism" implies a state of mind that allows for creative tension between cultural voices as they interact (e.g., Hwang, 1994; Marranca, 1991; Tanaka, 1993, 1994, 1995). In this regard, it is perhaps no surprise that Marranca (1991, p. 13) concludes in a book on performed art that America's intercul-

turalism is growing "out of . . . the country's own geography and changing demographics" (emphasis added).

In fact, it is the close resemblance that fragmentation from changing campus demographics bears to work *across* difference in the arts that leads me to want to apply "interculturalism" to student development theory now. The need for this had surfaced earlier. At a large public university, a dance department's transition from Eurocentrism to multiculturalism had left white students without a way to connect to the new milieu (Tanaka, 1996). It was not enough merely to add new voices. In another study, the transformation of a liberal arts college into a multicultural campus ran into problems when it did not provide a way for white students and alumni to feel a part of the new campus community (Tanaka, 1997). At another institution, white students complained that a required course in American Cultures led to "white male bashing" (Tanaka, in press). Similar problems were encountered when urban K-12 school teachers entered a rural setting in Chile (Arratia, 1997).

A. Three Current Interpretations of Interculturalism

Interculturalism has at least three current interpretations. One is "hybridity" analysis (Bhabha, 1994) examining points of contact between cultures when they interact. Presuming a hybrid result, this framework can help researchers track the merging or overlapping of different cultures on a campus. Hybridity, however, tends to leave power out of the analysis, presume an end result of assimilation, and overlook what might occur when cultures interact but do not merge.

A second approach, "border theory" (Anzaldua, 1987), examines the two-way impact of cultures that come into contact, as when Latinos move north across the United States border and both impact and are impacted by the Eurocentric culture they find there. Using the metaphor of border crossing, this approach can separate out the different perspectives of power that come into play when two cultures mutually impact one another on a university campus. However, border theory has most often been limited to a binary analysis of two interacting cultures, and this does not match the campus context in which more than two cultures and social locations are interacting at the same time.

A third form of interculturalism (and the version I prefer) is "intersubjectivity" (Bakhtin, 1929/1984; Burbeles & Rice, 1991, p. 409; Flores, Tanaka, & McLaren, 2001; Tanaka & Cruz, 1998). Under one interpretation of intersubjectivity (Lenkersdorf, 1996, p. 28; Radhakrishnan, 1996, p. 120), emphasis is on cultivating "subject position" for each individual—the ability of each student to have voice and a forum to tell his or her story. In an ideal interchange, each student acquires subject position without turning anyone else into an object of his or her speech. This exchange is subject-to-subject (de Certeau, 1986, p. 217; contra Prus, 1997, p. 6; Jackson, 1998, p. 6) and builds relations of interdependence, collaboration, and complementarity that can lead to a greater sense of identity and belonging (Malaguzzi, 1993, pp. 62–63; Merleau-Ponty, 1964). In effect, "I am me through you."

Under a second interpretation of intersubjectivity, emphasis is placed on evaluating the meanings attached to abstract social identifiers like gender, ethnicity, and sexual orientation—one's "subjectivities" (Bakhtin on religion, 1929/1984, pp. 88–97; contra Schutz, 2000, p. 226; Tanaka & Cruz, 1998, pp. 144–151). Under this perspective, researchers can examine historical differences in power associated with each subjectivity, research how to create "positive subjectivities" out of ethnicity, gender, and sexual orientation, and delimit "negative subjectivities" like race and class, or explore whether a student's subjectivities are supported (or suppressed) in the student's major. The challenge will be to avoid letting this analysis wind up with tinier reductionistic categories for meanings that are in reality quite textured, shifting, overlapping, and complex (Kaplan, 1997; Shohat, 1997).

What I want to suggest is that *both* interpretations are called into play in the increasingly complex U.S. college campus. With so many identifiers like race, ethnicity, and gender all swirling and evolving in one space, intersubjectivity must now take into account the ability of every person on campus to have "subject position" *and* have her or his "subjectivities" nurtured in positive ways. With a nurturing of personal and social intersubjectivity, human development becomes more nearly a process of *"remaking the subject"* (e.g., de Certeau, 1986, p. 92, 217; Crapanzano, 1992, pp. 74, 83; Foucault, 1983, p. 208; contra Chun, 2000, pp. 572–576; Orellana, 1999, p. 64) in which the harsh effects of "objectification" (de Certeau, 1986, p. viii; Said, 2000, p. 448; Strathern, 1996, p. 177) are reversed and superseded by a kind of "resubjectification" that marks the end of the poststructural turn.

Under intersubjective analysis, education researchers can study tensions caused by differences in power between social locations of each student, the faculty, and the dominant cultures of a campus and build "interconnectiveness" (Greer-Jarman, 2001). The ideal would be to overlay intersubjective analysis upon an existing survey instrument like Astin's Cooperative Institutional Research Program (CIRP) or Pace's College Student Experiences Questionnaire (CSEQ).

In the end, some combination of hybridity, border theory, and intersubjectivity will likely be needed to fully interpret, comprehend, and assess the transnational, gender enriched, and otherwise polyvocal text of student experiences on U.S. campuses today. I favor the third—intersubjectivity—as an initial framework for higher education research, because it helps me see the power issues inherent in cultural interactions, does not presume a merger or assimilation of one culture into another, and reasserts the importance of a personal and social analytical framework in lieu of one based on institutionalized impacts or essentialized categories like "race."

B. Interculturalism and Student Development

The following design therefore builds upon the strengths of modern student development theory. Second, it adds to that base some of the important lessons from recent social theory. Third, it imports hope for responsible reconstitution of academic structures, practices, and reward mechanisms. Most importantly, this design reflects my own history and tradition as a third generation Japanese-American male traveling through higher education research, looking for but not finding toeholds and meaning. Linked to this, the design reflects my self-interest in not marginalizing European Americans but rather in promoting for them an enhanced ability to participate as equals (who find meaning) in "intersubjective" exchanges. On today's polycultural campuses, one might hypothesize that European Americans will undergo new identity formation in stages, similar to what Cross had found with African Americans, (see also Helms, 1990; Helms & Cook, 1999).

How would an intercultural theory of student development be translated into new research methods? Under an intercultural framework, the interactions between student, college, student major, family and close friends, and society are all considered important. Questions will avoid culturally loaded terms that might imply assimilation into a dominant culture, like "persistence," "integration," "institutional departure," "underprepared," or "mainstream." What these words share with Tinto's use of "social and academic integration" is not an overt sense of ethnocentrism but rather a more dangerous research assumption that a student no matter his or her subjectivities must survive an institutional culture that is nowhere made a part of the analysis. The fact that many students of color, or gays or lesbians, do "survive" and go on to rewarding careers does not lessen the harm they may have experienced during that survival process. The point is to evaluate those differential experiences in relation to sources of culture and power within the institution.

So rather than assign to European American culture the status of a neutral standard, the new perspective places all cultures and social positions under the same microscope, including the complex, shifting social locations of each European American male. New questions will allow a researcher to assess the extent to which all cultural voices—based on ethnicity, gender, or sexual orientation for example—get validated on a campus. Now we ask, "Does the faculty in your major support learning about your own cultural identity?" or "Do professors in your major promote an understanding of power relations on campus?" or "Do you feel the campus nurtures your sexual orientation?"

For example, though not meant to be exhaustive, an "intercultural theory of student development" might be reflected in survey questions added to Pace's CSEQ categories that examine distinctions in student perceptions about the social and cultural environment (specifically coded for this) that inhibit or nurture student effort in these ways:

Under "Experience with Faculty," add:

- The professors in your major provide a safe environment in which to discuss your cultural identity or identities.

- The professors in your major openly make their own power and authority a part of the discussion.

- The dominant racial or ethnic culture in your department major closely matches yours.

- The professors in your major support the study of issues you consider most important.

- I have experienced racial discrimination in grading.

- The gender make-up of professors in your major is appropriate.

- The racial make-up of professors in your major is diverse.

- At least one professor has changed his or her thinking because of something I wrote or said in class.

Under "Course Learning," add: ("Have you . . . ")

- Critiqued what counts as history and knowledge?

- Openly discussed the dominant culture on your campus?

- Learned how differences in power between men and women are sometimes overlooked in society?

- Discussed how power operates in race relations on your campus?

- Studied how power operates in business, government and education?

- Discussed gay and lesbian issues in a safe environment for such a dialogue?

- Learned from people from economic backgrounds different from yours?

- Been able to participate in class discussions about gender differences?

- Had the opportunity to give input into the make-up of a course syllabus?

Under "Personal Experience," add: ("Have you . . . ")

- Learned about your own privilege or disadvantage based on your racial identity?

- Found your campus a safe place in which to discuss differences in power with people of the opposite sex?

- Been able to affirm the positive value of your sexual orientation?
- Dated a person of a different race?
- Found that differences in economic class shape the way classmates behave toward you?
- Experienced gender discrimination by another student?
- Had the chance to view art that empowers women?
- Found that senior professors and deans support the nurturing of all cultural identities?

Still other questions can be added to address power relations in the department major regarding race, ethnicity, gender, sexual orientation, class, and physical "ableness." Others can be added to examine interaction effects between institutional priorities, the student's family history, and personal growth in college. A reconstituted instrument can also inquire into issues of legitimacy or systemic collapse in the student's major field, the institution, or society, and whether the student feels he or she can make a difference. These are not just "add on" questions, but questions that change the whole thrust of the instrument away from a presumption of assimilation and toward a perspective that makes difference the core orientation, as urged earlier by McCarthy (1993). A reconstituted instrument would make a student's subject position and subjectivities the point of departure.

Here it should be noted that the questions I propose are presented to trigger debate and change. Appearing as a "hodge-podge" of questions, they are intended to show the range of issues that need to be taken into account; they will need to be rewritten for clarity and conceptual coherence by redesigners of the instruments. Thus, where Pace had originally stressed a student's "quality of effort," the questions posed here would extend the conceptual underpinnings of his instrument to encompass a "context-based analysis" (Hymes, 1996, p. 212; Baxter Magolda, 1996, pp. 298–299; Voloshinov, 1929/1973, pp. 20–22) of student effort. Added to student behavior are now various measures of that context: perceptions of environment, new outcomes, views of people other than students, and so on. It remains to be seen, however, whether a single instrument will be able to accommodate both theories of college impact and student development. The breadth of questions listed above may radically alter the psychometrics of an instrument. A revised instrument would have to be tested over time, and if the cost of making trade-offs is too high, a new instrument may be needed altogether.

What I want to suggest is that a decision to maintain the conceptual integrity of a limited instrument may now be *more* harmful to future research than the risk of altering the psychometric properties that might come from broadening the scope of an instrument. Instead of adding to existing categories in Pace's questionnaire, an entirely new section could be added. Here, caution will need to be taken to avoid assuming that by simply adding a section dealing, for example, with power and gender, it will remove all responsibility to correct for culture bias in the rest of the instrument. Alternatively, the instrument could contain one or two short answer essay questions or be administered in conjunction with focus groups (see e.g., Levine & Cureton, 1998).

C. Implications for Future Research

Seeking to combine lessons from social theory with strengths from modern student development theory, the above design features can give a researcher greater ability to track the cognitive and affective development of a student while deconstructing the play of power on college campuses. The intention thus is not to bring to an end modernist efforts at assessing student development—which have already achieved the aims identified as important in the '70s and '80s—but to re-articulate them in the complex, shifting space of colleges and universities where issues of culture, power, and knowledge are increasingly salient. In this *poly*cultural world, new methods are needed to reflect the fact that zones of intercultural contact are increasingly fecund.

What this also means is that questions of construct validity may be mounting. Researchers can no longer be confident about present measures of cognitive and social development without examining, for example, how a white student's learning is being impacted by diversity. In fact, dividing students into simplistic categories like "Chicanos" or "Whites" or "gays and lesbians" may already be outdated. New ways of contemplating research are now needed that reveal the *intersections* of multiple, shifting subjectivities and historical contexts for each student. This may even equate one day to examining connections between higher education policy and the forces of global capitalism. In other words, the five probes in this paper surface the possibility that there might be some benefit to launching a renewed examination of tropes for analysis in higher education research as a whole.

Ultimately, the concept of intelligence may need to be revised to encompass a student's ability to make decisions and share knowledge in an increasingly intercultural human society. Research itself will need to become more dialogical. In this vein, collaborative teams and co-authorships across difference might yield co-writings that are more illuminating than lone writer efforts (e.g., Leonardo, 1998; but see Anderson & Herr, 1999, p. 16). Further, it appears that researchers will now need to be careful about the *kind* of power they examine in relation to college student development. With the social terrain of today's campuses shifting and so complex, traditional definitions of power are also in flux. What definitions of power might be best for college campuses that are becoming intercultural? Will this represent a sharing of control in a Western sense of power—or a more generalized and inchoate feeling of interconnectiveness molded out of intersubjective participation?

Once the door is opened to analysis of multiple, shifting, and intersecting subjectivities and subject positions, new questions must ultimately be raised about the usefulness of culture itself. As a trope for analysis, "culture" seems too rigid, too binary, too awkwardly applied in the complex social terrain of the urban campus. Indeed, an intersubjective approach might help shift the focus of research beyond monolithic notions of culture (and race) to the underlying forces of privilege and victim status that may hinder egalitarian learning in a polycultural space.

There are also broader implications for how colleges and universities might reconstitute themselves in response to increasingly diverse student bodies. At an "intercultural campus," institutional leaders might employ concepts from recent social theory to create spaces specifically for intersubjective exchange (e.g., Alfaro, Coleman & McLaren, 1999; Edwards, Gandini & Forman, 1993; Pratt, 1995, pp. 188–189; Tanaka & Flores, in press; Tharp, Estrada, Dalton &

Yamauchi, 2001). At one university, $800,000 in grants was used to create intersubjective moments for what could become "the first intercultural university campus" in the United States (Tanaka, in press; Tanaka, Johnson, & Hu, 2001). In the wake of school shootings at Columbine and Santee, intersubjective storytelling could lead to a renewed sense of identity formation and belonging through teacher education.

Conclusion

In questioning the assumptions underlying Tinto's research, Tierney may have signaled an even wider turn in higher education research than he might have imagined. Having raised a legitimate question about who holds power to publish theories of student retention and development, he indirectly surfaced this larger concern. Now squarely at issue is the question of whether higher education research is fast becoming an ethnocentric practice in the face of changing campus conditions, and if so, whether it might soon complete a "self-reflexive turn" by locating the power and culture of the researcher within the analysis. In other words, from now on researchers *must locate themselves* within their analysis or risk being perceived as ethnocentric *and* monological. Having pushed debate about the legitimacy of research on college student learning to the next level, Tierney thus leaves to other researchers the responsibility to examine *just how* their own positionalities (regarding voice, power, authenticity, self-reflexivity, and reconstitution) will affect the way in which new theory is constructed, knowledge is produced, and assessment is made. In this press he is asking higher education research to critique itself.

In view of these developments, this writing should be taken to heart as a call for higher education researchers to rearticulate the work of modern theorists and give fresh impetus to the field's future practice. The recent willingness of a leading modernist to examine issues of power and authenticity lends a note of optimism to this project, and I am myself a beneficiary of that willingness.

References

Aaron, M. (1988). *The academic and social environment at UCI: Quality of student life survey on ethnic differences and similarities regarding perceptions about the UCI undergraduate experience.* Irvine: University of California, Irvine MCA, Academic Affairs.

Alfaro, L., Coleman, W., & McLaren, P. (1999, December 5). *Intersubjective performance held at open house for Unity & Difference.* Los Angeles: Self-Help Graphics.

Altman, I., & Haythorn, W. (1967). The ecology of isolated groups. *Behavioral Science, 12,* 169–182.

Amos, A. K., Jr. (1988). *The Davis academic environment: A report on student opinions.* Davis: University of California, Davis Student Affairs Research and Information Office.

Amos, A. K., Jr. (1990). *Effort and gain: The UC Davis undergraduate experience.* Davis: University of California, Davis Student Affairs Research and Information Office.

Anderson, G. L., & Herr, K. (1999). The new paradigm wars: Is there room for rigorous practitioner knowledge in schools and universities? *Educational Researcher, 28*(5), 12–21.

Antonio, A. L. (1998). *The impact of friendship groups in a multicultural university.* Unpublished doctoral dissertation, University of California, Los Angeles.

Anzaldua, G. (1987). *Borderlands/la frontera: The new Mestiza.* San Francisco: aunt lute books.

Arias, T. L. (1989). *UC Riverside student opinion survey: A report of the university environment.* Riverside: University of California, Riverside Counseling Center.

Arratia, M. I. (1997). Daring to change: The potential of intercultural education in Aymara communities in Chile. *Anthropology and Education Quarterly, 28*(2), 229–250.

Astin, A. W. (1975). *Preventing students from dropping out.* San Francisco: Jossey-Bass.

Astin, A. W. (1984). Student involvement: A developmental theory for higher education. *Journal of College Student Personnel, 25,* 297–308.

Astin, A. W. (1991). *Assessment for excellence.* New York: Macmillan.

Astin, A. W., Astin, H. S., Antonio, A. L., Astin, J., & Cress, C. (1999). *Meaning and spirituality in the lives of college faculty: A study of values, authenticity, and stress.* Los Angeles: Higher Education Research Institute.

Astin, A. W., Trevino, J. G., & Wingard, T. L. (1991). *The UCLA campus climate for diversity: Findings from a campuswide survey conducted for the chancellor's council on diversity.* Los Angeles: Higher Education Research Institute.

Bakhtin, M. M. (1929/1984). *Problems of Dostoevsky's poetics.* Minneapolis: University of Minnesota Press.

Banning, J. H., & Aulepp, L. (1971). University community mental health services survey. In *Program activities and student utilization of campus mental health facilities in the West.* Boulder, CO: Western Interstate Commission for Higher Education, Monograph 3.

Baxter Magolda, M. B. (1992). Students' epistemologies and academic experiences: Implications for pedagogy. *Review of Higher Education, 15,* 277–291.

Baxter Magolda, M. B. (1996). Epistemological development in graduate professional education. *Review of Higher Education, 19,* 283–304.

Bhabha, H. K. (1994). *The location of culture.* London: Routledge.

Bischoping, K., & Bell, S. (1998). Gender and contradictory definitions of university accessibility. *Review of Higher Education, 21,* 179–194.

Bloland, H. G. (1995). Postmodernism and higher education. *Journal of Higher Education, 66,* 521–560.

Burbeles, N. C., & Rice, S. (1991). Dialogue across differences: Continuing the conversation. *Harvard Educational Review, 61,* 393–416.

California Postsecondary Education Commission OnlineData: www.cpec.ca.gov/On-LineData/GenReport.asp.

Cherryholmes, C. H. (1988). *Power and criticism: Poststructural investigations in education.* New York: Teachers College Press.

Chun, A. (2000). From text to context: How anthropology makes its subject. *Cultural Anthropology, 15,* 570–595.

Clinchy, B., & Zimmerman, C. (1993). Epistemology and agency in the development of undergraduate women. In J. S. Glazer, E. M. Bensimon, & B. K. Townsend (Eds.), *Women in higher education: A feminist perspective* (pp. 263–276). Needham Heights, MA: Ginn Press.

Cornwell, G. H., & Stoddard, E. W. (1994, Fall). Things fall together: A critique of multicultural curricular reform. *Liberal Education,* 40–51.

Crapanzano, V. (1992). *Hermes' dilemma & Hamlet's desire: On the epistemology of interpretation.* Cambridge, MA: Harvard University Press.

Cross, W. E., Jr. (1971). Toward a psychology of black liberation: The Negro-to-black conversion experience. *Black World, 20*(9). 13–24.

Cross, W. E., Jr. (1991). *Shades of black: Diversity in African-American identity.* Philadelphia: Temple University Press.

Darder, A. (1991). *Culture and power in the classroom: A critical foundation for bicultural education.* New York: Bergin & Garvey.

De Certeau, M. (1986). *Heterologies: Discourse on the other.* Minneapolis: University of Minnesota Press.

Dey, E. L., & Hurtado, S. (1996). Faculty attitudes toward regulating speech on college campuses. *Review of Higher Education, 20,* 14–32.

Duster, T. (1990). *The diversity project: An interim report to the chancellor.* Berkeley: Institute for the Study of Social Change, University of California, Berkeley.

Edwards, C., Gandini, L., & Forman, G. (Eds.). (1993). *The hundred languages of children: The Reggio Emilia approach to early childhood education.* Norwood, NJ: Ablex.

Evans, N. J., Forney, D. S., & Guido-DiBrito, F. (1998). *Student development in college: Theory, research, and practice.* San Francisco: Jossey-Bass Publishers.

Fabian, J. (1983). *Time and the other: How anthropology makes its object.* New York: Columbia University Press.

Flores, R., Tanaka, G., & McLaren, P. (2001). Autonomy and participatory democracy: An ongoing discussion on the application of Zapatista autonomy in the U.S. *International Journal of Education Reform, 10,* 130–144.

Foster, M. (1994). The power to know one thing is never the power to know all things: Methodological notes on two studies of black American teachers. In A. Gitlin (Ed.), *Power and method: Political activism and educational research* (pp. 13–35). New York: Routledge.

Foster, M. (1997, June 21). *Insider research: What counts as critical.* Paper presented at conference Reclaiming Voice: Ethnographic Inquiry and Qualitative Research in a Postmodern Age. Los Angeles: University of Southern California Rossier School of Education.

Foucault, M. (1972). *Power/knowledge: Selected interviews and other writings.* New York: Pantheon Books.

Foucault, M. (1976). *The history of sexuality: An introduction.* New York: Vintage Books.

Foucault, M. (1983). Afterword. The subject and power. On the genealogy of ethics: An overview of work in progress. In H. L. Dreyfus & P. Rabinow (Eds.), *Michel Foucault: Beyond structuralism and hermeneutics* (pp. 208–252). Chicago: University of Chicago Press.

Gilligan, C. (1977/1982). *In a different voice: Psychological theory and women's development.* Cambridge, MA: Harvard University Press.

Gitlin, A. (1994). The shifting terrain of methodological debates. In A. Gitlin, A. (Ed.), *Power and method: Political activism and educational research* (pp. 1–7). New York: Routledge.

Gramsci, A. (1977). *Selections from the prison notebooks of Antonio Gramsci.* New York: International Publishers.

Greer-Jarman, C. (2001, March 2). *Our diverse community: The impact of racism, classism, ableism, and sexism on young children.* Paper presented at the For the Love of Children Conference, Pasadena, CA.

Helms, J. E. (1990). Toward a model of white racial identity development. In J. E. Helms (Ed.), *Black and white racial identity: Theory, research and practice* (pp. 49–66). Westport, CN: Greenwood Press.

Helms, J. E., & Cook, D. A. (1999). *Using race and culture in counseling and psychotherapy: Theory and process.* Boston: Allyn and Bacon.

Henson, J., & Shepard, C. (1989). *1988 CIRP freshmen data report: Attitudes and values regarding intergroup tolerance and diversity.* Los Angeles: UCLA Student Affairs Information & Research Office.

hooks, b. (1984). *Feminist theory: From margin to center.* Boston: South End Press.

Hu, N. B., & Tanaka, G. (2000, November 1). *Does interculturalism affect campus values for a favorable learning and teaching environment?* Paper presented at the 25th annual conference of the California Association for Institutional Research, Pasadena, CA.

Hymes, D. (1996). *Ethnography, linguistics, narrative inequality: Toward an understanding of voice.* London: Taylor & Francis.

Hwang, D. H. (1994). Facing the mirror. Foreword to K. Aguilar-San Juan, K. (Ed.), *The state of Asian America: Activism and resistance in the 1990s* (pp. ix–xii). Boston: South End Press.

Jackson, M. (1998). *Minima ethnographica: Intersubjectivity and the anthropological project.* Chicago: University of Chicago.

Jacobi-Gray, M. (1990). *The freshman year experience in the college of letters and science: Results of student survey.* Los Angeles: UCLA Student Affairs Information and Research Office.

Kaplan, C. (1997, February 21). *The romance of distance and the comforts of home: Demystifying spatial metaphors in an era of globalization.* Paper presented at the conference Hybrid Cultures and Transnational Identities, UCLA Faculty Center, Los Angeles.

Kerlinger, F. N. (1979). *Behavioral research: A conceptual approach.* New York: Holt, Rinehart & Winston.

Kondo, D. (1990). *Crafting selves: Power, gender, and discourses of identity in a Japanese workplace.* Chicago: University of Chicago Press.

Kondo, D. (1997). *About face.* New York: Routledge.

Kraemer, B. A. (1997). The academic and social integration of Hispanic students into college. *Review of Higher Education, 20,* 163–180.

Kuh, G. D., & Vesper, N. (1997). A comparison of student experiences with good practices in undergraduate education between 1990 and 1994. *Review of Higher Education, 21,* 43–62.

Lenkersdorf, C. (1996). *Los hombres verdaderos: Voces y testimonios Tojolabales.* Mexico: Siglo Veintiuno Editores.

Leonardo, Z. (1998, March 14). *On co-writing and writing.* Paper presented at the UCLA Graduate School of Education Reading Room, Los Angeles.

Levine, A., & Cureton, J. S. (1998). Student politics: The new location. *Review of Higher Education, 21,* 137–150.

Love, P. G. (1998). Cultural barriers facing lesbian, gay, and bisexual students at a Catholic college. *Journal of Higher Education, 69,* 298–323.

Low, J. M. (1991). *The Davis social environment—1990: A report of student opinions.* Davis: University of California, Davis Student Affairs Research and Information.

Malaguzzi, L. (1993). History, ideas, and basic philosophy. In C. Edwards, L. Gandini, & G. Foreman (Eds.), *The hundred languages of children: The Reggio Emilia approach to early childhood education* (pp. 41–89). Norwood, NJ: Ablex Publishing.

Marcus, G. E., & Fischer, M. M. J. (1986). *Anthropology as cultural critique: An experimental moment in the human sciences.* Chicago: University of Chicago Press.

Marranca, B. (1991). Thinking about interculturalism. In B. Marranca & G. Dasgupta (Eds.), *Interculturalism & performance.* New York: PAJ Publications.

Marranca, B., & Dasgupta, G. (Eds.). (1991). *Interculturalism & Performance.* New York: PAJ Publications.

Maslach, C. (1991). *Promoting student success at Berkeley: Guidelines for the future.* Report of the Commission on Responses to a Changing Student Body. Berkeley: University of California, Berkeley.

Mau, R. Y. (1993). Barriers to higher education for Asian/Pacific-American females. In J. S. Glazer, E. M. Bensimon, & B. K. Townsend (Eds.), *Women in higher education: A feminist perspective.* Needham Heights, MA: Ginn Press.

McCarthy, C. (1993). After the canon: Knowledge and ideological representation in the multicultural discourse on curriculum reform. In C. McCarthy & W. Crichlow (Eds.), *Race, identity and representation in education.* New York: Routledge.

McDonough, P. M., Korn, J. S., & Yamasaki, E. (1997). Access, equity, and the privatization of college counseling. *Review of Higher Education, 20,* 297–318.

Mercer, J. R. (1990). *The campus climate for women graduate students at UCR, 1989–1990.* Riverside, CA: The Chancellor's Advisory Committee on Sexual Harassment Prevention and The UCR Affirmative Action Committee.

Merleau-Ponty, M. (1964). *Signs.* Evanston, IL: Northwestern University Press.

Morrell, D., & Lare, C. (1988). *Measuring the quality of student experiences at UCSD.* San Diego: University of California, San Diego Student Research & Information Office.

Morrison, T. (1992). *Playing in the dark: Whiteness and the literary imagination.* Cambridge, MA: Harvard University Press.

Mourad, R. P., Jr. (1997). Postmodern interdisciplinarity. *Review of Higher Education, 20,* 113–140.

Murguia, E., Padilla, R. V., & Pavel, M. (1991). Ethnicity and the concept of social integration in Tinto's model of institutional departure. *Journal of College Student Development, 32,* 433–439.

National Center for Education Statistics (1977). *First followup survey design, instrument preparation, data collection, and file development—National longitudinal study of the high school class of 1972* (77–262). Washington, DC: NCES.

Nelson, R., & Baker, H. (1990). *The educational climate for gay, lesbian and bisexual students.* Santa Cruz: University of California at Santa Cruz, Office of Analysis and Planning.

Nora, A. (1987). Determinants of retention among Chicano college students: A structural model. *Research in Higher Education, 26,* 31–59.

Nozaki, Y. (2000). Essentializing dilemma and multiculturalist pedagogy: An ethnographic study of Japanese children in a U.S. school. *Anthropology & Education Quarterly, 31*(3), 355–380.

Orellana, M. F. (1999). Good guys and "bad" girls: Identity construction by Latina and Latino student writers. In M. Bucholtz, A. C. Liang., & L. A. Sutton (Eds.), *Reinventing identities: The gendered self in discourse* (pp. 64–82). London: Oxford University Press.

Pace, C. R. (1979, 1990). *College student experiences questionnaire.* Los Angeles: UCLA Graduate School of Education.

Pace, C. R. (1984). *Measuring the quality of college student experience.* Los Angeles: UCLA Higher Education Research Institute.

Pace, C. R. (1990). *College student experiences questionnaire* (3rd ed.). Los Angeles: UCLA Graduate School of Education.

Pace, C. R. (1991). *College student experiences questionnaire: Information report.* Los Angeles: UCLA Graduate School of Education.

Pace, C. R. (1992). Interview, Los Angeles: UCLA Graduate School of Education.

Pascarella, E. T., & Terenzini, P. T. (1991). *How college affects Students.* San Francisco: Jossey-Bass.

Pascarella, E. T., & Terenzini, P. T. (1998). Studying college students in the 21st century: Meeting new challenges. *Review of Higher Education, 21,* 151–166.

Popkewitz, T. S. (1997). A changing terrain of knowledge and power: A social epistemology of educational research. *Educational Researcher, 26*(9), 18–30.

Popkewitz, T. S. (1998). Dewey, Vygotsky, and the social administration of the individual: Constructivist pedagogy as systems of ideas in historical spaces. *American Education Research Journal, 35,* 535–570.

Pratt, M. L. (1995). Arts of the contact zone. In D. Bartholome & A. Petrosky (Eds.), *Reading the lives of others* (pp. 179–194). New York: St. Martin's Press.

Prus, R. (1997). *Subcultural mosaics and intersubjective realities: An ethnographic research agenda for pragmatizing the social sciences.* Albany, NY: SUNY Press.

Radhakrishnan, R. (1996). *Diasporic meditations: Between home and location.* Minneapolis: University of Minnesota Press.

Richardson, R. C., Jr., & Skinner, E. F. (1990). Adapting to diversity: Organizational influences on student achievement. *Journal of Higher Education, 61,* 485–511.

Rogers, R. F. (1980). Theories underlying student development. In D. G. Creamer (Ed.), *Student development in higher education* (pp. 10–95). Cincinnati, OH: American College Personnel Association.

Rosaldo, R. (1989). *Culture & truth: The remaking of social analysis.* Boston: Beacon Press.

Said, E. W. (2000). *Reflections on exile and other essays.* Cambridge, MA: Harvard University Press.

Schutz, A. (2000). Teaching freedom? Postmodern perspectives. *Review of Educational Research, 70,* 215–251.

Shohat, E. (1997, February 21). *Nationalism, multiculturalism, feminism.* Paper delivered at the Transnationalism Conference. Los Angeles: UCLA Faculty Center.

Strange, C. C., & King, P. M. (1990). The professional practice of student development. In D. G. Creamer & Associates (Eds.), *College student development: Theory and practice* (pp. 9–24). Alexandria, VA: American College Personnel Association.

Strathern, A. J. (1996). *Body thoughts.* Ann Arbor: University of Michigan Press.

Tanaka, G. (1993). Book review of *Multicultural teaching in the university. Amerasia Journal, 19*(3), 173–175. Los Angeles: UCLA Asian American Studies Center.

Tanaka, G. (1994). Toward unity and difference: The traveling art of cultural explainers. In *Cultural explainers: Portals, bridges, and gateways.* Venice, CA: The Social and Public Art Resource Center.

Tanaka, G. (1995). Deconstructing Christmas. *Taboo: The Journal Of Culture and Education, 1,* 38–47.

Tanaka, G. (1996). Dysgenesis and white culture. In J. Kincheloe, S. Steinberg, & A. Gresson III (Eds.), *Measured lies: The Bell Curve examined* (pp. 304–314). New York: St. Martin's Press.

Tanaka, G. (1997). Pico college. In W. G. Tierney & Y. Lincoln (Eds.), *Representation and the text: Reframing the narrative voice* (pp. 259–304). Albany, NY: SUNY Press.

Tanaka, G. (1999). Ressentiment. *Anthropology and Humanism, 24,* 75–77.

Tanaka, G. (in press). *The intercultural campus: Transcending culture and power in American higher education.* New York: Peter Lang.

Tanaka, G., Bonous-Hammarth, M., & Astin, A. W. (1998). Rethinking college admissions criteria to fit a changing society. In G. Orfield & E. Miller (Eds.), *Chilling admissions: The affirmative action crisis and the search for alternatives* (pp. 123–130). Cambridge, MA: Harvard Civil Rights Project and Harvard Education Publishing Group.

Tanaka, G., & Cruz, C. (1998). The locker room: Eroticism and exoticism in a polyphonic text. *International Journal of Qualitative Studies in Education, 11*(2), 137–153.

Tanaka, G., & Flores, R. (in press). Caminando juntos: On intersubjective storytelling and the promise of participatory democracy. In J. Herrera (Ed.), *Chile con karma: Investigations on the new borderlands and other questions.* Philadelphia: Temple University Press.

Tanaka, G., Johnson, P., & Hu, N. B. (2001). Creating an intercultural campus: A new approach to diversity. *Diversity Digest, 5*(2), 6–7.

Tate, W. F. (1997). Critical race theory and education: History, theory, and implications. *Review of Research in Education, 22,* 195–247.

Tharp, R. G., Estrada, P., Dalton, S. S., & Yamauchi, L. (2001). *Teaching transformed: Achieving excellence, fairness, inclusion, and harmony.* Boulder, CO: Westview Press.

Thompson, C. E., & Fretz, B. R. (1991). Predicting the adjustment of black students at predominantly white institutions. *Journal of Higher Education, 62,* 437–450.

Tierney, W. G. (Ed.). (1991). *Culture and ideology in higher education: Advancing a critical agenda.* New York: Praeger.

Tierney, W. G. (1992). An anthropological analysis of student participation in college. *Journal of Higher Education, 63,* 603–618.

Tierney, W. G. (1997). *Academic outlaws: Queer theory and cultural studies in the academy.* Thousand Oaks, CA: Sage.

Tierney, W. G., & Rhoads, R. A. (1993). Postmodernism and critical theory in higher education: Implications for research and practice. In J. C. Smart (Ed.), *Higher education: Handbook of theory and research* (Vol. 9). New York: Agathon.

Tinto, V. (1975). Dropout from higher education: A theoretical synthesis of recent research. *Review of Educational Research, 45,* 89–125.

Tinto, V. (1989). *Leaving college: Rethinking the causes and cures of student attrition.* Chicago: University of Chicago Press.

Tinto, V. (1993). *Leaving College: Rethinking the causes and cures of student attrition.* Chicago: University of Chicago Press.

Tinto, V. (1998). Colleges as communities: Taking research on student persistence seriously. *Review of Higher Education, 21,* 167–178.

Torres, C. (1998, February 12). *Presentation on sociology of education.* Los Angeles: Moore Hall Faculty Reading Room, UCLA Graduate School of Education and Information Studies.

Trinh, T. M. (1989). *Woman, native, other.* Bloomington, IN: Indiana University Press.

Tse, L. (1990). Seeing themselves through borrowed eyes: Asian Americans in ethnic ambivalence/evasion. *Multicultural Review, 7*(2), 28–34.

U.S. Department of Education. (1977). *National Longitudinal Survey of 1972 high school graduates.* Washington, DC: Author.

Voloshinov, V. N. (1929/1973). *Marxism and the philosophy of language.* Cambridge, MA: Harvard University Press.

Wolf-Wendel, L. E. (1998). Models of excellence: The baccalaureate origins of successful European American women, African American women, and Latinas. *Journal of Higher Education, 69,* 141–186.

Section 3

SPIRITUAL AND FAITH
DEVELOPMENT

Chapter 9

The Journey Toward Mature Adult Faith: A Model

Sharon Parks

I have studied many times
The marble which was chiseled for me—
A boat with a furled sail at rest in a harbor.
In truth it pictures not my destination
But my life.
For love was offered me and I shrank from its disillusionment;
Sorrow knocked at my door, but I was afraid;
Ambition called to me, but I dreaded the chances.
And now I know that we must lift the sail
And catch the winds of destiny
Wherever they drive the boat.
To put meaning in one's life may end in madness,
But life without meaning is the torture
Of restlessness and vague desire—
It is a boat longing for the sea and yet afraid.

—EDGAR LEE MASTERS
Spoon River Anthology, "George Gray"

The journey of faith can take us to new vistas of knowing, to deepened realms of trust, and to ever-widening circles of belonging. I wish to describe some of the perils and promises of this experience as it may occur in adulthood by tracing three discrete strands of development: form of cognition, form of dependence, and form of community. Woven together, these strands form a descriptive model of the journey of faith in adulthood that is strong without being unnecessarily complex. This model is anchored in a description of intellectual development because it is this dimension of young adult development that is most unambiguously the focus of higher education. The primary purposes of the model, however, are, first, to enable us to see the intimate relationship between cognitive development and the development of affect, community, and faith and, second, to set forth a picture of the broad contours of the path of adult faith. In the following chapter we will focus on the place of young adulthood.

Form of Cognition

As noted earlier, William Perry, during his years as a master listener, counselor, and teacher at Harvard's Bureau of Study Counsel, accompanied a good many students as they made their way as natural epistemologists coping with the puzzles of life in the context of higher education. Further, he and his associates have listened systematically to yet more students in order to confirm and better understand their emerging intuitions of a discernable pattern of development. They have identified nine positions, and their variants, through which persons seem to make their way. I have collapsed, modified, and extended these into four positions (below).

Authority-Bound and Dualistic

The first form of knowing Perry identifies is oriented to Authority and is dualistic in character. In this form of knowing, what a person really trusts, knows, and believes is finally based on some Authority "out there." Such Authority may take the form of a particular person or group, or it may take the more diffused but subtly powerful form of a person's conventional ethos: media, that is, films, television, newspapers, magazines, books, journals; culturally affirmed roles and personalities, such as parents, government officials, religious leaders, recognized artists and popular entertainers; and custom, that is, expected conventions of thought, feeling, and behavior. These various authorities are confirmed by the stories, myths, and symbols that hold the meanings of a people and their institution.

When persons compose their sense of truth in this form, they may assert deeply felt and strong opinion but, if they are asked to reveal the basis for their knowing, eventually they will reveal their uncritical, assumed trust in a source of authority located outside the self. In some way regarded as self-evident, this Authority is presumed to have access to Truth. This form of knowing may be characterized as "Authority-bound" (not Perry's term), in that this form of authority functions in an all-powerful, determi-native manner; the person cannot "stand outside of it" or otherwise have any critical leverage upon it. The person's knowing is inextricably bound up with the power of the trusted Authority.

This form of knowing also tends to be "dualistic." People who compose self, world, and "God" in this form can make clear divisions between what is true and untrue, right and wrong, "we" and "they." There is little or no tolerance for ambiguity. It is important to note, however, that *what* such persons hold absolute certainty about—the "content" of their sense of truth—will vary from person to person, though they share the same cognitive structure. Thus, even though the "structure" of this form of knowing is quite rigid, the "content" that is known so absolutely may itself be seemingly fluid. The language of "relativism," for example, is now commonplace enough to be part of the conventional ethos. Yet this Authority-bound and dualistic way of knowing may still be heard in declarations like "It is totally wrong for anyone to think that truth isn't merely relative," or "You *must* be tolerant."

In this form of knowing, even the truth of the self is composed by the authority of others. The power of that Authority is revealed in these words of a college senior reflecting on the changes he experienced in his college years:

> Some of the main things I can think of are like in high school everybody said, "Oh, you're tall, you must play basketball." So I translated it, "You must play basketball." I just hated basketball, but I turned out every year anyway (laugh). So finally . . . I said, "Hey, I'm tired of that. I don't want to." And I sort of stepped out of the role of being the tall sports figure and into just being myself. I liked that a lot more.

Another senior, reflecting on how he felt after his first exam of his freshman year, reveals the way in which the Authority-bound form of knowing is determined by authority outside the self. The values and criteria of others have the power to shape one's sense of self.

> In terms of studying, I didn't know how I would stand in a class. Like I remember the first test I took was in History and Culture

| Form of Cognition | Authority-bound Dualistic | → Unqualified relativism | → Commitment in relativism | → Convictional commitment |

of the Orient. I didn't know at all what I would get on the test . . . anything from a C to an A. I didn't think I had flunked because I had studied for it, but I didn't know quite how I stood. And I got the test back and I got an A. And that seemed to set a precedent, you know, what goals I set for myself. It's kinda strange. I look back, if I'd gotten maybe a B or a C on that test I might have . . . set lower standards for myself.

A key insight from a constructive-developmental perspective, however, is the recognition that this uncritical, Authority-bound, and dualistic form of knowing is characteristic, not only of children and adolescents, but also of some persons throughout the whole of biological adulthood. From a constructive-developmental point of view, development of cognition beyond this Authority-bound form of knowing does not inevitably occur.

Some who go to college or university arrive with this mode of composing meaning very much intact; for others this form of knowing, this form of faith, has already begun to dissolve. In either case, the journey that follows (for which higher education at its best has been a primary sponsor) is the journey from this uncritical form of certainty to another kind of knowing.

A transformation of Authority-bound knowing typically occurs in the discomfort of finding that established patterns of thinking do not accommodate lived experience. For example, while taking notes from several different yet trusted professors, a student may begin to recognize that one professor's point of view seriously conflicts with another professor's. The student will then either compartmentalize them, place them in some hierarchy of value, or begin to recognize the validity of competing points of view that cannot easily be reconciled into simple either-or forms of true and untrue, good and evil. For a time the student may trust that there is still a "right" answer that some Authority has or will surely discover, since the existence of such a right answer cannot be in question. But the cataclysmic shift occurs in the revolutionary moment when the relative character of *all* knowledge becomes the only "truth."

Unqualified Relativism

Now the student can no longer avoid the awareness both that the human mind acts upon its world to compose it (rather than simply receiving it "as it is") and that all knowledge is relative, meaning that all knowledge is conditioned by the particularity of the relation or context in which it is composed. This requires the student to recognize that the most trusted adults and the most venerable disciplines of knowledge (even the natural sciences) must each compose reality in a pluralistic and relativized world, now perceived as a universe in which every perception leads to a different "truth," and, therefore, every opinion and judgment may be as worthy as another. This form of knowing is Perry's "position 5," and in its most robust form it might appropriately be termed "unqualified relativism."

This shift may occur gradually or abruptly in the context of ongoing lived experience. It may be precipitated by a "lead from the head," as when a person is intentionally introduced to competing perspectives in a stimulating seminar. Authority-bound and dualistic thinking, however, is not besieged only in the seminar room; it may also come unraveled outside the classroom. Wherever one undergoes experience that does not fit the assumptions of one's conventional world, there is an invitation to begin to recognize the relative character of all knowing and to develop critical thinking. Sometimes the reordering of meaning is initiated in forming or losing relationships. For instance, in the pluralistic setting of a typical college or university (or in the military or in prison or in moving to a new place), a person is apt to associate with someone he or she had always defined as "they." When it is discovered that "they" neither fit the stereotypes nor can be assimilated as a mere "exception" into an assumed system of meaning, the dualistic world of "we" and "they" begins to decline in power, and the Authority by which it was composed is called under review. For a time, a person may cope by saying things like, "I have my truth; you have your truth; they have their truth. It doesn't matter what you think, as long as you are sincere." "The Truth" seems to become one truth among many. But this sort of statement discloses, on one hand, the hope that absolute certainty still dwells somewhere (in this case in sincerity), while, on the other hand, it reveals a sort of bravado that serves as a defense against the increasing awareness that conventional certainty just isn't holding well at all. Doubt is deepened when someone points out that both Martin

Luther King, Jr. and devotees of Adolf Hitler were in a sense "sincere."

Likewise, a person may be involved in a romance, or some other close association, that is assumed to be trustworthy because it fits the myths that the person holds about life and how it will be. Under these conditions, when "the" romantic relationship or "the" career opportunity collapses, the person suffers, not only the obvious loss, but also the shipwreck of self, world, and "God,"—the truth of life itself betrayed.

The balance or the pattern of subject and object shifts. The person is no longer "subject to" the assumptions of his or her conventional world; these assumptions may now be held as possible points of view among others—"objects" of reflection. This new balance may offer some new power and freedom, but it is achieved at the cost of an earlier certainty. Perry expresses the experience as it may be felt from the "inside":

> Soon I may begin to miss those tablets in the sky. If this [one possible interpretation among others] defines the truth for term papers, how about people? Principalities? Powers? How about the Deity . . . ? And if this can be true of my image of the Deity, who then will cleanse my soul? And my enemies? Are they not *wholly* in the wrong?
>
> I apprehend all too poignantly now that in the most fateful decisions of my life I will be the only person with a first-hand view of the really relevant data, and only part of it at that. Who will save me then from that "wrong decision" I have been told not to make lest I "regret-it-all-my-life"? Will no one tell me if I am right? Can I never be sure? Am I alone?

Perry then observes:

> It is not for nothing that the undergraduate turns metaphysician.

A position of unqualified relativism is, however, difficult to sustain over time. One discovers that there is a difference between just any opinion and an opinion that is grounded in careful and thoughtful observation and reflection. One may move into a more qualified relativism, increasingly aware that discriminations can be made between arguments based on such principles as internal coherence, the systematic relation of an argument to its own assumptions, external data, and so forth. But the dilemma remains: If thinking doesn't bring us to certainty, why think? The answer usually comes from the imperative of ongoing life.

Commitment in Relativism

Certainty may be impossible, but choices must be made that have consequences for oneself and those one loves. Particularly in relation to issues of moral choice, a person may begin to look for a place to stand, a way of composing truth more adequate to lived reality than other possibilities are. This search for a place to stand is the search for a place Perry terms *commitment in relativism.*

To form commitment in relativism is to begin to take self-conscious responsibility for one's own knowing. One now joins with other adults in discerning what is adequate, worthy, valuable—while aware of the finite nature of all judgments. Fowler speaks of this form of knowing as the composing of an "explicit system" because the person has shifted from a form of world coherence that is "tacit" in its character and assumptions to a form of world coherence that is formed in a desire to make explicit the meaning of life as best one may. As we shall see, it is this movement that is most characteristic of the young adult in the university years.

Convictional Commitment

Fowler describes the development of yet another form of knowing on the other side of commitment in relativism. With Fowler, I believe that typically it does not emerge until well after the ordinary college years, indeed, not until after midlife. It is a place I wish to term *convictional commitment.* It seems to me that this form of knowing was expressed by Carl Jung in a film made near the end of his life. The interviewer asked, "Do you believe in God?" Jung immediately responded, "No." I happened to watch this film with a large university audience, mostly undergraduate, and many spontaneously laughed, assuming, "Of course Jung was too sophisticated to believe in God." Jung, however, continued his response, saying, "I don't have to believe in God, I know God." This time, no one laughed.

Jung exemplified a strength of knowing that is quite other than the Authority-bound, dualistic knowing described earlier. Aware that all knowledge is relative, he knew that what he knew on any given day could be radically altered by something he might learn the next day. Yet he embodied a deep conviction of truth—the sort of knowing that we recognize as wisdom. This wisdom is also reflected in a statement of Oliver Wendell Holmes, who is reported to have said: "I do not give a fig for the simplicity on this side of complexity. But I would give my life for the simplicity on the other side of complexity." Mature wisdom manifests the simplicity on the other side of complexity. Mature wisdom is not an escape from, but an engagement with, complexity and mystery. Our response to this form of knowing is not necessarily agreement, but it does arrest our attention and compel our respect. Such knowing does not put us off the way Authority-bound and dualistic knowing may; rather, we seek it out, or sense that we are sought by it.

Convictional commitment corresponds with Fowler's fifth stage, which he has described as "multi-systemic" in contrast to either the tacit or the explicit forms of world coherence characteristic of earlier places in the epistemological journey. This form of knowing represents a "second naïveté" (Recoeur) that, without abandoning the centered authority of the self and a disciplined fidelity to truth, has a new capacity to hear the truth of another. This form of knowing "resists forced syntheses or reductionist interpretations and is prepared to live with ambiguity, mystery, wonder, and apparent irrationalities" (p. 81).

Cognitive development, as I have described it here, moves from Authority-bound, dualistic, and tacitly held forms of cognition through the development of intellectual thought (the capacity and desire to reflect critically upon the relationship of thought to value and action) toward responsible and convictional commitments. Observed in a distanced fashion from the outside, it may appear to describe a cognitive development of the mind, occurring independently from the affective, emotional life of the person. As experienced from the inside, however, this is decidedly not the case.

When a person undergoes the transformation of his or her sense of truth and reorders "how things really are," such a repatterning of life may involve feelings of curiosity, awe, fascination, delight, satisfaction, exuberance, and joy. But inevitably there is also some degree of challenge, threat, bewilderment, confusion, frustration, fear, loss, emptiness, or other suffering. There is some element of the "shipwreck" described earlier. This suffering dimension and its relationship to cognitive-intellectual development is focused in an account given to William Perry by a young woman about her experience in a physics class. There was, she said, a particular apparatus that appeared to revolve in a circle; however, when the light cast upon it was changed, it then appeared instead to be oscillating. This change in perception, which occurred with only the flick of a light switch, catalyzed her recognition of the relative character of all perception. She concluded her telling of the incident, which had happened many months earlier, by remarking that in the midst of the experience her physics professor had been very helpful to her. When asked how, she said, "Well, now that I think about it, I realize that he didn't say anything; but the way he looked at me, I knew that he knew what I had lost."

To undergo the loss of assumed certainty, to have to reorder what can be trusted as true and real at the level of one's ultimacy, involves emotion as well as cognition. Cognition and affect are intimately woven together in the fabric of knowing. To travel along the epistemological journey that Piaget, Perry, and Fowler describe is to be affected and moved. Kegan has stated it nicely: "A change in how we are composed may be experienced as a change in our own composure." This is to say that there is development in affective life also, for the evolution of meaning is simultaneously a consequence of evolving cognitive power and the ongoing experience of being affected in interaction with one's world. The experience of the motion of life is manifest as emotion—even if constrained by the conventions of "reasonableness" within the academy or some other social context. Indeed, all our deepest emotions may originate in the felt experience of continual meaning-making activity, the experience of our participation in the motion of life itself.

In other words, if, as Piaget observed, the discovery of knowledge occurs in an interaction between self and world, then, since the self represents an intimate relation between body, mind, and heart, developments in intellectual awareness are one with a reordering of feelings and relationships. Relation, power, and vulnerability are dynamically repatterned with every insight. The splitting of the atom, for example, is reordering our relationship to the earth and to each other, enlarging our power and our vulnerability, and fundamentally changing those matters that ultimately concern us. We have been affected. Whether we cope by means of psychic numbing or a resolute engagement with the potential terror which has become our daily reality, we are moved and feel a new wave of emotion upon us. Our concern with the "balance of powers" between nations reflects our personal sense of being moved "off balance." Our inner sense of a dependable balance of trust and vulnerability has precariously shifted. Within this motion we are recomposing our sense of what is ultimately dependable (or our sense of "God"), as we begin to live with a new awareness that more depends upon us than we had previously supposed. We are moved to recompose more interdependent and, therefore, more dependable patterns of knowing and being.

Since it is apparent that the dynamic of dependence is integral to the relation within which cognition develops, I turn now to a consideration of the forms of dependence, an affective strand of development in the weaving of mature faith.

Form of Dependence

Dependence is a manifestation of relationship. Dependence is an inevitable dimension of the power of the relation of self and other. To depend is to be "held by" or "subject to," but it is also "to hold" (as object). A focus on cognition gives us access to how a person *thinks* in her or his composing of meaning at the level of faith. A focus on dependence gives us access to what a person *feels*. For holding, being held, depending and being depended upon at the level of ultimacy (even in the conceptual dimension, even in adulthood) touches the core of the self so profoundly that emotions such as confidence, fear, vulnerability, and strength are inevitably evoked—emotions that undergo transformation and development. Humans are always and necessarily interdependent beings, but the form, experience, and awareness of dependence

changes. I propose, therefore, that we add "form of dependence" as a strand of adult development (see below).

Dependence

At the time of Authority-bound knowing, it follows logically that a person's sense of world is dependent upon an uncritically assumed Authority (though, particularly in adulthood, this may take subtle forms that mask the profound dependence that is, in fact, in place). A person may be able to give a variety of logical reasons for holding a particular position or point of view but, if pressed, will eventually reveal an unexamined trust in some form of Authority that that person is held by. The self quite literally hangs in a balance of self and other in which the self is uncritically dependent upon an authoritative other outside the self. Feelings of assurance, rightness, hope, fear, loyalty, disdain, or alarm can be determined by Authority—whether in the voice of Walter Cronkite, the Pope, a government official, a person's "always there and always right" parent, a minister, a spouse, or others who serve individually or collectively as trusted mediators of Truth.

Kegan quite-fittingly names this era in development "interpersonal," for here a person's sense of truth depends upon his or her relational and affectional ties. Fowler, with equal fittingness, names this era (stage three) "conventional," for here the person uncritically accepts the conventions of group and societal norms. The boundaries of the group may be rather narrowly drawn, as in the case of a "conventional" cult or club member, or more broadly construed, as in the case of a "conventional" Democrat, Republican, Protestant, Roman Catholic, marine, hippie, yuppie, activist, or Hell's Angel. In each instance, the person's sense of reality and what is fitting and true is dependent upon a sense of felt relationship to an ethos of assumed Authority.

Form of Cognition	Authority-bound Dualistic (tacit)	→ Unqualified relativism	→ Commitment in relativism (explicit)	→ Convictional commitment (paradoxical)
Form of Dependence	Dependence/Counter dependent		→ Inner-dependent	→ Inter-dependent

Counterdependence

A person's feelings will continue to be shaped by this assumed Authority until the day when there is the yearning (or the absolute necessity) to explore and test truth for oneself. This may occur in the midst of the utter shipwreck of the truth one has depended upon (in which it may be accompanied by feelings of devastation, betrayal, bewilderment, or the like), or it may emerge as a manifestation of just a restlessness arising as a sort of readiness for more being. In the latter instance, it is as though a strength has been established which can now "push away from the dock" of that which has been sure moorage, to move out into the deep waters of exploring for oneself what is true and trustworthy. Initially, however, this move is essentially another form of dependence, since this pushing away from the dock takes the form of counter-dependence.

Counterdependence is the move, in opposition to Authority, that provides momentum for the passage into the unknown. It is a dimension of the earlier dependence, because Authority is still in control in that the person can push against the pattern that is, but is not yet able to create a new one. Here, the "I" dwells in negative tension with every "truth." One is dependent upon moving apart, dependent upon creating some distance. Indeed, the very need for distance merely obscures continuing participation in a relation that is still (and in most instances will continue to be) quite powerful.

This move can occur in relatively nontraumatic forms if the person is in an environment of wise parents, sponsoring teachers, or others who consciously encourage or nurture it. Little "pushing against" is necessary, because one is encouraged to explore and is supported in doing so. However, when this motion is not understood and when the bond of relation has been particularly good and trustworthy, the person may have to push against the dock with greater force if a new relationship is to take form. In contrast, people with the least experience of positive trust may suffer counterdependence over an extended period of time, for relationships of negative tension may feel most fitting or truthful when one has had little experience of knowing a worthy truth grounded in positive relationship.

In any case, this may be a complicated time for parents, teachers, administrators, or students (or spouses trying to repattern their marriage bond). For example, when a student moves in the opposite direction from Authority, Authority may recognize this and may suggest the opposite of what is really intended. Clever students figure this out, however, and any real meeting or collaboration becomes quite impossible for everyone, even when the forms of this distancing motion are subtle rather than overt. (This is particularly the case when Authority resists the now necessary recomposing of the relationship and becomes authoritarian.) Frustrations abound as earlier forms of communication seem to dissolve and alternative patterns of relationship have not yet taken form (and cannot as long as connection feels like a return to earlier patterns of dependence).

Yet, in time, a person may begin to recompose Authority and recognize that, indeed, Authority doesn't hold ultimate truth or power. The counterdependent pilgrim is compelled, therefore, to begin to look less toward resisting Authority and more toward the self as an act of responsibility in relation to self, world, and truth. The person begins to move toward inner-dependence.

Inner-dependence

The term *inner-dependence* is used here to signify something different from independence. Western culture places an extraordinary value on individuality and autonomy—a sort of independence that implies, not only strength of self, but also the utter absence of a fundamental recognition of the adult's need for affectional relation with others. The presumed needs of industrial societies have conspired with Freud's insights so as to cast suspicion on all forms of dependence. Dependence is regarded as infantile, particularly those forms of dependence that have religious justification. Partaking in the same industrial and Enlightenment influence, Protestant religious faith has simultaneously fostered a cultural ethos in which the individual conscience and independent action tend to have ultimate value. Yet, as William Rogers observes, "while there is solid conviction as well as psychological wisdom in both religious and general cultural manifestations of independence, the excess of such claims easily leads us to the suspicion that they may betray more underlying anxiety about forms of dependence." Not all forms of dependence are appropriately equated solely with weakness, immaturity, or a dynamic of regression to infantile relationships. Dependence also points toward the relational dimension of all being, a dimension neglected to the impoverishment of our cultural myths and our over-individualized lives.

Inner-dependence, in contrast to the common associations we make with notions of independence or autonomy, is not intended to connote a "standing all by oneself." Rather, the motion into inner-dependence occurs when one is able to self-consciously include the self within the arena of authority. In other words, other sources of authority may still hold credible power, but now one can recognize and value also the authority of the self. Carol Gilligan's study suggests a corresponding motion in the dimension of care. People (especially women) who have previously tended to extend care almost exclusively to others to the neglect of the self (because only others had the authority to claim care) can now extend care also to the self (who now also has the authority to claim care).

Responsibility to authority outside the self is thereby relativized (but not demolished). With the term *inner-dependence,* then, I wish to signify, not a negation of the essential relatedness upon which all human life depends, but a new consciousness of the authority of the inner life of the self in the composing of truth and of choice. A person begins to listen within, with a new respect and trust for the truth of his or her "own insides." That is, the person begins to listen and be responsive to the self as a source of authority and as an object of care. Again, this does not mean that sources of insight outside the self or the claims of others for care necessarily become irrelevant; it does mean, however, that the self takes conscious responsibility for adjudicating competing claims for truth and care.

In this movement of the soul, there emerges the possibility of a new quality of correspondence between inner and outer realities—and the potential for new bonds of relation between self and world. There is sometimes also a new vulnerability that comes with a heightened awareness of the discrepancies between the claims of the self and the capacity of the social structures of one's world to respond to those claims. Before a new relation between self and world is created, the claims of each may threaten the other.

After inner-dependence is established and the trustworthiness of the inner self is confirmed, there seems to be yet another movement toward the further enlargement of trust and conviction of promise. This movement again expands the arena of authority and of care.

Interdependence

In the mid-life period, a person may simply move through a transition from the first half of his or her life to the second half. (It is my sense that "mid-life" occurs at different times for different persons, because it is determined by one's own inner sense that one has probably lived half of one's life. The future is no longer infinitely revisable. One's sense of "lifetime" becomes more focused. This is a transition in consciousness, usually marked by physical changes as well.) But transitions can be occasions for transformation. The transformative potential of the mid-life transition lies in the strength of the inner-dependent self. For only when one has become strong enough can the "deep self" emerge to be re-known as a resource for the further repatterning of truth of faith.

The "deep self" is composed of those buried dimensions of oneself—particularly the sufferings of childhood, the unresolved issues of adolescence, and, as well shall see, the most luminous dreams and hopes of young adulthood. This deep self may now surface to be healed, to be realized, or at least to be known and lived with nondefensively. This movement may be resisted, but, if allowed, it may lead not only to a deeper knowing and trust of the self but also to a more profound awareness of one's relatedness to others.

This transformation constitutes another qualitative shift in the balance of vulnerability, trust, and faith. Now more at home with the limitations and strengths of the self, one can be more at home with the truth embedded in the strengths and limitations of others. A person's locus of primary trust now resides neither in the assumed authority of another nor in the courageously claimed authority of the inner self. Rather, trust is now centered in the meeting of self and other, recognizing the strength and finitude of each and the promise of the truth that emerges in relation. This trust is the self-conscious expression of interdependence.

When meaning-making moves into an interdependent form, it is not the fact of interdependence that is new. As we are beginning to recognize more adequately, from infancy through adulthood a person is always interdependent, always dependent in varying ways upon faithful relationships with others. What is new, however, is one's awareness of the depth and pervasiveness of the interrelatedness of all of life. One now may become increasingly angered and saddened by assertions of truth that exclude the authority of the experience of others. A dean, for example, may earlier have been tolerant of shared inquiry and decision making, and even have affirmed the notion ideologically—all the while silently harboring a sense that his or her inner synthesis of experience, knowledge, and intuition would more efficiently achieve an adequate enough "truth." Now, however, he or she perceives dialogue to be not merely politically expedient, but essential. Yet one brings to that dialogue the strength of one's own capacity to author truth—a strength to which one now is no longer subject, but that one can now hold as object in dialogue with others to whom one can now listen with new attention. The person can depend upon others without fear of losing the power of the self. When this motion occurs within the marriage relation a yet more profound intimacy becomes possible, for the person not only is a self, but can hold even that self as object to be given to another. This is to say that the person now participates in a freedom allowing both weakness and strength, needing and giving, tenderness and assertiveness—without anxiety that in the recognition and even enlargement of the other the self will be diminished.

A person who has composed and is composed by this form of dependence—interdependence—comfortably dwells in the truth that the needs of nurturance, affection, and belonging extend throughout life and into every domain of being, both public and private. Interdependence can now be profoundly "owned" at the affective level. The person now most trusts the truth that emerges in the dialectic, or, better, in the communion between self and other, self and world, self and "God." The person can recognize and know with the whole self the truth of the interdependence that we are. This knowing involves the feelings of delight, wonder, freedom—and often a deep sense of the tragic arising from the capacity to see what others cannot or will not.

Attention to the development of dependence gives us some access to the ebb and flow of the feelings of trust, constraint, threat, fear, confidence, and communion. These are feelings rooted in inner experience. But the motion of affective life and its development emerges neither in a merely private inner world nor in abstract reflections upon relationship but only in the frustrations and transformations of relationships lived out in the everyday. The importance of relationship brings us to reflect upon a third strand of development, form of community.

Form of Community

One of the distortions of most psychological models is that their attention to the particular and inner experience of the individual obscures the power of social dynamics in the shaping of personal reality. The reifications of the disciplines of psychology and sociology reflect the split in modern thought between subject and object, private and public, and do not serve to cultivate the strength of understanding required to interpret a world increasingly requiring our recognition of the interdependence of all of life.

A potential (but yet unrealized) strength of the Piagetian paradigm is its conviction that human becoming absolutely depends upon the quality of the interaction between the person and his or her environment. The human being does not compose meaning all alone. The individual person is not the sole actor in the drama of human development. Just as the infant is dependent upon others for the confirmation of a universe of care and promise, even so is everyone throughout life dependent upon a *network of belonging*. Every person needs a psychological "home." This home is constituted by the patterns of connection and interaction between the person and his or her environment. The composing of ultimate meaning is determined, in part, by our relationship with "those who count." Faith as a patterning, connective, relational activity is embodied, not in the individual alone, but in the social fabric of life.

Networks of belonging may take the form of an obviously present and easy to identify circle of relationships, membership in which confirms identity and security. In other instances, the network of belonging may be scattered geographically or otherwise dispersed among arenas of involvement and may include people both living and dead. For example, one may live in a strong sense of association with a historical figure one has never met, but who serves as a touchstone for one's life and values. Or one may live and work far from colleagues who share one's vision and commitments and yet be able to sustain committed action, even when criticized in the immediate situation, because of the felt linkage with others who confirm one's very being. Even those who choose the life of solitude dwell in a dependence upon others who have formed and confirmed the self.

The power of the network of belonging is two-fold. First, the security it offers bestows the gift of freedom to grow and become. Second, every network of belonging has composed norms and boundaries that one cannot cross and still belong. The network of belonging is simultaneously a freedom and a constraint. Thus social norms may manifest a collective wisdom that protects and nourishes the individual, but the same social norms may also distort and/or in time unnecessarily limit the promise of human life. Transformations in the meaning of the self, therefore, not only occur in the interaction with the social world, but may require a mutual recomposing.

It is this awareness that has prompted Dwayne Huebner to insist that the most worthy point of any developmental theory lies not in its capacity simply to diagnose an individual; rather, developmental theorists find their most fitting vocation in enabling us to respond to the question, What do the developing person and his or her community now mean to each other? This is to say that the story of human development is also the story of the transformation in a person's experience of the meaning of community. Thus an understanding of adult development depends upon attention to forms of community (see below).

We never outgrow our need for others, but what others mean to us undergoes transformation. It is precisely at the point of becoming adult, however, that the form and role of community in our lives may become confused. Due to both the domination of the notion of independence in our understanding of adult psychology and the corresponding cultural perception that dependence is infantile, we are apt to feel uncomfortable if our need for community is strong.

The importance and the power of the social milieu has been somewhat more adequately acknowledged in psychological descriptions of children and adolescents. It is recognized that children are profoundly affected by parents, families, chums, and school groups; "peer groups" are well factored into the story of adolescent development. But when the mark of psychological adulthood is "autonomy," and maturity is measured in terms of degrees of "individuation," the ongoing and essential role of community in adult life becomes obscured.

The communion features of the psyche remain in focus, however, if we remember that the motion of meaning-making is located in the oscillation between "two great yearnings" of human beings: the yearning to be distinct—to exercise one's own action in the world, to stand alone, to differentiate the self from the other— and the yearning for connection, inclusion, belonging, relation, intimacy, and communion. The current revisioning of constructive-developmental theory does well in reminding us that every new equilibrium "represents a kind of temporary compromise between the move toward differentiation and the move toward integration; every developmental era is a new solution to this universal tension" (pp. 412, 413).

Conventional Community

Fowler, building on the insights of Robert Selman has attended to this social aspect of faith by describing the development of the "bounds of social awareness." At Fowler's stage three (typically, the era of adolescence and often beyond),

Form of Cognition	Authority-bound Dualistic (tacit)	Unqualified → relativism		Commitment → in relativism (explicit)		Convictional → commitment (paradoxical)
Form of Dependence	Dependence/Counter dependent			Inner- → dependent		Inter- → dependent
Form of Community	Conventional →	Diffuse →		Self-selected class or group	→	Open to "others"

the composing of self and world is located within and dependent upon "membership in a group or groups characterized primarily by face-to-face relationships." These groupings are "conventional" because they conform to class norms and interests and are "ascriptive," meaning that one belongs because one is located by birth or other circumstance in that assumed context. Such groups and their prevailing ethos tend to "be defined by any one or some combination of the following: ethnic-familial ties, social-class norms, regional perspectives and loyalties, religious system, technoscientific ethos, peer values and pressures, and sex role stereotypes" (p. 63).

This boundary of social awareness is drawn so as to include only "those like us." People from out-groups may be appreciated as individuals for virtues and qualities determined by the values and norms of the in-group (pp. 63, 64). This form of community corresponds to the Authority-bound and dualistic form of cognition, in which Authority defines "we" and "they."

Diffuse Community

But as one begins to want to know for oneself, often it is precisely this social ordering that is brought under examination. An experience of "other" that is contradictory to previous assumptions may recompose one's perceptions of the social order.

In the initial relinquishing of the assumed norms of relationship and the expanding of the boundaries of the social horizon, the form of community may become diffuse. An expansive, exploratory, experimental, and tentative character may predominate, for when any one truth or perspective is as good as another, there is some corresponding sense that any sort of relationship may be as good as any other. This is not to say that relationships become a matter of indifference. Quite the contrary may be the case when the person, now feeling a bit "at sea," has both a new freedom to explore the horizon of life and a new vulnerability to the potential power of every possible relationship. Rather, it is to say that when unqualified relativism prevails, the sustaining of any particular relationship becomes problematic. Ironically, however, the person awash in the sea of unqualified relativism may be sustained, nevertheless, only by the subjective experience of the importance of human connectedness, which may become "the spar we

cling to" when the shipwreck of certainty dumps us into a seemingly meaningless world.

It is thus that people are typically dependent upon community for the formation of commitment within relativism, a community that will both represent and confirm a new pattern of knowing and being. Fowler describes the new social constellation that emerges at this time as a "self-selected class or group."

Self-Selected Group

I became aware of the power of these dynamics to shape and reshape forms of community when I was teaching in a liberal arts college that encouraged off-campus study, particularly during its month long mini-term in January. With another colleague, I led a group of students to San Francisco, where they studied "the city" for a month. As an instructor in religion and a chaplain, I noted with interest that some students who had little or nothing to do with religion on campus were exploring the cathedrals in San Francisco as well as particular religious communities. They were also at times asking questions about religion, in contrast to their behavior on campus. At first, I assumed that this was simply because of a change in environment—that is, there were more cathedrals and more religious diversity in San Francisco. Only later did I recognize another dynamic at play with us in San Francisco—a change in the students' network of belonging.

On campus, students tended to choose patterns of affiliation based partly on their religious orientation. Once these were established, significant deviation was a threat to belonging. This meant that, for some, religion was "out of bounds" and, for others, "required." But when they were in a new social constellation, new questions and new behavior became possible.

We had expected that when students returned to campus those who had not traveled would benefit from association with those who had. We discovered, however, that the travelers tended to form new patterns of affiliation. They formed community—a self-selected group—with those who had also traveled and with whom they could confirm a new perception of the world.

The "self-selected class or group" not only confirms the adult's new world of meaning that is composed on the other side of critical awareness, it also confirms a particular form of meaning. Even the most "cosmopolitan and liberal of mind" often discover, upon making a close examination of their own network of belonging, that at least initially, "those who count" are "of like mind"—though they may represent an expansion of previously held boundaries of ethnicity, class, geography, and so on. For example, one's network of belonging may be constituted by those who, though diverse in many respects, nevertheless hold similar political, religious, and philosophical views and values.

Community Open to Others

Fowler's description of the evolution of the bounds of social awareness finds its most profound implication in the last stage he describes, a picture of mature faith manifest in a commitment to inclusive community marked by justice and love. But it is Ronald Marstin, building on the work of Fowler, who has most forcefully elaborated the essential linkages between the development of faith and the development of the capacity to move beyond provincial perceptions and conventional forms of community.

In his book, *Beyond our Tribal Gods*, Marstin is not shy about acknowledging that implicit in developmental theory is the assumption that each succeeding stage is "better" in that each succeeding stage can account for more. Each stage offers the capacity to handle greater complexity and thereby to be more inclusive. Marstin's boldness comes, not from an indifferent or arrogant elitism, but from a commitment to social justice. He sees clearly that not only is complex perspective taking essential to adequate moral reasoning (Kohlberg and Selman) but the character of one's composition of the whole of reality (one's faith) will condition what one finds tolerable and intolerable. He recognizes that the press to compose a fitting meaning in its most comprehensive dimensions becomes the press toward both truth and justice. Most fundamentally, he underscores the Piagetian insight that human beings develop "because we need to." We recompose meaning when we encounter the "other" in such a way that "we are left with no other choice, short of blocking out what we can no longer block out with any honesty. If we pass to a new way of interpreting the world, it is because the new way can account for things that the old way no longer could. We are now able to acknowledge considerations previously

ignored, to account better for all the facts, to embrace a wider range of perspectives. We couldn't have reached the new stage without having first passed through the former stage. But the new one is not simply different; it is better" (p. 34). Development creates the capacity to embrace a more adequate truth and an expanded community.

Marstin celebrates the promise for human life inherent in a person's ongoing encounter with a world inhabited by other selves with their own needs, an encounter continually requiring the recomposing of what is true for the self in relationship to a world of others. As he does so, he shows that the process of cognitive development will surely require a relativizing of the tribal gods—one will be required to recognize the limitations of one's provincial ultimacy. But he is sobered by the recognition that, for many, leaving tribal gods appears to lead only to a new set of tribal gods. This is the case when people settle into a self-selected class or group that offers an easy ecumenism and the leisure to experiment, and shapes a private truth—while the earth remains sick (p. 44). This is to say that a "critically aware" movement to a "self selected class or group" may not necessarily represent an advance in inclusiveness. "Those of critical but like mind" may even represent a diminished concern for others, if critical awareness leads only to the formation of a network of belonging marked by cynicism and/or an ideology marked by exclusion (two conditions to which the young adult is particularly vulnerable).

Marstin quite rightly and compellingly sees two things: First, the content—the ideas and images that cognitive structures hold—is as important as the structures themselves (a matter we will take up in chapter 6) and, second, that yet another transformation in community is required for a faith that is mature in love and justice. When the conversation with "otherness" is sustained, when one continues to bump up against those who are different, the inner-dependent self begins to find a more adequate truth in a dialectic with the "other" both within and without. A yearning for community (not just association) with those who are profoundly other than oneself emerges. The form of a person's community is transformed into a more profound inclusiveness, because it is truer. Ongoing meaning-making necessarily comes to challenge the system that protects some while neglecting others. "Issues of social justice are essentially about who is to be cared for and who neglected, who is to be included in our community of concern and who excluded, whose point of view is to be taken seriously and whose ignored. As faith grows, it challenges all the established [assumed and conventional] answers to these questions."

This challenge becomes embodied in a form of community that recognizes the "other" as "other." In the Fowler data, this form of community appears to be composed in the post-mid-life period. Perhaps this is because this capacity, not only to participate in, but to demand and create inclusiveness is nurtured, in part, by the capacity to include the "otherness" within.

Gordon Allport described the character of a faith that embodies convictional commitment, interdependence, and the creating and maintaining of a community that is genuinely open to others:

> Maturity is never merely a matter of age, but one of development. A mature sentiment has a way of handling doubt, of realizing . . . that personal commitment is possible even without absolute certainty, that a person can be half-sure without being half-hearted.
>
> The mature religious sentiment is dynamic in its desire to be truly comprehensive; it is not called upon only in fear, sorrow, and mystical moments; it saturates one's life. It joins a person's religion, which is deeply solitary, to social living.

A Model

When we weave these three strands of development together, we are able to see some of the interrelated dynamics that shape the journey toward mature faith. The strands of cognition

and dependence in their mutual resonance may assist us in recognizing that how we think about what concerns us ultimately and how we feel in the most intimate elements of our lives are dynamically interdependent. The strand of community begins to reveal that this telling of the journey toward mature faith represents a potential not necessarily realized in adult life; for the development of faith is a communal process dependent, not only upon the capacities and yearnings of the self, but also upon teachers, friends, mentors, colleagues, and neighbors who together form the social context that nourishes and enhances or diminishes and blocks the cultivation of the life of faith.

This model portrays a motion by which we may journey from Authority-bound forms of meaning-making anchored in conventional assumed community through the wilderness of counterdependence and unqualified relativism to a committed, inner-dependent mode of composing meaning, affirmed by a self-selected class or group. This model, furthermore, challenges the provincial character of much of adult faith by requiring attention to the possibility of further movement toward a yet more mature faith, marked by an engaged wisdom that manifests a conviction of interdependence and seeks communion with those who are profoundly other than the self.

Since the purpose of this model drawn with the tools of social science is to describe something true about the journey of faith in adult experience, we should also be able to find some resonance between this model and the ancient tales of our people. If the model illumines something that is true, we should be able to hear it echoed in the traditions of human faith. And we do. What is described here seems to correspond

Form of Cognition	Authority-bound Dualistic (tacit)	Unqualified → relativism	→	Commitment in relativism (explicit)	→	Convictional commitment (paradoxical)
Form of Dependence	Dependence/Counter dependent			Inner- → dependent	→	Inter- dependent
Form of Community	Conventional	Diffuse →		Self-selected class or group	→	Open to "others"
Form of Faith	Egypt God as Parent	Wilderness → The Far Country	→ Spirit Within			Promised Land Many members, one body

with the story in the Hebrew Scriptures of a movement from Egypt (initially a place of salvation, which becomes a bondage ill fitted to the promise of life) through a wilderness to a promised land.

This model also suggests that if a person's sense of ultimacy is recomposed in these modes, then the experience of God would also undergo transformation. Differing images of God might be more resonant at one place in the journey than another. For example, in the language of the Christian Scriptures, at the time of Authority-bound and dependent faith, one might know and experience God primarily as the loving parent or good shepherd "who cares for me and guides me"; the journey into unqualified relativism might be felt as a journey into the "far country" and away from God the Parent; a more inner-dependent commitment might be expressed in the imagery of the Spirit within; and interdependent, convictional commitment may have been something of what Saint Paul attempted to describe in the imagery of "many members . . . one body."

Looking briefly at Eastern traditions, we may note that Confucian teaching holds the conviction that all human beings have the heart-mind that cannot bear to see the suffering of another, but that this feeling-knowing can be lost unless cultivated by an education that is a learning to be human. Hindu wisdom has recognized stages of life in the imagery of a journey from apprentice (the dependent one), to householder (the responsible one), to seeker of spiritual truth (the wise one). The Buddhist vision begins in a story of a young person who went forth and found wisdom only on the other side of an encounter with suffering. Indeed, virtually all religious traditions have some story of pilgrimage.

The voice of faith, in this instance drawing on Christian imagery, perhaps captures the heart of the model of faith that has been offered here, saying:

> Our greatest truths are but half-truths. Think not to settle down forever in any truth, but use it as a tent in which to pass a summer's night, but build no house for it or it will become your tomb. When you first become aware of its insufficiency, and descry some counter-truth looming up in the distance, then weep not, but rejoice: it is the voice of the Christ saying, "Take up your bed and walk."

With this model to serve us as a broad framework describing the motion of adult faith, we are now prepared to focus on the experience of young adult faith and its significance in the formation of mature adult faith.

Chapter 10

Defining Spiritual Development: A Missing Consideration for Student Affairs

Patrick Love and Donna Talbot

Spirituality and spiritual development have been conspicuously absent from student development theories and ignored by many student affairs professionals. The authors argue for consideration of spiritual development by student development theorists, provide a definition and framework through which to consider spirituality and spiritual development, examine Maslow's (1971) and Chickering and Reisser's (1993) work through a spiritual lens, and suggest directions for future practice and research.

Spirituality and spiritual development are topics that do not appear very often in higher education and student affairs literature. In fact, only one short essay addressing spirituality or spiritual development (Collins, Hurst, & Jacobsen, 1987) has appeared in any of the major student affairs journals (i.e., *Journal of College Student Development, The NASPA Journal, College Student Affairs Journal,* and *College Student Journal*) in the past 15 years. Reluctance to address spirituality in the field of student affairs is neither surprising nor unusual given the context in which it exists: higher education. One reason for this reluctance is that spirituality is often associated with religion and is, therefore, an uncomfortable topic to discuss in society (Bolman & Deal, 1995) and on college campuses (Collins et al., 1987). Cultural norms in the United States dictate that issues related to religion or spirituality are private matters (Collins et al., 1987). This is most evident in the constitutional mandate for "separation of church and state" so often championed by politicians, educators, and others, and of such a concern on public college campuses (Moberg, 1971). Beyond cultural norms, the Western paradigm of empirical, positivistic, objective, "value-free" knowledge so cherished in traditional academia had no room for issues of faith, hope, and love (Palmer, 1993). Academe, however, is moving increasingly toward a postmodern perspective in which values, assumptions, and beliefs play a central role in the social sciences (Tierney & Rhoads, 1993). With this in mind, student affairs professionals must understand the role that such values as faith, hope, and love play in the structure and persistence of communities, in the construction of knowledge, in the understanding of truth, and in developmental processes of students.

The purpose of this article is to provide information about the intentional inclusion of spirituality and spiritual development in the discourse of the student affairs field and the area of student development. The article begins by providing a rationale for the inclusion of spirituality and spiritual development in the scholarship of student affairs. Propositions are then provided as a basis for a definition and conceptual framework of spiritual development. Finally, the spiritual aspects of two student development theories are discussed and a course for future practice and research is suggested.

Why Spirituality and Spiritual Development?

There are several reasons for including spirituality in the discourse and scholarship of the student affairs profession. The first is based on a very traditional and closely held assumption of the profession: the value of holistic student development (American Council for Education, 1937; 1949). By failing to address students' spiritual development in practice and research we are ignoring an important aspect of their development. Another reason is that these concepts are being addressed in other related helping professions and in academic disciplines that have traditionally informed our practice, such as psychology (Ferrucci, 1982; Helminiak, 1996; Tart, 1990), health (Allen & Yarian, 1981; Banks, 1980), social work (Canda, 1988; Sermabeikian, 1994), counseling (Chandler, Holden, & Kolander, 1992; Hinterkoff, 1994; Ingersoll, 1994; Maher & Hunt, 1993), nursing (Henderson, 1989; Krohn, 1989; Piles, 1990; Sims, 1977), and teaching and learning (Benally, 1994; Farber, 1995; Palmer, 1993). This widening discussion not only signals a challenge to the cultural assumption that spirituality is a taboo topic in academe, but also provides an interdisciplinary foundation of knowledge upon which a definition of spiritual development can be devised. There also continues to be a surge in the quest for spiritual or religious fulfillment both within society and among traditional-aged college students. This trend is evident in the increasing emphasis on community service and service learning (Jacoby, 1996; Lankard, 1995), the rise of new age spirituality (Walz-Michaels, 1996), the growing emphasis on servant-leadership (Fraker & Spears, 1996), and the continued attraction to cults and cult-like groups (Blunt, 1992).

A void has existed on campus and in academe related to spirituality and spiritual development. There are few places to talk about these topics other than religious studies programs and campus ministry offices, which can be narrow avenues for discussing issues of spirituality. Traditional-aged college students often experience a period of displacement, confusion, and discomfort as they develop cognitively and emotionally. During this time, students may be attracted to traditional and fundamentalist religions, cults, and cult-like groups that promise definitive answers, especially in this area of spirituality and spiritual development. For many educators and student affairs professionals, the fear is that these groups require, often vehemently, a convergence of thoughts and beliefs from their followers. This expectation necessarily works against values such as free inquiry, exploration and questioning. However, during a period of time when students struggle to make meaning in and of their lives, they will seek support and stability. Unfortunately, the profession's failure to engage in discussions of spirituality and spiritual development may contribute not only to foreclosure on matters of spirituality, but also to a general narrowness of perspective and an inability or unwillingness to think critically, explore value-related issues, and question authorities.

Toward a Definition of Spiritual Development

There is no commonly accepted definition of spirituality. Ingersoll (1994) noted that others have described it as communication with God (e.g., Fox, 1983), a movement towards union with God (e.g., McGill & McGreal, 1988), a focus on ultimate concerns and meanings of life (e.g., Tillich, 1959), and belief in a force greater than oneself (e.g., Booth, 1992; Wittmer, 1989). In trying to define spirituality, others have introduced concepts and language that focus on a particular outcome or state of being (Hawks, 1994), or on the process of spiritual development (Chandler et al., 1992). Still others have grounded aspects of spiritual development in traditional student development theory. For example, Fowler's (1981) stages of faith development are based in part on Perry's (1970) stages of intellectual development. In our efforts to incorporate spirituality into the discussion of student development in higher education, we have developed a set of propositions that can guide discussion in the field and provide a framework through which to research the topic.

Several assumptions underlie the propositions we describe. First, the quest for spiritual development is an innate aspect of human development (Chandler et al., 1992), though one "cannot cause experiences of a spiritual nature to occur; one can only create certain conditions in which spiritual experiences are more likely to occur"(Chandler et al., 1992, p. 169). Also, while innate, motivations toward spirituality can be repressed (Haronian, 1972). Second, spiritual development and spirituality are interchangeable concepts in that both represent a process (i.e., movement, interaction, transcendence) with no endpoint.

A third assumption is that openness is a prerequisite to spiritual development. Chandler et al. (1992) describe a balanced openness. Optimal openness exists between the extremes of repressing spiritual elements in one's life (being closed to spiritual experiences or spiritual aspects of experiences) and being obsessed by spiritual experiences. Being open to spiritual development need not be conscious, intentional, or defined as openness to spiritual development. In fact, Helminiak (1996) argued that a dynamic openness of spirit is behind human curiosity and longing and is, therefore, the root of ongoing development in human beings. Openness to spiritual development can include being in awe of one's surroundings, having a sense of wonder about the world, being receptive to the as yet unexplained, being alert and sensitive to changes in one's relationships, or being curious as to the root of our emotions.

The propositions listed below acknowledge a wide range of belief systems that may or may not incorporate organized religions. Some of the components cited in these propositions, such as spiritual development's focus on connectedness to self and others, transcending locus of centricity, and deriving meaning, are aspects of traditional psychosocial and cognitive development theory. This relates to the contention that spiritual development is an important and integral aspect of students' development. These five propositions are not stages, nor are they listed in a linear, chronological order. They are processes that are interrelated and often are in evidence concurrently.

1. *Spiritual development involves an internal process of seeking personal authenticity, genuineness, and wholeness as an aspect of identity development.*

   Seeking personal authenticity, genuineness, and wholeness involves the process of developing a sense of self that is unitary (as opposed to fragmented), consistent, congruent with our actions and beliefs, and true to our sense of self. This process can be motivated by the unrest or dissatisfaction individuals feel when their sense of values and meaning are not clear or not congruent with the way they live their lives. Benner (1988) describes the pursuit of authenticity, genuineness, and wholeness as "the response to a deep and mysterious human yearning (p. 104). This unsettled feeling encourages individuals to be introspective about their lives and the conditions under which they have chosen to exist. This self-examination, in many ways, is inevitable developmentally as individuals struggle with identity issues—and questions of who they are.

2. *Spiritual development involves the process of continually transcending one's current locus of centricity.*

   To transcend means to go beyond one's current limits. Leean (1984) describes spiritual development as the ongoing process of learning and growing through life's challenges in the direction of self-transcendence. According to Maslow (1971), "transcendence refers to the very highest and most inclusive or holistic levels of human consciousness" (p. 269). Helminiak (1996) describes the transcendent dimension of spirituality as being aware of something beyond the spatial-temporal world.

   When discussing "locus of centricity," Chandler et al. (1992) differentiate among an unhealthy egocentricity (self-centered and narcissistic), a healthy egocentricity (enlightened self-interest), humanicentricity (centered in humanity), geocentricity (centered in the planet), and cosmocentricity (centered in the cosmos). Certainly, between egocentricity and humanicentricity there exist other levels of centeredness related to the communities we experience and of which we are a part, such as family, neighborhood, school, and church. Within each of these communities there can be various levels, such as nuclear family and extended family.

3. *Spiritual development involves developing a greater connectedness to self and others through relationships and union with community.*

"Spirituality is personal [and] intimate. . . . All human existence has a spiritual aspect" (Jones, Wainwright & Yarnold, 1986, pp. xxiv, xxvi), yet spirituality is also rooted in connectedness, relationship, communion, and community with the spirit, and the sense of spirit that often exists in true communities (Fowler, 1981). Bolman and Deal (1995) address the issue of "community" in relationship to spirit:

Historically, humans have found meaning in work, family, community, and shared faith. They have drawn upon collective resources to do what they could not do alone. United efforts—raising a barn, shoring a levee, rescuing earthquake victims, or singing a hymn—have brought people together, created enduring bonds, and exemplified the possibilities of collective spirit. (p. 6)

The paradox of spirituality is that its experience is personal and unique, but only finds its fullest manifestation in the context of an ever broadening, mutually supportive community (Helminiak, 1996). Community also relates to the notion of increased knowledge and love, the contents of spiritual development. Palmer (1993) asserts that knowledge is love; however, he also indicates that:

Scholars now understand that knowing is a profoundly communal act. Nothing could possibly be known by the solitary self, since the self is inherently communal in nature. In order to know something, we depend on the consensus of the community—a consensus so deep that we often draw upon it unconsciously. (p. xv)

4. *Spiritual development involves deriving meaning, purpose, and direction in one's life.*

Canda (1989) refers to spirituality as the basic human drive for meaning and purpose. The content of spirituality and the focus of the process of spiritual development is greater knowledge and greater love (Chandler et al., 1992); it is knowledge and love that help provide meaning, purpose, and direction in one's life. Helminiak (1996) describes the directionality of spiritual development:

The . . . openness of spirit is oriented in a particular direction. The ideal goal of spirit is being, all that there is to be known (and loved). So the openness of spirit entails a movement toward that all. . . . Spirit's nature is continually to move, to reassess, to rework, until it attains its ultimate goal, the complete and coherent appropriation of all reality. This dynamism of spirit is behind the unending curiosity and insatiable longings of the human heart. This dynamism is at the root of ongoing development in human beings. (p. 68)

In these postmodern times, knowledge relates not only to a greater worldview (Chandler et al., 1992), but to the recognition of the role of power, values, and assumptions on the fabrics of our communities. Benally (1994) explains that knowledge is spiritual according to the Navajo philosophy of learning and pedagogy. The purpose of gathering knowledge, which must be internalized as guiding principles for life, is to "draw one closer to a state of happiness, harmony, and balance" (p. 30). In the context of spirituality, love refers to the Greek notion of agape. Agape is the unselfish love of one person for another, a love that reaches out to others without expectation of return. It is the "acceptance of what is, and a motivation to bring about change that results in the greater good. Together with greater knowledge, this implies an evolving sense of life purpose with its increasingly comprehensive and constructive systems of ethics and values" (Chandler et al., 1992, p. 169). It is a "growth in good will toward one's fellows" Jones et al., 1986, p. 565). Love provides direction for the process of spiritual development and for the spiritually developed person. Most of our cognitive development theories focus on the process of meaning making; spirituality gives focus and direction to those processes and a context in which to apply one's love, increasing knowledge, and advanced cognitive skills.

5. *Spiritual development involves an increasing openness to exploring a relationship with an intangible and pervasive power or essence that exists beyond human existence and rational human knowing.*

Spirituality also relates to the relationship with and openness to the influence of forces that exist beyond oneself (Opatz, 1986). Related to transcendence, as one develops spiritually there is a growing recognition of a spirit or force larger than oneself; a force accessible only through faith, hope, love, and other nonrational aspects of human experience. This spirit is often referred to—especially in Western tradition and religions—as God, but its experience and definition has varied throughout time and across cultures. For example, Buddhism, Taoism, and Confucianism are profoundly spiritual traditions, yet make no reference to God.

Kennedy (1997) cites Elkins, Hedstrom, Hughes, Leaf, and Saunders' (1988) description of individuals who are at advanced levels of spiritual development:

These individuals . . . know that there is more than what they can see and that it is important to stay in touch with this other world. Spiritual individuals know that life has meaning and that there is a purpose to their lives. They have a sense that they need to accomplish a mission or fulfill a destiny in their lives. Spiritual individuals believe that all life is sacred. They can find wonder in even ordinary things. . . . Spiritual individuals are aware of the tragedies of life. While this gives their lives a serious side, it also makes them see their lives as more valuable. Spiritual individuals have evidence of spirituality in their lives. Their spirituality will affect their relationships with themselves and with everyone and everything around them. (p. 7–8)

Taken together the five propositions describe spiritual development as an interrelated process of seeking self-knowledge and centeredness, transcending one's current locus of centricity, being open to and embracing community, recognizing an essence or pervasive power beyond human existence, and having that sense of spirit pervade one's life.

Spirituality and Student Development Theory

In order to substantiate the assertion that spiritual development needs to be considered by student development theoreticians and practitioners, the work of psychosocial theorists Maslow (1971) and Chickering and Reisser (Chickering & Reisser, 1993) is examined to highlight spiritual elements already present in traditional student development theory. This examination provides support to the suggestion that introducing spirituality to the discussion and research of student development is not as big a leap as some might assume.

Maslow's Hierarchy of Needs

In Maslow's (1971) hierarchy of needs the pinnacle of development is self-actualization. What is rarely mentioned is that Maslow differentiated between "mere" self-actualization and self-actualization that is self-transcendent. In his work, he appeared to use the terms self-transcendence and spirituality synonymously. Maslow also identified non-self-actualized individuals who had transcendent experiences, proposing that spirituality is evident throughout the developmental process. In fact, human development is incomplete without consideration of spiritual development:

The spiritual life is . . . part of the human essence. It is a defining characteristic of human nature, without which human nature is not full human nature. It is part of the Real Self, of one's identity, of one's inner core, of one's specieshood, of full humanness. (p. 314)

Maslow addressed issues that have since come to be known as postmodern—rejection of the concept of "value-free" knowledge, the inability to "objectively" study and know something and the critical importance of examining subconscious culture—and linked these to spiritual development:

The value life and the animal life are not in two separate realms as most religions and philosophies have assumed, and as classical, impersonal science has assumed. The spiritual life . . . is within the jurisdiction of human thought and is attainable in principle by man's own efforts. . . . Let me also make quite explicit the implication that metamotivation is species-wide, and is, therefore, supracultural, common-human, not created arbitrarily by culture. . . . Culture is definitely and absolutely needed for their actualization; but also culture can fail to actualize them, and indeed this is just what most known cultures actually seem to do. . . . Therefore, there is implied here a supracultural factor which can criticize any culture from outside and above that culture, namely, in terms of the degree to which it fosters or suppresses self-actualization. (p. 314–15)

Therefore, spiritual development, like student development, can either be fostered or inhibited by the environmental context in which students live, grow, and develop. Maslow (1971) also spoke to the intentional development of the spiritual elements of the human experience. Ultimately, Maslow argued for an integration of spiritual development practices into other aspects of our work focused on learning and development.

Chickering and Reisser's Vectors

Within the vector of "Developing Integrity," Chickering and Reisser (1993) presented three interrelated aspects: humanizing values, personalizing values, and developing congruence. Much of the discussion of humanizing values in *Education and Identity* focused on issues and experiences related to religion and church. Again, it is important to distinguish between spiritual development and religious values, beliefs, and behaviors. Pascarella and Terenzini (1991) found that most of the research done in the area of religious attitude change fell into two categories: general religiosity and religious activities. Most studies in the past 30 years have shown significant declines in religious attitudes, values, and behaviors. However, the specific practices often addressed are church attendance, prayer, grace before meals, identification with a particular religious denomination, and beliefs in a supreme being. While some of these, it may be argued, relate to rejection of spirituality, most do not address issues of spirituality at all; they are merely external measures or practices associated with religion.

On the other hand, changes in students identified in the literature of the past 30 years not often associated with religion, but congruent with the propositions related to spirituality and spiritual development, include a movement toward greater altruism, humanitarianism, and social conscience, more social, racial, ethnic, and political tolerance, greater support for the rights of individuals and for gender equality, and increasing openness and other-person orientation (Pascarella & Terenzini, 1991). Each of these changes can be argued as being at least somewhat spiritual in nature.

Viewed from the lens of spirituality, Chickering and Reisser's (1993) notion of humanizing values takes on a distinctly spiritual tone:

In the earlier developmental stages, moral rules and religious teachings are interpreted literally. But if the stories are seen to contradict each other or if the teachings contradict life experience, literalism breaks down. New teachers may be found, but sooner or later, interpreters are bound to differ. As students deal with tensions between ancient traditions and new ideas, conformity and questioning, guilt and freedom, self-interest and unselfishness, they slowly recognize the need to take responsibility for defining their own positions, to commit to beliefs that ring true to their deepest selves, while remaining open and tolerant. (pp. 240–241)

This description reflects the propositions presented earlier in that spirituality, while developed within a community or tradition, is, ultimately, personal and idiosyncratic; it is a process, and it is punctuated by crises.

Only these two brief examples of developmental theories have been viewed through a spiritual lens. In this case, they were both psychosocial theories. Certainly, additional insights can be gained by examining the work of moral development theorists, such as Kohlberg (1971) and Gilligan (1982), as well as the work of other cognitive-structural theorists, through a spiritual lens. But beyond the examination of current theory, there is the need to explore the spiritual development of college students as a primary focus.

Continuing the Exploration

The challenges of studying spirituality from a scholarly perspective are many. As Collins et al. (1987) point out,

Spirituality does not lend itself to scientific study alone. . . . Spirituality requires different methods of consideration and investigation than those used through scientific approaches in most subject areas. Spirituality rests on the balance of faith and experience, on both revelation and reason. Openness to traditional and nontraditional approaches to investigation and understanding must be considered. (p. 275)

The time has come when nontraditional approaches to the study of spirituality and spiritual development among college students is warranted. Qualitative research has moved from the periphery of social science methodologies to acceptance as a legitimate form of research.

Assumptions related to the epigenetic nature of development (Erickson, 1968) may be another obstacle to the study of spirituality. While a "ground plan" may be somewhat genetically predetermined for cognitive development and while mainstream and middle-class societal influences may affect the relative similarity of psychosocial and identity development among college students, perhaps the variations in students' spiritual experiences make it difficult to develop parsimonious theories of spiritual development. Another possible challenge to the study of spiritual development among college students is related to the nature of the college experience for traditional-aged students (especially those living at college). With its movement away from family and community of origin, its challenges to previous ways of thinking and believing and its assault on a variety of "authorities," going away to college may be experienced as a form of spiritual emergency or crisis, a time when "one is overwhelmed or preoccupied with spirituality" (Chandler et al., 1992, p. 170). While spiritual emergencies, due to their overwhelming nature, often cause a temporizing of spiritual development, they do provide the grist for future development.

Jones et al. (1986) argue that "spiritual development is no steady, regular advance, but is punctuated by crises in which growth appears to have come to a stop for a time; old battles have to be refought and old experiences relived at a deeper lever" (p. 566). As evidenced by Chickering and Reisser's (1993) description of the crises faced by college students as they struggle to develop integrity, college may be a time when for some traditional-aged students growth in spirituality may appear stopped, a time when beliefs need to be reexamined and prior experiences relived. The challenges to their current spirituality may be overwhelming. Therefore, in the case of some traditional-aged college students, spiritual development may temporize and appear to be not occurring at all or even regressing. Frankly, we just do not know, because we have not looked at students' experiences through the lenses of spirituality and spiritual development.

Implications for Practitioners

Despite the relative lack of knowledge or understanding of, as well as the potential discomfort with, college students' spiritual development and the research that needs to be done, there are practical implications from the information presented. These implications relate to incorporating the recognition of spirituality into interactions with students:

1. Student affairs professionals need to reflect on their own spiritual development. This means considering how they derive meaning, purpose, and direction in their lives, how they are growing in connectedness with self and others, and how they are or are not growing toward a greater openness to a relationship with an intangible and pervasive essence beyond human existence and rational knowing.

2. Student affairs professionals must be open to issues of spiritual development in students. This may mean looking beyond issues of religion and differentiating between religion and spirituality. It may also entail the recognition of religion as a manifestation of students' search for spirituality.

3. Student affairs professionals must recognize that emotional crises in a student's life may have a spiritual element or, in fact, may be a spiritual emergency or crisis. Failure to recognize this possibility may result in misdirected advice or counseling, or a misdirected referral.

4. Student affairs professionals need information and training related to spirituality and spiritual development. Until spiritual development is incorporated into the canon of student development theory, it may be up to professional organizations to encourage this information dissemination through workshops and conference programs.

Implications for Researchers

The propositions have been structured in such a way as to encourage and focus research on the spiritual development of college students and can be viewed as a starting point. Additional questions to aid in this exploration include:

What is the relationship between spiritual development and the role of spirituality in development?

What are the processes of spiritual development?

Can spirituality be intentionally developed?

How is spiritual development similar or distinct from faith development, cognitive development, moral development, or psychosocial development? How do these interact?

Can a student reach a higher level of cognitive, moral, or psychosocial development without having developed somewhat spiritually?

Conclusion

This article, like that of Collins et al. (1987) over 10 years ago, represents a call for a focus on the exploration of students' spiritual development. At a time when college students are faced with more challenges than ever before, continuing to neglect this aspect of development makes us less effective as educators. As a profession, however, we need to know much more about spiritual development. This promises to be a rich and valuable exploration.

References

American Council for Education (1937, 1949). *The student personnel point of view.* Washington, DC: Author.

Allen, R. J., & Yarian, R. A. (1981). The domain of health. *Health Education, 12*(4), 3–5.

Banks, R. (1980). Health and the spiritual dimension: Relationships and implications for professional preparation programs. *Journal of School Health, 50,* 195–202.

Benally, H. J. (1994). Navajo philosophy of learning and pedagogy. *Journal of Navajo Education, 12*(1), 23–31.

Benner, D. G. (1988). *Psychotherapy and the spiritual quest.* Grand Rapids, MI:Baker Book House.

Blunt, D. H. (1992). Cults on campus: Awareness is key. *AGB Reports, 34*(1), 31–33.

Bolman, L . G., & Deal, T. E. (1995), *Leading with the soul: An uncommon journey of the spirit.* San Francisco: Jossey-Bass.

Booth, L. (1992). The stages of religious addiction. *Creation Spirituality, 8*(4), 22–25.

Canda, E. R. (1988). Spirituality, religion, diversity, and social work practice. *Social Casework: The Journal of Contemporary Social Work, 69,* 238–247.

Canda, E. R. (1989). Edward Canda's response. *Social Casework: The Journal of Contemporary Social Work, 70,* 572–574.

Chandler, C. K., Holden, J. M., & Kolander, C. A. (1992). Counseling for spiritual wellness: Theory and practice. *Journal of Counseling and Development, 71*(2), 168–175.

Chickering, A., & Reisser, L. (1993). *Education and identity* (2nd Ed.). San Francisco: Jossey-Bass.

Collins, J. R., Hurst, J. C., & Jacobsen, J. K. (1987). The blind spot extended: Spirituality. *Journal of College Student Personnel, 28*(3), 274–76.

Elkins, D. N., Hedstrom, L. J., Hughes, L. L., Leaf, J. A., & Saunders, C, (1988). Toward a humanistic-phenomenological spirituality: Definitions, description, and measurement. *Journal of Humanistic Psychology, 28*(4), 5–17.

Erickson, E. (1968). *Identity: Youth and crisis.* New York: Norton.

Farber, P. (1995). Tongue tied: On taking religion seriously in school. *Educational Theory, 45*(1), 85–100.

Ferrucci, P. (1982), *What we may be: Techniques for psychological and spiritual growth thvough psychosynthesis.* Los Angeles: Jeremy P. Thatcher.

Fowler, J. W. (1981). *Stages of faith: The psychology of human development and the quest for meaning.* San Francisco: HarperCollins.

Fox, M. (1983). *Original blessing.* Santa Fe, NM:Bear & Co.

Fraker, A., & Spears, L. (1996). *Seeker and servant.* San Francisco: Jossey-Bass.

Gilligan, C. (1982). *In a different voice.* Cambridge, MA: Harvard University Press.

Haronfian, F. (1972). *Repression of fhe sublime.* New York: Psychosynthesis Research Foundation.

Hawks, S. R. (1994). Spiritual health: Definition and theory. *Wellness Perspectives, 10,* 3–13.

Helminiak, D. A. (1996). *The human core of spirituality: Mind as psyche and spirit.* Albany, NY: SUNY Press.

Henderson, K. J. (1989). Dying, God, and anger: Comforting through spiritual care. *Journal of Psychosocial Nursing, 27*(5), 17–21, 31–32.

Hinterkoff, E. (1994). Integrating spiritual experiences in counseling. *Counseling and Values, 38, 165–175.*

Ingersoll, R. E. (1994). Spirituality, religion, and counseling: Dimensions and relationships. *Counseling and Values, 38,* 98–111.

Jacoby, B., & Associates. (1996). *Service-learning in higher education: Concepts and practices.* San Francisco: Jossey-Bass.

Jones, C., Wainwright, G., & Yarnold, E. (1986). *The study of spirituality.* New York: Oxford University Press.

Kennedy, D. B. (1997). *Spiritual development.* Unpublished manuscript. Kent State University, Ohio.

Kohlberg, L. (1971). Stage of moral development. In C. M. Beck, B. S. Crittenden, & E. V. Sullivan (Eds.), *Moral education* (pp. 23–92). Toronto: University of Toronto Press.

Kramnick, I., & Moore, R. L. (1996, November/December). The Godless university. *Academe, 82,* 18–23.

Krohn, B. (1989). Spiritual care: The forgotten need. *NSNA/Imprint, 36(l),* 95–96.

Lankard, B. A. (1995). *Service learning: Trends and issues alerts.* Washington, DC: Office of Educational Research and Improvement. ERIC reproduction number—ED 384737.

Leean, C. (1984). Spiritual and psychological life cycle tapestry. *Religious Education, 83*(1), 45–51.

Maher, M. F., & Hunt, T. K. (1993). Spirituality reconsidered. *Counseling and Values, 38,* 21–28.

Maslow, A. H. (1971). *The farther reaches of human nature.* New York: Penguin Books.

McGill, F. N., & McGreal, I. P. (Eds.) (1988). *Christian spirituality: The essential guide to the most influential spiritual writings of the Christian tradition,* San Francisco: Harper & Row.

Moberg, D. O. (1971). *Spiritual well-being: Background.* Washington, D. C.: White House Conference on Aging.

Opatz, J. P. (1986). Stevens Point: A longstanding program for students at a Midwestern university. *American Journal of Health Promotion, 1*(1), 60–67.

Palmer, P. J. (1993). *To know as we are known: Education as spiritual journey.* San Francisco: Harper.

Pascarella, E., & Terenzini, P. (1991). *How college affects students.* San Francisco: Jossey-Bass.

Perry, W. G. (1970). *Forms of intellectual and ethical development in the college years: A scheme.* New York: Harcourt Brace Javanovich College Publishers.

Piles, C. (1990). Providing spiritual care. *Nurse Educator, 15(1).,* 36–41.

Sermabeikian, P. (1994). Our clients, ourselves: The spiritual perspective and social work practice. *Social Work, 39*(2), 178–183.

Sims, C. (1977). Spiritual care as part of holistic nursing. *NSNA/Imprint, 24*(4), 63–65.

Tart, C, T. (1990). Adapting Eastern spiritual teachings to Western culture. *Journal of Transpersonal Psychology, 22*(2), 149–166.

Tierney, W. G., & Rhoads, R. A. (1993). Postmodernism and critical theory in higher education: Implications for research and practice. In J. C. Smart (Ed.), *Higher education: Handbook for theory and research, vol 9* (pp. 308–343). New York: Agathon.

Tillich, P. (1959). *Theology of culture.* New York: Oxford University Press.

Walz-Michaels, G, (April, 1996). The spiritual and educational dimensions of the New Science movement. Paper presented at the annual meeting of the American Educational Research Association, New York. ERIC reproduction number—ED 394–822.

Wittmer, J. M. (1989). Reaching toward wholeness: An integrated approach to well being over the life span. In T. J. Sweeney (Ed.), *Adlerian counseling: A practical approach for a new decade.* Muncie, IN: Accelerated Press.

Chapter 11

The Role of Faith in the Development of an Integrated Identity: A Qualitative Study of Black Students at a White College

Dafina Lazarus Stewart

Using phenomenology and portraiture as a framework, the awareness and integration of multiple sociocultural identities, such as race, class, and gender were investigated in the experiences of five Black students at a predominantly White college. This article focuses on the particular findings concerning the role of faith and spirituality in this development.

Identity integration and wholeness are critical concepts for all people and especially Blacks and members of other cultural minorities, who hope to attain "true self-consciousness" in defiance of the "symbolic violence" (Lutrell, 1996) of schooling and educational practice. At the beginning of the 20th century, DuBois wrote, "The history of the American Negro is the history of this strife,—this longing to attain self-conscious [selfhood], to merge his [sic] double self into a better and truer self" (1903/1994, pp. 2–3). This longing also represents a spiritual consciousness that recognizes the interrelated nature of human existence and the desire to be whole within oneself (Baker-Fletcher, 1998). Researchers studying the experiences of Black students on predominantly White campuses have repeatedly pointed to the fragmented, disjointed nature of that experience (Allen, Epps, & Haniff, 1991; Fleming, 1984; Gibbs, 1974; Hughes, 1987; Parham, 1989; Sedlacek, 1987). Moreover, this research has pointed to the reliance on spirituality by Black students as a means of navigating through their educational experiences and developing a positive racial identity in the midst of a culturally hostile environment (Fleming; Hughes; Sedlacek). Drawing on this previous work, the author studies identity development in Black students to capture stories that are related to the social and cultural influences that help us to answer the question, "Who am I?"

Much of the previous work done on identity development in Black students has been focused on the process of developing a mature racial identity (Atkinson, Morten, & Sue, 1993; Cross, 1971, 1991; Helms, 1993; Parham, 1989; White & Parham, 1990). Identity integration, akin to racial identity development, represents an internal process of self-development. However, this level of cross-cultural, psychosocial development reflects an understanding of the self as inherently composed of multiple facets, in which the different forms or facets of self (race being only one of those forms or facets) come together and impact each other in potentially transformative ways. For example, a Black woman's understanding of her racial identity is transformed by her lived reality as a woman, and vice versa. Definitions of the self as raced, gendered, and educated move from being externally imposed limitations to internalized, interlocking components through which self-actualization may be more fully realized. Such a symbiotic relationship means that each different sociocultural identity facet is identifiable and salient in all areas of the individual's life. Hearkening to DuBois, "In this merging [the better and truer self] he wishes neither of the older selves to be lost. He would not Africanize America. . . . He would not bleach his Negro [sic] soul in a flood of White Americanism. . . . He simply wishes to make it possible for a man [sic] to be both a Negro [sic] and an American" (1903/1994, p. 3).

Identity integration provides a way to transcend the societal tendency to compartmentalize everything, including the self, to smooth out the supposed contradictions between these faces or facets of self (i.e., sociocultural identities), and to provide a sense of coherency about who one is and how one lives in social context. The symbiotic resolution of these three sociocultural identities (i.e., race, gender, and class) represents one vision of identity integration and wholeness. To accomplish this task in an environment that may be hostile to certain resolutions of one or all of these sociocultural identities presents psychosocial and psychocultural identity challenges for Black students.

The purpose of this study was to investigate the awareness and integration of multiple sociocultural identities among upper-class Black students on a predominantly White campus. Sociocultural identities should be understood as those aspects or facets of self-identity that are shaped and influenced by the larger society and personal cultures of individuals. Sociocultural identities such as race and gender, which are biologically rooted, have inscribed meanings that are socially or culturally determined. The research focus on participants who were upper class refers to the students' collegiate standing, not their socioeconomic position. The following presentation and discussion of findings focus on one research question which was part of the much broader study, "In what ways did spirituality impact the perception of multiple sociocultural identities and the development of an integrated and whole sense of self for these Black students?"

Literature Review

Developmental psychology, womanist theology, and student affairs practice combine to inform the interpretive analysis that follows. One of the inherent propositions of spirituality and faith is an understanding of the self and nature as inherently whole. As Joy James (1993) wrote, "Spirit is inseparable from the mundane or secular and bridges artificially and socially constructed dichotomies" (p. 35). The foundation of spirituality, then, is to deconstruct the fragmentation we have created in our lives. Wholeness and identity integration are not only consistent with faith and spirituality but are the core of it. Parker J. Palmer (1983) wrote about the role of spirituality in education. He describes Western educational institutions as places where students are taught to understand themselves as fragmented and incoherent as they learn the same thing about the world in which they live.

Love and Talbot (1999) wrote that spiritual development involved an internal process of seeking personal authenticity, continually transcending one's current locus of centricity, and developing greater connectedness to self and others. Moving from external definitions of self to internal ones (see also Baxter Magolda, 1999) and finally to divine definitions of self is critical for the development of an identity that is impervious to external criticism and hostility. As Jones (1997) found, self-definition was a critical step in moving away from confining and fragmenting notions of the self toward selfconcepts that were authentic and liberating. Connectedness to self and others is ideologically synonymous with the Afrocentric ethos that Nobles (1980) expressed and that McEwen, Roper, Bryant, and Langa (1990) used. Interconnection within the myriad forms of self-identity encourages connection with the myriad forms of humanity.

Womanism, emerging out of and parallel to Black feminism, is attuned to the intersections of identity because women of color are often situated in multiple locations within society and experience oppression in multiple ways (Cole, 1995). Within this tradition, womanist theologians emphasize the interconnectedness of body, mind, and spirit and the intersections of identity (Baker-Fletcher, 1998; Wade-Gayles, 1995). As Karen Baker-Fletcher wrote, they are "integrated and interconnected deeply and densely within each other like the molecules of a rock" James Fowler (1981) has done extensive research on the development of faith throughout a person's life cycle. Fowler described faith as people's ultimate support when the other things they depend on in their lives collapse around them. Faith enables one to find meaning in the world and in one's life, and is about making a commitment to what is known and living in a way that is informed by that commitment. Moreover, Fowler described faith as shaping who people are and how they see themselves.

It is from this last point that Fowler (1981) moved on to introduce the deep interconnections between faith and identity. He began with acknowledging that each human being has many "triads," or centers of value and meaning, that operate in people's lives and shape how they see themselves. People live their lives in "dynamic fields of forces" that pull them in many different directions, and they are faced with the challenge of making meaning of their lives by composing some kind of "order, unity, and coherence in the force fields of [their] lives" (Fowler, p. 24). These layers of relationship between faith and identity inform a typology of faith-identity patterns that were initially conceived by theologian H. Richard Niebuhr (as cited in Fowler). These faith-identity patterns are clearly progressive and hierarchical, which is consistent with other developmental theories.

Sharon Daloz Parks (2000) built from the framework laid by James Fowler (1981) and other cognitive-structural developmental theorists to discuss faith as a way of making meaning for young adults. Parks highlighted the important ways that different social contexts such as higher education can influence and "mentor" that development for young adults. Parks, in a manner similar to Fowler, described faith as more transcendent than religion or spirituality: Faith is the primary meaning-making activity that all human beings share. Parks also defined faith as the "capacity and demand for meaning," the self-conscious discovery of what is ultimately true and dependable in life (p. 6). Parks also theorized the interrelationship between faith and identity commitments through the lens provided by Niebuhr's faith-identity patterns. Part of the meaning-making task is "to become at home in the universe," to be at home within one's self, place, and community in such a way that you know that you belong and that you can be who you are. "To be human is to desire relationship among the disparate elements of existence" (Parks, p. 19).

Despite the differing points of origin into this framework of faith, spirituality, and meaning making, it is significant to note that all of the scholars mentioned here agree that issues of faith and spirituality are ultimately issues that involve seeking coherence and wholeness among the myriad identities, responsibilities, and relationships that all human beings possess. Identity integration or wholeness is supported as a spiritual concept that is related to faith and the commitments that are made to certain roles, relationships, and concepts, and that is deeply relevant to the development of young adults. The work of Fowler (1981) and Parks (2000) were particularly helpful in analyzing the student interviews.

Methodological Framework

As Jones states in her article in this volume, there are four essential elements that construct and shape how research is done. Further, shaping the "how" of research begins not with the decision to use interviews over questionnaires, but rather with the deep consideration of what view(s) of knowledge and philosophical position(s) provide the clearest pathway(s) to knowledge(s) about our subjects. Likewise, this study was grounded in particular epistemological positions and theoretical perspectives that informed the selection of portraiture and phenomenology as a research methodology and the semistructured interview as a research method.

Epistemology. Afrocentrism understands the world as divinely ordered, inherently coherent, and the marriage of material (temporal) and spiritual realities (Myers, 1993; Nobles, 1980). An Afrocentric epistemology considers knowledge accessible to all individuals and shared within community. Constructivism, along with Afrocentrism, privileges the interaction of individuals with each other and with their environments as fundamentally shaping how individuals understand themselves and their social worlds. Such an epistemology requires a subject-centeredness in the approach to research questions, data collection, and data analysis.

Theoretical Perspective. The theoretical perspective that follows from these epistemologies is heavily influenced by hermeneutics. Such a perspective results in a research attitude that privileges the voices of the subjects and their ability to make sense of their own lives and experiences and "looks for assumptions and meanings beneath the texture of everyday life" (Schubert, 1986, p. 181). Language use and meaning receive a primary focus and, logically coherent with the governing epistemologies above, view reality as "intersubjectively constituted and shared within a historical, political, and social context" (Schubert, p. 181). Further, the nature of an Afrocentric approach is critical and emancipatory and seeks to expose dominating and oppressive social and mental structures, while enabling both researchers and participants to reconnect to the core of their identity.

Methodology. Based on such an epistemology and theoretical perspective, the methodology employed in this study was a hybrid of portraiture and phenomenology, grounded in Afrocentric philosophy (Myers, 1993). It can be best described as a snapshot of experiences that is developed by both subject and researcher. The portrait becomes a place to voice and express the intuitive sociocultural realities of both researcher and subject, while making evident the ways that these lived realities interact to influence how the subject tells the story, how the researcher hears the story, as well as the narrative of the story. Central to this methodology is the tenet that an in-depth authentic understanding of the particular is key to understanding the general (Chase, in press; Lawrence-Lightfoot & Davis, 1997; Myers, 1993; Stake, 1994).

Methods. Through in-depth, individual interviews (Seidman, 1998), I sought to make implicit knowledges explicit and to transform habit to knowing as these students discussed the meaning they made of their identities through story. The larger aim here was to create a "vital text" (Denzin, 1994), one that enabled the expression of multiple identities and their intersections and interconnections (Peterson, 1998).

Participants

This study dealt with how 5 individual students negotiated and integrated their multiple sociocultural identities in their selfimages. The students selected for this study were all Black students at Rosse College (a pseudonym), a rural, selective liberal arts college in the Midwestern United States. Rosse enrolls approximately 1,600 students in a residential setting. Founded by a cleric in the early 19th century as a seminary for young men, women were not admitted until the latter half of the 20th century. Beset with a conflicted history of both opportunity and exclusion, Rosse College has an enrollment of 54.6% women, 9.2% students of color (i.e., Asian Americans, Hispanic Americans, Native Americans, African Americans) and 2.3% international students. Moreover, according to Sage (one of the participants), Rosse is the kind

of place that knows it is an elite institution and wears that elite status with a sense of pride that is paradoxically unaware of how that elitism implicitly labels others as inferior. Nevertheless, Rosse seems to be attempting to fashion a marriage of its isolated and distinctive character with the educative needs of a diverse intellectual community to produce a democratic elite with the same high idealism and stubborn determination of its clerical founder. The close examination of this "microworld," created by narrowing my focus to students at one type of institution, afforded me the opportunity for greater in-depth study and understanding of the phenomenon investigated (i.e., identity integration and wholeness), and was consistent with the tenets of portraiture and phenomenology.

Student participants were selected using the following rationale. I first sought to recruit students at the junior or senior levels. This decision was supported by student development theory, which demonstrated that the capacity for critical self-reflection is connected to the duration of one's college experience and general maturity levels. Secondly, within this group of Black students, maximum variation sampling and intensity sampling were used to select the participants for the study.

Maximum variation sampling was used to ensure the inclusion of Black students who were male and female, from working-class and more privileged backgrounds, from suburban and urban neighborhoods, and from public and private educational backgrounds. The data gathered through this sampling technique "document unique or diverse variations that have emerged in adapting to different conditions and will identify important common patterns that cut across variations" (Patton, 1990, p. 182). Intensity sampling was then employed to narrow this pool of students to those "information-rich" cases that represented those students most likely to have engaged thoughtfully and intensely (but not extremely) with issues of sociocultural identities and identity integration and wholeness (1990). Based on a pilot study conducted during Winter semester 2000, I believed that students who were leaders of organizations or active in campus activities would provide the best "information-rich cases" for engagement with issues of race, gender, and class. With a sample of 5 students, I sought a more open range of experiences among a smaller number of people to achieve my purpose: the investigation of the awareness and integration of multiple socio-cultural identities among Black college students (Patton). The students chose the following pseudonyms to refer to themselves to protect their anonymity: K.B., Kashmir, Ophelia, Poke, and Sage.

Procedure

Four semistructured, individual interviews were used to collect data from each participant. A demographic survey was also administered to the participants. The interviews were audio-taped with the consent of the students and took place on campus at Rosse College. The interviews were conducted between February and May 2001. The purpose of the first interview was to get a picture of the life history of each partic-ipant, clarifying and expanding upon responses given in the survey. The aim in the second inter-view was to procure the students' descriptions of their own identities and to investigate the stu-dents' understanding and acknowledgment of their multiple sociocultural identities and progress toward identity integration or whole-ness. The third interview focused on the respon-dents' self-knowledges of the ways in which race, gender, and class intersected and intercon-nected in their lives as Black college students on their campus. The last interview centered more specifically around the issues of dependency and home place that Parks (2000) discussed. The first three interviews lasted 60 minutes on average and the fourth took 30 minutes to complete on average. Trustworthiness of the data was ensured through member checks and an inquiry auditor, who reviewed the data and subsequent analysis.

Findings and Analysis

Although Fowler's (1981) and Parks's (2000) faith-identity typology theory is presented as a means of interpreting and understanding the stu-dents individually and collectively, the faith-identity typology was not used as an a priori framework; rather, in the midst of the interviews, I searched for more literature related to the area of faith and spiritual development. The faith-identity typology stood out as being the most responsive to the stories that the students were telling me. Therefore, the students' identity com-mitments and self-images are discussed herein as spiritual issues.

Student Portraits

Kashmir. Kashmir is a biracial woman, the child of an African American mother and Caucasian father. She grew up in a predominantly White suburb and attended the affluent, public, pre-dominantly White high schools in her area. Kash-mir views her world through a Black/White prism and her identity commitments reflect that. Kashmir's current pattern of identity commit-ments is different from what it was in high school and from what it looks like when she goes home. At Rosse, Kashmir's world and the focus of her most intense commitment was very solidly African American. Her relationships with the Black sorority and her African American boyfriend helped to cement her tie to the Black community at Rosse.

Kashmir confessed that she came to Rosse anticipating and expecting the opportunity to "change" to "be something [she had] never expe-rienced before," to be Black. In our first inter-view, Kashmir shared that she was never considered to be Black by her friends in high school, who were all White, until they met her mother. As she said,

> I didn't associate much with Black students in high school. . . . A lot of the girls didn't like me . . . and a lot of the guys didn't want to talk to me because all I dated was the White guys. So that was a big issue, very much like I wasn't Black at my school.

She generally was assumed to be White and therefore was related to as a White person. Rosse offered the possibility of a different experience, of exploring the other side of her racial identity in a way that had never been afforded her, despite her close connection with her mother's family.

As resolute as Kashmir's identity may seem as a Black female, further conversation with her during the second interview, particularly, demonstrated that this was indeed a transient identity. Her attachment to that Black female identity was dependent on others' feelings and attitudes, and her persistence in that identity was also dependent on her perception of others' atti-tudes and her relationships with certain indi-viduals, particularly her boyfriend. This abrupt and discontinuous shift in identity from high school to college is reflected in the following quote. Here, Kashmir discussed what might have happened if her first interactions with the Black community at Rosse had been different.

> If I wouldn't have felt the warmth and the welcome of the Black community from the jump, I probably wouldn't have been so close and part of the community . . . and I would have been one of those, those "I think she's Black, but we're not sure, she doesn't associate with Black people," it would have been like that.

The disassociation that Kashmir is referring to is what she felt in high school toward the Black community. Her identification with the Black community at Rosse and her corollary self-identification as a Black female were grounded reflexively in the reaction of the Black community to her as a visitor during her senior year in high school.

Secondly, her relationship to her Black female identity is acknowledged as completely external to herself.

> So, ownership over being a Black female it would, it was a title given to me when I came here and, I've carried it with me over the last 3 years here . . . but I don't know how much it really is going to be with me when I leave here.

Again, Kashmir's comments strongly suggest that once she leaves Rosse, whether she carries the "title" Black female with her will be fully dependent on whether other Black females see her and relate to her as such. She has not internalized this identity, although she has over the last 3 years adopted it as part of her self-concept and credits it with having had influence over her developmentally: "It has made me stronger."

Despite her current attachment to her identity as a Black female, Kashmir knew that this was a very unsteady rock on which she sat. She recognized the fact that she had been tossed to and fro with every wind, as it were, and had come to a peace about the process and had found an internal monitor by which to assess her development by the end of our time together.

Ophelia. Race and gender were the two primary value centers for Ophelia, along with her personal identity as a writer. However, her commitment to these two centers of meaning making was not consistent. Unlike Kashmir, who found

her identity through her social relationships and then switched back and forth in an effort to please whoever was closest to her at the time, Ophelia rather consistently identified both race and gender as important ways that she made meaning of her life and of the world around her. As she said, "It's intuitively obvious that I'm a Black woman." Nevertheless, she was very loosely attached to those centers of meaning.

> He'll voice some issue about Blackness to me, and I'll be like, you know what, it's not time for me to be Black today, today I'm a feminist, [Interviewer: right] and tomorrow I'll talk about Black stuff, and the day after that I'm off, I'm not going to talk about any of that stuff, I'm going to talk about fashion and makeup that day . . . , I just . . . I don't know what to do with myself, and those are the days when I say, no, just screw it, I'm going to talk about Britney Spears' clothes today or something.

Ophelia also confessed that although synthesizing the pieces of her identity was important to her, she was "seeing" the impossibility of it. This was resonant of Kashmir as well, and likewise was reflective of Ophelia's lack of a more universal transcendent center of meaning to use to synthesize these subordinate identities.

Ophelia elaborated on her need to be cohesive, and this elaboration warranted further analysis. When I asked her how she wove together all the pieces of herself that others assumed to be contradictory, her answer revealed a deep sense of frustration, confusion, and displacement.

> I really don't know how to synthesize everything. I don't know what I want people to think of me as . . . at my worst . . . you know, I just, I don't care about being a woman, I don't care about being Black, I don't care about being anything except for being in the bed and asleep and not worrying about any of it.

Despite Ophelia's confusion, frustration, and "Britney Spears" days, she did recognize that the process of weaving herself together is important to her and that she "would really like to be able to do it." She continued, "I think that's part of the reason why I'm crazy because it's kind of like I'm trying to figure out where my priorities should lie, you know . . . particularly where race and gender are concerned." To achieve her goal, however, Ophelia will need to search for a center of meaning and value that is capable of transcending and including her identities as woman and Black.

Poke. Poke seemed to rely on his openness and ability to function as the "man in the middle," as a bridge between White and Black students, as the primary mode of meaning making for his life and the center of his dependency. This is illustrated in the following quotes. Discussing his reason for choosing Rosse, Poke commented, that if he and other Black students decided not to go to Rosse because of the lack of cultural and ethnic diversity on the campus, then the situation would never improve:

> But I figured if everybody who gets in, like me, decides they're not going to go . . . , nobody'll be there, so if I go somebody else will say they will go. You know what I mean? So I was like if we all . . . get there and really have a good time, like we can leave our mark, change some minds and that'd be cool.

Later in the interview, he posited that "God" put him here to be "a teacher." Specifically, he said,

> I've noticed all throughout my life I've been in the situation of being the man in the middle. I have friends on this side, friends on this side and then I'm in the middle and through that I'm teaching these people.

Through these examples and numerous others in the interviews, Poke relayed his consistent trust in his own ability to act as an ambassador to White people and to bridge Black and White people together through educating each group about their commonalities. This is augmented by his feeling that the reason he was born may have been to be just such an ambassador. Particularly in assessing his decision to attend Rosse College, paramount in his mind was his responsibility and ability to be an effective change agent, and he cited this as the real reason he decided to attend Rosse, although he also described it as "the corniest." Further, he treated another question about whether he ever felt conflict about his identity completely as an issue of his ability to make and maintain relationships. This suggested that Poke put a great deal of value and power in his openness and "man in the middle" status as a locus of his identity. One could infer that if he were to suddenly find himself in a situation in which he was not able to make friends, his identity might begin to lose focus as well.

However, Poke also seemed to recognize the insufficiency of this value center. During the inter-

views, he often pointed to a more transcendent center of meaning making that is capable of sustaining him when his ability to be a bridge or to be the "man in the middle" fails him. Poke relayed two stories of when he should have died or at least gotten into pretty serious trouble, but did not "for some reason." One of these experiences was a very bad car accident that nearly totaled his car; he hadn't been wearing his seat belt, but yet he was able to walk away from the accident with "no scratches, no bruises, no soreness, no nothing." He told me that as the car was spinning, before he finally crashed, trunk first, into a tree, that he was praying to God. Also, Poke was aware that his ability to form friendships even "under the ocean" is totally irrelevant in the face of possible injury or death, "like in serious times." Nevertheless, he did not seem to see the relevance of God in negotiating his relationships with others. He remained "frustrated" by the fact that he will be incapable of teaching some people or protecting the people he cared about from other's closed-mindedness. Moreover, he seemed to explain that closed-mindedness as defying his best efforts at being "well liked" or financially successful. The issue of financial success came up earlier in his second interview when Poke described what it meant to him to be a Black male and that, in spite of the Black comedian Chris Rock's wealth, there were no White people who would be willing to trade places with him. Further, he seemed to feel that there was no hope for those people who remained unswayed by the force of his personality.

K.B. For his first 2 years at Rosse, K.B. described himself as "doing everything." Now, since his return from a semester abroad experience at another institution, he has limited himself to only three organizational involvements: the Black fraternity, the Black student organization, and the campus multicultural center.

K.B. seemed to have a transcendent value center in racialized discourses and had committed himself to what could be termed a "Black agenda" for his time at Rosse. However, this noble commitment was joined with what appeared to be a very diffuse orientation to understanding both himself and the world around him. Like Kashmir, K.B. was also very dependent on receiving positive affirmation from others and filtered his self-assessments through how he felt he was being perceived by others. K.B. pursued his involvement with "anything multicultural" to the point that he was suffering from overexhaustion. This narrowly focused commitment was reflective of his worldview.

> The way that I look at things or see things in terms of issues or things that we're talking about, things that [happen] on campus is different than some people, because I definitely see things through a "racial lens."

According to K.B., the primary difference between himself and most of the other students at Rosse was that he saw things in a racialized context. This also was the foundation of one of his main reasons for joining the Black fraternity. "I think it's important to showcase that we could all still be Black men unified under that moniker, but still be diverse within themselves, I think it was important to showcase that." K.B.'s "Black agenda" represented his primary way of making meaning at Rosse and is his primary, if not sole, analytical lens of his experiences there.

Yet, as described earlier, the racial lens was not the orienting structure for his sense of affirmation in the area of his identity he feels most strongly tied to now, being a Black male. In fact, K.B. admitted that he also joined the fraternity because "to an extent it largely did feel like it was expected of me, that I [was] looked at and hoped I would do it." Along with this, it was a close friendship he had formed with another Black male that also "had a lot to do" with him deciding to pledge. The importance of external expectations resonated throughout my sessions with K.B. and was reflected in the following passage, in which he told me about a time when he thought seriously about deactivating from the group but chose not to because it was also a time of great organizational stress.

> I thought of deactivating and everything and, but I just couldn't . . . they wouldn't have taken it very well at all. I really think my brothers would have taken it as a snub and that would have been the end of our friendship period. I would not have been able to talk with them or anything like that for the remainder of my time here. And I mean honestly, I care about them a lot, so I couldn't abandon them.

Despite his final comment that recentered his decision to remain in the group as an internal resolution of his attachment to them and concern for his fraternity brothers, the major impetus of the passage cannot be ignored. The major reason he maintained his membership in the group was that he could not face losing that connection with them. Their opinion of him was more important than his own mental fatigue or the lack of care they showed him by letting him do all the work of the organization alone.

In our last session together, K.B. did express to me that his dependence on other people was shifting. He acknowledged that he had become too dependent on the Black man who was his best friend here and that he was beginning to "try to solve [his] problems [him]self." Nevertheless, there was still a struggle with relying on and trusting in other people.

Sage. The all-encompassing and foundational center of value and power for Sage was her faith in the ultimate purpose of her life and her belief that God's hand was directing her. This was not a fatalistic faith, where she believed that she had no choice in the direction her life took her. Unlike Poke, she did not simply fall into decisions because "there was nothing I could do," as Poke indicated in his first interview. Rather, she fully believed that everything had a purpose to it and that everything she did must also have a purpose. "I think things should have a purpose, not just necessarily for the sake of doing whatever," as she stated. This purpose was God's will for her life, as she saw it.

My conversations with Sage continually revolved around the importance of being whole, of being able to weave the pieces of herself together, of finding herself constantly having to explain groups of people to each other, and thereby constantly explaining pieces of herself, because "people . . . pick and choose what they like to see." She almost relished the opportunity to discuss these issues because, as she stated in her second interview,

> This has not been a good semester for weaving things together." Sage also stated that "a lot of the way that I reinforce [my spirituality] is by being among other people who encourage me to think about it [pause] and if I feel out of sync with those people, then I'm out of sync with myself, and it just perpetuates problems I'm having elsewhere.

Sage had trouble maintaining her faith in God's purposefulness as the primary and prioritizing center of value and meaning in her life. For Sage, the priority she placed in relationships and her need to be in sync with the Christian community at Rosse continually threatened to pull her away from her central commitment to her identity as a Christian, into a faith commitment and selfidentity that would be reliant on maintaining positive, harmonious relationships with the Rosse Christian community. Later in the interview, Sage revisited this theme, specifically regarding how her faith impacted her ability to see herself as integrated and whole.

> It's just a feeling of not in it [i.e., not a part of the Christian community at Rosse] and as long as I feel out of discord with people that I relate with spiritually, as far as I can't communicate openly and honestly with people that I look to for guidance, for discourse about where I am in my faith, I think in a lot of ways [that] hampers my ability to look at myself.

Sage clearly acknowledged that this struggle with her relationships with other people was problematic, but she was unclear as to how to make them less important and was not sure if she really wanted them to be less important. Sage continued from the last quote, "Maybe that's part of the point, that I'm focusing too much on the people and need to stop, like, holding onto people." At the end of our last conversation, Sage reflected on her desire to have the kind of outlook where "you could be poor and buttnaked in the middle of winter with nowhere to live and you wouldn't care" and her inability to attain that state of what she called "joyfulness."

An Analytical Lens

Individuals accentuate those facets of themselves with which they are most comfortable or that they have more fully developed. An extension of this is that they gravitate toward friendships and organi-zations that voice those aspects or facets of their identities. For instance, a woman who has a strong commitment to her identity as a gendered being is likely to become highly involved in a feminist organization or club. Therefore, the students' organizational commitments provided some clues as to what facets of their sociocultural identities were central for them in their daily lives at Rosse. Also, the degree of "crossover" and overlap between and among those organizational commitments indicated their abilities to integrate their multiple worlds, and thus integrate their own self-identities.

As introduced in the literature review, a three-fold typology of faith-identity patterns has been used to discuss the differing ways that individuals negotiate the multiple commitments in their lives (Fowler, 1981) and prioritize their sources of

dependency and meaning making in their lived experiences (Parks, 2000). There are several theoretical frameworks that could be used to understand these students' identity developments; however, the faith-identity typology is used here because of the unique connection made between relationships with others and the ability to integrate multiple roles, contexts, and identities within one's own self-image or identity.

The patterns (polytheist, henotheist, and radical monotheist) represent increasingly theocentric and more optimal value centers and modes of meaning making. Fowler (1981) demonstrated the progressive development implied by this typology when he asserted that radical monotheism is of "extreme importance" for the future of humankind, which "[will require] our learning to live in an inclusive, global community" (p. 23).

The first pattern of faith and identity is characterized as polytheistic faith. As its name implies, this pattern of faith and identity is exhibited by persons who have interests in many nontranscendent centers of value and power (Fowler, 1981). Parks (2000) further described the polytheist as one who may comprehend the whole of his or her life, but has only been capable of composing an "assortment of isolated wholes" (p. 22). Kashmir and Ophelia represent polytheistic faith and identity patterns. Polytheism has two possible manifestations in the patterns of faith and identity. The first was described through an analysis of Kashmir's commitments. Kashmir is an individual whose value commitments are transient and shifting, moving from one faith-relational triad to another depending on her circle of associates. Fowler described the second as a diffuse attachment to several relational triads and centers of value. This diffuse attachment is not intense; the diffused polytheist can withdraw from any of those commitments at any given time (Fowler). Ophelia's many value commitments lack the intensity of Kashmir's and thus she exhibits a more diffuse form of polytheism (Fowler; Parks).

Although I have suggested that both Kashmir and Ophelia are most appropriately read as polytheists in the faith-identity typology, this should not be taken to mean that Kashmir and Ophelia's life experiences are similar or overlapping. By contrast, Kashmir and Ophelia have led very different lives, with the exception of their admitted discomfort and estrangement from other Black students before coming to Rosse. Indeed, it is this very differences in their life histories that makes their parallel faithidentity relationships both compelling and significant.

The second faith-identity pattern discussed by Fowler (1981) and Parks (2000) is called henotheism. Henotheism, from the Greek for "one god," suggests that the individual has identified a single source of value, meaning, and dependency. In other words, as Fowler characterized it, the henotheistic pattern of faith and identity reflects a deep investment in a transcending center of value and meaning making through which one focuses his or her personality and outlook, but this center is inappropriate and incapable of supporting the individual in the face of crises and loss (Parks). Among this group of students, both Poke and K.B. stand out as reflections of faith and identity grounded in henotheism.

Poke described his social relationships through the character of his relationships with people as family, friends, or associates, and not through his organized campus involvements. The one exception to this was his membership in the Black fraternity on campus, which he firmly positions as part of his circle of family on campus. Within this, Poke identified his involvements as either with Black people or with White people. He describes himself as the man in the middle in these relationships. Yet, Poke also acknowledged that this ability was not adequate to sustain him in times of crisis. It was Poke's inordinate faith in his own ability to serve as a teacher and connection between diverse people that warranted his categorization as a henotheist in the faith-identity typology.

At the time of our discussions during the winter and early spring of 2001, K.B.'s comments suggested to me that he would be more accurately interpreted as falling between two faith and identity patterns, instead of fitting neatly within one. His dependence on race as an interpretive lens for his social world combined with his reliance on external support and validation for his self-image and decision supports such an interpretation. Nevertheless, K.B. definitely seemed to be heading more firmly away from a polytheistic faith-identity pattern. Indeed, he still had another year at Rosse, and there were more challenges ahead for him. He told me that our sessions were "therapeutic" for him, yet, he admitted that he was still holding back. He had not told me everything. It was clear, however, that K.B. internalized his feelings and emotions a

great deal and so I was not surprised that our interviews, although they almost always went over time, barely scratched the surface of his feelings, reflections, and hopes about the issues that we discussed.

As stated above in relation to Kashmir and Ophelia, the categorizing of Poke and K.B. as henotheists should not be used to obviate the very deep differences in their perspectives and life histories. These two young men have almost nothing in common beyond their involvement in their fraternity, and the motivations for their involvement differed as well. Nevertheless, as was said earlier, the very difference between them makes their commonality within this interpretive frame significant.

Radical monotheism, in contrast to both polytheism and henotheism, displays an ultimate trust and loyalty in a center of value and power that is neither an extension of individual or organizational ego, nor can be inhabited within any finite cause or institution (Fowler, 1981). In other words, that center of commitment is the lens through which all other commitments are analyzed. It reveals a consciousness of the foundation of the universe, of something that not only transcends us but also inhabits our very being (Parks, 2000). This is not to say that radical monotheists negate the importance of other less encompassing commitments and value centers, but rather that these centers are prioritized according to their ability to commune with an all-encompassing, foundational center of meaning (Fowler).

Consistent with the typology, my reading of Sage as an exemplar of emergent radical monotheism is not based in her Christian faith or in her active involvement with the Christian community at Rosse. Instead, it is based in her trust and loyalty to something both transcendent and intimate. However, as Fowler (1981) explained, this pattern of faith, radical monotheism, is rarely consistently actualized in persons or communities. Instead, it is too easy to lapse into henotheistic or even polytheistic forms of faith and identity because those pulls constantly surround people (Fowler). Sage believed that God created her Black and female and working class and spiritually centered, and she recognized that the intersection of all those identities had made her who she was. Yet, it was logical that Sage vacillated between allowing the opinions of others to determine how much of herself she gave voice to in particular settings and standing firm in the multiplicity of her identity.

Through the patterns of faith and identity, very interesting portraits of the students were developed. However, this was only one way to read these students' lives. Indeed, this was just one of three analytical frameworks that were initially applied to the data. This particular lens, like the others, made a different and unique understanding of the students more accessible. However, no one lens could provide the most complete or definitive analysis (Honan, Knobel, Baker, & Davies, 2000).

Discussion

Literature in spiritual development and womanist theology suggest that an integrated perception of the multiple aspects of one's identity is related to a mature and developed sense of spirituality and concept of God (Baker-Fletcher, 1998; Cannon, 1995; Fowler, 1981; Love & Talbot, 1999; Parks, 2000). In this study, therefore, I included a focus on the ways in which the students' understandings of their spirituality impacted or influenced their perception and development of integrated or whole identities. Four out of the 5 students indicated that spirituality was a central component of their identity make-up, which supports earlier findings by Fleming (1984), Hughes (1987), and Sedlacek (1987). However, there was wide variation in what spirituality meant to each of them and how it operated in their lives for the goal of identity integration.

There are two related assertions I would like to make based on these findings. The first assertion is that there is a general lack of mature spiritual development as assessed according to Fowler (1981) and Love and Talbot (1999) among these students. The students tended to portray their spirituality as merely oppositional to religious observances or organized forms of corporate worship. Some of the students spoke of being "forced" to attend church as children and still when they returned home from college. For instance, Poke stated, "When I was real little, I was in church a lot; as I got older, it was more just the Sunday, [until] now." Similarly, Ophelia commented,

> Well, because my mom is a reverend she has a lot of involvement in the church and

because of that, that really affects where I'm going to be on Sunday. . . . I think the only time I think about church in my life here is when my mom calls and asks, "Did you go to church this Sunday?"

These experiences with religious dogma have pushed them to resist formal or organized expressions of faith and spirituality in favor of individualized articulations that are expressed as cultural ties, emotionality, or individual moral codes. Generally, the students confirmed the existence of a supreme being that they referred to as "God," but spirituality was generally an amorphous variable that did not live for them as a central organizing principle, as Fowler has theorized mature faith.

However, Sage disconfirmed this assertion and demonstrated a more developed understanding of the difference between faith and religion, and wove a spiritual perspective into her understanding of herself and her relationships with others. As she said in this quote, "It's faith on one hand . . . and on the other hand, I think there's something to be said for religion, for having a concrete mode of expressing." Although she also admitted that spirituality was closely knit to ethnicity for her, she had not allowed the different modes of religious expression at Rosse to keep her from continuing her pursuit of God. She said that her "faith ha[d] done some interesting things," among them investigating what it was she really believed about God and why. Yet, she "still judge[d] what she [saw] through her understanding of what God want[ed] her to be." The self-reflexivity of Sage's spirituality represented a more mature approach than what was suggested by the other students.

Perhaps as a consequence of their generally amorphous grasp on spirituality, K.B. and Ophelia saw little relationship between spirituality and their perception and development of themselves as integrated, whole beings. As K.B. stated,

> It works, see that, it's not like, it's not like it helps me put it together, it's kind of like I'm giving my problems to God in that sense, and He would just handle it and it would get done, not that it has anything to do with me.

The following comment from Ophelia also supports this interpretation:

> So it [spirituality] doesn't really seem to factor in. . . . I guess you can think of it in this

way, that when I'm here I don't go to church, I don't think about going to church.

Again, Sage and Poke stand out from the group in their more firm belief in a spiritual or divine purpose to how they were put together as individuals. Sage and Poke both firmly believed that there was rhyme and reason to everything in the universe, including themselves, although for Poke this was more fatalistic. Interestingly, the other students also tended to share the hope and trust that everything would all work out, including their present confusion or frustrations with their identities. As Kashmir stated,

> Everything happens for a reason and things are going to work out the way they need to and just kind of evolve into what they need to be and I'm going to eventually be at a point where I know me and I have an identity.

In sum, the students recognized that there was a more optimal way of being and seemed to innately trust that they would eventually reach that point.

These conflicting findings could be used to suggest any of three things. These findings could suggest that spirituality is not a critical factor in the perception or development of an integrated self-identity and that Sage's example stands as an anomaly. This interpretation would contradict the assertions made by the spiritual development theorists mentioned earlier. Secondly, these findings could also suggest that the lack of a mature spiritual sensibility is masking the possible impact spirituality could actually be having on this issue. Such an interpretation would call for an assessment of spiritual development correlated with the student's degree of identity integration, which may assist in sifting out any relationship between these two variables (a limitation of this study). However, a third interpretation is suggested by these findings. A certain level of spiritual maturity may be required for an individual to appreciate and integrate multiple identity facets. Such an interpretation would be consistent with the spiritual development literature, especially Fowler's (1981) work. After talking with these students over an extended period and reviewing the literature, I posit that this third interpretation is the most reasonable one and best fits the data that I have collected and presented. Nevertheless, a more thorough inventory of spiritual development that could be correlated with levels of identity integration is

warranted and would provide more support for this interpretation of the data.

This study has several limitations. The small sample size, though justified in both portraiture and phenomenology, restricts the generalizability of these findings beyond the variation of experiences represented. Also, the focus on student leaders silences the relevant experiences of other members of the campus community. Lastly, only Black students were included in this study. Identity integration is relevant for individuals of all racial and ethnic backgrounds. The inclusion of racial and ethnic variation among the sample would likely reveal important themes.

Implications for Practicce

What do these findings suggest for student affairs administrators and others involved in the lives of college students? The stories told by Sage, Poke, Kashmir, K.B., and Ophelia suggest some courses of contemplation and action for higher education. "Space" was a recurring theme for the students. The students often spoke of a hunger for a space to talk about themselves with someone who could help to nurture and mentor them and space to weave together the multiple facets of their identities. The lack of adults who were willing and capable of serving as mentors was highlighted by several of these students. This resonates with Hughes's (1987) findings that PWIs were often unprepared to deal with the differing needs of Black students. This finding also resonates with Parks' (2000) work, which showed the central role that institutions of higher education should and do play in the mentoring of young people's lives.

Moreover, these students bemoaned the dearth of spaces—in organizations, in campus recognitions, and in classrooms—in which multiple aspects of their identities were acknowledged and welcomed. Sage and Kashmir spoke particularly of their sorority as the only space where such a sanctuary was available to them. Further, the students were hungry for a space to discuss spirituality and the meaning of having a center of value and meaning that is transcendent. All these students leapt at the opportunity to discuss these issues and several of them indicated that they had not considered these issues before, because they had never been asked.

The application of spirituality and spiritual development is necessary and important within student affairs research and theory. As Love and Talbot (1999) pointed out, attention to all the salient aspects of an individual's development will afford those who work with students a better and more well-rounded understanding of them.

References

Allen, W., Epps, E., & Haniff, N. (1991). *College in Black and White: African American students in predominantly White and in historically Black public universities.* New York: SUNY Press.

Atkinson, D. R., Morten, G., & Sue, D. W. (1993). *Counseling American minorities: A cross-cultural perspective* (4th ed.). Madison, WI: Brown & Benchmark.

Baker-Fletcher, K. (1998). *Sisters of dust, sisters of spirit: Womanist wordings on God and creation.* Minneapolis, MN: Fortress Press.

Baxter Magolda, M. (1999). *Creating contexts for learning and self-authorship: Constructive-developmental pedagogy.* Nashville, TN: Vanderbilt University Press.

Cannon, K. (1995). *Katie's canon: Womanism and the soul of the Black community.* New York: Continuum.

Chase, S. (in press). Taking narrative seriously: Consequences for method and theory in interview studies. In R. Josselson & A. Lieblich (Eds.), *Interpreting experience: The narrative study of lives* (Vol. 3, pp. 1–26). Newbury Park, CA: Sage.

Cole, J. (1995). Jesus is a sister. In G. Wade-Gayles (Ed.), *My soul is a witness: African American women's spirituality* (pp. 150–155). Boston: Beacon Press.

Cross, W. E., Jr. (1971). Toward a psychology of Black liberation: The Negro-to-Black conversion experience. *Black World, 20*(9), 13–27.

Cross, W. E., Jr. (1991). *Shades of Black: Diversity in African American identity.* Philadelphia: Temple University Press.

Denzin, N. (1994). The art and politics of interpretation. In N. Denzin & Y. Lincoln (Eds.), *Handbook of qualitative research* (pp. 500–515). Thousand Oaks, CA: Sage.

DuBois, W. E. B. (1994). *The souls of Black folk.* New York: Dover. (Original work published 1903)

Fleming, J. (1984). *Blacks in college.* San Francisco: Jossey-Bass.

Fowler, J. (1981). *Stages of faith: The psychology of human development and the quest for meaning.* San Francisco: Harper & Row.

Gibbs, J. T. (1974). Patterns of adaptation among Black students at a predominately White university: Selected case studies. *American Journal of Orthopsychiatry, 44,* 728–740.

Helms, J. E. (Ed.). (1993). *Black and White racial identity: Theory, research, and practice.* Westport, CT: Praeger.

Honan, E., Knobel, M., Baker, C., & Davies, B. (2000). Producing possible Hannahs: Theory and the subject of research. *Qualitative Inquiry, 6*(1), 9–32.

Hughes, M. S. (1987). Black students' participation in higher education. *Journal of College Student Personnel, 28,* 532–545.

James, J. (1993). African philosophy, theory, and "living thinkers." In J. James & R. Farmer (Eds.), *Spirit, space, and survival: African-American women in (White) academe,* (pp. 31–44). New York: Routledge.

Jones, S. (1997). Voices of identity and difference: A qualitative exploration of the multiple dimensions of identity development in women college students. *Journal of College Student Development, 38*(4), 376–385.

Lawrence-Lightfoot, S., & Davis, J. H. (1997). *The art and science of portraiture.* San Francisco: Jossey-Bass.

Love, P., & Talbot, D. (1999). Defining spiritual development: A missing consideration for student affairs. *NASPA Journal, 37*(1), 361–375.

Luttrell, W. (1996). Becoming somebody in and against school: Toward a psychocultural theory of gender and self-making. In B. Levinson, D. Foley, & D. Holland (Eds.), *The cultural production of the educated person: Critical ethnographies of schooling and local practice* (pp. 93–118). Albany: SUNY Press.

McEwen, M. K., Roper, L. D., Bryant, D. R., & Langa, M. J. (1990). Incorporating the development of African-American students into pyschosocial theories of student development. *Journal of College Student Development, 31,* 429–436.

Myers, L. J. (1993). *Understanding an Afrocentric world view: An introduction to optimal psychology.* Dubuque, IA: Kendall/Hunt.

Nobles, W. W. (1980). African philosophy: Foundations for Black psychology. In R. L. Jones (Ed.), *Black psychology* (pp. 23–36). New York: Harper & Row.

Palmer, P. J. (1983). *To know as we are known: Education as a spiritual journey.* San Francisco: Harper & Row.

Parham, T. A. (1989). Cycles of psychological nigrescence. *Counseling Psychologist, 17*(2), 187–226).

Parks, S. D. (2000). *Big questions, worthy dreams: Mentoring young adults in their search for meaning, purpose, and faith.* San Francisco: Jossey-Bass.

Patton, M. Q. (1990). *Qualitative evaluation and research methods* (2nd ed.). Newbury Park, CA: Sage.

Peterson, P. (1998). Why do educational research? Rethinking our roles and identities, our texts and contexts. *Educational Researcher, 27*(3), 4–10.

Schubert, W. (1986). *Curriculum: Perspective, paradigm, and possibility*. New York: Macmillan.

Sedlacek, W. E. (1987). Black students on White campuses: 20 years of research. *Journal of College Student Personnel, 28,* 484–495.

Seidman, I. (1998). *Interviewing as qualitative research: A guide for teachers in education and the social sciences*. New York: Teachers College Press.

Stake, R. (1994). Case studies. In N. Denzin & Y. Lincoln (Eds.), *The handbook of qualitative research* (pp. 236–247). Thousand Oaks, CA: Sage.

Wade-Gayles, G. (Ed.). (1995). *My soul is a witness: African-American women's spirituality*. Boston: Beacon.

White, J. L., & Parham, T. A. (1990). *The psychology of Blacks: An African American perspective* (2nd ed.). Englewood Cliffs, NJ: Prentice Hall.

UNIT III

Intrapersonal/Interpersonal Dimensions of Development

Section 4

PSYCHOSOCIAL DEVELOPMENT

CHAPTER 12

THE SEVEN VECTORS

ARTHUR W. CHICKERING AND LINDA REISSER

Our model does not portray development as one predominant challenge or crisis resolution after another, each invariably linked to specific ages. Development for college students, which today includes persons of virtually all ages, is a process of infinite complexity. Just as students are notorious for not proceeding through the institution according to schedule, they rarely fit into oversimplified paths or pigeonholes. We propose the seven vectors as maps to help us determine where students are and which way they are heading. Movement along any one can occur at different rates and can interact with movement along the others. Each step from "lower" to "higher" brings more awareness, skill, confidence, complexity, stability, and integration but does not rule out an accidental or intentional return to ground already traversed. We assume that "higher" is better than "lower," because in adding the skills and strengths encompassed by these vectors, individuals grow in versatility, strength, and ability to adapt when unexpected barriers or pitfalls appear.

We also recognize that developmental patterns described by psychosocial theorists may have been skewed by the exclusivity of their samples, as was the case for cognitive theorists. Women were less prominent in Erikson's thinking, and males were initially excluded from Loevinger's sample. Nontraditional students and members of minority groups often were left out altogether. These deficiencies are now being corrected. For example, there have been studies on identity formation for women (Josselson, 1987), on nonwhite students (Cross, 1971; Helms, 1990, Sue and Sue, 1971; Martinez, 1988; Johnson and Lashley, 1988; Atkinson, Morten, and Sue, 1983; Ho, 1987; Branch-Simpson, 1984), and on homosexual students (Cass, 1979; Coleman, 1981–1982; Dank, 1971; Minton and McDonald, 1983–1984; Plummer, 1975; Troiden, 1979). Many of these studies seem to be turning up variations in style and sequence, but the fundamental themes reappear and continue to serve as foundations for the seven vectors.

The vectors describe major highways for journeying toward individuation—the discovery and refinement of one's unique way of being—and also toward communion with other individuals and groups, including the larger national and global society. We propose that while each person will drive differently, with varying vehicles and self-chosen detours, eventually all will move down these major routes. They may have different ways of thinking, learning, and deciding, and those differences will affect the way the journey unfolds, but for all the different stories about turning points and valuable lessons, college students live out recurring themes: gaining competence and self-awareness, learning control and flexibility, balancing intimacy with freedom, finding one's voice or vocation, refining beliefs, and making commitments.

Since we refrained from describing development in terms of Erikson's age-specific crises, we are hesitant to portray it as movement from one stage or position to the next. Rest (1979) differentiated between "simple-stage models" and "complex-stage models." Using simple-stage models, a typical assessment question was, "What stage is a person in?" Assuming one stage at a time with no overlapping, no skipping of stages, and no steps backward, it should be easy to pinpoint where a student is and design challenges to foster the next step. Loevinger, Perry, and Kohlberg, following Piaget's lead, envisioned cognitive structures that evolved in an orderly fashion. Like windows built into a house, they became relatively fixed lenses for interpreting reality and screening input. Major remodeling was needed to change the windows. Once the new model was installed, it was as hard to go back to the old structure as to replace stained glass with a plain windowpane. Furthermore, the brain would not move from windowpane to stained glass in one leap. A sliding glass door had to come next, and then beveled, leaded designs, perhaps with inset mirrors and magnifying glasses. Perry differed from his colleagues in allowing for escape, retreat, and delay in his theory of intellectual development. For others, it was onward and upward, and while it was easy for a student to look back with disdain on an earlier way of thinking, it was hard to see beyond the next level of complexity, let alone understand an instructor who was teaching two or more stages ahead.

King (1990, pp. 83–84) warns against an overly simplified description of cognitive processes, which are inconsistent with many research findings. "For example, people don't seem to change from the exclusive use of one set of assumptions to the exclusive use of those of the next adjacent stage; rather, the use of assumptions characteristic of several stages at once often has been found. Stage usage seems to be influenced by a variety of individual factors (e.g., consolidation of existing structures, fatigue, readiness for change) and environmental factors (e.g., whether one is asked to create one's own solution to a problem or to critique someone else's solution, explaining one's beliefs verbally or in writing)." Different test characteristics and demands call forth different cognitive structures. Rest (1979, p. 63) proposes that instead of trying to assess what stage the person is in, we should ask, "To what extent and under what conditions does a person manifest the various types of organizations of thinking?"

A linear perspective may also frustrate those who want to help students achieve the upper reaches of stage theories. Pascarella and Terenzini (1991, p. 35) found no evidence of college students functioning at any of the final three stages of Loevinger's model. Kohlberg (1972) found that stage 4 (law and order) was the predominant stage in most societies. Perry (1970) was more optimistic, saying that perhaps 75 percent of the seniors in his study had reached positions 7 and 8. Subsequent research found Perry position scores ranging from 2 to 5, with no students scoring at the committed positions (Kurfiss, 1975; Pascarella and Terenzini, 1991, p. 30). This does not mean that higher levels are not present or possible. In fact, as our student populations diversify, the likelihood that all the stages will be represented increases. It may mean that the strategies for assessing developmental levels still need refining, or it may mean that the journey is a more logical priority than the destination.

Given the limitations of sequential models, we have proposed a sequence in order to suggest that certain building blocks make a good foundation. Some tasks are more likely to be encountered early in the journey. College students, regardless of age, will be challenged to develop intellectual competence. If the college does nothing else, it will try to move students along this vector. If it requires physical education or encourages athletics and if it supports participation in music, art, drama, or dance, it will foster physical and manual competence. Unless the new student makes a serious effort to remain isolated, the experience of meeting new people inside and outside of class will stimulate interpersonal competence. Whether leaving home for the first time or returning to college late in life, students will face loneliness, anxiety, frustration, and conflict. They will be required to make decisions, set goals, and develop greater autonomy. While younger students may be more obsessed with sex and romance, older students may be forming new relationships and perhaps reexamining earlier ones in light of what they are reading and whom they are meeting. Therefore, it is likely that a college will move students along these first four vectors, and growth in each area helps construct identity. Most students also experience greater clarity about purposes, values, and ways of thinking. If they are lucky, they will discover interests and people they care deeply about and will make lasting commitments. And they will expand their awareness of who they are and of how valuable they are.

Few developmental theories have paid much attention to emotions and relationships. More work has been done on thoughts and values. Our theory assumes that emotional, interpersonal, and ethical development deserve equal billing with intellectual development.

TABLE 1
The Seven Vectors: General Developmental Directions

From	To
Developing Competence	
Low level of competence (intellectual, physical, interpersonal)	High level of competence in each area
Lack of confidence in one's abilities	Strong sense of competence
Managing Emotions	
Little control over disruptive emotions (fear and anxiety, anger leading to aggression, depression, guilt, and shame, and dysfunctional sexual or romantic attraction)	Flexible control and appropriate expression
Little awareness of feelings	Increasing awareness and acceptance of emotions
Inability to integrate feelings with actions	Ability to integrate feelings with responsible action
Moving Through Autonomy Toward Interdependence	
Emotional dependence	Freedom from continual and pressing needs for reassurance
Poor self-direction or ability to solve problems; little freedom or confidence to be mobile	Instrumental independence (inner direction, persistence, and mobility)
Independence	Recognition and acceptance of the importance of interdependence
Developing Mature Interpersonal Relationships	
Lack of awareness of differences; intolerance of differences	Tolerance and appreciation of differences
Nonexistent, short-term, or unhealthy intimate relationships	Capacity for intimacy which is enduring and nurturing
Establishing Identity	
Discomfort with body and appearance	Comfort with body and appearance
Discomfort with gender and sexual orientation	Comfort with gender and sexual orientation
Lack of clarity about heritage and social/cultural roots of identity	Sense of self in a social, historical, and cultural context
Confusion about "who I am" and experimentation with roles and lifestyles	Clarification of self-concept through roles and lifestyle
Lack of clarity about others' evaluation	Sense of self in response to feedback from valued others
Dissatisfaction with self	Self-acceptance and self-esteem
Unstable, fragmented personality	Personal stability and integration
Developing Purpose	
Unclear vocational goals	Clear vocational goals
Shallow, scattered personal interests	More sustained, focused, rewarding activities
Few meaningful interpersonal commitments	Strong interpersonal and family commitments
Developing Integrity	
Dualistic thinking and rigid beliefs	Humanizing values
Unclear or untested personal values and beliefs	Personalizing (clarifying and affirming) values while respecting others' beliefs
Self-interest	Social responsibility
Discrepancies between values and actions	Congruence and authenticity

How does this revision differ from the earlier version of *Education and Identity*?

1. The fifth vector, *freeing interpersonal relationships,* had been retitled *developing mature interpersonal relationships* and moved back in sequence, prior to *establishing identity.* We did this primarily to recognize the importance of students' experiences with relationships in the formation of their core sense of self.

2. The chapter on the *Managing Emotions* vector has been broadened beyond the earlier focus on aggression and sexual desire to address anxiety, depression, anger, shame, and guilt, as well as more positive emotions.

3. We have placed more emphasis on the importance of interdependence, while not denying the significance of learning independence and self-sufficiency. Instead of retaining the term *developing autonomy,* we have renamed this vector *Moving through autonomy toward interdependence.*

4. More emphasis has been placed on the intercultural aspects of tolerance as a component of developing mature interpersonal relationships, which also entails a growing capacity for intimacy.

5. We have added more complexity to the *developing identity* vector. We have noted issues raised by recent researchers concerning differences in identity development based on gender, ethnic background, and sexual orientation.

6. More current research findings have been cited as they relate to the vectors (although this book is not meant to contain a thorough review of the literature).

7. We have added illustrative statements from students to reflect greater diversity. Where earlier statements reinforce the text, they have been left in.

Like many humanistic models, this one is founded on an optimistic view of human development, assuming that a nurturing, challenging college environment will help students grow in stature and substance. Erikson believed in an epigenetic principle. Rogers saw a benign pattern at work in human beings, similar to the process that turns acorns into oak trees. The ancient Greeks had a concept alien to our modern-day emphasis on specialization and fragmentation between body and mind, between the physical and the spiritual. It is called *aretê.* According to the Greek scholar H.D.F. Kitto (1963, pp. 171–172), it was their ideal:

> When we meet it in Plato we translate it "Virtue" and consequently miss all the flavour of it. "Virtue," at least in modern English, is almost entirely a moral word; *aretê* on the other hand is used indifferently in all the categories and means simply "excellence." It may be limited of course by its context; the *aretê* of a race-horse is speed, of a cart-horse strength. If it is used, in a general context, of a man it will connote excellence in the ways in which a man can be excellent—morally, intellectually, physically, practically. Thus the hero of the Odyssey is a great fighter, a wily schemer, a ready speaker, a man of stout heart and broad wisdom who knows that he must endure without too much complaining what the gods send; and he can both build and sail a boat, drive a furrow as straight as anyone, beat a young braggart at throwing the discus, challenge the Phraecian youth at boxing, wrestling, or running; flay, skin, cut up, and cook an ox, and be moved to tears by a song. He is in fact an excellent all-rounder; he has surpassing *aretê.*

Kitto says that "this instinct for seeing things whole is the source of the essential sanity in Greek life" (p. 176). Institutions that emphasize intellectual development to the exclusion of other strengths and skills reinforce society's tendency to see some aspects of its citizens and not others. Just as individuals are not just consumers, competitors, and taxpayers, so students are not just degree seekers and test takers. To develop all the gifts of human potential, we need to be able to see them whole and to believe in their essential worth. In revising the seven vectors, we hope to offer useful tools to a new generation of practitioners who want to help students become "excellent all-rounders." We also hope to inspire experienced faculty, administrators, and student services and support staff to recommit to the mission of nurturing mind, body, heart, and spirit.

The Seven Vectors: An Overview

Lasting personality changes may not occur in a blinding flash. As Dylan Thomas (1939, pp. 29–30) said, "Light breaks where no sun shines . . . Dawn breaks behind the eyes . . . Light breaks on secret lots . . . On tips of thought. . . ." While some epiphanies are dramatic and sudden, most occur gradually and incrementally. We may not know for years that a single lecture or conversation or experience started a chain reaction that transformed some aspect of ourselves. We cannot easily discern what subtle mix of people, books, settings, or events promotes growth. Nor can we easily name changes in ways of thinking, feeling, or interpreting the world. But we can observe behavior and record words, both of which can reveal shifts from hunch to analysis, from simple to complex perceptions, from divisive bias to compassionate understanding: Theory can give us the lenses to see these changes and help them along.

The challenges students, faculty, and administrators face today can be overwhelming. While the 1960s brought protest marches, drug busts, demands for curricular relevance, and students insisting on shared power, it was also an era of expanding budgets, new construction, and innovative programs. The boom lasted through the 1970s, and longer in some states. The resources were there to support adequate staffing, burgeoning specialization, and bold experiments. Perhaps we should have foreseen the pendulum swinging backward. Now administrators spend a great deal of time stretching dollars, consolidating services, and managing crises. Faculty are teaching larger classes or worrying about too few enrollees, fretting about retirement, relying on adjunct instructors, scrutinizing contracts, and going to union meetings. Students are facing higher tuition, longer lines, and fewer seats in the classroom. With higher costs, bleaker job prospects, and more evident crime statistics, students may focus more on security than on self-improvement.

Student development theory must apply to this generation of students as well as to future ones. It must be useful to institutional leaders as they cope with retrenchment as well as expansion. Without a developmental philosophy at the core of the college, it can become a dispensary of services, a training ground for jobs that may not exist, or a holding tank for those not sure what to do next. Institutions that impart transferable skills and relevant knowledge, bolster confidence and creativity, and engender social responsibility and self-directed learning are needed more then ever. To be effective in educating the whole student, colleges must hire and reinforce staff members who understand what student development looks like and how to foster it.

The seven vectors provide such a model. Though they were originally proposed as major constellations of development during adolescence and early adulthood, we have attempted to apply the vectors to adults as well. We have tried to use language that is gender free and appropriate for persons of diverse backgrounds. The vectors have stood the test of time as conceptual lenses. They have enabled higher education practitioners to view their students, their courses, and their programs more clearly and to use them as beacons for change. Those who have kept up to date on research, or who want more specificity and complexity, may be frustrated by our level of generality. Yet we believe that the original version of the model has been useful precisely because of its broad conceptual nature, leaving practitioners the options of putting their own understanding and interpretation into it and applying it within their own contexts.

We have also attempted to tie this model to student perceptions of their experience. We have drawn excerpts from student self-assessments, short reflection exercises, and papers on developmental theories where autobiographical examples were included. Over a period of three years, I (Reisser) invited students in my classes and professionals attending my presentations to complete a "developmental worksheet" by writing anonymous responses to the following:

1. Briefly describe a change in yourself that had a major impact on how you lived your life. What was the "old" way of thinking or being, vs. the "new" way? What did you move *from* and what did you move *to*? How did you know that a significant change had occurred?

2. What were the important things (or persons) that *helped* the process? What did the person *do*? What was the experience that catalyzed the shift? Were there any *feelings* that helped or accompanied the process?

In all, 120 worksheets were collected, and though they were not based on carefully designed sampling procedures, the statements excerpted from them bring to life the potentially dry formality of theory. When students' research or reflection papers included relevant examples; I (Reisser) asked to keep copies for future writing projects on student development. Students' statements from the 1969 edition were also used here to illustrate developmental stages.

The seven vectors are summarized below.

1. *Developing competence.* Three kinds of competence develop in college—intellectual competence, physical and manual skills, and interpersonal competence. Intellectual competence is skill in using one's mind. It involves mastering content, gaining intellectual and aesthetic sophistication, and, most important, building a repertoire of skills to comprehend, analyze, and synthesize. It also entails developing new frames of reference that integrate more points of view and serve as "more adequate" structures for making sense out of our observations and experiences.

Physical and manual competence can involve athletic and artistic achievement, designing and making tangible products, and gaining strength, fitness, and self-discipline. Competition and creation bring emotions to the surface since our performance and our projects are on display for others' approval or criticism. Leisure activities can become lifelong pursuits and therefore part of identity.

Interpersonal competence entails not only the skills of listening, cooperating, and communicating effectively, but also the more complex abilities to tune in to another person and respond appropriately, to align personal agendas with the goals of the group, and to choose from a variety of strategies to help a relationship flourish or a group function.

Students' overall sense of competence increases as they learn to trust their abilities, receive accurate feedback from others, and integrate their skills into a stable self-assurance.

2. *Managing emotions:* Whether new to college or returning after time away, few students escape anger, fear, hurt, longing, boredom, and tension. Anxiety, anger, depression, desire, guilt, and shame have the power to derail the educational process when they become excessive or overwhelming. Like unruly employees, these emotions need good management. The first task along this vector is not to eliminate them but to allow them into awareness and acknowledge them as signals, much like the oil light on the dashboard.

Development proceeds when students learn appropriate channels for releasing irritations before they explode, dealing with fears before they immobilize, and healing emotional wounds before they infect other relationships. It may be hard to accept that some amount of boredom and tension is normal, that some anxiety helps performance, and that impulse gratification must sometimes be squelched.

Some students come with the faucets of emotional expression wide open, and their task is to develop flexible controls. Others have yet to open the tap. Their challenge is to get in touch with the full range and variety of feelings and to learn to exercise self-regulation rather than repression. As self-control and self-expression come into balance, awareness and integration ideally support each other.

More positive kinds of emotions have received less attention from researchers. They include feelings like rapture, relief, sympathy, yearning, worship, wonder, and awe. These may not need to be "managed" so much as brought into awareness and allowed to exist. Students must learn to balance self-assertive tendencies, which involve some form of aggressiveness or defensiveness, with participatory tendencies, which involve transcending the boundaries of the individual self, identifying or bonding with another, or feeling part of a larger whole.

3. *Moving through autonomy toward interdependence.* A key developmental step for students is learning to function with relative self-sufficiency, to take responsibility for pursuing self-chosen goals, and to be less bound by others' opinions. Movement requires both emotional and instrumental independence, and later recognition and acceptance of interdependence.

Emotional independence means freedom from continual and pressing needs for reassurance, affection, or approval. It begins with separation from parents and proceeds through reliance on peers, nonparental adults, and occupational or institutional reference groups. It culminates in diminishing need for such supports and increased willingness to risk loss of friends or status in order to pursue strong interests or stand on convictions.

Instrumental independence has two major components: the ability to organize activities and to solve problems in a self-directed way, and the ability to be mobile. It means developing that volitional part of the self that can think critically and independently and that can then translate ideas into focused action. It also involves learning to get from one place to another, without having to be taken by the hand or given detailed directions, and to find the information or resources required to fulfill personal needs and desires.

Developing autonomy culminates in the recognition that one cannot operate in a vacuum and that greater autonomy enables healthier forms of interdependence. Relationships with parents are revised. New relationships based on equality and reciprocity replace the older, less consciously chosen peer bonds. Interpersonal context broadens to include the community, the society, the world. The need to be independent and the longing for inclusion become better balanced. Interdependence means respecting the autonomy of others and looking for ways to give and take with an ever-expanding circle of friends.

4. *Developing mature interpersonal relationships.* Developing mature relationships involves (1) tolerance and appreciation of differences (2) capacity for intimacy. Tolerance can be seen in both an intercultural and an interpersonal context. At its heart is the ability to respond to people in their own right rather than as stereotypes or transference objects calling for particular conventions. Respecting differences in close friends can generalize to acquaintances from other continents and cultures. Awareness, breadth of experience, openness, curiosity, and objectivity help students refine first impressions, reduce bias and ethnocentrism, increase empathy and altruism, and enjoy diversity.

In addition to greater tolerance, the capacity for healthy intimacy increases. For most adolescent couples, each is the pool and each the Narcissus. Satisfying relationships depend on spatial proximity, so that each can nod to the other and in the reflection observe himself or herself. Developing mature relationships means not only freedom from narcissism, but also the ability to choose healthy relationships and make lasting commitments based on honesty, responsiveness, and unconditional regard. Increased capacity for intimacy involves a shift in the quality of relationships with intimates and close friends. The shift is away from too much dependence or too much dominance and toward an interdependence between equals. Development means more in-depth sharing and less clinging, more acceptance of flaws and appreciation of assets, more selectivity in choosing nurturing relationships, and more long-lasting relationships that endure through crises, distance, and separation.

5. *Establishing identity.* Identity formation depends in part on the other vectors already mentioned: competence, emotional maturity, autonomy, and positive relationships. Develop-

ing identity is like assembling a jigsaw puzzle, remodeling a house, or seeking one's "human rhythms," a term that Murphy (1958) illustrated by photic driving. A person watching an instrument that emits flashes at precise intervals eventually hits a breaking point—the point at which the rhythm induces a convulsion. If, for example, the number is sixteen, the observer may rapidly lose consciousness as this number is presented in the standard time interval. Seventeen and fifteen, however, are safe numbers. It is not until thirty-two or some other multiple of sixteen is reached that a breakdown recurs. Like the piano wire that hums or like the glass that shatters, we will have our critical frequencies in a variety of areas. Development of identity is the process of discovering with what kinds of experience, at what levels of intensity and frequency, we resonate in satisfying, in safe, or in self-destructive fashion.

Development of identity involves: (1) comfort with body and appearance, (2) comfort with gender and sexual orientation, (3) sense of self in a social, historical, and cultural context, (4) clarification of self-concept through roles and life-style, (5) sense of self in response to feedback from valued others, (6) self-acceptance and self-esteem, and (7) personal stability and integration. A solid sense of self emerges, and it becomes more apparent that there is an *I* who coordinates the facets of personality, who "owns" the house of self and is comfortable in all of its rooms.

College student concern with appearance is obvious. Though gowns no longer prevail except at Oxford and Cambridge, town residents recognize students, especially younger ones who don emblems of student culture. Whatever the limitations or prescriptions, experimentation occurs. With clarification of identity, however, it diminishes. By graduation, most of the early creative—or bizarre—variations are given up. Experimentation with dress and appearance herald pathways to sexual identity. Looking at old high school yearbooks confirms the evolution of hairstyles. Macho, androgynous, or femme fatale "looks" come and go, but identity hinges on finding out what it means to be a man or a woman and coming to terms with one's sexuality.

Establishing identity also includes reflecting on one's family of origin and ethnic heritage, defining self as a part of a religious or cultural tradition, and seeing self within a social and historical context. It involves finding roles and styles at work, at play, and at home that are genuine expressions of self and that further sharpen self-definition. It involves gaining a sense of how one is seen and evaluated by others. It leads to clarity and stability and a feeling of warmth for this core self as capable, familiar, worthwhile.

6. *Developing purpose.* Many college students are all dressed up and do not know where they want to go. They have energy but no destination. While they may have clarified who they are and where they came from, they have only the vaguest notion of who they want to be. For large numbers of college students, the purpose of college is to qualify them for a good job, not to help them build skills applicable in the widest variety of life experiences; it is to ensure a comfortable life-style, not to broaden their knowledge base, find a philosophy of life, or become a lifelong learner.

Developing purpose entails an increasing ability to be intentional, to assess interests and options, to clarify goals, to make plans, and to persist despite obstacles. It requires formulating plans for action and a set of priorities that integrate three major elements: (1) vocational plans and aspirations, (2) personal interests, and (3) interpersonal and family commitments. It also involves a growing ability to unify one's many different goals within the scope of a larger, more meaningful purpose, and to exercise intentionality on a daily basis.

We use the term *vocation* in its broadest sense—as specific career or as broad calling. Vocations can include paid work, unpaid work, or both. We discover our vocation by discovering what we love to do, what energizes and fulfills us, what uses our talents and challenges us to develop new ones, and what actualizes all our potentials for excellence. Ideally, these vocational plans flow from deepening interests, and in turn, lend momentum to further aspirations that have meaning and value. Considerations of life-style and family also enter the question. As intimate relationships increasingly involve the question of long-term partnership and as formal education and vocational exploration draw to a close, next steps must be identified. It is difficult to construct a plan that balances life-style considerations, vocational aspirations, and avocational interests. Many compromises must be made, and clearer values help the decision-making process.

7. *Developing integrity.* Developing integrity is closely related to establishing identity and clarifying purposes. Our core values and beliefs provide the foundation for interpreting experience, guiding behavior, and maintaining self-respect. Developing integrity involves three sequential but overlapping stages: (1) humanizing values—shifting away from automatic application of uncompromising beliefs and using principled thinking in balancing one's own self-interest with the interests of one's fellow human beings, (2) personalizing values—consciously affirming core values and beliefs while respecting other points of view, and (3) developing congruence—matching personal values with socially responsible behavior.

Humanizing values involves a shift from a literal belief in the absoluteness of rules to a more relative view, where connections are made between rules and the purposes they are meant to serve. Thus, the rules for a ball game can change to accommodate limited numbers of players or other unusual conditions; rules concerning honesty, sex, or aggressiveness can vary with circumstances and situations, while overriding principles (such as the Golden Rule) become more important. This change has also been called "liberalization of the superego" or "enlightenment of conscience"—the process by which the rigid rules received unquestioned from parents are reformulated in the light of wider experience and made relevant to new conditions (Sanford, 1962, p. 278).

Students bring to college an array of assumptions about what is right and wrong, true and false, good and bad, important and unimportant. Younger students may have acquired these assumptions from parents, church, school, media, or other sources. When others' values are internalized, most behavior conforms even when the judge is absent. Disobedience produces either diffuse anxiety or specific fear of discovery and punishment. Most of the values are implicit and unconsciously held; therefore, they are hard to identify or explain. With humanizing of values, much of this baggage comes to light. The contents are examined. Many items are discarded on brief inspection, sometimes with later regret. Some items are tried and found unsuitable. A few are set aside because they still fit and can be incorporated into a new wardrobe.

Personalizing of values occurs as the new wardrobe is assembled. Ultimately, the items selected are those required by the characteristics of the wearer, by the work expected to be done, by the situations to be encountered, and by the persons who are seen as important. In short, individuals select guidelines to suit themselves and to suit the conditions of their lives. In time, the components of this wardrobe are actively embraced as part of the self and become standards by which to flexibly assess personal actions.

Personalizing of values leads to the development of congruence—the achievement of behavior consistent with the personalized values held. With this final stage, internal debate is minimized. Once the implications of a situation are understood and the consequences of alternatives seem clear, the response is highly determined; it is made with conviction, without debate or equivocation.

These, then, are the seven major developmental vectors for college students. Each has additional components, and more detailed study reveals further ramifications. This overview, however, suggests the major configurations. The following chapters consider research and theory relevant to each vector in more detail.

Chapter 13

Identity

Ruthellen Josselson

Identity is the ultimate act of creativity—it is what we make of ourselves. In forming and sustaining our identity, we build a bridge between who we feel ourselves to be internally and who we are recognized as being by our social world. When we have a secure sense of our identity, we take ourselves for granted as being who we are. We feel at home in ourselves and in our world, and have an inner experience of coherence and purpose.

The psychologist Erik Erikson brought this central aspect of our existence to our attention, and his ideas about the "identity crisis" have resonated deeply in Western culture. Identity represents knowing who we are in the context of all that we might be. The sense of crisis is the experience of questioning what we have taken as a given: "I have always been like this, but perhaps I could still be otherwise. I could make and live out different choices."

Most people would become confused and confounded if asked what their identity is. Identity emerges; it is greater than the sum of its parts—much like a cake is the product of its ingredients and not a simple compound. Although composed of discrete, conscious elements, identity is bound and organized internally and unconsciously and cannot be easily contained in words. In forming a core of who we "are," identity weaves together all the aspects of ourselves and our various locations of ourselves with others and with the larger society. What we connect ourselves to feels part of ourselves; the world is imbued with self: *my* project, *my* husband, *my* cause. Identity also excludes all the things we are not (and often it is easier to identify ourselves by naming what we are not). Usually, we include in our identity an economic function in society, a set of meanings we have for others, a place in a sequence of generations, and a set of beliefs and values. We may also have an unusual genetic makeup, an atypical early history or family background, an eccentric temperament or psychological structure, or we may have special abilities or disabilities. Any of these may channel our lives in one way and not another.

The *experience* of identity is one of meaningful continuity over time and place. We recognize more and more what it means to be who we are, rather than someone else. "To be adult," Erikson said, "means among other things to see one's own life in continuous perspective, both in retrospect and in prospect." Identity, then, proclaims our sameness-as-ourselves in containing our life story, but identity also evolves and changes over time as we grow. It is, therefore, our continuity in the process of revision.

People, of course, grow within a culture. Identity is what we make of ourselves within a society that is making something of us. Identity "makes sense" only within the context of a particular social and historical time.

Societies limit what is possible for the individual. We might question why things are the way they are, but there are boundaries imposed by our society on the desires and ambitions we might realize and on the choices we might make. The more open the society, the more choices possible.

In modern Western society, there is much latitude in how we might earn our living, how we construct our relationships with others, what we may believe spiritually and politically, how we spend discretionary time, and how we care for our physical well-being. We differ from one another in how we arrange these elements of our lives, to what we give priority, and how we interpret what we have created. Some people do all this without giving it much thought, experiencing their identities as "natural," as givens, as lives unfolding according to inevitability, a plan constructed elsewhere. Others are self-conscious about who they are, analyzing their choices, carefully considering a plethora of possibilities, envisioning alternate selves.

Crisis in identity can be spurred either by inner change or social dislocation. We might arrive at periods in our lives where our past ways of being feel no longer gratifying, and we may then cast about for means of transformation. Or social change may lead us to have to rearticulate ourselves in the social world—we can no longer maintain our customary position in relation to others by being just as we have always been. What is acceptable and valued in one place and time may be scorned in another.

When we move about our world harmoniously, taking ourselves and our meaning to others for granted, identity functions as a silent gatekeeper. We are who we are and occupy ourselves with being rather than with creating ourselves. Erikson has said that we are most aware of our identity when we are just about to make its acquaintance. Living our identities is much like breathing. We don't have to ask ourselves each morning who we are. We simply are. As life progresses, we may add new elements and find room for them in the mixture. We may discard others through disuse. Identity is never fixed; it continually evolves. But something in it stays constant; even when we change, we are recognizably who we have always been. Identity links the past, the present, and the social world into a narrative that makes sense. It embodies both change and continuity.

As I track the identities of the women I have followed for twenty years, I am impressed by how the woman of 43 is unmistakably like the young woman of 21, yet very different. If I were to scramble the tapes and remove all identifying information, a thoughtful listener would still be able to match them up. It is also true, however, that some women have changed more than others.

"Who Are You?" Said the Caterpillar

When we feel we are "getting to know" someone, we are in the process of becoming aware of another's identity. What matters to you? What goals do you pursue? How do you want others to think of you? What do you believe in? What guides your actions? Whom do you love? What values do you hold dear? Where do you expend your passion? What causes you pain? These are the central questions of knowing another and knowing ourselves—the questions of identity.

We know ourselves both through our shared identities and our distinctiveness from others. We identify ourselves with others who share our goals or values and thereby feel affirmed in who we are. But we also know ourselves through contrasting ourselves with others, feeling the edges of our individuality in noting what so uniquely belongs to us.

Each of us confronts a different challenge in fashioning our identity. We begin with different pieces, different experiences and realities. Natural talents, physical attractiveness, social privilege, temperament, social ease, physical limitations, and traumatic early experiences—all these are building blocks that we must fit into the design. Each of us has been offered different puzzle pieces with which we must assemble a complete picture. We must each make something of ourselves. If we don't, our society will provide us an identity from the bag of deviant labels it has for people who don't create it for themselves.

Identity, however, is complex and cannot be stated simply. We are not the same in all regions of our lives, and how we make meaning may change across situations or over time. Identity is what integrates our own diversity, gives meaning to the disparate parts of ourselves, and relates them to one another. Identity is how we interpret our own existence and understand who we are in our world. I am a woman, but my identity as a woman is my unique way of being a woman in the culture in which I live. And so on with other aspects of my (or your) identity.

Identity and Society

Society, in making certain ways of being possible and others impossible or very difficult, is a powerful agent in shaping identity. "Cultures," say Shotter and Gergen (1989), "lay out an array of enabling potentials and also establish a set of constraining boundaries beyond which selves cannot be easily made" (p. ix). On the other hand, we, as a society, create these enabling potentials and boundaries and thereby shape the individuals who will compose our social world. We create them and we can change them. We have a vested interest in what kinds of identity we make possible. When we worry together about social influence, we are concerned with what sort of individuals our social conditions are likely to foster. We ask, for example, what it means to have so much violence on TV? What kinds of people will this make in the future? Or we wonder about changes in family structure. What will individual identities look like if family attachment erodes as a keystone of social life? What we create together as a society forms the framework for identity for the next generation.

Although modern Western industrial society embraces individualistic values, upholding the ideals of individual self-determination and the right to self-definition, we must have something in common with one another, some shared beliefs, goals, and attitudes in order to have a society at all. We cannot escape being affected by what each of us chooses. We are bound together, and the identities of each individual both limit and empower the identities of others.

While the context of identity is, in part, the larger culture, for each particular person, identity is understood, evaluated, and transmuted by the people around her—family, friends, colleagues, neighbors, and so on. Social influence occurs in thousands of ways, some at a general level, such as the media, but others closer to home, through people and experiences in one's immediate world. A chance conversation with an old friend can have profound impact on identity. Recognizing that someone else—someone we know and accept—is taking a risk or living a dream that we desire for ourselves can give us permission to do what we had been afraid to do. These local, personal influences are largely responsible for the rapid shift in our society's ideas about how women might live in our soci-

ety. Identity, then, is not just a private, individual matter. Instead, it is a complex negotiation between the person and a society.

Identity and Women

Nowhere in the modern age has the issue of identity been more vexing than in our society's confusion over the roles it is willing to allot to women. Women born after World War II spent their girlhoods in a world where women's possibilities were sharply defined and clearly delimited and seemed to have been that way since history began. A woman's mission was to marry and raise children, though she might also be a teacher or a nurse before having children or after her children were grown. Her social place and value were defined by her husband, and young girls dreamed of one day becoming "Mrs. Someone." The idea of a woman retaining her name, symbolically maintaining her own selfhood, was not to emerge until women of this (my) generation were in their late adolescence in the late 1960s. Erikson, in 1968, mindful of the social limits imposed on women, said, "I think that much of a young woman's identity is already defined in her kind of attractiveness and in the selective nature of her search for the man (or men) by whom she wishes to be sought."

That identity for women derives from marriage was a theme pervading the literature of the times—and of previous times as well. In most novels, the path to marriage is the only real drama in a woman's life, the only realm of decision, of possibility, of surprise. The cultural narrative of women's lives, told in literature, was a story of growth, events, and choices leading to marriage. Carolyn Heilbrun, in her book, *Writing a Woman's Life*, discusses the way in which the courtship plot has dominated literary portrayal of women: "The woman must entrap the man to ensure herself a center for her life. The rest is aging and regret."

But women of the postwar generation could extend this plot, could create lives beyond marriage, aging, and regret. These women came of age in a time of social rearrangement about what was expected of or permissible for women. They came of age in a society that was in the throes of beginning to take women seriously, as productive workers, voters with independent minds, forces within the social order, as people with a right to self-fulfillment. The society began to wonder whether women might be equivalent to men, with similar needs and deserving of equal rewards and recognition. Instead of having to resign themselves to constricted, narrow options, the women of this generation, led by the rising chorus of feminism, were prepared to demand that locked doors be opened to them.

Psychology and Woman

Psychology, the intellectual discipline that explores—and shapes—our understanding of human life, also had to come to terms with a revolution in how it might regard women. Most psychological studies before 1970 merely disregarded women altogether or, with a wave of the hand, assumed that women were probably pretty much like men in terms of universal psychological principles. At least, the "laws" of human behavior that psychology adduced were derived from studies of men and applied to "people."

But women have always constructed their identities in different phrasing from men and, except for Erikson's comment that women readied themselves for the men they wished to be sought by, on this topic psychology was largely silent. The early efforts of psychologists to investigate identity in women, which began in the 1970s, tended to try to find "male" patterns in women or at least to discover women who were sufficiently "masculine" in their orientation that they would behave on psychological tests much like men did. Only in the 1980s did psychology begin to embrace the fact that women have a definable identity, but that they construct this identity in relational terms, different from men, but not simply as selves defined by husbands or children. Women construct themselves in the voice of care and of connection, to use psychologist Carol Gilligan's words. This led to the quest for a new vocabulary for women's identity, an effort to find ways of thinking about women that were beyond the "marriage plot," but did not merely translate women into the familiar lexicon of the male sense of self.

Identity expresses both our separateness from others (who we are within our individuality) and our ways of connecting ourselves to others (who and how we are with other people). In women, identity tends to be phrased more in relational, pattern-building terms than in the language of separateness. A woman forms her sense of herself through connections with others—at home, at work, and in her values and beliefs. Identity in women is more rooted in "being" than in "doing," and a woman's life story is often centered on how she experiences herself, or wishes to experience herself, with others. Love is a way of delineating the self, not of losing the self, as many have wrongly concluded.

How a woman comes to define her identity is a process of articulating herself with others, bridging what feels inner and necessary with what opportunities she has for expressing herself in interaction. With the wider social choices available to women after 1970, a woman had the task of finding her place in a more complex way than ever before. She could marry, but how she defined her marriage was open to vast possibility. She could work in the field of her choice, in domains that had been closed just years before, and she was challenged to take up these roles in her own voice. She could have children or not and, if she had children, she had to mother in a way quite different from the way in which her mother had. She could continue her professional ambitions and still raise a family. Spirituality and religion became matters of choice rather than acceptance of authority, and the defining of ideology became both more pressing and more diffuse than it had ever been. In all these spheres, a woman had the opportunity to locate herself, to define herself in ways newly available, often with no models to guide her.

Women and Choice

Some women embraced this opportunity for choice and tried to expand the framework in which they were raised in order to allow for greater self-expression. Others tended to take things pretty much as they found them, hoping only to "fit in." Still others tried to burst through whatever structure had contained them as girls, to experiment with themselves and try to create new selves or new worlds. Some women became heroines of their own lives, to paraphrase Dickens; others allowed circumstance or other people to fill that station.

How identity is formed determines its nature as much or more than the particular roles or values we may include. Rita and Jean, for example, may both be 40-year-old working mothers, and if this is all we are to know about them, we may regard them as similar. But if we also know that Rita went through a long process of choice and change before deciding to become an actress and delayed having children until she was professionally established, we understand that she is quite different from Jean who became a nurse without really thinking about it and had her children within a year of her marriage after college. These differences in the *process* of choosing an identity have been at the center of my study. How does a woman come to be who she is—with what consideration, what anguish, what commitment, and with what regret? What does she leave aside and relinquish and how does she decide to do this? How does a woman gather the reins of her life?

Pathways to Identity

"I didn't have my adolescence until my late twenties," said Grace, one of the women I have been interviewing, "not until after my divorce. After that, I became a whole different person." Grace is reflecting on how she has changed, the way in which her identity has evolved, and she is noting that her progression to identity seems to her different from what she assumes has been true for most people. People differ in whether and how they experiment with and organize their sense of identity—and this itself changes with time and development.

Initially, identity is ascribed to each of us. Babies are "identified" immediately—"she looks like your family"; "she has a bad temper just like my mother"; and so on. We are born to a certain family in a given social time, to a social class, a race and, of course, to a gender. In our families we learn what it is acceptable to do or to believe, we are given a religious framework and a set of values that form our way of viewing the world. This is the identity we carry through childhood into adolescence.

Modern industrialized societies that make available a variety of adult roles also allow young people a period in which they are granted permission to rework the identities ascribed to them through childhood. Erikson called this period a "moratorium," a time out for an "identity crisis" in which the young person is encouraged to become aware that familiar childhood ways of being and believing are not the only ones possible. With this sense of "I could be different," the young person tries out new possibilities, does some things she (or he) might never

have imagined doing before, and, in general, explores a range of possible selves. But this phase has a limit, and, at a certain point, the society indicates its readiness to "identify" a person, to take her seriously as being who she has chosen to be. The individual is then expected to declare herself by adopting particular ways of being and believing—in short, to commit herself to an identity.

The young person envisions, considers, explores, and then chooses. Identity commitments are sometimes made consciously with a lot of thought; at other times, they seem to "creep up" on the person who comes to take seriously aspects of herself that she thought she was just playing at. Who she chooses as friends, what interests she pursues, how hard she studies, whether she takes drugs or plays the flute or wins at tennis—all these might become significant elements of her identity.

But there are pitfalls and byways in this process. Some people are afraid to relinquish their childhood certainty about things; they strive to stay as much as possible the same as they have always been. Others are awash in choice, and no matter how much significant people in their life pressure them, they cannot commit themselves to a way of being.

I build on the work of psychologist James Marcia who found a way to study Erikson's theory of identity formation as a process that different people undertake in different ways. He reasoned that we could determine how far late adolescents have come in the course of their identity development by investigating whether or not they have experienced a period of exploration and whether or not they have made firm identity commitments. By interviewing late adolescents about their decision-making with regard to occupational choice, religious and political beliefs, and concerns about relationships, psychologists who followed his method could divide people into four distinct groups that placed them in one track or another along the path to identity formation (see Figure 1).

Guardians have made identity commitments without a sense of choice, carrying forward the plans for their life mapped out in childhood or designed by their parents. They are likely to feel, "This is how I am because it's how I was raised or how I've always been."

Pathmakers are people who have experienced a period of exploration or crisis and then made

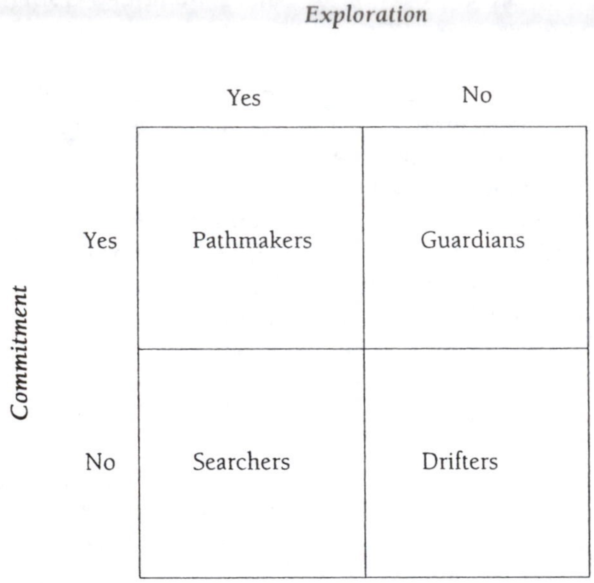

Exploration

	Yes	No
Yes	Pathmakers	Guardians
No	Searchers	Drifters

Commitment

Figure 1 Exploration

identity commitments on their own terms. Their orientation to their identity is, "I've tried out some things, and this is what makes most sense for me."

Searchers are still in an active period of struggle or exploration, trying to make choices but not yet having done so. They feel, "I'm not sure about who I am or want to be, but I'm trying to figure it out."

Drifters are without commitments and not struggling to make them, either feeling lost or following impulses of the moment. These people are likely to say, "I don't know what I will do or believe, but it doesn't matter too much right now."

Nearly thirty years of research and hundreds of studies have been conducted on college students using these four groups. They have been found to be groups who can be reliably assessed and groups that share predictable personality characteristics and ways of behaving.

I interviewed the women I have been studying when they were college seniors, a time when the future loomed ahead unwritten, no longer structured by their parents or the academic calendar. This was a time, as Erikson suggests, when the society was exacting choice from them, drawing the curtain on the era of preparation. What will I do next? was a pressing, urgent question. I used Jim Marcia's interview method to determine where they were in forming their

identities by asking them about four areas—occupation, religion, politics, and sexual standards—in which they might be deciding, areas central to identity. I evaluated whether they had had a period of exploration in deciding on their goals and values, and whether they had yet made clear choices. Had they considered options and experimented with possibilities for themselves, or had they stayed within the molds cast for them by their families? And, if they had explored, had they made some commitment, choices that would guide their next steps? Or, alternatively, were they leaving their future open to fate, avoiding choice, waiting to see where the currents might take them?

The differences among the four groups—those with and without exploration, those with and without commitment—reflect different ways of dealing with the challenges of adolescence. The four groups represent types or stances, different positions on the path to identity. And women who were following each of these paths had commonalities. Aspects of their personality structure, the deeper regions of their emotional makeup rooted in their early histories, in part determined the pathway they had followed to this point. But the style in which they were approaching identity dilemmas was not fixed forever. I interviewed and classified them at the end of college at an important moment, but I expected that they would continue to change, that their choices were only relatively firm rather than solid and unchangeable. But I didn't know and couldn't predict how they would change as their adulthood unfolded.

The end of college marks the close of the period that our society grants young people to experiment, to play with identity. After that, as Erikson says, society takes the person seriously—and young people feel the pressure of declaring themselves as in pursuit of certain ways of being while relinquishing others. Some of these women felt more ready to take a place than others—and this readiness was in part what distinguished these four groups.

The Four Pathways to Identity

The *Guardians* knew where they were going without having considered alternatives. Fern, for example, at the end of college, was sure of her goals and beliefs and answered all questions about her plans and her values by referring to how she had been raised. "My parents instilled these ideas in me," or "It's what I've *always* wanted to be when I grew up" were typical Guardian phrases. The Guardians had, as little girls, absorbed the values and attitudes of their families and still held fast to them or, as adolescents, found someone else to cling to who would define what was right for them. Many had childhood occupational dreams; all had strong moral or religious guideposts. Little or none of any of this was ever questioned; the crisis of exploration was avoided. These women leapfrogged over the challenges of adolescence, clutching what was safe and familiar. Moralistic and value-dominated, most of them held to an unassailable sense of what was right and wrong. They regarded the options of the times as threatening to their sense of certainty; they never rebelled or challenged. Reluctant to "leave home" emotionally, they wanted their adult lives, as much as possible, to be a continuation of the warmth and comfort of childhood in their families.

The *Pathmakers*, by contrast, were women who had followed Erikson's progression from exploration into commitment. After making the discovery, during college, that her parents' values and assumptions "were not necessarily the only way to be," Andrea set out to investigate other ways of situating herself in life and found herself wanting to become a kind of woman—a

professional woman, a nonreligious woman—that neither she nor her family had ever encountered. Some of the Pathmakers had had intense identity crises; some had only mild, but psychologically significant ones. All, however, had considered some options, tried out alternate ways of being or believing, and then made choices that they intended to be the basis for their adult sense of themselves. They were women who had taken some risks and tried out new ways of experiencing themselves that led them to integrate a stable sense of personal independence and make choices on their own terms. These choices were often formed in the context of important new relationships, but the choices felt self-authored—what I want for myself, what I have designed. These women charted their own course. They had enough inner strength to tolerate crisis and uncertainty and to design their lives to suit themselves. They stood on the threshold of adulthood with a plan, with a template of how they wanted to realize the identity they had sculpted. But, having relinquished childhood certainty, they were often anxious, worried that their plans might not work out, afraid sometimes of their own capacity for change. They had made compromises to achieve closure, but wondered if they hadn't perhaps given away more than was necessary.

Those women who were *Searchers* at the end of college were in the midst of crisis. Uncertain, sometimes intensely confused, they were struggling among possibilities, and were finding it hard to decide which road to take. These are women who fought their families and left their churches to march in anti-war protests, experimented with mind-altering drugs, had sex—and felt guilty about it all. They were critical of society and the obvious roles available to them and wanted something different for themselves—but what? The choices seemed overwhelming. How could they know what was Right? Highly perceptive, lively, and engaging, these women daydreamed of experiencing many things and finding a way of being that felt authentic. Other times, rent by ambivalence, they felt great anxiety about the future. No choice or value seemed completely comfortable, but they were wrestling to make choices nonetheless. Millie, for example, felt herself on a bumpy road and described her experience of searching like this: "It starts when you're little. You think your parents are gods. Then you find out they're only human, but you still believe what they say because they're your parents. I really don't want to hurt my parents, but I've got to live my own life. The more I learn, the more middle of the road I become. I learn that there are two sides of every story and it's hard that way because I like to have the Answers. But it seems like that's the way it's going—that you just can't say that this is right and this is wrong. It's hard to make decisions about things because there are so many avenues to go down."

Many Searchers felt guilty about having forsaken the values of their childhood and fearful that they weren't quite sure what they were doing with themselves. At the end of college, they were still wrestling with choice in the areas of their lives most significant to them. As graduation approached, however, the Searchers were still unable to choose.

The women I classified as *Drifters* were women who were neither in crisis nor had they made commitments. They were like leaves blown by the wind, living each day, sometimes happily, sometimes despairingly, but they tried to ignore the approach of the future. There were many different kinds of women in this group— no one person exemplifies it—but what they had in common was that they avoided decision-making. The daily choices they made were choices of the moment, and they didn't require themselves to be consistent or to make sense. Asked about her future, Debbie said offhandedly with a shrug, "When the time comes, I'll do something." Many had occupational dreams that lasted for a short time only to disappear until another might take its place; their relationships seemed equally unpredictable. Their values or standards shifted with each situation. They seemed to feel they would "go with the flow" wherever the flow might take them. When I got to know the Drifters better as college seniors, I found that many of these women had early inner conflicts that made it difficult to grapple with the developmentally more advanced issues of identity. While a few were simply "free spirits" who were exploring intensely and refusing to tie themselves to any post, others were preoccupied with unresolved emotional problems that showed themselves in impulsivity, depression, or personality fragmentation. As a group, the Drifters were swept along, sometimes enjoying themselves, sometimes in great pain, but they thought of the future as something that would organize itself when the time came.

No categorizing system, of course, can contain everyone. People always more or less fit into any grouping. These four groups represented an effort to sort people based on their ability to tolerate uncertainty and change, their readiness to imagine possibilities for themselves, their ability to use what they gained from their families without being enslaved to it, and their capacity for commitment at the end of college. When other colleagues listened to the tapes, we were able to agree about where each woman best fit, so this seemed to be a reliable as well as a meaningful form of classification.

These categories were designed to be descriptive rather than evaluative. Each style has both its advantages and its costs. The *Guardians*, for example, in their steadfastness can be regarded as either loyal or rigid, the *Pathmakers* as independent or prematurely certain of themselves. The *Searchers*, depending on one's point of view, can seem flexible and philosophical or anxious and indecisive. Similarly, one might respond to the *Drifters* as creative and free-spirited or irresponsible and disaffected. I mean only to name their characteristics and to explore what awaits the women who follow each path. I am not suggesting that one path is necessarily better or worse than another.

Identity and Revision

These four groups represent gateways to adulthood. Where a woman was on the path to identity determined how she would enter her adult life and this, in turn, would influence how the next chapters of her life might be written. The pathway she was following at the end of college served as a portal to the future, a way of entering adulthood, with conviction and direction, with openness and flexibility, or with confusion and tentativeness.

Although Erikson showed that identity is the central task of late adolescence, he did not suggest that identity, once formed, is inscribed in stone or, if not formed in adolescence, never will be. Identity continues to be modified throughout adult life; it builds on and incorporates earlier choices. Identity is always both product and process; it embodies continuity and change.

Never again in life is identity as malleable as it is in adolescence. As we progress through life, our own decisions limit what we may decide later. If I have spent ten years as a psychologist, it is much more difficult for me to decide to become an art historian than if I had set out on that road in the beginning. Similarly, getting married or having children bonds one to relationships that may limit mobility or time. Nevertheless, we continue to make changes, to better understand ourselves, to better know the social world in which we live. The woman of 40 knows herself, experiences herself, and expresses herself differently from the woman of 21.

And, as the life course progresses, the social world is itself changing: choices become available that may not have been there before. Ideas that have been around for some time may not be taken up as a part of someone's personal biography until years after others have incorporated them. People of the same social and historical period derive different meanings from the same events that occur in the larger society—adopting change, resisting it, or remaining indifferent to it. What is least to be expected is that, over twenty years, people will remain the same.

These four groups greeted their adulthood in different ways. About to graduate from college, these women entered their future from one of these four doors—some with a clear sense of themselves that came of experimentation with their own possibility, some with a sense of self rooted in the authority of the past, some uncertain of how or what they wished to become, and some avoiding the question altogether. These were important gateways in that they opened out onto avenues that phrased the questions of life in different ways. The next stages would have to unfold distinctively. What became of the women who backed into grown-up life holding fast to the past? And what of those who were living only the present, hoping to stave off the future? And what would happen to those who still, at the end of college, felt unable to choose? How would they ultimately decide and what would their openness gain them—or cost them?

These groups, then, represent starting points rather than lifelong categories. I have followed these women for twenty-two years. All of them, by age 43, have carved a more or less reliable sense of identity, or circumstance has provided them one. In the intervening years, they have continued to revise themselves. At age 43, some are in the midst of midlife questioning and reworking; others are content with who they have

become and feel themselves to be pretty much who they expect to be for the rest of their lives. There is continuity and change—both within the groups and over time. In order to tell their stories, I continue to group them in terms of the exit door they took from their adolescence. As the complexity of life increases after college, so do the differences among them, and they divide less neatly into well-marked groups. (To reorder them at each ten-year interval would become too confusing and, in any case, we lack the psychological instruments to categorize the identity process in adulthood.) I therefore use the group names to refer to where these women were at the end of college but not to label their adult identities.

I am interested in exploring the ways in which these women's lives unfold. Thinking of the four groups as different starting points, representing different personalities and orientations to life, is a useful conceptual vantage point for identifying the different courses that women follow as they continue to grow. At the outset, we cannot know if one or the other path may be the more direct or certain route to adult fulfillment and satisfaction. Or whether each path may lead to a unique form of adult life experience. I wanted to discover what became of women who took each of these different identity routes. I hoped to learn about how these differences play out as women encounter and respond to the challenges of living.

Above all, I hoped to discover what the differences among these women could teach me about identity in women. What are its components and what are its crucial determinants? How can we name and appreciate both the commonalities and the differences among women as they construct their identities and, in doing so, weave their lives?

In the next part, I introduce the women in the four groups, one group at a time, and explore the way in which they have pursued their lives. I highlight the way in which the identity pathway taken at the end of college affected the course of their adulthood. In this part, I look for communalities within each group and point out the differences I find between them. I also look at the ways in which people, in making and remaking their identities, carry elements of their beginnings while taking on new attributes—intermingling continuity and change.

CHAPTER 14

THE RELATIONSHIP BETWEEN PSYCHOSOCIAL DEVELOPMENT AND RACIAL IDENTITY OF COLLEGE STUDENTS OF COLOR

RAECHELE L. POPE

This nationwide study was conducted to examine the relationship between psychosocial development and racial identity of 539 Black American, Asian American, and Latino American traditional-aged undergraduate college students. Note that the broader racial category Black American *was used when describing this study's sample rather than the term* African American, *a term which describes ethnicity that would be inaccurate since both African American and Caribbean American students were included in the sample. The findings suggest that both race and racial identity are clearly related to the combined tasks of psychosocial development. Implications for practice are explored.*

Student affairs professionals are primarily responsible for the out-of-class education and development of college students (Miller & Winston, 1991). To the degree that their practice is grounded in developmental theories and concepts, these professionals are often effective in meeting the needs of a diverse student body (Rodgers, 1991). A variety of student development theories have been offered as a means of understanding students' intellectual, personal, and social growth (Knefelkamp, Widick, & Parker, 1978; Rodgers, 1980). These theories have been categorized into a number of families, namely; psychosocial, cognitive, typology, and person-environment (Evans, Forney, & Guido-DiBrito, 1998; Knefelkamp et al., 1978; Rodgers, 1980). Issues of social identity (e.g., ethnicity, race, gender, sexual orientation) have been considered less frequently when examining how students change and develop during their college years. Although some scholars have urged the incorporation of ethnic, racial, and other cultural influences into student development research and practice (Jones, 1990; McEwen & Roper, 1994; Miller & Winston, 1990; Wright, 1987), limited research has been conducted in this area. Where such studies exist, they tend to focus on African American students or, to a lesser degree, international students (see for example, Branch-Simpson, 1984; Cheatham, Slaney, & Coleman, 1990; Gibson, 1995; Itzkowitz & Petrie, 1986; Jordan-Cox, 1987; Sheehan, 1995; Taub & McEwen, 1991). The few studies that focus on students of color other than African American students have been dissertations with limited circulation (e.g., Testa, 1994; Utterback, 1992).

Since the early 1970s, a number of racial identity development models that share similar conceptualizations of how growth and development occur have been proposed (Atkinson, Morton, & Sue, 1979; Cross, 1971, Helms, 1984; Jackson & Hardiman, 1983; Myers et al., 1991; Phinney, 1996; Root, 1990; Sue & Sue, 1971). By definition, racial identity models examine one's sense of belonging to a particular racial group and the impact that sense of belonging has on one's thinking, perceptions, feelings, and behavior (Rotheram & Phinney, 1987). More recent conceptualizations of racial identity development (Helms & Piper, 1994) have suggested:

1. Racial identity development is applicable to all racial groups including Whites;

2. Racial identity involves how one views and understand one's own racial group as well as members of other racial groups;

3. Racial identity development reflects a cognitive worldview ranging from less mature (simplistic, inaccurate, and externally defined) to more mature (complex, accurate, and internally derived).

Helms (1990) suggested that the movement from a less mature worldview to a more mature one is segmented not by stages, but rather by statuses. *Statuses* implies that a person may possess multiple worldviews with associated feelings, attitudes, and behaviors, but that one worldview dominates. A fundamental assumption of racial identity development models is that movement from less mature to more mature statuses is associated with more positive interactions and a greater degree of personal adjustment (Helms).

Having a clear understanding of race and racial identity, and their impact on the experiences and worldview of college students of color, is vital to providing developmentally appropriate and meaningful support and services. As stated previously, almost no information is available on the developmental issues and needs of Asian American, Latino American, and Native American college students, and limited information is available concerning African American students, which can hinder efforts to provide such vital services. The purpose of this study was to enhance understanding of the developmental needs and issues of college students of color and the impact of race and racial identity on their development. Specifically, this study was conducted to determine the relationship between psychosocial development and racial identity of undergraduate, traditional-aged African American, Asian American, and Latino American college students. Two research questions were investigated:

1. Is racial identity predictive of psychosocial development of college students of color?

2. What differences, if any, in psychosocial development and racial identity exist between the three racial groups?

Method

Participants

Black American, Asian American, and Latino American traditional-aged (17 to 24) undergraduate college students enrolled in 44 colleges and universities participated in the study. Of 583 surveys returned, 43 were judged unusable due to: (a) extensive omissions, (b) age ineligibility (younger than 17 or older than 24), (c) response-bias scale concerns (25 students answered three or more response-bias scale items in the keyed direction), or (d) ineligible race, ethnicity, or foreign-student status (i.e., 9 Native American, 4 White, and 3 foreign students responded). Hence, 539 student responses were deemed usable.

Of the 539 usable participants, 349 (65%) were women and one participant did not identify gender. The racial classification of the participants were as follows: 115 (21%) were Asian American, 309 (57%) were Black American, and 115 (21%) were Latino American. The mean age of the respondents was 19.85 years. Full-time students comprised the overwhelming majority (526; 98%) of the participants. Ninety-three (17%) of the participants were seniors, 101 (19%) were juniors, 121 (22%) were sophomores, 153 (28%) were freshmen, and 71 (13%) did not respond to this question. Approximately 27% (148) of the participants were natural science or engineering majors; 36% (194) were social science and humanities majors; education majors were 7% (38); 12% (65) were business majors; "other" and "undecided" comprised 17% (89) of the respondents; and .1% (5) did not respond to this question.

Instruments

The following instruments were used in this study: (a) the Student Development Task and Lifestyle Inventory (SDTLI) (Winston & Miller, 1987), (b) the Racial Identity Attitudes Scale-B (RIAS-B) (Parham & Helms, 1981), (c) the Visible Racial and Ethnic Identity Scale (VREI) (Helms & Carter, 1986), and (d) a personal data form constructed for this study.

The SDTLI (Winston & Miller, 1987), designed to measure aspects of Chickering's (1969) theory of student development, was selected to measure patterns of psychosocial development. Substantially different from its predecessors, the 140-item SDTLI is a major revision of SDTLI-2. The SDTLI consists of three developmental task areas—Establishing and

Clarifying Purpose Task, Developing Mature Interpersonal Relationships Task, and Developing Academic Autonomy Task—and three scales: Intimacy, Salubrious Lifestyle, and Response Bias. Two of the tasks have additional subtasks. The Establishing and Clarifying Purpose Task is divided into five subtasks: Educational Involvement, Career Planning, Lifestyle Planning, Life Management, and Cultural Participation. The Mature Interpersonal Relationships Task is divided into three subtasks: Peer Relationships, Tolerance, and Emotional Autonomy.

Winston (1990) presented internal consistency reliability estimates for the tasks of the SDTLI on the basis of a sample of 1,200 undergraduate students. Reported estimates ranged from .45 to .90 all tasks, and scales were .70 or higher suggesting, according to Winston, that the tasks and scales are sufficiently homogeneous for research with groups of students. Henning-Stout (1992) reported that the validity of the SDTLI is also well established. However, Winston did report that caution should be exercised in using some of the subtasks because of relatively low alpha coefficients for specific subtasks (i.e., Cultural Participation, Tolerance, and Emotional Autonomy) and found the more reliable measures to be the total task scores. Hence, Winston suggested that the total task scores be used.

The RIAS-B (Parham & Helms, 1981) was designed to assess attitudes associated with African American identity development and was initially based in the Cross's (1978) four-stage model (Preencounter, Encounter, Immersion, and Internalization) of psychological *Nigrescence* (defined as the process of becoming Black) and has since been extensively revised and expanded. The instrument consists of 50 items to which participants respond using a Likert-type scale ranging from 1 (*strongly disagree*) to 5 (*strongly agree*).

Helms (1990) reported internal consistency reliability coefficients for the four scales from .51 to .80 (n = 175). Importantly, Helms recommended using the scores on all four scales to describe an individual's racial identity attitude profile rather than to assign that individual to a single stage based on highest score. Construct, content, and criterion validity studies generally have been supportive of the RIAS-B (Helms & Parham, in press).

The VREI (Helms & Carter, 1986) was designed to assess attitudes associated with racial or ethnic identity development of Asian American, Latino American and Native American indi-viduals. The scale is based on the Helms and Carter four-stage model of visible racial-ethnic identity (Conformity, Dissonance, Resistance, and Awareness), which was adapted from the Atkinson, Morton, and Sue (1979) Minority Identity Development (MID) five-stage model. The scale consists of 43 items to which participants respond using a Likert-type scale ranging from 1 (*strongly disagree*) to 5 (*strongly agree*). Although this instrument was developed over 10 years ago and is one of the few racial identity instruments available for use with Asian American, Latino American, and Native American individuals, it has not yet been widely used in research. For the current study, the internal consistency reliability coefficients for the four scales from .87 to .95 (n = 240).

For this study, the researcher used the RIAS-B to explore racial identity development of Black American students and the VREI for Asian American and Latino American students. Although both racial identity instruments identify four statuses, the statuses are labeled differently. Nonetheless, the description of the process within both models is similar. Both Preencounter and Conformity are associated with positive feelings for the dominant race and negative feelings toward one's own race. Encounter and Dissonance both reflect confusion and conflict brought on by experiences that challenge the attitudes held in the previous status. Immersion– Emersion and Resistance are characterized by positive feelings toward one's own racial group, which are advanced by immersion in one's race through books, movies, friends, and activities. During this period, some negative feelings toward the dominant group often emerge. And finally, both Internalization and Awareness involve the absence of negative feelings and attitudes as a result of resolution of the confusion and conflict from previous statuses. The person at this level is able to function within the dominant society without sacrificing racial pride and heritage.

The personal data form was used to gather participants' demographic data (e.g., age, gender, racial group, family's socioeconomic status) and academic status (e.g., year in school, grade point average, full- or part-time). The personal data form was constructed by the author for this study.

Procedures

Participants were initially solicited via the use of electronic mail (E-mail), primarily through student affairs electronic listservers. A request for student affairs practitioners to assist in the collection of data on the psychosocial development and social attitudes of college students of color was posted on a variety of electronic listservers in the student affairs field (e.g., residence hall directors listservers, various multicultural affairs listservers, a first-year program listserver). Interested student affairs practitioners were asked to contact the author for additional information. After receiving additional information, also via E-mail, practitioners who agreed to serve as site coordinators for their campus were asked to identify a small number of college students of color (identified as Asian American, Black American, Latino American, and Native American) willing to participate in the study.

Packets containing a cover letter, detailed instructions (including a return date), a statement to be read to the participants, instruments, and a return envelope were mailed to the site coordinators. Site coordinators were asked to select a convenient time (for both site coordinator and students) to meet with a group of students (preferably 10 to 15 students) and coordinate the data collection. Upon the completion of the data collection, site coordinators were asked to return all completed and unused materials.

Results

The means and standard deviations of the psychosocial development tasks for this study are: Establishing and Clarifying Purpose (43.06, SD 11.56), Developing Mature Interpersonal Relationships (19.73, SD 4.95), and Developing Academic Autonomy (4.77, SD 2.73). The means reflect the means of the norm sample as reported by Winston and Miller (1987). Table 1 contains the means and standard deviations scale values of each racial group from the statuses of racial

identity. However, in the actual analysis, the scores for racial identity were converted to z scores to account for differences in the racial identity scales for Black American students and for non-Black students of color.

A multivariate analysis of covariance was performed on the tasks of psychosocial development: Establishing and Clarifying Purpose, Developing Mature Interpersonal Relationships, and Developing Academic Autonomy. The four covariates included the four statuses of racial identity, referred to as statuses 1 through 4. The one grouping variable was race, with three levels: Black American, Asian American, and Latino American. Although data was collected from Native American students, there were too few respondents to include in data analysis.

SPSS MANOVA was used for the analysis on a total $N = 539$. With the use of Wilks's criterion, racial identity was significantly related to the combined tasks of psychosocial development, approximate $F(12, 1402.54) = 3.24$, $p < 0.01$, indicating an association between the construct of psychosocial development and the development of racial identity. After adjusting for racial identity, race was also significantly related to the combined tasks of psychosocial development, approximate $F(6, 1060) = 2.56$, $p = 0.02$ indicating that the psychosocial development varied by race.

Univariate tests were used to further investigate the association between racial identity and the tasks of psychosocial development. Racial identity was significantly associated with Establishing and Clarifying Purpose, $F(4, 532) = 3.50$, $p = 0.01$; Developing Mature Interpersonal Relationships, $F(4, 532) = 6.23$, $p < 0.01$; and Developing Academic Autonomy, $F(4, 532) = 2.87$, $p = 0.02$. These results indicated that each task of psychosocial development was clearly related to racial identity.

TABLE 1
Scores on Four Statuses of Racial Identity

Four Statuses of Racial Identity	ASIAN AMERICAN (N = 115) M (SD)	BLACK AMERICAN (N = 309) M (SD)	LATINO/A AMERICAN (N = 115) M (SD)
Status 1	12.31 (4.69)	24.45 (8.09)	10.89 (4.97)
Status 2	38.59 (9.34)	11.38 (4.10)	34.82 (12.91)
Status 3	18.11 (5.53)	19.16 (6.97)	16.93 (6.50)
Status 4	39.03 (6.16)	47.61 (12.96)	36.57 (11.33)

TABLE 14.2
Univariate Tests of Racial Identity and Psychosocial Development

Dependent Variable	F, (DF)	Independent Variable	β	t
PUR	3.50 (4, 532)*	Status 1	−.69	−3.56**
		Status 2	.07	0.49
		Status 3	.21	0.94
		Status 4	.39	2.17*
MIR	6.23 (4,532)**	Status 1	−.76	−3.94**
		Status 2	.19	1.22
		Status 3	−.06	−0.25
		Status 4	.51	2.92 **
AA	2.87 (4,532)*	Status 1	−.52	−2.65*
		Status 2	−.06	0.37
		Status 3	−.14	−0.64
		Status 4	.51	3.23**

*$p < .05$.   **$p < .01$.

The univariate analysis indicated that Statuses 1 and 4 of racial identity were related to the three tasks of psychosocial development. The first status, characterized by strong positive feelings regarding the dominant race and negative (conscious or unconscious) feelings towards one's own race, was negatively related to each of the tasks; however, the fourth status, characterized by the realization that the dominant race and one's own race have both positive and negative aspects, were positively related to each of the tasks. In the regression equations with Establishing and Clarifying Purpose, Developing Mature Interpersonal Relationships, and Developing Academic Autonomy, these results indicated that as scores in Status 1 decreased and scores in Status 4 increased, development in each of the tasks of psychosocial development increased (see Table 2).

To determine whether step-down analysis was appropriate, pooled within-cell correlations among dependent variables were examined. Pooled within-cell correlations provide the degree to which the dependent variables are correlated, adjusting for the covariate variables. If the correlations are in excess of .30, step-down analysis is appropriate, when investigating the relationships between the race and the tasks of psychosocial development. Pooled within-cell correlations among the dependent variables—

the psychosocial development tasks—are presented in Table 3.

To examine the pure relationship between race and psychosocial development it was necessary to control for racial identity. The relationship between race and psychosocial development, after adjusting for racial identity, was investigated in univariate and step-down analysis in which Establishing and Clarifying Purpose was given highest priority (priority was established by empirical degree of relationship), Developing Mature Interpersonal Relationships second priority (so that adjustment was made for Establishing and Clarifying Purpose and racial identity), and Developing Academic Autonomy third priority (so that adjustment was made for Establishing and Clarifying Purpose, Developing Mature Interpersonal Relationships, and Racial Identity). Results of this analysis are summarized in Table 4.

After adjusting for differences on racial identity, race had a significant relationship with the combined tasks of psychosocial development. The step-down tests demonstrated that Establishing and Clarifying Purpose best distinguishes between the three racial groups, step-down $F(2, 532) = 4.86, p < 0.01$. Greater development was found among Black American students and Latino American students than Asian American students (adjusted means 44.24, 42.18, and 40.53 respectively) on this task. Step-down tests

TABLE 14.3
Pooled Within-Cells Correlations Among Three Dependent Variables After Controlling for Racial Identity (Standard Deviations on the Diagonals)

	Establishing and Clarifying Purpose	Developing Mature Interpersonal Relationships	Academic Autonomy
Establishing and Clarifying Purpose	11.40		
Developing Mature Interpersonal Relationships	0.24	4.84	
Developing Academic Autonomy	0.35	0.41	2.72

demonstrated no significant differences between the Black American, Asian American, and Latino American students on Developing Mature Interpersonal Relationships nor Developing Academic Autonomy after controlling for differences on racial identity.

Discussion

The purpose of this study was to investigate the relationship between psychosocial development and racial identity of Black American, Asian American, and Latino American college students. Specifically, this study focused on two primary questions:

1. Is racial identity status predictive of psycho-social development of college students of color?

2. What differences, if any, in psychosocial development exist between the three racial groups selected for this study?

Analysis of the data revealed that the construct of racial identity was significantly related to the combined tasks of psychosocial development. Furthermore, significant relationships were found between racial identity development and the individual tasks of Establishing and Clarifying Purpose, Developing Mature Interpersonal Relationships, and Academic Autonomy. The analysis indicated that as scores progressed in the statuses of racial identity development, they also increased on each of the tasks of psychosocial development. In other words, as students moved from Status 1 to Status 4, they demonstrated increased psychosocial development. The results do not imply a causal relationship. The results do not indicate that development in racial identity causes development in psychosocial development or vice versa.

TABLE 4
Tests of Racial Identity and Race

Independent Variable	Dependent Variable	Univariate F	DF	Step-down F	DF	Significance
Race Identity	PUR	3.50[a]	4,532	3.50	4,532	.008
	MIR	6.23[a]	4,532	4.69	4,531	.001
	AA	2.87[a]	4,532	1.56	4,530	.188
Race	PUR	4.86[a]	2,532	4.86	2,532	.008
	MIR	4.62[a]	2,532	2.72	2,531	.067
	AA	1.05	2,532	0.12	2,530	.883

[a] Analysis would achieve significance at the .05 level in an univariate test.

Instead, the results demonstrate that racial identity and psychosocial development are clearly related. This has important implications for practitioners working with students of color. This finding seems to suggest that racial identity and psychosocial development are equally important and concurrent developmental concerns for students of color. Students of color may be required to devote additional energy to the resolution of racial identity development issues while progressing through the tasks of psychosocial development. The energy they commit to the development of their racial identity may, at times, hinder their ability to focus on psychosocial development. Therefore, additional attention to racial identity is critical when attempting to facilitate the psychosocial development of students of color. This finding may, in fact, help explain why some traditional developmental interventions are not always successful with students of color. Focusing on psychosocial development to the exclusion of racial identity realities may make such interventions seem less relevant and meaningful.

Additionally, a significant relationship was found between race and the combined tasks of psychosocial development. However, further investigation indicated Establishing and Clarifying Purpose was most pivotal in understanding that relationship. On this task, Black American and Latino American students scored higher than Asian American students. This finding means that Black and Latino American students, in this study, were further along in the development of their academic career or life goals and plans, or perhaps further along in the necessary integration of academic, vocational or recreational activities, than were Asian American students. Perhaps obviously, this study again indicates that racial differences, even among students of color, must be viewed as essential. With regards to this specific study, the findings involving Asian American students warrant special note. Asian American students scored significantly lower on this task than did the Black American and Latino American students and the reported norm sample (Winston & Miller, 1987). This finding could be of particular interest to practitioners because it appears to contradict the stereotype of Asian Americans as the "model minority" needing little to no assistance in areas of academic, career, or life-planning skills. Many researchers have criticized the model minority

stereotype because it does not take into account important social and historical information and daily realities of the diverse Asian American community (Lee & Zane, 1998). Another interpretation of these results could be that Asian Americans' experiences and skills in academic, career, and life planning are culturally influenced. Some research has described Asian Americans as being more dependent in their decision-making style, less autonomous, and more deferent to authority, especially their parents (Lee & Zane, 1998; Leong, 1985). Other studies have identified social anxiety and discomfort as a possible factor affecting the career aspirations of Asian Americans. Understanding potential cultural influences and realities is important to ensure that Asian American students are not viewed as deficient in particular areas of development. Regardless of why Asian American students may score differently on this task, the results of this study indicate that Asian American students may benefit from programs that address the skills associated with educational involvement, career and lifestyle planning, life management, and cultural participation. How these programs are advertised and presented will determine whether or not they will be attended or viewed as relevant or meaningful by Asian American students.

As with all empirical research, this study does have some limitations, which are based primarily in sampling concerns. The sample for this study was obtained primarily by identifying site coordinators who contacted groups of Black American, Asian American, Native American, and Latino American students on various campuses across the country. Although this method did not emphasize random sampling, the size of the sample ($N = 539$) as well as having participants from all over the country may help to minimize the effect of that limitation. Finally, more extensive efforts must be made to collect data on Native American students as their needs have not been effectively incorporated into this or other studies.

Implications

This study has provided an empirically documented profile of group similarities and differences in the psychosocial development for students of color. The results of this study encourage student affairs practitioners to carefully design and implement programs that are specifically sensitive to the differences between students of color. The results indicated that Asian American students scored lower than Black American and Latino American students on the Establishing and Clarifying Purpose Task. Establishing and Clarifying Purpose is composed of the following subtasks: Educational Involvement, Career Planning, Lifestyle Planning, Life Management, and Cultural Participation. Thus, programs targeted toward assisting students in the development of these areas should reflect consideration for Asian American student differences on this task. This means that student affairs professionals may need to seek out Asian students to ensure proper attention to this developmental task. Practitioners may especially want to focus on individual interactions like advisement and career counseling sessions to pass on important information and skills for this developmental task.

Student affairs professionals need to also take the coexisting relationship between racial identity development and psychosocial development into account when working with students of color. Student affairs practitioners must not make assumptions about the students' level of psychosocial development without first considering their racial identity and how they perceive themselves as racial beings. And when psychosocial development is targeted for interventions, the unique concerns of students of color need to be incorporated into such interventions. Without such considerations, the personal support or programmatic efforts targeted towards students of color may miss their mark because they may not be focused on the most pressing concerns.

Another vital consideration that comes out of the results of this research is the importance of looking at differences between students of color. To meet their needs as developing individuals, both in terms of racial identity and psychosocial development, the unique history, cultural values, and perspectives of the different racial groups must be addressed. Different types of workshops, personal approaches, mentoring, and advising or counseling efforts may be required in any interventions targeted towards students of color. Only through extensive reading and interactions with various cultural groups will student affairs practitioners be prepared to incorporate important and unique cultural understandings into their interactions with and interventions towards various students of color groups. Campus-wide discussions about these concerns should occur among student affairs professionals so individual and group interactions are meaningful and productive. Brainstorming and piloting new types of programs and interventions would be the goal for such dialogues.

Finally, the results of this study highlighted the importance of considering both race and racial identity as important factors in understanding the development of students of color. Although some scholars have cautioned to not over interpret the significance of race, factors such as racial identity may be more helpful in understanding the experiences and perspectives of people of color. These results indicate the value in examining the importance of both race and racial identity in creating interventions for students of color.

To effectively meet the developmental needs of students of color, student affairs professionals need to be creative in their programmatic and intervention efforts. Expanding their repertoire, consulting with cultural experts, and increasing their sensitivity to cultural nuances between racial groups are all necessary to enhance their effectiveness. Pope and Reynolds (1997) described these and similar tasks as multicultural competence. Further, they suggested that as college campuses become increasingly diverse, multicultural competence has become a requisite core competency area for ethical and efficacious practice (Pope & Reynolds). For many campuses this means additional training and skill building for student affairs practitioners. An example of a creative approach would be to develop a series of focus groups with students of color to assess their psychosocial development and willingness to participate in a variety of interventions targeted toward their self understanding and skill development. Campuses should not just rely on the same old interventions; they may need to use training or outreach models from other disciplines like community psychology or social work that may more regularly target interventions toward people of color.

The paucity of research into the experiences and development of Asian American, African American, Latino American, and Native American students underscores the importance of continuing this line of research. The results of this study are not definitive, and further research is needed; however, the implications of this study indicate that the practitioner ought to assume that psychosocial development may be influenced by an individual's identity and environment. Thus, practitioners should be sensitive to possible group differences when applying student development theories to students of color. Withingroup differences do exist and not all students of color necessarily have the same experiences, attitudes, and beliefs as White students. Many research questions have been raised by the results of this study as well as the lack of available data on the students of color. More information is needed to understand why Asian American students score lower on Establishing and Clarifying Purpose. Further investigation that more clearly distinguishes between statuses two and three of racial identity is important to enhance our understanding of racial identity. Examining the racial identity of all students is important to better understand psychosocial development. Over the past 20 years extensive research has been done on the developmental issues and needs of White students. The student affairs profession must expand the research agenda to incorporate the study of the development of students of color to create an optimal environment for understanding their needs and concerns.

References

Atkinson, D. R., Morton, G., & Sue, D. W. (1979). *Counseling American minorities: A cross-cultural perspective*. Dubuque, IA: W. C. Brown.

Branch-Simpson, G. (1984). A study of the patterns in the development of black seniors at The Ohio State University (Doctoral dissertation, The Ohio State University, 1984). *Dissertations Abstract International, 45-08A*, 2422.

Carter, R. T. (1995). *The influence of race and racial identity in psychotherapy*. New York: Wiley.

Cheatham, H. E., Slaney, R. B., & Coleman, N. (1990). Institutional effects on the psychosocial development of African-American college students. *Journal of Counseling Psychology, 37*, 453–458.

Chickering, A. W. (1969). *Education and identity*. San Francisco: Jossey-Bass. Cross, W. E. (1971). Negro-to-Black conversion experience. *Black World, 20*, 13–27.

Cross, W. E. (1978). The Cross and Thomas models of psychological Nigrescence. *Journal of Black Psychology, 5*, 13–19.

Evans, N. J., Forney, D. S., & Guido-DiBrito, F. (1998). *Student development in college: Theory, research, and practice*. San Francisco: Jossey-Bass.

Gibson, G. (1995). Chickering's model of student development and the academic performance of African-American college students on a predominantly White campus. *Dissertation Abstracts International, 56(10)*, 3848A.

Helms, J. E. (1990). *Black and White racial identity: Theory, research, and practice*. Westport, CT: Greenwood Press.

Helms, J. E. (1984). Toward an explanation of the influence of race in the counseling process: A Black-White model. *The Counseling Psychologist, 12*, 153–165.

Helms, J. E., & Carter, R. T. (1986). Manual for the Visible Racial/Ethnic Identity Attitude Scale. Paper presented at the annual convention of the American Psychological Association, Washington, D.C.

Helms, J. E., & Parham, T. A. (in press). The development of the Racial Identity Attitude Scale. In R. L. Jones (Ed.), *Handbook of tests and measurements for Black populations* (Vols. 1-2). Berkeley, CA: Cobb & Henry.

Helms, J. E., & Piper, R. E. (1994). Implications for racial identity theory for vocational psychology. *Journal of Vocational Behavior, 44*, 124–138.

Henning-Stout, M. (1992). Review of the Student Development Task and Lifestyle Inventory. In J. Kramer & J. Close Conoley (Eds.), *The 11th mental measurements yearbook* (pp. 879–881). Lincoln, NE: The Buros Institute of Mental Measurement.

Itzkowitz, S. A., & Petrie, R. D. (1986). The Student Development Task Inventory: Scores of Northern versus Southern students. *Journal of College Student Personnel, 27*, 406–412.

Jackson, B. W., & Hardiman, R. (1983). Racial identity development: Implications for managing the multiracial work force. In R. A. Ritvo & A. G. Sargent (Eds.), *NTL manager's handbook* (pp. 107–119). Arlington, VA: NTL Institute.

Jones, W. T. (1990). Perspectives on ethnicity. In L. V. Moore (Ed.), *Evolving theoretical perspectives on students* (pp. 59–72). San Francisco: Jossey-Bass.

Jordan-Cox, C. A. (1987). Psychosocial development of students in traditionally Black institutions. *Journal of College Student Personnel, 28*, 504–512.

Knefelkamp, L., Widick, C., & Parker, C. A. (Eds.). (1978). *Applying new developmental findings*. San Francisco: Jossey-Bass.

Lee, L. C., & Zane, N. W. S. (Eds.). (1998). *Handbook of Asian American Psychology*. Thousand Oaks, CA: SAGE.

Leong, F. T. L. (1985). Career development of Asian Americans. *Journal of College student Personnel, 26*, 539–546.

McEwen, M. K., & Roper, L. D. (1994). Incorporating multiculturalism into student affairs preparation programs: Suggestions from the literature. *Journal of College Student Development, 35*, 46–53.

Miller, T. K., & Winston, R. B. (Eds.). (1991). *Administration and leadership in student affairs*. Muncie, IN: Accelerated Development.

Miller, T. K., & Winston, R. B. (1990). Assessing development from a psychosocial perspective. In D. Creamer (Ed.), *College student development: Theory and practice for the 1990s* (pp. 99–126). Alexandria, VA: American College Personnel Association.

Myers, L. J., Speight, S. L., Highlen, P. S., Cox, C. I., Reynolds, A. L., Adams, E. A., & Hanley, C. P. (1991). Identity development and worldview: Toward an optimal conceptualization. *Journal of Counseling and Development, 70*, 54–63.

Parham, T. A., & Helms, J. E. (1981). The influence of Black students' racial identity attitudes on preference for counselor's race. *Journal of Counseling Psychology, 28*, 250–257.

Phinney, J. (1996). When we talk about American ethnic groups, what do we mean? *American Psychologist, 51*, 918–927.

Pope, R. L. & Reynolds, A. L. (1997). Student affairs core competencies: Integrating multicultural awareness, knowledge, and skills. *Journal of College Student Development, 38*, 266–277.

Rodgers, R. F. (1980). Theories underlying student development. In D. G. Creamer (Ed.) *Student development in higher education: Theories, practices, and future directions*. Washington, DC: American College Personnel Association.

Rodgers, R. F. (1991). Using theory in practice in student affairs. In T. K. Miller & R. B. Winston (Eds.), *Administration and leadership in student affairs* (pp. 203–251). Muncie, IN: Accelerated Development.

Root, M. P. (1990). Resolving "other" status: Identity development of biracial individuals. In L. S. Brown, & M. P. Root (Eds.), *Diversity and complexity in feminist therapy* (pp. 185–206). New York: Harrington Park Press.

Rotheram, M. J. & Phinney, J. S. (1987). Ethnic behavior patterns as an aspect of identity. In J. S. Phinney & M. J. Rotheram (Eds.), *Children's ethnic socialization: Pluralism and development*. Newbury Park, CA: Sage. Sue, S., & Sue, D. W. (1971). Chinese-American personality and mental health. *Amerasia Journal, 1*, 36–49.

Sheehan, O. T. O., & Pearson, F. (1995). Asian international and American students' psychosocial development. *Journal of College Student Development, 36*, 522–530.

Taub, D. J., & McEwen, M. K. (1991). The relationship of racial identity attitudes to autonomy and mature interpersonal relationships in Black and White undergraduate women.

Testa, A. M. (1994). A study of psychosocial development of African American, Hispanic, and White university students: A comparison of scores between first-year and upper- division students on the Student Development Task and Lifestyle Inventory (SDTLI) at a Western University (Doctoral dissertation, University of Nevada at Reno, 1994). *Dissertation Abstracts International, 55-07A*, 1833.

Utterback, J. W. (1992). Interactive effects of gender and ethnicity on levels of intimacy in college students (Doctoral dissertation, University of Northern Colorado, 1992). *Dissertation Abstracts International, 5, 53-06A*, 1820.

Winston, R. B. (1990). The Student Task Development and Lifestyle Inventory: An approach to measuring students' psychosocial development. *Journal of College Student Development, 31*, 108–120.

Winston, R. B., & Miller, T. K. (1987). *Student Development Task and Lifestyle Inventory Manual*. Athens, GA: Student Development Associates.

Wright, D. J. (1987). Minority students: Developmental beginnings. In D. J. Wright (Ed.), *Responding to the needs of today's minority students* (New directions for student services No. 4, pp. 5–22). San Francisco: Jossey-Bass.

Chapter 15

Incorporating the Development of African-American Students into Psychosocial Theories of Student Development

Marylu K. McEwen, Larry D. Roper,
Deborah R. Bryant, and Miriam J. Langa

Nine dimensions that address the development of African-American students are proposed for inclusion in psychosocial theories of college student development.

Colleges and universities in the United States have a tradition and mission of transforming and enriching the lives of students (Boyer, 1987). This mission is consistent with the goals of preserving, enriching, and transmitting culture, as was identified by the Student Personnel Point of View (SPPV) (American Council on Education [ACE], 1937, 1949). The SPPV suggests that college personnel, especially student affairs professionals, should fulfill their mission by responding to the whole person, acknowledging individual differences, and meeting students at their level of development (Saddlemire & Rentz, 1986). In addition, college and university programs help students to make "significant life transitions" (National Association of Student Personnel Administrators [NASPA], 1987). Implied in all three of these statements (ACE, 1937, 1949; NASPA, 1987) is that student affairs professionals also have a responsibility of responding to all students, which includes both majority and racial and ethnic minority students.

For much of the history, however, higher education in the United States was racially segregated. Beginning in the 1960s, large numbers of Black students began attending predominantly White institutions (Fleming, 1984). The sudden influx of Black students created an educational dilemma for college and university professionals—how could they respond to the educational needs of students for whom their institutions were not designed? Predominantly White institutions (PWIs) were founded for the intention of educating the White middle class (Kovel, 1970). These institutions, based on Anglo-Saxon, Euro-American values, are like all social institutions; they survive because they are symbolically related to the culture values of the broader American society.

The cultural values of PWIs also influence how students are viewed and how education is approached. The cultural values of institutions affect what students are taught, how they are taught, and how student learning is evaluated. Most important, cultural values influence the direction that educators attempt to move students, how student behavior is evaluated, and what knowledge base is used to explain student (human) development. Because educators at PWIs have historically relied upon a body of knowledge that supports and reinforces Euro-American values, they often prove unsuccessful in responding to the educational and cultural needs of African-American students (Bulhan, 1985). Black students at PWIs are taught and evaluated from an Anglo-Saxon perspective.

Those responsible for teaching and helping Black students must create models of human and student development that take into account the unique needs and experiences that Black students bring to the college campus. Issues specific to African-American students that are not accounted for in the traditional theories of human development are (a) the unique psychohistory of Blacks in this country and the adaptations that Blacks must make (Essien-Udom, 1971); (b) the "colonized" nature of Black existence in this country (Fanon, 1967); (c) the extended nature of the Black family and Black homelife (Willie, 1976); (d) the unique educational/socialization role of the Black family (Willie, 1976); (e) the oral tradition within the Black community (Hall & Freedle, 1975); (f) the impact of racial hostility and environmental press (Ogbu, 1981); (g) the unique character of Black Americans (Essien-Udom 1971); (h) the psychological dynamics that accompany being "a caste-like minority" (Ogbu, 1981), representing a "rejected strain" in society (Cruse, 1967), being "codified" (Scruggs, 1971), and attempting to reconcile two identities (DuBois, 1953); and (i) the philosophical connections to African tradition, such as oral tradition, action/belief connection, elastic concept of time, kinship tradition/group consciousness, survival focus (collective versus individual), spiritual disposition, and view of people as an integrated whole (Baldwin, 1981; Nobles, 1980). Among other issues to be considered are the limitations of Euro-American definitions of normalcy (Bulhan, 1985) for African-American students.

Black scholars suggest that the Black experience in American society requires that Blacks interact with and participate in White institutions. This participation results in *oppression, dehumanization*, and *deracialization*. Deracialization occurs through a process by which people are required/forced to abandon "cultural forms, . . . [one's] language, . . . [one's] food habits, . . . [one's] sexual behavior, . . . [one's] way of sitting down, of resting, of laughing, of enjoying [oneself]" (Fanon, 1972, pp. 20–21). Student affairs professionals must concern themselves with whether or not, through the use of traditional theories and practices, they are participating in the dehumanization of African-American students. One way of responding is by expanding psychosocial theories of college student development to address the experience of African-American students.

Psychosocial theories, one of five clusters of student development theories (Knefelkamp, Widick, & Parker, 1978, p. xi), are those based directly or indirectly on Erikson's (1968) theory of human development. Examples of psychosocial theories/models include those of Chickering (1969), Sanford (1962), Keniston (1971), Coons (1970), and King (1973). Roy Heath's (1964) typology model and Douglas Heath's (1968) maturity model can also be included in the psychosocial framework.

The purpose of this discussion is to offer ways in which proponents of psychosocial theories of student development can incorporate more effectively the developmental issues of African-American students. A number of different dimensions must be added to extend the boundaries of student development theories. Nine such dimensions for inclusion in psychosocial theories are proposed below. These issues have been identified both through theoretical literature and essays on the Black experience and through quantitative and qualitative research conducted with African-American students in higher education.

Developmental Issues

Nine factors relate to developmental tasks of African-American students. These issues, which either have not been addressed adequately in the psychosocial theories or need to be considered in more complex ways for African-American students, include developing ethnic and racial identity, interacting with the dominant culture, developing cultural aesthetics and awareness, developing identity, developing interdependence, fulfilling affiliation needs, surviving intellectually, developing spiritually, and developing social responsibility.

A number of authors have cited the need to expand the notion of identity development to include attitudes about the race to which one belongs, that is, the role of racial or ethnic identity (Baldwin, 1981, 1984: Baldwin & Bell, 1985; Baldwin, Duncan, & Bell, 1987); Cross, 1971, 1978; Fleming, 1984; Helms, 1981; Parham, 1989; Parham & Helms, 1981, 1985a, 1985b; Pounds, 1987). Fleming (1984) indicated that Black students may hold doubts about their ethnic identity and that they must put psychological energy into protecting themselves against identity loss. Helms (1984) contrasted this issue for Black students with that of Whites, in which many Whites do not see themselves as White and thus may not hold a set of attitudes about the racial group to which they belong.

Cross (1971, 1978) offered a useful model from which to consider the development of racial identity. He proposed five stages, namely, (a) Preencounter, in which the Black student has not yet encountered the issue of one's own racial identity; (b) Encounter, in which one has a significant experience and begins to develop a Black identity; (c) Immersion-Emersion, in which one becomes intensely focused upon one's new Black identity; (d) Internalization, in which one resolves the conflicts between the old and new worldviews; and (e) Internalization Commitment, encompassing the previous stage but adding commitment to resolution of problems shared by one's racial group. In discussing cycles of psychological Nigrescence, Parham (1989) suggested that the racial identity of a Black person is "potentially influenced by his or her life stage and the developmental tasks associated with that period of life" (p. 196). Parham (1989) also described "how the stages of racial identity may be manifested at three phases of life (late adolescence/early adulthood, middle adulthood, and late adulthood)" (p. 197).

Parham and Helms (1981, 1985a, 1985b) have extended Cross's (1971, 1978) model by developing the Racial Identity Attitude Scale (Parham & Helms, 1981) and by conducting research with Black college students on the relationship between racial identity and self-esteem (1985a), self-actualization (1985b), and counselor preference (1981). In Parham and Helm's study of counselor preference, preencounter attitudes were negatively related and encounter attitudes positively related to preference for Black counselors; furthermore, preencounter attitudes were positively related to preference for White counselors (Parham & Helms, 1981). Parham and Helms (1981) summarized that (a) the preencounter stage is characterized by pro-White-anti-Black counselor preferences, (b) the encounter stage is characterized by pro-Black-anti-White counselor preferences, and (c) the immersion-emersion and internalization stages are similar in pro-Black attitudes but are not as anti-White as is the encounter stage (p. 254). In two studies, Parham and Helms found that both preencounter and immersion attitudes were significantly related to low self-esteem (1985a) and less self-actualization (1985b),

whereas encounter attitudes were associated with positive self-esteem and greater self-actualization.

In both cases, the variance explained by a combination of the racial identity attitudes was between 15% and 18%. Parham and Helms (1985b) concluded that (a) the racial identity process may be more complex than is expected and (b) both professionals and Black students should be aware that some of the feelings associated with particular racial identity attitudes may be unpleasant and require resolution, but may be a natural part of the Nigrescence process. Parham and Helms (1985a) also concluded that "self-concept may be governed by the way the student handles the conditions of the Black experience" (p. 145). In a later study, Carter and Helms (1988) found that socioeconomic status variables were not significant predictors of racial identity attitudes.

Baldwin (1981, 1984), Baldwin and Bell (1985), and Baldwin et al. (1987) discussed the concept of African self-consciousness as "central to normal and healthy Black personality functioning" (Baldwin et al., 1987, p. 28). According to their theory, African self-consciousness involves (a) the recognition of oneself as "African" and what being "African means," (b) the recognition of African survival and pro-active development as one's first priority value, (c) respect for and active perpetuation of all things African, and (d) having a standard of conduct toward all things "non-African" and "anti-African" (Baldwin et al., 1987, p. 29). Baldwin and Bell (1985) have developed the African Self-Consciousness (ASC) Scale that measures competency in the four areas of African self-consciousness identified previously. In a study of the relationship of background characteristics and social cultural setting to African self-consciousness, Baldwin et al. (1987) found that Black students at a predominantly Black college had significantly higher ASC scale scores than did Black students attending a predominantly White institution.

They also found that older students and upper-class students had higher ASC scores than did younger students and underclass students, with the class difference being more pronounced for students in the predominantly Black college. Baldwin et al. (1987) concluded that a predominantly Black academic setting may have a more positive influence on the development of African self-consciousness than will a predominantly White academic setting.

Interacting With the Dominant Culture

Another aspect of culture is the role that assimilation and acculturation play in the development of racial and ethnic minority students. Because White students are part of the majority and dominant culture, this issue of assimilation/acculturation does not emerge for students of the dominant culture. For African-American students, however, the task of "adjusting to living/learning in a campus environment that varies from the accustomed cultural frame of reference" (Wright, 1987, p. 11) is a most important issue.

Gibbs (1974) cited numerous studies in which Black students suffer from a series of identity problems resulting from culture conflict. Through clinical experience with Black students experiencing ethnic or cultural conflicts, Gibbs identified four modes of adaptation to the college and university environment. These four modes are withdrawal, described as movement away from the dominant culture and is characterized by apathy and depression; separation, described as movement against the dominant culture and is characterized by anger, hostility, and conflicts with the dominant culture; assimilation, described as movement toward the dominant culture and is characterized by social anxiety and desire for acceptance; and affirmation, described as movement with the dominant culture and is characterized by self-acceptance, high achievement, and a positive ethnic identity. Three of these modes of adaptation are similar to Pettigrew's (1964) three major modes of response to oppression. Among the 41 students in Gibbs's study, withdrawal was the most frequent response mode. Gibbs found that 70% of those students who described themselves as feeling adequate were in the affirmation category, and 61% of those who felt inadequate were in the withdrawal category.

In examining four different categories of socioeconomic class, class differences were found among three of the four response categories. For students of the two highest socioeconomic classes, affirmation and assimilation were the second and third most frequent response modes. There were no students in the separation category among the highest class, and none in the assimilation or affirmation categories among the lowest class. Among working-class students (third lowest class), there were "fewer in the affirmation category and more in the separation and assimilation categories" (p. 738) than there were students in the top two socioeconomic classes.

Developing Cultural Aesthetics and Awareness

Developing cultural aesthetics and awareness is an additional developmental issue for African-American students (Jones, 1987; Stikes, 1984; Wright, 1987). This relates to an appreciation of one's own culture, and of other cultures, especially in addition to the dominant culture, and also developing ways in which African-American students can express and celebrate their own cultures.

Developing Identity

The general concept of identity must also be expanded and viewed from a different perspective for African-American students. Sedlacek (1987) addressed this in terms of the importance of self-concept and self-appraisal. Erikson (1968) noted the message of lost, confused and "surrendered identity" contained in the writings of revolutionary Black authors. These same authors speak of inaudibility, namelessness, facelessness, and invisibility that Blacks have been made to experience. Knefelkamp and Golec (1985) echoed the invisibility that certain persons in American society have had to face. Others (Anson, 1987; DuBois, 1953; Wright, 1987) addressed the duality or even multiplicity with which Black students must struggle, an identity consideration not typically faced by majority students. As Wright (1987) indicated, many minority students live and learn in bicultural/biracial/bilingual environments, which are different from and frequently in conflict with those experienced at college. According to Bradley and Stewart (1982), Blacks experience depersonalization, which brings with it a loss of one's sense of identity, pride, and accomplishment. Cummins (1986) talked about bicultural ambivalence. Brown-Collins and Sussewell (1986) raised the issue of multiple self-referents for African-American students, especially Black women, and suggested at least three self-referents, that of the psychophysiological (Gilligan, 1982), the African American, and oneself (self-knowledge). All of these authors suggest the multiplicity of roles or identities, the implication of contextual identities for students of nondominant cultures, and the intense struggle for African-American students at PWIs to develop identity when the environment seems to work at cross-purposes to such development.

Furthermore, identity development, according to Erikson (1968), relates both to a developmental stage in the life of an individual and to a period in history. Thus, his statement provides strong support for DeVos's (1980) notion of the importance of considering the current social environment. Gurin and Epps (1975), in a series of studies conducted in several historically Black colleges between 1964 and 1970, found that the Black student's sense of identity involves both uniquely personal and collective elements that result from social interaction and group identifications and demonstrated that the students used being Black as the basis for collective elements of identity.

Developing Interdependence

For African-American students, developing independence and autonomy seems to occur within the context of interdependence and relationships, contrasted with the developmental issue of separating oneself from family and significant others as suggested by the literature (Chickering, 1969; Erikson, 1968). Hughes (1987), based on her qualitative research with 79 Black students, found patterns of individuation unique to Black students resulting from the close relationship that Black students maintain with their families. She highlighted the importance of interdependence in individuation and suggested that "it is likely that Black individuation helps to integrate Afrocentric cultural values, commonly referred to as the 'extended family'" (p. 540). Hughes's findings are supported by the literature on the extended nature of the Black family and Black homelife (Willie, 1976) and the unique educational/socialization role of the Black family (Willie, 1976). The roles of family and community are also strongly tied to philosophical connections with the African tradition, such as kinship tradition/group consciousness, survival focus (collective versus individual) and view of people as an integrated whole (Baldwin, 1981; Nobles, 1980).

Fulfilling Affiliation Needs

The role of affiliation needs is also highlighted by Hughes (1987). Affiliation opportunities play a significant role in the survival, success, and development of African-American students at PWIs. On predominantly White campuses, affiliations can counter the social isolation experienced by Black students. In Hughes's (1987) study, Black students' needs were fulfilled external to the university campus, through the Black community, Black churches, and the extended family. DeVos (1980) also addressed the importance of peers or a reference group in the development of Black students, especially in the development of ethnic identity.

Surviving Intellectually

The intellectual survival of African-American students on predominantly White campuses must also be addressed. Fleming (1984) eloquently discussed, based on her research, the impoverished environment for Black students in terms of their cognitive development and the intense struggle that many Black students face in developing the most basic intellectual competence, which is necessary for survival on the college campus. Others (DeVos, 1980; Hughes, 1987) also provide evidence in support of this issue. Hughes goes even further when she indicates that many Black students realize that development in other areas will be delayed or postponed because of their preoccupation with intellectual survival.

Developing Spiritually

The role of religion and spiritual development are two related dimensions that are frequently important to African-American students but that have not been accounted for adequately in most student development theories. Religion not only remains an important activity for African-American students throughout the college years (Wright, 1987) but the church is often an important support for African-American students (Erikson, 1968; Hughes, 1987). Similarly, spiritual development needs to be incorporated in student development theories for a better understanding of African-American students. An additional support reported by Black students in Hughes's (1987) study was reliance on spiritual strength, with spirituality being a deeply rooted aspect of Afrocentric culture (Hughs, 1987). Baldwin (1981) and Nobles (1980) also address the spiritual disposition of African Americans.

Developing Social Responsibility

Wright (1987) suggested that the development of social responsibility is a special psychosocial issue for racial and ethnic minority students. Because of their ethnic status and their exposure to real and perceived social injustice, African-American students frequently assume major responsibility for social advocacy roles on campus. Wright suggests that the greatest dilemma for racial/ethnic minority students in relation to social responsibility is not whether to assume it, but rather how it relates to other multiple responsibilities they hold.

Summary

The following recommendations are offered:

1. Student affairs professionals must develop out of the experiences of African Americans workable theories of student development. When traditional theories are used in working with Black students, conclusions are often reached that are not accurate. Traditional theories are based on the values, philosophical assumptions, and experiences of European Americans.

2. The philosophical connections to Africa have created a distinct African-American ethos. There are many additional factors that contribute to the unique experience and psychological disposition of African Americans. These issues must be taken into account if there is to be created an accurate working model to understand the attitudes, behaviors, feelings, and development of African-American students.

3. Because of the diversity in the Black community, there is no such thing as a "typical Black person." The shared experience of being Black in American Society, however, provides a link in the experiences of all African Americans. The link consists of a core of behavioral/dispositional variables upon which theories of the development of African-American students may be developed.

4. Student affairs professionals can work with Black students neither meaningfully nor successfully without understanding their philosophical assumptions and their life experiences.

5. Black student development must not be viewed/approached as "deficit development." There are at least two approaches that may be taken to look at Black student developmental issues. One approach focuses on the negative experiences that African Americans have in American society and at PWIs; the other approach focuses on the positive traits that connection to the African tradition brings to Black students and their efforts to succeed in an Anglo-Saxon social structure. Focus on the former causes a person to view the Black student from a deficit-deficiency perspective. By focusing on the latter, African-American students are approached based on the positive skills and personal characteristics that they bring to the campus community, and subsequent programs will build on those values, traditions, and attitudes.

6. One way of creating a workable theory of college student development is to incorporate the nine issues identified above into an existing psychosocial theory. Chickering's (1969) theory, as one of the most comprehensive of the psychosocial theories and also as one of the best known and most frequently applied theories, offers a good possibility. Some of the nine developmental issues discussed earlier, such as developing identity in multicultural environments, developing cultural aesthetics and awareness, and fulfilling affiliation needs, could be incorporated into a more comprehensive understanding of Chickering's seven vectors. One example would be expanding Chickering's conceptualization of developing identity with the notions of invisibility (Erikson, 1968; Knefelkamp & Golec, 1985), multiple identities (Anson, 1987; Cummins, 1986; DuBois, 1953; Wright, 1987), and African-American psychohistory (Essien-Udom, 1971). Other issues, such as developing racial and ethnic identity, interacting with the dominant culture, and developing spiritually, could become additional vectors in Chickering's theory. With such an approach, an empirical base would need to be developed to determine the appropriateness of such a rationally derived theory.

A real danger, however, is involved in taking an existing theory, such as Chickering's theory, which is based upon the values and philosophical assumptions of European Americans and upon research with predominantly Caucasian samples. The problem in revising an existing theory is making the assumption that the theory, such as Chickering's, is indeed appropriate for African-American students, although not sufficient. Straub and Rodgers (1986) and Taub (1989) have already raised questions about the applicability of the order of Chickering's vectors of female students. Taub (1989) also has reported findings that challenge the appropriateness of Chickering's theory for Black female students. Thus, as student affairs professionals attempt to make theories of human and student development more inclusive of other populations, it seems more important to create new theories rather than to modify or revise existing ones.

In conclusion, if colleges and universities are to achieve the lofty ideals that they have set forth in their various mission statements, they must begin to approach the education of African-American students in a more positive manner. This approach must include seeing the strengths that African-American students bring to the campus, understanding the influence of various life situations on the educational/developmental process, and treating the campus environment as the deficit in the deficit-deficiency model.

References

American Council on Education. (1937). *The student personnel point of view*. Washington, DC: Author.

American Council on Education. (1949). *The student personnel point of view* (rev. ed.). Washington, DC: Author.

Anson, R. S. (1987). *Best intentions: The education and killing of Edmund Perry*. New York: Vintage Books.

Baldwin, J. A. (1981). Notes on an Afrocentric theory of personality. *The Western Journal of Black Studies, 5*, 172–179.

Baldwin, J. A. (1984). African self-consciousness and the mental health of African-Americans. *Journal of Black Studies, 15*, 174–194.

Baldwin, J. A., & Bell, Y. (1985). The African self-consciousness scale: As Africentric personality questionnaire. *The Western Journal of Black Studies, 9*, 61–68.

Baldwin, J. A., Duncan, J. A., & Bell, Y. (1987). Assessment of African self-consciousness among Black students from two college environments. *The Journal of Black Psychology, 13*, 27–41.

Boyer, E. L. (1987). *College: The undergraduate experience in America*. New York: Harper & Row.

Bradley, L. R., & Stewart, M. A. (1982). The relationship between self-concept and personality development in Black college students: A developmental approach. *Journal of Non-White Concerns, 10*, 114–125.

Brown-Collins, A. R., & Sussewell, D. R. (1986). The Afro-American woman's emerging selves. *The Journal of Black Psychology, 13*, 1–11.

Bulhan, H. A. (1985). *Frantz Fanon and the psychology of oppression*. New York: Plenum Press.

Carter, R. T., & Helms, J. E. (1988). The relationship between racial identity attitudes and social class. *Journal of Negro Education, 57*, 22–30.

Chickering, A. W. (1969). *Education and identity*. San Francisco: Jossey-Bass.

Coons, F. (1970). The resolution of adolescence in college. *The Personnel and Guidance Journal, 48*, 533–541.

Cross, W. E., Jr. (1971). The Negro-to-Black conversion experience: Toward a psychology of Black liberation. *Black World, 20*(9), 13–27.

Cross, W. E., Jr. (1978). The Thomas and Cross models of psychological Nigrescence: A review. *The Journal of Black Psychology, 5*, 13–31.

Cruse, H. (1986). Empowering minority students: A framework for intervention. *Harvard Educational Review, 56*, 18–36.

DeVos, G. A. (1980). Ethnic adaptation and minority status. *Journal of Cross-Cultural Psychology, 11*, 101–124.

DuBois, W. E. B. (1953). *The souls of Black folks*. Greenwich, Ct: Fawcett Publications, Inc.

Erikson, E. H. (1968). *Identity: Youth and crisis*. New York: Norton.

Essien-Udom, E. U. (1971). Black identity in the international context. In N. I. Huggins, M. Kilson, & D. M. Fox (Eds.), *Key issues in the Afro-American experience* (Volume 2, pp. 233–258). New York: Harcourt Brace Jovanovich.

Fanon, F. (1967). *Black skin, White Masks*. New York: Grove Press.

Fanon, F. (1972). Racism and culture. In W. King & E. Anthony (Eds.), *Black poets and prophets: The theory, practice, and esthetics of the Pan-Africanist revolution* (pp. 13–25). New York; Mentor Books.

Fleming, J. (1984). *Blacks in college*. San Francisco: Jossey-Bass.

Gibbs, J. T. (1974). Patterns of adaptation among Black students at a predominantly white university: Selected case studies. *American Journal of Orthopsychiatry, 44*, 728–740.

Gilligan, C. (1982). *In a different voice*. Boston: Harvard University Press.

Gurin, P., & Epps, E. (1975). *Black consciousness, identity, and achievement*. New York: Wiley.

Hall, W. S., & Freedle, R. O. (1975). *Culture and language: The Black American experience*. Washington, DC: Hemisphere Publishing.

Heath, D. H. (1968). *Growing up in college: Liberal education and maturity*. San Francisco: Jossey-Bass.

Heath, R. (1964). *The reasonable adventurer*. Pittsburgh: University of Pittsburgh Press.

Helms, J. E. (1984). Toward a theoretical explanation of the effects of race on counseling: A Black and White model. *The Counseling Psychologist, 12*(4), 153–165.

Hughes, M. S. (1987). Black students' participation in higher education. *Journal of College Student Personnel, 28*, 532–545.

Jones, W. T. (1987). Enhancing minority-white peer interactions. In D. J. Wright (Ed.), *Responding to the needs of today's minority students* (pp. 81–94). San Francisco: Jossey-Bass.

Keniston, K. (1971). *Youth and dissent*. New York: Harcourt Brace Jovanovich.

King, S. H. (1973). *Five lives at Harvard: Personality change during college*. Cambridge: Harvard University Press.

Knefelkamp, L. L., & Golec, R. R. (1985). *A workbook for using the P-T-P model*. College Park, MD: University Book Store.

Knefelkamp, L., Widick, C., & Parker, C. A. (Eds.). (1978). *Applying new developmental findings*. San Francisco: Jossey-Bass.

Kovel, J. (1970). *White racism: A psychohistory*. New York: Vintage Books.

National Association of Student Personnel Administrators. (1987). *Perspective on student affairs*. Washington, DC: Author.

Nobles, W. W. (1980). African philosophy: Foundations for Black psychology. In R. L. Jones (Ed.), Black psychology (pp. 23–36). New York: Harper & Row.

Ogbu, J. U. (1981). Black education. In H.P. McAdoo (Ed.), *Black Families* (pp.139–153). Beverly Hills: Sage.

Parham, T. A. (1989). Cycles of psychological Nigrescence. *The Counseling Psychologist, 17*, 187–226.

Parham, T. A., & Helms, J. E. (1981). The influence of Black students' racial identity attitudes on preferences for counselor's race. *Journal of Counseling Psychology, 28*, 250–257.

Parham, T. A., & Helms, J. E. (1985a). Attitudes of racial identity and self-esteem of Black students: An exploratory investigation. *Journal of College Student Personnel, 26*, 143–147.

Parham, T. A., & Helms, J. E. (1985b). Relation of racial identity attitudes to self-actualization and affective states of Black students. *Journal of Counseling Psychology, 32*, 431–440.

Pettigrew, T. F. (1964). *A profile of the Negro American*. Princeton: Van Nostrand.

Pounds, A. W. (1987). Black students' needs on predominantly white campuses. In D. J. Wright (Ed.), *Responding to the needs of today's minority students* (pp. 23–38). San Francisco: Jossey-Bass.

Saddlemire, G. L., & Rentz, A. L. (Eds.). (1986). The student personnel point of view. In *Student affairs: A profession's heritage* (rev. ed., pp. 122–140). Alexandria, VA: American College Personnel Association.

Sanford, N. (1962). Developmental status of the entering freshman. In N. Sanford (Ed.), *The American college* (pp. 253–282). New York: Wiley.

Scruggs, O. M. (1971). The economic and racial components of Jim Crow. In N. I. Huggins, M. Kilson, & D. M. Fox (Eds.), *Key issues in the Afro-American experience* (Volume 2, pp. 70–87). New York: Harcourt Brace Jovanovich.

Sedlacek, W. E. (1987). Black students on White campuses: 20 years of research. *Journal of College Student Personnel, 28*, 484–495.

Stikes, C. S. (1984). *Black students in higher education*. Carbondale, IL: Southern Illinois University Press.

Straub, C., & Rodgers, R. F. (1986). An exploration of Chickering's theory and women's development. *Journal of College Student Personnel, 27*, 216–224.

Taub, D. G. (1989). *The patterns of development of autonomy and mature interpersonal relationships in Black and White undergraduate women*. Unpublished master's thesis, University of Maryland, College Park.

Willie, C. V. (1976). *A new look at Black families*. New York: General Hall Inc.

Wright, D. J. (1987). Minority students: Developmental beginnings. In D. J. Wright (Ed.), *Responding to the needs of today's minority Students* (pp. 5–22). San Francisco: Jossey-Bass.

CHAPTER 16

AN ASIAN AMERICAN PERSPECTIVE ON PSYCHOSOCIAL STUDENT DEVELOPMENT THEORY

CORINNE MAEKAWA KODAMA, MARYLU K. MCEWEN,
CHRISTOPHER T. H. LIANG, AND SUNNY LEE

Psychosocial student development theory based on predominantly white student populations may not be appropriate for Asian American students. The authors propose a new model of psychosocial development for Asian American students that takes racial identity and external influences into account.

In recent years, discussion in higher education has centered on how practitioners can provide more effective and inclusive services for all students. Given that these services are often based on theoretical foundations that have been narrowly normed, it makes sense to examine some of these theories and their relevance to today's student populations. Arguments about developmental theories not reflecting the voices of women students (Belenky, Clinchy, Goldberger, and Tarule, 1986; Gilligan, 1982; Straub and Rodgers, 1986), African American students (McEwen, Roper, Bryant, and Langa, 1990), and gay and lesbian students (Levine and Evans, 1991) have been made. Similarly, we contend that the psychosocial development of Asian American students is not reflected adequately in the psychosocial theory of Chickering and Reisser (1993) and propose a model of psychosocial development that accounts more effectively for the experiences and development of Asian American students.

This model was developed from an examination of psychosocial themes and issues discovered in the research literature in combination with a critique of traditional student development theory, primarily Chickering's psychosocial student development theory (1969; Chickering and Reisser, 1993; for a more detailed critique, see Kodama, McEwen, Liang, and Lee, 2001). Although we are assuming some knowledge of Chickering's developmental model, a brief introduction to psychosocial theory and Chickering may be helpful.

Psychosocial development, according to Parker, Widick, and Knefelkamp (1978), addresses "what students will be concerned about and what decisions will be primary" (p. xii). However, to date there has been no research examining psychosocial theory with Asian American students (Evans, Forney, and Guido-DiBrito, 1998).

Chickering's theoretical frame of student development (Chickering and Reisser, 1993) has been adopted widely and used by student affairs practitioners. In Chickering's model, developmental tasks are presented as seven core issues or challenges that the college student encounters: developing competency, managing emotions, moving through autonomy toward interdependence, developing mature interpersonal relationships, developing identity, developing purpose, and developing integrity. Chickering presents a typical pattern to the seven vectors, with the first four vectors providing the foundation for the fifth vector, which then leads to the final two vectors.

Most of the themes that emerged in this theoretical research as psychosocial issues for Asian American students mirrored the *content* areas of Chickering's seven vectors, though the specific *tasks* associated with those vectors, that is, *how* students negotiate or address those content areas, did not fit well. For example, emotions are an area of development that Asian American students are dealing with, but not necessarily learning how to "manage," as Chickering suggests. We frame our model in the context of two external domains that exert influences on Asian American students' development: Western values and racism from U.S. society and Asian values from family and community. How students are able to negotiate this tension of dominant societal norms and familial and cultural values influences the development of their identity.

External Influences and Domains

Life in the United States is dominated by Western values such as individualism, independence, and self-exploration, each of which underlies the development of traditional psychosocial theory. Another influence from dominant society is that of racism, which is often overlooked in terms of its influence on an individual's psychosocial development. Like many nonwhite groups in the United States, Asian Americans are often not exposed to the history of contributions and struggles of their own communities. Although their heritage is rendered invisible in education, their identity may have incorporated a variety of stereotypes from society and the media of who they are and what they should be. Hamamoto (1994) explains that these images serve to perpetuate "psychosocial dominance" (Baker, 1983, p. 35), as Asian Americans may begin to disdain their racial or ethnic background and even themselves. Essentially, "psychosocial dominance" refers to how racial minorities internalize racism and accept the primacy of Euro-American cultural values and social institutions (Espiritu, 1997). Identity, then, becomes a process of negotiating the mores of the dominant culture.

Racial identity, tied to the experience of all people of color with oppression (Helms, 1995), becomes central to a student's overall sense of identity and psychosocial development. Racial identity theories (Atkinson, Morten, and Sue, 1993; Helms, 1995), as Alvin Alvarez shows in Chapter Four, can help explain the various ways that students approach, negotiate, and understand their identity as racial beings and how it affects other aspects of their lives.

The second domain of influence on Asian American college students is traditional Asian familial and cultural values. These include the values of collectivism, interdependence, placing the needs of the family above the self, interpersonal harmony, and deference to authority, which often contradict those of the dominant Western society (Kim, Atkinson, and Yang, 1999). For example, Asian collectivism contrasts with Western individualism, which influences identity, as Western cultures view identity as the development of a self-actualized, autonomous individual, while Asian cultures view the identity of the individual as connected to the family unit (Huang, 1997). This presents a dilemma for Asian American students who are trying to negotiate and reconcile these conflicting influences with their own experiences at home and around peers.

Family and dominant white society may exert opposing forces on an Asian American student that both constrain and influence the student's development. However, some research indicates that Asian Americans are influenced strongly in their identity by others (Leong, 1985; Yeh and Huang, 1996), so external influences may have a greater impact on Asian American students than acknowledged in traditional theories, which portray identity development primarily as an individual process.

The degree of polarization between these two domains of familial and cultural values and dominant societal mores differs from student to student, based on generational status, level of acculturation, geographical location, peer groups, and proximity to Asian American political movements (Yeh and Huang, 1996). For instance, a first-generation Laotian American student whose family recently immigrated to the United States may experience more dissonance between Asian and Western values than a fourth-generation Chinese American student whose family has been in the United States since the early 1900s and has grown up with the dominant culture's values.

A Psychosocial Model for Asian American Students

In this new model of psychosocial development for Asian American students, we use much of the language of Chickering's theory, including ideas of competency, emotions, interdependence versus independence, identity, purpose, and integrity. However, we apply these terms to general content areas of development rather than associate them with specific tasks, and the order and emphasis on these areas differs from Chickering's original theory. A visual representation of this model is presented in Figure 1.

Central to the model is identity. Identity, according to Erikson (1968), embraces not only a sense of who one is as an individual but also a sense of self within one's family and community and some degree of congruence between one's view of oneself and others' views. Also central to this model is purpose, which includes vocational plans and aspirations as well as plans for college and the future.

In Figure 1, identity and purpose are represented as concentric circles, closely interrelated and as foundations for other areas of development. Since Asian Americans' pursuit of higher education is often pragmatic, goaloriented, and job-related (Hune and Chan, 1997), purpose may be central to students' reasons for attending college as well as how they identify themselves. The interface between identity and purpose is semipermeable, suggesting that an Asian American college student's identity may be filtered through the student's educational and vocational purpose; purpose may even serve as a protection against developing identity. For example, for a student whose identity is defined primarily by personal career goals and family commitments, new experiences and points of view may have little influence in challenging the student's devel-

opment around purpose or identity if they do not fit into this already established self-definition.

A change in identity for a student may result in a change of purpose (or vice versa) and may subsequently cause changes in other areas of development such as competency, emotions, interdependence, relationships, and integrity (visually portrayed as vectors, a term used by Chickering, 1969). The circular pattern of these vectors represents their nonhierarchical and fluid nature, not assigning primacy to one over another.

This model of psychosocial development takes place in the context of external influences from dominant U.S. society and traditional Asian values from family. This is represented visually by an axis on which the student's development is situated, with the two domains located at either end. This representation shows that a student's development can shift toward one side or the other, depending on which domain is exerting a stronger influence at a particular time or on a particular issue. For some students, the distance between the two ends may be great, representing much incongruence between the dominant society and the values of their family. For others, the distance may be short, particularly if the student is relatively acculturated and feels little conflict between the domains of family and society.

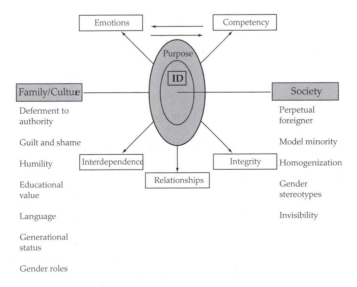

Figure 1 Asian Americans: Negotiating Identity and
Developmental Tasks

Increased awareness of the relationship of self to the two domains promotes the development of identity and purpose, which in turn influences change and growth among the other five developmental tasks. This sense of empowerment can lead to greater self-efficacy, congruence, and holistic development. The further a student moves in her or his development, the better able the student is to negotiate the dissonance between the two domains.

Identity. Identity centers our model of understanding Asian American students' psychosocial development, as it involves development of an increasingly complex self. Identity development means that there is increasing congruence between one's own sense of self and external feedback (Erikson, 1968).

Developing a racial identity provides a foundation for Asian American students' overall identity development because of the primacy of racism on psychosocial development. Although Chickering and Reisser (1993) and other psychosocial theorists do not single out racial or ethnic identity in much detail, we find it crucially important for the identity development of Asian Americans. As Noel, a Pilipino American student, suggests, race "is such a key part of my identity . . . that to separate the racial or ethnic component from the rest of me would be to slice myself in half."

Asian American students face racism and stereotypes that may influence the way they see themselves. Asian Americans often report having encounters that create a sense of otherness— surprise at their fluent English speech, assumptions that they are not American, and stereotypes such as computer geek, martial arts expert, and exotic woman. Such incidents teach Asian Americans that people make assumptions about who they are based on their physical appearance, which may be incongruent with their own self-perceptions. Michelle, a Chinese-Japanese American, provides a good example of this contradiction: "I don't think I've ever seen myself as looking Asian, though other people do. I just thought I had a regular face. . . . It seemed weird to me that people make judgments about who I am just because of how I look. . . . Just because I look Asian or Asian American to others doesn't mean that I understand the Asian culture."

Identity issues may be even more complex for multiracial students of Asian descent, who face additional questions about their appearance, identity, and loyalties. They may experience conflicting messages about the importance of their racial and ethnic identities within their families, and they may question where they fit in due to the often mutually exclusive groupings of race and ethnic identification (King and DaCosta, 1996; Root, 1997). Multiracial students struggle not only with how others perceive them but also with how they view themselves and construct their identity.

Gender and sexual identity are often overlooked but are important to Asian American students' identity development in college. Gender identity is particularly salient for Asian American college-age women, who may be encountering peers or role models who have a more feminist point of view. This can be a dramatic identity issue if these new points of view conflict with family expectations and values (Bradshaw, 1994; Homma-True, 1997). Being gay or lesbian can be a complex identity issue for Asian Americans as people of color who are already dealing with an oppressive society (Wall and Washington, 1991). Coming-out issues for gay and lesbian Asian Americans may be especially difficult in a culture where sexuality is rarely talked about, much less homosexuality (Aoki, 1997; Chan, 1989, 1997; Huang, 1997; Leong, 1996). Further, being gay may be perceived as bringing shame to oneself and one's family, conflicting with Asian cultural values of family heritage, honor, and passing on the family name (Aoki, 1997; Chan, 1989).

Purpose. For many Asian Americans, purpose is often connected closely with the issue of academic achievement. To the extent that segments of the Asian American community subscribe to an academic- and economic-based definition of success, Asian Americans may decide early in their college career on a major that leads to a prestigious or high-paying job, resulting in respect and economic security for their family (Leung, Ivey, and Suzuki, 1994). Concerned about prestige and financial security, many Asian Americans study the sciences, engineering, health care fields, and business (Lee, 1996; Hune and Chan, 1997). However, for students who are not interested in these fields, family expectations may make it difficult to choose another major or career path. Thus it seems that Asian Americans may come to college with a clearer sense of purpose in terms of majors and careers but may be less likely to change that original goal despite shifts in academic and personal interests.

Another issue for Asian Americans related to purpose is developing an awareness and understanding of various career opportunities. Because of stereotyping, lack of role models, and an economic-based definition of success, Asian American students may not see the full range of options available for their future. A lack of Asian American role models may result in students not being able to envision themselves in particular careers, regardless of interest.

Interdependence affects purpose and career choice (Leong, 1995; Wong and Mock, 1997), as Asian Americans have expressed higher levels of dependent decision making (Leong and Gim-Chung, 1995). In fact, Leong (1995) found that Asian Americans were the only ethnic group to rank parental pressure as one of the five most influential reasons in career choice. Thus traditional career counseling, focusing primarily on exploration of individual interests, may not fit well. However, relevant tasks around purpose for Asian Americans might be developing an understanding of personal interests in terms of career and lifestyle, recognizing that one can change majors and career paths, reconciling individual interests with family expectations, and integrating career goals within the scope of a larger, more meaningful purpose.

Competency. Competency as developed by Chickering (1969; Chickering and Reisser, 1993) is a relevant developmental task for Asian American college students. However, for Asian American students, the focus seems to be on intellectual competency rather than the other types of competency (physical and manual, interpersonal) that Chickering highlights in his theory. This may relate to a cultural value on education (Hune and Chan, 1997; Wong and Mock, 1997), perceived by many Asian Americans not only as an economic necessity but also as a primary vehicle by which to achieve success in a racist society (Hune and Chan, 1997). Asian Americans may also internalize the myth of the "model minority", whereby they are expected to do well intellectually. As a result, these students may experience "achievement stress" (Yamagata-Noji, 1987) as they place great pressure on themselves.

However, both interpersonal competency and physical competency may be challenges for Asian American students who have been taught to emphasize educational talents and goals (Wong and Mock, 1997). Social and interpersonal competency may be an even greater challenge for firstgeneration students, who may struggle with language barriers, cultural adjustments, or feelings of alienation, which contribute to a lack of confidence about their interpersonal abilities (Kiang, 1992).

Emotions. Asian cultural values include emotional discipline, inhibition of strong feelings, and use of restraint in interactions with others. Guilt and shame are often used as powerful controls (Lee, 1997; Liem, 1997; Uba, 1994) that affect how Asian Americans deal with emotions and behaviors. Further, there is some evidence that the long hours of hard work by Asian American parents (particularly recent immigrants) and a cultural tendency not to talk about discrimination and racism may result in neglect of children's emotional needs (Hong, 1993; Hongo, 1995; Lee, 1992).

Since withholding free expression of feelings is considered an important part of maintaining harmony (Chew and Ogi, 1987), Asian American college students may have had minimal modeling of emotional awareness and expression. Because the Asian cultural value places others' feelings above one's own (Wong and Mock, 1997), emotions may be an area of "untested waters" for many Asian American students. In a predominantly white college environment, however, expressiveness is often the norm, and Asian Americans may not be comfortable with others' openness (Chew and Ogi, 1987). Thus "exploring" or "understanding" emotions might be more appropriate tasks for Asian American students as they develop an awareness of a range of emotions, the appropriate expression of them, and which emotions are valued in a college environment (William Ming Liu, personal communication, Apr. 1998). This contrasts with Chickering's idea of "managing" emotions, which is based primarily on students' learning how to control "unruly" emotions (Chickering and Reisser, 1993, p. 83).

Interdependence Versus Independence. Interdependence is central to Asian cultures and families, with the Confucian values of filial piety and obligation to the family taking precedence over individual identity, wants, and desires (Lee,

1997). Western notions of adolescence as a time of separation and individuation (for example, separating psychologically and physically from parents) may consequently not fit the cultural values or life pattern of Asian Americans (Huang, 1997; Wong and Mock, 1997). Physical separation from Asian American parents often occurs only after marriage, and emotional separation, if it ever occurs, usually happens well into one's thirties rather than during the college years (Wong and Mock, 1997).

Family responsibility and support are central to interdependence for Asian Americans, particularly for students who serve as cultural brokers between their immigrant parents and the Western world. Asian American parents often exert strong parental guidance, particularly in terms of decisions to attend college (Choe, 1998) and career issues (Leong and Serafica, 1995). However, it is important to note that acculturation levels and generational statuses are influential variables in the development of autonomy and interdependence (Wong and Mock, 1997).

Asian Americans may need to learn how to see themselves as individuals outside their family group, which contrasts with students described by Chickering who are "looking out primarily for themselves" (Chickering and Reisser, 1993, p. 142) and focused on gaining independence and autonomy from their families. In a sense, Asian American students are moving through this area of development in a sort of reverse order from what is posited in Chickering's theory.

This interdependence with family may have a significant influence on students' social and emotional lives in college (Wong and Mock, 1997). Because of familial interdependence, Asian American students may be more likely to live at home than with peers (Yamagata-Noji, 1987) or attend college closer to home than move across the country (except to attend prestigious private schools). However, living at home or close to home can make it difficult for a student to become involved in the social life of the college and develop friendships or support networks outside the family.

Relationships. Maintaining harmonious interpersonal relationships is important in Asian cultures based on collectivism. Valued behaviors and personality traits include cooperation and accommodation, patience, humility, and nonconfrontation (Uba, 1994), along with respect for

elders and deference to authority. As a result, relationships with family, peers, romantic partners, and authority figures may be different from one another, and so the development of interpersonal relationships can be quite complex.

A challenge for Asian American students is developing relationships with faculty and staff. Given the hierarchical nature of relationships and respect for elders in many Asian cultures, Asian American students may be more comfortable deferring to authority rather than approaching faculty to introduce themselves or ask questions. This affects classroom interactions, where verbal expression and interaction are valued and even necessary for evaluation purposes. This also has implications for Asian American students' relationships with student affairs staff, as Asian Americans may be more formal with their elders, more concerned about doing something wrong, and less likely to challenge an adviser's perspective. Thus an important task for Asian American students may be developing relationships with faculty and staff that may be culturally different from their relationships with elders within their families.

A significant variable to consider in Asian Americans' development of relationships is the demographics of the college environment, particularly if it is different from a student's home environment. For example, a student who grew up in a predominantly Asian American neighborhood may need to learn how to adjust to a white majority on campus, while students who grew up in predominantly white neighborhoods may be unaccustomed to seeing many other Asian Americans. Many students experience pressure to choose between Asian American and non–Asian American friends and frequently deal with issues of integration versus segregation (Choe, 1998; Lee, 1996).

Furthermore, developing quality relationships, both platonic and romantic, may become more complex as Asian American students address their racial identity and learn the impact of racism and racial identity on their relationships (Helms, 1995). Michelle provides an example of these challenges:

> I do face a milder form [of racism and discrimination] . . . ; I've gotten bad vibes from [my classmates]; they've been hesitant to make friends with me, though I've tried very hard . . . It's an awkward situation . . . I just go to class, sit by myself, get the most out of it that I can, and leave. It's just the fifty min-

utes I have to deal with them . . . I haven't really approached them . . . I feel very uncomfortable with it, as it's very awkward having people speculate . . . and look at you like you're an animal in a zoo.

An important relationship issue that occurs often in college for Asian American students is the dynamics around dating issues, particularly interracial dating (Mock, 1999; Wang, Sedlacek, and Westbrook, 1992). Stereotypes of Asian American women and men may influence perceptions by the opposite sex, both within and outside their own ethnic or racial group. In particular, dating between white men and Asian American women is common and often causes tension between Asian American men and women about community and racial identity. Interracial relationships can also give rise to family tension and conflicts related to identity, grandchildren, and carrying on the family name (Lee, 1997; Wong and Mock, 1997).

Integrity. For Asian Americans, integrity is determined within the context of one's family and community by how individuals represent their families, respect their ancestors, and uphold the family name. Thus Asian Americans may be negotiating integrity for self versus integrity of family. According to Chickering (Chickering and Reisser, 1993), increasing congruence between behavior and values and consistency in applying ethical principles are keys to developing integrity. Asian American students, because of the differences between traditional Asian values and those of the dominant society, may find it difficult to develop congruence in these ways. Thus learning how to maintain balance and congruence between these two often competing sets of cultural values is a likely challenge.

This idea of a contextual integrity contrasts with Chickering's discussion of "humanizing values" as the ability to "detach, to withhold judgment, while staying in touch with persistent feelings" (Chickering and Reisser, 1993, p. 243) and "personalizing values" as students find their own way and clarify values and principles of their own apart from those of peers, family, and society. Because emotional restraint is a value in many Asian cultures, being "in touch with one's feelings" may be challenging. Furthermore, because of the interdependent nature of Asian Americans, making a clear distinction between individual values and those of the family can be difficult. Thus Chickering's framework of under-

standing integrity may not be appropriate for use with Asian Americans, who may not be trying to separate their own values from others' values as much as to maintain a sense of self within the context of values from family and society.

Implications for Professional Practice

The model of psychosocial development presented in this chapter has been designed to broaden the perspective of the ways that students may develop throughout the college years. Despite growing diversity on today's campuses, student affairs professionals, in developing programs and services, tend to rely on traditional psychosocial theories based on assumptions that may not fit current student populations.

Student affairs professionals should consider the importance of racial identity development in working with Asian American students and how racial identity can affect other areas of development. A change in racial identity may alter how students see themselves, their relationships, and their purpose in life, resulting in a renegotiation of other aspects of development.

The centrality of identity and purpose, as well as the focus on academic and economic variables in defining success, is important to consider in Asian Americans' pursuit of higher education. The interrelationship between identity and purpose is also crucial: if identity and purpose are one and the same for highly career-path-focused individuals, perhaps deep reflection or a set of challenging experiences such as not doing well in one's major may be necessary for students to challenge their established identity and to develop an identity beyond that of a specific vocational focus.

An understanding of familial interdependence and expectations and their impact on decision making for Asian Americans may help reevaluate practice, particularly in academic advising, career counseling, and even leadership development. Traditional methods of focusing primarily on students' individual interests and desires may not be appropriate, and it is important to consider the role of family expectations and pressures as the student negotiates his or her future.

An awareness of Asian Americans' perspectives on emotions can help student affairs practitioners understand and work better with Asian

American college students and perhaps identify some of the reasons for challenge in interpersonal settings. It is also a reminder that student affairs professionals cannot always rely on emotional cues to signal distress or difficulty and assume that the lack of emotional expression means that Asian American students are doing fine.

The impact of racism and the effect of cultural values should be considered in designing programming and services for Asian American students. Offering contextual experiences that address the impact of race and culture on student development increases Asian American students' ability to better navigate racism, understand clashing cultural values, and gain insight into why they may experience conflicts. The model minority stereotype is important to keep in mind because of its impact not only on educators' perceptions of Asian Americans but also on Asian American students themselves (Chun, 1995). Student affairs professionals should consider how challenged or burdened Asian American students are by this stereotype of success. Noel speaks about the effect of the model minority stereotype: "The model minority stereotype really bothers me . . . I think it makes people want to rebel against achieving more . . . because they're pigeonholed, they're told that you have to be a model minority . . . and that makes people want to rebel against that . . . and as a result against their racial identity."

In addition, providing and supporting Asian American studies programs, culturally and ethnically based student organizations, and a diverse student body, faculty, and staff help students understand their cultural heritage and learn from role models. Furthermore, these structures provide students with environments to explore the effects of the negotiation between familial and cultural influences and dominant cultural values on the students' sense of self and weaken the effects of psychosocial dominance. Angela, a Pilipina American, describes her experience: "I never knew our Asian American history. I knew about Pilipino history, but not about the contributions of Pilipinos here in America. I can finally see all the reasons for all those theories in my head about the way [we are] . . . This is talking about my grandfather or my dad . . . talking about my history, for once. I finally understood . . . why I felt the way I did growing up. I was really able to identify with the issues and with the people in class."

As a broader implication for theory and practice, the development of this new psychosocial model underscores the need to examine traditional theories critically in light of new and changing populations. It is important to look at the underlying assumptions of developmental theories that may be inapplicable to students from cultures with contrasting values. In the case of Chickering's theory, for example, the content areas of his theory make sense, but we challenge their specific meanings, associated tasks, and use in explaining Asian American students' development. In addition, descriptions that may seem to have negative connotations (for example, lack of experience with emotions and having an external locus of control) may not necessarily be negative in themselves but are perceived that way because of the Western biases inherent in student affairs professionals' understanding and application of a particular theory. Finally, external forces like racism and cultural values can greatly affect students' development, a perspective that contrasts with traditional views that development is an individual process. Thus it is not appropriate to continue to view diverse populations all through the same lens and rely on traditional theories to explain their development.

We suggest in this model of psychosocial student development that Asian American students will develop more fully as they understand themselves in the contexts of U.S. society, their families, and their communities. Understanding themselves in these contexts implies that parts of themselves are no longer silenced or denied, thereby enabling students to develop to their fullest potential. By creating more opportunities for students to explore themselves in college, socially imposed definitions of who and what is normal or developed are challenged. Knowing and taking into account students' familial and cultural contexts and helping them draw on their strengths and values, rather than viewing them as deficient in relation to dominant society ideals, will assist Asian American students in greater and more meaningful psychosocial development.

References

Aoki, B. K. "Gay and Lesbian Asian Americans in Psychotherapy." In E. Lee (ed.), *Working with Asian Americans: A Guide for Clinicians.* New York: Guilford, 1997.

Atkinson, D. R., Morten, G., and Sue, D. W. *Counseling American Minorities: A Cross-Cultural Perspective.* (4th ed.) Dubuque, Iowa:Brown/Benchmark, 1993.

Baker, D. G. *Race, Ethnicity, and Power: A Comparative Study.* London: Routledge & Kegan Paul, 1983.

Belenky, M. F., Clinchy, B. M., Goldberger, N. R., and Tarule, J. M. *Women's Ways of Knowing: The Development of Self, Voice, and Mind.* New York: Basic Books, 1986.

Bradshaw, C. "Asian and Asian American Women: Historical and political considerations in psychotherapy." In L. Comas Diaz and B. Greene (eds.), *Women of color: Integrating ethnic and gender identities in psychotherapy.* New York: Guilford, 1994.

Chan, C. S. "Issues of Identity Development Among Asian American Lesbians and Gay Men." *Journal of Counseling and Development,* 1989, *68,* 16–20.

Chan, C. S. "Don't Ask, Don't Tell, Don't Know: The Formation of a Homosexual Identity and Sexual Expression Among Asian American Lesbians." In B. Greene (ed.), *Ethnic and Cultural Diversity Among Lesbian and Gay Men.* Thousand Oaks, Calif.: Sage, 1997.

Chew, C. A., and Ogi, A. Y. "Asian American College Student Perspectives." In D. J. Wright (ed.), *Responding to the Needs of Today's Minority Students.* New Directions for Student Services, no. 38. San Francisco: Jossey-Bass, 1987.

Chickering, A. W. *Education and Identity.* San Francisco: Jossey-Bass, 1969.

Chickering, A. W., and Reisser, L. *Education and Identity.* (2nd ed.) San Francisco: Jossey-Bass, 1993.

Choe, Y. L. "Exploring the Experience of Asian Students at the University of Virginia." Unpublished paper, University of Virginia, 1998.

Chun, K. T. "The Myth of Asian American Success and Its Educational Ramifications." *IRCD Bulletin,* 1980, *1 and 2,* 1–12. Reprinted in D. T. Nakanishi and T. Y. Nishida (eds.), *The Asian American Educational Experience: A Source Book for Teachers and Students.* New York: Routledge, 1995.

Erikson, E. H. *Identity: Youth and Crisis.* New York: Norton, 1968.

Espiritu, Y. L. *Asian American Women and Men: Labor, Law, and Love.* Thousand Oaks, Calif.: Sage, 1997.

Evans, N. J., Forney, D. S., and Guido-DiBrito, F. *Student Development in College: Theory, Research, and Practice.* San Francisco: Jossey-Bass, 1998.

Gilligan, C. *In a Different Voice: Psychological Theory and Women's Development.* Cambridge, Mass.: Harvard University Press, 1982.

Hamamoto, D. Y. *Monitored Peril: Asian Americans and the Politics of TV Representation.* Minneapolis: University of Minnesota Press, 1994.

Helms, J. E. "An Update of Helms's White and People of Color Racial Identity Models." In J. G. Ponterotto, J. M. Casas, L. A. Suzuki, and C. M. Alexander (eds.), *Handbook of Multicultural Counseling.* Thousand Oaks, Calif.: Sage, 1995.

Homma-True, R. "Asian American Women." In E. Lee (ed.), *Working with Asian Americans: A Guide for Clinicians.* New York: Guilford, 1997.

Hong, M. (ed.). *Growing Up Asian American.* New York: Avon, 1993.

Hongo, G. (ed.). *Under Western Eyes: Personal Essays from Asian America.* New York: Anchor, 1995.

Huang, L. N. "Asian American Adolescents." In E. Lee (ed.), *Working with Asian Americans: A Guide for Clinicians.* New York: Guilford, 1997.

Hune, S., and Chan, K. S. "Special Focus: Asian Pacific American Demographic and Educational Trends." In D. J. Carter and R. Wilson (eds.), *Fifteenth Annual Status Report on Minorities in Higher Education, 1996–1997.* Washington, D.C.: American Council on Education, 1997.

Kiang, P. N. "Issues of Curriculum and Community for First-Generation Asian Americans in College." In L. S. Zwerling and H. B. London (eds.), *First-Generation Students: Confronting the Cultural Issues.* New Directions for Community Colleges, no. 80. San Francisco: Jossey-Bass, 1992.

Kim, B.S.K., Atkinson, D. R., and Yang, P. H. "The Asian Values Scale: Development, Factor Analysis, Validation, and Reliability." *Journal of Counseling Psychology,* 1999, *46,* 342–352.

King, R. C., and DaCosta, K. M. "Changing Face, Changing Race: The Remaking of Race in the Japanese American and African American Communities." In M.P.P. Root (ed.), *The Multiracial Experience.* Thousand Oaks, Calif.: Sage, 1996.

Kodama, C. M., McEwen, M. K., Liang, C.T.H., and Lee, S. "A Theoretical Examination of Psychosocial Issues for Asian Pacific American Students." *NASPA Journal,* 2001, *38,* 411–437.

Lee, E. "A Multicultural Coup at U-Md." *Washington Post,* Aug. 30, 2000, p. B1.

Lee, J.F.J. *Asian Americans: Oral Histories of First-to Fourth-Generation Americans from China, the Philippines, Japan, India, the Pacific Islands, Vietnam, and Cambodia.* New York: New Press, 1992.

Lee, S. J. *Unraveling the "Model Minority" Stereotype.* New York: Teachers College Press, 1996.

Leong, F.T.L. "Career Development of Asian Americans." *Journal of College Student Development,* 1985, *26,* 539–546.

Leong, F.T.L. (ed.). *Career Development and Vocational Behavior of Racial and Ethnic Minorities.* Mahwah, N.J.: Erlbaum, 1995.

Leong, F.T.L., and Gim-Chung, R. H. "Career Assessment and Intervention with Asian Americans." In F.T.L. Leong (ed.), *Career Development and Vocational Behavior of Racial and Ethnic Minorities*. Mahwah, N.J.: Erlbaum, 1995

Leong, F.T.L., and Serafica, F. C. "Career Development of Asian Americans: A Research Area in Need of a Good Theory." In F.T.L. Leong (ed.), *Career Development and Vocational Behavior of Racial and Ethnic Minorities*. Mahwah, N.J.: Erlbaum, 1995.

Leong, R. (ed.). *Asian American Sexualities: Dimensions of the Gay and Lesbian Experience*. New York: Routledge, 1996.

Leung, S. A., Ivey, D., and Suzuki, L. "Factors Affecting the Career Aspirations of Asian Americans." *Journal of Counseling and Development*, 1994, 72, 404–410.

Levine, H., and Evans, N. J. "The Development of Gay, Lesbian, and Bisexual Identities." In N. J. Evans and V. A. Wall (eds.), *Beyond Tolerance: Gays, Lesbians, and Bisexuals on Campus*. Washington, D.C.: American College Personnel Association, 1991.

Liem, R. "Shame and Guilt Among First- and Second-Generation Asian Americans and European Americans." *Journal of Cross-Cultural Psychology*, 1997, 28, 365–392.

McEwen, M. K., Roper, L. D., Bryant, D. R., and Langa, M. J. "Incorporating the Development of African-American Students into Psychosocial Theories of Student Development." *Journal of College Student Development*, 1990, 31, 429–436.

Mock, T. A. "Asian American Dating: Important Factors in Partner Choice." *Cultural Diversity and Ethnic Minority Psychology*, 1999, 5, 103–117.

Parker, C. A., Widick, C., and Knefelkamp, L. "Editors' Notes: Why Bother with Theory?" In L. Knefelkamp, C. Widick, and C. A. Parker (eds.), *Applying New Developmental Findings*. New Directions for Student Services, no. 4. San Francisco: Jossey-Bass, 1978.

Root, M.P.P. "Multiracial Asians: Models of Ethnic Identity." *Amerasia Journal*, 1997, 23(1), 29–41.

Straub, C. A., and Rodgers, R. F. "An Exploration of Chickering's Theory and Women's Development." *Journal of College Student Development*, 1986, 27, 216–224.

Uba, L. *Asian Americans: Personality Patterns, Identity, and Mental Health*. New York: Guilford, 1994.

Wall, V. A., and Washington, J. "Understanding Gay and Lesbian Students of Color." In N. J. Evans and V. A. Wall (eds.), *Beyond Tolerance: Gays, Lesbians, and Bisexuals on Campus*. Washington, D.C.: American College Personnel Association, 1991.

Wang, Y., Sedlacek, W. E., and Westbrook, F. D. "Asian Americans and Student Organizations: Attitudes and Participation." *Journal of College Student Development*, 1992, 33, 214–221.

Wong, L., and Mock, M. R. "Asian American Young Adults." In E. Lee (ed.), *Working with Asian Americans: A Guide for Clinicians*. New York: Guilford, 1997.

Yamagata-Noji, A. "The Educational Achievement of Japanese-Americans." Unpublished doctoral dissertation. Claremont Graduate School, 1987.

Yeh, C. J., and Huang, K. "The Collectivistic Nature of Ethnic Identity Development Among Asian American College Students." *Adolescence*, 1996, 31, 645–661.

Section 5

Dynamics of Race and Ethnicity in Development

CHAPTER 17

INTRODUCTION:
REVIEW OF RACIAL IDENTITY TERMINOLOGY

JANET E. HELMS

In discussing racial identity development, theorists have used diverse terminology, sometimes to describe the same or similar phenomena and sometimes not. Reconciling this linguistic diversity is beyond the scope, intent, or capability of this book. Rather it might be more useful and parsimonious to explain how various racial identity concepts are used in this work, particularly since in many instances, this usage represents the first time that such constructs have been used to describe the racial identity development of Whites as well as Blacks.

Many people erroneously use a person's racial categorization (e.g., Black versus White) to mean racial identity. However, the term "racial identity" actually refers to a sense of group or collective identity based on one's *perception* that he or she shares a common racial heritage with a particular racial group. Racial designation or category and ethnicity per se are confusing issues in the United States. As McRoy and Zurcher (1983) have pointed out, one needs only to have one-sixteenth black African ancestry or some physical features deemed typical of such ancestry in order to be classified as Black. Nevertheless, for the sake of simplicity, Casas's (1984) definition of race will be used. Quoting Krogman (1945), he defines race accordingly: "a sub-group of peoples possessing a definite combination of physical characters, of genetic origin, the combination of which to varying degrees distinguishes the sub-group from other sub-groups of mankind [sic] (p. 49)" (p. 787). As Casas further points out, this biological definition has no behavioral, psychological, or social implications ipso facto. However, what people believe, feel, and think about distinguishable racial groups can have such implications for individuals' intrapersonal as well as interpersonal functioning. Racial identity development theory concerns the psychological implications of racial-group membership; that is, belief systems that evolve in reaction to perceived differential racial-group membership.

Dizard (1970) indicates that the two significant contributors to a perceived collective or group identity are: "[a] a common thread of historical experience and a sense that each member of the collectivity, regardless of how distinct he [or she] may be, somehow shares in this historical experience, and [b] a sense of potency or strength inhering in the group" (p. 196). In partial agreement with Dizard's analysis, racial identity theories generally postulate a common thread of historical experiences; that is, they agree with the first part of Dizard's definition. However, in such theories, whether or not group identification is assumed to result in "a sense of group potency" depends on one's manner of identifying.

In distinguishing ethnicity from race, Casas (1984) defined ethnicity "as a group classification of individuals who share a unique social and cultural heritage (customs, language, religion, and so on) passed on from generation to generation" (p. 787). As he points out, ethnicity is not biologically defined and, therefore, race and ethnicity are not synonymous. Conceivably, members of different racial groups could belong to the same ethnic group; members of different ethnic groups need not belong to different racial groups. In contemporary social science literature, the mental health issues of Blacks typically have been examined without regard to ethnicity, and those of Whites typically have been examined without regard to race. That is, in the former case, one rarely finds analyses of how different categories of Black ethnics differ (e.g., how descendants of free and freed people or slaves in the United States differ from those of Haitians or Cape Verdeans or Black Hispanics and so on). Rather one's ostensible "Africanness" is assumed to account for one's psychosocial development regardless of ethnicity. On the other hand, though one occasionally finds analyses of how White ethnics (e.g., Irish, Polish, etc.) differ from one another (cf. Giordano & Giordano, 1977), with few recent exceptions (e.g., P. Katz, 1976), one rarely finds scholarly consideration of how the condition of being White influences Whites' psychosocial development.

Black and White racial identity theories examine psychological development from the level of racial rather than ethnic similarity. Therefore, although various theorists (cf. Helms, 1987) have proposed group identity theories to account for the psychosocial development of various ethnic groups (usually of color), it should be emphasized that ethnic group theories are *not* the focus of this book. Moreover, some writers use the term "ethnicity" as a euphemism for "race." So as not to distort these authors' language too severely, ethnicity will be used in this manner when an author's perspective seems to be better represented by such usage.

In this instance, racial identity and, by implication, racial identity theory in general refers to a Black or White person's identifying or not identifying with the racial group with which he or she is generally assumed to share *racial* heritage. In other words, racial identity partially refers to the person of black African ancestry's acknowledgment of shared racial-group membership with others of similar race as previously defined or the person of white European ancestry's acknowledgment of shared racial-group membership with others of similar race as previously defined.

Additionally, racial identity refers to the quality or manner of one's identification with the respective racial groups. Therefore, racial identity theories generally describe a variety of modes of identification. More specifically, Black racial identity theories attempt to explain the various ways in which Blacks can identify (or not identify) with other Blacks and/ or adopt or

abandon identities resulting from racial victimization; White racial identity theories attempt to explain the various ways in which Whites can identify (or not identify) with other Whites and/or evolve or avoid evolving a nonoppressive White identity.

Additionally, one's quality of adjustment has been hypothesized to result from a combination of "personal identity," "reference group orientation," and "ascribed identity" (cf. Cross, 1987; Erikson, 1963; 1968). Personal identity concerns one's feelings and attitudes about oneself, in other words, generic personality characteristics such as anxiety, self-esteem, and so on. Reference-group orientation refers to the extent to which one uses particular racial groups; for example, Blacks or Whites in this country, to guide one's feelings, thoughts, and behaviors. One's reference-group orientation is reflected in such things as value systems, organizational memberships, ideologies, and so on. Ascribed identity pertains to the individual's deliberate affiliation or commitment to a particular racial group. Typically one can choose to commit to one of four categories if one is Black or White: Blacks primarily, Whites primarily, neither, or both. Hence, a person who considers one race or the other to be the important definer of Self has a mono-racial ascribed identity; a person who feels a connectedness to both racial groups has a bi-racial ascribed identity; and the person who commits to neither group has a marginal ascribed identity.

It seems possible that each of these components varies relatively independently. So, for example, a Black or White person might feel positively about himself or herself, treat the experiences of racial group members as irrelevant to her or his own life circumstances, and feel a commitment to neither racial group. The "assimilating" Black (i.e., the Black person who wants to become a nondistinguishable member of White society), for instance, might feel good about herself or himself (i.e., positive personal identity), consider her or his racial-group membership to be irrelevant to her or his life circumstances (e.g., marginal ascribed identity), while attempting to live according to "White" beliefs about the world (i.e., White reference-group orientation). Similarly, a "melting pot" White (i.e., the person who believes everyone should be defined by the tenets of White socialization experiences) might feel good about herself or himself (i.e., positive personal identity), use White as a reference group for defining appropriate behavior (i.e., White reference-group orientation), and feel a commitment only to other White (i.e., White ascribed identity).

Nevertheless, the three components—personal identity, reference-group orientation, and ascribed identity—undoubtedly interact with each other. For instance, to the extent that society stereotypes one racial group as "dirty," "shiftless," and "ignorant" and another group as "clean," "industrious," and "intelligent" and can enforce with stereotypes, then it is likely that the individual will find it easier to use the second than the first group as both a reference group and source of ascribed identity. Relatedly, if one identifies with the positively characterized group, then it is likely that one will feel more positively about oneself than if one does not. However, such identifications become problematic to the extent that they require denial or distortions of oneself and/or the racial group(s) from which one descends.

From the discussion so far, it might be apparent that one's racial identity can involve various weightings of the three racial identity components. Racial identity theories attempt to describe the potential patterns of the personal, reference group, and ascribed identities, though not always so explicitly. Such theories also attempt to predict the varied feelings, thoughts, and/or behaviors that correspond to the differential weightings of components. The resulting variations might be called racial identity resolutions. Two different kinds of racial identity models have been used to describe potential resolutions. These can be characterized as "type" or "stage" perspectives.

Type models propose that potential racial identity resolutions can be grouped into one of several or a few categories (e.g., Dizard, 1970; Kovel, 1970). A basic supposition of such theories is that it is by appropriately "diagnosing" the person's category membership that one comes to understand the person's behavior. Seemingly, according to this perspective, one's racial identity category is assumed to be a fairly stable aspect of one's personality. Stage theories (e.g., Cross, 1971; Thomas, 1971) describe racial identity as a developmental process wherein a person potentially, though not necessarily, moves from one level of identity to another. According to stage theorists, one comes to understand a person's present behavioral dispositions by analyzing his or her identity at the present time, though the present identity may or may not have long-term implications for the person's future characteristics. Whether or not one's present level of racial identity development influences one's later development seems to depend on a complex mixture of environmental forces (e.g., economic factors), individual attributes (e.g., general cognitive development), and personal life experiences (e.g., the extent to which racism was a recognized element of the environment in which one grew up).

With regard to other common terminology, as used herein, racial identity and racial consciousness are considered to be interrelated but not synonymous, although such usage differs from that of other theorists (e.g., Caplan, 1970; Terry, 1977). Racial consciousness refers to the awareness that (socialization due to) racial-group membership can influence one's intrapsychic dynamic as well as interpersonal relationships. Thus, one's racial awareness may be subliminal and not readily admitted into consciousness or it may be conscious and not easily repressed. Racial identity pertains to the quality of the awareness or the various forms in which awareness can occur, that is, identity resolutions. Awareness of race may be accompanied by positive, negative, or neutral racial-group evaluations. The major racial identity theories propose that, within racial groups, various kinds of racial identity resolutions can exist, and consequently, racial consciousness per se usually is not considered to be dichotomous, present, or absent, but rather is polytomous.

In a similar vein, "cultural" is often used as a substitute for "racial" or "ethnic." Since one's racial-group designation does not necessarily define one's racial, cultural, or ethnic characteristics if racial identity theory is accurate, the interchangeable usage of these three terms will be avoided as much as possible.

CHAPTER 18

MODELS OF RACIAL OPPRESSION AND SOCIORACE

JANET E. HELMS AND DONELDA A. COOK

It is impossible for us to provide a thorough review of the socioracial group issues of each of the five major groups. Nevertheless, in previous chapters, we sought to provide enough of a flavor of the tensions so that therapists can have a basis for thinking about possible socioracial tensions that might impact the therapy process with themselves as the symbolic catalyst. Social scientists of various theoretical persuasions and orientations have attempted to provide explanations of racism's impact on individuals and/or intergroup relations, but rarely (with the possible exception of psychoanalytic theorists) have they considered the impact of racial factors on the therapy process per se.

Most contemporary theories of race and culture have tended to focus on the societal structural dynamics and implications of race and (occasionally) culture, but have rarely examined their intrapsychic and interpersonal consequences at the level of the individual. Yet therapists ought to be concerned about the interplay between the person's objective reality or circumstances (e.g., conditions of oppression) and her or his subjective well-being (e.g., manner in which experiences are interpreted).

Moreover, it is important to realize that although both race and culture involve person-environment socialization, for each individual client, psychorace and psycho-culture may be differentially salient to the client in any given situation (see Table 1). For some people, racial socialization will be a more important aspect of their personality development, and for others, cultural socialization will be more important. In this chapter, we examine models of racial oppression and sociorace for their usefulness in assessing client dynamics.

Socioracial Racial Theory

In order to maintain control over a group, it is necessary for the group in power to psychologically debilitate the target group's members. Not only must the members of the VREGs (in this case) be convinced that the inferior status of their group is pre-ordained or deserved, but the benefactors, beneficiaries, and perpetrators of the psychological and systemic oppression must also convince members of their own group that their superior status is justly deserved and that they bear no personal responsibility for the inferior status of the other socioracial out-groups.

Of course, one set of strategies that White Americans collectively have used to achieve and maintain functional control over visible racial and ethnic groups (VREGs) is differential dispensation and allotment of social, political, and economic power according to White-defined racial criteria. The efficient use of such strategies requires that mutually exclusive racial categories be created, regardless of whether these categories have any biogenetic basis in fact.

Moreover, members of the oppressed group(s) must be "de-cultured," by which we mean exposed to pervasive, systematic, ongoing indoctrination to the effect that their traditional culture as well as the members of that cultural group are inferior and worthless. The resulting cultural vacuum is then filled with the dominant group's stereotypical depictions of the various socioracial groups.

Also, members of the deculturated groups must be taught to which "racial" group they belong, and what observable socially undesirable characteristics define their group membership. That is, they must be "racinated" (see Cross, Parham, & Helms, 1991). This sequence of events makes it possible for the dominating group to maintain control over those groups considered to be threats to the status quo. In this society, groups of color (ALANAs) have been the primary focus of societies' demoralizing deculturation and racination tactics.

Whites, the preservers of the racial status quo and definers of the dominative group, must also be taught the fabricated observable criteria for innately belonging to or earning membership in the privileged group. As mentioned in the previous chapter, the racination process for them involves learning the sociopolitical rules of the dominant group (a process that presumably begins at birth); it also requires replacement of traditional European and Asian cultures with amalgamated (White) American culture. In addition, they must create and/or learn the rationale for why VREGs do not have or deserve equivalent status in this country.

For both Whites and VREGs, a discernible manifestation of the deculturation-racination process is the internalization of racial stereotypes. The mental health professions as well as politicians have contributed mightily to the content of existing racial stereotypes. Thus, in their analysis of racism in the mental health literature, Thomas and Sillen (1972) outlined the following racial stereotypic assumptions: (a) Blacks are endowed with "less gray matter" and smaller brains and consequently, are more prone (than Whites) to "insanity"; (b) social protest by People of Color is an infallible symptom of mental derangement; (c) less evolved or "lower races" (on the racial hierarchy) have not evolved sufficiently beyond their "simian past" to practice appropriately the conventions of civilized society (e.g., monogamous marriage); (d) VREGs cannot control their emotions and demonstrate a lack of morality, particularly with respect to sexuality; (e) VREGs are inappropriate candidates for psychoanalysis because of their "simplistic minds," but make excellent research specimens; and (f) living in close proximity to Blacks and other "lower races" (especially Asians and Native Americans) contaminates Whites, and so forth.

Perhaps not surprisingly, these stereotypes do not differ markedly from the racial stereotypes that prevail in contemporary society more widely. However, perhaps more surprising is the fact that the themes underlying the stereotypes are still a strong aspect of the conceptualization of racial dynamics in mental health and psychotherapy literature.

Interestingly, as Axelson (1993) noted, there is no consensual derogatory stereotype of Whites as a *racial* group. Their superiority is assumed. White stereotypes, such as they are, pertain to particular "deviant" ethnic groups (e.g., Polish jokes) or White subgroups who otherwise are assumed (without evidence) to differ in major ways from most White people (e.g., "rednecks").

For both the oppressors and oppressed, internalized racial stereotypes about oneself as well as others are a major component of what is meant by the term *internalized racism*, or psychological reactions to racial oppression. Among mental health practitioners, personalized psychological reactions are assumed to have major therapeutic implications, although they typically only discuss these implications as they pertain to Blacks and other VREGs.

For example, Landrum and Batts (1985) proposed a variety of related symptoms including poor self-concept, misdirected anger, in-group discord, drug addiction, and so forth as the potential focus of race-related interventions. When internalized racism is expressed overtly, it can have implications for the quality of a person's interactions with others. In the case of therapists and clients, in particular, the quality of the therapy process may be detrimentally influenced by the nature of the psychological reactions to race that each party has internalized.

Models of Racial Oppression

Feagin (1984) divides the existing explanatory models of racism and ethnocentricism into two categories—*order* and *power-conflict*. The focus of these models tends to differ depending on whether they were intended to explain the life circumstances of the dominative group (Whites) or one or more of the dominated groups. In the former case, one typically sees a greater emphasis on describing White people's negative reactions to "non-White" or "non-American" others; in the latter, one sees most emphasis on explaining adaptations of African, Latina/Latino, Asian, and Native Americans (ALANAs) to societal racism and ethnocentricism.

According to Feagin (1984), order theories generally emphasize the outcomes of assimilation and/or racism, that is, the manner by which nondominant groups adapt to or become like the dominant group. Power-conflict theories focus on the social control and conflict associated with subordinating other groups, in this case, White strategies for controlling other groups.

Nevertheless, virtually none of the models discussed by Feagin is of much use in analyzing the psychological implications of race in the psychotherapy process because they tend to treat race as group or structural dynamic rather than individual-difference dimensions. Structural dynamics pertain to societal conditions of racial classification (such as racial integration in housing and schools), and differential access to power (such as voting patterns and numbers of elected officials), whereas individual difference dimensions pertain to subjective reactions to one's conditions of racism (such as depression, exhilaration, and so forth). Using our terminology, structural models identify distal or sociological characteristics, whereas psychological models describe psychological (subjective) or proximal reactions to race.

In this chapter, some models that pertain specifically to issues of structural conditions of racism and ethnocentricism, that is, power-conflict and order models, are briefly summarized. We think these models are most useful for forming hypotheses about the societal racial conditions under which individual members of the various socioracial groups may exist. We also present models of racial identity development (Helms, 1990a) as one manner of conceptualizing clients' psychological adaptations to racism that we have found useful for explaining client and therapist racial dynamics in individual and group psychotherapy.

White Power-Conflict Models

The central question driving the quest for White models of racial oppression has concerned the group's propensity to seek and maintain dominative relationships with people who are assumed to be of a different race. At least up until 1964, when the first Civil Rights Act was signed, the relationship of Whites to groups of color was unapologetic domination, segrega-

tion, and oppression. Again the details of the domination differed depending on which group one considers.

However, the common thread running through race relations involving Whites as the protagonists is that Whites considered themselves to be superior to *all* non-White groups, and therefore entitled by birthright to "life, liberty, and the pursuit of happiness." Naturally, all groups of color were considered subservient and inferior and were expected to earn any of the rights to life, liberty, or justice that White society was willing to accord them.

Even the White people who are often portrayed as being sympathetic to the causes of people of color often were practitioners of racism. Abraham Lincoln, the "Great Emancipator," reveals his level of personal and institutional racism in the following quote: "I will say, then that I am not, nor ever have been, in favor of bringing about in any way the social and political equality of the white [sic] and black [sic] races (applause); that I am not, nor ever have been, in favor of making voters or jurors of Negroes [sic], nor of qualifying them to hold office, nor to intermarry with white [sic] people . . .

And inasmuch as they cannot so live, while they do remain together there must be the position of superior and inferior, and I as much as any other man am in favor of having the superior position assigned to the white [sic] race" (cited in Zinn, 1980, p. 184).

Most social scientists have been unable to explain why Whites have adhered to the principles of White supremacy, privilege, and domination for so long and so consistently with so many socioracial groups. Several theoretical explanations have been offered and we briefly summarize them here, not necessarily because we subscribe to them, but because therapists should be aware of the theories that may underlie their clients' expectations of them.

Theoretical explanations of Whites' dominative status can be categorized approximately as follows: (a) racial superiority; (b) racial inferiority; and (c) circumstantial. We intend only to describe these perspectives briefly, and consequently, in the case of those perspectives that are purported to be theories of "development" or "evolution," we may have done the perspectives a disservice. Therefore, the reader is referred to the original sources for a fuller elaboration of the perspectives.

White Racial Superiority

The general premise of White superiority explanations is that Whites deserve their dominant sociopolitical status because they are genetically, intellectually, and/or culturally superior to those whom they have dominated. Consequently, the characteristics of the White group are the standards by which members of other groups are evaluated.

In psychology more specifically, White superiority explanations have existed in both implicit and explicit versions. To the extent that they are based on the experiences of White people and their culture, universalistic perspectives are implicit White superiority perspectives (see Wrenn, 1962). Explicit models typically are founded on principles of sociobiology and directly base their premises on racial classifications, but not necessarily measurable physiological "racial" characteristics.

Universalistic Perspectives

In a sense most of the traditional theories of counseling and psychotherapy are based on universalistic principles. According to Ridley, Mendoza, and Kanitz (1994), universalistic perspectives are of two types—*generic* and *etic* or *true universalistic*. Proponents of generic perspectives argue that there are principles, aspects, or processes of human existence that transcend (socio)racial and cultural boundaries and, therefore, are applicable to all human beings. Proponents of etic universalistic frameworks contend that aspects of traditional theories are universally applicable to all people or that new culturally inclusive models can be created that will be applicable to everyone regardless of socioracial and/or cultural boundaries.

Generic models, theories, and principles are implicitly White racial and/or cultural superiority perspectives because they typically are explanations of human adaptations using the socialization experiences of White westerners and Europeans ás the basis of such interpretations. Such perspectives rarely consider the possibility that different life circumstances might contribute to alternate adaptations, which might be equally "healthy" for members of those groups to whom they pertain.

Consequently, the behavior of Whites is considered to be normative for other groups, and deviations from such norms are considered to be deficits. Explanations for these alleged deficits are then presumed to lie in the group's genetic makeup (in reality, racial classifications) or environmental deprivation. Hypothetical "group deficiencies" then become the justification for a wide range of dominative behaviors on the part of Whites.

With regard to the history of intergroup racial and cultural relations in general, group deficiencies of various sorts were used to justify the domination of all of the visible racial and ethnic groups. According to Hacker (1992), "From the premise of genetic inferiority, there follows the corollary that members of a lesser race should be content to perform tasks unsuited to other strains. This was the rationale for slavery, and it has by no means disappeared. (There are even hints of this in the plea to create more blue-collar jobs for black [sic] men.)" (p. 28). In the mental health professions more specifically, alleged ALANA inferiority has been used consistently to explain why ALANAs' behaviors supposedly do not conform to White-based standards in most aspects of the helping process.

Sociobiology

The basic premise of race-related sociobiological theory is that the racial-classification groups can be aligned along a superiority/inferiority hierarchy based on their presumed ancestry regardless of national or continental boundaries. Franklin (1991) contends that the underlying "scientific" basis of this perspective is Social Darwinism, and suggests that it was the philosophy underlying much of the "founding fathers'" and their descendants' mistreatment of VREGs in this country (see Helms, 1994).

According to Hutnik (1991) and Spikard (1992), some of the earliest spokespersons in U.S. society for this perspective were Madison Grant (1916), Henry Pratt Fairchild (1926), Howard C. Hill (1919), and Ellwood P. Cubberly (1929). In psychology, some spokespersons have been G. Stanley Hall (1904), J. Phillip Rushton (1990, 1995), and Arthur Jensen (1969). Originally, as previously noted, advocates of the racial sociobiological perspective argued that the northern and western European "races" were superior to all other racial groups, including southern and eastern Europeans. Although the order of the alignment of the racial categories shifted slightly over the ensuing decades, with Asians occasionally replacing Whites at the top of the hierarchy (see, for example, Rushton, 1995), according to Spikard (1992, p. 14), the typical order devised by the dominant European group was as follows: ". . . Caucasians at the top, Asians next, then Native Americans, and Africans at the bottom—in terms of both physical abilities and moral qualities [such as dishonesty, poverty, uncleanliness]."

The notion that psychological characteristics (e.g., physical abilities, personality characteristics) were inherited provided the justification for White Americans' domination and exploitation of other groups. Each racial group was assumed to be defined by a distinctive combination of psychological characteristics, and consequently, to occupy a different rung on the Darwinian evolutionary ladder. Since they were presumably the most evolved, Anglo-Saxon Americans had the right to force other groups to conform to their standards and/or to take from misfits that which was necessary (e.g., land, life, personhood, culture) to ensure the dominance and unity of the White American group.

White Racial Inferiority Models

White inferiority models attribute Whites' history of other-group domination to inherent aspects of the condition of being White, such as physiological or environmental deficits relative to other socioracial groups. Both psychoanalytic and cultural explanations of the "White personality" have been offered, according to which the sociopolitical characteristics of the White group are attributed to physiological or evolutionary deficiencies, and consequent psychological impairment resulting therefrom.

As is true of the other perspectives, our rationale for presenting these perspectives is not necessarily because we endorse them wholeheartedly, but rather because many clients will have internalized them as a form of folk psychology, a way of ameliorating the pain of institutional and cultural racism. The therapist who first hears about these views of White people from the mouths of her or his client is likely to be caught unawares.

Psychoanalytic. Although psychoanalytic theory often has been used to account for White racism (comer, 1991; P. Katz, 1976), psychiatrist Frances Cress Welsing (1974) is probably the first person to use this theoretical orientation to account for Whites' propensity to dominate other socioracial groups. Psychoanalytic theory origi-

nated with Sigmund Freud. In general, psychoanalytic theorists locate the motivation for human behavior in (usually) unconscious drives and instincts as Freud did. In many versions of psychoanalytic theory, these motivations have themes of sexuality and/or aggression.

For Welsing, the conscious or unconscious force that motivates Whites' domination of others is the drive to compensate for their whiteness; that is, their "color inadequacy" or "albinism." Thus, the basic premises of Cress's "Color-Confrontation Theory" are as follows: (a) When white people encounter any part of the massive numbers of peoples of color of the world, they become painfully aware of their minority status with respect to their own relative lack of color and number; and (b) in response to the wounded sense of identity that is based on an unchangeable part of themselves—their external appearance—they develop a number of defensive reactions and mechanisms to protect themselves from their own feelings of inadequacy.

Among the reactions are uncontrollable hostility and aggression, and defensive feelings that continuously have had peoples of color as their target throughout history. Among the defense mechanisms are repression of feelings and awareness of their genetic color inferiority; reaction formation in which the valued and desired skin color is psychologically imbued with opposite characteristics such as dirtiness, evil, and so forth; and "compensatory logic" (also a form of reaction formation) in which the lack of color or genetic deficiency is transformed into White supremacy. Thus, according to Welsing, White supremacy then becomes Whites' justification for their participation in the varieties of institutional and cultural racism that prevail in the society.

Environmental. Micheal Bradley (1978), an anthropologist, proposed the theory of the "iceman inheritance." According to his theory, White people are the descendants of Africans of color who migrated into the Northern Hemisphere, where their efforts to survive during the Ice Age (from 100,000 to 10,000 years Before the Present, B.P., which he defines as beginning in 1950) resulted in the evolution of definitive physiological and psychological characteristics, vestiges of which were transmitted to successive generations.

Thus, Bradley (1978, p. 26) contends that "glacial evolution demanded certain special adaptations of Neanderthal man [sic] and that present-day Caucasoids still show vestiges of these adaptations. *These special adaptations had incidental side effects which resulted in an exceptionally aggressive psychology, an extreme expression of the cronos complex, and a higher level of psychosexual conflict compared to all other races of men* [sic]."

In Bradley's thesis, "Caucasoid" refers to "White peoples." By *cronos complex*, he means territorial behaviors designed to protect one's identity and status across time (past, present, and future). In other words, people compete with their ancestral past (i.e., one must achieve more than one's ancestors), the present (i.e., one should accomplish more than the living including one's own offspring), and the future (i.e., one attempts to leave a legacy that others cannot surpass). Whereas Bradley contends that the cronos complex is a theme in all human societies, he argues that it is stronger in White groups because they were the only group to have evolved in a glacial environment, and consequently, they alone developed the exceptionally high level of aggression used to impose their identity on others. Unlike other racial groups, evolution in such austere circumstances allegedly narrowed the range of physical (e.g., sexual enjoyment) and psychological (e.g., empathy) options available to Whites for sublimating their self-protective aggressiveness.

Circumstantial

These explanations generally attribute Whites' exploitation of other groups to the circumstance of Whites' being the political majority in the country. Most such perspectives tend to begin the search for descriptions of the White condition post Civil War. More often than not, some simplistic form of racism or other manner of out-group prejudice is seen as the cause of Whites' self-aggrandizement. Richardson (1989) pointed out that these theories of racism generally treat VREG people as stressors to White people rather than conversely. Nevertheless, based on their reviews of racism literature, various authors (e.g., Allport, 1958; Katz, 1976; Richardson, 1989; Singer, 1962) have classified existing power-conflict racism-prejudice theories as follows:

Historical. The root causes of contemporary interracial-group conflict are located in the histories of the visible racial and ethnic groups (VREGs) that are participants in the conflict. Recall that the opportunity to convert and save the souls of African and Native Americans was frequently used as a rationale for slavery, an option that presumably is no longer available. Therefore, if ALANAs are discriminated against, it is because the options to civilize them are no longer readily available, and/or they no longer take maximal advantage of existing remedies. In other words, to understand Whites' anti-Black or anti-Native sentiments, then one needs to examine the histories of enslavement of these groups. Typically such perspectives do not explicate the reasons why or the manner in which the historical experiences of VREGs are responsible for shaping White people's feelings, attitudes, or behaviors.

Sociocultural. Societal and cultural (actually racial) trends cause people's individual racism. So, for example, urbanization (the tendency of large groups of especially People of Color to move into cities) has been hypothesized to account for Whites' antipathy toward Blacks because it promotes racial isolation and segregation, and because the incoming group does not share the same cultural values as the host group. Yet as Richardson (1989) notes, such explanations disregard the fact that even people who are not involved in the societal trend (e.g., urbanization) may express or experience the same types and levels of racism as those who are involved.

Earned Reputation. Alleged offensive characteristics of VREGs (e.g., bad odor, diminishment of property values, intellectual deficits) may provoke White people's abhorrence and aggression. Then these racial stereotypes may be used to justify Whites' negative attitudes toward other socioracial groups. This perspective is implicit in much of the psychotherapy literature pertaining to racial factors.

White Order Models

Although race- and culture-focused theorists have tended to be oblivious to the impact of White racism and Anglo-Saxon ethnocentrism on White people, if we stretch our imaginations some, we can adapt a couple of the existing frameworks to discuss Whites' potential adaptations to racism at the individual level.

Frustration-Aggression Hypothesis. Originally proposed by Dollard (1957; Dollard, Doob, Miller, Mowrer, & Sears, 1939), this explanation of the causes of racism and ethnocentrism continues to exist in the psychotherapy literature in sometimes modified forms. The basic premise here is that people respond to frustration, hostility, or unpleasant feelings of day-to-day arousal by taking them out on (displacing) convenient substitutes (scapegoats) for the more powerful aggressors or uncontrollable events. In this case, people of other perceived races or cultures become the scapegoats or targets for the frustration-reducing expressions of racism-ethnocentricism.

According to McLemore (1983), any guilt aroused by recognition that one is displacing aggression is assuaged by using racial stereotypes to rationalize former behaviors as well as new feelings of adverse arousal to daily frustrations, resulting in a cycle of out-group aggression. Since Whites are in the numerical majority and hold the institutional power, it is more likely that their frustration-aggression cycle will be overtly expressed, whereas VREGs are assumed to use convert forms of expression such as passive aggression or urban riots (Simpson & Yinger, 1972).

Although the frustration-aggression hypothesis was proposed as a universally applicable explanation of the manner by which people acquire personal racism, we think it may be more useful for understanding some, but not all, White people's racial reactions. In our experience, some White clients use a race-specific lay version of the frustration-aggression hypothesis to explain their antipathy toward other groups. "Some (fill in the socioracial group) person was mean (fill in a specific act) to me and ever since then, I have hated (or other appropriate affective verb) all (fill in the blank) people."

Obviously, certain amount of personal racism and inadequate skills for managing one's emotions underlie such assertions. The therapist can use the frustration-aggression hypothesis to aid her or him in identifying the client's specific manner of resolving daily frustrations, and to assist the client in learning more competent strategies for coping explicitly with life in general, and incidentally, other racial groups.

VREG Models

Interestingly, theories of VREGs' adaptation to their group's particular conditions of exploitation and domination have generally focused on describing the circumstances of African Americans. This singular focus on African Americans when addressing matters of race, and the other groups (i.e., Asian Latino/Latina, and Native Americans) when examining issues concerning cultural adaptation, probably has occurred for two reasons.

Throughout mental health history until the mid-1970s, all of the groups of color were generally considered to be no different than Black for all practical purposes (Thomas & Sillen, 1972). Consequently, theoretical formulations that pertained to one group were considered to be applicable to members of the other socioracial groups as well.

As it became expedient for economic and political reasons to expand the varieties of socioracial groups to accommodate differential prejudices and discrimination against immigrants of color and/or from undesirable parts of Europe and Asia, mental health theorists, practitioners, and researchers joined the rest of society in focusing on cultural differences as the justification for their alleged psychopathology rather than the maladaptive racial climate. Moreover, because Native Americans were generally considered to have a distinct culture whereas African Americans were not the effect of racism on Native people's well being has been as absent as the study of cultural incompatibility has been for people of African descent in the United States.

Thus, with respect to theoretical perspectives, one finds some allegedly racial psychological models with Black Americans as their focus, and some cultural models with Native, Latino/Latina, and Asian Americans as their focus. One rarely sees cultural factors addressed with respect to African Americans or racial factors addressed vis-à-vis the other groups of color. Consequently, in our experience, we have found that many of our colleagues and students have difficulty realizing that both cultural and racial factors might be of concern to VREG clients, regardless of their particular socioracial membership group.

In this chapter, we discuss racial sociological and psychological models. In the next chapter, we focus more explicitly on group-relevant cultures.

Sociological Perspectives

Most of these theories are intended to explain the psychological consequences of and/or the psychological motivations (i.e., internal mechanisms) for what is considered to be group-specific antisocial or deviant behavior. Most locate the stimuli for these consequences in the conditions of institutional racism and personality deficits of African Americans.

Geschwender (1968; cited in McLemore, 1983) proffered three theoretical models based on the proposition that civil disturbances is a reaction to people's increased dissatisfaction as they compare their real circumstances to their ideal circumstances. They are as follows: (a) Rising-expectation hypothesis—in response to improving group-related conditions, people begin to hope and believe that significant change is possible. Discontent occurs when the hoped-for ideal and one's reality are too discrepant, and consequently, collective action may occur; (b) Relative-deprivation hypothesis—People of Color compare their lives to those of Whites and if the gap between one's group's real status and the status of Whites is not perceived to be narrowing, then discontent may occur. Such discontent would not be based entirely on one's group's objective circumstances, but rather one's circumstances relative to the more advantaged group(s); (c) Rise-and-drop hypothesis—if an era of improvement for one's group is perceived as being followed by a period of stagnation or decline, then frustration and anger may result from unfulfilled expectations, even if individual members of the group are better off than before.

Note that each of these models infers individual psychological reactions (e.g., frustration, discontent, anger) from one's ascribed sociocracial membership group.

Psychological Models

Some theorists have presented the perspective that all Black people are irrevocably scarred by their circumstances of being the victims of the societal conditions of racism (see Helms, 1990b, for an overview). Contemporary versions of this perspective conceivably can find their antecedents in the work of Kardiner and Ovesey (1951). Therefore, we believe that it might be useful to examine their formulation in some detail.

Mark of Oppression. Kardiner and Ovesey contend that the "central problem" of personality adaptation for "Negro" people is racial discrimination. Racial discrimination creates chronically low self-esteem among members of this population because they are constantly receiving negative images of themselves from other people's behavior toward them. Because the pain of racial discrimination is unremitting and constant, the person adopts "restitutive maneuvers" (defense mechanisms) to maintain internal equilibrium. Some of these defenses protect the person's intrapsychic status by preventing her or him from being overwhelmed by the pain of discrimination; some enable the person to present an acceptable social façade so that he or she can interact with the relevant social environments, albeit in a maladaptive manner. All of this self-management requires a constant expenditure of psychic energy that deprives the person of the psychological resources necessary to build a more healthy personality structure.

Figure 1 illustrates the personality structure of Black people as conceptualized by Kardiner and Ovesey. In the model, (racial) discrimination fuels development of the Black personality constellation of low self-esteem (the self-focused consequence of discrimination) and aggression (the other focused reaction to discrimination).

The figure portrays the primacy of low self-esteem and aggression in the Black personality, but was intended to be only a skeletal outline of the ways in which these dynamics manifest themselves. Thus, not only is low self-esteem evident in Black people's allegedly high levels of anxiety and tendencies to have higher aspirations than society will permit them to realize, but also in their self-contempt, idealization of Whites, and "frantic efforts to be white [sic]," hostility, apathy, hedonism, "living for the moment," "criminality," and hatred of oneself and other members of one's racial group.

Similarly, not only are anxiety, ingratiation, simplistic thinking, and denial of aggression symptoms of Black people's underlying aggression, but so too are the following: (a) rage and fear, which eventually become interchangeable because of the societal prohibitions against expressing the former if one is Black; (b) submission or compliance, which become increasingly more abject with greater levels of rage and hatred; (c) laughter, gaiety, or flippancy, which, of course, are evidence of denied rage; and (d) masochism, depression, migraine headaches, and hypertension resulting from repressed rageful feelings toward a loved object.

It is fairly easy to find the psychological themes proposed by Kardiner and Ovesey reverberating throughout the mental health literature in which visible racial and ethnic groups are depicted. For example, Smith (1980) noted the

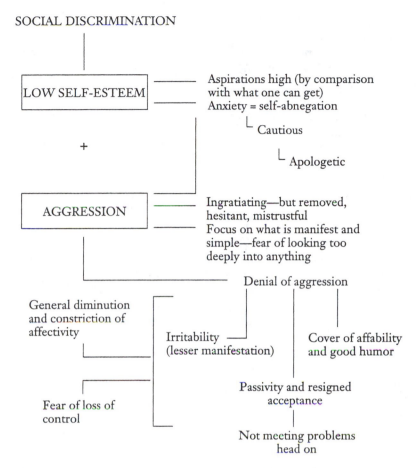

Figure 1 Kardiner and Ovesey's (1951) Model of the Black Personality

overwhelming focus on the alleged psychopathology of Black people rather than of society in the career development literature.

Moreover, even the cursory overview of Kardiner and Ovesey's perspective that we have presented reveals that their (and similar) perspectives make "healthy personality" and (especially) Black people oxymorons. In addition, although we will not present the rest of their perspective here, suffice it to say that the contemporary themes of restricted emotionality, family pathology, absentee fathers, emotionally ungratifying mothers, lack of positive Black "role models," and so forth may not necessarily have begun with Kardiner and Ovesey, but were certainly embellished by them.

In addition, Kardiner and Ovesey believed that their depictions pertained to Black people regardless of social class or any other life conditions. According to them, ". . . the Negro [sic] has no possible basis for a healthy self-esteem and

every incentive for self-hatred. The basic fact is that in the Negro [sic] aspiration level, good conscience and even good performance are irrelevant in face of the glaring fact that the Negro [sic] gets a poor reflection of himself [or herself] in the behavior of whites [sic], no matter what he [or she] does or what his [or her] merits are" (Kardiner & Ovesey, 1951, p. 197, underlines added).

Racial identity theorists were the first to offer the perspectives that healthy personality development is possible for People of Color, White people are not necessarily the main objects of identification and reinforcement for People of Color, and that racism in its various forms has implications for the personality development of White people.

Racial Identity Models

In actuality, racial (in fact "socioracial") identity models are psychological models because they intend to explain individuals' intrapsychic and interpersonal reactions to societal racism in its various manifestations. That is, they are descriptions of hypothetical intrapsychic pathways for overcoming internalized racism and achieving a healthy socioracial self-conception under varying conditions of racial oppression. We find these models useful for assessing the influence of racial factors on the client's concerns as well as the reactions of the client and therapist to one another.

Table 1 summarizes some of the models that have been proposed to describe the socioracial adaptations of specific socioracial groups. Most of these models are "typologies" that propose static character types, which develop in response to being deprived by or benefiting from racism in its various forms. A few are stage theories that propose a sequential process by which an individual's growth toward healthy adjustment occurs.

Many of the models purport to be descriptions of "ethnic" or "cultural" development or adaptation. However, if to us, the particulars of the models seemed to pertain more to socioracial dynamics as we have defined them than to culture, then they were included in Table 1. In some instances, we modified the original theorists' language to reflect our interpretation. Therefore, we include them here as exemplars of racial rather than cultural psychological models.

The majority of the models summarized have single socioracial groups as their focus (either African American or White American). Although some models attempt to describe the adaptations of a variety of groups exposed to similar conditions of oppression (e.g., Atkinson, Morten, & Sue, 1989; Myers et al., 1991), these latter theories presumably are examples of what Ridley et al. (1994) mean by etic-universal perspectives.

Still other theories not summarized in Table 1 are either efforts to integrate existing theories with similar themes and constructs (e.g., Sabnani, Ponterotto, & Borodovsky, 1991) or derivatives or restatements of those theories (e.g., Rowe, Bennett, & Atkinson, 1994). Despite the many versions of racial identity theory from which one might choose, we will use Helm's (1984; 1990a; 1994) version of racial identity theory because that is the perspective that we have found most useful in our own work with therapists, clients, and ourselves.

Helms's Racial Identity Theory

Helms (1984; 1990a) originally proposed White and Black racial identity models and used them to describe the psychotherapy process involving these two groups. Subsequently, she expanded the Black model to pertain to other VREGs in recognition of the commonalities of experience with respect to racial (but not necessarily cultural) societal forces.

Thus, as is our central premise, the models are based on the assumption that racial classifications are sociopolitical constructions whose existence signals socioracial groups' differential rankings or access to resources in the political and economic societal hierarchy. Predictable psychological consequences (e.g., internalized racism) are assumed to result from being socialized as a member of one group rather than another; that is, either a dominant or nondominant collective.

The racial identity models are intended to describe the process of development by which individual members of the various socioracial groups overcome the version of internalized racism that typifies their group in order to achieve a self-affirming and realistic racial-group or collective identity. The need for such development exists because society differentially rewards or punishes members of societally ascribed racial groups according to their racial classifications.

Common Themes

The two racial identity models (as well as her gender identity model) share some common themes, which are summarized in Table 2. However, to discuss these, it is necessary to take note of another alteration in Helms's Black/White model, which is the replacement of the construct of "stages" with "ego statuses" (Helms, 1996). Statuses are cognitive-affective-conative intrapsychic principles for responding to racial stimuli in one's internal and external environments. Helms (1996) contends that the change was necessary to encourage mental health workers who use racial identity models to conceive of the process of development as involving dynamic evolution rather than static personality structures or types. Therapists presumably cannot modify types whereas they may be able to alter processes.

TABLE 1
Selected Summary of Visible Racial or "Ethnic" Group (VREG)

Author	Kind	Group	Description of Types/Stages
Banks (1981)	Stage	African American	**Ethnic Psychological Captivity**—Person internalizes society's negative view of his/her socioracial group.
			Ethnic Encapsulation—Person participates primarily with own socioracial group, which is idealized. Ethnic Identity Clarification—Person learns self-acceptance.
			Biethnicity—Person possesses healthy sense of socioracial identity and can function in own group and in White culture.
			Multiethnicity—Person is self-actualized and can function beyond superficial levels in many cultures.
Cross (1971)	Stage	African American	**Preencounter**—Person identifies with White people and culture, and rejects or denies kinship with Black people and culture.
			Encounter—Person repudiates previous identification with Whites, seeks identification with Blacks.
			Immersion-Emersion—Person completely identifies with Black and abhors Whites.
			Internalization—Person incorporates a positive Black identity and transcends psychological effects of racism.
			Internalization-Commitment—Person maintains Black identity while resisting the various forms of societal oppression.
Dizard (1970)	Typology	African Americans	**Assimilated**—Person moves as comfortably and easily in White environments as White prejudice will permit.
			Pathological—Person exhibits some form of psychopathology as the primary response to life's hardships.
			Traditional—Person attempts to preserve one's own-group identity, integrity and dignity.
Gay (1984)	Stage	African American	**Preencounter**—Person's socioracial identity is subconscious or subliminal or dominated by Euro-American conceptions of one's group.
			Encounter—Person's perceptions of her/his socioracial group are shattered by an event, which initiates search for new group conceptions.
			Post-Encounter—Person experiences and exudes inner security, self-confidence, and pride in one's socioracial group.
Carney & Kahn (1984)	Stage	White American	**Stage 1**—Person's perceptions of VREG people are based on societal stereotypes.
			Stage 2—Person recognizes own-group embeddedness, but deals with other groups in a detached scholarly manner.
			Stage 3—Person either denies the importance of race or expresses anger toward one's own group.
			Stage 4—Person attempts to blend aspects of White culture with aspects of VREG cultures.
			Stage 5—Person has commitment to promoting social equality and cultural pluralism.

(*continued*)

TABLE 1 (*continued*)

Author	Kind	Group	Description of Types/Stages
Hardiman		White American	**Acceptance**—Person shows active or passive endorsement of White superiority.
			Resistance—Person has initial conscious awareness of racial identity.
			Redefinition—Person attempts to redefine Whiteness from a nonracist perspective.
			Internalization—Person internalizes nonracist White identity.
Terry		White American	**Cold blind**—Person equates acknowledgment of color with racism; feels one can exonerate oneself from being White by asserting one's "human-ness."
			White Blacks—Person abandons Whiteness by overidentifying with Blacks and rejecting one's Whiteness.
			New Blacks—Person recognizes that racism is a White problem and ascribes to a pluralistic racial world view.

Note: More extensive versions of this table appear in Helms (1990a, 1990b).

For both models, the developmental process involves successive differentiations of increasingly more sophisticated racial identity ego statuses whose objective or measurable manifestations are schema or information-processing strategies. The maturation or evolution of the more sophisticated statuses makes it possible for the person to perceive and respond to racial information in one's internal and external environments in increasingly more complex ways.

Thus, Helms makes a distinction between racial identity *development* and racial identity *expression*. Development or maturation refers to the sequence by which racial identity statuses potentially become available for self-expression, and schema or expression is the manner(s) in which a person's available statuses actually are manifested.

Although the general process of developing a racial identity (that is, self-referential commit-

---

TABLE 2
Summary of Common Ego Status Themes in Helm's Racial Identity Models

Themes

Person must overcome societal definitions of one's socioracial group by redefining oneself in personally meaningful terms.

Self redefinition involves a sequential differentiation or maturation of ego statuses.

Simplest or least complex statuses develop first.

The seeds of more complex statuses are inherent in earlier statuses.

Statuses that are most consistently reinforced in the environment become strongest and potentially dominant.

A status is dominant when it occupies the largest percentage of the ego and is used most frequently for interpreting racial material.

Statuses that are not reinforced recede in importance and become recessive.

Recessive statuses are infrequently used to govern responses to racial stimuli.

Ego statuses are hypothetical constructs that cannot be measured.

The strength of ego statuses is inferred from their behavioral expressions—schemata.

Schemata typically reflect the themes that are present in the person's socioracial environment(s).

Environments can be internal (psychological) or external (environmental).

ment to a societally ascribed racial group) is considered to share some similarities, the content of the developmental process within the two models differs markedly because of group differences in access to social, economic, political, and numerical resources. Thus, although the underlying thematic content of the models as described is susceptible to change as the racial dynamics of the global society change, it seems to require major societal cataclysms for societal racial dynamics to be transformed—at least in positive directions.

People of Color (POC) Racial Identity

In the POC model, a basic assumption is that, in the United States, the symptoms or consequences of racism directed toward one's racial group are a negative conception of one's racial group and oneself as a member of that group. In this model, *POC* refers to Asian, African, Latino/Latina, and Native Americans of color living in the United States regardless of the original continental origins of their ancestry. Even our cursory overview of the history of race (rather than ethnic) relations in the United States (e.g., Takaki, 1993; Zinn, 1990) reveals that peoples of the so-designated groups have been subjected to similar (but not necessarily identical) deplorable political and economic conditions because they were not perceived to be "pure" white.

Moreover, as Alba (1990) notes, the conditions of oppression that "undesirable" White ethnic immigrants to this country originally faced virtually had disappeared by their third generation in this country. Yet racism continues to follow members of the visible racial groups well beyond the third generation in this country, and has become a "tradition" that they must learn to survive.

Thus, a primary collective identity developmental task for them all is to overcome or abandon socialized negative racial-group conceptions (that is, internalized racism) as previously discussed in order to develop a realistic self-affirming collective identity. Therefore, abandonment of internalized racism involves similar processes for each of the groups of color, regardless of the specific group to which they have been relegated.

Helms's model to explain the process by which this adaptation potentially occurs is a derivative and integration of aspects of Cross's (1971) Negro-to-Black conversion model, Atkinson et al.'s (1989) Minority Identity Development

model, and Erikson's collective identity model, with some influence from Kohut's (1971) self psychology. Table 6.3 summarizes the sequence by which the ego statuses as well as the correlated schema become differentiated for VREGs. The labels for the ego statuses in parentheses are the names appropriated from Cross (1971), and Helms tends to use them when only African American people are the population being assessed.

Conformity. Accordingly, *Conformity*, the original or least sophisticated status and schema, involves the person's adaptation and internalization of White society's definitions of one's group(s), either by conforming to the existing stereotypes of one's own group(s) or attempting to become White and assimilated into White culture. Thus, this status tends to foster information processing in which White people and their culture are idealized and anything other than White is denigrated. When the person is using the Conformity schema or information processing strategy (IPS), he or she is oblivious to the racial dynamics in her or his environment, and if they are forced into the person's awareness, he or she may respond with selective perception in which information is nonconsciously distorted and minimized to favor the White group.

The Conformity speaker in Table 3 illustrates the manner in which those aspects of oneself that are perceived to be White (heritage, culture) are elevated and those that are not are devalued or ignored. However, she also demonstrates a basic principle of racial identity development—the seeds of latter statuses are present in the original status. Thus, that part of herself that is proud of her White heritage will still be present if she develops the status of Integrative Awareness, but she will be able to demonstrate equal pride in her African American heritage.

Dissonance. *Dissonance*, the ego status characterized by disorientation, confusion, and unpredictable responses to racial events, begins to evolve as the person begins to acknowledge her or his lack of fit in the White world. Notice that the speaker in Table 3 seems to be caught between two cultures, Black and White, in this instance. A common theme underlying the Dissonance schema is the ambivalence and anxiety caused by the lack of familiarity with the nature of one's own group's cultural and sociopolitical battles and accomplishments and the lack of positive mate-

TABLE 3

Summary of ALANA Racial Identity Ego Statuses, Examples, and Information Processing Strategies (IPS)

Status and Example

Conformity (Pre-encounter)—External self-definition that implies devaluing of own group and allegiance to White standards of merit. Person probably is oblivious to socioracial groups' sociopolitical histories. IPS: Selective perception, distortion, minimization, and obliviousness to socioracial concerns.

Example: "If you are a mixed race [Black-White] person, don't deny your European heritage just because Black people [in the U.S.] try to force you to choose. We are special because of our White heritage! We can be mediators of peace between these two warring peoples."

Dissonance (Encounter)—Ambivalence and confusion concerning own socioracial-group commitment and ambivalent socioracial self-definition. Person may be ambivalent about life decisions. IPS: Repression of anxiety-evoking racial information, ambivalence, anxiety, and disorientation.

Example: "I talked 'white,' moved 'white' most of my friends were white. . . . But I never really felt accepted by or truly identified with the white kids. At some point, I stopped laughing when they would imitate black people dancing. I distanced myself from the white kids, but I hadn't made an active effort to make black friends because I was never comfortable enough in my 'blackness' to associate with them. That left me in sort of a gray area. . . ." (Wenger, 1993, p. 4).

Immersion—Idealization of one's socioracial group and denigration of that which is perceived as White. Use of own-group external standards to self-define and own-group commitment and loyalty is valued. May make life decisions for the benefit of the group. IPS: Hypervigilence and hypersensitivity toward racial stimuli and dichotomous thinking.

Example: "So there I was, strutting around with my semi-Afro, studiously garbling the English language because I thought that 'real' Black people didn't speak standard English, . . . contemplating changing my name to Malika, or something authentically black . . ." (Nelson, 1993, p. 18).

Emersion—A euphoric sense of well-being and solidarity that accompanies being surrounded by people of one's own socioracial group. IPS: Uncritical of one's own group, peacefulness, joyousness.

Example: "A jubilant [Black] scream went up . . . we had a feeling, and above all we had power . . . So many whites [sic] unconsciously had never considered that blacks [sic] could do much of anything, least of all get a black [sic] candidate this close to being mayor of Chicago" (McClain, 1983, cited in Helms, 1990, p. 25).

Internalization—Positive commitment to and acceptance of one's own socioracial group, internally defined racial attributes, and capacity to objectively assess and respond to members of the dominant group. Can make life decisions by assessing and integrating socioracial group requirements and self-assessment. IPS: Intellectualization and abstraction.

Example: "By claiming myself as African-American and Black, I also inherit a right to ask questions about what this identity means. And chances are this identity will never be static, which is fine with me" (L. Jones, 1994, p. 78).

Integrative Awareness—Capacity to value one's own collective identities as well as empathize and collaborate with members of other oppressed groups. Life decisions may be motivated by globally humanistic self-expression. IPS: Flexible and complex.

Example: "[I think of difference not] as something feared or exotic, but difference as one of the rich facts of one's life, a truism that gives you more data, more power and more flavor . . . [you need a variety of peoples in your life.] . . . so you won't lapse into thinking you're God's gift to all knowledge as North American Negro" (L. Jones, 1994, p. 80).

Note: Descriptions of racial identity statuses are adapted from Helms (1994). Statuses are described in the order they are hypothesized to evolve.

rial about one's own group with which to replace one's waning idealization of the White group.

Immersion. The *Immersion* status evolves in response to the person's need to replace the group-specific negativity that resides in her or his identity constellation with positive group information, and thereby alleviate the anxiety triggered by awareness of the lack of a viable racial self-definition in a society that so values racial classifications. When a person is using the Immersion status, he or she idealizes everything considered to be of his or her group and denigrates everything considered to be of the "White world." When this schema is operative, the person maintains stability and predictability by indulging in simplistic thinking in which race or racism is virtually always a central theme, and one's own group members are always right as long as they conform to externally defined standards of group-appropriate behaviors. In Table 3, Nelson demonstrates the seemingly mindless conformity to stereotypic ideals of Blackness, whether or not those ideals are personally meaningful.

Emersion. Thematically, community, communalism, and commitment to one's own group are the driving forces of the *Emersion* status. The appearance of this status is the recognition of the person's need for positive group definition. When the person is using this status, he or she feels grounded when surrounded by members of her or his own group. As is the case for the Dissonance status, Emersion is primarily an affective status (e.g., joyousness and euphoria in response to the presence or accomplishments of one's own group).

The example in Table 3 demonstrates the joyousness that may be experienced when a member of one's groups accomplishes something of note. The solidarity is often evident in people's clustering with people of their own group, particularly in predominantly White environments.

Internalization. A positive commitment to one's group, internally defined racial attributes and perspectives, as well as the capacity to objectively assess and respond differentially to members of one's own as well as the dominant racial group characterize the *Internalization* status. When using this status, the person uses abstract reasoning or intellectualization and is capable of weighing and integrating complex racial information.

The speaker using the Internalization schema in Table 3 illustrates the person's ability to be self-analytic, self-exploratory, and flexible with respect to her identity. She also illustrates the principle that one's manner of resolving racial dilemmas becomes more complex as one gains access to increasingly more sophisticated ego statuses.

Integrated Awareness. The most sophisticated status and schema (i.e., *Integrative Awareness*) involve the capacity to express a positive racial self and to recognize and resist the multiplicity of practices that exist in one's environment to discourage positive racial self-conceptions and group expression. In addition, when this status is accessible, the person is able to accept, redefine, and integrate in self-enhancing ways those aspects of herself and himself that may be deemed to be characteristic of other socioracial and cultural groups. Furthermore, her or his conceptualization of other people and environmental events can be as complex as needed to ensure healthy intrapsychic and interpersonal functioning. When speaking from this status, L. Jones demonstrates the thirst for diversity that often characterizes this status.

Summary. To summarize, the evolution of ego statuses for People of Color begins with the most primitive status whereby the person primarily interprets and responds to racial information in a manner that suggests negative own-group identification, endorsement of societal prejudices toward one's group, and uncritical esteem for the White group. The last status to evolve permits the person to resist many types of oppression of ones own and others' collective identity groups without abandoning one's primary commitment to one's own group(s). The end goal of the maturational process is to acquire the latter status and be able to use it most of the time in coping with a racially complex world in which one's integrated and positive sense of self is frequently at risk.

White Racial Identity

In the White model, it is assumed that being a member of the acquisitive socioracial group contributes to a false sense of racial-group superiority and privilege. Thus, the process of overcoming internalized racism for Whites is assumed to require the individual to replace societally ordained racial group entitlement and privilege with a nonracist and realistic self-affirming collective (racial) identity. Helms and Piper (1994) define *White people* as follows: "those Americans who self-identify or are commonly identified as belonging exclusively to the White racial group regardless of the continental source (e.g., Europe, Asia) of that racial ancestry" (p. 126).

As a consequence of growing up and being socialized in an environment in which members of their group (if not themselves personally) are privileged relative to other groups. Whites learn to perceive themselves (and their group) as being entitled to similar privileges. In order to protect such privilege, individual group members and, therefore, the group more generally, learn to protect their privileged status by denying and distorting race-related reality, and aggressing against perceived threats to the racial status quo. Consequently, healthy identity development for a White person involves the capacity to recognize and abandon the normative strategies of White people for coping with race.

Helms's (1984, 1990a, 1994) theory proposes a process by which White people develop racial identity. As shown in Table 4, for White people, the maturation process of recognition and abandonment of White privilege begins with the ego's avoidance or denial of the sociopolitical implications of one's own and others' racial-group membership (Contact status) and concludes with its capacity to strive for nonracist own-group membership and humanistic racial self-definition and social interactions (Autonomy status).

Contact

The racial identity evolutionary process for whites begins with *Contact*, a primitive status, primarily characterized by simplistic reactions of denial and obliviousness to the ways in which one benefits from membership in the entitled group and only superficial acknowledgement of one's membership in the White group. Thus, when this status is dominant, the person reacts to racial stimuli with denial, obliviousness, or avoidance of anxiety-evoking racial information, especially when such information implies something derogatory about the White group or the person as a member of that group.

Notice that in the example, the historian's family rejects him when he attempts to move from the family's pie-in-the-sky romanticization of its ancestors' slave ownership. Their obliviousness serves a protective function in that those family members who can avoid facing their ancestors' history of ownership of Black people can also avoid present-day responsibility for doing something to make amends.

Disintegration. *Disintegration* begins to evolve when one can no longer escape the moral dilemmas of race in this country and one's participation in them. Sometimes it is initiated by People of Color's reactions to one's naivete or superfi-

ciality, but usually it evolves and becomes stronger as one is continuously exposed to circumstances where one cannot afford to ignore one's Whiteness and the socialization rules that characterize the group because of the risk of ostracism by the White group.

The basic nature of the moral dilemmas is that one is continuously forced to disassociate with respect to race and racism while acting toward People of Color in inhumane ways in order to be loved, accepted, and valued by significant members of the White group. When this status is in charge of the person, it is expressed as disorientation, confusion, general (sometimes debilitating) distress, and nonreceptivity to anxiety-evoking information.

In the example in Table 4 the speaker illustrates the type of disintegration that frequently follows the White person's rebuffed attempts to "do good" for People of Color. Whereas the speaker thinks his turmoil is attributable to a Black person's animosity, a more likely explanation is that family members' antipathy is causing him to question whether the costs of being beneficent outweigh the benefits.

Reintegration. The *Reintegration* status evolves as a system for mitigating the anxiety that occurs when one's Disintegration status is dominant. The person reduces pain and avoids personal anxiety by adopting the version of racism that exists in her or his socialization environments, which then relieves her or him of the responsibility for doing anything about it. The general theme of this status and correlated schema is idealization of one's own socioracial group, denigration and intolerance toward other groups, and protection and enhancement of the White group and thereby the maintenance of the racism status quo. Thus, selective perception and distortion of information in an own-group enhancing and out-group debasing manner describe this status and correlated schema.

The need to avoid personal responsibility for racism is evident in the Reintegration example. By minimizing the significance of his family's role in perpetuating slavery, and consequently, his personal advancement because of it, he eliminates his own and his entire family's responsibility to do anything about it.

Pseudo-Independence. The *Pseudo-Independence* status is characterized by an intellectualized

TABLE 4
Summary of White Racial Identity Ego Statuses, Examples, and Information Processing Strategies (IPS)

Status and Example

Contact—Satisfaction with racial status quo, obliviousness to racism and one's participation in it. If racial factors influence life decisions, they do so in a simplistic fashion. IPS: Obliviousness, denial, superficiality, and avoidance.

Example: ". . . The Balls have prided themselves on the ancestral image of compassion, emphasizing that masters tried as best they could not to separate slave families in sale; that no Ball masters perpetrated violence or engaged in master-slave sex. Ed Ball's research is viewed by some family members, especially the elderly ones, as a threat to long-held beliefs. Some would prefer not to know too many details about their ancestors' slave practices, one relative says" (Duke, 1994, p. 12).

Disintegration—Disorientation and anxiety provoked by unresolvable racial moral dilemmas that force one to choose between own-group loyalty and humanism. May be stymied by life situations that arouse racial dilemmas. IPS: Suppression, ambivalence, and controlling.

Example: "I was upset. I couldn't do anything for a couple of weeks . . . Was I causing more pain than healing? Was this somebody else's history, not mine? Was I an expropriator, as Stefani Zinerman [a Black woman newspaper editor] accuses me of being? Should I just stop [investigating my family's history of slave ownership] and let black [sic] people do their own history?" (Duke, 1994).

Reintegration—Idealization of one's socioracial group; denigration and intolerance for other groups. Racial factors may strongly influence life decisions. IPS: Selective perception and negative outgroup distortion.

Example: "When someone asks him, 'Don't you feel bad because your ancestors owned slaves?' his response is 'No, I don't feel bad because my ancestors owned slaves. I mean, get over it. If Ed wants to go around and apologize, Ed's free to go around and apologize. But quite frankly, Ed didn't own any slaves. He isn't responsible for slavery or anybody's misfortunes . . .'" (Duke, 1994, p. 24).

Pseudo-Independence—Intellectualized commitment to one's own socioracial group and subtle superiority and tolerance of other socioracial groups as long as they can be helped to conform to White standards of merit. IPS: Selective perception, cognitive restructuring, and conditional regard.

Example: "He has also said to them [the descendants of his family's slaves]: I am sorry . . . his mother, brother and a few other relatives believe the apology had a healing effect . . ." (Duke, 1994, p. 12).

Immersion—The searching for an understanding of the personal meaning of Whiteness and racism and the ways by which one benefits from them as well as a redefinition of Whiteness. IPS: Hypervigilance, judgmental, and cognitive-affective restructuring.

Example: "I'm interested to look at whiteness [sic] as carefully as white [sic] people look at blackness [sic]. As a white [sic] person, I'm interested to understand how my ethnicity [sic] has produced me as an individual . . . and how whiteness [sic] produces the majority experience of Americans. My plantation research might be a way for me to do this intellectually as a writer" (Duke, 1994, p. 12).

Emersion—A sense of discovery, security, sanity, and group solidarity and pride that accompanies being with other. White people who are embarked on the mission of rediscovering Whiteness. IPS: Sociable, pride, seeking positive group-attributes.

Example: "But Ed's apology [for his family's ownership of slaves] produced positive reactions as well. Janet and Ted Ball, Ed's mother and brother, both were moved by [his apology]: 'I was crying too,' says Janet Ball . . . Ted Ball . . . says he whispered a private 'thank you' to his little brother. . . . He feels grateful to Ed 'for doing the hard work it took to get to the apology.'" (Duke, 1994, p. 24).

Autonomy—Informed positive socioracial-group commitment, use of internal standards for self-definition, capacity to relinquish the privileges of racism. Person tries to avoid life options that require participation in racial oppression. IPS: Flexible and complex.

Example: ". . . It's [the exploration of his familial history of slave ownership] about me personally trying to find some way as a white [sic] person, quite apart from my family's history, to acknowledge what's happened in this country. I mean during the time that English-speaking people have been in this country, for more years were black [sic] people enslaved than not enslaved" (Duke, 1994, p. 25).

Note: Descriptions of racial identity statuses are adapted from Helms (1994). Racial identity ego statuses are listed in the order that they are hypothesized to evolve.

commitment to one's racial group in which one identifies with the "good" nonracist Whites and rejects the "bad" racists. Identification and commitment are made possible by acknowledgement of superficial group (rather than personal) culpability for Whites' racial wrongdoing, and by not necessarily conscious efforts to resolve "the race problem" by assisting People of Color to become more like Whites. Schematic expression or information-processing strategies involve reshaping racial stimuli to fit one's own "liberal" societal framework, avoidance of negative information about oneself, and selective perception.

Immersion. The *Immersion* status involves the search for a new, humanistic, nonracist definition of Whiteness. When this status is operative, the person attempts to recover from prior distorted racial socialization and seeks accurate information about race and racism and their pertinence to oneself. The information-processing strategies operative here are searching for internally defined racial standards or reeducating oneself, hypervigilence, and activism.

In Table 4 the Immersion schema is expressed by the person's frenetic search for the meaning of Whiteness to himself or herself as well as to other White people in society. Although he or she is not certain where his or her inquiry will end, it is fueled by the inexplicable belief that such self- and other exploration is virtually ordained. This sensation of being on a mission of recovery characterizes the Immersion status and its schematic expression.

Emersion. The *Emersion* status is the appreciation of and withdrawal into the community of reeducated White people for the purposes of rejuvenating oneself and solidifying one's goals of seeking new self-knowledge. This is primarily an affective status and so one finds a variety of emotional themes including the joyous tears and prayerful gratitude toward kindred sojourners described in Table 4.

Autonomy. The last and most advanced status to evolve permits complex humanistic reactions to internal and environmental racial information based on a realistic, nonracist self-affirming conception of one's racial collective identity. When a person is operating from the *Autonomy* status, he or she no longer has to impose arbitrary racial definitions on others nor must succumb to oth-

ers' arbitrary racial criteria. The Autonomy schema permits flexible analytic self-expression and responses to racial material.

Racial Identity Expression

As previously discussed, the model describes the development or process by which the statuses come into being. Consequently, the highlights or distinguishable aspects of the statuses and related schemata are described. However, most individuals develop more than one status, and if multiple statuses exist, then they can operate in concert. That is, they may each influence a person's reactions to racial stimuli.

Thus, in Tables 3 and 4, although we have categorized the examples according to what appears to be the strongest status-schema theme, it seems to us that aspects of other status-schema are present in virtually every instance. For example, in Table 4 the Reintegration segment is classified as *primarily* Reintegration because of the person's subtle dehumanizing and unwillingness to acknowledge even his ancestors' role in perpetuating slavery and racism. However, the minimization and intellectualization of racial tensions that characterize the Contact and Pseudo-Independence statuses also waft through this example. Similar blends of statuses can be found in the other examples as well, and presumably blends describe people's reactions more often than do "pure" statuses.

Also apparent in the examples in Table 3 is the fact that racial identity themes may be blended in the individual's reactions to racial catalysts regardless of their socioracial classification. As we just observed with respect to White identity development, most people probably do not express their racial identity in pure forms. Thus, the second example in Table 3 illustrates expression of both the Conformity and Dissonance statuses in that the VREG speaker acknowledges his White cultural socialization and consequent greater familiarity with White people on one level (Conformity), but also is able to describe his lack of fit with either the Black or White socioracial group (Dissonance).

Nevertheless, each of the examples has a racial identity theme that seems to be stronger than the others, and to determine which is a person's strongest status, one would need to analyze the themes inherent in several samples of a person's race-related behavior. Themes that frequently occur presumably signal stronger underlying statuses, and conversely, stronger statuses conceivably contribute to more consistent thematic race-related expressions. Insight 1 should give the reader an opportunity to try her or his hand at this type of qualitative analysis of racial identity.

However, more often than not, researchers have attempted to develop quantitative paper-and-pencil inventories for assessing racial identity. Burlew and Smith (1991) and Ponterotto and Casas (1991) critically reviewed some of them. Of these measures, the ones used most frequently are the Black and White racial identity research scales developed by Helms and her associates (Helms & Parham, 1996; Helms & Carter, 1990; Carter, 1996; Corbett, Helms, & Reagan, 1992). From these measures, Helms (1996) proposed racial identity assessment inventories, which she suggests might be useful in mapping the person's racial identity expression.

Using the scoring procedures Helms proposed for the assessment of Whites' racial identity expression (WRIAS Social Attitudes Inventory), we generated a racial identity profile for the White female group leader. The profile suggests that this person's racial identity resting-state expression is characterized by equally strong Contact, Pseudo-Independent, and Autonomy schemata. Thus, she does not have a clearly dominant schemata, although Disintegration and Reintegration appear to be recessive for her. In response to race-related stimuli other than the paper-and-pencil inventory, one would expect her to be rather naïve about such matters, but to express her naivete in a liberal and intellectualized manner with traces of personal independence and non conformity to derogatory group norms.

INSIGHT

A Proud American

Whoopi Goldberg doesn't hesitate when filling out nationality questions on census forms.

> "I wouldn't put 'African-American.' I just put down 'American,' because that's what I am," she says.
>
> "Yes, I've been criticized by the black [sic] community, and loudly. But I'm fifth- or sixth-generation American, and I also have Chinese and white [sic] in me.
>
> "I'm not culturally from Africa. I've been in Africa—I know better. I'm real proud that

I helped build America, so I'm not going to let anybody call me anything accept American.

Note: This excerpt is reprinted from "A proud American," The Kansas City Star, August 30, 1994, p. E-6.

Conclusions and Implications for Therapy

It is possible to add some depth to our discussion of socioracial and psychoracial characteristics. As symbolized in Figure 3, the first question one needs to ask is whether issues of commitment to a socioracial group are germane to the problem for which the client is seeking assistance. The possibilities are: (a) yes, either implicitly or explicitly the client's problem involves race, racism, or racial identity; (b) maybe, the possibility exists that such factors are relevant, but if so, their manner of influence is not unambiguously evident; (c) no, the person is experiencing a "universal" life problem for which racial tensions and/or dynamics in particular do not seem to be relevant.

In the case of the first two options, the general sociological models of oppression *might* provide some insight into the racial life conditions experienced by clients and/or therapists. However, inferring that any particular circumstances or characteristics of a group necessarily pertain to individual members of the group is ill-advised. Rather one might use such perspectives to form hypotheses about the relevant dynamics in the person's life, but these should be confirmed or disconfirmed in one's actual interactions.

Moreover, the content of one's own or one's client's racial stereotypes might reveal the racial perspective on which they are based. It may be easier to countermand such stereotypes when one understands their origins. In any case, one dimension of our perspective concerns examining whether the client has *personally* experienced socioracial oppression or benevolence because of her or his racial classification, and, if so, in what form. Remember that cues to such experiences can be factors so subtle as differential treatment due to skin color differences within and between socioracial groups, or so overt as job promotions accorded on the basis of racial classification.

The psychological perspectives might be more useful in conceptualizing the race-related dynamics of clients with respect to any of the three options, although we think that the early

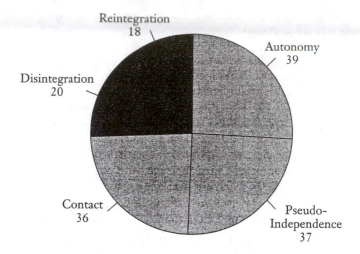

Figure 2 Linda's White Racial Identity Profile

Linda's profile suggests that her strongest expressed statuses are a combination of Contact, Autonomy, and Pseudo-Independence. Her weakest statuses are Disintegration and Reintegration. Subscales followed by asterisk(s) are higher (single) or very much higher (double) than the subsequent subscale. The ordering of Linda's scores is similar whether one examines subscale scores relative to her immediately adjacent clockwise raw score (see pie), or her scores as compared to Carter's (1996) percentile norms (% tile column). Pie slices of the same shade do not differ significantly. Contact (i.e., lack of sophistication about the significance of race) appears to be a strong influence in her interpretation and reaction to racial information. For more information about interpreting racial identity profiles, see Helms (1996).

Mode of Expression	Raw Score	% tile	Comment
Contact	36*	81	Contact is stronger than Disintegration
Disintegration	20	19	Disintegration does not differ significantly from Reintegration
Reintegration	18**	11	Reintegration is much weaker than Pseudo-Independence
Pseudo-Independence	37	70	Pseudo-Independence does not differ significantly from Autonomy
Autonomy	39	70	Autonomy does not differ significantly from Contact
Total	150		Profile appears to be valid

historical perspectives that we summarized (e.g., frustration-aggression) might pertain to certain clients rather than all clients. For example, if one's client is clearly aggressing against someone of another socioracial group, then one should look initially toward daily life frustrations to identify provocations or socialization experiences.

However, if the client is the target of the aggression, then it is not certain that any of the power-conflict or most of the traditional psychological race-related models will be of benefit to her or him. Particularly, if the client is a VREG person, such models may be inapplicable because for the most part, they were created to assist White people in comprehending People of Color.

In our experience, client's reactions to socioracial dynamics tend to be complex on the cognitive, affective, and behavioral levels regardless of the person's socioracial group. Therefore, we tend to prefer the more complex psychological (i.e., racial identity) theories for making sense of these dynamics because they make it possible to conceptualize racial reactions as common human responses in the racial environment(s) of the United States rather than as inexplicable peculiarities of the visible racial and ethnic groups.

If one thinks that history of oppression-domination is relevant, then one needs to specify the kinds that are relevant for this particular client and perhaps her or his social system. Next, one

Excerpt: 'We're special because of our European ancestry."
Therapist considerations: ARE SOCIORACIAL DYNAMICS RELEVANT?

YES	MAYBE	NO
Relevant Sociological Factors		
Psychological Reactions		
Interventions		

Relevant Sociological Factors	Psychological Reactions	Interventions
Apparent racial classification	Anger	Empathy
Skin color	Defensiveness Conformity status	Factual race-related information
Parents' differential experiences of sociorace	Naivete	Communication skills

Figure 3 Some socioracial dimensions of clients and therapists

attempts to move inside the client by choosing some psychological model (e.g., racial identity) for describing her or his reactions to these stimuli. Then one shapes one's interventions according to what seems appropriate for the client's conditions. Several authors, some of whom are summarized in Table 2, have proposed interventions matched to the client's levels of expressed racial identity (Carney & Kahn, 1984; Gay, 1984; Helms, 1990a; Sabnani et al., 1991). These may need to be modified somewhat to match the client's needs.

Figure 3 is an example of how one might perform such an analysis using the first example in Table 3. The comment suggests that the person is experiencing anxiety, anger, and perhaps confusion (psychological reactions) apparently in response to others' communications about her racial classification (sociological), and perhaps her own manner of communicating about her socioracial group allegiances.

Others might intuit from her statement that she devalues membership in the African American group, and that she is ignorant of the racial histories of both of her parents' socioracial

groups. Moreover, she is attempting to resolve her Conformity status issues with respect to the two groups—Blacks and Whites—that have the longest continuous history of racial conflict in this country, perhaps without the conceptualization and communication skills necessary to do so.

Thus, in her case, a racially sensitive therapist would need to understand the multiple ways in which issues of racial oppression and dominance might be expressed within the client (e.g., Does she perceive that she acquires higher or lower status because of her parentage?) as well as her significant socialization environments (e.g., How does each parent cope with race?), and communicate this understanding to the client in an empathic manner. Moreover, since the client may be caught in a familial and societal war that is not of her making, the therapist will need to help her acquire information and teach her communication strategies to help her disentangle herself, as well as help her learn to explore and recognize the complex racial dynamics that seem to be playing themselves out in her environment.

The issues presented in the figure for discoursive purposes are based on a rather small excerpt of this person's behavior and may not be accurate even for her. Therefore, they should not automatically be generalized to someone else who makes a similar comment. Rather the framework should be used to suggest the kind of investigation in which the therapist should engage in order to be appropriately responsive to racial dynamics.

Also, at the risk of being redundant, let us remind the reader that information about a person's racial identity does not reveal anything about her or his cultural socialization, except perhaps how much the person values her or his socioracial group's traditional culture. That is, a person may have developed a positive racial identity (e.g., have positive feelings about her or his socioracial group) without ever having been socialized in the relevant culture. Conversely, a person may have been socialized in a particular culture, and consequently, be capable of practicing its customs, traditions, and so forth without having any understanding of the sociopolitical racial dynamics that the groups consider to be central to their survival.

REFERENCES

Alba, R. D. (1990). *Ethnic identity: The transformation of White America*. New Haven: Yale University Press.

Allport, G. (1958). *The nature of prejudice* (abridged edition). New York: Doubleday Anchor Books.

Atkinson, D. R., Morten, G., & Sue, D. R. (1989). *Counseling American minorities: A cross-cultural perspective* (3rd ed.). Dubuque, IA: Wm. C. Brown.

Axelson, J. A. (1993). *Counseling and development in a multicultural society* (2nd ed.). Pacific Grove, CA: Brooks/Cole Publishing Company.

Banks, J. A. (1981). The stages of ethnicity: Implications for curriculum reform. In J. A. Banks (Ed.), *Multi-ethnic education: Theory and practice* (pp. 129–139). Boston: Ally & Bacon.

Bradley, M. (1978). *The iceman inheritance: Prehistoric sources of Western man's racism, sexism, and aggression*. New York: Warner Books.

Burled, A. K., & Smith, L. R. (1991). Measures of racial identity: An overview and a proposed framework. *Journal of Black Psychology, 17*(2), 53–71.

Carney, C. G., & Kahn, K. B. (1984). Building competencies for effective cross-cultural counseling: A developmental view. *The Counseling Psychologist, 12*(1), 111–119.

Carter, R. T. (1996). Exploring the complexity of racial identity attitude measures. In G. R. Sodowsky & J. Impara (Eds.), *Multicultural assessment* (pp. 193–223). Lincoln, NE: Buros Institute of Mental Measurement.

Comer, J. P. (1991). White racism: Its root, form, and function. In R. L. Jones (Ed.), *Black psychology* (pp. 591–596). Berkeley, CA: Cobb & Henry.

Corbett, M., Helms, J. E., & Regan, A. (1992). The development of a White racial identity immersion scale. Paper presented at the American Psychological Association Convention, Washington, D.C.

Cross, W. E., Jr. (1971). The Negro-to-black conversion experience: Toward a psychology of Black liberation. *Black World, 20*(9), 13–27.

Cross, W. E., Jr., Parham, T. A., & Helms, J. E. (1991). The stages of Black identity development: Nigrescence models. In R. L. Jones (Ed.), *Black Psychology* (pp. 319–338). Berkeley, CA: Cobb & Henry Publishers.

Cubberly, E. P. (1929). *Changing conceptions of education*. Boston: Houghton & Mifflin.

Dizard, J. E. (1970). Black identity, social class, and Black power. *Journal of Social Issues, 26*(1), 195–207.

Dollard, J. (1957). *Caste and class in a Southern town* (3rd ed.). Garden City, NY: Doubleday.

Dollard, J., Doob, L., Miller, N., Mowrer, O. H., & Sears, R. R. (1939) *Frustration and aggression*. New Haven: Yale University Press.

Duke, L. (1994, August 28). This harrowed ground. *The Washington Post Magazine*, pp. 8–13; 20–25.

Fairchild, H. P. (1926). *The melting pot mistake*. Boston: Little, Brown and Company.

Feagin, J. R. (1984). *Racial and ethnic relations*. Englewood Cliffs, NJ: Prentice-Hall, Inc.

Franklin, V. P. (1991). Black social scientists and the mental testing movement, 1920-1940. In R. L. Jones (Ed.), *Black Psychology* (pp. 207–224). Berkeley, CA: Cobb & Henry.

Gay, G. (1984). Implications of selected models of ethnic identity development for educators. *The Journal of Negro Education, 54*(1), 43–52.

Geschwender, J. A. (1968). Explorations in the theory of social movements and revolutions. *Social Forces, 47*, 127–135.

Grant, M. (1916). *The passing of the great race*. New York: Scribner.

Hacker, A. (1992). *The nations: Black and White, separate, hostile, unequal*. New York: Charles Scribner's Sons.

Hall, G. S. (1904). *Adolescence*. New York: Appleton.

Hardiman, R. (1982). *White identity development: A process oriented model for describing the racial consciousness of White Americans*. Unpublished doctoral dissertation, University of Mass-achusetts, Amherst.

Helms, J. E. (1984). Toward a theoretical explanation of the effects of race on counseling: A Black and White model. *The Counseling Psychologist, 12* 153–165.

Helms, J. E. (1990a). *Black and White racial identity: Theory, research, and practice.* Westport, CT: Greenwood Press.

Helms, J. E. (1990b). Three perspectives on counseling and psychotherapy with visible racial/ethnic group clients. In F. C. Serafica, A. I. Schwebel, R. K. Russell, P. D. Isaac, & L. B. Myers (Eds.), *Mental Health of Ethnic Minorities* (pp. 171–201). New York: Praeger.

Helms, J. E. (1994). Racial identity and other "racial" constructs. In E. J. Tricketr, R. Watts, & D. Birman (Eds.), *Human Diversity* (pp. 285–311). San Francisco: Jossey Bass.

Helms, J. E. (1996). Toward a methodology for assessing "racial identity" as distinguished from "ethnic identity." In G. R. Sodowsky & J. Impara (Eds.), *Multicultural Assessment.* Lincoln, NE: Buros Institute of Mental Measurement.

Helms, J. E., & Carter, R. T. (1990). Development of the White racial identity attitude scale. In J. E. Helms (Ed.), *Black and White racial identity: theory, research, and practice* (pp. 67–80). Westport, CT: Greenwood Press.

Helms, J. E., & Parham, T. A. (1996). The Racial Identity Attitude Scale. In R. L. Jones (Ed.), *Handbook of tests and measurements for Black populations* (Vol. 2), (pp. 167–174). Hampton, VA: Cobb & Henry Publishers.

Helms, J. E., Piper, R. E. (1994). Implications of racial identity theory for vocational psychology. *Journal of Vocational Psychology, 44,* 124–138.

Hutnik, N. (1991). *Ethnic minority identity: A social psychological perspective.* Oxford: Oxford University Press.

Jensen, A. R. (1969). How much can we boost IQ and scholastic achievement? *Harvard Educational Review, 39,* 1–123, 126.

Jones, L. (1994, May). Mama's White. *Essence Magazine,* pp. 78, 80, 148.

Kardiner, A., & Ovesey, L. (1951). *The mark of oppression: Explorations in the personality of the American Negro.* Cleveland, OH: Meridian Books.

Katz, P. A. (1976). The acquisition of racial attitudes in children. In P. A. Katz. (Ed.), *Toward the elimination of racism* (pp. 125–150). New York: Pergamon.

Kitano, H. H. (1982). Mental health in the Japanese American community. In E. E. Jones & S. J. Korchin (Eds.), *Minority Mental Health* (pp. 149–164). New York: Praeger.

Kohut, H. (1971). *Analysis of the self.* New York: International University Press.

Landrum, J., & Batts, V. A. (1985). *Internalized racial oppression.* Unpublished working piper. Cited in J. Landrum-Brown, Black mental health and racial oppression. In D. S. Ruiz (Ed.), *Handbook of mental health and mental disorder among Black Americans* (pp. 113–132). New York: Greenwood Press.

McClain, L. (1983, July 24). How Chicago taught me to hate Whites. *Washington Post, Section C,* 1, 4.

McLemore, S. D. (1983). *Racial and ethnic relations in America.* Boston, MA: Allyn and Bacon.

Myers, L. J., Speight, S. L., Highlen, P. S., Cox, C. I., Reynolds, A. L., Adams, E. M., & Hanley, C. P. (1991). Identity development and worldview: Toward an optimal conceptualization. *Journal of Counseling and Development, 70,* 54–63.

Ponterotto, J. G., & Casas, J. M. (1991). *Handbook of racial/ethnic minority counseling research.* Springfield, IL: Charles C. Thomas.

Richardson, T. Q. (1989). White racial consciousness and the counseling profession. Unpublished paper, LeHigh University, Bethlehem, PA.

Ridley, C. R., Mendoza, D. W., & Kanitz, B. E. (1994). Multicultural training: Reexamination, operationalization, and integration. *The Counseling Psychologist, 22,* 227–289.

Rowe, W., Bennett, S. K., & Atkinson, D. R. (1994). White racial identity models: A critique and alternative proposal. *The Counseling Psychologist, 22,* 129–146.

Rushton, J. P. (1990). Differential K theory: The sociobiology of individual and group differences *Personality and Individual Differences, 6,* 441–452.

Rushton, J. P. (1995). *Race, evolution, and behavior: A life history perspective.* New Brunswick, NJ: Transaction Publishers.

Sabnani, H. B., Ponterotto, J. G., & Borodovsky, L. G. (1991). White racial identity development and cross-cultural counselor training: A stage model. *The Counseling Psychologist, 19* (1), 76–102.

Shuffleton, F. (1993). *A mixed race: Ethnicity in early America.* New York: Oxford University Press.

Simpson, G. E., & Yinger, J. M. (1972). *Racial and cultural minorities* (4th ed.).New York: Harper and Row.

Singer, L. (1962). Ethnogenesis and Negro Americans today. *Social Research, 29,* 419–432.

Smith, E. J. (1980). Profile of the Black individual in vocational literature. In R. L. Jones (Ed.), *Black Psychology* (pp. 324–357). New York: Harper & Row.

Spikard, P. R. (1992). The illogic of American racial categories. In M. P. P. Root (Ed.), *Racially mixed people in America* (pp. 12–23). Newbury Park, CA: Sage Publications.

Takaki, R. (1993). *A different mirror: A History of multi-cultural America*. Boston: Little, Brown.

Terry, R. W. (1977). *For Whites only*. Grand Rapids, MI: William B. Erdmans.

Thomas, A., & Sillen, S. (1972). *Racism and Psychiatry*. New York: Brunner/Mazel, Inc.

Welsing, F. C. (1974). The Cress theory of color-confrontation. *The Black Scholar, May*, 32–40.

Wenger, J. (1993). Just part of the mix. *Focus, 21* (9), 3, 4.

Wrenn, G. C. (1962). The culturally e encapsulated counselor. *Harvard Educational Review, 32*(4), 444–449.

Zinn, H. (1980). *A history of the United States*. New York: Harper & Row.

CHAPTER 19

NIGRESCENCE AND EGO IDENTITY DEVELOPMENT—ACCOUNTING FOR DIFFERENTIAL BLACK IDENTITY PATTERNS

WILLIAM E. CROSS, JR. AND PEONY FHAGEN-SMITH

PRIMARY OBJECTIVE: To describe the process of Black identity development across the life span

SECONDARY OBJECTIVES: To critique the application of an Eriksonian perspective in mapping the unfolding of a Black person's identity

To account for those African Americans who make race central to their self-conceptions as well as those with a "nonethnic" frame of reference

To show how Nigrescence may enter the picture as early as adolescence or after the establishment of one's foundational adult identity

To show how this type of model helps counter any tendency toward overgeneralization and stereotyping

Over the past 10 to 15 years, the discourse on Black identity, which once turned on simple-minded and ubiquitous notions of Negro self-hatred (Gordon, 1980; Kardiner & Ovesey, 1951), has been recentered on an axis that balances diverse and normative, as well as deviant, trends (Cross, 1991; Hecht, Collier, & Ribeau, 1993; Helms, 1990; Spencer, Brookins, & Allen, 1985). This expanded orientation is revealed in the empirical literature as a shift away from studies involving the administration of a single measure of Black identity, and toward investigations that are multidimensional in scope and execution (Bat-Chava, Allen, Aber, & Seidman, 1995; Connell, Spencer, & Aber, 1994; McAdoo, 1985). The intent of the current work is to further expand the discourse on Black identity by comparing the stages of Nigrescence with the stages embedded in Erik Erikson's (1968) perspective on adolescent identity development. It will be argued that the parallels between the two orientations can be overstated and that an interpretation of certain empirical findings is possible only when the two processes are differentiated. The chapter ends with a model that reconceptualizes the relationship between Nigrescence and ego identity development.

Ericksonian Stages of Ethnicity Identity Development

The United States' changing demographics have stoked interest in the unique psychological experiences of women and various racial and ethnic groups. One type of response has been the formulation of identity development models that are specific to each group, resulting in as many identity development models as there are ethnic and racial groups. Not surprisingly, some researchers (Atkinson, Morten, & Sue, 1983; Phinney, 1989) have tried to extract the core elements that are common to the identity development of all minority groups, in hopes of articulating a pan-ethnic identity development perspective that might lead to the construction of a paper-and-pencil measure for simultaneous administration to a broad range of racial and ethnic groups, including Whites. A panethnic schema and a common way to measure it are needed by researchers conducting studies in urban centers, where a plethora of ethnic groups reside, go to school, and work (Bat-Chava et al., 1995; Spencer, 1995).

One of the latest attempts at pan-ethnic theorizing has gone a step further (Phinney, 1989). This new approach not only collapses the identity development experiences of a variety of racial and ethnic groups into a set of common stages, but it also spells out the linkages between ethnicity and the identity development struggles of human beings in general. Application of the theory makes it possible for scholars and students of human development to (a) discuss generic notions of identity development, (b) explore race and ethnicity as issues that are linked to, rather than divorced from, generic theory, and (c) easily swing the focus back to the generic stages of development after ethnic case studies have been explored. In this chapter, we describe and eventually critique a pan-ethnic identity perspective (Phinney, 1989) that uses the works of Erikson (1968) as the conduit for moving back and forth between generic notions of identity development and racial/ethnic identity dynamics.

Erik Erikson's ideas have found wide application in discussions of human development across the life span. According to Erikson (1968), adolescence marks the developmental period when the healthy integration of one's personal identity, general personality, and social or group identity is achieved. Explicated as stages (Marcia, 1966), Erikson's ideas suggest that young people enter adolescence with ideas about themselves that are unclear (*diffused identity*) or that they may derive an untested clarity by uncritically absorbing parental teachings (*foreclosed identity*). Erikson stated that to take ownership of one's self-concept, the young person must enter a period of exploration that may engender an identity crisis (*identity moratorium*). Under optimal conditions, the phase of moratorium is followed by a state of resolution, clarity of thinking, and commitment to a well-thought-out notion of "who I am." The person is said to have "achieved her or his identity," and the final stage is labeled, appropriately, *achieved identity*.

The ethic identity development (EID) model, crafted by Jean Phinney (1989), distills the unique identity experiences of different social groups into the four stages of Erikson's model. Her transracial and transethnic developmental scheme suggests that the psychodynamics of each stage are the same whether one is studying adolescents who are coming to grips with being Jewish, Black, White, or Asian American, to mention a few instances in point. Phinney believes it is possible to integrate fully the discourse on ethnic identity with the general literature on adolescent identity. Having a "poorly" developed ethnic identity, for Phinney, is a special case of "identity diffusion." Likewise, being in the midst of changing one's ethnic identity is tantamount to an identity crisis, which is the central characteristic for the moratorium phase of the generic model. Summarized more completely, the EID model incorporates the following four identities:

1. *Diffused identity:* Person shows little or no evidence of having explored his or her ethnicity; there is no clear understanding of the issues; there may be little interest in the topic.

2. *Foreclosed identity:* Person evidences little exploration of ethnicity; however, his or her ideas about ethnicity are very clear; parental ideas have been internalized, without much questioning; depending on his or her socialization experiences, the ethnic ideas may have a negative or positive valence.

3. *Moratorium identity:* There is evidence of ongoing exploration, and the person may actually be in the midst of an ethnic identity crisis.

4. *Achieved identity:* There are signs that the person's exploration period is a thing of the past and that the ethnic identity has been achieved; the habituated identity shows signs of being effectively integrated into the person's overall self-concept and worldview.

In summary, the EID model states that ethnic and racial minorities enter adolescence with poorly developed ethnic identities (diffusion) or with an identity "given" to them by their parents (foreclosure). They may sink into an identity crisis, during which the conflicts and challenges associated with their minority status are sorted out (moratorium), and should all go well, they achieve an ethnic identity that is positive and gives high salience to ethnicity (achieved ethnicity).

Part of the research associated with the EID model has been the refinement of a paper-and-pencil test called the Multigroup Ethnic Identity Measure or MEIM ((Phinney, 1992). Applying the MEIM and other measures in studies that typically included Black, Asian, and Hispanic subjects, Phinney and her students (Phinney, 1992; Phinney & Alipuria, 1990; Phinney & Chavira, 1992) reported that poorly formed (diffuse) and seldom explored (foreclosed) ethnic identities are linked to lower levels of self-esteem and lower performance on measures of general ego development. Minorities failing into the moratorium stage show signs of exploration and conflict, and achieved minority status correlates with high levels of self-esteem and strong ego development.

Nigrescence Theory

Black identity development theory, or Nigrescence theory (*nigrescence* is a French word that means, in a cultural-psychological sense, the process of becoming Black), is also a multistage construct. It is not a generic model, but is designed to reveal the nuances of identity development that are unique to the experiences of Black people. Nevertheless, the stages of Nigrescence have provided the foundation for thinking about Asian American identity development (Kim, 1981), feminist identity development (Downing & Roush, 1985), and gay/lesbian identity development (Finnegan & McNally, 1987). We will focus on the Cross model of psychological Nigrescence, which has two versions: the original (Cross, 1971) and the recently published revised version (Cross, 1991).

Both versions incorporate five developmental stages: Pre-Encounter, Encounter, Immersion-Emersion, Internalization, and Internalization-Commitment. Delaying for the moment a description of the revised version, we note that in the original model:

1. *Pre-Encounter* defines the identity that will become the target of personal change; it is out-group oriented, somewhat negative in valence, and, perhaps, self-hating in essence.

2. *Encounter* describes the event or events that lead a person to conclude that he or she needs to change in the direction of greater cultural self-awareness and racial self-acceptance.

3. *Immersion-Emersion* is the transition stage, during which the old identity and the emergent identity struggle for dominance.

4. *Internalization* marks the point at which the new identity becomes accepted and habituated.

5. *Internalization-Commitment* marks the stage at which person continue to show high race and culture salience in the organization of their daily lives, well beyond the point at which they initially internalized a Black identity.

As in our earlier description of the EID model, Nigrescence begins with a person who has a poorly developed ethnic sense of self. After an encounter that unleashes change, the person is steeped in an Immersion-Emersion stage that has the characteristics of a moratorium episode, and the process culminates in a periods of synthesis and improved mental health, Internalization, that is clearly the equivalent of an "achieved identity."

Reviews of Nigrescence research (Cross, 1991; Cross, Parham, & Helms, 1995; Helms, 1990) reveal a pattern of results linking (a) Pre-encounter to low self-esteem, elevated depression, hypersensitivity, hostility, increased anxiety, a defeatist attitude, and lower levels of self-actualization; (b) Immersion-Emersion to a state of flux; and (c) Internalization to high self-esteem, low depression, hopeful vision for the future, high levels of personal efficacy, and a greater sense of self-actualization.

From a certain angle, the theoretical and empirical parallels between the Cross and Phinney perspectives are obvious. One can speak of diffusion and Pre-Encounter in the same breath, which is equally true of the overlap between Immersion-Emersion and Moratorium. Similarly, Internalization and achieved identity provide essentially the same analysis of advanced identity development. Both models depict persons in the early stages as low in self-esteem, behind in their ego-identity development, and weak in their racial-cultural development. With advances in Nigrescence and ethnic identity development, ego identity is said to increase, self-esteem becomes more optimal, and one's racial/ethnic frame takes on a more positive valence. In a direct test of the association between Nigrescence and ego identity status, Wiggins (1989) administered a separate measure for each construct to a large sample of female and male Black college students. Students showing signs of diffusion and foreclosure on the ego identity measure had high Pre-Encounter scores on the Nigrescence measure. There was a match for moratorium and Immersion-Emersion, and persons at the achieved status (highest level of ego development) stored high on Internalization (stage of advanced Nigrescence).

Revising Nigrescence Theory

A growing body of research calls into question particular dimensions of the Nigrescence theory and, by implication, the EID model. Research on Nigrescence has produced findings that give credence to the theory as a whole and the dynamics of the Pre-Encounter, Immersion-Emersion, and Internalization stages. But other findings have led to a revamping of the Nigrscence theory. (For a thorough review of the research that drove the revision, and a full explication of the changes, see Cross, 1991.) For example, although the original 1971 model suggested a commonality in the identity dynamics of all persons who reach Internalization, empirical findings point to the existence of ideological "splits" among persons positioned at Internalization. Consequently, the new 1991 version of the theory takes into account the range of identities found at Internalization. In the reformulated model, all persons at the advanced stage are shown to place high salience on issues of race and Black culture in their everyday lives. However, persons at Internalization are also depicted as differing in the degree to which they stress race and culture. In the revised model, some persons at Internalization are said to embrace an Afrocentric worldview (categorical salience placed on race and culture); others, a bicultural frame of reference (multiple reference group orientation). These differences attempt to capture the "real-world" identity conflicts and ideological splits found among contemporary Black leaders (Early, 1993).

Taking these differential Internalization profiles into account does not require extensive reworking of the Nigrescence theory. However, more problematic is the discovery of a way to reconfigure Pre-Encounter that effectively addresses the following research trends:

1. A basic premise of Nigrescence theory is that self-esteem and racial identity are highly correlated; this is why the theory predicts low self-esteem and poor ego identity at Pre-Encounter and higher levels of esteem and ego functioning at Internalization. A number of studies have recorded such a relationship; however, exceptions are not difficult to come by. In a review of 45 Black identity studies that explored the relationship between self-esteem and various measures of group identity, the majority of investigations failed to confirm a relationship. This held true whether the subjects were children, adolescents or adults (Cross, 1991). Even in those studies reporting a relationship between self-esteem and Black identity, the amount of variance explained by the correlation was typically modest. Other patterns may be embedded in the data, including profiles that link low race identification with high self-esteem and adequate ego development (Taylor, 1995).

2. Two ongoing studies of urban adolescent youth (Bat-Chava et al., 1995; Spencer, 1995), both incorporating sizable African American adolescent subsamples, have found that Black identity varies from one context to another. There are human ecological niches that allow Blacks to achieve high self-esteem even though their worldview and self-concept place little salience on race.

3. In a reexamination of a handful of Nigrescence studies that originally reported an increase in self-esteem and ego functioning with advanced progress through the stages, it was found that the Pre-Encounter stage may encompass two prototypes, not one (Cross, 1991; Cross et al., 1995). One cluster reflects alienation from other Blacks, evidence of internalized racism, and a Eurocentric worldview, which are factors associated with lower self-esteem and degrees of psychopathology. Such a self-hating profile is classic to the original notion of Pre-Encounter. However, another group positioned at Pre-Encounter feels attached to

other Blacks, evidence little internalized racism, and records a healthy profile across a number of personality variables, inclusive of average levels of self-esteem. Persons located within the second Pre-Encounter cluster do not use ethnicity to frame their identities, yet their positive self-concepts suggest that, in its place, something other than ethnicity is driving their healthy Pre-Encounter perspectives. This raises the possibility that some persons at Pre-Encounter may be operating with an identity that is "achieved" in its psychodynamics, but not "Black or ethnic" in its content and focus.

These findings suggest that the self-concept of African Americans may be configured in a number of ways. In some configurations, positive self-esteem and strong ego development may be associated with a strong Black identity. However, in other instances, positive self-esteem and strong ego development may be linked to an identity that is based on something other than race. One of the best examples of this complicated pattern can be found in a brilliant, but seldom cited, unpublished study of Black gays, Julius Johnson (1981) studied the psychological characteristics and reference group orientation of 51 Black men, all of whom were gay. Thirty-one of the Black homosexuals affirmed a primary identity that centered on race and culture, leading to their classification as "Black identified." The 20 Black homosexuals who placed greater salience on being gay than Black were classified by Johnson as "gay identified." The two groups were fairly well matched for age, education, and income. Each subject was given 10 psychological measures—psychometric complaints, happiness, exuberance, self-acceptance, loneliness, depression, tension, paranoia, suicidal feelings and impulses, and acceptance of professional help—and eight reference group or social measures—interactions with homosexuals, acceptance of homosexuality, interactions with Blacks, racial esteem (i.e., attitudes toward Blacks), interactions with Whites, attitudes toward Whites, attitudes toward overt expressions of homosexuality (general), and attitudes toward overt expressions of homosexuality (familial).

Johnson found important differences between the gay- and Black-identified groups on various social or group identity measures. The gay-identified Black men were more likely to live in the gay community, tended to have White lovers, felt comfortable and welcomed in the gay community, and felt uncomfortable in and mildly estranged from the Black community. The gay-identified men felt less inhibited about public displays of affection toward their made friends and lovers.

A very different picture evolved for the Black-identified gays. For them, being Black was highly salient to their private and public affairs. They enjoyed living and partaking in the traditional aspects of the Black community, most of their friends were Black, as was also true of their lovers, and, in line with their Black allegiance, they felt estranged from the predominantly White gay community. Given the salience of Black traditionalism to their lives, it should come as no surprise that the Black-identified gays preferred private, and even felt uncomfortable with public, displays of affection between gays.

Johnson's study was premised on neither the Nigrescence theory nor the EID model, but had either been the case, he would have predicted lower mental health scores for the gay-identified groups and higher mental health scores for those Black men who stressed their Blackness over their gayness. As it happened, Johnson recorded minimal mental health differences between the two groups, and each group showed good adjustment. In other words, whether one's group identity was positive and Black oriented or positive but gay oriented neither enhanced nor negatively affected personal adjustment. Each chosen social identity was equally efficacious in helping members of the two groups achieve mental health. Consequently, neither type of group identity provided a mental health advantage. Both identities provided a way for reaching the status of "achieved identity," despite being divergent in content and focus. This suggests that, like anyone, a mentally healthy Black person must show signs of having successfully explored and cemented a sense of connection with some type of reference group. However, it is not a given that the emotional health of any particular Black person will be tied to issues of Blackness (ethnicity).

The Johnson study is an excellent example of the diversity to be found in contemporary Black life (Early, 1993). There are Black people with strong, well-developed social identities that are Black oriented, and there are those who achieve strength and resilience through something other than race (e.g., religion, politics, social status, gang affiliation, occupation). This variation in identity development can be traced in individual differences as well as situational factors that define a person's context, such as family structure, socioeconomic status, and neighborhood quality and dynamics. In some contexts, affiliation with Blackness may be appropriate for optimal psychological functioning. But it other contexts, an affiliation with something besides race and culture may explain healthy adjustment. The context in which the person finds him- or herself seems to be the explanatory or moderating variable.

Any update of the Nigrescence theory must show Pre-Encounter incorporating healthy personality profiles, for the reasons just outlined, as well as profiles that reveal self-denigration. With such changes in Pre-Encounter in mind, and with our reconceptualization of Internalization outlined earlier, the overall changes in the 1991 version of the Cross Nigrescence model can be summarized as follows:

1. *Pre-Encounter:* Some Black persons at this stage place low salience on Blackness, but, because they have achieved a strong identity that is grounded in something other than race, may evidence high self-esteem and advanced ego development. Others at this stage show signs of having internalized racist notions about Black people, low self-esteem, and weak ego development. Both types may undergo Nigrescence, one to increase the salience of race in his or her life, the other as a corrective to racial self-negativity.

2. *Encounter* (unchanged from original version): The event or events that lead a person to conclude that he or she needs to change in the direction of greater cultural self-awareness and racial self-acceptance.

3. *Immersion-Emersion* (unchanged from original version): This is the transition stage, during which the old and emergent identities struggle for dominance.

4. *Internalization:* Persons at this stage show high salience for race and culture; however, they cluster into divergent ideological camps. Some persons may embrace a nationalist worldview, others a bicultural perspective, and still others a multicultural perspective. Persons at Internalization can be expected to have higher self-esteem and healthier ego identity development than those persons at Pre-Encounter who show signs of internalized racism. However, no differences in ego identity or self-esteem should be expected in comparisons between persons at Internalization and Pre-Encounter when the Pre-Encounter persons are those who exhibit low race salience but little evidence of internalized racism.

Implications for Altering the Ethnic Identity Development Model

If the EID model were simply a variant of the Nigrescence theory, needed adjustments might be manageable. But although it is an ethnic identity model, it also seeks to show linkages between ethnicity and ego identity development. In its current form, the EID model states that achieved identity can take place only at the final stage, when the person has an explicitly race-or ethnic-oriented achieved identity. We have seen that persons with achieved identity can be found at either Pre-Encounter or Internalization. Where, within the EID model, would one place those Blacks, such as today's Black conservatives or the gay-identified Blacks from the Julius Johnson study, who have an "achieved identity" that is not based on race and ethnicity? The inability to account for minority persons possessing healthy identities not grounded in their ethnic perspectives logically destroys the link between race identity theory and ego identity development that the EID model attempts to forge. If a relationship exists, it is not as straightforward as the EID model would suggest.

Indeed, the correlations that researchers are finding between ethnic identity and ego development are real. But when all is said and done, a great deal of variance remains unexplained by the correlation. Obviously, other trends are embedded in the data. When such trends are eventually confirmed and identified, probably through research that is sensitive to contextual variations (Bat-Chava et al., 1995; Spencer, 1995), diversity in Black identity will be better appreciated. Any minority identity model that is applied to the Black experience must be able to explain how the status of "achieved identity" can be found in Blacks who either do or do not make race salient to their worldview.

An Alternative Way to Linking Nigrescence to Erikson's Stages

Our discussion of the limitations of the EID model in no way signals that we think the search for the link between Nigrescence theory and generic models of human development should be abandoned. There are no sections in either the original or revised versions of the Cross model that explicitly link Nigrescence and ego identity development. This criticism probably applies to all group-specific identity development models. In attempting to fill the void, Phinney and her students have correctly isolated one of the most important gaps in the discourse on minority identity development. However, we believe that, as currently constructed, the EID model cannot predict and explain the diverse and healthy identities to be found among Black Americans. An alternate approach to the EID model is presented in Figure 1. It builds on the ideas of Margaret Spencer, Urie Bronfenbrenner, J. Lawrence Aber, and Thomas Parham, as well as Jean Phinney. The alternative model has six sectors:

Sector 1. As Spencer et al. (1985) would say, a Black infant is born into a context defined by (a) family and kinship factors; (b) family socioeconomic status; (c) neighborhood, school, and church characteristics, inclusive of local cultural traditions: and (d) macro forces, such as national political tends, national social policies, and historical trends (the drift to the far right today, and the civil rights movement of yesterday). These contextual variables interact in complex ways to create an "identity niche" for the growing child, providing early form and substance to her or his emerging identity. The majority of Black children are likely to be raised in human ecologies that steer identity development toward high race salience. However, a significant number of other Black children will exist in niches for which something other than race is given preference (Taylor, 1995).

Sector 2. During preadolescence, each Black child's identity begins to flower. Depending on family preferences and the multitude of ways context may affect self-concept development,

some Black children will show signs of an emergent identity that gives high salience to race and culture, and others will not. In Sector 2 of the model, identity content variability is represented as Identity A, Identity B, Identity C, and so on.

Sector 3. At adolescence, Black youth will burst onto the scene with a broad spectrum of identity agendas; some will be attached to religious issues, others to sexual preference, and still others to their social class status or school affiliation. Because of housing segregation and the prominence of race in American society, race and culture are likely to be a high priority in the self-concept struggles for many Black children. For those Black youth who make race a central organizing feature of their identities, the moratorium experience will be very Nigrescence-like in dynamics. This is shown by the line that connects adolescence (Sector 3) and Nigrescence (Sector 5). However, because Blacks are living and growing in a multitude of circumstances, the identity content of Black youth will vary from context to context. Consequently, the moratorium stage for some Black youth will focus on their religious ideas, for others on their gang membership, and for still others, on issues that have little race content. Most Black adolescents will go through the various Eriksonian stages, yet the content of each young person's identity crisis will not always center on race. Studies showing a relationship between level of Blackness and self-esteem indicate that most Black youth live in contexts in which optimal adjustment requires that they address race matters. On the other hand, the limited amount of variance explained by such correlations reveals, in part, that the context for many Black children allows issues other than race to drive their movement toward an achieved identity.

Sectors 4 and 5. At late adolescence and early adulthood, each person will be "stuck" with whatever identity status has unfolded to this point. This identity (in the model it is called one's "foundational identity") defines one's psychological foundation for adult living; this is the identity frame that will both define the person and guide his or her emotions, ideas, and actions. A psychological analysis may show that one's foundational identity is diffused, foreclosed, or achieved in its characteristics and psychodynamics. Black persons who research this point with a foundational identity that is low in race

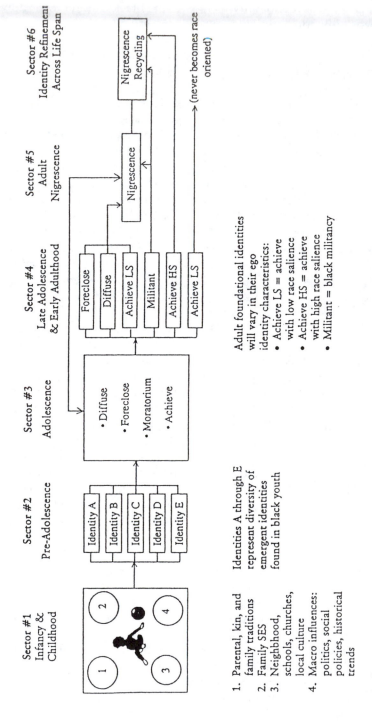

Figure 1 Model depicting the relationship between ego identity development and Nigrescence

content or anti-Black in nature are prime subjects for Nigrescence. What sets the stage for Nigrescence is not one's identity status per se (foreclosed, diffused, or achieved), but one's identity content (race salience). A Black person with a foundational identity that is "achieved" but low in Black content may become susceptible to Nigrescence in the face of an encounter. As the model shows, however, a person with low race salience may go through life and never experience Nigrescence. One exception to the content rule pertains to Blacks who have a foundational identity that is foreclosed in nature. Such a person may have been taught to have positive ideas about the Black experience; however, if the person never questioned or explored such teachings, he or she may go through Nigrescence, not to "become Black," but as a substitute for the missed "moratorium" experience.

Sector 6. The last sector highlights Thomas Parham's concept of Nigrescence recycling (Parham, 1989). Parham suggested that whether one develops a Black identity at adolescence or at some later point in life, certain questions or unexpected challenges lie in waiting. As Parham explained, a youthful person's inexperience makes it impossible to anticipate all of the issues that are related to Blackness. Consequently, as one progresses through the life cycle, certain questions and challenges take on new significance. These new challenges or questions are experienced by the person as a new Encounter. If the Encounter triggers a strong emotional response in the person the recycling may take on the intensity of the person's first spin through Immersion-Emersion and Internalization. The response to a less striking Encounter may be a cognitive "walk through" of the stages. Periodic recycling will likely lead the person to a sense of "wisdom" about the self and Black life in general. (There are gerontological issues that might be addressed there, but that must wait for another essay.)

Conclusion

The model captures our impressions of Black identity development across the life span. For each life span interval, the dual themes of identity development and identity variability are synthesized. In addition, the model applies an Eriksonian perspective to map the unfolding of any Black person's identity from one status to the next, independent of the content of that identity. We account for those African Americans who make race central to their self-conceptions, as well as those who progress to the status of achieved identity despite having a "nonethnic" frame of reference. We show how Nigrescence may enter the picture as early as adolescence or after the establishment of one's foundational adult identity. The possibility for refinement and growth into the status of "wisdom" is reflected in the sector on Nigrescence recycling. Finally, we think this type of model helps counter any tendency toward overgeneralization and stereotyping. In terms of personalities and racial frames of reference, Blacks have been, and remain, a diverse group of individuals. The search for overarching trends need not blind one to coexisting "counterintuitive" trends. We think our model will have value in interpreting the pattern of results emerging from two important studies of urban adolescence: the Adolescent Pathways Project (Bat-Chava et al., 1995) and a multisite project on adolescent development being conducted by Spencer (1995) out of the University of Pennsylvania. Preliminary results from both projects reveal the diverse, normative, and negative ways Black identity can be, and is being, configured in everyday life across a variety of contexts.

Furthermore, variations in adaptive and maladaptive manifestations of Black identity have strong implications for counseling and clinical practices with African American clients. Mental health providers should guard against presuming that a Black client whose identity is not centered on race is maladjusted to her environment. For example, one could be (a) Black and living in the inner city; or (b) Black and residing in a wealthy suburb; or (c) gay and Black and living in a working-class environment; or (d) gay, Black, and disabled and living with a biracial family in a rural, southern community! The combinations and permutations of Black life are as infinite as the imagination, and healthy Black adjustment should be expected to vary from one context to another.

Finally, it is imperative that providers understand the client's frame of reference and the contextual variables associated with the development of that frame. Lumping all Black problems into "self-esteem" or "self-hatred" categories does a grave injustice to the rich and varied psyches of African Americans. Likewise, social interventions with Black clients, whether young or old, should be premised on a multidimensional model of Black psychological functioning. Repairing racial self-images and increasing self-esteem are legitimate objectives of many programs, but they can be applied as "cure-alls" when the actual needs of Black clients may lie elsewhere.

References

Atkinson, D., Morten, G., & Sue, D. (1983). *Counseling American minorities*, Dubuque, IA: William C. Brown.

Bat-Chava, Y., Allen, L., Aber, J., & Seidman, E. (1995, February). *Ethnic identity in the context of neighborhoods and schools: Preliminary report on data analysis from Adolescent Pathways Project*. Paper presented at the Conference on Identity in Context, School of Education, University of Pennsylvania, Philadelphia.

Connell, J. P., Spencer, M. B., & Aber, J. L. (1994). Educational risk and resilience in African American youth: Context, self, action, and outcomes in school. *Child Development, 64*, 493–506.

Cross, W. E. Jr. (1971). The Negro-to-Black conversion experience. *Black World, 20*, 13–26.

Cross, W. E., Jr. (1991). *Shades of Black: Diversity in African American identity*. Philadelphia: Temple University Press.

Cross, W. E., Jr., Parham, T., & Helms, J. (1995). Nigrescence revisited: Theory and research. In R. Jones (Ed.), *Advances in Black psychology* (pp. 1–69). Hampton, VA: Cobb & Henry.

Downing, N. E., & Roush, K. L. (1985). From passive acceptance to active commitment: A model of feminist identity development for women. *Journal of Counseling Psychology, 13*, 695–709.

Early, G. (1993). *Lure and loathing*. New York: Allen Lane.

Erikson, E. H. (1968). *Identity: Youth in crisis*. New York: Norton.

Flnnegan, D. G., & McNally, E. B. (1987). *Dual identities: Counseling chemically dependent gay men and lesbians*. Center City, MN: Hazelton.

Gordon, V. V. (1980). *The self-concept of Black Americans*, Lanham, MD: University Press of America.

Hecht, M. L., Collier, M. J., & Ribeau, S. A. (1993). *African American communication: Ethnicity and cultural interpretation*. Newbury Park, CA: Sage.

Helms, J. E. (1990). *Black and White racial identity: Theory, research and practice*. Westport, CT: Greenwood.

Johnson, J. M. (1981). *The influence of assimilation on psychosocial adjustment of Black homosexual men*. Unpublished doctoral dissertation, California School of Professional Psychology at Berkeley.

Kardiner, A. K., & Ovesey, L. (1951). *The mark of oppression*. New York: Norton.

Kim, J. (1981). *The process of Asian-American identity development*. Unpublished doctoral dissertation, University of Massachusetts, Amherst.

Marcia, J. (1966). Development and validation of ego identity status. *Journal of Personality and Social Psychology, 3*, 551–558.

McAdoo, H. P. (1985). Racial attitudes and racial preferences in young Black children. In H. P. McAdoo & J. L. McAdoo (Eds.), *Black children: Social, educational and parental environments* (pp. 213–242). Newbury Park, CA: Sage.

Parham, T. (1989). Nigrescence: The transformation of Black consciousness across the life cycle. In R. Jones (Ed.), *Black adult development and aging* (pp. 187–226). Berkeley, CA: Cobb & Henry.

Phinney, J. (1989). Stages of ethnic identity development in minority group adolescents. *Journal of Early Adolescence, 9*, 34–49.

Phinney, J. (1992). The multigroup ethnic identity measure. *Journal of Adolescent Research, 7*, 156–176.

Phinney, J., & Alipuria, L. (1990). Ethnic identity in college students from four ethnic groups. *Journal of Adolescence, 13*, 171–183.

Phinney, J., & Chavira, V. (1992). Ethnic identity and self-esteem: An exploratory longitudinal study. *Journal of Adolescence, 15*, 271–281.

Spencer, M. B. (1995, February). *Identity as coping: The search for self in African American youth. Preliminary report on data analysis from Multicity Project on the Identity Development of Male and Female Adolescent Youth*. Paper presented at the Conference on Identity in Context, School of Education, University of Pennsylvania, Philadelphia.

Spencer, M. B., Brookins, G. K., & Allen, W. R. (1985). *Beginnings: The social and affective development of Black children*. Hillsdale, NJ: Lawrence Erlbaum.

Taylor, R. (1995, February). *The social construction of racial identity in a changing environment*. Paper presented at the Conference on Identity in Context, School of Education, University of Pennsylvania, Philadelphia.

Wiggins, F. (1989). *The relationship between racial identity attitudes and ego identity status in Black college students*. Unpublished paper, Illinois State University.

CHAPTER 20

RESOLVING "OTHER" STATUS: IDENTITY DEVELOPMENT OF BIRACIAL INDIVIDUALS

MARIA P. P. ROOT

Half-breed, mulatto, mixed, Eurasian, mestizo, amerasian. These are the *"other,"* biracial individuals, who do not have a clear racial reference group (Henriques, 1975; Moritsugu, Foerster, & Morishima, 1978) and have had little control over how they are viewed by society. Because of their ambiguous ethnic identity and society's refusal to view the races as equal, mixed race people begin life as *marginal people*. Freire (1970) observes that *marginality is not a matter of choice, but rather a result of oppression of dominant over subordinate groups.*

The challenge for a nonoppressive theory and therapy, feminist perspectives attempt, is twofold. First, racism must be recognized and challenged within the therapist's and theorist's world. Without meeting this challenge, it is unlikely that nonpathological models of mental health for mixed race persons can be developed. Second, theoretical conceptualization and application to therapy must become multiracial and multicultural to accurately reflect the process of more than a single racial group. New templates and models for identity development are needed which reflect respect for difference. Necessarily, these theories will need to deviate from traditional linear or systemic models which both have singular endpoints to define mental health. These models are based upon male mental health or, more recently, alternative models define white women's mental health. Current models of mental health do not accommodate the process by which individuals who have "other" identities, such as biracial and or gay/lesbian, arrive at a positive sense of self-identity or maintain a positive identity in the face of oppressive attitudes.

In this essay, the phenomenological experience of "otherness" in a biracial context is described and its socio-political origins explored. The integration of biracial heritage into a positive self-concept is complicated and lengthy. An alternative model for resolution of ethnic identity is offered which takes into account the forces of socio-cultural, political, and familial influences on shaping the individual's experience of their biracial identity. The uniqueness of this essay's approach is that several strategies of biracial identity resolution are offered with no inherent judgment that one resolution is better than another. Instead, the problems and advantages inherent with each type of resolution are discussed. It is proposed that individuals may shift their resolution strategies throughout their life-time in order to nurture a positive identity.

While early sociological theory might suggest that such a model as proposed here describes a "marginal personality" (Stonequist, 1935), or in DSM-III-R nosology inadequate personality or borderline personality, recent research suggests that biracial young adults are generally well adjusted (Hall, 1980; Pouissaint, 1984). Thus, the resolution of major conflicts inherent in the process of racial identity development may result in a flexibility to move between strategies which may reflect positive coping and adaptive abilities and be independent of the integrity of the individual's personality style.

Assumptions About the Hierarchy of Color in the United States

Several general assumptions are made throughout this essay which are important for understanding the origins and dynamics of conflict surrounding the biracial individual. These dynamics further influence the developmental process of identity resolution.

First, in the United States, despite our polychromatic culture, we are divided into white and non-white. The positive imagery created by the "melting-pot" philosophy of the United States is relevant to white ethnic groups of immigrants such as the Irish, French, and Scandinavian people and not Africans, Asians, Hispanics, or even on home territory, American Indians. Cultural pluralism is neither appreciated nor encouraged by the larger culture.

Second, white is considered superior to non-white: the privileges and power assumed by whites are desired by non-whites. It is from this assumption attempts are made to prevent racial mixing because free interaction assumes equality. A corollary of this assumption is that mixed race persons who are part white and can pass as such will be very likely to strive for this racial identity in order to have maximum social power and to escape the oppression directed towards people of color.

The third assumption is that there is a hierarchy of racial/cultural groups based upon their similarity to middle-class white social structure and values. Thus, in general, Asian Americans have a higher social status than Black Americans in white America.

The hierarchical social status system based upon color has oppressed biracial people in two major ways. Both reasons stem from American society's fear of "racial pollution" (Henriques, 1975) (an attitude that was acutely reflected in Hitler's Germany). First, biracial persons have been given little choice in how they are identified. Any person with non-white ethnic features or traceable non-white blood is considered non-white (cf. Henriques, 1975). As a result, Poussaint (1984) notes than any individual with one black and one non-black parent is considered black. Because Asian ethnic groups can be equally oppressive in their fear of "racial pollution" (cf. Murphy-Shigematsu, 1986; Wagatsuma, 1973), a child that is half Asian and half anything else, particularly black, is identified by the blood of the non-Asian parent. Mixed race persons from two minority groups are likely to experience oppression from the racial group of heritage which has higher social status. This method of "irrational," incomplete racial classification has made identity resolution for the biracial individual very difficult and oppressive.

The second source of oppression stems from society's silence on biracialism as though if it is ignored, the issue will go away. It was only as recently as 1967 that the Supreme Court ruled in the *Lovings* case of Virginia that anti miscegenation laws were unconstitutional, a ruling based on an interpretation of the 14th amendment (1868) to the Constitution that could have been made any time in the previous 100 years (Sickels, 1972). Subsequently, the last 12 states with anti-miscegenation laws were forced to overturn them. However, this ruling does not change attitudes. Society still prohibits interracial unions (Petroni, 1973).

The last assumption about the hierarchy of color is necessary for understanding the marginality of biracial persons who are part white. Because whites have been the oppressors in the United States, there is a mistrust by people of color of those accepted by or identified as white. Subsequently, those biracial individuals who are part white (and look white) will at times find it harder to gain acceptance by people of color by virtue of the attitudes and feelings that are projected onto them because of their white heritage and the oppression it symbolizes to people of color (Louise, 1988).

Being mixed race, like interracial marriages, has meant different things at different times (e.g., whether it reflects sexual oppression of a minority group, or equity and similarity of racial groups). Nevertheless, mixed race persons have always has an ambiguous ethnic identity to resolve. *It is the marginal status imposed by society rather than the objective mixed race of biracial individuals which poses a severe stress to positive identity development.* There are few if any role models due to the lack of a clear racial reference group. Friends, parents, and other people of color usually do not comprehend the unique situation and intrapersonal conflict inherent in the resolution of an ambiguous ethnic identity for mixed race persons.

The Beginnings of "Otherness"

The themes described in the development of awareness of otherness in biracial persons have been highlighted in several recent research reports, e.g., Asian-White (Murphy-Shigematsu, 1986), Black-Asian (Hall, 1980), and Black-White mixes (Pouissaint, 1984). The themes of the early years are around race, family, acceptance, difference, and isolation. It is suggested that the intrapersonal and interpersonal conflicts which merge out of these themes are circular and transitory. They reemerge at different points in development with a chance for a greater depth of resolution and understanding with each cycle.

The awareness of "otherness," or ambiguous ethnicity begins early when a child starts to be aware of color around age three (Goodman, 1968) but before a sense of racial identity is formed. An ethnic name or non-ethnic name, which may not be congruent with how a child is perceived, can intensify this awareness. Initially this awareness develops from being identified as different from within any ethnic community. Questions and comments such as, "Where are you from?" "Mixed children are so attractive," and "You are so interesting looking," heighten the feeling of otherness. This acknowledgment of a child's ethnic mix or differentness is natural and not in and of itself harmful or particularly stressful. In fact, the special attention initially may feel good. It is the combination of inquisitive looks, longer than passing glances to comprehend unfamiliar racial-ethnic features (an "unusual or exotic look"), and comments of surprise to find out that the child is one or the other parent's biological child *along with* disapproving comments and nonverbal communication that begin to convey to the child that this otherness is "undesirable or wrong." Suddenly, previously neutral acknowledgement or special attention is interpreted as negative attention. It is with these reactions that the child in her or his dichotomous way of knowing and sorting the world may label her or his otherness as bad. The child's egocentrism can result in assuming blame or responsibility for having done something wrong related to their color; subsequently, one may notice in young children peculiar behaviors to change racial characteristics such as attempts to wash off their dark color. Because the child is not equipped to resolve this conflict at such as early age, the conflict in its complexity is suppressed. It emerges only when negative experiences force the conflict to the surface.

During the early grade school years, children start comprehending racial differences consciously (Goodman, 1968). Self-concept is in part internalized by the reflection of self in others' reactions. Subsequently, a significant part of identification of self in reference to either racial group is influenced by how siblings look, their racial identification, and people's reactions to them. Racial features can vary greatly among the children of the same parents; for example in a Black-White family, one child may look white, one may look black and one may look mixed.

They are teased by their schoolmates, called names, and/or isolated—all the result of the prejudice that is transmitted by relatives, the media, and jokes. For these children who are products of interracial unions during foreign wars (i.e., WW II, Korean War, Vietnam War), fear of the "enemy," translated into national hatred towards the "enemy," translated into national hatred towards the "enemy," may be projected onto interracial families and their children.

Once the child comprehends that there is a concept of a concept of superiority by color, she or he may attempt to achieve acceptance by embracing membership in the "hierarchically superior" racial group of their heritage, and rejecting the other half of their heritage. For example, black-white children may want their hair straightened if it is kinky; Asian-white children may want blue eyes.

A teacher's oppressive assumptions and projections can also contribute to the marginality of the biracial child. This child may be singled out in ways that set her or him apart from peers. Unrealistic expectations of the child may be assumed, and misperceptions of the child's environment perpetuated. For example, in assuming that the child identifies with a culture unfamiliar to the teacher, she or he may be asked to "teach" the class about their racial/cultural group (while other children are not asked to do the same). By her or his action, the teacher is likely to project stereotypes onto the child with which they may not identify.

During the process of ethnic identity development, the biracial child from mid-grade school through high school may be embarrassed to be seen with one or both parents. This embarrassment reflects internalized oppression of societal attitudes towards miscegenation, possible internalized family oppression, as well as more typical American adolescent needs to appear independently functioning of their parents.

The Role of Family

The family environment is critical in helping the child and teenager to understand their heritage and value both races. A positive self-concept and view of people is promoted in interracial partnerships and extended families in which a person's value is independent of race though race is not ignored. This environment, whether it be as a single- or two-parent household, gives the individual a security that will help them weather the stress of adolescence. It is this unusual objectivity about people which determines the options the biracial person has for resolving their identity.

Unfortunately, the stress that has been experienced by interracial families, particularly those that have developed during wartime (e.g., Vietnam and the Korean wars), has often resulted in a lack of discussion of race, discrimination, and coping strategies for dealing with discriminatory treatment. This silence has perhaps reflected these families' needs for a sanctuary from the painful issue of racial differences. Similar to issues of sexuality, the silence may also reflect the difficulty most people appear to have in discussing race issues.

Being identified with a minority group that is oppressed can generate feelings of inferiority within the biracial person, particularly if this parent if treated as such in the extended family. If the extended family is primarily composed of the socially dominant racial group, overt or covert prejudicial remarks against the parent with less racial social status will increase the child's insecurity about their acceptance. He or she may subsequently also devalue cultural and racial features associated with this parent in an attempt to be accepted.

Outright rejection of the parent with less racial social status, in the aspiration of being conditionally accepted by the dominant cultural group, reflects internalization and projection of discriminatory, oppressive attitudes towards one's own racial heritage (Sue, 1981) and creates tremendous intrapersonal conflict in resolving

racial identity. Rejection at this age stems from the awareness that one is judged by those with whom they affiliate; color is a social issue that regulates acceptance and power.

In general, the intensity of the child's reaction is mediated by the racial diversity present in the community, the amount of contact the individual has with other biracial individuals, and the presence of equity among racial groups in their community (Allport, 1958). A child is much less likely to be embarrassed or to reject that part of their heritage that is judged negatively by society if there are ethnic communities which live side by side, if the parent with less racial social status has pride in themselves, and if parents have equal social status within the family. (It is important to be aware that persons of different races in relationships are not exempt from acting prejudicially or in an oppressive manner towards each other.) Based upon the pervasiveness of racism and the widespread oppression of women in American culture, it hard to imaging equity in an interracial, heterosexual marriage.

Some families have a difficult start when an interracial relationship results in the severing of emotional and physical ties by the extended family such as in refusals to visit or accept a marriage or the children. It is a type of abandonment which contributes to mixed race children feeling more different and insecure from other children. Emotional cutoffs are more subtle than physical ones and can be equally damaging, e.g., biracial grandchildren are treated negatively compared to the rest of the grandchildren. This type of discrimination can be very subtle such as loving treatment of biracial child combined with a simultaneous refusal to acknowledge biracial features. Cutoffs can also occur by non-white families and communities. For example, more traditional Japanese grandparents may refuse to accept grandchildren who are any other race *and* ethnic background (e.g., Chinese). Rigid, impermeable physical, emotional, and psychological boundaries communicate hatred and judgment; they mirror to a greater or lesser extent community feelings.

The estrangement and isolation described above encourage denial and rejection of the part of self that has been unaccepted by the extended family; it is very difficult not to internalize this oppression and rejection. As in the case of people who are emotionally deprived of acceptance, some mixed race persons will subsequently try to obtain the approval or acceptance of those persons who are least willing to give it. In the case of biracial children, they may place extra importance on the opinions of persons whose race is the same as their grandparents who initiated the cutoff. Alternatively, they may displace anger towards the extended family onto strangers of the same race.

Summary

The process of identity development so far mirrors what Atkinson, Morten, and Sue (1979) describe in their first two states of minority identity development. In the first stage (Conformity Stage), there is a preference for the dominant culture's values (which in the case of the biracial person may be part of their heritage). In the second stage (Dissonance Stage), information and experiences are likely to create confusion and challenge the individual's idealization of the dominant culture. It is at this point that the individual is usually reaching the end of elementary school and entering junior high school.

Due both to the adolescent's motivation to belong to a community or group and to the adolescent's reaction to a sense of injustice, the biracial individual may seek refuge and acceptance with the group that represents the other half of their heritage. The Minority Identity Development Model predicts that in the third stage (Resistance and Immersion) there will be a simultaneous rejection of the other part of their racial heritage, e.g., being angry and distrustful towards whites (Atkinson et al., 1979) or the racial-social group with greater status. However, this is where models for identity development are not adequate for the biracial individual's unique situation.

For the biracial individual to reject either part of their racial heritage continues an internalized oppression. In reality, it appears that some biracial persons attempt to do this, but the attempts are likely to be very shortlived due to powerful reminders of both sides of their racial heritage. To reject the dominant culture is to reject one parent and subsequently, an integral part of themselves that is unchangeable, particularly if it is the same sex parent. And because racial groups other than white have their prejudices and fears, biracial individuals may feel neither fully accepted nor fully privileged by their other reference group. The individuals are

harshly reminded of their ambiguous ethnic/racial status; they are an *other*. They are *marginal* until they achieve a unique resolution of themselves that accepts both parts of their racial heritage. In order to move out of marginal status they need to place less importance on seeking social approval and even move beyond the dichotomy of thinking about the world and self as white versus non-white, good versus bad, and inferior versus superior. This strategy towards resolution requires the child to do something that in all likelihood they have few models to emulate.

Facing Racism: The End of Childhood

In retrospective reports, biracial adults report differing degrees of awareness of the extent to which their biracial heritage increased the stress of adolescence (Hall, 1980; Murphy-Shigematsu, 1986; Seattle Times, April 1988). This awareness seems to be affected by the communities in which they have lived, parental support, acceptance by the extended family, racial features, and friends.

Junior high and high school are difficult developmental years as teenagers seek a balance between establishing a unique identity while pursuing conformity to peer values. For many biracial individuals, the teenage years appear to be encumbered by a more painful process than the monoracial person. Racial identity conflict is forced to the surface through increased peer dependence, cliques, dating, and movement away from the family.

Turmoil is generated when acceptance at home is not mirrored in the community. At an age that one depends on peers' reactions as the "truth," the teenager may be angry at their parents for failing to prepare them, or for leading them to believe that they are wonderful, lovable, and likable. This inconsistency results in confusion, grief, and anger. Subsequently, conflicts of vague origin increase between children and parents; the adolescent sentiment, "You don't understand; no one understands!" takes on added meaning. Teenagers feel increasingly isolated when they do not know who to trust and as a result may become vulnerable to interpreting environmental cues. For those biracial individuals who feel a tremendous amount of alienation, they may dismiss the positive feedback about self and become extra sensitive to negative feedback. They may overcompensate academically and or in social relationships in order to prove their worth.

A dual existence may be reported by the biracial person; they may appear to be accepted and even popular, but may simultaneously continue to feel different and isolated. Morishima (1980) suggests there may be more identity conflicts for Asian/White children because of their ambiguous appearance. Many White-Asians reflect feeling different regardless or growing up in predominantly white or Asian neighborhoods (Murphy-Shigematsu, 1986). In contrast, Black-White and Black-Asian persons' racial identities appear to be more influenced by their neighbors' color (Hall, 1980), though this difference may simply reflect the continuing, strong oppression of Blacks leading to less freedom of choice for persons who are part Black. However, the biracial adolescent may not relate their feelings of alienation to their biracial status, particularly in the case of those persons who have appeared to move well between and among racial groups. For therapists working with biracial persons, this source of alienation should always be kept in mind, especially with vague complaints of dissatisfaction, unhappiness, and feelings of isolation.

Dating brings many of the subtle forms of racism to the surface. For mixed race persons, all dating is interracial and can be fraught with all the tensions that have historically accompanied it (Petroni, 1973). For the teenager who has seemingly been accepted by different racial groups and has friends of different races they may be confronted with the old slur, "It's okay to have friends who are Black (Asian, White, etc.), but it's not okay to date one, and definitely not okay to marry one." A more subtle form of this racism occurs with parental encouragement of interracial friendships and even dating. However, more covert communication imparts the message, "you can date one, but don't marry one." For those biracial persons who can "pass" as white on the exterior, but do not identify as such, their attraction to non-whites may be met with statements such as, "You can do better than that." This statement is interpreted as a prejudicial comment towards their internal perception and identification of themselves. For some biracial persons this will be the first time that they experience barriers because of color or their socially perceived ambiguous race. For the child who has grown up in an extended white family and has been encouraged to act white and identify white, dating is painful. The teenager or young adult may avoid much dating and or continue in their activities in which these conflicts are absents.

A form of racism which surfaces during adolescence and may continue throughout life is "tokenism," which occurs both personally and vocationally. The biracial person's racial ambiguity and partial similarity by values or appearance may be used by a dominant group as a way of satisfying a quota for a person of color who is less threatening than a monoracial person of color (despite how the biracial person identifies). What makes this type of recruiting oppressive is that the group is using this person to avoid dealing with their racism; furthermore, they are assigning racial identity for the person and not informing her or him of their purpose. The group or organization subsequently uses their association with this person as evidence of their affirmative action or antiracist efforts. As a result, they have actually made this person marginal to the group.

Gender Issues

Like women, non-white persons have had to work harder to prove themselves equal by white, male standards. This observation is true for mixed race persons who may have to fight misperceptions that mixed race persons may be abnormal. The arenas in which biracial men and women have particular difficulties are different. Non-white men, because they have moral social, economic, and political power than most women, are particularly threatening to White America. It is hypothesized that mixed race men will have a more difficult time overcoming social barriers than mixed race women; they will have to work harder to prove themselves and experience an oppression, which while shared by other minority group men, may exist also within their minority reference groups towards them.

On the other hand, because women in general are less threatening to the mainstream culture than men, mixed race women may not experience as much direct oppression as mixed race men. Biracial women may in fact be perceived as less threatening than monoracial women of color. They are likely to have difficulty comprehending, and then subsequently coping with pervasive myths that mixed race women are "exotic" and sexually freer than other women (Petroni, 1973; Wagatsuma, 1973). These myths appear to stem from myths that interracial relationships are based upon sex (cf. Petroni, 1973). Coupled with a lack of acceptance, some biracial women become sexually promiscuous in a search for acceptance (Gibbs, 1987). Mixed race women may also have more difficulty in relationship because of intersections of myths, lower status as women, and their search for an identity.

Summary

Racism challenges adolescent optimism. The young person's sensitivity to social approval and the human need for belonging make the resolution of biracial identity a long, uncharted journey. The path is determined by family, community, and peer values and environments. Racial features including skin color of self and family members also shape one's sense of racial identity.

To assume that the biracial person will racially identify with how they look is presumptive, but pervasive. Besides, the biracial person is perceived differently by different people. *Many persons make the mistake of thinking that the biracial person is fortunate to have a choice; however, the reality is that the biracial person has to fight very hard to exercise choices that are not congruent with how they may be visually and emotionally perceived.* She or he should have options to go beyond identifying with one or the other racial group of their heritage; the limitations of this dichotomy of options is oppressive and generates marginal status. To be able to have an expanded slate of options may shorten the journey and reduce the pain involved in resolution of biracial identity.

Strategies for Resolution of "Other" Status

Several models for identity development exist both in the psychological and sociological bodies of literature. Minority models for identity development share in common the rejection of white values in order to appreciate minority. However, as pointed out in the Atkinson et al.'s (1979) model, there is an inherent difficulty in rejecting "whiteness" if one is part white. In fact, the author proposes that for those individuals

who are part white to manifest hatred towards whiteness probably reflects oppression within the nuclear and extended family system. For biracial persons who are a minority-minority racial mix, it is not clear how to apply this model.

A Beginning Schematic for Identity Development

I am proposing a schematic metamodel that might be used to understand the process of identity development for persons with different types of "other" status. This model is schematically a spiral where the linear force is internal conflict over a core sense of definition of self, the importance of which is largely determined by socialization (e.g., race, gender). Different sources of conflict may move the individual forward. It is proposed, however, that in each person's life there are at least one or two significant conflicts during critical developmental periods that move them forward. The circular or system forces encompass the political, social, and familial environments.

I suggest that in the identity development of the biracial person, the strongest recurring conflict at periods of development will be the tension between racial components within oneself. Social, familial, and political systems are the environments within which the biracial person appears to seek a sense of self in a circular process repeatedly throughout a lifetime. Themes of marginality, discrimination, and ambiguity are produced by these systems.

At all times, biracial persons contend with both parts of their racial heritage. Early in the process of identity development, after the child has become aware of race, she or he is likely to compartmentalize and separate the racial components of their heritage. The attention they give to aspects of their heritage may alternate (though not necessarily equally) over time. This alternating represents conflict and lack of experience and strategies for integrating components of self. Resolution reflects the lack of need for compartmentalizing the parts of their ethnic heritage.

The rest of this essay is dedicated to outlining four general resolutions of biracial identity. That there is more than one acceptable outcome confronts the limitations of traditional psychological theory which allow for only a single healthy endpoint. If there is another step in the contribution that feminist theory can make to personality development, it might be to provide flexibility and tolerance for more than a single definition of mental health.

The factors and criteria that determine each resolution are outlines. All resolutions are driven by the assumption that an individual recognizes both sides of their heritage. The resolutions that are proposed are an articulation of what appears on the surface: acceptance of the identity society assigns; identification with a single racial group; identification with both racial groups; and identification as a new racial group.

Acceptance of the Identity Society Assigns. Biracial people growing up in more racially oppressive parts of the country are less likely to have freedom to choose their racial identity. They are likely to be identified and identified and identify as a person of color which will be equated with subordinate status. This strategy reflects the case of a passive resolution that is positive but may stem from an oppressive process. However, it is possible for it to be a positive resolution if individuals feel they belong to the racial group to which they are assigned. Affiliation, support, and acceptance by the extended family is important to this resolution being positive.

Individuals who have largely been socialized within an extended family, depending on them for friendship as well as nurturance are likely to racially identify with this group regardless of their visual similarity or dissimilarity to the extended family. One will tend to identify with the ethnic identity with which society views the family. The advantage of this identification is that the extended (well-functioning) family is a stable, secure reference group whose bonds go beyond visual, racial similarity.

This resolution is the most tenuous of the strategies outlined in that the individual may be perceived differently and assigned a different racial identity in a different part of the country. Because one's self-image in the mind's eye is stable across significant changes, the conflict and subsequent accumulated life experience would need to be tremendous to compel the individual to change their internally perceived racial identity. In the event of this challenge, the biracial person may work towards a more active resolution process. However, it is likely that she or he will still racially identify the same way but based on a different process such as identification with the extended family. Evidence of a pos-

itive resolution is that the individual would educate those persons with whom they interact of their chosen identity.

Identification with Both Racial Groups. Some biracial persons identify with both racial groups they have inherited. When asked about their ethnic background, they may respond, "I'm part Black and part Japanese," or "I'm mixed." This resolution is positive if the individual's personality remains similar across groups and they feel privileged in both groups. They may simultaneously be aware that they are both similar and different compared to those persons around them. However, they view their otherness as a unique characteristic of self that contributes to a sense of individuality.

This may be the most idealistic resolution of biracial status, and available in only certain parts of the country where biracial children exist in larger numbers and mixed marriages are accepted with greater tolerance by the community such as on the West Coast. This strategy does not change other people's behavior; thus, the biracial person must have constructive strategies for coping with social resistance to their comfort with both groups of their heritage and their claim to privileges of both groups.

Identification with a Single Racial Group. The result of this strategy sometimes looks identical to the strategy of assuming the racial identity that society assigns. It is different, however, by the process being active rather than passive and not the result of oppression. In this strategy, the individual *chooses* to identify with a particular racial/ethnic group regardless if this is the identity assumed by siblings, assigned by society, or matching their racial features. This is a positive strategy if the individual does not feel marginal to their proclaimed racial reference group and does not deny the other part of their racial heritage. This is a more difficult resolution to achieve in parts of the country which have the strongest prohibitions against crossing color lines (e.g., the South).

A major difficulty may be faced with this strategy when there is an incongruous match between how an individual is perceived by others and how they perceive themselves. With this strategy, the biracial person needs to be aware and accept the incongruity and have coping strategies for dealing with questions and suspicion by the reference group. Some individuals will need to make a geographic move to be able to live this resolution more peacefully.

Identification as a New Racial Group. This person most likely feels a strong kinship to other biracial persons in a way that they may not feel to any racial group because of the struggle with marginal status. Identification as a new race is a positive resolution if the person is not trying to hide or reject any aspect of their racial heritage. This individual may move fluidly between racial groups but view themselves apart from these reference groups without feeling marginal because they have generated a new reference group. There are few examples of biracial groups being recognized in a positive way. Hawaii perhaps sets one of the best examples with the Hapa Haole (White-Asian) (Yamamoto, 1973).

A clear problem with this resolution is that society's classification system does not recognize persons of mixed race. Thus, this individual would continually experience being assigned to a racial identity and would need to inform people of the inaccuracy when it felt important of them.

Summary

I suggest that these strategies are not mutually exclusive and may coexist simultaneously, or an individual may move among them. Such movement is consistent with a stable, positive sense of identity if the individual does not engage in denial of any part of their heritage (internalized oppression). Two themes are common to the resolutions listed above. First, it is important that biracial persons accept both sides of their racial heritage. Second, biracial persons have the right to declare how they wish to identify themselves racially—even if this identity is discrepant with how they look or how society tends to perceive them. Third, biracial persons develop strategies for coping with social resistance or questions about their racial identity so that they no longer internalize questions as inferring that there is something wrong with them. Rather, they attribute questions and insensitivities to ignorance and racism.

Resolution of biracial identity is often propelled forward by the internal conflict generated by exposure to new people, new ideas, and new environments. Subsequently, it is not uncommon that many individuals emerge out of college years

with a different resolution to their racial identity than when they graduated high school. Furthermore, geography plays a large part in the options the individual has. Living in more liberal parts of the country may be necessary to exercise a wider range of options with less social resistance.

Conclusion

The multiple strategies for resolution of other status in this essay constitute a proposal, challenge, and appeal to theorists of human personality development to be more flexible in considering the range of positive psychological functioning. Psychological theories have been oppressive by their narrow range of tolerance and allowance for positive mental health. As a result, many different types of people can relate to the search for a resolution of other status, though not necessarily based on racial/ethnic ambiguity. If theories of identity development allowed for a slate of equally valid resolutions of conflict around basic components of identity, fewer people may struggle with "identity crises." Because of the role that feminist theory has played in attempting to validate the experience of persons with "other" status by sexual orientation, religious/ethnic identity, etc., *it seems than feminist theorists and therapists may be the persons most able to develop flexible models of mental health that truly allow for diversity.* But first, more feminist theorists and therapists will have to reach out beyond their boundaries of cultural safety to understand issues of race.

Although it appears that the biracial person may have the best of both worlds, this is a naïve assumption which presumes that she or he has unopposed freedom to choose how she or he wishes to be perceived. In reality all racial groups have their prejudices which when projected onto the biracial person are the creators of marginal status. The biracial person does not have a guaranteed ethnic reference group if they leave it to the group to determine if they can belong.

The key to resolving other status derived from ethnic ambiguity requires an individual to move beyond the dichotomous, irrational categorization of race by white versus non-white in turn has been equated with degrees of worth and privilege in our culture. Towards this goal, three significant assumptions can be made about the experience of the biracial person which subsequently affects their process of identity resolution.

First, the biracial person does not necessarily racially identify with the way she or he looks (Hall, 1980). Because self-image is an emotionally mediated picture of the self, one's perception of self is governed by more than racial features. One's image of self is shaped by the presence or absence of other people similar to them, the racial features of siblings, exposure to people of both races which they inherit, identification with one parent over another, peer reactions, and how the extended family has perceived them as children.

Second, unlike monoracial people of color, the biracial person does not have guaranteed acceptance by any racial reference group. Thus, minority models of identity development do not reflect the resolution of this situation which is the crux of the biracial person's marginal status. *Looking for acceptance from others keeps the biracial person trying to live by the "irrational" racial classification rules which may keep her or him marginal to any group.*

The third assumption is that there is more than one possible, positive resolution of racial identity for biracial persons. This assumption reflects a departure from traditional European, male originated identity models which have a single, static, positive outcome. Furthermore, the *resolution strategies for biracial identity can change during a lifetime.* It is this ability to be flexible that may indeed determine both self-acceptance and constructive, flexible coping strategies.

Marginality is a state created by society and not inherent in one's racial heritage. *As long as the biracial person bases self-acceptance on complete social acceptance by any racial reference group, they will be marginal.* Freire (1970) clearly articulates the origin and subsequently difficult resolution of marginality:

> marginality is not by choice, (the) marginal (person) has been expelled from and kept outside of the social system. . . . *Therefore, the solution to their problem is not to become "beings inside of," but . . . (people) . . . freeing themselves; for, in reality, they are not marginal to the structure, but oppressed . . . (persons) . . . within it* (author's emphasis). (pp. 10-11)

Notes

Maria P. P. Root is half Asian (Filipino) and half white, born in the Philippines and raised in California. This bicultural context has been the

catalyst for many interests which appear diverse but are related through integration of the diversity represented in her cultural background, e.g., psychosomatic symptomatology, family therapy, identity development, and issues of underserved populations.

The author wishes to acknowledge feedback from Carla Bradshaw, PhD, Laura Brown, PhD, Christine C. Iijima Hall, PhD, and Christine Ho, PhD which helped shape revisions of this paper.

References

Allport, Gordon W. (1958). *The nature of prejudice.* Reading, MA: Addison-Wesley.

Atkinson, D., Morten, G., & Sue, Derald W. (1979). *Counseling American minorities: A cross cultural perspective.* Dubuque, IA: Brown Company.

Dien, D. S., & Vinacke, W. E. (1964). Self-concept and parental identification of young adults with mixed Caucasian-Japanese parentage. *Journal of Abnormal Psychology, 69*(4), 463–466.

Freire, Paolo (1970). *Cultural action for freedom.* Cambridge: Harvard Educational Review Press.

Gibbs, Jewelle Taylor (1987). Identity and marginality: Issues in the treatment of biracial adolescents. *American Journal of Orthopsychiatry, 57*(2), 265–278.

Goodman, M. E. (1968). *Race awareness in young children.* New York: Collier Press.

Hall, Christine C. Iijima (1980). *The ethnic identity of racially mixed people: A study of Black-Japanese.* Doctoral Dissertation, University of California, Los Angeles.

Henriques, Fernando (1975). *Children of conflict: A study of interracial sex and marriage.* New York: E. P. Dutton & Co., Inc.

Louise, Vivienne (1988). Of Color: What's In a Name? *Bay Area Women's News, 1*(6), 5, 7.

Morishima, James K. (1980). *Asian American Racial Mixes: Attitudes, Self-Concept, and Academic Performance.* Paper presented at the Western Psychological Association convention, Honolulu.

Moritsugu, John, Foerster, Lynn, & Morishima, James K. (1978). *Eurasians: A Pilot Study.* Paper presented at the Western Psychological Association convention, San Francisco, 1978.

Murphy-Shigematsu, Stephen (1986). *The voices of amerasians: Ethnicity, identity, and empowerment in interracial Japanese Americans.* Doctoral Dissertation, Harvard University.

Petroni, Frank A. (1973). Interracial Dating—The Price is High. In I. R. Stuart and L. Edwin (Eds.), *Interracial marriage: Expectations and Realities.* New York: Grossman Publishers.

Poussaint, Alvin F. (1984). Benefits of Being Interracial. In the Council on Interracial Books for Children, *Children of interracial families, 15*(6).

Sickels, Robert J. (1972). *Race, marriage, and the law.* Albuquerque, NM: University of New Mexico Press.

Stonequist, Everett. (1935). The problem of the marginal man. *The American Journal of Sociology, 41,* 1–12.

Sue, Derald W. (1981). *Counseling the culturally different: Theory and practice.* New York: John Wiley & Sons.

Wagatsuma, Hiroshi (1973). Some Problems of Interracial Marriage for the Japanese. In I. R. Stuart and L. Edwin (Eds.), *Interracial Marriage: Expectations and Realities.* New York: Grossman Publishers.

Yamamoto, George (1973). Interracial Marriage in Hawaii. In I. R. Stuart and L. Edwin (Eds.), *Interracial Marriage: Expectations and Realities.* New York: Grossman Publishers.

CHAPTER 21

ASIAN AMERICAN IDENTITY DEVELOPMENT THEORY

JEAN KIM

The primary purpose of this chapter is to share the Asian American Identity Development (AAID) Model.[1] This model provides insight into how Asian Americans resolve the racial identity conflicts they face as Americans of Asian ancestry in a predominantly White society. The chapter beings with a discussion of White racism and the way it impacts the experience of Asian Americans. This material provides a societal context for examining the racial identity conflicts of Americans of Asian heritage. The next section presents the AAID theory and discusses the assumptions underlying the model and the model's five conceptually distinct, sequential, and progressive[2] stages. These stages are *Ethnic Awareness White Identification, Awakening to Social Political Consciousness, Redirection to Asian American Consciousness,* and *Incorporation*. The review of the AAID is followed by a section that reflects on the relevance of the AAID theory to Asian Americans today, and an outline of current issues for future research in the area of racial identity development for Asian Americans.

Social Context and Asian Americans

One cultural trait that Americans of Asian heritage share and that distinguishes them from the majority White population is the group orientation through which they learn to be sensitive to the expectations of the group and their social environment.[3] For example, Asian people's view of themselves (the private self) is primarily influenced by what other people (the public), and particularly what a specific group of people (the collective) think of them. Consequently, the development of the self is largely influenced by messages that are external to Asian Americans' in both the collective and public environments. Given Asian Americans' tendency to be externally rather than internally focused, their racial identity development is especially affected by the social environment. In particular, the impact of White racism and the attendant oppression of Asian Americans by European Americans are critical factors in Asian American identity development (Kim 1981; Moritsugu and Sue 1983; Smith 1991; Chan and Hune 1995). However, before we can discuss the impact of racism on Asian Americans, it may be helpful to clarify how race is conceptualized in the United States and how racism is defined.

Discussions about race tend to be very emotional, and it is difficult to have a common understanding of what race is and why it matters. But many scholars, especially those associated with the Critical Race Theory movement (Crenshaw 1995; Delgado 1995; Begley 1995) have argued persuasively that the phenomenon of race is a social and legal construct.[4] A growing number of Asian American legal scholars also support this view, arguing that race is not simply an immutable biological attribute (as in skin color) but represents a complex set of social meanings which are affected by political struggle (Omi and Winant 1994). Understanding that race is socially and politically, rather than biologically, determined may help us to understand how racial prejudice and racial dominance operate in U. S. society.

Racial prejudice is created by inaccurate and/or negative beliefs that rationalize the *superiority* or *normalcy* of one race, (in this case Whites over people of color). Racial dominance, on the other hand, describes the control of societal structures by a single racial group which enforces that group's racial prejudice and maintains its privileges. Racism occurs when racial prejudice and racial dominance occur simultaneously (Wijeyesinghe, Griffin, and Love 1997). In the United States the White race is racially dominant and racial prejudice is taught to everyone, including members of racially oppressed groups. In addition, race tends to be seen in Black and White terms, and we are most familiar with racial prejudices directed against Black Americans. We are less aware of the experiences of other groups of color (Asian, Latino, and American Indian). We also assign a specific set of stereotypes to each racial group (Wijeyesinghe, Griffin, and Love 197).

Since the mid-1960s, when the Black civil rights movement was gaining momentum, the media began depicting Asian Americans as the "model minority." Articles appeared in popular magazines portraying Asian Americans as one minority group who had made it in this country through hard effort (Kasindorf 1982; Chan and Hune 1995). These works cited higher academic attainments and combined family earnings of Asian Americans as indicators that Asians are a model minority. Therefore, several positive generalizations—such as, Asians work hard, are technological nerds, are good at math, focus on education, and the like—were added to the negative stereotypes of Asians—such as, Asians are sly, ruthless, untrustworthy, submissive, quiet, foreigners, and lack communication skills and leadership potential. Given this "model minority" myth and the so-called "positive" stereotypes of Asian Americans, some people are unaware of the fact that White racism is also directed against Asian Americans. In fact, the history of racism against Asians began with the first wave of Asian immigrants from China almost one hundred fifty years ago. Subsequent to this early period, Asians have been subjected to massive and intense discrimination, including the denial of citizenship, the segregation of schools and housing, lynching, massacres, internment in concentration camps, random acts of violence, and subtle forms of unfair treatment in employment.[5]

In spite of this history, there is a pervasive myth accepted by many, including Asian Americans themselves, that Asian Americans have overcome all these obstacles and succeeded in finding a place for themselves in the American dream through hard work, perseverance, and quiet suffering. It is true that many Asian Americans have obtained higher levels of education than the general population and have achieved middle-class status (Carnevale and Stone 1995). However, the model minority myth[6] ignores both the significant psychological cost of acculturation into a White racist society and the reality of continuing discrimination against Asian Americans. One such psychological cost is racial identity conflict.

Racism and Identity Conflict

Of the many problems faced by Asian Americans in the psychological arena, racial identity conflict is the most critical and severe (Sue and Sue 1971; Suzuki 1975; Sue and Sue 1990). Conflict about one's identity can be said to exist when individuals perceive certain aspects or attributes of themselves which they simultaneously reject. In the case of Asian Americans, awareness of one's self as an Asian person is rejected in favor of the White models that are so pervasive in our society. The issue here is not the lack of awareness of one's racial self but rather how one feels about and values that part of oneself.[7]

This phenomenon of identity conflict is manifested in a number of ways, with varying degrees of severity (Kohatsu 1993; Huang 1994)/ An Asian American may experience identity conflict as a belief in his or her own inferiority (as well as the inferiority of other Asian Americans) perhaps coupled with deep-seated feelings of self-hatred and alienation. At some point in their lives, many Asian Americans have either consciously or unconsciously expressed the desire to become White, and tried to reject their identity as Asians (Kim 1981; Suzuki 1975; Huang 1994). A painful expression of this identity conflict among Asian American women is the practice of creating double-folded eyelids (many Asians have single-folded eyelids) either through surgery or by using scotch tape in a vain attempt to meet the beauty standards to White society. This practice of "Americanizing" Asian eyes in reminiscent of the practice among Blacks of straightening their hair and bleaching their skin to look Whiter in appearance (Suzuki 1975). Such experiences of denial and/or rejection of their Asian heritage contribute toward Asian Americans' negative self-concept and low self-esteem, both hallmarks of negative racial identity (Sue and Sue 1990).

The experience of identity conflict among Asian Americans is a direct result of living in a society that has institutionalized racism throughout its major structures, cultures, and value systems (Knowles and Prewitt 1969). An example of institutional racism are stereotypes of Asians evident in film and television. The history of the U.S. legal and political system also contains voluminous pages of violence and discrimination directed at Asian Americans (Takaki 1989; Chan and Hune 1995). Although the racism experienced by Asian Americans today may be more subtle than in prior decades, its effects have been shown to have a negative impact on Asian Americans' psychological well-being (Chin 1970; Sue and Kitano 1973; Sue and Sue 1971, 1990). Various manifestations of identity conflict can be seen as the result of Asian Americans' attempts to make it in a White society, which, for the most part, devalues racial minorities and considers people of color to be aliens and foreigners even though many have been here for generations. Identity conflict as experienced by Asian Americans seems inevitable in a society where being different is synonymous with being inferior.

Asian American Identity Development (AAID) Theory: Assumptions

Before we being to discuss the actual AAID model, it is important to discuss some of its underlying assumptions. These assumptions stem from the fact that racial minorities in our society have to deal with the daily realities of White racism, whether or not they are managing this challenge consciously. The first assumption states that White racism cannot be separated from Asian American identity development due to racism's pervasive nature and the fact that the social environment (the public and collective self) has such a huge impact on the way Asian Americans determine who they are (the private selves).

The second assumption is that Asian Americans cannot shed their negative racial identity automatically. It involves a conscious decision to unlearn what Asian Americans have learned about themselves. This unlearning process requires that Asian Americans become conscious of the stereotypes about themselves that they have internalized, and get rid of perceptions that they accepted unconditionally in the past.

The third assumption is that the psychological well-being of Asian Americans is dependent on their ability to transform the negative racial identity they experience as a result of identity conflict and to acquire a positive racial identity.

These assumptions about AAID are similar to the general principles found in the racial identity development theories of other racial minorities (Helms 1990; Bernal and Knight 1993). This is not surprising, as all racial minorities experience White racism in this country. As Gay notes:

Positive ethnic identification for most American racial minorities does not happen automatically nor does it happen for all individuals. When it does happen, it is learned . . . Second, the psychological well-being of ethnic minorities [is] contingent upon this rebirth or resynthesization of ethnic identity. Part of this rebirth is the replacement of feelings of ethnic shame and denigration with self ethnic pride and acceptance. . . . Third, the reformation of ethnic identity is a progressional process. . . . Fourth, a dialectical interaction exists between the personal processes of ethnic identity development and the sociocultural contexts in which they occur. (1985:49–50)

Asian American Identity Development Theory: The Model

Within the AAID, the process of acquiring a positive Asian American racial identity occurs through five stages.[8] Each stage is characterized by the basic components of an identity, that is, a self-concept that includes evaluation and meaning attribution (ego identity). Experiencing the various stages lead in turn to specific behaviors and a social consciousness about being an Asian American. The five stages are sequential in nature, although the process is not linear or automatic. For example, it is possible for an Asian American to get stuck in a certain stage and never move to the next stage. Whether Asian Americans move on to the next stage in their racial identity development is dependent primarily on their social environment, and various factors in this environment determine both the length and the quality to experience in a given stage.

Stage One: Ethnic Awareness

Ethnic Awareness is the first stage of AAID, and represents the period prior to Asian Americans entering the school system. Awareness of their ethnicity comes primarily from interactions with family members and relatives. Asian Americans who live in predominantly Asian or mixed neighborhoods have greater exposure to ethnic activities and experience more ethnic pride and knowledge of their cultural heritage. One benefit of membership in a larger Asian community is that Asian Americans experience what it is like to be in the majority and have a sense of security and positive ethnic awareness. Asian Americans who live in predominately White neighborhoods and have less exposure to ethnic activities are not sure what it means to be a member of an Asian ethnic group and feel neutral about their ethnic membership. Furthermore, greater exposure to Asian ethnic experiences at this stage leads to a positive self-concept and clearer ego identity while less exposure is related to a neutral self-concept and confused ego identity (Kim 1981). For most Asian Americans, this stage lasts until they enter the school system. By the time they being school, Asian Americans' social environment changes from a protective secure home and family setting to a more public arena. More significantly, this change social environment heralds a period of increased contact between Asian Americans with the dominant White society. This is a key factor that moves individuals to the next stage.

Key features of the Ethnic Awareness Stage include:

Social environment: mostly at home with family.

Critical factor: extent of participation in Asian ethnic activities.

Self-concept: greater participation leads to positive self-concept; less participation leads to neutral self-concept.

Ego identity: greater participation leads to clear sense as a person of Asian heritage, less participation leads to less clear meaning about being a person of Asian heritage.

Primary reference group: family.

Hallmark of the stage: discovery of ethnic heritage.

Stage Two: White Identification

The beginning of the White Identification stage is marked by Asian Americans' strong sense of being different from their peers. They acquire this sense mostly through painful encounters, for example, being made fun of, being the object of name-calling, and the like. At this stage, Asian Americans are not sure what makes them different from their peers, and they are not prepared to handle these negative reactions. The following words by a second-generation Chinese American woman illustrates this phase.

> When I was younger I was always obsessed with my shadow. I used to look at it and then at my other school peers' shadows and realize that there was no differences from that perspective. Unfortunately, as soon as I heard the name "eggroll," or "gook," I was reminded all over again of my racial differences and set back in a state of self-consciousness.

Such experiences tell Asian Americans that being different is bad. Given the Asian cultural values of quiet suffering and avoiding public shame, most Asian parents are not able to help their children other than telling them to ignore these slights and hurts. The children, however, find this difficult to do. The Asian cultural tendency toward group or collective orientation has taught them to attend to the reactions of others in their social circle and to try to fit in rather than stick out.

In addition to group orientation, the significance of shame in Asian cultures may influence Asian Americans to try at all costs to fit into White society in order to avoid publicly embarrassing themselves. All these influences cause Asian Americans to gradually internalize White societal values and standards and see themselves through the eyes of White society, especially regarding standards of physical beauty and attractiveness. The following statement by a second-generation Korean American college student is illustrative of this stage.

> Junior high was a time in my life where image was everything and I didn't fit into that image. To, me the blonde-haired, blue-eyed girls were the lucky ones. I believed that I wouldn't have a boyfriend because I was Korean. Everyone assumed I was super smart, especially in math. But the only thing I really wanted to be was "the image." I was as White as a sheet. All of my friends were

White. I had such a difficult time dealing with my different appearance. I would just freak out when someone would point out that I was Korean.

The hallmark of the White Identification stage are experiences of alienation from self and other Asian Americans. Although their reference group is White, Asian Americans in this stage often feel socially isolated from their White peers and enjoy little closeness or meaningful friendships with them. Many Asian Americans compensate for this by becoming involved in formal organizational roles and responsibilities within school such as becoming class presidents, class officers, club leaders, and by excelling academically.

This is a very painful time, a period when Asian Americans' self-concept begins to change from positive or neutral to negative. Consequently, Asian Americans' ego identity is centered on being inferior and being at fault and responsible for things that happen to them.

Active White Identification

There is some variation as to how the White Identification stage is experienced, depending on the degree to which Asian Americans identify with White people. Asian Americans who grow up in predominantly White environments are more likely to experience what is called Active White Identification, and repress negative feelings and experiences associated with their Asianness. In actively identifying with White people, such Asian Americans consider themselves to be very similar to their White peers and do not consciously acknowledge any differences between themselves and Whites. They do not want to be seen as an Asian person and do all they can to minimize and eliminate their Asian selves. The following statement by a first-generation Korean American man is a good example of a person in Active White Identification:

> In time I learned to speak and write just like a White person, leaving no traces that my mouth had ever formed the words of another language. I was so proficient that oftentimes people who I had only spoken to on the phone were shocked when they met me, and discovered me to be something other than White.

Passive White Identification

Asian Americans who experience a positive self-concept during the first stage of Ethnic Awareness and who grow up in predominantly Asian or mixed neighborhoods are more likely to experience Passive White Identification. They also enter the White Identification stage later on in life, in junior high rather than in elementary school, for example. In Passive White Identification, Asian Americans do not consider themselves to be White and do not distance themselves from other Asians. However, they do experience periods of wishful thinking and fantasizing about being White. Like Asian Americans in Active White identification, Asian Americans in Passive White Identification also accept White values, beliefs, and standards, and use Whites as a reference group.

The White Identification stage is most likely to be experienced in a passive way by first-generation Asian Americans who arrive in the United States as adults with a developed sense of themselves from their mother country, even when they reside in predominantly White neighborhoods. However, the neighborhood environment will influence how children who emigrated to the United States prior to their teens (also known as the 1.5 generation) (Harklau, Losey, and Siegal 1999) experience his stage. Although these Asian Americans were born elsewhere, their primary reference growing up is the United States. Thus, they resemble second-generation Asian Americans. If these 1.5 generation folks grow up in predominantly White neighborhoods, they will likely experience the White Identification stage actively. However, if they grow up in predominantly mixed or Asian neighborhoods, they will experience this stage more passively.

Whether experienced actively or passively, White Identification is a stage marked by negative attitudes and evaluations of self as Americans of Asian ancestry and includes behaviors that reflect turning one's back on other Asian Americans and on other minorities. These behaviors and attitudes are accompanied by a lack of political understanding, or a context that could enable them to make sense of their experiences. At this stage, Asian Americans personalize their experiences and are not conscious of social injustice or racism. They are likely to say that there is no racism and that they have not encountered any discrimination. The goal of Asian Americans at this stage is to fit in, to be treated like White people, and to pass for a White person. As long as Asian Americans believe they can be fully assimilated into White society, they remain in this stage of White Identification.

Key features of the White Identification Stage include:

Social environment: public arenas such as school systems.

Critical factor: increased contact with White society which leads to acceptance of White values and standards.

Self-concept: negative self-image, especially body image.

Ego identity: being different, not fitting in, inferior to White peers, feel isolated and personally responsible for any negative treatment.

Primary reference group: White people and dominant society.

Hallmark of the stage: feelings of being different, alienation from self and other Asian Americans, and inability to make connections between personal experience and racism.

Stage Three: Awakening to Social Political Consciousness

It is during the stage of Awakening to Social and Political Consciousness that some Asian Americans are able to shift their worldview and realize that they are not personally responsible for their situation and experiences with racism. In moving their paradigm from personal responsibility to social responsibility, Asian Americans acquire social and political understanding that transforms their self-image. While there is some variation as to how these shifts occur, they are a critical factor in changing Asian Americans' self-concept from negative to positive. It is also apparent that Asian Americans must acquire an awareness of White racism and develop a resistance to being subordinated if they are to move out of the White identification stage.

How then, does the awareness of White racism bring about change? First, the new awareness leads to a realistic assessment of Asian Americans' social position, that is, a clear realization of the existence of societal blocks and the futility of trying to "pass" or to strive for acceptance within the White world. Second, the political awareness of White racism provides alternative

perspectives, a new paradigm for Asian Americans. This new worldview allows people to reinterpret their lives and lets them know that things could be different. Prior to the awakening to Social Political Consciousness stage, Asian Americans blamed themselves for their negative experiences and believed these were the result of personal failings. An alternative perspective in stage Three is that these negative encounters have societal rather than personal roots. This understanding releases the individual from unnecessary guilt and feelings of inferiority. Similarly, having a different analysis of the past and present facilitates the generation of new solutions, which lead to a belief that change is possible.

In my original study underlying the AAID (Kim 1981), this paradigm shift occurred through participants' involvement in the political movements of the 1960s and 1970s.[9] A family member's or a close friend's interest in a sociopolitical issue initiated the political involvement of some participants. Others were influenced by the campus politics of the late 1960s and early 1970s when student activism was high and centered around the issues of war, Black studies, and women's rights. A significant theme among Asian Americans' experience in the original study (Kim 1981) was that their political consciousness was initially centered on being a minority and they became politically conscious about being Asian Americans later. Asian Americans often enjoyed greater support for their fledgling political consciousness from other minority groups than from White Americans.

Another major change that occurs during Stage Three is a reaction against White people. For Asian Americans at this stage, White people are no longer the reference group to which they aspire. Rather, White people become the antireferent group, people they don't want to be like. For example, one Asian American at the stage of Awakening to Social and Political Consciousness noted that:

> Most of our friends were Black, so there were a lot of antiWhite feelings. It was the political atmosphere that made us feel alienated from Whites. We would say anti-White things because we were looking at White people in terms of the society. They were responsible for the things that were happening in the world. I put Whites in a general grouping and they were more the "enemy." Of course, we always had a number of White friends. I guess I saw them as exceptions.

In summary, through political involvement, Asian Americans at Stage Three find meaningful support systems and a new paradigm, which enables them to reinterpret their past negative experiences of personal shame and take ownership of their identities in light of the societal illness called racism. Asian Americans also realize that regardless of what they achieve, they will never be fully accepted into the dominant society as long as White racism exists. They no longer blame themselves for the discrimination and racial prejudice they have encountered. Ego identity at this stage is centered on being a minority and being oppressed. Asian Americans no longer feel inferior to Whites, and they relate to the experiences of other racial minorities. A third-generation Japanese American woman recalled her feelings at the time as follows:

> I had a context for the first time to think about it. In racism and stereotypes, I had a whole context. It was a really nice opening time for me in a lot of ways. I had friends. I felt like I had friends for the first time in ages. I felt safer to deal with things like racism.

Key features of the Awakening to Social Political Consciousness Stage include:

Social environment: social political movements and/or campus politics.

Critical factor: gaining political consciousness related to being a racial/political minority and awareness of White racism.

Self-concept: positive self-concept, identification as a minority in the United States.

Ego identity: accepts being a minority but resists White values and White domination, feels oppressed but not inferior to Whites.

Primary reference group: individuals with similar social political philosophy and antiestablishment perspective.

Hallmark of the stage: gaining new political perspective and sociological imagination, political alienation from Whites.

Stage Four: Redirection to an Asian American Consciousness

Although in the preceding stage Asian Americans changed their affiliation from Whites to minorities, they had not yet identified with Asian Americans. This change occurs at the fourth stage of AAID, *Redirection to an Asian American Con-*

sciousness. With support and encouragement from friends, Asian Americans begin to feel secure enough in themselves to look at their own experiences. Some Asian Americans are motivated to develop this orientation by observing and learning from other political movements. This point is aptly illustrated by the words of a fourth-generation Japanese American woman:

> The civil rights movement was the vehicle to express our concern. That's when I became concerned with Asian identity. We were involved in the Black Nationalist movement and people would talk a lot about Africa, or about culture, and returning to your tradition. Because most of our friends were Black and changing their names to African names, at that point everyone in our family started to think more about being Asian and what that meant. I started to feel for the first time proud to be an Asian. That was because of the civil rights movement.

A critical step taken by Asian Americans during this stage is an immersion in the Asian American experience. Through related activities, Asian Americans discover that while they had some knowledge of their Asian cultural heritage, they don't really know very much about the Asian American experience. As they learn more about the real experience of Asian Americans, they feel anger and outrage toward the dominant White system for the acts of racism directed toward Asians. Eventually Asian Americans are able to move out of this reactionary state into a more realistic appraisal of both themselves and other Asian Americans and to figure out what parts of themselves are Asian and what parts are American.

The ego identity of Asian Americans at this stage is centered on being an Asian American, which entails knowing they belong here, having a clear political understanding of what it means to be Asian American in this society, and no longer seeing themselves as misfits. They finally acquire racial pride and a positive self-concept as Americans with Asian heritage. The following statement by a third-generation Japanese American woman is a good illustration of this outcome.

In the context of America, it's a good feeling to have an Asian American identity finally. Until we got to that point, we didn't know where we fit. We weren't Black, we weren't White, and we weren't Japanese. Having an Asian American identity means that you share an experience that other Asians experience. It's a positive side to your makeup.

Key features of the Redirection to an Asian American Consciousness Stage include:

Social environment: Asian American community.

Critical factor: immersion in Asian American experience.

Self-concept: positive self-concept, and identification as Asian American.

Ego identity: proud of being Asian American, experience a sense of belonging.

Primary reference group: Asian Americans, especially those at similar stage of identity development.

Hallmark of the stage: focus on personal and Asian American experience, feel anger against Whites about treatment of Asian Americans.

Stage Five: Incorporation

The key factor in Stage Five, *Incorporation,* is confidence in one's own Asian American identity. This confidence allows Asian Americans to relate to many different groups of people without losing their own identity as Asian Americans. Having been immersed in an Asian American experience in the previous stage and resolving their racial identity conflict, Asian Americans in Stage Five no longer have a driving need to be exclusively with other Asian Americans. They also recognize that while racial identity is important, it is not the only social identity of importance to them. The hallmark of this last stage is the blending of individuals' racial identity with the rest of their social identities, as evidenced in the following words:

> What I also discovered was that my needs got less driving. That I had a lot more in common with people who were Caucasians in some cases. I accepted that. That just because we're Asian American doesn't mean we're going to be kindred spirits. I'd say that writing that book was a commitment to seeing it through to really try to get some blood flowing in that part of myself and find that missing limb, that missing corner of my heart and spirit.

Key features of the Incorporation Stage include:

Social environment: general.

Critical factor: clear and firm Asian American identity.

Self-concept: positive as a person.

Ego identity: whole person with race as only a part of their social identity.

Primary reference group: people in general.

Hallmark of the stage: blending of Asian American identity with the rest of an individual's identities.

Current Issues and Future Research

When this theory was developed in the 1980s, there were no other theories of Asian American racial identity development. Two decades later, this theory continues to be relevant to Asian Americans. Research has been done on specific ethnic groups and specific aspects of the ethnic and racial identity development of Asian Americans.[10] There is research that examines whether it is possible for different Asian ethnic groups to view themselves as a racial group and under what circumstances this unity might occur.[11] The general conclusion that one can draw from these works is that racial unity among Asian Americans is possible when it is politically and economically advantageous to do so, often in response to adversity. Examining how and when a racial group might come together is a different discourse than exploring the psychological processes that lead to a person's racial identity formation.

The Asian American Identity Development theory specifically focuses on racial identity development rather than ethnic identity development. This focus was fueled by the belief that much of what influences AAID is Asian Americans' status as a racial minority in the United States and the social and psychological consequences of this status. This is not to deny the existence of real cultural diversity among Asian ethnic groups. In fact, a study of college students by Yeh and Huang (1996) which focused on ethnicity, found that Asian Americans explicitly separate race and ethnicity and focus on ethnicity. Their research indicated that Asian Americans are largely affected by external forces and relationships in determining their affiliation with their cultural group and ultimately in forming ethnic identity. Yeh and Huang highlight the importance of acknowledging the collectivistic nature of ethnic identity development among Asian Americans.

However, the reality of everyday experience is that all Asian ethnic groups are perceived and treated from a common set of racial prejudices and stereotypes (Chan and Hune 1995). For the most part, we do not accord different status or treat an Asian person differently depending on the ethnic group (Chinese, Japanese, Korean, Vietnamese, and the like) he or she represents. The murder of Vincent Chin[12] in 1982 is a painful example of this reality. In fact one of the stereotypes of Asian Americans is that they all look alike. Just as a Black person is treated primarily on the basis of the color of his or her skin in this country regardless of ethnic membership (for example, African, Jamaican, Cape Verdean, mixed race, and so on), Asian Americans experience a similar social dynamic. It is their racial membership, not their ethnic membership, that impacts how Asian Americans feel about themselves in this country. This is the primary reason for formulating AAID as a racial identity theory.

While I have received much anecdotal information from Asian Americans of different ethnic backgrounds that the theory is applicable to their personal experience, it has not been tested by research among different Asian ethnic groups. This could be a fruitful area of future research. Relatedly, on college campuses today, there are more Asian ethnic associations, such as organizations for Korean students or Chinese American students, than Asian American associations. This shift implies a greater ethnic than racial orientation among modern college students. Future research could examine why this is so.

Although Ethnic Awareness is a stage of AAID, Asian American identity development is not primarily a process for finding one's heritage, although this does occur for some Asian Americans. As evident in the AAID theory, understanding and proclaiming one's Asian heritage is a necessary but not a sufficient condition for developing an Asian American racial identity. A critical factor is the acquisition of a coherent political point of view and a new paradigm, which are often gained though involvement in political movements. That new perspective recognizes the subordination of people of color in this country, including Asian Americans.

The political climate in the United States has changed significantly since the 1960s and the 1970s. There is more acceptance of the racial status quo, more political backlash about affirmative action, and more resistance to dealing with social oppression and injustice.[13] Given the importance of the sociopolitical environment in facilitating the development of an Asian American identity, how will the current, politically

less progressive, environment affect Asian Americans? Will Asian American identity still evolve as outlined in the AAID theory if there are fewer opportunities to become involved in political movements that challenge current racial dynamics and institutions? Responses to the AAID theory from college students I've worked with indicate that the shifting of their paradigm during the third stage is much more subtle and at times hard to distinguish from the fourth stage. That is, the Awakening to Social Political Consciousness and Redirecting to Asian American Consciousness seem to blend into one stage. It will be important to study current college students and those in their mid- to late twenties to see how they resolve their racial identity conflict, and how similar or different their experience of racial identity conflict resolution is to the stages of AAID. Future research in this area could lead to a modification of the AAID theory.

Another potential impact of the post-1960s and 1970s political environment is that the importance of racial identity is beginning to be questioned. Two recent books by Asian American writers, *Native Speaker* by Change-rae Lee (1995) and *The Accidental Asian* by Eric Liu (1998), provide some evidence of this. In his own way each author focuses more on the American part of his experience than on the Asian. Both authors are second-generation Asian American males in the White Identification stage, albeit passively, but they do not deny the existence of racial discrimination. One consequence of the changed political environment may be that Asian Americans spend more time in the White Identification stage, and perhaps never leave it. If this outcome is documented by future research, it would support one of AAID's theoretical assumptions of the importance of shifting one's paradigm by enhancing one's sociopolitical understanding, without which one remains in the White Identification stage.

Future research on Asian American racial identity must explore the length of time it takes for racism to affect the racial identity of Asian Americans, and whether this effect is the same for all generations of Asian Americans. Differences between the experiences of foreign-born and native-born Asian Americans warrant additional attention.

Responses gained from sharing the AAID model with different generations of Asian Americans indicate that the theory primarily fits the experience of the 1.5 plus generation. The first generation of immigrants, who come to this country as adults, seem less affected psychologically by racism. Since the theory was developed using second-, third-, and fourth-generation Asian Americans, it may not accommodate the experiences of the immigrant generation. This is an important group to research, especially since fully 62 percent of Asian Americans in this country are immigrants.

Another significant social change that has occurred since the AAID theory was developed relates to the marriage patterns of Asian Americans. Specifically, more Asian Americans are marrying out of their Asian ethnic groups (for example, Chinese Americans marrying Korean Americans) and especially marrying out of their racial group (for example, Asians with White partners, Asians with Black partners, and so on). The AAID as currently written does not account for the experiences of interracial and interethnic people. Therefore, future research needs to examine the kinds of identity conflict that arise for Asian Americans who are in interracial marriages, or who are children of interracial or interethnic marriages. How these conflicts are resolved by these populations should also be studied. I believe the identity conflict issues are greatest for interracial people, especially if their background includes a blending of Asian and another race of color (that is, Black, Latino, or American Indian) because of their physical appearance. On the other hand, the mixed Asian ethnic families and children would probably have similar experiences as Asian Americans in general and would follow the AAID model because of the saliency of race over ethnicity that was discussed earlier. Additional research is needed to explore these topics more fully.

Summary: Synthesis

In summary, the Asian American Identity Development (AAID) theory is comprised of five stages which explore how Asian Americans gain a positive racial identity in a society where they must deal with various negative messages and stereotypes about who they are. The cultural tendency for Asian Americans to have a group and public orientation and to avoid shame contributes to the assimilation strategy evident in the White Identification Stage. Access to infor-

mation and increased understanding about White racism can help an Asian American to move out of the White Identification Stage and start on the road to a positive racial identity.

While there are a number of research topics that could shed light on Asian Americans' racial identity conflict and its resolution, the AAID theory still seems very relevant today. This is due in part to the fact that as a society we have not made significant progress toward eliminating White racism, and therefore the societal setting in which Asian Americans experience life has not changed significantly. If anything, our society seems to be more reactionary toward issues of affirmative action and politically more conservative about race relations now than a few decades ago. In such an environment, there is a shortage of progressive social political movements and agendas. Consequently, it may be more difficult than before for Asian Americans to work through the AAID stages and positively resolve their racial identity conflicts.

NOTES

1. The AAID was created in the 1980s, based on doctoral dissertation research on the experiences of Japanese American women.
2. I have shared the AAID theory with many Asian Americans professionals in large corporations, both male and female. On one such occasion, a Chinese American woman rose up in a crowded room of over two hundred people to say how much of her own life experience was reflected in the AAID stages. Through her tears she talked about the pain of spending many years in the White Identification stage. In 1999, I taught an undergraduate course composed primarily of Asian American students from various ethnic backgrounds. The AAID theory was discussed as a part of the course. I wasn't sure how relevant the AAID stages would be for young people who grew up in the post-civil rights and the race pride movement era. However, I was pleasantly surprised by their recognition of AAID stages in their young lives.
3. Studies that have compared culturally diverse groups found that Asian American subjects provide more collective responses, 20 to 52 percent, than European American subjects who only gave 15 to 19 percent collective responses (Higgins and King 1981). When compared to European Americans,

Asian Americans tend to depend more heavily on the situation and values of the society to define who they are (Triandis 1989).

4. Specifically, Critical Race theorists believe that race is a conceptual mechanism by which power and privileges are distributed in this country. Furthermore, the concept of race was constructed as a political device to keep people of color subordinated to Whites. Therefore Critical Race theorists believe that progressive racial identity must reflect more than appreciation of common ancestry and include a common political agenda based on a shared worldview. This agenda should seek to terminate the subordination of people of color in this country (Iijima 1997).

5. There are a few books that chronicle the experience of Asian Americans in this country. Ronald Takaki (1989) is a great primer that describes the experiences of the major Asian ethnic groups in America. Another good source is a report of the U.S. Commission on Civil Rights (1992).

6. For further information on the history of racial discrimination suffered by Asian Americans and a critique of the model minority thesis, see Chin et al. (1996: 13–23).

7. Much research done in the area of racial identity concludes that a child between the ages of three and six becomes aware of different ethnic groups and begins to identify with the appropriate one. However, both minority and majority children develop preferences for White racial stimuli (Clark 1955; Clark and Clark [1947] 1958; Clark 1980; Brand, Ruiz, and Padilla 1974)

8. Since completing the original study, I have processed the results with hundreds of Asian Americans in different adult stages of development, generations, ethnic backgrounds, and social environments. These encounters have illustrated that for the most part the theory of five stages is still viable. However, I have become more aware of the interplay between the way Asian Americans experience the various stages and Asian cultural values, especially of *group orientation* resulting in greater focus on the external social environment and the role of *shame* as a preferred control mechanism among Asian cultures.

9. Major political influences of this era were the Black liberation movement and Black nationalism. These movements believed that the way to reduce racial domination was to directly transform the power relationship between Blacks and Whites. The birth of the Asian American movement itself coincided with these movements for Black liberation. Asian American activists focused on raising questions of oppression and power and not so much on racial pride. To them, Asian American identity was primarily a means of uniting for political struggle rather than acquiring racial identity solely for its own sake (Iijima 1997).

10. Two unpublished theses, Ray (1996), Alvarez (1996), document the experiences of Asian Americans as they adjust to living in this country. Others who have written on Asian American identity development are Phinney (1989), Lee (1989), Yeh and Huang (1996), DesJardins (1996), Oyserman and Sakamoto (1997), Ponpipom (1997), Ibrahim, Ohnishi, and Sandhu (1997), Sue, Mak, and Sue (1998), Lee (1999), Tse (1999), and Sodowsky, Kwan, and Pannu (1995).

11. Espiritu (1996) contains many chapters that examine various Asian ethnic group experiences and the circumstances under which Asian Americans unite and view themselves as a racial group. The book does not contain any theories of racial identity development of Asian Americans but does examine various circumstances under which Asian ethnic groups come together. The dominant examples are in the areas of national politics, responding to social service agency funding requests, responses to violence directed against Asian Americans, reactions to discrimination, and so on.

12. In 1982 Vincent Chin was murdered by a group of laid-off auto workers in Detroit. His Asian appearance made him a target. In an area where there was a lot of anti-Japanese feeling due to competition in the auto industry, Vincent was thought to be Japanese, though he was Chinese American. The fact that the White men who murdered Chin received minimum sentences of probation is an example of institutional racism directed against Asian Americans in our legal system.

13. It was during the 1990s that we saw the passage of proposition 206 in California that eliminated affirmative action in contracting, selection, and hiring in businesses, and admissions to universities. A number of other states, including Washington State, have followed suit. Other evidence of this changing social climate are the Texas Law school case and the Maryland scholarship case, both of which questioned the legality of affirmative action and the value of diversity in higher education in professional school admissions.

REFERENCES

Alvarez, Alvin N. 1996. "Asian American Racial Identity: An Examination of Worldviews and Racial Adjustment." Doctoral dissertation, Department of Psychology, University of Maryland, College Park.

Begley, Sharon. 1995. "Three Is Not Enough: Surprising New Lessons from the Controversial Science of Race." *Newsweek* (February 3):67–69.

Bernal, Martha E., and George P. Knight. 1993. *Ethnic Identity: Formation and Transmission among Hispanic and Other Minorities*. Albany: State University of New York Press.

Brand, Elaine S., Rene A. Ruiz, and Amado M. Padilla. 1974. "Ethnic Identification and Preference: A Review." *Psychological Bulletin* 81(11):860–890.

Carnevale, Anthony P., and Susan C. Stone. 1995. *The American Mosaic: An In-Depth Report on the Future of Diversity at Work*. New York: McGraw-Hill.

Chan, Kenyon S., and Shirley Hune. 1995. "Racialization and Panethnicity: From Asians in America to Asian Americans." Pp. 205–233 in *Toward a Common Destiny: Improving Race and Ethnic Relations in America*, ed. W. D. Hawley, A. W. Jackson, et al. San Francisco: Jossey-Bass.

Chin, Gabriel J., Sumi Cho, Jerry Kang, and Frank Wu. 1996. *Beyond Self Interest: Asian Pacific Americans, Towards a Community of Justice: A Policy Analysis of Affirmative Action*. Los Angeles: UCLA Asian-American Studies Center.

Chin, Pei-Ngo. 1970. "The Chinese Community in L.A." *Social Casework* (51)(10):591–598.

Clark, Kenneth B. 1955. *Prejudice and Your Child*. Boston: Beacon Press.

——. 1980. "What Do Blacks Think of Themselves?" *Ebony*: 176–182.

Clark, Kenneth B., and M. P. Clark. [1947] 1958. "Racial Identification and Preference in Negro Children." Pp. 169–178 in *Readings in Social Psychology*, ed. T. Newcomb and E. L. Hartley. New York: Holt.

Crenshaw, Kimberle. 1995. *Critical Race Theory: The Key Writings That Formed the Movement*. New York: New Press.

Delgado, Richard. 1995. *Critical Race Theory: The Cutting Edge*. Philadelphia: Temple University Press.

DesJardins, Kunya S. 1996. "Racial Identity Development and Self Concept in Adopted Korean Women." Doctoral dissertation, Boston University.

Espiritu, Yen Le. 1996. *Asian American Panethnicity*. Los Angeles: Asian American Studies Center, UCLA.

Gay, Geneva. 1985. "Implications of the Selected Models of Ethnic Identity Development for Educators." *Journal of Negro Education* 54(1):43–55.

Harklau, Linda, Kay M. Losey, and Meryl Siegal, eds. 1999. *Generation 1.5 Meets College Composition: Issues in the Teaching of Writing to U.S.-Educated Learners of ESL*. Mahwah, N.J.: Lawrence Erlbaum.

Helms, Janet E. 1990. *Black and White Racial Identity: Theory, Research and Practice*. Westport, Conn.: Greenwood.

Higgins, E. Tory, and Gillian King. 1981. "Accessibility of Social Constructs: Information-Processing Consequences of Individual and Contextual Variability." Pp. 69–121 in *Personality, Cognition and Social Interaction*, ed. N. Cantor and J. F. Kihlstrom. Hillsdale, N.J.: Lawrence Erlbaum.

Huang, Larke N. 1994. "An Integrative View of Identity Formation: A Model for Asian Americans." Pp. 43–59 in *Race, Ethnicity, and Self: identity in Multicultural Perspective*, ed. E. P. Salett and D. R. Koslow. Washington , D.C.: National MultiCultural Institute.

Ibrahim, Farah, Hifumi Ohnishi, and Data Singh Sandhu. 1997. "Asian American Identity Development: A Culture Specific Model for South Asian Americans." *Journal of Multicultural Counseling and Development* 25(1):34–50.

Iijima, Chris K. 1997. "The Era of We-Construction: Reclaiming the Politics of Asian Pacific American Identity and Reflections on the Critique of the Black/White Paradigm." *Human Rights Law Review* 29:47.

Kasindorf, Martin. 1982. "Asian-Americans: A "Model Minority.'" *Newsweek* (December 6):39.

Kim, Jean. 1981. "Process of Asian American Identity Development: A Study of Japanese American Women's Perceptions of Their Struggle to Achieve Positive Identities as Americans of Asian Ancestry." Doctoral dissertation, School of Education, University of Massachusetts, Amherst.

Knowles, Louis L., and Kenneth Prewitt, eds. 1969. *Institutional Racism in America*. Englewood Cliffs, N.J.: Prentice-Hall.

Kohatsu, Eric L. 1993. "The Effects of Racial Identity and Acculturation on Anxiety, Assertiveness, and Ascribed Identity among Asian American College Students." Doctoral dissertation, University of Maryland, College Park.

Lee, Chang-rae. 1995. *Native Speaker*. New York: Riverhead Books.

Lee, Sally R. 1989. "Self-Concept Correlates of Asian American Cultural Identity Attitudes." Doctoral dissertation, University of Maryland, College Park.

Lee, Stacey J. 1999. "'Are you Chinese or what?' Ethnic Identity among Asian Americans." Pp. 107–121 in *Racial and Ethnic Identity in School Prac-*

tices: Aspects of Human Development, ed. R. Hernández and E. R. Hollins. Mahwah, N.J.: Lawrence Erlbaum.

Liu, Eric. 1998. The Accidental Asian. New York: Random House.

Moritsugu, John, and Stanley Sue. 1983. "Minority Status as a Stressor." Pp. 162–173 in Preventive Psychology: Theory, Research, and Practice, ed. R. D. Felner, L. A. Jason, J. N. Moritsugu, and S. S. Farber. Elmsford, N.Y.: Pergamon.

Omi, Michael, and Howard Winant. 1994. Racial Formation in the United States: From the 1960s to the 1990s. New York: Routledge.

Oyserman, Daphna, and Izumi Sakamoto. 1997. "Being Asian American: Identity, Cultural Constructs, and Stereotype Perception." Journal of Applied Behavioral Science 33(4):435–453.

Phinney, Jean S. 1989. "Stages of Ethnic Identity Development in Minority Group Adolescents." Journal of Early Adolescence 9(1):34–49.

Ponpipom, Ada. 1997. "Asian-American Ethnic Identity Development: Contributing Factors, Assessment, and Implications for Psychotherapy." Doctoral dissertation, Institute for Graduate Clinical Psychology, Widener University, Chester, Pennsylvania.

Ray, Indrani E. 1996. Racial and Ethnic Identity: South Asian American Youth's Experiences and Perceptions, a Thesis. Doctoral dissertation, University of Massachusetts, Boston.

Smith, Elsie J. 1991. "Ethnic Identity Development: Toward the Development of a Theory within the Context of Majority/Minority Status." Journal of Counseling and Development 70:181–188.

Sodowsky, Gargi R., Kwong-Liem K. Kwan, and Raji Pannu. 1995. "Ethnic Identity of Asians in the United States." Pp. 123–154 in Handbook of Multicultural Counseling, ed. J. G. Ponterotto, J. M.

Casas, L. A. Suzuki, and C. M. Alexander. Thousand Oaks, Calif.: Sage.

Sue, Stanley, and Harry H. Kitano. 1973. "Stereotypes as a Measure of Success." Journal of Social Issues 29(2):83–98.

Sue, David, Winnie S. Mak, and Derald W. Sdue. 1998. "Ethnic Identity." Pp. 289–323 in Handbook of Asian American Psychology, ed. L. C. Lee, N. W. S. Zane et al. Thousand Oaks, Calif.: Sage.

Sue, Stanley, and Derald W. Sue. 1971. "Chinese-American Personality and Mental Health." Amerasia Journal 1:36–49.

———. 1990. Counseling the Culturally Different: Theory and Practice. New York: John Wiley.

Suzuki, Bob J. 1975. "The Broader Significance of the Search for Identity by Asian Americans." Lecture presented at the AA Conference held at Yale University, New Haven, Conn. (April 12).

Takaki, Ronald. 1989. Strangers from a Different Shore: A History of Asian Americans. Boston: Little Brown.

Triandis, Harry C. 1989. "The Self and Social Behavior in Differing Cultural Contexts." Psychological Review 96(3), 506–520.

Tse, Lucy. 1999. "Finding a Place to Be: Ethnic Identity Exploration of Asian Americans." _Adolescence 34(133):121–138.

United States Commission on Civil Rights. 1992. Civil Rights Issues Facing Asian Americans in the 1990s. Washington, D.C.: The Commission.

Wijeyesinghe, Charmaine L., Pat Griffin, and Barbara Love. 1997. "Racism Curriculum Design." Pp. 82–109 in Teaching for Diversity and Social Justice: A Sourcebook, ed. M. Adams, L. A. Bell, and P. Griffin. New York: Routledge.

Yeh, Christine J, and Karen Huang. 1996. "The Collectivistic Nature of Ethnic Identity Development among Asian American College Students." Adolescence 96(31):645–661.

CHAPTER 22

ETHNIC IDENTITY IN ADOLESCENTS AND ADULTS: REVIEW OF RESEARCH

JEAN S. PHINNEY

Ethnic identity is central to the psychological functioning of members of ethnic and racial minority groups, but research on the topic is fragmentary and inconclusive. This article is a review of 70 studies of ethnic identity published in refereed journals since 1972. The author discusses the ways in which ethnic identity has been defined and conceptualized, the components that have been measured, and empirical findings. The task of understanding ethnic identity is complicated because the uniqueness that distinguishes each group makes it difficult to draw general conclusions. A focus on the common elements that apply across groups could lead to a better understanding of ethnic identity.

The growing proportion of minority group members in the United States and other Western countries has resulted in an increasing concern with issues of pluralism, discrimination, and racism in the media. However, psychological research on the impact of these issues on the individual is uneven. Most of the research dealing with psychological aspects of contact between racial or ethnic groups has focused on attitudes toward racial or ethnic groups other than one's own and particularly on stereotyping, prejudice, and discrimination. The emphasis has been on attitudes of members of the majority or dominant group toward minority group members; this is a research area of great importance in face of the daily evidence of ethnic tensions and racial violence.

A far less studied aspect of diversity has been the psychological relationship of ethnic and racial minority group members with their own group, a topic dealt with under the broad term *ethnic identity*. The study of attitudes about one's own ethnicity has been of little interest to members of the dominant group, and little attention has been paid by mainstream, generally White researchers to the psychological aspects of being a minority group member in a diverse society.

Recent concern with ethnic identity has derived in part from the ethnic revitalization movements in the 1960s. Growing awareness in society of differences associated with ethnic group membership (e.g., lower educational and occupational attainment) has been accompanied by social movements leading to increased ethnic consciousness and pride (Laosa, 1984). Attitudes toward one's ethnicity are central to the psychological functioning of those who live in societies where their group and its culture are at best poorly represented (politically, economically, and in the media) and are at worst discriminated against or even attacked verbally and physically; the concept of ethnic identity provides a way of understanding the need to assert oneself in the face of threats to one's identity (Weinreich, 1983). The psychological importance of ethnic identity is attested to by numerous literary writings of ethnic group members about the struggle to understand their ethnicity (e.g., Du Bois, 1983; Kingston, 1976; Malcolm X, 1970; Rodriguez, 1982).

The issue of ethnic identity has also been brought to the fore by changing demographics, including differential birthrates and increasing numbers of immigrants and refugees throughout the world. Projections suggest that by the mid-1990s, minority youth will constitute more than 30% of the 15- to 25-year-olds in the United States (Wetzel, 1987). The topic not only has important implications within psychology (e.g., Ekstrand, 1986) but also has broad political significance. In response, Canada has developed an explicit policy of multiculturalism and supports continuing study of the issue (Berry, Kalin, & Taylor, 1977). Many European countries will be dealing for years to come with struggles of ethnic minorities to maintain or assert their identities (Kaplan, 1989).

Within the social sciences, many writers have asserted that ethnic identity is crucial to the self-concept and psychological functioning of ethnic group members (e.g., Gurin & Epps, 1975; Maldonado, 1975). Critical issues include the degree and quality of involvement that is maintained with one's own culture and heritage; ways of responding to and dealing with the dominant group's often disparaging views of their group; and the impact of these factors on psychological well-being. These issues have been addressed conceptually from a variety of perspectives (e.g., Alba, 1985; Arce, 1981; Atkinson, Morten, & Sue, 1983; Dashefsky, 1976; DeVos & Romanucci-Ross, 1982; Frideres & Goldenberg, 1982; Mendelberg, 1986; Ostrow, 1977; Parham, 1989; Staiano, 1980; Tajfel, 1978, 1981; Weinreich, 1988; Yancey, Ericksen, & Juliani, 1976; Zinn, 1980).

However, the theoretical writing far outweighs empirical research. Most of the empirical work on ethnic identity has concentrated on young children, with a focus on minority children's racial misidentification or preference for White stimulus figures. This work has been widely discussed and reviewed (e.g., Aboud, 1987; Banks, 1976; Brand, Ruiz, & Padilla, 1974) and is not addressed here. Far less work has been done on ethnic identity beyond childhood and particularly the transition from childhood to adulthood; this gap has been recently noted (Kagitcibasi & Berry, 1989). In published studies on ethnic identity in adolescents and adults, researchers have generally focused on single groups and have used widely discrepant definitions and measures of ethnic identity, which makes generalizations and comparisons across

studies difficult and ambiguous. The findings are often inconclusive or contradictory.

The topic is of sufficient importance to warrant serious research attention, but in order for the research to yield useful and meaningful results, greater conceptual and methodological clarity is needed. The primary goal of this article is to provide such clarity through a review of the empirical literature on ethnic identity in adolescents and adults. I describe the definitions and conceptual frameworks that have guided empirical research, the way in which the construct has been defined and measured, and the empirical findings. The article concludes with recommendations for future research.

In order to review the literature, an extensive search was carried out to locate journal articles from psychology, sociology, and allied social sciences, published since 1972, that dealt empirically with ethnic or racial identity in adolescents (12 years or older) or adults. The material reviewed was limited in several ways. In order to focus on research that had been subject to peer review and that was accessible to readers, only published journal articles were included. Books, chapters, dissertations, and unpublished papers were excluded, with some noted exceptions. Also excluded were (a) articles that dealt only with social identity (social class, political affiliation, national and religious identity) and did not include ethnicity and (b) articles in which the term *ethnic identity* was used to mean simply the ethnic group membership of the subjects (e.g., Furnham & Kirris, 1983). Only English-language articles were examined. Conceptual articles that included no empirical data were reviewed and are referred to but are not included in the analyses.

Seventy empirical articles dealt substantively with ethnic identity beyond childhood. The authors of those articles examined many ethnic groups and presented widely differing approaches to the meaning, the measurement, and the study of ethnic identity in adolescents and adults. The articles varied widely both in conceptualization and in the terminology applied to ethnic identity and its components. They differed in whether ethnic identity was simply described or was considered a variable whose antecedents, correlates, or outcomes were studied. However, all dealt with ethnic identity in minority or non-dominant group members, including White ethnics. Ethnic identity among members of a dominant group in society, although it can be conceptualized (Helms, 1985), has apparently not been studied empirically. The next section is an overview of the studies.

Overview: Studies of Ethnic Identity

The articles reviewed focused on a variety of ethnic groups. The largest group of studies, nearly half the total, dealt with White ethnic groups, such as Greek and Italian Americans or French Canadians. These articles included (in order of frequency) studies from the United States, Canada, the United Kingdom, Israel, and Australia. Within White ethnic groups, Jews have been the subgroup most studied. In a few studies, White subjects were included primarily as a group in contrast to an ethnic minority group (Hispanic, Black, or Asian); in these cases the White subjects were undifferentiated as to ethnic origin.

The second largest group of studies involved Black subjects; these studies were mostly from the United States. A smaller group of studies, entirely from the United States, dealt with Hispanic subjects. A few studies focusing on Asians were primarily from the United States, but some were from Canada and Great Britain; the studies from Great Britain dealt with East Indians, mostly Pakistanis. The distribution of studies has been very uneven; many studies focused on White ethnic groups and Black Americans, but few on Asian Americans, Hispanics, or American Indians.

The articles represented research from a diversity of fields, published in 36 different journals; the minority were from psychology but some were from sociology, anthropology, social work, and education. Researchers often appeared unaware of previous work; that is, they did not cite relevant prior work. Therefore, there was much duplication of effort as researchers developed new measures independently.

The research overall presented a picture of fragmented efforts by many researchers working individually with particular ethnic groups and developing measures of limited generality. Rarely have researchers conducted follow-up studies to develop or extend a measure or to elaborate on concepts developed in a study. Nevertheless, the studies provided a starting point for understanding how different researchers have sought to understand and study ethnic identity.

Definitions of Ethnic Identity

Ethnic identity was defined in many ways in the research reviewed. The fact that there is no widely agreed-on definition of ethnic identity is indicative of confusion about the topic. A surprising number of the articles reviewed (about two thirds) provides no explicit definition of the construct. The definitions that were given reflected quite different understandings or emphases regarding what is meant by *ethnic identity*.

In a number of articles, ethnic identity was defined as the ethnic component of social identity, as defined by Tajfel (1981): "that part of an individual's self-concept which derives from his knowledge of his membership of a social group (or groups) together with the value and emotional significance attached to that membership" (p. 255). Some writers considered self-identification the key aspect; others emphasized feelings of belonging and commitment (Singh, 1977; Ting-Toomey, 1981; Tzuriel & Klein, 1977), the sense of shared values and attitudes (White & Burke, 1987, p. 311), or attitudes toward one's group (e.g., Parham & Helms, 1981; Teske & Nelson, 1973). In contrast to the focus by these writers on attitudes and feelings, some definitions emphasized the cultural aspects of ethnic identity: for example, language, behavior, values, and knowledge of ethnic group history (e.g., Rogler, Cooney, & Ortiz, 1980). The active role of the individual in developing an ethnic identity was suggested by several writers who saw it as a dynamic product that is achieved rather than simply given (Caltabiano, 1984; Hogg, Abrams, & Patel, 1987; Simic, 1987).

In summary, researchers appeared to share a broad general understanding of ethnic identity, but the specific aspects that they emphasized differed widely. These differences are related to the diversity in how researchers have conceptualized ethnic identity and in the questions they have sought to answer; these issues are reviewed in the next section.

Conceptual Frameworks for the Study of Ethnic Identity

About a quarter of the studies suggested no theoretical framework, but most of the studies were based on one of three broad perspectives: social identity theory, as presented by social psychologists; acculturation and culture conflict, as studied by social psychologists, sociologists, or anthropologists; and identity formation, drawn from psychoanalytic views and from developmental and counseling psychology. There is considerable overlap among the frameworks on which the studies were based, as well as great variation in the extent to which the relevant framework or theory was discussed and applied to the research. However, these three approaches provide a background for understanding the empirical research.

Ethnic Identity and Social Identity Theory

Much of the research on ethnic identity has been conducted within the framework of social identity as conceptualized by social psychologists. One of the earliest statements of the importance of social identity was made by Lewin (1948), who asserted that individuals need a firm sense of group identification in order to maintain a sense of well-being. This idea was developed in considerable detail in the social identity theory of Tajfel and Turner (1979). According the theory, simply being a member of a group provides individuals with a sense of belonging that contributes to a positive self-concept.

However, ethnic groups present a special case of group identity (Tajfel, 1978). If the dominant group in a society holds the traits or characteristics of an ethnic group in low esteem, then ethnic group members are potentially faced with a negative social identity. Identifying with a low-status group may result in low self-regard (Hogg, Abrams, & Patel, 1987; Ullah, 1985). An extensive literature deals explicitly with the notion of "self-hatred" among disparaged ethnic groups, generally with reference to Black Americans (Banks, 1976; V. Gordon, 1980). Much of the research reviewed was concerned with this issue: that is, whether or to what extent membership in, or identification with, an ethnic group with lower status in society is related to a poorer self-concept. A number of studies addressed these issues (Grossman, Wirt, & David, 1985; Houston, 1984; Paul & Fischer, 1980; Tzuriel & Klein, 1977; White & Burke, 1987); the specific findings are discussed later in the article.

Tajfel (1978) asserted that members of low-status groups seek to improve their status in various ways. Individuals may seek to leave the group by "passing" as members of the dominant group, but this solution may have negative psychological consequences. Furthermore, this solution is not available to individuals who are racially distinct and are categorized by others as ethnic group members. Alternative solutions are to develop pride in one's group (Cross, 1978), to reinterpret characteristics deemed "inferior" so that they do not appear inferior (Bourhis, Giles, & Tajfel, 1973), and to stress the distinctiveness of one's own group (Christian, Gadfield, Giles, & Taylor, 1976; Hutnik, 1985).

Social identity theory also addresses the issue of potential problems resulting from participation in two cultures. Both Lewin (1948) and Tajfel (1978) discussed the likelihood that identification with two different groups can be problematic for identity formation in ethnic group members because of the conflicts in attitudes, values, and behaviors between their own and the majority group (Der-Karabetian, 1980; Rosenthal & Cichello, 1986; Salgado de Snyder, Lopez, & Padilla, 1982; Zak, 1973). The issue in this case is whether individuals must choose between two conflicting identities or can establish a bicultural ethnic identity and, if so, whether that is adaptive.

A distinct but related approach to ethnic identity is based on symbolic interactionism and identity theory (Stryker, 1980). Research in this framework emphasizes the importance of shared understandings about the meaning of one's ethnic identity, which derive both from one's own group and from a "countergroup" (White & Burke, 1987).

Acculturation as a Framework for Studying Ethnic Identity

Ethnic identity is meaningful only in situations in which two or more ethnic groups are in contact over a period of time. In an ethnically or racially homogeneous society, ethnic identity is a virtually meaningless concept. The broad area of research that has dealt with groups in contact is the acculturation literature.

The term *ethnic identity* has sometimes been used virtually synonymously with *acculturation*, but the two terms should be distinguished. The concept of acculturation deals broadly with changes in cultural attitudes, values, and behaviors that result from contact between two distinct cultures (Berry, Trimble, & Olmedo, 1986). The level of concern is generally the group rather than the individual, and the focus is on how minority or immigrant groups relate to the dominant or host society. Ethnic identity may be thought of as an aspect of acculturation, in which the concern is with individuals and the focus is on how they relate to their own group as a subgroup of the larger society.

Two distinct models have guided thinking about these questions: a linear, bipolar model and a two-dimensional model. In the linear model, ethnic identity is conceptualized along a continuum from strong ethnic ties at one extreme to strong mainstream ties at the other (Andujo, 1988; Makabe, 1979; Simic, 1987; Ullah, 1985). The assumption underlying this model is that a strengthening of one requires a weakening of the other; that is, a strong ethnic identity is not possible among those who become involved in the mainstream society, and acculturation is inevitably accompanied by a weakening of ethnic identity.

In contrast to the linear model, an alternative model emphasizes that acculturation is a two-dimensional process, in which both the relationship with the traditional or ethnic culture and the relationship with the new or dominant culture must be considered, and these two relationships may be independent. According to this view, minority group members can have either strong or weak identifications with both their own and the mainstream cultures, and a strong ethnic identity does not necessarily imply a weak relationship or low involvement with the dominant culture.

This model suggests that there are not only the two acculturative extremes of assimilation or pluralism but at least four possible ways of dealing with ethnic group membership in a diverse society (Berry et al., 1986). Strong identification with both groups is indicative of integration or biculturalism; identification with neither group suggests marginality. An exclusive identification with the majority culture indicates assimilation, whereas identification with only the ethnic group indicates separation. Table 1 is an illustration of this model and some of the terms that have been used for each of the four possibilities in empirical research. A number of the studies reviewed were based on this model (e.g., M. Clark, Kaufman, & Pierce, 1976; Hutnik, 1986; Ting-Toomey, 1981; Zak, 1973), and in some the authors explored empirical evidence for the bipolar versus the two-dimensional models (e.g., Elias &

Blanton, 1987; Zak, 1976). Research on this issue is summarized later.

An important empirical issue in this area has been the question of the extent to which ethnic identity is maintained over time when a minority ethnic group comes in contact with a dominant majority group (DeVos & Romanucci-Ross, 1982; Glazer & Moynihan, 1970; M. Gordon, 1964) and the impact of the process on psychological adjustment (e.g., Berry, Kim, Minde, & Mok, 1987). Underlying both these issues is the theme of culture conflict between two distinct groups and the psychological consequences of such conflicts for individuals. How such conflicts are dealt with at the individual level is part of the process of ethnic identity formation.

Ethnic Identity Formation

Both the social identity and the acculturation frameworks acknowledge that ethnic identity is dynamic, changing over time and context. In a similar vein, several of the definitions cited earlier include the idea that ethnic identity is achieved through an active process of decision making and self-evaluation (Caltabiano, 1984; Hogg et al, 1987; Simic, 1987). In a conceptual chapter, Weinreich (1988) asserted that ethnic identity is not an entity but a complex of process by which people construct their ethnicity. However, in research based on the social identity or acculturation frameworks, investigators in general have not examined ethnic identity at the level of individual change—that is, developmentally.

TABLE 1

Terms Used for Four Orientations, Based on Degree of Identification With Both One's Own Ethnic Group and the Majority Group

Identification with majority group	Identification with ethnic group	
	Strong	Weak
Strong	Acculturated Integrated Bicultural	Assimilated
Weak	Ethnically identified Ethnically embedded Separated Dissociated	Marginal

A developmental framework was provided by Erikson's (1968) theory of ego identity formation. According to Erikson, an achieved identity is the result of a period of exploration and experimentation that typically takes place during adolescence and that leads to a decision or a commitment in various areas, such as occupation, religion, and political orientation. The ego identity model, as operationalized by Marcia (1966, 1980), suggests four ego identity statuses based on whether people have explored identity options and whether they have made a decision. A person who has neither engaged in exploration nor made a commitment is said to be *diffuse*; a commitment made without exploration, usually on the basis of parental values, represents a *foreclosed* status. A person in the process of exploration without having made a commitment is in *moratorium*; a firm commitment following a period of exploration is indicative of an *achieved identity* (see Table 2). Although Erikson alluded to the importance of culture in identity formation, this model has not been widely applied to the study of ethnic identity.

The formation of ethnic identity may be thought of as a process similar to ego identity formation that takes place over time, as people explore and make decisions about the role of ethnicity in their lives. A number of conceptual models have described ethnic identity development in minority adolescents or adults. Cross (1978) described a model of the development of Black consciousness in college students during the Civil Rights era. In a dissertation, Kim (1981) described Asian-American identity development in a group of young adult Asian-American women. A model of ethnic identity formation based on clinical experience was proposed by Atkinson et al. (1983), and Arce (1981) conceptualized the issues with regard to Chicanos.

In a recent article, Phinney (1989) examined commonalities across various models and proposed a three-stage progression from an unexamined ethnic identity through a period of exploration to an achieved or committed ethnic identity (see Table 2). According to this model, early adolescents and perhaps adults who have not been exposed to ethnic identity issues are in the first stage, an unexamined ethnic identity. According to Cross (1978) and others (e.g., Atkinson et al., 1983; Kim, 1981), this early stage is characterized for minorities by a preference for the dominant culture. However, such a preference is not a necessary characteristic of this stage. Young people may simply not be interested in ethnicity and may have given it little thought (their ethnic identity is diffuse). Alternatively, they may have absorbed positive ethnic attitudes from parents or other adults and therefore may not show a preference for the majority group, although they have not thought through the issues for themselves—that is, are foreclosed (Phinney, 1989).

A second stage is characterized by an exploration of one's own ethnicity, which is similar to the moratorium status described by Marcia (1980). This may take place as the result of a significant experience that forces awareness of one's ethnicity ("encounter," according to Cross, 1978, or "awakening," according to Kim, 1981). It involves an often intense process of immersion in one's own culture through activities such as reading, talking to people, going to ethnic museums, and participating actively in culture events. For some people it may involve rejecting the values of the dominant culture.

The stage model suggests that as a result of this process, people come to a deeper understanding and appreciation of their ethnicity—that is, ethnic identity achievement or internalization. This culmination may require resolution or coming to terms with two fundamental problems for ethnic minorities: (a) cultural differences between their own group and the dominant group and (b) the lower or disparaged status of their group in society (Phinney, Lochner, & Murphy, 1990). The meaning of ethnic identity achievement is undoubtedly different for different individuals and groups because of their different historical and personal experiences. However, achievement does not necessarily imply a high degree of ethnic involvement; one could presumably be clear about the confident of one's ethnicity without wanting to maintain one's ethnic language or customs. A recent conceptual article suggested that the process does not necessarily end with ethnic identity achievement but may continue in cycles that involve further exploration or rethinking of the role or meaning of one's ethnicity (Parham, 1989). A similar idea has been suggested with regard to ego identity (Grotevant, 1987).

Empirical research based on these models has involved describing changes over time in a person's attitudes and understanding about his or her ethnicity. In addition, researchers have looked

TABLE 2
Marcia's Ego Identity Statuses (Top) and Proposed Stages of Ethnic Identity (Bottom)

Marcia (1966, 1980)	Identity diffusion	Identity foreclosure	Identity crisis*	Moratorium	Identity achievement
			Encounter	Immersion/ emersion	Internalization
Cross (1978)		Pre-encounter			
Kim (1981)		White identified	Awakening to social political awareness	Redirection to Asian American consciousness	Incorporation
Atkinson et al. (1983)		Conformity: Preference for values of dominant culture	Dissonance: Questioning and challenging old attitudes	Resistance and immersion: Rejection of dominant culture	Synergetic articulation and awareness
Phinney (1989)	Unexamined ethnic identity		Ethnic identity search (Moratorium): Involvement in exploring and seeking to understand meaning of ethnicity for oneself		Achieved ethnic identity
	Lack of exploration of ethnicity. Possible subtypes:				Clear, confident sense of own ethnicity
	Diffusion: Lack of interest in or concern with ethnicity	Foreclosure: Views of ethnicity based on opinions of others			

*Identity crisis is not one of Marcia's original four statuses.

at factors related to ethnic identity formation, such as parental attitudes and social class, and at correlates, including self-esteem or adjustment and attitudes toward counselors. Results of research on these questions are discussed later.

Components of Ethnic Identity

In order to examine questions that derive from theory or to address research questions of current interest, it is necessary to begin with a measure of ethnic identity. In this section, the various aspects of ethnic identity that were selected for study are reviewed. The majority of the studies focused on components related to what might be called the *state* of ethnic identity—that is, a person's identification at a given time. In studies of this type, the components most widely studied were self-identification as a group member, a sense of belonging to the group, attitudes about one's group membership, and ethnic involvement (social participation, cultural practices and attitudes). A much smaller group of studies emphasized *stages* of ethnic identity, or changes over time in a person's identification. In the following section, I examine these components and the ways in which they have been assessed.

Ethnicity and Ethnic Self-Identification

Self-identification (also called *self-definition* or *self-labeling*) refers to the ethnic label that one uses for oneself. Research with children has been concerned largely with the extent to which children "correctly" label themselves—that is, whether the label they choose corresponds to the ethnicity of their parents (Aboud, 1987). A related issue has been whether "incorrect" labeling is associated with a poor self-concept (Cross, 1978). Beyond childhood, the concerns are different. Adolescents and adults can be assumed to know their ethnicity; the issue is thus one of choosing what label to use for oneself. Although this appears to be a simple issue, it is in fact quite complex, inasmuch as one's ethnicity, as determined by descent (parental background), may differ from how one sees oneself ethnically.

In countries settled by Europeans (where much of the research under review was conducted), the use of an ethnic label, for example, Polish American, is for the most part optional for people of European descent. Many Whites under

these circumstances use no ethnic label and may in fact be unable to identify their country of origin (Singh, 1977).

However, among those who are racially distinct, by features or skin color, or whose culture (language, dress, customs, etc.) clearly distinguishes them from the dominant group, self-identification is at least partly imposed. Calling oneself Black or Asian American is less-categorization than recognition of imposed distinctions, and the issue is less *whether* to use an ethnic label than *which* ethnic label to adopt. For example, people whose parents or grandparents came from Mexico can call themselves Mexican American, Hispanic, Latino, or Chicano (among others), each of which has a different connotation (Buriel, 1987).

Regardless of whether an ethnic label is chosen or imposed, people may feel that a single label is inaccurate, inasmuch as they are part of two or more groups. Ethnic groups members may identify themselves as only partly ethnic and partly mainstream. For example, among a group of second-generation Irish adolescents in England, about half considered themselves part English and part Irish; the remainder called themselves either English or Irish (Ullah, 1985, 1987). Selection of a label is particularly problematic for those whose parents are from two or more distinct groups; they may, for example, call themselves mixed, such as half Hispanic and half White, or they may ignore part of their heritage and call themselves either White or Hispanic (Alipuria & Phinney, 1988).

Although ethnic self-identification is clearly an essential starting point in examining ethnic identity, it was not specifically assessed in about half the studies reviewed. In some cases, subjects were recruited from groups whose ethnicity was known to the researchers (e.g., Jewish student groups were recruited by Davids, 1982, and by Lax & Richards, 1981; students at Armenian schools were recruited by Der-Karabetian, 1980). In other studies, the subjects were simply defined as group members without explanation of how this was determined. None of the studies with Black subjects included self-identification. The failure to assess self-definition with any group raises the possibility that the studies included subjects who did not consider themselves members of the group in question.

When self-identification was assessed, items were presented in a variety of ways. If the participants were assumed to be from a given group or groups, it was possible to provide multiple-choice items appropriate for the particular group (e.g., Ullah, 1985, 1987) or to have subjects rate themselves or match labels of themselves in terms of similarity to individuals with particular labels (Christian et al., 1976; Giles, Llado, McKirnan, & Taylor, 1979; Giles, Taylor, & Bourhis, 1977; Giles, Taylor, Lambert, & Albert, 1976; Rosenthal & Hrynevich, 1985).

However, to use these sorts of questions, the researcher must preselect participants of known ethnicity. Determining ethnicity for research purposes is in itself a methodological problem that has often been ignored. An alternative is to use an unselected sample and determine ethnicity by asking participants about their parent's ethnicity. Ethnic self-identification can then be assessed with open-ended questions or multiple-choice items with a wide range of possible alternative labels, or both. However, the responses of some subjects will vary, depending on whether they are forced to choose from a list of labels provided or are simply given a blank to fill in.

In summary, ethnic self-identification is an important but complex aspect of ethnic identity, and the way in which it is assessed needs to be considered when the results obtained are interpreted.

Sense of Belonging

People may use an ethnic label when specifically asked for one and yet may not have a strong sense of belonging to the group chosen. Therefore, it is important to assess the feeling of belonging. However, a sense of belonging was evaluated in only about a quarter of the studies reviewed, perhaps because of the difficulty of accurately tapping this subtle feeling. Researchers have devised a number of approaches to this problem; some examples are the following: "I am a person who (never, seldom, sometimes, often, very often) feels strong bonds toward [my own group]" (Driedger, 1976); "My fate and future are bound up with that of [my own group]" (Der-Karabetian, 1980; Zak, 1973, 1976); "I feel an overwhelming attachment to [my own group]" (Krate, Leventhal, & Silverstein, 1974; Parham & Helms, 1981, 1985a, 1985b). The subject may express a sense of "peoplehood" (Lax & Richards, 1981) or present self with an ethnic label (M. Clark et al., 1976; Elizur, 1984). A variation of this attitude is the importance attributed to one's ethnicity (Davids, 1982; Zak, 1973, 1976) or a feeling of concern for one's culture (Christian et al., 1976).

A sense of belonging to one's own group can also be defined in contrast to another group—that is, the experience of exclusion, contrast, or separateness from other group members (Lax & Richards, 1981): for example, "How much difference do you feel between yourself and [members of another group]?" (Ullah, 1987) or "[How similar are you to] kids from other countries who don't fit in well?" (Rosenthal & Hrynevich, 1985).

Positive and Negative Attitudes Toward One's Ethnic Group

In addition to their self-identification and a sense of a belonging, people can have both positive and negative attitudes toward their own ethnic group. These attitudes were examined in more than half the studies reviewed. Positive attitudes include pride in and pleasure, satisfaction, and contentment with one's own group. They are assessed by items such as "[I am] proud to identify with [my own group]" and "[I] consider [my own] culture rich and precious" (Driedger, 1976) and "[I am similar to] people who feel good about their cultural background" (Rosenthal & Hrynevich, 1985) or by questions such as "How much pride do you feel toward [your own group]?" (Phinney, 1989; Ullah, 1987).

The term *acceptance* is frequently used for positive attitudes, particularly in studies involving Black subjects (Paul & Fischer, 1980). Typical items include "I believe that being Black is a positive experience" and "I believe that because I am Black I have many strengths" (Parham & Helms, 1981, 1985a, 1985b) and "I feel excitement and joy in Black surroundings" (Krate et al., 1974; Parham & Helms, 1981, 1985a, 1985b). Acceptance of being Black is often phrased in contrast to White culture: "When I think of myself as a Black person, I feel I am more attractive and smarter than any White person" (Morten & Atkinson, 1983). Acceptance of being Black has been assessed indirectly, through having subjects draw figures and determining whether they include Black characteristics. Although this method has been used commonly with children, it has also been employed in studies with adults (Bolling, 1974; Kuhlman, 1979).

Two indirect ways of measuring positive (and negative) attitudes are to have subjects rate themselves and their group in relation to adjectives with good and bad connotations (Grossman et al., 1985) or to rate a speech that had been tape-recorded in different languages and accents (Bourhis et al., 1973). The latter case included adjectives such as "arrogant," "friendly," "self-confident,", and "snobbish".

The absence of positive attitudes, or the presence of actual negative attitudes, can be seen as a denial of one's ethnic identity. They include "displeasure, dissatisfaction, discontentment' with one's ethnicity (Lax & Richards, 1981); feelings of inferiority; or a desire to hide one's cultural identity (Driedger, 1976; Ullah, 1985). An item used to tap negative feelings is "[I am like/unlike] kids from other countries who try to hide their background" (Rosenthal & Hrynevich, 1985). Negative feelings may be a normal aspect of ethnic identity for some groups; Lax and Richards (1981) stated that "Jewish identity by itself does not imply acceptance of one's Jewishness . . . . being Jewish stirs up many ambivalent feelings" (pp. 306–307). An indirect but presumably powerful way of assessing negative attitudes is to determine whether the subject would remain a group member if given the choice. Several researchers asked whether the subject, if given a chance to be born again, would wish to be born a member of their ethnic group (Der-Karabetian, 1980; Tzuriel & Klein, 1977; Zak, 1973).

In studies with Black subjects, the negative attitudes are phrased both as denial of Blackness and as preference for White culture (Morten & Atkinson, 1983; Paul & Fischer, 1980; Phinney, 1989); "Most Black people I know are failures" (Parham & Helms, 1981, 1985a, 1985b); "I believe that large numbers of Blacks are untrustworthy" (Krate et al., 1974); "Sometimes I wish I be-longed to the White race"; and "I believe that White people are intellectually superior to Blacks' (Krate et al, 1974; Parham & Helms, 1981, 1985a, 1985b).

In summary, the terms and phrasing vary with the groups under study, particularly in assessments of negative attitudes. Items for most White ethnic groups are more likely to make reference to hiding or denying one's group; for Blacks and Jews, lack of acceptance or wishing to change groups suggest negative attitudes.

Ethnic Involvement (Social Participation and Cultural Practices)

Involvement in the social life and cultural practices of one's ethnic group is the most widely used indicator of ethnic identity but also the most problematic. As long as measures are based one specific practices that distinguish an ethnic group, it is impossible to generalize across groups; this issue is explored in detail later. The indicators of ethnic involvement that are most commonly assessed are language, friendship, social organizations, religion, cultural traditions, and politics.

Language. Language is the most widely assessed cultural practice associated with ethnic identity, but it was included in less than half of the studies. Language was most intensively assessed in studies of White subjects. Most of these studies dealt with subjects who had emigrated from Continental Europe to an English-speaking country (the United States, Canada, England, or Australia) and had the option of retaining their language; some were living in their country of origin (Wales) where English is dominant. Language was also assessed in a study involving American Jews in Israel, and of the nine studies of Hispanics in the United States, seven included assessment of the use of Spanish. In addition, several researchers examined the desire of adults to have their children learn their ethnic language (Caltabiano, 1984; Leclezio, Louw-Potgieter, & Souchon, 1986; Teske & Nelson, 1973).

Although language has been considered by some as the single most important component of ethnic identity, its importance clearly varies with the particular situation, and it is inappropriate for some groups. None of the studies of Black identity have included language, even though familiarity with Black English is considered an important marker of Black identity (Kochman, 1987).

Friendship. In roughly a fourth of the studies, the researchers assessed friendship, using items such as ratings of "importance of ingroup friends" and "ingroup dating" (Driedger, 1975), "ethnic background of friends" (Garcia, 1982), or other measures of ethnic friendships. Friendship was included as an aspect of ethnic identity in studies with most groups; however, only a few studies with Black subjects include this component.

Religious affiliation and practice. This component was assessed in less than a fourth of the studies; the researchers used items related to church membership, attending religious ceremonies, parochial education, and religious preference. The subjects of those studies came largely from White ethnic groups, from some Hispanic groups, and from one Jewish group; no studies of Blacks included religion as an aspect of ethnic identity.

Structured ethnic social groups. Participation in ethnic clubs, societies, or organizations was included as a component of ethnic identity in studies involving primarily White subjects; Asians and Hispanics were also represented, but no Black groups were.

Political ideology and activity. Involvement in political activities on behalf of one's ethnic group was included in a few studies; a disproportionately large number of those studies focused on Blacks. Typical items were "I frequently confront the system and the man" (Krate et al., 1974; Parham & Helms, 1981, 1985a, 1985b). "A commitment to the development of Black power dominates my behavior" (Krate et al., 1974); and "I constantly involve myself in Black political and social activities" (Parham & Helms, 1981, 1985a, 1985b). One measure of Black identity focused primarily on political ideology (Terrell & Taylor, 1978).

A study of Mexican-Americans included the question "Are you active in any political organization which is specifically Mexican-American oriented?" (Teske & Nelson, 1973). Some studies with White ethnics mentioned involvement with the politics of one's country of origin as an indicator of ethnic identity (Constantinou & Harvey, 1985).

Area of residence. In a few studies, the subject's area of residence was included. In some cases, the geographical region was assessed (Giles et al., 1977, 1976; Taylor, Bassili, & Aboud, 1973). In others, items tapped the number of proportion of in-group members in one's neighborhood (Der-Karabetian, 1980)—for example, "[Subject] chooses to live in an area where others [ingroup members] have settled' (Caltabiano, 1984)—or

were worded to assess "[subject's] readiness to live in an integrated neighborhood" (Tzuriel & Klein, 1977). This component has not been included in studies of Blacks.

Miscellaneous ethnic/cultural activities and attitudes. In addition to those elements already mentioned, a wide variety of specific cultural activities and attitudes were assessed. Half the studies, distributed across all the groups studied, included one or more of the following miscellaneous cultural items: ethnic music, songs, dances, and dress; newspapers, periodicals, books, and literature; food or cooking; entertainment (movies, radio, TV, plays, sports, etc.); traditional celebrations; traditional family roles, values, and names; visits to and continued interest in the homeland; the practice of endogamy or opposition to mixed marriages; and knowledge about ethnic culture or history. These items were most often assessed by direct questions. However, in one study (of Chinese Americans), subjects were asked to rate themselves on attitudes or values that were presumed to be characteristic of a group: for example, agreement with the statement that "A good child is an obedient child" (Ting-Toomey, 1981).

Reliability of Measures

Specific measures of ethnic identity as a state have included various combinations of the aforementioned elements; differing numbers of items have been used to assess each one. The reliability of measures is often not reported or is low enough to raise questions about conclusions based on the measure. Of the studies analyzed, less than a fifth furnished reliability information on the measures used. The reliability coefficients cited (usually Cronbach's alpha) ranged widely (from .35 to .90), and many were quite low. Rarely was the same measure used in more than one study in order to establish reliability with different samples, and in no studies was there evidence for test-retest reliability with the same subjects. A reliable measure of ethnic identity is clearly essential to the further study of this topic.

Ethnic Identity Development

Measuring stages of ethnic identity development presents quite different problems. In only a small number of the studies reviewed did researchers attempt to deal with individual changes in ethnic identity over time; they used one of two basic approaches.

One group of studies was based on the model of Black identity formation described by Cross (1978). The researchers used variations of the Racial Identity Attitude Scale (RIAS), developed by Parham and Helms (1981) on the basis of Cross's earlier work. This scale is essentially an attitude scale, aimed at tapping negative, positive, or mixed attitudes of Blacks toward their own group and toward the White majority, attitudes that are assumed to change as the person moves through the stages. Items tap each of the four proposed stages—pre-encounter, encounter, immersion, and internalization—with reliabilities of .67, .72, .66, and .71, respectively (Parham & Helms, 1981). Issues related to the reliability of the scale were addressed in two articles (Helms, 1989; Ponterotto & Wise, 1987). Ponterotto and Wise found support for the existence of all the stages except the second, the encounter stage. However, Akbar (1989) questioned whether ethnic or racial identity, as a core personality trait, could be assessed by an attitudinal measure such as the RIAS.

A second group of studies were aimed at developing measures of stages of ethnic identity that can be applied across ethnic groups. This approach, which was based on the ego identity measures of Marcia (1966) and Adams, Bennion, and Huh (1987), focused on the two components of the process of identity formation: (a) a search for the meaning of one's ethnicity and (b) a commitment or a decision about its place in one's life. A questionnaire used with college students from four groups (Asian American, Black, Mexican, American, and White) yielded reliabilities of .69 for ethnic identity search and .59 for ethnic identity commitment (Phinney & Alipuria, 1990). In a subsequent study, interviews were used to assess ethnic identity among high school students from three minority groups (Asian American, Black, and Mexican American); raters then judged each subject as being in one of the three stages of ethnic identity (Phinney, 1989). Absolute agreement between raters on stage assignment was .80 (Cohen's kappa = .65).

The variety of components of ethnic identity in the research reviewed makes it diffi-cult to summarize or draw conclusions about exactly what ethnic identity consists of. Most researchers have acknowledged its complex, multidimensional nature and have tried to understand this complexity in some way, as is examined in the next section.

Interrelationship, Salience, and Generality of Components

Researchers have approached the complexity of ethnic identity by attempting to identity its essential components, their interrelationships, and their relative salience. One common approach has been factor analysis. However, because of the variety of types and the numbers of items used, factor analysis has yielded widely discrepant results in different studies. Researchers have found a single factor for ethnic identity (Garcia & Lega, 1979); two factors, differing widely among the studies (Constantinou & Harvey, 1985; Driedger, 1976; Leclezio et al., 1986); three factors (Hogg et al., 1987); or four or more factors, again different in each study (Caltabiano, 1984; Driedger, 1975; Garcia, 1982; Makabe, 1979; Rosenthal & Hrynevich, 1985). When several groups were studied, the factors varied, depending on the group (Driedger, 1975; Rosenthal & Hrynevich, 1985).

Interrelationships of Components

A specific questions that has concerned researchers is the relationship between what people say they are (ethnic self-identification) and what they actually do (ethnic involvement) or how they feel (ethnic pride). In a study of Irish adolescents in England, Ullah (1987) found a close relationship between ethnic self-definition and indices of ethnic group behavior, as did Der-Karabetian (1980) in a study with Armenian Americans. In contrast, a study of East Indian adolescents in England (Hutnik, 1986) revealed little relation between ethnic identification and behavior. In a comprehensive study in which a variety of components of ethnicity for Chicanos were measured separately, Garcia (1982) found a complex set of relationships, including a negative relationship between ethnic self-identification and preference for various ethnic practices. Pride in their Irish background, among second-generation Irish adolescents in England, was related to self-identification as Irish; those who called themselves English were more likely to hide the fact of their Irish background (Ullah, 1985).

Salience of Components

Assumptions regarding salience were implicit in the components of ethnic identity selected for study with particular groups, and these components differed widely among groups. For White ethnic groups, language and a variety of miscellaneous cultural activities were most widely used as indicators of ethnic identity, and attitudes were considered somewhat less important. In the assessment of Jewish identity, ethnic affirmation and denial were included far more than with other White groups, whereas language was less frequently included. In studies with Hispanics, language was treated as a dominant component. A distinctive pattern emerges from the studies of American Blacks: Attitudes were the most widely used element, and the measures generally included both pro-Black and anti-White attitudes. Also, political activity was more evident as a criterion for Black identity than for the other groups, but assessment of language, friends, social groups, and neighborhood were almost completely absent.

A number of studies have suggested that language is one of the most important elements of ethnic identity (Giles et al., 1976, 1977; Leclezio et al., 1986; Taylor et al., 1973). However, a study carried out in a different setting showed that language was not salient (Giles et al., 1979). Language was seldom included in studies involving particular groups, such as Black.

Furthermore, salience can be manipulated. When salience of ethnicity was increased through an experimental manipulation, Welsh subjects expressed closer affiliation with their group (Christian et al., 1976).

General Versus Specific Aspects of Ethnic Identity

The widely differing results from attempts to define the components and structure of ethnic identity raise a fundamental conceptual question: Is it possible to study ethnic identity in general terms, or, because each group and setting is unique, must each be studied separately? It is interesting that in the theories and definitions presented by researchers, ethnic identity was treated as a general phenomenon that is relevant across groups. Yet researchers have attempted to answer theoretical and definitional questions almost exclusively in terms of one group or, sometimes, a few specific groups.

A starting point in resolving this dilemma is to recognize that there are elements that are both common across groups and unique to ethnic identity for any group. On the basis of the research reviewed, it appears that self-identification, a sense of belonging, and pride in one's group may be key aspects of ethnic identity that are present in varying degrees, regardless of the group. Furthermore, the developmental model postulates that all ethnic group members have the option to explore and resolve issues related to their ethnicity, although they may vary in the extent to which they engage in this process, at both the individual and the group levels. A focus on these common elements would allow for comparisons across groups and permit one to determine whether general conclusions can in fact be drawn. A measure aimed at assessing common aspects of ethnic identity requires both selection of common components and wording of items in general rather than specific terms. Such a measure has recently been proposed as a start toward studying ethnic identity as a general phenomenon (Phinney, 1990).

On the other hand, the specific cultural practices, customs, and attitudes that distinguish one group from another are essential for understanding individual groups and the experience of members of those groups in particular settings and time frames (e.g., Keefe & Padilla, 1987). The study of ethnic identity at this more specific level may be of particular value for education, counseling, and therapeutic applications.

Empirical Findings

Because of the different conceptualizations, definitions, and measures that have been used in the study of ethnic identity, empirical findings are difficult or impossible to compare across studies. Not surprisingly, the findings are often inconsistent.

Self-Esteem, Self-Concept, and Psychological Adjustment

A key issue in conceptual writing about ethnic identity has been the role of group identity in the self-concept: Specifically, does a strong identification with one's ethnic group promote a positive self-concept or self-esteem? Or, conversely, is identification with an ethnic group that is held in low regard by the dominant group likely to lower one's self-esteem? Furthermore, is it possible to hold negative views about one's own group and yet feel good about oneself?

Early interest in these questions stemmed from the work of K. Clark and Clark (1947), which showed that young Black children tended to prefer White dolls to Black dolls. The meaning of such findings continues to be debated, and a number of reviewers have discussed the findings (Aboud, 1987; Banks, 1976; Brand et al., 1974; V. Gordon, 1980). However, this controversy has been dealt with almost entirely in studies with children, and there has been little extension of the work into adolescence and adulthood, the topic of the current review. Given the theoretical importance of this issue, it is surprising that in only 11 of the studies reviewed, the researchers assessed self-esteem or a related construct and examined its relationship to some measure of ethnic identity. The researchers who did address this question presented conflicting results.

Three of the studies suggested positive effects of ethnic identity, although the measures used were different in each case. Among Black early adolescents (ages 13–14) of low socioeconomic status (SES), "acceptance of racial identity," as measured by six items (no reliability given), was found to be significantly related to self-concept as measured by the Tennessee Self Concept Scale (Paul & Fischer, 1980). A study with Anglo-American and Mexican-American junior high school students revealed a positive relationship between self-esteem, assessed by Rosenberg's (1979) Self-Esteem Scale, and ethnic esteem, as measured by adjective ratings of one's own group (Grossman et al., 1985). Among Israeli high school students, ego identity, which is suggestive of good adjustment, was higher among those with high ethnic group identification than among those with low identification (on a scale with reliability of alpha equal to .60), especially among the Oriental Jews, a minority group in Israel (Tzuriel & Klein, 1977).

Four studies revealed no relationship between ethnic identity and various measures of adjustment. A study of Black and White college students revealed no relationship between self-esteem (Rosenberg scale) and ethnic identity, measured in terms of similarity-to-group scores on semantic differential ratings of Blacks and Whites—that is, similarity to a stereotype of one's own group (White & Burke, 1987). Also, for Black college students, "Black consciousness," measured by attitudes toward Blacks and Whites, was unrelated to two measures of self-esteem (Houston, 1984). Among Arab-Israeli college students, self-esteem (Rosenberg scale) was not related to measures of Arab identity (scale reliability = .81) or Israeli identity (scale reliability = .83; Zak, 1976). Finally, a study of Italian Australians revealed "Italian identity" (scale reliability = .89) to be unrelated to psychosocial adjustment, according to the Offer Self-Image Questionnaire and the Erikson Psychosocial Stage Inventory (Rosenthal & Cichello, 1986). In summary, these studies of ethnic identity, in which a variety of measures of ethnic identity as a state were used, permit no definitive conclusion about its role in self-esteem.

In contrast to the preceding studies, researchers in four studies examined self-esteem in relation to the stage model of ethnic identity. By analogy with the ego-identity literature, in which positive psychological outcomes have been associated with an achieved identity (Marcia, 1980), the developmental model predicts higher self-esteem in subjects with an achieved ethnic identity. This prediction was supported in a study with 10th-grade Black, Asian-American, and Mexican-American adolescents, in which subjects at higher stages of ethnic identity, as assessed by interviews, were found to have significantly higher scores on all four subscales of a measure of psychological adjustment (self-evaluation, sense of mastery, family relations, and social relations), as well as on an independent measure of ego development (Phinney, 1989). A similar relationship between ethnic identity search and commitment (scale reliabilities = .69 and .59, respectively) and self-esteem was found among college students from four ethnic groups (Asian American, Black, Mexican American, and White); the relationship was stronger among minority group students than among their White peers (Phinney & Alipuria, 1990). A study with Black college students, which was based on Cross's

(1978) process model, revealed that low self-esteem was related to the earliest (pre-encounter) stage and to the immersion (moratorium) stage, whereas high self-esteem was associated with the encounter stage, which involves events that precipitate a search or immersion (Parham & Helms, 1985a). In a related study, the pre-encounter and immersion stages were found to be related to feelings of inferiority and anxiety (Parham & Helms, 1985b). These studies suggest that a positive self-concept may be related to the process of identity formation—that is, to the extent to which people have come to an understanding and acceptance of their ethnicity.

Ethnic Identity in Relation to the Majority Culture

The acculturation framework for studying ethnic identity suggests that for understanding ethnic identity, it is necessary to consider also the individual's relationship to the dominant or majority group. Whereas a number of the studies reviewed focused on a single ethnic group, without reference to the dominant group (i.e., Asbury, Adderly-Kelly, & Knuckle, 1987; Constantinou & Harvey, 1985; Garcia & Lega, 1979; Keefe, 1986; Masuda, Hasegawa, & Matsumoto, 1973), many researchers took into consideration the relationship to the dominant group.

A central question, as discussed earlier, is whether ethnic identity is directly related to degree of acculturation or whether, conversely, it is independent, so that, for example, one could have a strong ethnic identification and also have strong ties to the dominant culture (see Table 1). Several studies suggest that the two are independent. In a study with adolescent girls of East Indian extraction who were living in England, Hutnik (1986) assessed separately self-identification (as Indian or British) and Indian and British cultural behaviors; the results showed the two dimensions to be unrelated. A similar picture emerged from a study of seven White ethnic groups in Canada (Driedger, 1976). Group scores demonstrated varying degrees of ethnic affirmation and denial for each group, which resulted in three types of ethnic identity, depending on degree of ethnic identification or denial: majority assimilator, ethnic identifiers, and ethnic marginals. Similarly, studies of Armenian Americans (Der-Karabetian, 1980), Jewish Americans (Zak, 1973), and Chinese Americans (Ting-Toomey, 1981) revealed ethnic identity and American identity to be independent dimensions.

However, other studies gave different results. A comparison of bipolar and orthogonal models of ethnic identity among Israelis living in the United States suggested that attitudes and behaviors relative to being Israeli, Jewish, or American were not independent (Elias & Blanton, 1987). Affective measures of the three aspects of identity were positively intercorrelated, whereas behavioral measures were negatively related; subjects who engaged in many typical American behaviors showed fewer Israeli behaviors. In another study of Israelis residing in the United States (Elizur, 1984), Jewish and American identity tended to be negatively related.

More complex results emerged from two studies in which qualitative data were used. An extensive study of Mexican-American and Asian-American adults (M. Clark et al., 1976) revealed six profiles representing different combinations of attitudes, behaviors, and knowledge relative to one's own culture and American culture. A qualitative study of Mexican-American high school students (Matute-Bianchi, 1986) demonstrated five types of ethnic identity, depending on the students' degree of involvement in their own ethnic culture and in the main-stream culture of the high school. Moreover, the types of identity were related to school achievement. Those students who were more embedded in the barrio culture were the least successful academically.

The value of studies such as these, in which mainstream as well as ethnic orientation is assessed, has been in emphasizing that ethnic identity is not necessarily a linear construct; it can be conceptualized in terms of qualitatively different ways of relating to one's own and other groups. A problem in using this more complex conceptualization is in assessing the attributes of the contrast group. The characteristics of mainstream culture are far more difficult to define than those of a particular subculture. The issue of measurement of mainstream attitudes belongs properly to the topic of acculturation; these measurement issues were thoroughly discussed by Berry et al. (1986).

The two-dimensional model provides some clarification of the importance of ethnic identity to the self-concept. Some of the contradictions and inconsistencies noted in this review may be a function of differences in the degree to which researchers have considered identification with both the ethnic group and the mainstream culture. For example, although ethnic identity, in the sense of identification with one's ethnic group, can range from strong to weak, an understanding of how ethnic identity is related to self-concept may require also determining an individual's relationship to the majority group. There is some evidence that the acculturated or integrated option may be the most satisfactory and the marginal, the least (Berry et al., 1987). However, the other two possibilities, assimilation and separation, may also provide the basis for a good self-concept, if the person is comfortable with these alternatives and is in an environment that supports them (Phinney et al., 1990).

Changes in Ethnic Identity Related to Generation of Immigration

A second focus of research within the acculturation frame-work is the way in which ethnic identity changes with contact with another group. Writers generally have agreed that ethnic identity is a dynamic concept, but relatively few have studied it over time. However, a number of researchers have examined changes related to generational status among immigrant groups.

Studies of generational differences in ethnic identity have shown a fairly consistent decline in ethnic group identification in later generations descended from immigrants (Constantinou & Harvey, 1985; Fathi, 1972). Ethnic identity was found to be similarly weaker among those who arrived at a younger age and had lived longer in the new country (Garcia & Lega, 1979; Rogler et al., 1980) and among those with more education (Rogler et al., 1980). However, a study of third- and fourth-generation Japanese-American youth revealed virtually no generational difference (Wooden, Leon, & Toshima, 1988), and a study of Chinese Americans suggests a cyclical process whereby ethnic identity became more important in third- and fourth-generation descendents of immigrants (Ting-Toomey, 1981). A recent study (Rosenthal & Feldman, in press) found that among adolescent Chinese immigrants, ethnic knowledge and behavior decreased between the first and second generations, but that there was no change in the importance or positive valuation of ethnicity. The authors suggest that although some behavioral and cognitive elements of ethnic identity decline,

immigrants retain a commitment to their culture. Furthermore, specific programs can foster ethnic identity (Zisenwine & Walters, 1982).

A study of three age groups in Japan (Masuda et al., 1973) illustrates the possible confounding of generation with age and cultural change. Older Japanese scored higher than did younger people in a measure of Japanese identification, in results similar to the generational differences among Japanese immigrants. Comparisons between younger (second-generation) and older (first-generation) subjects may thus tap age as well as cohort differences. In a retrospective interview study with elderly Croatians, Simic (1987) noted an intensification of ethnic sentiments during later life.

Ethnic Identity and Gender

Gender may be a variable in acculturation in those cultures in which men are more likely to get jobs in the mainstream culture while the women remain at home. There may also be different cultural expectations for men and women, such as the assumption that women are the carriers of ethnic traditions. The very little research that addresses this issue suggests a greater involvement in ethnicity by women than by men. Research with Chinese-American college students revealed women to be more oriented to their ancestral culture than were men (Ting-Toomey, 1981), and a drawing study showed higher Black identification in women (Bolling, 1974). Among Irish adolescents in England, girls were significantly more likely than boys to adopt an Irish identity (Ullah, 1985). Japanese girls and women tended to score higher than boys and men on Japanese ethnic identity (Masuda et al., 1973).

In contrast, Jewish boys in Canada were found to show greater preference for Jewish norms than did girls (Fathi, 1972), a fact that the author suggested may be related to the Jewish emphasis on male dominance. Among East Indian and Anglo-Saxon adolescents in England, girls were more inclined than boys to mix with their own groups, but they were also more willing to invite home someone from a different group (Hogg et al., 1987). Gender was found to interact with ethnic identity on attitudes toward counseling (Ponterotto, Anderson, & Grieger, 1986) and on a measure of visual retention (Knuckle & Asbury, 1986).

In the sparse literature on identity formation, Parham and Helms (1985b) found that Black men were more likely than Black women to endorse attitudes from the earliest stages and less likely to show evidence of the highest stage. A similar trend among Black adolescents was noted by Phinney (1989). These fragmentary results clearly allow no conclusions about sex differences in ethnic identity.

Contextual Factors in Ethnic Identity

Ethnic identity is to a large extent defined by context; it is not an issue except in terms of a contrast group, usually the majority culture. The particular context seems to be an essential factor to consider, yet relatively few researchers have examined it in any detail. There is some evidence that ethnic identity varies according to the context (e.g., Vermeulen & Pels, 1984) and the characteristics of the group (Rosenthal & Hrynevich, 1985). Adolescents report that their feelings of being ethnic vary according to the situation they are in and the people they are with (Rosenthal & Hrynevich, 1985). Ethnic identity is positively related to the ethnic density of the neighborhood (Garcia & Lega, 1979) and negatively to the occupational and residential mobility of subjects (Makabe, 1979); it varies among communities within the same state (Teske & Nelson, 1973).

Some writers have suggested that ethnic identity is less likely to be maintained among middle-SES than among lower-SES ethnic group members. Among second-generation Irish adolescents in England, those from lower socioeconomic backgrounds were significantly more likely to identify themselves as Irish than were middle-SES youth, perhaps because they lived in areas with a higher concentration of Irish immigrants. However, research based on the developmental model has revealed no relationship between stages of ethnic identity and social class among high school students (Phinney, 1989) or college students (Phinney & Alipuria, 1990), and racial identity attitudes were not predictive of socioeconomic status among Black college students (Carter & Helms, 1988).

The impact of the context on Black identity has been investigated through studies of transracial adoption. Racial identity was more of a problem for Black children and adolescents adopted into White homes than for those adopted by Black parents, although the self-esteem of the two groups did not differ (McRoy, Zurcher, Lauderdale, & Anderson, 1982). Transracially adopted Hispanic adolescents were similarly likely to identify themselves as Americans, whereas those adopted by Mexican-American couples overwhelmingly called themselves Mexican American (Andujo, 1988). Furthermore, the parental attitudes and perceptions had an important impact on the racial identity of transracial adoptees (McRoy, Zurcher, & Lauderdale, 1984).

There has been little research on such presumably important factors as the relative size of the ethnic group (at the local or the national level) or its status in the community.

Ethnic Identity Formation

The developmental model assumes that with increasing age, subjects are more likely to have an achieved ethnic identity. Although there is little empirical support for this assumption, some results suggest that there is a developmental progression. In an interview study with Black and White 8th graders, about a third of the subjects showed evidence of ethnic identity search (Phinney & Tarver, 1988); among 10th graders in a related study, the comparable figure was about half (Phinney, 1989). Thus it appeared that the older students had done more searching. In a study based on Cross's (1978) model, Black college students reported their perceptions of themselves over the past, present, and future as shifting from lower to higher levels of Black identity (Krate et al., 1974). Both longitudinal and cross-sectional studies are needed to examine changes toward higher levels of ethnic identity formation.

Although the process model of ethnic identity has not been validated, it provides an alternative way of thinking about ethnic identity. Both attitudes and behaviors with respect to one's own and other groups are conceptualized as changing as one develops and resolves issues and feelings about one's own and other groups. Differing ethnic attitudes and behaviors may therefore reflect different stages of development, rather than permanent characteristics of the group or the individuals studied. Some discrepancies in the findings regarding relationships among components of ethnic identity, reported earlier in this review, may result from studying subjects at different stages of development.

Another topic of interest in this area has been the impact of ethnic identity stages on attitudes regarding the ethnicity of counselors. Black college students in the early stages preferred White counselors (Parham & Helms, 1981), whereas those in the intermediate stages showed a preference for Black counselors (Morten & Atkinson, 1983; Parham & Helms, 1981). Results for subjects at the highest stage are mixed; they may show Black preference (Parham & Helms, 1981) or no preference (Morton & Atkinson, 1983). Stages of ethnic identity development in Blacks are also related to perceptions of White counselors (Pomales, Claiborn, & LaFromboise, 1986).

In examining the relationship of stages of Black identity to Black value orientations, Carter and Helms (1987) found that certain values could be predicted from the stages; for example, the highest stage, internalization, was associated with a belief in harmony with nature.

The study of stages of ethnic identity is at present rudimentary; however, a developmental perspective may be able eventually to provide a more complete understanding of this phenomenon across age.

Recommendations for Future Research

The most serious need in ethnic identity research is to devise reliable and valid measures of ethnic identity. To accomplish this, it is important to distinguish between general aspects of ethnic identity that apply across groups and specific aspects that distinguish groups. General measures would be valuable in addressing the important questions about ethnic identity that are raised by theory.

A key question is the implication of ethnic identity for psychological adjustment. The relationship is complex, and a clarification requires consideration not only of the strength of ethnic identity but also of the relationship to the majority culture, as outlined in Table 1, and of the stages of ethnic identity development suggested in Table 2. A specific question to be answered is whether self-esteem can be equally high in people who are acculturated, ethnically embedded (or dissociated), or even assimilated. The extent to which these alternatives are equally healthy forms of ethnic identity may depend on whether a person has an achieved ethnic identity—that is, has explored the issues and made a conscious decision.

Another critical issue is the impact of ethnic identity on attitudes toward both the dominant group and other minority groups. Is it the case that feeling good about one's own group is associated with positive attitudes toward other groups? The answer to this question could have important policy implications, as is seen in the case of Canada (Berry et al., 1977).

The role of the context—family, community, and social structure—needs further study. In particular, past researchers have generally neglected socioeconomic status as a variable and, like most psychological researchers, has mostly used middle-SES samples. Because some ethnic minority groups are substantially underrepresented in the middle class, findings based on college students or other middle-class samples may lack generality. Even data from high school surveys may be distorted because lower-class students are more likely not to obtain parental permission to participate, to be absent from school, or to have reading problems (Phinney & Tarver, 1988). The confounding of socioeconomic status and ethnicity as a personal identity issue was eloquently stated by Steele (1988).

The vast majority of the research on ethnic identity is descriptive or correlational; only a very few investigators have used experimental manipulations (e.g., Rosenthal, Whittle, & Bell, 1988). As long as purely descriptive approaches are used, ethnic identity may be confounded with other personality characteristics, and it will be impossible to identify the effect of ethnic identity on behavior and attitudes.

A significant problem that has been virtually ignored in research is that of people from mixed backgrounds. There has been little documentation of this growing phenomenon, and it has been difficult to study, as many subjects identify themselves as members of one group even though they in fact have a mixed background (Alba & Chamlin, 1983; Salgado de Snyder et al., 1982; Singh, 1977). Anecdotal evidence indicates that in some cases women who have married Hispanics are considered to be Hispanic because of their surnames, as are children whose father is Hispanic, regardless of their mother's ethnicity. In general, persons with one minority-group parent are considered to belong to that group. The responses of all such persons to items assessing aspects of ethnic identity may well distort the findings. Collecting data on the ethnicity of both parents and distinguishing subjects who are from mixed backgrounds is an essential step in dealing with this problem.

Summary

In a world where the populations of most countries are increasingly diverse, both ethnically and racially, it is essential to understand the psychological impact of such diversity (Albert, 1988). Although attitudes of the majority toward minority ethnic groups have received most attention, it is equally important to understand how ethnic group members deal with being part of a group that may be disparaged or discriminated against, that must struggle to maintain its own customs and traditions, and that is not well represented in the media, among other problems. The task of understanding ethnic identity is complicated by the fact that the uniqueness that distinguishes each group and setting makes it difficult to draw general conclusions across groups.

There are important research questions to be addressed, such as the role of ethnic identity in self-esteem, its relationship to acculturation, and its place in the development of personal identity. Currently, researchers can offer few answers to these questions because of widely differing approaches to the study of ethnic identity, including lack of agreement on what constitutes its essential components, varying theoretical orientations that have guided the research, and measures that are unique to each group. It is hoped that this article brings some conceptual clarity to this important area and stimulates further research on ethnic identity.

References

Aboud, F. (1987). The development of ethnic self-identification and attitudes. In J. Phinney & M. Rotheram (Eds.), *Children's ethnic socialization: Pluralism and development* (pp. 32–55). Newbury Park, CA: Sage.

Adams, G., Bennion, L., & Huh, K. (1987). *Objective measure of ego identity status: A reference manual*. Logan: Utah State University Laboratory for Research on Adolescence.

Akbar, N. (1989). Nigrescence and identity: Some limitations. *The Counseling Psychologist, 17,* 258–263.

Alba, R. (1985). *Ethnicity and race in the U.S.A.* London: Routledge & Kegan Paul.

Alba, R., & Chamlin, M. B. (1983). A preliminary examination of ethnic identification among Whites. *American Sociological Review, 48,* 240–242.

Albert, R. (1988). The place of culture in modern psychology. In P. Bronstein & K. Quina (Eds.), *Teaching a psychology of people: Resources for gender and sociocultural awareness* (pp. 12–18). Washington, DC: American Psychological Association.

Alipuria, L., & Phinney, J. (1988, April). *Ethnic identity in mixed-ethnic college students in two settings.* Paper presented at the meeting of the Western Psychological Association, Burlingame, CA.

Andujo, E. (1988). Ethnic identity of transethnically adopted Hispanic adolescents. *Social Work, 33,* 531–535.

Arce, C. (1981). A reconsideration of Chicano culture and identity. *Daedalus, 110*(2), 177–192.

Asbury, C., Adderly-Kelly, B., & Knuckle, E. (1987). Relationship among WISC-R performance categories and measured ethnic identity in Black adolescents. *Journal of Negro Education, 56,* 172–183.

Atkinson, D., Morten, G., & Sue, D. (1983). *Counseling American minorities*. Dubuque, IA: Wm. C. Brown.

Banks, W. (1976). White preference in Blacks: A paradigm in search of a phenomenon. *Psychological Bulletin, 83,* 1179–1186.

Berry, J., Kalin, R., & Taylor, D. (1977). *Multiculturalism and ethnic attitudes in Canada*. Ottawa, Canada: Minister of Supply and Services.

Berry, J., Kim, U., Minde, T., & Mok, D. (1987). Comparative studies of acculturative stress. *International Migration Review, 21,* 491–511.

Berry, J., Trimble, J., & Olmedo, E. (1986). Assessment of acculturation. In W. Lonner & J. Berry (Eds.), *Field methods in cross-cultural research* (pp. 291–324). Newbury Park, CA: Sage.

Bolling, J. (1974). The changing self-concept of Black children. *Journal of the National Medical Association, 66,* 28–31, 34.

Bourhis, R., Giles, H., & Tajfel, H. (1973). Language as a determinant of Welsh identity. *European Journal of Social Psychology, 3,* 447–460.

Brand, E., Ruiz, R., & Padilla, A. (1974). Ethnic identification and preference: A review. *Psychological Bulletin, 86,* 860–890.

Buriel, R. (1987). Ethnic labeling and identity among Mexican Americans. In J. Phinney & M. Rotheram (Eds.), *Children's ethnic socialization: Pluralism and development* (pp. 134–152). Newbury Park, CA: Sage.

Caltabiano, N. (1984). Perceived differences in ethnic behavior: A pilot study of Italo-Australian Canberra residents. *Psychological Reports, 55,* 867–873.

Carter, R., & Helms, J. (1987). The relationship of Black value-orientations to racial identity attitudes.

Measurement and Evaluation in Counseling and Development, 19, 185–195.

Carter, R., & Helms, J. (1988). The relationship between racial identity attitudes and social class. *Journal of Negro Education, 57,* 22–30.

Christian, J., Gadfield, N., Giles, H., & Taylor, D. (1976). The multidimensional and dynamic nature of ethnic identity. *International Journal of Psychology, 11,* 281–291.

Clark, K., & Clark, M. (1947). Racial identification and preference in Negro children. In T. Newcomb & E. Hartley (Eds.), *Readings in social psychology* (pp. 551–560). New York: Holt.

Clark, M., Kaufman, S., & Pierce, R. (1976). Explorations of acculturation: Toward a model of ethnic identity. *Human Organization, 35,* 231–238.

Constantinou, S., & Harvey, M. (1985). Dimensional structure and intergenerational differences in ethnicity: The Greek Americans. *Sociology and Social Research, 69,* 234–254.

Cross, W. (1978). The Thomas and Cross models of psychological nigrescence: A literature review. *Journal of Black Psychology, 4,* 13–31.

Dasheksky, A. (Ed.) (1976). *Ethnic identity in society.* Chicago: Rand McNally.

Davids, L. (1982). Ethnic identity, religiosity, and youthful deviance: The Toronto computer dating project. *Adolescence, 17,* 673–684.

Der-Karabetian, A. (1980). Relation of two cultural identities of Armenian-Americans. *Psychological Reports, 47,* 123–128.

DeVos, G., & Romanucci-Ross, L. (1982). *Ethnic identity: Cultural continuities and change.* Chicago: University of Chicago Press.

Driedger, L. (1975). In search of cultural identity factors: A comparison of ethnic students. *Canadian Review of Sociology and Anthropology, 12,* 150–161.

Driedger, L. (1976). Ethnic self-identity: A comparison of ingroup evaluations. *Sociometry, 39,* 131–141.

Du Bois, W. E. B. (1983). *Autobiography of W. E. B. Du Bois.* New York: International Publishing.

Ekstrand, L. (1986). *Ethnic minorities and immigrants in a cross-cultural perspective.* Lisse, Netherlands: Swets & Zeitlinger.

Elias, N., & Blanton, J. (1987). Dimensions of ethnic identity in Israeli Jewish families living in the United States. *Psychological Reports, 60,* 367–375.

Elizur, D. (1984). Facet analysis of ethnic identity: The case of Israelis residing in the United States. *Journal of General Psychology, 111,* 259–269.

Erikson, E. (1968). *Identity: Youth and crisis.* New York: Norton.

Fathi, A. (1972). Some aspects of changing ethnic identity of Canadian Jewish youth. *Jewish Social Studies, 34,* 23–30.

Frideres, J., & Goldenberg, S. (1982). Myth and reality in Western Canada. *International Journal of Intercultural Relations, 6,* 137–151.

Furnham, A., & Kirris, R. (1983). Self-image disparity, ethnic identity and sex-role stereotypes in British and Cypriot adolescents. *Journal of Adolescence, 6,* 275–292.

Garcia, J. (1982). Ethnicity and Chicanos: Measurement of ethnic identification, identity, and consciousness. *Hispanic Journal of Behavioral Sciences, 4,* 295–314.

Garcia, M., & Lega, L. (1979). Development of a Cuban ethnic identity questionnaire. *Hispanic Journal of Behavioral Sciences, 1,* 247–261.

Giles, H., Llado, N., McKirnan, D., & Taylor, D. (1979). Social identity in Puerto Rico. *International Journal of Psychology, 14,* 185–201.

Giles, H., Taylor, D., & Bourhis, R. (1977). Dimensions of Welsh identity. *European Journal of Social Psychology, 7,* 165–174.

Giles, H., Taylor, D., Lambert, W. E., & Albert, G. (1976). Dimensions of ethnic identity: An example from northern Maine. *Journal of Social Psychology, 100,* 11–19.

Glazer, N., & Moynihan, D. (1970). *Beyond the melting pot.* Cambridge, MA: Harvard University Press.

Gordon, M. (1964). *Assimilation in American life.* London: Oxford University Press.

Gordon, V. (1980). *The self-concept of Black Americans.* Lanham, MD: University Press America.

Grossman, B., Wirt, R., & Davids, A. (1985). Self-esteem, ethnic identity, and behavioral adjustment among Anglo and Chicano adolescents in West Texas. *Journal of Adolescence, 8,* 57–68.

Grotevant, H. (1987). Toward a process model of identity formation. *Journal of Adolescent Research, 2,* 203–222.

Gurin, P., & Epps, E. (1975). *Black consciousness, identity, and achievement.* New York: Wiley.

Helms, J. (1985). Toward a theoretical explanation of the effects of race on counseling: A Black and White model. *The Counseling Psychologist, 12,* 153–165.

Helms, J. (1989). Considering some methodological issues in racial identity counseling research. *The Counseling Psychologist, 17,* 227–252.

Hogg, M., Abrams, D., & Patel, Y. (1987). Ethnic identity, self-esteem, and occupational aspirations of Indian and Anglo-Saxon British adolescents. *Genetic, Social, and General Psychology Monographs, 113,* 487–508.

Houston, L. (1984). Black consciousness and self-esteem. *Journal of Black Psychology, 11,* 1–7.

Hutnik, N. (1985). Aspects of identity in a multi-ethnic society. *New Community, 12,* 298–309.

Hutnik, N. (1986). Patterns of ethnic minority identification and modes of social adaptation. *Ethnic and Racial Studies, 9*, 150–167.

Kagitcibasi, C., & Berry, J. (1989). Cross-cultural psychology: Current research and trends. In M. Rosenzweig & L. Porter (Eds.), *Annual review of psychology* (Vol. 40, pp. 493–531). Palo Alto, CA: Annual Reviews.

Kaplan, R. (1989, July). The Balkans: Europe's third world. *The Atlantic, 263*, 16–22.

Keefe, S. (1986). Southern Appalachia: Analytical models, social services, and native support systems. *American Journal of Community Psychology, 14*, 479–498.

Keefe, S., & Padilla, A. (1987). *Chicano ethnicity.* Albuquerque: University of New Mexico Press.

Kim, J. (1981). *The process of Asian-American identity development: A study of Japanese American women's perceptions of their struggle to achieve Positive identities.* Unpublished doctoral dissertation, University of Massachusetts.

Kingston, M. (1976). *The woman warrior.* South Yarmouth, MA: J. Curley.

Knuckle, E., & Asbury, C. (1986). Benton revised visual retention test: Performance of Black adolescents according to age, sex, and ethnic identity. *Perceptual and Motor Skills, 63*, 319–327.

Kochman, T. (1987). The ethnic component in Black language and culture. In J. Phinney & M. Rotheram (Eds.), *Children's ethnic socialization: Pluralism and development* (pp. 219–238). Newbury Park, CA: Sage.

Krate, R., Leventhal, G., & Silverstein, B. (1974). Self-perceived transformation of Negro-to-Black identity. *Psychological Reports, 35*, 1071–1075.

Kuhlman, T. (1979). A validation study of the Draw-a-Person as a measure of racial identity acceptance. *Journal of Personality Assessment, 43*, 457–458.

Laosa, L. (1984). Social policies toward children of diverse ethnic, racial and language groups in the United States. In H. Stevenson & A. Siegel (Eds.), *Child development research and social policy* (pp. 1–109). Chicago: University of Chicago Press.

Lax, R., & Richards, A. (1981). Observations on the formation of Jewish identity in adolescents: Research report. *Israel Journal of Psychiatry and Related Sciences, 18*, 299–310.

Leclezio, M. K., Louw-Potgieter, J., & Souchon, M. B. S. (1986). The social identity of Mauritian immigrants in South Africa. *Journal of Social Psychology, 126*, 61–69.

Lewin, K. (1948). *Resolving social conflicts.* New York: Harper.

Makabe, T. (1979). Ethnic identity scale and social mobility: The case of Nisei in Toronto. *The Canadian Review of Sociology and Anthropology, 16*, 136–145.

Malcolm X. (1965). *Autobiography of Malcolm X.* New York: Golden Press.

Maldonado, D., Jr. (1975). Ethnic self-identity and self-understanding. *Social Casework, 56*, 618–622.

Marcia, J. (1966). Development and validation of ego-identity status. *Journal of Personality and Social Psychology, 3*, 551–558.

Marcia, J. (1980). Identity in adolescence. In J. Adelson (Ed.), *Handbook of adolescent psychology* (pp. 159–187). New York: Wiley.

Masuda, M., Hasegawa, R., & Matsumoto, G. (1973). The ethnic identity questionnaire: A comparison of three Japanese age groups in Tachikawa, Japan, Honolulu, and Seattle. *Journal of Cross-Cultural Psychology, 4*, 229–244.

Matute-Bianchi, M. (1986). Ethnic identities and pattern of school success and failure among Mexican-descent and Japanese-American students in a California high school: An ethnographic analysis. *American Journal of Education, 95*, 233–255.

McRoy, R., Zurcher, L., & Lauderdale, M. (1984). The identity of transracial adoptees. *Social Casework, 65*, 34–39.

McRoy, R., Zurcher, L., Lauderdale, M., & Anderson, R. (1982). Self-esteem and racial identity in transracial and inracial adoptees. *Social Work, 27*, 522–526.

Mendelberg, H. (1986). Identity conflict in Mexican-American adolescents. *Adolescence, 21*, 215–222.

Morten, G., & Atkinson, D. (1983). Minority identity development and preference for counselor race. *Journal of Negro Education, 52*, 156–161.

Ostrow, M. (1977). The psychological determinants of Jewish identity. *Israel Annals of Psychiatry and Related Disciplines, 15*, 313–335.

Parham, T. (1989). Cycles of psychological nigrescence. *The Counseling Psychologist, 17*, 187–226.

Parham, T., & Helms, J. (1981). The influence of Black student's racial identity attitudes on preferences for counselor's race. *Journal of Counseling Psychology, 28*, 250–257.

Parham, T., & Helms, J. (1985a). Attitudes of racial identity and self-esteem of Black students: An exploratory investigation. *Journal of College Student Personnel, 26*, 143–147.

Parham, T., & Helms, J. (1985b). Relation of racial identity attitudes to self-actualization and affective states of Black students. *Journal of Counseling Psychology, 32*, 431–440.

Paul, M., & Fischer, J. (1980). Correlates of self-concept among Black early adolescents. *Journal of Youth and Adolescence, 9*, 163–173.

Phinney, J. (1989). Stages of ethnic identity in minority group adolescents. *Journal of Early Adolescence, 9*, 34–49.

Phinney, J. (1990). *The Multigroup Ethnic Identity Measure: A new scale for use with adolescents and adults from diverse groups.* Manuscript submitted for publication.

Phinney, J., & Alipuria, L. (1990). Ethnic identity in older adolescents from four ethnic groups. *Journal of Adolescence, 13*.

Phinney, J., Lochner, B., & Murphy, R. (1990). Ethnic identity development and psychological adjustment in adolescence. In A. Stiffman & L. Davis (Eds.), *Ethnic issues in adolescent mental health*. Newbury Park, CA: Sage.

Phinney, J., & Tarver, S. (1988). Ethnic identity search and commitment in Black and White eighth graders. *Journal of Early adolescence, 8*, 265–277.

Pomales, J., Claiborn, C., & LaFromboise, T. (1986). Effect of Black students' racial identity on perceptions of White counselors varying in cultural sensitivity. *Journal of Counseling Psychology, 33*, 57–61.

Ponterotto, J., Anderson, W., & Grieger, I. (1986). Black students' attitudes toward counseling as a function of racial identity. *Journal of Multicultural Counseling and Development, 14*, 50–59.

Ponterotto, J., & Wise, S. (1987). Construct validity study of the Racial Identity Attitude Scale. *Journal of Counseling Psychology, 34*, 218–223.

Rodriguez, R. (1982). *Hunger of memory*. Boston: Godine.

Rogler, L., Cooney, R., & Ortiz, V. (1980). Intergenerational change in ethnic identity in the Puerto Rican family. *International Migration Review, 14*, 193–214.

Rosenberg, M. (1979). *Conceiving the self*. New York: Basic Books.

Rosenthal, D., & Cichello, A. (1986). The meeting of two cultures: Ethnic identity and psychosocial adjustment of Italian-Australian adolescents. *International Journal of Psychology, 21*, 487–501.

Rosenthal, D., & Feldman, S. (in press). The nature and stability of ethnic identity in Chinese youth: Effects of length of residence in two cultural contexts. *Journal of Cross-Cultural Psychology*.

Rosenthal, D., & Hrynevich, C. (1985). Ethnicity and ethnic identity: A comparative study of Greek-, Italian-, and Anglo-Australian adolescents. *International Journal of Psychology, 20*, 723–742.

Rosenthal, D., Whittle, J., & Bell, R. (1988). The dynamic nature of ethnic identity among Greek-Australian adolescents. *Journal of Social Psychology, 129*, 249–258.

Salgado de Snyder, N., Lopez, C. M., & Padilla, A. M. (1982). Ethnic identity and cultural awareness among the offspring of Mexican interethnic marriages. *Journal of Early Adolescence, 2*, 277–282.

Simic, A. (1987). Ethnicity as a career for the elderly: The Serbian-American case. *Journal of Applied Gerontology, 6*, 113–126.

Singh, V. (1977). Some theoretical and methodological problems in the study of ethnic identity: A cross-cultural perspective. *New York Academy of Sciences: Annals, 285*, 32–42.

Sommerlad, E., & Berry, J. (1970). The role of ethnic identification in distinguishing between attitudes towards assimilation and integration of a minority racial group. *Human Relations, 13*, 23–29.

Staiano, K. (1980). Ethnicity as process: The creation of an Afro-American identity. *Ethnicity, 7*, 27–33.

Steele, S. (1988). On being Black and middle class. *Commentary, 85*, 42–47.

Stryker, S. (1980). *Symbolic interactionism: A social structural version*. Menlo Park, CA: Benjamin Cummings.

Tajfel, H. (1978). *The social psychology of minorities*. New York: Minority Rights Group.

Tajfel, H. (1981). *Human groups and social categories*. Cambridge, England: Cambridge University Press.

Tajfel, H., & Turner, J. (1979). An integrative theory of intergroup conflict. In W. Austin & S. Worchel (Eds.), *The social psychology of intergroup relations* (pp. 33–47). Monterey, CA: Brooks/Cole.

Taylor, D. M., & Bassili, J. N., & Aboud, F. E. (1973). Dimensions of ethnic identity: An example from Quebec. *Journal of Social Psychology, 89*, 185–192.

Terrell, F., & Taylor, J. (1978). The development of an inventory to measure certain aspects of Black nationalist ideology. *Psychology, 15*, 31–33.

Teske, R., & Nelson, B. (1973). Two scales for the measurement of Mexican-American identity. *International Review of Modern Sociology, 3*, 192–203.

Ting-Toomey, S. (1981). Ethnic identity and close friendship in Chinese-American college students. *International Journal of Intercultural Relations, 5*, 383–406.

Tzuriel, D., & Klein, M. M. (1977). Ego identity: Effects of ethnocentrism, ethnic identification, and cognitive complexity in Israeli, Oriental, and Western ethnic groups. *Psychological Reports, 40*, 1099–1110.

Ullah, P. (1985). Second generation Irish youth: Identity and ethnicity. *New Community, 12*, 310–320.

Ullah, P. (1987). Self-definition and psychological group formation in an ethnic minority. *British Journal of Social Psychology, 26*, 17–23.

Vermeulen, H., & Pels, T. (1984). Ethnic identity and young migrants in The Netherlands. *Prospects, 14,* 277–282.

Weinreich, P. (1983). Emerging from threatened identities. In G. Breakwell (Ed.), *Threatened identities* (pp. 149–185). New York: Wiley.

Weinreich, P. (1988). The operationalization of ethnic identity. In J. Berry & R. Annis (Eds.), *Ethnic psychology: Research and practice with immigrants, refugees, native peoples, ethnic groups and sojourners* (pp. 149–168). Amsterdam: Swets & Zeitlinger.

Wetzel, J. (1987). *American youth: A statistical snapshot.* Washington, DC: William T. Grant Foundation.

White, C., & Burke, P. (1987). Ethnic role identity among Black and White college students: An interactionist approach. *Sociological Perspectives, 30,* 310–331.

Wooden, W., Leon, J., & Toshima, M. (1988). Ethnic identity among Sansei and Yonsei church-affiliated youth in Los Angeles and Honolulu. *Psychological Reports, 62,* 268–270.

Yancey, W., Ericksen, E., & Juliani, R. (1976). Emergent ethnicity: A review and reformulation. *American Sociological Review, 41,* 391–403.

Zak, I. (1973). Dimensions of Jewish-American identity. *Psychological Reports, 33,* 891–900.

Zak, I. (1976). Structure of ethnic identity of Arab-Israeli students. *Psychological Reports, 38,* 239–246.

Zinn, M. (1980). Gender and ethnic identity among Chicanos. *Frontiers, 5,* 18–24.

Zisenwine, D. & Walters, J. (1982). Jewish identity: Israel and the American adolescent. *Forum on the Jewish People, Zionism, and Israel, 45,* 79–84.

CHAPTER 23

INFLUENCES ON ETHNIC IDENTITY DEVELOPMENT OF LATINO COLLEGE STUDENTS IN THE FIRST TWO YEARS OF COLLEGE

VASTI TORRES

In this qualitative study, I use grounded theory methodology to investigate the influences on the ethnic identity development of 10 Latino/a students during their first two years at a highly selective college. The findings indicate that two categories were salient in the first two years: Situating Identity (conditions: environment where they grew up, family influence and generational status, and self-perception of status in society) and Influences on Change (conditions: psychosocial and cognitive development). Conditions and subprocesses involved in each of the categories are discussed.

Higher education researchers have been forecasting an increase in the diversity of students for many years and predicting that Latinos will be the largest minority group by 2020 (Day, 1996). The 2000 census confirmed this increase by reporting that from 1990 to 2000, the percentage of Latinos in the United States increased dramatically, making it the largest minority group many years ahead of the prediction. Although non-Latino Whites increased 5.9%, the Latino population increased by 57.9%. This is the largest increase of any racial or ethnic group in the United States (Asian American population increased by 48.3%; American Indians, 26.4%; and African Americans, 15.6%; U.S. Census Bureau, 2000).

This increase in population has heightened the need to understand the experiences of Latino college students. One of the important theoretical tools that practitioners have to help them understand diverse populations is identity development theory, through which researchers attempt to explain the developmental process that students encounter. There is general acceptance that identity development during college influences how students adapt to and manage their college experiences, but how this process differs for ethnically diverse students is not as clear (Chickering & Reisser, 1993). Few researchers have explored the development of Latino ethnic identity specifically during the college years (Phinney, 1993). The formation of ethnic identity is based on one's sense of self as part of an ethnic group (Bernal, Knight, Ocampo, Garza, & Cota, 1993). This self-identification is mitigated by the choices made between the American and Latino cultures and is therefore an important aspect of development that demands closer examination (Garza & Gallegos, 1995; Torres, 1999).

Few identity development theories have considered the ethnic identity development of students under the broad category of Latino. Despite much diversity among Latinos, "the unique historical and sociological context of the United States creates the backdrop for Latino identity" (Ferdman & Gallegos, 2001, p. 37). This historical and sociological context is illustrated by data from the Department of Education indicating that approximately 45% of Latino students are enrolled in Hispanic serving institutions (Stearns, Watanabe, & Snyder, 2002). Attendance at an Hispanic serving institution may provide a critical mass from one country of origin, but that is not guaranteed because the criteria for the Hispanic serving institution designation is that the Latino student enrollment be approximately 25%. In reality the majority (55%) of Latino students attend institutions where they are the minority and as a result often associate with other Latinos (Stearns, Watanabe, & Snyder, 2002). The diversity within the term *Latino* requires that the literature that informs this study also consider this diversity.

This study was informed by Phinney's (1993) model of ethnic identity development, which was created using multiple groups of ethnic students, and the work of Torres (1999) on cultural orientation of Latino students. Care was taken so that the influence of this previous research informed, but did not "hinder the creativity" needed to conduct grounded theory research (Strauss & Corbin, 1998, p. 53).

For the purposes of this study, ethnicity is narrowly defined by the distinguishing differences of a group that are based on national or cultural characteristics (Atkinson, Morten, & Sue, 1993). These differences are multidimensional and include language, food, behavior, and other customs (Phinney, 1995). Some of the literature on Latinos uses content measures of ethnicity, such as language, to determine ethnic identification. Yet research indicates that pride in one's ethnicity is maintained even when these content measures are not present (Keefe & Padilla, 1987). Because Latino college students tend to be highly acculturated (Sanchez & Fernandez, 1993; Torres, 1999) using ethnic identity models focused only on content measures are not optimal.

Phinney (1993) developed a model based on interviews with adolescents from multiple ethnic groups. In this model, the researcher focuses on the formation of ethnic identity and how an individual comes to understand his or her ethnicity. The model has three distinguishable stages that develop sequentially (Phinney & Chavira, 1992). The first stage, Unexamined Ethnic Identity, indicates a lack of probing into the concept of ethnicity. Like other racial identity models, individuals in this stage tend to accept the values and attitudes of the majority culture. The second stage is Ethnic Identity Search/Moratorium, which occurs when individuals are faced with a situation that forces them to "initiate an ethnic identity search" (Phinney, 1993, p. 69). The third stage is Ethnic Identity Achievement and is characterized by a clear and confident sense of one's ethnicity (Phinney, 1993).

Using Phinney's model as a framework, Torres (1999) validated the Bicultural Orientation Model (BOM). The conceptual idea behind cultural orientation is to understand the nuances among the Latino college student population by looking at the choices they have made between two cultures. This model is focused on identifying the choices that Latino students make between their culture of origin and the majority culture. In the Torres model there are four cultural orientations that distinguish the Latino students. The first is a Bicultural Orientation, which indicates a comfort level with both cultures. The second is a Latino/Hispanic Orientation, which indicates greater comfort with the culture of origin. The third is an Anglo Orientation, which indicates a greater comfort with the majority culture. And finally the Marginal Orientation indicates discomfort with both cultures and may indicate conflict within the individual (Torres). Individuals are placed in the model through acculturation and ethnic identity scales. Acculturation looks at the choices made about the majority culture, whereas ethnic identity looks at the maintenance of the culture of origin (Torres). However, this model does not explain the process involved in choosing a cultural orientation. In this study, the scales were not used in the analysis, and only the construct of cultural orientation was considered (Torres & Baxter Magolda, 2002).

The fact that multiple ethnic groups were included in the validation of Phinney's (1993) model makes this an attractive model to consider with the broad group of individuals included under the term "Latino." Yet, Phinney did not concentrate solely on college students or Latinos and thus questions remain of how Latino college students fit into the model and begin college at the first stage (Unexamined). In this study I sought to investigate this gap in the research and inform practitioners in student affairs about the development of Latino identity development in college students. The Phinney (1993) and Torres (1999) models raised particular questions that inform this inquiry. Literature was used as a tool to "stimulate thinking about properties and for asking conceptual questions" (Strauss & Corbin, 1998, p. 47). This study adds to the knowledge by looking at a different context and by using a longitudinal research design. The longitudinal nature of this study allows exploration of individual development. This study is ongoing and this article will focus only on the first two years of college.

Research Design

I used a constructivist (Lincoln & Guba, 1985; Schwandt, 1994) approach to inquiry and grounded theory methodology (Strauss & Corbin, 1998) to guide design and analysis decisions. By using constructivist grounded theory I recognize that meaning arises from the experiences of participants as they are shared during the interaction between participants and myself; therefore the relationship between participants and researcher is valued, rather than avoided (Charmaz, 2000). I selected grounded theory methodology for two reasons: first, because the goal of the research is to ground theory in the data and therefore "offer insight, enhance understanding, and provide a meaningful guide to action" (Strauss & Corbin, 1998, p. 12); and second, because grounded theory acknowledges that the "combining [of] methods may be done for supplementary, complementary, informational, developmental, and other reasons" (p. 28). For the purpose of this study only qualitative methods were used; during sampling procedures participants were asked to self-select from four descriptions that corresponded to cultural orientations (Torres, 1999). At this point in the study, the participants have not been placed in the Bicultural Orientation Model because I did not want to be biased by their placement (Torres & Baxter Magolda, 2002).

The context for this study is an independent, urban, research university located on the East Coast. In the Fall 1999 semester 43% (8,168) of the student population were undergraduate students and 5% (569) of the undergraduates self-identified as Hispanic (term used by institution to represent Latino students). The freshman class consisted of 2,120 students with a median SAT of 1240. Latino students made up 3.7% (82) of the freshman class. Overall 18.6% (394) of the freshman class came from non-White ethnic or racial groups.

Procedures

Participants. All first-time freshmen who self-identified with Latino backgrounds to the university were invited to participate in this study.

Open sampling techniques (Strauss & Corbin, 1998) were initially used. With this technique, the researcher accepts any participant willing to participate as long as he or she fits the sampling need (selfidentified Latino/a). The use of this sampling method was advantageous because of the loose structure in data gathering; at this point in the research process a tight data-gathering technique could "mislead the analysis or foreclose on discovery" (Strauss & Corbin, p. 206). On the interview response form, students were also asked to select from four cultural orientation descriptions the one that best represented them. Once the interviews were conducted, I reviewed the characteristics of the participants to determine if inviting others would enhance the sample. After looking at characteristics that previous research identified as providing variety in the sample (i.e., country of origin, generation in the United States, region where students came from, and self-selected cultural orientation), I determined that this sample reasonably represented the theoretical diversity of the Latino students in this context (Glaser & Strauss, 1999). Because institutions do not collect data on Latin country of origin, generation in the United States, or cultural orientation, an exact comparison was not feasible; this required me to use my judgment and theoretical sensitivity to determine the diversity of the sample.

Initially, 12 students volunteered in their first year. This article is based on data from the 10 students who continued to participate in their second year. The sample consists of 7 women and 3 men; 8 were born in the United States; and 8 were bilingual. Participants' cultural or ethnic backgrounds were as follows: 3 Mexican, and 1 each Puerto Rican, Cuban, Venezuelan, El Salvadorian, Guatemalan, Nicaraguan, and Colombian.

Method. Interviews were the primary method used to gather the qualitative data. The interview protocol in the first year was semistructured and was focused on constructs that previous research indicated were relevant to the development of ethnic identity (Phinney, 1993; Torres, 1999). The areas covered in the interview included selfidentification, cultural orientation, family influence, and the college environment. Although theoretical sensitivity requires that previous knowledge and research be considered, I was open to other issues and framed the interview so that appropriate probes and follow-ups could be done in an easy manner. This protocol was piloted with two older Latino students who I knew well and who had a sense of their ethnic identity and cultural orientation. These students were asked to comment on clarity, comfort with the items, appropriateness of follow-up probes, and completeness of the interview. Feedback from these two students was incorporated into this study.

In the second year, the interviews were less structured and focused on the process of changes in the participants' perceptions of their self-identification, cultural orientation, and college experiences. During the second-year interviews, I asked participants about their self-selected cultural orientation and if that had changed. The taped interviews were conducted during the Spring semester each year and lasted 30 to 60 minutes.

Establishing trustworthiness. The notion of trustworthiness refers to the internal and external validity of the qualitative research process (Lincoln & Guba, 1985). Several methods were used to establish the trustworthiness of the research. First, because this is a longitudinal study there was sufficient time to test misinformation and to allow participants to correct misinformation. This process was achieved through member checks (Lincoln & Guba) at the end of each year. In the first year, I shared with the participants the emerging categories among the all the participants. In the second year, I created a case report for each participant that included quotes illustrating how their interview fit into some of the emerging themes. Participants were asked if the reports accurately reflected their experiences and if they found any incorrect information. At this time the participants were asked permission for the possible use of these quotes in scholarly publications.

The second method used for establishing trustworthiness was to intentionally conduct debriefing (Lincoln & Guba, 1985) with a Latina whose experiences differed from my own. A debriefer is a professional peer who can hold conversations with the researcher and challenge the process when he or she feels other interpretations should be considered (Lincoln & Guba). I chose to debrief with a Latina who was third generation in the United States and whose ancestors came from a different country of origin than mine did. The peer debriefing challenged or confirmed

impressions about the developmental process and provided insight from another perspective.

The third method was to maintain a researcher's journal that both chronicled research decisions and noted times when I felt that my interpretations could be based on my own experiences, thus possibly not reflective of the student's voice. Because I am a Latina, this process is important to note. Researcher positioning as a Latina required me to reflect and use peer debriefing to intentionally evaluate my own interpretations of the students' stories.

Analysis

The interviews were transcribed verbatim and analysis of the data began with a microscopic (line-by-line) examination of each interview (Strauss & Corbin, 1998). The microscopic examination was the first step in the open coding process used to create initial categories for comparisons among the cases. During open coding, "data are broken down into discrete parts, closely examined, and compared for similarities and differences" (Strauss & Corbin, p. 102). The similarities are then grouped into abstract concepts called categories. Once initial categories emerged, the analysis moved into axial coding, thus connecting categories to subcategories, which explain the concepts in the categories. This is all done in order to reassemble the data in such a manner that can better explain the complete phenomenon. Because this study is ongoing, I did not include a discussion of selective coding in this article. Instead, I chose to focus on coding for process, identifying the connections between the categories, and identifying the components of the change process (Strauss & Corbin).

Findings

The two major categories that emerged during the first two years of interviews are the focus of this paper. The categories are: Situating Identity (the starting point of identity development in college) and Influences on Change in identity development. These categories are being shared at this point in the research process because these categories emerged from these first two years of interviews and can be considered saturated because they occurred during a specific time frame in the longitudinal study (Strauss & Corbin, 1998). Each category is discussed separately along with the conditions that explain the why and how of the phenomenon.

Situating Identity

Because this research is focused on the identity development process it is important to evaluate the different starting points and how those differences influence the phenomenon of ethnic identity or cultural orientation. Consistent with grounded theory methodology, analysis of data reveals three conditions that help explain the Situating Identity category and help answer questions about the phenomenon (Strauss & Corbin, 1998). The conditions are related to the how and why issues of the category. In this case they identify the influences that distinguish the different starting points of the participants. The conditions are: the environment where they grew up, family influences and generation in the United States, and selfperception of status in society.

Environment where they grew up. The makeup of the environment where the students came from influenced both how they ethnically self-identified and their cultural orientation. The major property of this condition is the existence or nonexistence of diversity in their environment. The diversity of the environment should be seen as a continuous dimension rather than dichotomous. For illustrative purposes the ends of the dimensional continuum will be used to demonstrate differences. Students who came from diverse environments tended to have a strong sense of ethnicity and were more likely to enjoy the diversity around them. Jackie described the environment where she grew up and its influence on her by saying:

> There's a lot of different cultures [in my high school], and we get a lot of international students and stuff. So I have always . . . participated in Asian programs, African American programs. It hasn't been only Hispanic. But I am very proud of being Hispanic, but I don't think anything less of other races just because they are another race.

Students from areas where Latinos are a critical mass did not see themselves as in the minority until they arrived on the predominantly White campus. This change in their environment prompted a stronger tie to their ethnicity rather than assimilation. Carlos described his reaction like this:

> Before, when I was at home, everybody knew I was Hispanic . . . Everybody knows I am Mexican, and it is just part of everyday life. Ninety percent of the students where I was going to school were of Hispanic background. Now I come and I have to say my name differently. Instead of saying [Spanish pronunciation], I say [Americanized pronunciation], because everybody is like, "What did you say?" You know, . . . I have to educate people about who I am, where I am from, what the reality of my life is, in contrast to what they think the reality of my life is.

On the other end of the dimension are those who came from environments where there was mainly a White European influence. These students tended to define their ethnicity as where they are from—using a geographic definition. Juan, who in his first year identified himself as an American or Texan (northern area), stated that this selfidentification was "just that—that is my location on the map." Or in Elizabeth's case, whose father is Latino and mother is Anglo, she described herself with a: "Spanish background. Like a Latina. Have a Latin background."

These students tended to associate with the majority culture and found the diversity in the college environment as presenting some conflict for them. Elizabeth described it this way:

> I have felt that I have been more segregated [in college] because when I was in high school, there weren't many Hispanics, and so like I [being Cuban] . . . would be neat, like, "Yes, I am Cuban, and this is how we do things."
>
> And here there are so many Hispanics, but most of them have grown up with both Hispanic parents, or in a Hispanic neighborhood, or in a Hispanic country, and so they are like very, very cultural, and I am like half and half, so sometimes I feel like a . . . an outsider in the Hispanic group, but then like I don't want to be, because that is like my culture, but I don't speak fluent Spanish anymore, and they [other Latino students] do things different than I would.

Family influence and generation in the United States. Differences among the generational status of the participants began emerging in the first year of interviews because of the types of issues these students were dealing with. By looking at the generation in the United States, I explored the properties associated with level of acculturation of the student as well as the parents and the dimensions of this condition within the context of the college environment.

The most obvious dimension that emerged is that students identified themselves using the same terms and language their parents used. This was evident by the term they selected to describe themselves and their reaction to the college environment. For example students who chose to describe themselves using their familial country of origin, such as Mexican American, talked about how their parents talked about their Mexican culture. Other students who used more generic terms like *Hispanic* also talked about how their parents used that term. This dimension became obvious when I asked students what influence their family had on how they see themselves. All of the students credited their parents for their views on ethnicity and its role in their life. They also talked about their Latino ethnicity in a positive manner and attributed this positive meaning of ethnicity to their parents. The more parents participated in culturally relevant activities, such as speaking Spanish at home and attending Latino social functions, the more students identified with their ethnic identity. Those students who came from families where one parent was Latino and the other was not tended to talk about their desire to learn more about the culture.

The second dimension is the generational status of the participants and their parents. Students who are the first generation in the United States struggled with the unknown expectations of the college environment. Though all students make some adjustments, first generation in the United States students also struggled to balance the college expectations with those of their parents. For example, Sara exemplified this dimension when she talked about the issues she had to deal with from her parents: "That is one thing I don't like about my roots, because my parents are so strict. That is how their parents grew up." Sara's parents held on to many of the traditions of their country of origin and therefore expected Sara to live by their rules even when she was on her own in college. Her mother called daily and expected Sara to be in her residence hall room to receive the phone call. Freedom was seen as an American value and Sara's parents had not acculturated to the majority culture in a manner that would make them feel comfortable with the freedoms associated with college life.

This balancing of acculturation levels seemed to have two consequences. First, students like Sara, who tried to please her parents by being in her room every night when they called, ended up feeling a little alienated from their peers because they would not tell them what they were dealing with. This consequence could cause conflicts and be stressful. Sara described her feelings of alienation:

> When someone asked me, "What is going on?" I am just, oh, this, this, and that. . . . So I am trying to isolate myself a little from them, because I don't want them to think that I am nuts or something. . . . I have a lot of pressure [from my parents] now.

The second consequence was that students kept things from their parents. Diana, was born in the United States, but she and her family returned to their country of origin when she was still a baby. She did not tell her parents she was engaged. She felt they would be upset by this information. This consequence seemed to come from a desire to respect and protect parents rather from a desire to rebel or reject.

Students who are the first generation in the United States also sometimes feel alienated from the mainstream because they do not understand things that are taken for granted by others in the majority culture. They feel caught between the two cultures, not completely fitting in with either culture. Diana described it like this:

> I always feel like I am left out, and I think that I'm going to be for the rest of my life. I am left out here because—everybody talks about their experience before I came here, like elementary school, and middle school— I have no idea about that. I can't even . . . know songs they used to [sing] when they were little. . . . And when I go [back to my family's country of origin] I feel left out because of the things that I have missed [since] I came here. So I am never going to be settled anywhere.

These students are caught between the expectations, traditions, and knowledge from the majority culture and their culture of origin.

At the other end of the array in this dimension are the students who are second and third generation in the United States who assume the mingling of the two cultures. When I asked Carlos, a second-generation student, about the values he felt his mother had instilled in him and if they were connected to the Latino culture, he responded by saying:

> I would say half of them are consistent with the Latino culture, because a lot of what she has instilled in me is a sense of family, a sense of community. But the rest just has to do with who [I am as] a person and the experiences that a person has had.

These students tend to have less conflict with parents and are comfortable with the role their parents play in their identification. This condition points out the unclear transition from issues of acculturation to development of ethnic identity. All of these students can be seen as highly acculturated and have no accent when they speak English. Yet, as in the case of the first-generation students, they were continuing to deal with issues of acculturation to the majority culture. Their parents' views of American values associated with freedom, for example, created additional stressors for these students.

Self-perception of status in society. This condition is often associated with social economic status, but here it is more generally described as students perceiving some advantage or privilege as compared to others. The basic dimension of this condition is the perception or nonperception of privilege. Those who talked about privilege tended to believe in the negative stereotypes associated with Latinos; they just did not see themselves as associated with those negative stereotypes. For example, Juan, who came from an economically privileged family, elaborated on his interpretation of the term *Tejano* by saying:

> It's like you are Mexican, and you were born and raised in Texas, and you have loyalties to the Mexican people, which I have never had. Because growing up in my city, the Mexican people were in the ghettos, or in the bad parts, and if there was vandalism, that is where you kind of thought of.
> But I lived in the White part of town, because my dad is a doctor. And all my friends were White, and . . . in my high school . . . I [had] the highest male GPA. And that completely separated me from the rest of them.

On the other end of this dimensional range, Diana, who did not perceive any privilege or advantage over others, described her interpretation of the differences between her culture of origin and the American culture like this:

> Having gone through a different way of living over there, especially . . . when I was little, it helps me see things in a different way. It makes me more openminded about other people and other ways of living.

This condition was focused more on how the participants reacted to others and their ability to recognize racism when it is occurring to them or around them. Juan seemed to believe the negative stereotypes, but did not see them as including him, whereas Diana expressed that her experiences with different cultures made her more open. In other parts of the interview Diana was able to identify when she experience racism, whereas Juan did not see racism at all.

Influences on Change in Identity Development

This category emerged while I was coding for process between the first and second-year interviews. This type of coding emphasizes the relationship between process and structure while connecting the categories (Strauss & Corbin, 1998). Two subprocesses of cultural dissonance and change in relationships within the environment emerged as relevant conditions and influenced change in the participant's ethnic identity.

Cultural dissonance. The behaviors that are expressed within this condition refer to the experience of dissonance or conflict between one's own sense of culture and what others expect. Though this type of conflict with the culture intersected with other conditions mentioned earlier, there was sufficient evidence to consider it a condition of change (see Figure 1). For the students who came from first generation in the United States families, conflicts with their parents' cultural expectations led them to desire more association with the majority culture. This is exemplified by Sara in her second-year interview:

> I am not as comfortable with [the Latino culture], because . . . I won't accept some of the things that my parents believe, and I know that is part of my culture, I just don't think it is right. I think that my parents shouldn't totally stick with the culture that they grew up with because that is not where we live, and that is not like the influences that I have. So they expect me to kind of live by that culture . . . [even though] I am not living anywhere near it right now.

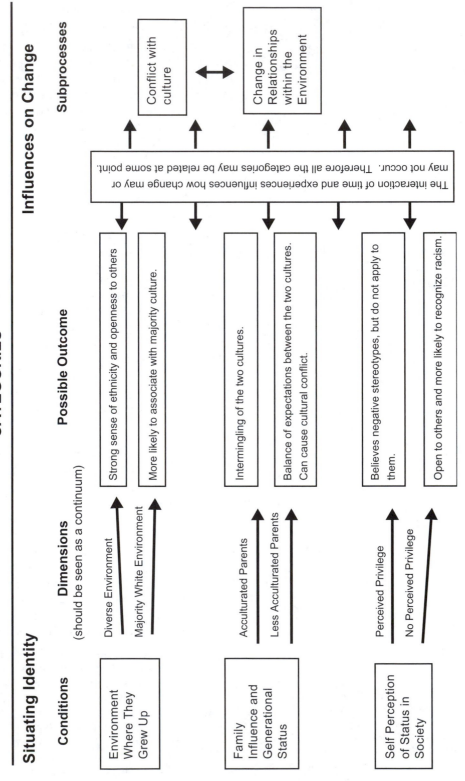

Figure 1 Conceptual figure of the categories influencing ethnic identity development in the first two years of college. Arrows represent connections and interactions.

The magnitude of the dissonance forced the change to occur. In her first year, Sara had self-selected the Bicultural Orientation description and in her second year she described herself as having an Anglo Orientation (Torres, 1999). Her change focused on retreating from the cultural dissonance her parents created with their rules. Sara began to associate ethnicity with her parents' strictness. Though Sara's self-selected cultural orientation description changed, her pride in ethnicity had not lessened; she sought out an internship with a Latino organization in the city. Though this pride was intact, her movement towards more ethnic awareness was clearly on standby. The dissonance between her own and what she perceived as her parents' definition of culture had created a type of critical moment that had not been resolved and seemed to cause stagnation in her development.

Elizabeth experienced a different type of cultural dissonance, which produced a different type of change in her self-identification. In her first-year interview Elizabeth had mentioned that her lack of speaking Spanish made her feel alienated from other Latinos on the campus. In her second year, her attempt to make meaning of this issue was described like this:

> I was in a class this past semester with a professor.... And there are a lot, like tons, of Hispanic kids in that class. And my last name is [common Spanish surname], so everyone looks at me, even at [the food court on campus], the people that work there will speak Spanish to me, and I'm just like, I can understand them but I can't really speak back, I mean I could, but it would take me a while. . . . So, in that class, I just really felt Whiter than White, like more American than ever, and they would stay afterwards with the professor and speak Spanish and . . . oh, I just hurt. I really want to be able to do that and that's like a really big deal why I am studying [abroad] the entire year, because my Spanish is horrendous and . . . I want to be fluent by the time I get back. I want to be able to read in Spanish, write in Spanish and be good at it. And it's been really hard because the Hispanic kids don't look at me as very Hispanic. But the White kids or the American kids, . . . [with] their racism issue, they'll look at me and they'll hear me sing a Spanish song or listen to Spanish music or, you know, things like that, or I want to eat Spanish food and they look at me like, "Oh, God, she is so Spanish," you know, and I'm not. It's just because it's so different to them. So, I don't know, it's hard.

The change that happened to Elizabeth revolved around her quest to know about her ethnicity and the language. She described the meaning behind her search:

> My quest or journey to learn Spanish is a really big deal but also the education I get and the different classes in Latin America . . . they all kind of deal with like the same things, like cultural identity, and that's why I am really, really interested in anthropology. But that's like a really big deal, how people see themselves, how people [selfidentify] because it really has an effect on your whole outlook on life.

This passage illustrates the search Elizabeth has begun and her own descriptions of a cultural orientation that changed from an Anglo Orientation in her first year to a Bicultural Orientation in her second year.

Change in relationships within the environment. The prominent dimension of this condition is the peer group that the individual seeks out while in college. In the case of Carlos, who was already comfortable with his ethnicity and self-selected the Bicultural Orientation description, the change he saw in himself and his environment came by seeking out the diverse group of friendships he valued, but had not found in his first year of college. He described how much better adjusted he felt in his second year by saying:

> I definitely found my place. I know a lot more Hispanic students. That's great; I can speak Spanish with them a lot and love that. Also I've learned to live with like the fact that I am different culturally, myself. I've learned to integrate myself and I've culturalized [adapted].

I focused the follow-up questions on further exploring how that adjustment happened and he responded with:

> The way I found it is not by trying to change others, but just by trying to understand and making them understand more about me. The Mexican culture within the Hispanic culture is different and I talk about it in conversation, but I also learned not to focus on the fact that my skin may be a different color or my name might be a lot different than others, but rather that all our blood is red. In a way I have become blind to it, but not completely blind to it. . . . In a way I accept it more.and I think that through me accepting it like that, I think others accept.

Carlos never expressed "a critical moment" in his development and that may be because he grew up in an environment where he was the majority; thus providing him with a strong sense of ethnicity and strong coping skills for issues that emerged in the college environment. Carlos' cultural orientation remained bicultural for the two years. Carlos keeps up with the Latino student group on campus, but does not participate in the group's activities. When asked about that he indicated it was an issue of time rather than interest.

The experiences of Sarah also exemplified change, but from a different perspective. (Note that because two students selected the same pseudonym, this name is spelled with an *h* to differentiate from the other participant.) Sarah is half Latina, and her Latino father was not part of her growing up years. Prior to starting college, Sarah visited her father's country of origin and felt a need to further explore this side of her. In her second-year interview, Sarah talked about joining the Latino student group on campus and meeting a friend she related to and enjoyed spending time with. When I asked what kinds of things she had learned about herself, Sarah responded:

> Just about my heritage, and just how because as I was growing up, I never really thought of myself as a Latina. Like it wasn't very important in life, and I am just realizing how important it is, and how I want to learn more about the culture, and just to learn more about my family, and my ancestors, and what not. . . . It broadened my horizon, and it made me want to explore, and that is very important.

Sarah illustrated the beginning of the search process and was cautious about her exploration. For example, Sarah also talked about wanting to learn Spanish, but had not taken any active steps to fulfill that desire. In her first year, Sarah self-selected the Anglo Orientation description and in her second-year interview she selected the Bicultural Orientation description (Torres, 1999). This illustrated the change in her identity, yet this needs to be considered along with her safe progression into the search for ethnic identity.

Both of these examples illustrate how changes in personal relationships and involvement in Latino student groups can influence personal growth and identity development. As the students progress during their college years, these conditions may become even more salient.

Discussion

This study clearly illustrates that not all Latino students begin college with Unexamined Ethnic Identities (Phinney, 1993). The influences of where they grew up, their generational status in the United States, and self-perception of societal status play a major role in situating their identity in their first year of college.

The students who came from diverse environments self-selected the descriptions associated with the Bicultural or Latino Orientations (Torres, 1999). Their selection seems to depend on how they perceived the campus' diversity. The students who found the college environment as not accepting of diversity would identify with a Latino Orientation wanting to focus their orientation towards those who share their interest in diversity. The other students who acknowledged the lack of diversity, but were not as critical of the environment, would self-select the bicultural description in their orientation. In general, these students did not take on the values of the majority culture, but they were also not in a search of their ethnic identity, indicating that there is not a clear fit with Phinney's (1993) first stage of Unexamined Identity. It is important to note that students who come from environments where they have been the majority may come to college without ever going through the Unexamined Ethnic Identity or Ethnic Identity Search stages (Phinney).

The students from majority-White environments tended to identify with an Anglo Orientation or Bicultural Orientation (Torres, 1999) and seemed to fit the description of Stage 1: Unexamined Ethnic Identity (Phinney, 1993). The environment where they grew up did not provide extensive exposure to their own culture, or diversity in general, thus prompting them to mainly identify with the majority culture. Even though these students were more likely to associate with the majority culture, they still maintained a positive view of their Latino background. This draws into question the use of deficiency models of identity development with college students. There was no evidence that these students had negative views about being Latino.

It should be noted that though students who are first generation in the United States may have a stronger tie to their country of origin, they are also the ones that experienced more dissonance with their culture of origin. This dissonance was a result of the acculturation level of their parents and their desire to balance their parents' expectations with their own. The salience of generational status seems evident, but the resulting behavior can have much variation (Garza & Gallegos, 1995).

This finding also brings to light the possibility of some type of retreat or escape, as Perry (1970) might consider it, during the developmental process. This deflection may be the outcome of the strong dissonance felt by the students in their ethnic identity development. This interpretation connects ethnic identity with cognitive development and illustrates the process of meaning making in the process of identity development (Baxter Magolda, 2001; Chickering & Reisser, 1993).

Although first-generation-in-the-United-States students experience cultural dissonance, the evidence seems to indicate that later generations resolve those conflicts and emerge with strong ethnic identities. In the case of the students in this study, those from the later generations seem to be more active in acknowledging the influence of their ethnicity and in wanting to express their ethnicity. This finding provides further insight into the work of Keefe and Padilla (1987) who found that between the first and second generation of Mexican Americans there was a drop in Ethnic Loyalty, a concept similar to ethnic identity, yet later generations of Mexican Americans maintained a fairly consistent level of Ethnic Loyalty. The concept of the melting pot does not seem to be as salient today as in previous generations.

The condition of self-perceived status illustrates the intragroup differences among the Latino population. In several cases, the students with self-perceptions of privilege could be placed in Stage 1 (Unexamined Ethnic Identity; Phinney, 1993); they tended to select the Anglo Orientation description. Those who did not perceive privilege varied in their starting points on Phinney's model and were more likely to recognize and talk about how racist behaviors have impacted their sense of identity. Their cultural orientation tended to be dependent on other issues and therefore no clear conclusions can be made.

Influences on Change illustrated the process of identity development. The students who in their first year wanted to know more about their culture tended to selfidentify themselves as Anglo Orientation (Torres, 1999) and were likely to be in Stage 1 of Phinney's (1993) model. Yet as illustrated in the quoted passage by Elizabeth, a desire to explore cultural background can create movement towards Phinney's Stage 2 (Ethnic Identity Search). The cultural dissonance can also change students in other ways, as was illustrated by Sara, who changed her choice of descriptions from Bicultural to Anglo Orientation as a result of the magnitude of dissonance she felt between her own beliefs and those of her parents. This internal process requires us to be aware of many factors that may not be readily acknowledged by the student, yet these factors (such as generation in the United States) can cause stress for these students.

Implications for Practitioners and Researchers

Student affairs practitioners need to reflect on their own assumptions about the Latino students on their campus and identify how they are applying ethnic identity development theories. To serve all Latino students intentionally, it is important for practitioners to understand how these factors will affect the experiences of Latino students on their campus. Ethnic identity development is another tool in a practitioner's toolbox of developmental theories and should help administrators better understand Latino students. The same way a practitioner gets to know a student to gain insight as to where he or she is developmentally could be used to explore the factors that could influence how a Latino student's ethnic identity may evolve. This understanding could broaden conversations to be more intentional and allow non-Latinos glimpses of the issues that are relevant in the Latino student experience. Participants who were first generation in the United States shared how difficult it was to talk to non-Latinos about the pressure they feel from their parents. The level of stress can be an underlying issue for students with academic or social problems. Practitioners must have sensitivity to these issues when dealing with Latino students.

There is much more research that can be done in the area of Latino ethnic identity development. One issue that emerged during data analysis and deserves further exploration is the transition from acculturation to the ethnic identity development. Much of the growth in the Latino population comes from new immigrants who will soon be first-generation-in-the-United-States college students. At what point do these students transition from acculturating to the majority culture into a process of developing an ethnic identity? There is probably no clear-cut answer to this question, but further understanding is clearly needed to serve the Latino students coming into higher education.

Different contexts should also be considered for further research. The context of this study does not reflect all institutions in the United States. There is a great need to better understand the role of ethnic identity development at community colleges, where the majority of Latino students enroll. In addition, different social environments need to be investigated. If a student does not leave a geographic area where Latinos are a critical mass, would his or her development differ from students who relocate? Researchers have only begun to scratch the surface of the experiences of Latino college students and each study brings forth more information that can inform practice and improve the experiences of Latino students in college.

Limitations

The findings of this study are limited to the context of the study and the participants in the study. These students are probably similar to many other college students, yet their stories are unique to their experiences. The diversity among the Latino population is also a limitation because it is difficult to represent all the cultures incorporated under this label. The students who participated in this study clearly illustrate a variety of experiences and in turn reflect some of the diversity in the Latino college student population. In an effort to respect this diversity, I have tried to draw out findings that truly reflect their stories and experiences. Despite this effort, in qualitative studies the researcher is the instrument of the research and therefore this should be noted as a possible limitation.

Conclusion

Because this is a longitudinal study using grounded theory methodology, this article should be seen as a first installment on the theory-building process concerning the ethnic identity development of Latino college students. By sharing the categories that emerged in the first two years of this study, I hope to provide information that practitioners in higher education can use immediately and in turn create a better environment for Latino college students. My responsibility as a Latina researcher is to interpret the student stories and to formulate meaning around those stories. It is up to practitioners and other researchers to implement the knowledge and improve the experiences of Latino students.

References

Atkinson, D. R., Morten, G., & Sue, D. W. (1993). *Counseling American minorities: A cross-cultural perspective* (4th ed.). Madison, WI: Brown & Benchmark.

Baxter Magolda, M. (2001) *Making their own way: Narratives for transforming higher education to promote self-development*. Sterling, VA: Stylus.

Bernal, M. E., Knight, G. P., Ocampo, K. A., Garza, C. A., & Cota, M. K. (1993). Development of Mexican American identity. In M. E. Bernal & G. P. Knight (Eds.) *Ethnic identity: Formation and transmission among Hispanics and other minorities* (pp. 31–46). Albany: SUNY Press.

Charmaz, K. (2000). Grounded theory objectivist and constructivist methods. In N. K. Denzin & Y. S. Lincoln (Eds.) *Handbook of qualitative research* (2nd ed., pp. 509–536). Thousand Oaks, CA: Sage.

Chickering, A., & Reisser, L. (1993). *Education and identity*. San Francisco: Jossey-Bass.

Day, J. C. (1996). *Population projections of the United States by age, sex, race, and Hispanic origin: 1995 to 2050*. (Current Population Reports, P25–1130). Washington, DC: U.S. Bureau of the Census.

Ferdman, B. M., & Gallegos, P. I. (2001). Racial identity development and Latinos in the United States. In C. L. Wijeyesinghe & B. W. Jackson III (Eds.), *New perspectives on racial identity development: A theoretical and practical anthology* (pp. 32–66). New York: New York University Press.

Garza, R. T., & Gallegos, P. I. (1995). Environmental influences and personal choice: A humanistic perspective on acculturation. In A. M. Padilla (Ed.), *Hispanic psychology: Critical issues in theory and research* (pp. 3–14). Thousand Oaks, CA: Sage.

Glaser, B. G., & Strauss, A. L. (1999). *The discovery of grounded theory: Strategies for qualitative research.* New York: Aldine De Gruyter.

Keefe, S. E. & Padilla, A. M. (1987). *Chicano ethnicity.* Albuquerque: University of New Mexico Press.

Lincoln, Y. S. & Guba, E. G. (1985). *Naturalistic inquiry.* San Francisco: Jossey-Bass.

Perry, W. G. (1970). *Forms of intellectual and ethical development in the college years: A scheme.* Troy, MO: Holt, Rinehart & Winston.

Phinney, J. S. (1993). A three-stage model of ethnic identity development in adolescence. In M. E. Bernal & G. P. Knight (Eds.), *Ethnic identity: Formation and transmission among Hispanics and other minorities* (pp. 61–79). Albany: SUNY Press.

Phinney, J. S. (1995). Ethnic identity and self-esteem: A review and integration. In A. M. Padilla (Ed.), *Hispanic psychology: Critical issues in theory and research* (pp. 57–70). Thousand Oaks, CA: Sage.

Phinney, J. S., & Chavira, V. (1992). Ethnic identity and self-esteem: An exploratory longitudinal study. *Journal of Adolescence, 15,* 271–281.

Sanchez, J. I., & Fernandez, D. M. (1993). Acculturative stress among Hispanics: A bidimensional model of ethnic identification. *Journal of Applied Social Psychology, 23*(8), 654–688.

Szapocznik, J., & Kurtines, W. (1980). Acculturation, biculturalism and adjustment among Cuban Americans. In A. M. Padilla (Ed.), *Acculturation, theory, models, and some new findings* (pp. 139–159). Boulder, CO: Westview Press.

Schwandt, T. A. (1994). Constructivist, interpretivist approaches to human inquiry. In N. K. Denzin & Y. S. Lincoln (Eds.), *Handbook of qualitative research* (pp. 118–137). Thousand Oaks, CA: Sage.

Solis, E., Jr. (1995). Regression and path analysis models of Hispanic community college students' intent to persist. *Community College Review, 23*(3), pp. 3–15.

Stearns, C., Watanabe, S., & Snyder, T. D. (2002). *Hispanic serving institutions: Statistical trends from 1990 to 1999* (NCES Publication No. 2002-051). Washington, DC: U.S. Department of Education, National Center for Education Statistics.

Strauss, A. L., & Corbin, J. (1998). *Basics of qualitative research: Techniques and procedures for developing grounded theory* (2nd ed.). Thousand Oaks, CA: Sage.

Torres, V. (1999). Validation of the bicultural orientation model for Hispanic college students. *Journal of College Student Development, 40,* 285–298.

Torres, V., & Baxter Magolda, M. B. (2002). The evolving role of the researcher in constructivist longitudinal studies. *Journal of College Student Development, 43,* 474–489.

U.S. Census Bureau, U.S. Department of Commerce. (2001, April 2). *Census 2000* [Electronic version]. Retrieved from http://www.census.gov/population/cen2000/phc-t1/tab04.pdf

CHAPTER 24

HOW WE FIND OURSELVES: IDENTITY DEVELOPMENT AND TWO-SPIRIT PEOPLE

ALEX WILSON

Psychological theorists have typically treated sexual and racial identity as discrete and independent developmental pathways. While this simplifying division may make it easier to generate theory, it may also make it less likely that the resulting theory will describe peoples' real-life developmental experiences. In this article, Alex Wilson examines identity development from an Indigenous American perspective, grounded in the understanding that all aspects of identity (including sexuality, race, and gender) are interconnected. Many lesbian, gay, and bisexual Indigenous Americans use the term "two-spirit" to describe themselves. This term is drawn from a traditional worldview that affirms the inseparability of the experience of their sexuality from the experience of their culture and community. How can this self-awareness and revisioning of identity inform developmental theory? The author offers her personal story as a step toward reconstructing and strengthening our understanding of identity.

The interconnectedness of sexual identity and ethnicity contributes to the complex nature of the process of identity development. As educators, we must acknowledge that fact in the supports and services we offer to our students. Although the research on lesbian, gay, and bisexual Indigenous Americans is extensive, these inquiries are typically from an anthropological perspective.[1] Much of this research is based on the rereading and reinterpretation of early field notes, testimony, and biographical sketches, twice removed from Indigenous American experiences, and twice filtered through non-Indigenous eyes (C. McHale, personal communication, March 21, 1996). Anthropologists and historians such as Evelyn Blackwood (1984), Beatrice Medicine (1983), Harriet Whitehead (1981), Walter Williams (1986), and Will Roscoe (1988, 1991) have contributed to a body of work that describes and documents the construction of sexuality and gender in Indigenous American communities. Their work provides a critique of Western assumptions about sexuality and gender, but generally fails to recognize the existence of and to acknowledge the contributions of "two-spirit" Indigenous Americans today.[2] From my perspective as a two-spirit Swampy Cree woman, I will critically assess current theory in identity development through reflection on my life and identity development.[3] This reassessment has implications for developmental theorists, counselors, and educators who engage with two-spirit people.

I have chosen the terms "two-spirit" and "Indigenous American" carefully. Until recently, anthropologists claimed authority to name two-spirit people by labeling them the *berdache* (Blackwood, 1984; Jacobs & Cromwell, 1992; Jacobs & Thomas, 1994; Weston, 1993). *Berdache* described anthropological subjects who did not fit neatly into European American gender and sex role categories, meaning a category of (gendered and sexual) "other." The term was imported to North America by

Europeans who borrowed it from the Arabic language. Its use, to describe an "effeminate" (Blackwood, 1984, p. 27) or "morphological male who does not fill a society's standard man's role, who has a non-masculine character" (Williams, 1986, p. 2), spoke articulately about European assumptions about gender roles and sexuality (Weston, 1993). The metaphoric power of the term grew over time; the role of *berdache* acquired, at least within gay history and storytelling, considerable spiritual power. In Tom Spanbauer's (1991) revisionist story of the American West, his narrator explains:

> Berdache is what the Indian word for it is.... I don't know if berdache is a Bannock word or a Shoshone word or just Indian. Heard tell it was a French word but I don't know French so I'm not the one to say.
>
> What's important is that's the word Berdache. "B. E. R. D. A. C. H. E. means holy man who fucks with men." (Spanbauer, 1991, p. 5)

Because of the historical and spiritual connotations that had been vested in the term, some members of Indigenous American communities embraced it as their self-descriptor (Roscoe, 1988). More recently, in recognition of the poor fit of the term *berdache*, we have looked for language that more accurately describes our historic and present-day realities.

The growing acceptance of the term two-spirit as a self-descriptor among lesbian, gay, and bisexual Indigenous American peoples proclaims a sexuality deeply rooted in our own cultures (Brant, 1995; Fife, 1993). Two-spirit identity affirms the interrelatedness of all aspects of identity, including sexuality, gender, culture, community, and spirituality. That is, the sexuality of two-spirit people cannot be considered as separate from the rest of an individual's identity (Jacobs & Thomas, 1994). Two-spirit connects us to our past by offering a link that had previously been severed by government policies and actions.

Pueblo psychologist and educator Terry Tafoya (1990) states that there have been "direct attempts [by] the federal government to regulate, control, and destroy Native American behavior patterns. . . . There are more than 2,000 laws and regulations that only apply to American Indians and Alaskan Natives and not to other American Citizens" (p. 281). The religious freedom of Indigenous peoples in the United States was not legally supported until 1978 (Tafoya, 1990). The

Canadian federal government made a similar effort to separate Indigenous peoples from their cultural traditions (York, 1990). Two-spirit reconstitutes an identity that, although misstated by anthropologists, had been based on the recognition of people with alternative genders and/or sexualities as contributing members of traditional communities. In contemporary European American culture, sexuality is perceived as a discrete aspect of identity, constructed on the basis of sexual object choice (Almaguer, 1993; Whitehead, 1981). This conception stands in sharp contrast to two-spirit identity.

There are over five hundred Nations (tribes) in the United States and Canada. In spite of the vast physical distances between the autochthonous people of North America, few ideological barriers exist between these Nations (Sioui, 1992). Each of our traditional worldviews recognizes the deep interdependency between humans and nature, that our origin is in the soil of the land, and that we are bound to each other in an intimately spiritual way. This shared understanding of the world shapes the life experiences of North America's Indigenous peoples and, in turn, their identity development.

The existence and value of two-spirit people's difference is recognized in most Indigenous American cultures, oral histories, and traditions. In some cultures, two-spirit people were thought to be born "in balance," which may be understood as androgyny, a balance of masculine and feminine qualities, of male and female spirits. In many Indigenous American cultures, two-spirit people had (have) specific spiritual roles and responsibilities within their community. They are often seen as "bridge makers" between male and female, the spiritual and the material, between Indigenous American and non-Indigenous American. The term two-spirit encompasses the wide variety of social meanings that are attributed to sexuality and gender roles across Indigenous American cultures. Many gay historians, anthropologists, and other researchers have struggled with the "epistemological differences in Native American concepts of gender and sexual behaviors" (Tafoya, 1990, p. 287) and veered into dangerous generalizations about the specialness and spiritual power of two-spirit people. Today, academics argue over whether or not two-spirit people had a "special" role or were special people in Native societies. In my community, the act of declaring some people special threatens to separate them from their community and creates an imbalance. Traditionally, two-spirit people were simply a part of the entire community; as we reclaim our identity with this name, we are returning to our communities.

Since European contact with the Americas, many of these Indigenous American traditions have been misrepresented and misinterpreted. Within an imposed construct based on eighteenth-century European values, difference became deviance (D'Emilio & Freedman, 1988; Jacobs & Cromwell, 1992; Tafoya, 1990; Williams, 1986). It is difficult to understand the concept of two-spirit from these perspectives. Within the European American perspective, the male and female genders are the only two acknowledged. Transsexuals who surgically alter their bodies to become physically the "opposite" sex, individuals who choose to dress in clothing thought to be only appropriate for the "opposite" gender, or those who choose not to adhere to either of the dichotomous gender types are seen as abnormal and, therefore, as deviant.

Cartesian definitions of gender, which impose dual roles defining the respective "acceptable behaviors" for women and men, have procreation as their ultimate goal (Jacobs & Cromwell, 1992). These notions of gender categorization have been misapplied to Indigenous Americans. For European explorers, philosophers, and anthropologists, too many Indigenous American people did not fit into the two categories found in Cartesian theories.

The anthropologist Sue-Ellen Jacobs has reconstructed her own notions about gender and sexual identity. In her ethnographic observations of Tewa Pueblo people, she observed a number of gender categories reflecting an individual's "sexuality, sexual identity and sociocultural roles" (Jacobs & Cromwell, 1992, p. 48). This conception of gender reflects a fluid understanding of sexual identity that has persisted for many present-day Indigenous Americans who consider themselves bisexual, rather than strictly lesbian or gay (Tafoya, 1990).

Traditional teachings, however, have also been influenced by events that have altered the construction of sexual identity in contemporary Indigenous American communities. In an attempt to assimilate Indigenous Americans, government policy has been directly involved in the destruction of many aspects of Indigenous American life (Ross, 1992; York, 1990). For almost one hundred years it was illegal to practice traditional religion in both the United States (Delo-ria, 1969) and Canada (Cardinal, 1969; Miller, 1989). Generations of children were forcibly removed from their families and placed in residential schools, where they were punished for speaking their own language, for practicing their own religion, or for any other expressions of their "Indian-ness" (Berkhofer, 1978; Ing, 1991; York, 1990). In spite of these assaults on traditional values, they still shape the lives and communities of Indigenous American people. Today, most leaders in Indigenous communities express a commitment to traditional spirituality and an Indigenous worldview.

Indigenous Ethics

Our worldviews are shaped by our values, our ideologies, theories, and assumptions about the world. They circumscribe our encounters with the world, creating and re-creating our cultures and our epistemologies, pedagogies, psychologies, and experiences. How are Indigenous American worldviews constructed?

The Mohawk psychiatrist Clare Brant, in his work with Iroquois, Ojibway, and Swampy Cree people, has identified five ethics that, he believes, underpin these Indigenous peoples' worldview (1990). These cultural ethics and rules of behavior include: an Ethic of Non-Interference, an Ethic That Anger Not Be Shown, an Ethic Respecting Praise and Gratitude, the Conservation-Withdrawal Tactic, and the Notion That Time Must Be Right. As Brant himself points out, these Ethics cannot be assumed to describe all Indigenous American people. At the same time, these Ethics resonate deeply with me and describe the emotional substance of much of my own experiences in the Cree community. Although Indigenous American cultures have changed since first contact with Europeans, and continue to change, it is important to realize that these traditionally based Ethics exist in some form today and will persist in some form into the future. Brant's Ethics are further developed by Rupert Ross (1992) in his book *Dancing with a Ghost: Exploring Indian Reality*, which includes an important reminder:

> Until we realize that Native people have a highly developed, formal, but radically different set of cultural imperatives, we are likely to continue misinterpreting their acts, misperceiving the real problems they face, and imposing, through government policies, potentially harmful "remedies." (p. 42)

These Ethics shape our worldview and direct our behavior. The Ethic of Non-Interference refers to the expectation that Indigenous Americans should not interfere in any way with another person. This has shaped culturally distinctive child-rearing practices in Indigenous American communities. Generally, children are allowed to explore the world without the limitations of punishment and praise, or of privileges withheld and rewards promised by members of the community. Children are taught through the patient practice of modeling, by stories, and by example. There are unwritten rules against giving advice or telling someone what to do (Ross, 1992; B. Wilson, personal communication, ongoing).

The Ethic That Anger Not Be Shown is demonstrated by the absence of emphasis on or displays of emotions in speech and other forms of communication by Indigenous American people. Implicit in this ethic is a prohibition against showing grief and sorrow. Ross goes so far as to say that it is not acceptable even to *think* about one's own confusion and turmoil; in this way, one does not "burden" others with one's own personal emotional stress. The Ethic Respecting Praise and Gratitude may appear as a lack of affect to a non-Indigenous observer. Rather than vocally expressing gratitude to someone, a person might simply ask the other to continue their contribution, because voicing appreciation may be taken by an Indigenous American as creating an embarrassing scene. Because the idea of community is inherent in the Indigenous American philosophy and existence, an egalitarian notion of place within a society exists. To call attention to one person is to single them out and to imply that they have done better or are better in some way or at something than others are.

The Conservation-Withdrawal Tactic emphasizes the need to prepare mentally before choosing to act. Thinking things through before trying them or thinking thoughts through before voicing them is seen as a well-calculated preservation of physical and psychic energy. According to Ross (1992), the more unfamiliar the new context, the more pronounced a withdrawal into stillness, silence, and consideration may become. This concern that time should be taken to reflect on the possible outcomes of a particular action and to prepare emotionally and spiritually for a chosen course of action is reflected in the Notion That Time Must Be Right. Attention to the spiritual world gives a person the opportunity to examine her or his state of mind before initiating or participating in the task at hand (Ross, 1992).

Additionally, an important part of Indigenous American traditional spirituality is paying respect to our ancestors, to those who died tens of thousands of years ago as well as those who have just recently entered the spirit world. The land that we live on today is made up of our ancestors; the food that we eat (for the most part) is grown from the soil that our ancestors went back to when they died; and the animals and plants in our world have also grown out of and been nourished by this soil. We thank the spirits of animals, minerals, and plants, and turn to them for strength and continuity. This gratitude helps to maintain or regain the balance that is necessary to be a healthy and complete person. We understand that the spiritual, physical, emotional, and intellectual parts of ourselves are equally important and interrelated. When one aspect of a person is unhealthy, the entire person is affected. This too is true for the entire community; when one aspect of the community is missing, the entire community will suffer in some way.

Some Current Models of Sexual Identity and Development

Within the context of these basic principles, identity development can be examined. How do these ethics become incorporated into who we are or whom we identify as? What impact do they have on our responses to experiences? How do they shape our identities? For Indigenous American Nations now in contact with European American culture, racism and homophobia are inevitably present to some degree. Currently, the way some Indigenous Americans deal with homophobia and racism and the way that they construct their sexual and racial identity is framed by an Indigenous American spirituality and worldview.

This traditional Indigenous worldview can inform current theories of sexual and racial identity development for theorists and educators. I will examine three developmental theories, one of which addresses sexual identity, another racial identity, and a third sexual and/or racial identity. Sexual identity formation is typically presented in stage theory models. In her book *Psychotherapy with Lesbian Clients: Theory into*

Practice, psychologist Kristine Falco (1991) presents a review of theory on lesbian identity formation.[4] Finding many similarities in the five models she examines, Falco sketches a generalized model for the sexual identity development of lesbians by combining and summarizing others' models. In the first stage, a person is aware of being different and begins to wonder why. In the second phase, she begins to acknowledge her homosexual feelings and may tell others. Sexual experimentation marks the next stage, as the person explores relationships while seeking a supportive community. She then begins to learn to function in a same-sex relationship, establishing her place in the lesbian subculture while passing as heterosexual when needed. In the final stage, she integrates her private and social identities.

Racial identity development theory examines the psychological implications of membership in a racial group and the resultant ideologies. William Cross's Black Racial Identity Development model is often assumed to represent the racial identity formation experience of people of color in general (Tatum, 1992, 1993). Cross's model representing the racial identity formation experience of people of color in general doesn't hold for Indigenous Americans. In the Preencounter stage, which is described in the model as the initial point, an individual is unaware or denies that race plays any part in the definition of who they are. Thereafter, they move through a predictable series of stages: Encounter, after a sequence of events forces them to realize that racism does affect their life; Immersion/Emmersion, as they respond by immersing themselves in their culture, and reject with anger the values of the dominant culture; Internalization, as they develop security in their identity as a person of color; and Internalization/Commitment, when they have acquired a positive sense of racial identity (Cross, Parham, & Helms, 1991; Tatum, 1992, 1993).

Susan Barrett (1990) offers a developmental theory that attempts to encompass the experiences of all "others," including those of us who have been "othered" because of racial and sexual identity. This is the five-stage Minority Identity Development Model, which Barrett suggests can be applied to anyone who is not part of the dominant European American male heterosexual culture. In the Conformity stage, a person is ashamed of her membership in a minority culture, and accepts the devaluing judgments of the dominant culture. In the Dissonance stage, she wants to express her membership in a minority culture, but is still restricted by discomfort with it. She then moves into a Resistance and Immersion stage, as she becomes aware of the positive value of her membership in a minority culture and rejects the dominant culture. Following immersion in her minority culture, she enters an Introspective period, as she realizes that she cannot express herself fully within the constraints of an isolated minority identity. Finally, in the stage Barrett calls Synergetic Articulation and Awareness, she finds self-fulfillment when she integrates her minority identity into all aspects of her life.

Each of the above identity development models was constructed in an attempt to fill some gaps in developmental psychology. They attempt to recognize the diversity of human experience by describing the developmental sequences that occur in response to the experience and context of homophobia or racism. They do not, however, describe the effects of the *simultaneous* experience of homophobia and racism. These models assume an availability of supportive experiences that provide the means for an individual to progress from one stage to the next. Although each of these models is claimed to be nonlinear and nonhierarchic, each posits a final stage that represents a developmental peak of mental health. In this self-actualized stage, a person's sexual identity is no longer problematic and their bicultural adaptation (comfortably being the "other" within the dominant culture) has become a source of empowerment. Therefore, the underlying assumption is that a supportive bicultural experience is available to all "others." We (two-spirits) become self-actualized when we become what we've always been, Empowered by our location in our communities (versus the micro-management of an individuated identity).

Indigenous American Perspectives on Sexual and Racial Identity

Despite the reationship between sexual and racial identity development presented in European American models, for Indigenous American lesbian, gay, or bisexual people, the effect of racism and homophobia cannot be separated from each other or form the rest of their experiences. The emphasis of the Indigenous American worldview on the interconnectedness of all aspects of an individual's life challenges the compartmentalized structure of developmental stage models. As Pueblo psychologist and educator Terry Tafoya states, "[D]etermination of an individual's identity on the basis of sexual behavior makes no conceptual sense to many American Indians" (1989, p. 288). That is, any presentation of sexual and racial identity development as two distinct phenomena and any analysis proceeding from that assumption cannot adequately describe the experiences of Indigenous American people.

Furthermore, Indigenous Americans may respond to homophobia and racism in markedly different ways than people from other cultures. For example, if she respects the Ethic That Anger Not Be Shown, she may appear not to react to the "-isms" that affect her. If she uses the Conservation-Withdrawal Tactic or the Notion That Time Must Be Right in her response, the strength of her resistance might not be recognized. Also, the Ethic of Non-Interference would require her friends and family to respect and trust the choices she makes.

Two-Spirit Identity Formation

Because there is limited research and few case studies available on the developmental experiences of gay and lesbian Indigenous Americans, in the following section I will use my life experiences to illustrate both the impact of racism and homophobia (including sexism) on identity development, and the ill fit between current identity development theory and an Indigenous American reality.[5]

I grew up in northern Canada in a very small, isolated Cree community that could only be reached by boat in the summer or by plane in the winter. After I was born, as was the custom, elders came to visit, bringing gifts and blessing me as the newest member of their community. We returned to my father's home community, a reserve on the edge of a pulp mill town, before I was five. Some of my first memories of that town are of racism, although at the time I did not have a name for the meanness I experienced. I knew that unfair things were happening to me because I was an Indian, but I couldn't make the conceptual leap required to understand that racism meant, for example, that I was not allowed to play inside the homes of some of my White school friends. My family was

a place of strength and support, where we spoke, listened, and answered with respect. I was never made to feel wrong there. As I grew older, I dreamt of hockey and minibikes. I preferred to play with "boy's toys," so my parents sensibly brought me Hotwheels instead of Barbies. Later, I was allowed to hunt with a gun, and *moosum*, my grandfather, taught me and my brothers how to make snares to trap ermines and rabbits on the frozen creek behind our house. In my family, I was taught what I wanted to learn.

I remember dancing at a gathering when I was ten or eleven. Everyone was dancing around and around the reserve hall to the powwow music that was piped in over the bingo loudspeaker system. Back then the dance was an ordinary thing. Some people wore bits of regalia. Most of us, though, just wore jeans and sweatshirts. I was really enjoying myself, dancing the way that I wanted to. I was picking up my feet and even taking spinning steps at times. The old people were watching from the chairs on the side in encouraging silence, clapping their knees and smiling, inviting us to continue. Everything seemed so natural. I was learning new steps by watching what others were doing and learning the Cree songs in my head.

Then a friend danced up along side of me and told me to quit dancing like a boy. Confused, wondering how I could dance the wrong steps, I stopped. After that evening, I became self-conscious about the toys I wanted to play with. Knowing became not knowing, and the sureness of my experience was replaced by a growing certainty that I could not be the girl that was wanted outside of my family. Being "different" was no longer a gift, and my self-consciousness led me to learn ways to pretend and ways to hide myself. I would play sports with my younger brothers and their friends but was wary around kids my own age. When I was fourteen, I was given the hockey skates I wanted, but when we had skating at school, rather than showing up in "boy's skates, I pretended that I didn't have any. By that age, I understood that sexist judgments directed at me had a homophobic subtext, but I did not grasp the extent of their effect on me. I sat alone on the sideline benches that winter.

As I grew older, racism continued to erode my self-confidence and pride. Eventually I refused to identify as Cree, acknowledging only my Scottish heritage, although everyone in our small community knew my family. When I was in town I would avoid my relatives. I would even pass right by *moosum* without saying hi, acknowledging him only out of the corner of my eye. He knew what was going on: I was embarrassed to be related to him. At the same time as I struggled with my Cree identity, I was beginning to realize that I was a lesbian. The combination of racism and homophobia, much of it internalized, was very devastating for me; I didn't finish high school. I moved to the nearest city, in part to get away from the racism of the small town that surrounded our community, and in part to explore my new-found sexuality in a more anonymous way. I was looking for the idealized gay world that I had caught sight of in movies, in books, and on television. Somehow, I had lost my place in my own community as a result of the move, combined with how I felt.

In the city, I began a pre-medical study program at a university by enrolling as a mature student.[6] There were twelve Indigenous students in the program; six of us were two-spirit. However, we did not acknowledge it, and it was only when most of us had quit university that we realized we had experienced the same struggles at the same time. The "coming out" process was not easy for any of us. For example, as an Indigenous woman, I could not find a positive place for myself in the predominantly White, gay scence. I looked there for support in my lesbian identity, and instead found another articulation of racism. Although a large number of gay and lesbian Indigenous people live in the city, the Indigenous community remains segregated from the mainstream, non-Indigenous gay and lesbian community.

Immersion in the White, gay party scene became a way to numb a growing depression. I remember the excitement of getting ready to go out for the evening. I studied the culture: the way people danced, dressed, talked, moved, and even the way everyone greeted each other with a hug. This was all new to me, and I dove into that culture with anthropological zeal, hoping to uncover the secrets of it strangeness. I cut my hair, as though proclaiming a new identity was enough to make me belong in the lesbian and gay community. I know that, in Cree tradition, we cut our hair when we are in mourning. When someone we are related to or someone we love dies, a part of ourselves dies. It is a personal ceremony. The hair, usually a braid, is buried in a quiet safe place where no people or animals can step on it or disturb it. There I was with a flat-top, shaved on the sides and short, spiky, and flat on the top. My hair was everywhere on the floor of the flashy salon of a new-found friend. People were stepping on it, walking through it, and eventually it just ended up in the garbage along with everyone else's. A connection with my community was buried in that garbage can.

The support of my family, culture, and spiritual traditions helped me through this period. When I "came out" to my parents, they were not shocked by my confession and told me that they already knew. This puzzled me. How could they know and I didn't? I understand now that they respected me enough not to interfere, and enough to be confident that I would come to understand my sexuality when the time was right. Throughout my life, my family had acknowledged and accepted me without interference: my grandfather gave me hunting lessons and my parents brought me the toys that I would enjoy. As I was told by another child that I danced the "wrong" dance, the elders of my community smiled and clapped, quietly inviting me to continue. My development has obviously been shaped by a traditional Indigenous worldview.

I came to be empowered by who I was, rather than disempowered by who I wasn't. In the context of Native spirituality, I learned about the traditions of two-spirit people. I acquired strength from elders and leaders who were able to explain that as an Indigenous woman who is also a lesbian, I needed to use the gifts of my difference wisely.

Even my "maladaptive" responses to homophobia and racism can be understood as at least in part shaped by traditional values. The Conservation-Withdrawal Tactic and the Ethic That Anger Not Be Shown are both resistive responses that can easily be misread as passive acceptance. In Cree culture, "Silence" does not equal "Death," and to "Act Up" should not lead us to remove ourselves from our community. If it does, we seem most often to quietly find our way back home.[7] When confronted with racism and homophobia, I had internalized many of the devaluing judgments of the dominant culture. As I struggled with my racial and sexual identity, I had looked for affirmation by immersing myself in the minority cultures to which I belonged. Most significant, though, is the fact that when I sought support in the mainstream lesbian and gay community, it simply was not there.

This struggle is very typical of the "coming out" experiences of Indigenous people. As I reflect on the lives of my Indigenous friends, I realize that those of us who are happy have achieved our presence within the Indigenous American community. Two-spirit identity is rarely recognized in the mainstream lesbian and gay community unless it is accompanied by romantic notions that linger from the concept of the *berdache*. We are either Spanbauer's "holy man who fucks" or "just a fuckin' Indian."[8]

What this means, then, is that the positive bicultural adaptation that sexual and racial identity development models prize is simply not available to most of us. Although elements of my life could be neatly arranged into these identify models, this partial fit does not mean that a model expresses a life story, or even a simple developmental sequence.

It is possible for psychological theory to illuminate our understanding of the identity development of two-spirit people. Unlike the three theories discussed earlier, Robinson and Ward's (1991) work with African American adolescent girls uncovered an important distinction between strategies for survival and strategies for liberation. While survival strategies move the girls further from their true selves, liberation strategies strengthen their voices because they are "alternative avenues to personal empowerment and positive change" (p. 96). Robinson and Ward place the girls' experiences within a worldview that emphasizes an identity that is strengthened by a sense of interconnectedness with others.

This extended sense of self that Robinson and Ward offer is similar to an Indigenous worldview and includes a sort of timelessness, one that includes not only those of us here now, but also those who have come before us and those who will follow. Within this worldview, the girls' strategies are forms of resistance. Within Robinson and Ward's construct, the choices I made throughout my adolescence and early adulthood could be seen as short-term survival strategies. For two-spirit people, this can emerge from a commitment to community and collective experience, to creative and courageous action, and to an intimately spiritual worldview. This is how I have negotiated my own identity in the distance that stretches between the values of my culture and the values of Western culture.

Gloria Anzaldua (1990), in the introduction to her collection of writing by women of color, calls such survival stretegies "making face," the way that we must become "like a chameleon, to change color when the dangers are many and the options few" (p. xv). Quick fixes, like wishing away my skates, dropping out of school, and walking past *moosum*, were strategies that pushed me away from my sense of self and my sense of community. Did racism force me out of my home town, or did I choose to distance myself from my community? When confronted with racism and homophobia, I internalized many of the devaluing judgments of the dominant culture. Leaving my home community was an attempt to leave behind my devalued status, to become "raceless." However, it removed me from the strength and support I found in my community. I was even more of an "other" in the city than I was at home, even farther from a place where my self could be found.

Returning Practice to Theory

Last summer, I was part of a gathering of two-spirit people. When I first arrived, I was cautious. Everyone seemed cautious, as though we were all unsure of how we should act. On the wall of the main cabin a sign was posted; it said, "pow-wow, Saturday night." When I read it, I felt dizzy, overwhelmed by my imagining what the dance might be. Two-spirit people dancing. I have lived with dreams of dancing, dreams where I spin around, picking up my feet. I have many feathers on my arms and my body and I know all the steps. I turn into an eagle. Arms extended, I lift off the ground and begin to fly around in big circles. Would this be my chance?

For the rest of the week I listened for tidbits about the pow-wow. I learned that a local drum group would be singing. I heard about a woman who was collecting her regalia—"Her regalia . . ." —and wondered, did that mean men's? I waited patiently for Saturday night to come. Listening.

When the drumming started, I was sitting still, listening and watching. The first people to dance were women. They had their shawls with them. Next, some men came in; they were from different Nations, but still danced in distinctively male styles. I watched with disappointment in my heart but said to myself that I would still enjoy the pow-wow. And then a blur flew by me and landed inside the circle of dancers that had formed. It was a man in a jingle dress. He was beautiful and he knew how to dance and he danced as a woman. It was a two-spirit dancing as it should be. After that, more two-spirits drifted into the circle. I sat and watched, my eyes edged with tears. I knew my ancestors were with me; I had invited them. We sat and watched all right, proud of our sisters and brothers, yet jealous of their bravery. The time for the last song came. Everybody had to dance. I entered the circle, feeling the drumbeat in my heart. The songs came back to me. I circled the dance area, in my most humble moment, with the permission of my ancestors, my eleven-year-old two-spirit steps returned to me.

The aspect of my own experience (and that of my two-spirit friends) that current sexual and racial identity development models cannot encompass is that my strength and identity, along with the strength and identity of my peers, is inseparable from our culture. Educators and school counselors need to acknowledge that this is the reality for our community. This means that we need to stop assuming that all lesbian and gay people can find support in mainstream gay culture, and that we make a point of creating opportunities for two-spirit Indigenous people to find their place in their traditional communities. There has been little research done on the developmental experiences of Indigenous American people, and there is almost no research on the experiences of two-spirit people, despite grim statistics that reveal the urgency of addressing the needs of these groups. Gay and lesbian youth are two to six times more likely to attempt suicide than heterosexual teens (Kroll & Warneke, 1995), and Indigenous Canadians have the highest suicide rate of any racial group in the world (York, 1990).

Whenever possible, we need to ensure that two-spirit youth have access to the history and unwritten knowledge of their community, and that it is available to them in a culturally congruous way. Educators can also easily access written texts by important Indigenous American leaders, such as Beatrice Medicine (1983), Terry Tafoya (1989, 1990), Chrystos (1988, 1991, 1993), Connie Fife (1992, 1993), and Beth Brant (1985, 1988, 1991, 1993, 1995). These authors ground their work in their identities as Indigenous Americans, and they offer insight into the historic and present-day realities of two-spirit people. Tafoya's work as a psychologist and educator has made invaluable contributions to an effective approach to AIDS education for Indigenous American people. Two-spirit writers such as Chrystos, Connie Fife, and Beth Brant provide stories and narrative texts that record the contemporary life of two-spirit people. Their body of work is a rich resource for identity development theorists, and an invaluable affirmation for two-spirit youth.

Educators and developmental theorists need to study the resistance, strength, and liberation strategies two-spirit people employ as part of their development of an empowered identity. By examining the meaning of these strategies relative to an Indigenous American worldview, educators and theorists can increase their awareness in a way that will inevitably have a spill-over effect. They will learn to look beyond the limits inscribed by mainstream lesbian and gay culture and into the lives of the women, men, and children who are lesbian, gay, and two-spirit. We, whether educators, Indigenous Americans, or two-spirit people, must abandon the assumptions of a European American worldview in order to understand the identity development of two-spirit Native American and Canadian First Nations people, and to develop our theory and practice from within that understanding.

Notes

1 The term "Indigenous American" in this article refers to Canadian First Nations and Native American peoples. I acknowledge that, in a sense, this term presents our diverse cultures and communities as monolithic. However, my use of the term here is an appeal to the commonality of our origins and colonial/post-colonial experiences.

2 The term "two-spirit" will be used in this article to describe lesbian, gay, and bisexual Indigenous Americans.

3 The Cree Nation spreads in a wide swath across central Canada, from Quebec in the East, west through Ontario and Manitoba along the James and Hudson Bays, across Saskatchewan to the plains of Alberta, and South from there into northern Montana. Most of these communities are located in remote areas. I am from the Opaskwayak Cree Nation, located five hundred miles north of the border between the United States and Canada. The Cree Nations form one of the largest groups of Indigenous people in North America. There are over twenty-three Cree dialects.

4 I choose Falco because lesbian identity formation theory is the most appropriate focus for the use of my own narrative as a critique of contemporary developmental theory. Theorists who describe the developmental stages of gay men's sexual identity use similarly structured models (e.g., Coleman, 1982).

5 Sexism, when directed at children, is often a homophobic attempt to regulate or direct the development of their sexual identities.

6 "Mature student" is a category similar to "non-traditional," referring to students who have been out of high school for a few years before entering university.

7 In last year's "Indian Days" celebration at a reserve neighboring my own, the community celebration included a drag show by two-spirit people in traditional clothing.

8 These words were hurled at me by a lesbian who had been, I thought, one of my closest friends for ten years.

References

Almaguer, T. (1993). Chicano men: A cartography of homosexual identity and behavior. In H. Abelove, M. Barale, & O. Halperin (Eds.), *The lesbian and gay studies reader* (pp. 225–273). New York: Routledge.

Anzaldua, G. (1990). *Haciendo caras, una entrada, Making face, making soul.* San Francisco: Aunt Lute.

Barrett, S. E. (1990). Paths toward diversity: An intrapsychic perspective. In L. S. Brown & M. P. P. Root (Eds.), *Diversity and complexity in feminist therapy* (pp. 41–52). New York: Harrington Park Press.

Berkhofer, R. F. Jr. (1978). *The White man's Indian.* New York: Vintage Books.

Blackwood, E. (1984). Sexuality and gender in certain Native American tribes: The case of cross-gender females. *Signs: Journal of Women in Culture and Society, 10,* 27–42.

Brant, B. (1985). *Mohawk trail.* Ithaca, NY: Firebrand Books.

Brant, B. (Ed.) (1988). *A gathering of spirit: A collection by North American Indian Women.* Ithaca, NY: Firebrand Books.

Brant, B. (1991). *Food and spirits.* Ithaca, NY: Firebrand Books.

Brant, B. (1993, Summer). Giveaway: Native lesbian writers. *Signs: Journal of Women in Culture and Society, 18,* 944–947.

Brant, B. (1995). Lesbian writers. *Aboriginal Voices, 2*(4), 42–42.

Brant, C. (1990). Native ethics and rules of behavior. *Canadian Journal of Psychiatry, 35,* 534–539.

Cardinal, H. (1969). *The unjust society: The tragedy of Canada's Indians.* Edmonton: M. G. Hurtig.

Chrystos. (1988). *Not vanishing.* Vancouver: Press Gang.

Chrystos. (1991) *Dream on.* Vancouver: Press Gang.

Chrystos. (1993). *In her I am.* Vancouver: Press Gang.

Coleman, E. (1982). Developmental stages of the coming-out process. In W. Paul, J. Weinrich, J. Gonsiorels, & M. Hotvedt (Eds.), *Homosexuality: Social, psychological, and biological issues* (pp. 149–158). Beverly Hills: Sage.

Cross, W. E., Parham, T., & Helms, J. (1991). The stages of Black identity development: Nigrescence models. In R. Jones (Ed.), *Black psychology* (pp. 319–338). Berkeley: Cobb & Henry.

Deloria, V. Jr. (1969). *Custer died for your sins: An Indian manifesto.* Norman: University of Oklahoma Press.

D'Emilio, J., & Freedman, E. B. (1988). *Intimate matters: The history of sexuality in America.* New York: Vintage Press.

Falco, K. (1991). *Psychotherapy with lesbian clients: Theory into practice.* New York: Brunner/Mazel.

Fife, C. (1992). *Beneath the naked sun.* Toronto: Sister Vision Press.

Fife, C. (Ed.) (1993). *The colour of resistance.* Toronto: Sister Vision Press.

Ing, N. R. (1991). The effects of residential schooling on Native child rearing practices. *Canadian Journal of Native Education, 18*(Supplement), 65–118.

Jacobs, S., & Cromwell, J. (1992). Visions and revisions of reality: Reflections on sex, sexuality, gender, and gender variance. *Journal of Homosexuality, 23,* 43–69.

Jacobs, S., & Thomas, W. (1994, November 8), Native-American two-spirits. *Anthropology Newsletter, 7.* Arlington, VA: American Anthropological Association.

Kroll, I., & Warneke, L. (1995, June). *The dynamics of sexual orientation and adolescent suicide: A comprehensive review and developmental perspective.* Calgary, Canada: University of Calgary.

Medicine, B. (1983). "Warrior women": Sex role alternatives for Plains Indian women. In P. Albers & B. Medicine (Eds.), *The hidden half: Studies of Plains Indian women* (pp. 267–280). Lanham, MD: University Press of America.

Miller, J. R. (1989). *Skyscrapers hide the heavens: A history of Indian-White relations in Canada.* Toronto: University of Toronto Press.

Robinson, T., & Ward, J. V. (1991). "A belief in self far greater than anyone's disbelief": Cultivating resistance among African American female adolescents. In C. Gilligan, A. Rogers, & D. Tolman (Eds.), *Women, girls and psychotherapy: Reframing resistance* (pp. 87–103). New York: Harrington Park Press.

Roscoe, W. (Ed.). (1988). *Living the spirit: A gay American Indian anthology.* New York: St. Martin's Press.

Roscoe, W. (1991). *The Zuni man-woman.* Albuquerque: University of New Mexico Press.

Ross, R. (1992). *Dancing with a ghost: Exploring Indian reality.* Markham, Ontario: Octopus.

Sioui, G. (1992). *For an Amerindian autohistory: An essay on the foundations of a social ethic*. Buffalo, NY: McGill-Queen's University Press.

Spanbauer, T. (1991). *The man who fell in love with the moon*. New York: Harper Perennial.

Tafoya, T. (1989). Dancing with Dash-Kayah. In D. M. Dooling & P. Jordan-Smith (Eds.), *I become part of it: Sacred dimensions in Native American life* (pp. 92–100). New York: Parabola Books.

Tafoya, T. (1990). Pulling coyote's tail: Native American sexuality and AIDS. In V. Mays (Ed.), *Primary prevention issues in AIDS* (pp. 280–289) Washington, DC: American Psychological Association.

Tatum, B. (1992). Talking about race, learning about racism: The application of racial identity development theory in the classroom. *Harvard Educational Review, 62*, 1–24.

Tatum, B. (1993). *Racial identity development and relational theory: The case of Black women in White communities* (Work in Progress Series). Wellesley, MA: Stone Center for Research on Women.

Weston, K. (1993). Lesbian/gay studies in the house of anthropology. *Annual Review of Anthropology, 22*, 339–367.

Whitehead, H. (1981). The bow and the burden strap: A new look at institutionalized homosexuality in Native North America. In S. B. Ortner & H. Whitehead (Eds.), *Sexual meanings* (pp. 80–115). Cambridge, Eng.: Cambridge University Press.

Williams, W. L. (1986). *The spirit and the flesh: Sexual diversity in American Indian culture*. Boston: Beacon Press.

York, J. (1990). *The dispossessed: Life and death in Native Canada*. Boston: Little, Brown.

Section 6

DYNAMICS OF GENDER
IN DEVELOPMENT

CHAPTER 25

THE RELATIONAL SELF:
A NEW PERSPECTIVE FOR UNDERSTANDING
WOMEN'S DEVELOPMENT

JUDITH V. JORDAN

In traditional Western psychological theories of development, the "self" has long been viewed as the primary reality and unit of study. Typically, the self has been as separated out from its context, a bounded, contained entity that has both object and subject qualities. Clinical and developmental theories generally have emphasized the growth of an autonomous, individuated self. Increasing self-control, a sense of self as origin of action and intention, an increasing capacity to use abstract logic, and a movement toward self-sufficiency characterize the maturation of the ideal Western self. Although most theorist have struggled with the issue of reification of the self, all have to some degree succumbed to the powerful pull to de-contextualize, abstract, and spatialize this concept. I will examine some of these models in terms of their limited applicability to the psychology of women and suggest an alternative conceptualization of self, a "rational self" or, as Jean Miller has suggested, a model of "being in relation" (Miller, 1984).

Established Theory

Several biases have prominently shaped clinical-developmental theory about the self. Psychology as a discipline emulated Newtonian physics, seeking thus to be recognized as a bona fide "hard" science rather than as an arm of philosophy, theology, or other humanistic traditions. Newtonian physics posited discrete, separate entities existing in space and acting on each other in predictable and measurable ways. This easily led to a study of the self as a comparably bounded and contained "molecular" entity, a notion most visibly supported by the existence of separate body-identities. It became very seductive to equate self with embodied person. As Helen Lynd notes:

> This assumption that understanding proceeds by means of first seeking the discrete, supposedly unchanging elements into which a phenomenon under study can be analyzed and only later turning attention to the changes going on in the elements and to the relations among them is still very much with us. (Lynd, 1958, p. 67)

> The separation having been initially assumed, the problems of relation and integration are posed. (Lynd, 1958, p. 81)

A further influence on theory building about the self was provided by the social-political context in Western, democratic societies, where the sanctity and freedom of the individual greatly overshadowed the compelling reality of the communal and deeply interdependent nature of human beings. In this societal paradigm, as represented particularly in the American culture, there is an imperative in socializing children to wean the "helpless" and "dependent" infant toward greater self-sufficiency and independence; so engrained is this bias that it is hard for most of us to appreciate that other cultures may in fact perceive the infant as born independent and needing acculturation toward dependency!

Major support for the "separate self" model came from Freudian theory. While Freud did not explicitly theorize about the self, his original "das Ich," later translated as "ego," had much in common with the subject "I" aspect of self delineated by James (1890/1968). Certainly, many of his ideas have been influential in subsequent concepts of the self. Specifically, his understanding of the psyche grew from a view of pathology in which the ego was seen as coming into being to protect the person from assaults both by internal impulses and external demands. Its relational function was obscured. Freud commented that, "Protection against stimuli is an almost more important function for the living organism than reception of stimuli" (Freud, 1920/1955, p. 27). Derivative psychoanalytic theories view the individual as growing from an undifferentiated, then embedded and symbiotic phase into an ultimately separate, individuated state (Mahler, Pine, & Bergman, 1975). Until quite recently in psychoanalytic theories, healthier, more mature modes of functioning were predicated on greater separation of self and other.

Furthermore, Freudian theory stressed the power of innate instinctual forces and the development of increasing internal structure and freedom from dependence on others for gratification of needs. Relationships were seen as secondary to or deriving from the satisfaction of primary drives (e.g. hunger or sex). Intrapsychic development was seen as the ultimate area of interest; and "self development" (or ego development) was seen as a process internalization of resources from caretakers and others to create an increasingly unique, separate, self-sufficient structure: the self. Connotations of control, ownership of action, and mastery over both impulses and outer reality abound in this model.

Pivotal to this individualistic picture of human beings is the pleasure principle (Freud, 1920/1955; Jordan, 1987) Attainment of satisfaction, motivated by desire or need, is framed as the primary goal of behavior and therefore shapes the self. In this tradition (both psychoanalytic and behaviorist) "the self" is the personal history of gratifications and frustrations of desire and the projection of these into the future in the form of intention (Jordan, 1987).

Although disagreements with Freudian theory occurred as quickly as the theory was put forth, the dissenters never gained a hold on the cultural vision of "Man" or on the imagination of clinical practitioners in the way that Freud's original ideas did. Sullivan (1953), in this country, took a major step away from the instinct–drive model, as did Horney (1926/1967) and Thompson (1941). In addition, Sullivan placed the development of the self directly within the interpersonal realm: "A personality can never be isolated from the complex of interpersonal relations in which the person lives and has his being" (1953, p. 10). While this was an enormous contribution and gave impetus to the movement away from construction of the self as separate being, the basic inactivity of the self and the unidirectional quality of development survived in his model. The self was seen as being constructed of "reflected appraisals" (1953).

Erikson's ego identity (1963), comparable in many ways to what others call a sense of self, is importantly constructed as an outcome of a psychosocial line of development; this represents a definite and important move beyond the earlier Freudian psychosexual model. But in Erikson's schema, identity is early predicated on establishment of autonomy. Intimacy is established later, only after identity is consolidated. As such, the basic relationality of development is lost in much of this model.

The object relations theorists in Britain advanced our understanding of the centrality of relationships in human development. But they, unfortunately, were unable to free themselves of many of the core premises of Freudian psychology and continued to view the other person as "object" to the subject; that is, defined by drive factors in the subject. The language and naming of this theory perpetuate the biological approach these theorists struggled against. The bias of an instinctually driven and basically selfish and aggressive being is also carried forward in this theory. Melanie Klein (1953) thus traces the development of a capacity for love to the infant's wish to make reparations to the mother for harm inflicted.

Fairbairn (1946/1952) and Guntrip (1973) distance themselves most clearly from the Freudian model of the developing organism. Fairbairn stated, "It is impossible to gain any adequate conception of the nature of an individual organism if it is considered apart from its relationship to its natural objects, for it is only in its relationship to these objects that its true nature is displayed " (1946/1952, p. 39)

Most recently in the clinical realm, Kohut (1984) has emphasized the ongoing need for relationships throughout life. His concept of the "selfobject" pertains to the importance of others in shaping our self image and maintaining self esteem. But this theory, too, is built on a model of drives, with others used as objects to perform some function for a self that still remains intrinsically and ideally separate, if at best empathically connected.

In a study both psychoanalytic and developmental, Daniel Stern has creatively delineated modes of "being with the other." Early patterns of differentiation and relatedness, in which mother and infant participate in a mutually regulated relationship, are traced in his work (Stern, 1986). Trevarthan (1979) has pointed to a "primary intersubjectivity" in human development, which is innate and unfolding. Earlier, George Klein posited the existence of "we" identities in the development of a concept of self, an "aspect of one's self construed as a necessary part of a unit transcending one's autonomous actions." (G. Klein, 1976, p. 178).

A contextual-relation view of self also has much in common with the earlier work of the symbolic interactionists (Baldwin, 1897/1968; Cooley, 1902/1968; Mead 1925/1968), typified by Mead's idea that "selves exist only in relation to other selves" (Mead, 1925/1968). Cooley addressed the relation of the self to context in noting: "It [the self] might also, and perhaps more justly, be compared to the nucleus of a living cell, not altogether separate from the surrounding matter, out of which indeed it is formed, but more active and definitely organized" (Cooley, 1902/1968, p. 89). A relational model also resembles the existential approach in which the "being-with-others" (*Mitsein*) is stressed as fully as the concrete existence (*Dasein*) (Tiryakian, 1968).

The change in emphasis involved in a relational point of view is comparable to what other theorists have described as a movement to dialectical schemata. Basseches (1980), writing about dialectical thinking, captures the quality of the shift in perspective:

> Conceptualizing entities as forms of existence rather than as elements of existence emphasizes the sense of coherence, organization, and wholeness implicit in the notion of form

over against the sense of separateness implicit in the notion of elements. Secondly since these entities are viewed as temporary rather than immutable, the entities themselves are deemphasized relative to that process of existence as a whole, which is viewed as characterized by continual differentation and integration. (Basseches, 1980, p. 404)

Existence ceases to be seen as being "composed of independent monads" (Basseches, 1980).

Piaget's (1952) model of adaptation, with accommodation and assimilation in an ever shifting process of equilibration, is helpful in conceptualizing the changing, active, ongoing, and interactive quality of a relational model of development.

Relational Being

In the past decade, an important impetus for shifting to a different paradigm of "the self" in developmental-clinical theory has come from feminist psychologists who have been increasingly vocal and articulate about their dissatisfaction with existing models of female development and the "female self." Although not always explicitly stated, the adequacy of old models for describing male development is also questioned.

> Feminist thought [has been described as] different in every respect: as a practical, particular, contexted, open, and nonsystematic knowledge of the social circumstances in which one has one's being, concerned with achieving a heterachy of times and places for a plurality of otherwise conflicting voices (Shotter & Logan, 1988, pp. 75–76)

Miller (1976), Chodorow (1978), and Gilligan (1982) are the most notable of the new wave of women challenging existing conceptualizations of women's development and personal organization. All note the male (phallocentric) bias in clinical-developmental theory.

Miller's works takes a broad psychological-cultural approach to the problem; she explicitly notes, "As we have inherited it, the notion of 'a self' does not appear to fit women's experience" (Miller, 1984, p. 1). More recently, she has been drawing on clinical work to broaden and deepen her alternative perspective of "being in relation."

Gilligan's ideas about the nature of female development derived from her awareness that prevailing theories of moral development (Kohlberg, 1984) were not applicable to women but were being used in such a way that women consistently appeared as defective or deficient moral selves. As Gilligan notes: "The disparity between women's experience and the representation of human development, noted throughout the psychological literature, has generally been seen to signify a problem in women's development. Instead, the failure of women to fit existing models of human growth may point to a problem in the representation, a limitation in the conception of human condition, an omission of certain truths about life" (Gilligan, 1982, pp. 1–2). An important truth being omitted was the power of the ethic of caretaking and relationship in women's lives.

Chodorow (1978) re-examined object relations theory and found that traditional theory failed to acknowledge the importance of the early and longer lasting bond between the girl and her mother. This bond leads to a different experience of boundaries and identity than what the boy, as objectified other, experiences with mother.

What all of these theorist allude to, and seek to begin to correct, in psychological theory reflects an old tradition, captured in Aristotle's statement that: "The female is a female by virtue of a certain lack of qualities; we should regard the female nature as afflicted with a natural defectiveness" (Sanday, 1988, p. 58). When men are studied, when men do the studying, and when male values hold sway in the culture, one cannot expect any other outcome; the "other" will always be defined in the terms of the subject, and differences will be interpreted as deficiencies, especially in a hierarchical system. (Broverman, Broverman, Clarkson, Rosenkrantz, & Vogel, 1970). Very specifically, all of these theorists note the failure of previous theories of "human development" to appreciate the relational nature of women's sense of themselves. Miller (1976) and Gilligan (1982) also explicitly or implicitly posit a more contextual, relational paradigm for the study of all self experience.

One perspective of the "interacting sense of self," sometimes called "self-in-relation" (Jordan & Surrey, 1986; Surrey, 1985), "relational-self" (Jordan, 1985), or "being in relation" (Miller, 1984), is currently being developed by Miller (1984), Jordan (1984, 1985, 1987), Kaplan (1984), Stiver (1984), and Surrey (1985) at the Stone Center at Wellesley College. New relational theory of self, perhaps like the "new physics" of quantum theory and uncertainty, emphasizes the contextual, approximate, responsive and process factors in experience. In short, it emphasizes relationship and connection. Rather than a primary perspective based on the formed and contained self, this model stresses the importance of the intersubjective, a relationally emergent nature of human experience. While there is still a "felt sense of self," which is acknowledged by this point of view, it is a "self inseparable from a dynamic interaction" (Miller, 1984, p. 4), an "interacting sense of self", (Miller, 1984). From this intersubjective perspective, the movement of relating, of mutual initiative and responsiveness, are the ongoing central organizing dynamics in women's (but probably all people's) lives (Jordan, 1989). This goes beyond saying that women value relationships; we are suggesting that the deepest sense of one's being is continuously formed in connection with others and is inextricably tied to relational movement. This primary feature, rather than structure marked by separateness and autonomy, is increasing empathic responsiveness in the context of interpersonal mutuality.

Empathy, the dynamic cognitive-affective process of joining with and understanding another's subjective experience, is central to this perspective (Jordan, 1984). Mutual empathy, characterized by the flow of empathic attunement between people, alters the traditional boundaries between subject and object and experientially alters the sense of separate self in a profound way. In true empathic exchange, each is both object and subject, mutually engaged in affecting and being affected, knowing and being known. In interpersonal language, in a mutually empathic relationship, each individual allows and assists the other in coming more fully into clarity, reality, and relatedness; each shapes the other (Jordan, 1987)

Thus, in mutual empathic understanding, the inner conviction of the "separate self" is challenged. Description of the empathic process refer to the "sharing in and comprehending the momentary psychological state of another person" (Schafer, 1959, 345) or "trial identification" (Fliess, 1942), which occur during empathy. The boundaries as well as functional differences between subject and object, knower and known, cognitive and affective are altered in the process of empathy. As two people join in empathic subjectivity, the distinctions between "subject" and "object" blur; knower and known connect and join in mutual empathy. The other's subjective experience becomes as one's own; this is at the heart of "relational being." Action, creativity, and intentionality occur within this context.

Empirical work on empathy demonstrates that in addition to cognitive awareness of another's inner subjective state, in empathic attunement people resonate emotionally and physically with the other's experience (this mirroring physiological arousal is sometimes called vicarious affective arousal). Women typically demonstrate more emotional-physical resonance with others' affective arousal than do men (Hoffman, 1977). Also of note, is that 1- to 2-day-old infants demonstrate distress cries to other infants' wails of distress; sex differences exist at that time as well, with girls showing more resonant distress. (Sagi & Hoffman, 1976; Simmer, 1971), The sex differences at this age are not easily explained, and the greater import of this study is to suggest that intrinsic empathic responsiveness exists in all human beings. This is a simple, yet dramatic example of the deep interconnectedness between people that "separate self" theory overlooks. Not just at the level of goals, values, and beliefs do women experience a sense of connected self but at the very concrete and compelling level of feelings and body experience. The study of the development of empathy, then, may provide a route to the delineation of relational development and intersubjective processes, slighted for so long in Western psychology.

The Question of Boundaries

In moving from a theory of separate self to a perspective of relational being, the question of how we experience and depict boundaries becomes very important. Our metaphors for "being" are heavily spatialized. Thus, the self typically is portrayed as existing in space, characterized by the "possession" of various unique attributes (a particular organization of physical, cognitive, psychological, and spiritual attributes), demarcated or bounded in some way (typified either by "open boundaries" or closed boundaries") and interacting from a place of separation or containment with "the world out there." This is a profoundly de-contextualized self. The emphasis on boundary functions as protecting and defining, rather than as meeting or communicating, reinforces especially the self as "separate"

entity rather than "being" as a contextual, interactional process.

The way one conceptualizes one's "place" in the world broadly affects interpretive, meaning-making, value-generating activity. The nature of relatedness, the nature of the boundary concept shapes the openness to new experience and the quality of revelations about inner experience that occur between people. If "self" is conceived of as separate, alone, "in control," personally achieving and mastering nature, others may tend to be perceived as potential competitors, dangerous intruders, or objects to be used for the self's enhancement. A system that defines the self as separate and hierarchically measurable is usually marked in Western cultures by power-based dominance patterns. In such systems, the self-boundary serves as protection from the impinging surround and the need for connection with, relatedness to, and contact with others is subjugated to the need to protect the separate self. Abstract logic is viewed as superior to more "connected knowing" (Belenky, Clinchy, Goldberger, & Tarule 1986). Safety in a power-based society seems to demand solid boundaries; self-disclosure is carefully monitored, lest knowledge about the inner experience be used against one. As caricatured in this way, this actually prescribes much of the socialization of Western males.

If, on the other hand, self is conceived of as contextual and relational, with the capacity to form gratifying connections, with creative action becoming possible though connection, and a greater sense of clarity and confidence arising within relationship, others will be perceived as participating in relational growth in a particular way that contributes to the connected sense of self. In empathic resonance, the person experiences, at a cognitive and physical level, the powerful sense of connection. Further, if mutuality prevails, not only will I be influenced, moved, changed by context, and most importantly by my relational context, but I will also be shaping and participating in the development of others' "selves." This growth and movement is participatory and synergistic. This view of "self with other" typifies much of the socialization toward care-taking and empowerment of others that occurs for females in Western cultures.

Hence, it should be no surprise to find important differences between men's and women's experiences of boundaries, contributing to vastly different experiences of "self with other" or the "interacting sense of self." As Carol Gilligan notes, women "define themselves in the context of human relationship" (1982, p. 17). For men, wht is crucial is "separation as it defines and empowers the self" (Gilligan, 1982, p. 156). Women feel most themselves, most safe, most alive in connective, men . . . in separation (Gilligan and Pollack, 1982).

Chodorow (1978) gives one explanation for gender differences in the sense of identity vis-à-vis boundaries. She suggests that Western cultures allow a much longer pre-oedipal period for the girl, in which the immediate and close attachment and consequent identification with mother is uninterrupted for an extended time. The boy's experience is marked, on the other hand, by an abrupt interruption of the earliest identification with the mother and a shift of the identification to father when he discovers the "defective," penis-less state of the mother and the superior power of the father. He is further treated as an object rather than as an identified-with subject by the mother. This difference in intrapsychic development, in Chodorow's opinion, leads to more "permeable boundaries" in girls and a greater premium on separation and protection from other in boys. Lynn (1962) hypothesized that the nature of the identification process is quite different in boys and girls by virtue of the very different roles mothers and fathers traditionally play in raising children; that is, mothers are present in an ongoing way while fathers are typically more absent. Thus, it is suggested, boys are left having to identify with an "abstract role" rather than a specific, particular, interacting person. This dynamic, alone, would shed light on the greater contextuality of girls and the greater tendency toward abstracted and separate functioning of boys. I would also like to suggest that boys are actively socialized toward a power-dominance experience of selfhood, while girls are socialized toward a love-empathy mode of being in the world (Jordan, 1987). The former stresses discontinuity between self and other, decreased empathic resonance; the latter enhances the movement of mutual impact and growth. These two very different approaches to organizing "self with other" experience also have far-reaching effects on every aspect of our lives, including the theories of self and science that we construct. Psychological theories of self, especially value-laden notions of the ideally functioning self, in turn broadly affect our expe-riences of ourselves. And they are saturated with gender bias.

Bias in Science and Language

Evelyn Fox Keller delineates what I think are the consequences of this bias in the realm of science, pointing out that there are two basic approaches in science: the Baconian model, where knowledge leads to "power over" nature, and the Platonic approach, where knowledge occurs through entering into the world of the studied (Keller, 1985, p. 34). The former lauds the capacity to abstract and objectify, while the latter suggests a much more contextual orientation. The Baconian approach might be thought of as fitting the power–dominance mode, which I suggest is the ruling ethic for Western male socialization. It leads to what Belenky et al. (1986) refer to as "separate knowing." In contrast, the Platonic model represents the empathic mode or "connected knowing," encouraged in traditional female development.

In no science is the bias of the scientist about these issues more likely to affect the material she or he studies than in psychology. I submit that we are at all times, even in the most rigorous empirical studies, trying to learn something about ourselves; at worst, we are trying to "prove" something about or for ourselves. Our efforts at being objective are limited by our prejudices, needs, and conditioning. The enterprise is fraught with contradiction. If we could accept this contradiction and acknowledge it, perhaps we could come a step closer to the complex flow of life. But I think psychology as an enterprise has suffered from a sense of shame about the limits on its "objective powers" and therefore has become even more heavily invested in extolling the separation of subject and object, denying the subjective nature of its own being. This pressure can lead away from a study of human process as movement and mutual influence to celebration of the dualism implied in subject versus object and contributes heavily to the metaphor of "separate self." As Keller notes, "the relation between knower and known is one of distance and separation. It is that between a subject and an object radically divided, which is to say, no worldly relation" (Keller, 1985, p. 79). Belenky et al. (1986) point to the differences between knowledge and understanding, a difference which is familiar to clinicians. Knowledge "implies separation from the object and mastery over it", while "understanding involves intimacy and equality between self and object" (Belenky et al, 1986, p. 101)

Nevertheless, the tendency to objectify and "it-ify" or render into "thingdom" is powerful in psychological theory. As Robert Kegan notes: "We are greatly tempted and seduced by our language into experiencing ourselves and the world as *things* that move" (Kegan, 1982, p. 8 [emphasis mine]). I think this is in part because of our culturally induced need to control and predict. The material world, the person as discrete body in space, is a compelling reality. And language is used to both express and create this reality. Unfortunately, the effort to transcend these biases often fails, particularly with language. Thus, even in Kegan's very fine attempt to move psychology out of this bind ("This book is about human being as activity" [1982, p. 8]), his ultimate definition of subjectivity relies on "having" rather than "being," whether actions, sensations, impulses, and so on. "Having", again, falls into the old paradigm of things that are possessed by a possessor, that is, structured, "owning" self. In his approach, "having" is a more mature mode than "being."

Our language, so neatly split into discrete words, nouns, and verbs, further makes discussion of this material almost impossible. The drift toward abstracted entities occurs again and again as I struggle with these ideas. Nevertheless, in shifting from a study of separate knowledge to connected knowing (Belenky et al., 1986) or from "self-development" to "relational development" (Jordan, 1989), I attempt to leave a language of structure and dualism for one of process. I look beyond the polarities of egoism versus altruism, self versus other. Concretely, I see that people move into relationship, not just as a means toward self-development or to acquire something for the self (be it love, money, or sex) but to contribute to the growth of something that is of the self but beyond the self . . . the relationship.

Self, other, and the relationship—no longer clearly separated entities but mutually forming—are interconnected rather than in competition in a model of relational movement. Growth occurs in becoming a part of relationship rather than apart from relationship (Jordan, 1990). The enhancement of the relationship may constitute a greater goal than individual gratification and ironically may lead to greater individual fulfill-

ment (Jordan, 1987). Stated more strongly, perhaps the most basic human need is the need to participate in relationship (Kaplan, 1984). It is movement, growth in connection, differentiation and integration in the evolving context that characterize this view of Life.

Central to any discussion of self is the dilemma of process and structure. Our language does impose limits on our ability to delineate modes of being, to trace continuities of intention, memory, energy, and sensation; we quickly resort to reifications, making solid that which is fluid, changing and ongoing. One reason I prefer the term *relational being* to *relational self* or *self-in-relation* is that it is purposely true to the process nature of experience. The ambiguity of the term *being* (noun or verb, structure or process?) nicely captures the paradox of the process–structure interface. The experience of being "real," central to the sense of self, then emerges in an ongoing relational context. The metaphor of "voice" so often used to characterize the experience of self, is apt, for one's voice is vividly shaped by the quality of listening provided, whether with a real audience or an imagined one.

In Hazel Markus's terms, "the dynamic interpretive structure," it seems to me, is shaped importantly in relational contexts. Markus notes "the self concept can no longer be explored as if it were a unitary, monolithic entity" (Markus & Wurf, 1987, p. 300). Some have gone so far as to argue that there is no integrative self-process but that the individual is a separate and new self in each context in which he or she participates (Sorokin, 1947), or as Goffman notes, the individual can be thought of as a constant "mummer" (Goffman, 1959). If we posit a model of contextual, dialogic movement, the constancies and patterns of interpersonal interactions and the ways they shape our sense of ourselves become the focus for understanding personal integration. Study of relationality is needed to supplement intrapsychic investigation.

To summarize, from a relational perspective, human beings are seen as experiencing a primary need for connection and essential emotional joining. This need is served by empathy, which is authentic relatedness, is characterized by mutuality. Further, in relationships one comes to experience: clarity about one's own experience and the other's; the capacity for creating meaningful action; and increased sense of vitality; and capacity for further connection (Jordan, 1987;

Miller, 1986). Relational capabilities and processes exist from the time of birth and develop over the course of one's life. In our culture, there has been a split along gender lines between the ideal of a separate, autonomous, objective male self and a relational, connected, and empathic female self. Notably, different values, motivational patterns, ways of knowing (Belenky et al., 1986), moral systems (Gilligan, 1982), primary ways of organizing interpersonal experience (Jordan, 1987), and spheres of influence have been delineated by gender. Scientific inquiry itself has been aimed toward "objective truth," mastery over nature; as such, it represents a masculine ideal (Keller, 1985). Despite the revelations of modern physics of the interpenetrability of all movement and structure, the myth, and possibly the arrogance, of this notion of impersonal, objective truth perseveres. In psychology, we must be very cautious with our language, for in naming, we give form. We shape areas of study; we eliminate others. Needed is a move toward a psychology of relationship and exploration of intersubjective reality, expressed by a relational language that supports relational understanding. Although we can most easily see the importance of this in the depiction of women's lives, the exploration of "relational being" should not stop with women. A larger paradigm shift from the primacy of separate self to relational being must be considered to further our understanding of all human experience.

References

Baldwin, J. (1968). The self-conscious person. In C. Gordon & K. Gergen (Eds.), *The self in social interaction* (pp. 161–171). New York: John Wiley and Sons. (Original work published 1897)

Basseches, M. (1980). Dialectical schemata: A framework for the empirical study of the development of dialectical thinking. *Human Development, 23,* 400–421.

Belenky, M., Clinchy, B., Goldberger, N., & Tarule, J. (1986). *Women's way of knowing: The development of self, voice, and mind.* New York: Basic Books.

Broverman, I., Broverman, D., Clarkson, F., Rosenkrantz, P., & Vogel, S. (1970). Sex role stereotype and clinical judgments of mental health. *Journal of Consulting and Counselling Psychology, 43,* 1–7.

Chodorow, N. (1978). *The reproduction of mothering: Psychoanalysis and the sociology of gender.* Berkeley: University of California Press.

Cooley, C. H. (1968). The social self: on the meanings of "I." In C. Gordon & K. Gergen (Eds.), *The self in social interaction,* (pp. 87–93). New York: John Wiley and Sons. (Original work published 1902)

Erikson, E. (1963). *Childhood and society* (2nd ed.). New York. W. W. Norton.

Fairbairn, W. (1952). *An object relations theory of personality* New York: Basic Books. (Original work published 1946)

Fliess, R. (1942). The metapsychology of the analyst. *Psychoanalytic Quarterly, 11,* 211–227.

Freud, S. (1955). Beyond the pleasure principle. In J. Strachey (Ed. and Trans.), *The standard edition of the complete psychological works of Sigmund Freud* (Vol. 18, pp. 3–64). London: Hogarth Press. (Original work published 1920)

Gergen, M. (1988). *Feminist thought and the structure of knowledge.* New York: New York University Press.

Gilligan, C. (1982). *In a different voice.* Cambridge, MA: Harvard University Press.

Goffman, E. (1959). *The presentation of self in everyday life.* Garden City, NY: Doubleday Anchor.

Guntrip, H. (1973). *Psychoanalytic theory, therapy and the self.* New York: Basic Books.

Hoffman, M. (1977). Sex differences in empathy and related behaviors. *Psychological Bulletin, 84*(4), 712–722.

Horney, K. (1967). The flight from womanhood. In H. Kelman (Ed.). *Feminine psychology* (pp. 54–70). New York: W. W. Norton. (Original work published 1926)

James, W. (1968). The self. In C. Gordon and K. Gergen (Eds.), *The self in social interaction* (pp. 41–51). New York: John Wiley Sons. (Original work published 1890)

Jordan, J. (1984). Empathy and self boundaries. *Work in progress. No. 16.* Wellesley, MA: Stone Center Working Paper Series.

Jordan, J. (1985). The meaning of mutuality. *Work in progress, No. 23.* Wellesley, MA: Stone Center Working Paper Series.

Jordan, J. (1987). Clarity in connection: Empathic knowing, desire and sexuality. *Work in progress, No. 29.* Wellesley, MA: Stone Center Working Paper Series.

Jordan, J. (1989). Relational development: Therapeutic implications of empathy and shame. *Work in progress. 39* Wellesley, MA: Stone Center Working Paper Series.

Jordan, J. (1990). Relational development through empathy: Therapeutic applications. *Work in progress. 40* Wellesley, MA: Stone Center Working Paper Series.

Jordan, J. & Surrey, J. (1986). The self-in-relation: Empathy and the mother-daughter relationship. In T. Bernay and D. Cantor. *The psychology of today's woman: New psychoanalytic visions.* New York: Analytic Press.

Kaplan, A. (1983). Women and empathy. *Work in progress, No. 2.* Wellesley, MA: Stone Center Working Paper Series.

Kaplan, A. (1984). The "self-in-relation": Implications for depression in women. *Work in progress, No. 14.* Wellesley, MA: Stone Center Working Paper Series.

Kegan, R. (1982). *The evolving self: Problem and process in human development.* Cambridge, MA: Harvard University Press.

Keller, E. (1985). *Reflections on gender and science.* New Haven, CT: Yale University Press.

Kohlberg, L. (1989). *The psychology of moral development: The nature and validity of moral stages.* San Francisco, CA: Harper & Row.

Klein, G. (1976). *Psychoanalytic theory: An explanation of essentials.* New York: International Universities Press.

Klein, M. (1953). *Love, hate and reparation,* with Joan Riviere. London: Hogarth Press.

Kohut, H. (1984). *How does analysis cure?* Chicago: University of Chicago Press.

Lynd, H. (1958). *On shame and the search for identity.* New York: John Wiley and Sons.

Lynn, D. (1962). Sex role and parental identification. *Child Development, 33*(3), 555–564.

Mahler, M. S., Pine, F., & Bergman, A. (1975). *The psychological birth of the human infant: Symbiosis and individuation.* New York: Basic Books.

Markus, H., & Wurf, E. (1987). The dynamic self-concept: A social psychological perspective. *Annual review of psychology, 38,* 299–337.

Mead, G. H. (1968). The genesis of the self. In C. Gordon & K. Gergen (Eds.), *The self in social interaction.* (pp. 51–61). New York: John Wiley and Sons. (Original work published 1925)

Miller, J. B. (1976). *Toward a new psychology of women.* Boston: Beacon Press.

Miller, J. B. (1984). The development of women's sense of self. *Work in progress, No. 12.* Wellesley, MA: Stone Center Working Paper Series.

Miller, J. B. (1986). What do we mean by relationships? *Work in progress, No. 22.* Wellesley, MA: Stone Center Working Paper Series.

Piaget, J. (1952). *The origins of intelligence in children.* New York: W. W. Norton.

Pollak, S. & Gilligan, C. (1982). Images of violence in thematic apperception test stories. *Journal of Personality and Social Psychology, 42,* (1), 159–167.

Sagi, A., & Hoffman, M. (1976). Empathic distress in newborns. *Developmental Psychology, 12,* 175–176.

Sanday, P. R. (1988). The reproduction of patriarchy in feminist anthropology. In M. Gergen (Ed.), *Feminist thought and the structure of knowledge.* (pp. 49–69). New York: New York Universities Press.

Schafer, R. (1959).Generative empathy in the treatment situation. *Psycho-analytic Quarterly, 28,* 342–373.

Shotter, J., & Logan, J. (1988). The pervasiveness of patriarchy: On finding a different voice. In M. Gergen (Ed.), *Feminist thought and the structure of knowledge* (pp. 69–87). New York: New York University.

Simner, M. (1971). Newborn's response to the cry of another infant. *Developmental Psychology, 5,* 135–150.

Sorokin, P. (1947). *Society, culture and personality: Their structure and dynamics.* New York: Harper.

Stern, D. (1986). *The interpersonal world of the infant.* New York: Basic Books.

Stiver, I. (1984). The meanings of "dependency" in female-male relationships. *Work in Progress, No. 11.* Wellesley, MA: Stone Center Working paper Series.

Sullivan, H. S. (1953), *The interpersonal theory of psychiatry.* New York: W. W. Norton.

Surrey, J. (1985). Self-in-relation: A theory of women's development. *Work in Progress, No. 13.* Wellesley, MA: Stone Center Working Paper Series.

Thompson, C. (1941). Cultural processes in the psychology of women. *Psychiatry, 4,* 331–339.

Tiryakian, E. (1968). The existential self and the person. In C. Gordon & K. Gergen (Eds.), *The self in social interaction* (pp. 75–87). New York: John Wiley & Sons.

Trevarthan, C. (1979). Communication and cooperation in early infancy: A description of primary intersubjectivity. In J. M. Bullower (Ed.), *Before speech: The beginning of interpersonal communication.* New York: Cambridge University Press.

Turner, R. (1968). The self-conception in social interaction. In C. Gordon & K. Gergen (Eds.), *The self in social interaction* (pp. 93–107). New York: John Wiley and Sons.

CHAPTER 26

VOICES OF GENDER ROLE CONFLICT: THE SOCIAL CONSTRUCTION OF COLLEGE MEN'S IDENTITY

TRACY L. DAVIS

The purpose of this constructivist inquiry was to explore the impact of socially prescribed gender roles on college men's identity development. Ten White, traditionally-aged students were interviewed and data from the interviews were analyzed using hermeneutic phenomenology. Students discussed communication restrictions associated with scripted gender roles, fear of femininity, feelings of being overly challenged, and a sense of confusion about masculinity.

Gilligan's (1982) landmark self-in-relation theory of women's development inspired important challenges to traditional views of human development and led to the reevaluation of many of the theories that undergird the practice of student development. Student affairs scholars and practitioners no longer rely solely on theories that have been constructed primarily by and about men. Belenky, Clinchy, Goldberger, & Tarule (1986), for example, developed a conceptual framework that helped student affairs practitioners better understand women's cognitive development. Josselson's (1987, 1996) and Jones's (1997) investigations allow student affairs professionals to hear women's voices in the context of identity development. The findings in these studies demonstrate the need for student affairs practitioners to become familiar with the ways that gender affects development.

Although researchers have begun to investigate how gender affects women's identity development, there has been relatively little written about such impact on the psychosocial development of college men. One reason for this lack of research may be based on a faulty assumption that most traditional scholarship regarding human development has already been about men. At first glance, this assumption seems obvious and well-founded. After all, Gilligan (1982) and others have convincingly argued that developmental research has too often viewed the male sex as representative of humanity. However, as Meth and Pasick (1990) point out,

> although psychological writing has been androcentric, it has also been gender blind [and] it has assumed a male perspective but has not really explored what it means to be a man any more than what it means to be a woman. (vii)

Researchers need, therefore, to more closely examine the development of men through the lenses of gender.

Researchers' understanding of identity formation is commonly attributed to Erikson's (1968) developmental theory. According to Erikson, individuals gain a sense of who they are by confronting a universal sequence of challenges or crises (e.g., trust, intimacy, etc.) throughout their lives. Marcia (1966) operationalized Erikson's original theory and similarly suggested that identity formation is the most important goal of adolescence. Marcia viewed identity development as a process of experiencing a series of crises with one's ascribed childhood identity and subsequently emerging with new commitments. That is, as individuals consider new ideas that are in conflict with earlier conceptions, they weigh possibilities, potentially experiment with alternatives, and eventually choose commitments that become the core of a newly wrought identity. Those successfully transcending crises and making commitments are said to have an achieved identity. Individuals avoiding the process altogether, neither experiencing crises nor making commitments, are in a state of identity diffusion. Individuals may also be somewhere between these two possibilities by either simply maintaining a parentally derived ideology (foreclosed) or by actively experimenting with and resolving identity related questions prior to commitment (moratorium).

Josselson's longitudinal research (1987, 1996), based upon Marcia's framework, investigated women's identity development. Josselson (1987) categorized participants into all four identity statuses and found that women

> internalize the central priorities of their mothers as the issues to feel the same or different about. As college-age, late adolescents, these women judge their distance from their families by whether and how much they carry on family religious traditions, whom they choose as friends, what sexual values they adopt, how they dress, whether and when and whom they plan to marry. These were the central points of negotiation in the separation-individuation drama. (p. 172)

For the women in her study, relationships with primary family, partners, children, and friends were what Josselson (1987) called key "anchors" (p. 176) that mediated making new commitments.

Whereas Marcia (1966) found decisions involving occupational choice, religious beliefs, and political ideology to be predictive of overall identity statuses, especially with men, Josselson (1987) and Schenkel and Marcia (1972) each found that crises and commitments in the areas of religion and sexual values to be more indicative of women's identity statuses.

Recent models of identity development have gone beyond these more epigenetic conceptualizations, with their emphasis on cognitive processes of development, to increasingly focus on the dynamic interaction between individuals and the social systems in which they function. Chickering and Reisser (1993), for example, in an update of Chickering's (1969) work, added a section to the establishing identity chapter entitled "sense of self in a social, historical, and cultural context" (p. 181). In addition, Josselson (1996) recently suggested that identity is "not just a private, individual matter . . . [but] a complex negotiation between the person and society" (p. 31). Similarly, D'Augelli (1994) conceived identity as "the dynamic processes by which an individual emerges from many social exchanges experienced in different contexts over an extended historical period" (p. 324). The construction of identity also depends, therefore, on the cultural, social, and political context in which these processes occur. A recent model offered by Jones and McEwen (2000) reinforces this idea. In their model, sexual orientation, race, culture, class, religion, and gender are identity dimensions that circulate around one's core identity. The salience of a particular dimension to one's core identity depends on changing contexts that include current experiences, family background, sociocultural conditions, career decisions, and life planning. In the current investigation, we examined one of these dimensions—gender—in an attempt to understand how college men internally experience externally defined gender roles.

Gender role conflict is defined as "a psychological state occurring when rigid, sexist, or restrictive gender roles learned thorough socialization, result in personal restriction, devaluation, or violation of others or self" (O'Neil, 1990, p. 25). Numerous studies using a common measure of men's gender role conflict, the Gender Role Conflict Scale (GRCS) (O'Neil, Helms, Gable, David, & Wrightsman, 1986) resulted in four underlying Factors: Restrictive Emotionality; Success, Power, and Competition; Restrictive Affectionate Behavior Between Men; and Conflict Between Work and Family Relations. In a review of the gender role literature, Thompson, Pleck, and Ferrera (1992) concluded that "gender role conflict provides an important link between societal norms scripting traditional masculinities and an individual's adaptation" (p. 598). Exploring men's gender role conflict, therefore, may provide rich information about college men's identity development.

Gender role conflict has been correlated with higher levels of anxiety and lower capacity for intimacy (Sharpe & Heppner, 1991). In addition, research has found that gender role conflict is related to negative attitudes toward seeking help (Good & Wood, 1995), low self-esteem (Cournoyer & Mahalik, 1995), negative attitudes and intolerance toward homosexuals (Rounds, 1994), depression (Good & Mintz, 1990), and endorsement of a traditional masculine ideology (Good, Braverman, & O'Neil, 1991). Results of these studies illustrate the importance of understanding male gender role conflict and its effects on the healthy development of men.

The purpose of this study was to explore conflicts related to socially constructed gender roles that may impact men's identity development. Given the increasing emphasis on the social construction of identities and the negative impacts that gender role conflict have on men, it seemed critical to examine how college men are coping with culturally defined notions of what it means to be a man. That is, assuming identity develops as one interacts with society and that gender is a central dimension of one's conception of self, it would be helpful to investigate how societal gender role expectations are influencing college men. Although the underlying concepts of identity development and gender role conflict assisted in making sense of the interviews, interpretations were allowed to emerge from the data.

Method

General identity development models and theories offer descriptions of a wide array of experiences for diverse populations of individuals. To more clearly understand how gender roles influence college men's identity development, unconstrained by current deterministic conceptualizations, I used a constructivist approach (Lincoln & Guba, 1985). The purpose of constructivist inquiry is "to produce depth of understanding about a particular topic or experience" (Manning, 1999, p. 12). The constructivist perspective, based largely on the research of Piaget (1954) and Vygotsky (1978), suggests that knowledge does not and cannot produce representations of an independent reality, but instead is rooted in the perspective of the knower. As such, identity development is not the result of stage development related to maturation; rather, it is understood as a construction by the individual through social learning and interpretive reorganization. There has been a recent debate about

constructivism among those who place more emphasis on the individual cognitive structuring processes and those who emphasize the sociocultural effects of learning. In this study, I assumed a more social constructivist approach with emphasis on (a) the social context in which development occurs and (b) the importance of social interaction and negotiation.

Consistent with the epistemological assumptions of constructivism is the phenomenological methodology employed in this study. Phenomenology addresses experience from the perspective of the individual and is based on the assumption that people have a unique way of making meaning of their experience. That is, for people to understand a phenomenon, they must grasp it from another's perspective.

In addition to constructivist epistemological assumptions and a phenomenological methodology, this investigation is informed by a hermeneutic philosophical position. Hermeneutics is the science of interpretation. According to van Manen (1990), meanings are often hidden and must be brought to the surface through reflection. Hermeneutic phenomenology, thus, can "bring explicitness out of implicitness, to unveil the essence of the lived experience of a few, which allows for insight into the possible lived experience of others" (p. 316).

Consistent with these paradigmatic assumptions, interviews were conducted at Western Illinois University (WIU). Western Illinois University enrolls approximately 12,000 students, about half of whom are men. WIU is a public regional institution with popular ROTC and law enforcement programs, and high student participation in Greek life and intramurals. WIU is also a politically conservative and rural campus. Interviews were conducted between Spring 2000 and Spring 2001.

Participants

Participants in this study were 10 male undergraduate students who ranged in age from 18 to 21 years old. Five were in their last semester of their senior year, 4 were juniors, and 1 was a sophomore. All participants in this study were White and heterosexual. Three individuals were enrolled in the College of Liberal Arts, two in Business, two in Communications, one in Education, one in Agriculture, and one in Law

Enforcement. Each participant was extensively involved in leadership of at least one of the following organizations: Interfraternity Council, Student Alumni Council, University Housing and Dining Services, or the Bureau of Cultural Affairs.

Procedure

Participants were purposefully selected through snowball or chain sampling (Patton, 1990). This approach "identifies cases of interest from people who know people who know people who know what cases are information-rich, that is, good examples for study" (p. 182). These exemplar cases were identified based on the recommendations of student affairs professionals and graduate assistants who work directly with students. The referral contact people were asked to identify students who were reflective about gender or currently struggling with gender-related issues. They were also given a description of gender role conflict and asked if they knew men who might be grappling with socially scripted gender expectations.

Interviews were conducted by a male investigator and three graduate students (one male and two female). Each researcher was skilled at conducting interviews and trained in microcounseling and listening skills. Interviewers were also knowledgeable about gender-related developmental issues in general and men's issues, in particular.

Interviews

Prior to individual interviews, prospective participants were given a description of the study and its methods, a clarification of the commitment required for participation, and an informed consent form describing procedures to ensure confidentiality. After consent was given, participants provided basic demographic information.

Individual interviews were conducted in a private room by one of the four interviewers. According to Lincoln and Guba (1985), interviewing is one strategy for examining an individual's constructions and reconstructions of "persons, events, activities, organizations, feelings, motivations, claims, concerns, and other entities" (p. 268). Interviews lasted between 45 minutes and 70 minutes and were tape-recorded.

Following each session, interviewers noted their experience and specifically commented on general impressions of the meeting, their reactions to the participant, and any notable or peculiar aspects of the interview. These journals were included in the data set and used in the analysis.

The interviewers used a set of questions adapted from Josselson's (1996) study of women's identity development. The protocol focused on how participants see themselves, important factors in their lives that shape who they are, how they have changed and what has stimulated that change, how they imagine their future, and what it is like being a man on campus. According to Kavale (1996), "an interview is literally an *inter view*, an inter-change of views between two persons conversing about a theme of mutual interest" (p. 14). Although the interview protocol was structured, interviewers were given latitude to explore responses in more depth. This open-ended questioning helps to "minimize the imposition of predetermined responses when gathering data" (Patton, 1990, p. 295).

Data Analysis

One of the greatest difficulties I had in analyzing the data was negotiating the Self-Other dynamic (discussed at length in this issue by Susan Jones). Jones warns qualitative researchers to check their "own subjectivity and theoretical stance so that decisions are indeed rooted in the research process as it unfolds rather than in the researchers' own points of view." For me, this meant being aware that I might try to make the interview data fit my preconceptions (Self) rather than allowing the participants (Other) to speak for themselves. I am drawn to the study of gender and men due to my own curiosity about the impact of gender on men's development, but I also have political, social, and cultural views related to this topic. I also clearly have biases associated with my own development as a White, heterosexual, Italian American male. As I read transcripts and listened to participants, for example, I had to intentionally avoid relying on initial intuitive interpretations rooted in my own experience. Negotiating interpretations with other interviewers helped me routinely assess whose story was being told. My own theoretical filter of knowledge, based in developmental gender role conflict and identity theory, also influenced my interpretations. In addition to the fact that these interpretations were subjected to the scrutiny of other members of the research team, I use participants' own language to illustrate our interpretations. These and several strategies listed below are aimed at "working the hyphen" (Fine, 1994, p.72) in the Self-Other split to try to maintain the integrity of the participants' stories.

The data set for this study consisted of the 10 interviews, which were transcribed verbatim, and the interviewer journals. Following procedures outlined by Coffey and Atkinson (1996), the first step in the analysis was for each investigator to independently read the interview transcripts and mark concepts, words, phrases, or sentences that seemed interesting or important. We then met to compare categories, negotiate and reconcile discrepancies, and develop a set of meaning categories or themes. As the transcripts were read and reread, the meaning categories were refined by analyzing the concepts that the data were organized around, comparing concepts across transcripts, and adding new themes that emerged only after seeing similar concepts in multiple transcripts. As Miles and Huberman (1994) pointed out, this refinement process illustrated critical nuances and generated awareness of previously unnoticed and seemingly unremarkable units of data.

This technique of reexamination (similar to Arminio and Hultgren's description of unloosening and uncovering in this volume) continued throughout the data analysis and interpretation processes. The major themes that emerged from this process were identified, discussed among analysts, and compared to literature related to men's psychosocial development. These themes and comparisons are reported in the following sections.

Trustworthiness of these findings was enhanced through peer debriefing, keeping a methodological journal, and member checking. Lincoln and Guba (1985) defined peer debriefing as "a process of exposing oneself to a disinterested peer in a manner paralleling an analytic session and for the purpose of exploring aspects of the inquiry that might otherwise remain only implicit within the inquirer's mind" (p. 308). The peer debriefer for this study was a doctoral candidate in the University of Iowa College of Education. Lincoln and Guba also maintained that member checks, a process through which participants verify data and the resulting interpre-

tations, are necessary to establish credibility. Participants in this study were given an opportunity to review the categories and summative interpretations for review, clarification, and suggestions. Due to the length of the study, graduation, and in one case, failure to show up for scheduled sessions, only two respondents participated in member checks.

Dependability and confirmability added to the trustworthiness of this study and were assessed through an auditor. According to Lincoln and Guba (1985), dependability can be established as the auditor examines the processes by which the various stages of the study, including analytic techniques, were conducted. The auditor, an advanced doctoral candidate well versed in qualitative methodologies, confirmed that the analytic processes were applicable to this study and that the data analysis strategies were applied consistently. To demonstrate confirmability, a journal of the inquiry process, copies of all taped interviews, notes from interviewer reflections and discussions, and hard copies of all transcripts were maintained.

In addition to peer debriefing, limited member checks, auditor review, and keeping a methodological journal, this study provided information regarding transferability of findings. The standard of transferability is a measure of whether or not the reader is given enough information about the setting to evaluate the extent to which the study's findings might be transferred to other contexts (Lincoln & Guba, 1985). According to Patton (1990), this can be accomplished through "thick description" and solid descriptive data. In this article, the context of the investigation is described and readers are given rich descriptions of participants' characteristics, including direct quotes from the interviews.

Results

Five themes emerged from the data: the importance of self-expression, code of communication caveats, fear of femininity, confusion about and distancing from masculinity, and a sense of challenge without support.

Importance of Self-Expression

Contrary to the popular image of the inexpressive male, participants felt that self-expression and communication were very important to them. It was clear, however, that being comfortable with self-expression was something recently learned and not a behavior that was routinely practiced earlier in life. For example, one man reflected,

> What I enjoy the most is having good conversations with people, like interacting with people. It's something I really enjoy—especially—this is a really new thing for me too. I didn't really do it a lot in the past and it's something I'm starting to [do] a little more. I'd say right now that's probably something that I enjoy most.

Moreover, participants rarely mentioned how they communicate with others without indicating some awareness that what they were doing was somehow outside of the boundaries of traditional masculinity. One participant reported:

> It just seems like it's amazing how different men and women are regarding handling stress and things. It's kind of a role confusion for me, because I'm the kind of person that likes to talk it out. It's difficult when you're supposed to keep things in.

Whereas verbal interaction was seen as personally important, the awareness of how others might view expressivity seemed to shape these participants' reflections on their behavior.

Code of Communication Caveats

There were three important caveats that seemed to affect these students' styles and levels of communication. These caveats are related to feelings of safety, worrying about how others will perceive them, and learned, socially appropriate ways of interacting, particularly with other men.

Communication with women. Men seemed to be able to express themselves more freely with women than with other men. One participant put it this way, "I like to talk to friends. I like to talk and chat—I'll talk about anything, I'm especially a chatterbox with girls [sic]. We'll just sit around and watch TV, we'll discuss like relationships, life, anything." Opening up to women as friends was seen as safer and easier than being vulnerable to other men. Although this appeared to be true with female friends, there was some fear that expressive and relational behavior might be penalized if women were seen as potential partners. According to one man:

> You've got to be jerky to women, I know that. They say they want nice guys but they really don't. The thing that bugs me is that I've always been the ideal husband rather than the ideal boyfriend, which bothers me. They're like, "you're the type of guy I'd like to marry, not the type of guy I'd want to date." I just think it's because I'm too nice.

Messages that these men received from women affected their attitudes about dating. Although communication was less inhibited with female friends than with male friends, it appears to be more affected by sex-typed assumptions with potential female mates.

One-on-one communication with other men. Participants also felt that their style of communication was quite different in groups than it was with one other person. When these men were with a group of other men, even friends, there was some level of performance associated with their communication. Humorous comments and "put-downs" were the norm. On the other hand, respondents felt able to become more intimate and direct in the context of just one other friend. One man commented:

> Men don't communicate unless they have their secure circle of friends and they can talk with this one guy. I mean they all hang out and drink beer and have a good time, but after everyone leaves, Stan's going to stay behind and we're going to have a great talk. There's always that one guy that stays behind and there's always going to be that connection too.

These students sent a strong message that they were conscious of gendered rules associated with when and how relational communication can occur. Another student talked about limiting what he said during discussions with groups of men until he was confident they were accepting and that he would not have to worry about what they were going to think.

Nonverbal and side-by-side communication. The way that participants communicated affection to other men took a form that could easily be missed or misunderstood. These men talked about indirectly showing affection through both verbal and nonverbal means. One participant, for example, discussed how he relates to his father.

The way I show affection, like the first thing I do is come in the house and he just grabs a hold of my shoulder, squeezes it a little bit and then I punch him in the stomach a little bit and that's—I mean I've told my dad I love him like maybe four times in my entire life—I mean that's just how we show affection. And that's basically the way I am with all guys too, like if I don't feel like I can punch you, you're not my friend. . . . It's like a love tap, you know, that's basically what it amounts to.

When participants did verbally express themselves with other men, they often did so in a "side-by-side," as opposed to a "face-to-face," manner. One student shared that his most memorable bonding experience with his best friend occurred as they sat next to each other and talked about their fears and problems during a long trip in the car. Similarly, other participants discussed taking a trip to a casino or getting together to watch World Wrestling Federation (WWF) as activities that created opportunities to communicate and relate to other men. On the surface, these activities might appear to be anything but relational, but note *how* two participants described their activity: "One of the big things me and Nick do is play Playstation. We get out of class and we can play for like 8 hours and just—it's kind of like a bonding experience between us." or "Like when I go gambling. It's the trip down and talking with somebody that kind of knows at the same level as what I'm doing, it's sorting things out, you know at the same level as me." These men discussed their connection to and relationship with other men in the context of an activity, but their story was not about the activity itself.

Fear of Femininity

Although participants described ways that they were able to express themselves to other men, some communicated both fear and frustration related to the narrow boundaries of that expression. At the root of this frustration was a fear of being seen as "feminine" or somehow "unmanly." One student said, "You know if at the bar someone bumps into you, you have to be the tough guy. You can't have guys thinking weird things about you, you know you got to prove yourself." Participants also discussed how even seemingly nongendered activities raised questions about how others interpret their sex-

ual orientation. Openness to talking, wearing a lot of cologne, and clothing choices were each actions mentioned by participants that made other people question their sexual orientation. One student, for example, said, "People have thought I am gay. I think it's because I talk, but, I'll sit there and listen too, and I'll put input into other people's problems like friends do or gay guys do." This connection between ostensibly feminine activities and being gay sent a clear message to these students that to avoid certain labels, they had to restrict their behavior.

Confusion About and Distancing From Masculinity

Each participant was asked about what it was like being a man on campus. This question, more than any other, was generally met with a long silence before a response was given. It was as if these men had given very little thought to this part of their identity. Several students replied by saying, "I really don't think about it too much," or, "I really don't pay attention to differences." Students were clear, however, that they did not see themselves as typical of most men. One man said, for example, "I'm not a stereotypical male macho kind of person. I talk about lots of things, and I really value my relationships with people." Participants communicated a general sense of unease with masculinity. They were simultaneously unreflective about what being a guy means and aware that masculinity was something with which they did not want to identify.

Sense of Challenge Without Support

For those respondents who did answer the question about what it was like being a man on campus, there was a common theme of feeling left out. Several students mentioned the existence of support services designed specifically for women (e.g., women's center, women's leadership programs) without a corresponding focus on men. One student gave a specific example of feeling challenged, whereas female students were supported.

> I know a lot of men because I'm in a lot of math and physics classes and there are not a whole lot of girls [sic] in them. It seems like they get more attention, I don't know why. Our male teachers, it seems like they are more apt to give them help. If we don't get it, it's like "I don't understand how you don't

understand this—you should be understanding this." I'm like "OK, fine, I don't understand." Then the girl goes up there and he talks quieter and he's more apt to listen to her. I don't know, it just seems he's more understanding of why a girl would not understand. I don't see why girls and guys are different that way.

Discussion

The finding that these men did not often think of themselves in terms of their gender is not surprising. This is consistent with Levine and Cureton's (1998) study, which found that "males were neither as eloquent nor as thoughtful in describing gender differences. In the main, it was simply not on the male radar screen" (p. 111). It is, however, problematic if men do not see themselves as men. If identity development is fostered by experiencing crises and choices, as Marcia (1966) suggested, gender and sex need to at least be a blip on the radar screen before reflective commitment can occur. The lack of gender awareness may also be explained by Jones and McEwen's (2000) multiple identity model. According to this model, privilege and inequality are least visible and least understood by those who are most privileged by cultural systems. Like White people who do not see themselves as having a race (Helms, 1992), these men may not have been conscious of their sex. This may be particularly true within university cultures like WIU, where profeminist influences are not as visible as they are on many college campuses.

It was similarly noticeable that these men did not mention anything about their racial identity in the interviews. Existing in a cultural context where their gender and race are not "on the radar screen" is both a privilege and a problem. That is, being in an environment where one's race and gender are routinely affirmed promotes a foreclosed identity where crisis is absent and commitments are not explored. To reach an achieved identity, important aspects of one's identity (such as race, gender, and religion) need to be explored.

Although gender and race identity issues were generally unconsidered, men in this study had a sense that they were not being supported. Consistent with Pollack's (1999) research, this study found that men felt pushed or challenged without sufficient empathy or support. One participant's story about feeling that female students

were supported whereas male students were challenged is particularly poignant. Not only is it outside the traditional male role for an individual to express a need for help (Good & Wood, 1995), but also educators may misunderstand this lack of expression as a lack of need. Osherson (1986), moreover, described the archetypal scene of a distressed little boy crying out for emotional soothing only to experience both the minimizing of his pain and disapproval for showing such unmanly behavior. The common phrase "take it like a man" is an artifact of this deeper cultural script.

This research also illuminates the importance of gender role conflict on college men's identity development. Students described several instances where they were fearful about how other people might interpret their behavior. According to O'Neil (1981), fear of femininity is at the center of men's gender role conflict. In this study, fear manifested itself through stories of homophobia, restricted emotional expression (e.g., no crying), and limits on verbal expression and communication. These heterosexual men were afraid, essentially, that others would view them as feminine, gay, or somehow other than a man. Thus, when others' assumptions about their sexual orientation did not fit with their own sense of self, participants felt a need to alter their behavior. Men's self-expression may be mediated by what this behavior means, or might mean, to other people. In other words, being less expressive had the benefit of helping to avoid labels they wanted to evade. This may also help to explain findings that male students tend to exhibit more homophobic attitudes and perpetrate significantly more hate-motivated assaults than women do (D'Augelli, 1991).

The finding that participants felt restrictions associated with expression is problematic in a number of ways. First, gender-related limits on men's self-expression have been linked to negative emotional outcomes (Blazina, 2001; Brody, 1996). Second, one of the central findings in this study was that these students clearly felt that self-expression was important to them. The fact that they valued self-expression even though they were aware that this behavior was sometimes penalized illustrates one the tensions causing gender role conflict. In other words, these men wanted to give voice to certain emotions but were acutely cognizant of the parameters in which these feelings could be expressed. The expression of certain feelings or certain behaviors is quite simply outside of what Pollack (1999) calls "the boy code." Not wanting to appear vulnerable to other men, fear of being seen as gay, and wanting to avoid the "just friend-not boyfriend" label all shaped how and what men in this study communicated.

Students also described communication with their male friends in a way that could easily be misunderstood. Stories about playing video games, traveling in a car to go gambling, and watching WWF wrestling were initially overlooked by investigators. When, however, we suspended our assumptions and more carefully listened to the participant's descriptions, it became clear that they were describing these activities in relational terms. Although communication was "side-by-side" and "doing oriented," the stories being told were about relationship building and connection. This finding is similar to Pollack's (1999) investigation into male development which found that "many mothers find that if they engage in action-oriented activities with their sons, their boys began to open up and talk" (p. 101). Although various activities that men do together may appear on the surface to be incongruent with intimacy, the actions may in fact be rooted in forging relationships and building "buddyship."

Interestingly, the interviewers felt that some of these communication patterns were evident during the interviews. The female researchers noted that men were generally more comfortable expressing themselves than the interviewers anticipated. Several men in this study felt that expressing themselves to women was generally easier than talking with men, as long as the women were viewed as friends and not potential partners. This was true about most topics, although female interviewers felt that discussions about sex and relationships were sometimes awkward. The male interviewers felt that the participants were generally very expressive. This may be, in part, due to the one-on-one nature of the interaction. Men in this study mentioned that it was easier to express themselves with just one other male as opposed to groups of men.

Implications for Student Affairs

Results of this study suggest that student affairs professionals need to provide programming and learning interventions aimed at putting gender on the radar screen for men. Just as we need to help White students see themselves as racial beings, we need to facilitate men learning about themselves as men. Helping men become more aware of their gender should help to promote identity development to the extent that unconsidered gender roles are keeping them from making reflective identity commitments. One strategy that I have used with undergraduate men is to show commercial, movie, and sitcom video clips that have gender-related messages. I then follow these clips with questions to focus attention on both how gender roles are constructed and how to become a critical consumer of these messages. The goal is to help students select for themselves who they are and who they want to become.

In addition to the need for student development professionals to facilitate reflection regarding gender identity, participants' stories also suggest that we may need to give college men more support. In a patriarchal culture, men are privileged, but that should not keep us from treating men developmentally. Pollack (1990), for example, challenged us to "be sensitively aware (and less countertransferentially critical) of the particular forms of affiliative needs and capacities shown by men" (p. 318). Student affairs professionals need to be alert to any disposition to rely on sex role expectations in deciding on developmentally appropriate challenges and supports. Similarly, in this study, several men noticed institutional supports for women, but no such safety net or safe harbor for men on campus. It is important to offer direct services to men, as men, on campus.

Student affairs professionals should also understand that certain forms of men's communication might be more relational than we initially realize. Gender-related restrictions regarding verbal expression clearly influenced *how* men in this study communicated. The students generally preferred one-on-one communication, felt more comfortable communicating with women, and expressed intimacy "side-by-side" or in the context of doing. Certain developmental interventions may, therefore, be more effective outside of the context of groups. For example, resident assistants (RAs) trying to confront a male student may meet less resistance if the confrontation is handled one-on-one.

It is similarly important for male RAs to be aware that men may have a hard time expressing certain feelings to them. Activity-based or "doing" strategies may help facilitate such expression. According to Pollack (1999), the following approaches are critical to facilitating discussion with men: create a safe space, give men time to feel comfortable with expression, seek out and provide alternative pathways for expression (i.e., relate while engaging in action-oriented activities), listen without judging, and give affirmation and affection. Student affairs professionals should consider engaging men in action-oriented activities such as going for a walk or some other "doing" activity in order to get beyond the mask of masculinity.

Conclusion

Research into women's identity development grew out of a belief that women must be understood within the context of their role expectations and restrictions. To understand men's identity development, student affairs professionals need to explore how men see themselves as men within "the context of the restraints, constraints, and expectations of the male gender role" (Scher, 1990, p. 325). Identity models that are focused on naturally occurring developmental tasks may tell only a portion of the story. Researchers and student affairs practitioners would be well advised to consider models that reflect the idea that identities are also socially constructed (e.g., Jones & McEwen, 2000). Participants in this research clearly articulated conflicts between behaviors that they personally valued (e.g., self-expression) and how they felt others interpreted that behavior. To the extent that people accept scripted gender roles either blindly or due to perceived sanctions for acting outside of these roles, their identity is less self-authored and more socially constructed.

O'Neil's (1981) concept of gender role conflict provides a useful framework for understanding how a man may see himself in the context of culturally transmitted role expectations. Fear of femininity, restricted expression, and restricted affectionate behavior among men were evident in the stories told by students in this study. The themes emerging from these stories suggest ways for student affairs professionals to design developmentally appropriate interventions for men, especially those experiencing gender role conflict.

The findings from this study must be interpreted within the limitations of the phenomenological methodology, participants, and context in which the research was conducted. Consistent with the constructivist tradition, the participants' voices and research team's interpretations are not intended to be representative of all men. Clearly, the fact that the research was based on a nondiverse group of men, especially in terms of important identity dimensions of sexual orientation and race, limits the transferability of findings. Information is given, however, regarding the research context and participant interviews to assist the reader in applying the results.

Future researchers should consider implementing longitudinal qualitative studies to get a sense of the events that promote or inhibit development, how other components of self (e.g., sexual orientation, cultural heritage, etc.) might impact growth, and how identity development progresses over time. It is also important to vary the contexts in which studies are implemented. In addition, more research is clearly necessary for various populations of men, including gay men, men with disabilities, and men from various cultural backgrounds.

References

Belenky, M. F., Clinchy, B. M., Goldberger, N. R., & Tarule, J. M. (1986). *Women's ways of knowing.* New York: Basic Books.

Blazina, C. (2001). Analytic psychology and gender role conflict: The development of the fragile masculine self. *Psychotherapy, 38*(1), 50–59.

Brody, L. R. (1996). Gender, emotional expression, and the family. In R. Kavanaugh, B. Zimmerberg-Glick, and S. Fein (Eds.), *Emotion: Interdisciplinary Perspectives.* Hillsdale, NJ: Lawrence Erlbaum.

Chickering, A. W., (1969). *Education and identity.* San Francisco: Jossey-Bass.

Chickering, A. W., & Reisser, L. (1993). *Education and identity (2nd ed.).* San Francisco: Jossey-Bass.

Coffey, A., & Atkinson, P. (1996). *Making sense of qualitative data: Complementary research strategies.* Thousand Oaks, CA: Sage.

Cournoyer, R. J., & Mahalik, J. R. (1995). Cross-sectional study of gender role conflict examining college-aged and middle-aged men. *Journal of Counseling Psychology, 42*(1), 11–19.

D'Augelli, A. R. (1991). Gay men in college: Identity processes and adaptations. *Journal of College Student Development, 32,* 140–146.

D'Augelli, A. R. (1994). Identity development and sexual orientation: Toward a model of lesbian, gay, and bisexual development. In E. J. Trickett, R. J. Watts, & D. Birman (Eds.), *Human diversity: Perspectives on people in context* (pp. 312–333). San Francisco: Jossey-Bass.

Erikson, E. (1968). *Identity, youth, and crisis.* New York: Norton.

Fine, M. (1994). Working the hyphens: Reinventing self and other in qualitative research. In N. R. Denzin & Y. S. Lincoln (Eds.), *Handbook of Qualitative Research* (pp. 70–82). Thousand Oaks, CA: Sage Publications.

Gilligan, C. (1982). *In a different voice.* Cambridge, MA: Harvard University Press.

Good, G. E., Braverman, D., & O'Neil, J. M. (1991). *Gender role conflict: Construct validity and reliability.* Paper presented at the annual meetings of the American Psychological Association, San Francisco, CA.

Good, G. E., & Mintz, L. B. (1990). Gender role conflict and depression in college men: Evidence for compound risk. *Journal of Counseling and Development, 69,* 17–21.

Good, G. E., & Wood, P. K. (1995). Male gender role conflict, depression, and help seeking: Do college men face double jeopardy? *Journal of Counseling & Development, 74*(1), 70–75.

Helms, J. E. (1992). *A race is a nice thing to have: A guide to being a White person or understanding the White persons in your life.* Topeka, KS: Content Communications.

Jones, S. R. (1997). Voices of identity and difference: A qualitative exploration of the multiple dimensions of identity development in women college students. *Journal of College Student Development, 38*(4), 376–385.

Jones, S. R., & McEwen, M. K. (2000). A conceptual model of multiple dimensions of identity. *Journal of College Student Development, 41*(4), 405–414.

Josselson, R. (1987). *Finding herself: Pathways to identity development in women.* San Francisco: Jossey-Bass.

Josselson, R. (1996). *Revising herself: The story of women's identity from college to midlife.* New York: Oxford University Press.

Kavale, S. (1996). *Interviews: An introduction to qualitative research interviewing.* Thousand Oaks, CA: Sage.

Levine, A., & Cureton, J. (1998). *When hope and fear collide.* San Francisco: Jossey-Bass.

Lincoln, Y., & Guba, E. (1985). *Naturalistic inquiry.* Thousand Oaks, CA: Sage.

Manning, K. (1999). *Giving voice to critical campus issues: Qualitative research in student affairs.* Lanham, MD: University Press of America.

Marcia, J. (1966). Development and validation of ego-identity status. *Journal of Personality and Social Psychology, 3,* 551–559.

Meth, R. L., & Pasick, R. S. (1990). *Men in therapy: The challenge of change.* New York: Guilford Press.

Miles, M. B., & Huberman, A. M. (1984). *Qualitative data analysis.* Beverly Hills, CA: Sage.

O'Neil, J. M. (1981). Patterns of gender role conflict and strain: Sexism and fear of femininity in men's lives. *The Personnel and Guidance Journal, 60,* 203–210.

O'Neil, J. M. (1990). Assessing men's gender role conflict. In D. Moore & F. Leafgren (Eds.), *Problem-solving strategies and interventions for men in conflict* (pp. 23–38). Alexandria, VA: American Counseling Association.

O'Neil, J. M., Helms, B. J., Gable, R. K., David, L., & Wrightsman, L. S. (1986). Gender role conflict scale: College men's fear of femininity. *Sex Roles, 14,* 335–350.

Osherson, S. (1986). *Finding our fathers.* New York: Fawcett Columbine.

Patton, M. Q. (1990). *Qualitative evaluation and research methods* (2nd ed.). Newbury Park, CA: Sage.

Piaget, J. (1954). *The construction of reality in the child* (M. Cook, Trans.). New York: Basic Books.

Pollack, W. S. (1990). Men's development and psychotherapy: A psychoanalytic perspective. *Psychotherapy, 27,* 316–321.

Pollack, W. S. (1999). *Real boys: Rescuing our sons from the myths of boyhood.* New York: Holt.

Rounds, D. (1994). *Predictors of homosexual intolerance on a college campus: Identity, intimacy, attitudes toward homosexuals and gender role conflict.* Unpublished master's thesis, Department of Psychology, University of Connecticut.

Schenkel, S., & Marcia, J. E. (1972). Attitudes toward premarital intercourse in determining ego identity status in college women. *Journal of Personality, 40*(1), 472–482.

Scher, M. (1990). Effect of gender role incongruities on men's experience as clients in psychotherapy. *Psychotherapy, 27,* 322–326.

Sharpe, M. J., & Heppner, P. P. (1991). Gender, gender-role conflict, and psychological well-being in men. *Journal of Counseling Psychology, 38,* 323–330.

Thompson, E. H., Pleck, J. H., & Ferrera, D. L. (1992). Men and masculinities: Scales for masculinity ideology and masculinity-related constructs. *Sex Roles, 27,* 573–607.

van Manen, M. (1990). *Researching the lived experience: Human Science for an Action Sensitive Pedagogy* (SUNY Series in the Philosophy of Education). Albany, NY: State University of New York Press.

CHAPTER 27

FROM PASSIVE ACCEPTANCE TO ACTIVE COMMITMENT: A MODEL OF FEMINIST IDENTITY DEVELOPMENT FOR WOMEN

NANCY E. DOWNING AND KRISTIN L. ROUSH

This article presents a model of feminist identity development for women. The model is derived, in part, from Cross's (1971) theory of Black identity development and is based on the premise that women who live in contemporary society must first acknowledge, then struggle with, and repeatedly work through their feelings about the prejudice and discrimination they experience as women in order to achieve authentic and positive feminist identity. The stages in this process include passive acceptance, revelation, embeddedness-emanation, synthesis, and active commitment. Implications of the model are outlined for women, nonsexist and feminist psychotherapies and contemporary society.

Much of the literature on feminist counseling and psychotherapy has focused on definitions (e.g., Rawlings & Carter, 1977) and comparisons with traditional paradigms. Inherent in many of these writings is an adherence to the "uniformity myths" of psychotherapy (Keisler, 1966), the assumption that a particular approach will work for most, if not all, clients, presenting problems, and under most circumstances. Feminist authors have attended minimally, if at all, to issues of appropriateness for different clients and client receptiveness to feminist interventions. The purpose of this article is to address these issues by describing a developmental model of feminist identity and delineating the implications of this model for women, feminist and nonsexist psychotherapies, and contemporary society.

This model has been developed by drawing upon the authors' clinical and personal experience, the meager literature in the area (Avery, 1977; Gurin, 1982; Moreland, 1976), and the developmental theories describing the acquisition and maintenance of a positive minority (specifically, Black) identity. The authors wrote this article from a feminist perspective, believing that any model that attempts to describe accurately events in women's lives must acknowledge the prejudice and discrimination that are a significant part of their life experiences. Hence, the authors feel that in contemporary society women share some of the developmental experiences of a minority population (as defined by Yetman & Steele, 1975); therefore, the literature on the identity development of minorities is considered relevant for women as well.

Specifically, this article will describe (1) a representative theory of positive Black identity development (Cross, 1971), (2) the application of Cross's theory to a developmental model of feminist identity, (3) the interface between this model and other selected developmental theories, and (4) the implications of this model for women, feminist and nonsexist psychotherapies, and contemporary society.

Theories of Positive Black Identity Development

Of the major theories of positive Black identity development (Cross, 1971, 1978; Jackson, 1976/1977; Thomas, 1970, 1971), the one most relevant and applicable to a model of feminist identity is that outlined by Cross (1971). He delineates a five-stage theory: preencounter, encounter, immersion-emersion, internalization, and internalization-commitment.

In Cross's first stage, that of *preencounter*, individuals consciously or unconsciously support individual, institutional, and cultural oppression and accept their oppression as if it were justified. This acceptance of oppression often results in a very negative self-concept. In addition, people in this stage believe that the minority group should strive to assimilate itself into the majority culture. Jackson (1976/1977) describes a similar phenomenon that he labels the passive acceptance stage.

The second stage, *encounter*, is actually a two-step process. First, the individual has a profound experience, a crisis, and, second, the person begins to reinterpret the world as the result of this experience. Cross points to the slaying of Martin Luther King as just such a significant catalyzing experience for many Blacks in the later 1960s. The predominant feelings experienced during this stage are guilt over previous passive acceptance of cultural oppression and anger for being "brainwashed" by society. Cross's second stage is similar to Jackson's (1976/1977) active resistance stage in which the individual consciously rejects the manifestations of oppression and experiences intense anger.

The third stage, *immersion-emersion*, is inevitable because individuals cannot tolerate the intensity of their feelings generated in the encounter stage for prolonged periods of time. Individuals in this stage initially withdraw from the dominant culture, and immerse themselves in the minority subculture. The theme "Black is beautiful" is characteristic of Afro-Americans in the immersion stage; they develop "an idealistic, superhuman expectancy toward practically anything Black" (Cross, 1971, p. 21).

During the emersion phase of this stage, feelings of guilt and anger begin to dissipate, ego involvement in "being Black" begins to decrease, and there is an increasing sense of pride. The emersion phase is also characterized by a greater openness to alternate viewpoints. The individ-ual's perspective begins to mellow from the dualistic thinking that "Black is good; non-Black is bad" to a more relativistic perspective. We again find parallels with Jackson's theory; he describes this stage as one of redirection in which individuals define their minority identity in positive terms independent of the values of the dominant culture and sublimate their anger by immersing themselves in the minority subculture and heritage.

Cross's fourth stage, *internalization*, is characterized by the resolution of the conflicts between the old and new identities, an increased self-confidence about one's Blackness, and movement toward a "pluralistic, nonracist perspective." Jackson's fourth stage, which he also labels internalization, is similar, with the addition that individuals integrate the positive aspects of their newly found minority identity with their unique, individual qualities.

Cross adds a fifth stage, *internalization-commitment*, which is characterized by the struggle to translate one's new, integrated identity into meaningful action for the benefit of the minority community. Implicit in this stage is Cross's belief that the development of a positive minority identity cannot remain an individual experience in isolation from a commitment to the minority community.

A Model Of Feminist Identity

Cross's theory has heuristic value for the development of a model of positive feminist identity. The proposed model, outlined in Table 1, has five stages: passive acceptance, revelation, embeddedness-emanation, synthesis, and active commitment. The model addresses feminist identity development specifically for women; implications for men are included when relevant.

Stage I, passive acceptance. Our first stage, passive acceptance, parallels Cross's theory and describes the woman who is either unaware of or denies the individual, institutional, and cultural prejudice and discrimination against her. As Schaef (1981) describes it, this is the woman who accepts the white male system, the perspective of the dominant, majority culture. This woman carefully selects associates and experiences so as to avoid contact with ideas that may upset her sense of equilibrium as a woman (Avery, 1977). Traditional sex-role stereotypes are

TABLE 1
Parallels Between the Identity Development Stages for Women and Blacks

		Stages for Women		
Passive Acceptance	*Revelation*	*Embeddedness-Emanation*	*Synthesis*	*Active Commitment*
Passive acceptance of traditional sex roles and discrimination; belief that traditional roles are advantageous; men are considered superior.	Catalyzed by a series of crises, resulting in open questioning of self and roles and feelings of anger and guilt; dualistic thinking; men are perceived as negative.	Characterized by connectedness with other select women, affirmation and strengthening of new identity. Eventually more relativistic thinking and cautious interaction with men.	Development of an authentic and positive feminist identity; sex-role transcendence; "flexible truce" with the world; evaluate men on an individual basis.	Consolidation of feminist identity; commitment to meaningful action, to a nonsexist world. Actions are personalized and rational Men are considered equal but not the same as women.

		Stages for Blacks		
Preencounter	*Encounter*	*Immersion-Emersion*	*Internalization*	*Internalization-Commitment*
The unaware person; acceptance of oppression as justified; values assimilation into majority culture; negative self-concept.	Catalyzed by profound event(s) resulting in increased awareness, rejection of oppression, and feelings of guilt and anger.	Initially characterized by withdrawal from the dominant culture, immersion in one's heritage and hostility toward whites. Eventually greater cognitive flexibility and pride emerge.	Development of an integrated, more positive self-image; adoption of a pluralistic, nonracist perspective.	Commitment of the new self to meaningful action for the benefit of the minority community.

Note: The data on the stages for Black women were adapted from Cross (1971).

accepted (Moreland, 1976); the Stage I woman believes the traditional roles to be advantageous and considers men to be superior to women. An example of a woman in this stage is a student enrolled in one of the author's "Psychology of Women" courses who, after the instructor encouraged class members to use the terms "men" and "women" for college-age males and females, responded by saying that she did not want to consider herself a woman because she liked the advantages of thinking of herself as a girl.

Toward the end of this stage there appears to be an important element of readiness (e.g., Erickson, 1950; Helms, 1984), a receptivity or openness to change or risk. Denial and selective perception diminish and the woman becomes increasingly open to alternative conceptualizations of herself and the world. This readiness helps facilitate the transition into the revelation stage and may be related to higher levels of ego development and/or self-esteem.

Stage II, revelation. Stage II, revelation, is precipitated by one or a series of crises or contradictions that the woman can no longer ignore or deny. Although the events that precipitate this stage vary widely, some typical ones include consciousness-raising groups, realization of discrimination against female children, ending of a relationship, divorce, or denial of credit or job application, or involvement in the women's movement (Cherniss, 1972). It is likely that movement from passive acceptance to revelation is a function of not only the quality, frequency, and intensity of such significant events but also the readiness of the individual to change her frame of reference.

Some women make the transition into the revelation stage suddenly, but for most it is a gradual and difficult shift. Unlike the process for Blacks in the late 1960s, as outlined by Cross, most women make the transition through a series of events less monumental than the death of a major leader like Martin Luther King. In fact, it may be the absence of generally agreed-upon, highly publicized, significant events relevant to women that has contributed to the difficulty of this transition and the seemingly small percentage of women who enter the revelation stage (Gurin, 1982). Transition may be further complicated by the perceptual distortions so characteristics of women in the passive acceptance stage. Traditional female socialization includes a dis-

trust of one's perceptions, a mechanism that helps perpetuate the woman's subordinate status (Miller, 1976). A growing sense of trust in one's perceptions is necessary to begin the process of questioning oneself and one's role in order to make the transition to the revelation stage.

During revelation, women experience primarily feelings of anger and secondarily feelings of guilt. "Women describe themselves as having been duped, sold out, betrayed and raped by the universe," and their response is often anger and rage in cosmic proportions (Avery, 1977). Women in this stage often experience feelings of guilt over the ways they have participated in their own oppression in the past. Another characteristic is very dualistic thinking (Knefelkamp, Widick, & Stroad, 1975). They see all (or most) men as negative and all women as positive; one woman labeled these perceptions as "female chauvinism." Frequently, a woman in this stage restricts her social contacts to a small number of people who are comfortable and accepting of her intense feelings (Moreland, 1976).

Often women in the revelation stage are perceived by other women in this stage as having a mature, positive identity, when in reality they have developed a "pseudo-identity" based on the negation of traditional femininity and the dominant culture. In Erickson's (1968b) terms, these women have developed a negative identity rather than an identity based on an affirmation of the strengths of being female (see Miller, 1976; Moreland, 1976, for clarification).

Stage III, embeddedness-emanation. The embeddedness phase of the third stage is most likely more difficult for Caucasian women than for Blacks in this culture. The barriers for women to attainting this stage seem more subtle in nature, are chronic in duration, and may be posed by significant others as well as by society. Most women are so integrally involved in the dominant culture through marriage, work, and children that it is difficult for them to withdraw and to find and embed themselves in a "female is beautiful" subculture. As Gurin (1982, p. 5) writes, "And this [development of gender consciousness] is very uncomfortable because women are, after all, the mothers, wives, lovers, sisters and daughters of men. There is no other subordinate group that has such an intimate relationship with the dominant group." Some marriages end in divorce when the woman feels the need to withdraw from the dominant culture in order to immerse herself, feeling that she cannot do so within the context of her marriage. Women's centers, women's studies classes, and women's support groups are some of the few havens that exist for women experiencing embeddedness.

This phase is a time for "discovery of sisterhood" (Avery, 1977) and for much creative activity (art, music, drama) depicting the oppressed role of women. When a woman is able to experience embeddedness, she often develops a close emotional connection with other, similar women. This connectedness provides the woman with a reflection of her new frame of reference, the opportunity to discharge her anger in a supportive environment, and affirmation and strength in her new identity. Lesbians who have a supportive female-oriented subgroup with which to identify may often have an easier transition to the embeddedness phase.

Although embeddedness may be more difficult for Caucasian women than for Blacks, their continued interconnection with the dominant culture may result in the greater ease with which women seem to experience the latter part of this stage, emanation—the beginnings of an openness to alternate viewpoints and to a more relativistic versus dualistic perspective. Although the need to reduce dissonance between one's newly emerging identity and the repeated experience of being treated as subordinate may result in women reverting to earlier stages, some women are able to tolerate these discrepancies and emerge from this uncomfortable state with a healthier, multidimensional, and adaptive perspective. Women in the emanation phase typically interact cautiously with men.

Factors that likely influence the transition to emanation include the realization that one's rage has limited effects upon the factors that produce and maintain the oppressive dominant culture, an awareness that one has adopted as rigid a belief system in the embeddedness phase as one assumed during the passive acceptance stage, a willingness to grieve the loss of the self as defined by either traditional sex roles or the rigid beliefs of the embeddedness phase, and the capacity to separate from the strong female friendships developed in Stage III.

Stage IV, synthesis. Women in Stage IV, synthesis, increasingly value the positive aspects of

being female and are able to integrate these qualities with their unique personal attributes into a positive and realistic self-concept. They are able to transcend traditional sex roles, make choices for themselves based on well-defined personal values, and evaluate men on an individual, rather than stereotypic, basis. Women in this stage accept both oppression-related explanations for events and other causal factors and are able to make accurate attributions. They have struck "a flexible truce" (Avery, 1977) with the world, one that allows them to channel their energies productively but also to respond appropriately to experiences of oppression and discrimination. Miller (1976) alludes to internalization when she writes about the "new way" (p. 41) women can value their psychological qualities and live life with authenticity, and Moreland (1976) labels this stage as one of celebration.

Stage V, active commitment. The fifth stage, active commitment, involves the translation of the newly developed consolidated identity into meaningful and effective action. There is a "deep and pervasive commitment to social change" (Avery, 1977) aimed at creating a future in which sex-role transcendence is a valued and encouraged goal. Women in this stage select issues carefully based on their unique talents and the possibility of both personal gratification and effecting societal change. Few women truly evolve to the active commitment stage, and the authors believe that most women who are dedicated to working for women's rights may actually be functioning out of needs from earlier stages, particularly revelation and embeddedness-emanation.

As with some more recent development theories (e.g., Loganbill, Hardy & Delworth, 1982), it is assumed that women may recycle through these stages, each time experiencing the challenge of that stage more profoundly and using previously learned skills to work through the particular stage again. It is also assumed that women may stagnate in a specific stage, most often in the revelation or embeddedness periods. In addition, women may revert to earlier stages when their skills are insufficient to respond to the demands of current life stresses. Furthermore, progress from stage to stage is determined not only by the woman's readiness, but also by the unique interpersonal and environmental context of her life (see Helms, 1984, for clarification).

Research

There has been virtually no research directly addressing the development of a positive feminist identity. The most closely related research is on group consciousness for women. Gurin (1982) identified four essential components of group consciousness: (1) group identification, (2) discontentment with the group's power, (3) recognition of the disparity in status between one's group and other groups, and (4) approval of collective action. She collected data from representative national samples in 1972, 1976, and 1979 and found (1) increased group identification for women over time; (2) low and unchanged feelings of discontentment with the group's power; (3) increased recognition of the disparity between groups (e.g., in 1972, 33% of the women surveyed attributed status differences to discrimination rather than to individual deficiencies; by 1979 the proportion had risen to 55%); and (4) low and unchanged endorsement of collective action. In addition, Gurin found that greater labor force participation, education, and political activism were related to higher levels of group consciousness, whereas religious activism and marital status (being married or widowed) were related to lower group consciousness. Overall, Gurin's sociological study suggests that some progress has been made in women's collective journey toward a positive feminist identity, but the road ahead appears to be a long and difficult one.

Research is sorely needed that explicitly addresses the development of a positive feminist identity. Specifically, future research should address (1) the development of assessment methods to identify and distinguish the stages; (2) longitudinal studies to discover the optimal sequence of stages and the predicted length of each stage; (3) the identification of precipitating events and moderator variables that maximize and impede movement through the stages; and (4) the impact of various therapist-client stage combinations on a variety of psychotherapeutic process and outcome variables.

Interface with Other Developmental Theories

The proposed model of feminist identity development is most closely related to the general literature on identity development, with Erickson's (1950) work, "The Eight Stages of Man (sic)," being central to this literature. According to Erickson, identity versus role confusion (Stage 5) precedes intimacy versus isolation (Stage 6). Although not clearly states, Erickson's stages focused on male, not female, development (Downing, 1983). More recently, numerous authors (Chodorow, 1973; Douvan & Adelson, 1966; Gilligan, 1982; Josselson, 1973; Marcia & Friedman, 1970; Williams, 1977) have concluded that identity and intimacy are concurrent, not sequential stages for females and that females find their identity within the context of relationships. Thus Erickson's stage theory cannot serve as a broader developmental context in which to place the proposed model of feminist identity development.

More germane to this model is Erickson's (1968a) notion of a "passive-identity," a total reliance on personal identity in an effort to transcend the culture and its available psychosocial identity patterns, expectations, and constraints (e.g., social identity). Passive identity can be non-adaptive or pathological when a new coherent social identity fails to be established and one remains absorbed within a personal world (see Marcia & Friedman's [1970] descriptions of moratorium, foreclosed, and diffused identity statuses for clarification). Passive identity can also be an adaptive regression, leading to an ability to forge actively a new social identity through redefining the existing world and one's role within it in ways that allow for congruence with one's personal identity (Lichtenstein, 1977). The proposed model of feminist identity development serves as a blueprint for women to transcend their passive identity and to integrate both personal and social identities into a coherent whole (Stage IV, synthesis).

Unlike Erickson, Kegan (1982) provides a broader developmental framework in which to place this model of feminist identity development. He proposes a six-stage model of the development of the self, which he describes as a lifelong process of differentiation from embeddedness. Of interest here is Kegan's description of Stages 5 and 6: institutional balance and interindividual balance. With the attainment of institutional balance, individuals lose their embeddedness in relationships (similar to the latter part of the emanation phase) and develop a coherent self across space and time and apart from others (necessary for successfully completing the synthesis stage). Institutional balance is followed by interindividual balance, in which one can acknowledge being an individual among individuals and in which groups are important to meeting the needs of people, rather than being an end in themselves (similar to the latter part of the synthesis and the active commitment stages). Although further elaboration of these parallels is needed, it seems quite likely that movement through the feminist identity stages is dependent, in part, on successful mastery of the stages of general identity development as outlined by Kegan.

In addition, this model of feminist identity development appears to overlap and have implications for Rebecca, Hefner, and Oleshansky's (1976) theory of sex-role transcendence. Their three-stage theory describes the evolution from a nondiscriminating position to a polarized stage and finally to a transcendent sex-role identity. Individuals in the polarized stage adopt and value traditional sex-role attitudes and behaviors (similar to the women in the passive acceptance stage). Individuals who have reached sex-role transcendence are described as feeling "free to express their human qualities without fear of retribution for violating sex-role norms. There has been a transcendence of stereotypes and a reorganization of possibilities learned in Stage II (polarized) into a more personally relevant framework" (p. 204). The characteristics of this sex-role transcendence stage are strikingly similar to those ascribed to Stage IV, synthesis. Thus the proposed feminist identity model may prove useful in further elaborating the transition between a polarized and a transcendent sex-role identity.

Implications for Psychotherapy

This model has a number of implications for psychotherapy with women. First, viewing female clients' presenting problems within the context of this developmental framework will add richness to the therapist's understanding of clients' concerns. For example, a woman in the embeddedness-emanation stage who presents with feelings of loneliness and isolation, of feeling unconnected to a similar peer group, is likely to have a very different phenomenological field than a woman in the passive acceptance stage who describes herself as isolated and lonely. Thus this model provides a useful assessment tool for therapists to gain a greater contextual understanding of their clients' experiences.

The model also has implications for intervention strategies. Therapists who are familiar with the sequence of stages can better plan interventions, using such techniques as plus-one staging (Knefelkamp et al., 1975), thereby lessening client resistance and confusion and increasing the possibility of successful therapeutic outcome. For example, encouraging the isolated, lonely woman who is in the embeddedness-emanation stage to seek out a woman's support group or to get involved in her local chapter of NOW will most likely be effective interventions. Similar suggestions for the passive acceptance woman who lacks the readiness to move on to revelation are more likely to be counterproductive. Likewise, if a female client wishes to work through her intense feelings of anger at all men, the model provides guidance regarding the sequence of feelings and experiences necessary for the client to gain a more flexible, individualistic perspective on this issue. In addition, therapists who are familiar with this model can provide anticipatory guidance to clients regarding the sequence of stages they will likely experience. By providing a clear goal, an understandable endpoint, the model may also assist both the therapist and client to tolerate better the erratic progress (two steps forward, one step back) that is so characteristic of psychotherapy.

Furthermore, the theory suggests that clients who progress from one stage to the next may experience some feelings of loss as they discard the familiarity and security of an earlier stage for the unknown, new stage. The therapist can be alerted to these feelings of loss and facilitate the grieving process.

In addition to having implications for assessment and intervention, this model also provides a developmental framework for feminist therapy. The tenets of feminist therapy as outlined by Rawlings and Carter (1977) can be viewed as reactions to the predominant paradigms of psychotherapy. Thus many of the principles of feminist therapy have evolved antithetically to these traditional paradigms, rather than from a thorough understanding of the life experiences of women (Gilligan, 1982, is a notable exception). In contrast, this theory represents a proactive, observation-based contribution to the theory of feminist therapy.

Finally, the model provides one yardstick to measure therapists' potential effectiveness when working with particular client issues. Cross

(1971) and Helms (1984) both believe that individuals who have experienced Stage V, internalization-commitment, have a greater capacity for understanding, supporting, and showing compassion for individuals who are struggling with earlier stages. In our opinion, female therapists can be most beneficial to female clients with sex-role issues when they themselves have cycled through the first five stages at least once. In addition, this model has implications for feminist therapy training programs; such programs should consider this developmental sequence in the design and implementation of the curriculum and its experiential components in order to produce well-qualified feminist therapists.

Implications for Contemporary Society

In addition to having important implications for psychotherapy with women, this model is also relevant to the women's movement and society in general. Although the five-stage process has been described in the context of individual life experience, the women's movement could also be viewed as experiencing these stages. Considering recent history, the 1950s were a time of passive acceptance of the feminine mystique. The 1960s and early 1970s constituted the revelation stage in which women in the movement expressed anger and demanded that their rights be unrestricted (Rosenthal, 1984). The late 1970s and the beginning of this decade have brought with it a realization that the expression of anger is not the ultimate goal (*Notes from the Third Year*, 1970) and an increasing, yet tentative, sense of pride in what it means to be female (e.g., Miller, 1976; Schaef, 1981). The movement appears to be immersing itself in its cultural roots and heritage. This model suggests that emanation is the next task for the movement to master collectively; it is likely to take many years before great numbers reach the synthesis or active commitment stages (Gurin, 1982).

This model also has implications for men. Specifically, males who are familiar with this model may be more understanding and supportive of the feelings and needs of women with whom they are intimately involved. Knowledge of this model may also help the unfortunate male who becomes the focus of the anger of the Stage II woman. Understanding the revelation experience may help the male separate his responsibility for the woman's anger from that which is the result of many years of prejudice and discrimination. In addition, this theory may have some relevance for the development of gender consciousness in males, although extensive work is needed to discern the similarities and differences between the sexes in this area.

There are also several limitations of this model as it has been proposed. First, the issue of possible class, age, racial, and ethnic differences in the development of a feminist identity has not been addressed here (e.g., Giddings, 1984; Malson, 1983) and requires much more attention. Second, greater attention needs to be focused on the intrapersonal, interpersonal, institutional, and cultural forces that both catalyze and impede progress through the stages. Third, a better understanding of the recycling process through the stages (what Schaef [1981] would call "a higher level of truth" [understanding]) is needed. Fourth, greater elaboration of the similarities and differences between our proposed model and other developmental theories is needed. Finally, and most important, much research is needed to substantiate the various components of this theory. It is hoped that future theoretical and empirical efforts will address these and other important implications of the model.

Cross (1971, p. 25) points out that until Blacks understand, control, and direct the process of positive identity development they "will continue to rely on the jolting consequences of fortuitous events"; the same applies to women. It is our hope that continued exploration of this model will increase our collective understanding of the process and lessen "the jolting consequences of fortuitous events" in women's lives.

References

Avery, D. M. (1977). The psychosocial stages of liberation. *Illinois Personnel and Guidance Association Quarterly, 63,* 36–42.

Cherniss, C. (1972). Personality and ideology: A personological study of women's liberation. *Psychiatry, 35,* 190–225.

Chodorow, N. (1973). *The reproduction of mothering.* Berkeley: University of California Press.

Cross, W. E. (1971). Negro-to-Black conversion experience: Toward a psychology of Black liberation. *Black World, 20*(9), 13–27.

Cross, W. E. (1978). The Thomas and Cross models of psychological nigrescence: A review. *Journal of Black Psychology, 5,* 13–31.

Douvan, E., & Adelson, J. (1966). *The adolescent experience.* New York: John Wiley.

Downing, S. D. (1983). *The emerging female self: An exploration of personal identity, social identity and the conflict of coalescence.* Unpublished manuscript, University of Denver, School of Professional Psychology.

Erickson, E. H. (1950). *Childhood and society.* New York: Norton.

Erickson, E. H. (1968a). *Identity, youth and crisis.* New York: Norton.

Erickson, E. H. (1968b). *Young man Luther: A study in psychoanalysis and history.* New York: Norton.

Giddings, P. (1984). *When and where I enter: The impact of Black women on race and sex in America.* New York: Morrow.

Gilligan, C. (1982). *In a different voice: Psychological theory and women's development.* Cambridge: Harvard University Press.

Gurin, P. (1982). Group consciousness. *Institute for Social Research Newsletter, 10*(1,2), 4–5.

Helms, J. E. (1984). Toward a theoretical explanation of the effects of race on counseling: A Black and White model. *The Counseling Psychologist, 12,* 153–165.

Jackson, B. W. (1977). The function of a Black identity development theory in achieving relevance in education for Black students (Doctoral dissertation, University of Massachusetts, Amherst, 1976). *Dissertation Abstracts International, 37,* 5667A.

Josselson, R. (1973). Psychodynamic aspects of identity formation in college women. *Journal of Youth and Adolescence, 2,* 3–52.

Kegan, R. (1982). *The evolving self: Problem and process in human development.* Cambridge: Harvard University Press.

Keisler, D. (1966). Some myths of psychotherapy research and the search for a paradigm. *Psychological Bulletin, 65,* 110–136.

Knefelkamp, L. L., Widick, C. C., & Stroad, B. (1975). Cognitive-developmental theory: A guide to counseling women. In L. Harmon, J. Birk, L. Fitzgerald, & M. Tanney (Eds.), *Counseling women.* Monterey, CA: Brooks/Cole.

Lichtenstein, H. (1977). *The dilemma of human identity.* New York: Jason Aranson.

Loganbill, C., Hardy, E., & Delworth, U. (1982). Supervision: A conceptual model. *The Counseling Psychologist, 10,* 3–42.

Malson, M. R. (1983). Black women's sex-roles: The societal context for a new ideology. *Journal of Social Issues, 39,* 101–113.

Marcia, J. E., & Friedman, M. L. (1970). Ego identity status in college women. *Journal of Personality, 38,* 249–263.

Miller, J. B. (1976). *Toward a new psychology of women.* Boston: Beacon.

Moreland, J. R. (1976). Facilitator training for consciousness raising groups in an academic setting. *The Counseling Psychologist, 6*(3), 66–68.

Notes from the third year. (1970). New York: The Herstory Collection [Microfilm].

Rawlings, E. T., & Carter, D. K. (1977). Feminist and nonsexist psychotherapy. In E. I. Rawlings & D. K. Carter (Eds.), *Psychotherapy for women.* Springfield, IL: Charles C Thomas.

Rebecca, M., Hefner, R., & Oleshansky, B. (1976). A model of sex-role transcendence. *Journal of Social Issues, 32,* 197–206.

Rosenthal, N. B. (1984). Consciousness raising: From revolution to re-evaluation. *Psychology of Women Quarterly, 8,* 309–326.

Schaef, A. W. (1981) *Women's reality: an emerging female system in a white male society.* Minneapolis: Winston.

Thomas, C. (1970). Different strokes for different folks. *Psychology Today, 4*(4), 48–53, 78–80.

Thomas, C. (1971). *Bays no more.* Encino, CA: Glencoe.

Williams, J. (1977). *Psychology of women: Behavior in a biosocial context.* New York: Norton.

Yetman, N., & Steele, C. (Eds.). (1975). *Majority and minority: The dynamics of racial and ethnic relations.* Boston: Allyn & Bacon.

Chapter 28

Transgenderism and College Students: Issues of Gender Identity and its Role on our Campuses

Kelly A. Carter

A number of specific assumptions guide the college student affairs profession, one being the concept of the "whole student." By definition, the goal of student development is promoting the growth of the whole student in both the cognitive and psychosocial domains (Brown, 1989; Rogers, 1989). The awareness of identity as a part of social and personal development is apparent in many development theories used in the student affairs profession. For example, "identity versus role confusion" is one of Erikson's (1950, 1968) eight stages of development. This stage occurs while traditional students are attending college. Chickering also recognized the importance of identity development (Chickering, 1969; Chickering & Reisser, 1993). Other theories of majority and minority student development directly focus on identity awareness (Cass, 1979; Cross, 1991; Helms, 1990; Sue & Sue, 1990).

When we think of students establishing their identities, we rarely think of gender identity as an issue. We might think of specific male identity issues, "What does it mean to be a real man?" (Levinson, 1986) or specific female identity issues, "What does it mean to be a professional woman?" (Levinson, 1996). But an issue that faces some students is their actual gender identity, "Am I a man, woman or something else?" (Feinberg, 1998). Sometimes this question arises due to physical vagueness: having both male and female genitalia. More often, students struggle with their assigned gender. Some students may feel more comfortable functioning outside of their gender roles either part-time or full-time. For others, the identity issue is even more pressing: they experience discomfort with their physical body. Some may question if, cognitively and emotionally, they truly are the other gender. A few students question if they are yet another gender, neither male nor female. All of these students can be considered transgendered (Feinberg, 1998).

Students with these identity issues bring a number of concerns to their college or university settings. On issues of gender, most of our society functions dualistically (Lips, 1997) and as a microcosm of society, so does higher education. Not only are our living facilities and rest rooms segregated by gender, but so are many student groups, athletic teams, and even our daily language. Tinto (1987, as cited in Love, Jacobs, Boschini, Hardy, & Kuh, 1993) recognized that, "students who identify with marginal or loosely connected groups (e.g., commuters on a residential campus) usually feel less connected to the overall student culture; those who feel unconnected are less likely to graduate" (p. 60). Marginalized transgendered students across the nation have been demanding comfortable living space, representation in organizations, and support from higher education administration and staff (Reitz, 1995; B. Zemsky, personal communication, November 15, 1996). Student affairs professionals, who are responsible for the development of all students, must see that the needs of transgendered students are met.

In order to understand transgendered students and their issues, four major topics must be addressed. First, educators must understand common terminology and the issues surrounding the use of various terms. Second, they must be familiar with the history of the phenomena surrounding transgenderism. Third, the psychology of transgenderism needs to be reviewed to eliminate stereotypical misconceptions. Fourth, the relationship between LGB issues and transgenderism needs to be discussed.

Terminology

Agreement on a common language or vocabulary would be helpful in communicating about transgender issues. The transgender movement is relatively new, however, and many transgendered individuals are still deciding how they want to define themselves. Feinberg (1996) raised a concern that many publications produced in the early stages of the movement will soon be outdated, due to changed vocabulary. There are some generally accepted terms, but understandably there are criticisms associated with these terms as well.

Originally the term *transgenderist* was meant to refer to a person who lives full time as the other gender, but who has not made any anatomical changes. Virginia Prince, a pioneer gender researcher, coined the term to refer to people like herself (Feinberg, 1996; MacKenzie, 1994). While many still use the word with Prince's intent, the community at large now views the term *transgendered* more generally, meaning an individual who bends or blends gender. It encompasses terms such as cross-dresser, transvestite, transsexual, and intersexual (Ekins & King, 1996; Raymond, 1996). Feinberg (1996) noted that the term *trans* is increasingly being used in a uniting way to make the term *transgenderist* available for those who are still identifying as such. In this chapter, *transgender* will be used as an umbrella term.

The terms *cross-dresser* and *transvestite* are often used interchangeably (Brown & Rounsely, 1996; Hirschfeld, 1910/1991; King, 1996), although some writers assert a distinction (Feinberg, 1996; MacKenzie, 1992). Many entirely reject the term transvestite due to its clinical origin (Garber, 1992). Others claim that both terms are legitimate, but have different meanings. These critics would claim the distinction lies in causality. A cross-dresser is motivated by social results, while a transvestite has a genuine emotional need to cross-dress. Most sources agree that the term cross-dresser refers to anyone who wears the sex role clothing of another gender, generally on a part-time basis. While cross-dressers tend to be very diverse, Brown and Rounsley (1996) asserted that a typical transvestite is heterosexual, married, and well educated. Benjamin (1953) proposed a continuum of cross-dressing that encompassed issues of causality, ranging from transsexuals to part-time cross-dressers. Rothblatt (1995) claimed that most modern women could certainly be referred to as cross-dressers because some wear clothing that was originally intended for males (such as pants, jeans, and even blazers and ties). In this chapter, the term *cross-dresser* will be used to indicate persons who wear clothing identified with a gender other than their own, regardless of the reason.

Gender dysphoria is a clinical label coined by Fisk in 1974 to refer to a gender identity crisis (Fisk, 1974). It has been incorporated into the *Diagnostic and Statistical Manual of Mental Disorders-IV* (American Psychiatric Association, 1994), a guidebook used by psychologists and psychiatrists to identify disorders exhibited by their clients. Although *gender dysphoria* is rejected as a social identity label, because few people are aware of any language associated with gender identity issues, the clinician's office is often the first place persons learn terminology and this label may be the first one they apply to themselves.

Transsexualism is yet another clinical tem, although it is more widely used as an identity label. The term was first used in 1953 by Benjamin. Transsexuals identify a distinct difference between their physical sex and their internal sense of gender. Bolin (1988) described the male-to-female transsexuals in her study as "women who have male genitals . . . not hyperfeminine in gender identity or role" (p. 2, xii). Some transsexuals choose to undergo hormone therapy, often, but not always, followed by sex reassignment surgery (SRS). Those who have decided to undergo SRS, but haven't yet, or are in the process of transition, are considered *pre-operative*. Transsexuals who have completed SRS are considered *post-operative*. Some are either content with no physical alterations or cannot afford the change and are thus referred to as *non-operative* or *no-op*. Some in the latter group, such as Virginia Prince, prefer to be called *transgenderist*.

Consideration of physical versus emotional phenomena leads to the question: What determines sex and gender? Is there a difference? Feinberg (1996) and Lips (1997) explained that *sex* refers to physical make up. There are three criteria that distinguish an individual's sex: genitalia, chromosomes, and hormone levels. Some examples of sex are male, female, or *intersexual*. An *intersexual* is one whose genitalia, chromosomes, and hormone levels are not congruent with each other. Intersexuality does not occur in only one way; therefore there are many sexes. Some people have both male and female genitalia, while others may have vaguely defined genitalia matched with vague chromosome pairings such as XXY. By contrast, the term *gender* refers to internal identity (Bolin, 1988; Feinberg, 1996; Grimm, 1987; Lips, 1997). Some genders include masculine, feminine, and androgynous. Because gender is an internal identity, some transsexuals have defined their own gender. Therefore there are endless variations on gender as well. Arguably, every individual could represent a unique gender.

When making the distinction of which way a cross-dresser is dressing or with what gender a transsexual identifies, the terms *female-to-male (F to M)* and *male-to-female (M to F)* are often used, the first word being their sex and the second being the gender they present or with which they identify. There are two strong criticism of these terms. MacKenzie (1992) asserted that if the second term refers to one's gender then better terminology would be female-to-man and male-to-woman. Feinberg (1996) also noted that "terms like cross-dresser, cross-gender, male-to-female, and female-to-male reinforce the idea that there are only two distinct ways to be—you're either one or the other—and that's just not true" (p. xi).

As one of Hirschfeld's (1910/1991) mottoes states, "There are more emotions and phenomena than words" (p. 17). A major point to remember when using terminology is that people are free to identify as they choose. Understanding existing phenomena and associated terminology is necessary, however, if student affairs professionals are to learn more about how these issues can affect their students and their institutions.

Why Does "Gender Blending" Make Us Uncomfortable?

Transgenderism does make people uncomfortable. It is important to acknowledge that nearly every person raised in this nation, including those who are transgendered, was socialized to believe in the existence of only two sexes: male and female. A distinction between sex and gender is rarely made. Children are not born with the ability to distinguish what is male and what is female. Society works very hard to teach children the differences and by age three the goal is usually met (Lips, 1997).

Most people also are given fairly strict guidelines within which the two sexes function. Feminist rhetoric suggests that these rigid expectations are a result of sexism in the culture of this and other countries (Raymond, 1996). Certain emotions, communication styles, careers, and clothing choices are socially limited to one sex or the other. Violations of the social rules have serious implications. Picture a career-oriented male engineer wearing a smart tailored skirt with his jacket and tie to an interview. Even optimists who hope he would have a shot at the job know that bias will definitely be at work during his interview. Family, schools, media, and/or culture have taught gender role rules to nearly every American. Some people are actively attempting to unlearn them, but the socialization is strong. It is this socialization plus the prevalence of two common myths that perpetuate discomfort with transgender issues. The two myths are that (1) transgenderism is a new fad and (2) transgendered people are crazy.

History of Transgenderism

Many people believe that transgenderism is a new topic and perhaps the newest fad in sexuality development. This myth has been fueled by the increasing visibility of transcending celebrities: Michael Jackson, Madonna, David Bowie, Annie Lennox, RuPaul, and Dennis Rodman. Because of the relatively recent origin of the transgender movement, it is tempting to believe that these phenomena are new and that this issue is trendy and will soon pass. In fact, the concept of gender bending is as old as gender roles themselves. The transgender phenomena can be accounted for in nearly every culture throughout history. Some societies and cultures even accounted for more than two gender roles (Feinberg, 1996).

During mid-3000 BCE (before the common era) in parts of Europe, the Middle East, northern Africa, and western Asia, male to female transsexual priestesses were reported as having important religious roles. These priestesses served as liaisons to a goddess most often called the Great Mother. This Great Mother has been described as an intersexual deity. The priestesses would castrate themselves and wear women's clothing (Besnier, 1993; Feinberg, 1996).

Many Greek mythological heroes and gods cross-dressed at one time or another and others even changed their sex. Intersexuals are represented in Greek mythology and Greek art (Feinberg, 1996; Herdt, 1993). One example is Eros the goddess of love, whose parents were Hermes and Aphrodite. Their names are the source of the word hermaphrodite, an outdated term meaning intersexual. Cupid is the Roman equivalent of Eros. The Greek gods or heroes Dionysus, Athena, Achilles, Theseus, and Heracles were all reported to have cross-dressed at some time (Feinberg, 1996).

Although there are many accounts of the Amazons, no two seem to be quite the same. Most sources agree that these women were brave warriors either defending their territory or invading others' lands. Some accounts tell of male slaves who attended to domestic responsibilities and occasionally helped with procreation. Sources have placed them in numerous locations, including the north side of Asia Minor, Syria, Benin, and the banks of the Baltic Sea (Feinberg, 1996, Hirschfeld 1910/1991; Wheelwright, 1989). One source historically places their existence at around 1050 AD (Hirschfeld 1910/1991). According to Greek legend, Amazons were paired up in battles with such warriors as Achilles, Theseus, and Heracles. The Greeks made reference in their writings to an androgynous race they encountered during travels in Abomey, Benin in western Africa. These people were believed to also be the Amazons. In 1576, a Spanish explorer, Pedro de Magalhaes, wrote about a culture in northeastern Brazil in which the women lived as men and were accepted as such. It was he who named the "Amazon River" after the Amazons he had read about (Feinberg, 1996).

During the Byzantine Empire (200s–1100s), eunuchs were fairly common in eastern Europe. Eunuchs were men who chose to withdraw from the world and refused to procreate; thus the term means something more than just a castrated male. Some men chose to engage in these actions for religious reasons while others wanted to achieve status through court positions that were usually reserved for eunuchs. Others did not

have a choice; they became sterile through illness, birth defect, or accident. Some peasant families had their infant sons castrated so they could be sold into slavery. The castration of men was an early form of sex reassignment surgery. The physiology of a woman was defined in relation to the male physiology (without a penis), hence the eunuch was viewed by many as a woman. However, most often in the Byzantine Empire, castration was performed by the mutilation of the testicles (removal, crushing, or tying off). In many cases, then, eunuchs were viewed as neither male nor female, just eunuchs. But the Roman society did not include a language for such a third sex option, so the masculine pronoun was applied to eunuchs. Eunuchs castrated in adulthood retained most of their secondary sex characteristics, and continued to be sexually active. Eunuchs castrated as boys never experienced puberty and therefore lacked body hair, musculature, and a deep voice (Ringrose, 1993).

Legend speaks of a female Pope Joan or John Anglicus during the mid-800s. She attended university with her lover, disguised as a man. She so loved the knowledge and critical thinking she was exposed to, that she never stopped passing as a man. "She recognized that her intellect was strong and she was drawn by the sweetness of learning" (Hotchkiss, 1996, p. 75). Joan pursued a career in the church and was elected as pope unanimously by the voting body. During a ceremonial procession Pope Joan dropped to the ground and gave birth. Stories say she died in childbirth or was killed by the mob there. Her reign was said to have lasted two years, seven months, and four days. To this day, the pope does not proceed down the alleyway where Pope Joan is said to have died (Dekker & van de Pol, 1989; Feinberg, 1996; Garber, 1991; Hotchkiss, 1996).

The story of Joan of Arc is well known. Born in the early 1400s, she came from a French peasant family and wore men's clothing. She became a warrior and was instrumental in leading other peasants in defending France against the English in the Hundred Years War. The peasants deemed her a scared figure, while the French ruling class and church abhorred her heroism. As a peasant she accomplished what the people in power could not. For this reason the French aristocracy sought to execute her. They arrested her on charges of paganism and cross-dressing. The paganism became hard to prove, so they prosecuted her for cross-dressing. Because there were no laws against cross-dressing, they had her sign an agreement to never wear men's clothing again. However, as the French ruling class knew, Joan was illiterate and did not understand what she was signing. Since she continued to cross-dress, they executed her based on disobedience. It is evident in the accounts of her trial that Joan's decision to wear men's clothes was a spiritual one. When Joan had to make a decision of whether to burn alive tied to a stake at the age of 19 or wear women's clothing, Joan said "Not for anything would I take an oath not to arm myself and wear men's clothing in order to do our Lord's pleasure!" (Trask, 1996, p. 122). Her spirituality was event to the French; some thought of her as a witch who used her powers for evil while others considered her a messenger from god (Dekker & van de Pol, 1989; Hotchkiss, 1996; Trask, 1996).

Dekker and van de Pol (1989) cited 119 cases of female to male cross-dressing in western Europe between the years of 1550 and 1839. They noted, "Whatever the personal motives for dressing as a man, an important consideration was that the women knew that they had predecessors, that other women had made the same decision" (p. 100).

In the 1700s, European seafarers recorded information about transgendered Polynesians. Journals noted boys being raised as females with an by women. Other times seafarers noted being attracted to a girl dancer who later turned out to be a young boy. Besnier (1993) cited examples in contemporary Polynesia of transgendered men taking on female roles in various societies. He also reported some cross-dressing, especially during festive occasions. There is no known religious connection for the transgendered Polynesians (Besnier, 1993).

In modern day India the hijras are considered neither male nor female. Hijras are vehicles of divine power to Bahuchara Mata, a version of the Mother God. A hijra is considered man plus woman. Born as interseuxal or transsexual, hijras feel a calling to Bahuchara Mata. "It is by virtue of their sexual impotence (with women) that men are called on by Bahuchara Mata to dress and act like women and undergo emasculation" (Nanda, 1993, p. 373).

"Berdache" is an American anthropological word that was coined in the 1600s. Feinberg (1996) noted that many Native people consider the term offensive. Europeans used the word in a derogatory way to describe any Native person who did not fit narrow European definitions of gender. Feinberg used instead the respectful term, "Two-Spirit." The role of the Two-Spirit person is documented in nearly 150 North American societies. Roscoe (1993) explained three major roles of the Two-Spirit people: specialized production, supernatural sanction, and gender variation. "Berdaches were accepted and integrated members of their communities, as their economic and religious reputations indeed suggest . . . In a few cases they were feared because of the supernatural power they were believed to possess" (p. 335). Gender roles are loosely defined in many Native cultures and the Two-Spirit tradition continues today (Bolin, 1993; Feinberg, 1996; Katz, 1976; Roscoe, 1993).

Psychology of Transgenderism

The question of pathology verses identity comes up quite often when modern day transgendered media characters are considered. Two predominant stereotypes persist. Either transgendered people are introduced for comic relief *(Mrs. Doubtfire, Tootsie,* and *The Bird Cage)* or portrayed as being pathologically crazy *(Silence of the Lambs).* With such images in the media, it is easy to believe that transgendered people have a psychological disorder. But these images come from an even more powerful place. As noted previously, strict gender roles have been extremely influential in setting up norms for people's behaviors. Once any behavioral norm is violated, the person is labeled as abnormal and consequently mentally unhealthy (Lips, 1997).

Even though the concept of transgenderism has been known since antiquity (Dekker & van de Pol, 1989; Feinberg, 1996; Herdt, 1993; Hotchkiss, 1996), it wasn't until 1830 that Friedreich first described the condition in the medical literature. In 1980, the American Psychiatric Association included under psychosocial disorders a section on gender identity disorders in its third edition of the *Diagnostic and Statistical Manual of Mental Disorders* (DSM-HI). Three different types of diagnoses were outlined: *transsexualism, non-transsexualism type,* and *not otherwise specified.* This was the first time the medical literature listed the transgender phenomena as a psychological disorder. This listing required insurance carriers to cover any services rendered to such persons, from psychotherapy to sex reassignment surgery (SRS).

Since 1980 there have been two more editions of the DSM: DSM-III-R (American Psychiatric Association, 1987) and DSM-IV (American Psychiatric Association, 1994). Within these newer documents, gender identity disorders (GID)) have been rearranged into various categories and even given a category of their own. Diagnoses and treatments vary as well.

Opinions within the transgender community vary greatly as to whether these identities should be included in the DSM. Some transgendered people believe that the inclusion is important to maintain insurance coverage. As long as gender identity disorders are included, there will be financial support for therapy, hormones, and full sex reassignment surgery (Pauly, 1992). However, many insurance companies refuse to cover costs regardless of the DSM inclusion of transgendered identities (Knox, 1989; Millenson, 1989).

Others argue that in order to have treatments covered, a person would have to be documented as having a mental illness. This labeling can be traumatic on many levels, but perhaps the most damaging is the cost to one's career (Goodavage, 1994; Johnson, 1994; Mazanec, 1993; Paddock, 1994; Pratt, 1995). Job discrimination against transgendered people in the United States is prohibited in only one state and three cities: Minnesota, Santa Cruz, Seattle, and San Francisco (Feinberg, 1996; Goodavage, 1994; Johnson, 1994; Paddock, 1994).

Many individuals believe that having a transgendered identity is not a mental disorder. A transsexual protester at an American Psychological Association meeting in 1993 said, "Transsexuality is not a disease. I am not crazy. It is who I am" (Olezewski, 1993, p. 13). Pressure to remove gender identity disorders from the DSM has been compared to the 1973 removal of homosexuality as a mental illness classification (Olezewski, 1993; Pauly, 1992).

During the early 1970s, research was based on the dualistic question, are transsexuals mentally sound or do they suffer from a psychopathological conflict? Two early studies (Finney, Bransdsma, Tondow, & Lemaistre, 1975; Stinson, 1972) showed a correlation between male-to-female transsexualism and a significant ego deficit, which implied some degree of psychopathology. Other researchers (Roback,

McKee, Webb, Abramowitz, & Abramowitz, 1976; Rosen, 1974; Tsushima & Wedding, 1979) studied male-to-female transsexual mental health in relation to other psychiatric populations. They found that mental health adjustment is an issue; however, there was no evidence of a correlation to psychopathology (Johnson & Hunt, 1990).

As every dualistic question is investigated, gray areas are discovered. Research shifted to an investigation of variables that may predict psychiatric adjustment depending on the type of transsexuals being considered. Studies in the 1980s (Freund, Steiner, & Chan, 1982; Green 1987; O'Gorman, 1982) focused on determining two separate etiologic tracks leading to transsexualism: male transsexuals whose gender orientation was rooted in a heterosexual cross-dressing fetishism and male transsexuals who first identified as gay men with feminine ideologies. Correlation was sought between the length of time the transsexuals spent in the feminine role and their mental health. O'Gorman (1982) theorized that late onset of transsexualism is correlated with a history of psychiatric illness. O'Gorman also assumed that late onset was correlated with heterosexual cross-dressing fetishism. Hence he theorized that transsexuals whose identity proceeded from heterosexual cross-dressing fetishism are more prone to psychiatric illness.

A study by Johnson and Hunt (1990) included 25 male-to-female transsexuals who were either post-operative or in the process of transition. They found a low correlation between the two typological features and psychological disturbance. The study also revealed that transsexualism manifests itself in both heterosexuals and homosexuals around the same time.

Bloom (1994) discussed two studies. The first involved a psychological test aimed at revealing a person's feelings of masculinity and femininity. The study compared female-to-male transsexuals before hormone therapy to genetic females. Findings showed that the transsexuals "tested high masculine/low feminine before the treatment and afterward as well-adjusted men who accept their feminine side" (p. 46). A second study compared the psychological personality of female-to-male transsexuals with genetic men and women. The transsexuals before treatment are not too far from the norm for women; but after treatment, they are completely in the normal range for men.

In November of 1995, headlines hit the world's papers, "Possible Transsexual Brain Trait Found" (Suplee, 1995). Dr. Dick F. Swaab and some of his colleagues in the Netherlands conducted a biological study of the brain. They looked at corpse brains of male-to-female transsexuals, heterosexual genetic men, homosexual genetic men, and heterosexual genetic women. A region of the hypothalamus, called the central division of the bed nucleus of the stria terminalis (BSTc), is thought to be responsible for sexual behavior. This area is 44% larger in men than in women, yet all 6 transsexual brains observed had female-sized BSTc. The researchers discovered that this area said nothing about sexual orientation, as the gay men's BSTc was the same size as the straight men's and the transsexuals varied in sexual orientation. (In an earlier study, LeVay, 1991 discovered another part of the hypothalamus that seems to be related to sexual orientation.) Further research into possible biological links to transgenderism is needed to confirm these findings.

With a better understanding of the history and psychology of transgenderism as a base, the implications of the transgender movement for LGB communities will be considered. What does gender identity have to do with sexual orientation?

Implications for the Lesbian, Gay, and Bisexual Communities

Although, by definition, gender identity and sexual orientation are two completely different issues, there are elements of each that bring them together. Gender identity refers to whether one is a man, woman, or person who transcends gender. Sexual orientation concerns the gender of the object of one's affections, such as heterosexual, gay, lesbian, or bisexual. Three concerns unite sexual orientation and gender identity in distinct ways: overlapping identities, mistaken identities, and the sexual orientation of transgendered people.

Individually, as transgendered people begin to define themselves, many first identify as lesbian, gay, or bisexual. They know that their life experience is different from others. Either lack of information about transgendered identities or internalized oppression can prevent transgendered people from embracing the accurate terminology. Many transgendered people find an accepting community among LGB people under the premise that they "belong" (Bloom, 1994). After identifying as transgendered, however, some people have been ostracized by their previously supportive LGB community.

While some individuals make a distinction between their sexual orientation and their gender identity, there is some overlapping of identities as well. An example is a drag queen, a cross-dressing man. Some men impersonate females only for the purpose of entertaining others, some cross-dress for comfort on occasion, and others incorporate women's clothing into their everyday wardrobe. Most drag queens are gay. There are LGB-identified people who identify as transgendered as well (Burana, Roxxie, & Due, 1994). Some post-operative transsexuals have reported experiencing attraction to the sex that they have transitioned to, and therefore identify as lesbian or gay (Bornstein, 1994).

Based on our popular culture stereotypes of LGB people (Lips, 1997), transgendered people are often mistakenly assumed to be the same as LGB people. Transgendered people are perhaps more vulnerable to random homophobic attacks than LGB people. Even though many members of the transgender community are not readily identifiable on the street, some are. As a male-to-female cross-dresser walks down the street in women's apparel, the shouts out of the passing car are not, "Hey, freaky transgendered guy." The shouts are most likely fueled by homophobia, like, "Faggot!" When a pre-operative female-to-male transsexual walks out of a store, the group who pulls him into an alley and beats him is not doing so because this person has transcended gender. This person is perceived as gay or lesbian, and is being gay bashed. It's not only strangers who attack transgendered people. Those who are not clearly identified have been attacked as well by people they have trusted and to whom they have acknowledged their identity. Contrary to media portrayal, transgendered people are quite often the victims of assaults and rarely are the perpetrators (Denny & Schaffer, 1992). Many transgendered people feel a connection to the LGB communities because they are all targets of the same hate—homophobia.

If gender identity concerns an individuals' gender and sexual orientation concerns the gender of the object of one's affections, what happens when a transgendered person is involved in an affectionate relationship? What is the sexual orientation of the transgendered person? What is the sexual orientation of the person who is attracted to a transgendered person? Currently, there is no answer to that question. The premise upon which the transgender movement is based is freedom from gender, and yet when individuals identify their sexual orientation a rigid definition of gender is required. With limited options in our language many have become creative, using terms such as omnisexual or transdyke. However, these terms are by no means universal. The critical point to remember is that when the intent is to include all sexual orientations, the sexual orientations of transgendered people and the objects of their affections must be included. The safest way to accomplish this is to include the term transgendered when referring to all sexual orientation minorities; i.e., lesbian, gay, bisexual, and transgendered, or LGBT.

In summary, the transgender movement has the following implications for the LGB communities: (a) Some transgendered people have identified themselves, or currently identify themselves, as gay, lesbian, or bisexual; (b) Transgendered people are also targets of homophobia; and (c) Transgendered sexual orientation should be included when referring to all minority sexual orientations. The LGB movement and the transgender movement, although not the same, have too much in common to ignore.

Implications and Recommendations for Student Affairs

After reviewing the facts around two common myths about transgendered people (that transgenderism is a new phenomena and that transgendered people are crazy) and the relationship between transgendered individuals and LGB people, implications for the field of student affairs can now be discussed in an informed manner. Practitioners need to know what sort of incidents involving transgender issues are occurring on college campuses and how to proactively address potential issues.

Some practitioners may question whether transgender issues are prevalent enough within higher education to even warrant concern. Although transsexuals who seek sex reassignment surgery make up less than .01% of the population in Europe and the United States, "experts

say that it is reasonable to assume that there are scores of unoperated cases for every operated one" (Brown & Rounsley, 1996, p. 9). Given that transsexuals are only part of the transgendered spectrum, it is likely that at least a few transgendered students will be found on most college campuses. If transgender issues are prevalent at all, they are relevant enough to address. There are three primary ways for student affairs administrators to address the needs of transgendered students: work towards an elimination of administrative gender division, provide support resources that specifically target transgendered students, and educate the university community about transgender issues.

Any segregation of students by gender presents a problem for individuals who transcend gender. Restrooms, sports teams, and some student organizations are segregated by gender. Daily language, including use of pronouns, demands that assumptions be made about the individuals people are talking to or about. In addition, society has normative expectations about men and women that, when violated, have serious social implications. Student affairs departments face these types of questions: Where does college housing assign a preoperative female-to-male transsexual? Which rest room is he allowed to use? For which track team does a male-to-female transsexual run, women's or men's? Is a cross-dressing male able to be admitted into a sorority? Can a cross-dressing student be dismissed from a classroom for being a disturbance? How should university records for transsexual students who change their names reflect these changes? In addition to these administrative questions, questions of support exist: Do LGB student resources also provide support for transgendered students? What will be the reaction of university officials who are asked to console a beaten cross-dresser? Does the university's definition of diversity include gender diversity? Which pronouns are to be used when staff speak to transgendered students? Does the university have certain expectations of each gender, behaviorally or otherwise?

Idealistically, once gender classification is eliminated from society, all of these questions will be resolved. During a talk given after her performance, "Opposite Gender Is Neither," at the Pennsylvania State University, Kate Bornstein explained her theory that there is absolutely no reason to categorize gender other than to discriminate and oppress (personal communication, April, 4, 1995). She sees a future where gender is chosen, and there are so many genders that oppression will not be an option. Rothblatt (1995) also argued against the necessity for gender definition. She equated gender categorization with racial apartheid.

While doing away with gender categorization seems fantasy-like and at best only a future solution, there are measures that can be taken now toward that end. Consider that co-educational housing, single occupancy rooms, unisex rest rooms, and open admission policies for all student groups are measures that many institutions are presently practicing (Winston, 1993). However, even if an institution of higher education established an intention to do away with all divisions based on gender, the school would still exist in a dualistic society and schools do not function independently of societal norms.

Despite this limitation, policies and common practices should be examined. Any gender segregation that can be eliminated, should be eliminated. If a policy, such as visitation restrictions, cannot be changed due to the politics or values of the institution, student affairs practitioners need to think about the implications of the policy for their transgendered student population. How would a school with a visitation policy react if a male-to-female cross-dresser walked into a women's residence hall after hours? Is there a procedure in place? How can the transgendered student be supported in such an environment? Being unprepared for such a situation can leave student affairs practitioners fumbling for an appropriate response. Institutions should identify the policies that transgendered students would find the most challenging to navigate around. Proactive measures, such as anticipating potential problems and appropriate responses (with regard to the student and the institution) would be helpful when and if the need arises.

For an institution of higher education realistically to meet the development needs of its transgendered students, support services must be provided. Any resources on campus that address LGB students' needs can be expanded to include transgendered students' needs as well. This effort should entail more than a name change for the established programs and offices.

Staff members must be introduced to the meaning of terms and the issues of transgendered students. Some institutions have broadened the mission of their LGB student centers to include addressing the needs of their transgendered student population (Barnett, 1997) but many others have yet to consider this step.

To improve the campus climate, not only should support services be extended to transgendered students, but the college or university community must be educated on issues of transgenderism. In order for transgendered students to function comfortably, all students, faculty, staff, and administrators need to understand the concept that people have a right to be free from gender. This challenge extends beyond higher education environments and into the very core of society.

At the University of Minnesota, the mission of the Gay, Lesbian, and Bisexual Programs Office is to educate the university community. Director Betz Zemsky (personal communication, November 15, 1996) defines the problem as the campus climate, not the transgendered community. The University of Minnesota deals with a large open transgender community in comparison with many other universities due to the inclusion of gender identity in Minnesota's state civil rights law and the location of many clinics and services for transgendered people in Minneapolis. When the Gay, Lesbian and Bisexual Programs Office opened in 1993, one of its' first goals was to educate the community about the meaning of "transgender." In January 1995, a planning committee made up of transgendered people from the university community put together a week of programming focused on transgender issues. The tone of the week's activities was, "Let's look at deconstructing gender; let's learn about ourselves!" (B. Zemsky, personal communication, November 15, 1996). Zemsky felt that this effort reached out to the transgender community and established the institution as an ally.

Language remains one of the biggest challenges. Even if society could accept freedom from gender, pronouns demand definition. The word "people" can be used in place of "men and women." Many gendered words can be neutralized: however, pronouns provide a limitation. In general, it is good practice to refer to people as the gender they are presenting. For example, a male-to-female cross-dresser would be referred to as "she" only when cross-dressing. However, the *best* practice is to respect the wishes of the person to whom one is referring. It is helpful to remember the advice given to allies of LGB people: don't assume the gender of the object of the person's affections. The same could be said for transgendered people: don't assume their gender identity.

There is absolutely no research on transgendered students. The size of the transgendered student population has not been determined. There is no documented method for recording incidents of harassment involving transgendered victims. While theorists and researchers have examined the identity development of LGB individuals (Cass, 1979; Zinik, 1985) there has been little research on the development of a transgendered identity. Bolin (1993) did study the psychosocial development of male-to-female transsexuals and proposed a four-stage model of development. However, male-to-female transsexuals make up a very small part of the transgendered population. For practitioners interested in the study of gender identity development, it would seem advantageous to study people who function on both sides of the dichotomous gender line. After talking to a few transsexuals, it is obvious that there is more to gender than social roles. One person compared the feeling to that of a phantom limb. They feel something that physically just isn't there. For a greater understanding of all transgendered identities, further research is needed.

But institutions cannot wait for definitive research to address the needs of the transgendered student population. Transgendered students are attending colleges and universities and deserve consideration in the development of policies and in the provision of services. If student affairs professionals ignore this population that are failing to carry out their role as educators and advocates for all students.

References

American Psychiatric Association. (1980). *Diagnostic and statistical manual of mental disorders* (3rd ed.). Washington, DC: Author.

American Psychiatric Association. (1987). *Diagnostic and statistical manual of mental disorders* (3rd ed., rev.). Washington, DC: Author.

American Psychiatric Association. (1994). *Diagnostic and statistical manual of mental disorders* (4th ed.). Washington, DC: Author.

Barnett, D. (1997, January 24). *LGBT campus resource centers* [On line]. Available: http://www.uic.edu/orgs/lgbt/LGBT directors_list.html.

Benjamin, H. (1953). Transvestism and transsexualism. *International Journal of Sexology, 7,* 12–14.

Besnier, N. (1993). Polynesian gender liminality though time and space. In G. Herdt (Ed.), *Third sex, third gender: Beyond sexual dimorphism in culture and history* (pp. 285–328). New York: Zone Books.

Bloom, A. (1994, July 18). The body lies. *The New Yorker,* pp. 38–49.

Bolin, A. (1988). *In search of Eve: Transsexual rites of passage.* South Hadley, MA: Bergin & Garvey.

Bolin, A. (1993). Transcending and transgendering: Male-to-female transsexuals, dichotomy and diversity. In G. Herdt (Ed.), *Third sex, third gender: Beyond sexual dimorphism in culture and history* (pp. 447–486). New York: Zone Books.

Bornstein, K. (1994). *Gender outlaw: On men, women, and the rest of us.* New York: Routledge.

Brown, M. L., & Rounsley, C. A. (1996). *True selves: Understanding transsexualism—for families, friends, coworkers, and helping professionals.* San Francisco: Jossey-Bass.

Brown, R. D. (1989). Fostering intellectual and personal growth: The student development role. In U. Delworth & G. R. Hanson (Eds.), *Student services: A handbook for the profession* (2nd ed., pp. 284–303). San Francisco: Jossey-Bass.

Burana, L., Roxxie, & Due, L. (1994). *Dagger: On butch women.* Pittsburgh, PA: Cleis Press.

Cass, V. C. (1979). Homosexual identity formation: A theoretical model. *Journal of Homosexuality, 4* (3), 219–235.

Chickering, A. W. (1969). *Education and identity.* San Francisco: Jossey-Bass.

Chickering, A. W., & Reisser, L. (1993). *Education and identity* (2nd ed.). San Francisco: Jossey-Bass.

Cross, W. E., Jr. (1991). *Shades of Black: Diversity in African-American identity.* Philadelphia: Temple University Press.

Dekker, R. M., & van de Pol, L. C. (1989). *The tradition of female transvestism in early modern Europe.* London: MacMillan.

Denny, D., & Schaffer, M. (1992, April 21). Do transgender issues affect the gay community? *Advocate: The National Gay & Lesbian Magazine,* p. 114.

Ekins, R., & King, D. (1996). Blending genders—an introduction. In R. Ekins & D. King (Eds.), *Blending genders: Social aspects of cross-dressing and sex-changing* (pp. 1–4). New York: Routledge.

Erikson, E. H. (1950). *Childhood and society*. New York: Norton.

Erikson, E. H. (1968). *Identity: Youth and crisis*. New York: Norton.

Feinberg, L. (1996). *Transgender warriors*. Boston: Beacon Press.

Feinberg, L. (1998). *Transliberation: Beyond pink or blue*. Boston: Beacon Press.

Finney, J. C., Bransdsma, J. M., Tondow, M., & Lemaistre, G. (1975). A study of transsexuals seeking gender reassignment. *American Journal of Psychiatry, 132*, 962–964.

Fisk, N. (1974). Gender dysphoria syndrome. In D. Laub & P. Gandy (Eds.), *Proceedings of the second interdisciplinary symposium on gender dysphoria syndrome* (pp. 7–14). Ann Harbor, MI: Edwards Brothers.

Freund, K., Steiner, B. W., & Chan, 5. (1982). Two types of cross gender identity. *Archives of Sexual Behavior, 11*, 49–63.

Garber, M. (1992). *Vested interests: Cross-dressing and cultural anxiety*. New York: Routledge.

Goodavage, M. (1994, December 19). San Francisco tough on transgender protection. *USA Today*, p. 7A.

Green, R. (1987). *The "Sissy Boy Syndrome" and the development of homosexuality*. New Haven, CT: Yale University Press.

Grimm, D. E. (1987). Toward a theory of gender. *American Behavioral Scientist, 31* 66–85.

Helms, J. E. (1990). *Black and white racial identity: Theory, research, and practice*. New York: Greenwood.

Herdt, G. (1993). *Third sex, third gender: Beyond sexual dimorphism in culture and history*. New York: Zone Books.

Hirschfeld, M. (1991). *Transvestites: The erotic drive to cross-dress* (M. A. Lombardi-Nash, Trans.). Buffalo, NY: Prometheus Books. (Original work published in 1910)

Hotchkiss, V. R. (1996). *Clothes make the man: Female cross-dressing in medieval Europe*. New York: Garland.

Johnson, C. (1994, December 13). 'Transgender' bias is banned in S. F.: Supervisors create a new civil right. *San Francisco Chronicle*, pp. A15, A18.

Johnson, S. L., & Hunt, D. D. (1990). The relationship of male transsexual typology to psychosocial adjustment. *Archives of Sexual Behavior, 19*, 349–360.

Katz, J. (1976). *Gay American history: Lesbians and gay men in the U.S.A.* New York: Thomas Y. Crowell.

King, D. (1996). Gender blending: Medical perspectives and technology. In R. Ekins & D. King (Eds.), *Blending genders: Social aspects of cross-dressing and sex-changing* (pp. 79–98). New York: Routledge.

Knox, R. A. (1989, March 17). Transsexual blames insurer for plight. *Boston Globe*, pp. 15, 16.

LeVay, S. (1991). A difference in hypothalamic structure between heterosexual and homosexual men. *Science, 253,* 1034–1037.

Levinson, D. J. (1986). *The seasons of a man's life*. New York: Alfred A. Knopf.

Levinson, D. J. (1996). *The seasons of a woman's life*. New York: Alfred A. Knopf.

Lips, H. M. (1997). *Sex and gender: An introduction* (3rd ed.). Mountain View, CA: Mayfield.

Love, P. G., Boschini, V. J., Jacobs, B. A., Hardy, C. M., & Kuh, G. D. (1993). Student culture. In G. D. Kuh (Ed.), *Cultural perspectives in student affairs work* (pp. 59–79). Lanham, MD: ACPA.

MacKenzie, G. O. (1994). *Transgender nation*. Bowling Green, OH: Bowling Green State University Popular Press.

Mazanec, J. (1993, February 12). Transsexual joins ban on gays fray. *USA Today*, p. A3.

Millenson, M. L. (1989, May 25). Transsexual twilight zone. *Chicago Tribune*, section 5, pp. 1, 4.

Nanda, S. (1993). Hijras: An alternative sex and gender role in India. In G. Herdt (Ed.), *Third sex, third gender: Beyond sexual dimorphism in culture and history* (pp. 373–418). New York: Zone Books.

O'Gorman, E. C. (1982). A retrospective study of epidemiological and clinical aspects of twenty-eight transsexual patients. *Archives of Sexual Behavior, 11*, 231–236.

Olezewski, L. (1993, May 24). Transsexuals protest at psychiatry meeting. *San Francisco Chronicle*, p. 13.

Paddock, R. C. (1994, December 26). S. F. targets anti-transgender bias. *Los Angeles Times*, pp. A3, A46.

Pauly, I. B. (1992). Terminology and classification of gender identity disorders. In W. O. Bockting & E. Coleman (Eds.), *Gender dysphoria: Interdisciplinary approaches in clinical management* (pp. 1–14). New York: Haworth.

Pratt, C. (1995, June 18). The perilous times of transgender youth. *New York Times*, p. CY7.

Raymond, J. (1996). The politics of transgenderism. In R. Ekins & D. King (Eds.), *Blending genders: Social aspects of cross-dressing and sex-changing* (pp. 215–224). New York: Routledge.

Reitz, J. E. (1995, January 24). Proposal to add 'transgender' to LGBSA debated, voted down. *The Daily Collegian* (The Pennsylvania State University), p.1.

Ringrose, K. M. (1993). Living in the shadows: Eunuchs and gender in Byzantium. In G. Herdt (Ed.), *Third sex, third gender: Beyond sexual dimorphism in culture and history* (pp. 85–110). New York: Zone Books.

Roback, H. B., McKee, E., Webb, W., Abramowitz, C. V., & Abramowitz, S. L. (1976). Comparative psychiatric status of male applicants for sexual reassignment surgery, jejunoileal bypass surgery, and psychiatric outpatient treatment. *Journal of Sex Research, 12,* 315–320.

Rogers, R. F. (1989). Student development. In U. Delworth & G. R. Hanson (Eds.), *Student services: A handbook for the profession* (2nd ed., pp. 117–164). San Francisco: JosseyBass.

Roscoe, W. (1993). How to become a berdache: Toward a unified analysis of gender diversity. In G. Herdt (Ed.), *Third sex, third gender: Beyond sexual dimorphism in culture and history* (pp. 329–372). New York: Zone Books.

Rosen, A. C. (1974). Brief report of MMPI characteristics of sexual deviation. *Psychological Reports, 35,* 73–75.

Rothblatt, M. (1995). *The apartheid of sex: A manifesto on the freedom of gender.* New York: Crown.

Stinson, B. (1972). A study of twelve applicants for transsexual surgery. *Ohio State Medical Journal, 68,* 245–249.

Sue, D. W., & Sue, D. (1990). *Counseling the culturally different: Theory and practice* (2nd ed.). New York: Wiley.

Suplee, C. (1995, November 2). Possible transsexual brain trait found. *The Washington Post,* p. A3.

Trask, W. (1996). *Joan of Arc: In her own words.* New York: BOOKS & Co.

Tsushima, W. T., & Wedding, D. (1979). MMPI results of male candidates for transsexual surgery. *Journal Personality Assessment, 43,* 385–387.

Wheelwright, J. (1989). *Amazons and military maids: Women who dressed as men in the pursuit of life, liberty, and happiness.* London: Pandora.

Winston, R. G. (1993). *Student housing and residential life: A handbook for professionals committed to student development goals.* San Francisco: Jossey-Bass.

Zinik, G. (1985). Identity conflict or adaptive flexibility? Bisexuality reconsidered. In F. Klein & T. J. Wolf (Eds.), *Bisexualities: Theory and research* (pp. 7–19). New York: Haworth.

Section 7

DYNAMICS OF SEXUAL ORIENTATION
IN DEVELOPMENT

CHAPTER 29

IDENTITY DEVELOPMENT AND SEXUAL ORIENTATION: TOWARD A MODEL OF LESBIAN, GAY, AND BISEXUAL DEVELOPMENT

ANTHONY R. D'AUGELLI

Traditional notions of psychological identity stress the ontogenesis of personal coherence, with individuals moving slowly, if not always surely, toward a particular developmental end-state. Conventional wisdom holds that identity is normatively achieved at a certain point in chronological time, usually during late adolescence or early adulthood, and then endures. Such an essentialist position has dominated psychological models of development, reflecting a philosophical position that privileges certain kinds of individual action, reflection, and accomplishment while marginalizing others.

In contrast is the view that identity is a social construction. In this view, notions of personal consistency are no more fundamental than any other social reflection, custom, or script. Our awareness of the degree to which we are shaped by social circumstances varies over time as well; our images of identity are transient and malleable. Such a view is deeply suspicious of essentialist views of identity, seeing such constructions as disguised efforts at social moralism. Exemplifying the essentialist view, Erikson wrote of our "accrued confidence to maintain inner sameness and continuity" (Erikson, 1959, p, 89). Nearly twenty years later, Zurcher (1977) proposed an alternative, a "mutable self," an identity that is (and should be) fundamentally plastic. More recently, Gergen (1991) described the "saturated self" of contemporary postmodern society, an identity subject to perpetual scrutiny and redefinition. The self as multiple identities is well demonstrated in an analysis of lesbians, gay men, and bisexual people.

Being lesbian, gay, or bisexual in our culture requires living a life of multiple psychological identities. At the very least, lesbians, gay men, and bisexually identified people live in a predominantly heterosexual society that demands adherence to certain personal, relational, and social norms. On the other hand, difference becomes expressed in its own lesbian, gay, or bisexual coherence or identity, its own set of relational norms, its own communities, and its own culture (Herdt & Boxer, 1992). "Becoming" lesbian, gay, or bisexual requires two processes. On the one hand, it involves a conscious distancing from heterosexist essentialism—the person must become "ex-heterosexual" and cast off the mandated identity of mainstream culture. She or he must also create a new identity oriented around homosocial and homosexual dimensions. Constructing a complex "essence" is the task.

Living as a lesbian, gay, or bisexual person in our society demands identity diffusion in the traditional Eriksonian sense; at the same time, a lesbian, gay, or bisexual life exemplifies the functionality of identity differentiation and plasticity. In their analysis of sexual scripts, Simon & Gagnon (1986) state it well: "Recent considerations of the Eriksonian model have required increasing emphasis to dimensions of personality 'off the diagonal' of his epigenetic chart: the emphasis shifts from the linear developmental line to the maintenance of the self process with multiple sources of uncertainty. . . . What was once understandably perceived as a failure of socialization, a failure of identity crystallization, increasingly comes to be seen as the flexibility whose dialectical partner is cohesiveness" (p. 114).

In this chapter, I will use the example of sexual orientation and the development of lesbian, gay, and bisexual identities to point out how psychological views of identity function to reinforce heterosexist privilege. Heterosexism is the belief that "normal" development is heterosexual and that deviations from this identity are "unnatural," "disordered," or "dysfunctional." The general concepts underlying my analysis are these: (1) concepts of identity are rooted in a sociopolitical context, although this is seldom articulated; (2) this dynamic is demonstrated in historical views of lesbian and gay sexual orientation; (3) a model of lesbian, gay, and bisexual identity development based on a human development metatheory overcomes the fundamentally oppressive structure of earlier identity development views; and (4) such a model provides generative power for research and thinking about the development of sexual orientation and may be useful as well for other analyses of identity. A review of theoretical and metatheoretical issues related to sexual orientation is beyond the scope of this chapter. For such analyses, the reader is referred to McWhirter, Sanders, and Reinisch (1990), Sedgwick (1990), Stein (1992), and Weeks (1989).

Development of Sexual Orientation

Women and men who come to define themselves as lesbian, gay or bisexual must create their own consistencies in the face of two powerful barriers—the *social invisibility of the defining characteristic* and the *social and legal penalties* attached to its overt expression. Many writers on cultural diversity stress the process of self-acknowledgement—the proclamation of existence as the first critical step in personal and, later, social change. This simple proclamation is a revolutionary act in its repudiation of a socially imposed, majority identity and its silencing of difference. Lesbian, gay, and bisexual people are unique in that their defining difference—their sexual orientation—is invisible. Since they can literally hide their difference from others' gaze, the affirmation

of their existence is delayed. To the degree that identity is a socially mediated subjectivity, lesbians and gay men develop their identities in a uniquely private way. Consolidation of identity is driven by internal processes, with few positive and many negative social facilitators. The universal "coming-out" story is nearly always one of difficult *personal* discovery, of slowly and painfully appreciating a personal consistency that cannot be explored through routine socialization mechanisms.

Not only is lesbian and gay identity development intensely personal and private, but it is also conditioned by fear and shame. Even in early childhood, individuals learn that such an identity is problematic. Homophobic comments are routine in elementary schools, and exploration of same-sex physical and emotional closeness is severely punished by parents and others as soon as it appears. (More extreme sanctioning is applied to affection between boys.) The "hidden curriculum" of heterosexism is taught to all, even those children who as adults will self-identify as lesbian, gay, or bisexual. In contrast to other groups, lesbians, gay men, and bisexual people have grown up absorbing a destructive mythology before they appreciate that it is meant for them.

Homophobia at such an early age is unusually resistant to change. Lesbian, gay, and bisexual people have been socialized from birth in the normalcy of heterosexual identity and have been trained to reject any homosocial characteristics, especially those involving serious emotional or sexual expression. Becoming conscious of the pervasiveness of heterosexual socialization is difficult, since it demands as awareness of the historical nature of personal identity and an appreciation of the arbitrariness of identity concepts. Ultimately, as lesbians, gay men, and bisexual people acknowledge their difference, the introjected stereotypes that have silently directed their lives for many years become clearer. The disentangling of introjected identity concepts from personal history and individual characteristics is an enormously difficult task.

For this reason, the process of creating a lesbian-gay-bisexual identity is a prolonged one. Existing from the heterosexual identity that has been etched into consciousness since birth is profoundly unsettling and is greatly complicated by the many real societal barriers. The task is so difficult because heterosexual identity is not considered socially constructed but is rather viewed as natural. No self-consciousness exists about sexual orientation—unless one deviates from the unstated natural order. Our cultural script is that we must (painfully) create a non-heterosexual identity; heterosexuality exempts us from this kind of identity struggle, though surely contemporary heterosexual women and men confront some complex issues of sex-role articulation. Heterosexuality, in fact, has its own social history (Katz, 1990). Heterosexual men and women, however, do not need to create a sexual identity by *resistance*—by rejection of a cultural heritage that renders them suspect, deprives them of intimacy, and deracinates them from society. The other task of lesbian-gay-bisexual identity—the creation of a life that affirms one's nonheterosexual identity—is also profoundly difficult, yet it is less complex than existing heterosexual identity.

The need for lesbians, gay men, and bisexual people to struggle to proclaim their identity—first internally and privately in early adolescence, and then more and more publicly in early adulthood—contrasts with the degree to which core sexual identity remains unquestioned in most heterosexual women and men. This contrast highlights the power of achieved identity as a cultural concept that is to be developed by late adolescence—with emotional, vocational, and spiritual pieces all in place. But for lesbian, gay, and bisexual people, a critical piece—sexual identity—has resisted the heterosexist imperative and remains discordant, rendering other identity dimensions unstable.

This distinction forms the conceptual basis for heterosexism—the privileging and normalizing of one set of socioaffective characteristics. The entire dynamic is possible only because sexual identity is removed from its historical and political context. As a result, lesbian, gay, and bisexual lives are assumed to be unrelated and unresponsive to social circumstances, history, or culture, allowing for the image of an "essential homosexual" with mythic identity characteristics. This construction of an "essential" sexual identity prevents the fluidity of lesbian, gay, and bisexual sexual development from disturbing the achieved heterosexual statuses of the majority. Monolithic concepts of sexual identity, which assume that achieved psychological coherence is accomplished before adulthood, perpetuate heterosexist hegemony and fuel the many layers of very real victimization that nonheterosexual people must tolerate.

Scholars, theorists, and researchers have historically colluded in promoting an essentialist, unidimensional, and ahistorical perspective on lesbian-gay identity. For example, the view that homosexuality is a psychiatric disorder, which has dominated cultural concepts for most of this century, dismisses the historical, community, or social factors that shape the expression, repression, suppression, or denial of same-sex attractions. When the context is assumed to be irrelevant, homosexuality becomes a treatable reification, a dysfunctional *individual* identity detached from common experience. Presumed difference is transformed into distinct deviance. Such analyses readily lead to therapeutic methods to alter the deviant identity and to social policies and laws that institutionalize the stigma. The entire oppressive sequence is driven by a normative heterosexual pattern of identity development that constructs homosexuality as deviant, pathological, and illegal. The social opprobrium and criminalization attached to the deviant identity is consistent with the metatheoretical model that underlines these analyses.

The Human Development View

Lesbian and gay identity processes must be described using a conceptual model that explicates the complex factors influencing the development of people in context over historical time. The most powerful metatheoretical model for these processes is a life-span human development perspective (Baltes, 1987; Lerner, 1991). This general view, which has many individual variants, involves the explication of patterns of dynamic interaction of multiple factors over time in the development of an individual person. The developing woman or man must be understood in context; simultaneous descriptions of the person's social network, neighborhood and community, institutional settings, and culture are complemented by descriptions of individual physical and psychological change and stability. In contrast with earlier developmental views, the human development model stresses the impact of historical time on processes of development, whether the processes are observed during an individual's life, over the lives of family members, within a community, or in a culture. The human development perspective is an effort to discover variations among individuals as they move in time through social situations, the community, culture, and history. Moreover, they are not passive recipients of social history but shape circumstances and contexts as well.

A model for analyzing the development of sexual orientation must account for several broad sets of factors: individual changes from birth through adulthood to death, patterns of social intimacy across the life span, and linkages between the person, his or her significant others, and his or her proximal and distal environments. The first set of variables helps describe *personal subjectivities and actions,* the second set involves *interactive intimacies,* and the third set concerns *sociohistorical connections.* In contrast to either essentialist or constructivist models in which one set of explanatory constructs is deemed sufficient, a more appropriate framework must link the following three sets of factors:

1. How individuals feel about their sexual identities over their lives, how they engage in diverse sexual activities with different meanings, and how they construct their sexual lives and feel about them (*subjectivities and actions*). This element is influenced by and influences the second set of factors.

2. How sexuality is developed by parental and familial factors, how age-peer interactions shape and modify the impact of early parental and familial socialization, and how this learning affects and is affected by intimate partnerships of different kinds (*interactive intimacies*). All of this results from and affects the third set of factors.

3. Social norms and expectations of various geographic and subcultural communities; local and national social customs, politices, and laws; and major cultural and historical continuities and discontinuities (*sociohistorical connections*).

The goal is to locate an individual's life within a dynamic matrix of these three sets of factors. The life-span human development view is sufficiently comprehensive to meet the challenge of organizing these factors into a coherent system. This model, shown in Figure 1 presents the six identity processes that will be described later in this chapter.

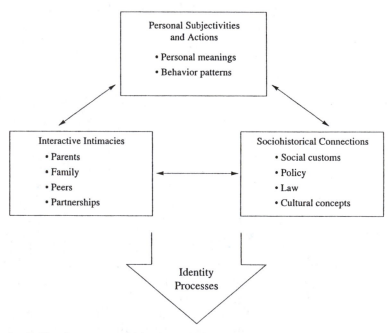

1. Exiting heterosexual identity
2. Developing a personal lesbian-gay-bisexual identity status
3. Developing a lesbian-gay-bisexual social identity
4. Becoming a lesbian-gay-bisexual offspring
5. Developing a lesbian-gay-bisexual intimacy status
6. Entering a lesbian-gay-bisexual community

Figure 1 Model of Lesbian-Gay-Bisexual Development

The major characteristics of a human development model are described below, this brief descriptions of their relevance to lesbian, gay, and bisexual identity development.

The first perspective is that *individuals develop and change over the entire course of their life spans.* This means that psychological, cognitive, behavioral, emotional, and physical change does not stop after the achievement of socially defined "adulthood" (usually heterosexual marriage and occupational stability). The development of sexual orientation is a lifelong process. This concept strikes at the heart of a view of sexual orientation as fixed early in life. Such a view is a historical anachronism, although it may be currently consistent with women's and men's phenomenological perceptions of their sexual identity. That sexual and affectional feelings can change in varying degrees over the course of one's life must be assumed; efforts to suggest otherwise are disguised social constructions. For instance, for an older man or woman to focus his or her emotional life on someone of the same gender late in life does not necessarily imply repression of *earlier* homosexual feelings. Feelings of physical and emotional closeness for an individual of the same gender can evolve throughout life; they are highly conditioned by social, family, and personal normative expectations.

The labels *lesbian* and *gay* and their negative connotations for older adults create a powerful barrier to the expression of intense closeness to same-sex others. Likewise, individuals who define themselves as lesbian or gay may experience affectional and sexual interest in people of the opposite sex across the span of their lives, though the plasticity of this process is limited by the current scripts about how to become lesbian or gay in contemporary society.

The human development model also embodies the importance of *developmental plasticity.* Plasticity suggests that human functioning is highly responsive to environmental circumstances and to changes induced by physical and other biological factors. The human development model makes few assumptions about the fixed nature of human functioning, but it suggests that plasticity is a prime characteristic of human behavioral development. Plasticity may change over chronological time: at different ages, certain components of human behavioral functioning are resistant to or responsive to differing circumstances. The implication for the development of sexual orientation is that sexual identity may be very fluid at certain times in the life span and more crystallized at others.

Given the role of hormonal development in sexual identity development, for instance, the likelihood is that the years in which changes in hormonal development in men and women occur are periods in which cognitive concepts of sexual orientation become especially salient. Sexual cues may be heightened and may have a greater impact on the individual because of her or his cognitive development. Yet this is not an inevitable, "natural" process. Adolescent peer culture in our society forces a social definition of sexual interests so that "expected" dating behavior can occur. This dating behavior happens with increasing distance from family monitoring and thus becomes increasingly subject to peer and distal sociocultural influences.

Self-awareness of lesbian-gay identity occurs for many during early adolescence (Herdt, 1989; Hetrick & Martin, 1987). However, the negative consequences of any homosocial-homosexual feelings are heightened because peer relationships would likely be threatened by the expression of these feelings. For many young people, the combination of cues, expectancies, and social circumstances are such that their sociosexual feelings remain diffuse, consciousness of their meaning is not well developed, and social circumstances, including pervasive homophobia, make the emergence of same-gendered affect or behavior improbable. The consequences of early disclosure for those teens whose feelings crystallize, however, are risky (Remafedi, Farrow, & Deisher, 1991).

The human development model emphasizes *interindividual difference in the development of intraindividual behavior.* In other words, the perspective focuses on behavioral variation; individual women and men are unique in their own development over the life span. The nature of interindividual differences in intraindividual functioning varies at different points in life, in different settings and in different historical periods. The issue of variability is essential to the development of sexual orientation. Indeed, the concept strikes directly at the trichotomization of sexual life, in which individuals are assumed to be heterosexual, gay or lesbian, or bisexual. The human development perspective suggests a continuum of sexual feelings and experience, but it would predict less variance in individual sexual self-definitions at certain phases of life (for example, in later adulthood), in certain kinds of families (for instance, those that do not value difference), in certain communities (such as those with strongly traditional values and those that are highly homogeneous in nature), and at certain historical times (like the 1950s). That sexual diversity increases during adulthood is the result not only of postadolescent experiential factors, but also of exposure to less restrictive expectations and of the availability of an increased range of behavioral models for diversity.

Finally, the human development perspective suggests that the deterministic views of behavior that often are seen in traditional models of development underestimate *the impact that individuals have on their own development.* The actions of an individual shape his or her development. Individuals and their families are not passive respondents to social circumstances; behavioral development also results from conscious choice and directed action. Individual acts and the acts of family members (in consort or in varying degrees of coordination) have an impact on the developmental process of the individual person and on the family unit. If we assume that development involves differentiation, then individuals who are likely to be more highly "developed" are those who possess refined abilities to behave in diverse ways, whose psychoemotional responsiveness allows for behavioral complexity, and whose social skills allow for competent performance in a wide range of social settings. These abilities to act in differentiated ways and to manipulate one's own development are at the core of lesbian, gay, and bisexual life.

But this power to self-create is also rooted in context. Lesbians and gay men shape their own development out of necessity in a heterosexist culture that provides no routine socialization practices for them. Because of this historical need, lesbians and gay men have created social institutions that provide socialization experiences. For example, the primary structure for urban gay men has been the gay bar, while earlier cohorts of gay men were socialized in urban bathhouses designed for multiple, anonymous sexual partnerings. (These have nearly dis-appeared as a result of the human immunodeficiency virus (HIV) epidemic.) In the past, lesbian socialization occurred more often in small, nonpublic informal groups or in women's "communities."

The increasing number of nonsexual opportunities for gay men and the greater number of expressive options for lesbians today will have a tremendous impact on their distinctive, "normative" development. Surely contemporary lesbian and gay youths face far more opportunities to share their adult identities than did their predecessors. These opportunities will counteract the prior identities shaped by the gay bar and women's communities: that gay men are sexual machines unable to form lasting attachments, lesbians are relationship-bound and disinterested in sexual pleasure, and bisexuals are ambivalent (for histories, see Faderman, 1991; Herdt, 1992; Hutchins & Kaahumanu, 1991).

Thus, the tenet that individuals help to direct their own development is extraordinarily powerful for understanding lesbian and gay development at different historical times. For an adult in 1954 to decide that she or he had strong lesbian or gay feelings and to publicly say this was an extremely different event than it would be today, although the actions may seem similar. One area where such changes are vivid involves disclosure to family.

In earlier days families could fear their offspring's arrest, loss of employment, social censure, and isolation. By definition, disclosure of lesbian or gay status was admission of criminal status and mental illness. The typical familial response was shame, and many lesbians and gay men chose to relocate to supportive urban communities without telling their families about their sexual orientation. In pursuing self-definition under the conditions of the time, they were forced into dual identities—the emerging lesbian-gay identity of their new context and the ongoing heterosexual identity presumed by their families. For many lesbian and gay adults, they self-development thus yielded two nonoverlapping "families"—their family of origin and their family of creation (Weston, 1991).

Though disclosure to family remains a highly stressful part of lesbian and gay development, it is now facilitated by increased cultural acceptance, more positive imagery in media, and many more affirmative resources, including parental support networks. These changes have moderated the intense familial rejection of earlier generations by increasing social acceptance and by the erosion of prevalent myths about parental responsibility for sexual orientation. Families have fewer realistic fears of horrific negative consequences for their off-spring, with the exception that parents of gay men report considerable worry about HIV infection (Robinson, Walters, & Skeen, 1989).

Yet powerful barriers to self-development remain. Because of the lack of legal protection that lesbians and gay men experience in asserting their rights in housing, adoption of children, military service, and so on, self-development remains compromised. Identity development and integration must be influenced if it jeopardizes employment and careers, family relationships, and personal safety. Historical, institutional, and cultural practices still negatively influence the self-development of lesbians, gay men, and bisexual people with multiple levels of victimization (Herek, 1992; Berrill & Herek, 1992).

The human development model serves as a powerful alternative to the pathologizing influences of the past and to approaches emphasizing one set of influencing factors to the exclusion of others. It suggests a very different psychological model from the traditional identity development view. In the next section, I will show one use of the human development model to explicate the processes of lesbian, gay, and bisexual identities.

Steps Toward a Model of Lesbian and Gay Male Development

The preceding section suggests that many current models of lesbian and gay male identity formation suffer from an excessive emphasis on the internal processes of personal development, usually conceived of in stage-model terms. In contrast, from a human development perspective, identity is conceived of as the dynamic processes by which an individual emerges from many social exchanges experienced in different contexts over an extended historical period—the years of his or her life. Several processes must be considered in studying lesbian and gay lives, using a human development metatheory as a guide. These processes are mediated by the cultural and sociopolitical contexts in which they occur.

Exiting Heterosexual Identity

This set of concerns involves personal and social recognition that one's sexual orientation is not heterosexual. Generally, this includes understanding the nature of one's attractions and labeling them. Initially, the breadth of meaning for the new label is uncertain: Does this mean a new life or no change at all? Historically, the label connoted a new identity, but this surely has changed. Exiting from heterosexuality also means telling *others* that one is lesbian, gay, or bisexual. This "coming out" begins with the very first person to whom an individual discloses and continues throughout life, decreasing only to the extent that the person is consistently and publicly identified with a non-heterosexual label. The pervasiveness of heterosexist assumptions makes the development of a continuing method for asserting non-heterosexuality a necessity.

Developing a Personal Lesbian-Gay-Bisexual Identity Status

An individual must develop a sense of personal socioaffective stability that effectively summarizes thoughts, feelings, and desires. Surely, such an initial status may be subject to revision as more experience is accumulated. This personal status functions as a mobilizing force, bringing along with it directives for action. Given that sexual orientation is fundamentally social in character, a lesbian, gay, or bisexual label propels people toward social interaction. To a large degree, they cannot confirm their sexual-orientation status without contact with others. Thus, they must learn how to be gay, lesbian, or bisexual, with these constructs defined by their proximal community of lesbians, gay men, or bisexual people.

In addition, a critical part of personal identity status is coming to an appreciation of internalized myths about non-heterosexuality. Some of these myths are the obvious stereotypes about inversion and dysfunctional development. Others are less well articulated, maintaining that lesbians and gay men do not have long-lasting relationships, that their families reject them, that they can never be engaged in child-rearing, and that they cannot have positions of power in society. To the degree that these views have been consciously incorporated, they are easy to challenge, but they must be challenged by demythologizing personal contact. Such occurrences as recognizing long-term lesbian and gay couples, talking to parents who warmly accept their children, and interacting with gay men and lesbians with children slowly modify the more deeply entrenched myths.

Developing a Lesbian-Gay-Bisexual Social Identity

This involves creating a large and varied set of people who know of the person's sexual orientation and are available to provide social support. This, too, is a lifelong process that has a profound effect on personal development. Ideally, one's social network is *affirmative*; that is, the people in it actively, continually, and predictably treat the person as lesbian, gay, or bisexual. A network composed of people who would prefer the person to hide his or her sexual orientation or who do not discuss it at all is not an affirming one. Tolerance is indeed harmful in this regard, in that it subtly reinforces societal interest in lesbian, gay, and bisexual invisibility. The process of creating a support network is long-lasting for this very reason. It takes times for a person to truly know the nature of others' reactions. These reactions are not uniform and may change over time. Also, many reactions are hypothetical: the reality of the person's orientation has not been translated into a real difference. For example, some may not find the person's orientation problematic until a dating partner emerges. The reality of sexual orientation in others' eyes is a complex process too: members of the individual's social network must also "come out" in their acknowledgement to others about her or his orientation.

Becoming a Lesbian-Gay-Bisexual Offspring

Parental relationships are often temporarily disrupted with the disclosure of sexual orientation. All available research suggests a return to the predisclosure state, though possibly only after the passage of some time (Cramer & Roach, 1988; Robinson, Walters, & Skeen, 1989; Strommen, 1989). Reintegration into the family of origin is the preferred outcome of the process, and the family (as a support network) must also be affirmative. Generally, families show complex patterns of adaptation, with parents, siblings, and members of the extended family coming to overlapping, but not identical, approaches. Much of the responsibility for movement from tolerance falls to the lesbian, gay, or bisexual person; families generally prefer to "contain" the deviance as much as possible (Boxer, Cook, & Herdt, 1991). This maneuver reinforces stigmas and myths and keeps the person in a distinct (nonheterosexual) category. While it is surely still the case that the burden will fall on the individual, more and more parents are taking active steps to reintegrate the person and to understand and affirm his or her life.

Developing a Lesbian-Gay-Bisexual Intimacy Status

The psychological complexities of same-sex dyadic relationships are made much more problematic by the invisibility of lesbian and gay couples in our cultural imagery. The view that gay men are solitary and cannot form relationships of any duration because of sexual excesses has surely dominated our views, even of lesbians. It is the case that our social and cultural apparatuses for heterosexual bonding are not available to lesbians and gay men (thus producing fewer examples of committed relationships and/or "marriage," for instance); this is a good example of how social structure reinforces heterosexism. The lack of cultural scripts directly applicable to lesbian, gay, and bisexual people leads to ambiguity and uncertainty, but it also forces the emergence of personal, couple-specific, and community norms, which should be more personally adaptive. (Note how the norms have radically changed in urban, gay male communities in the wake of the HIV epidemic.)

Entering a Lesbian-Gay-Bisexual Community

This set of identity processes involves the development of commitments to political and social action. For some who believe their sexual orientation to be a purely private matter, this never happens. For others, public engagement in social or political action is literally risky, in that jobs or housing may be jeopardized. However, an understanding of one's own identity development as a lesbian, gay, or bisexual person generally involves confrontation with current social and political barriers to development. The inequities become clearer as the person becomes more and more open or learns how much hiding is needed and why. To be empowered as a lesbian, gay, or bisexual person involves awareness of the structure of heterosexism, the nature of relevant laws and policies, and the limits to freedom and exploration. To be lesbian, gay, or bisexual in the fullest sense—to have a meaningful identity—leads to a consciousness of the history of one's own oppression. It also, generally, leads to an appreciation of how the oppression continues, and a commitment to resisting it.

Conclusion

The processes of lesbian, gay, or bisexual identity formation are very different for a 20-year-old in 1994 than they were for a person aged twenty in 1974. In the twenty years spanning the two lives, major events have occurred in lesbian-gay history, events that *fundamentally* restructure the processes of identity development. The changes have been dramatic—from mental illness to alternative life-style to sexual variation to diverse minority. In 1974, a young man who felt attracted to other men would label himself homosexual; the label was equivalent to self-diagnosis of mental illness. Management of this mental illness in a positive way—asserting it at all—involved entering into the marginal world of the gay ghettos of large metropolitan areas. If disclosure of sexual orientation occurred, the probability of familial rejection was exceedingly high. Out migration to certain metropolitan areas often occurred without disclosure to the family, so that the new urban dwellers created a local gay identity while maintaining their former heterosexual identity for their family, many friends, and most co-workers.

Many people, of course, unconsciously repressed their feelings, entering heterosexual marriage; many consciously suppressed their feelings as well. The societal concept of gay identity was sufficiently repellent to thwart the formation of a positive identity. The sociological reality of the times directed men into highly secretive and highly sexualized settings for their socializations. Despite twenty years' progress, our culture is hardly lesbian- and gay-affirming. Explicit discrimination is legal in most places, and severe penalties for lesbian (and gay male) sex can be imposed in nearly half of the states (Rivera, 1991). All evidence points to the general acceptance in our culture of antilesbian and antigay views, feelings, and action (Berrill & Herek, 1992; Comstock, 1991).

Lesbian identity development was even more invisible in our culture twenty years ago, though considered no less pathological in nature. Within the gay urban neighborhoods, women

were less visible—there were fewer bars and no female version of gay baths, and cultural stereotypes of lesbian behavior never evolved to the precision of gay male stereotypes. Because of these factors and others related to their status as women, lesbians had a much harder time exiting heterosexual identities. The time to awareness of their sexual orientation was prolonged because their sexual feelings were generally devalued. Same-gendered feelings between women could be readily assimilated as emotional, not sexual. Without the cultural salience of the lesbian label and without a meshing to internal feelings and social anchors, women's identity formation was considerably more complex. Fortunately, lesbians could find some support within the women's movement, although this support was never entirely unambiguous.

For a woman aged twenty who is coming out in 1994, some aspects of creating a lesbian identity may seem similar, but much is different. As of May 1987, "ego-dystonic homosexuality" has been deleted from the *Diagnostic and Statistical Manual of Mental Disorders* (DSM-III-R) (American Psychiatric Association, 1987); professional groups have stressed the normality of diverse sexual identities, and a rich lesbian culture of literature and music is relatively accessible. Yet context remains crucial. A young woman in Berkeley, California, comes out very differently from one in rural central Pennsylvania, so much so that one might consider these women as inhabiting different psychological worlds. Thus, the young woman in central Pennsylvania who tells her mother that she is dating her female college friend may unleash a psychological storm that nongay people will never experience, though its consequences will probably be less traumatic than her 1974 counterpart's would have been. Many will not tell their fathers or mothers, but those that do may be told not to tell the extended family and to keep it to themselves.

Women can still create an identity for themselves more easily than in the past, since more helping resources exist, even in geographical areas formerly without such resources (D'Augelli, 1989). The process of "becoming lesbian" is far more psychologically manageable, yet it is still compromised by pervasive social and institutional stigmatization that cannot be simply relegated to the background. The risk of loss of employment, housing, family relations, and so on is still fundamental to the *psychologi-*

cal processes of identity, and these realities cannot be left out. How can someone achieve identity when to do so may lead to job loss, eviction from housing, and even arrest?

In the future, research on lesbian, gay, and bisexual life must start with the assumption that identity is mutable. Although individuals' views of their identity status are perceived as fixed, they are flexible; this should become the focus of study in itself (see Kitzinger, 1987, for an excellent example of this). Identity is heuristically conceived as a dynamic process of interaction and exchange between the individual and the many levels of social collectives during the historical period of her or his life. For many (including lesbian, gay, and bisexual researchers), the achievement of a sense of integrated affectional identity may *seem* to be the end-point of affectional development. This view is surely fueled by the emotional strains of heterosexual exiting and the heterosexist barriers that must be faced daily. Our concepts and research may unintentionally replace conceptual heterocentrism with homocentrism and may preclude the analysis and study of continued evolution and process in identity in lesbian and gay populations. The elimination of the concept of identity as a predetermined, implicitly heterosexual developmental goal would help us explore how humans continue to develop.

A revision of our operational definition of sexual orientations must occur, allowing for study of the continuities and discontinuities, the flexibilities and cohesiveness, of sexual and affectional feelings across the life span, in diverse contexts, and in relationship to culture and history. Any model of sexual orientation that does not address the influence of heterosexism, homophobia, and disenfranchisement will provide unintended corroboration for oppression. A lifespan human development model can, in principle, mitigate this by its simultaneous analysis of exogenous and endogenous variables over time. This approach reflects complexities of lesbian, gay, and bisexual lives and allows analysis of how these lives will change in the future. It is also a model that insists on addressing diversity—so that crucial dimensions that were once "off the diagonal," such as gender, race, ethnicity, and class, are considered fundamental to an analysis of sexual orientation as well as other aspects of human development. How these dimensions affect the many processes of personal development, however, cannot be assumed, but must be studied. Much of this is fundamentally uncharted territory. As Fuss (1991) comments, "Interrogating the position of 'outsiderness' is where much recent lesbian and gay theory begins, implicitly if not always directly raising the questions of the complicated processes by which sexual borders are constructed, sexual identities assigned, and sexual politics formulated. Where exactly . . . does one identity leave off and the other begin" (p.2).

References

American Psychiatric Association (1987). *Diagnostic and Statistical Manual of Mental Disorders* (3rd ed.). Washington, DC: Author.

Baltes, P. B. (1987). Theoretical perspectives on life-span developmental psychology: On the dynamics between growth and decline. *Developmental Psychology, 23,* 611–626.

Berrill, K. T., & Herek, G. M. (1992). Primary and secondary victimization in anti-gay hate crimes: Official response and public policy. In G. M. Herek & K. T. Berrill (Eds.), *Hate crimes: Confronting violence against lesbians and gay men* (pp. 289–305). Newbury Park, CA: Sage.

Boxer, A. M. Cook, J. A., & Herdt, G. (1991). Double jeopardy: Identity transitions and parent child relations among gay and lesbian youth. In K. Pillemer & K. McCartney (Eds.), *Parent-child relations throughout life* (pp. 59–92). Hillsdale, NJ: Erlbaum.

Comstock, G. D. (1991). *Violence against lesbians and gay men.* New York: Columbia University Press.

Cramer, D. W., & Roach, A. J. (1988). Coming out to mom and dad: A study of gay males and their relationships with their parents. *Journal of Homosexuality, 15,* 79–92.

D'Augelli, A. R. (1989). The development of a helping community for lesbians and gay men: a case study in community psychology. *Journal of Community Psychology, 17,* 18–29

Erikson, E. H. (1959). *Identity and the life cycle.* New York: International Universities Press.

Faderman, L. (1991). *Odd girls and twilight lovers: A history of lesbian life in twentieth-century America.* New York: Columbia University Press.

Fuss, D. (1991). Inside/out. In D. Fuss (Ed.), *Inside/our: Lesbian theories, gay theories* (pp. 1–10). New York: Routledge & Kegan Paul.

Gergen, K. J. (1991). *The saturated self: Dilemmas of identity in contemporary life.* New York: Basic Books.

Herdt, G. (1989). Gay and lesbian youth: Emergent identities and cultural scenes at home and abroad. *Journal of Homosexuality, 17,* 1–42.

Herdt, G. (Ed.). (1992). *Gay culture in America: Essays from the field.* Boston: Beacon Press.

Herdt, G., & Boxer, A. (1992). Culture, history, and life course of gay men. In G. Herdt (Ed.), *Gay culture in America: Essays from the field* (pp. 1–28). Boston: Beacon Press.

Herek, G. M. (1992). The social context of hate crimes: Notes on cultural heterosexism. In G. M. Herek & K. T. Berrill (Eds.), *Hate crimes: Confronting violence against lesbians and gay men* (pp. 89–104). Newbury Park, CA: Sage.

Hetrick, E. S., & Martin, A. D. (1987). Developmental issues and their resolution for gay and lesbian adolescents. *Journal of Homosexuality, 14,* 25–43.

Hutchins, L., & Kaahumanu, L. (Eds.). (1991). *Bi any other name.* Boston: Alyson.

Katz, J. N. (1990). The invention of heterosexuality. *Socialist Review, 21,* 7–34.

Kitzinger, C. (1987). *The social construction of lesbianism.* London: Sage.

Lerner, R. M. (1991). Changing organism-context relations as the basic process of development: A developmental contextual perspective. *Developmental Psychology, 27,* 27–32.

McWhirter, D. P., Sanders, S. A., & Reinisch, J. M. (1990). *Homosexuality/heterosexuality: Concepts of sexual orientation.* New York: Oxford University Press.

Remafedi, G., Farrow, J. A., & Deisher, R. W. (1991). Risk factors for attempted suicide in gay and bisexual youth. *Pediatrics, 87,* 869–875.

Rivera, R. R. (1991). Sexual orientation and the law. In J. C. Gonsiorek & J. D. Weinrich (Eds.), *Homosexuality: Research implications of public policy* (pp. 81–100). Newbury Park, CA: Sage.

Robinson, B. E., Walters, L. H., & Skeen, P. (1989). Response of parents to learning that their child is homosexual and concern over AIDS: A natural survey. *Journal of Homosexuality, 18*(1–2), 59–80.

Sedgwick, E. K. (1990). *Epistemology of the closet.* Berkeley: University of California Press.

Simon, W., & Gagnon, J. H. (1986). Sexual scripts: Permanence and change. *Archives of Sexual Behavior, 15*(2), 97–120.

Stein, E. (1992). (Ed.). *Forms of desire: Sexual orientation and the social constructionist controversy.* New York: Routledge & Kegan Paul.

Strommen, E. F. (1989). "You're a what?": Family members' reactions to the disclosure of homosexuality. *Journal of Homosexuality, 18,* 37–58.

Weeks, J. (1989). *Sexuality.* New York: Routledge & Kegan Paul.

Weston, K. (1991). *Families we choose: Lesbians, gays, kinship.* New York: Columbia University Press.

Zurcher, L. A. (1977). *The mutable self: A self-concept for social change.* Newbury Park, CA: Sage.

CHAPTER 30

LESBIAN, GAY, AND BISEXUAL IDENTITY AND STUDENT DEVELOPMENT THEORY

RUTH E. FASSINGER

Student Affairs professionals utilize a wide variety of developmental theories and models in their work (McEwen, 1996; Moore & Upcraft, 1990). There is a basic assumption that a campus environment that offers both challenge and support will help students to redefine themselves gradually in complex, distinct, and integrated ways across a variety of intellectual, affective, and behavioral domains (McEwen, 1996). Theoretical perspectives commonly used include models of intellectual development (Baxter Magolda, 1992), spiritual development (Fowler, 1981; Parks, 1986), moral development (Gilligan, 1982; Kohlberg, 1981), psycho-social development (Chickering, 1969; Chickering & Reisser, 1993), career development (Brown & Brooks, 1996), learning styles, and other identity development models, particularly racial/ethnic identity development (Atkinson, Morten, & Sue, 1993; Helms, 1990; McEwen, 1996).

Identity models are thought to be particularly important in understanding student development because students' experiences of their own identities create a lens through which all cognitive, affective, and behavioral events are filtered (McEwen, 1996). Students also experience multiple aspects of identity simultaneously, and the environmental context appears to be a critical factor in determining which aspects of identity are most important to an individual at any given time (Evans & Levine, 1990). One might expect, then, in this context of pervasive heterosexism and homophobia characterizing many college campuses, that sexual orientation will be the most salient aspect of identity for many lesbian, gay, and bisexual (LGB) students. Moreover, on some college campuses, LGB individuals compose a significant minority group, and receive considerably less attention and limited services than do other groups (Wall & Evans, 1991). To be helpful, Student Affairs professionals need to be aware of the models of LGB identity development and the "coming out" process, as well as the potential impact of LGB identity on other theories and models of student development (Fassinger, 1994; Washington & Evans, 1991). The purpose of this chapter is to address those two points by presenting a brief overview of existing models of LGB identity development and by presenting examples of the way LGB identity may impact the applicability of student development theories.

Theories of Lesbian, Gay and Bisexual Identity Formation

Theories of lesbian and gay identity development, or "coming out" to self and others (Cass, 1979, 1984; Chapman & Brannock, 1987; Coleman, 1982; Fassinger & Miller, 1997; McCarn & Fassinger, 1996; Sophie, 1986; Troiden, 1989), are important theoretical growths of the past two decades. These models are grounded in the assumption that oppressive contextual influences exert impact on normative developmental processes and attempt to articulate a common sequence of recognizing, accepting, and affirming a stigmatized sexual identity that is unique to lesbians and gay men in this culture at this time (Fassinger, 1994; Gonsiorek & Rudolph, 1991; McCarn & Fassinger, 1996). These models are primarily concerned with the development and expression of same-sex attractions and behaviors; thus they focus on the homophilic aspects of one's sexual orientation. Although recent work has begun to address apparently unique aspects of bisexual identity (Pope & Reynolds, 1991), the focus of existing models is relevant to the same-sex attractions of bisexual orientation. Therefore, LGB terminology is used inclusively throughout this chapter.

Existing models focus on social versus psychological aspects of identity (Cox & Gallois, 1996) and generally assume a somewhat linear progression of discrete, discernible stages or phases. The number of stages varies from three to seven, but all articulate a similar sequence in identity formation. Each begins with a lack of awareness of same-sex inclinations and proceeds to dawning awareness of same-sex preferences and the LGB community. The individual then experiences a gradual firming of same-sex lifestyle and intimacy choices and increased immersion in the LGB community (often with deliberate withdrawal from heterosexuals). Finally, the developmental process culminates in identity affirmation and successful integration of sexual orientation into one's life. The final stages of these models explain that developmental maturity involves relatively permanent homophilic identification and at least some public disclosure of identity.

Cass's (1979, 1984) model of lesbian and gay identity development was one of the first to be published with an empirical measure (1984). It remains the most widely cited and used of the existing models and forms the foundation for subsequent work in this area. The six stages integrating lesbian and gay identity into the self-concept are useful in examining other LGB identity theories. The stages are: identity confusion involves questioning assumptions about one's sexual orientation; identity comparison involves feelings of isolation and alienation, both from prior assumptions as well as from nongay others; identity tolerance involves seeking out other gay people and merely tolerating a lesbian or gay identity; identity acceptance involves

selective disclosure of identity to others; identity pride involves immersion in lesbian and gay culture and rejection of heterosexual values; and, identity synthesis takes place when lesbian or gay identity becomes one aspect of the self rather than an independent, overriding identity. Although there has been criticism of Cass's model (McCarn & Fassinger, 1996), its familiarity to many and the brevity of its assessment instrument suggest that it will remain widely used within Student Affairs as a model for understanding LGB students.

Although the Cass model and other identity models have wide appeal and appear intuitively to capture an important process, they have limitations. Most of the existing models were developed based on clinical and anecdotal data, and few have been tested adequately (Fassinger, 1994). Common problems in the limited research that has been conducted include small or biased samples (individuals who belong to gay social or political groups) and measures that are psychometrically undeveloped or unsound (using two or three brief sentences to depict a complex stage location). In addition, many of the models were developed based on the experiences of gay men and then generalized to include lesbians. The growing body of literature in LGB issues suggests that many of the important differences between the experiences of men and women in current United States culture are mirrored in the LGB community and therefore implies critical distinctions between lesbians and gay men that must be taken into account in identity development models (Fassinger, 1994; McCarn & Fassinger, 1996).

From the point of view of Student Affairs professionals who respect and value student diversity, the most serious limitation of the existing models is that they ignore demographic or cultural factors that influence the LGB identity formation process (Fassinger, 1991, 1994). The models do so by confusing two separate developmental paths: One is concerned with the internal clarification of same sex desire, and the other focuses on fostering identification with an oppressed group (Fassinger, 1991, 1994; Fassinger & Miller, 1997; McCarn & Fassinger, 1996). The melding of these two processes in existing models is not surprising, since they grew out of the models of the 1970s—the influences of the Stonewall riots, the subsequent gay rights movement, and the women's movement, all of which have contributed to an interest in the politics of identity pride (Fassinger, 1994).

LGB identity development exhibits a critical distinction from other kinds of minority identity development (based on race, ethnicity, gender, etc.) in that LGB identity usually is not visible to oneself or others (Wall & Evans, 1991). For most minority groups, identity transformation involves changed attitudes toward the meaning of an identity already known, whereas according to McCarn and Fassinger (1996), LGB individuals must pursue two goals simultaneously: They must personally deal with a sexual identity that they previously considered reprehensible and/or irrelevant; and they must acknowledge their membership in, and change their attitudes toward, a largely invisible minority group that they also previously considered reprehensible and/or irrelevant (McCarn & Fassinger, 1996). Thus, identity development is a mixture of self-categorizations related to both personal and social identities (Cox & Gallois, 1996).

The confusion of these two separate (but related) processes in existing models results in highly politicized frameworks that tend to focus on the internal developmental tasks in the beginning stages but then shift to the more group-oriented tasks in the later stages. Developmental maturity thus becomes synonymous with public disclosure of identity, and less public ("closeted") behaviors are viewed as developmental arrest. Not only does the importance of homoerotic intimacy disappear altogether in the focus on accommodation to minority group membership, but the linking of public disclosure and involvement in the LGB community with integrated identity ignores the social realities of many LGB people who feel compelled to maintain the privacy of their sexual identity for pressing contextual reasons. For example, LGB individuals who are members of racial/ethnic, religious, or occupational groups in which homophobia is especially virulent are likely to experience strong pressure to hide their identities in order to maintain needed and valued ties to those groups. For these individuals, coming out publicly may not be a reasonable option, and developmental models must theorize maturation possibilities that are sensitive to diverse demographic realities (Fassinger, 1991, 1994; Fassinger & Miller, 1997; McCarn & Fassinger, 1996).

The work of Fassinger and colleagues (Fassinger & Miller, 1997; McCarn & Fassinger, 1996) represents an attempt to create a model of LGB development that is more inclusive of demographic and cultural influences and less reliant on identity disclosure as a marker of developmental maturity. This model (Table 1) espouses two separate but reciprocal processes of identity formation: One that involves an internal, individual process of awareness and identification with a homophilic intimacy orientation (Am I lesbian or gay?) and one that involves changed identification regarding group membership and group meaning (What does it mean, to me and to other LGB people, to be lesbian or gay in this society at this time?). A four-phase sequence (preceded by non-awareness) characterizes both the individual (I) and group (G) branches of the model. In Phase 1 there might be an *awareness* of feeling or being different as an individual (I) or of the existence of different sexual orientations in a group (G). Phase 2. denotes *exploration* of strong/erotic feelings for same sex people or a particular same sex person by an individual (I) or of one's position regarding lesbians or gays as a group (G), in terms of both attitudes and possible membership. Phase 3 is a *deepening commitment* to self-knowledge, self-fulfillment, and crystalization of choices about sexuality as an individual (I) or to personal involvement with the reference group, including awareness of oppression and consequences of choices (G). Phase 4 is *internalization/synthesis* of love for same sex people and sexual choices into overall identity as an individual (I) or of identity as a member of a minority group, across contexts (G).

The model assumes that because the branches are separate and not necessarily simultaneous, an individual could be located in a different phase in each branch—for example, a young woman actively involved in campus gay rights advocacy (G3) who is just coming to realize that she has strong erotic feelings for a female friend (I2). The branches of the model also are assumed to be mutually catalytic, in that addressing the developmental tasks in either branch is likely to produce some movement in the other branch. Moreover, a cyclical process is assumed, in which recycling through phases occurs as developmental pathways shift in response to the demands of external circumstances; an individual, for example, who has resolved conflicts about how "out" to be in college classes may be forced to revisit those decisions with a change of major. Finally,

TABLE 1

Inclusive Model of Lesbian/Gay Identity Formation

Individual Sexual Identity (I)	*Group Membership Identity (G)*

1. Awareness

*of feeling or being different	*of existence of different → sexual orientations in people

Self-Statement Examples (for women):

"I feel pulled toward women in ways I don't understand." (I)

"I had no idea there were lesbian/gay people out there." (G)

2. Exploration

*of strong/erotic feelings for same sex people or a particular same sex person	*of one's position re: gay people as a → group (both attitudes and membership)

Self-Statement Examples (for men):

"I want to be closer to men or to a certain man." (I)

"I think a lot about fitting in as a gay man and developing my own gay style." (G)

3. Deepening/Commitment

*to self-knowledge, self-fulfillment, and crystallization of choices about sexuality	*to personal involvement with a reference group, with → awareness of oppression and consequences of choices

Self-Statement Examples (for women):

"I clearly feel more intimate sexually and emotionally with women than with men." (I)

"Sometimes I have been mistreated because of my lesbianism."(G)

4. Internalization/Synthesis

*of love for same sex people, sexual choices into overall identity	*of identity as a member of a → minority group, across contexts

Self-Statement Examples (for men):

"I feel a deep contentment about my love of other men." (I)

"I rely on my gay/lesbian friends for support, but I have some good heterosexual friends as well." (G)

Source: Fassinger & Miller, 1997; McCarn & Fassinger, 1996

---

self-disclosure in this model is not viewed as an index of developmental advancement, allowing for diverse paths to an integrated LGB identity (Fassinger & Miller, 1997; McCarn, 1991; McCarn & Fassinger, 1996).

This model has been empirically validated on samples of diverse lesbians (N = 38) and gay men (N = 34) using a Q-sort methodology (Fassinger & Miller, 1997; McCarn, 1991; McCarn & Fassinger, 1996). In these studies, support for the two branches of the model was strong, and support also was found for the four-phase sequence, particularly the first and last phases. Self-report measures based on the model also have been developed (40 item Likert scales, available from

the author) and currently are being tested. It is hoped that this model will provide an additional resource for those interested in culturally sensitive models of LGB identity formation. The implications of LGB identity development models for theories of student development are discussed in the following section.

LGB Identity and Student Development Theories

A comprehensive review of all theoretical frameworks used by Student Affairs professionals in terms of their applicability to LGB individuals is not possible in this limited space. The aim here is to present examples of ways in which LGB identity development models have important implications for the use of developmental theories in the daily work of Student Affairs professionals. The examples, discussed in the form of questions about the viability of theoretical assumptions, are presented for two broad classes of student development theories involving psychosocial and cognitive development.

Psychosocial Development

Chickering's theory of seven developmental vectors (Chickering, 1969; Chickering & Reisser, 1993) represents the most current, comprehensive, and widely used theory of student psychosocial development (McEwen, 1996a). The vectors include the developmental tasks of developing competence, managing emotions, moving through autonomy toward interdependence, developing mature interpersonal relationships, establishing identity, developing purpose, and developing integrity. A close examination of these vectors reveals theoretical assumptions that put LGB students at considerable disadvantage in terms of achieving successful resolution of developmental tasks.

Consider, for example, the first four tasks, which provide a foundation for later, more advanced tasks (Chickering & Reisser, 1993). These first tasks all center in some way around developing competency in handling interpersonal relationships and issues, including emotional expression, capacity for intimacy, and appreciation of differences among people. One might ask, How can a young gay man who is feeling alienated from his nongay peers but fearfully hiding his identity seek out other gay people and learn to become part of a community that is appropriate for him? In other words, how can this individual achieve interpersonal competence in a context of isolation, lack of an appropriate reference group, and unknown reference group norms? Similarly, how can a young lesbian deal with her dawning physical and emotional attraction to her roommate or teammate when to reveal those feelings would likely result in hysteria and ostracism? In other words, how can this individual learn to recognize and manage complex emotions in a context of homophobia and repression?

Similar questions can be raised regarding the development of autonomy and mature relationships. How does a young bisexual woman deal with the disapproval she is likely to experience in both the gay and nongay communities? In other words, how is this individual's development of autonomy and interdependence affected by lack of an appropriate community or marginalization in existing communities? Interpersonally, what lessons does a young gay man learn about tolerance of differences when he is physically assaulted by other students? How does he learn to trust others and develop intimacy in relationships when he is consistently regarded with fear and hatred? In other words, how can this individual possibly develop mature interpersonal relationships in an environmental context of oppression and prejudice?

Clearly, the difficulties encountered by LGB students in resolving these preliminary developmental tasks are, as Chickering's theory posits, likely to lead to difficulties in resolving more advanced tasks related to identity, purpose, and integrity (Chickering & Reisser, 1993). One might ask, for example, how an individual can possibly establish a secure identity in the face of marginalization, invisibility, and societal censure. Moreover, one might expect that developing purpose—clarifying vocational, avocational, and lifestyle plans and goals—is very likely to be ignored or stalled in the face of more pressing identity concerns related to safety, acceptance, and belonging (Fassinger, 1995, 1996a). Finally, one might ask how the process of developing a personally relevant set of beliefs and values by which to live—such as integrity—is influenced by invisibility and stigmatization of lifestyle.

The point, of course, is not that Chickering's theory is irrelevant or useless but simply that the unique needs of LGB students must be taken into account very consciously in implementing programs and interventions based on its assumptions. If, for example, we truly wish our students to develop awareness and tolerance of differences and we do not want any student ignored or mistreated based on his or her differences, then we must be sure that LGB issues are included in all of our campus programming, not just interventions targeted toward "gay awareness." Programs on dating that are oriented toward heterosexual couples should be noted as such and comparable programs offered for LGB students. Similarly, career workshops should include attention to the special problems of representing gay-related activities in resumes or job interviews or dealing with a two-career job search when the relationship is not public. Commitment to optimal psychosocial development for *all* students in Chickering's theoretical terms (Chickering, 1969; Chickering & Reisser, 1993) would suggest the need for vigorous efforts to address the unique and pressing emotional, interpersonal, and social needs of LGB students.

Cognitive Development

Cognitive student development theories focus on how students think and reason, with moral thinking included as a special kind of cognitive process (McEwen, 1996a). The cognitive theories most widely used by Student Affairs professionals are Perry's (1970, 1981) and Belenky et al.'s (1986) schemes of intellectual development, and the moral development theories of Kohlberg (1975) and Gilligan (1982). The assumptions in these theories raise critical questions about their applicability to LGB students, but in this case, LGB students may experience some advantages over their nongay peers.

Consider, for example, the intellectual progression posited in the theories of both Perry (1970, 1981) and Belenky et al. (1986). These theories assume early positions in which knowledge and discourse are largely molded by external others whose ultimate authority is to be accepted, gradually maturing to positions in which multiple realities and options are considered and evaluated by an increasingly self-referential thinker. It is a maxim in the LGB community that "coming out is a crash course in how relative everything is," a reference to the cognitive shifts that occur as one negotiates a new identity and lifestyle that often are at odds with the larger community in which one lives. The extensive reeducation and resocialization that occur during LGB identity formation often result in the recognition that authority figures—parents, teachers, and clergy as examples—can be wrong about issues fundamental to one's being, an increasing degree of reliance on oneself and one's own needs to guide experiences, and a live-and-let-live attitude of acceptance regarding others' lifestyles and beliefs. These cognitive shifts clearly parallel those posited in theories of intellectual development.

Consider also the moral/ethical positions that are theorized by Kohlberg (1975) and Gilligan (1982). Kohlberg (1975) explained a sequence

in which moral reasoning matures from positions focused on personal safety and approval from others to positions increasingly motivated by higher principles of social order, universality, and conscience. Gilligan (1982) noted a mode of moral reasoning focused on an ethic of care in which responsibility toward others increasingly becomes integrated with responsibility toward oneself. It is interesting to note that the maturation point in both theories involves balancing commitment to self with a responsibility toward others in society. This also is the inherent tension in the identity formation process for LGB people—to reconcile personal needs and desires with the (usually conflicting) demands of society.

Taking these theoretical assumptions into account, we might ask such questions as: How do the personal awareness and acceptance of a stigmatized identity affect an LGB student's cognitive shifts from dualistic through multiplistic to relativistic points of view (Perry, 1970, 1981)? How do LGB individuals committed to social justice manage to express and maintain that commitment in a context of personal and societal oppression (as in Perry, 1970, 1980)? In terms of moral/ethical-development, we might ask: How is the development of an ethic of care influenced by same-sex commitments, and is it different for lesbians versus gay men (Gilligan, 1982)?

Scholars (Friend, 1987; Kimmel & Sang, 1995) have argued that LGB individuals are forced to learn an array of cognitive, interpersonal, and emotional coping skills during the process of coming out in a heterosexist and homophobic environment that provide them with uncommon resiliency and flexibility in managing other life stresses and developmental tasks. Services to LGB students might be targeted toward strengthening and building upon existing cognitive strengths, for example, support groups that focus on cognitive coping strategies. LGB students might be invited to assist in campus programming targeted toward prejudice reduction and awareness of differences, sharing their own experiences and coping strategies with others.

Implications and Conclusion

It seems clear that the development of LGB identity has important implications for student development theory and practice. This author has argued elsewhere (Fassinger, 1996a) that assumptions regarding optimal development based on maturational markers attainable only by small segments of the population are not particularly helpful in guiding practice. Student development theories, like most mainstream developmental theories, have not given adequate attention to the unique ways in which LGB individuals traverse the maturational maps posited in those theories (Evans & Levine, 1990a; Fassinger, 1994; McEwen, 1996b; Wall & Evans, 1991). Clearly, scholars need to be actively addressing the paucity of research in this area (Wall & Evans, 1991) in order to provide more inclusive theories from which professionals can work. Student Affairs professionals can begin the important task of raising questions about the theories that guide their practice. They can examine the myriad ways in which those theories may be inadequate or inappropriate for use with LGB students, either because they ignore the difficulties in developing a healthy LGB identity and therefore inadvertently pathologize lengthy or deviating paths to psychosocial maturation, or because they fail to acknowledge and draw upon the cognitive and emotional strengths developed by LGB individuals during the identity formation process. We have much to learn from and about LGB students—their unique experiences can inform and sharpen our understanding of the development of *all* students with whom we work.

CHAPTER 31

REVISIONING SEXUAL MINORITY IDENTITY FORMATION: A NEW MODEL OF LESBIAN IDENTITY AND ITS IMPLICATIONS FOR COUNSELING AND RESEARCH

SUSAN R. MCCARN AND RUTH E. FASSINGER

This article describes a new, inclusive model of lesbian identity formation. A rationale for the model is presented, which includes a review of relevant literature in lesbian/gay identity, racial/ethnic identity, and gender issues related to identity development. Three case studies are presented to elucidate the applications of the model to counseling, and the article concludes with a discussion of the implications of the model for research.

Although societal awareness of the existence of lesbian and gay people has increased dramatically over the past decade or so, most lesbians and gay men still grow up within a context of pervasive environmental and internalized homophobia and expectation to be heterosexual. This fosters a specific struggle with identity awareness, acceptance, and affirmation, a process known as *coming out to self and others* (see Fassinger, 1991, for more detailed discussion). Models of the identity formation or coming out process, an important recent theoretical development, assume the primacy of oppressive contextual influences on normative developmental and psychological processes (Gonsiorek & Rudolph, 1991). These models can help counseling psychologists in their work with lesbian and gay clients because they seek to predict, articulate, and normalize common experiences in developing and managing a stigmatized identity. If, for example, identifiable phases of the coming out process are found to be predictive of specific problems of living (career indecision, depression, sexual acting out), they may be properly recognized and treated as normative developmental issues, rather than as indications of pathology.

Although a common general progression of identity development is implied in all of the existing lesbian/gay models, many have been conceptualized around the experiences of White men, and the extent to which they deliberately incorporate gender, race, and other demographic differences is variable (Gonsiorek & Rudolph, 1991). Most existing lesbian/gay models also tend to ignore the critical difference between personal and reference group components of identity, a distinction that is central to conceptualizations of identity found in general theories of the development of the self (e.g., Greenwald & Pratkanis, 1984; Taylor & Dube, 1986; Triandis, 1989). The model presented in this article is an attempt to address some of the limitations in the current lesbian/gay identity literature. It is intended be inclusive of the diverse experiences of self-identification in lesbians and differs from previous models in that it posits a dual nature of lesbian identity as an *individual sexual identity* that results in *membership in an oppressed minority group.*

This article begins with a review of existing models of lesbian and gay identity, followed by a brief examination of literature and research in racial minority and women's identity development, from which our model is derived. We then present our model, offering several case examples that elucidate the application of the model to practice and conclude with recommendations for future research.

Models of Lesbian/Gay Identity Development

Perhaps the most widely cited of the existing models of lesbian/gay identity development and one that has formed a foundation for much of the subsequent work in this area is that of Cass (1979). Intended to apply to both women and men, her model encompasses cognitive, affective, and behavioral components into a six-stage process of integrating a lesbian/gay identity into the self-concept:

1. identity confusion, involving questioning assumptions about one's sexual orientation;
2. identity comparison, involving feelings of isolation and alienation from both prior assumptions and nongay others;
3. identity tolerance, involving seeking out other gay people and tolerating a lesbian/gay identity;
4. identity acceptance, involving selective identity disclosure to others;
5. identity pride, involving immersion in lesbian/gay culture and rejection of heterosexual values; and
6. identity synthesis, in which lesbian/gay identity becomes one aspect of the self instead of an overriding independent identity.

Cass (1984) attempted to validate this model using a questionnaire she developed, conclud-

ing that individuals can be distinguished by stage characteristics, that they follow the order predicted in the model, and that blurring present in earlier and later stages suggested four developmental stages rather than six. Cass' pioneering attempt to quantify and validate a model of lesbian/gay identity formation is important because few such studies exist even at present. Problems inherent in Cass' work, however, include the methodological confounding of self-designated stage allocation and instrument completion in the implementation of the study, the conceptual limitation of exceptional political awareness and identity disclosure required in the final stage of the model, and the fact that her work using Australian samples has been widely utilized in the United States with little discussion of contextual differences.

Based on many of the assumptions in Cass' work, Coleman (1982) outlined a similar five-stage model:

1. precoming out
2. coming out
3. exploration
4. first relationships
5. integration

Like Cass, he included widespread identity disclosure as a developmental task of the final stage but without the overt politicization of Cass's model. Coleman also discussed the force of social pressure at different stages of the coming out process, articulated the need to return to earlier stages repeatedly throughout adulthood, and described clear counseling implications associated with each stage. This model, however, has not been empirically validated.

Troiden (1989) synthesized several models of lesbian/gay identity formation into a sociological model with four stages:

1. sensitization
2. identity confusion
3. identity assumption
4. identity commitment

Troiden noted the critical importance of a supportive lesbian/gay environment in facilitating self-definition and self-acceptance within the context of social stigma and postulated identity disclosure as an option rather than a characteristic of any specific developmental stage, allowing for social realities that may prevent disclosure. He also acknowledged the differential effect of gender role socialization on identity formation in lesbian women and gay men. However, like Coleman's (1982) model, no empirical support exists at present for Troiden's model.

In another synthesis of existing models, Minton and McDonald (1984) used ego development theory to build a model based primarily on males and consisting of three stages, labeled egocentric, sociocentric, and universalistic. Like Coleman, Minton and McDonald implied the need for circularity in coming out models because changing life situations always hold anew the possibility of rejection, and they discussed the costs and benefits of disclosure. Problems with their model, however, include the collapsing of many developmental tasks into one final ego-identity stage and the lack of empirical validation.

Faderman (1984) critiqued the Minton and McDonald (1984) model based on lesbian feminist literature, asserting that "new gay" lesbians exist who begin with a critical evaluation of heterosexual social norms, which they then internalize in a commitment to women that includes lesbianism as an active choice. Thus, although Faderman's conceptualization is not a formal model, she implied a developmental trajectory for new gay lesbians that directly reverses the process described in the Minton and McDonald model. Faderman accurately notes the unique sociopolitical context existing in women's communities that supports lesbianism as a creative choice for women and thus has made an important contribution to a literature that has been built largely on the experiences of men. However, Faderman's equation of political and sexual identities may be inappropriate in that the philosophy of feminism, which may equip some women with prolesbian beliefs facilitative of the coming out process, probably has little influence on the affective power of internalized homophobia that hinders development of a positive sexual and relational self-concept (MacCowan, 1987).

Attempting to synthesize existing gay identity theory into the first known model developed specifically for women, Sophie (1985–1986) proposed and tested four stages:

1. first awareness
2. testing and exploration
3. identity acceptance
4. identity integration

Results obtained through structured interviews with 14 women experiencing sexual orientation confusion indicated that although many participants' experiences fit the early stages of the model, later changes were less closely linked to theoretical predictions and some women did not fit the model at all. Predictions supported by the interviews included late rather than early disclosure to nongays, exploration of the lesbian/gay community preceding acceptance, and acceptance characterized by a preference for lesbian/gay social interaction. However, contrary to prediction, first awareness did not always precede lesbian/gay contact or lead to alienation, identity disclosure and entering relationships occurred in the second stage for some women (suggesting that first relationships occur earlier in the developmental process for lesbians than for gay men), negative identity did not always precede positive identity, disclosure levels in the third stage were mixed, and little support was found for movement to an integrated worldview or of lesbianism as a static identity. Sophie concluded that the linearity of existing models may be useful for describing early stages, but there is a great variety in the order and timing of events further into the process, rendering a linear model inadequate. However, although Sophie's use both qualitative and quantitative approaches is commendable, the adequate testing of her model is compromised by a small sample of what appear to be homogeneous, predominantly feminist women who are unusually free of predicted conflicts associated with coming out.

A second model developed specifically for women is that of Chapman and Brannock (1987), who described a five-stage conscious process by which lesbians come to self-label (vs. come to terms with attraction to same-sex people, as in other models):

1. same-sex orientation
2. incongruence
3. self-questioning/exploration
4. identification
5. choice of lifestyle

They tested their model by surveying a sample of 197 self-identified lesbians regarding their experiences from first awareness of same-sex inclinations to their status at the time of the research. The majority of participants referred to strong emotional or physical bonds with women as the reason they first questioned their sexual orientation, indicating that most of these women experienced self-questioning in relation to others. Although 89% had had sexual contact with men and heterosexuality was not abandoned until an average of 4 years after first same-sex experiences, most (82%) also believed they had always been lesbians; the duration of heterosexual involvements suggests support for the authors' inclusion of these as part of a lengthy period of self-questioning/exploration in their model. Chapman and Brannock concluded from their results that sexual orientation precedes awareness, that awareness is the first step in self-labeling, and that labeling results from interaction with the heterosexual environment. However, although the survey information in this study is useful in understanding women's experiences, it is not clear how it coincides with the model being tested.

All of these models describe a lengthy process of coming to terms with homoerotic desire and changes in self-concept required to act upon, accept, and internalize that desire. Each begins with a phase in which the nature of attraction is unclear to the individual, a turning point that involves recognizing a difference, and progressive movement toward self-affirmation and disclosure to others. All describe a linear path in three to six stages, along which lesbian/gay identity moves from the recesses of the self-concept to the very center and finally emerges as one acknowledged part of the self. Whereas empirical validation of these models is scant and methodologically compromised, attempts to put these ideas to test are useful in providing a foundation for further theoretical efforts, such as the present work. In addition, lesbian/gay identification is linked to other forms of minority identity by their common roots in the context of societal prejudice and oppression. Little has been written explicitly about these interconnections, particularly the integration of diverse gender and racial/ethnic experiences into models of the coming out process. In an effort to begin to articulate the interplay of these forces, we next briefly explore racial/ethnic and gender issues in identity development.

Expanding the Inquiry: Related Research

Racial/Ethnic Issues in Identity Development

There have been attempts in the literature to document the complications of multiple oppressions in the coming out experiences of racial/ethnic minority group members. Loiacano (1989), for example, conducted structured interviews with six Black lesbians and gay men and identified several themes related to dual identity. Because of difficulty in finding validation as Blacks in the predominantly White gay/lesbian community and the lack of support as lesbians/gays in the predominantly heterosexual Black community, a need was expressed to find life contexts in which to integrate dual identities. Loiacano also noted that Blacks may place less emphasis on coming out than Whites because of a need to maintain support within their racial communities and that lesbian/gay identity formation in Blacks is likely to be related to racial identity. Unfortunately, although these are interesting results, the sample consisted of a very small number of unusually well-educated and politically active individuals, suggesting that Loiacano (like Cass, 1984, and Faderman, 1984) may have mistaken politicization for self-acceptance.

In another study of dual identities, Chan (1989) conducted a survey of 35 Asian American lesbians and gay men who were attending race-specific lesbian/gay events. Similar to participants in Loiacano's (1989) study, Chan's sample reported conflict between needs associated with their two identities. Though 26 of the 35 subjects indicated attending lesbian/gay-only events, none reported attending Asian-only events, and over half noted that the existence of lesbians/gays was denied in their culture. Unfortunately, Chan's sample (like Loiacano's) was unusually political, limiting the generalizability of her findings.

Morales (1989) proposed an identity model for visible racial/ethnic gay and lesbian individuals that attempts to incorporate their dual statuses. This model proposed five states (vs. stages) possible for an individual in integrating multiple identities:

1. denial of conflicts
2. bisexual vs. gay/lesbian
3. conflicts in allegiances

4. establishing priorities in allegiance

5. integrating various communities

This model builds upon the strengths of previous models of identity development (e.g., Cass, 1979), highlights the notion of flexible states or statuses (vs. linear stages), focuses on family and cultural issues, and clearly addresses the irony of invisibility within two (or more) communities faced by lesbian/gay people who also are members of visible racial/ethnic groups. However, the model has not yet been tested in empirical studies and its heuristic and practical usefulness is unclear.

Although there is scant empirical work regarding racial/ethnic minority lesbians and gay men, a growing literature addressing general racial identity issues exists and contributes to understanding the role of oppression in shaping identity formation in stigmatized groups. Moreover, Cross's (1971) seminal model of racial identity formation influenced Cass's early (1979) work, thus having indirect influence on much subsequent gay/lesbian identity scholarship. Cross's model, developed within the context of the civil rights movement, described the stages of liberation traversed by Black activists in moving from devaluation to affirmation of Black identity and has sparked considerable research and theoretical work.

Cross (1971) described the "Negro-to-Black conversion" as consisting of five stages:

1. pre-encounter, involving political naivete and dependence on White dominance;

2. encounter, involving a challenge to the individual's view of self and other Blacks;

3. immersion-emersion, involving immersion in the Black world and hostility toward Whites;

4. internalization, involving the incorporation of learnings into the self-concept; and

5. internalization-commitment, representing a transformation to conscious anger, self-love, Black communalism.

This model was validated using a Q-sort methodology, and support was found for the existence and ordering of the stages (Hall, Cross, & Freedle, 1972). Further empirical work based on this original model has produced increasingly refined theoretical statements regarding racial/ethnic identities, measures of racial identity attitudes,

studies of the effects of racial identity on counseling, and increased interest in multicultural research, counseling, and training (see Helms, 1990; Mio & Iwamasa, 1993; Parham, 1989; Pedersen, 1991; Ponterotto & Sabnani, 1989; Ridley, Mendoza, & Kanitz, 1994). It seems clear that the heuristic richness of the Cross (1971) model provides a useful template for generating, operationalizing, and testing models of identity development related to race, ethnicity, and culture.

Attempting to apply Cross's (1971) ideas to the identity development of any cultural minority, Atkinson, Morten, and Sue (1979) offered a similar five-stage model that addresses four attitude areas at each stage: views of self, others of the same minority, those of another minority, and majority group individuals. The five stages are

1. conformity

2. dissonance

3. resistance and immersion

4. introspection

5. synergetic articulation and awareness

Their final stage of minority identity development involves self-fulfillment regarding cultural identity, characterized by individual control, objectivity, flexibility, and the willingness to fight all oppression.

Myers and her colleagues (1991) offered a general, holistic model of self-identification in oppressed people. Based on optimal theory, this model represents an attempt to address the oversimplification of linear developmental models. The Myers et al. model configures the identity process as an expanding spiral of six phases (rather than stages), representations, and language choices that are intended to reflect the fluidity of integrating and expanding one's sense of self, the core process described in their model.

The final conceptual framework presented in this section is that of Reynolds and Pope (1991), who proposed a multidimensional identity model built on Root's (1990) work in biracial identity. This model offers four possible options for identity resolution in those who are members of multiple oppressed groups:

1. passive acceptance of societally assigned identification with one aspect of self;

2. conscious identification with one aspect of self;

3. segmented identification with multiple aspects of self; and

4. intersecting identification with multiple aspects of self.

Reynolds and Pope indicate clearly that these options are dynamic and fluid, as well as strongly linked to personal needs, reference groups, and environmental demands. This model is notable in its attempt to build upon racial identity work that is specifically focused on the intersection of dual statuses. However, like the models of Atkinson et al. (1979) and Myers et al. (1991), it has not yet been subjected to empirical validation.

As is evident in the selected models described here, the process of racial/ethnic minority identity development is thought to be similar to the process of sexual minority identity development. Common to both processes is moving the reality of the experience of oppression from unconsciousness to consciousness, then addressing the issues raised by a changed awareness of oppression. For women, who also experience pervasive oppression and discrimination, similar processes regarding the development of gender consciousness are likely to occur and are discussed in the following section.

Gender Issues in Identity Development

Models depicting the process of psychological development of women vis-à-vis their gender recently have been formulated. Peck (1986), for example, offered a model of women's self-definition in adulthood that, although untested, is one of the few attempts to translate theoretically the assertion that linear models do not adequately describe the multiplex nature of self-creation. Her model, illustrated in conical form, describes a dialectical relationship among myriad forces in a woman's life to shape an emerging identity, rather than a series of discrete tasks and stages. These forces include sociohistorical time (era and age), influences of the woman's relationships, and an emerging core self-definition. Peck's model contributes to conceptualizing lesbian identity development in its explicit attention to the interplay of external and internal forces. Sociohistorical time, for example, indeed defines the context for establishment of an oppressed identity, and flexibility or rigidity in family relationships is likely to determine whether a developing lesbian identity will be released or strangled.

Downing and Roush (1985) offered a model of feminist identity development explicitly based on Cross's (1971) work and consisting of five stages:

1. passive acceptance of discrimination against women;

2. revelation of contradictions being avoided;

3. embeddedness-emanation in close connection with other women and caution with men;

4. synthesis of positive aspects of womanhood, gender role transcendence, and evaluation of men individually; and

5. active commitment to a role-transcendent future through personal action.

This model is useful in expanding the conceptual framework of lesbian identity development in its attention to the uniquely intimate relations between subordinate and dominant group members that exist for lesbians in relation to heterosexual family members. In addition, as a model of political identity change, this model relates closely to Faderman's (1984) work rooting lesbianism in feminist identity development, again suggesting that it may be easier for feminist than nonfeminist women to develop lesbian identities because of the valuing of woman-identified choices.

Ossana, Helms, and Leonard (1992) proposed a model that is similar to the Downing and Roush (1985) work in using as its foundation the Cross (1971) model but focuses on the development of "womanist" identity, which the authors define as movement from external to internal standards of gender identity. This model also differs from the Downing and Roush model in its deemphasis of a feminist political orientation. The four stages in the model are

1. pre-encounter

2. encounter

3. immersion-emersion

4. internalization

Using a measure of womanist identity attitudes based on Helms' work in racial identity (see Helms, 1990), the authors found relationships among womanist identity, self-esteem, and environmental gender bias in a study of college women; this suggests the usefulness of the model in empirical studies, particularly as a conceptual alternative to more politicized notions of women's development.

An important area of crossover between lesbian and feminist/womanist identity development is the experience of sexism that affects women's identities. Although many of the existing models of lesbian/gay identity development describe a process thought to be common to both women and men, most rest on androcentric assumptions; that is, they were attempts to document male experience, they represent syntheses of earlier (male-biased) models, or they simply do not attend to women's experience and thus perpetuate the oft-noted invisibility of lesbians in the sexual orientation literature. Little rationale has been offered for either the inclusion or separation of the sexes in these models, but we believe that there are elements of female socialization that uniquely and profoundly affect the experience of lesbian identity formation: the repression of sexual desire, the interrelationship of intimacy and autonomy, and the recent availability of reinforcement for nontraditional role behavior.

Much has been written regarding the repression/expression of women's sexuality and the complex interrelationship between intimacy and autonomy in both lesbian and heterosexual women (Butler, 1993; Daniluk, 1993; Fassinger & Morrow, 1995; Frye, 1992; Gilligan, 1982; Vance, 1984). A few models, such as Peck's (1986), explicitly incorporate these ideas. In addition, some writers have begun questioning the very foundation of accepted views of human sexuality based on attention to the unique features of lesbian relationships (e.g., Fassinger & Morrow, 1995; Frye, 1992). This new theoretical work offers insight into commonly noted differences in the identity development process for lesbians and gay men. Women attempting to incorporate a lesbian sexual identity face a struggle that their male counterparts do not: First, they have been taught that sexual desire itself is dangerous and wrong, then they find that the object of their desire is devalued. This may help to explain why women tend to come out later in life than men and why women are more likely to come out in the context of a relationship as opposed to an independent process of articulating and acting on sexual desire (Fassinger & Morrow, 1995; Troiden, 1989). Accurate models of lesbian iden-

tity development must therefore account for the generation of sexual identity in women in relation to intimacy with others, rather than in relation to sex.

A final element affecting the developmental process of lesbians is a context that now exists whereby nontraditional role behaviors (e.g., working in traditionally male jobs, initiating sex, showing strength) are somewhat reinforced and supported in women. Whereas the common stereotype that only nontraditionally sex-typed women become lesbians is inaccurate, it may be true that the presence and expression of same-sex desire requires some nontraditional role behavior (Browning, Reynolds, & Dworkin, 1991; Fassinger & Morrow, 1995). In models of identity development, this might be manifested in feeling fundamentally different from other girls or women, although this awareness would not necessarily provoke the intense role anxiety suggested in models of gay male development, again indicating the overriding salience of gender in sexual identity development.

Summary and Critique of Existing Literature

The identity models outlined above describe a process that begins by questioning previously held, socialized assumptions regarding the self, one's place in society, and dominant and minority group attributes. In the case of lesbian identity development, a two-fold process occurs: On the one hand, desire is becoming articulated in the self and a personal sexual identity is developing; on the other hand, that experience is causing a shift in self-defined group membership and group meaning. Existing models of lesbian/gay identity formation conflate these personal and social developmental trajectories, a weakness Cross (1987) has written about extensively in regard to racial identity models, as well. Indeed, Cross recently (1987) has described racial identity as having two different sectors: personal identity, including self-evaluation and self-esteem; and reference group orientation, which includes race awareness and racial identity and which can be self-defined or ascribed. Moreover, Cross criticized existing racial identity research for not adequately distinguishing between personal or reference group sectors of identity, positing this problem as an explanation for the mixed and confusing outcomes that pervade the racial identity literature.

This confounding of two different developmental trajectories also may be one reason why the lesbian/gay models tend to be less reliable descriptors in the later stages and why they do not overlap more with other minority identity models; the individual sexual identification process falls into the first two or three stages of existing lesbian/gay models, whereas the group identification process tends to fall in later, more sociopolitical stages. First, there is a process that involves individual sexual awareness and identification (Am I lesbian/gay?); then there is a process involving reference group identification (What does it mean to be lesbian/gay in society?) that is similar to other minority identity development.

The conflation of these two processes in existing models results in an odd tyranny in which political activism and universal disclosure become signs of an integrated lesbian/gay identity (e.g., Cass, 1979). The models deal little with the meaning of homoerotic intimacy, addressing mostly accommodation to minority group membership. There is, of course, merit in the idea that social activism and interpersonal openness are positively associated with mental health and successful internalization of lesbian/gay identity as well as some evidence for the benefits of being out to others, at least selectively (see Fassinger, 1991; Gonsiorek & Rudolph, 1991). However, the implication that lacking these qualities signals developmental arrest fails to account for the social realities of diverse groups of lesbians and gay men. Such factors as occupational environment, geographical location, racial/ethnic group membership, family situation, legal and economic realities, and support systems determine the extent to which disclosure and politicization are even possible for many lesbians and gay men (Fassinger, 1991). Models of lesbian/gay identity formation that describe a common developmental process must be inclusive of diversity in these populations.

Moreover, both the process and the content of lesbian/gay identity development are oversimplified in linear models that postulate immutable same-sex relational orientation as the final stage. As identity research suggests, individuals may be in several stages of development simultaneously, not all individuals will negotiate all stages, and the process of moving from early awareness to identity integration is a lengthy one (e.g., Sophie, 1985–1986). Linear models tend to ignore the paths of those who do not progress predictably through the stages or to view alternative outcomes (bisexuality, heterosexuality) as developmental arrest (Sophie, 1985–1986). Models of racial/ethnic minority identity development do not place the burden of political awakening on the individual and imply negative judgment of members who have not reached advanced stages in quite the same way that the lesbian/gay models do. This may be due to an element that these identities do not share: Lesbians/gays in the early stages of sexual minority identity formation can deny membership in the minority group (both to self and others), which members of visible racial/ethnic groups may not find possible. Other minorities step onto the path toward raised consciousness with an identity that usually is apparent to themselves and others, and the transformation involves changing attitudes toward the meaning of that identity. Lesbians and gay men step onto two paths at once—they must acknowledge their membership in an invisible minority group and change their attitudes toward the meaning of a group that was not previously relevant. Accurate models must account for these dual demands.

Proposed Model of Lesbian Identity Formation

The model described here represents an attempt to address the deficits noted in existing models and is intended to be broadly inclusive of the diverse paths one may take to comfortable, integrated lesbianism. We clearly distinguish between the two processes of personal development of same-sex sexual orientation and redefinition of group membership and group meaning; our work is thus somewhat similar to the attempt of Ossana et al. (1992) to separate internal from sociopolitical processes. We propose a four-phase model with two parallel branches that are reciprocally catalytic but not simultaneous: individual sexual identity and group membership identity. An initial state of nonawareness precedes both branches of the model, and the four subsequent phases follow in the same progression for each branch (see Table 1).

The model is built on several assumptions held in common with other identity models. We prefer the term *phases* to *stages* because of the greater flexibility implied, and although we outline phases in a progression, we conceptualize the process as continuous and circular; every new relationship raises new issues about individual sexuality, and every new context requires renewed awareness of group oppression. We borrow from the racial/ethnic minority identity literature the concept of three relevant attitude areas at each phase of group identity development: attitudes toward self, other lesbians/gays, and nongays. Also, based on current conceptions of women's identity and gender effects in the coming out process, this model reflects the self-definition of homoerotic desire in terms of a relational identity. Unlike most other lesbian/gay identity models, however, our model does not assume disclosure behaviors as evidence of developmental advancement, except, to some extent, at the last phase of group identity. We believe that disclosure is so profoundly affected by environmental oppression that to use it as an index of identity development directly forces an individual to take responsibility for her own victimization. The model is outlined in the following section.

TABLE 1
Proposed Model of Lesbian Identity Formation

Individual Sexual Identity	*Group Membership Identity*
(Nonawareness)	

1. Awareness

–of feeling or being different	–of existence of different sexual orientations in people

Self-Statement Examples:

"I feel pulled toward women in ways I don't understand." (I)
"I had no idea there were lesbian/gay people out there." (G)

2. Exploration

–of strong/erotic feelings for women or a particular woman	–of one's position regarding lesbians/gays as a group (both attitudes and membership)

Self-Statement Examples:

"The way I feel makes me think I'd like to be sexual with a woman." (I)
"Getting to know lesbian/gay people is scary but exciting." (G)

3. Deepening/Commitment

–to self-knowledge, self-fulfillment, and crystallization of choices about sexuality	–to personal involvement with reference group, with awareness of oppression and consequences of choices

Self-Statement Examples:

"I clearly feel more intimate sexually and emotionally with women than with men." (I)
"Sometimes I have been mistreated because of my lesbianism." (G)

4. Internalization/Synthesis

–of love for women, sexual choices, into overall identity	–of identity as a member of a minority group, across contexts

Self-Statement Examples:

"I am deeply fulfilled in my relationships with women." (I)
"I feel comfortable with my lesbianism no matter where I am or who I am with." (G)

Individual Sexual Identity Development

Phase 1: Awareness. The dawning of a minority sexuality is likely to begin with awareness of a difference, a general feeling of being different or awareness of feelings or desires that are different from the heterosexual norm and therefore from the predicted self. Nonconscious ideologies become conscious; the previously held assumption that all persons, including the self, are heterosexual is called into question. Same-sex thoughts and feelings, however, do not imply self-labeling. This phase encompasses experiences similar to Coleman's (1982) Stage 2, Sophie's (1985–1986) Stage 1, and Cass's (1984) Stage 1.

Phase 2: Exploration. The second phase involves active examination of questions arising in the first phase. For women, it is explicitly hypothesized that this phase involves strong relationships with or feelings about other women or another woman in particular. This phase will involve exploration of sexual feelings but will not necessarily involve exploration of sexual behaviors or a variety of partners. Some issues from Sophie's (1985–1986) Stages 2–3 and Chapman and Brannock's (1987) Stage 3 will be addressed by women in this phase, as well as some from Stages 3–4 (particularly 4) of Coleman (1982).

Phase 3: Deepening/commitment. Exploration leads to a deepening of self-knowledge and to the crystallization of some choices about sexuality. Some may see relationships with women as only one possibility and identify as bisexual, and others may decide in favor of men as sexual partners. It is here that the emerging lesbian is likely to recognize her desire for other women as within herself and, with deepening self-awareness, will develop sexual clarity and commitment to her self-fulfillment as a sexual being. Intimacy and identity become meshed as the woman recognizes that her forms of intimacy imply certain things about her identity and then moves toward accepting and further examining those aspects of herself. The commitment to self-fulfillment transcends previous assumptions about the self and will necessarily intersect with the woman's socialization to be heterosexual, heterosexist, and homophobic. This commitment, therefore, probably affects the group identity process described in the other branch of this model, implying that com-pletion of this phase of sexual identity development may require addressing some group membership tasks; this may elucidate Sophie's (1985–1986) findings that women in her study waited to identify as lesbian until they had acquired a positive concept of lesbianism. Thus it is at this stage that we would most expect to see the anger and sadness described by Coleman's (1982) Stage 3 and the acceptance and pride of Cass's (1984) Stages 4–5.

Phase 4: Internalization/synthesis. In this last phase, a woman experiences fuller self-acceptance of desire/love for women as a part of her overall identity. Women at this phase of lesbian identity development are likely to have completed many years of emotional and sexual self-exploration and to have resolved difficult decisions about their desires and practices. This internal process of clarification will involve the synthesis of role identity into ego identity (Minton & McDonald, 1984), creating a sense of internal consistency and certainty that may be manifested in unwillingness to change lesbian preferences (Sophie, 1985–1986).

Having examined and transformed the internal concept of self, reformulation of public identity will be necessary as well. Choices will be made about where and how to be open about sexuality, and we believe that it is the process of resolving these questions that creates integration, not the content of their resolution. That is, a woman may choose to be professionally "closeted" for important contextual reasons; as long as the choice has been addressed, this woman may be as developmentally integrated as the woman who is professionally open. However, at some point, as the woman lives in society with a clearly defined alternative sexual preference, she will have to address the meaning of lesbianism in that society. Therefore, we believe that it is unlikely that one could reach the final phase of individual sexual identity development without beginning to address the group membership questions in the parallel branch of the model.

Group Membership Identity Development

Although the previously described branch of this model focuses on the internal process of clarifying and incorporating same-sex emotional and sexual desires, this separate but reciprocal branch consists of tasks that result from the context in which the internal process occurs; that is, it involves addressing social attitudes toward those desires and the tasks of self and group labeling. Because this branch of the model addresses identification as a member of a minority reference group, it resembles the racial/ethnic identity models discussed earlier. Also (as mentioned previously), each phase describes feelings and attitudes towards the self, other lesbians/gays, and nongays.

It must be remembered that both branches of this model emerge from the common root of nonawareness of homoerotic preference and socialized ideologies regarding sexual norms. The content of each individual's non-awareness is very specific—it may range from total ignorance to virulent antigay beliefs—and therefore will shape the process of group identification uniquely for each woman. It is almost certain in present society that strong training in heterosexism and homophobia will have occurred, and the process of group identification involves the unlearning of both. Thus, although a common sequence of development is postulated here, the emotional intensity and difficulty of the process will be determined by the degree of heterosexism and homophobia within each individual.

Phase 1: Awareness. The first phase of group identity is set into motion by a new awareness that heterosexuality is not a universal norm and that people exist who have different sexual orientations. Realization that a community of lesbians/gays exists may force the woman to acknowledge that heterosexism exists and that she has lived under heterosexist assumptions. This initial awareness is likely to resemble the disintegration (Helms, 1990) or revelation (Downing & Roush, 1985) described in other minority identity models. However, the disintegration here is more likely to produce confusion and bewilderment than rage. Unlike the initial phase of other minority identity models, this initial discovery pertains to the very existence of the group, not yet to the meaning or oppression of the group; thus it may be more like an epiphany than a confrontation.

Phase 2: Exploration. At this phase, a woman seeks to define her position in relation to the reference group along two dimensions: attitudes and membership. The phase is characterized by active pursuit of knowledge about lesbian/gay people,

in terms of both the group as a whole and the possibility of one's belonging in the group. For example, a woman developing feminist consciousness may move through this phase of group identity, develop increased knowledge and a positive view of lesbians, and yet not self-identify as a member of that reference group. Moreover, clarification of attitudes toward lesbians may be a complex, affectively charged process for a woman who has held strong homophobic feelings or who has limited access to information and resources. As in the Downing and Roush (1985) model, women in this phase are likely to feel anger and guilt for being "duped" by and participating in heterosexism. On the other hand, exploring the existence of other lesbians also will be likely to produce driving curiosity and exhilarating joy.

Phase 3: Deepening/commitment. This phase involves a deepening awareness of both the unique value and oppression of the lesbian/gay community. It involves a commitment to create a personal relationship to the reference group, with awareness of the possible consequences entailed. Some women deepening their commitment to lesbian identity are likely to experience the ideological and emotional transformation described in immersion or embeddedness stages of other models (e.g., Cross, 1971; Downing & Roush, 1985), including an intense identification with lesbian culture and rejection of heterosexual society. Not all, however, will pass through such an intensely dichotomous phase (Sophie, 1985–1986). Whether coupled with a rejection of the dominant group or not, this phase will include some version of the "discovery of sisterhood" (Avery, 1977, cited in Downing & Roush, 1985, p. 701), and this experience is likely to be affectively reflected in a combination of excitement, pride, rage, and internal conflict.

Phase 4: Internalization/synthesis. In this final developmental phase, the lesbian woman has moved through a process of conflict and reevaluation, identified herself as a member of a minority group, redefined the meaning of that group, internalized this new identity, and synthesized it into her overall self-concept. This synthesis will be reflected in feelings of fulfillment, security, and an ability to maintain her lesbian sense of self across contexts. This does not necessarily mean that she has become politicized, though it does mean that she has become socially aware of her own oppression as a lesbian. If she experienced a dichotomized worldview in the previous phase, she will now move toward a more integrated view, and it is likely that some identity disclosure will have occurred. It is assumed that women at this phase will evaluate both gays and nongays individually rather than stereotypically (Downing & Roush, 1985) and also may be sensitive to the distinction Cross (1971) makes between individuals and institutions. She will have traversed the path from rage, anxiety, insecurity, and rhetoric to directed anger, dedication, and self-love as a lesbian woman.

As previously noted, the two branches of the model, though reciprocal and mutually catalytic, are not necessarily simultaneous. Some lesbians living in isolation, for example, may have fully developed lesbian relationships long before coming to understand that there are other women in the world doing the same. We believe, however, that it probably is not possible to proceed completely through either branch of this model without to some degree addressing the other (e.g., it is unlikely that an individual could be fully integrated into the lesbian community without having clarified her emotional and sexual feelings for other women), and one process may trigger the other at almost any point. For example, suddenly falling in love with a woman (individual, Phase 2) may spark the beginning realization that a population of persons with same-sex orientation exists and is of personal relevance (group, Phase 1); or, a woman who is politically and socially involved in the lesbian community (group, Phase 3) may only later realize that she is sexually attracted to women (individual, Phase 2).

Implications for Counseling: Case Examples

In this section, we explore the implications and usefulness of the proposed model in planning counseling interventions, particularly in facilitating accurate assessment. Conceptualizations of identity that distinguish between the developmental tasks of individual sexual identity formation and group membership identity formation can help therapists select more appropriately and efficiently targeted interventions. For example, without noting this distinction, it is easy to assume that confusion signaling early phases of individual sexuality development implies lack of experience with lesbian/gay culture, as well, or that strong ties to lesbian/gay people are

indicative of internal struggles with homoerotic preferences. Planning counseling interventions around presumed parallel internal and reference group developmental trajectories can lead to, at best, wasted time and energy by both therapist and client and, at worst, perceptions of therapist insensitivity and lack of knowledge on the part of clients. We present here several fictional case examples to further elucidate the important distinction between individual and group identity development and to suggest possibilities for treatment implied by our model.

Case 1: Carol

Carol's dearest friend has just come out to her, and Carol is slowly realizing that she is in love with her friend. Carol, a 22-year-old African American woman attending a conservative Christian college, is confused because her strong religious background has taught her that these feelings are wrong. However, she cannot shake them and has sought a counselor's advice. Carol appears unaware of the existence of lesbian/gay people as a group and would not label her current feelings as anything but strong, loving feelings for her friend. She is reluctant to tell her friend of these feelings because she is terrified of their losing control over the situation.

In terms of the model, it is clear that Carol is just becoming aware of her strong feelings for a specific woman (individual, 2). She has no awareness or experience of a lesbian/gay community (group, 1), and added to her burden of ignorance is a homophobic religious background. Carol faces important challenges in the intersection of her individual and group identities. She has several group affiliations that may feel contradictory to her nascent inner feelings, and in whichever arena she acts, her actions affect both her relationship to herself and her experience of her community. Clients often feel trapped into inaction in such situations, and much therapeutic benefit can result from maintaining separation of developmental tasks related to individual and group identities until feelings are clarified, accurate information is provided, and reality testing regarding consequences has occurred.

Carol is confused and afraid; it may help her simply to know that these are common feelings in the first phases of questioning as assumed identity. This, of course, is an appropriate, affirming therapeutic response to any client questioning her individual sexuality, as is the provision of accurate information, resources, and referrals regarding reference groups, particularly those that support dual minority status for women of color. Our model suggests, however, that caution and sensitive timing are critically important to group identity interventions in a case such as Carol's, in which fears regarding reference group identification can swiftly destroy fragile sexual and emotional feelings or bonds. Moreover, Carol's case makes clear the assumption in our model that emerging sexual identity is likely to be relationally defined, and there is much therapeutic work to be done in clarifying those feelings and locating them within the self, to strengthen individual identity and prepare for the considerable risks of involvement in the lesbian/gay community and possible ostracism from existing reference groups. Carol's case also points to the need for counseling psychologists to broaden their arenas of intervention (Fassinger, 1991) to include those crucial to healthy group identity development; that is, to create a context in which Carol (and others like her) may grow, it is important to work proactively within religious and other cultural communities to change attitudes and build contacts with sympathetic and informed leaders in those communities.

Case 2: Carla

Carla, a 31-year-old Latina, has served in the military for 10 years. She has been with her lover, Angela, for 4 years, and they live off-base, restricting physical intimacy to their home. Carla has been aware of her same-sex attraction since childhood and has been comfortable maintaining a sense of privacy about this aspect of her life. Recently, however, the media attention to gays in the military triggered many new emotions in Carla. At first, she was frightened and angered by her more open peers, then she began to imagine the possibilities of a freer lifestyle. Carla began reading lesbian books and talked to Angela about having a holy union in the presence of selected friends. Carla was furious with the presidential "don't ask, don't tell" mandate, has become belligerent and resistant at work, and has provoked conflict with Angela. Carla reveals to the counselor that she "can't stand hiding anymore," is angry at Angela for "acting ashamed of who we are," and does not feel she can be herself anywhere.

In terms of our model, Carla is in an ongoing relationship with another woman and has accepted her orientation for some time (individual, 4). She is currently experiencing a heightened awareness of her position in society as a lesbian and has changing feelings about her commitment to that group, including a mixture of conflict, anger, and pride (group, 3). Carla's deepening commitment to her lesbianism has resulted in a widespread dissatisfaction with life choices she made at a time when she was comfortable being more closeted; as a result she is in conflict both at work and at home. She has just become more acutely aware of a pressure she has lived with all her life, but Angela and the military appear to be the sources of constriction, and Carla likely feels that the only choices that will allow her to feel congruent are options that many threaten her career and her relationship.

Our model suggests that developmental tasks related to group identity present the most pressing foci for intervention in Carla's case. In fact, sharing the model with Carla may help her to understand the process she is moving through and to caution her against making decisions about her life that she may regret at a later phase, much as she now regrets the constriction she feels from the demands of an earlier phase. In exploring ways to meet Carla's growing need to identify with other lesbians/gays within the context of her realistic job concerns, there may be arenas in which she can begin to lead a more overtly lesbian lifestyle, for example, immediate and extended family, selected co-workers, or safe lesbian support groups and events. Of course, Carla's increased disclosure poses a challenge for the couple in that it threatens Angela's privacy, as well, and each may newly experience the other as a source of painful personal and social pressure. This case thus demonstrates clearly our assumptions regarding the reciprocal nature of the individual and group identity processes described in our model and suggests that this, too, is an area that can be addressed by helping both members of the couple understand the developmental process in which they are engaged and clarifying the position of each person to facilitate negotiation and compromise. Finally, it would be useful to further explore Carla's anger, which may obscure underlying guilt. As we have suggested in our model, lesbians embracing their community also face the history of their own heterosexism and homophobia and may have many experiences and relationships to reevaluate as their vision shifts.

Case 3: Emily

Emily's mate of 18 years recently has died. She was Emily's first and only relationship, and the two women lived a private life in the rural Midwest, isolated from any kind of lesbian community. Emily, a 52-year-old Caucasian woman, has always accepted her lesbianism as an integral part of her identity, without much notice paid to it. Now she reluctantly seeks out a counselor because she is feeling extremely lonely and in need of support and does not know where else to turn.

In terms of our model, it would appear that to have sustained this primary relationship for so long, Emily probably has fully integrated her sense of herself as lesbian in terms of her personal sexuality (individual, 4). Her attitude toward lesbians as a group is less clear and seems characterized either by ignorance or by avoidance (group, 1–2). In her group identity development, Emily faces a challenge both internal and external, because of the unique strain of having had only her mate as a group referent. Thus, as our model suggests in positing a relational identity, Emily may be grieving both the loss of a mate and a loss of safety in her identity. Also congruent with our model's assumption of reciprocal individual and group identity processes, Emily may well have to address hitherto unexamined aspects of her group identity to gain support for grieving the personal loss of her mate.

Clearly, our model suggests that group identification represents a major developmental task for Emily. However, careful assessment must first identify the components of Emily's loneliness. Her isolation may be rooted in deeply internalized homophobia and secrecy despite availability of lesbian community, or it may result from simple lack of awareness of or access to other lesbians. Each of these possibilities requires a different kind of intervention and will determine how she is introduced to the lesbian community. Moreover, it is likely that immediate individual grief work with Emily initially will take precedence over concerns related to group identity, except insofar as involvement in the community facilitates her healing.

As the foregoing cases illustrate, each woman has experienced a strong connection to another woman that has strongly affected her individual sense of self. In addition, all three women are coping with some form of social isolation related to that personal identity, although the form and effects differ for each. Carol has no awareness of a social context that could be supportive of her dawning individual feelings, and she is not yet able to internally support them herself. Emily and Carla are comfortable with their personal sexual orientation but face different types of social isolation; Emily's loss confronts her with the unique aloneness of grieving, and Carla's changing awareness has left her a feeling alone within a set of life circumstances that no longer fit. All three women face challenges to both individual and group identity, dividing their life talks into questions about how they will understand themselves and how they will achieve a sense of belonging in the world. Although interventions for these women may include commonly used activities, such as individual and couples counseling, psychoeducation, group treatment, bibliotherapy, and referral to lesbian/gay community resources, it is important to note that accurate assessment and appropriate attention to distinct developmental needs inherent in individual and group identity processes can help counseling psychologists to plan their interventions more efficiently and effectively.

Implications for Research

In terms of theory and research, accurate models of lesbian/gay identity development are necessary to help clarify within- and between-group similarities and differences, as well as to assess the needs and predict the challenges facing the population. Sexual minority models first must be validated then further this population. Sexual minority models first must be validated then further tested through research designed to relate phases of the coming out process to other mental health variables, such as relationship satisfaction, career development, and self-esteem. Future research also must focus on elucidating intragroup differences among lesbians, so that the models we use are truly inclusive of the diverse experiences of women in our society.

The model of lesbian identity proposed here represents an effort to advance scientific work with this population by positing and articulating a dual process of identity formation and by explicitly grounding lesbian/gay identity theory in work in race/ethnicity and gender. The model already has been initially validated using the Q-sort methodology recommended for early work in model development (Hall et al., 1972).

Preliminary results suggest its usefulness in describing the experiences of diverse lesbians, as expected (McCarn, 1991). Perhaps surprisingly, the model, somewhat modified to reflect greater sexual exploration and activity, appears to describe the experiences of diverse gay men, as well (Fassinger & Miller, in press); this may be due to the increasingly relational orientation of gay men being anecdotally reported in the literature or to the general utility of a model that distinguishes between group and individual processes. Instrument development based on the model is needed (and already under way by the present authors); an assessment tool that distinguishes individual sexual identity from group membership identity could enhance research efforts—for example, by aiding in the formulation and evaluation of more specifically targeted interventions with this population.

One area requiring research attention is the relationship between disclosure and lesbian/gay identity development. The present model, unlike most models, does not implicitly assume a strong relationship between these variables. However, empirical research in this area is virtually nonexistent, in part because of the lack of instrumentation to measure identity disclosure. If we organize our interventions around disclosure as an index of identity development and personal maturity, we may unwittingly exacerbate internal and social tensions already experienced by lesbian/gay individuals. Again, strong research base in this area would be helpful in guiding intervention efforts.

Burgeoning empirical work in the area of multicultural awareness and mass-cultural psychology suggests another possibility for the use of lesbian/gay identity models. As the research foundation regarding models of racial/ethnic identity has grown, Helms and colleagues (see Helms, 1990) have begun writing with increased clarity about the absence of cultural identity awareness in members of dominant racial/cultural groups. Similarly, it is important to speculate about what our theoretical and empirical explorations of lesbians and gay men can teach us about nongays. How might a deepened understanding of this area change the lenses through which we view adult development generally? Have we adequately explored the development of a fully integrated sexual identity that is not associated with strong social stigma? How might our developmental understanding of human sexuality and intimacy be affected if we attended to the relational experiences of same-sex individuals? Brown (1989, p. 451) described the "normative creativity" necessary in choosing and living a lifestyle that requires formulating rules as they are lived. Greater empirical attention to the personal and social behavior of lesbians and gay men in designing and living their lives can teach us developmental lessons that have important implications for understanding all people.

Conclusion

We have presented what is intended to be an inclusive, heuristically useful model of the development of lesbian identity. It is our hope that the present model begins to address the complexity of developing self-acceptance and comfortable group membership in sexual minority people. By separating the experience of clarified internal desire from that of altered group definitions, we remove from the model an onus of pressure and politicization applied to the individual in other models. We must at all times remain aware that it is the context of homophobia that defines the meaning of lesbian or gay identity. We would hope that all persons in our society eventually move through a process of reevaluating the meaning of the groups *gay* and *lesbian*, but it is the discovery of their potential membership in those groups that forces lesbians and gay men to begin this process more urgently than heterosexuals. We look forward to a day when models for internalizing self-acceptance will be irrelevant and obsolete because we will have ceased to perpetuate a context that fosters self-loathing—to a day when the word *homosexual* has lost its power to label and stigmatize people and has become merely a descriptor of one of a wide variety of acceptable forms of loving.

Notes

This article is based, in part, on the master's thesis of the first author in consultation with the second author, under the departmental advisement of Mary Ann Hoffman. The authors gratefully acknowledge Dr. Hoffman for her help in preparing this manuscript for publication. Correspondence may be addressed to Ruth E. Fassinger, Ph.D., Department of Counseling and Personnel Services, 3214 Benjamin Building, University of Maryland, College Park, MD 20742, or by electronic mail to RF36@UMAIL.UMD.EDU

References

Atkinson, D. R., Morten, G., & Sue, D. W. (1979). *Counseling American minorities: A cross-cultural perspective*. Dubuque, IA: W. C. Brown.

Avery, Donna M. (1977). The psychosocial stages of liberation. *Illinois Personal and Guidance Association Quarterly, 63*, 36–42.

Brown, L. S. (1989). New voices, new visions: Toward a lesbian/gay paradigm for psychology. *Psychology of Women Quarterly, 13*, 445–458.

Browning, C., Reynolds, A. L., & Dworkin, S. H. (1991). Affirmative therapy for lesbian women. *The Counseling Psychologist, 19*, 177–196.

Butler, J. (1993). *Bodies that matter: On the discursive limits of "sex."* New York: Routledge.

Cass, V. C. (1979). Homosexual identity formation: A theoretical model. *Journal of Homosexuality, 4*, 219–235.

Cass, V. C. (1984). Homosexual identity formation: Testing a theoretical model. *Journal of Sex Research, 20*, 143–167.

Chan, C. (1989). Issues of identity development among Asian-American lesbians and gay men. *Journal of Counseling and Development, 68*, 16–20.

Chapman, B. E., & Brannock, J. C. (1987). Proposed model of lesbian identity development: An empirical examination. *Journal of Homosexuality, 14*, 69–80.

Coleman, E. (1982). Developmental stages of the coming out process. In J. Gonsiorek (Ed.), *Homosexuality and psychotherapy: A practitioner's handbook of affirmative models* (pp. 31–44). New York: Haworth Press.

Cross, W. E., Jr. (1971). The negro-to-black conversion experience: Toward a psychology of Black liberation. *Black World, 20*, 13–27.

Cross, W. E., Jr. (1987). A two-factor theory of Black identity: Implications for the study of identity development in minority children. In J. S. Phinney & M. J. Rotheram (Eds.), *Children's ethnic socialization: Pluralism and development* (p. 117–133). Newbury Park, CA: Sage.

Daniluk, J. C. (1993). The meaning and experience of female sexuality: A phenomenological analysis. *Psychology of Women Quarterly, 17*, 53–69.

Downing, N. E., & Roush, K. L. (1985). From passive acceptance to active commitment: A model of feminist identity development for women. *The Counseling Psychologist, 13*(4), 695–709.

Faderman, L. (1984). The "new gay" lesbians. *Journal of Homosexuality, 10*, 85–95.

Fassinger, R. E. (1991). The hidden minority: Issues and challenges in working with lesbian women and gay men. *The Counseling Psychologist, 19*, 157–176.

Fassinger, R. E., & Miller, B. A. (in press). Validation of a model of homosexual identity formation on a sample of gay men. *Journal of Homosexuality*.

Fassinger, R. E., & Morrow, S. L. (1995). OverCome: Repositioning lesbian sexualities. In L. Diamant & R. McAnulty (Eds.), *The psychology of sexual orientation, behavior, and identity: A handbook* (pp. 197–219). Westport, CT: Greenwood.

Frye, M. (1992). *Willful virgin*. Freedom, CA: Crossing.

Gilligan, C. (1982). *In a different voice*. Cambridge, MA: Harvard University Press.

Gonsiorek, J. C., & Rudolph, J. R. (1991). Homosexual identity: Coming out and other developmental events. In J. C. Gonsiorek & J. D. Weinrich (Eds.), *Homosexuality: Research implications for public policy* (p. 161–176). Newbury Park, CA: Sage.

Greenwald, A. G., & Pratkanis, A. R. (1984). The self. In R. S. Wyer & T. K. Srull (Eds.), *Handbook of social cognition* (Vol. 3, pp. 129–178). Hillsdale, NJ: Lawrence Erlbaum.

Hall, W. S., Cross, W. E., & Freedle, R. (1972). Stages in the development of a Black identity. *American College Testing Program Report, 50*.

Helms, J. S. (Ed.). (1990). *Black and White racial identity: Theory, research, and practice*. Westport, CT: Greenwood.

Lolacano, D. K. (1989). Gay identity issues among black Americans: racism, homophobia, and the need for validation. *Journal of Counseling and Development, 68*, 21–25.

MacCowan, L. (1987). Review of "The 'new gay' lesbians" by Lillian Faderman. *Journal of Homosexuality, 14*, 173–178.

McCarn, S. R. (1991). *Validation of a model of sexual minority (lesbian) identity development*. Unpublished master's thesis, University of Maryland at College Park.

Minton, H. L., & McDonald, G. J. (1984). Homosexual identity formation as a developmental process. *Journal of Homosexuality, 9*, 91–104.

Mio, J. S., & Iwamasa, G. (1993). To do or not to do: That is the question for white cross-cultural researchers. *The Counseling Psychologist, 21*, 197–212.

Morales, E. S. (1989). Ethnic minority families and minority gays and lesbians. *Journal of Homosexuality, 17*, 217–239.

Myers, L. J., Speight, S. L., Highlen, P. S., Cox, C. I., Reynolds, A. R., Adams, E. M., & Hanley, C. P. (1991). Identity development and worldview: Toward an optimal conceptualization. *Journal of Counseling and Development, 70*, 54–63.

Ossana, S. M., Helms, J. E., & Leonard, M. M. (1992). Do "womanist" identity attitudes influence college women's self-esteem and perceptions of environmental bias? *Journal of Counseling and Development, 70*, 402–408.

Parham, T. A. (1989). Cycles of psychological nigrescence. *The Counseling Psychologist, 17*, 187–226.

Peck, T. (1986). Women's self-definition in adulthood: From a different model. *Psychology of Women Quarterly, 10*, 274–284.

Pedersen, P. (Ed.). (1991). Special issue: Multiculturalism as a fourth force in counseling. *Journal of Counseling and Development, 70*, 4–250.

Ponterotto, J. G., & Sabnani, H. B. (1989). "Classics" in multicultural counseling: A systematic five-year content analysis. *Journal of Multicultural Counseling and Development, 17*, 23–37.

Reynolds, A. I., & Pope, R. L. (1991). The complexities of diversity: Exploring multiple oppressions. *Journal of Counseling and Development, 70*, 174–180.

Ridley, C. R., Mendoza, D. W., & Kanitz, B. E. (1994). Multicultural training: Reexamination, operationalization, and integration. *The Counseling Psychologist, 22*, 227–289.

Root, M. P. (1990). Resolving "other" status: Identity development of biracial individuals. In L. S. Brown & M. P. Root (Eds.), *Complexity and diversity in feminist theory and therapy* (p. 185–205). New York: Haworth.

Sophie, J. (1985–1986). A critical examination of stage theories of lesbian identity development. *Journal of Homosexuality, 12*, 39–51.

Taylor, D. M., & Dube, L. (1986). Two faces of identity: The "I" and the "We." *Journal of Social Issues, 42*, 81–98.

Triandis, H. C. (1989). The self and social behavior in differing cultural contexts. *Psychological Review, 96*, 506–520.

Troiden, R. R. (1989). The formation of homosexual identities. *Journal of Homosexuality, 17*, 43–73.

Vance, C. S. (1984). *Pleasure and danger: Exploring female sexuality*. London: Routledge & Kegan Paul.

Section 8

MULTIPLE DIMENSIONS
OF DEVELOPMENT

CHAPTER 32

A CONCEPTUAL FRAMEWORK FOR UNDERSTANDING RACE, CLASS, GENDER, AND SEXUALITY

LYNN WEBER

Since the mid-1980s, scholarship and college courses that address multiple dimensions of inequality under the rubric of race, class, gender, and (recently) sexuality studies have grown rapidly. Most courses now employ a set of readings, many of which are drawn from a growing number of anthologies. A strength of this approach is its presentation of the diversity of human experiences and the multiplicity of critical perspectives. A weakness is its failure to convey the commonalities in race, class, gender, and sexuality analyses of social reality. To aid in teaching and research on race, class, gender, and sexuality, this article presents six common themes that characterize this scholarship. Race, class, gender, and sexuality are historically and globally specific, socially constructed power relations that simultaneously operate at both the macro (societal) and micro (individual) levels of society. Scholarship in this tradition emphasizes the interdependence of knowledge and activism.

People's real life experiences have never fit neatly into the boundaries created by academic disciplines: Lives are much more complex and far reaching. Just as the social, political, economic, and psychological dimensions of everyday life are intertwined and mutually dependent, so too are the systems of inequality—race, class, gender, and sexuality—that limit and restrict some people while privileging others. Increasingly, interdisciplinary studies, including Women's Studies and multicultural studies, are extending the range of the curriculum; such programs are critical sites for the development of meaningful commentaries on human social and psychological realities that reflect such complexities (Magner, 1996).

It is in Women's Studies—not in racial or ethnic studies, not in social stratification (class) studies in sociology, not in psychology or in other traditional disciplines—that race, class, gender, and sexuality studies first emerged.[1] Because of its critical stance toward knowledge in the traditional disciplines, its interdisciplinary approach, and its orientation toward social change and social betterment, Women's Studies has been most open to self-critique for its exclusion of multiply oppressed groups, such as women of color, working-class women, and lesbians (Baca Zinn, Weber Cannon, Higginbotham, & Dill, 1986; Weber Cannon, Higginbotham, & Leung, 1988).

Since these initial writings, scholarship and college courses that simultaneously address these multiple dimensions of inequality under the rubric of race, class, gender, and, increasingly, sexuality studies have grown rapidly. Texts in most courses now consist of a set of readings selected by individual faculty and/or of one of a growing number of anthologies on the topic (Andersen & Collins, 1995; Anzaldúa, 1987a, 1987b; Baca Zinn & Dill, 1994; Chow, Wilkinson, & Baca Zinn, 1996; Cyrus, 1993; Rothenberg, 1995). The strength of these anthologies is that they demonstrate the significance of race, class, gender, and sexuality by presenting a wide array of diverse human experiences and analyses across these dimensions. Students are encouraged to move beyond thinking about major social and personal issues solely from their own viewpoints or from dominant group perspectives. The major limitation is that anthologies provide little direction in identifying the themes and assumptions that pull these diverse perspectives together. We are given little guidance about what constitutes a race, class, gender, and sexuality analysis of social reality. In part, this omission parallels the development of the field of race, class, gender, and sexuality studies, which began by revealing diverse experiences across these dimensions to counter the monolithic views of the social world put forth in both mainstream and Women's Studies scholarship.

Now, however, scholars are beginning to search for and to identify common themes and approaches that characterize the work in race, class, gender, and sexuality studies (cf. Baca Zinn & Dill, 1996). This process should invite debate and critique, further the development of the scholarship, and help provide one or more frameworks for teaching about this work. This article presents six themes that currently characterize this scholarship. By reminding us of some questions that need to be asked in any analysis of human society, these themes can guide the race, class, gender, and sexuality analyses we conduct for our research, our teaching, and our social activism.

A Brief History of Race, Class, Gender, and Sexuality Studies

In the 1970s and 1980s, women of color, the majority of whom were poor or working class, were especially vehement in voicing their opposition to theories of and perspectives on social reality that focused on a single dimension—especially on gender, but also on race, class, or sexuality. They argued that the multidimensionality and interconnected nature of race, class, gender, and sexuality hierarchies are especially visible to those who face oppression along more than one dimension of inequality. Patricia Hill Collins (1990), author of *Black Feminist Thought*, identifies the "interlocking nature of oppression" as one of three recurring themes in the work of Black feminists. Collins notes that this theme dates back at least to Sojourner Truth, who in the

mid-19th century said: "There is a great stir about colored men getting their rights, and not colored women theirs. You see the colored men will be masters over the women, and it will be just as bad as before" (cited in Loewenberg & Bogin, 1976, p. 238).

When Black women began to critique recent gender scholarship for its exclusionary practices, they focused on conducting analyses that began from the experience of Black women, putting them at center stage. *The Black Woman* (Cade, 1970), *Ain't I a Woman* (hooks, 1981), *The Black Woman* (Rodgers-Rose, 1980), "The Dialectics of Black Womanhood" (Dill, 1979), and "Race, Class, and Gender: Prospects for an All Inclusive Sisterhood" (Dill, 1983) were among the first critical perspectives on Black women published as books or articles in major feminist journals.

The irony of ignoring groups whose experiences typically reflected the confluence of multiple major dimensions of inequality was captured in the often-cited title of one of the first anthologies in Black Women's Studies: *All the Women Were White, All the Blacks Were Men, But Some of Us Are Brave: Black Women's Studies* (Hull, Scott, & Smith, 1982). Since that time, the critique of the White middle-class bias in Women's Studies has been joined by a critique of the male bias in racial ethnic studies, harkening back to the words of Sojourner Truth. And the study of race, class, gender, and sexuality has been expanded by studies of other groups of women of color (cf. Amaro & Russo, 1987; Anzaldúa, 1987b; Baca Zinn & Dill, 1994); of other oppressed groups, such as gays and lesbians (cf. Barale & Halperin, 1993; D'Emilio & Freedman, 1988; Greene, 1994); and, more recently, of privilege itself: for example, studies of the social construction of whiteness (cf. Frankenberg, 1993; McIntosh, 1995; Roediger, 1991) or of masculinity (cf. Brod & Kaufman, 1994; Connell, 1995; Messner, 1992).

As a recently developing field, race, class, gender, and sexuality studies has not yet produced a wise range of competing theories about the nature of race, class, gender, and sexual hierarchies. Rather, it has begun to generate debates about the most productive ways of conceptualizing race, class, gender, and sexuality; about the nature of their relationships to one another; and about their manifestations in everyday life (see, e.g., Collins et al., 1995, pp. 491–513; West & Fenstermaker, 1995, pp. 8–37).

The scholarship has been characterized more by diversity of content and commonalities in perspective than by competing or conflicting interpretations. Perhaps these common themes arise because the field is young and the research and writing has come primarily from women of color and other marginalized groups who share an "outsider within" perspective (Collins, 1991). Although inside the academy by virtue of their status as professors, writers, researchers, and scholars, these groups also have an outsider's view of the knowledge that the academy has produced because they are women of color, come from working-class backgrounds, and/or are gays and lesbians. Much of the new scholarship follows the tradition established by early writers who made women of color the center of attention, describing their everyday lives. Seeing the world through the eyes of oppressed groups raises new questions about our preconceived notions of many aspects of social reality—from the social relations of domestic work to what it takes to be a "good" mother to the American Dream that talent and hard work will produce material success (Dill, 1988; Glenn, 1992; Hochschild, 1995; Rollins, 1985).

At the same time that it questions traditional scholarship and interpretations of the lives of oppressed as well as dominant groups, the scholarship on race, class, gender, and sexuality also tends to avoid grand theorizing about the essential natures of these hierarchies. Scholars instead emphasize that these social constructs cannot be understood outside of their context in the real lives of real people. And, in part, because examining race, class, gender, and sexuality simultaneously forces one to acknowledge the multiple angles of vision that are brought to bear in any social situation, scholars in the field are reluctant to put forth a single unifying theory of the dynamics of these processes (Collins, 1990).

Some of the dominant themes in the new scholarship, which are also emerging in gender, sexuality, and race scholarship, can be broadly subsumed under the label of social constructionist theories and in recent work on "multiracial feminism" (Baca Zinn & Dill, 1996). They emphasize the historical and social contingencies of these dimensions and, to some extent, their macro social structural character and their basis in power relations (cf. Brod & Kaufman, 1994; Connell, 1985, 1995; Frankenberg, 1993; Omi & Winant, 1994; Thorne, 1993; West & Fenstermaker, 1995; West & Zimmerman, 1987).

Common Themes in Race, Class, Gender, and Sexuality Scholarship

I have identified six common themes in this new scholarship. Five of them describe the way that race, class, gender, and sexuality are conceptualized as systems of oppression; the sixth is an epistemological assumption.

1. Contextual. Race, class, gender, and sexuality are contextual. Although they persist throughout history, race, class, gender, and sexuality hierarchies are never static and fixed, but constantly undergo change as part of new economic, political, and ideological processes, trends, and events. Their meanings vary not only across historical time periods, but also across nations and regions during the same period. Because race, class, gender, and sexuality must always be understood within a specific historical and global context, research tends to avoid the search for common meanings that would apply to all times and all places.

For example, in the post-Civil Rights era in the United States, the racial signifiers "Latino/a," "Asian American," "People of Color," and "Native American" developed when people from different cultures, tribes, and national origins were treated as a single racial group by a dominant culture that failed to recognize differences among "racial" ethnic groups. Many members of these groups subsequently organized politically to resist their joint oppressions, and out of those political movements new racial identities were forged (Omi & Winant, 1994). These labels did not exist before the 1960s, and even today some people identify with them and others do not, signifying the fluid, political, historically specific, and social meaning of race.

Additionally, during the mid-19th century, dominant cultural conceptions of femininity became associated with the warm, personal, "private" sphere of home, whereas masculinity became associated with the cold, "public" sphere of the labor market. As Carol Tavris (1992, p. 265) notes:

People began to attribute to inherent male and female characteristics what were actually requirements of their increasingly separate domains. Thus, women were expected to provide warmth, nurturance, and care, and forgo achievement; men were expected to provide money and success, and forgo close attachments. The masculine ideal, tailored to fit the emerging economy, was to be an independent, self-made, financially successful man. Masculinity now required self-control: no gaudy displays of emotion; no weakness; no excessive self-indulgence in feelings. Femininity required, and soon came to embody, the opposite.

Despite the pervasiveness the these images, numerous race, class, and gender scholars have noted that not *all* women and men were included in these ideals of masculinity and femininity. Men of color were not extended a family wage, and women of color were already in the paid labor market, doing domestic work, other low-wage service work, or agricultural work. Further, the ideal traits held up for men and women of color contrasted sharply with those for White women and men. For example, after Reconstruction the ideal dominant culture image of the "good" African American man was the Sambo image: a happy-go-lucky, silly, and stupid person who was often afraid of the dark (Goings, 1994). The image provided a justification for slavery and at the same time reduced the perceived physical and sexual threat posed by real African American men. The Mammy image was the female parallel to Sambo: a happy asexual slave who so loved the master's family—and slavery itself—that she would willingly give over her life to the care and nurturance of slave-owning White families (Collins, 1990; Going, 1994). As the ideal White man was strong, independent, and emotionless, Sambo—like White women—was weak, dependent, and full of emotion. White women were to nurture their families, whereas emotionally strong Mammies could have no families of their own, just as they could have no sexuality. In sum, the meanings of masculinity and femininity are differently constructed throughout history for different social groups through social processes that produce and maintain a racialized, class-bound, heterosexist patriarchy.

2. Socially constructed. Race, class, gender, and sexuality are social constructs whose meaning develops out of group struggles over socially valued resources. The dominant culture defines the categories within race, gender, and sexuality as polar opposites—White and Black (or non-White), men and women, *heterosexual* and *homosexual*—to create social *rankings*: good and bad, worthy and unworthy, right and wrong (Lorber, 1994). It also links these concepts to biology to imply that the rankings are fixed, permanent, and embedded in nature. That is, dominant groups define race, gender, and sexuality as ranked dichotomies, where Whites, men, and heterosexuals are deemed superior. Dominant groups justify these hierarchies by claming that the rankings are a part of the design of nature—not the design of those in power. Subordinate groups resist the binary categories, the rankings associated with them, and the biological rationales used to justify them. Critical examination of either process—polarizing or biologizing—reveals that race, gender, and sexuality are based neither in polar opposites nor in biology but are social constructs whose meanings evolve out of group struggles (Garnets & Kimmel, 1991; King, 1981; Lorber, 1993; Omi & Winant, 1994).

When we say that race, gender, and sexuality are social constructs, not fixed biological traits, we also mean that we cannot *fully* capture their meaning in everyday life in the way that social scientists often attempt to do by employing them as variables in traditional quantitative research. When race, gender, and sexuality are treated as discrete variables, individuals are typically assigned a single location along each dimension, which is defined by a set of presumably mutually exclusive and exhaustive categories. This practice reinforces the view of race, gender, and sexuality as permanent characteristics of individuals, as unchangeable, and as polarities—people can belong to one and only one category. The practice cannot grasp the relational character, the historical specificity, or the conflicting meanings that arise in everyday life (Omi & Winant, 1994.) "Mixed race" people, for example, often have no place in the schemas provided. And what of the people who see themselves as bisexual or as heterosexual at one time of life and gay or lesbian at another?

The case of social class provides an instructive contrast to race, gender, and sexuality ideologies. The dominant ideology of social class is that it is not binary, polarized, or biological. Instead, the United States is seen as having an open economic system where talent and hard work—not inherited physical traits—are the primary determinants of one's economic location (Hochschild, 1995). Our system is not seen as polarized between rich and poor, capitalists and workers, or middle and working classes. Rather, it is viewed as a continuous ladder of income and resources, where people can slide up and down based on their own efforts and abilities—not on their biology (Vanneman & Weber Cannon, 1987). In the final analysis, the real power of the middle and upper classes is reinforced through this ideology as well as through the race, gender, and sexuality ideologies because all obscure the forces that underlie the social hierarchy. In the case of social class, however, unfair hierarchy is obscured by referring to ability and effort rather than by referring to biological superiority. Social class ideology disavows biology and categorical binaries, yet justifies hierarchy and dominance nonetheless. The case of social class makes very clear that ideologies are created to justify hierarchies and need not be based in binaries or biology, nor need they be internally consistent or logical. To justify the power and control of the dominant group, ideologies of dominance develop in different ways over time and in different social contexts and can rest on fundamentally very different—even seemingly contradictory—beliefs.

For over a century, social expectations of women's work and family roles, for example, have been rationalized by the biological fact that women can bear children. Middle-class mothers who stay at home to care for their children are often viewed by the dominant culture as "good mothers," yet poor women who do the same are viewed as lazy or "welfare queens." How can women's reproductive capacities prescribe their roles as mothers when we have different expectations for mothers of different classes, races, and sexual orientation?

Furthermore, the biological relationship of women to children is far more complex than ever before and is even now being challenged as a basis for legally defining motherhood. Today, when women and men have so many different biological and social relationships to their children, the courts are increasingly being asked to mediate questions of who should rear children. Consider the following "mothers:"

- *traditional mothers:* women who have a genetic, gestational, and legally sanctioned social relationship to the child

- *lesbian mothers:* women whose biological relationship may be the same as that of traditional mothers, yet whose legal status as mothers is often challenged because of their sexual orientation

- *surrogate mothers:* either genetic mothers who provide an egg, but do not bear the child; or gestational mothers (as in the case of Baby M) who have no genetic relationship to it, but bear the child

- *social mothers:* foster mothers, adoptive mothers, or "other" mothers who have no direct genetic or gestational relationship to the child, but play a significant role in raising the child (cf. Collins, 1990).

Each of these ways of mothering is constructed in race, class, gender, and sexual hierarchies that prescribe the meanings attached to them and shape the legally prescribed rights of these mothers to rear children. Chesler (1986, p. 280) discusses why we have the phenomenon of surrogate mothers at all:

> Racism is the issue, and why thousands of babies are "unsuitable" (for adoption). Ownership is the issue, and the conceit of patriarchal genetics. "Barren women" are the issue, and why some women must come to feel an excruciating sense of failure because they cannot bear a child. . . . And guilt and money, and how women can earn both, are the issues that need honest attention.

Race, class, gender, and sexuality are social constructions that are constantly undergoing change both at the level of social institutions and at the level of personal identity. They are not fixed, static traits of individuals, as is implied when they are treated either as biological facts or as categorically fixed variables in a research model. They are, however, deeply embedded in the practices and beliefs that make up our major social institutions. The permanence and pervasiveness they exhibit illustrate their significance as major organizing principles of society and of personal identity.

3. Systems of power relationships. Perhaps the single most important theme is that race, class, gender, and sexuality are historically specific, socially constructed hierarchies of domination—they are power relationships. They do not merely represent different lifestyle preferences or cultural beliefs, values, and practices. They are power hierarchies in which one group exerts control over another, securing its position of dominance in the system, and in which substantial material and nonmaterial resources—such as wealth, income, or access to health care and education—are at stake (Baca Zinn & Dill, 1996; Connell, 1987, 1995; Glenn, 1992; Vanneman & Weber Cannon, 1987; Weber, 1995; Weber, Hancock, & Higginbotham, 1997; Wyche & Graves, 1992). Race, class, gender, and sexuality are thus fundamental sources of social conflict among groups.

The centerpiece of these systems is the exploitation of one group by another for a greater share of society's valued resources. That they are based in social relationships between dominant and subordinate groups is key to understanding these systems. There can be no controlling males without women whose options are restricted; there can be no valued race without races that are defined as "other"; there can be no owners or managers without workers who produce the goods and services that the owners own and the managers control; and there can be no heterosexual privilege without gays and lesbians who are identified as "abnormal" or as "other."

Race, class, gender, and sexuality are not just rankings of socially valued resources—who has more income or prestige. They are power relationships—who exerts power and control over whom (Baca Zinn & Dill, 1996; Connell, 1987, 1995; Glenn, 1992; Griscom, 1992; Kahn & Yoder, 1992; Vanneman & Weber Cannon, 1987; Weber, 1995; Weber et al., 1997; Yoder & Kahn, 1992)? The groups that have power in a social system influence the allocation of many types of resources. In one sense, then, the procurement of socially valued resources can be seen as the end product—the spoils to the victors—of struggles for power. To maintain and extend their power and control in society, dominant groups can and do use the resources that they command. So socially valued resources, such as money and prestige, accrue to those in power and, once procured, serve as tools for maintaining and extending that power into future social relations.

Although scholars studying race, class, gender, and sexuality tend to see them as power relations, this perspective is not universally accepted. Ethnic approaches to race (cf. Glazer & Moynihan, 1975), gradational perspectives on class (reviewed in Vanneman & Weber Cannon, 1987),

sex/gender differences, and gender roles (for a review, see West & Fenstermaker, 1995), and moral or biological approaches to sexual orientation all conceive of these dimensions as differences that are not ultimately power based. Differences between woman and men, gays and straights, and among racial and ethnic groups are taken as primarily centered in women's and men's social roles and in cultural variations in traditions such as food, clothing, rituals, speech patterns, leisure activities, child-rearing practices, and sexual practices.

These perspectives often downplay or ignore the very real struggles over scarce resources that accompany location in these different groups. A similar tradition in the field of stratification—the gradational approach—sees class inequality as represented by relative rankings along a scale of prestige or income (a ladder image), not by the struggle between opposing groups for scarce resources (for reviews see Lucal, 1994; Vanneman & Weber Cannon, 1987). In the gradational perspective, no oppositional relationships exist between positions on a scale; it is a continuum along which some people simply have more than others.

Perhaps because race, class, gender, and sexuality studies primarily emerged from the experiences and analyses of groups who face multiple dimensions of oppression, and perhaps because power relationships are simply much more apparent when more than one dimension of inequality is addressed, the cultural difference, gradational, or ranking perspective is almost nonexistent in race, class, gender, and sexuality studies. The view that power relations are central is almost universal.

Looking at the *relational* nature of these systems of inequality rather than the differences in rankings of resources that accompany these systems forces us to focus on privilege as well as on oppression. Because the one cannot exist without the other, any analysis of race, class, gender, and sexuality must incorporate an understanding of the ways in which the privilege of dominant groups is tied to the oppression of subordinate groups. Consequently, the scholarships in this field has begun to explore the social constructions of Whiteness (cf. Frankenberg, 1993; McIntosh, 1995; Roediger, 1991), of masculinity (cf. Brod & Kaufman, 1994; Connell, 1995; Messner, 1992), and of heterosexual privilege (Giuffre & Williams, 1994; Rich, 1980).

4. Social structural (macro) and social psychological (micro). Race, class, and gender relations are embedded and have meaning at the micro level of individuals' everyday lives as well as at the macro level of community and social institutions. To grasp the significance of race, class, gender, and sexuality in society, we must examine their meaning in both contexts. In fact, a key aspect of such analyses involves explicating the linkages between broad societal level structures, trends, and events and the ways in which people in different social locations live their lives. In the last 25 years, for example, U.S. society has undergone major shifts in the distribution of wealth, income, jobs, and housing and in the health status of its people. Race, class, gender, and sexuality power relations structure the ways in which these societal trends develop and play out among different groups of people.

Macro social structural trends are often represented analytically as a set of lifeless statistics about different populations. When we look at statistics summarizing national trends in economic or health indicators, for example, it is difficult to know exactly what they mean for the way people live their lives. But when we closely follow the everyday lives of a group of people, we can learn how they live with financial constraints, how they feed their families, how they deal with the stresses they face, how they manage work and family life how they stay healthy.

It is in families and individual lives where race, class, gender, and sexuality scholarship has made perhaps its most important contributions. This work has begun to identify the ongoing struggles of subordinate groups to resist negative and controlling images of their group—to resist internalizing the limits to self-esteem, self-valuation, and collective identity imposed by the dominant group (cf. Bookman & Morgen, 1987; Collins, 1990; Comas-Díaz & Greene, 1994; Weber et al., 1997).

Because of the distorted images of subordinate groups that pervade society's institutions such as education and the media, subordinate groups are viewed by many as weak human beings who passively accept—and even deserve—a lesser share of society's valued resources. However, subordinate groups actively resist oppression and devaluation in numerous ways every day. Although, as a consequence of their location in subordinate social locations, they often lack institutional power, subordinate

groups members can and do use other forms of personal power and collective action to resist unfair treatment and to struggle for group power. Daily acts of resistance can range from the individual psychological process of rejecting negative group images and affirming positive group images to group activities designed to produce social change. Acts of resistance also range from passive forms such as work slow-downs or excessive and carefully planned use of sick leave (to ensure maximum disruption of the workplace) to active measures such as public protests, marches on Washington, strikes, or violence (Bookman & Morgen 1987). For example, through public protest and persistent demand for civil rights laws, which made racial discrimination in education, housing, employment, and other areas of society illegal, African Americans were able to shift greater educational and economic opportunity and earning power in their direction.

Although the barriers of oppression are material and ideological, the resources associated with one's social location in the matrix of dominance and subordination are both material and psychological (Collins, 1990; Weber et al., 1997). Nonmaterial psychosocial resources have important consequences for social and psychological well-being that in turn affect one's ability to secure material resources. Psychosocial resources associated with one's social location include positive feelings of well-being and self-respect that result from a strong connection to and identity with a group of people who share a common history and life experiences (Comas-Díaz & Greene, 1994). Developing a positive identity and feelings of self-respect is easier for dominant groups whose own experiences serve as the public model for how all people should live their lives. Because social institutions such as schools are structured to support the White middle class, such children are usually raised in families with greater access to resources to help them succeed in school. They enter school with greater expectations for success; teachers expect their success and, therefore, give them more attention. Teacher's positive orientations enhance the children's sense of self-worth, thus further improving their performance and their chances for school success (Oakes, 1985; Ornstein & Levine, 1989; Polakow, 1993).

Occupying a subordinate location in the race, class, gender, and sexuality systems, however, does not necessarily equate with a lack of psychosocial resources (Comas-Díaz & Greene, 1994). Working-class, Latino/a children, for example, growing up in the barrio may develop such intangible resources if they are surrounded by loving family members and neighbors who convey a sense of each child's special worth as an individual and as a Latino/a. And this psychosocial resource can serve as the foundation for a healthy defense against negative or rejecting messages from the dominant society. Resistance to the pressures of structured inequality within subordinate group communities can, in fact, be a psychosocial resource that can be used in a collective struggle against oppression and in a personal journey toward self-appreciation and good mental health.

The key aspect of dominance, then, is not whether people have access to psychosocial resources but whether the social order supports or constrains people's development. The concept of hegemonic ideologies refers to beliefs about what is right and proper, which reflect the dominant group's stance and pervade society. Controlling images refer to dominant culture beliefs about subordinate groups; these images serve to restrict their options and to constrain them. Although society has many conceptions of working women, for example, only one is hegemonic, taking precedence over other conceptions and serving as the standard against which the value or worth of all other conceptions of working women is measured.

When you hear the phrase "today's working woman" mentioned in the media or in a popular magazine, what kind of woman comes to mind? In all likelihood, no matter what your race, class, gender, or sexual orientation, you think of a White, heterosexual, professional woman working hard in a position of some power in the labor force. She is most likely married, but if she is single, she is certainly young. This image of today's working woman is not only atypical, it is antithetical to the reality of work for most women today. Only 28.7% of working women are in professional, managerial, or administrative positions, and many of those hold little real power in the workplace (U.S. Bureau of Labor Statistics, 1995).

Why would such an atypical image come to mind? Because this image is the dominant, hegemonic conception of working women. It represents the image of the most powerful race, class,

and sexual orientation group of women. It is grossly overrepresented in the media, because it is set up as the model, the ideal against which other working women are to be judged. By its repeated presentation in the media (e.g., most women seen on television are White, middle-class, professional women), the image distorts the public perception, leaving the impression that the attainment of positions of power among women is far more possible than is actually the case. By masking the true nature of race, class, gender, and sexuality oppression, the image helps to preserve the status quo. The image further sets up a standard for judgment that most women cannot attain. If they come to believe that their failure to measure up is a result of their personal limitations—a lack of talent, desire, or effort—they internalize the oppression. If, on the other hand, they are aware of the dominant belief system nature of and the structural barriers to attaining the "ideal," they resist internalizing the oppression and have the potential for self-definition and self-valuation, a process critical to the survival of oppressed groups.

To comprehend the human agency, resilience, creativity, and strength of oppressed group members, one must view the actions and motivations of subordinate group members through their own lenses, not through the lenses of the controlling images of the dominant culture. Recognition of the history of subordinate group resistance helps to counter the cultural myths and beliefs in the dominant culture that the subordinate place of these groups is a "natural" aspect of society.

Race, class, gender, and sexuality scholarship has clarified the notion of internalized oppression, as well as the processes within communities that enable them to survive and the individuals within them to define themselves, value themselves, and build community solidarity (Collins, 1990; Weber et al., 1997). The Civil Rights Movement, racial and ethnic pride, gay pride, and women's movements are collective manifestations of resistance to negative and controlling images of and structures constricting oppressed groups. Interestingly, the American labor movement has been too weak and invisible to provide a positive counterimage that workers can employ to resist oppression.

5. **Simultaneously expressed.** Race, class, gender, and sexuality simultaneously operate in

every social situation. At the societal level, these systems of social hierarchies are connected to each other and are embedded in all social institutions. At the individual level, we each experience our lives and develop our identities based on our location along all dimensions, whether we are in dominant groups, subordinate groups, or both.

That almost all of us occupy both dominant and subordinate positions and experience both advantage and disadvantage in these hierarchies means that there are no pure oppressors or oppressed in our society. Thus, race, class, gender, and sexuality are not reducible to immutable personality traits or other seemingly permanent characteristics. Instead, they are social constructions that often give us power and options in some arenas while restricting our opportunities in another.

From his principle we cannot argue that we are all oppressed or that our oppressions can simply be added up and ranked to identify the most oppressed group or the most victimized individuals. We cannot say that disadvantage on any two dimensions is the same as on any other two. No simple mathematical relationship can capture the complexity of the interrelationships of these systems. And yet recognizing that each of us simultaneously experiences all of these dimensions—even if one is foregrounded in a particular situation—can help us see the often obscured ways in which we benefit from existing race, class, gender, and sexuality social arrangements, as well as the ways in which we are disadvantaged. Such an awareness can be key in working together across different groups to achieve a more equitable distribution of society's values resources.

The final characteristic describes a common epistemology of race, class, gender, and sexuality scholarship.

6. Interdependence of knowledge and activism. Race, class, gender, and sexuality scholarship emphasizes the interdependence of knowledge and activism (Baca Zinn & Dill, 1994, 1996; Collins, 1990). These analyses developed as a means of understanding oppression and of seeking social change and social justice. The "truth value" or merit of this knowledge depends on its ability to reflect back to social groups their experiences in such a way that they can more effectively define, value, and empower themselves to seek social justice.

When we think of race, class, gender, and sexuality as historically specific, socially constructed power relations that simultaneously operate at both macro and micro levels, a more complex set of questions arises than from analyses of a single dimension. The following is an example from everyday life that illustrates the simultaneous impact of these hierarchies on a fundamental social identity in the United States today.

Race, Class, Gender, Sexuality and the Construction of Masculinity

Consider how masculinity is differently defined by and for heterosexual, White middle-class males and for other groups of men, such as gays, working-class White men, and men of color. When you hear about such groups as the Michigan Militia or the Ku Klux Klan, you likely think of White working-class men. If you hear of the Crips or the Bloods, you likely think of Black or Latino, working-class, male gang members. Research by Kathleen Blee (1991) on *Women of the Ku Klux Klan* and by Karen Joe and Meda Chesney-Lind (1995) on female gang members has clearly documented that women are active participants in both worlds. Nonetheless, in the dominant culture ideology, these worlds are almost exclusively associated with working-class men.

How is masculine identity socially constructed for working-class males? The dominant culture portrays men in these groups as valuing physical strength, aggressive behavior, and dominance over women and as devaluing emotional sensitivity and intellectual development.

Consider now the dominant image of White professional/middle-class males. These men are deemed superior based on their positions of power and authority in the labor force, by their financial or material wealth, by their intellectual prowess and knowledge, and, increasingly today, by their emotional sensitivity—but *not* by their physical strength or aggressiveness.

In the popular documentary *Hoop Dreams* (Marx, Gilbert, Gilbert, & James, 1994) and in Michael Messner's (1992) *Power at Play: Sport and the Problem of Masculinity.*, we see the difference in how schools steer athletically talented working-class men toward careers in athletics. Sports represent a career that fits with racialized conceptions of what is suitable for working-class men. And because they represent one of the few legitimate avenues for upward social mobility, sports careers are sought by working-class and lower class men—despite the almost insurmountable odds against making a lifelong career in sports. Only 6% or 7% of high school football players ever play in college, and only 2% of eligible college football or basketball athletes ever sign a professional contract. The chances of attaining professional status in a sport are 4 in 100,000 for a White man, 2 in 100,000 for a Black man, and 3 in 1,000,000 for a U.S.-born Latino (Messner, 1992, p. 45).

Athletically talented, White, middle-class men, in contrast, are steered into college to achieve the academic credentials to work in the middle class—as professionals, owners, managers, or administrators. Athletics are seen as a way of building positive character traits, such as competitiveness, camaraderie, and determination, and of providing valuable avenues for social networking in the middle class. Sports are almost never considered as a career in themselves.

The dominant conception of masculinity in capitalist economies portrays "real men" as those who have power in the economic realm, where ownership, authority, competitiveness, and mental—not physical—labor are values. Physical strength or physically aggressive behavior is not a valued method of maintaining power and control.

Sports do, however, serve an important role in constructing masculine identities for the many men who play them. As Messner's (1992) research shows, sport is an institution created by and for men. Misogyny and homophobia, as exhibited in extremely derogatory language toward women and gay men in the context of sports, serve as bounding agents for heterosexual men by separating them from anything "feminine." Expressing strong antigay sentiments enables men to be intimate without being sexual. And objectifying women through derogatory language enables men to be sexual without being intimate, a process that fits with maintaining a position of control over women and men of lower status in the race, class, gender, and sexuality hierarchies (Messner, 1992).

In sum, many masculinities operate in the United States today. What it means to be a man—or a woman, a husband or a wife, a father or a mother—depends on one's *simultaneous* location in the race, class, gender, and sexuality hierarchies.

Conclusions

This conceptual framework for understanding race, class, gender, and sexuality can support our teaching by guiding the content we select for classes, the questions we bring to the analysis of course readings and materials, and the ways in which we promote positive interaction across race, class, gender, and sexuality hierarchies in the classroom. First, it provides a framework for conceptualizing and assessing the diverse readings that currently constitute courses on gender and diversity. To convey the complexities of these intersections we need to select course content—readings, lectures, films—that highlight the intersections of multiple dimensions of oppression. Providing students with a set of themes to help them review the diverse materials they read can be a useful pedagogical tool.

Second, rather than providing a set of answers, I hope these themes raise some questions and issues to consider in our analyses of social reality. I am increasingly convinced that the most important tools we bring to the analytical processes are the questions we ask.

Race, class, gender, and sexuality are contextually rooted in history and geography. Ask how the dynamics we study might vary in different places and at different times. It is important to take account of the histories and global contexts of particular groups to understand their current situations. Taking a broad historical and global view also enables us to see the tremendous changes that have taken place in each of these systems over time and the diversity across social geography and thus to recognize the potential for change in situations we face every day.

These systems are socially constructed, not biologically determined. Ask if gender and race are taken to determine how people should act out of some notion of biological or social imperative. Is seeing gender or race as an immutable fact of people's lives either privileging them or relegating them to certain inferiority? How might we view a situation differently if someone of a different race, class, gender, or sexual orientation were in it?

The race, class, gender, and sexuality systems operate at the social structural (macro) and the social psychological (micro) levels. When we analyze a particular social event, the interpersonal and psychological manifestations of oppression are often more readily apparent. The broad macro-level forces that shape events are more remote and abstract and are, therefore, more difficult to see. Ask about those structures.

In looking at the case of White male backlash against affirmative action, for example, we can easily see angry White men out to push back gains made by women and people of color and to maintain their position of power and control. We can dismiss them as "oppressors" or bad people. When we ask about the broader race, class, gender, and sexuality forces that shape this situation, however, we also see that the recent decline in our economy has rendered many White men vulnerable to loss of jobs, income, and health. White men's anger in part comes out of their different expectations—out of their sense of privilege. If we are to collaborate to achieve economic change that benefits most people, we must recognize the ways in which many White men, as well as other people, are vulnerable in the present economy.

These systems are simultaneously experienced. All operate to shape every one's lives at all times. Ask about all of the systems in every situation. Although one dimension may appear to be in the foreground, go beyond the obvious and ask about the less visible dimensions.

Make the connection between activism for social justice and the analyses you conduct. Ask about the implications for social justice of the perspectives you employ, the questions you ask, and the answers you obtain. Does the analysis provide insights that in a political context would likely serve to reinforce existing power relations? Or does it illuminate processes of resistance or avenues for self-definition or self-valuation that could transform the race, class, gender, and sexuality hierarchies? How might people in different social locations react to and employ this analysis? To what ends?

Race, class, gender, and sexuality hierarchies are power relationships. Always ask who has the socially sanctioned power in this situation. What group gains and what group loses? Try not to confuse personal power with social power. Individuals can be powerful by virtue of their insight, knowledge, personalities, and other traits. They can persuade others to act in ways they want. But personal power can be achieved in spite of a lack of socially sanctioned power. It is the power that accrues from occupying a position of dominance in the race, class, gender, and sexuality hierarchies that enables large numbers of people in sim-

ilar locations to have privileges/advantages in a situation. And it is their systematic and pervasive embeddedness in all our major institutions that makes race, class, gender, and sexuality such critical systems to understand.

Finally, when we change the content that we teach to be more inclusive and to address the complexities of race, class, gender, and sexuality, we need to change our pedagogy as well. Learning about diversity is most likely to take place when classroom interactions and activities promote positive intergroup interaction across race, class, gender, and sexuality. Themes in the scholarship suggest some strategies for shaping positive classroom dynamics across difference.

That race, class, gender, and sexuality are socially constructed, not fixed traits of individuals, means that we cannot accept group membership as a guarantee of the privileged knowledge or experience of any dominant or subordinate group member in our classes. The socially constructed nature of these dimensions means that the experiences and perspectives that students have—for example, even in the same racial group—vary by their age and the region and community they grew up in, as well as by their gender, class, and sexual orientation.

Acknowledging the diversity of experiences among our students need not, however, lead to an unfettered relativism that denies the significance of group membership or the greater impact of some dimensions than others on life chances and options. Because we recognize that power is the foundation on which these systems rest, we must acknowledge the differential power that dominant and subordinate groups wield in the classroom as well as in society at large. Members of dominant groups are less likely to know about subordinate groups and are more likely to rely on stereotypes (Fiske, 1993), speak in class, receive eye contact, have their opinions correctly attributed, and have their contributions shape group responses to tasks (cf. Webster & Foschi, 1998). Teaching strategies that acknowledge these tendencies and contradict them can upset the normative balance of power in the classroom and can increase understanding. They include ground rules to guide classroom discussion; introductions of students that acknowledge their race, ethnicity, and other statuses while identifying them as unique individuals; equal time for talking; and group projects (see Weber Cannon, 1990, for discussion).

Having students address the simultaneity of race, class, gender, and sexuality can help them to understand that there are no pure oppressors nor oppressed people, and that each of them must reflect on their own privilege as well as on their experiences of oppression. They cannot deny their privilege of claim absolute victim status. Recognizing their own multiple locations can open them to the complexities in the lived realities and experiences of others.

And finally, the interdependence of knowledge and activism that is central to race, class, gender, and sexuality scholarship suggests that certain kinds of learning activities can be especially effective. Active learning projects, particularly those that involve students in working together toward solutions to social problems, are especially likely to engage students and to facilitate positive group interaction.

Note

1. Although many scholars still refer to this growing field of study as race, class, and gender studies, I include sexuality because, as I argue, these structures of inequality and the meanings they engender are socially constructed in historically specific time frames and regional locations. Their meanings are not fixed, immutable, or universal but instead arise out of group struggles over socially valued resources, self-determination, and self-valuation. In recent years, the mass movement of gays, lesbians, and bisexuals for social power and self-determination has precipitated significant scholarly attention to sexuality. Our growing awareness and understanding of the pervasiveness and comprehensiveness of the system of compulsory heterosexuality has begun to place it at the center of political and intellectual attention along with race, class, and gender as essential elements in a comprehensive understanding of contemporary human social relationships and psychological processes. To date, however, the scholarship on sexuality is much less developed than work addressing the other dimensions, and race, class, and gender research is only beginning to integrate this new dimension.

References

Amaro, H., & Russo, N. F. (Eds.). (1987). Hispanic women and mental health: Contemporary research and practice [Special issue]. *Psychology of Women Quarterly, 11*(4).

Andersen, M., & Collins, P. H. (1995). *Race, class, and gender: An anthology.* Belmont, CA: Wadsworth.

Anzaldúa, G. (1987a). *Borderlands/la frontera: The new mestiza.* San Francisco: Spinsters/AuntLute.

Anzaldúa, G. (Ed.). (1987b). *Making faces, making soul/haciendo caras: Creative and critical perspectives by women of color.* San Francisco: Spinsters/Aunt-Lute.

Baca Zinn, M., & Dill, B.T. (1994). *Women of color in U.S. society.* Philadelphia: Temple University Press.

Baca Zinn, M., & Dill, B. T. (1996). Theorizing difference from multiracial feminism. *Feminist Studies, 22,* 321–331.

Baca Zinn, M., Weber Cannon, L., Higginbotham, E., & Dill, B. T. (1986). The costs of exclusionary practices in women's studies. *Signs: Journal of Women in Culture and Society, 11,* 290–303.

Barale, M., & Halperin, D. M. (Eds.). (1993). *The lesbian and gay studies reader.* New York: Routledge.

Blee, K. M. (1991). *Women of the klan: Racism and gender in the 1920s.* Berkeley: University of California Press.

Bookman, A., & Morgen, S. (1987). *Women and the politics of empowerment: Perspectives from the workplace and the community.* Philadelphia: Temple University Press.

Brod, H., & Kaufman, M. (1994). *Theorizing masculinities.* Thousand Oaks, CA: Sage.

Cade, T. (Ed.). (1970). *The Black woman.* New York: Signet.

Chesler, P. (1986). *Mothers on trial: The battle for children and custody.* New York: McGraw-Hill.

Chow, E. N. Wilkinson, D., & Baca Zinn, M. (1996). *Race, class, and gender; Common bonds, different voices.* Thousand Oaks, CA: Sage.

Collins, P.H. (1990). *Black feminist thought: Knowledge, consciousness and the politics of empowerment.* New York: Routledge.

Collins, P. H. (1991). Learning from the outsider within: The sociological significance of Black feminist thought. In M. M. Fonow & J. A. Cook (Eds.), *Beyond methodology: Feminist scholarship as lived research* (pp. 35–59). Bloomington, IN: Indiana University Press.

Collins, P. H., Maldonado, L. A., Takagi, D. Y., Thorne, B., Weber, L., & Winant, H. (1995). Symposium on West and Fenstermaker's "Doing difference." *Gender & Society, 9,* 491–513.

Comas-Díaz, L., & Greene, B. (1994). *Women of color: Integrating ethnic and gender identities in psychotherapy.* New York: Guilford.

Connell, R. W. (1985). Theorising gender. *Sociology, 19,* 260–272.

Connell, R. W. (1987). *Gender and power: Society, the person, and sexual politics.* Stanford, CA: Stanford University Press.

Connell, R. W. (1995). *Masculinities.* Berkeley: University of California Press.

Cyrus, V. (1993). *Experiencing race, class and gender in the United States.* Mountain View, CA: Mayfield.

D'Emilio, J., & Freedman, E. (1988). *Intimate matters; A history of sexuality in America.* New York: Harper & Row.

Dill, B. T. (1988). Our mother's grief: Racial ethnic women and the maintenance of families. *Journal of Family History, 13,* 415–431.

Dill, B. T. (1983). Race, class and gender: Prospects for an all-inclusive sisterhood, *Feminist Studies, 9,* 131–150.

Dill, B. T. (1979). The dialectics of Black womanhood, *Signs: Journal of Women in Culture and Society, 4,* 543–555.

Fiske, S. T. (1993). Controlling other people: The impact of power on stereotyping. *American Psychologist, 48,* 621–628.

Frankenberg, R. (1993). *The social construction of whiteness: White women, race matters.* Minneapolis, MN: University of Minnesota Press.

Garnets, L., & Kimmel, D. (1991). Lesbian and gay male dimensions in the psychological study of human diversity. In J. Goodchilds (Ed.), *Psychological perspectives on human diversity in America* (pp. 143–189). Washington, DC: American Psychological Association.

Giuffre, P. A., & Williams, C. L. (1994). Boundary lines: Labeling sexual harassment in restaurants. *Gender & Society, 8,* 378–401.

Glazer, N., & Moynihan, D.P. (Eds.). (1975). *Ethnicity: Theory and experience.* Cambridge, MA: Harvard University Press.

Glenn, E. N. (1992). From servitude to service work: Historical continuities in the racial division of paid reproductive labor. *Signs: Journal of Women in Culture and Society, 18,* 1–43.

Goings, K. (1994). *Mammy and Uncle Moses: Black collectibles and American stereotyping.* Bloomington: Indiana University Press.

Greene. B. L. (1994). Lesbian and gay sexual orientations: Implications for clinical training, practice, and research. In B. Greene & G. M. Herek (Eds.), *Lesbian and gay psychology: Theory, research, and clinical applications* (pp. 1–24). Thousand Oaks, CA: Sage.

Griscom, J. L. (1992). Women and power: Definition, dualism, and difference. *Psychology of Women Quarterly, 16,* 389–414.

Higginbotham, E., & Webber, L. (1992). Moving up with kin and community: Upward social mobility for Black and White women. *Gender & Society, 6,* 416–440.

Hochschild, J. (1995). *Facing up to the American dream: Race, class, and the soul of the nation.* Princeton, NJ: Princeton University Press.

hooks, b. (1981). *Ain't I a woman.* Boston: South End Press.

Hull, G., Scott, P. B., & Smith, B. (Eds.). (1982). *All the women were White, all the Blacks were men, but some of us are brave: Black women's studies.* Old Westbury, NY: Feminist Press.

Joe, K. A., & Chesney-Lind, M. (1995). "Just every mother's angel": An analysis of gender and ethnic variations in youth gang membership. *Gender & Society, 9,* 408–431.

Kahn, A. S. & Yoder, J. D. (Eds.) Women and power [Special issue]. *Psychology of Women Quarterly, 16,* Whole No. 4.

King, J. (1981). *The biology of race.* Berkeley: University of California Press.

Loewenberg, B. J., & Bogin, R. (Eds.). (1976). *Black women in the nineteenth-century life.* University Park: Pennsylvania State University.

Lorber, J. (1994). *Paradoxes of gender.* New Haven, CT: Yale University Press.

Lucal, B. (194). Class stratification in introductory textbooks: Relational or distributional models? *Teaching Sociology, 22,* 139–150.

Magner, D. (1996, September 16). Fewer professors believe western culture should be the cornerstone of the college curriculum. *Chronicle of Higher Education,* pp. A12–A15.

Marx, F., Gilbert, J., Gilbert, P. [Producers], & James, S. [Director]. (1994). *Hoop dreams* [Film]. (Available from Facets Video, 1518 W. Fullerton, Chicago, IL 60614)

McIntosh, P. (1995). White privilege and male privilege: A personal account of coming to see correspondences through work in women's studies. In M. Andersen & P. H. Collins (Eds.), *Race, class, and gender: An anthology* (pp. 76–86). Belmont, CA: Wadsworth.

Messner, M. (1992). *Power at play: Sports and the problem of masculinity.* Boston: Beacon.

Oakes, J. (1985). *Keeping track: How schools structure inequality.* New Haven, CT: Yale University Press.

Omi, M., Winant, H. (1994). *Racial formation in the United States from the 1960s to the 1990s.* New York: Routledge.

Ornstein, A. C., & Levine, D. U. (1989). Social class, race, and school achievement: Problems and prospects. *Journal of Teacher Education, 40,* 17–23.

Polakow, V. (1993). *Lives on the edge: Single mothers and their children in the other America.* Chicago: University of Chicago Press.

Rich, A. (1980). Compulsory heterosexuality and lesbian existence. *Signs: Journal of Women in Culture and Society, 5,* 631–660.

Rollins, J. (1985). *Between women: Domestics and their employers.* Philadelphia: Temple University Press.

Rodgers-Rose, L. (Ed.). (1980). *The black woman.* Beverly Hills, CA: Sage.

Roediger, D. (1991). *The wages of whiteness: Race and the making of the American working class.* London: Verso.

Rothenberg, P. S. (1995). *Race, class, and gender in the United States: An integrated study.* New York: St. Martin's Press.

Tavris, C. (1992). *The mismeasure of woman.* New York: Touchstone.

Thorne, B. (1993). *Gender play: Girls and boys in school.* New Brunswick, NJ: Rutgers University Press.

U.S. Bureau of Labor Statistics (1995). *Employment and earnings* (Vol. 45). Washington, DC: U.S. Government Printing Office.

Vanneman, R., & Weber Cannon, L. (1987). *The American perception of class.* Philadelphia: Temple University Press.

Weber Cannon, L. (1990). Fostering positive race, class, and gender dynamics in the classroom. *Women's Studies Quarterly, 17,* 126–134.

Weber Cannon, L., Higginbotham, E., & Leung, M. (1988). Race and class bias in qualitative research on women. *Gender & Society, 2,* 449–462.

Weber, L. (1995). Comment on "Doing difference." *Gender & Society, 9,* 499–503.

Weber, L., Hancock, T., & Higginbotham, E. (1997). Women, power, and mental health. In S. Ruzek, V. Olesen, & A. Clark (Eds.), *Women's health: Complexities and differences* (pp. 380–396). Columbus, OH: Ohio State University Press.

Webster, M., Jr. and Foschi, M. (1988). Status generalization: New theory and research. Palo Alto, CA: Stanford University Press.

West, C., & Fenstermaker, S. (1995). Doing difference. *Gender & Society, 9,* 8–37.

West. C., & Zimmerman, D. H. (1987). Doing gender. *Gender & Society, 1,* 125–151.

Wyche, K. F., & Graves, S. B. (1992). Minority women in academia: Access and barrier to professional participation. *Psychology of Women Quarterly, 16,* 429–438.

Yoder, J. D., & Kahn, A. S. (1992). Toward a feminist understanding of women and power. *Psychology of Women Quarterly, 16,* 381–388

CHAPTER 33

A CONCEPTUAL MODEL OF MULTIPLE DIMENSIONS OF IDENTITY

SUSAN R. JONES AND MARYLU K. MCEWEN

A conceptual model of multiple dimensions of identity depicts a core sense of self or one's personal identity. Intersecting circles surrounding the core identity represent significant identity dimensions (e.g., race, sexual orientation, and religion) and contextual influences (e.g., family background and life experiences). The model evolved from a grounded theory study of a group of 10 women college students ranging in age from 20–24 and of diverse racial-ethnic backgrounds.

Development of socially constructed identities has received increasing attention within literature and research in psychology and student affairs within the past decade. Racial identity (e.g., Cross, 1995; Helms, 1990, 1992, 1995), ethnic identity (Phinney, 1990, 1992), sexual identity (Cass, 1979; McCarn & Fassinger, 1996), and gender identity (Ossana, Helms, & Leonard, 1992; O'Neil, Egan, Owen, & Murry, 1993) have received primary focus. Yet, most developmental models and related research have addressed only a single dimension of identity, such as race or sexual orientation. Atkinson, Morten, and Sue (1993), in their well-known Minority Identity Development model, do not specify type of minority status (e.g., race or gender or sexual orientation or disability could apply) and also do not address how an individual may simultaneously develop and embrace multiple minority statuses. Although research has frequently considered differences according to gender, age, or other particular social conditions, the models and research have generally not addressed intersecting social identities. In addition to racial, ethnic, sexual, and gender identities, college students may have other identity orientations, such as social class, religious, geographic or regional, and professional identities (McEwen, 1996).

Not only have researchers placed increasing emphasis upon identity development, but the number of identity development models has also increased. In terms of models regarding multiple identities, the only frequently acknowledged model is that of Reynolds and Pope (1991). However, Reynolds and Pope's model concerns primarily multiple oppressions (not identities in general) and possible ways that one can negotiate multiple oppressions. McEwen (1996) has proposed a theoretically driven model concerning development of multiple identities, but this model has not been empirically tested. A small number of studies have addressed multiple identities, and some theoretical and autobiographical essays speak to the experience of multiple identities (e.g., Bridwell-Bowles, 1998; Espiritu, 1994; Moraga, 1998; Thompson & Tyagi, 1996). So, although existing literature can inform discussions on multiple identities, no models specifically concerning multiple identities have been developed.

Reynolds and Pope (1991) drew attention to the importance of multiple identities through their discussion of multiple oppressions. They used several case studies to provide examples of how individuals might deal with their multiple oppressions and then extended Root's (1990) model on biracial identity development to multiple oppressions. Specifically, Reynolds and Pope (1991), in creating the Multidimensional Identity Model, suggested four possible ways for identity resolution for individuals belonging to more than one oppressed group. These four options were created from a matrix with two dimensions—the first concerns whether one embraces multiple oppressions or only one oppression, and the second concerns whether an individual actively or passively identifies with one or more oppressions. Thus, the four quadrants or options become:

1. Identifying with only one aspect of self (e.g., gender or sexual orientation or race) in a passive manner. That is, the aspect of self is assigned by others such as society, college student peers, or family.

2. Identifying with only one aspect of self that is determined by the individual. That is, the individual may identify as lesbian or Asian Pacific American or a woman without including other identities, particularly those that are oppressions.

3. Identifying with multiple aspects of self, but choosing to do so in a "segmented fashion" (Reynolds & Pope, 1991, p. 179), frequently only one at a time and determined more passively by the context rather than by the individual's own wishes. For example, in one setting the individual identifies as Black, yet in another setting as gay.

4. The individual chooses to identify with the multiple aspects of self, especially multiple oppressions, and has both consciously chosen them and integrated them into one's sense of self.

The value of Reynolds and Pope's (1991) work lies in their focus on the topic of multiple identities, their attention to the possible danger of considering an individual's identity development too narrowly by only using identity development models that address singular dimensions of one's identity, and their attention to identity resolution in the context of multiple oppressions. Yet, in the decade since the publication of Reynolds and Pope's model, researchers have only minimally addressed multiple identities, contributing no application or testing of their model and little follow-up to their work.

McEwen (1996), drawing on her education in mathematics and physics, considered how such dimensions and developmental processes regarding multiple identities might be represented. She suggested that the interaction and intersection of multiple identity development could be viewed as a conical structure with varying radii and heights. The conical structure is similar to a helix. The increasing length and circumference of the cone represent the greater complexity of an individual's development as one's age, experiences, education, and reflection change. A two-dimensional cross section of the cone, similar to a circle or ellipse, would represent an individual's development at that particular point in time. Thus, an examination of many horizontal cross sections of the cone would provide a comprehensive picture of one's development at various points in time. These horizontal cross sections, however, would not provide any sense of one's developmental patterns over time.

On the other hand, vertical cross sections might incorporate only one or two dimensions of identity. However, a vertical cross section would suggest how an individual's identity in that particular dimension or dimensions has developed over the span of one's lifetime. A vertical "slice" would represent just one part of the picture of an individual at multiple points in time. Other kinds of cross sections of this conical representation could be considered. McEwen's model, through various cross sections, enables a portrayal of intersections or interactions among identity development dimensions or between multiple identities not seen in other models.

In addition, theoretical discussions by Deaux (1993), a social psychologist, relate to the conceptual model of multiple dimensions of identity presented here. She conceptualized identity as both defined internally by self and externally by others, which provides a foundation for understanding multiple identities. Other recent research (Ferguson, 1995; Finley, 1997; Kiely, 1997) underscored the importance of relative salience, sociocultural context, and overlapping identities. A strength in these studies lies in examining multiple identities; however, none provided a model of multiple identities nor suggested a process by which multiple identities are developed and negotiated.

In an effort to extend existing work on multiple identities, the researchers attempted to advance a more complex understanding of identity and present a model of multiple dimensions of identity development. The model evolved from a qualitative study conducted at a large public university on the East Coast. Using the grounded theory approach of Glaser and Strauss (1967), the researchers explored the self-perceived identities and the multiple dimensions of identity from the perspective of women college students. The focus of the study was on students' understandings of their own identity and experiences of difference and of the influence of multiple dimensions of identity on an evolving sense of self.

Methodology

Participants

Participants were 10 undergraduate women all enrolled at a large East Coast university and diverse in race, cultural background, and academic major. They ranged in age from 20 to 24 and were predominantly of junior or senior class standing. The racial and ethnic backgrounds of participants included 5 who were White, 2 who identified themselves as African American or Black, 1 woman who identified herself as African, 1 as Sri Lankan, and 1 as Asian Indian. A variety of religious affiliations were also represented: Jewish, Buddhist, Hindu, Catholic, Presbyterian, and Holiness Pentecostal.

Participants were drawn to the study using "purposeful sampling" (Patton, 1990), which emphasizes sampling for information-rich cases. The criterion for constructing the sample in this study was evidence of variation along identity dimensions such as race, culture, sexual orientation, and religion. An initial group of 5 participants was chosen from among those who responded to an invitation to take part in the study and who met sampling criteria for maximum variation and ability to participate. Consistent with grounded theory methodology and theoretical sampling (Strauss & Corbin, 1990) 5 participants were added as the study progressed. These participants were identified through snowball sampling strategies or through responses to invitations to participate extended at a campus leadership program. Sampling decisions were guided by initial data analysis, the opportunity for information-rich cases, and a commitment to a diverse sample. Saturation was achieved and sampling was ended when patterns and themes in the data emerged and a diverse sample had been accomplished.

Procedure

Data were collected through in-depth, open-ended interviews. The central purpose of the interviews was to engage in dialogue with participants to elicit their descriptions and perceptions of themselves and their understandings of identity development. This phenomenological approach emphasized the importance of providing a structure for participants to communicate their own understandings, perspectives, and attribution of meaning. Interviews were open-ended to permit and encourage participants' use of their own words in describing the internal and interpersonal processes by which they defined their identities and made sense of difference.

Three interviews were conducted with each participant. Interview protocols were developed in response to emerging patterns and themes for all participants as well as to pick up on experiences and perceptions particular to an individual. Initial questions were broad enough to create room for individual response and freedom. Subsequent interviews were more structured and focused specifically on particular identity dimensions identified in the previous interview. Interviews lasted between 30 and 75 minutes and all were audiotaped.

Several strategies to assure trustworthiness of findings were employed. These included member checking by providing participants an opportunity to read transcripts and check initial analysis, and the use of an inquiry auditor to verify the work by essentially conducting a parallel process of data analysis and comparing notes.

True to grounded theory methodology, data analysis was conducted using three levels of coding: open coding, axial coding, and selective coding. The first stage of coding involves breaking down data and beginning the process of categorization. Axial coding takes initial categories and makes further comparisons that describe relationships between categories. Using selective coding, saturation of categories is examined, which means that further analysis produces no new information or need for additional categories. In short, all the data are captured and described by key categories, and a core category emerges that tells the central story of all participants as a group. This core category then is used to develop an emerging theory and conceptual model that is considered grounded in the data and reflective of the lived experiences of all participants.

In this study, data analysis produced over 2,000 concepts from raw data, 71 categories from initial comparison, 10 key categories, and 1 core category (Jones, 1997). The conceptual model was developed to provide a visual representation of the findings from the study.

Results

Because the focus of this article is on the conceptual model developed from the findings, only a brief description of the 10 key categories is included. More detailed descriptions may be found elsewhere (Jones, 1997). The key categories that emerged from analysis of data from the interviews with participants were (a) relative salience of identity dimensions in relation to difference; (b) the multiple ways in which race matters; (c) multiple layers of identity; (d) the braiding of gender with other dimensions; (e) the importance of cultural identifications and cultural values; (f) the influence of family and background experiences; (g) current experiences and situational factors; (h) relational, inclusive values and guiding personal beliefs; (i) career decisions and future planning; and (j) the search for identity. The key categories represent themes and constructs that are interrelated and when integrated define the core category.

The core category provides an integrative function by weaving together the key categories in a way that tells the central story of all the participants. In this study, the core category was defined as the contextual influences on the construction of identity. The contextual influences that emerged as significant included race, culture, gender, family, education, relationships with those different from oneself, and religion. The core category also reflects the finding that identity was defined and understood as having multiple intersecting dimensions. The particular salience of identity dimensions depended upon the contexts in which they were experienced. Therefore, both difference and privilege worked to mediate the connection with and salience of various identity dimensions (i.e., race was not salient for White women; religion was very salient for Jewish women; culture was salient for the Asian Indian woman).

A Conceptual Model for Multiple Dimensions of Identity

The conceptual model presented here (see Figure 1) is intended to capture the essence of the core category as well as the identity stories of the participants. The model represents multiple dimensions of identity development for a diverse group of women college students. The model is a fluid and dynamic one, representing the ongoing construction of identities and the influence of changing contexts on the experience of identity development. Therefore, the model is illustrative of one person's identity construction at a particular time. The model is also drawn to depict the possibility of living comfortably with multiple identities, rather than simply describing multiple dimensions of identity.

At the center of multiple dimensions of identity is a core sense of self. This center, or core identity, is experienced as a personal identity, somewhat protected from view, which incorporates "valued personal attributes and characteristics" (Jones, 1997, p. 383). The core was frequently described by participants as their "inner identity" or "inside self" as contrasted with what they referred to as their "outside" identity or the "facts" of their identity. Outside identities were easily named by others and interpreted by the participants as less meaningful than the complexities of their inside identities which they guarded and kept close to themselves and made less susceptible to outside influence. The words these women used to describe their core included intelligent, kind, a good friend, compassionate, independent. They resisted using terms that conveyed external definition and identity categories to describe their core sense of self. To these young women, labels lacked complexity, accuracy, and personal relevancy. They believed that labels rarely touched the core of an indi-vidual's sense of self. For them, individual identity was experienced and lived at far greater depth than such categories suggested or permitted. Surrounding the core, and at times integrally connected to the core, were what they experienced as more externally defined dimensions such as gender, race, culture, and religion.

The intersecting circles of identity in the model (see Figure 1) represent the significant identity dimensions and contextual influences identified by participants in this study. These

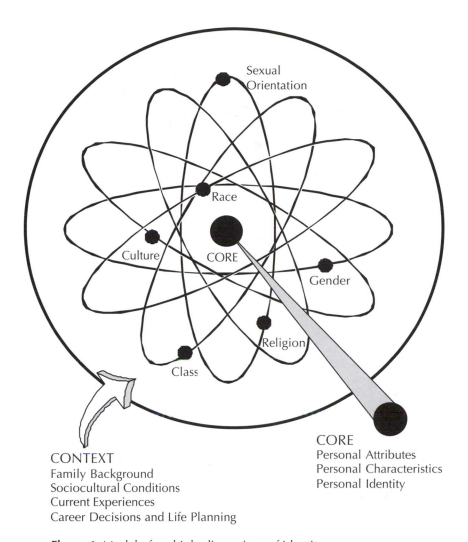

Figure 1 Model of multiple dimensions of identity

dimensions were variously experienced and included race, culture, gender, sexual orientation, religion, and social class. The circles intersect with one another to demonstrate that no one dimension may be understood singularly; it can be understood only in relation to other dimensions. For example, for all the participants, gender was an identity dimension to which they related. However, the description of what being female meant to them was quickly connected with other dimensions (e.g., Jewish woman, Black woman, lesbian, Indian woman). For those participants for whom culture was most salient, family and culture were inextricably connected.

The importance, or relative salience, of these identity dimensions is indicated by dots located on each of the identity dimension circles. The

location of the dot and its proximity to the core represents the particular salience of that identity dimension to the individual at that time. For example, if culture is particularly salient to an individual, the placement of the dot on that dimension is closer to the core. If sexual orientation is not particularly salient to an individual at that point in time, the dot is farther away from the core. The model does, however, illustrate that various identity dimensions are present in each individual, yet experienced in different ways as more or less salient. For example, race was found to be very salient for the Black women in the study, and rarely salient for the White women. Similarly, culture was salient for the Asian Indian woman and religion for the Jewish women.

The intersecting circles and the various locations indicating salience of particular identity dimensions also represent that more than one identity dimension can be engaged by the individual at any one time. Identity dimensions then may be experienced simultaneously as well as more or less salient than other dimensions.

The context within which the individual experiences multiple dimensions of identity is represented by the larger circle that includes both the core and intersecting identity dimensions. These dimensions become more or less salient as they interact with contextual influences such as family background, sociocultural conditions, current life experiences, and career decisions and life planning. Participants perceived identity dimensions as both externally defined and internally experienced, and also influenced by different contexts. When identities are imposed from the outside, dimensions are not seen as integral to core. However, when interacting with certain sociocultural conditions such as sexism and racism, identity dimensions may be scrutinized in a new way that resulted in participants' reflection and greater understanding of a particular dimension.

Influences of sociocultural conditions, family background, and current experiences cannot be underestimated in understanding how participants constructed and experienced their identities. The conceptual model presented in Figure 1 is drawn to illustrate the relationship of these factors to the identity development process. Salience of identity dimensions was rooted in internal awareness and external scrutiny (e.g., race for Black women), and lack of salience seemed prevalent among those more privileged identity dimensions (e.g., sexual orientation for heterosexual women). These findings suggested that systems of privilege and inequality were least visible and understood by those who are most privileged by these systems. Thus, when difference was experienced, identity was shaped. When difference was not experienced, participants attributed these dimensions as relevant to others. Both privilege and difference mediated the connection with and relative salience of various dimensions of identity and shaped the connection to identity dimensions by the individual.

Discussion

Interest in understanding multiple identities emerges from a growing awareness of the non singular nature in which individual identities are constructed and self-perceived. Extending Erikson's (1980) description of identity, more recent research draws attention to the importance of considering the influences of dimensions such as race, culture, social class, and sexual orientation, as well as the need for examination of the sociocultural and sociopolitical contexts in which identities are constructed (Trickett, Watts, & Birman, 1994). The conceptual model of multiple dimensions of identity presented in Figure 1 is drawn from the words and understandings of a diverse group of women college students and depicts the complexities of identity development when multiple dimensions are considered. The model reflects an acknowledgment that different dimensions of identity will be more or less important for each individual given a range of contextual influences. It also presents identity development as a fluid and dynamic process rather than a more linear and static stage model.

The findings from this study and the resulting model reflect Deaux's (1993) conceptualizations of identities as both defined internally by self and externally by others. She suggested that "social and personal identity are fundamentally interrelated. Personal identity is defined, at least in part, by group memberships, and social categories are infused with personal meaning" (p. 5). More specifically, according to Deaux (1993):

> *social identities* are those roles [e.g., parent] or membership categories [e.g., Latino or Latina] that a person claims as representative. . . . *Personal identity* refers to those traits and behaviors [e.g., kind or responsible] that the person finds self-descriptive, characteristics that are typically linked to one or more of the identity categories. (p. 6)

Thus, the core identity in this conceptual model might be described as "personal identity" in Deaux's language, and the multiple identities (intersecting circles) characterize Deaux's "social identities." Further, and particularly important to this discussion of multiple identities, Deaux (1993) indicated that, within the tradition of sociology, "multiple identities are assumed" (p. 5). An articulated assumption of multiple identities, however, does not seem to be the case within theories of student development.

Despite a complex discussion of identity development, Deaux (1993) provided no specific attention to how multiple identities are formed. Her research does, however, underscore the importance of the context in which social identities exist, distinctions between selfperceived inside self and outside identity, and the ongoing negotiations and relationships between one's personal and social identities that contribute to the experience of multiple identities. This model of multiple dimensions of identity goes beyond Deaux's work in suggesting how multiple identities develop and change.

Although Reynolds and Pope (1991) focused on multiple oppressions, their model suggests an expanded understanding of multiple identities and the idea of relative salience, as supported by the findings of this study. The model proposed here extends the work of Reynolds and Pope (1991) by contributing to an understanding of "the multidimensional nature of human identity" (p. 179) and providing a more integrativeframework for understanding identity. Specifically, our conceptual model addresses multiple identities more broadly than multiple oppressions and provides a dynamic representation of the fit of the core self with other identities and the changing relative salience of particular dimensions of identity. Further, as Reynolds and Pope suggested through their examples, this model also incorporates the importance of contexts to how multiple identities are formed and shaped.

Finley (1997), in a qualitative study of 6 women with multiple minority statuses, used the Optimal Theory Applied to Identity Development model (Myers et al., 1991) and the Multidimensional Identity Model (Reynolds & Pope, 1991), and found that "multiple identities followed overlapping, interweaving spirals of development" (p. 3921B). Finley also underscored both the importance of environmental influences on identity development and the complexity of the process. This complexity is typically not represented in other models. The model of multiple dimensions of identity and Finley's findings share an understanding of the identity development process as dynamic, non linear, and complex.

This conceptual model complements and elaborates upon McEwen's (1996) emerging model of multiple identities by portraying how one's personal identity and other multiple identities might relate at any one point in time. Both this model and McEwen's model suggest the presence and interaction of multiple dimensions of identity. This conceptual model, however, shows how identity can be understood and expe-

rienced differently at different points in time, particularly in relation to one's personal identity and in terms of relative salience of each dimension. McEwen also suggested the importance of considering and representing the separate developmental processes of each individual's social identity over time.

The representation in the model of the relationship of the dots on the intersecting circles to the core identity suggests the evolving nature of identity and the changing salience of the various multiple identities. This aspect of the model that emerged from Jones's qualitative study (1997) also reflects Ferguson's (1995) findings in a quantitative study of the relationship of race, gender, sexual orientation, and selfesteem in 181 lesbians of African descent. Ferguson suggested that the women in her study "may be in a continual recycling process in which they retain ties with all three social identities and communities [lesbian, woman, and African American], but to greater or lesser degrees" (p. 4565).

Kiely (1997), in a study of racial identity, womanist identity, and social class variables in Black ($n = 173$) and White ($n = 163$) women college students, found that students' incorporation of multiple aspects of their identity was more common among Black women than White women in her sample. Kiely's research supports the description in this conceptual model that the relative salience of multiple identities is influenced by those identities that are privileged and by those that are externally scrutinized.

The conceptual model for multiple dimensions of identity represents the researchers' attempt to capture the complexity of the identity development process. This model offers another option for thinking about multiple identities and the importance of contextual influences to the development of identity. The model does not portray a developmental process, although it incorporates the importance of the interaction and interface among one's multiple identities and hints at factors that contribute to the development of identity (e.g., contextual influences). It does provide a developmental snapshot of the most salient dimensions of an individual's identity, how the individual experiences those dimensions, and directions for the individual's future growth and development.

This conceptual model suggests the importance of understanding the complexities of identity development. Student affairs educators must not presume what is most central to individuals, but must instead listen for how a person sees herself. This study underscores the importance of seeing students as they see themselves or as they reveal themselves to others. The participants in this study wanted to be understood as they understood themselves and as the totality of who they were, rather than be understood through externally imposed labels and by a singular dimension. Reynolds and Pope (1991) stated that the professional's responsibility is to conceptualize, "understand and facilitate this integration of [college students'] identity" (p. 179).

In addition, the results of this study suggest that educators have a responsibility to help students from majority identity statuses understand the implications of taken-for-granted identities. More specifically, student affairs educators can encourage students who are members of groups whose identity is not examined to consider these aspects of their identity. Similarly, educators must exercise caution in making assumptions about the relative salience of particular identity dimensions for students in traditionally marginalized groups.

The findings of this study suggest the importance of additional research on multiple identities and the development of models that depict this process. The model presented here has not been tested or widely applied. The inclusion of students' voices in this kind of research cannot be understated. Although this study was limited by a small sample, at one institution, of women who indicated an interest in talking about their identity development, the presence of diverse voices and identities contributed to the richness of the data and an understanding of the complexity of the process. Future research that explores this process and incorporates Deaux's suggestion that with "shifting contexts . . . people must continually work at their identities" (p. 10) will add greater clarity to understanding multiple identities. As one participant in the study articulated, the process of identity development when multiple dimensions are considered is an "ongoing journey of self-discovery."

References

Atkinson, D. R., Morten, G., & Sue, D. W. (1993). *Counseling American minorities: A cross-cultural perspective* (4th ed.). Dubuque, IA: Brown & Benchmark.

Bridwell-Bowles, L. (Ed.) (1998). *Identity matters: Rhetorics of difference*. Upper Saddle River, NJ: Prentice Hall.

Cass, V. C. (1979). Homosexual identity formation: A theoretical model. *Journal of Homosexuality, 4* , 219–235.

Cross, W. E., Jr. (1995). The psychology of Nigrescence: Revising the Cross model. In J. G. Ponterotto, J. M. Casas, L. A. Suzuki, & C. M. Alexander (Eds.), *Handbook of multicultural counseling* (pp. 93–122). Thousand Oaks, CA: Sage.

Deaux, K. (1993). Reconstructing social identity. *Personality and Social Psychology Bulletin, 19*, 4–12.

Erikson, E. H. (1980). *Identity and the life cycle*. New York: Norton (Original work published 1959).

Espiritu, Y. L. (1994). The intersection of race, ethnicity, and class. The multiple identities of second-generation Filipinos. *Identities: Global Studies in Culture and Power, 1*, 249–273.

Ferguson, A. D. (1995). The relationship between African-American lesbians' race, gender, and sexual orientation and self-esteem (Doctoral dissertation, University of Maryland, College Park, 1995). *Dissertation Abstracts International, 56*, 4565A.

Finley, H. C. (1997). Women with multiple identities: A qualitative search for patterns of identity development among complex differences (Doctoral dissertation, The Ohio State University, 1997). *Dissertation Abstracts International, 58*, 3921B.

Glaser, B., & Strauss, A. (1967). *The discovery of grounded theory: Strategies for qualitative research*. Chicago: Aldine.

Helms, J. E. (1990). Toward a model of White racial identity development. In J. E. Helms (Ed.), *Black and White racial identity: Theory, research, and practice* (pp. 4966). New York: Greenwood Press.

Helms, J. E. (1992). *A race is a nice thing to have: A guide to being a White person, or Understanding the White persons in your life*. Topeka, KS: Content Communications.

Helms, J. E. (1995). An update of Helms's White and People of Color racial identity models. In J. G. Ponterotto, J. M. Casas, L. A. Suzuki, & C. M. Alexander (Eds.), *Handbook of multicultural counseling* (pp. 181–198). Thousand Oaks, CA: Sage.

Jones, S. R. (1997). Voices of identity and difference: A qualitative exploration of the multiple dimensions of identity development in women college students. *Journal of College Student Development, 38*, 376–386.

Kiely, L. J. (1997). An exploratory analysis of the relationship of racial identity, social class, and family influences on womanist identity development (Doctoral dissertation, University of Maryland, College Park, 1997). *Dissertation Abstracts International, 58*, 2086A.

McCarn, S. R., & Fassinger, R. E. (1996). Revisioning sexual minority identity formation: A new model of lesbian identity and its implications. *The Counseling Psychologist, 24*, 508–534.

McEwen, M. K. (1996). New perspectives on identity development. In S. R. Komives & D. B. Woodard Jr. (Eds.), *Student services: A handbook for the profession* (3rd ed., pp. 188–217). San Francisco: Jossey-Bass.

Moraga, C. (1998). La güera. In M. L Andersen & P. Hill Collins (Eds.), *Race, class and gender: An anthology* (pp. 26–33). Belmont, CA: Wadsworth.

Myers, L. J., Speight, S. L., Highlen, P. S., Cox, C. I., Reynolds, A. L., Adams, E. M., & Hanley, C. P. (1991). Identity development and worldview: Toward an optimal conceptualization. *Journal of Counseling & Development, 70 ,* 54–63.

O'Neil, J. M., Egan, J., Owen, S. V., & Murry, V. M. (1993). The Gender Role Journey Measure: Scale development and psychometric evaluation. *Sex Roles, 28*, 167–185.

Ossana, S. M., Helms, J. E., & Leonard, M. M. (1992). Do "womanist" identity attitudes influence college women's self-esteem and perceptions of environmental bias? *Journal of Counseling & Development, 70*, 402–408.

Patton, M. Q. (1990). *Qualitative evaluation and research methods* (2nd ed.). Newbury Park, CA: Sage.

Phinney, J. S. (1990). Ethnic identity in adolescents and adults: Review of research. *Psychological Bulletin, 108*, 499–514.

Phinney, J. S. (1992). The Multigroup Ethnic Identity Measure: A new scale for use with diverse groups. *Journal of Adolescent Research, 7*, 156–176.

Reynolds, A. L., & Pope, R. L. (1991). The complexities of diversity: Exploring multiple oppressions. *Journal of Counseling & Development, 70*, 174–180.

Root, M. P. P. (1990). Resolving "other" status: Identity development of biracial individuals. In L. S. Brown & M. P. P. Root (Eds.), *Complexity and diversity in feminist theory and therapy* (pp. 185–205). New York: Haworth Press.

Strauss, A., & Corbin, J. (1990). *Basics of qualitative research: Grounded theory procedures and techniques.* Newbury Park, CA: Sage.

Thompson, B., & Tyagi, S. (Eds.). (1996). *Names we call home: Autobiography on racial identity.* New York: Routledge.

Trickett, E. J., Watts, R. J., & Birman, D. (Eds.). (1994). *Human diversity: Perspectives on people in context.* San Francisco: Jossey-Bass.

CHAPTER 34

THE COMPLEXITIES OF DIVERSITY:
EXPLORING MULTIPLE OPPRESSION

AMY L. REYNOLDS AND RAECHELE L. POPE

There has been a growth of identity development models in multicultural psychology for the past 20 years; these frameworks, however, rarely acknowledge the complexities of multiple identities and multiple oppressions. The purpose of this article is to challenge our understanding of cultural diversity beyond its current simplistic frameworks. Alternative worldviews, such as Afrocentric psychology, can broaden our comprehension of human diversity and are used to examine the identity development literature. Several case examples of individuals experiencing multiple identities and multiple oppressions are explored to illustrate the complexities of cultural diversity. Implications for counseling, training, and research are briefly discussed.

Although there has been growing interest in cultural diversity and multicultural counseling since the early 1970s, the dynamics of the literature and t he perspectives used continue to change (Heath, Neimeyer, & Pedersen, 1988; Lee, 1989; Smith & Vasquez, 1985). Initially, the literature focused on how mainstream psychology was not meeting the needs of people of color (Sue & Sue, 1971; Vontress, 1971). Throughout the 1970s, many authors explored how people of color differed from Whites and what effect those racial differences had in therapy. A later development in multicultural counseling focused on the differences that existed within oppressed groups including the creation and expansion of racial-ethnic identity development models during the 1980s.

During the late 1970s and early 1980s, there was increasing interest in other aspects of cultural diversity such as gender and affectional-sexual orientation. Feminism challenged the effect of counseling on women's lives and began offering alternative perspectives. Identity development models were created for women (Avery, 1977; Downing & Roush, 1985) as well as for gays and lesbians (Cass, 1979). Since the early 1980s, some authors have become increasingly aware of the similarities among oppressed groups and have offered frameworks to help understand the commonalities of oppression (Atkinson, Morten, & Sue, 1989; Banks, 1984; Highlen et al., 1988; Sue & Sue, 1990).

Although the growth of these identity development models has been fairly recent, much parallel work has already been done across a variety of groups (Highlen et al., 1986). The creation of these frameworks seems to reflect the social movements in this country (Reynolds, 1989). The first identity development models focused on Black identity and seemed to follow and describe the civil rights movements of the 1960s. Feminist identity as well as lesbian and gay identity models grew out of the late 1970s while the women's and gay rights movements were being established.

Durante los últimos veinte años ha habido un aumento de modelos de desarrollo de identidad en la consejería multicultural; sin embargo, estos cuadros no suelen reconocer las complejidades de identidades múltiples y opresiones múltiples. El propósito de este artículo es desafiar a nuestro conocimiento de diversidad yendo más allá de sus simplistas cuadros actuales. Visiones universals alternativas, como la consejería afrocéntrica, pueden ampliar nuestra comprensión de la diversidad humana y pueden ser usadas para examinar la literatura del desarrollo de identidad. Para ilustrar las complejidades de diversidad, se exploran varios ejemplos de individuos que sufren de identidades múltiples y de oppressions múltiples. Se discuten las implicaciones para la conserjería, el entrenamiento y la investigación.

The Minority Identity Development (MID) model by Atkinson et al. (1989), along with the multiethnic model by Banks (1984) and other inclusive frameworks, reflected a trend in the 1980s toward unification as in the "rainbow coalition."

The available identity development theories as well as the general literature about culturally diverse groups have rarely examined or acknowledged the multiple layers of diversity and identity and instead offer one-dimensional images of culturally diverse individuals (Highlen et al., 1986). Within these models little attention has been demonstrated toward within-group differences such as sex, age, race/ethnicity, affectional-sexual orientation, and religion and their effect on the developmental process. A common example of this frequent dichotomization or segmenting of human identities is found in many job advertisements—"Minorities and women are encouraged to apply"—which implies two separate and unrelated groups and ultimately makes women of color invisible. Clearly, many individuals in our culture have multiple identities and are members of more than one oppressed group, thus making such dichotomization both inaccurate and limiting. Although this multiplicity of identities and its inherent challenge to current identity development models also applies to individuals who are not members of oppressed groups, this article focuses on the effects and implications of multiple oppression rather than multiple identities.

Although there is much discussion as to what entails or defines an oppressed group and more complex definitions and discussions of oppression have been offered in the literature (Myers et al., 1991), for the purpose of this article, *oppression* is defined as a system that allows access to the services, rewards, benefits, and privileges of society based on membership in a particular group. According to Highlen, Speight, Myers, and Cox (1989), "Within the United States, the generally accepted norm by which people are evaluated or against which they measure themselves is how close one comes to being anglo, middle class, male, Christian, heterosexual, English speaking, young, and mentally, physically, and emotionally unimpaired" (p.8).

Nature does not create discrete categories of human traits or identities. People create these categories to simplify the complexity of multiple identities and multiple realities. There are many women who are also people of color; many people of color who are also lesbian, gay, or bisexual; many lesbian, gay, or bisexual people who may also have physical disabilities; and so on. According to Highlen et al. (1988), a multiple oppression is when an individual is a member of two or more oppressed groups. For example, an Asian American woman who is also a lesbian is a member of three oppressed groups. Each of her oppressions is unique and must be addressed separately (being Asian American, a lesbian, and a woman), as well as the combined oppressions (Asian American woman or Asian American lesbian) with their own issues.

The purpose of this article is to challenge and expand the definitions and comprehensions of human diversity in multicultural counseling beyond its current simplistic frameworks. As the field of multicultural counseling grows our understanding of the dynamics of human diversity becomes increasingly complicated. Although a few of the current models of identity development offer measurable construct, they create an incomplete and, therefore, inaccurate picture of the multiple layers of identity and oppression. Although these frameworks add much to our appreciation of human diversity, they also simplify the complexities of identity development and group identification.

This article presents a brief review and critique of some of the available identity development and acculturation models. These issues are examined through the lens of afrocentric psychology, which offers a broader perspective of human diversity and identity. Such alternative models are necessary to understand the ever-changing and continually expanding groups of oppressed people in the 21st century. Several case examples of individuals experiencing multiple identities and multiple oppression are explored to illustrate the complexities of identity. Implications for counseling, training, and research are briefly discussed.

Literature Review

During the past decade, identity development frameworks have become a major consideration in multicultural counseling. Historically, this work began in anthropology during the 1920s in the study of acculturation. Primarily, these acculturation studies have examined the experiences of people of color when they came in contact with the dominant White culture in United States (U.S.). Many acculturation theories contend that contact and interaction among several autonomous cultural groups may cause change in one or both groups (Mena, Padilla, & Maldonado, 1987). Until recently, most acculturation research was primarily anthropological in nature (Olmedo, 1979). In multicultural psychology, however, research on acculturation, primarily with Asian American and Chicano/Latino people has been occurring more frequently (Keefe & Padilla, 1987; Mendoza & Martinez, 1981; Suinn, Rickard-Figueroa, Lew, & Vigil, 1987). Although the acculturation research continues to clarify the impact of contact with another culture, this research seems to describe the participants as one-dimensional. Although variables such as socioeconomic class, education level, and language may be explored as part of defining acculturation level, other factors such as gender or affectional-sexual orientation are rarely mentioned or explored.

Within the racial-ethnic identity literature, developmental stage models have focused primarily on African Americans (Cross, 1971; Jackson, 1975; Parham, 1989; Parham, & Helms, 1981; Thomas, 1971). In addition, there has been a growth of models exploring White identity (Hardiman, 1979; Helms, 1984, 1990; Ponterotto, 1988). Despite the growing available literature on racial/ethnic identity, other identities or differences within these racial/ethnic groups have rarely been explored. In fact, several authors (Akbar, 1989; Nobles, 1989) have begun to challenge the underlying assumptions of the racial-ethnic identity development models.

Although these racial-ethnic identity models often have been one-dimensional in their view of individuals, some authors have examined the intersections of gender or age with racial/ethnic identity. Cross (1974) discovered gender differences in the Immersion-Emersion stage in a study of his Black identity model. Williams (1975), in a study of the Cross model, found differences in the distribution of women and men in the various stages. Although several racial/ethnic identity studies have included gender as a variable, such distinctions were not explored in the actual development of the models.

More recently, Parham (1989), in an expansion of the Cross (1971) model, incorporated the effects of age and the developmental process on Black identity, yet his examples of W.E. DuBois and Malcolm X offered only a male point of view. Carter (1990) explored the relationship between racism and racial identity among Whites and found significant gender differences. His results suggested that gender socialization has an impact on the development of racial attitudes. Delworth (1989) examined the relationship between racial/ethnic and gender identity for college students and encouraged a reexploration of student development theories, constructs, and practices with the notions of both gender and race/ethnicity in mind.

Other models of identity development have not fared much better in their exploration of human diversity. Downing and Roush (1985) modeled their feminist identity framework on the Black identity model by Cross (1971), yet acknowledged their lack of attention to diversity among women (e.g., class, race/ethnicity, age) as a major limitation. In many respects, their model might best be renamed as an identity development model for middle-class, nonlesbian White women (Reynolds, 1989). Hess (1983) explored the similarities and differences in the identity development of lesbians and feminists although her analysis often implies and described them as separate rather then overlapping groups.

Although there has been much psychological literature examining the "coming out" process for gay and lesbian people, Cass (1979) offered a stage model most similar to the previously described identity development frameworks (Highlen et al., 1986). This model groups gay men and lesbians together in this process even though other authors describe significant gender differences (DeMonteflores & Schultz, 1978; Faderman, 1984). In addition, Case (1979) did not acknowledge or examine the issues related to bisexuality despite strong support in the literature for a bisexual orientation (Golden, 1987; Klein, 1978; Schuster, 1987). Some authors have explored the identity development dynamics of being a person of color as well as gay or lesbian, although not in context of a specific identity model (Chan, 1989; Cochran & Mays, 1986; Loiacano, 1989).

Although on the surface the models that focus on the similarities among oppressed people might seem most open to exploring the complexities of diversity, such as the MID model by Atkinson et al. (1989), their framework discusses how members of culturally diverse groups must struggle with how to relate to members of other oppressed groups as if implying that they might not also be members of other oppressed groups. Although the Optimal Theory Applied to Identity Development (OTAID) model has challenged the tendency of the identity development literature to ignore the effects of multiple oppression (Highlen et al., 1986), it has done little to offer specifics about the impact of such complexities on the identity development process.

Little research has been done to examine the internal process of dealing with multiple oppressions and identities; several possible options, however, exist (Highlen et al., 1988). An individual may address her or his multiple oppressions at the same time (e.g., deal with being an American Indian and a woman simultaneously). Or such work may occur separately where, for example, one might face aspects of being an American Indian first, then experience a similar process for being a woman. The shift in focus may be affected by one's environment, reference group, or individual needs (Highlen et al., 1988). Often a person is most likely to focus on which ever oppression is most salient in her or his life (Reynolds, 1989).

The only paradigms available to aid in the exploration of this phenomenon of multiple identities can be found in biracial and bisexual identity development theories and models. Inherent in their self-definition process, bisexual and biracial individuals must face the realities of multiple identities. Although the literature in these areas is still scarce, the past several years have brought increasing interest in exploring the identity issues of these groups.

In examining bisexuality, a common definition is an individual who connects with both women and men in terms of attraction, love, and desire. There are different types of bisexual identification or routes through which bisexual individuals understand their sexuality (Schuster, 1987). Contemporaneous bisexuals are in intimate relationships with both women and men. Sequential bisexuals have a series of intimate relationships with women and men. Other bisexual individuals may be monogamous in their involvement with a woman or a man yet may define themselves as bisexual.

Like gays and lesbians, bisexual individuals go through both an internal and external process of self-definition, although "the diversity of bisexuals' individual histories makes it difficult to generalize about those processes" (Schuster, 1987, p. 59). According to Schuster, "By definition, bisexuals defy categorization" (p.57). Although there is often an expectation that identity development occurs in a predictable manner, "there is not a bisexual prototype: that is the center of both their significance and their challenges" (Schuster, 1987, p. 57).

Because of this complexity, bisexuals are often hidden among gay and nongay individuals. There are myths, stereotypes, and biases that keep bisexual people marginal and make it difficult for them to find a supportive community. Many women who self-define as bisexual may publicly define themselves as lesbian and may be strongly connected to the lesbian community (Golden, 1987; Schuster, 1987). Golden articulated how many bisexual women come out as lesbians first and then realize that their sexual identity is more accurately defined as bisexual. The nongay culture sees bisexuals as gay and, therefore, subjects them to homophobia and discrimination. Meanwhile, in gay and lesbian communities, there is fear and distrust of bisexual individuals. Golden stated that a bisexual identity may have more stigma than a lesbian identity. Clearly, to self-define as bisexual, these individuals must be willing to challenge the notion of dichotomous sexuality and identity (Schuster, 1987).

Similar struggles occur for individuals of mixed racial heritage. Brandell (1988) noted that the "formation of ethnic/racial identity in the biracial child seems to be a complex and variable developmental process" (p.179). According to Root (1990), "Theoretical conceptualization and application to therapy must become multiracial and multicultural to accurately reflect the process of more than one single racial group" (p. 192). Biracial individuals have always been viewed as marginal people and have had to resolve an ambiguous ethnic identity (Poston, 1990; Root, 1990). The traditional racial/ethnic identity models do not encompass the reality of biracial people, especially if their racial heritage involves both oppressed and dominant racial groups (e.g., Asian American and White). As such, biracial individuals cannot reject either part of their racial heritage without continuing a process of internalized oppression (Root, 1990). Somehow they must be able to reach a resolution that allows the diverse parts of their racial heritage to coexist.

Root (1990) allowed even more diversity to complicate the issues of biracial individuals by examining gender issues. She suggested that biracial men may have more difficulty overcoming social barriers because they are often viewed as more threatening because of their male status. Biracial women have to deal with myths, such as being exotic, which they may not be as prepared to do because of their invisibility as women.

Root (1990) offered a new framework of identity resolution for biracial individuals that challenges the linear notions found in traditional identity development models. She described this process as facing "internal conflict over a core sense of definition of self" (p. 204). The strongest tension occurs between the racial components within the biracial individual in the context of the family and society. In her model there is more than one acceptable outcome, which contradicts the tenet found in mainstream psychological theories that allows for only one healthy option.

The first possible resolution, "acceptance of the identity society assigns," is a passive resolution in which the individual usually accepts a definition as a person of color. Because of racism in this culture, most individuals with any non-White racial heritage are usually defined exclusively by that heritage (Poussaint, 1984; Root, 1990). This process is similar to the effects of homophobia that cause bisexual individuals to be perceived as gay by the dominant nongay culture. A second option for resolution, "identification with both racial groups," means that the individual actively identifies with both racial groups. They may often realize their similarities and differences to others around them and work to connect with both groups.

"Identification with a single racial group" is a third option for resolution of a biracial identity. Unlike the first option, this individual makes an active choice to identify with a particular group. In doing so, this individual may or may not deny the other aspects of her or his racial identity. The final option for resolution is called "identification as a new racial group. "This identification means that the individual's strongest connection is to other biracial people. This strategy may be the most challenging because there is little acceptance of a biracial identity and not any visible community.

According to Root (1990), all of these options have opportunities for both positive and negative outcomes. These options are not mutually exclusive; individuals may move among them during different parts of their lives. All of these choices can be positive unless individuals deny any aspect of their heritage.

Clearly, this framework offers a flexible and dynamic view of identity development within a nonlinear process. In challenging the core beliefs of psychology, Root (1990) has made way for alternative theoretical models. Her theory illustrates some of the complexities of multiple identities such as addressing the implications of when those identities are from oppressed groups and when they are from dominant groups. Being biracial and a member of more than one oppressed group, such as being both African American and Japanese American, has a different meaning than being biracial and identifying with both oppressed and dominant groups such as being both Chicano and White. Such complexities demand further exploration and in-depth research before any true understanding can occur.

Alternative Models

According to Root (1990), "Current models of mental health to not accommodate the process by which individual who have 'other' identities, such as biracial and/or gay/lesbian, arrive at a positive sense of self-identity or maintain a positive identity in the face of oppressive attitudes" (p. 186). Mainstream psychology must consider alternative frameworks to better meet the needs of culturally diverse clients and professionals who continue to test the limits and generalities of psychological theories (Sue et al., 1982). Alternative perspectives, such as those offered by afrocentric psychology, can broaden our understanding of human diversity. Afrocentric psychology is a conceptual system or worldview that challenges the core assumptions of Western psychological theory and creates an optimal and holistic conceptualization of human being and the universe in which we live (Myers, 1988).

A major tenet of this optimal conceptualization or worldview centers on the inseparability of the spiritual and material aspects of reality (Myers, 1988). In other words, our spiritual essence and our physical and material realities are completely interwoven and as one. In a Western worldview, the nature of reality is primarily material, which supports the notion that there are limited material resources and we must compete for these resources in order to survive. The materialistic, and often competitive, perspective causes individuals to emphasize their individuality and separateness from others.

Alternative perspectives about who we are in relation to others do exist. Nobles (1976) described the African concept of extended self in which self includes all ancestors, the yet unborn, all of nature, as well as the surrounding community. This optimal conceptualization honors and emphasizes connections among all of life and denounces separation of individuals.

According to Afrocentric epistemology, self-knowledge is the basis of all knowledge (Myers, 1988). Reasoning in this mindset is based on diunital logic or the union of opposites (Myers, 1988). Diunital reasoning challenges the dualistic and either-or beliefs found in the dominant Western worldview and is centered on the notion that all things or beliefs can occur simultaneously and in harmony with each other. In other words, the dualities commonly known to our culture (i.e., mind-body, theory-practice, science-art) are the result of a segmented worldview (Myers, 1988). According to Myers, "An optimal conceptual system yields a world view that is holistic, assuming the interrelatedness and interdependence of all things" (p.13).

Western culture, however, supports the notion that knowledge occurs outside of us and that we are inherently separate from all others (Myers, 1988). According to Myers et al. (1991), "To be oppressed is to be socialized into a worldview that is suboptimal and leads to a fragmented sense of self" (p. 56). As such, it is difficult for individuals to embrace all of who they are when they internalize a worldview based on fragmentation and dichotomization. Therefore, science, in which psychology is based, views individuals in one-dimensional ways, thus making the notion of multiple identities and multiple realities inconceivable. By comparison, an Afrocentric worldview places a premium on self-knowledge as the basis of all knowledge which in turn encourages individuals to define their own realities and embrace their entire beings (Myers, 1988).

Afrocentric psychology is but one alternative worldview that can expand our visions and understanding of human realities. Obviously, new perspectives and definitions are needed if we are to embrace the complexities of identity. To further highlight and understand the nature of identity and multiple oppressions, several case examples are explored.

> John is a 20-year-old Mexican American man who is gay and has been involved in a gay relationship for the past year. He is a junior in college and is studying business. He entered therapy because he was feeling ambivalent about his relationship. He was feeling depressed and unmotivated, and his alcohol use had increased during the past several months.

John was born in Mexico and lived there until he was in the fifth grade. His parents speak only Spanish and have little formal education. John resents his parents' lack of comfort and ability to live in Anglo culture and has expressed feeling ashamed of them. John has never strongly identified as Mexican American or Chicano and changed his name from Juan to John when he was in junior high. He identified as gay in high school and has had several relationships that never lasted more than 1 year.

John has always sought out stable and committed relationships yet has had difficulty maintaining them because he feels "crowded." He seems uncomfortable with emotions and intimacy yet feels a strong sense of isolation and emptiness. He is highly self-critical and feels a strong need to be better than others.

John's interpersonal and intrapersonal struggles seem strongly connected to unresolved developmental issues of identity, autonomy, and intimacy. He seems to have made a choice to submerge his Chicano identity. His depression, perfectionism, and difficulty in interpersonal relationships may all be related to his inability to integrate and accept all of who is he is. John has internalized the dominant worldview by choosing to believe his different identities are incompatible.

If John chose to integrate his multiple identities, he might experience rejection on all fronts. If he is strongly Chicano identified within the gay community, he must face racism directly. If he is strongly gay identified in the Chicano community, he must face homophobia. Instead, he has chosen to live in a gay world as a gay man with little notice of his ethnicity. His choice to be highly acculturated occurs in a specific context unique to his multiple oppressions.

Within therapy, efforts were made to examine the underlying issues that fueled John's depression, low self-esteem, and discomfort with intimacy. His core belief is that he is unacceptable. Obviously, he has internalized his oppression and, therefore, has a fragmented sense of self. To accept all of who he is, John must be willing to embrace and understand his multiple identities.

> Judy is a 35-year-old African American woman who is a fourth-year doctoral student in political science. She has been experiencing much anxiety about school and her relationships. Judy entered therapy to help her deal more effectively with stress.

Judy is politically active and is strongly Black identified. In the past several years she has been exploring feminist theories and considers herself a feminist. Although she has always been involved in issues central to the African American community, she feels most strongly connected to African American women. Judy, however, has felt increasingly isolated and alienated from many African American women who believe that sexism is a White women's issue.

Because of her strong feminist beliefs, Judy's community of friends is predominantly women, which has limited her romantic options as a heterosexual woman. On the outside, Judy says she has accepted the possibility that her values and education may decrease her chances of finding a compatible life partner yet she seems to be more ambivalent than she reports.

Judy's anxiety over relationships seems connected to the roles and expectations in her life. She seems to have a strong identity as a woman and as an African American, yet she may be struggling with the intersection between those two identities and their impact on her hopes for a supportive community and possibly even a long-term romantic relationship. The alienation and isolation she experiences adds to the level of stress in her life and creates barriers to any available inner resources.

Within therapy, Judy explored her image and expectations of herself and what she wanted out of her life. She identified conflicting goals that she had between some values that she was taught (e.g., support the struggle against racism no matter what) and her belief in paying attention to her own needs. She explored how her feminism and racial identity clashed at times as she struggled to find a community where she felt she belonged. In the African American community she was frustrated with a lack of attention to sexism and women's issues, yet she was even more fed up with the White feminist community and its unwillingness to examine its own racism. Judy may need to look inward to find a place where she can integrate and accept all of who she is.

> Megan is a 24-year-old White woman who is also blind. She recently graduated with a degree of women's studies and political science. During the past several years, she became strongly involved at the women's center. Megan came to therapy to deal with her low self-esteem and depression.

Because of Megan's parents had difficulty dealing with her disability, she was both sheltered and neglected as a child. She has internalized negative messages about being blind that affect every aspect of her life. When she was introduced to the women's community, she embraced the positive acceptance she found and began to focus on her identity as a woman.

Although Megan acknowledges difficulty dealing with her disability, she has been hesitant to form relationships with other people with disabilities. Whenever she examines her blindness, she feels it is ugly.

Megan's low self-esteem and depression seem strongly linked to her difficulty in accepting her disability. She seems to have chosen to celebrate the female part of her because it is more acceptable, yet she is unable to shake the other unacceptable parts of her. Her discomfort is so high that she hesitates to seek out positive relationships or role models with other people with disabilities.

If Megan chose to integrate her multiple identities, she would have to face her fears about being blind and she would need to reexamine her beliefs about what blind people are capable of doing. Rather than face those possible barriers, Megan has chosen to embrace her female self. Somehow she is able to identify sexism and externalize her anger toward the inequalities that women face, yet she has difficulty transferring those notions to her disability. To address these conflicting messages about herself, Megan needs to explore the core roots of oppression that lead her to devalue the many diverse aspects of herself.

Counseling Implications

These case examples illustrate the complexity and importance of considering multiple identities and realities in multicultural counseling. Without exploration of the multidimensional aspects of identity, psychotherapists increase the likelihood of misunderstanding or misinterpreting their clients' perspectives and actions.

Just as many authors have challenged the notions of traditional developmental theories that have often labeled women as developmentally delayed (Gilligan, 1982; Miller, 1986), identity development theories also may make unjust assumptions about individuals' identity based only on their behavior. For example, an African American gay man who is strongly connected with both identities and is trying to be involved with these diverse communities might be perceived quite narrowly through current identity development theories. If he chose not to be very public with his gay identity with his family or within his church, he might be perceived as closeted. If at times he distanced himself from the African American community and associated with predominantly White-gay friends, he might be perceived as denying his African American

heritage. Neither of these identity development theories fully comprehends and allows for his multiple identities. If therapists base their understanding of identity on these available models, they can easily make assumptions about their clients' experiences and perspectives.

When therapists are able to identify and understand the complex nature of their clients' realities, they will be more equipped to help them deal with such issues as marginality, isolation, and internalized oppression. To clarify and expand understanding of existing multiple options for identity resolution for members of more than one oppressed group and to build on the biracial Identity Model by Root (1990), the Multidimensional Identity Model (MIM) has been created. Figure 1 shows the four possible options for identity resolution that occur within a dynamic process of self-growth and exploration.

As is seen in the first two options of the MIM, some individuals may choose to identify with just one aspect of their identity. This option may be passive (allowing society or one's community or family to determine one's primary group) or active (marking a conscious choice of self-identification). Part of this choice may cause individuals to suppress one aspect of themselves to feel more accepted in their family or community.

Another option involves individuals who decide to embrace all aspects of their identities by living in separate and sometimes unconnected worlds (e.g., a nonlesbian Puerto Rican

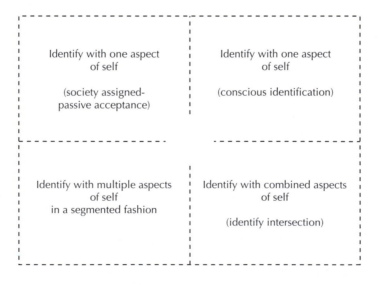

Figure 1 Multidimensional identity model

woman embracing her racial-ethnic heritage in her Puerto Rican community yet also becoming involved in predominantly White feminist groups where she can more fully celebrate her female self). In both of these communities she presents a one-dimensional, in complete, and segmented self.

A final option for identity resolution for members of more than one oppressed group is to identify as a new group. By focusing on the intersections of their identifies, these individuals may be able to integrate their multiple identities. In other words, rather than identifying as a woman or as person with a disability, a deaf woman might make connections with other women with disabilities so she no longer has to segment and dichotomize the different aspects of herself. These communities are appearing more frequently and offering new perspectives that challenge the status quo. Women of color, bisexual individuals, and gay and lesbian people of color are examples of communities that are embracing the intersections of their identities.

Within this model, all options are acceptable and create opportunities for positive self-esteem and pride as well as challenges to maintain an integrated sense of self. Figure 1 is drawn to exemplify the dynamic and fluid nature of this identity development process through its use of broken lines between the various options. Throughout one's life, movement among these options occurs based on personal needs, reference group, or environment.

If we are to be supportive of our clients, we must also be able to understand and facilitate this integration of identity. Psychotherapists must be willing to challenge their assumptions about identity development and group identification if they are to create a responsive environment for their clients. Encouraging self-awareness of the available options for identity resolution and creating a supportive relationship for exploration are two vital goals for therapy with individuals who are members of more than one oppressed group. Being nonjudgmental and open to the strategies chosen by one's clients is necessary to facilitate growth and insight. Such tasks are not easy in a culture and profession that often implies and directly states that healthy development occurs only in a specific manner.

Because such complexities have never been part of traditional psychological frameworks, we must make great efforts to retrain and reeducate ourselves. There are many unanswered questions to aid us in this process of fully understanding the complicated nature of human diversity. New training and research paradigms must be created to develop and perpetuate alternative perspectives or world views.

Training and Research Implications

Teaching the complexities of multicultural psychology is challenging at best when the field of psychology is still struggling to incorporate multicultural issues into the mainstream of the profession. So often, multicultural training occurs at the content level—teaching trainees and professionals about different oppressed groups and their perspectives. Such approaches segment and simplify the notations of diversity.

Process-oriented approaches allow for alternative models that emphasize self-knowledge, relationships, and worldviews (Myers, 1988; Speight, Myers, Cox, & Highlen, 1991; Sue & Zane, 1987). Speight et al. (1991) have encouraged the redefinition of multicultural counseling using optimal theory, which emphasizes self-knowledge and uses experiential and didactic learning. If our training examines the underlying principles and worldview of psychology that may lead to fragmented identities, we will be better prepared to help our clients understand their own struggles.

Like training, psychological research has yet to embrace the full complexity of human diversity. New research questions and methods need to be designed to expand our understanding of identity developments as well as traditional methodology (Helms, 1989; Speight et al., 1991). Exploring the realities of a multiple oppression from an *emic* perspective (using the worldview of the participants) that honors the experiences of those diverse individuals is crucial in order for us to comprehend the multidimensional nature of their lives.

Conclusion

The frameworks in this article illuminate the issues of multiple oppressions and their impact on the identity development process and offer new direction for multicultural counseling, training, and research. Although the issues presented challenge the universal claims of developmental theories and models, more research and exploration is needed to fully understand the multidimensional nature of human identity. We must expand our worldviews more broadly to understand and embrace the multiple realities of our clients and colleagues. By moving beyond simplistic frameworks, we inherently need to struggle with the challenges of changing the ways in which we view the world. This nexus of identities is a vital and necessary link to a more complete appreciation of the complexities of human diversity.

References

Akbar, N. (1989). Nigrescence and identity: Some limitations. *The Counseling Psychologist, 17*, 258–263.

Atkinson, D. R., Morten, G., & Sue, D. W. (Eds.). (1989). *Counseling American minorities: A cross-cultural perspective* (3rd ed.). Dubuque, IA: William C. Brown.

Avery, D. M. (1977). The psychological stages of liberation. *Illinois Personnel and Guidance Association Quarterly, 63*, 36–42.

Banks, J. A. (1984). *Teaching strategies for ethnic studies* (3rd ed.). Boston: Allyn & Bacon.

Brandell, J.R. (1988). Treatment of the biracial child: Theoretical and clinical issues. *Journal of Multicultural Counseling and Development, 16*, 176–187.

Carter, R. T. (1990). The relationship between racism and racial identity among White Americans: An exploratory investigation. *Journal of Counseling & Development, 69*, 46–50.

Cass, V. C. (1979). Homosexual identity formation: A theoretical model. *Journal of Homosexuality, 4*, 219–235.

Chan, C. S. (1989). Issues of identity development among Asian-American lesbians and gay men. *Journal of Counseling & Development, 68*, 16–20.

Cochran, S. D., & Mays, V. M. (1986, August). *Sources of support in the Black lesbian community*. Paper presented at the meeting of the American Psychological Association, Washington, D.C.

Cross, W. E. (1971). The Negro-to-Black conversion experience. *Black World, 7*, 13–27.

Cross, W. E. (1974, June). *Empirical analysis of the Negro-to-Black conversion experience*. Paper presented at the meeting of the First Conference on Empirical Research in Black Psychology, Ann Arbor, MI.

Delworth, U. (1989). Identity in the college years: Issues of gender and ethnicity. *National Association of Student Personnel Administrators, 26*, 162–166.

DeMonteflores, C., & Schultz, S. J. (1978). Coming out. Similarities and differences for lesbians and gay men. *Journal of Social Issues, 34*, 59–72.

Downing, N. E., & Roush, K. L. (1985). From passive acceptance to active commitment: A model of feminist identity development of women. *The Counseling Psychologist, 13*, 695–705.

Faderman, L. (1984). The "new gay" lesbians. *Journal of Homosexuality, 10*, 85–95.

Gilligan, C. (1982). *In a different voice: Psychological theory and women's development*. Cambridge, MA: Harvard University Press.

Golden, C. (1987). Diversity and variability in women's sexual identities. In Boston Lesbian Psychologies Collective (Eds.), *Lesbian psychologies. Explorations and challenges* (pp. 18–34). Urbana, IL: University of Illinois Press.

Hardiman, R. (1979). *White identity developmental theory*. Unpublished manuscript.

Heath, A. E., Neimeyer, G. J., & Pedersen, P. (1988). The future of cross-cultural counseling: A Delphi poll. *Journal of Counseling and Development, 67*, 27–30.

Helms, J. E. (1984). Toward a theoretical explanation of the effects of race on counseling: A Black and White model. *The Counseling psychologist, 12*, 153–165.

Helms, J. E. (1989). At long last-Paradigms for cultural psychology research. *The Counseling Psychologist, 17*, 98–101.

Helms, J. E. (Ed.). (1990). *Black and White racial identity theory, research, and practice*. Westport, CT: Greenwood Press.

Hess, E. P. (1983). Feminist and lesbian development: Parallels and divergencies. *Journal of Homosexuality, 23*, 67–78.

Highlen, P. S., Myers, L. J., Hanley, C. P., Speight, S., Reynolds, A. L., Adams, E. M., & Cox, C. (1986). *Seed grant proposal*. Unpublished manuscript.

Highlen, P. S., Reynolds, A. L., Adams, E. M., Hanley, C. P., Myers, L. J., Cox, C., & Speight, S. (1988, August). *Self-identity development model of oppressed people: Inclusive model for all?* Paper presented at meeting of the American Psychological Association, Atlanta, GA.

Highlen, P. S., Speight, S. L., Myers, L. J., & Cox, C. I. (1989). *Oppression: Understanding the chains that bind*. Unpublished manuscript.

Jackson, B. (1975). Black identity development. *MEFORM: Journal of Educational Diversity and Innovation, 2*, 19–25.

Keefe, S. E., & Padilla, A. M. (1987). *Chicano ethnicity*. Albuquerque, NM: University of New Mexico Press.

Klein, F. (1978). *The bisexual option: A concept of one hundred percent intimacy*. New York: Arbor House.

Lee, C. (1989). Editorial: Who speaks for multicultural counseling? *Journal of Multicultural Counseling and Development, 17,* 2–3.

Loiacano, D. K. (1989). Gay identity issues among Black Americans: Racism, homophobia, and the need for validation. *Journal of Counseling & Development, 68,* 21–25.

Mena, F. J., Padilla, A. M., & Maldonado, M. (1987). Acculturative stress and specific coping strategies among immigrant and later generation college students. *Hispanic Journal of Behavioral Sciences, 9,* 207–225.

Mendoza, R. H., & Martinez, J. L. (1981). The measurement of acculturation. In A. Baron (Ed.), *Explorations in Chicano psychology* (pp. 71–82). New York: Praeger Publishers.

Miller, J. B. (1986). *Toward a new psychology of women* (2nd ed.). Boston: Beacon Press.

Myers, L. J. (1988). *Understanding an Afrocentric world view: Introduction to an optimal psychology.* Dubuque, IA: William C. Brown.

Myers, L. J., Speight, S. L., Highlen, P. S., Cox, C. I., Reynolds, A. L., Adams, E. M., & Hanley, C. P. (1991). Identity development and worldview: Toward an optimal conceptualization. *Journal of Counseling & Development, 70,* 54–63.

Nobles, W. (1976). Extended self: Rethinking the so-called Negro self-concept. *Journal of Black Psychology, 2,* 15–24.

Nobles, W. W. (1989). Psychological nigrescence: An Afrocentric review. *The Counseling Psychologist, 17,* 253–257.

Olmedo, E. L. (1979). Acculturation: A psychometric perspective. *American Psychologist, 34,* 1061–1070.

Parham, T. A. (1989). Cycles of psychological nigrescence. *The Counseling Psychologist, 17,* 187–226.

Parham, T. A., & Helms, J. E. (1981). The influence of Black student's racial preferences for counselor's race. *Journal of Counseling Psychology, 28,* 250–257.

Ponterotto, J. G. (1988). Racial consciousness development among White counselor trainees: A stage model. *Journal of Multicultural Counseling and Development, 16,* 146–156.

Poston, W. S. C. (1990). The biracial identity development model: A needed addition. *Journal of Counseling & Development, 69,* 152–155.

Poussaint, A. F. (1984). Study of interracial children presents positive pictures. *Children of Interracial Books Bulletin, 15,* 9–10.

Reynolds, A. L. (1989). Asian-American and Black identity: Validation of a Self-Identity Development Model of Oppressed People. *Dissertation Abstracts International, 50,* 738B–739B.

Root, M. P. P. (1990). Resolving "other" status: Identity development of biracial individuals. In L. S. Brown & M. P. P. Root (Eds.), *Complexity and diversity in feminist theory and therapy* (pp. 185–205). New York: Haworth Press.

Schuster, R. (1987). Sexuality as a continuum: The bisexual identity. In Boston Lesbian Psychologies Collective (Eds.), *Lesbian psychologies. Explorations and challenges* (pp. 56–71). Urbana, IL: University of Illinois Press.

Smith, E. M., & Vasquez, M. J. (1985). Introduction: A special issue of cross-cultural counseling. *The Counseling Psychologist, 13,* 531–536.

Speight, S. L., Myers, L. J., Cox, C. I., & Highlen, P. S. (1991). A redefinition of multicultural counseling. *Journal of Counseling & Development, 70,* 29–36.

Sue, D. W., Bernier, J. E., Durran, A., Feinberg, L., Pedersen, P., Smith, E., & Vasquez-Nuttall, E. (1982). Position paper: Cross-cultural competencies. *The Counseling Psychologist, 10,* 45–51.

Sue, D. W., & Sue, D. (1990). *Counseling the culturally different: Theory and practice* (2nd ed.). New York: Wiley.

Sue, S., & Sue, D. W. (1971). Chinese-American personality and mental health. *Amerasia Journal, 1,* 36–49.

Sue, S., & Zane, N. (1987). The role of culture and cultural techniques in psychotherapy. *American Psychologist, 42,* 37–45.

Suinn, R. M., Rickard-Figueroa, K., Lew, S., & Vigil, P. (1987). The Suinn-Lew Asian Self-Identity Acculturation Scale: An initial report. *Educational and Psychological Measurement, 47,* 401–407.

Thomas, C. W. (1971). *Boys no more.* Beverly Hills, CA: Glencoa Press.

Vontress, C. E. (1971). Racial differences: Impediments to rapport. *Journal of Counseling Psychology, 18,* 7–13.

Williams, I. J. (1975). *An investigation of the developmental stages of Black consciousness.* Unpublished doctoral dissertation, University of Cincinnati, OH.

UNIT IV

COGNITIVE DIMENSIONS OF DEVELOPMENT

Section 9

INTELLECTUAL DEVELOPMENT

CHAPTER 35

DIFFERENT WORLDS IN THE SAME CLASSROOM: STUDENTS' EVOLUTION IN THEIR VISION OF KNOWLEDGE AND THEIR EXPECTATIONS OF TEACHERS

WILLIAM G. PERRY

I want to describe an orderly variety in the ways students in your classroom make sense—including their sense of what you should be doing to be a good teacher. We labor among our students' individual differences-daily, and yet the way these differences are categorized tends to mislabel the variables I have in mind. In the parlance of college pedagogy, the phrase "individual differences" usually refers to relatively stable characteristics of persons, such as academic ability, special talents or disabilities, or the more esoteric dispositions called "learning styles." We are, of course, expected to accommodate all such differences in our teaching, perhaps by broadening our teaching styles, and you may anticipate that I am about to add to our burden.

My hope, rather is to lighten our burden, or at least to enlighten it. The variations I wish to describe are less static; they have a logical order, and most students tend to advance from one to another in response to teachings or readings that impinge on the boundaries of their intelligible universe of the moment. These variables are therefore more fun to address, and in my opinion often more determinant of what goes out of our classrooms than all the other individual differences put together. At the very least, an understanding of them makes intelligible many of those aberrations of the pedagogical relation that we must otherwise ascribe to a student's stupidity or, more generously, to a clash of "personalities."

Let's start with one of the ordinary enigmas—students' persistent misreading of examination questions. Perhaps "unreading" would be a better term. We commonly struggle in staff meetings for nearly an hour over the wording of an essay question for the midterm. The choice of topic takes only five minutes. It is the wording of the intellectual issue we wish the students to address that takes the labor. At last the issue is stated clearly, concisely, and unambiguously. Yet, if the class contains a large contingent of freshmen, the blue books will reveal that a third of the students looked at the question to locate the topic and ignored all the rest of the words, so carefully crafted. It will seem as if these students read the question as saying, "Tell all you know about . . . ," and then did so, sometimes with remarkable feats of irrelevant memory.

Such evidence of misplaced diligence can be marvelously depressing, but the realize we should not be surprised. In their years of schooling what else have these students learned to suppose an examination question intends? Clearly we have an educational job ahead of us, and we undertake it with spirit in class and in office hours, student by student. We explain with patient clarity. The students assure us that they understand and thank us profusely.

At midyears, however, most of our grateful beneficiaries dismay us by doing just what they did before. Our instructions were quite simple, and when intelligent students cannot keep a simple idea in mind, we can suspect them of being diverted by more pressing considerations. I choose here an example, extreme for this community, in the hope that stark simplicity may lay a foundation for more general observations.

A top student from a good rural school came to Harvard at a young age, possibly a year too young. Since he had won a regional prize in history, he enrolled in a section of Expository Writing that focused on writing about history. He consulted me in a state of some agitation, having failed in three attempts to write a satisfactory response to a assignment: "Consider the theory of monarchy implied in Queen Elizabeth I's Address to Members of the House of Commons in 1601." Look," he says he doesn't want that. What is this 'theory of monarchy implied' stuff anyway? He says to read between the lines. So I try to read between the lines and—huh—there's nothing there."

The intellectual problem is not too obscure. The student cannot see a theory of monarchy because he has never been confronted with two. Until he sees at least two, a monarch is a monarch and who needs a theory? I was aware, of course, that his writing instructor had tried hard, but I decided said, " I can tell what she said—all her main points. I've done it three times, longer each time. But he to try once more. We devised alternative theories together, but the more he seemed to understand, the more agitated he became. Then he complained that his mind had gone blank. I shall return later to this student's shock to help us understand the courage required of more advanced students if they are to hear what we are saying about the world. After all, why should two theories of monarchy be so terrifying?

Such curious reactions are not limited to exceptional students. In Freshman Week over the years the staff of the Bureau of Study Counsel has asked entering students to grade two answers to an essay question. Again, fully a quarter of the class gives higher grades to the essay crowded with facts utterly devoid of relevance to the question. In response, we have tried to help these students see that college instructors consider relevance the sole justification for memorizing a fact. Accordingly, we try to teach them simple reading strategies, such as surveying for a sense of the author's purpose before starting to collect detail. Half the students catch on with enthusiasm; the other half accuse us of urging them to "cheat."

This brings me to the last enigma we need to share: the range of perception in students' evaluations of their teachers. Most evaluations are invited by rating scales. The computer will give the mean and the standard deviation. As a teacher I have never found the figures very informative, and on occasion I have ventured to inquire beyond them, inviting my students to write me anonymous "fee comments." I expect a range of opinion; I would not want to please everybody. But nothing ever prepares me for the range I get. How can I possibly be the one who has "opened the world to me. Now I know what learning is about; and the rest is up to me!"—and at the same moment "the most dishonest, hypocritical and careless teacher I've had the misfortune to meet—and Harvard pays you!"

Can differences in "personality" explain all this? Every student who came to us for counseling seemed, if we listened long enough, to be attending a different college; each student enrolled in a given course was in a different course, and the instructor was an angel, a dud, and a devil. Was this variety common only among the fifteen percent of undergraduates whose distress brought them to us? We thought not, and we set out to inquire of some students who had expressed no need of our wisdom.

We asked half the freshman class to submit to tests measuring aspects of personality we thought relevant, and in May we invited representatives of all dispositions to come to tell us about their year. They responded enthusiastically. We soon learned not to ask them questions that imposed frameworks of sense-making on a conversation that we intended to be an opportunity for the students to inform us of theirs. The individual variety then exceeded our expectations, the students enjoyed it, and we parted in agreement to meet again next spring, and also in junior and senior year.

It was in this setting that the students rewarded us. As we first listened to them as freshmen, they interpreted their experience in ways that seemed harmonious with those traits of "personality" our measures had ascribed to them. But then, in sophomore year, to our astonishment, most of these students changed their "personalities"—and did so again as juniors and as seniors. Each year they interpreted their educational experience through frameworks of assumptions and expectations that placed knowledge and learning, hope, initiative, responsibility, and their teachers, in new relations. Perhaps our original tests in freshman year had reflected not so much enduring bents of personality as temporary constellations of perceived relations. Gradually we came to see that these constellations through which the students made sense of their worlds followed one another in an orderly sequence. Finding that their current ways of making sense failed to comprehend the increasing complexities and uncertainties in their intellectual and social lives, the students "realized" (as they phrased it) that the world was other than they had thought; that only a new way of seeing and thinking could encompass the new set of discrepancies, anomalies, or contradictions. Each of these new realizations comprehended the old as the old could not encompass the new. This was development, a visible, even explicit broadening of the mind—not simply change, but evolution.

We sensed that each step in this evolution involved a challenge. We had yet to realize the depth of these challenges, but we could see that some students refused, at one point or another, to take the next step. We went so far as to dub the sequence a Pilgrim's Progress and made a map of it, Slough of Despond and all. Every student, as we saw it, spoke from some place or "position" on this journey.

But it is now time to enter your classroom. You, however, are late—unavoidably, but conveniently for our purpose. The last thing you said, on Friday, was, "Next week we'll consider three theories of the economic cycle" (or the equivalent in your particular field). As restlessness sets in this Monday morning a conversation begins, and I am going to cast it in the mold of our Pilgrim's Progress. That is, I shall label the dramatic personae First Student, Two, Three, etc., letting each express in sequence the outlook from the several positions of our map.

By this device I hope not only to convey a sense of the order in the varied perceptions and expectations that await your arrival, but also to make it possible for you to imagine that each of the speakers might be one and the same student speaking from outlooks attained sequentially over a number of years—perhaps in just the four years of college.

I have already mentioned the First Student— he of the history prize. He saw me on Saturday. He sits near the door watching for you. He is too anxious to speak or even to think well. His despair about theories of monarchy has probably left him so mute that if he heard you mention "three theories of the economic cycle" at all, it only added boundlessness to his terror. His inability to understand the nature of knowledge as Harvard sees it has become less an epistemological problem than an ontological horror. If there are several theories of monarchy, why shouldn't there be infinite theories of monarchy? So is there such a thing as a monarch Is the same true of all authority and so of all obedience? Of parents and sons? Of all meaning?

The camaraderie of the dorm might have carried him through this existential crisis, but this lad seems to lack the humor to become one of the boys. His is primitive shock, but we shall find in the class other, more sophisticated approaches to the abyss.

Several low-key conversations are now going on in the room. The voice of the second student—I shall call him Two—rises above the rest as he talks to his neighbor. "What's this rigmarole about three theories of the cycle anyway? Why doesn't he give us the right one and forget the bullshit?"

Someone laughs. "You're not in high school anymore, Joe."

"Yeah, I know. Here they give you problems, not answers, I see that. That's supposed to help us learn independent thought, to find the answer on our own. That's what he said when I asked him—or I guess it's what he said, along with the rigmarole. OK, but enough is enough. We gotta know what to learn for the exam." Two's voice has become plaintive, almost desperate; there is silence as he pauses. "My roommate's in the eleven o'clock. He says his instructor really knows and really answers your questions. Maybe I should go ask her."

It is hard to portray Two's thinking without seeming to caricature it. Do I need to assure you that he exists? He has brought with him from years of schooling a clear epistemology. Knowledge, he learned early, consists of right answers, and there is a right answer for every question: e.g., spelling words, arithmetic problems, dates. These truths are discrete items and can be collected by memorization; so some people know more, others know less. ("Better" or "worse" are not applicable.) Teachers know these answers in their own fields. The answers seem to exist up there somewhere, and the teacher is privy to them.

In the stage setting of this epistemology the roles of the actors are clearly prescribed. The teacher's duty is to "give" the student the truth, the right answers, in assimilable, graduated doses. Two's duty is to "absorb" them by honest hard work known as "study." Then the teacher will "ask for them back" in the same form in which they were originally given. Two's responsibility is then to re-present them unmodified and unabridged for the teacher's inspection.

The morals of this world are equally coherent. The teacher must not ask questions in a strange from—"trick questions." That teachers often give problems to solve, withholding the answers which they already know, can at first seem an anomaly in this world, something to make sense of. As the First Student might say, "I think they're hiding things." Two has made sense of it, acknowledging that beneficent Authority should help us learn "independent thought": i.e., to find the answer for ourselves. Assigning problems therefore falls within the bounds of the moral contract so long as the teacher makes the problems clear and the procedures for solving them memorizable.

As student, the, Two's reciprocal moral duty requires him to collect truth through honest hard work, never by guessing. Right answers hit by guesswork (including "thought") are false currency, and when he accepts credit for them he feel guilty.

Freshman Adviser Perry (after November hour exams): How'd it go?

Freshman: Four 'A's.

Adviser (swallowing praise): How do you feel about that?

Freshman: Terrible. I didn't deserve any of them.

Two's logical corollary, of course, is that if he's worked hard he should get some credit even when he comes up with the wrong answer. The gods and similar authorities have always been bound by the rituals they have established for their appeasement. This myth, to the extent that Authority shares it, provides safety to the weak. The vital requirement of ritual is that nothing be omitted—that it be completed. Since neglect of the smallest detail invalidates the whole, every detail is of equal import.

It is therefore of fundamental urgency for Two that you stipulate the nature of the ritual, particularly its length. He has been stopping you in the door at the end of class.

"You said three to five pages, sir. Does that mean four?"

Can Authority refuse to answer? "Well, whatever you need."

"Oh, then, four will be satisfactory?"

"OK, sure, if they make your point."

"Thanks, sir—oh, will that be double-space or single?"

I have more than once found myself pressed to the wall and settling, to my chagrin, for "1200 words." And I have received them, tallied in the margin, the final entry a smug "1204."

Quality and "coverage" are visible entities, making obedience palpable. "Organization and coherence"—meaning the logical subordination and sequencing of relationships in the service of an overarching theme—these are not yet visible to Two. A recent study has revealed that the students who think as Two thinks use "coverage" as their criterion for "coherence" as they write, sometimes going so far as to "organize" by putting "similar" details together. If you ask Two to rewrite his paper to improve its organization, he will therefore submit more of the same.

Two knows that there are Rights and Wrongs and a cold world outside of Eden. In Eden the only role is obedience; the only sin in arrogating to oneself the knowledge of good and evil (the power to make judgments). In the Bureau's class in strategies of learning, when we urge students to find the main theme of an article or chapter first (perhaps by starting at the end) so that they can judge the function of details, those who think like Two cry out, "Do you want us to be thrown out of here?" Two recognizes the college instructor who asks him to exercise his judgment as Serpent.

Two, then, construes the world (and teachers) dualistically. Along with right and wrong, he has come to see that some teachers know, and some do not. The truth is One and Invariable, yet teachers disagree about it. There is only one possible sense to make of this without disaster to Truth: just as there are right answers and wrong answers, so there are good teachers and frauds, beneficent teachers and those who are mean. ("My roommate says his instructor really knows.")

Two thinks in a noble tradition. A study of examination questions given to freshman at Harvard at the turn of the century reveals them all to be just the kind that Two expects questions to be. They ask for memorized facts and operations in a single assumed framework of Absolute Truth. It wasn't until midcentury that half the questions would require consideration of data from two or more perspectives. And surely today there are still many ways in which we confirm Two's vision.

Indeed, the meanings Two attributes to the educational world are so sensible—and he has such ready categories for dismissing incongruities—that his system seems almost closed. And if this system were as perfect as Locke portrayed it, then all knowledge, judgment and agency would reside out there in Authority, and the student's sole duty would be to absorb. Some Twos do indeed stay closed. Our Two, however, has unknowingly opened a door by conceding legitimacy to Authority's assigning problems instead of giving answers. Solving problems, he has found, is kind of fun, and he derives more satisfaction from doing than from memorizing. In arithmetic one can even check an answer for oneself to see if it's right or wrong. This temptation to agency and judgment is the first step in a path that will lead Two away from the safety he presumes to lie in obedience in Eden toward ultimate questions about the very nature of truth itself.

What is required next is for Authority to be allowed just a bit of legitimate uncertainty. Student Three supplies it: "Well, there may have to be some different theories for a while," she ventures "after all, Ec. is sort of a new science and there's lots they don't know the answers to yet—like some things in Physics even." By using the word "yet" she has legitimized present uncertainty without disturbing her vision of an orderly Laplacean universe out there waiting to be known, bit by bit. Three's assimilation of temporary uncertainty makes the system even more vulnerable. A little temporary uncertainty legitimizes a little difference of opinion. "Temporary" can now reveal itself to extend longer and longer, and uncertainties can appear in wider domains. The mind is then likely to be overwhelmed by the sheer quantity of possibilities.

There are two Fours in the class, one a bit of a fighter, the other more trusting. I shall call them Four A (Adam) and Four B (Barbara). Four A makes sense out of the impending chaos by exploiting it. He "realizes" that the world, instead of being divided between right and wrong, is divided between those things about which right/wrong can be determined and those about which not even Authority knows. In this new domain of indeterminacy, where "Everyone has a right to his own opinion," he feels a new freedom. In this domain no one can be called wrong because the right in unknown. By implication all opinions are equally valid. This broad tolerance provides for peace in the dormitory before drawn. At the same time it means that Four A will feel outraged when you question his opinion, especially if you asked for it.

He says to Three: "Yeah, that's right. There's so much they won't know for a hundred years, so why only three theories? Anyone can have a theory, and if it's neat for them it's neat for them."

This ultimate individualism, when applied to the moral sphere, is of course absolute license, and since it is often spoken of as "relativism" it has given actual disciplined relativism a bad name. There is of course no relationship in sight, only solipsism: "My opinion is right because I have it." We called this view multiplicity, an awkward word we stole from Henry Adams. In any case, the view is not relative but absolute, just as absolute as the right/wrong dichotomy. What Four A has done is to save the dual character of the world by doubling it, leaving right/wrong on one side and if-I-can't-be-called-wrong-I'm right on the other. He feels no need as yet to relate opinions to their supporting data and limiting contexts.

Three's interest in how to solve problems and her realization of temporary uncertainty are leading her to a curiosity about "how" we know, or if we can't know yet, how we develop an opinion tenable on grounds other than "It's my opinion." Four B (Barbara) has taken a course in literary analysis in which she has discovered that "What they wanted wasn't just an answer but a 'way,' a 'how'. I came to see that what a poem means isn't just anybody's guess after all. The way they wanted us to think was maybe special to that course, but you had to put all kinds of evidence together to build an interpretation and then try it out against others. So we'd end up with a few good interpretations to choose from, like three theories maybe, but a lot of others turned out to be nonsense—at least that's how it was in that course. Maybe . . ."

Four B is on the brink. She has allowed a special case into the world of "right answers for credit." With this "way" she can be an agent in using relationships among data and contexts to generate interpretations. She realizes then that these interpretations may be compared to one another. Some few may appear most valid; others less so; others unacceptable. In the special case of this one course, Authority itself has introduced knowledge as qualitative. But a special case can be a Trojan horse. Its contents can burst forth to take over the whole fortress.

Four A (Adam) is entrenched in his efforts to expand the realm of indeterminacy at Authority's expense. If he is to discover a contextual qualitative world, he may do so more readily when the prodding comes from peers. In the bull sessions in the dorm a colleague more advanced than he may ask him, "Well, how do you substantiate that?" again and again until he discovers that things relate and that he can relate them.

Five: "Hell, everything's like that—like Barbie says, not just in one course. There isn't a thing on earth sensible people don't disagree about—and if they don't today they will tomorrow! Even the hard scientists: look what Godel did to math! It's not like Adam says, 'When no one knows anything goes.' Just because there's no single certainty in the end and individuals will have to choose—that's no reason to give up thinking. Maybe it's the reason to begin, I mean, you've gotta use all the analysis and critical thinking and stuff as advertised. Theories—they aren't the Whole Truth anyway, they're just models like they say, some of them pretty good. So you've got to know how each one works, inside with its logic and outside with the world. It's like different geometries . . . like games really."

Two interrupts. "I can't follow all this bull you're all talking. Isn't anyone going to help pin him down? How can you study for an exam with all that crap you're talking about?" Everyone looks at Two, but no one responds. "Well, maybe it's me. I mean I can learn things, but I can't seem to do what people do around here, whatever it is—interpret or something." He hangs his head.

Three attempts a rescue. "Well, I kind of agree. I mean he ought to tell us sooner or later. After all, there are right answers, right ways."

"Sure, there's rights and wrongs if you know the context," resumes Five. "It's all set by the context and the assumptions and all. Sure it gets complicated and some contexts are looser then others. Like in History and in Lit., there may be more different, defensible things to say. But still, idiot opinions, they're infinite. I thought everybody knew that."

Five "realized" all this only eighteen months ago, but he has so completely reorganized his view of the world, and in the process perhaps recatalogued his memory, that he has forgotten that the world ever seemed different from the way he now sees it to be. We wouldn't forget—or might we?

We should pause here. A rift has been revealed in the class, and the rest of the conversation will further our understanding of it. Five has taken us over a watershed, a critical traverse in our Pilgrim's Progress. On the first side of the watershed the students were preoccupied with the frightening failure of most college teachers to fulfill their assigned role as dispensers of knowledge. Even Barbara, who has mastered the initial processes of analytical, contextual, relativistic thought, has assimilated this form of thought by assigning it the status of an exception in the old context of What They Want. Five, in crossing the ridge of the divide, has seen before him a perspective in which the relation of learner to knowledge is radically transformed. In this new context, Authority, formerly source and dispenser of all knowing, is suddenly authority, ideally a resource, a mentor, a model, and potentially a colleague in consensual estimation of interpretations of reality. What-They-Want is now a special case within this context. As for the students, they are now no longer receptacles but the primary agents responsible for their own learning.

Not all teachers will fulfill these expectations, of course, but to Five, Six, Seven, and Eight their failures will not be so demoralizing—or preoccupying. Most students will turn their attention to the implications of the new perspective: choosing among interpretations in their studies, making decisions in a relativistic world, and deciding how to make commitments to career, persons, values and to what they "know" in a world in which even Physics changes its mind. Some, perhaps lacking support or stuck in old resentments, will opt out by shrugging off responsibility.

As students speak from this new perspective, they speak more reflectively. And yet the underlying theme continues: the learners' evolution of what it means to them to know.

Another student now speaks to Five. 'Well, I've just come to see what you're talking about and it helps. I've begun to be able to stand back and look at my thinking—what metaphors and stuff I'm using. Not just in my studies, I mean I find the same goes for people. I've begun to get the feel too of where the other guy is coming from and what's important to him—huh, this sounds corny, but I get along better with most people."

There's a silence, then Five speaks more tentatively in a lower voice. "Yeah, I can do this in my head. I like learning the games and seeing what model fits best where and all. But I can't see how to make any big decisions—there's always so many other possibilities. That's been a real downer. I list all the reasons for doing this and for doing that and all the reasons against and then I get depressed [laughs], so I go back to playing the games, 'cause that's something I can do well. I mean I get 'fine critical thinking' and jazz like that all over the margins of my papers and it keeps me going, but where to? I know it's I'm still trying to be too sure, but I can't let go, I don't want to just plunge."

A student is sprawled in the back of the room. "Games is right! So who cares? If they want independent thought, just give it to them. Always have an opinion, I say—but don't forget to be 'balanced' and all that crap."

"Yeah," replies Six, "and then when you get to General Motors, what's good for them will be good for you. I was lost a whole year, felt like copping out like that plenty—then thought what'll that be like when I'm forty? Now I've got it narrowed down some. I don't see how some guys seem to know from age two—always knowing they'll be doctors. Did they ever have a doubt? Or will it hit 'em Later? Like midlife crisis, huh? Anyway guys like me—you gotta plunge, I think. I'm not quite there yet, but I can see there's different ways of plunging. You can jump in just to get away from the agony—or you can do your thinking, and when your guts tell you 'this is it,' you listen. They're your guts. I mean you gotta plunge, in a way, because you know you can't be sure—you're risking it—but it'll be sort of a positive plunge. And once I'm in, I think everything else will fall in line."

"I did that last spring," says Seven, "and now that I'm getting deeper into things—I'm in Bio—it helps, feeds on itself I guess and I see it isn't narrowing down like I thought it would but spreading out bigger than I can handle. But I wouldn't say—I wouldn't say."

"That it straightens everything else out?" The prompting comes from Eight. She laughs ruefully, "I got everything straightened out last spring. I'd gone round and round. There was premed I've been in forever, I'd got more and more into Linguistics, and here was this guy I'd been going with who wanted to get married. So I thought all my thoughts and everyone else's and then one day told my parents, 'Sorry, Linguistics is it. I've really listened, but this has to be mine.' And then I let the guy go to the Amazon to study birds without me. Did everything straighten out? Like hell it did, and then it did, in a funny way. I mean there was the thesis in Linguistics; I still love that guy and don't want to marry him; I'm all wound up in this day care thing; my father's sick in Francisco, and I met this intern who's taking care of him, and and and. Before, it seemed there was just premed or Linguistics, marriage or no marriage, so now I ought to feel worse, all divided up, but it's better. I find I even believe in some things, like they're really true." She pauses; no one says anything. "It's like with the thesis, somehow. Seems I hit on something new-well, not new, just joining a couple of old procedures to tackle an old problem they'd never been used on before. My tutor says I'm really on to something—we can't find anything wrong about it or too far out. I've never known something new to be mine like this before. And the feeling goes over into all the rest in a way, only I don't have my tutor to check me out. It's all bits and pieces with cracks in it, but I'm the center of something, a place from where I see things as I see them and all that jazz. Get things together—that's it I guess, not getting everything I want but getting things together. Oh hell, maybe all that holds me together is irony."

After a moment, somebody, laughs, "Nice try, nice try, but these verities seem a long way from those three theories of the economic cycle, whatever they are. Anybody done the reading?"

"Sure the reading's important," says Six, "but what we've all been saying does connect. What I want to know is what he does with those three theories. As a person, I mean, an economist-type person. I mean he seems to care about Ec.—he's kind of zestful about it really. I want to know what he does with all this. Not just which he thinks is right but does he, or if all three are valid, then what? I don't think he's kidding himself, so what does he do? Let's some of us ask him for lunch someday [laughs]. See if he's for real."

At this point you hurriedly enter the room. Under your arm you carry a sheaf of forms from University Hall. They are questionnaires for students' evaluation of teaching—an experimental form, it says, for trial at midterm. You have been assured that giving them out is purely voluntary.

You—and I—are at "Nine" (so we hope), the farthest reach of our map. At Nine we have had time to realize that growth is not linear as the metaphor of our map implies, but recursive. We turn and turn again, and when we come across our own footsteps we hope it will be with the perspective of some altitude and humor. We have also seen that in the several areas of their lives, such as their work, politics, social relationships, family, or religion, people (including ourselves) often employ somewhat different levels of thought. As teachers, we often use these variations by finding the areas of students most sophisticated thought and helping them to move by analogy into areas in which they are less advanced. Indeed, students, will often do so spontaneously.

But first, you may ask, "An I supposed to do something about all this development?" I must state my premise. I do believe that the purpose of liberal education is to assist students to learn to think the way Eight is thinking. The goals are stated in the catalogues of all liberal arts colleges. In these terms the development the students reveal is a Good, and we are enjoined to promote it. You may disagree, sensing that I am loading on you a trip into personality development; your responsibility, you may say, is to teach History. I hope you have sensed that this makes no difference. Students who have not progressed beyond the outlook of Three will be unable to understand what you as a modern historian want them to understand about History. To the extent that you wish your subject to become accessible to as many students as reasonably possible, the development we have been tracing remains a Good, and you have already been promoting it.

After all, the students who told us of this adventure were not taking a course in cognitive development complete with maps. They came to "realize" through the necessities of the intellectual disciplines as you taught them. This is not to say, however, that as teachers we have nothing to gain from a more explicit awareness of the steps in the students' progression. At the very least, an understanding of Two's expectations somewhat reduces the personal abrasion of his anger. Similarly, we can feel less assaulted by the outrage of Four when he feels we do not accept his "opinion." Beyond saving our energies, this awareness extends the possibility of our staying in communication long enough for seeds to take root.

Our outline of the successive ways in which students make sense throws some light on the potentials and constraints of this communication. It has been observed for two millennia that in any learning situation the learner requires the support of some elements that are recognizable and familiar. Then, if the experience is to be anything more than drill, the second requirement is a degree of challenge. In the decade since the publication of our scheme, a younger generation of teacher-researchers has spelled out the characteristics of learners at each position and traced the sequential changes in the conditions students experience as support and challenge as they progress. Two, for instance, feels supported by explicit directions—supported enough to tolerate the challenge of being directed to read contradictory authorities. Looking back at the First Student we see him overwhelmed by challenge; he may make it through, but only with the community's support—and time. Looking ahead, Five feels supported in being turned loose on the reserve shelf to find and write up an interesting problem, and can be challenged afterward by such a question as "And what did doing all that mean to you?"

This question of personal meaning leads toward the concerns voiced by Six, Seven, or Eight, who are searching to orient themselves in the profusion of legitimate possibilities they discovered in the relativism of position Five. They seek a way to make commitments to career, companions, values, and to make them wholeheartedly in a world in knowledge and meaning are tentative. In the midst of this challenge they seek support in models, especially in their teachers. In providing this support, the best we can do is to let them see that see that we share with them the risks that inhere in all commitments. Then their sense of ultimate aloneness in their affirmations becomes itself a bond of community.

It is revealing to observe what happens when the teacher's and the students' ways of making sense are uncompromisingly disparate by two or more levels. If students Five through Eight are taught in the manner expected by Two, they may be bored or frustrated, by they understand what the teacher is doing. In the reverse of this mismatch, however, when students at the level of Two are taught in a manner that is good teaching only for Five and above, they panic and retreat. Over the past twenty-five years the position of the modal entering freshman at Harvard has advanced from around Three to nearly Five. Yet many Twos and Threes and Fours are among us. Since we tend as teachers to address the more responsive students at and above the mode, we can be concerned about the remainder, who feel they are outsiders to the enterprise. I hope, if only for their learning, that they are fortunate in their advisers and their friends, and that their instructors, if opportunity permits, confirm the legitimacy of their bewilderment.

This concern has brought me to my last observation. What powers do we not have? Clearly (if we remember), we cannot push anyone to develop, or "get them to see" or "impact" them. The causal metaphors hidden in English verbs give us a distracting vocabulary for pedagogy. The tone is Lockean and provocative of resistance. We can provide, we can design opportunities. We can create setting in which students who are ready will be more likely to make new kinds of sense.

But what happens to the old kinds of sense? Where do yesterday's certainties go? Are Two and Three and Four the only ones in need of support? Five and Six and Seven and Eight (and you and I) have dared at each step to approach the abyss where the First student has stumbled into meaninglessness. For the advancing students a new world has opened from each new perspective, to be sure, but the mind is quicker than the guts. The students had invested hope and aspiration and trust and confidence in the simpler design of their world of yesterday. How long will it take them to dig out their vitality and reinvest it in the new, problematical vision? And all the while they are told that these are the happiest days of their lives.

The students do find their gains expensive and fulfilling, but does no one see the losses? If no one else does, can they? They can but wonder: "What is this cloud, this reluctance?" It can't be grief, can it? I believe that students will not be able to take a next step until they have come to terms with the losses that inhere in the step just taken.

In ordinary daily work, our understanding of how students see, whether we agree or not,

legitimizes their being as makers of sense. If they make overly simple sense, we must ask them to look further. But by acknowledging that making sense as they used to do was legitimate in its own time, and even a necessary step, we empower them to learn new and better sense. Our recognition is most encouraging in moments when the student is moving from one level of sense-making to another. When the transition happens right in front of us, we will see the eager realization and then, perhaps very shortly, the shadow of the cloud. We say something like, "Yes, you've got the point all right . . . but we do wish it made things simpler." The most heartening leaven for the mind can come from just such a brief acknowledgment as this.

Note

WILLIAM G. PERRY has taught in school and college, and, as the first Director of the Harvard University Bureau of Study Counsel, has listened to students for thirty-four years. He is the author, with his associates, of *Forms of Intellectual and Ethical Development in the College Years.*

References

Copes, Larry (compiler), Bibliography and Copy Service Catalog: Perry Development Scheme. SIP. Paul, MN (10429 Barnes Way, 55075), ISEM, Oct. 1984.

Knefelkemp L. Lee and Janet L. Cornfeld. "Combining Stages and Style in the Design of Learning Environments." Address to American College Personnel Association, 1979. Reprints obtainable from author at College of Education, University of Maryland, College Park, MD 20742.

Perry, William, G. (and associates), *Forms of Intellectual and Ethical Development in the College Years.* NY: Holt, Rinehart and Winston, 1970

Perry, William, C., "Cognitive and Ethical Growth: The Making of Meaning" in Chickering, Arthur (editor). *The Modern American College.* San Francisco: JosseyBass, 1981.

Perry, William G. "Examsmanship in the Liberal Arts: A Study in Educational Epistemology." Harvard College, 1963. Reprints available at the Harvard-Danforth Center. Also reprinted in Zeender, Karl and Linda Morris (editors), *Persuasive Writing: A College Reader* (NY: Harcourt Brace Jovanovich, 1981).

Chapter 36

Sharing in the Costs of Growth

William G. Perry, Jr.

During my visits to the conference groups and workshops, I had a feeling that developmental this and that (e.g., Perry's Scheme, whatever *that* might be) had been pushed onto people a bit these three days. In one group, a person suddenly broke into the conversation to say, "I don't know what's going on! I wish I knew what this conference was all about. All I'm doing is sitting wondering all the time whether I should sell my house. I shouldn't worry so about such a thing. My parents bought and sold lots of houses when I was young and never thought anything about it. I don't see why I'm so upset about it, but I am. And I can't seem to see how this fits into the Perry Scheme."

I am not about to fit such an experience into anything, much less the Perry Scheme. However, I want to put that experience up on the shelf, for a minute, because I think it may help us to understand something important about development, no matter whose scheme one uses to look at development—something we have not mentioned at this conference.

First, let me review three or four of those little discoveries of the obvious that we all make in life. When we first come into this world, it is obvious that there are authorities and that they know what they are doing, or at least so it seems. They tell us what to do and what not to do, and so they know what they are doing. That is discovery 1.

Discovery 2 is that they do not know what they are doing after all. And since they do not seem to know what they are doing and do not have all the answers, we think, "Hurray! As soon as I can get out from under their tyranny I'm free, and any opinion is as good as any other, mine included."

Discovery 3 is that when I get out from under their tyranny I walk smack into a plate-glass wall and find that I am still subject to a tyranny, not of *they*, but of *fact*. And in that tyranny of reality I discover that, although there are a lot of differences of opinion among reasonable people, not every opinion is as good as any other, including some which I have that are no good at all. And then I have to get to work and start thinking about all these things. I think about various ways in which very reasonable people disagree very reasonably in wide areas. For instance, I am told that all the Euclidian geometry I learned was just a nice little game with its own rules. Of course, one can be right or wrong within the rules of Euclidian geometry, but the chances that Euclidian geometry conforms to anything in this universe, I am now told, are only about one in three billion; there are other geometries that have a better probability of conforming to something in the universe. I also find that in such important matters as religion very reasonable people disagree very intensely. I examine various religions and I find that some of them have as much claim to be more than superstition as anything I believe. Suddenly I realize that it is a little questionable to go around killing other people to the glory of the particular god I believe in. So I have discovered the obvious 3.

Then I make one more discovery, another obvious one, that I am faced with the challenge of affirming myself and my life as a person. Given so many differences of opinion among reasonable people, differences which reason alone cannot resolve, I see that I can never be sure I am making the "right" decisions in life. And yet I must decide. Oh, I have been told never to make a wrong decision lest I regret it all my life, but now I see I have no protection against regret. Unless I am going to weasel out of really living, I must choose what I believe in and own the consequences, and never know what lay down the roads I did not take. I have discovered what Robert Frost meant, and what it means to commit.

Why have I just rehearsed these four obvious discoveries? There has been all this talk at this conference about the Perry Scheme, and if some of you are in doubt about what it is—that is it. I mean, students reported to us about making these discoveries, and that is what the Perry Scheme is, nothing more. It took thirty of us, listening to students for fifteen years to make these obvious discoveries, and then we looked at each other and said, "Fifteen years for *this*?"

So the next questions are, "What's so good about advancing along such a series of discoveries (or any other scheme of development we have been considering)? Why should we educators devote ourselves to promoting discoveries like that? Why should we push or entice or seduce people to go along with discoveries like that?" I know of one reason, and that is that since the world is, indeed, complicated, it is better to have a matching set of complicated ideas to deal with it than to try to use a simple idea that does not fit. Perhaps something more can be said for these discoveries, however. One is that by a considerable study of the different ways in which reasonable people see things, we are put in the position to learn that the most valuable of all the qualities of maturity of which Doug Heath talked this morning is compassion.

I am not about to expand on the social utility of compassion. I want to ask some special questions about this conference: "If development is all so obvious, then *why is it so hard*? If it's all that simple and all that obvious, then what in the world are we here for? Why *is* it so hard to grow? Why is it even harder to help *other* people grow? What have we been talking about for three days?"

Over the past several months, some of the staff in our little office have been asking students about how they learn. We just ask, "Tell us about how you experience learning." The usual response is, "You mean *really* learning?" There seems to be a distinction between "just" learning and "really" learning, which is what the students want to talk about. "Really" learning invariably refers to experiences in which one sees

the world and onself in a new and broader light—in short, to those very discoveries that mark the major steps into maturity I have been talking about.

I want to share with you the response of a young woman, a freshman. She said that so far she had been just learning more things at Harvard—"kind of flat"—and that the last time she had really learned was back in high school. She had a social science teacher whom she admired and he introduced to the class one of the Ames experiments with the revolving window. (You know it: There is this odd-shaped window that revolves on an axis and you see it revolve and you *know* it revolves; but then the lighting is changed and the window does not revolve; it oscillates from side to side, and you *know* it oscillates; and then the lighting is changed back and there the window is, revolving.) She said her teacher looked around and said to no one in particular, "So what do you make of *that*?" and no one said anything. "And all of a sudden I *saw*. I mean I saw how much we bring with us to our perception of things, how much we construct our worlds. And I realized that if this was true of windows, how about people? parents? myself, too? The whole world opened up to me, sort of, how everybody makes their own meanings, how different things can look in a different light so to speak."

She then went on to say how the same experiment had been demonstrated at Harvard as just one more gimmick of perceptual illusion. The interviewer, bored with this complaint, brought her back to that moment in high school: "How did you feel then?" "Oh, it was awful. I mean, my world was shattered. I guess it's sort of naïve to use a word like this here, but it was like I lost my innocence. I mean nothing could ever be for sure—like it seems—I mean, again."

Our interviewer then asked, "How come you stayed with it instead of just laughing it off and forgetting it?"

"Oh, that was because of the teacher! You see, I trusted him, and I knew he knew. I mean, we didn't talk about it really, but he just looked at me and I knew he knew—what I'd learned—and what I'd lost! I guess because he knew what I'd lost, I could stay with what I'd seen."

So what I am talking about is something that we have left out in our talk of promoting development: What do we do about the house we leave when we go to a new place? When we leave the way we saw the world, in which everything was just so and just as we thought, and we see it all differently, we move into a world where all of what was solid and known is crumbling. And the new is untried. What do we do about the house we just sold out of? What do we do about the old simple world? It may be a great joy to discover a new and more complex way of thinking and seeing, but what do we do about all the hopes that we had invested and experienced in those simpler terms? When we leave those terms behind, are we to leave hope, too?

Does the teacher have a responsibility here, not only to promote growth and development, but to help people to do something with the losses?

I want to go back to the words: "Because he knew what I'd lost, I could stay with what I'd seen." If a loss has been known, if a pain of mine has been known and shared by somebody, if somebody has been aware of one of my pains, then I can go on. I can let that pain die in some way and go on to reinvest the hope. (Not that I ever really get entirely over it, you understand. What happens to the wounds of the past? Theodore Reik was asked that question, you remember. He said, "Well, they ache in bad weather.") But still, if these things have been known and shared, then somehow it is possible for me to do a strange thing called grieving, which I do not pretend to understand. It seems all right to let it hurt.

But if it is not allowed to grieve or to hurt, I have to deny the truth to have my chin up. If my loss has never "lived," socially, then I must keep it alive myself, protect it like a responsibility, even. Then I do not know why it is that I get stuck. It comes to me as a sort of theorem, that when you have taken one step in development, you cannot take another until you have grieved the losses of the first. I wonder how that hypothesis would look in testing. Jessie Taft, who was a therapist, wrote, "The therapist becomes the repository of the outworn self." So too, this teacher of social sciences became the repository of this young woman's innocence.

What about the losses in what we have been calling "career development"? In good times, when there is a world of plenty out there, students can be butcher, baker, candlestick maker; they can be anything. All they have to do is choose. It feels like a narrowing down. It feels as if you are losing all the other selves that you

could have been. So I have always wanted to write vocational theory all over again; not about how you choose what you are going to do, but about how you give up all the other selves you are not going to be.

Nowadays, of course, fewer of those opportunities are available out there. So, in the last few years, we have had a different kind of feeling, one of desperation. In order to make it in this competitive world everything becomes contingent on what I do right now. It is an unbroken chain. If I slip any place, I have had it. My whole life rests on this one sentence that I am trying to write, so I cannot finish the sentence.

I do not know what to say about grieving and the teaching of grieving, because I do not understand it. I know it goes by waves. I know that when you take yourself off someplace, and say, "Now I will face this, and grieve," nothing happens. But when you open up a bureau drawer and see something there that reminds you of something, then you have had it. I do not understand it, but I know that we do not allow it enough in our culture and we do not have the legitimizing rituals for the experience; therefore our people cannot grow well. They have to leave parts of themselves behind. Although I do not know how to teach people how to grieve, I have found that the teacher or counselor can make it clear that the pain is legitimate.

Such, then, is surely our responsibility: to stay, as it were, with the student's past and to the very extent that we invite the student to grow beyond it. It is a challenging trask. Yet, just as our students can tell us why the obvious is so difficult (were we only to listen), so they may also tell us how we can help them to learn that the pain of growth is not a shame of youth that separates them from us.

I am reminded of a privileged moment I was given recently. A young woman had given me a lovely time all year. This woman, a freshman, is very accomplished; she was the president of her class in school and captain of the swimming team, and she had straight As in one of the most challenging schools in the country. But something was all wrong at college. She came to see me, we chatted, and she worked things out. I found that it was not only my privilege but my duty to enjoy her and to appreciate the trip she gave me on the roller coaster of adolescence. It was marvelous and sometimes very painful, but always somehow beautiful. Of course, she sometimes scared me by carrying too much sail. But I was enjoying it; I knew who I was supposed to be—the good uncle who listened. Then there came a day when she seemed profoundly moved, so I fastened my seatbelt. She had decided to transfer, she said, and she was feeling sad about leaving friends she had taken so long to make. There was a pause. Then she said, "Yesterday I was walking to class, and all of a sudden it came over me, that my days are numbered." I did my best not to stir. She looked at me. "Then it came to me that these days with you are numbered, too. Like there comes a time when you have to move over and make room for others who need the time more." And then I thought of her as an older sister with her four younger sisters. And I said, "Well, gee, yeh, I know. And I've been thinking how I'll *miss* you." And she said, "Oh, really? Have you been thinking that way, too?" And so she just kept looking at me. It was one of those silences that went on for about fifteen minutes. About every five minutes or so she said softly, "Yes." Now I realized

that she was a bright person and was putting things together. One of the things she was looking at was a guy whose days also were numbered, and by a lot smaller number than hers, and she looked me right in the eye for a long time. After a long time we got up. Somehow I decided it was time to say something, and I heard my voice say, "Growing is so bitter, so *bittersweet.*"

I did not hear the condescension in that remark until too late, and my inner critic turned on me in fury. "There you go, ruining the most beautiful moments again with your sappy platitudes." Well, I have learned that when I have made a mistake I am not the best person to try picking up the pieces, so I bit my tongue and waited. She looked at me without wavering and said gently, "And bittersweet for you, too." With that she touched my hand and left.

I have been finding that growing at this conference is bitter, bittersweet, and if I may let that young woman speak for all of us, I think she would say, gently, "And for you, too."

CHAPTER 37

REFLECTIVE JUDGMENT: THEORY AND RESEARCH ON THE DEVELOPMENT OF EPISTEMIC ASSUMPTIONS THROUGH ADULTHOOD

PATRICIA M. KING AND KAREN STROHM KITCHENER

The reflective judgment model (RJM) describes the development of complex reasoning in late adolescents and adults, and how the epistemological assumptions people hold are related to the way they make judgments about controversial (ill-structured) issues. This article describes the theoretical assumptions that have guided the development of the RJM in the last 25 years, showing how these ideas influenced the development of assessment protocols and led to the selection of research strategies for theory validation purposes. Strategies discussed here include a series of longitudinal studies to validate the proposed developmental sequence, cross-sectional studies examining age/educational level differences, and studies of domain specificity. Suggestions for assessing and promoting reflective thinking based on these findings are also offered here.

Do the benefits of inoculating health care workers against smallpox outweigh the risks? Will a proposed urban growth policy protect farmland without sacrificing jobs? Is affirmative action an effective tool for promoting genuine access to higher education? Controversial problems such as these about which "reasonable people reasonably disagree" are called ill-structured problems (Churchman, 1971; Wood, 1983); they are characterized by two features: that they cannot be defined with a high degree of completeness, and that they cannot be solved with a high degree of certainty. In the last 25 years, we have investigated how late adolescents and adults come to understand and make judgments about these kinds of controversial problems. In examining the responses that hundreds of individuals across a wide range of age and educational levels have given to such questions, we have made three major observations: (a) there are striking differences in people's underlying assumptions about knowledge, or epistemic assumptions; (b) these differences in assumptions are related to the way people make and justify their own judgments about ill-structured problems; and (c) there is a developmental sequence in the patterns of responses and judgments about such problems. The reflective judgment model (RJM; King & Kitchener, 1994; K. S. Kitchener & King, 1981) provides a theoretical framework for understanding and organizing these observations.

In this article, we begin by presenting the original theoretical grounding and underlying assumptions that have guided the development of the RJM, as well as the influence of subsequent theoretical developments, and then show how these assumptions guided the development of assessment protocols and led to the selection of research strategies for theory validation purposes. The next major section of this article summarizes research on the RJM that tested the theoretical claims about the development of reflective judgment. Last, we explore some of the implications for practice and research based on the theoretical ideas and empirical findings presented here.

Reflective Judgement Model

The RJM is a model of the development of reflective thinking from late adolescence through adulthood. This construct was first defined by Dewey (1933), who argued that reflective judgments are initiated when an individual recognizes that there is controversy or doubt about a problem that cannot be answered by formal logic alone, and involve careful consideration of one's beliefs in light of supporting evidence. This kind of reasoning remains a central goal of education, especially higher education; this is evident in several recent national reports on undergraduate education, each of which reiterated the need for college graduates to think reflectively (American Association of Colleges and Universities [AAC&U], 2002; American Association of Higher Education, American College Personnel Association [ACPA], & National Association of Student Personnel Administrators, 1998; ACPA, 1994). The RJM describes a progression of seven major steps in the development of reflective thinking leading to the capacity to make reflective judgments; each step represents a qualitatively different epistemological perspective. In defining these perspectives, we use K. S. Kitchener's (1983) definition of epistemic cognition (as distinguished from cognition and metacognition), focusing on individuals' underlying assumptions about knowledge and how it is gained. For each step in this progression (which we call stages, as defined below) the RJM includes a description of individuals' views of knowledge and concepts of justification, showing the relationship between the epistemological assumptions people hold and the way they make judgments about controversial (ill-structured) issues. The model shows how the assumptions are interrelated and how they reflect an internal logic within each stage. (See Table 1.) In the following description, we offer a general overview of these seven stages and offer examples from Stage 4, which is characteristic of the reasoning of a majority of college students, and Stage 7, which is indicative of the kind of reasoning many colleges aspire to teach (AAC&U) and which has been associated with the kind of thinking skills adults need to function effectively in today's complex societies (Baxter Magolda, in press; Kegan, 1994). These examples illustrate how qualitatively different sets of epistemic assumptions are associated with distinctly different ways

of justifying beliefs in adulthood. Because a detailed descriptions of each stage is available elsewhere (King & Kitchener, 1994), here we offer only a brief summary of the seven stages.

As an introduction to this developmental progression, consider the seven stages grouped into three levels: prereflective thinking (Stages 1–3), quasi-reflective thinking (Stages 4–5), and reflective thinking (Stages 6–7). We are aware that labels such as these (e.g., "absolutist") risk being interpreted as overly simplistic reflections of complex epistemological perspectives and that similar terms are used to refer to quite different epistemologies (as documented by Hofer & Pintrich, 1997). For this reason, we use numbers to reflect the order in which the epistemological perspective typically emerges and offer these broader categories as a more general introduction to the model. Although clustering qualitatively different stages into levels reduces complexity by collapsing stages within levels and highlighting similarities, this strategy also risks obscuring within-level differences. Thus, the summaries that follow should be read with the understanding that important differences exist between stages, both within and across levels.

A major hallmark of *prereflective thinking* is that knowledge is assumed to be certain, and accordingly, that single correct answers exist for all questions and may be known with absolute certainty, usually from authority figures. Welland ill-structured problems are not differentiated, as all problems are assumed to be well structured. Further, those using prereflective assumptions do not use evidence to reason toward a conclusion, relying instead on a restatement of beliefs or on unsubstantiated personal opinions. With *quasi-reflective thinking* comes the recognition that uncertainty is a part of the knowing process, the ability to see knowledge as an abstraction, and the recognition that knowledge is constructed. This is a major advance, as it lays a foundation for the construction of beliefs that are internally derived, not simply accepted from others. Further, evidence is now understood as a key part of the knowing process, as it provides an alternative to dogmatic assertions that are characteristic of prereflective thinking. Those using quasi-reflective assumptions are aware that different approaches or perspectives on controversial issues rely on different types of evidence and different rules of evidence, and that factors like these contribute to different ways of framing issues. Here are two examples of Stage 4 reasoning:

Stage 4 Reasoning, Example 1

Interviewer (I): "Can you say that one point of view is better and another worse?"

Respondent (R): "No, I really can't on this issue. It depends on your beliefs since there is no way of proving either one."

I: "Can you say that one is more accurate than the other?"

R: "No, I can't. I believe they're both the same as far as accuracy."

Stage 4 Reasoning, Example 2

I: "Can you say one view of creation is right and one is wrong?"

R: "No, because no one can prove how the world was created or how man evolved. Scientists can get close to it—an actual answer. When it comes right down to it, as to the actual change, they don't know because they can't draw a straight relationship between apes and man. There isn't a straight relationship . . . "

In quasi-reflective reasoning, the link between gathering evidence and making a conclusion is tenuous; this link becomes explicit in reflective thinking, the third level of the RJM.

Reflective thinkers consistently and comfortably use evidence and reason in support of their judgments. They argue that knowledge claims must be understood in relation to the context in which they were generated, but that they can be evaluated for their coherence and consistency with available information. Because new data or new perspectives may emerge as knowledge is constructed and reconstructed, individuals using assumptions of reflective thinking remain open to reevaluating their conclusions and knowledge claims.

Stage 7 Reasoning, Example 1

I: "Can you ever say you know for sure?"

R: "It's [the view that the Egyptians built the pyramids] very far along the continuum of what is probable."

I: "Can you say one is right and one is wrong?"

R: "Right and wrong are not comfortable categories to assign to this kind of item—more or less like or reasonable—more or less in keeping with what the facts seem to be."

Stage 7 Reasoning, Example 2

R: "It's my belief that you have to be very skeptical about what you read for popular consumption . . . even for professional consumption."

I: "How do you ever know what to believe?"

R: "I read widely . . . of many points of view. Partly [it's] reliance on people you think you can rely on, who seem to be reputable journalists, who make measured judgments. Then reading widely and estimating where the reputable people line up or where the weight of the evidence lies."

These examples illustrate the kinds of developmentally ordered differences in the way people reason about ill-structured problems that are described in the RJM.

Theoretical Assumptions Underlying the RJM

We turn next to one of the questions that is the focus of this volume, the paradigmatic assumptions underlying each theory of personal epistemology. Because research on the RJM spans more than 25 years, we will introduce the theoretical assumptions from both historical and contemporaneous perspectives.

Developmental traditions. The RJM evolved out of a careful examination of the few models of late adolescent and adult intellectual development that existed in the late 1970s. Our initial conceptualization (K. S. Kitchener & King, 1981) was grounded in the cognitive-developmental tradition of Piaget (1965; Piaget & Inhelder, 1969) and Kohlberg (1969). Other developmental theorists in this tradition whose work informed our early conceptualization of the RJM were Perry (1968, 1970), Broughton (1975, 1978), Loevinger (1976), and Harvey, Hunt, and Schroder (1961). The cognitive-developmental tradition has much in common with more recent constructive-developmental perspectives (e.g.,

TABLE 1
Summary of Reflective Judgment Stages

Preflective Thinking	Quasireflective Thinking	Reflective Thinking
Stage 1	**Stage 4**	**Stage 6**
View of knowledge: Knowledge is assumed to exist absolutely and concretely; it is not understood as an abstraction. It can be obtained with certainty by direct observation.	*View of knowledge:* Knowledge is uncertain, and knowledge claims are idiosyncratic to the individual because situational variables (such as incorrect reporting of data, data lost over time, or disparities in access to information) dictate that knowing always involves an element of ambiguity.	*View of knowledge:* Knowledge is constructed into individual conclusions about ill-structured problems on the basis of information from a variety of sources. Interpretations that are based on evaluations of evidence across contexts and on the evaluated opinions of reputable others can be known.
Concept of justification: Beliefs need no justification because there is assumed to be an absolute correspondence between what is believed to be true and what is true. Alternate beliefs are not perceived.	*Concept of justification:* Beliefs are justified by giving reasons and using evidence, but the arguments and choice of evidence are idiosyncratic (e.g., choosing evidence that fits an established belief).	*Concept of justification:* Beliefs are justified by comparing evidence and opinion from different perspectives on an issue or across different contexts and by constructing solutions that are evaluated by criteria such as the weight of the evidence, the utility of the solution, or the pragmatic need for action.
"I know what I have seen."	*"I would be more inclined to believe evolution if they had proof. It is just like the pyramids: I do not think we will ever know. Who are you going to ask? No one was there."*	*"It is very difficult in this life to be sure. There are degrees of sureness. You come to a point at which you are sure enough for a personal stance on the issue."*
Stage 2	**Stage 5**	**Stage 7**
View of knowledge: Knowledge is assumed to be absolutely certain or certain but not immediately available. Knowledge can be obtained directly through the senses (as in direct observation) or via authority figures.	*View of knowledge:* Knowledge is contextual and subjective because it is filtered through a person's perceptions and criteria for judgment. Only interpretations of evidence, events, or issues may be known.	*View of knowledge:* Knowledge is the outcome of a process of reasonable inquiry in which solutions to ill-structured problems are constructed. The adequacy of those solutions is evaluated in terms of what is most reasonable or probable according to the current evidence, and it is reevaluated when relevant new evidence, perspectives, or tools of inquiry become available.

(continued)

TABLE 1 (continued)

Prereflective Thinking	Quasireflective Thinking	Reflective Thinking
Stage 2 (continued)	Stage 5 (continued)	Stage 7 (continued)
Concept of justification: Beliefs are unexamined and unjustified or justified by their correspondence with the beliefs of an authority figure (such as a teacher or parent). Most issues are assumed to have a right answer, so there is little or no conflict in making decisions about disputed issues.	*Concept of justification:* Beliefs are justified within a particular context by means of the rules of inquiry for that context and by context-specific interpretations of evidence. Specific beliefs are assumed to be context specific or are balanced against other interpretations, which complicates (and sometimes delays) conclusions.	*Concept of justification:* Beliefs are justified probabilistically on the basis of a variety of interpretive considerations, such as the weight of the evidence, the explanatory value of the interpretations, the risk of erroneous conclusions, consequences of alternative judgments, and the interrelationsof these factors. Conclusions are defended as representing the most complete, plausible, or compelling understandingof an issue on the basis of the available evidence.
"If it is on the news, it has to be true."	*"People think differently and so they attack the problem differently. Other theories could be as true as my own, but based on different evidence. "*	*"One can judge an argument by how well thought-out the positions are, what kinds of reasoning and evidence are used to support it, and how consistent the way one argues on this topic is as compared with how one argues on other topics."*
Stage 3		
View of knowledge: Knowledge is assumed to be absolutely certain or temporarily uncertain. In areas of temporary uncertainty, only personal beliefs can be known until absolute knowledge is obtained. In areas of absolute certainty, knowledge is obtained from authorities.		
Concept of justification: In areas in which certain answers exist, beliefs are justified by reference to authorities' views. In areas in which answers do not exist, beliefs are defended as personal opinion because the link between evidence and beliefs is unclear.		
"When there is evidence that people can give to convince everybody one way or another, then it will be knowledge; until then, it is just a guess."		

Note. From *Developing Reflective Judgment* (p. 14–15), by P. M. King and K. S. Kitchener, 1994, San Francisco: Jossey-Bass. Copyright 1994 by John Wiley & Sons, Inc. Reprinted with permission.

Fischer & Pruyne, 2002; Kegan, 1982, 1994). What these two approaches share are (a) the underlying assumption that meaning is constructed, (b) the emphasis on understanding how individuals make meaning of their experiences, and (c) the assumption that development (not just change) occurs as people interact with their environments. Another central defining feature is that patterns of meaning-making are described in developmental terms, that is, the frameworks people use for interpreting their experiences (e.g., categories and organizing principles) are described as becoming more complex, integrated, and complete over time. These changes do not occur automatically but rather through interaction with an environment that both challenges and supports growth.

However, our data led us to reject two well-known assumptions espoused by prominent theorists from this tradition. First, unlike Piaget, we do not assume that cognitive development is best measured by deductive reasoning, nor do we assume that it is complete with the emergence of formal operations at age 16 (indeed, our data show that this is not the case). And in contrast to Kohlberg, we do not claim cross-cultural universality, and we endorse Rest's (1979) concept of a complex rather than a simple stage model of development.

Stage theory. At the time the RJM was being developed in the1970s, Rest (a faculty member who supervised our initial research) was also working within the cognitive-developmental tradition. As a researcher of moral development, he was beginning to raise questions about the adequacy of what he called the "simple stage" model being advanced by Kohlberg (1969), a critique Rest (1979) later published in his first book. We took the opportunity to ask similar questions based on our initial study (K. S. Kitchener & King, 1981), such as whether there was stage variability or consistency among an individual's responses. Our scoring procedures were intentionally designed to allow for this question to be tested (i.e., allowing raters to record multiple stages if several were apparent in a given interview protocol). We found that Rest's alternative, the "complex stage" model of development, provided a good explanatory framework for our data. That is, we observed that development in reasoning about ill-structured, controversial problems has stage-like properties, but not that it evolves in a lock-step, one-stage-at-a-time fashion. Hence, we refer to the major categories of thinking and interrelated clusters of assumptions as stages, but our use of this term is qualified, based on specific assumptions and definitions that fall outside more traditional usage. Below, we offer data illustrating development across stages that support this approach.

We acknowledge that stage models within the cognitive-developmental tradition have been criticized as providing inadequate conceptual frameworks for describing development (e.g., Flavell, 1971). Two underlying assumptions about stages (traditionally defined) have drawn considerable criticism. The first is that individuals utilize only one organizing framework (stage) at a time and, therefore, that development from stage to stage is abrupt with any overlap between stages occurring briefly only during transitions between stages. At the time of stage consolidation, stage usage is assumed to peak at 100%, consistent with the common phrase used when referring to stage theories, being "in a stage." The second criticism is that the stages constitute an invariant sequence that exists across all cultures. Kohlberg's (1969, 1984) claim to the universality of his sequence of stages of moral development was based on his refutation of moral relativism as an inadequate philosophical framework (Kohlberg, 1991) and on cross-cultural studies indicating that the pattern of development he proposed was also apparent among individuals across several cultures. We do not make these claims. We do, however, support the other claims within this tradition (that meaning is constructed, that these constructions are developmentally ordered, and that development is the result of person-environment interactions).

Rest's (1979) complex stage model better captures the nature of development of reflective judgment because it accounts for the observed patterns in data gathered using the Reflective Judgment Interview (RJI). For example, it is common to find an individual who relies heavily on Stage 4 assumptions while reasoning about a controversial problem, but who also makes statements that are consistent with Stage 3 and Stage 5 assumptions. By contrast, someone who relies heavily on Stage 2 assumptions rarely uses assumptions of any stage higher than Stage 3. As Rest noted, this approach suggests a "much messier and complicated picture of development" (p. 65) than does a simple stage approach.

Does the complex stage model proposed by Rest accurately capture reflective judgment data? We examined variability of scores of those in our 10-year longitudinal sample (described later in the review of RJM research) to answer this question. In only two cases were the RJI ratings limited to a single stage; in the vast majority of cases, a subdominant score was assigned, and this was almost always an adjacent stage. In a small proportion of cases, more than two stage scores were assigned. Wood (1997) examined the variability of RJI scores using data from 15 studies for which raw data were available (n = 1,995 problem scores; reported in Wood, 1993). He constructed a "percent stage utilization score" based on all responses across the four problems; this score indicated the proportion of time each stage was assigned. He then calculated a series of spline regressions (Darlington, 1990), which predicted stage utilization on the basis of overall RJI score. (A graph of these may be found in King & Kitchener, 1994, Figure 6.2.) Here, development is pictured as a series of uneven, overlapping waves, where usage of given stage assumptions rises and falls in different proportions over time. As this figure shows, for those whose modal score was Stage 2, 70% of the ratings were for Stage 2, with less than 20% at Stage 3. About two-thirds of the ratings were at Stage 3 for those with a modal Stage 3 rating, with the remainder fairly equally distributed between Stages 2 and 4. A similar pattern was obtained for those with a modal Stage 4 rating; here, the remaining ratings were split fairly equally between Stages 3 and 5. However, the shape of the "wave" was much flatter for Stage 5, with only about half of the ratings at Stage 5; the remainder were spread two stages higher and lower than the mode. The shape of the curve for Stage 6 was more similar to those for Stages 3 and 4. In other words, variability in reasoning across stages was the norm and not the exception in these ratings. No individuals evidenced non-adjacent utilization patterns (3/5, 4/6, etc.). This evidence is consistent with the assumptions of complex stage theory (Rest, 1979) and adds further evidence that characterizing individuals as being "in" or "at" a single stage is misleading. Based on these patterns, King, Kitchener, and Wood (1994) suggested that development in reflective thinking be characterized as

> . . . waves across a mixture of stages, where the peak of a wave is the most commonly used set of assumptions. While there is still an observable pattern to the movement between stages, this developmental movement is better described as the changing shape of the wave rather than as a pattern of uniform steps interspersed with plateaus. (p. 140)

This shift from simple to complex stage theory represents a radical change in how development is conceptualized; indeed, it may be considered a change of paradigmatic proportions within stage theory.

Skill theory. The second theoretical model that has affected our thinking about RJM research is Fischer's skill theory. Fischer and his colleagues (Fischer, 1980; Fischer, Bullock, Rosenberg, & Raya, 1993; Fischer & Lamborn, 1989; K. S. Kitchener & Fischer, 1990) identified seven developmental levels that emerge between ages 2 and 30. These levels are divided into two overlapping tiers, the representational tier and the abstract tier. The focus of the representational tier is on individuals' ability to manipulate concrete representations, objects, people, or events; the focus of the abstract tier is on individuals' ability to integrate, manipulate, and reason using abstract concepts. This portion of skill theory has much in common with Kegan's (1982, 1994) theory of the development of mature capacity toward self-authorship. The upper levels of Fischer's model also have much in common with the RJM; in fact, the seven stages of the RJM can be readily mapped onto Representational Levels 1–4 and Abstract Levels 2–4 (Fischer & Pruyne, 2002; King, 1985; K. S. Kitchener, 2002; K. S. Kitchener & Fischer, 1990). Reflective thinking requires the ability to think abstractly, which explains the correspondence between the abstract levels of skill theory and Stages 4–7. K. S. Kitchener (2002) also suggested that skill theory provides a framework for comparing the multiple models of folk epistemology (R. Kitchener, 2002) and personal epistemology, such as those in Hofer and Pintrich's (1997, 2002) comprehensive reviews.

Another important and influential aspect of Fischer's work is his assumption that no skills exist independent of the environment and that the skill levels a person demonstrates will vary depending on the conditions under which they are assessed. (Notably, the acknowledgement that performance varies with task demands is incompatible with the simple stage assumption that individuals are "in" one stage at a time.)

Fischer and his colleagues (Fischer & Pipp, 1984; Lamborn & Fischer, 1988) posited that variability in individuals' responses across tasks reflects the degree of "contextual support" (e.g., memory prompts, feedback, opportunity to practice) available at the time of the assessment. He suggested that tasks that require performance without support elicit a person's *"functional level"* capacity, but that tasks that provide contextual support can elicit performance at levels that are closer to the upper limit of the person's cognitive capacity, called *"optimal level."* Contextual support can be provided by offering participants a high-level example of the skill, the opportunity to ask questions about the example, the chance to practice the skill in a variety of settings, and so on:

> It is the emergence of this general capacity [for abstract thinking] that establishes an upper limit on the level of independent functioning an individual can potentially achieve in reflective thinking or other domains involving advanced abstract thinking. This upper limit of skill development is termed the *optimal* level. (Fischer & Pruyne, 2002, p. 169; italics in original)

The space between functional and optimal levels is called one's "developmental range" and reflects the range of skills that an individual can access and produce depending on the circumstances. That is, the nature of the person's experience—including the structure of the learning and assessment tasks—affects where within this developmental range a per-son's performance will fall. If courses and other opportunities for student learning do not provide contextual support for developing the skills associated with forming abstract concepts like reflective thinking (a criticism commonly levied at both schools and colleges), students will be more likely to perform at functional rather than optimal levels. Further, those who have access to higher levels of development would also have access to a larger repertoire of responses from which to choose, explaining Fischer's (1980; Kitchener & Fischer, 1990) hypothesis that optimal and functional level will diverge to a greater degree as the person approaches higher levels of development.

Fischer (1980; Kitchener & Fischer, 1990) also hypothesized that functional level performance would improve in a slow, steady fashion, resulting in a gradual, even slope if graphed over time. By contrast, he hypothesized that optimal level performance would be less even and instead be characterized by spurts at given age levels, followed by plateaus between spurts. Thus, researchers would expect different developmental trajectories depending on whether their measures yield data on functional or optimal level performance.

The ability to operate at an optimal level is influenced not only by support and practice, but also by changes in brain activity and the reorganization of neural networks (Fischer & Pruyne, 2002; Fischer & Rose, 1994). The emergence of abstractions and reflective thinking appears to involve brain development that does not occur until late adolescence and early adulthood.

As this brief summary shows, skill theory provides an innovative approach to the study of human development in general and the development of reflective thinking (with its grounding in epistemic cognition) in particular. For example, the concept of developmental range provides an alternative way of addressing the question of being "in" or "at" a single stage on the RJM, and a way of targeting educational interventions to students' developmental levels. Further, its differentiation of functional and optimal level suggests the need to analyze measures of cognitive development or personal epistemology for degree of contextual support, and to develop measures that assess both levels. And although skill theory is certainly consistent with the person-environment interaction assumptions inherent in the cognitive-developmental paradigm, it specifies particular environmental variables (e.g., contextual support) that appear to affect how students learn to engage in the production of more advanced behaviors (here, reflective thinking).

Measuring Reflective Judgment

Over the last 25 years, we have experimented with several assessment procedures to measure reflective judgment and its underlying epistemic assumptions. In order to illustrate the links between theoretical assumptions stemming from our research paradigm and our assessment approaches, we describe how the development of several assessment procedures was grounded in theoretical considerations.

The Reflective Judgment Interview. The RJI was initially designed to measure reflective thinking as described by the RJM and to inform theory development. We used an iterative process between theory development and assessment ("boot-strapping") for much of the first decade of research on the RJM, moving back and forth between theory development and validation efforts. The RJI uses a semistructured interview format to elicit responses from participants regarding how they reason about ill-structured problems. A trained and certified interviewer asks a series of predetermined but open-ended questions regarding their reasoning in order to get at their fundamental assumptions concerning knowledge and how it is gained. The original interview consisted of four controversial problems (the accuracy of news reporting, the creation of human beings, the safety of chemical additives to foods, and the building of the Egyptian pyramids). A dilemma on the safety of nuclear power was added for the 10-year longitudinal retest, and several discipline-specific dilemmas have been used in subsequent studies (business, chemistry, and psychology). The RJI also includes a standardized series of probe questions; each question is designed to elicit comments that reflect individuals' epistemic assumptions (specifically, their assumptions about knowledge, how it is gained, how they decide what to believe). Probe questions ask about the basis for their point of view, the certainty with which they hold that view, whether differing opinions on the topic are right or wrong or better or worse, and how it is possible people (including experts) disagree about the topic. The one-hour interview was designed to yield a picture of how people approach the task of knowing and making judgments about controversial intellectual issues by looking at ways they understand and make meaning of concepts such as evidence, differences of opinion, uncertainty, and interpretation. (For a detailed description of the RJI, see King & Kitchener, 1994, Chapter 5 and Resource A.)

The RJI is scored by trained and certified raters using the Reflective Judgment Scoring Rules (K. S. Kitchener & King, 1985). Consistent with the complex stage assumptions noted above, raters can assign three scores to each dilemma to reflect whatever characteristics of reasoning they observe in the interview; these typically range across two adjacent stages. The stage most clearly or frequently observed is coded first as the dominant stage, followed by the subdominant stage(s). Occasionally, one dilemma includes statements that reflect three different stages; this is rare, but recording all

three is on option available to raters if they determine that this best captures the reasoning in the interview. The point here is that scoring is designed to reflect whatever stage-characteristic responses are evident in the transcript and not to assume a priori that consistency (or inconsistency) will be observed. Assigned scores are then weighted across dominant and subdominant stages, and an overall dilemma score is calculated. The training and certification programs for interviewers and raters were put into place to assure comparability across studies and researchers. (We have recently discontinued these programs in order to focus on the development of other measures.)

Fischer's (Fischer & Pruyene, 2002; Kitchener & Fischer, 1990) differentiation of functional and optimal levels of performance raised several questions for research on the RJM. In particular, it called for the consideration of the level of performance characterized by the RJI: because no contextual support is offered, the RJI may be considered a measure of functional level. As such, it may underestimate a person's capacity to engage in reflective thinking, yielding a score at the lower rather than the higher end of the individual's developmental range. Implications of this insight for research and teaching are explored later in the article.

The Prototypic Reflective Judgement Interview (PRJI). As noted earlier, there are several points of correspondence between Fischer's skill theory and the RJM. In order to evaluate whether the developmental patterns Fischer (1980) had predicted occurred for the development of reflective thinking as defined by the RJM (K. S. Kitchener & Fischer, 1990), a measure of optimal level performance was needed. Fischer argued that optimal measures required two qualities: first, there had to be an independent assessment for each step in the developmental sequence. Second, the research design had to vary relevant characteristics of the participants (especially age) as well as characteristics of the environment (e.g., the amount of environmental support provided for a response). Using these criteria, K. S. Kitchener, Lynch, Fischer, and Wood (1993) designed a new measure, the prototypic reflective judgment interview (PRJI) to assess reflective judgment under conditions of support and practice. The study measured both functional level (using the RJI) and optimal level (using the PRJI) to determine whether scores differed between the two measures of reflective thinking and whether there was evidence for age-related spurts and plateaus using the optimal level measure. Because of its theoretical significance, this study is summarized here.

To construct the PRJI, two problems from the RJI were selected, and stage-prototypic responses were written for reflective judgment Stages 2 through 7. These responses were based on answers given by people for the same problems used in the RJI; they were presented in order to give contextual support for high-level responses to the reflective judgment problems. Participants were first asked to complete the RJI, then to read one of the prototypic statements, and to respond to a series of questions that directed their attention to key elements of the statement. They were then asked to explain the prototypic statement in their own words; each answer was scored as a "hit" if it accurately paraphrased the statement and as a "miss" if it did not. This procedure was repeated for each reflective judgment stage and both of the problems. They were then given two prototypic statements addressing a different ill-structured problem; the statements were selected to correspond with the highest and second highest stages they had paraphrased in the interview. Participants were asked to think about these statements prior to the next testing, which took place two weeks later; this strategy provided contextual support in the form of exposure to and the opportunity to think about higher stage responses to ill-structured problems. The procedure was repeated at the next testing, fulfilling the practice component of contextual support.

Three findings from the study are relevant for the current discussion of how stage theory and skill theory as complementary theoretical models have informed research on the RJM. First, participants scored higher on the PRJI than on the RJI. This supports the idea that individuals are not "in" a stage but rather that they have access to several stages, and that this reflects the effects of contextual support and practice. In other words, contextual support appears to increase the individuals' access to higher stage functioning, yielding more advanced levels of performance (here, higher reflective thinking scores). Second, there was an age-related ceiling in the PRJI even after practice, suggesting that optimal levels are age-related. This is consistent with the developmental trends observed in RJM research (described later) but offers new

information about the nature and limits of age-related trends. Third, there was evidence of age-related developmental spurts on the PRJI at reflective judgment Stages 4 to 6. This is consistent with Fischer's hypothesis that the emergence of optimal levels is marked by spurts in performance and then plateaus. It also helps explain the growth in reflective thinking that has been observed with samples of traditional-age college students (whether this growth is consistent with collegiate goals is discussed later).

The Reasoning About Current Issues Test (RCI). Although the RJI and PRJI provided extremely rich information for theory development, their expense both in time and money was problematic in terms of conducting the kind of validation and application studies that were of interest to researchers and educators alike. In the process of developing an objectively scored measure of reflective thinking, we developed and tested several different approaches; these are described by Wood, Kitchener, and Jensen (2002). Here, we discuss the most recent measure, the Reasoning About Current Issues Test (RCI). This is an objectively scored instrument that was built on research using prior measures, but using a format that is amenable to large-scale administration. Because this is described elsewhere, the focus of this discussion is on ways our theoretical assumptions guided measurement development.

The RCI was modeled after Rest's Defining Issues Test (DIT) of moral judgment (Rest, 1979, 1986; Rest, Narvaez, Bebeau, & Thoma, 1999). The DIT has been found to be a highly reliable measure of moral judgment, able to detect developmental change over time, and sensitive to macrolevel changes in reasoning about social issues among adults. (For reviews of research using the DIT among college students, see King & Mayhew, 2002, in press.) In the RCI, respondents are asked to read a dilemma similar to those used in the RJI. In addition to the chemicals in foods dilemma, several others have been used that reflect contemporary issues (causes of alcoholism, workforce preparation, immigration policy, determinants of sexual orientation). The RCI first asks respondents to write a short statement describing their response in their own words. These written statements served to "prime the pump" by encouraging respondents to start thinking about their views on the given topics. Respondents are then asked to rate and rank in order a series of short statements to indicate the statements' similarity to the respondents' own views; each statement reflects the epistemic assumptions of one of the reflective judgment stages.

Each statement was based on responses made by respondents taking the RJI and modified from the statements developed for the PRJI. By merit of being a recognition task, this format provides contextual support (in contrast to the RJI). These brief statements are not written to capture an individual's whole network of underlying assumptions on which a judgment is based, nor to yield a nuanced articulation of how the individual approaches making judgments about controversial issues. Rather, it appears that responding to short items serves to activate the internal organizing schemas that individuals use to make judgments about the given issue, but without filling in the details about the specific rationale used and strategies employed, and without articulating the specific epistemic principles underlying the approach. (For a more detailed description of this rationale as applied to the DIT, see Rest et al., 1999.)

In addition, we wished to control for the possibility that the respondents would endorse statements that sounded impressive (e.g., that used sophisticated vocabulary) but that were not similar to the approach they used, or even to an approach they aspired to use. To address this concern, we created a series of statements that are grammatically correct but nonsensical. When these are selected, the responses for that problem are excluded from the analyses. The RCI score is calculated across all dilemma topics based on the statements most often ranked as similar to the participant's own view. Internal consistency reliabilities have been in the low to mid-.70s (depending on the sample). It takes 30 to 45 minutes to complete (Wood et al., 2002).

There are many trade-offs to be made when moving from a production task with open-ended questions (the RJI) to a recognition task where respondents are asked to choose from a limited set of predefined options (the RCI). Although both approaches are designed to tap into related skills required for the production of reflective thinking, the two are not simply different formats that yield comparable scores; rather, each serves a different purpose, makes different demands on respondents, and yields a different "snapshot" of the development of reflective thinking. Having participants evaluate state-

ments provides more contextual support than responding to open-ended interview questions; therefore, we would anticipate that individuals would score higher on the RCI than the RJI, and this has been the case.

Research on the RJM

In the last 25 years, we have learned a great deal about reflective thinking and how it develops. The centerpiece of our book, *Developing Reflective Judgment* (King & Kitchener, 1994), is a review of this research base. It reports both the results of our 10-year longitudinal study of the development of reflective judgment using three age/educational level cohorts (*n* = 80 at Time 1), other longitudinal studies of 120 other respondents, as well as a review of cross-sectional studies in which more than 1,700 people (high school students, college students, graduate students, and nonstudent adults) completed the RJI. Since the publication of that volume, Wood (1997) has completed a comprehensive secondary analysis of these data, and an updated literature review was published (King & Kitchener, 2002). Interested readers should consult these works for details. Here, we will summarize the major findings from this body of research, especially as they pertain to the focus of this special issue, how our theoretical framework has guided research on reflective judgment.

Validating the developmental sequence. RJM was proposed as a model of reflective thinking in the cognitive-developmental tradition, where the major claim is that the stages constitute a developmental sequence. Documenting the existence of this sequence and validating the model requires longitudinal data. Toward this end, we conducted a 10-year longitudinal study using three age/educa-tional cohorts (*n* = 80 at Time 1, *n* = 53 at Time 4). At Time 1, the three gender-balanced cohorts included high school juniors, college juniors, and third-year doctoral students; the younger two groups were matched to the doctoral students on gender and academic aptitude (based on scores from the Minnesota Scholastic Aptitude Test). This was designed as a check of the competing hypothesis that obtained cohort differences on the RJI (e.g., if graduate students scored higher than college students) could be attributed to differences in aptitude. Even with this control, age and educational level remained confounded in this study. By the time of the last testing, all but one of the high school cohort had completed a bachelor's degree, and about half of the college cohort had completed post-baccalaureate degrees. This yielded a well-educated sample and served as a leveling factor for the age/educational level confounding at Time 1.

Mean RJI scores were significantly different between groups at Time 1 (1977), with the doctoral students scoring the highest ($M = 5.67$), followed by the college students ($M = 3.76$), and the high school students ($M = 2.77$). The RJI mean score increased consistently for the high school and college student groups at each subsequent testing (1979, 1983, and 1987). Over the 10-year period, the former high school students' RJI scores increased over 2.5 stages to 5.29, the former college students' scores rose an average of 1.29 stages to 5.05, and the mean scores of the former doctoral students increased an average of .54, to 6.21. The overall rate of increase (less than two stages in two years) suggests that reflective thinking evolves slowly and steadily, even among those engaged in postsecondary education.

To determine whether a developmental sequence existed, we carefully examined the pattern of scores over time—and even reprinted the list of individual RJI scores in their entirety for other researchers to examine (King & Kitchener, 1994, Table B6.2). We found that during the 10 years of this study, the use of higher stage reasoning increased, and the use of lower stage reasoning decreased. This is evident in the individual examples reported by King and Kitchener (1994). For example, listed below are RJI scores for three individuals (a high school student, #105; a college student, #417; and a doctoral student, #310) at Times 1 (1977), 2 (1979), 3 (1983), and 4 (1987). The mean score is given first, followed by the mode (dominant/subdominant stage observed):

105, T1: 3.17; 3(4); T2: 3.96; 4(3); T3: 5.67; 6(5); T4: 6.59; 7(6)

417, T1: 3.92; 4(3); T2: 3.63; 4(3); T3: 4.54; 4(5); T4: 4.96; 5(6/4)

310, T1: 5.29; 5(6); T2: 5.63; 6(5); T3: 5.71 6(5); T4: 6.02; 6(7/5)

Both types of analyses offer strong support for the claim that the posited reflective judgment stages form a developmental sequence.

Similar patterns of change were obtained in six other longitudinal studies involving an additional 180 individuals who took the RJI (Brabeck & Wood, 1990; Polkosnik & Winston, 1989; Sakalys, 1984; Schmidt, 1985; Van Tine, 1990; Welfel & Davison, 1986) and ranging in duration from 3 months to 4 years. The most noteworthy finding among these studies is that the pervasive pattern is one of growth or stability. As King and Kitchener (1994) reported, "in every sample tested, the scores either stayed the same or increased over time. Further, with two exceptions, the mean score increased significantly for all groups tested at 1- to 4-year intervals" (p. 156). The amount of change was smallest in studies of short duration (3–4 months); significant increases were consistently observed in studies of at least a year's duration. In studies reporting incidence of regressions (Brabeck & Wood; King & Kitchener; Sakalys; Schmidt; Welfel & Davison), 0–16% of the mean scores declined between testings, while 84–100% of the mean scores either remained consistent or increased. This suggests that change in reflective thinking over time is better reflected as stability or development rather than decline, and that earlier stage assumptions are rarely used once they are replaced with more advanced assumptions.

Similarly, longitudinal data based on RCI scores obtained at the beginning and end of the first year of college yielded significant increases of about one third of a standard deviation, with comparable gain scores by gender and ethnicity (K. S. Kitchener, Wood, & Jensen, 2003). These freshmen were tested again as sophomores, and a sample of juniors was retested as seniors; RCI scores again increased significantly over time. These findings provide additional evidence that the RJM describes a developmental sequence. However, the growth correlation coefficient was significantly and negatively correlated with scores at Time 1 for the entire sample, by class and by gender: Those who had the lowest scores at Time 1 gained the most, and those who entered with the highest scores gained the least. The pattern was similar for a small subset of the participants who also completed the RJI (K. S. Kitchener et al., 2003).

Differences by age/educational level. Another desirable characteristic of a model of reflective thinking is that it can detect predictable changes in thinking across educational levels (e.g., that graduate students score higher than undergraduate students). Over two dozen cross-sectional studies have been used to examine educational level differences in reflective judgment; these studies include samples of high school students, traditional- and nontraditional-age college students, graduate students, and nonstudent adults. Questions related to educational level differences have been of particular interest to those interested in using reflective thinking as a college outcomes variable. Because promoting intellectual development (and especially skills associated with complex reasoning) is a common goal of higher education, studies documenting complex reasoning among college students have been of interest among many higher education researchers. As these studies have been summarized elsewhere, we present only a brief review of these findings.

King et al. (1994) reviewed 25 studies in which more than 1,500 respondents from across the United States took the RJI. Student RJI scores increased slowly but steadily across educational levels, from high school (M =3.2) to the first year of college (M = 3.6) to the senior year of college (M = 4.0) to early graduate study (M =4.6) to advanced doctoral study (M =5.3). The average RJI scores for nonstudent adults with and without college degrees were 4.3 and 3.6, respectively. The high school students consistently evidenced the assumptions associated with prereflective thinking, such as making decisions on the basis of beliefs that are not subject to evaluation, especially when a conclusion was consistent with what they wanted to believe. Among the college samples, the shift to Stage 4 reasoning indicates that the students had accepted uncertainty as part of the knowing process and were using evidence more consistently to make judgments. Kroll (1992) eloquently captured the shift from prereflective to quasi-reflective thinking as the movement from "ignorant certainty" (the dogmatic assertions characteristic of prereflective thinking) to "intelligent confusion" (acknowledging what you don't know, and why). Although this represents an important step toward reflective thinking, it is not the kind of thinking that is consistent with intended college outcomes (Brabeck, 1983; King, 1992). Only advanced doctoral students consistently used the assumptions of reflective thinking.

A similar pattern of findings was reported based on studies that used the RCI. Wood, Kitchener, and Jensen (2003) conducted a meta-analysis based on all available studies using RCI data; this yielded a sample of 8,537 students who were enrolled in college, graduate, and professional programs at seven different colleges or universities. They found significant differences by educational level, even after controlling for academic aptitude and prior academic achievement. Graduate students scored significantly higher than did medical students, who scored significantly higher than did undergraduate students ($p < .001$). Among the undergraduate students, significant differences were found between early level college students (freshmen and sophomores) and more advanced students (seniors). Thus, the educational level differences in reflective thinking that were found using the RJI were also found using the RCI; however, scores by educational level were about one stage higher on the RCI than on the RJI.

Data from cross-sectional studies showing upward trends in reflective judgment scores across age/educational levels offer corroborating evidence that the RJM describes a developmental sequence. In addition, this collection of studies (especially those that controlled for age) offers evidence that development in reflective thinking is associated with participation in educational programs.

Domain specificity. Do individuals reason using similar sets of epistemic assumptions across domains? That is, do respondents score similarly or differently when reasoning about controversies of different content? We have analyzed score variability using several indices. Internal consistency, as measured by coefficient alpha, has been high, with the median scores in the low .80s (King & Kitchener, 1994). Inter-dilemma correlations have been lower, varying with the heterogeneity of scores in the sample, typically in the mid .40s. King, Kitchener, Wood, and Davison (1989) examined individual modal RJI scores and found that the modal score was consistent across dilemmas 75% of the time. However, Wood et al. (2003) reported a significant main effect for dilemma topic using the RCI, as well as an interaction of topic by education level. Students in all four collegiate class levels (freshman through senior) plus graduate students tended to score higher on the two psychology dilemmas (origins of alcoholism and of homosexuality) than on the other three (artificial sweeteners, curricular reform, and immigration policy); however the class difference was accounted for by the higher scores of the seniors and graduate students. That is, the magnitude of the dilemma differences was more pronounced for the more advanced students. Whether this is an artifact of sampling (e.g., representation of behavioral science majors among the seniors) is not known. Interestingly, the scores within the two sets of dilemmas (psychology and nonpsychology) were quite similar.

These findings suggest that there is a relatively high rate of consistency in people's use of epistemic assumptions when reasoning about ill-structured problems. This could be because the RJM describes development in molar rather than fine-grained terms, and therefore is less sensitive to differences in dilemma content. Alternatively, it may be that epistemic assumptions themselves provide a guiding framework for making interpretive judgments that individuals use across a variety of problems such as those measured by the RJI and RCI.

Another way to consider questions related to domain specificity is to look at whether people reason similarly in terms of reflective thinking as compared with how they reason about issues in other areas. Data from several studies that have examined this question (reviewed in King & Kitchener, 1994) strongly suggest that development in reflective judgement is related to but distinct from development in other aspects of cognitive development (verbal aptitude, formal operations, academic ability, critical thinking) and from moral and identity development, and strongly predictive of tolerance for diversity (Guthrie, King, & Palmer, 2000).

Implications for Practice and Research

How can educators apply their understanding of the nature of the development of reflective thinking as described by the RJM to educational practice? The theory and research presented here offer many possibilities for answering this question. First, the strong effects associated with education offer a hopeful sign that the educational experiences for many students are effective in promoting growth toward reflective thinking. However, the nature of these practices remains largely unexplored, and there is considerable concern (e.g., Baxter Magolda, in press; King, 1992) that the observed reflective thinking skills are not as developed as those called for in the national reports mentioned at the beginning of this article. Nor are they at the level consistent with college goals for students, nor at the level associated with the complex issues and decisions college students will face upon graduation, whether as employees, citizens, consumers, or parents.

Second, consider the consistent finding that development in reflective thinking appears to unfold in a slow, steady manner following the sequence of stages outlined in the RJM. Without data on specific educational experiences affecting this growth curve, it is reasonable to assume that theoretically grounded interventions would yield increases in performance, but probably not in dramatic proportions. Given that stage assumptions are organizing categories for viewing knowledge and knowing, and given that each stage is more like a molar than a fine-grained unit of analysis for development, slow, steady progress is a more reasonable expectation; after all, each stage is a dramatic shift in world view and one's role as a knower. We have offered a number of suggestions elsewhere for promoting reflective thinking (King, 1992, 2000; King & Kitchener, 1994, 2002; K. S. Kitchener et al., 2003; Wood & Lynch, 1998). These range from intentionally incorporating ill-structured problems into the curriculum to improving discipline-specific contextual support, to structuring opportunities for practice and feedback to stimulate optimal level thinking. In each of these practices, students are encouraged to examine their assumptions, gather and interrogate the available evidence from multiple perspectives, and be responsible for offering their own conclusions of the evidence.

Third, it is noteworthy that virtually all the studies that comprise the database for the RJM have measured functional level, not optimal level. In only one study (Kitchener et al., 1993) did the measure of reflective judgment offer contextual support, and probably not at a level that would elicit performance at the upper reaches of a participant's developmental range. According to skill theory, functional level measures offer a low estimate of individuals' ability to engage in reflective thinking. If the average educational level scores are low estimates, then the concerns indicating deficits in student performance around reflective thinking may be overstated. Kroll (1992) also discouraged educators from directing their efforts toward a student's average performance; instead, he encouraged teachers to focus on the leading edge of development, which would be at a higher level within the student's developmental range. Similarly, the finding of differences in performance with and without contextual support suggests that educators should be encouraged to evaluate the amount and kind of contextual support they offer when assessing reflective thinking, for example, in student papers.

K. S. Kitchener et al. (2003) provided new information on the role of student involvement in an assortment of campus activities in promoting reflective thinking. In addition to the RCI, they also administered the College Student Experiences Questionnaire (CSEQ; Pace, 1990), which asks students to indicate on a 4-point scale how frequently they participated in particular collegiate activities. Findings from the freshman sample highlight the complexity of the relationship between participation in college activities and epistemological thinking. Predictably, those who entered college with higher reflective judgment scores also graduated with higher scores. For freshmen, the relationship between Time 1 and Time 2 scores are consistent with expectations about students with higher and lower reflective scores scores: Those who entered with higher scores endorsed an appreciation for challenging courses, a willingness to work harder in classes, and a commitment to thinking through ideas themselves. They expressed enthusiasm for being in college and indicated an appreciation for the scientific method and further growth in understanding of science. By contrast, the amount of growth in RCI scores for freshmen was almost always negatively correlated with the educational college activities on the CSEQ, including almost all items having to do with seeking out experiences that were different from prior experiences, or seeking out others who were different from themselves. That is, those who relied on prereflective assumptions were less open to experiences that involved talking about different points of view or interacting with others who are different. These students simply may not seek out these experiences as frequently as students who enter with more advanced epistemological assumptions. Studies such as this that link types of collegiate experiences to patterns of college student growth would be particularly helpful in advancing our understanding of the mechanisms of development in reflective thinking. Baxter Magolda's (1999, 2001) pedagogical framework for promoting development

offers a promising conceptual tool for designing interventions to promote not only reflective thinking but also advanced capacities in identity and interpersonal domains (for examples in higher education contexts, see Baxter Magolda & King, in press).

Educators have often reported that they are puzzled by how students defend their beliefs—for example, why some reduce complex controversies to simple, black-and-white terms, and why others are so appreciative of the value of multiple perspectives that they are unable to make their own judgments. Our hope here is that educators can better interpret their observations about student behaviors by understanding how such behaviors are grounded in their epistemic assumptions, and how these assumptions about knowledge and how it is gained are related to the ways students justify their own judgments about controversial issues.

References

American Association of Colleges and Universities (2002). *Greater expectations: A new vision for learning as a nation goes to college*. National Panel Report. Washington, DC: Author.

American Association of Higher Education, American College Personnel Association, National Association of Student Personnel Administrators (1998). *Powerful partnerships*. Washington, DC: Author.

American College Personnel Association (1994). *The student learning imperative*. Washington, DC: Author.

Baxter Magolda, M. B. (1999). *Creating contexts for learning and self-au-thorship: Constructive-developmental pedagogy*. Nashville, TN: Vanderbilt University Press.

Baxter Magolda, M. B. (2001). *Making their own way: Narratives for transforming higher education to promote self-development*. Sterling, VA: Stylus Publishing.

Baxter Magolda, M. B. (in press). Self-authorship as the common goal of 21st century education. In M. B. Baxter & P. M. King (Eds.), *Learning partnerships: Educating for self-authorship*. Sterling, VA: Stylus Publications.

Baxter Magolda, M. B., & King, P. M. (Eds.). (in press). *Learning partnerships: Educating for self-authorship*. Sterling, VA: Stylus Publications.

Brabeck, M. (1983) Critical thinking skills and reflective judgment development: Redefining the aims of higher education. *Journal of Applied Developmental Psychology, 4*(1), 23–34.

Brabeck, M., & Wood, P. K. (1990). Cross-sectional and longitudinal evidence for differences between well-structured and ill-structured problem solving abilities. In M. L. Commons, C. Armon, L. Kohlberg, F. A. Richards, R. A. Grotzer, & J. D. Sinnott (Eds.), *Adult development 2: Models and methods in the study of adolescent and adult thought* (pp. 133–146). New York: Praeger.

Broughton, M. (1975). *The development of natural epistemology in years 11 to 16.* Unpublished doctoral dissertation, Graduate School of Education, Harvard University, Cambridge, MA.

Broughton, M. (1978). Development of concepts of self, mind, reality, and knowledge. In W. Damon (Ed.), *Social cognition. New directions for child development* (Vol. 1, pp. 75–100). San Francisco: Jossey-Bass.

Churchman, C. W. (1971). *The design of inquiring systems: Basic concepts of systems and organization.* New York: Basic Books.

Darlington, R. B. (1990). *Regression and linear models.* New York: McGraw-Hill.

Dewey, J. (1933). *How we think: A restatement of the relations of reflective thinking to the educative process.* Lexington, MA: Heath.

Fischer, K. W. (1980). A theory of cognitive development: The control and construction of hierarchies of skills. *Psychological Review, 87,* 477–531.

Fischer, K. W., Bullock, D., Rosenberg, E. J., & Raya, P. (1993). The dynamics of competence: How context contributes directly to skill. In R. Wozniak & K. W. Fischer (Eds.), *Development in context: Acting and thinking in specific environments* (pp. 93–117). Hillsdale, NJ: Lawrence Erlbaum Associates, Inc.

Fischer, K. W., & Lamborn, S. D. (1989). Mechanisms of variation developmental levels: Cognitive and emotional transitions during adolescence. In A. de Ribaupierre (Ed.), *Transitions mechanisms in child development: The longitudinal perspective* (pp. 33–670). Cambridge, England: Cambridge University Press.

Fischer, K. W., & Pipp, S. L. (1984). Processes of cognitive development: Optimal level and skill acquisition. In R. J. Sternberg (Ed.), *Mechanisms of cognitive development* (pp. 45–80). New York: Freeman.

Fischer, K. W., & Pruyne, E. (2002). Reflective thinking in adulthood: Emergence, development, and variation. In J. Demick & C. Andreoletti (Eds.), *Handbook of adult development* (pp. 169–198). New York: Plenum.

Fischer, K. W., & Rose, S. P. (1994). Dynamic development of coordination of components of brain and behavior. In G. Dawson & K. W. Fischer (Eds.), *Human behavior and the developing brain* (pp. 2–66). New York: Guilford.

Flavell, J. (1971). Stage related properties of cognitive development. *Cognitive Psychology, 2,* 421–453.

Guthrie, V. L., King, P. M., & Palmer, C. J. (2000). Cognitive capabilities underlying tolerance for diversity among college students. Manuscript submitted for publication.

Harvey, L. J., Hunt, D., & Schroder, H. M. (1961). *Conceptual systems and personality organization.* New York: Wiley.

Hofer, B. K. & Pintrich, P. R. (1997). The development of epistemological theories: Beliefs about knowledge and knowing and their relation to learning. *Review of Educational Research, 67,* 88–140.

Hofer, B. K., & Pintrich, P. R. (2002). Personal epistemology: The psychology of beliefs about knowledge and knowing. Mahwah, NJ: Lawrence Erlbaum Associates, Inc.

Kegan, R. (1982). *The evolving self.* Cambridge, MA: Harvard University Press.

Kegan, R. (1994). *In over our heads: The mental demands of modern life.* Cambridge, MA: Harvard University Press.

King, P. M. (1985). Choice-making in young adulthood: A developmental double-bind. *Counseling and Human Development, 18*(3), 1–12.

King, P. M. (1992). "How do we know? Why do we believe?" Learning to make reflective judgments. *Liberal Education, 78*(1), 2–9.

King, P. M. (2000). Learning to make reflective judgments. In M. B. Baxter Magolda (Ed.), *Linking student development, learning, and teaching: New directions for teaching and learning* (Vol. 82, pp. 15–26). San Francisco: Jossey-Bass.

King, P. M., & Kitchener, K. S. (Eds.). (1994). *Developing reflective judgment: Understanding and promoting intellectual growth and critical thinking in adolescents and adults.* San Francisco: Jossey-Bass.

King, P. M., & Kitchener, K. S. (2002). The reflective judgment model: Twenty years of epistemic cognition. In B. K. Hofer & P. R. Pintrich (Eds.), *Personal epistemology: The psychology of beliefs about knowledge and knowing* (pp. 37–61). Mahwah, NJ: Lawrence Erlbaum Associates, Inc.

King, P. M., Kitchener, K. S., & Wood, P. K. (1994). Research on the reflective judgment model. *Developing reflective judgment: Understanding and promoting intellectual growth and critical thinking in adolescents and adults.* San Francisco: Jossey-Bass.

King, P. M., Kitchener, K. S., Wood, P. K., & Davison, M. L. (1989). Relationships across developmental domains: A longitudinal study of intellectual, moral and ego development. In M. L. Commons, J. D. Sinnott, F. A. Richards, & C. Armon (Eds.), *Adult development: Vol. 1. Comparisons and applications of developmental models* (pp. 57–72). New York: Praeger.

King, P. M., & Mayhew, M. J. (2002). Moral judgement development in higher education: Insights from the Defining Issues Test. *Journal of Moral Education, 33,* 247–270.

King, P. M., & Mayhew, M. J. (in press). Theory and research on the development of moral reasoning among college students. *Handbook of Higher Education.*

Kitchener, K. S. (1983). Cognition, metacognition and epistemic cognition: A three-level model of cognitive processing. *Human Development, 4,* 222–232.

Kitchener, K. S. (2002). Skills, tasks, and definitions: Discrepancies in the understanding and data on the development of folk epistemology. *New Ideas in Psychology, 20,* 309–328.

Kitchener, K. S., & Fischer, K. (1990). A skill approach to the development of reflective thinking. In D. Kuhn (Ed.), *Contributions to human development: Developmental perspectives on teaching and learning thinking skills* (Vol. 21, pp. 48–62). Basel, Switzerland: Karger.

Kitchener, K. S., & King, P. M. (1981). Reflective judgment: Concepts of justification and their relationship to age and education. *Journal of Applied Developmental Psychology, 2*(2), 89–116.

Kitchener, K. S., & King, P. M. (1985). *The reflective judgment scoring manual.* Unpublished manuscript.

Kitchener, K. S., Lynch, C. L., Fischer, K. W., & Wood, P. K. (1993). Developmental range of reflective judgment: The effect of contextual support and practice on developmental stage. *Developmental Psychology, 29*(5), 893–906.

Kitchener, K. S., Wood, P. K., & Jensen, L. (2003). *Individual differences in gains in reflective judgment and their relationship to college experiences.* University of Denver, CO.

Kitchener, R. (2002). Folk epistemology: An introduction. *New Ideas in Psychology, 20*(2/3), 89–105.

Kohlberg, L. (1969). Stage and sequence: The cognitive-developmental approach to socialization. In D. Goslin (Ed.), *Handbook of socialization theory and research.*(pp. 347–450). Chicago: Rand McNally.

Kohlberg, L. (1984). *The psychology of moral development: The nature and validation of moral stages.* San Francisco: Harper & Row.

Kohlberg, L. (1991). My personal search for universal morality. In L. Kuhmerker (Ed.), *The Kohlberg legacy for the helping professions.* Birmingham, AL: R.E.P. Books.

Kroll, B. (1992). *Teaching hearts and minds: College students reflect on the Vietnam War through literature.* Carbondale, IL: Southern Illinois University Press.

Lamborn, S. D., & Fischer, K. W. (1988). Optimal and functional levels in cognitive development: The individual's developmental range. *Newsletter of the International Society for the Study of Behavioral Development, 2*(Serial No. 14), 1–4.

Loevinger, J. (1976). *Ego development: Conceptions and theories.* San Francisco: Jossey-Bass.

Pace, R. (1990). *College Student Experience Questionnaire: Norms for the third edition.* Bloomington, IN: Center for Postsecondary Research and Planning, Indiana University.

Perry, W. (1968). *Patterns of development in thought and values of students in a liberal arts college: A validation of a scheme* (Final Report, Project No. 5-0825, Contract No. SAE-8973). Washington, DC: Department of Health, Education, and Welfare.

Perry, W. (1970). *Forms of intellectual and ethical development in the college years: A scheme.* Troy, MO: Holt, Rinehart & Winston.

Piaget, J. (1965). *The moral judgment of the child.* New York: Free Press.

Piaget, J., & Inhelder, B. (1969). *The psychology of the child.* New York: Basic Books.

Polkosnik, M. C., & Winston, R. B. (1989). Relationships between students' intellectual and psychological development: An exploratory investigation. *Journal of College Student Development, 30*(1), 10–19.

Rest, J. R. (1979). *Development in judging moral issues.* Minneapolis: University of Minnesota Press.

Rest, J. R. (1986). *Moral development: Advances in research and theory.* New York: Praeger.

Rest, J. R., Narvaez, D., Bebeau, M., & Thoma, S. (1999). *Postconventional moral thinking: A neo-Kohlbergian approach.* Mahwah, NJ: Lawrence Erlbaum Associates, Inc.

Sakalys, J. (1984). Effects of an undergraduate research course on cognitive development. *Nursing Research, 33,* 290–295.

Schmidt, J. A. (1985). Older and wise? A longitudinal study of the impact of college on intellectual development. *Journal of College Student Personnel, 26,* 388–394.

Van Tine, N. B. (1990). The development of reflective judgment in adolescents. *Dissertation Abstracts International, 51,* 2659.

Welfel, E. R., & Davison, M. L. (1986). How students make judgments: Do educational level and academic major make a difference? *Journal of College Student Personnel, 23,* 490–497.

Wood, P. K. (1983). Inquiring systems and problem structure: Implications for cognitive development. *Human Development, 26,* 249–265.

Wood, P. K. (1993). *Context and development of reflective thinking: A secondary analysis of the structure of individual differences.* Unpublished manuscript, University of Missouri at Columbia.

Wood, P. K. (1997). A secondary analysis of claims regarding the Reflective Judgment Interview: Internal consistency, sequentiality and intra-individ-ual differences in ill-structured problem solving. In J. C. Smart (Ed.), *Higher education: Handbook of theory and research* (Vol. 12, pp. 243–312). Edison, NY: Agathon Press.

Wood, P. K., Kitchener, K. S., & Jensen, L. (2002). Considerations in the design and evaluation of a paper-and-pencil measure of epistemic cognition. In B. K. Hofer & P. R. Pintrich (Eds.), *Personal epistemology: The psychology of beliefs about knowledge and knowing* (pp. 277–294). Mahwah, NJ: Lawrence Erlbaum Associates, Inc.

Wood, P. K., Kitchener, K. S., & Jensen, L. (2003). College students' concepts of belief justification regarding open-ended controversies. Manuscript submitted for publication.

Wood, P. K., & Lynch, C. L. (1998). Using guided essays to assess and encourage reflective thinking. *Assessment Update, 10*(2), 14–15.

CHAPTER 38

REVISITING WOMEN'S WAYS OF KNOWING

BLYTHE McVICKER CLINCHY

When Mary Belenky, Nancy Goldberger, Jill Tarule, and I began the project that led eventually to our book on *Women's Ways of Knowing* (WWK, 1986/1997), we called it Education for Women's Development. We set out to interview women varying widely in age, ethnicity, and social class, women who had attended or were attending a variety of educational institutions ranging from small, selective liberal arts colleges to inner city community colleges, as well as several "invisible colleges," social agencies serving mothers of young children living in rural poverty. The question that guided our research continues to guide my research today. I like the way Mary Belenky words the question: "How come so many smart women feel so dumb?" Based on our own experiences in college and graduate school, and experiences recounted by our friends and our students, the four of us suspected that part of the answer might lie in the structure and practices of these educational institutions. Thus, we shared with earlier psychologists such as G. Stanley Hall a concern that higher education might be harmful to women's health. Hall worried that college might shrink women's wombs, rendering them infertile or "functionally castrated" (1917, p. 634); we worried that it might shrink their minds, or at least fail to expand them to their full potential.

In an attempt to explore the nature of the problem and to consider how institutions might be modified to better serve the needs and interests of women, we developed an extensive interview and administered it to 135 women, along with several standard developmental measures. The interview included sections dealing with self-concept, moral judgment, relationships, and educational experiences, as well as one ultimately labeled "ways of knowing." Although, like all of the contributors to this volume, we were familiar with William Perry's "scheme" tracing epistemological development in the college years (1970), and Nancy Goldberger (1981) and I (Clinchy & Zimmerman, 1982; 1985) had used it in previous longitudinal research, epistemology was at first no more salient in our thinking than any other aspect of development. Gradually, however, as we coded responses to what we then called the "Perry part" of the interview and then re-read the rest of each woman's interview in the light of the coding, we came to believe, as we say in the preface to the second edition of the book, "that the women's epistemological assumptions were central to their perceptions of themselves and their worlds," and so "epistemology became the organizing principle for our data analysis and for the book that we were beginning to imagine" (WWK, 1997, xviii).

In the book we describe five different perspectives from which women view the world of truth, knowledge, and authority. Perry's scheme provided the scaffolding we used in coding the women's responses, and the perspectives we present are deeply grounded in his "positions," although we emphasize slightly different aspects of epistemology. Perry's positions are defined mainly in terms of the nature of knowledge and truth (truth as absolute, for example, versus multiple), whereas we stress the women's relation to knowledge and truth, their conceptions of themselves as knowers. For instance, do they conceive of the source of knowledge as internal or external, and do they experience themselves as receiving or as creating truth? We listened, too, for deviations from Perry's scheme, for one would not expect the responses of women varying widely in age, class, and educational background to be identical to those of Perry's largely privileged and largely male undergraduate sample. Indeed, we found that while the general outline of Perry's scheme survived, many of the answers the women gave could not be wedged into it, and so, "In this instance, as in others, when the data the women provided diverged from the theories we had brought to the project, we forced ourselves to believe the women and let go of the theories" (WWK, 1997, pp. xii–xiv).

The book plunged us into a lively, wide-ranging conversation: It drew serious attention, often intensely critical, among scholars and researchers from a variety of disciplines, as well as moving testimonials from hundreds of "ordinary" women who saw parallels between their own stories and the stories in the book. I intend this chapter to be a contribution to this continuing conversation. I shall discuss some salient and controversial aspects of each of the perspectives we defined, drawing on the original text and also on research and theoretical speculations that have emerged in the years since its publication.

Silence

We named this, the least adequate perspective we could discern, "Silence," signifying the voicelessness of women at this position. Asked, "How do you fell about speaking?" Trish responds, "Um. I wonder if I'm using the right words. I can't do it anywhere." These women have difficulty hearing as well as speaking. As Belenky writes, they "see words more as weapons than as a means of passing meanings back and forth between people. They do not believe themselves capable of understanding and remembering what the authorities or anyone else might say to them" (Belenky, 1996, p. 394). Lacking "the most basic tools for dialogue, the Silenced feel voiceless and excluded from the community" (Belenky, 1996, p. 394). They have been excluded, also, from theories of epistemological development, for these theories are based on words—

oral or written accounts—produced mainly by people with considerable formal education. Silent women, feeling "incapable of articulating their own thoughts and feelings to others," (Belenky, 1996) make poor research subjects, and they rarely wend their way into institutions of higher learning. All of the women who taught us about Silence came from the invisible colleges, not the visible ones, and most of them could describe the position only because, having moved somewhat beyond it, they could view it retrospectively. For example, Ann said:

> I could never understand what they were talking about. My schooling was very limited. I didn't learn anything. I would just sit there and let people ramble on about something I didn't understand, and I would say "Yup, yup." I would be too embarrassed to ask, "What do you really mean?". . . I had trouble talking. If I tried to explain something and someone told me that it was wrong . . . I'd just fall apart. (WWK, p. 23)

In fact, the Silence perspective does not belong in accounts of epistemological "development." Silence grows out of a background of poverty, isolation, subordination, rejection, and often, violence. It is not a step in "normal" development but a failure to develop. "a position of not knowing" (Goldberger, 1996b, p. 4) imposed by a society inattentive to the needs of its members.[1] It should not be seen, as some readers have interpreted it, as the first stage in a developmental sequence.

Still, since the publication of WWK, I have learned that the position, although "abnormal," may not be as rare as I once thought. A few years ago, while outlining the WWK positions for a group of community college faculty, I remarked that we could skip quickly over "Silence" because such people were unlikely to appear in their classes. A flurry of hands went up, and the participants proceeded to disabuse me of my assumption. The position was heavily represented, they said, among the many very poor people who had recently entered their colleges, mostly perforce, as a result of changes in welfare regulations.

Even highly educated articulate women, some of whom make a profession of speaking and writing, have testified to us in hundreds of letters that they resonate to the description of this perspective. Although they are by no means entrapped in (capital "S") Silence, they report that they frequently find themselves in situations in which they are (lowercase "s") silenced. Lewis and Simon offer a fascinating account of a graduate course taught by Simon in which Lewis and the other women students felt silenced by the males in the class. They quote an account by one student that is remarkably similar to Ann's:

> I don't understand what they [the men] are talking about. I feel like I'm not as well educated as them. I haven't done too much reading in this area. They know so much more than I. I just feel that if I said anything, they'd say, what is she doing in this class, she doesn't know anything, so I keep my mouth shut. (Lewis & Simon, 1986, p. 466)

As Simon says.

> Being muted is not just a matter of being unable to claim a space and time within which to enter a conversation. Being muted also occurs when one cannot discover forms of speech within conversation to express meanings and to find validation from others. (Lewis & Simon, 1986, p. 464)

The muting of the women in Simon's class was confined to a particular (although not uncommon) situation, and the women were able to devise strategies for eliminating it. The muting of the profoundly Silent women pervades their entire lives and is much less tractable, but it is not irreversible: The invisible colleges and programs like the "Learning Partners" project directed by Belenky and her colleagues (Belenky, 1996; Belenky, Bond, & Weinstock, 1998), have succeeded in providing settings in which Silent women can "express meanings and find validation from others."

Received Knowing[2]

From this perspective, built on Perry's (1970) Dualism, truth is absolute and unambiguous. Received Knowers[3] believe that for every question there is a single, correct answer. They see the world in terms of black and white, right and wrong, true and false, good and bad; there is no room for ambiguity. "The stars twinkle for one reason." A student said, "That's why they do it. If something is proven, then there is no other way it could happen." Truth is external; it lies in the hands of Authorities, and one is utterly dependent on Them to dispense it:[4] "How can you learn if the teacher isn't telling you?" In the course of

a longitudinal study of epistemological development in young women, based on Perry's scheme. (Clinchy & Zimmerman, 1982; 1985.) Claire Zimmerman and I asked Wellesley undergraduates, "Suppose two people disagree on the interpretation of a poem. How would you decide which one is right?" A sophomore replied, "You'd have to ask the poet. It's his poem."

Like many of my colleagues, I grow impatient with students who behave as Received Knowers. These are the students who sit, pencils poised, prepared to record the truths I dispense, the ones who ask exactly how long the paper should be, and exactly which topics will appear on the exam. These students are willing to regurgitate the information they have stored in their heads on a test, but they don't like being asked to apply it. They tend to see knowledge as something to be stored and reproduced, but not to be used and never to be questioned. They like multiple choice exams, and I don't. I can muster some compassion for Received Knowers by recalling how I revert to this position whenever I am faced with something novel, complex, and incomprehensible, like the first time I saw a game of cricket or heard a piece of atonal music. On such occasions I yearn for an expert who will just tell me what it all means.

It was not until I embarked on the WWK research however, that I came to feel genuine respect for Received Knowing. I teach at an academically selective, academically rigorous college, and I see it as my task to help students move beyond received knowing and on to more active, reflective models of thinking. But through this project we met women for whom Received Knowing and on to more active, reflective modes of thinking. But through this project we met women for whom Received Knowing was an achievement, rather then something to be "got over," like measles or chicken pox or adolescence. They showed us that the position has virtues. The chief virtue of the Received Knower is that she is receptive. She can listen, even if the listening seems hardly more active than the listening a tape recorder does. Women who rely on received knowledge can take in information, while Ann, looking back on a life in Silence, recalls that she "could never understand what they were talking about." Received Knowers can appreciate expertise and make use of it. Silent women do not perceive authorities as sources of knowledge. "Authorities bellow but do not explain;" although they must be obeyed; they cannot be understood.

Ann began to emerge as a knower when she became a mother. She needed to know how to take care of her baby, and she was lucky enough to live in an area serviced by a Children's Health Program, where the staff "knew all the answers," and took the time to spell them out in language she could understand. Unlike many professionals, they continually emphasized her competence, rather than their own.

> I'd walk in there and they would say, "You're wonderful. You're a great mother.". . . I'd walk out of there feeling so good. I'd feel like I could tame the world. . . . I feel like I could go in there and they could hire me, you know, that's how much knowledge they have given me.

While recognizing the virtues of Received Knowing, it is important, also to see its limitations. For Received Knowers, as we defined the position. Authority is the only source of knowledge. Judging by the comments of some of our critics, we did not make the "only" point clear. The feminist literary theorist Patrocinio Schweickart, for instance, recalls herself as listening intently and taking careful notes in college and graduate school. We "miss something important," she says, if we assume that in this case she was behaving as a Silent woman or a Received Knower. But the authors of WWK would make no such assumption; we would agree with Schweickart that "silence" in this case might well be "a sign not of passivity, but of the most intense intellectual engagement" (1996, p. 307). It is important to distinguish between (lowercase) received knowing as a "strategy" (Goldberger, 1996a) that one chooses to deploy in a particular situation (during a lecture, say, or a cricket game), because of its adaptive value, and (uppercase) Received Knowing as a compulsory position from which authorities are viewed as the sole source of knowledge, knowledge that is assumed to be absolutely true, and which one simply ingests "as is" without any awareness of active processing. Similarly, we do not assume, of course, that simply because a person is not speaking, she is operating from a position of Silence.

As Goldberger points out, "Relying on experts or yielding to the knowledge of others is not necessarily indicative of the narrowly defined version of Received Knowing we pre-

sent in WWK. . . . It is the way in which a person 'constructs' authority and expert that helps us understand more fully his or her epistemological stance" (1996a. p. 347). For instance, in her own research with "bicultural" Americans, Goldberger found that although African Americans stressed in their stories the importance of relying on God, "their construal of God as authority is more one of Collaborator and Coknower than Dictator" (1996a. p. 347). Goldberger implies that WWK's treatment of Received Knowledge is culture bound: "Yielding to authorities external to oneself is often characterized in Western culture, which values autonomy and independent judgment, as 'childlike,' 'passive,' or 'dependent'" (1996a, p. 347). I agree, and I think, too, that we were "bound" by the limits of our sample. Most of the women we coded as Received Knowers occupied relatively subordinate positions in terms of age or social class, being either very young undergraduates or very poor older women. Received Knowing might take a different form among, say, a sample of prosperous middle-aged people.

I believe, now, that we paid too little attention to distinctions within our sample of Received Knowers. As it is, our construction of this and the other positions partakes of what might be called "epistemological (or perhaps "positional") essentialism," lumping into the same category perspectives that may differ in significant ways. Received Knowing cannot be quite the same for a first-year student in an elite college who depends on the words of a presumably benign professor, and a fifty-year-old with minimal formal education who is at the mercy of the "information" supplied by an abusive mate. Or consider a milder, but not insignificant contrast: the experiences of a male and a female Received Knower in Perry's sample (Harvard undergraduates in the 1960s) might also differ, for the male knew that he might someday be one of Them, while the female could envision no such possibility.[5]

Subjectivism

Subjective knowing is in some respects the opposite of received knowledge. Received Knowers believe in universally valid Absolute Truths. Subjectivists adhere to the doctrines of "Multiplicity" (Perry, 1970) and "Subjective Validity" (Clinchy & Zimmerman, 1982): truth (lowercase

t) is personal and individual, all opinions are equally valid, and everyone's opinions are right for them. While Received Knowers see knowledge as external and utterly objective, subjectivists look inside themselves for knowledge; for them, truth springs from the heart or the gut. In WWK we tell the story of Inez, a young single mother of three, who (in our terms), had lately moved out of Received Knowing into Subjectivism. She told us, "There's a part of me that I didn't even know I had until recently—instinct, intuition, whatever. It helps me and protects me. It's perceptive and astute. I just listen to the inside of me and I know what to do."

Unlike Received Knowers, Subjectivists tend to be deeply suspicious of the information dispensed by authorities. For most of her life Inez had been abused and exploited by powerful males, first her father and brothers, then her husband. She grew up believing that, as she put it, no woman could "think and be smart." Inez no longer pays any attention to external authorities; she is her own authority. "I can only know with my gut," she said. "I've got it tuned to a point where I think and feel all at the same time and I know what is right. My gut is my best friend—the one thing in the world that won't let me down or lie to me or back away from me."

For Inez, Subjectivism spells liberation, but for Kim, a first-year African American student at a traditional elite college, it almost certainly spells trouble. I asked Kim to read and respond to the following statement: "In areas where the rights answers are known, I think the experts should tell us what is right. But in areas where there are no right answers I think anybody's opinion is as good as another's." Kim didn't just agree with the second sentence; she also *disagreed* with the first, the notion that there are in any area "right answers" that are "known." "I don't like that," she said. "I just don't like that. Who's to say what answer is right and what answer is wrong? They could have been given the wrong information. I'm sure there are a helluva lot of teachers who are walking around being misinformed. . . . I very seldom go by what people say."

Like other Subjectivists, Kim relied on the data supplied by first-hand experience rather than the second-hand information offered by authorities:

If they were to tell me that there was going to be an earthquake tomorrow, that scientists had gone and studied all the scales and said this, I wouldn't believe them. I'd have to wait and see. The only way I could believe it is for it to actually happen. It is said that the earth goes around the sun. I don't have any proof. It is written in books, sure. But the person who wrote it in books could have been misinformed.

A Subjectivist would not dream of "asking the poet" how to interpret his poem. In her view, it isn't "his poem;" it's hers, and "there isn't any right or wrong. We're all allowed to read into a poem any meaning we want." As one woman said, "Whatever you see in the poem, it's got to be there." Here, the external world seems almost to disappear. The words on the page dissolve into a sort of Rorschach inkblot exerting little constraint on the meaning the reader projects onto the page. What the Subjectivist reader "sees" is likely to resemble closely what she already "knows." Asked how she decided among competing interpretations being discussed in English class, one student said, "I usually find that when ideas are being tossed around I'm usually more akin to one than another. I don't know—my opinions are just sort of there." And another said, "Well, with me it's almost more a matter of liking one more than another. I mean, I happen to agree with one or identify with it more"

Unless she can "identify" with a phenomenon, the Subjectivist cannot deal with it. "I cannot relate to an atom," Kim told me. Asked what she meant by "relate," she said, "I can comprehend it, I can feel it." Some of her classmates, she said, "can see why two positives would connect. I can't see that force, but I can see anger and emotions." How, I wondered, was this young woman going to pass the science distribution requirement?

Subjectivists "just know" what they know; their knowledge is based not on words or inferences but on the immediate apprehension of reality. Mrs. Spender, a character in Angela Thirkell's novel, *Growing Up*, says, "You only have to mention a thing to me and I seem to see it . . . I don't need to read, I just sense what things are about." Mrs. Spender does not question the validity of her perceptions, nor does she leave room for others to question them. "A person's experience can't be wrong," as one young woman said, and "an idea is right if it feels right"—right for herself, although not necessarily for anyone else.

Subjectivists are as tolerant of others' opinions as they are of their own: judge not, that ye not be judged. When Kim told me that she didn't like to call people wrong, I asked, "Would that extend to people like Hitler?" "Absolutely," she replied. "I would never, no—I wouldn't call him wrong. Whatever he has done, I would not call bim wrong . . . I value my opinion. I value what I do. I have no right whatsoever to go out and call somebody wrong because it is different from what I do."

At first glance, this passage may strike the reader, as it did me, as amoral mindless relativism. But Kim's next sentence makes it clear that she does have values of her own: "Now I think that the extermination of the Jews was wrong. I am not saying that he was wrong." It is not clear whether Kim means that Hitler's opinion is wrong in some objective or absolute sense, or whether it is simply wrong for her, but it is clear that she distinguishes between persons and the opinions they hold. She knows that, as the anthropologist Clifford Geertz puts it, differences of opinion are not just "clashes of ideas," that "there are people attached to those ideas" (Geertz, quoted in Berreby, 1995). Only if you realize that, Geertz maintains, can you be "open to dialogue with other people."

Kim realizes it, but she is not open to dialogue with other people. She disagrees with Hitler, but she would see no point in exploring the issue with him. She is not interested in why he believes in the extermination of Jews, nor would she care to argue the point: Hitler's opinion may be right for him, but it is irrelevant to her. Subjectivists do not see values—their own or anyone else's—as a subject for reflection, and without reflection there can be no genuine dialogue. Their anemic "discussions" are like parallel play: based on "mere unlikeness" of views, in Geertz's phrase, they are characterized by a "vacuous tolerance that, engaging nothing, changes nothing" (Geertz, 1986, p. 133). As the philosopher Elizabeth Spelman wrote:

> Tolerance is . . . the least of the virtues of people who really want to learn about others and about their lives: to tolerate someone is simply to let her have her say; I needn't listen to her, I needn't respond to her, I needn't engage with her in any way at all. All I have to do is not interfere with her. Prior to and after I've allowed her to make her presence known, I can blot her out of my consciousness. (Spelman, 1988, p. 181)

Although Subjectivists preach "openness," they actually practice a sort of aloof tolerance toward other points of view; they listen politely, but they do not really hear. As the philosopher Iris Murdoch might put it, they are unable to love. "Love," Murdoch said, "is the extremely difficult realization that something other than oneself is real. Love . . . is the discovery of reality" (1970/1985, p. 51). Genuine dialogue, Geertz says, requires the realization that "other people are as real as you are" (quoted in Berreby. 1995). In some sense, the Subjectivist lacks this realization; she is lost in her own subjectivity. Although she acknowledges in theory the existence and validity of other realities, only her own is really real to her. She can only look out through this subjective reality; she cannot transcend it or detach herself from it.

Subjectivists perceive the world in terms of themselves, ignoring its otherness. The writer/teacher Peter Elbow calls this "projection in the bad sense" (Elbow, 1973, p. 149). They hear a person (or a poem) meaning what they would mean, if they said those words, or else they do not hear it at all. In order to perceive otherness, one must acquire a degree of objectivity. To avoid projection in the bad sense. Subjectivists need to acquire techniques for "imaginative entry . . . into an alien turn of mind" (Geertz, 1986, p. 118). They need to learn how to explore and examine ideas—their own and other people's. They must rediscover on a higher plane the insight achieved by children of four and five, that belief and reality do not always coincide.

The Limits of Preprocedural Knowing

At my college, many students, especially in the first year or two, exhibit a split epistemology. Typically, they perceive science and mathematics from a Received Knowing perspective, and the humanities from a Subjectivist perspective. Students with a strong proclivity for Received Knowledge gravitate toward the first domain, and those who are strongly tilted toward Subjectivism gravitate toward the latter.[6] If they persist in these positions, both groups will run into trouble, especially in advanced courses: Received Knowers may be confronted with Heisenberg's uncertainty principle and Bohr's principle of complementary, and Subjectivists will certainly encounter teachers who insist that only those interpretations that are thoroughly grounded in the text deserve consideration. Unless they are to find themselves "in over their heads" in the psychologist Robert Kegan's (1994) phrase, in college and beyond, they will need to develop more powerful ways of knowing, for both these perspectives, although seemingly so different, share similar serious deficiencies.

Both are uncritical ways of knowing. Ann, the Received Knower, perceives the staff at her invisible college to be infallible, and Inez, the Subjectivist, perceives her own gut as infallible. They do not examine their knowledge; they simply accept it as true and act on it with unquestioning obedience. Both modes are relatively passive. Ann and Inez do not create their knowledge. Ann's opinions come ready-made from the agency; Inez's opinions are, as that student put it, "just there." People who rely solely on received or subjective knowledge are in some sense not really thinking. They have no systematic, deliberate procedures for developing new ideas or for testing the validity of ideas. Judging from longitudinal data and the women's retrospective accounts, this "Procedural Knowing" is for some the next step in development.

Procedural Knowing

Procedural Knowers no longer believe that one can acquire knowledge or arrive at truth through immediate apprehension. Knowledge does not consist of facts to be stored "as is," nor of the static residue of direct experience. Knowledge is a process, and it requires work. Although no single "answer" may be "right," all interpretations are not equally valid. Knowing requires the application of procedures for comparing and contrasting and constructing interpretations, and the quality of the knowledge depends on the skill of the knower.

In WWK we described two sorts of procedures that we called "separate" and "connected" knowing. Separate Knowing is a detached, impersonal, objective, critical approach, best typified, perhaps, by the model of "hard science." Many people would call it simply "thinking," or maybe "good thinking." Once upon a time, so did I. Elsewhere, I have told how Zimmerman and I stumbled on what we now call "connected knowing" while searching for evidence of what we now call "separate knowing" among Wellesley undergraduates. Some of our interview questions were designed to ascertain whether the

students had acquired an appreciation of critical thinking, a component of Perry's Position 4. For example, we asked them to respond to a statement another student had made in an earlier interview that seemed to provide evidence of critical thinking: "As soon as someone tells me his point of view, I immediately start arguing in my head the opposite point of view. When someone is saying something, I can't help turning it upside down" (Clinchy, 1998, p. 770).

Although some of the women agreed heartily with the quotation, some disagreed. One said, "When I have an idea about something, and it differs from the way another person's thinking about it. I'll usually try to look at it from that person's point of view, see how they could say that, why they think they're right, why it makes sense." And another said,

> If you listen to people and listen to what they have to say, maybe you can understand why they feel the way they do. There are reasons. They're not just being irrational. When I read a philosopher I try to think as the author does. It's hard, but I try not to bias the train of thought with my own impressions. I try to just pretend that I'm the author. I try to really just put myself in that person's place and feel why is it that they believe this way.

This young woman would agree with Virginia Woolf (1932/1948) that in reading a book one should "try to become" the author, his "fellow worker" and "accomplice."

In time, as my colleagues and I accumulated more and more responses like these, we began to think that connected knowing might constitute a genuine procedure, and this is how we present it in WWK. In retrospect, this seems to me to have been an audacious, perhaps presumptuous move. Because we had little empirical data of our own to use in constructing the concept, having never asked a single question designed to elicit it, in a sense we "made it up"— not out of whole cloth, to be sure, but out of a necessarily eclectic assortment of ideas. Since the publication of the book, along with various collaborators, I have been attempting through systematic research and conversations with colleagues (alive and dead, in person and in print) to define the components of connected knowing and separate knowing more clearly and to ascertain how the two procedures (or various versions thereof) play out in actual practice. Annick Mansfield and I (1992) developed an interview designed to elicit the ways in which men and women define the two procedures, how they feel about them, what they see as their benefits, drawbacks, and purposes, when and where and with whom they do and do not use each procedure, and how their use of them has changed over time. A number of researchers, including my own students as well as other investigators at various institutions working with widely varying populations, have also used some version of this interview. Because most of this research is still in progress, and because of limitations of space, I shall not dwell on it in detail here, but I have drawn on it in developing the description of the two procedures that I present here.

Table 1 summarizes some contrasting features of separate and connected knowing. The two modes have somewhat different purposes: while Connected Knowers are primarily inter-ested in understanding the object of attention. Separate Knowers are primarily oriented toward its validity. The Connected Knower asks. "What does this poem (person, idea, etc.) mean?" The Separate Knower might ask. "How good is this poem? What are its strengths and weaknesses?"

"What is the evidence for and against this theory?" In attempting to get at the meaning of an idea, the Connected Knower adopts a "believing" stance (Elbow, 1973; 1986), using empathy in an attempt to share the experience behind the idea, "feeling with" and "thinking with" the author of the idea. One woman told us that in counseling undergraduates, she is "usually a bit of a chameleon. I try to look for pieces of the truth in what the person's saying instead of going contrary to them, sort of collaborate with them." In contrast, Separate Knowers take a critical stance, acting as adversaries rather than allies.

TABLE 1
Characteristics of Connected and Separate Knowing

Aspect	Connected Knowing	Separate Knowing
The name of the game:	The "Believing Game": looking for what is right; accepting	The "Doubting Game": looking for what is wrong: critical
Goals:	Emphasis on meaning: to under-stand and be understood	Emphasis on validity: to justify, test, refine, convince, and be convinced
The relationship between the knowers:	Supportive: reasoning *with* the other	Adversarial, challenging: reasoning *against* the other
The knower's relation to the known:	Personal, Attachment & intimacy: "stepping in"	Impersonal, Detachment and distance: "stepping back"
The nature of agency:	Active surrender	Mastery and control
The nature of discourse:	Narrative	Argument
The role of emotion:	Feelings illuminate thought	Feelings cloud thought
Procedure for achieving (approximating) "objectivity"	Adopting the perspective of the particular other: empathy	Adopting a neutral perspective, "from no position in particular," adhering to rules for avoiding bias
Basis of authority:	Personal experience (own or vicarious)	Mastery of relevant knowledge and methodology
Strengths:	Holistic, inclusive	Narrowing, discriminating
Vulnerabilities:	Absence of conviction: loss of identity, autonomy, and power. Danger of always being the listener	Absence of conviction; alienation and absence of care and intimacy. Danger of never listening

Instead of stepping into the other's shoes they step back, measuring the quality of the object against impersonal criteria such as the logic of the argument or the fit between the theory and the data.

Both Separate and Connected Knowers exhibit objectivity, but of a different sort. Separate Knowers believe in separating the knower from the known, so as to avoid "contamination." In searching for truth, they try to "weed out the self" using Elbow's (1973, p. 149) phrase, putting their own feelings and values aside and adopting a neutral perspective, "from no position in particular." To avoid bias, they adopt procedures such as "double-blinding" in conducting experiments and "blind grading" in assessing students' work. Connected Knowers also attempt to suspend their own beliefs, but instead of adopting a neutral perspective, they adopt the perspective of the other. When we asked women what "objectivity" meant to them, and why one should be objective, they often said something like, "When you're trying to help a friend decide whether to get an abortion, you have to forget what you think about abortion and see it from her point of view, given her assumptions." Connected Knowers do not "extricate" (Elbow, 1973) the self: convinced that the knower and the known are inextricably related, they use the self to help them connect with the other. To "the strong democrat," wrote the political scientist Benjamin Barber:

> "I will listen" means not that I will scan my adversary's position for weaknesses and potential trade-offs, nor even . . . that I will tolerantly permit him to say whatever he chooses. It means, rather, "I will put myself in his place. I will try to understand, I will strain to hear what makes us alike (1984, p. 175; emphasis added).

Connected Knowers take this approach not only to people but to relatively "impersonal" objects. "To understand a poem." an undergraduate said. "You must let the poem pass into you and become part of yourself, rather than something you see outside yourself. . . . there has to be some parallel between you and the poem." And the biochemist portrayed by June Goodfield in *An Imagined World* says, "If you really want to understand about a tumor you've got to *be* a tumor" (Goodfield, 1991/1994, p. 226). In contrast, Separate Knowers adhere to what the feminist philosopher Susan Bordo calls "the Cartesian masculinization of thought;" for them

it is "the otherness of nature [that] allows it to be known," and "empathic, associational, or emotional response obscures objectivity, feeling for nature muddies the clear lake of the mind" (Bordo, 1986, p. 452). Connected Knowers, in contrast, believe that emotions can serve as clues. A nursery school teacher once told me that in trying to understand a particular child, she asks herself, "How does this child make me feel?" "I know my reaction says something about me," she says, "and I have to sort that out, but it also tells me something about him."

Separate and connected knowing, as presented here, are inventions, something like ideal types. In our work we have never encountered an individual who exhibited all the aspects of either mode, and it is possible that different categories of individuals will show different patterns, containing some components of a mode and excluding others. In a study of attitudes toward separate and connected knowing among Wellesley and MIT undergraduates, Mansfield and I found that many of the Wellesley undergraduates we interviewed embraced some aspects of Separate Knowing as we presented it (impartial analysis, for example) but strongly objected to its more oppositional aspects, such as playing "devil's advocate," and while most of the women included empathy in delineating their own versions of "connected knowing," not one of the men referred to empathy or, indeed, made any mention of affect (Rabin, 1994). (We suspect that the difference has as much or more to do with the cultural norms of the two institutions as with gender.)

Some of our research participants seem to express more complex versions of the modes than others. As the philosopher Sara Ruddick reminds us, "a 'position' or 'way' allows development within its modality" (Ruddick, 1996, p. 225). In an attempt to trace this development. Mansfield and I are looking for specific differences between versions that seem intuitively more or less sophisticated, and we are examining longitudinal data collected from adolescents in search of developmental change, asking, for instance, whether some components appear to come in earlier than others.

As work continues, particularly in different cultures and subcultures, researchers will surely deconstruct the crude dichotomy presented in Table 1, identifying configurations that contain elements from both its columns. Consider, for instance, Kochman's (1981) intriguing account of the distinctive ways in which urban community Black students and White middle-class students in his Chicago college classroom deal with conflict. The White students seem to adopt a prototypical detached Separate Knowing style: They "relate to their material as spokesmen, not advocates . . . They believe that the . . . merits of an idea are intrinsic to the idea itself. How deeply a person cares about or believes in the idea is considered irrelevant to its fundamental value." Blacks, on the other hand, use as approach that is adversarial, but neither disinterested nor unemotional. They "present their views as advocates. They take a position and show that they care about this position" (p. 20)." Whites believe that "caring about one's own ideas" makes a person "less receptive to opposing ideas," but Blacks see no contradiction between attachment to one's own ideas and openness to alternative ideas, which they also value; in fact, they are suspicious of people who present an argument as if they had no personal stake in it. "Whites believe that opinions should be evaluated on their own merits: they are taught to present ideas as though the ideas had an objective life, existing independent of any person expressing them," but Blacks, "because they feel that all views . . . derive from a central set of core beliefs that cannot be other than personal . . . often probe beyond a given statement to find out where a person is 'coming from' in order to clarify [its] meaning and value" (Kochman, 1981, pp. 20–23).

Connected Knowing Versus Subjectivism

Of all the themes presented in WWK, the concept of Connected Knowing has provoked the most interest, probably the most research, certainly the most controversy, and—in my defensive opinion—the most misunderstanding. As I have written:

> In WWK we defined connected knowing as a rigorous, deliberate, and demanding procedure, a way of knowing that requires work. Contrasting it with . . . "subjectivism," we said, "It is important to distinguish between the effortless intuition of subjectivism (in which one identifies with positions that feel right) and the deliberate imaginative extension of one's understanding into positions that initially feel wrong or remote." (WWK, 1986, p. 121). Many of our readers—friends and foes alike—have ignored the distinction,

conflating connected knowing with subjectivism by treating it more as a reflex than a procedure. (Clinchy, 1996, p. 209)

Connected Knowing builds on the positive qualities of Subjectivism, but it transcends its limits. Table 2 presents some of the similarities and differences between the two models. Connected Knowers retain the Subjectivist's respect for subjectivity and for the lessons that can be learned from first-hand experience, but they are not imprisoned within their own subjectivity or confined to their own narrow slice of experience; they develop techniques for entering into alien subjectivities and making use of vicarious experience. Connected Knowers, like Subjectivists, are reluctant to make judgments; they are in this sense "accepting," but theirs is not the passive acceptance, the "to-each-his-own-indifferentism" (Geertz, 1986, p. 122) of the Subjectivist. Fully developed Connected Knowing requires that one "affirm" or "confirm" the subjective reality of the other, and affirmation is not merely the absence of negative evaluation; it is a positive effortful act. Affirmation of a person or a position means "saying Yes to it" (Elbow, 1986, p. 279), rather than merely offering sympathetic understanding. Confirmation means, in the theologian Martin Buber's wonderful phrases, to "imagine the real," to "make the other present" (Buber, quoted by Friedman, 1985, p. 4). It involves "a bold swinging . . . into the life of the other" (Buber, quoted by Kohn, 1990, p. 112).

We saw that Subjectivists cannot engage in genuine dialogue; although they speak, often they cannot really hear. "What's the point of class discussion," one student asked, "when you have your own thoughts that feel right?" For Connected Knowers knowledge is neither absolutely private nor absolutely certain; hearing other voices becomes not only possible but, because truth is now problematic rather than transparent, essential. Connected Knowers begin to perceive other people's realities not just as "alternatives to" themselves, as Subjectivists do, but as "alternatives for " themselves (Geertz, 1986, p. 111, citing Bernard Williams). Other people's realities become possibilities for them.

Connected Knowers develop techniques for facilitating and eliciting these realities through "active listening" (Rogers & Farson, 1967). Active listening is not a natural capacity; but in Geertz's phrase, a "skill arduously to be learned" (Geertz, 1986, p. 122), one that is rarely practiced in daily

TABLE 2
Subjectivism and Connected Knowing Similarities and Differences

Subjectivism	Separate Knowing
reflexive, reactive, spontaneous	deliberate, effortful; midwifery
locked in one's own perspective	entering another perspective
often, "projection in the bad sense" (Elbow): egocentric assumption that others share one's view	suspending, "bracketing" one's own view
Everyone has a right to their own opinion and everyone's opinion is right for them.	Everyone has a right to a considered opinion. People are responsible for their options.
All opinions are equally valid; an opinion has validity simply because someone holds it. Assertion of validity of one's own opinion for one's self, but only for one's self.	Some opinions are better than others, but one should not evaluate an opinion unless one has tried hard to understand it.
Knowledge is derived from first-hand experience.	Knowledge can be acquired through vicarious experience.
Only my own subjectivity is really real to me.	One can enter into other subjectivities.
One should show tolerance and respect for views that differ from one's own.	One should try to imagine, explore, and understand views that differ from one's own.
Intuition and feeling are involved, but not empathy (feeling, but not feeling with)	Intuition and feeling may be involved, especially empathy.
little or no reasoning involved; the "gut" or "the heart" predominate.	"thinking with" as well as "feeling with" the other.
One need not entertain other views as possible options for the self. (Resistant to change)	One should entertain other people's opinions as possibilities for the self. (Open to transformation)

life. Having tried for years with more and less success to learn and to teach the art of interviewing, I know how difficult it is to listen "objectively" in the connected sense, that is, to hear the other in the other's own terms, to act, as the psychoanalyst Evelyne Schwaber puts it, as "an observer from within" (Schwaber, 1983, p. 274). Connected Knowers achieve skill, too, in making themselves understood by finding a route into the other's subjectivity: Kim, the African American student we met earlier, seemed to move outside her normally Subjectivist frame when, in the midst of describing an experience of racial discrimination, she suddenly leaned across the desk and asked, "Are you Jewish?"—searching, it seemed, for some "parallel" between us that would allow her experience to "pass into" me.

Connected Knowing, like Subjectivism (and unlike Separate Knowing), attends to feelings as sources of insight, but it also involves reason-ing—feeling with and thinking with. This point is often overlooked, perhaps because the dichotomy between separate and connected knowing that we present is assimilated into the dualism between thinking and feeling that pervades this culture, leading to a fallacious syllogism: If separate knowing involves thinking, and connected knowing involves feeling, connected knowing must not involve thinking. We say that although connected knowing is uncritical it is not unthinking, but in a culture in which the predominant view is that thinking *is* critical thinking, "uncritical thinking" becomes an oxymoron.

Issues of Gender

Although WWK is based entirely on interviews with women, it has been widely described as a study of "sex differences," perhaps partly because when male and female are perceived as binary opposites, as they typically are, it is difficult to see why one would speak of "women's" ways of knowing except to distinguish them from men's ways. We did not argue that the positions we described applied only to women, although we speculated that for various reasons, the positions might take somewhat different form in men; Marcia Baxter Magolda's research suggests that this might be so. In particular, we did not mean to imply that all women, and only women, are Connected Knowers or that all men, and only men, are Separate Knowers. Because we interviewed only women, the voices we used to illustrate both modes were largely, of course, women's voices. Indeed, we did not attempt to "code" participants as Connected or Separate Knowers, but only as Procedural Knowers, for, having not yet clearly defined the two modes when we began the research, we had asked no questions designed to elicit the relevant data.

Subsequent research, involving men as well as women, and using recently developed survey measures as well as interviews focusing directly on separate and connected knowing, suggests that the two modes may be gender-related, but not gender exclusive. For instance, in two studies involving undergraduates at academically selective colleges, females consistently rated connected knowing statements higher than separate knowing statements, while males' ratings of the two modes did not differ (Galotti, Clinchy, Ainsworth, Lavin, & Mansfield, 1999; Galotti, Drebus, & Reimer, 1999). I know of no studies comparing the frequency of use of the two modes by males and females except in terms of self-report; more objective (observer-based) data would be useful.

However, sex differences were not then and are not now a central interest for me. I resonate to the words of Carol Gilligan: "When I hear my work being cast in terms of whether women and men are really (essentially) different or who is better than whom, I know that I have lost my voice, because these are not my questions" (1993, xiii). They were not our questions either. We did not mean to assert that connected knowing was "better" than separate knowing, only that it was "a different voice," a legitimate and effective voice that deserved to be heard. Like Gilligan and other "different voice" theorists, we "wished to repair an omission in psychological theory and in the society, by bringing into public consciousness a way of seeing, speaking, and knowing that emphasized attachment and interdependence rather than detachment and autonomy" (Clinchy & Norem, 1998, p. 785).

Critics contend that connected knowing is essentially a powerless way of knowing. I argue that it can be a powerful way of constructing knowledge (Clinchy, 1998), but I acknowledge that a society that devalues it will devalue the person who uses it. Until the "omission" of that voice in the institutions of this society is repaired, those who use it will suffer. I was reminded of this recently when I heard a colleague in economics tell how she insists that her students develop "a public voice" for use in class, a confident, decisive, authoritative voice that differs from the hesitant, groping, and uncertain "private" voice they use in the residence hall. "I tell them," she said, "that if the CEO asks them how many factories they should build, and they say "F-i-i—I-ve. . . . ? (with rising inflection), while the guy next to her says firmly "Seven!," seven will be built and the guy will be promoted above them." A bit shaken, I recalled how that very morning I had been urging the students in my seminar not to conduct an interview as if it were an exam, but to say things like "So - o - - o, you mean . . . ? . . . I'm not sure I understand . . . I think maybe . . ." In effect I was asking them to bring their private voices into the public domain. Which of us was right, I asked myself, the economist or me? Both. One voice is more effective in one context, the other in the other. We know from research that these procedures are not mutually exclusive, indeed, measures of the two appear to be orthogonal (David, 1999; Galotti, Clinchy, Ainsworth, Lavin, & Mansfield, 1999; Galotti, Drebus, & Reimer, 1999). Students need to develop skill in both modes, so that they can deploy whichever is appropriate for a given occasion. In time, we might even envision their achieving a way of knowing that integrates the two voices into one. What would such a voice sound like? In WWK, we weren't sure, but, we began to sketch it out, and we called it Constructed Knowing.

Constructed Knowing

The chapter on Constructed Knowing in WWK was by far the most difficult to write. It passed from hand to hand among us for months, as we wrote and revised it, and I, for one, have never been satisfied with it. Because this is the most complex of the positions, it is the most difficult to construct, and because our sample contained so few Constructed Knowers, we had little data to work with. Since the publication of WWK, my students and I have sought out research participants who we believed might help us in constructing a richer portrait of the position—for instance, relatively privileged adults active in professional and community life, and a sample of undergraduates nominated by their professors as "complex thinkers" in their fields (Arch, 1998). In this section, I rely largely on their words, elaborating on several aspects of the position presented in WWK. This research is in its infancy, and my comments should be read as highly speculative.

Constructed knowing has much in common with Perry's Position 5. Complexity and ambiguity are assumed, and "right answers are a special case." Anna, a senior honors student majoring in history, said that in her field, although there were some questions such as "Did this happen on this day?" to which an answer could be true or false, "those aren't the questions that are the important questions." For Amy, another senior, the epistemological "revolution" described by Perry, has clearly occurred: "There's a state of creative confusion, or at least doubt. I think it's always going to be that way." When last she encountered math and science. Amy had assumed that they contained "Truth with a capital T:"

> My experience with [science and math] has been on such a basic level that it's almost like spelling. You can spell right and you can spell wrong . . . I have a sense, though, that [in] higher level mathematics and stuff you get into things where just one-answer isn't sufficient or isn't the only way. Things can sort of just diverge off, and there is more than one possibility. . . . I think that exists, you know, it must. Can't all be '2 and 2 is 4.'

When we ask Procedural Knowers to describe their ways of learning and thinking, they often enumerate a linear step-by-step program. Constructivists are less articulate; they struggle to find images to express the process, and the images are more often circular than linear. Amy says "it's hard to explain:"

> You proceed out of confusion. . . . There's just sort of a sense of a mixing bowl where you sort of let—where you are confused and you don't have any solid or stable. . . . I think it's sort of like a whirlpool or something like that. Where you've got a lot of ideas zooming around, and you haven't yet affixed any of them to being right or wrong in your head

yet or meshing with all the others. Things are still just sort of whirling around; then you start, pulling them out and filtering things out and making sense out of them.

Similarly, Marie said:

> A lot of it has been lots of passive and then 'Boom!', all of a sudden something comes and really sticks, and I'm very active, and [then] lots of passive again, and then 'Boom!' again. It's like I have to take in a whole lot and sift it all down. You know, put it all in a big sieve and sift it all down and the stuff that falls through I collect and start building with, and then 'Wham!'—all of a sudden the right piece will fall into the sieve and something will be completed.

We gave the Constructed Knowing chapter the subtitle, Integrating the Voices, to capture the women's tales of "weaving together the strands of rational and emotive thought and of integrating objective and subjective knowing" (WWK, p. 134). Amy and Marie weave together the "active surrender" of connected knowing with the "mastery and control" of separate knowing into a single way of knowing. In her practice as a family counselor, Sara tries to combine the empathy of connected knowing with the detachment of separate knowing. Recently, she told us, she canceled an appointment with a client in order to take a needed vacation with her daughter, and the client felt betrayed. "I'm working hard to get to a place where I can really understand how tortured she feels by this," she said. "I want to stay right with her as much as I can. I also have to keep monitoring this whole thing from a professional stance, trying to see it all and keep it all in perspective." Aware that she herself is tilted toward connection, she observes herself carefully: "If I find myself being too much into that close-up stance where I'm completely involved in that person's perspective and maybe lose touch with the professional stance, I need to scramble to get my professional stance back." Although Sara is aware that some therapists find an aggressive approach effective, she knows that it would not work for her. "Even if I have to confront sometimes, I still want to do that within a relationship that I feel is viable and trusting." She has evolved an approach that blends aspects of separate and connected knowing: she will "take an oppositional stance," voicing exceptions to a client's interpretations, but she phrases her comments in connected language, "in a way that hopefully isn't argumentative, but sort of like a confused statement." No one taught Sara this technique; she developed it herself to suit the sort of person she is. As Kegan might put it, while Procedural Knowers are "subject" to their procedures, Constructed Knowers are in control of them; they own them.

At the heart of constructed knowing, as is implicit in Perry's Position 5, is the belief that "All knowledge is constructed, and the knower is an intimate part of the known" (WWK, p. 137). Kegan asks, "Having put our world together, are we awake to the fact that it is an invented reality, a made world? Do we regularly look for some quite different way the same experience could cohere and so render a whole different meaning? "[W]e 'make sense,'" he goes on, "but we do not always take responsibility for it as made" (Kegan, 1994, p. 205). Although none of us, of course, is always conscious of inventing reality. Constructivists often are, and at least on reflection, they recognize that they are responsible for their constructions and that it is their duty—"an ethical imperative," as one woman put it—to consider alternative constructions. If truth is "an increasing complexity," as the poet Adrienne Rich (1979, p. 187) said, and as our Constructivists believe, there is never a single, crucial experiment or a perfect, "impregnable" argument that will settle the matter. Procedural Knowers stay within a given system—the viewpoint of a particular person or a particular discipline, for example. Constructivists move among systems. Amy, who worried during her sophomore year that she might "mix up" the material from one course with the material from another, and "say the wrong things on the exam," told us, as a senior:

> I think one of the most exciting things is when you're getting different insights into a similar thing. Like when you're taking seventeenth-century literature as well as art you have a sense of a lot of things coming together, a lot of different things that explain each other sometimes . . . And you start getting a much greater sense of what was happening, and why each thing in turn produced the other, and how they all interact.

In WWK we wrote, "[C]onstructivists show a high tolerance for internal contradiction and ambiguity" (p. 137). "'Dialogue' and 'balance' were key words in [the] epistemological vocabulary" of the "complex thinkers" interviewed by Joanna Arch (1998, p. 53). For example, Karen approaches history, her field of concentration, as

"a dialogue" between past and present; although it is important for historians to avoid projecting current assumptions and concerns "blindly back into the past," she said, it is important also to keep them in mind. Philosophers any psychologists refer to this sort of approach as "dialectical thinking" (e.g., Basseches, 1986; Clayton & Birren, 1980; also see Oser & Reich, 1987, on "complementarity"), Karen calls it "my little two-direction thing." (Notice that, like Sara, she "owns" the approach.)

When Constructed Knowers find their thoughts and feelings in conflict, they try to cultivate a "conversation" between the two, instead of allowing one to silence the other. In her "rational mind." Karen said, she is opposed to censorship, but, "intuitively," because of an experience involving the attempted suicide of a friend after reading an assigned book, she is in favor of it:

> There has to be a way for that experience to coincide with thought. And be more than a gut reaction, even though the gut reaction is the strongest thing about it. And I think that's true of all sorts of things. . . . I remain convinced . . . that what's truly right will work on both an emotional and a logical level. And maybe that's not true. But I'd like to think that and pursue that thought.

Although barely twenty one years old, Karen seems to have the beginnings of "wisdom," as defined by Labouvie-Vief: "While *logos* has insisted on the separation of such realms as reason and faith, thinking versus feeling, outer versus inner, or mind versus body, wisdom maintains that these two realms constitute but complementary and interacting poles of thought (1990, p. 78)."

Interviews with older, seemingly "wise" women like Sara have led me to suspect that when constructed knowing reaches its fullest development (probably not before middle age, I would guess), the construction of self and other might look something like Kegan's (1994) "fifth order consciousness." To illustrate the difference between fourth and fifth order consciousness, respectively, Kegan invents two couples, the Ables and the Bakers, both of whom have been married for many years. The Ables respect their differences, and most of the time they are "comfortable" with them. "We're probably more comfortable with each other," they said, "because we're a lot more comfortable with ourselves. . . . Anyway, we've become a good team. We find that our differences are often complementary. One picks up what the other one misses." For each of the Ables, the self is single and complete: "Mr. Able comes over to discover the world of Mrs. Able, but in all his respectful discovering he never questions the premise that this is not his world." For each of the Bakers, on the other hand, the self is multiple and incomplete, an "evolving self" (Kegan, 1982) composed of contradictory parts. The Bakers have come to seek that the differences within the self and the other. "When Mr. Baker comes over to try on the perspective he has identified with Mrs. Baker, . . . he is vulnerable to discovering another world within himself." For instance, to an outsider it may appear that one of the Bakers is an activist and the other a contemplative. But "when we are at our best," said the Bakers themselves, "we get a good glimpse of the fact that the activist . . . also has a contemplative living inside him." And when they have a fight, if it's a good fight, "the fight becomes a way for us to recover our own complexity, . . . to leave off making the other into our opposite and face up to our own oppositeness."

The Ables have learned to avoid destructive conflict by treating each other as complements rather than enemies; through respecting each other's points of view, compromising, and taking turns, they have become "a good problem-solving team." But their relationship is not a source of growth: "We are who we are," they say (Kegan, 1994, p. 308). The Bakers' relationship is a source of growth, "a context for a sharing and an interacting in which both are helped to experience their 'multipleness,' in which the many forms or systems that each self is are helped to emerge" (Kegan, 1994, p. 313). When differences between partners are acknowledged as differences within each of the partners, they become similarities between them, and the apparent opposition between similarity and difference is dissolved. Piaget was right, I think, in positing difference and contradiction as powerful forces in development, but I believe that similarity and coincidence can be equally powerful, and that the integration of the two, in constructed knowing, is more powerful still.

Conclusion

In WWK we could not assert with confidence that the epistemological positions we defined represented a developmental progression, for we had longitudinal data for only the small proportion of our sample whom we had also interviewed in earlier studies; otherwise, we had to rely on retrospective accounts. In any case, I now believe that we should be wary of moving too quickly to embrace theories that postulate a single, acontextual linear direction in epistemological development. Such global theories have been useful in the past, but the pervasiveness of "domain specificity" has led me to believe that we need to examine development within rather than across domains. For instance, it seems likely that, while in approaching the humanities, students often move from a Subjectivist to a Procedural position, in approaching science they may "skip" Subjectivism, going directly from Received to Procedural Knowing. I believe that microanalytic longitudinal investigations of individuals grappling with a particular discipline or set of issues can be especially illuminating, for example, studies of changes over months or years in students' conceptions of truth within a particular course, as revealed through interviews and essays (e.g., McCarthy, 1987; McCarthy & Fishman, 1991). Besides providing a more detailed account of the nature of development, longitudinal "case studies" of this sort can lead to hypotheses about the kinds of experiences that facilitate epistemological development, for example, Haviland and Kramer's (1991) analysis of the diary of Anne Frank suggests that intensity of emotion about a particular issue can serve as a stimulus to more complex constructions of the issue.

Notes

1 In this respect, Belenky's (1996) renaming of the position as Silenced seems appropriate.

2 In WWK we call this position "Received Knowledge." All four of the coauthors now prefer the more active verbal form for each of the positions.

3 For convenience, I refer to Received "Knowers" rather than "Knowing," but I do not mean to imply that a given individual always operates out of a single perspective.

4 I borrow the uppercase (A and T) from Perry to connote the power of Authority and the nature of Truth as conceived at this position.

5 Even today, women constitute only about 12% of Harvard's faculty of Arts and Sciences.

6 In a survey distributed as part of the "Pathways Project" (Rayman & Brett, 1993) at Wellesley, students were asked to respond to the statement, "I prefer subject matter with precise answers to subject matter with

multiple interpretations." This question discriminated significantly, and more than any other, (a) between those students who said on entering the college that they planned to major in math or science from those who said they planned to major in social sciences of humanities; and (b) between those who at the end of the sophomore year stuck with their plan to major in math or science and those who switched to a nonscience major.

References

Arch, J. (1998). Epistemological assumptions and approaches to learning in three academic disciplines. Unpublished undergraduate honors thesis, Wellesley College, Wellesley, MA.

Barber, B. (1984). *Strong democracy: Participatory politics for a new age.* Berkeley: University of California Press.

Basseches, M. (1986). Dialectical thinking and young adult cognitive development. In R. A. Mines & K. S. Kitchener (Eds.), *Adult cognitive development: Methods and models.* New York: Praeger.

Belenky, M. (1996). Public homeplaces: Nurturing the development of people, families, and communities. In *Knowledge, difference, and power: Essays inspired by* Women's Ways of Knowing, 393–440. New York: Basic Books.

Belenky, M., Bond, L., & Weinstock, J. (1997). *A tradition that has no name: Public homeplaces and the development of people, families, and communities.* New York: Basic Books.

Belenky, M., Clinchy, B., Goldberger, N., R., & Tarule, J. (1986/1997). *Women's ways of knowing: The development of self, mind, and voice.* New York: Basic Books.

Berreby, D. (1995, April 9). Unabsolute truths: Clifford Geertz. *The New York Times Magazine.*

Bordo, S. (1986). The Cartesian masculinization of thought. *Signs, 11,* 439–456. Reprinted in S, Harding, & J. O'Barr (Eds.) (1987). *Sex and scientific inquiry* (pp. 247–264). Chicago: University of Chicago Press.

Clayton, V. & Birren, J. (1980). The development of wisdom across the life span: A reexamination of an ancient topic. *Life span development and behavior, 3,* 103–135.

Clinchy, B. (1996). Connected and separate knowing: Toward a marriage of two minds. In N. Goldberger, J. Tarule, B. Clinchy, & M. Belenky (Eds.), *Knowledge, difference, and power: Essays inspired by* Women's Ways of Knowing (pp. 205–247). New York: Basic Books.

Clinchy, B. (1998). A plea for epistemological pluralism. In B. Clinchy and J. Norem (Eds.), *Readings in gender and psychology* (760–777). New York: New York University Press.

Clinchy, B. & Norem, J. (1998). Code: In-Conclusion . . . In B. Clinchy and J. Norem (Eds.), *Readings in gender and psychology* (778–798). New York: New York University Press.

Clinchy, B., & Zimmerman, C. (1982). Epistemology and agency in the development of undergraduate women. In P. Perun (Ed.), *The undergraduate woman: Issues in educational enquity.* Lexington, MA: D. C. Heath.

Clinchy, B., & Zimmerman, C. (1985). Growing up intellectually: Issues for college women. *Work in Progress.* No. 19. Wellesley, MA: Stone Center Working Papers Series.

David, C. (1999). Fear of success and cognitive styles in college women. Unpublished undergraduate honors thesis. Wellesley College, Wellesley, MA.

Elbow, P. (1986). *Embracing contraries.* New York: Oxford University Press.

Elbow, P. (1973). Appendix Essay: The doubting game and the believing game—An analysis of the intellectual enterprise. In *Writing without teachers.* London: Oxford University Press.

Friedman, M. (1985). *The healing dialogue in psychotherapy.* New York: Jason Aronson.

Galotti, K., Drebus, D., & Reimer, R. (1999, April). Ways of knowing as learning styles. Research Display presented at the Biennial Meeting of the Society for Research in Child Development, Albuquerque, NM.

Galotti, K., Clinchy, B., Ainsworth, K., Lavin, B., & Mansfield, A. (1999). A new way of assessing ways of knowing: The attitudes toward thinking and learning survey (ATTLS). *Sex Roles, 40,* 745–766.

Geertz, C. (1986, Winter). The uses of diversity. *Michigan Quarterly Review,* 105–123.

Gilligan, C. (1993). Letter to readers. 1993. In *In a different voice: Psychological theory and women's development,* 2nd ed., ix–xxvii. Cambridge: Harvard University Press.

Goldberger, N. (1981). *Meeting the development needs of college students.* Final report presented to the Fund for the Improvement of Post-Secondary Education (FIPSE), Simon's Rock of Bard College, Great Barrington, MA.

Goldberger, N. (1996a). Cultural imperatives and diversity in ways of knowing. In *Knowledge, difference, and power: Essays inspired by* Women's Ways of Knowing, 335–371. New York: Basic Books.

Goldberger, N. (1996b). Looking backward, looking forward. In *Knowledge, difference, and power: Essays inspired by* Women's Ways of Knowing, 1–21. New York: Basic Books.

Goodfield, J. (1991/1994). *An imagined world: A story of scientific discovery.* An Arbor: University of Michigan Press.

Hall, G. S. (1917). *Adolescence: Its psychology and its relations to physiology, anthropology, sociology, sex, crime, religion, and education.* New York: D. Appleton & Co.

Haviland, J. M., & Kramer, D. A. (1991). Affect-cognition relationships in adolescent diaries: The case of Anne Frank. *Human Development, 34,* 143–159.

Kegan, R. (1982). *The evolving self.* Cambridge, MA: Harvard University Press.

Kegan, R. (1994). *In over our heads: The mental demands of modern life.* Cambridge, MA: Harvard University Press.

Kochman, T. (1981). *Black and white styles in conflict.* Chicago: University of Chicago Press.

Kohn, A. (1990). *The brighter side of human nature: Altruism and empathy in everyday life.* New York: Basic Books.

Labouvie-Vief, G. (1990). Wisdom as integrated thought: Historical and developmental perspectives. In R. Sternberg (Ed.), *Wisdom: Its nature, origins, and development* (pp. 52–83). Cambridge: Cambridge University Press.

Lewis, M., & Simon, R. (1986). Discourse not intended for her: Learning and thinking within patriarchy. *Harvard Educational Review, 56,* 457–471.

Mansfield, A., & Clinchy, B. (1992, May 28). *The influence of different kinds of relationships on the development and expression of "separate" and "connected" knowing in undergraduate women.* Paper presented as part of a symposium, *Voicing relationships, knowing connection: Exploring girls' and women's development,* at the 22nd Annual Symposium of the Jean Piaget Society: Development and vulnerability in close relationships. Montreal, Québec, Canada.

McCarthy, Lucille P. (1987). A stranger in strange lands: A college student writing across the curriculum. *Research in the Teaching of English, 21,* 233–265.

McCarthy, Lucille P., & Fishman, Stephen M. (1991). Boundary conversations: Conflicting ways of knowing in philosophy and interdisciplinary research. *Research in the Teaching of English, 25,* 419–468.

Murdoch, I. (1970/1985). *The sovereignty of good.* London: ARK Paperbacks, Routledge & Kegan Paul.

Oser, F., & Reich, K. (1987). The challenge of competing explanations: The development of thinking in terms of complementarity of 'theories.' *Human Development, 30,* 178–186.

Perry, W. (1970/1999). *Forms of intellectual and ethical development in the college years.* New York: Holt, Rinehart, and Winston.

Rabin, C. (1994). *Separate and connected knowing in undergraduate men and women.* Unpublished undergraduate honors thesis. Wellesley College. Wellesley, MA.

Rayman, P., & Brett, B. (1993). *Pathways for women in science: The Wellesley report.* Wellesley, MA: Wellesley College.

Rich, A. (1979). *On lies, secrets, and silence: Selected prose (1966–1978).* New York: Norton.

Rogers, C. & Farson, R. (1967). Active listening. In Haney, W. *Communication and organizational behavior: Text and cases.* (81–97). Homewood, IL: Richard D. Irwin, Inc.

Ruddick, S. (1996). Reason's femininity: A case for connected knowing. In *Knowledge, difference, and power: Essays inspired by* Women's Ways of Knowing, 248–273. New York: Basic Books.

Schwaber, E. (1983). Schwaber, E. (1983). Construction, reconstruction, and the mode of clinical attunement. In A. Goldberg, *The future of psychoanalysis.* (pp. 273–291). New York: International University Press.

Schweickart, P. (1996). Speech is silver, silence is gold: The assymetrical intersubjectivity of communicative action. In *Knowledge, difference, and power: Essays inspired by* Women's Ways of Knowing. 305–331. New York: Basic Books.

Spelman, E. (1988). *Inessential woman: Problems of exclusion in feminist thought.* Boston: Beacon Press.

Woolf, V. (1932/1948). How should one read a book? In *The common reader, Series 1 and 2* (pp. 281–295). New York: Harcourt Brace.

CHAPTER 39

CONNECTED AND SEPARATE KNOWING: TOWARD A MARRIAGE OF TWO MINDS

BLYTHE MCVICKER CLINCHY

In *WOMEN'S WAYS OF KNOWING (WWK, 1986)* Mary Belenky, Nancy Goldberger, Jill Tarule, and I described an epistemological position we called *procedural knowledge,* which took two forms, encompassing two "procedures" that many of the women we interviewed seemed to use in searching for truth; we called them "separate" and "connected" knowing. In the ensuing years, observing the varied and often surprising meanings assigned to these notions by some who have befriended them and the abuse that has been heaped upon them by some of their foes, I have occasionally felt like the character played by Woody Allen in the film *Annie Hall,* who, returning to childhood as an invisible presence, observes his parents engaged in one of their customary and (to him) imbecilic arguments. Incensed by the absurdity of both their positions, he shouts, "You're both wrong!" but his shouts are inaudible. In this chapter I want to make my views on separate and especially connected knowing audible.

Connected knowing was originally a serendipitous discovery. We did not ask the women we interviewed to tell us about it; they did so spontaneously, and from their comments we constructed the procedure as a sort of "ideal type." Since then, I have been attempting through systematic research and conversations with colleagues (alive and dead, in person and in print) to ascertain how the two procedures (or various versions thereof) play out in actual practice. My colleague Annick Mansfield and I (1992) developed an interview designed to elicit the ways in which men and women define the two procedures; how they feel about them; what they see as their benefits, drawbacks, and purposes; when and where and with whom they do and do not use each procedure; and how their use of them has changed over time. A number of researchers, including my own students, as well as other investigators at various institutions working with widely varying populations, have also used some version of this interview. Drawing on this work, I shall try in this chapter to clarify and complicate the concepts of separate and connected knowing, and, along the way, contest misreadings of the two modes that seem to me especially pernicious.

Believing and Doubting

Let me begin by defining the two orientations as we intended to define them in *WWK.* If you approach this chapter as a separate knower, you examine its arguments with a critical eye, insisting that I justify every point. In the writer Peter Elbow's terms you "play the doubting game" (1973), looking for flaws in my reasoning, considering how I might be misinterpreting the evidence I present, what alternative interpretations could be made, and whether I might be omitting evidence that would contradict my position. The standards you apply in evaluating my arguments are objective and impersonal; they have been agreed upon and codified by logicians and scientists. You need not be a person to apply these rules; you could be a cleverly programmed computer.

If, on the other hand, you take a connected approach to this chapter, you read it with an empathic, receptive eye. Instead of inspecting the text for flaws, you play "the believing game" (Elbow, 1973): if something I say seems to you absurd, you do not ask, "What are your arguments for such a silly view as that?' but rather, 'What do you see? . . . Give me the vision in your head. You are having an experience I don't have; help me to have it?' "The focus," Elbow writes, "is not on propositions and validity of inferences but on experiences or ways of seeing" (1986, p. 261). In asking, "Why do you think that?" connected knowers are not demanding logical or empirical justification; they are asking, "What in your experience has led you to that point of view?" They are concerned not with the soundness of the position but with its meaning to the knower; their aim is not to test its validity but to understand it.[1] Given our present primitive grasp of the "rules" for connected knowing, it would be impossible to program a computer to practice it, and given its "personal" character, it may never be possible.

In fact, of course, you will probably approach this chapter with a mixture of the two orientations. Although for the sake of convenience I will cast separate and connected knowing into dualistic terms, I do not mean to suggest that the two modes are mutually exclusive. "Separate knowers" and "connected knowers" are fictional characters; in reality the two modes can and do coexist within the same individual. Later in the chapter I will try to deconstruct the dualities and complicate the picture. But for the moment, to paraphrase Virginia Woolf (1929/1989), let these lies flow from my lips, and remember that they are lies.

In separate knowing one takes an adversarial stance toward new ideas, even when the ideas seem intuitively appealing; the typical mode of discourse is argument. In WWK we used the following excerpt from an interview with a college sophomore to illustrate the orientation, and we have used it in research and in workshops to stimulate discussion of separate knowing:

> I never take anything someone says for granted. I just tend to see the contrary, I like playing the devil's advocate, arguing the opposite of what somebody's thinking,

thinking of exceptions, or thinking of a different train of thought.

People often use images of war in describing separate knowing. Consider, for example, a young man we call Mel,[2] who espouses a sort of Patriot missile epistemology: "If I could get a job shooting holes in other people's [ideas]," he said, "I would enjoy my life immensely."

> If somebody explains [his or her position] to me and I can . . . shoot holes in it, then I won't tend to believe it, and if they can explain away every misgiving that I have about the [position], then I'll tend to believe it . . . [And] if they seriously believe in something which you think is very wrong, if you—if you shoot enough holes in what they're saying, they'll start doubting it themselves. It could happen to you too. It happens the other way around.

In contrast, in connected knowing one tries to embrace new ideas, looking for what is "right" even in positions that seem initially wrongheaded or even abhorrent. An excerpt from another college sophomore illustrates this approach:

> When I have an idea about something, and it differs from the way another person is thinking about it, I'll usually try to look at it from that person's point of view, see how they could say that, why they think that they're right, why it makes sense.

As an undergraduate we call Cecily said, "If you listen to people and listen to what they have to say, maybe you can understand why they feel the way they do. There are reasons. They're not just being irrational." Virginia Woolf, posing the question "How should one read a book?" (1932/1948), advises the reader to "try to become" the author, and Cecily agrees:

> When I read a philosopher I try to think as the author does. It's hard, but I try not to bias the train of thought with my own impressions. I try to just pretend that I'm the author. I try to really just put myself in that person's place and feel why is it that they believe this way.

Connected knowers act not as adversaries, but as allies, even advocates, of the position they are examining. Become the author's "fellow worker," his "accomplice," Woolf says, and Sheila, one of our research participants, tells us that in counseling undergraduates she is "usually a bit of a chameleon": "I try to look for pieces of the truth in what the person's saying instead of going contrary to them. Sort of collaborate with them."

Some of our research participants and some of our readers perceive the separate knower's argumentative style as a pig-headed attempt to bully the opponent into submission, but I regard this as a primitive or degenerate form of separate knowing. Properly practiced, the procedure requires that one hold one's views loosely, remaining open to competing positions. For Mel, other people's ideas are fair game, but so too are his: "It happens the other way around too," he says. "It could happen to you." For mature separate knowers, the doubting game is a fair game.

Whereas separate knowers are sometimes perceived as stubbornly attached to their own opinions and deaf to the views of others, connected knowers are sometimes perceived as excessively open-minded—indeed, as having no minds of their own, like the "over-empathizers" characterized by the psychologist Robert Hogan as "equivocating jellyfish" (1973, p. 224). But the picture of the connected knower as merely a jellyfish, clone, chameleon, or wimp, like that of the separate knower as merely a bully, is a caricature. It portrays, perhaps, a primitive or regressive form of connected knowing, but it grossly distorts more mature forms. Sheila, one of our most proficient connected knowers, describes herself as only "a bit of a chameleon," and is careful to distinguish between understanding a point of view and agreeing with it. She is not gullible. She does not believe everything she hears—at least not for long. She "believes" in a point of view only in order to understand it. "Believing" is a procedure that guides her interaction with other minds; it is not the result of the interaction.

Connected Knowing as Procedure

Notice the recurrence of the word try in the descriptions connected knowers give of their approach; Cecily, for instance, uses it four times in four sentences. Although some people exhibit a proclivity toward connected knowing that appears to be "natural," those who really seem to understand and use the approach rarely describe it as effortless and often allude to its difficulties. The philosopher Elizabeth Spelman

refers to the "strenuousness of knowing other people, even people very much like ourselves" (Spelman, 1988, p. 181), and the poet Adrienne Rich, in a brilliant essay recounting her attempt to enter the mind and heart of Emily Dickinson by journeying to the poet's home, depicts herself as "an insect, vibrating at the frames of windows, clinging to the panes of glass, trying to connect" (Rich, 1979, p. 161). True connected knowing is neither easy nor natural. As the anthropologist Clifford Greertz says:

> Comprehending that which is, in some manner of form, alien to us and likely to remain so, without either smoothing it over with vacant murmurs of common humanity, disarming it with to-each-his-own indifferentism, or dismissing it as charming, lovely even, but inconsequent, is a skill we have arduously to learn, and having learnt it, work continuously to keep alive; it is not a connatural capacity, like depth perception or the sense of balance, upon which we can complacently rely. (Geertz, 1986, p. 122)

In WWK we defined connected knowing as a rigorous, deliberate, and demanding procedure, a way of knowing that requires work. Contrasting it with the epistemological position we called "subjectivism," we said, "It is important to distinguish between the effortless intuition of subjectivism (in which one identifies with positions that feel right) and the deliberate imaginative extension of one's understanding into positions that initially feel wrong or remote" (WWK, 1986, p. 121). Many of our readers—friends and foes alike—have ignored the distinction, conflating connected knowing with subjectivism by treating it more as a reflex than as a procedure; connected and procedural become antonyms (procedural apparently being synonymous with separate), thus seeming to render connected knowing nonprocedural. The philosopher Lorraine Code makes this error, when, in discussing WWK, she describes people behaving "connectedly or procedurally" (Code, 1991, p. 261), and so does a member of my own household, who has read, apparently with care, every draft of everything I have written on this topic.

My immediate reactions to such misreadings are decidedly oppositional: like Mel, I prepare to launch a few verbal missiles. But then I seem to hear Cecily's voice whispering in my ear that perhaps our readers and my housemate are "not being irrational"; perhaps "there are reasons" for their "silly ideas." I resolve to use connected knowing procedures to try to understand why people are unable to see connected knowing as a procedure, why they persistently confuse it with subjectivism. Utilizing one of my favorite defense mechanisms, I transform a source of irritation into a subject for research.

In qualitative research, as methodologist Grant McCracken says, "the investigator serves as a kind of 'instrument' in the collection and analysis of data:" "Detection proceeds by a kind of 'rummaging' process. The investigator must use his or her experience and imagination to find (or fashion) a match for the patterns evidenced by the data" (McCracken, 1988, pp. 18, 19). I did not need to rummage very deeply before coming up with a couple of matches, two occasions on which I had interpreted as subjectivist, and dismissed as relatively mindless, behavior that I now believe might have exemplified connected knowing.

First match: I began teaching at a women's college while still attending graduate school at Harvard, where class discussions followed the ballistic model favored by separate knowers. Although I sometimes found it hard to breathe in this atmosphere, I also found it stimulating, and it became for me the mark of a "good class." When I tried to create the same atmosphere in the classes I was teaching, however, I met with considerable resistance from students like Sue, who said to her interviewer, "In class, when you want to say something, you just want to have it float out in the air and just, you know, stand. You don't want to have it, like, shot down." My students spoke their piece and listened politely as others spoke theirs, but they would not take issue with one another, and, in my opinion, they spent far too much time exchanging anecdotes about their personal experiences. In *Professing Feminism*, Daphne Patai and Noretta Koertge speak scornfully of women's studies groups in which everyone agrees with everyone else, "and everybody feels validated and cozy" (Patai & Koertge, 1994, p. 174). That is how I regarded these classes: it is embarrassing to recall that in a piece written at the time, I dismissed them as "sewing circle classes." (How's that for gender stereotyping?)

A second "match" drawn out of the compost of memory came from a longitudinal study that preceded and overlapped with the *WWK* research in which my colleague Claire Zimmerman and I (Clinchy & Zimmerman, 1982, 1985)

were using Williams Perry's (1970) "scheme" (largely derived from the illustrated by interviews with Harvard males) to trace the epistemological and ethical development of a sample of undergraduate women. Some of the questions we asked were designed to ascertain whether the students had reached a position in Perry's scheme that involves critical thinking. Some clearly had. For instance, during the first year of the project a student made a comment we would now consider prototypical of separate knowing: "As soon as someone tells me his point of view, I immediately start arguing in my head the opposite point of view. When someone is saying something, I can't help turning it upside down. "The next year, we converted this response into a stimulus and asked the students to respond to it.[3] To our dismay, most of them said that they didn't much like that approach and they didn't use it much. Grace, for instance, said that even when she disagreed with someone she didn't start arguing in her head; she started trying to imagine herself in the person's situation. She said, "I sort of fit myself into it in my mind and then I say, 'I see what you mean'" She said, "There's this initial point where I kind of go into the story, you know? And become like Alice in Wonderland falling down the rabbit hole." Search as we might, we could find no place in Perry's scheme for falling down rabbit holes, and so we interpreted Grace's comment as evidence not of a particular way of thinking but of the absence of any kind of thinking. We saw it, as our critics often see connected knowing, as a sort of naïve credulity: Grace, we concluded, was the sort of person who would fall for anything.

It took me a long time to see that people like Grace and the students in those sewing-circle classes might be following some sort of (admittedly tacit) procedure, rather than simply wallowing in subjectivity. Because connected knowing has much in common with subjectivism, the difference can be difficult to discern. Both subjectivists and connected knowers show respect for views that differ from their own: they seem to listen and refuse to criticize. Both value the sort of knowledge that emerges from firsthand experience, and both draw on feelings and intuition as sources of information. In each of these respects, however, connected knowing does not simply incorporate features of subjectivism; it builds on them, and the resulting construction is quite different.

Validity, Understanding, and Trust in the Knower

Incidents of miscommunication between men and women like the ones the sociolinguist Deborah Tannen (1990) recounts in *You Just Don't Understand* often come about because the men are operating out of a separate knowing perspective, while the women are operating out of a connected knowing perspective. For instance, a wife listens intently and nods encouragingly as she draws from her husband his reasons for wishing to buy a new car; the next day he turns up with the new car and is hurt and astonished by her angry reaction. The husband has taken the wife's uncritical acceptance as evidence of her agreement and approval; the wife, however, was merely trying to understand. Miscommunications between the authors of *WWK* and their readers take a similar form, especially when the readers are schooled in philosophy, a discipline founded on adversarial reasoning (Moulton, 1983) and, according to the philosopher Richard Rorty, preoccupied with questions concerning the validity of knowledge.[4] This is the separate knowing perspective. Connected knowing is concerned with matters that, as Rorty (cited by Bruner, 1986, p. 12) says, Anglo American philosophy does not often address, questions about the meaning of experience. Lorraine Code believes, as do we, that in dealing with the formula "S knows that P," philosophers have paid too little attention to S, to characteristics of the knower and her situation that can affect what is known, but she argues that we go too far in the other direction, focusing exclusively on the knower—on how she knows—and ignoring *what* she knows, the content and validity of her views.

We invite that charge, I think, by using the word *know*[5] instead of, say, *believe* or *think* or *feel*. For most philosophers, to "know" something is to make some claim to validity. I may believe that Martians are filling my cellar with poison gas, but surely I do not "know" it. Although we were aware that the word *know* was ambiguous and possibly misleading, we decided, nonetheless, to use it, because it seemed the connected thing to do: we wanted as much as possible to hear the women in their own terms, and "knowing" seemed to come closest to what most of them meant. We rejected "thinking" because, given the dichotomy in this culture between cognition and affect, we were afraid that "thinking" might imply absence of feeling, and for many of the women

feeling was intimately involved in "knowing." We rejected "belief" because although some of the women we interviewed distinguished between believing and knowing, others did not: in subjectivism, for example, the terms are synonymous. The literary theorist Patrocinio (Patsy) Schweickart (see her chapter in this volume) writes, "One cannot assert meaningfully that something is true or valid only for oneself." This, of course, is precisely what subjectivists do assert. "Everyone's opinion is right for him or her," they say, and, although such a statement may not be meaningful in some discourse communities, it is meaningful to them. Schweickart goes on, "I have beliefs, prejudices, or presuppositions; but I *make* validity claims" (Schweickart, 1988, p. 299). Again, although this is a sensible distinction, it is not one that subjectivists make: "Anyone's interpretation is valid, if that's the way he or she sees it. I mean nobody can tell you that your opinion is wrong, you know."

In interviewing the women and poring over transcripts of their interviews, we relied predominantly on connected knowing, suspending judgment in an attempt to make sense of the women's ways of making sense of their experience. Code regards connected knowing as "epistemologically problematic" (Code, 1991, p. 253) because it precludes evaluation, and she notes with disapproval a presumption shared by subjectivists and connected knowers that, as one student said, "A person's experience can't be wrong." Although she is aware of the damage done in the past by "experts' telling women what they are really experiencing" (Code, 1991, p. 256) and acknowledges that our "quasi-therapeutic" techniques may be useful in "empowering women who have been 'damaged by patriarchal oppression'" (Code, 1991, p. 252), Code argues that our "acritical acceptance" of the women's autobiographical accounts "is not the only—or the best—alternative" (Code, 1991, p. 256). For us, however, at the data-collection stage of our research, there was no alternative. In order to hear a person in her own terms, the listener must suspend judgment. We may object to the lessons a woman has drawn from her experience. We may feel that she is a victim of "false consciousness," that she has been brainwashed by her oppressors, and that the terms in which she casts her experience are not "her own" but have been foisted on her by the patriarchy. Nevertheless, we must put these thoughts aside and accept her reality as her reality, not only accept it but collude with her in its construction. As the social scientist Stephanie Riger says,

> In contrast to traditional social science in which the researcher is the expert on assessing reality, an interpretive-phenomenological approach permits women to give their own conception of their experiences. participants, not researchers, are considered the experts at making sense of their world. . . . The shift in authority is striking. (Riger, 1992, p. 733)

Psychologist Jill Morawski and literary theorist R. S. Steele show how in traditional psychological research "the power of the psychologist is increased at the cost of the subjects" (Morawski & Steele, 1991, p. 112), offering as an illustration the psychologists Walter Mischel's (1969) pronouncement that while "subjects" perceive continuities in their personality traits over time, statistics prove them wrong.

> According to [Mischel], in so far as the subjects are numbers on "IBM sheets," that is, objects of scientific reductionism, they are reliable. However, as sentient subjects, that is, beings capable of self-reflection and of constructing a personal history, they are untrustworthy. (Morawski & Steele, 1991, p. 113)

Distrust of the "subject" also permeates accounts of traditional psycho-analytic psychotherapy. After perusing this literature, the psychoanalyst Evelyne Schwaber concluded that "analytic listening remains steeped in a hierarchical two-reality view" (Schwaber, 1983a, p. 390), "the one the patient experiences, and the one the analysts "knows" (Schwaber, 1983a, p. 386):

> My first supervisor listened by sifting the material through her own perspective—that is, from the vantage point of the analyst's reality—in trying to aid the patients observing ego to recognize the distortions in her perceptions. The second supervisor sharpened the focus from within the patient's perspective, to see in it a certain plausibility, however outlandish, unrealistic, entitled, it may have seemed to the outside observer. (Schwaber, 1983a, pp. 379–380)

Schwaber, like the "constructed knowers" in *WWK*, sees value in the more separate as well as the more connected approach and uses elements of both in her work, but she firmly rejects the notion that the analyst's view is more accurate than the patient's: the two realities, she says, are "relative" rather than hierarchical (1983a, p. 390).

Like the males in Tanner's anecdotes, readers sometimes interpret our "acritical acceptance" of the women's stories as implying approval of their views. To refrain from criticism, however, means to refrain from approval as well as disapproval. (Good critics, after all, illuminate the merits as well as the faults of the things they examine.) Connected knowing shares with subjectivism an appreciation of subjective reality, but it does not adhere to the subjectivist doctrine of "subjective validity," the view that all opinions are equally valid and "everyone's opinion is right for him or her."[6] Connected knowing does not imply relativism in this sense. When one is using techniques of connected knowing, as in the initial stages of our research, issues of validity are simply irrelevant.

Although both subjectivists and connected knowers might say that "experience can't be wrong," they mean different things when they say it. Subjectivists *are* unmitigated relativists. They do believe that whatever truths have emerged from a person's firsthand experience are valid for that person. They do believe that these truths are unambiguous, in the feminist philosopher M. E. Hawkesworth's (1989) terms. "transparent" and "unmediated" by personal or cultural preconceptions. Asked how she decides what a poem means, a student speaking from this perspective replies, "Whatever you see in the poem, it's got to be there." Although her teacher may feel that such a student has ignored the words on the page, treating the text as a mirror or an inkblot into which she projects the contents of her own mind, to the student the meaning is simply there on the page. Much (although not all) of Hawkesworth's critique of feminist positions based on intuition can be applied to subjectivism:

> The distrust of the conceptual aspects of thought, which sustains claims that genuine knowledge requires immediate apprehension, presumes not only that an unmediated grasp of reality is possible but also that it is authoritative. Moreover, appeals to intuition raise the specter of an authoritarian trump that precludes the possibility of rational debate. Claims based on intuition manifest an unquestioning acceptance of their own veracity. . . . Thus, intuition provides a foundation for claims about the world that is at

once authoritarian, admitting of no further discussion, and relativist, since no individual can refute another's "immediate" apprehension of reality. Operating at a level of assertion that admits of no further elaboration or explication, those who abandon themselves to intuition conceive and give birth to dreams, not to truth.[7] (Hawkesworth, 1989, p. 545).

Code (1991, p. 258, n. 74), persisting in reading *WWK* as an endorsement of subjectivism, quotes this passage from Hawkesworth in criticizing what she interprets as our position. In fact, we could have written the passage ourselves, and we nearly did, in describing Minna, a Hispanic woman enrolled in a community college who, in our view, was beginning to struggle out of subjectivism into procedural knowledge. Deserted by her husband and left with an eight-year-old daughter, no money, no employable skills, and no friends, Minna saw now that as Hawkesworth puts it, in abandoning herself to intuition she had "conceived and given birth to dreams, not to truth." "I was confused about everything," she said. "I was unrealistic about things. I was more in a fantasy world. You have to see things for what they are, not for what you want to see them. I don't want to live in a dream world." Now, she says, "I think everything out, and I want to make sure I understand exactly what's going on before I do anything" (*WWK*, 1986, p. 99). Code warns that "a subjective knower's 'gut' often lets her down," and subjectivism is not necessarily "conducive to empowerment" (Code, 1991, p. 254). This is not news to Minna, nor to the authors of *WWK*.

Unlike the feminist scholars who are the objects of Hawkesworth's critique, Sue, the student who wished that her words might float out into the air and just stand, does not *choose* to rely on private, intuitive truth; she has not yet developed an alternative method. Encapsulated in her own world, she can only assert her own truth. For many women who speak from a subjectivist perspective conversations, especially with like-minded people, are a source of great pleasure, but for Sue "discussion" in English class is futile: "Because I know I can't see where they're coming from, so why, you know, why keep trying at it if it doesn't feel comfortable to you, but you have your own thoughts that feel right?" With the advent of procedural knowing, epistemological isolation comes to an end, and collabo-

rative construction of knowledge through discussion becomes not only possible but, because truth is now problematic rather than transparent, essential. Separate knowers can engage in "rational debate," rather than mere assertion and counterassertion, in order to adjudicate truth claims. And connected knowers can obtain vicarious experience through mutual "elaboration and explication" of personal narratives.

This is the sort of interchange, I now believe, that was struggling to be born and may occasionally have emerged, although I could not hear it, in those sewing circle classes I perceived as utterly unproductive. It is easy to misperceive active listening as passive and polite, hard to see it as a genuine procedure, a "skill requiring arduously to be learned." Anyone who has tried to teach (or to learn) the art of connected interviewing.[8] however, knows how difficult it is to learn to listen "objectively," in the connected sense, that is, to hear the other in the other's own terms, to become "an observer from within" (Schwaber, 1983b, p. 274).

Affirming the Knower

In connected knowing it is essential to refrain from judgment "because," as the psychologist Carl Rogers says, "it is impossible to be accurately perceptive of another's inner world if you have formed an evaluative opinion of that person" (Rogers, 1980, p. 152). If you doubt that assertion, Rogers says, try to describe the views of someone you believe is definitely wrong in a fashion that the person will consider accurate. "In the believing game," Elbow writes, "the first rule is to refrain from doubting" (Elbow, 1973, p. 149). For her undergraduate honors thesis, Carolyn Rabin (1994) analyzed interviews on separate and connected knowing with undergraduates from the Massachusetts Institute of Technology and Wellesley College collected in the Clinchy–Mansfield project. She noted that for many of the MIT men this is what "connected knowing" meant—to refrain from criticism—and this is all it meant; they had not progressed beyond the first rule of the game. I argue, however, that fully developed connected knowing requires that one "affirm" or "confirm" the subjective reality of the other, and affirmation is not merely the absence of negative evaluation; it is a positive effortful act. Affirmation of a person or a position means, as Elbow says, "to say Yes to it" (Elbow, 1986, p. 279), rather than merely offering sympathetic understanding. Confirmation means, in the philosopher Martin Buber's wonderful phrases, to "imagine the real," to "make the other present" (Buber, quoted by Friedman, 1985, p. 4). It involves "a bold swinging . . . into the life of the other" (Buber, quoted by Kohn, 1990, p. 112), and as Alfie Kohn says, this other, for Buber, is a particular other, not an "interchangeable someone" (Kohn, 1990, p. 112), and the knower is "not merely avoiding objectification but affirmatively invoking, . . . addressing the other's status as a subject, . . . an actor, a knower, a center of experience" (Kohn, 1990, p. 100).

This "bold swinging into the life of the other" is a far cry from polite tolerance or "to-each-his-own indifferentism," but it is also not to be confused with approval or agreement. It should be obvious that, as Geertz puts it, "Understanding what people think doesn't mean you have to think the same thing" (Geertz, quoted in Berreby, 1995, p. 4). "Understanding,'" Geertz writes, "in the sense of comprehension, perception, and insight needs to be distinguished from 'understanding' in the sense of agreement of opinion, union of sentiment, or commonality of commitment. . . . We must learn to grasp what we cannot embrace" (Geertz, 1986, p. 122). From the connected knowing perspective, of course, we must first try very hard to embrace it.

Conversations involving mutual confirmation are not to be confused with the "relatively harmonious situations" described by Patai and Koertge and mentioned earlier, in which "everyone feels validated and cozy" (Patai & Koertge, 1994, p. 174). If "everyone feels validated" in this situation, it is not because they have been told they are right; it is because they have been heard. As one young woman said, "When people [are] interested in why I feel the way I do and why it makes sense to me, . . . I feel that what I have to say might mean something and has some impact." This sort of validation is especially welcome to procedural knowers. Whereas subjectivities are confident that they can arrive at the truth (the truth for them) simply by reading it off from experience (whatever you see in the poem, it's got to be there) or attending to their infallible guts, procedural knowers have no such assurance. Separate knowers need to know whether their views can survive the scrutiny of an outsider's critical eye, and connected knowers need

to know whether their thoughts can "mean something" to someone else, even, perhaps, "an attentive stranger" (Ruddick, 1984, p. 148).

In swinging boldly into the mind of another, truly saying yes to it, two perversions of "connected knowing" are prevented. One is to "use it as a weapon," as one woman said, as "when people say, 'Well, I can see how you would say that given your background,' . . . referring to my background as some wacky thing that nobody else has ever experienced," In this patronizing version, known, I am told, as "the California fuck off," one distances one's self from the other's experience, in effect saying "No" to it. A second perversion is to say yes too quickly, to assume without reflection that others feel as we do or as we would feel in their situation, that is, to assimilate the other to the self: "I know just how you feel!" We say, having, in fact, very little idea or quite the wrong idea.

The Self as Instrument

Where separate knowing requires "self-extrication," "weeding out the self," in Elbow's terms, connected knowing requires "self-insertion" or projection in the good sense" (Elbow, 1973, p. 149) or, to use a more feminine image, "receiving the other into [the] self" (Noddings 1984, p. 30). Procedures for minimizing "Projection in the bad sense" (Elbow, 1973, p. 149), or, as developmental psychologist Jean Piaget puts it, "excluding the intrusive self" (Piaget, 1972, quoted by Keller, 1983b, p. 134), have been well developed and are known to be effective, although of course not perfectly so. For instance, the effects of "bias" are reduced if observers in an experiment are "double-blinked," unaware of both the hypothesis being tested and the treatment to which the subjects have been assigned. Procedures for using the self as an instrument of understanding are less well developed, but practitioners of the increasingly prevalent "new paradigm" research have made considerable progress in developing and articulating them.

This is not the place to inventory these techniques, but I have already mentioned the procedure by which the investigator rummages through her experience in search of a "match." "The diverse aspects of the self," McCracken says, "become a bundle of templates to be held up against the data until parallels emerge" (McCracken, 1988, p. 19). "To understand a poem, an undergraduate said, "You must let the poem pass into you and become part of yourself, rather than something you see outside yourself. . . . There has to be some parallel between you and the poem." This is an active procedure: we must construct the parallels, by conjuring up "metaphorical extensions, analogies, association" (Elbow, 1973, p. 149), and we need not simply wait for a poem or a person or a patient to strike a chord, for by "fine turning" (Margulies, 1989, p. 16) the instrument of our subjectivity we can increase the likelihood of its "empathic resonance" (Howard, 1991, p. 189). Instead of simply "letting" the other in, we can prepare our minds to receive it by engaging in arduous systematic "self-reflection." McCracken advises, for instance, that in preparation for qualitative research, the investigator should construct a "detailed and systematic appreciation of his or her personal experience with the topic of interest. . . . The investigator must inventory and examine the associations, incidents and assumptions that surround the topic in his or her mind" (McCracken, 1988, p. 32), thus, "preparing the templates with which he or she will seek out matches' in the interview data. The investigator listens to the self in order to listen to the respondent" (McCracken, 1988, p. 33)

In conducting the interview, too, one uses the self as an instrument of understanding. The sociologist Marjorie DeVault, who has forcefully urged us to "analyze more carefully the specific ways that interviewers use personal experience as a resource for listening," describes her own procedure as focusing "on attention to the unsaid, in order to produce it as topic and make it speakable." It "involves noticing ambiguity and problems of expression in interview data, then drawing on my own experience in an investigation aimed at 'filling in' what has been incompletely said" (DeVault, 1990, p. 104).[9]

In using the self to understand the other, we risk imposing the self on the other; projection in the good sense can easily degenerate into projection in the bad sense. Patti Lather, a sympathetic practitioner of new paradigm research, worries that "rampant subjectivity" could prove to be its "nemesis" (Lather, 1986, p. 68). How are we to distinguish between the psychoanalyst Heinz Kohut's "empathy," defined as "the recognition of the self in the other" (Kohut, 1978, quoted by Jordan, 1991, p. 68), and the subjectivist's "Whatever you see in the poem, it's got to be there"?

How do we ensure that we are not treating the other as a mirror or a blot of ink, a mere receptacle for our own subjectivity? As the psychologist Alfred Margulies says, "Because empathy is by definition the 'imaginative projection of one's own consciousness into another being,' we will unavoidably find ourselves reflected within our gaze toward the other. I look for you and see myself" (Margulies, 1989, p. 58).

Clinicians and qualitative researchers agree that the matches one pulls from one's own experience should serve only as "clues" (DeVault, 1990, p. 104), "merely a bundle of possibilities, pointers, and suggestions that can be used to plumb the remarks of a respondent" (McCracken, 1988, p. 19). "Imagining how one would feel—or actually has felt," says Alfie Kohn, should be regarded as only a "provisional indication" (Kohn, 1990, p. 133), or as Margulies puts it, "a map constructed second-hand from another life's travels, a map that undergoes constant reworking, revision (re-vision), and clarification" (Margulies, 1989, p. 53). One must remain open to "subtle surprises," to emerging discrepancies between the map and the patient's "inscape." Qualitative researchers devise strategies for inviting surprise, often enlisting the cooperation of participants in reworking the map. Indeed, one must move beyond matching to achieve true understanding. In Kohn's terms we must move beyond "imagine-self" to "imagine-other." if we assume that we have reached full understanding once we run out of matches, we are indeed assimilating the other to the self. The psychiatrist Maurice Friedman calls this truncated procedure "identification":

> [T]he therapist resonates with the experience related by the client only to the extent that they resemble his or her own. It says, in effect, "I am thou," but misses the Thou precisely at the point where its otherness and uniqueness takes it out of the purview of one's own life stance and life experience. (Friedman, 1985, p. 197)

I, Thou, And It

Some of our readers and research participants conceive of connected knowing as useful only in dealing with people. At worst, they describe it as a way of "being nice," getting along with people," and "keeping the peace"; at best, they see it as a way of understanding directed only at live and present people. In *WWK*, however, we said, "When we speak of separate and connected knowing we refer not to any sort of relationship between the self and another person but [to] relationships between knowers and the objects (or subjects) of knowing (which may or may not be persons)" (*WWK*, 1986, p. 102). We said that "the mode of knowing is personal, but the object of knowing need not be," citing Cecily's comment (*WWK*, 1986, p. 121) that in reading a philosopher she "tries to think as the author does," and the comment of another student, who said that "you shouldn't read a book [in this case, Dante's *Divine Comedy*] just as something printed and distant from you, but as a real experience of someone who went through some sort of situation" (*WWK*, 1986, p. 113).

In connected knowing, the "it" is transformed into a "thou," and the "I" enters into relationship with the thou.[10] Scientists use this procedure. The biologist Barbara McClintock says, in words that have grown familiar, that you must have the patience to hear what the corn "has to say to you" and the openness "to let it come to you" (Keller, 1983a, p. 198), and the pseudonymous biochemist portrayed by June Goodfield in *An Imagined World* says, "If you really want to understand about a tumor you've got to *be* a tumor" (Goodfield, 1991/1994, p. 226). According to the psychologist Seymour Papert, even toddlers are capable of a sensorimotor version of connected knowing. Before the age of two, he says, he "fell in love with gears"; indeed, he became a gear; "You can *be* the gear," he writes. "You can understand how it turns by projecting yourself into its place and turning with it" (Papert, 1980, pp. vi–vii). Papert and his colleague Sherry Turkle found that some of the students they observed learning to construct computer programs—especially girls and women—also "reasoned form within" their programs. Anne, for instance, "psychologically places herself in the same space as the sprites" (the objects whose movements she is programming). "She is down there, in with the sprites. . . . When she talks about them her gestures with hand and body show her moving with and among them. When she speaks of them she uses languages such as 'I move here'" (Turkle & Papert, 1990, p. 144).[11] Anne treats the computer rather like "a person" (Turkle, 1984, p. 112), "allowing ideas to emerge in the give and take of conversation with it" (Turkle, 1984, p. 104).

Our research participants often describe their way of reading in similar terms. "You should treat the text as if it were a friend," a student said, and she meant, as Schweickart means, not just to treat it nicely, but to regard it as "not a mere object, like a stone, but the objectification of a subject" (Schweickart, 1989, p. 83). Adrienne Rich, Schweickart writes, aims to make the poet Emily Dickinson "live as the substantial palpable presence animating her works" (Schweickart, 1989, p. 50), to "make [her] present" as Buber (quoted by Friedman, 1985, p. 4) would say. Connected readings is an intersubjective procedure: "The reader encounters not simply a text, but a 'subjectified object': the 'heart and mind' of another woman. She comes into close contact with an interiority—a power, a creativity, a suffering, a vision—that is *not* identical with her own." Schweickart contrasts this feminist version of reader response theory with one put forth by literary theorist Georges Poulet. Poulet also takes a personal approach: "To understand a literary work . . . is to let the individual who wrote it reveal [herself] to us *in* us" (Poulet, 1980, p. 46, quoted by Schweickart, 1986, p. 52). But he portrays reader and author as opponents in a zero-sum game. The reader "becomes the 'prey' of what he reads. . . . His consciousness is 'invaded,' 'annexed,' 'usurped.' . . . In the final analysis, the process of reading leaves room for only one subjectivity" (Schweickart, 1986, pp. 52–53).

In the feminist version of the theory (we call it "connected reading"), on the otherhand, there is a "doubling" of subjectivity: "One can be placed at the disposal of the text while the other remains with the reader." Schweickart warns, however, that ultimately, because the reader constructs the meaning of the text, "there is only one subject present—the reader. . . . The subjectivity roused to life by reading, while it may be attributed to the author, is nevertheless not a separate subjectivity but a projection of the subjectivity of the reader" (Schweickart, 1986, p. 53). Projection in the bad sense is a very real danger when the author, being absent, cannot speak for herself.[12] Schweickart:

> In real conversation the other person can interrupt, object to an erroneous interpretation, provide further explanations, change her mind, change the topic, or cut off conversation altogether. In reading, there are no comparable safeguards against the appro-

priation of the text by the reader. (Schweickart, 1986, p. 53)

The best that can be done in connected reading is to encourage absent authors to speak and to join them in a semblance of collaboration. The writer and critic Doris Grumbach recounts a midlife change in her ways of reading that sounds like a transition from a relatively separate to a relatively connected approach. "It is hard work to read more slowly," she says. "But when I slow down, I interlard the writers' words with my own. I think about what they are saying. . . . I dillydally in their views" (Grumbach, 1991, p. 15). Reading becomes a kind of conversation, and the reader apprentices herself to the writer. "Reading in the new way now, I learn. Before I seemed to be instructing the book with my superior opinions" (Crumbach, 1991, p. 15).[11] ("Do not dictate to your author, try to become him" [Woolf, 1932, p. 282].)

"Subjectivist theories of reading," Schweickart says, "silence the text" (Schweickart, 1989, p. 83). This applies to the informal subjectivist theories of ordinary readers as well as to members of the lit-crit community: "We're all allowed to read into a poem any meaning we want," and "Whatever you see in the poem, it's got to be there," whether the poet likes it or not. Objectivist readings, on the other hand, such as the ones offered by people adhering to the epistemological position we call *received knowing,* silence the reader: to find out what a poem means, "you'd have to ask the poet; it's his poem." For connected readers it is different: A poem does not belong solely to its author. "Poems are written," a student explained, "but you also have to interpret them." A poem is not something "that sits there and does nothing. It has to be interpreted by other people, and those people are going to have their own ideas of what it means." Those ideas, however, must be grounded in the text: interpretation is "a two-person activity," involving the poet as well as the reader.

In sharing with the text the task of interpretation, instead of claiming it as solely their own, connected readers might seem to possess less authority than subjectivist readers. But the authority of subjectivism is, in fact, derivative, and, being derivative, it is fragile. Who is it who "allows" us to interpret poetry for ourselves, and if They have the power to allow it, might They not also have the power to take away the privilege? ("My English teacher lets me have my own opinions," a student said, but she worried that next semester's teacher might be less lenient.)

Authority in subjectivism is limited, as well as tenuous. In one of our studies, we asked students to tell us how they assessed the merits of a poem. "To me," one woman replied, "what makes one poem better than another one is that I can get something from it as a person. That says nothing about the poem itself. I mean, I have no authority." I hear in this comment an appropriate humility, a refusal to lay down the law and speak for the text. But I hear, too, a poignant diffidence: The student is saying that she has no public voice, that, although she is free to make her own judgments, there is no reason for anyone to listen to her. Her judgments have no objective value. They say nothing about the poem—they are just about her; there is no "it" here; subjectivist reading is a one-person activity.

In granting some voice to the text, the connected reader actually increases the power of her own voice. Although acknowledging that the authority of her interpretation is qualified, she asserts that it does have some authority, and, because she constructed the interpretation herself, no one can take it away (although she herself may decide to abandon it). Like the subjectivist, the connected reader speaks "as a person," but, because her words concern the poem as well as herself, they are comprehensible to others and worthy of attention. And, far from silencing the author, by speaking as a person the connected reader leaves space for the text to speak. Schweickart astutely observes that although Rich's "use of the personal voice . . . serves as a reminder that her interpretation is informed by her own perspective," it also "serves as a gesture warding off any inclination to appropriate the authority of the text as a warrant for the validity of the interpretation" (Schweickart, 1986, p. 54). Like the subjectivist, the connected reader does not presume to speak for the text, but, unlike the subjectivist, she does not speak only to herself; she assumes that her words might "mean something, and have some impact" on other readers.

Thinking and Feeling

To adopt the perspective of the other requires thinking (reasoning, inference) as well as empathy. Indeed, although the term *empathy* has come to connote merely an affective "feeling with," the

German word from which it was translated, *Ein-fühlung,* meant, literally, "feeling into," and referred, according to the psychologist M. F. Basch, to "the ability of one person to come to know first-hand, so to speak, the experience of another"; "inference, judgment, and other aspects of reasoning thought" were as central to its meaning as affect (Basch, 1983, p. 110). The loss in translation of these cognitive aspects can be seen as an instance of the Western tendency to treat thinking and feeling as mutually exclusive, the same tendency that has led readers of *WWK* to assume that because separate knowing involves reasoning, and connected knowing differs from separate knowing, then connected knowing must involve merely feeling. A tendency to place a "separate spin" on essentially connected notions is also evident here. To "feel with" seems to preserve the autonomy of knower and known: their feelings are parallel but not fused. "Feeling into," in contrast, suggests a more intimate relation. In any case, connected knowing and *Einfühlung*, in its original meaning, seem to be close relatives, if not twins.

Kohn writes that "without imagining the reality of the other, empathic feeling is ultimately self-oriented and thus unworthy of the name" (Kohn, 1990, p. 131), and imagining the reality of the other requires responding to its cognitive content as well as its affect. Kohn recalls an incident from his student days when he raised a concern with his instructor, a psychiatrist, about some aspect of the course. "I can see you're angry," the instructor said. Up to that point, Kohn says, he had not been angry, but the instructor's response did anger him, because "it referred only to what he believed was my mood, effectively brushing aside the content of what I had expressed. His exclusively affective focus felt dismissive, even infantalizing, rather than empathic or understanding" (Kohn, 1990, pp. 311–312).

Subjectivism is especially prone to this "non-inferential empathy" (Flavell, 1985, p. 139). "I'm very empathic," a student told us, "very sensitive to other peoples emotions, even if I don't know them. Somebody could be depressed across the room, and I'll be depressed all day because that person's depressed who I don't even know." Emotional contagion is not sufficient for mature connected knowing (although it may constitute a rudimentary basis for it).[14] nor is "situational role-taking," Kohn's "imagine-self," meaning, What would *I* do, given *my*

background, personality, values, and so on, in *his* situation? In connected knowing one must "imagine-other" (my rephrasing of Kohn's "imagine-him"), put one's self into the head and heart, as well as the shoes of the other. Kohn:

> The issue is not just how weepy I become upon learning that your spouse has died: it is also whether I am merely recalling and reacting to a comparable loss in my own life or whether I am resonating to your unique set of circumstances—the suddenness of the death, the particular features of this person you loved that are especially vivid for you, your rocky marital history and the resultant prickles of guilt you are now feeling, the way your initial numbness is finally giving way to real pain, the respects in which your unconscious fears of being abandoned are about to be freshly revived by this event, the relationship that you and I have had up to now, and so on. (Kohn, 1990, pp. 132–133)

It is this intense concentration on the unique aspects of the object that characterizes the objectivity of connected knowing. If you act as the author's accomplice, Woolf says, "if you open your mind as widely as possible, then signs and hints of almost imperceptible fineness, from the twist and turn of the first sentences, will bring you into the presence of a human being unlike any other. Steep yourself in this, acquaint yourself with this." In separate knowing one regards the object as an instance of a category (a type of person, say, or a genre) and measures it against objectives standards. In connected knowing, the focus is on the object in itself, in all its particularity of detail. Once having constructed a complex constellation of specific circumstances peculiar to the particular worlds of the novelist or the next-door neighbor, or who-or whatever, connected knowers are forced to acknowledge disjunctions between these worlds and their own, and the danger of imagining the other as the self is sharply diminished.

"Nonempathic inference" (Flavell, 1985, p. 139) seems as problematic as noninferential empathy. Kohn asks us to "imagine a continuum: on one side are universal experiences, where imagine-self will do (burning hand); on the other side are things one has not personally experienced, where imagine-him is obviously required (giving birth)" (Kohn, 1990, p. 134). ("Him" seems an odd choice of pronoun in this context.) "The interesting cases," Kohn writes, "are in the middle (death of spouse). One can get away with treating that example as a generic grief, but only at a considerable cost to the integrity of the empathic response" (Kohn, 1990, p. 134). It seems likely that we are especially prone to assimilation to the self concerning the "things in the middle," those "universal" events that appear to be similar but are experienced differently, like the ones listed by the philosopher Elizabeth Spelman: "birth, death, eating, cooking, working, loving, having kin, being friends" (Spelman, 1988, p. 179). Fully to "imagine-other" in these situations seems to me to require feeling as well as thinking, but the MIT men do not seem to think so: in delineating their versions of "connected knowing," not one of them—even among those who claimed to use the procedure—referred to empathy or, indeed, made any mention of affect, whereas many of the Wellesley women did. The difference is rooted not in gender but in epistemology (which, although related to gender, is not synonymous with it). Women who are predominantly separate knowers also practice nonempathic inference, and, perceiving their ideas as autonomous, independent of their persons, they wish that others would do the same with them. Roberta, for instance, said that although she welcomed the opportunity to defend her carefully constructed opinions, when people tried to delve into the experiences behind the opinions instead of treating them on their own merits, she tended to "push [them] away:" "I feel like they're belittling me. . . . Why don't they just ask me straight out why I think my idea, because I've thought my idea through. They don't have to like, beat around the bush about it" (Mansfield & Clinchy, 1992).

To people like Roberta, who present themselves as heavily tipped in the direction of separate knowing, it is especially important that people respond to the impersonal cognitive content of their ideas; they tend to be suspicious of more personal approaches, experiencing them as Kohn experienced his instructor's noninferential empathy, as "belittling" (Roberta), as "infantalizing" and "dismissive" (Kohn). People who present themselves as oriented toward connected knowing, on the other hand, are wary of *impersonal* approaches: like the women in Tannen's accounts, they feel bereft when their listeners (in Tannen's account, men) offer analyses and solutions to the painful problem they have recounted, instead of resonating to their pain. Some adolescent males, observing this response in girls of their acquaintance, have formed a theory about it. "Girls don't want you to fix their prob-

lems," eighteen-year-old David Constantine writes to *Parade* magazine. "They just want to talk about them, and they want you to listen. They don't want you to say, 'What do you care?' or 'It's nothing to worry about.' " David infers correctly that girls don't want their worries dismissed, but his grasp of empathy seems limited: "Girls want you to say things like, 'Hmmm . . .' and 'Really?' and 'Wow, I don't blame you." ' According to David, girls just want to feel validated and cozy. "A good 'Hmmm . . .' and a feigned interested look is more important to them than the greatest answer we could come up with to all their troubles" ("What Bothers Me about Girls," 1994). David would claim, as have several of our students and colleagues who appear to be oriented separate knowing, that it is not necessary to feel what a person is feeling in order to understand him. From the connected knowing perspective, however, thinking cannot be divorced from feeling. Those who practice fully developed connected knowing, like those who practice Kohn's fully developed empathy, "truly experience the other as a subject." Kohn uses the word *experience* rather than *understand*—and so, I think, should I—"because something more than an intellectual apprehension is required. . . . [T]he connection . . . must be felt viscerally" (Kohn, 1990, p. 150).

Connected Knowing with the Self

I first read the words "[T]he connection . . . must be felt viscerally" after teaching an especially intense session of my seminar, and they seemed to me just right, but the next phrase brought me up short: "The connection must be felt viscerally *as surely as one's own humanness and uniqueness are felt*" (Kohn, 1990, p. 150). Whoa. Was Kohn asserting that knowledge of the self is prerequisite to knowledge of others, that we experience others as subjects only by analogy to our experience of ourselves as subjects? My fifteen seminar students had asserted that afternoon with nearly perfect unanimity that they found it far easier to understand other people's beliefs and values and desires than to know their own. They would agree with Addie, an interviewee who said, "It's easy for me to see a whole lot of different points of view on things and to understand why people think those things. The hard thing is sitting down and saying, 'Okay, what do I think, and why do I think it?" When in our research we asked young women to "describe themselves to themselves," they said things like "I'm about average" and "My ideas are just sort of like the norms." They seemed often to respond not as compassionate observers from within, but as stern judges from without" "I'm too fat . . . fairly good with people . . . pretty smart . . . not as tolerant as I should be." Psychologists Lyn Brown and Carol Gilligan describe how in adolescence girls who come up against "a wall of shoulds" (Brown & Gilligan, 1992, p. 97); they "come to a place where they feel they cannot say or feel or know what they have experienced" (Brown & Gilligan, 1992, p. 4). For many adult women, the wall remains in place; they cannot seem to connect with their own humanness and uniqueness. Muttering aloud, I reported all this to Kohn, interlarding my words with his, and apparently he heard me, for he went on: "[T]his last formulation gives us pause . . . [I]t is not clear that everyone does experience his or her own subjectivity" (Kohn, 1990, p. 150). It is crystal clear from research results (as well as ordinary observation) that many do not.

In our interviews, Annick and I tried to determine whether our respondents used separate knowing with themselves. We asked, "Do you ever use this approach with yourself—with your own thinking? Play devil's advocate with yourself, or argue with yourself?" Almost all said that they did, some describing the internal critic as a destructive antagonist, others drawing a more benign picture of "a friend behaving as an enemy" (Torbert, 1976), like the one inhabiting the philosopher Alice Koller's head, "thinking up the strongest possible arguments against my own position" in order to "find the flaws in my reasoning, the blunt edges of the ideas I'm trying to sharpen" (Koller, 1990, p. 27). No one was baffled by our question; everyone could make some sense of it.

One day Annick happened to notice that we asked no comparable question about connected knowing, whereas in every other respect we had constructed parallel questions about the two approaches. Although we wanted to repair the omission, we were uncertain how to phrase such a question, or even whether such a question made sense. it seemed nonsensical to ask whether people tried to step into their own shoes; surely they were already in them. Bewildered, we asked our friends, "What would it mean to use connected knowing with yourself?" Ann Stanton (see her chapter, this volume)

instantly replied, "It means to treat your mind as if it were a friend." This seemed to make sense. After all, we had ample evidence that the women we had interviewed found it hard to befriend their ideas, hard to "believe" them, to "say yes" to them. And so we added to the interview a question that, after repeated rephrasing, emerged (still a bit awkwardly) as "Do you ever use this approach with yourself? Try to see why you think what you do, what's right about it?" Our respondents had as much trouble answering the question as we had had in formulating it. "Huh? What? What do you mean? I don't get it." Often, they heard the question as asking about not a friend but an enemy in the head: "oh, yeah," they said. "I'm forever second-guessing myself." Not one of our research participants managed to articulate with much clarity a practice of connected knowing with the self.

For most of the women we interviewed, then, connected knowing with the self was at least as difficult to achieve as connected knowing with the other, and possibly more so. These women were like the patient described by the psychotherapist Judith Jordan who, before therapy, "did not seem able to take her own inner experience as a serious object for interest and attention." "I care for others sometimes like a sheepherder," the woman said. . . . "I put myself in their place and I understand. With myself, though, I used to be like a lion tamer with a bull whip" (Jordan, 1991, p. 78). The clinical literature suggests that "intrapsychic empathy" (Schafer, 1964, p. 261) is a skill arduously to be learned, requiring discipline and practice, usually under the guidance of some sort of tutor (a therapist, perhaps, or a Zen master).

The psychoanalyst Joanna Field tells a compelling story of her own efforts to achieve intrapsychic empathy. Feeling "utterly at sea as to how to live my life," thinking second-hand thoughts, and "whipping" herself in pursuit of second-hand goals, she developed over a period of years her own "method" of "active passivity" that enabled her, ultimately, to step inside her own shoes, to "see through [her] own eyes instead of at second hand." The method requires that one take an active stance toward one's thoughts and feelings, rather than simply letting them run on as a sort of "unconscious monologue" in the background of one's mind, but the activity is the sort practiced by midwives rather than taskmasters. "I began to see," Field writes, "that I must play the Montessori teacher to my thought, must leave it free to follow its own laws of growth, my function being to observe its activities, provide suitable material to enchannel them, but never to coerce it into docility" (Field, 1936/1981, p. 7). The process has much in common with the modes of fostering growth used by the public leader Mary Belenky in her chapter in this volume. Field writes,

> By continual watching and expression I must learn to observe my thought and maintain a vigilance not against "wrong" thoughts, but against refusal to recognize any thought. Further, this introspection meant continual expression, not continual analysis, it meant that I must bring my thoughts and feelings up in their wholeness, not argue about them. (Field, 1936/1981, pp. 204–205)

Field found that one way of bringing her thoughts and feelings up in their wholeness was to let them "write themselves" into the friendly pages of her journal. The journal turns the "I" into an "it," objectifying the knower's subjectivity, and in perusing the journal the knower turns the "it" into a "thou," in effect practicing connected knowing with herself.

But it is difficult to penetrate the wall of shoulds and speak truly, even in the privacy of one's journal, and in public it is even harder. The novelist Mary Gordon says that in striving to develop her own voice as a writer she was haunted by "bad specters" who infused her with a fear of being "trivial" (Gordon, 1980, p. 27), two famous male poets, perhaps, peering over her shoulder as she sat at the typewriter, and murmuring, "Your experience is an embarrassment; your experience is insignificant" (Gordon, 1980, p. 28). "Do you talk much in class?" we asked an undergraduate. "It's hard," she said. "I think— I always think, 'Do I really want to say this or not? Is it important enough to say?'"

Given the presence of strangling self-doubt, most of us find it impossible to achieve intrapsychic empathy on our own. Lacking the skill and stamina to serve as Montessori teachers to ourselves, we depend on external "teachers"—friends and colleagues, as well as certified teachers—who help us to say what we want to say (*WWK*, 1986, p. 218), reading our early drafts as "sympathetic allies," "trying to see the *validity*" in what we have written, and telling us "the ways in which [it] makes sense" (Elbow, 1986, p. 287).

It is reasonable to argue that without intimate knowledge of one's self one cannot enter into intimacy with another, that one "who is essentially a stranger to himself is unlikely to forge an affective connection to someone else" (Kohn, 1990, p. 152). Without self-knowledge we cannot exploit genuine similarities between self and other, using "templates' in the self to guide us to "matches" in the other. Without self-knowledge we cannot preserve the otherness of the other; he, she, or it becomes a creature of our projections. But how *well* must we know another, and must self-knowledge always come first? After all, as the philosopher Iris Murdoch says, "Self is as hard to see justly as other things" (Murdoch, 1970, p. 67)—harder, for people like Addie.

Fear of Fusion

Addie reports that when she entered her friends' subjective frames of reference, she lost touch with her own: "I felt, 'My God, I'm becoming— I'm not me anymore. I'm not thinking my own ideas anymore.' I was becoming very affected by other people's opinions and ideas." Writers on empathy seem to live in dread of such an event; anxiety over the possibility of "fusion" pervades the literature, expressed at times in hyperbolic terms and seeming to my mind to reach near-phobic proportions. "What happens to the self when it feels into the other?" Kohn asks, and he answers, apparently in an effort to quell anxiety that I was not experiencing, "All is not lost" (Kohn, 1990, p. 153). Kohn reports that Buber rejected the word *empathy* because it connoted "lost of the self in the process of experiencing the other" (Kohn, 1990, p. 153), and Buber was at pains to emphasize that one could experience the other "without forfeiting anything of the felt reality of his [own] reality" (Buber, 1947, p. 62). Schweickart assures us that Adrienne Rich does not "identity" with Dickinson, but merely "establishes an affinity" (Schweickart, 1989 p. 64). Steele warns that "the reader must claim her or his independence as a subject, not allowing her or himself to be subjugated by the text" (Steele, 1986; p. 259). Carl Rogers advises therapists "[t]o sense the client's world as if it were your own, but without ever losing the 'as if quality" (Rogers, 1961, p. 284). Kohn asserts that empathy does not require that "the self become submerged in the other" or that "its subjectivity be demolished" (Kohn, 1990, p. 153), and Elbow reminds players of the believing game that "it's only a game"; they can quit at any time (Elbow, 1973, p. 174).

Although of course there is truth in the view that the empathic self can (indeed, must) maintain its integrity and need not (indeed, must not) allow itself to be consumed by the other, these statements raise the specter of reducing a paradox—"the paradox of separateness within connection," as Jordan defines it (Jorden, 1991, p. 69)—to a dichotomy: "seeing the self as *either* distinct and autonomous *or* merged and embedded" (Jordan, 1991, p. 72). Words like *forfeit, claim,* and *allow* seem to partake of a "justice" orientation, common among those who conceive of themselves as "separate" rather than "connected" in relationships (Lyons, 1983). Formulations of empathy seem often to begin from a premise of distance and difference—"strain[ing]" after similarity" (Barber, 1984, p. 175) across a divide over an "abyss" (Buber, 1947, p. 175)—rather than solidarity and similarity. Perhaps it is possible to "leave the self *intact* but also leave the self *transformed*" (Kohn; 1990, italics added) if *intact* is defined as "unimpaired," but the word carries traces of its root meaning of "untouched," and so in this context connotes an impregnable self. Indeed, if empathy is defined as projection into the other, as it is in the *Oxford Universal Dictionary* among many others, one may even detect a whiff of castration anxiety in forebodings of fusion.

The women we interviewed used images of reception rather than projection in describing connected knowing (*WWK*, 1986, p. 122). The biographer Elizabeth Young-Breuhl puts it this way:

> Empathizing involves . . . putting another person in yourself, becoming another person's habitat, without dissolving the person, without digesting the person. You are mentally pregnant, not with a potential life but with a person, indeed, a whole life, a person with her history. So the person lives on in you and you can, as it were, hear her in this intimacy. But this depends upon your ability to tell the difference between the subject and yourself, to appreciate the role that she plays in your psychic life. (Young-Breuhl, as quoted by Breslin, 1994, p. 19)

For Young-Breuhl "the other is incorporated as other" (Breslin, 1994, p. 19). There is a "doubling" of subjectivity, as in Schweickart's account of reading, in spite of the (paradoxical) fact that "there is only one subject present" (see my earlier discussion and Schweickart's chapter, this volume). In "caring," says the philosopher Nel Noddings, "I become a duality. . . . The seeing and feeling are mine, but only partly and temporarily mine, as on loan to me" (Noddings, 1984, p. 30). In this "receptive" conception of empathy one need never leave home, and so, perhaps, the risk of being stranded, like Addie, behind the eyes of the other, is diminished.[15] Although Buber's concept of "inclusion" (explicated by Friedman) contains images of moving out ("bold swinging into the life of another"), in (paradoxical) fact, it does not require that one leave one's home ground: "Inclusion . . . does not mean at any point that one gives up the ground of one's own concreteness [or] ceases to see through one's own eyes" (Friedman, 1985, p. 199) Inclusion means "making present." Through "mutual confirmation," Friedman says, "partners" make each other present in their "wholeness, unity, and uniqueness"[16] (Friedman, 1985, p. 4). in this context, connected knowing with the other and connected knowing with the self are reciprocal rather than oppositional processes: neither partner disappears into the other; each makes and keeps the other present.

Knowing Communities

Both separate and connected knowing achieve their full power when practiced in partnership with other like-minded knowers. Separate knowers benefit from partnership with friends willing to behave as enemies. Francis Crick, one of the discoverers of the structure of DNA, says, "A good scientists values criticism almost more highly than friendship; no, in science criticism is the height and measure of friendship. The collaborator points out the obvious, with due impatience. He stops the nonsense" (Crick, quoted by Bruffee, 1981, p. 178). An MIT student supplied a moving illustration of this process and, incidentally, of the detachment that is, for me, the heart and soul of separated knowing. Ed was one of several summer student interns working in a hospital laboratory on various projects. Each week the students met with the dozen or so scientists who were the "brains of the group," to present their problems and their ideas.

> I would say something like, "You know, we had this spike in the frequency plot here, and I think it's because of this," and before you could blink an eye one of the big older guys would go, "No, no, that's wrong." And I'm

like—"Uh, okay." I mean, like, for three or four days I've been thinking that it was this thing. And I thought I was so clever for figuring it out. And the guy will—in—in five seconds shoot it down and say, "no, that's absolutely wrong because of this." And of course he's right.

It took me a good part of the summer to realize how much it wasn't malicious. And that all these gentlemen were there for the purpose of science and for engineering. And they didn't mean anything personal, when they shot you down right away. But it was— the way they saw it is, they were dismissing a wrong proposition so it wouldn't have time to—They would—they would just take care of its right away.

I thought it was real neat. To see that happen—I mean, some of these doctors are some of the best doctors or bioengineers around. And they were able to—they didn't see ideas as possessions. They saw ideas as ideas. [pause] And ideas were sort of like the group's ideas. You sat there and you formulated something for a project that the group was working on. So it was a group idea. [pause] It just continues to amaze me.[17]

Collaboration may be more essential to connected than to separate knowing. We are better at playing solitaire in the doubting game than in the believing game, Elbow thinks, because we've had more practice at it (Elbow, 1973, p. 175), and certainly the women we've talked with seemed more adept at doubting than believing themselves. It is easier to internalize a partner in the doubting game, because the rules of that game are codified within discourse communities, and anyone who knows the rules will do: the partner, to borrow a phrase from Kohn, is an "interchangeable someone" (Kohn, 1990, p. 112). Psychologists Marvin Berkowitz and Fritz Oser (1987) found that once adolescents reached the highest stage of skill in argumentation, achieving the ability to integrate a partner's argument with their own and to anticipate weaknesses in both, the partner became "superfluous . . . because one can now fully anticipate the other and take a more objective perspective on one's own reasoning, critically examining it as if from an outside perspective" (Berkowitz & Oser, 1987, p. 9).[18]

Because the partners in connected knowing are not interchangeable someones, but particular persons whose unique perspectives cannot be anticipated and so cannot be internalized, connected collaboration would seem to be minimally a two-person activity, although, of course, the external collaborator need not be a real and present person. Jill Tarule examines processes of connected collaboration in detail in her chapter in this volume. Here, I offer only one example, drawn from a famous short story, "A Jury of Her Peers," written by Susan Glaspell and published in 1917. Ed's story illustrates the power of detachment in the collaborative construction of knowledge; Glaspell's story shows how attachment can be an equally powerful force.

In the story, Mrs. Wright, a farmer's wife, has been taken off to jail on suspicion of murder, after apparently tying a rope around her husband's neck and strangling him in his sleep. Mrs. Hale, a neighbor who knew Mrs. Wright as a girl, but has rarely visited her in recent years, and Mrs. Peters, the sheriff's wife, are collecting household articles to take to Mrs. Wright in jail, while their husbands search the bleak homestead for clues to the motive for the crime. It is the women who come upon two crucial clues: a birdcage with its door hinge ripped apart, suggesting that "someone must have been—rough with it" (Glaspell, 1917, p. 273), and a strangled canary, laid in a pretty box. "She liked the bird," Mrs. Hale says. "She was going to bury it in that pretty box.'" Mrs. Peters, recapturing feelings she has trained herself to disown, remembers, "When I was a girl . . . my kitten—there was a boy took a hatchet, and before my eyes—before I could get there—. . . If they hadn't held me back I would have—'—hearing the men's footsteps overhead she finished "weakly,"—'hurt him.'"
"'Wright wouldn't like the bird," Mrs. Hale says, "'a thing that sang. She used to sing. He killed that too.'" Thinking of the bleak, childless, cheerless household, dominated by the chilly presence of the stern and silent Mr. Wright, which she has loathed to visit, and recalling Mrs. Wright as "Minnie Foster, when she wore a white dress with blue ribbons and stood up there in the choir and sang" (Glaspell, 1917, p. 278), Mrs. Hale says, "'If there had been years and years of—nothing, then a bird to sing to you, it would be awful— still—after the bird was still." Glaspell writes, "It was as if something within her not herself had spoken, and it found in Mrs. Peters something she did not know as herself." "'I know what stillness is,' she said, in a queer, monotonous voice. 'When we homesteaded in Dakota, and my first baby died—after he was two years old—and me with no other then—'" (Glaspell, 1917, p. 278).

The empathic interchange seems to involve not just a "doubling" but at least a tripling of subjectivities: Each woman achieves greater understanding of herself and the other, and both come to understand a crime that had seemed initially inexplicable, especially to Mrs. Peters, a woman who is, after all, "married to the law." Digging down deep, the women find a commonality of experience that dissolves the distance between them and leads to the construction of knowledge. Although Glaspell is aware of distinctions among the three women, it is the similarities she emphasizes. Mrs. Hale says, "'We live close together and we live far apart. We all go through just a different kind of the same thing! If it weren't,—why do you and I *understand? Why do we know*—what we know this minute?'" (Glaspell, 1917, p. 279).

Transformation of Self and Other

Theories of empathy that stress preservation of an intact self seem irrelevant to Glaspell's story. They connote a conception of the self as "finished" as well as separate—a sort of packaged self that one carts about from one relationships to the next. My (partially) postmodern mind is more comfortable with a notion of selves-in-process, being coconstructed and reconstructed in the context of relationships, and this is the story Glaspell tells: Mrs. Peters, in particular, is transformed by the visions Mrs. Hale shares with her and by her own "retrospective self-empathy" (Blanck & Blanck, 1979, p. 251). Friedman's notion of "mutual confirmation" (adopted from Buber) does seem to imply such a conception: he says that "mutual confirmation is essential to becoming a self" (Friedman, 1985, p. 119), and confirmation, in Buber's terms means "accepting the whole potentiality. . . . 'I accept you as you are' [means that] I discover in you just by my accepting love . . . what you are meant to become'" (Buber, 1966, pp. 181 ff., quoted in Friedman, 1985, p. 136).

In highly developed forms of connected knowing with the other, it becomes possible to view the self from the perspective of the other. As Kohn says, "[i]n order to make the *other* into a subject by taking her perspective, one must . . . make the self into an object . . . come to see ourselves from the outside, the way others see us" (Kohn, 1990, p. 150). Schwaber describes how in becoming a more "connected" (my term) therapist, she moved from a traditional conception of the "transference" as "a phenomenon arising from internal pressures within the patient, from

which the analyst, as a blank screen, could stand apart and observe, to that in which the specificity of the analyst's contribution was seen as intrinsic to its very nature" (Schwaber, 1983. p. 381). Taking the patient's reality seriously, "believing" it, forced her to see herself as the patient saw her, and to own (take seriously) her own response, instead of seeing it as merely a reaction to the patient's view, as is implied in the term *counter-transference.*

In one sense, it is not easy to objectify the self, to see one's self as others see us, especially, as Spelman points out, if it means entertaining the view of those whom we have oppressed of ourselves as oppressors (Spelman 1988, p. 178). (Oppressors objectify the oppressed, of course, in order to prevent such relations.) In another sense, however, women often find it all too easy to turn themselves into objects: the critic in their heads speaks from a distance, and it speaks in "shoulds," telling them how they ought to be and preventing them from seeing who they are and how they want to be. "Healthy self-objectification," Kohn says, consists of allowing one's self to be "watched and weighed" (Kohn, 1990, p. 151), an uncomfortable experience, but one that can be borne by "someone confident in her subjectivity, unafraid of being object to another." Many of our research participants, however, confess that they are not confident in their subjectivity, and, given the unhealthy objectifications to which they have been subjected in the past, perpetrated by not-so-friendly enemies within and without, they are understandably wary of being "watched and weighed." It is true that we need to face up to friends acting as enemies, but we also need friends acting as friends (Marshall & Reason, 1993), people who will view us with a compassionate rather than a critical eye, and who will invite us to do the same with them. *Subjectification*—joint subjectification—seems a better term than *objectification* to describe this process.

Spelman contrasts people (such as Schwaber) who actively seek out another person's viewpoint, "taking seriously how it represents a critique" of their own, with people who practice mere "tolerance" (Spelman, 1988, p. 183). The former are open to transformation; the latter are not. The subjectivist's spontaneity, her tendency to trust her own judgment and "go with her gut," are sources of genuine power, but they may limit her capacity for transformation. She is likely to emerge from "interactions" with ideas with her own prior positions intact. Asked how she decides among competing interpretations of a poem, a student replied:

> I usually find that when ideas are being tossed around I'm usually more akin to one than another. I don't know—my opinions are just sort of there. . . . It's almost more a matter of liking one more than another. I mean, I happen to agree with one or identify with it more.

In connected learning, on the other hand, both the learner and the subject matter are, Elbow says, "deformed":

> Good learning is not a matter of finding a happy medium where both parties are transformed as little as possible. Rather, both parties must be maximally transformed—in a sense deformed. There is violence in learning. We cannot learn something without eating it, yet we cannot really learn it either without being chewed up. (Elbow, 1986, p. 147)

Subjectivism is a form of what the psychologist David Perkins (Perkins, Farady, & Bushey, 1991) calls "makes-sense epistemology." A makes-sense epistemologist "believes that the way to evaluate conclusions is by asking whether they 'make sense' at first blush." (Baron, 1991, p. 177). The person

> only has to get to the point of telling one story about the situation that weaves together the facts in one way, from one point of view, congruent with the person's prior beliefs. Then the model "makes sense." When sense is achieved, there is no need to continue. (Perkins et al., 1991, p. 99)

Both separate and connected knowing are procedures that transcend makes-sense epistemology and meet the criteria for Perkins's "critical epistemology." Both procedures contain the premise that "it is not enough for a particular story to match one's prominent prior beliefs" (Perkins et al., 1991, p. 100), and "it is not enough for a particular story about a situation to hang together. One must consider what other, rather different stories might also hang together " (Perkins et al., 1991, pp. 99–100). In separate knowing one generates arguments that compete with a given position—another person's or one's own—and looks for flaws beneath the apparently sensible surface. In connected knowing one enters into stories beyond the bounds of one's own meager experience, and attempts to make meaning out of narratives that "at first blush"

make little sense. Players in the believing game, Elbow says, are anything but credulous.

> The credulous person really suffers from *difficulty* in believing not ease in believing: give him an array of assertions and he will always believe the one that requires the least expenditure of believing energy. He has a weak believing muscle and can only believe what is easy to believe. . . . The fact that we call this disease credulity when it is really incredulity reflects vividly our culture's fear of belief. (Elbow, 1973, p. 183)

Perhaps it was my own fear of belief, and my addiction to doubt, that made it so hard for me to see that when Grace told us of "falling down the rabbit hole, like Alice in Wonderland," she might be describing a hard-won ability, rather than an involuntary swoon; that an uncritical way of knowing might qualify as a critical epistemology; and that "going into the story" could be a powerful strategy for discovering how "other stories, rather different" from one's own, "might also hang together."

A part of me would like to end this chapter here, leaving you with a picture of connected knowing as a tough-minded, counterintuitive way of knowing, a critical epistemology that is in some sense the absolute opposite of the subjectivist makes-sense epistemology with which it is so often confused. This is how Elbow presents the believing game, as a way of achieving "distance" from one's spontaneous beliefs. And this is how we represent connected knowing in our research: "When I have an idea about something, and it *differs* from the way another person is thinking about it." But I cannot leave it at that. Neither Elbow's concept of the believing game nor the quotation we use in our research captures the full meaning I would like the concept to have.

Although it is important to distinguish the connected knower from the make-sense epistemologist who accepts without further exploration whatever appears at first blush to be true, it is also important to remember that what appears to be true may in fact *be* true and should not be dismissed out of hand. This is a notion that frightens academicians, who greet with suspicion books like *WWK* and Gilligans's (1982) In *a Different Voice* precisely because the stories they tell "resonate so thoroughly" with the experience of women readers that they are accepted without further exploration as true and may serve to reinforce sexist stereotypes (Greeno & Maccoby, 1986, p. 315).

Of course it is dangerous to accept without further exploration ideas that seem intuitively right, but it is equally dangerous to dismiss out of hand knowledge gleaned from experience that fails to meet conventional standards of truth. That is what women and other groups marginal to the academy have done for years. We have been taught, to paraphrase Gilligan, "to forget what we know." It is well, I think, to remember what we know, or think we know; to preserve rather than abandon the respect for one's own intuition that is at the heart of subjectivism. Of course, what feels right may be wrong, but it may be right; "They" may be wrong. And although I agree that it is important to subject apparent truths to further exploration, I believe it is important to do so along connected as well as separate paths.

It took me a long time to recognize that there was a connected path. Separate knowing came easily to me, as I believe it does for most academic women, our proclivities in this direction being part of the reason we became academics: we like to argue and, as academics, we're allowed to. I first drifted into graduate school in search of the tough-minded reasoning I had known in college and had found largely missing during the years since college, spent mainly in the company of children under the age of eight and their mothers. I knew I had come to the right place when, at one of the first class meetings, the professor said, "Whenever an idea rings a bell with me, seems intuitively true, I'm immediately suspicious of it"–critical epistemology in a nutshell, and, to mix a couple of metaphors, just my cup of tea!

Like Sara Ruddick (this volume), I too have had a love affair with reason. The affair has endured, and although, as is often the case in long-term relationships, I have grown less starry-eyed and idealistic about this lover than I once was; like Ed, the MIT summer intern, I still find it "real neat" that a group of scientists can treat ideas "not as possessions" but "as ideas." On the twenty-fifth reading, Ed's story still sends thrills down my spine. I want my students, too, to fall in love and stay in love with separate knowing.

Once upon a time, this was my only wish. My pedagogical duty, as I saw it, was to stamp out any sign of reliance on firsthand experience and intuition, and instill a reliance on hard-headed critical thinking. For instance, when,

objecting to my pronouncement from on high that males proved to be more adept on tests of spatial intelligence than females, a student in development psychology argued that she had a terrific sense of direction, whereas her brother couldn't find his way out of a paper bag. I would explain, patiently, through gritted teeth (accompanied, sometimes, by a sickly smile, but it's hard to do both at once), that of course there were exceptions, that psychological laws were merely proababilistic statements—saying to the student, in effect, "Your experience is irrelevant; your experience is embarrassing." In a sense, of course, I was "right," but so, in another sense, was she. Elsewhere, I have told how an African American student taught me, before the psychologist Diana Baumrind (1972) did, that parental practices defined as "authoritarian" might have a different meaning and different consequences in African American than in White families (Clinchy, 1995). Experiences such as these have led me to see that my job is not to suppress the lessons students have gained from firsthand experience, but to help them build on them. The other day, a colleague said, "Anecdotes are not data." "Nonsense," I replied, in characteristically connected fashion. "Of course they are."

As this essay attests, my relationship with connected knowing has become a full-blown affair. The procedures that Glaspell's Mrs. Hale and Mrs. Peters bring to bear on their problem are as exciting to me as the ones Ed's bioengineers bring to bear on theirs, and the knowledge they construct is just as powerful; indeed, as Mary Belenky's chapter (this volume) suggests, the Mrs. Hales and Mrs. Peterses might even transform the world.

I now bring to my teaching a polygamous epistemology, and I find that far from disrupting the first marriage, the second has stabilized it: the two are complementary. My students and I are amenable to argument, if we know that people are really listening. We are willing to dilly-dally in one another's embryonic notions, aware that with careful cultivation, these notions might blossom into powerful ideas—possibly even testable hypotheses to be subjected to the rigors of the doubting game. And, whereas once I hoped only that my students might achieve competence in the skills of separate knowing, now I wish for them what has meant so much to me—a marriage of two minds.

Notes

1. Connected knowing differs in this respect from the believing game, the ultimate purpose of which is to test validity.

2. Unless otherwise indicated, quotation are from participants interviewed in various research projects, and names are pseudonyms.

3. In this research we frequently adopted responses given in one year as stimuli the next year, in an attempt to conduct as sort of quasi conversation among students across the period of the study.

4. Although there have always been less adversarial strains in philosophy and in social science (notably *verstehen*), they have not been dominant.

5. I thank my friend Margaret Osler for helping me to understand this.

6. We may invite misreading by careless use of the terms *subjective knowledge* and *subjectivism*, sometimes using them interchangeably, as Code (1991, p. 255) points out.

7. Subjectivists are not "authoritarian" in the usual sense, however, they make no claim that what is true for them should be true for others or that, as some standpoint theorists assert, their own views are privileged. They are honestly unmitigated relativists.

8. Separate (adversarial) interviewing also has its place, of course, and also requires skill, of a different sort.

9. In another instance of the perhaps inevitable failure of understanding across disciplinary divides, Code speaks of *WWK*'s researchers as taking their respondents' words "literally," "from the surface" (1991, p. 256), a characterization that scarcely does justice to the sort of procedures DeVault describes, nor, indeed, to the complexity of any decent qualitative research procedure.

10. I have borrowed the phrase "I, thou, and it" from the philosopher of science David Hawkins (1967), who uses it in a different but related fashion in discussion of primary education.

11. These "body syntonic" (Turkle & Papert, 1990, note, p. 144) forms of connected knowing should be explored further. Some cultures, Nancy Goldberger says (see her chapter in this volume), support these ways of knowing, but the computer culture does not. Turkle and Papert tell of a fourth-grade boy who, overhearing a classmate speaking of "getting down inside the computer," sneered: "That's baby talk." Instructors in a Harvard programming course were no more hospitable to these "primitive" modes.

12. Spelman (1988), following Jean-Paul Sartre, points out that the danger is not eliminated even when the subject is present. We can "imagine" the person sitting next to us instead of really trying to make her acquaintance.

13. Grumbach's description is reminiscent of Schwaber's account of the shift in her perspective as therapist from external expert, instructing the patient with her superior opinions, to "observer from within," dillydallying respectfully in their views.

14. In observations of very young children, psychologists Carolyn Zahn-Waxler and her colleagues found that "self-referential behaviors" such as "pointing to one's own injury when another is injured" and reproducing or imitating others' affective experiences" predicted later "empathic concern" (Zahn-Waxler, Radke-Yurrow, Wagner, & Chapman, 1992, pp. 133, 134).

15. Although this is sheer—perhaps wild—speculation, both "doubling" and the emphasis on receptivity versus projection may have precursors in early childhood. Doubling is reminiscent of the "double-voiced discourse" in which one attends simultaneously to one's own and one's playmates' agendas, observed by sociolinguist Amy Sheldon (1992) among preschoolers, especially girls. The spontaneous stories of preschool girls are often structured around domestic harmony, whereas boys' stories involve venturing forth into an often frightening and chaotic unknown (Nicoloupoulo, Scales & Weintraub, 1994).

16. In my view, of course, the partner need not be a person.

17. I thank the student who conducted this interview as part of her work for a seminar I teach. The student must remain anonymous in order to protect Ed's identity, but she knows who she is.

18. "I have always had in my head an adversary," Piaget says (1972, p. 222). Piaget's adversary, usually a logical positivist, seems to me to have been something of a pushover.

References

Barber, B. R. (1984). *Strong democracy: Participatory politics for a new age*. Berkeley: University of California Press.

Baron, J. (1991). Beliefs about thinking. In J. F. Voss, D. N. Perkins, & J. W. Segal (Eds.), *Informal reasoning and education*, 169–186. Hillsdale, NJ: Lawrence Erlbaum.

Basch, M. F. (1983). The concept of self: An operational definition. In B. Lee & G. Noam (Eds.), *Develop-*

mental approaches to the self. New York: Plenum Press.

Baumrind, D. (1972). An exploratory study of socialization effects on black children: Some black-white comparisons. *Child Development, 43,* 261–267.

Belenky, M., Clinchy, B., Goldberger, N., & Tarule, J. (1986). *Women's ways of knowing: the development of self, voice, and mind.* New York: Basic Books.

Berkowitz, M. W., & Oser, F. (1987, April). *Stages of adolescent interactive logic.* Paper presented at the Biennial Meeting of the Society for Research in Child Development, Baltimore, MD.

Berreby, David, (1995, April 9). Unabsolute truths: Clifford Geertz. *New York Times Magazine.*

Blanck, G. & Blanck, R. (1979). *Ego psychology II: Psychoanalytic developmental psychology.* New York: Columbia University Press.

Breslin, James, E. B. (1994, July 24). Terminating Mark Rothko: Biography is mourning in reverse. *The New York Times Book Review, 3,* 19.

Brown, L. M., & Gilligan, C. (1992). *Meeting at the crossroads: Women's psychology and girls' development.* Cambridge, MA: Harvard University Press.

Bruffee, K. A. (1981). The structure of knowledge and the future of liberal education. *Liberal Education, 67,* 177–186.

Bruner, J. S. (1986). Actual minds, possible worlds. Cambridge, MA: Harvard University Press.

Buber, M. (1947/1965). *Between man and man.* (Ronald G. Smith, Trans.). New York: Macmillan.

Buber, M. (1966). *The knowledge of man: A philosophy of the interhuman.* New York: Harper & Row, Torchbooks.

Clinchy, B. (1995). A connected approach to the teaching of developmental psychology. *Teaching of Psychology, 22,* 100–104.

Clinchy, B., & Zimmerman, C. (1982). Epistemology and agency in the development of undergraduate women. In P. Perun (Ed.), *The undergraduate woman: Issues in educational equity.* Lexington, MA: D. C. Heath.

Clinchy, B., & Zimmerman, C. (1985). Growing up intellectually: Issues for college women. *Work in Progress,* No. 19. Wellesley, MA: Stone Center Working Papers Series.

Code, L. (1991). *What can she know?* Ithaca, NY: Cornell University Press.

DeVault, M. L. (1990). Talking and listening from women's standpoint: Feminist strategies for interviewing and analysis. *Social Problems, 37,* 96–116.

Elbow, P. (1973). Appendix essay: The doubting game and the believing game—an analysis of the intellectual enterprise. In *Writing without teachers.* London: Oxford University Press.

Elbow, P. (1986). *Embroacing contraries.* New York: Oxford University Press.

Field, J. (1936/1981). *A life of one's own.* Los Angeles: J. P. Tarcher, St. Martin's Press.

Flavell, J. (1985). *Cognitive development* (2nd ed.).Englewood Cliffs, NJ: Prentice Hall.

Friedman, M. (1985). *The healing dialogue in psychotherapy:* New York: Jason Aronson.

Geertz, C. (1986, Winter). The uses of diversity. *Michigan Quarterly Review,* 105–123.

Gilligan, C. (1982). *In a different voice.* Cambridge, MA: Harvard University Press.

Glaspell, S. (1917). A jury of her peers. Reprinted in E. J. O'Brien (Ed.) (1918); *The best short stories of 1917 and the yearbook of the American short story,* 256–281. Boston: Small, Maynard.

Goodfield, J. (1991/1994). *An imagined world: A story of scientific discovery.* Ann Arbor: University of Michigan Press.

Gordon, M. (1980). The parable of the cave or: In praise of watercolors. In J. Sternburg (Ed.), *The writer on her work,* 27–32. New York: W. W. Norton.

Greeno, C. G., & Maccoby, E. E. (1986). On *In a different voice:* An interdisciplinary forum: How different is the "different voice"? *Signs, 11,* 310–316.

Grumbach, D. (1991). *Coming into the end zone: A memoir.* New York: W. W. Norton.

Hawkesworth, M. E. (1989). Knowers, knowing, known: Feminist theory and claims of truth. *Signs, 14,* 533–557.

Hawkins, D. (1967). *I, thou, it.* Reprint of a paper presented at the Primary Teachers' Residential Course , Loughborough, Leicestershire. Cambridge, MA: Elementary Science Study, Education Services, Inc.

Hogan, R. (1973). Moral conduct and moral character: A psychological perspective. *Psychological Bulletin, 70,* 217–232.

Howard, G. S. (1991) Culture tales: A narrative approach to thinking, cross-cultural psychology, and psychotherapy. *American Psychologist, 46,* 187–197.

Jordan, J. (1991). Empathy and self boundaries. In J. V. Jordan, A. G. Kaplan, J. B. Miller, I. P. Stiver, & J. L. Surrey (Eds.), *Women's growth in connection: Writings from the Stone Center,* 67–80. New York: Guilford Press.

Keller, E. F. (1983a). *A feeling for the organism.* New York: Freeman.

Keller, E. F. (1983b). Women, science, and popular mythology. In J. Rothschild (Ed.), *Machine ex dea,* 131–135. New York: Pergamon Press.

Kohn, A. (1990). *The brighter side of human nature: Altruism and empathy in everyday life.* New York: Basic Books.

Kohut, H. (1978). The psychoanalyst in the community of scholars. In P. Ornstein (Ed.), *The search for the self: Selected writings of Heinz Kohut,* Vol. 2,

685–724. New York: International Universities Press.

Koller, A. (1990). *The stations of solitude.* New York: William Morrow.

Lather, P. (1986). Issues of validity in openly ideological research: Between a rock and a soft place. *Interchange, 17,* 63–84.

Lyons, N. (1983). Two perspectives on self, relationships, and morality. *Harvard Education Review, 53,* 125–145.

McCracken, G. D. (1988). *The long interview. Qualitative research methods series* (vol. 13). Newbury Park: Sage.

McMillan, C. (1982). *Women, reason and nature.* Princeton, NJ: Princeton University Press.

Mansfield, A., & Clinchy, B. (1992, May 28). The influence of different kinds of relationships on the development and expression of "separate" and "connected" knowing in undergraduate women. Paper presented as part of a symposium, Voicing relationships, knowing connection: Exploring girls' and women's development, at the 22nd Annual Symposium of the Jean Piaget Society: Development and vulnerability in close relationships. Montreal, Québec, Canada.

Margulies, A. (1989). *The empathic imagination.* New York: W. W. Norton. Marshall, J. & Reason, P. (1993). Adult learning in collaborative action research: reflections on the supervision process. *Studies in continuing education, 15,* 117–133.

May, R. (1969). The emergence of existential psychotherapy. In R. May, E. Angel, & H. F. Ellenberger (Eds.), *Existence.* New York: Simon & Schuster.

Mischel, W. (1969). Continuity & change in personality. *American Psychologist, 24,* 1012–1018.

Morawski, J. G. & Steele, R. S. (1991). The one or the other? Textual analysis of masculine power and feminist empowerment. *Theory and Psychology, 1,* 107–131.

Moulton, J. (1983). A paradigm of philosophy: The adversary method. In Harding, S., & Hintikka, M. B. (Eds.), *Discovering reality.* Dordrecht, Holland: Reidel.

Murdoch, I. (1970/1985). *The sovereignty of good.* London: ARK Paper-backs, Routledge & Kegan Paul.

Nicolopoulou, A., Scales, B., & Weintraub, J. (1994). Gender differences and symbolic imagination in the stories of four-year-olds. In A. H. Dyson & C. Genish (Eds.), *The need for story: Cultural diversity in classroom and community.* Urbana, IL: Natioanl Council of Teachers of English.

Noddings, N. (1984). *Caring.* Berkeley, CA: University of California Press.

Papert, S. (1980). *Mindstorms.* New York: Basic Books.

Patai, D. & Koertge, N. (1994). *Professing feminism.* New York: Basic Books.

Perkins, D. N., Farady, M., & Bushey, B. (1991). Everyday reasoning and the roots of intelligence. In J. F. Voss, D. N. Perkins, & J. W. Segal (Eds.), *Informal reasoning and education.* HIllsdale, NJ: Lawrence Erlbaum.

Perry, W. (1970). *Forms of intellectual and ethical development in the college years.* New York: Holt, Rinehart, & Winston.

Piaget, J. (1972) *The child's conception of the world.* Totowa, NJ: Littlefield, Adams.

Poulet, G. (1980). Criticism and the experience of interiority (C. Macksey & R. Macksey, Trans.). In J. Tomkins (Ed.). *Reader-response criticism: From formalism to structuralism.* Baltimore: Johns Hopkins University Press.

Rabin, C. (1994). *Separate and connected knowing in undergraduate men and women.* Unpublished undergraduate honors thesis, Wellesley College, Wellesley, MA.

Rich, A. (1979). Vesuvius at home: The power of Emily Dickinson. In *On lies, secrets and silence: Selected prose, 1966–1978.* New York: W. W. Norton.

Riger, S. (1992). Epistemological debates, feminist voices: Science, social values, and the study of women. *American psychologist, 47,* 730–740.

Rogers, C. R. (1951). *Client-centered therapy.* Boston: Houghton Miffin.

Rogers, C. R. (1961). *On becoming a person: A therapist's view of psychotherapy.* Boston: Houghton Miffin.

Rogers, C. R. (1980). Empathic: An unappreciated way of being. In *A way of being* (pp. 137–163). Boston: Houghton Miffin.

Rogers, C. R., & Farson, R. E. (1967). Active listening. In Haney, W. V. *Communication and organizational behavior: Text and cases,* 81–97. Homewood, IL: Richard D. Irwin.

Ruddick, S. (1984). new combinations: Learning from Virginia Woolf. In Asher, C., DeSalvor, L., & Ruddick, S. *Between women,* Boston: Beacon Press.

Schafer, R. (1964). The clinical analysis of affects. *Journal of the American Psychoanalytic Association, 12,* 275–299.

Schwaber, E. (1983a). Psychoanalytic listening and psychic reality. *International Review of Psychoanalysis, 10,* 379–392.

Schwaber, E. (1983b). Construction, reconstruction, and the mode of clinical attunement. In A. Goldberg (Ed.), *The future of psychoanalysis,* 273–291. New York: International Universities Press.

Sechweickart, P. P. (1986). Reading ourselves:Toward a feminist theory of reading. In Elizabeth A. Flynn & P. P. Schweickart (Eds.), *Gender and reading: Essays on readers, texts, and contexts,* 31–62. Baltimore: Johns Hopkins University Press.

Schweickart, P. P. (1988). Engendering critical discourse. In C. Koelb & Victor Lokke (Eds.), *The cur-*

rent in criticism: Essays on the present and future of criticism, 295–317. West Lafeyette, IN: Purdue University Press.

Schweickart, P. P. (1989). Reading, teaching, and the ethic of care. In S. L. Gabriel & I. Smithson (Eds.), *Gender in the classroom: Power and pedagogy,* 78–95. Chicago: University of Illinois Press.

Sheldon, A. (1992). Conflict talk: Sociolinguistic challenges to self-assertion and how young girls meet them. *Merrill-Palmer Quarterly, 38,* 95–118.

Spelman, E. V. (1988). *Inessential woman: Problems of exclusion in feminist thought.* Boston: Beacon Press.

Steele, R. S. (1986). Deconstructing histories: Toward a systematic criticism of psychological narratives. In T. R. Sarbin, *Narrative psychology: The storied nature of human conduct,* 256–275. New York: Praeger.

Tannen, D. (1990). *You just don't understand: Women and men in conversation.* New York: Ballantine.

Torbert, W. (1976). *Creating a community of inquiry: Conflict, collaboration, transformation.* New York: Wiley.

Turkle, S. (1984). *The second self: The computer and the human spirit.* New York: Simon & Schuster.

Turkle, S. & Papert, S. (1990). Epistemological pluralism: styles and voices within the computer culture. *Sign, 16,* 128–157.

What bothers me about girls. (1994, March 13). *Parade.*

Woolf, V. (1929/1989). A *room of one's own.* New York: Harvest/HBJ Book, Harcourt Brace Jovanovich.

Woolf, V. (1932/1948). How should one read a book? In *The common reader, Series 1 and 2,* 281–295. New York: Harcourt Brace.

Zahn-Waxler, C., Radke-Yarrow, M., Wagner, E. & Chapman, M. (1992). Development of concern for others. *Development Psychology, 28,* 126–136.

Section 10

MORAL DEVELOPMENT

CHAPTER 40

MORAL STAGES AND MORALIZATION: THE COGNITIVE-DEVELOPMENTAL APPROACH

LAWRENCE KOHLBERG

In this chapter I shall present an overview of the cognitive-developmental theory of moralization as elaborated in studies of moral stages by myself and my colleagues. I shall first present a theoretical description of the six moral stages, followed by an account of the development of our methods for identifying or scoring stage. Having presented a picture of what moral development is and how to assess it, I shall go on to present the theory of moralization which can best account for this picture of moral development, and then to contrast this theory with approaches which see moral development as a result of socialization or social learning.

In a sense, this chapter represents an updating of earlier presentations of my theory of moral development stages (Kohlberg, 1969). In this chapter, however, there is no attempt to review research comprehensively, as research reviews have appeared earlier (Kohlberg, 1964, 1969) and are forthcoming (Kohlberg and Candee, in prep.). The philosophic assumptions and implications of our stages are also treated only briefly, having been thoroughly discussed elsewhere (Kohlberg, 1971b, 1981a.).

The Place of Moral Judgment in the Total Personality

To understand moral stage, it is helpful to locate it in a sequence of development of personality. We know that individuals pass through the moral stages one step at a time as they progress from the bottom (Stage 1) toward the top (Stage 6). There are also other stages that individuals must go through, perhaps the most basic of which are the stages of logical reasoning or intelligence studied by Piaget (1967). After the child learns to speak, there are three major developmental stages of reasoning: the intuitive, the concrete operational, and the formal operational. At around age 7, children enter the stage of concrete logical thought; they can then make logical inferences, classify things and handle quantitative relations about concrete things. In adolescence, many but not all individuals enter the stage of formal operations, at which level they can reason abstractly. Formal operational thinking can consider all possibilities, consider the relations between elements in a system, form hypotheses, deduce implications from the hypotheses, and test them against reality. Many adolescents and adults only partially attain the stage of formal operations; they consider all the actual relations of one thing to another at the same time, but do not consider all possibilities and do not form abstract hypotheses.

In general, almost no adolescents and adults will still be entirely at the stage of concrete operations, many will be at the stage of partial formal operations, and most will be at the highest stage of formal operations (Kuhn, Langer, Kohlberg, and Haan, 1977). Since moral reasoning clearly is reasoning, advanced moral reasoning depends upon advanced logical reasoning. There is a parallelism between an individual's logical stage and his or her moral stage. A person whose logical stage is only concrete operational is limited to the preconventional moral stages, Stages 1 and 2. A person whose logical stage is only "low" formal operational is limited to the conventional moral stages, Stages 3 and 4. While logical development is a necessary condition for moral development, it is not sufficient. Many individuals are at a higher logical stage than the parallel moral stage, but essentially none are at a higher moral stage than their logical stage (Walker, 1980).

Next after stages of logical development come stages of social perception or social perspective- or role-taking (see Selman, 1976). We partiallly describe these stages when we define the moral stages. These role-taking stages describe the level at which the person sees other people, interprets their thoughts and feelings, and sees their role or place in society. These stages are very closely related to moral stages, but are more general, since they do not deal just with fairness and with choices of right and wrong. To make a judgment of fairness at a certain level is more difficult than to simply see the world at that level. So, just as for logic, development of a stage's social perception precedes, or is easier than, development of the parallel stage of moral judgment. Just as there is a vertical sequence of steps in movement up from moral Stage 1 to moral Stage 2 to moral Stage 3, so there is a horizontal sequence of steps in movement from logic to social perception to moral judgment. First, individuals attain a logical stage, say, partial formal operations, which allows them to see "system" in the world, to see a set of related variables as a system. Next they attain a level of social perception or role-taking, where they see other people understanding one another in terms of the place of each in the system. Finally, they attain Stage 4 of moral judgment, where the welfare and order of the total social system or society is the reference point for judging "fair" or "right." We have found that individuals who move upward in our moral education programs already have the logical capacity, and often the social perception capacity, for the higher moral stage to which they move (Walker, 1980).

There is one final step in this horizontal sequence: moral behavior. To act in a morally high way requires a high stage of moral reasoning. One cannot follow moral principles (Stages 5 and 6) if one does not understand or believe in them. One can, however, reason in terms of such principles and not live up to them. A variety of factors determines whether a particular person will live up to his or her stage of moral reasoning in a particular situation, though moral stage is a good predictor of action in various experimental and naturalistic settings (Kohlberg, 1969).

In summary, moral stage is related to cognitive advance and to moral behavior, but our identification of moral stage must be based on moral reasoning alone.

Theoretical Description of the Moral Stages

The six moral stages are grouped into three major levels: pre-conventional level (Stages 1 and 2); conventional level (Stages 3 and 4), and postconventional level (Stages 5 and 6).

To understand the stages, it is best to start by understanding the three moral levels. The preconventional moral level is the level of most children under 9, some adolescents, and many adolescent and adult criminal offenders. The conventional level is the level of most adolescents and adults in our society and in other societies. The postconventional level is reached by a minority of adults and is usually reached only after the age of 20. The term "conventional" means conforming to and upholding the rules and expectations and conventions of society or authority just because they are society's rules, expectations, or conventions. The individual at the preconventional level has not yet come to really understand and uphold conventional or societal rules and expectations. Someone at the postconventional level understands and basically accepts society's rules, but acceptance of society's rules is based on formulating and accepting the general moral principles that underlie these rules. These principles in some cases come into conflict with society's rules, in which case the postconventional individual judges by principle rather than by convention.

One way of understanding the three levels is to think of them as three different types of relationships between the *self* and *society's rules and expectations*. From this point of view, Level I is a preconventional person, for whom rules and social expectations are something external to the self; Level II is a conventional person, in whom the self is identified with or has internalized the rules and expectations of others, especially those of authorities; and Level III is a postconventional person, who had differentiated his or her self from the rules and expectations of others and defines his or her values in terms of self-chosen principles.

Within each of the three moral levels, there are two stages. The second stage is a more advanced and organized form of the general perspective of each major level. Table 1 defines the six moral stages in terms of (1) what is right, (2) the reason for upholding the right, and (3) the social perspective behind each stage, a central concept to which our definition of moral reasoning now turns.

Social Perspectives of the Three Moral Levels

In order to characterize the development of moral reasoning structurally, we seek a single unifying construct that will generate the major structural features of each stage. Selman (1976) offers a point of departure in the search for such a unifying construct; he has defined levels of role-taking which parallel our moral stages and which form a cognitive-structural hierarchy. Selman defines role-taking primarily in terms of the way the individual differentiates his or her perspective from other perspectives and relates these perspectives to one another. From our point of view, however, there is a more general structural construct which underlies *both* role-taking and moral judgment. This is the concept of *sociomoral perspective*, which refers to the point of view the individual takes in defining both social facts and sociomoral values, or "oughts." Corresponding to the three major levels of moral judgment, we postulate the three major levels of social perspective as follows:

Moral Judgment	Social Perspective
I. Preconventional	Concrete individual perspective
II. Conventional	Member-of-society perspective
III. Postconventional, or principled	Prior-to-society perspective

Let us illustrate the meaning of social perspective in terms of the unity it provides for the various ideas and concerns of the moral level. The conventional level, for example, is different from the preconventional in that it uses the following reasons: (1) concern about social approval; (2) concern about loyalty to persons, groups, and authority; and (3) concern about the welfare of others and society. We need to ask,

What underlies these characteristics of reasoning and holds them together? What fundamentally defines and unifies the characteristics of the conventional level is its *social perspective*, a shared viewpoint of the participants in a relationship or a group. The conventional individual subordinates the needs of the single individual to the viewpoint and needs to the group or the shared relationship. To illustrate the conventional social perspective, here is 17-year-old Joe's response to the following question:

Q. *Why shouldn't you steal from a store?*

A. It's a matter of law. It's one of our rules that we're trying to help protect everyone, protect property, not just to protect a store. It's something that's needed in our society. If we didn't have these laws, people would steal, they wouldn't have to work for a living and our whole society would get out of kilter.

Joe is concerned about *keeping the law,* and his reason for being concerned is *the good of society as a whole.* Clearly, he is speaking as a member of society." It's one of *our* rules that *we're making* to protect everyone in *our* society." This concern for the good of society arises from his taking the point of view of "us members of society," which goes beyond the point of view of Joe as a concrete, individual self.

Let us contrast this *conventional member-of-society perspective* with the *preconventional concrete individual perspective*. The latter point of view is that of the individual actor in the situation thinking about his interests and those of other individuals he may care about. Seven years earlier, at age 10, Joe illustrated the concrete individual perspective in response to the same question:

Q. *Why shouldn't you steal from a store?*

A. It's not good to steal from the store. It's against the law. Someone could see you and call the police.

Being "against the law," then, means something very different at the two levels. At Level II, the law is made by and for "everyone," as Joes indicates at age 17. At Level I, it is just something enforced by the police, and accordingly, the reason for obeying the law is to avoid punishment. This reason derives from the limits of a Level I perspective, the perspective of an individual considering his or her own interests and those of other isolated individuals.

TABLE 1
The Six Moral Stages

	Content of Stage		
Level and Stage	What is Right	Reasons for Doing Right	Social Perspective of Stage
Level I: Preconventional Stage 1—Heteronomous Morality	To avoid breaking rules backed by punishment, obedience for its own sake, and avoiding physical damage to persons and property.	Avoiding of punishment, and the superior power of authorities.	*Egocentric point of view.* Doesn't consider the interests of others or recognize that they differ from the actor's; doesn't relate two points of view. Actions are considered physically rather than in terms of psychological interests of others. Confusion of authority's perspective with one's own.
Stage 2—Individualism, Instrumental Purpose, and Exchange	Following rules only when it is to someone's immediate interest; acting to meet one's own interests and needs and letting others do the same. Right is also what's fair, what's an equal exchange, a deal, an agreement.	To serve one's own needs or interests in a world where you have to recognize that other people have their interests, too.	*Concrete individualistic perspective.* Aware that everybody has his own interest to pursue and these conflict, so that right is relative (in the concrete individualistic sense).
Level II: Conventional Stage 3—Mutual Interpersonal Expectations, Relationships, and Interpersonal Conformity	Living up to what is expected by people close to you or what people generally expect of people in your role as son, brother, friend, etc. "Being good" is important and means having good motives, showing concern about others. It also means keeping mutual relationships, such as trust, loyalty, respect, and gratitude.	The need to be a good person in your own eyes and those of others. Your caring for others. Belief in the Golden Rule. Desire to maintain rules and authority which support stereotypical good behavior.	*Perspective of the individual in relationships with other individuals.* Aware of shared feelings, agreements, and expectations which take primacy over individual interests. Relates points of view through the concrete Golden Rule, putting yourself in the other person's shoes. Does not yet consider generalized system perspective.
Stage 4—Social System and Conscience	Fulfilling the actual duties to which you have agreed. Laws are to be upheld except in extreme cases where they conflict with other fixed social duties. Right is also contributing to society, the group, or institution.	To keep the institution going as a whole, to avoid the breakdown in the system "if everyone did it," or the imperative of conscience to meet one's defined obligations. (Easily confused with Stage 3 belief in rules and authority; see text.)	*Differentiates societal point of view from interpersonal agreement or motives.* Takes the point of view of the system that defines roles and rules. Considers individual relations in terms of place in the system.

(*continued*)

TABLE 1 (*continued*)

	Content of Stage		
Level and Stage	*What is Right*	*Reasons for Doing Right*	*Social Perspective of Stage*
Level III: *Postconventional, or Principled* Stage 5—Social Contract or Utility and Individual Rights	Being aware that people hold a variety of values and opinions, that most values and rules are relative to your group. These relative rules should usually be upheld, however, in the interest of impartiality and because they are the social contract. Some nonrelative values and rights like life and liberty, however, must be upheld in any society and regardless of majority opinion.	A sense of obligation to law because of one's social contract to make and abide by laws for the welfare of all and for the protection of all people's rights. A feeling of contractual commitment, freely entered upon, to family, friendship, trust, and work obligations. Concern that laws and duties be based on rational calculation of overall utility, "the greatest good for the greatest number."	*Prior-to-society perspective.* Perspective of a rational individual aware of values and rights prior to social attachments and contracts. Integrates perspectives by formal mechanisms of agreement, contract, objective impartiality, and due process. Considers moral and legal points of view; recognizes that they sometimes conflict and finds it difficult to integrate them.
Stage 6—Universal Ethical Principles	Following self-chosen ethical principles. Particular laws or social agreements are usually valid because they rest on such principles. When laws violate these principles, one acts in accordance with the principle. Principles are universal principles of justice: the equality of human rights and repect for the dignity of human beings as individual persons.	The belief as a rational person in the validity of universal moral principles, and a sense of personal commitment to them.	*Perspective of a moral point of view* from which social arrangements derive. Perspective is that of any rational individual recognizing the nature of morality or the fact that persons are ends in themselves and must be treated as such.

Let us now consider the perspective of the *postconventional level*. It is like the preconventional perspective in that it returns to the standpoint of the individual rather than taking the point of view of "us members of society." The individual point of view taken at the postconventional level, however, can be universal; it is that of *any rational moral individual*. Aware of the member-of-society perspective, the postconventional person questions and redefines it in terms of an individual moral perspective, so that social obligations are defined in ways that can be justified to any moral individual. An individual's commitment to basic morality or moral principles is seen as preceding, or being necessary for, his or her taking society's perspective or accepting society's laws and values. Society's laws and values, in turn, should be ones which any reasonable person could be committed to—whatever his or her place in society and whatever society he or she belongs to. The postconventional perspective, then, is *prior to society*; it is the perspective of an *individual who has made the moral commitments or holds the standards on which a good or just society must be based.* This is a perspective by which (1) a particular society or set of social practices may be judged and (2) a person may rationally commit him- or herself to a society.

An example is Joe, our longitudinal subject, interviewed at age 24:

Q. *Why shouldn't someone steal from a store?*

A. It's violating another person's rights, in this case, to property.

Q. *Does the law enter in?*

A. Well, the law in most cases is based on what is morally right, so it's not a separate subject, it's a consideration.

Q. *What does "morality" or "morally right" mean to you?*

A. Recognizing the rights of other individuals, first to life and then to do as he pleases as long as it doesn't interfere with somebody else's rights.

The wrongness of stealing is that it violates the moral rights of individuals, which are prior to law and society. Property rights follow from more universal human rights (such as freedoms which do not interfere with the like freedom of others). The demands of law and society derive from universal moral rights, rather than vice versa.

It should be noted that reference to the words *rights* or *morally right* or *conscience* does not necessarily distinguish conventional from postconventional morality. Orienting to the morally right thing, or following conscience as against following the law, need not indicate the postconventional perspective of the rational moral individual. The terms *morality* and *conscience* may be used to refer to group rules and values which conflict with civil laws or with the rules of the majority group. To a Jehovah's Witness who has gone to jail for "conscience," conscience may mean God's law as interpreted by his or her religious sect or group rather than the standpoint of any individual oriented to universal moral principles or values. To count as postconventional, such ideas or terms must be used in a way that makes it clear that they have a foundation for a rational or moral individual who has not yet committed him- or herself to any group or society or its morality. "Trust," for example, is a basic value at both the conventional and the postconventional levels. At the conventional level, trustworthiness is something you expect of others in your society. Joe expresses this as follows at age 17:

Q. *Why should a promise be kept, anyway?*

A. Friendship is based on trust. If you can't trust a person, there's little grounds to deal with him. You should try to be as reliable as possible because people remember you by this, you're more respected if you can be depended upon.

At this conventional level, Joe views trust as a truster as well as someone who could break a trust. He sees that the individual needs to be trustworthy not only to secure respect and to maintain social relationships with others, but also because as a member of society he expects trust of others in general.

At the postconventional level, individuals take a further step. They do not automatically assume that they are in a society in which they need the friendship and respect of other individuals. Instead they consider why any society or social relationship pre-supposes trust, and why the individual, if he or she is to contract into society, must be trustworthy. At age 24, Joe is postconventional in his explanation of why a promise should be kept:

I think human relationships in general are based on trust, on believing in other individuals. If you have no way of believing in someone else, you can't deal with anyone else and it becomes every man for himself. Everything you do in a day's time is related to somebody else and if you can't deal on a fair basis, you have chaos.

We have defined a postconventional moral perspective in terms of the individual's reasons *why* something is right or wrong. We need to illustrate this perspective as it enters into making an actual decision or defining *what is right*. The postconventional person is aware of the moral point of view that each individual in a moral conflict situation ought to adopt. Rather than defining expectations and obligations from the standpoint of societal roles, as someone at the conventional level would, the postconventional individual holds that persons in these roles should orient to a "moral point of view." While the postconventional moral viewpoint does also recognize fixed legal-social obligations, recognition of moral obligations may take priority when the moral and legal viewpoints conflict.

At age 24 Joe reflects the postconventional moral point of view as a decision-making perspective in response to Heinz's dilemma about stealing a drug to save his wife (see "The Nine Hypothetical Dilemmas," Appendix B):

It is the husband's duty to save his wife. The fact that her life is in danger transcends every other standard you might use to judge his action. Life is more important than property.

Q. *Suppose it were a friend, not his wife?*

A. I don't think that would be much different from a moral point of view. It's still a human being in danger.

Q. *Suppose it were a stranger?*

A. To be consistent, yes, from a moral standpoint.

Q. *What is this moral standpoint?*

A. I think every individual has a right to live and if there is a way of saving an individual, he should be saved.

Q. *Should the judge punish the husband?*

A. Usually the moral and the legal standpoints coincide. Here they conflict. The judge should weigh the moral standpoint more heavily but preserve the legal law in punishing Heinz lightly.

Social Perspectives of the Six Stages

This section will explain the differences in social perspective at each moral stage within each of the three levels. It will attempt to show how the second stage in each level completes the development of the social perspective entered at the first stage of the level.

We will start with the easiest pair of stages to explain in this way—Stages 3 and 4, comprising the conventional level. In the preceding section we quoted the isolated-individual perspective of Stages 1 and 2 and contrasted it with Joe's full-fledged member-of-society perspective at age 17, a perspective which is Stage 4. Joe's statements about the importance of trust in dealing with others clearly reflect the perspective of someone taking the point of view of the social system. The social perspective at Stage 3 is less aware of society's point of view or of the good of the whole of society. As an example of Stage 3, let us consider Andy's response to a dilemma about whether to tell your father about a brother's disobedience after the brother has confided in you.

> He should think of his brother, but it's more important to be a good son. Your father has done so much for you. I'd have a conscience if I didn't tell, more than to my brother, because my father couldn't trust me. My brother would understand; our father has done so much for him, too.

Andy's perspective is not based on a social system. It is rather one in which he has two relationships: one to his brother, one to his father. His father as authority and helper comes first. Andy expects his brother to share this perspective, but as someone else centered on their father. There is no reference to the organization of the family in general. Being a good son is said to be more important not because it is a more important role in the eyes of, or in terms of, society as a whole or even in terms of the family as a system. The Stage 3 member-of-a-group perspective is that of the average good person, not that of society or an institution as a whole. The Stage 3 perspective sees things from the point of view of shared relationships between two, or more individuals—relations of caring, trust, respect, and so on—rather than from the viewpoint of institutional wholes. In summary, whereas the Stage 4 member-of-society perspective is a "system" perspective, the Stage 3 perspective is that of a participant in a shared relationship or shared group.

Let us turn to the preconventional level. Whereas Stage 1 involves only the concrete individual's point of view, Stage 2 is aware of a number of other individuals, each having other points of view. At Stage 2, in serving my interests I anticipate the other person's reaction, negative or positive, and he or she anticipates mine. Unless we make a deal, we each will put our own point of view first. If we make a deal, each of us will do something for the other.

The shift from Stage 1 to Stage 2 is shown by the following change in another subject's response between age 10 and age 13 to a question about whether an older brother should tell his father about a younger brother's misdeed, revealed in confidence. At 10, the subject gives a Stage 1 answer:

> In one way it was right to tell because his father might beat him up. In another way it's wrong because his brother will beat him up if he tells.

At age 13, he has moved to Stage 2:

> The brother should not tell or he'll get his brother in trouble. If he wants his brother to keep quiet for him sometime, he'd better not squeal now.

In the second response, there is an extension of concern to the brother's welfare as it affects the subject's own interests through anticipated exchange. There is a much clearer picture of the brother's point of view and its relationship to his own.

Turning to the postconventional level, a typical Stage 5 orientation distinguishes between a moral point of view and a legal point of view but finds it difficult to define a moral perspective independent of contractual-legal rights. Joe, an advanced Stage 5, says with regard to Heinz's dilemma of whether to steal the drug to save his wife:

> Usually the moral and the legal standpoints coincide. Here they conflict. The judge should weigh the moral standpoint more.

For Joe, the moral point of view is not yet something prior to the legal point of view. Both law and morality for Joe derive from individual rights and values, and both are more or less on an equal plane. At Stage 6, obligation is defined in terms of universal ethical principles of justice. Here is a Stage 6 response to Heinz's dilemma:

> It is wrong legally but right morally. Systems of law are valid only insofar as they reflect the sort of moral law all rational people can accept. One must consider the personal justice involved, which is the root of the social contract. The ground of creating a society is individual justice, the right of every person to an equal consideration of his claims in every situation, not just those which can be codified in law. Personal justice means, "Treat each person as an end, not a means."

This response indicates a very clear awareness of a moral point of view based on a principle ("Treat each person as an end, not a means") which is more basic than, and from which one can derive, the sociolegal point of view.

Four Moral Orientations and the Shift Toward Greater Equilibrium Within Stages

In discussing social perspectives we have not differentiated *perception* of social fact (role-taking) from *prescription* of the right or good (moral judgment). What are the distinctive features of stages of moral judgment as opposed to social perspective in general?

To define the distinctively moral, we now turn to the moral categories analyzed by moral philosophy. These include "modal" categories (such as rights, duties, the morally approvable, responsibility) and "element" categories (such as welfare, liberty, equality, reciprocity, rules and social order). In describing moral philosophic theories by type, it is customary to analyze the primary moral categories of the theory from which the other categories derive. There are four possible groups of primary categories called *moral* orientations. Found at each of our moral stages, they define four kinds of decisional strategies, each focusing on one of four universal elements in any social situation. These orientations and elements are as follows:

1. *Normative order:* Orientation to prescribed rules and roles of the social or moral order. The basic considerations in decision making center on the element of *rules.*

2. *Utility consequences:* Orientation to the good or bad *welfare consequences* of action in the situation for others and/or the self.

3. *Justice or fairness:* Orientation to *relations* of liberty, equality, reciprocity, and contract between persons.

4. *Ideal-self:* Orientation to an image of actor as a *good self,* or as someone with conscience, and to the self's motives or virtue (relatively independent of approval from others).

In defining the distinctively moral, some writers stress the concept of rule and respect for rules (Kant, Durkheim, Piaget). Others identify morality with a consideration of welfare consequences to others (Mill, Dewey). Still others identify morality with an idealized moral self (Bradley, Royce, Baldwin). Finally, some (Rawls, and myself) identify morality with justice. In fact, individual persons may use any one or all of these moral orientations. As an example, we have the following orientations to the property issue at Stage 3:

Why shouldn't you steal from a store, anyway?

1. *Normative order:* It's always wrong to steal. If you start breaking rules of stealing, everything would go to pieces.

2. *Utilitarian:* You're hurting other people. The storeowner has a family to support.

3. *Justice:* The storeowner worked hard for the money and you didn't. Why should you have it?

4. *Ideal-self:* A person who isn't honest isn't worth much. Stealing and cheating are both the same, they are both dishonesty.

White all orientations may be used by an individual, my colleagues and I claim that the most essential structure of morality is a justice structure. Moral situations are ones of conflict of perspectives or interest; justice principles are concepts for resolving these conflicts, for giving each his or her due. In one sense, justice can refer to all four orientations. Sustaining law and order may be seen as justice (normative order), and maximizing the welfare of the group may be seen as justice (utility consequences). In the end, however, the core of justice is the *distribution of rights and duties regulated by concepts of equality and reciprocity*. Justice recognized as a "balance" or equilibrium corresponds to the structural moving equilibrium described by Piaget on logic (1967). Justice is the normative logic, the equilibrium, of social actions and relations.

A person's sense of justice is what is most distinctively and fundamentally moral. One can act morally and question all rules, one may act morally and question the greater good, but one cannot act morally and question the need for justice.

What are the actual developmental findings regarding the four moral orientations? And do they support our theory's assertion of the primacy of justice? A partial answer comes from our longitudinal data. For this purpose, we group the normative order and utilitarian orientations as interpenetrating to form Type A at each stage. Type B focuses on the interpenetration of the justice orientation with an ideal-self orientation. Type A makes judgments more descriptively and predictively, in terms of the given "out there." Type B makes judgments more prescriptively, in terms of what ought to be, of what is internally accepted by the self. A Type B orientation presupposes both awareness of rules and a judgment of their fairness.

Our longitudinal data indeed support the notion that the two types are relatively clear substages. The B substage is more mature than the A substage in the sense that a 3A may move to 3B, but a 3B can never move to 3A (though he or she may move to 4A). Individuals can skip the B substage, that is, move from 3A to 4A; but if they change substage, it is always from A to B. In a sense, then, the B substage is a consolidation or

equilibration of the social perspective first elaborated at the A substage. B's are more balanced in perspective. A 3A decides in terms of What does a good husband do? What does a wife expect? A 3B decides in terms of What does a husband who is a partner in a good mutual relationship do? What does each spouse expect of the other? Both sides of the equation are balanced; this is fairness. At 4A, the subject decides in terms of the questions What does the system demand? At 4B the, subject asks, What does the individual in the system demand as well as the system, and what is a solution that strikes a balance? Thus, a 4B upholds a system, but it is a "democratic" system with individual rights.

Because of this balance; B's are more prescriptive or internal, centering more on their judgments of what ought to be. They are also more universalistic, that is, more willing to carry the boundaries of value categories, like the value of life, to their logical conclusion. As an example, a Stage 3 subject responded to Heinz's drug-stealing dilemma by giving a standard A response, "A good husband would love his wife enough to do it." Asked whether a friend would steal a drug for a friend, he said, "No, a friend isn't that close that he has to risk stealing." He then added, "But when I think about it, that doesn't seem fair, his friend has just as much right to live as his wife."

Here we see a tendency, based on an orientation to justice, to universalize obligation to life and to distinguish it from role stereotypes. In summary, the full development and consolidation of moral judgment at each stage is defined by the categories and structures of justice, although stage development occurs in all four moral orientations.

Methodology in Assessing Moral Judgment Development

The Aspect-Scoring System

In our original formulation (Kohlberg, 1958, 1969), the moral stages were defined in terms of twenty-five "aspects," grouped, in turn, under the following major sets: rules, conscience, welfare of others, self's welfare, sense of duty, role-taking, punitive justice, positive justice, and motives. Each higher stage had a more internalized and autonomous idea of moral rules, a greater concern about the welfare of others, a broader conception of fairness, and so on.

Our first attempt to identify an individual's moral stage from his interview protocol used "aspect scoring." This was done with two methods: sentence scoring and story rating. Sentence scoring used a manual that listed prototypical sentences on each aspect in each moral dilemma. Every statement of a subject was scored by aspect and stage; and these statements were then converted into percentages, generating a profile of stage usage for each subject.

The second method of aspect scoring was story rating. Here the subject's total response to a story was assigned a stage on each aspect in terms of that stage's overall definition. Stage mixtures were handled by intuitively weighting a dominant and a minor stage of response. An example of a story-rating manual illustrating Stage 1 reasoning on seven aspects is presented in Table 2 which refers to the classic example of Heinz's dilemma:

> In Europe, a woman was near death from a rare form of cancer. There was one drug that the doctors thought might save her, a form of radium that a druggist in the same town had recently discovered. The druggist was charging $2,000, ten times what the drug cost him to make. The sick woman's husband, Heinz, went to everyone he knew to borrow the money, but he could only get together about half of what [the drug] cost. He told the druggist that his wife was dying and asked him to sell it cheaper or let him pay later. But the druggist said no. So Heinz got desperate and broke into the man's store to steal the drug for his wife.

> Q. *Should the husband have done that? Why?*

To illustrate the aspect-scoring procedure, we present an interview on the dilemma about Heinz and his dying wife, broken down into three statements and scored as Stage I by reference to Table 2.

Statement 1

Q. *Should Heinz have done that?*
A. He shouldn't do it.

Q. *Why?*
A. Because then he'd be a thief if they caught him and put him in jail.

In terms of Table 2, this statement reveals the following Stage 1 moral conceptions:

1. *Rules:* It's bad to steal or break rules whatever the reason, "he'd be a thief," it's a violation of law and police
2. *Conscience:* It's wrong because it leads to punishment.

Statement 2

Q. *Is it a husband's duty to steal?*
A. I don't think so.

TABLE 2
Aspect Scoring: Story Rating Manual with Prototypical
Stage 1 Statements on Drug-Stealing Dilemma

Stage I

1. *Rules:* Thinks Heinz Should not steal the drug, since it is bad to steal, whatever the motive; it's against external law and is a violation of the superior power of the police.
2. *Conscience:* Concern about the wrongness of stealing is in terms of fear of punishment.
3. *Altruism:* Thinks about his own welfare, not that of other people, like his wife.
4. *Duty:* Duty is only what he has to do, a husband doesn't have to steal for his wife.
5. *Self-interest:* Yields to power and punishment where rational self-interest would say to stick up for himself or to try to get away with it.
6. *Role Taking:* Since Stage I doesn't see things from other people's point of view, and doesn't expect them to see things from his, he expects punishment for stealing, no matter why he did what he did.
7. *Justice:* Justice in punishment is simply retribution for committing a crime, for breaking the law.

This statement indicates the following Stage 1 thinking:

3. *Altruism:* Doesn't focus on the welfare of the others, such as one's wife.

4. *Duty:* Obligation is limited on what one has to do because of superior power, not obligation to other people as such.

Statement 3

Q. *If you were dying of cancer but were strong enough, would you steal the drug to save your own life?*

A. No, because even if you did have time to take the drug, the police would put you in jail and you would die there anyway.

This statement indicates the following:

5. *Self-interest:* In thinking about his own welfare, he is not rational and does not stand up for himself or try to get away with a violation where it would be sensible to, because he believes he cannot escape the power and punishment system.

The limits of aspect scoring.

In a sense, aspect scoring by story is still the easiest introduction to the stages, and yields sufficient interjudge agreement (.89). This method turned out, however, to contain too much extraneous content to yield a measure or classification meeting the invariant sequence postulate of stage theory. This failure appeared in our original analysis of twelve-year longitudinal data gathered every three years on fifty males aged 10 to 26 (Kohlberg and Kramer, 1969; Kramer, 1968). The most outstanding inversion of sequence was an apparent shift from a Stage 4 society orientation to a Stage 2 relativistic hedonism in some subjects who became "liberated" and "relativized" in their college years. Based on the fact that these subjects eventually moved on to Stage 5 principled thinking, we eventually concluded that this relativistic egoism was a transitional phase, a "Stage 4 1/2"—a no-man's-land between rejection of conventional morality and the formulation of nonconventional or universal moral principles. The social perspective of Stage 4 1/2 was clearly different from that of naïve Stage 2. The Stage 4 1/2 questioned society and viewed himself and the rules from an "outside-of-society" perspective, whereas the Stage 2 saw things

as a concrete individual relating to other individuals through concrete reciprocity, exchange, and utilities.

A second inversion of sequence was found in a small proportion of individuals who "regressed" from Stage 4 to Stage 3, or skipped from Stage 3 to Stage 5. These inversions, in turn, could be seen as due to an inadequate definition of Stage 4, a definition which equated "law-and-order" ideas (content) with taking a social system perspective (stage structure). As a result, we redefined as Stage 3 (rather than Stage 4) any law-and-order thinking which did not display a social system perspective (for example, an Archie Bunker concept of law and order).

These changes in conceptions of the stages reflected a growing clarity in the distinction between structure and content which led us to abandon aspect scoring. Our aspect scoring was based not on "structure," but on certain statistical or probabilistic associations between structure and content. For example, a social system perspective tends to yield moral judgments whose content is law and order. One can, however, have much of this content at Stage 3 without the social system perspective, or one can have the social system perspective without this content. Accordingly, we decided to generate a new, more structural scoring method, which we call issue scoring.

Intuitive Issue Scoring

In order to develop a more structural scoring system, the first step was to standardize or analyze types of content used at every stage. These types of content, called issues or values, represent *what* the individual is valuing, judging, or appealing to rather than his *mode of reasoning* about that issue. To analyze stage differences, we must first make sure each stage is reasoning about or from the same values. We had attempted to do this with the aspects, but they were a mixture of formal or structural characteristics of judgment (for example, motives versus consequences and sense of duty) and direct issues or value content (for example, law and rules). Accordingly, we developed the following list of issues, values, or moral institutions found in every society and culture:

1. Laws and rules

2. Conscience

3. Personal roles of affection

4. Authority

5. Civil rights
6. Contract, trust, and justice in exchange
7. Punishment and justice
8. The value of life
9. Property rights and values
10. Truth
11. Sex and sexual love

The new content issues each embody several different moral aspects. For example, thinking about the issue of contract and trust involves formal aspects of altruism, duty, rules, role-taking, fairness, and so on.

Our classification of content in terms of issues also gave rise to a new unit to be rated. This unit is all the ideas a person uses concerning an issue in a story. The old system had rated each separate idea separately (sentence scoring) or else rated the story as a whole (story rating). But the sentence unit had proven too small for structural classification, and the story unit had proven too large for analytic, as opposed to ideal, typological scoring.

Having decided on issues, we then defined stage thinking on each issue. An example is the conception of life issue as worked out for Heinz's dilemma about stealing the drug (Table 3). To illustrate the use of this issue in scoring, here are excerpts from an interview with Tommy, a 10-year-old boy who spontaneously focuses on the life issue.

His wife was sick and if she didn't get the drug quickly, she might die. Maybe his wife is an important person and runs a store and the man buys stuff for her and can't gel it any other place. The police would blame the owner that he didn't save the wife.

> Q. *Does it matter whether the wife is important or not?*
>
> A.   If someone important is in a plane and is allergic to heights and the stewardess won't give him medicine because she's only got enough for one and she's got a sick friend in the back, they should put the stewardess in a lady's jail because she didn't help the important one.
>
> Q. *Is it better to save the life of one important person or a lot of unimportant people?*
>
> A.   All the people that aren't important, because one man just has one house, maybe a lot of furniture, but a whole bunch

of people have an awful lot of furniture and some of these poor people might have a lot of money and it doesn't look it.

Is Tommy's response Stage 1, Stage 2, or Stage 3 in terms of Why is life valuable? Tommy does not seem to fit Stage 1 in Table 3, since his response indicates that the wife's life does have a value justifying stealing. His response *is* Stage 1, however, because Tommy does not clearly recognize that life is more valuable to an individual than property. He says the lives of a lot of people who aren't important are worth more than the life of one important person because all the ordinary people together have more furniture or property. This is Stage 1 thinking, not Stage 2, because the value of life depends on a vague status of being important, not on the husband's or wife's interests or needs.

Standardized Issue Scoring

The procedure just discussed is called *intuitive issue scoring* and is theoretically the most valid method of scoring, since it is instrument free, that is, applicable to any moral dilemma. It is adequately reliable (90 percent interrater agreement) in the hands of thoroughly trained or experienced scorers. Reliable intuitive scoring, however, cannot be learned without personal teaching and supervised experience. It also is too intuitive to provide satisfactory test-construction characteristics of item independence, written versus oral interviews, and so on. We are therefore now developing a manual for standardized issue scoring (Colby and Kohlberg, 1984, in press). This manual is based on a standardized interview which probes only two issues on each of three stories. The standard form, Form A, contains three stories covering six issues as follows:

Story III: Heinz steals the drug
Issues: life, property
Story III: the judge must decide whether to punish Heinz
Issues: conscience, punishment
Story I: the father breaks a promise to his son
Issues: contract, authority

There is a second form for retest purposes, Form B, with different stories covering the same issues.

The manual for standardized issue scoring presents criterion judgments defining each stage on each issue for each story. A *criterion judgment*

TABLE 40.3
Issue Scoring Stages in Heinz's Dilemma

Stage	What is life's value in the situation?	Why is life valuable?
Stage 1	Wife's life has no clear value here to husband or others when it conflicts with law and property. Does not see that husband would value his wife's life over stealing.	Does not give a reason and does not indicate understanding that life is worth more than property.
Stage 2	It is its immediate value to the husband and to the wife, herself. Assumes the husband would think his wife's life is worth stealing for, but he isn't obligated to if he doesn't like her enough. Life's value to a person other than its possessor depends on relationship; you wouldn't steal to save the life of a mere friend or acquaintance.	Each person wants to live more than anything else. You can replace property, not life.
Stage 3	Life's value is its value to any good, caring, person like the husband. The husband should care enough to risk stealing (even if he does not steal), and a friend should care enough to save the life of a friend or another person.	People should care for other people and their lives. You're not good or human if you don't. People have much more feeling for life than for anything material.
Stage 4	Even though he may think it wrong to steal, he understands the general value or sacredness of human life or the rule to preserve life. Sacredness means all other values can't be compared with the value of life. The value of life is general; human life is valuable no matter what your relationship to the person is, though this doesn't obligate you to steal.	Life is valuable because God created it and made it sacred. Or life is valuable because it is basic to society; it is a basic right of people.
Stage 5	One recognizes that in this situation the wife's right to life comes before the druggist's right to property. There is some obligation to steal for anyone dying; everyone has a right to live and to be saved.	Everyone or society logically and morally must place each person's individual right to life before other rights such as the right to property.

is the reasoning pattern that is most distinctive of a given stage. Theoretically, such reasoning follows from the structural definition of the stage. Empirically, the criterion judgment is actually used by a substantial number of subjects at that stage (as defined by their global score) and not at other stages.

In the old sentence-scoring interview, sentences were matched to "prototypical" sentences of each stage in a manual. In some sense the new system returns to this procedure, but with controls. The first control is for the presence of the response in terms of the content or issue of response. The new system eliminates the problem of whether a criterion judgment at a given stage is not expressed because the subject does

not have a stage structure for that concept, or whether it is not expressed because the content (or issue) of response has not been elicited by the interview. The second control distinguishes between matching to a verbal sentence and matching to a criterion judgment. On the unit-of-response side, this implies that the unit of interpretation is bigger than the sentence. It also implies that the stage structure of the criterion judgment is clarified or distinguished from particular examples or exemplars.

The methodology of establishing standardized scoring is like Loevinger's methodology (Loevinger and Wessler, 1970) for scoring ego stage, in that criterion items are defined by reference to their use by individuals who have been intuitively staged. The difference, however, is that the criterion judgments are not the result of sheer empirical item analysis; rather, they must logically fit the theoretical stage description.

In my opinion, this standardized scoring system goes as far toward standardization as is possible while maintaining theoretical validity. We define "validity" as true measurement of development, that is, of longitudinal invariant sequence. A more common notion of test validation is prediction from a test to some criterion external to the test of which the test is presumed to be an indicator. Using the latter notion, some people assume that a moral judgment test should be validated by predicting "moral behavior." In this sense, Hartshorne and May's tests (1928–30) of "moral knowledge" fail to be valid, since they do not predict well to morally conforming behavior in ratings of experiments. We have argued that moral stage development predicts maturity of moral behavior better than Hartshorne and May's measures; but we have also argued that moral behavior is not a proper external criterion for "validating" a moral judgment test. From the point of view of cognitive-developmental theory, the relationship of the development of judgment to action is something to be studied and theoretically conceptualized; the issue is not one of "validating" a judgment test by a quantitative correlation with behavior.

Using the concept of external criterion validation, others have thought that a test of moral development should be validated by its relationship to age, a key meaning of the term *development*. While our measure of moral judgment maturity does correlate with chronological age in adolescents aged 10 to 18 ($r = +.71$), such a correlation is not "validating." Many adults are morally immature, so that a test which maximized correlation with age would ecologically relate to age but have little relation to *moral development*. The validity criterion of moral judgment development is construct validity, not prediction to an external criterion. *Construct validity* here means the fit of data obtained by means of the test to primary components of its theoretical definition. The primary theoretical definition of structural moral development is that of an organization passing through invariant sequential stages. The structural stage method meets this criterion in that longitudinal data so rated display invariant steplike change. The criterion for

validity for our new standard moral-reasoning test is congruence with, or prediction to, structural scoring.

The construct validity of a moral development measure has a philosophical or ethical dimension as well as a psychological dimension, that is, the requirement that a higher moral stage be a philosophically more adequate way of reasoning about moral dilemmas than a lower stage. This is a judgment about ways of thinking, not a grading of the moral worth of the individual. I claim (Kohlberg, 1971b) that each higher stage of reasoning is a more adequate way of resolving moral problems judged by moral-philosophic criteria. This claim is, again, made for structural scoring stages; a "standardized" test may be said to be valid insofar as it correlates with, or predicts to, structural stage.

An alternative approach to a standardizing measurement of moral development is set forth in Rest's presentation of his Defining-Issues Test (1976). Rest relies primarily on the more usual approach to empirical test construction and validation. Test construction is by empirical item analysis. The test is conceived as assessing a continuous variable of moral maturity rather than discrete qualitative stages. Test validation is primarily defined by correlations with various criteria, such as age, having studied moral philosophy, and so on. Rest, like my colleagues and myself, is interested in construct validity, not simply prediction to an external criterion. His conception of construct validity, however, is the notion of moderate-to-high correlations with other tests or variables expected to be associated with the test or variable in question. Instead, our conception of construct validity implies assignment of individuals to stages in such a way that the criterion of sequential movement is met. In our opinion, Rest's approach does provide a rough estimate of an individual's moral maturity level, as suggested by his reported correlation of .68 between his measure and an issue scoring of moral dilemma interviews.

We believe Rest's method is useful for exploratory examination of the correlates of moral maturity, but not for testing theoretical propositions derived from the cognitive-developmental theory of moral stages. Choice of various methods, then, must weight facility of data gathering and analysis against relatively error-free tests of structural theory.

In What Sense Are the Stages "True"?

In claiming that our stages are "true," we mean, first, that stage definitions are rigidly constrained by the empirical criterion of the stage concept: Many possible stages may be conceptualized, but only one set of stages can be manifested as a longitudinal invariant sequence. The claim we make is that anyone who interviewed children about moral dilemmas and who followed them longitudinally in time would come to our six stages and no others. A second empirical criterion is that of the "structured whole," that is, individuals should be consistently at a stage unless they are in transition to the next stage (when they are considered in mixed stages). The fact that almost all individuals manifest more than 50 percent of responses at a single stage with the rest at adjacent stages supports this criterion.

Second, in claiming that the stages are "true," we mean that the conceptual structure of the stage is not contingent on a specific psychological theory. They are, rather, matters of adequate logical analysis. By this we mean the following:

1. The ideas used to define the stages are the subjects', not ours. The logical connections among ideas define a given stage. The logical analysis of the connections in a child's thinking is itself theoretically neutral. It is not contingent on a psychological theory any more than is a philosopher's analysis of the logical connections in Aristotle's thinking.

2. The fact that a later stage includes and presupposes the prior stage is, again, a matter of logical analysis, not psychological theory.

3. The claim that a given child's ideas *cohere* in a stagelike way is a matter of logical analysis of internal connections between the various ideas held by the stage.

In short, the correctness of the stages as a description of moral development is a matter of empirical observation and of the analysis of the logical connections in children's ideas, not a matter of social science theory.

Although *the stages themselves are not a theory*, as descriptions of moral development they do have definite and radical implications for a social science *theory of moralization*. Accordingly,

we shall now (1) elaborate a cognitive-developmental theory of moralization which can explain the facts of sequential moral development and (2) contrast it with socialization theories of moralization.

Types of Moralization Theory: Cognitive-Developmental, Socialization, and Psychoanalytic Theories

A discussion of a cognitive-developmental moral theory immediately suggests the work of Piaget (1932). Piaget's concepts, however, may best be considered as only one example of the cognitive-developmental approach to morality represented in various ways by J. M. Baldwin (1906), Bull (1969), J. Dewey and J. H. Tufts (1932), Harvey, Hunt, and Schroeder (1961), Hobhouse (1906), Kohlberg (1964), McDougall (1908), and G. H. Mead (1934). The most obvious characteristic of cognitive-developmental theories is their use of some kind of stage concept, of some notion of age-linked sequential reorganizations in the development of moral attitudes. Other common assumptions of cognitive-developmental theories are as follows:

1. Moral development has a basic cognitive-structural or moral-judgmental component.

2. The basic motivation for morality is a generalized motivation for acceptance, competence, self-esteem, or self-realization, rather than for the meeting of biological needs and the reduction of anxiety or fear.

3. Major aspects of moral development are culturally universal, because all cultures have common sources of social interaction, role-taking, and social conflict which require moral integration.

4. Basic moral norms and principles are structures arising through experiences of social interaction rather than through internalization of rules that exist as external structures; moral stages are not defined by internalized rules but by structures of interaction between the self and others.

5. Environmental influences in moral development are defined by the general qual-

ity and extent of cognitive and social stimulation throughout the child's development, rather than by specific experiences with parents or experiences of discipline, punishment, and reward.

These assumptions contrast sharply with those of "socialization," or "social-learning," theories of morality. The work of Aronfreed (1968), Bandura and Walters (1959), Berkowitz (1964), Hoffman (1970), Miller and Swanson (1960), Sears, Rau, and Alpert (1965), and Whiting and Child (1953) may be included under this general rubric. The social-learning theories make the following assumptions:

1. Moral development is growth of behavioral and affective conformity to moral rules rather than cognitive-structural change.

2. The basic motivation for morality at every point of moral development is rooted in biological needs or the pursuit of social reward and avoidance of social punishment.

3. Moral development or morality is culturally relative.

4. Basic moral norms are the internalization of external cultural rules.

5. Environmental influences on normal moral development are defined by quantitative variations in strength of reward, punishment, prohibitions, and modeling of conforming behavior by parents and other socializing agents.

Research based on classical Freudian theory can also be included under the socialization rubric. While the classical Freudian psychoanalytic theory of moral development (Flugel, 1955) cannot be equated with social-learning theories of moralization, it shares with these theories the assumption that moralization is a process of internalization of cultural or parental norms. Further, while Freudian theory (like cognitive-developmental theory) postulates stages, these classical Freudian stages are libidinal-instinctual rather than moral, and morality (as expressed by the superego) is conceived as formed and fixed early in development through internalization of parental norms. As a result, systematic research based on Freudian moral theory has ignored stage components of moral development and has focused on "internalization" aspects of the theory (Kohlberg, 1963b).

A forthcoming book (Kohlberg and Candee, eds., in prep.) reports on forty studies which represent an accumulation of replicated findings firmly consistent with a cognitive-developmental theory of moralization and quite inexplicable from the view of socialization theories. The next section elaborates the cognitive-developmental view of how the social environment stimulates moral stage development.

How Does Cognitive-Developmental Theory Characterize Environmental Stimulation of Moral Development?

Moral development depends upon stimulation defined in cognitive-structural terms, but this stimulation must also be social, the kind that comes from social interaction and from moral decision making, moral dialogue, and moral interaction. "Pure cognitive" stimulation is a necessary background for moral development but does not directly engender moral development. As noted earlier, we have found that attainment of a moral stage requires cognitive development, but cognitive development will not directly lead to moral development. However, an absence of cognitive stimulation necessary for developing formal logical reasoning may be important in explaining ceilings on moral level. In a Turkish village, for example, full formal operational reasoning appeared to be extremely rare (if the Piagetian techniques for intellectual assessment can be considered usable in that setting). Accordingly, one would not expect that principled (Stage 5 or 6) moral reasoning, which requires formal thinking as a base, could develop in that cultural context.

Of more importance than factors related to stimulation of cognitive stage are factors of general social experience and stimulation, which we call *role-taking opportunities*. What differentiates social experience from interaction with things is the fact that social experience involves role-taking: taking the attitude of others, becoming aware of their thoughts and feelings, putting oneself in their place. When the emotional side of role-taking is stressed, it is typically termed *empathy* (or *sympathy*). The term *role-taking*, coined by G. H. Mead (1934), is preferable, however, because (1) it emphasizes the cognitive as well as the affective side, (2) it involves an organized structural relationship between self and others, (3) it emphasizes that the process involves understanding and relating to all the roles in the society of which one is a part, and (4) it emphasizes that role-taking goes on in *all* social interactions and communication situations, not merely in ones that arouse emotions of sympathy or empathy.

Although moral judgments entail role-taking—putting oneself in the place of the various people involved in a moral conflict—attainment of a given role-taking stage, as indicated earlier, is a necessary but not a sufficient condition for moral development. As an example, the role-taking advance necessary for Stage 2 moral reasoning is awareness that each person in a situation can or does consider the intention or point of view of every other individual in the situation. A child may attain this role-taking level and still hold the Stage 1 notion that right or justice is adherence to fixed rules which must be automatically followed. But if the child is to see rightness or justice as a balance or exchange between the interests of individual actors (Stage 2), he or she must have reached the requisite level of role-taking. Role-taking level, then, is a bridge between logical or cognitive level and moral level; it is one's level of social cognition.

In understanding the effects of social environment on moral development, then, we must consider that environment's provision of role-taking opportunities to the child. Variations in role-taking opportunities exist in terms of children's relation to their family, their peer group, their school, and their social status vis-à-vis the larger economic and political structure of the society.

With regard to the family, the disposition of parents to allow or encourage dialogue on value issues is one of the clearest determinants of moral stage advance in children (Holstein, 1968). Such an exchange of viewpoints and attitudes is part of what we term "role-taking opportunities." With regard to peer groups, children high in peer participation are more advanced in moral stage than are those who are low. With regard to status in the larger society, socioeconomic status is correlated with moral development in various cultures (Kohlberg and Candee, eds., in prep.). This, we believe, is due to the fact that middle class children have more opportunity to take the point of view of the more distant, impersonal, and influential roles in society's basic institutions (law, economy, government, economics) than do lower class children. In general, the higher an individual child's participation in a social group or institution, the more opportunities that child has to take the social perspectives of others. From this point of view, extensive participation in any particular group is not essential to moral development but participation in some group is. Not only is participation necessary, but mutuality of role-taking is also necessary. If, for instance, adults to not consider the child's point of view, the child may not communicate or take the adult's point of view.

To illustrate environments at opposite extremes in role-taking opportunities, we may cite an America orphanage and an Israeli kibbutz. Of all environments we have studied, the American orphanage had children at the lowest level, Stages 1 and 2, even though adolescence (Thrower, in Kohlberg and Candee, eds., in pep.). Of all environments studied, an Israeli kibbutz had children at the highest level, with adolescents mainly at Stage 4 and with a considerable percentage at Stage 5 (Reimer, 1977). Both orphanage and kibbutz environments involved low interaction with parents, but they were dramatically different in other ways. The American orphanages not only lacked parental interaction but involved very little communication and role-taking between staff adults and children. Relations among the children themselves were fragmentary, with very little communication and no stimulation or supervision of peer interaction by the staff. That the deprivation of role-taking opportunities caused a retardation in role-taking as well as in moral judgment was suggested by the fact that the orphanage adolescents failed a role-taking task passed by almost all children of their chronological and mental age. In contrast, children in the kibbutz engaged in intense peer interaction supervised by a group leader who was concerned about bringing the young people into the kibbutz community as active dedicated participants. Discussing, reasoning, communicating feelings, and making group decisions were central everyday activities.

Obviously, the kibbutz differed as a moral environment from the orphanage in other ways as well. Beyond provision of role-taking opportunities by groups and institutions, how do we define the *moral atmosphere* of a group or institution? We have said that the core of specifically moral component of moral judgment is a sense of justice. While role-taking defines the conflicting points of view taken in a moral situation, the "principles" for resolving conflicting points of view at each moral stage are principles of justice, of giving each his or her due. The core of the moral atmosphere of an institution or environment, then, is its justice structure, "the way in which social institutions distribute fundamental rights and duties and determine the division of advantages from social cooperation" (Rawls, 1971, p. 7).

It appears from our research that a group or institution tends to be perceived as being at a certain moral stage by its participants. Our empirical work on this has been primarily based on the perception by inmates of the atmospheres of various prisons in which they were incarcerated (Kohlberg, Hickey, and Scharf, 1972). Although for reasons of comprehension inmates cannot perceive an institution as being at a higher level than a stage above their own, they can perceive it as being at lower stages. Thus, Stage 3 inmates perceived one reformatory as Stage 1, another as Stage 2, and a third at Stage 3. An example of a Stage 3 prisoner's perception of staff in the Stage 3 institution is, "They are pretty nice and they show interest. I get the feeling that they care a little more than most people do." An example of a Stage 3 inmate's perception of staff as being Stage 2 in the Stage 2 institution is, "If a guy messes up in a certain way or doesn't brown-nose as much as he should, the counselor won't do a job for him. It's all favoritism. If you go out of your way for a guy, he will go out of his way for you."

Even more extreme perceptions of the subjects' world for institution as being low stage were shown in the orphanage study. With regard to parents, here is a 15-year-old boy's response:

Q. *Why should a promise be kept?*

A. They aren't. My mother called up and says, "I will be up in two weeks," then I don't see her for eight months. That really kills you, something like that.

On the moral judgment test this boy was beginning to show some Stage 3 concern about affection promises, and so on; but his world was one in which such things meant nothing. This boy's mother is Stage 2, but the orphanage environment presents no higher-stage moral world. While the nuns who direct this particular orphanage are personally conventionally moral, their moral ideology translates into a justice structure perceived as Stage 1 by this boy. He says:

It really breaks your heart to tell the truth because sometimes you get in trouble for it. I was playing and I swung a rock and hit a car. It was an accident, but I told the sister. I got punished for it.

Obviously, prisons and orphanages are exceptional in representing monolithic or homogeneous lower-stage environments. It is plausible in general, however, that the moral atmosphere of environments is more than the sum of the individual moral judgments and actions of its members. It is also plausible that participation in institutions that have the potential of being seen as at a higher stage than the child's own is a basic determinant of moral development.

A notion that a higher-stage environment stimulates moral development is an obvious extension of experimental findings by Turiel (1966) and Rest (1973) that adolescents tend to assimilate moral reasoning from the next stage above their own, while they reject reasoning below their own. The concept of exposure to a higher stage need not be limited to a stage of reasoning, however; it may also include exposures to moral action and to institutional arrangements. What the moral atmosphere studies we have quoted show is that individuals respond to a composite of moral reasoning, moral action, and institutionalized rules as a relatively unified whole in relation to their own moral stage.

Using the notion that creation of a higher-stage institutional atmosphere will lead to moral change, Hickey and Scharf (1980) and I developed a "just community" in a women's prison involving democratic self-government through community decisions as well as small-group moral discussion. This program led to an upward change in moral reasoning as well as to later changes in life-style and behavior.

In addition to the role-taking opportunities and the perceived moral level provided by an institution, a third factor stressed by cognitive-developmental theory is cognitive-moral conflict. Structural theory stresses that movement to the next stage occurs through reflective reorganization arising from sensed contradictions in one's current stage structure. Experiences of cognitive conflict can occur either through exposure to decision situations that arouse internal contradictions in one's moral reasoning structure or through exposure to the moral reasoning of significant others which is discrepant in content or structure from one's own reasoning. This principle is central to the moral discussion program that we have implemented in schools (Blatt and Kohlberg, 1975; Colby 1972). While peer-group moral discussion of dilemmas leads to moral stage change through exposure to the next stage of reasoning, discussion without such exposure also leads to moral change. Colby (1972) found, for example, that a program of moral discussion led to some development of Stage 5 thinking on a posttest in a group of conventional level students who had shown no Stage 5 reasoning on the pretest.

Real-life situations and choices vary dramatically in their potential for moral-cognitive conflict of a personal nature. This conclusion comes from our longitudinal data on the movement of individuals from conventional to principled morality (see chapter 6). One factor that appears to have precipitated the beginning of this shift was the college moratorium experience of responsibility and independence from authority together with exposure to openly conflicting and relativistic values and standards. The conflict involved here was between the subject's own conventional morality and a world with potentials for action that did not fit conventional morality. Some of our other subjects changed in more dramatic moral situations which aroused conflict about the adequacy of conventional morality. One subject, for example, moved from conventional to principled thinking while serving as an officer in Vietnam, apparently because of awareness of the conflict between law-and-order "Army morality" and the more universal rights of the Vietnamese.

Moral Development and Ego Development

As we move from general characteristics of environments to the more individual life experiences that seem to promote moral change, a cognitive-developmental theory begins to seem limited and abstract. At this point, one begins to draw upon theories like Erikson's (1964), which present age-typical emotional experiences as they relate to a developing personality or self. It then becomes useful to look at the individual's ego level as well as his or her moral stage. In this sense, ego-development theories represent possible extensions of cognitive-developmental theory as it moves into the study of individual lives and life histories. There is a broad unity to the development of social perception and social values which deserves the name of "ego development." This unity is perhaps better conceived as a matter of levels than of structural stages, since the unity of ego levels is not that of logical or moral stage structures. The requirements for consistency in logic and morals are much tighter than those for consistency in personality, which is a psychological, not a logical, unity. Furthermore, there are relatively clear criteria of increased adequacy in logical and moral hierarchies, but not in ego levels.

Because moral stages have a tighter unitary structure, it would be a mistake to view them as simply reflections of broader ego levels. Writers such as Peck and Havighurst (1960) and Loevinger and Wessler (1970) have nevertheless treated moral development as part of general stages of ego or character development—indeed, as a bench mark for such development. If ego development is seen as the successive restructuring of the relationship between the self and standards, it is natural for ego-development theorists to use changes in the moral domain as bench marks. Similar restructurings are assumed to hold in the relations of the self to values in other areas, such as work achievement, sociability, art, politics, religion, and so on.

We hold, however, that there is a unity and consistency to moral structures, that the unique characteristics of moral structures are defined by formalistic moral philosophy, and that to treat moral development as simply a facet of ego (or of cognitive) development is to miss many of its special problems and features. We believe that

1. Cognitive development or structures are more general than, and are embodied in, both self or ego structures and in moral judgment.

2. Generalized ego structures (modes of perceiving self and social relations) are more general than, and are embodied in, moral structures.

3. Cognitive development is a necessary but not sufficient condition for ego development.

4. Certain features of ego development are a necessary but not sufficient condition for development of moral structures.

5. The higher the moral stage, the more distinct it is from the parallel ego stage.

While these propositions suggest a high correlation between measures of ego development and measures of moral development, such a correlation does not imply that moral development can be defined simply as a division or area of ego development. Moral structure distinct from ego structures can be found, however, only if moral stages are first defined in way more specific than the ways used to characterize ego development. If this specification is not made in the initial defined of moral development, one is bound to find moral development to be simply an aspect of ego development, as Peck and Havighurst (1960) and Loevinger and Wessler (1970) have. Loevinger's inability to differentiate moral items from normal items in her measure of ego development simply demonstrates that her criteria of moral development were not more specific than her general criteria of ego development.

In summary, a broad psychological cognitive-developmental theory of moralization is an ego-developmental theory. Furthermore, in understanding moral functioning, one must place the individual's moral stage within the broader context of his or her ego level. To see moral stages as simply reflections of ego level, however, is to lose the ability to theoretically define and empirically find order in the specifically moral domain of the human personality.

CHAPTER 41
TWO MORAL ORIENTATIONS

CAROL GILLIGAN AND JANE ATTANUCCI

Recent discussions of sex differences in moral development have confused moral stage within Kohlberg's justice framework with moral orientation, the distinction between justice and care perspectives. Studies by Kohlberg (1984), Walker (1984), Baumrind (1986), and Haan (1985) address the question of whether women and men score differently in Kohlberg's scale of justice reasoning and report contradictory findings. In the present study, we address the question of moral orientation and examine evidence of two moral perspectives in people's discussions of actual moral conflicts. In addition, we ask whether there is an association between moral orientation and gender.

The distinction made here between a justice and a care orientation pertains to the ways in which moral problems are conceived and reflects different dimensions of human relationships that give rise to moral concern. A justice perspective draws attention to problems of inequality and oppression and holds up an ideal of reciprocity and equal respect. A care perspective draws attention to problems of detachment or abandonment and holds up an ideal of attention and response to need. Two moral injunctions—not to treat others unfairly and not to turn away from someone in need—capture these different concerns. From a developmental standpoint, inequality and attachment are universal human experiences; all children are born into a situation of inequality and no child survives in the absence of some kind of adult attachment. The two dimensions of equality and attachment characterize all forms of human relationship, and all relationships can be described in both sets of terms—as unequal or equal and as attached or detached. Since everyone has been vulnerable both to oppression and to abandonment, two moral visions—one of justice and one of care—recur in human experience.

This article reports the results of three studies undertaken to investigate the two moral orientations and to determine to what extent men and women differentially raise concerns about justice and care in discussing moral conflicts in their lives. Lyons (1983) operationalized the distinction between justice and care in terms of the perspective toward others which they imply, contrasting a perspective of reciprocity with a perspective of response. Evidence of these perspectives appeared in the kinds of considerations people raised in discussing real-life moral dilemmas. Lyons created a reliable procedure for identifying moral considerations and assigning them to categories. She defines a morality of justice as: fairness resting on "an understanding of relationships as reciprocity between separate individuals, grounded in the duty and obligations of their roles." Reciprocity is defined in terms of maintaining standards of justice and fairness, understood differently at different development levels (Kohlberg, 1981, 1984). A morality of care "rests on an understanding of relationship as response to another in their terms" (Lyons, 1983, p. 136). A care perspective involves the question of how to act responsively and protect vulnerability in a particular situation.

The examples presented in Table 1, drawn from discussions of real-life dilemmas, illustrate the concept of moral orientation. Each pair of dilemmas reveals how a problem is seen from a justice and from a care perspective. In each pair of examples, the justice construction is the more familiar one, capturing the way such problems are usually defined from a moral standpoint. In **1J** a peer pressure dilemma is presented in terms of how to uphold one's moral standards and withstand pressure from one's friends to deviate from what one knows to be right. In **1C** a similar decision (not to smoke) is cast in terms of how to respond both to one's friends and to oneself; the rightness of the decision not to smoke is established in terms of the fact that it did not break relationships—"my real friends accepted my decision." Attention to one's friends, to what they say and how it will affect the friendship is presented as a moral concern.

In the second pair of examples, a dilemma— whether to report someone who was violated the medical school's alcohol policy—is posed differently from the justice and care perspectives; the decision not to tell is reasoned in different ways. A clear example of justice tempered by mercy is presented in **2J**. The student clearly believes that the violator should be turned in ("I was supposed to turn her in") and justifies not doing so on the grounds that she deserved mercy because "she had all the proper level of contriteness" appropriate for the situation. In **2C** a student decides not to turn a proctor in because it would "destroy any relationship you have" and therefore, would "hurt any chance of doing anything for that person." In this construction, turning the person in is seen as impeding efforts to help. The concern

about maintaining relationship in order to be able to help is not mentioned in **2J**; similarly the concern about maintaining the honor board policy is not mentioned in **2C**. A further illustration of how justice and care perspectives restructure moral understanding can be seen by observing that in **2J** the student justifies not turning in the violator because of questions about the rightness or justification of the alcohol policy itself, while in **2C** the student considers whether what was deemed a problem was really a problem for the other person. The case of **2C** illustrates what is meant by striving to see the other in the other's terms; it also exemplifies the contrast between this endeavor and the effort to establish, independently of persons, the legitimacy of existing rules and standards. It is important to emphasize that these examples were selected to highlight the contrast between the justice and the care perspectives and that most people who participated in this research used considerations of both justice and care in discussing a moral conflict they faced.

Validity for Lyons' distinction between justice and care considerations was provided by Langdale (1983), who adapted Lyons' procedure in order to code hypothetical dilemmas. Langdale found that Kohlberg's justice-oriented Heinz dilemma elicits significantly more justice

TABLE 1

Examples of Justice and Care Perspectives in Real-Life Moral Dilemmas

Justice	Care
1J. [If people were taking drugs and I was the only one who wasn't, I would feel it was stupid. I know for me what is right is right and what's wrong is wrong . . . It's like a set of standards I have.] (High School Student)	1C [If there was one person, it would be a lot easier to say no. I could talk to her, because there wouldn't be seven others to think about. I do think about them, you know, and wonder what they say about me and what it will mean . . . I made the right decision not to, because my real friends accepted my decision.] (High School Student)
2J [The conflict was that by all rights she should have been turned into the honor board for violation of the alcohol policy.] [I liked her very much.] [She is extremely embarrassed and upset. She was contrite. She wished she had never done it. She had all the proper levels of contriteness and guilt . . .] [I was supposed to turn her in and didn't.] (Medical Student)	2C [It might just be his business if he wants to get drunk every week or it might be something that is really a problem and that should be dealt with professionally; and to be concerned about someone without antagonizing them or making their life more difficult than it had to me. Maybe there was just no problem there.] [I guess in something like a personal relationship with a proctor you don't want to just go right out there and antagonize people, because that person will go away and if you destroy any relationship you have, I think you have lost any chance of doing anything for a person.] (Medical Student)

considerations than either a hypothetical care-oriented abortion dilemma or subject-generated real-life moral dilemmas. Langdale demonstrated further that the hypothetical Heinz and abortion dilemmas as well as recurrent types of real-life dilemmas are construed by some people predominantly in terms of justice and by others predominantly in terms of care. This negates the suggestion that concerns about justice and care arise from different kinds of moral problems. Instead, Langdale's analysis of moral orientation indicates how the same problem can be seen in different ways. At the same time her study reveals that hypothetical moral dilemmas can "pull": for the justice or the care orientation.

In the present study, we ask the following three questions: (1) Is there evidence of both justice and care concerns in people's discussion of real-life moral conflict? (2) Do people represent both sets of concerns equally or do they tend to focus on one and minimally represent the other? (3) Is there a relationship between moral orientation and gender?

Method

Subjects

Subjects were drawn from three research studies conducted over the past six years. As part of each study, the subjects were asked to describe a real-life moral dilemma. All three samples consisted of men and women matched for levels of education; the adults were matched for professional occupations. The decision was made to sample from an advantaged population, since sex differences in adult moral reasoning have

been attributed to women's typically lower occupational and educational status (Kohlberg & Kramer, 1969).

Study 1. The design of this study matched participants for high levels of education and professional occupation to examine the variables of age, gender, and type of dilemma. The adolescents and adults included eleven women and ten men. The racial composition (nineteen white and two minority) was not statistically random, as race was not a focal variable of the study.

Study 2. In this study first-year students were randomly selected from two prestigious northeastern medical schools to be interviewed as part of a longitudinal study of stress and adaptation in physicians.[1] The twenty-six men and thirteen women students represented the proportions of each gender in the class at large. The nineteen white and twenty minority students (Black, Hispanic, and Asian Americans) were selected to balance the sample's racial composition (the only sample in the present study with such a design). The students ranged from twenty-one to twenty-seven years of age.

Study 3. The ten female and ten male participants were randomly selected from a coeducational private school in a midwestern city. The nineteen white and one minority student ranged in age from fourteen to eighteen years.

See Table 2 for the distribution of subjects by sample in age and gender categories.

Research Interview

All participants were asked the following series of questions about their personal experience of moral conflict and choice.

TABLE 2
Gender and Age of Subjects by Study (Moral Orientation Studies)

	15–22 years	23–34 years	35–77 years
Study 1			
Women (N = 11)	4	2	5
Men (N = 10)	4	1	5
Study 2			
Women (N = 13)	9	4	0
Men (N = 26)	12	14	0
Study 3			
Women (N = 10)	10	0	0
Men (N = 10)	10	0	0

1. Have you ever been in a situation of moral conflict where you have had to make a decision but weren't sure what was the right thing to do?

2. Could you describe the situation?

3. What were the conflicts for you in that situation?

4. What did you do?

5. Do you think it was the right thing to do?

6. How do you know?

The interviewer asked questions to encourage the participants to clarify and elaborate their responses. For example, participants were asked what they meant by words like responsibility, obligation, moral, fair, selfish, and caring. The interviewers followed the participants' logic in presenting the moral problem, most commonly querying, "Anything else?"

The interviews were conducted individually, tape recorded, and later transcribed. The moral conflict questions were one segment of an interview which included questions about morality and identity (Gilligan *et al.*, 1982). The interviews lasted about two hours.

Data Analysis

The real-life moral dilemmas were analyzed using Lyons' coding procedure.[2] The three coders trained by Lyons were blind to the gender, age, and race of the participants and achieved high levels of intercoder reliability (a range of 67–95 percent and a mean of 80 percent agreement across samples on randomly selected cases).

The Lyons procedure is a content analysis which identifies moral considerations. The unit of analysis is the consideration, defined as each idea the participant presents in discussing a moral problem. The units are designated in Table 1 with brackets. To reach an acceptable level of reliability in identifying considerations required extensive training; the coders in these studies were all trained by Lyons and achieved reliability at acceptable levels (Lyons, 1983). Typically, a real-life moral dilemma consists of seven considerations with a range of 4 to 17.[3] The coder classifies these considerations as either justice or care. The Lyons score indicates the predominant, most frequent mode of moral reasoning (justice or care). For the present analysis predominance has been redefined, such that a real-life moral dilemma consisting of only care or justice considerations is labeled Care Only or Justice Only (Table 3). A dilemma consisting of 75 percent or more care or justice considerations is labeled Care Focus or Justice Focus, respectively. A dilemma in which both orientations are present but neither orientation accounts for 75 percent of the codable considerations is placed in the Care-Justice category. Thus, dilemmas are described as focused only when more than 75 percent of the considerations fall into one mode.

Results

This article summarizes the real-life dilemma data from three studies with comparable designs, that is, samples with male and female subjects matched for high socioeconomic status. Frequencies and statistical tests are presented across samples.[4]

Looking at Table 3, two observations can be made. First, the majority of people represent both moral orientations: 69 percent (55 out of 80) compared to the 31 percent (25 out of 80) who use Care or Justice Only. Second, two-thirds of the dilemmas are in the Focus categories (Care Only, Care Focus, Justice Only, Justice Focus), while only one-third are in the Care-Justice category. The question addressed by Table 3 is do people

TABLE 3
Moral Orientation of Participants by Category

	Care Only	Care Focus	Care-Justice	Justice Focus	Justice Only
Observed	5	8	27	20	20
Expected*	0.64	4	70	4	0.64

Note: For the typical case, the ratio of care to justice considerations is Care Only, 7:0; Care Focus, 6:1; Care-Justice, 5:2, 4:3, 3:4, 2:5; Justice Focus, 0:7; and Justice Only, 0:7. Since the range of consideration is 4-17, percentages are used to define comparable categories across cases.

*Expected values are based on binomial distribution for $N = 7$, $p = 0.5$.

tend to focus their discussion of a moral problem in one or the other orientation? Using a binomial model, if one assumes an equal probability of care and justice orientations in an account of a real-life moral dilemma ($p = 0.5$), then a random sampling of moral considerations (typically $N = 7$) over eighty trials (eighty participants' single dilemmas) would result in an expected binomial distribution. To test whether the distribution of scores fits the expected distribution, the $\chi2$ goodness-of-fit test is applied. The observed distribution differs significantly from the expected, $\chi2$ (4, N = 80) = 133.8, p < 0.001,[5] and provides supporting evidence for our contention that an individual's moral considerations are not random but tend to be focused in either the care or justice orientation.

In Table 4, the relationship between moral orientation and gender can be examined. The test of statistical significance, $\chi2$ (2, N = 80) = 18.33, p < 0.001, demonstrates a relationship between moral orientation and gender such that both men and women present dilemmas in the Care-Justice category, but Care Focus is much more likely to occur in the moral dilemma of a woman, and Justice Focus more likely in the dilemma of a man. In fact, if one were to exclude women from a study of moral reasoning, Care Focus could easily be overlooked.[6]

We did not test the relationship between moral orientation and age, because the majority of participants were adolescents and young adults, providing little age range. Furthermore, in the present analysis, age is confounded with sample (i.e., the young adults are the medical students), making interpretation difficult.[7]

The medical student data (Study 2) raised further questions of interpretation which bear on the issues addressed in this analysis. First, the dilemmas from the medical students when tested separately do not show the same relationship between gender and moral orientation, $\chi2$ (2, N = 39) = 4.36, n.s. However, consistent with the overall findings, the two Care Focus dilemmas were presented by women.

Examining the pattern of difference in the dilemmas, the Care Focus dilemmas were presented by one white and one minority woman. The relationship between moral orientation and race for both men and women is that the dilemmas presented by white students are more likely to fall in the Care-Justice category and dilemmas of minority students in the Justice Focus category (Fisher's Exact p = 0.045 for women and p = 0.0082 for men).

Discussion

The present exploration of moral orientation has demonstrated that (1) concerns about justice and care are *both* represented in people's thinking about real-life moral dilemmas, but people tend to focus on one set of concerns and minimally represent the other; and (2) there is an association between moral orientation and gender such that both men and women use both orientations, but Care Focus dilemmas are more likely to be presented by women and Justice Focus dilemmas by men.

Our findings indicate that the selection of an all-male sample for theory and test construction in moral judgment research is inherently problematic. If women were eliminated from the present study, Care Focus would virtually disappear. Furthermore, most of the dilemmas described by women could be scored and analyzed for justice considerations without reference to the considerations of care. Thus, the interpretive question hinges on the understanding of the care perspective.

Our analysis of care and justice as distinct moral orientations that address different moral concerns leads us to consider both perspectives as constitutive of mature moral thinking. The tension between these perspectives is suggested by the fact that detachment, which is the mark of mature moral judgment in the justice perspective, becomes *the* moral problem in the care perspective—the failure to attend to need. Conversely, attention to the particular needs and

TABLE 4
Moral Orientation by Gender of Participation

	Care Focus	Care–Justice	Justice Focus
Women	12	12	10
Men	1	15	30

circumstances of individuals, the mark of mature moral judgment in the care perspective, becomes *the* moral problem in the justice perspective—failure to treat others fairly, as equals. Care Focus and Justice Focus reasoning suggest a tendency to lose sight of one perspective in reaching moral decision. The fact that the focus phenomenon was demonstrated by two-thirds of both men and women in our study suggests that this liability is shared by both sexes. The virtual absence of Care Focus dilemmas among men in these samples of advantaged North Americans is the surprising finding of this research.

This finding provides an empirical explanation for the equation of morality with justice in theories of moral development derived from all-male research samples (Piaget, 1932/1965; Kohlberg, 1969, 1984). In addition, the Care Focus dilemmas presented by women offer an explanation for the fact that within a justice conception of morality, moral judgments of girls and women have appeared anomalous and difficult to interpret; Piaget cites this as the reason for studying boys. Furthermore, finding Care Focus mainly among women indicates why the analysis of women's more thinking elucidated the care perspective as a distinct moral orientation (Gilligan, 1977) and why the considerations of care noted in dilemmas presented by men did not seem fully elaborated (Gilligan & Murphy, 1979). The evidence of orientation focus as an observable characteristic of moral judgment does not justify the conclusion that focus is a desirable attribute of moral decision. However, careful attention to women's articulation of care concerns suggests a different conception of the moral domain and a different way of analyzing the moral judgments of both men and women.

The category Care-Justice in our findings raises important questions that merit investigation in future research. Dilemmas in this "bifocal" category were equally likely among men and women in our study, but it is possible that interviews involving more dilemmas and further questioning might reveal the focus phenomenon to be more common and eliminate the bi-focal category. But it is also possible that such studies might find and elucidate further an ability to sustain two moral perspectives—an ability which according to the present data seems equally characteristic of women and men.

If people know both moral perspectives, as our theory and data suggest, researchers can cue perceptions in one or the other direction by the dilemmas they present, by the questions they raise, or by their failure to ask questions. The context of the research study as well as the interview itself must be considered for its influence on the likelihood of eliciting care or justice reasoning. In the case of the medical student data (Study 2), the findings raise just such contextual questions. In this large-scale study of stress and adaptation which included extensive standard, evaluative inventories as well as the clinical interview, is it possible that the first-year medical students might have been reluctant to admit uncertainty? A large number could not or would not describe a situation in which they were not sure what the right thing to do was. Also, is it possible that the focus on justice represents efforts by the students to align themselves with the perceived values of the institution they are entering? The focus on justice by minority students is of particular interest since it counters the suggestion that a care orientation is the perspective of subordinates or people of lower social power and status.

Evidence that moral orientation organizes moral judgment as well as the discovery of the focus phenomenon has led us to make the following changes in our research procedures which we offer as suggestions for other researchers:

1. That interviewers proceed on the assumption that people can adopt both a justice and a care perspective and that they encourage participants to generate different perspectives on a moral problem ("Is there another way to think about this problem?") and to examine the relationship between them.

2. That interviewers seek to determine the conception of justice and the conception of care that organizes the moral thinking in the discussion of a particular dilemma. Kohlberg's stages describe the development of justice reasoning. We have described different ways women think about care and traced changes over time in care reasoning. Our work offers guides to thinking about development and the nature of transitions in two perspectives.

Evidence of two moral perspectives suggests that the choice of moral standpoint, whether implicit or explicit, may indicate a preferred way of seeing. If so, the implications of such a preference need to be explored. Orientation preference may be a dimension of identity or self-definition, especially when moral decision becomes more reflective or "post-conventional" and the choice of moral principle becomes correspondingly more self-conscious. Interviewers should attend to where the self stands with respect to the two moral orientations. In our present research we have included the question, "What is at stake for you in the conflict?" to encourage subjects to reveal where they see themselves in the dilemmas they describe and how they align themselves with different perspectives on the problem.

The promise of our approach to moral development in terms of moral orientation lies in its potential to transform debate over cultural and sex differences in moral reasoning into serious questions about moral perspectives that are open to empirical study. If moral maturity consists of the ability to sustain concerns about justice and care, and if the focus phenomenon indicates a tendency to lose sight of one set of concerns, then the encounter with orientation difference can tend to offset errors in moral perception.

Notes

1. Nineteen medical students could not (two would not) describe a situation of moral conflict and were not, therefore, included in the present study. This unprecedented high number may reflect the pressures on first-year medical students in a context which discourages the uncertainty of not knowing what is the right thing to do. Generalizations about physicians from this specific study would be unwarranted, however, as several physicians who participated in Study 1 provided both care and justice perspectives on their experiences of conflict and choice.

2. Lyons' coding sheet (1983) specifies five categories that establish whether the consideration is assigned to justice or care. In the present study most of the considerations coded fit categories 2 and 3 under justice and care. When we ran our analysis using only these categories, some subjects were lost due to an insufficient number of considerations, but the direction of the findings reported in the results section remained. This is significant because categories 2 and 3 under justice and care best capture the distinction between justice and care: concern with fulfilling obligations, duty, or commitments; maintaining standards or principles of fairness (justice); concern with maintaining or restoring relationships, or with responding to the weal and woe and others (care). Lyons' categories 1, 4, and 5 under justice and care are consistent with her focus on the perspective taken toward others. In addition, they are suggestive of different stages or levels of justice and care reasoning as defined by Kohlberg (1984) and by Gilligan (1977, 1982). Yet categories 1, 4, and 5 can readily be confused with a conception of justice and care as bipolar opposites of a single dimension of moral reasoning where justice is egoistic and uncaring, and caring is altruistic and unjust. Since these categories were rarely evident in the current data, these questions, although important for other researchers to consider, are only marginally relevant to the present discussion.

3. A minimum of four considerations was required for the present analysis. When only four considerations were present, in all but one case, the four considerations were in one orientation. This provides additional support for the interpretation of justice and care as distinct orientations.

4. The statistical comparison of samples on moral orientation is not significant ($\chi2$ (4, N = 80) = 9.21, n.s.). The medical student sample does show fewer Care Focus and more Justice Focus than the other two samples. Parallel tests have been performed for each sample, and discrepancies from the overall pattern were reported and discussed.

5. The distribution was compared to theoretical distributions for N = 4 and N = 10, p = 0.5, and the difference remained highly significant.

6. Though Care Focus dilemmas are raised by women, it is important to emphasize that the focus phenomenon in two moral orientations is replicated in an all-female sample of students in a private girls' high school. The moral dilemmas of these forty-eight adolescent girls are distributed as follows: Care Focus, twenty-two; Care-Justice, seventeen; and Justice Focus, nine. This distribution differs significantly from the expected binomial distribution as well $\chi2$ (2, N = 48) = 154.4, p < 0.001.

7. The test for relationship between moral orientation and age (grouping fifteen to twenty-two-year-olds as Adolescents and twenty-three to seventy-seven-year-olds as Adults) is not significant, $\chi2$ (2, N = 78) = 1.93, n.s.

CHAPTER 42

LETTER TO READERS, 1993

CAROL GILLIGAN

I began writing *In a Different Voice* in the early 1970s, at a time of resurgence in the Women's Movement. College students now are incredulous when I say that in the spring of 1970, at the height of the demonstrations against the Vietnam war, after the shooting of students at Kent State University by members of the National Guard, final exams were canceled at Harvard and there was no graduation. For a moment, the university came to a stop and the foundations of knowledge were opened for reexamination.

In 1973, when the U.S. Supreme Court in *Roe v. Wade* made abortion legally available, the underpinnings of relationships between women and men and children were similarly exposed. When the highest court made it legal for a woman to speak for herself and awarded women the deciding voice in a complex matter of relationship which involved responsibility for life and for death, many women became aware of the strength of an internal voice which was interfering with their ability to speak. That internal or internalized voice told a woman that it would be "selfish" to bring her voice into relationships, that perhaps she did not know what she really wanted, or that her experience was not a reliable guide in thinking about what to do. Women often sensed that it was dangerous to say or even to know what they wanted or thought—upsetting to others and therefore carrying with it the threat of abandonment or retaliation. In the relational context of my research, where conversations with women were protected by confidentiality agreements, and where the usual structure of authority was reversed in that I had come to learn from them, many women in fact did know what they wanted to do and also what they thought would be the best thing to do in what often were painful and difficult situations. But many women feared that others would condemn or hurt them if they spoke, that others would not listen or understand, that speaking would only lead to further confusion, that it was better to appear "selfless," to give up their voices and keep the peace.

"If I were to speak for myself," a graduate student said one day in the middle of her oral exam—and then stopped. Hearing the sound of dissociation—the separation of herself from what she was saying, she began to question her relationship to what she was saying and what she was not saying. For whom was she speaking, and where was she in relation to herself? In the immediate aftermath of the *Roe v. Wade* decision, many women were openly questioning the morality of the Angle in the House—that nineteenth-century icon of feminine goodness immortalized by the poet Coventry Patmore: the woman who acts and speaks only for others. Discovering through experience the consequences of not speaking in relationships—the trouble that selfless behavior can cause—women were exposing the morality of the Angel as a kind of immorality: an abdication of voice, a disappearance from relationships and responsibility. The voice of the Angel was the voice of a Victorian man speaking through a woman's body. Virginia Woolf's realization that she had to strangle this Angel if she were to being writing illuminates women's need to silence false feminine voices in order to speak for themselves.

It was this choice to speak which interested me. Women's discovery of the problems that ensue from rendering oneself selfless in order to have "relationships" was momentous in releasing women's voices and making it possible to hear what women know. It was like seeing under the surface or picking up the undercurrents of the human conversation: what is known, and then not known, felt but not spoken. Women's choices not to speak or rather to dissociate themselves from what they themselves are saying can be deliberate or unwitting, consciously chosen or enacted through the body by narrowing the passages connecting the voice with breath and sound, by keeping the voice high in the head so that it does not carry the depths of human feelings or a mix of feelings and thoughts, or by changing voice, shifting to a more guarded or impersonal register or key. Choices not to speak are often well-intentioned and psychologically protective, motivated by concerns for people's feelings and by an awareness of the realities of one's own and others' lives. And yet by restricting their voices, many women are wittingly or unwittingly perpetuating a male-voiced civilization and an order of living that is founded on disconnection from women.

From Erik Erikson, I learned that you cannot take a life out of history, that life-history and history, psychology and politics, are deeply entwined. Listening to women, I heard a difference and discovered that bringing in women's lives changes both psychology and history. It literally changes the voice: how the human story is told, and also who tells it.

Now, twenty years after I began writing *In a Different Voice*, I find myself and also this book in the midst of an active and lively and often contentious discussion about women's voices, about difference, about the foundations of knowledge or what is currently called "the cannon," about relationships between women and men, and about women's and men's relationships with children. Within psychology, these questions have led to a serious reconsideration of research methods and the practices of psychological assessment and psychotherapy. Within education, these questions are radical and far-reaching. From people whose lives are very different from mine or who work in very different fields, I have learned to hear my own voice in new ways. For example, it seems obvious to me, as a

psychologist, that differences in the body, in family relationships, and in societal and cultural position would make a difference psychologically. Listening to legal scholars, in particular Martha Minnow in her book *Making All the Difference,* I have come to appreciate the legal ramifications of different ways of talking about or theorizing differences and to understand the reluctance of some people to talk about differences at all.

I find a strong resonance also in Ronald Dworkin's recent essay "Feminism and Abortion" in the *New York Review of Books* (June 10, 1993). Dworkin was led by the work of feminist legal scholars to the women whom Mary Belenky and I interviewed—the women whose voices are recorded in the third and fourth chapters of this book. Writing twenty years later, he also is struck by what at the time I found so striking: the difference between these women's voices and the terms of the public abortion debate ("the screaming rhetoric about rights and murder"). Listening closely to the voices of adolescent and adult women, he finds them deeply illuminating, so that he also reaches the conclusion which I reached at a time when it seemed a radical and difficult-to-support position: "deciding about abortion is not a unique problem, disconnected from all other decisions, but rather a dramatic and intensely lit examples of choices people must make throughout their lives."

In the years since *In a Different Voice* was published, many people have spoken to me about their lives, their marriages, their divorces, their work, their relationships, and their children. I am grateful for the many letters, books, and papers which people have sent me, often from places where I have never been, sometimes from places where I could not go. Their experiences, their examples of different voices, and their ideas expand and complicate that I have written, often in highly creative ways. During this time I have been working collaboratively with Lyn Mikel Brown, Annie Rogers, and other members of the Harvard Project on Women's Psychology and the Development of Girls. We formed this project to connect women's psychology with girls' voices and to develop a new voice for psychology—to "find new words and create new methods," as Virginia Woolf put it in the 1930s, expressing the hope that women's lives and women's education and women's entry into the professions might break the historical cycle of violence and domination. In working toward this vision, I feel a profound affinity with the work of Jean Baker Miller and draw inspiration from her radical insight that "women's situation is a crucial key to understanding the psychological order."

As I have continued to explore the connections between the political order and the psychology of women's and men's lives, I have become increasingly aware of the crucial role of women's voices in maintaining or transforming a patriarchal world. By becoming actively involved in this process of change, I have found myself and this book at the center of a psychologically and politically volatile debate in which sanity as well as power is at stake.

In listening to people's responses to *In a Different Voice*, I often hear the two-step process which I went through over and over again in the course of my writing: the process of listening to women and hearing something new, a different way of speaking, and then hearing how quickly this difference gets assimilated into old categories of thinking so that it loses its novelty and its message: is it nature or nurture? are women better than men, or worse? When I hear my work being cast in terms of whether women and men are really (essentially) different or who is better than whom, I know that I have lost my voice, because these are not my questions. Instead, my questions are about our perceptions of reality and truth: how we know, how we hear, how we see, how we speak. My questions are about voice and relationship. And, my questions are about psychological processes and theory, particularly theories in which men's experience stands for all of human experience—theories which eclipse the lives of women and shut out women's voices. I saw that by maintaining these ways of seeing and speaking about human lives, men were leaving out women, but women were leaving out themselves. In terms of psychological processes, what for men was a process of separation, for women was a process of dissociation that required the creation of an inner division of psychic split.

These are not simply abstract speculations on my part. My work is grounded in listening. I was picking up the sounds of disconnection and dissociation in men's and women's voices. I began to wonder: How is it that men in speaking of themselves and their lives, or speaking more generally about human nature, often speak as if they were not living in connection with women, as if women were not in some sense

part of themselves? I also asked: How do women come to speak of themselves as though they were selfless, as if they did not have a voice or did not experience desire? Women's discovery that to be selfless means not to be in relationship is revolutionary because it challenges the disconnection from women and the dissociation within women that maintain and are maintained by patriarchy or civilization. The justification of these psychological processes in the name of love or relationships is equivalent to the justifications of violence and violation in the name of morality.

The different voice in resisting such justifications is a relational voice: a voice that insists on staying in connection and most centrally staying in connection with women, so that psychological separations which have long been justified in the name of autonomy, selfhood, and freedom no longer appear as the *sine qua non* of human development but as a human problem.

If it is good to be responsive to people, to act in connection with others and to be careful rather than careless about people's feelings and thoughts, empathic and attentive to their lives, then why is it "selfish" to respond to yourself, I would ask women, counterposing the logic of my question against the force of their self-condemnation, the readiness of their self-abnegation and self-betrayal. "Good question," many women replied. When I was working with Erik Erikson and Lawrence Kohlberg at Harvard, teaching psychology in the traditions of Freud and Piaget, I remember moments in classes when a women would ask a question that illuminated with sudden brilliance the foundations of the subject we were discussing. And now, remembering those moments, I also can hear the sounds of my own inner division: my saying to the woman, "That's a good question," and then saying, "but that's not what we are talking about here."

In asking about my own and other women's relationship to the "we" that was for so long unselfconscious, I asked about men's relationship to this "we" as well. Were the *Odyssey* and the *Iliad* or other versions of the hero legend—stories about radical separation and violence—exemplary stories for men to tell themselves? The most basic questions about human living—how to live and what to do—are fundamentally questions about human relations, because people's lives are deeply connected, psychologically, economically, and politically. Reframing these questions to make these relational realities explicit—how to live in relationship with others, what to do in the face of conflict—I found that I heard women's and men's voices differently. Women's voices suddenly made new sense and women's approaches to conflict were often deeply instructive because of the constant eye to maintaining relational order and connection. It was concern about relationship that made women's voices sound "different" within a world that was preoccupied with separation and obsessed with creating and maintaining boundaries between people—like the New Englanders in Robert Frost's poem who say that "good fences make good neighbors." When I began writing, however, concerns about relationships were seen for the most part as "women's problems."

Within the context of U.S. society, the values of separation, independence, and autonomy are so historically grounded, so reinforced by waves of immigration, and so deeply rooted in the natural rights tradition that they are often taken as facts: that people are by nature separate, independent from one another, and self-governing. To call these "facts" into question is seemingly to question the value of freedom. And yet this is not at all the case. The questioning of separation has nothing to do with questioning freedom but rather with seeing and speaking about relationships. To take a current example, whatever one thinks about Columbus—however one judges the man and his mission—the fact is that he did not discover America: people were already there. In a very different vein, however one hears Anita Hill's testimony about her relationship with Clarence Thomas, the fact is that many women felt that they knew exactly what she was talking about because they had experienced similar incidents in their own lives. As with the revised story about Columbus, an illusion of autonomy was dispelled by a radical shift in voice or point of view: America Indians were Native Americans; sexual talk in the workplace was harassment. At the core of my work was the realization that within psychology and the larger society, values were being taken as facts.

Of the many questions people have asked me in the years since *In a Different Voice* was published, three kinds come up frequently and go to the heart of my writing: questions about voice, questions about difference, and questions about

women's and men's development. In thinking about these questions and learning from the work of other people, I have come to understand voice, difference, and development in ways that go beyond what I knew at the time when I wrote this book. I have also come to see more clearly the book's two-part structure: the relationship between psychological theory and women's psychological development, including the ways in which psychological theory becomes prescriptive. I introduce a relational voice and develop its counterpoint with traditional ways of speaking about self, relationship, and morality, as well as the potentials for misunderstanding, conflict, and growth. I reframe women's psychological development as centering on a struggle for connection rather than speaking about women in the way that psychologists have spoken about women—as having a problem in achieving separation.

I will begin with voice. The work of Kristin Linklater, one of theater's leading teachers of voice, has led me to a new understanding of voice and also to a far deeper understanding of my own work. Her analysis of the human voice has given me a physics for my psychology—a way of understanding how the voice works in the body, in language, and also psychologically, and therefore a way of explaining some of the psychological processes I have described. I have learned about resonance and come to a new way of understanding how the voice speaks in relationship—how it is expanded or constricted by relational ties—from Normi Noel, an actor, director, and voice teacher who builds on Linklater's work and that of Tina Packer. These women, all of whom work in the theater, have an understanding of voice which is physiological and cultural as well as deeply psychological. Linklater speaks of "freeing the natural voice," the title of her first book, and what she means is that you can hear the difference between a voice that is an open channel—connected physically with breath and sound, psychologically with feelings and thoughts, and culturally with a rich resource of language—and a voice that is impeded or blocked. Having worked with Linklater, I have heard and experienced the differences she describes. I also have learned from working with Noel to pick up relational resonances and follow the changes in people's voices that occur when they speak in places where their voices are resonant with or resounded by others, and when their voices fall into a space where there is no resonance, or where the reverberations are frightening, where they begin to sound dead or flat.

With this dramatic expansion of the empirical base of my work, I find it easier to respond when people ask me what I mean by "voice." By voice I mean voice. Listen, I will say, thinking that in one sense the answer is simple. And then I will remember how it felt to speak when there was no resonance, how it was when I began writing, how it still is for many people, how it still is for me sometimes. To have a voice is to be human. To have something to say is to be a person. But speaking depends on listening and being heard; it is an intensely relational act.

When people ask me what I mean by voice and I think of the question more reflectively, I say that by voice I mean something like what people mean when they speak of the core of the self. Voice is natural and also cultural. It is composed of breath and sound, words, rhythm, and language. And voice is a powerful psychological instrument and channel, connecting inner and outer worlds. Speaking and listening are a form of psychic breathing. This ongoing relational exchange among people is mediated through language and culture, diversity and plurality. For these reasons, voice is a new key for understanding the psychological, social, and cultural order—a litmus test of relationships and a measure of psychological health.

In an introduction to *Love's Labour's Lost* in the Riverside edition of Shakespeare's plays, Anne Barton makes an observation about language which rings true in the current discussion of culture and voice: "Language cannot exist in a vacuum. Even on what may seem to be its most trivial and humorous levels, it is an instrument of communication between people which demands that the speaker should consider the nature and feelings of the hearer. In love above all, this is true—but it is also true in more ordinary relationships." In this play about love and language, heterosexual love requires a change in language, following the demonstration that the men do not know the women whom they say they love: "Gently, but firmly, the men are sent away to learn something that the women have known all along: how to accommodate speech to facts and to emotional realities, as opposed to using it as a means of evasion, idle amusement, or unthinking cruelty."

Elizabeth Harvey, in *Ventriloquized Voices*, explores the question of why and when men, in the English Renaissance and also at present, have chosen to create feminine voices or to speak through female bodies, to ventriloquize their voices in this way. I find her analysis extremely helpful because she is so clear about the difference between the epistemological question of whether a man can know what it is to be a woman and therefore can speak on women's behalf and the ethical and political questions: what are the ethics and politics of men speaking for women or creating a feminine voice? When I have spoken with women about experiences of conflict, many women have a hard time distinguishing the created or socially constructed feminine voice from a voice which they hear as their own. And yet women *can* hear the difference. To give up their voice is to give up on relationship and also to give up all that goes with making a choice. It was partly because of the link between voice and choice that the *Roe v. Wade* decision initiated or legitimized a process of psychological and political growth for many women and men.

Which brings me to the question of difference. In the early 1970s, when I was working with Lawrence Kohlberg as a research assistant, I found his argument very powerful: in the aftermath of the Holocaust and the Middle Passage, it is not tenable for psychologists or social scientists to adopt a position of ethical neutrality or cultural relativism—to say that one cannot say anything about values or that all values are culturally relative. Such a hands-off stance in the face of atrocity amounts to a kind of complicity. But the so-called objective position which Kohlberg and others espoused within the canon of traditional social sciences research was blind to the particularities of voice and the inevitable constructions that constitute point of view. However well-intentioned and provisionally useful it may have been, it was based on an inerrant neutrality which concealed power and falsified knowledge.

I have attempted to move the discussion of differences away from relativism to relationship, to see difference as a marker of the human condition rather than as a problem to be solved. Robert Alter, in *The Art of Biblical Narrative*, has observed that the ancient Hebrew writers developed a narrative art because only through narrative could they convey a view of human life as lived reflectively, "in the changing medium of time, inexorably and perplexingly in relationship with others." At present, I find that women writers, and especially African-American poets and novelists who draw on an oral/aural tradition and also on searing and complex experiences of difference, are taking the lead in voicing an art that responds to the question which now preoccupies many people: how to give voice to difference in a way that recasts our discussion of relationship and the telling of truth.

One problem in talking about difference and the consequent theorizing of "difference" lies in the readiness with which difference becomes deviance and deviance becomes sin in a society preoccupied with normality, in the thrall of statistics, and historically puritanical. Toni Morrison, in *The Bluest Eye*, shows how the choice of a Platonic standard of beauty, or an ideal type of "the mother" or "the father" or "the family," affects children whose bodies do not conform to the standard and whose parents or families do not fit the ideal. In this early novel, Morrison gives voice to a father who rapes his daughter, drawing the psychological line that makes it possible to understand and speak about how such a violation could happen not only from the point of view of the daughter but from the father's point of view as well. In *Beloved*, Morrison gives voice to a mother who has killed her daughter rather than see her be taken back into slavery, and in this way explores a psychological and ethical question that has eluded the literature on psychological and moral development: what does care mean, or what could it potentially mean or entail, for a woman who loves her children and is living in a racist and violent society—a society damaging to both women and men?

When I find myself troubled by the current arguments about difference is where I find them unvoiced and hauntingly familiar—where it is not clear who is speaking, where those spoken about have no voice, where the conversation heads toward the endless circle of objectivism and relativism, veering off into the oldest philosophical or ontological question as to whether there is or is not an Archimedean position, whether or not there is a God. A friend, quoting Stendhal, remarked that "God's only excuse is that he doesn't exist," and even this conversation in contemporary circles leads back to gender and difference, dominance and power. I find

the question of whether gender differences are biologically determined or socially constructed to be deeply disturbing. This way of posing the question implies that people, women and men alike, are either genetically determined or a product of socialization—that there is no voice—and without voice, there is no possibility for resistance, for creativity, or for a change whose wellsprings are psychological. At its most troubling, the present reduction of psychology either to sociology or biology or some combination of the two prepares the way for the kind of control that alarmed Hannah Arendt and George Orwell—the hand over the mouth and at the throat, the suffocation of voice and the deadening of language which ripen the conditions for fascism and totalitarian rule, the psychic numbing which is associated with that now curiously unspoken word "propaganda."

Moral problems are problems of human relations, and in tracing the development of an ethic of care, I explore the psychological grounds for nonviolent human relations. This relational ethic transcends the age-old opposition between selfishness and selflessness, which have been the staples of moral discourse. The search on the part of many people for a voice which transcends these false dichotomies represents an attempt to turn the tide of moral discussion from questions of how to achieve objectivity and detachment to how to engage responsively and with care. Albert Hirschman, the political economist and author of *Exit, Voice, and Loyalty*, contrasts the neatness of exit with the messiness and heartbreak of voice. It is easier to step out than to step in. Relationship then requires a kind of courage and emotional stamina which has long been a strength of women, insufficiently noted and valued.

Relationship requires connection. It depends not only on the capacity for empathy or the ability to listen to others and learn their language or take their point of view, but also on having a voice and having a language. The differences between women and men which I describe center on a tendency for women and men to make different relational errors—for men to think that if they know themselves, following Socrates' dictum, they will also know women, and for women to think that if only they know others, they will come to know themselves. Thus men and women tacitly collude in not voicing women's experiences and build relationships around a silence that is maintained by men's not knowing their disconnection from women and women's not knowing their dissociation from themselves. Much talk about relationship and about love carefully conceals these truths.

Current research on women's psychological development speaks directly to this problem. The Harvard Project on Women's Psychology and the Development of Girls, in its investigation of women's lives, moves backward through developmental time, from adulthood to adolescence, and from adolescence to childhood. Taking the voices of adult women as its starting point, including the women who speak in this book, we have now listened in depth to the voices of adolescent girls in girls' schools and to girls and boys in coeducational school and after-school clubs. Once we found ourselves at home in the halls of adolescence, we moved with some measure of confidence and with new questions into the world of younger girls, initiating a five-year study of girls ages seven to eighteen and a three-year exploratory prevention project involving girls and women.

In the course of this research, Lyn Mikel Brown, Annie Rogers, and I came to a place where we heard a distinct shift in girls' voices and observed that this change in voice coincided with changes in girls' relationships and their sense of themselves. For example, we began to hear girls at the edge of adolescence describe impossible situations—psychological dilemmas in which they felt that if they said what they were feeling and thinking no one would want to be with them, and if they didn't say what they were thinking and feeling they would be all alone, no one would know what was happening to them. As one girl put it, "no one would want to be with me, my voice would be too loud." Hearing what she was saying, she compounded her conundrum by explaining, "But you have to have relationships."

Listening to these girls in relational impasse, we found ourselves rethinking psychological theory and listening anew to ourselves and other women. We were struck by the frankness and fearlessness of these young girls, their determination to speak truthfully, and their keen desire to remain in relationship. At the same time, we began to witness girls edging toward relinquishing what they know and what they have held fast to, as they come face to face with a social construction of reality that is at odds with

their experience, so that some kind of dissociation becomes inevitable. Girls' initiation or passage into adulthood in a world psychologically rooted and historically anchored in the experiences of powerful men marks the beginning of self-doubt and the dawning of the realization, no matter how fleeting, that womanhood will require a dissociative split between experience and what is generally taken to be reality.

While our research provided evidence of girls' resistance to dissociation, it also documented the initiation of girls into the psychological divisions that are familiar to many women: the coming not to know what one knows, the difficulty in hearing or listening to one's voice, the disconnection between mind and body, thoughts and feelings, and the use of one's voice to cover rather than to convey one's inner world, so that relationships no longer provide channels for exploring the connections between one's inner life and the world of others.

Suddenly it became clear why Amy's voice in this book was so striking to so many women and also why it left some women with a profound sense of unease. Amy's phrase "it depends" has been repeated by many women who also resist formulaic solutions to complex human problems. But her very insistence on the limitations of such formulas for resolving human conflicts led some women to hear her voice as it was heard by conventional psychologists: as wishy-washy, as indecisive, as evasive, and naive. The psychologist who interviewed Amy knew that her responses to the questions she was asked would result in her being assessed as not very "developed"—as not having a clear sense of self, as not being very advanced in her capacity for abstract thinking or moral judgment—which is why she kept repeating the questions to Amy, to give her another chance.

At fifteen, Amy carried that doubtful voice within herself and consequently struggled between two voices which kept running in and out of one another. The interview at fifteen caught her in the midst of an active process of dissociation, of knowing and then not knowing what she knew. For example, she saw that there was something deeply troubling about saying that a person should steal medicine to save the life of someone who is poor and dying, when she knew that in the city where she lived, poor people were dying every day for lack of medicine and she had no intention of stealing medicine to save them. At eleven, she said simply that stealing was not a good solution to this problem, that in fact it was likely to compound the problem by leaving the sick person not only without medicine and dying but also potentially all alone, without relationship and possibly with diminished economic resources as well. At fifteen, however, she could see the logic in a way of speaking about moral conflicts that she also saw as threatening to relationships and out of touch with reality, a way of reasoning that required making a series of separations, that began to alter her relationship with herself and to cloud her sense of reality. Misremembering what she had said at eleven, swaying back and forth between one way of approaching the problem and another, Amy at fifteen was in the process of changing her mind.

This change of mind and also of heart, which we observed repeatedly among girls in adolescence, led my colleague Annie Rogers to speak of girls' losing their "ordinary courage," or finding that what had seemed ordinary—having a voice and being in relationship—had now become extraordinary, something to be experienced only in the safest and most private of relationships. This psychological seclusion of girls from the public world at the time of adolescence sets the stage for a kind of privatization of women's experience and impedes the development of women's political voice and presence in the public world. The dissociation of girls' voices from girls' experiences in adolescence, so that girls are not saying what they know and eventually not knowing it as well, is a prefiguring of many women's sense of having the rug of experience pulled out from under them, or of coming to experience their feelings and thoughts not as real but as a fabrication.

At the same time, by recording girls' strong and courageous voices and by documenting girls' search for good ways of maintaining their voices and their relationships, the research of the Harvard Project provides evidence that grounds the questions raised in this book in a new way. The ongoing human conversation about separation and connection, justice and care, rights and responsibilities, power and love, takes a new turn when it is joined to evidence of girls' resistance to entering the conversation in terms of these dichotomies at just the time when they are reaching maturity and in many societies also gaining

a public voice or vote. Separations and detachments, which previously have been taken as the marks of development in adolescence and presented as psychological facts, no longer seem necessary or inevitable, natural or good. The road back from "selflessness" which many of the women in this book travel, often at great cost to themselves and to others, is no longer an inevitable journey. The disconnection in this book between the resistance and courage of eleven-year-old Amy and the more desultory voices of some of the teenagers in the abortion-decision study may well reflect a loss of relationship rather than a failure to develop relationships—the loss of relationship that becomes audible when women construct moral conflicts as choices between selfish and selfless behavior.

Joining this understanding of women's psychological development with theories of human development which turn out to be theories about men, I have arrived at the following working theory: that the relational crisis which men typically experience in early childhood occurs for women in adolescence, that this relational crisis in boys and girls involves a disconnection from women which is essential to the perpetuation of patriarchal societies, and that women's psychological development is potentially revolutionary not only because of women's situation but also because of girls' resistance. Girls struggle against losing voice and against creating an inner division or spit, so that large parts of themselves are kept out of relationship. Because girls' resistance to culturally mandated separations occurs at a later time in their psychological development than that of boys, girls' resistance is more articulate and robust, more deeply voiced and therefore more resonant; it resonates with women's and men's desires for relationships, reopening old psychological wounds, raising new questions, new possibilities for relationship, new ways of living. As girls become the carriers of unvoiced desires and unrealized possibilities, they are inevitably placed at considerably risk and even in danger.

Coming to the study of women's psychological development from her vantage point as a psychiatrist and psychoanalyst working with women in therapy, Jean Baker Miller observes that girls and women in the course of their development, in their attempt to make and maintain relationships, paradoxically keep large parts of themselves out of relationship. Miller's formulation of this paradox is central to a new understanding of the psychology of women and leads to a powerful rethinking of psychological suffering and trouble.

Miller and I have been struck by the fact that although we have approached the study of women and girls from different directions and worked in different ways, we have arrived at much the same insight into the relationship between women's psychology and the prevailing social order. A new psychological theory in which girls and women are seen and heard is an inevitable challenge to a patriarchal order that can remain in place only through the continuing eclipse of women's experience. Bringing the experiences of women and girls to full light, although in one sense perfectly straightforward, becomes a radical endeavor. Staying in connection, then, with women and girls—in teaching, in research, in therapy, in friendship, in motherhood, in the course of daily living—is potentially revolutionary.

In the course of teaching psychology, I often read Freud's essay "Civilization and Its Discontents," the essay in which he asks the question, why have men created a culture in which they live with such discomfort? And I talk with students about the liar paradox—"Romans always lie, said the Roman" —which becomes fascinating to many people at adolescence, the time when Freud sees detachment from childhood relationships and opposition to the previous generation as necessary for the progress of civilization and when Piaget says that the hypothetical takes precedence over the real. It is only recently that I have come to hear this paradox differently. "Romans always lie, said the Roman," contains a factual truth about imperialism: that there is a lie at the center of any imperial order.

This is the point of Joseph Conrad's prophetic and controversial novel *Heart of Darkness*. As Marlow travels into the heart of what was then the Belgian Congo, he begins to search for Mr. Kurtz, who was sent by "the gang of virtue," the Europeans who saw themselves as bringing enlightenment and progress or civilization to the Africans. Marlow believes that Kurtz will restore his faith in the vision of enlightened imperialism that is at odds with the pervasive evidence of corruption, lethargy, violence, and disease. As he reaches the interior, Marlow learns that Kurtz is dying. And meeting the dying Mr. Kurtz, he discovers the ultimate corruption. At the bottom of the report which Kurtz has prepared to send back to the Company in Belgium along with his shipment of ivory, he has scrawled the words which were to be enacted repeatedly in the twentieth century: the final solution to the problem of difference— "Exterminate all the brutes." The dying Mr. Kurtz himself offers the commentary: his last words are, "The horror! The horror!"

Marlow says that he cannot bear a lie, that lies deaden the world, "like biting into something rotten." And yet at the end of the book he lies to the woman who was Mr. Kurtz's Intended, the nameless European woman who waits for Kurtz and keeps alive his image. When Marlow visits her in Belgium, to return her portrait which was among Kurtz's possessions, she asks about Kurtz's last words, and Marlow lies to her: "The last word he pronounced was—your name."

This white lie is literally a white lie, because it covers the presence of the black woman with whom Mr. Kurtz was living—the woman who was actually with him. This issue of racial difference in the body of a woman goes to the heart of what is currently one of the most painful and difficult differences between women: war crimes in which white women have been directly involved.

Over the past two years, I have been a member of a group composed of eleven women—five black, five white, and one Hispanic—to ask about our relationship to the future by asking about our relationships with girls. Where are we as black, white, and Hispanic women in relation to black, white, and Hispanic girls? How can we create and maintain connections that cross the lines of racial division and in this way move toward breaking rather than perpetuating the cycle of racial domination and violence?

In an extraordinary passage in Conrad's novel, Marlow justifies his lie to Kurtz's Intended—as much of himself as to the men on shipboard who are listening to his story while waiting for the tide to turn:

> I heard a light sigh and then my heart stood still, stopped dead short by an exulting and terrible cry, by the cry of inconceivable triumph and of unspeakable pain. "I knew it— I was sure!". . . She knew. She was sure. I heard her weeping; she had hidden her face in her hands. It seemed to me that the house would collapse before I could escape, that the heavens would fall upon my head. But nothing happened. The heavens do not fall for

such a trifle. Would they have fallen, I wonder, if I had rendered Kurtz that justice which was his due? Hadn't he said he wanted only justice? But I couldn't. I could not tell her. It would have been too dark—too dark altogether.

This intersection between race and gender, colonialism and masculine narrative, also marks the convergence between the liar paradox and the relationship paradox: the place where women's and men's lives join and "civilization" makes its iron grip felt. A lie about progress joins with a lie about relationship, trapping both women and men and obliterating relationships among women. It is this intersection which joins the two parts of this book—the lie in psychological theories which have taken men as representing all humans, and the lie in women's psychological development in which girls and women alter their voices to fit themselves into images of relationship and goodness carried by false feminine voices.

Lies make you sick: an insight common to feminism and psychoanalysis. I wrote *In a Different Voice* to bring women's voices into psychological theory and to reframe the conversation between women and men. It has been astonishing for me to discover, in the time since this book was published, how my experiences resonate with the experiences of other women and also in different ways with the experiences of men. So that now the themes of voice and relationship, and the concerns about connection and the costs of detachment, which seemed so new in the 1970s, have become part of a growing conversation.

"You feel the need for giants," Madame Ranevskaya says to Lopahin in the scene from *The Cherry Orchard* which opens this book. Chekhov hears this observation about the hero legend and its story about development as a woman's commentary, or casts it in a female voice. These alternative formulations reveal a tension which remains unresolved in this book: whether there is an endless counterpoint between two ways of speaking about human life and relationships, one grounded in connection and one in separation or whether one framework for thinking about human life and relationships

which has long been associated with development and with progress can give way to a new way of thinking that begins with the premise that we live not in separation but in relationship.

Theories of psychological development and conceptions of self and morality that have linked progress or goodness with disconnection or detachment and advocated separation from women in the name of psychological growth or health are dangerous because they cloak an illusion in the trappings of science: the illusion that disconnection or dissociation from women is good. Women's voices constantly bring to the surface of the human conversation this underlying problem of failed relationship which is a seedbed for lies. The rash of questions about relationship and difference which become inescapable once women enter the conversation are now the most urgently pressing questions on the local, national, and international scene. The political has become psychological in the sense that men's disconnection and women's dissociation perpetuate the prevailing social order. Psychological processes and also the capacity to resist these separations and dissociations become political acts.

I have not revised *In a Different Voice* because it has become part of the process that it describes—the ongoing historical process of changing the voice of the world by bringing women's voices into the open, thus starting a new conversation.

Cambridge, England
June 1993

Note

I am grateful to Mary Hamer, Mary Jacobus, Teresa Brennan, and Onora O'Neill for generous and perceptive responses to earlier drafts of this preface. To Dorothy Austin and Annie Rogers I owe a debt of immense gratitude. I also want to thank the people who attended the Cambridge Women's Studies Forum at King's College, the Women's Speaker Series at Newnham College, and the lecture organized by Sandera Krol and Selma Sevenhuijsen at the University of Utrecht, where I read earlier versions of this work and benefited from the discussion.

CHAPTER 43

MORAL JUDGEMENT DEVELOPMENT IN HIGHER EDUCATION: INSIGHTS FROM THE DEFINING ISSUES TEST

PATRICIA M. KING AND MATTHEW J. MAYHEW

This article reviews 172 studies that used the Defining Issues Test to investigate the moral development of undergraduate college students and provides an organisational framework for analysing educational contexts in higher education. These studies addressed collegiate outcomes related to character or civic outcomes, selected aspects of students' collegiate experiences related to moral judgement development and changes in moral reasoning during the college years as they related to changes in other domains of development. Findings suggest that dramatic gains in moral judgement are associated with collegiate participation, even after controlling for age and entering level of moral judgement. Although many studies used gross indicators of collegiate context (e.g. institutional type or academic discipline), studies that examine specific collegiate characteristics and educational experiences are better suited to identifying factors that contribute directly or indirectly to changes in moral judgement during the college years. Implications for student development practice and future research are discussed.

The Defining Issues Test (DIT) has been widely used with samples of undergraduate college students to investigate a broad range of moral issues. Consequently, this instrument has played a major role in shaping our understanding of the development of moral judgement among college students. In their major review (over 2600 studies) of the effects of college on students, Pascarella and Terenzini (1991) devoted a whole chapter to moral development, and noted that there exists impressive evidence of moral development in the college years, both in terms of the sheer number of studies conducted and in the diversity of samples tested. As they are currently updating this book (Pascarella & Terenzini, in preparation) we wished to complement rather than replicate their efforts, so our guiding question for this essay was, "How has the DIT been used in higher education?" Starting here allows for a broader vantage-point from which to examine how the DIT has informed our understanding of moral development among college students. As Rest (1984) and others in this *JME* Special Issue point out, (Bebeau, 2002; Rogers, 2002; Thoma, 2002 issue), the domain of morality is much broader than the moral judgement component that the DIT is designed to measure; this review is limited to one aspect of moral development, moral judgement.

This student population is important for several reasons. First, it is common for both traditional- and non-traditional-age students to enroll in college at times in their lives when they are making important life transitions, many of which have moral implications. This is often accompanied by a new readiness to examine the moral dimension of their lives in preparation for their new life roles. Secondly, most American colleges and universities embrace a mission that arguably includes moral development (such as preparation for citizenship, character development, moral leadership, service to society). Most colleges offer courses in religion, ethics, or what Gaurasci (2001) calls "the democratic arts", and most offer opportunities for students to participate in community service and service learning projects, all of which have a moral dimension. Thirdly, college graduates often take leadership positions in both their employment settings and in their communities, positions in which they make decisions affecting the lives of others. Thus, there are many reasons to examine moral development in the college years, whether from an individual perspective (e.g. documenting the evolution of moral development among adults attending college), from a college cultural perspective (e.g. examining moral experiences across different institutional subcultures) or from a societal perspective (e.g. assessing the effectiveness of colleges in preparing citizens and workers for their societal roles). Clearly, it is important and valuable to understand how a major assessment tool has influenced our understanding of these important questions.

The impact of the DIT is reflected in the sheer number of studies in which it has been used with college samples. In preparation for writing this essay, we reviewed over 500 published articles, conference presentations and dissertations in which the DIT was used with college students. From this search, we discovered that many of the articles that used both the DIT and a college student sample were not designed intentionally to investigate the moral judgement of college students. Instead, many studies appeared to use college students as convenience samples or as proxies for reasonably bright young adults, but with no particular emphasis on college as an educational context nor on college students as a purposeful sample. As a result, we chose to include in this review only those studies that were intentionally designed to investigate the moral development of undergraduate college students. We also chose to delimit our review to US college samples because a discussion of international students and contexts was beyond the scope of this article. In addition, we omitted samples of college students that were used only to contrast college students with professional samples, as the use of the DIT in the professions is discussed by Bebeau (2002) in this issue. Last, with the exception of original pieces written by James Rest (Rest *et al.*, 1974; Rest, 1979a, 1979b), we chose to limit our review to articles published

since 1980, as many of the findings from Rest's early articles (1974–1979) are subsumed and/or replicated by more recent studies. Accordingly, the 172 studies reviewed here used the DIT to measure the degree to which students achieved intended collegiate outcomes related to character or civic outcomes, studies that focused on selected aspects of students' collegiate experiences related to moral judgement development (i.e. curricular and co-curricular activities), and studies that documented changes in moral reasoning during the college years as they related to changes in other domains of development.

We began our investigation of how the DIT had been used in collegiate studies of moral development by identifying the types of topics that have been addressed using the DIT and the kinds of variables that have been addressed in these studies. For example, differences in DIT scores by year in college, academic discipline and institutional type have been frequently researched. For each major topic included here, we ask, "What general conclusions can we draw from this body of research?" It is beyond the scope of this paper to provide a detailed review of the findings for each study and each major variable; instead, we offer a general review, and focus on those variables that are distinctive to higher education, or that are of particular interest to educators who work with college students or researchers investigating moral issues.

Moral Judgement Development in Higher Education

The purpose of this section is to examine how the DIT has been used to establish the relationship between the development of moral reasoning and participation in higher education. Intentionally or unintentionally, moral development is an outcome of higher education, at least as measured by the DIT (Rest *et al.*, 1974; Rest, 1979a,b, 1987, 1988; Gongre, 1981; Whiteley, 1982; Mentkowski & Strait, 1983; Hood, 1984; Kitchener *et al.*, 1984; King *et al.*, 1985; Rest & Thoma, 1985; Shaver, 1985; Gfellner, 1986; Shaver, 1987; Bouhmama, 1988; Buier *et al.*, 1989; Icerman *et al.*, 1991; Paradice & Dejoie, 1991; Burwell *et al.*, 1992; Jeffrey, 1993; Thoma & Ladewig, 1993; King & Kitchener, 1994; Quarry, 1997; Foster & LaForce, 1999; Loviscky, 2000; Mentkowski *et al.*, 2000; Stroud, 2000; Cummings *et al.*, 2001). With that said, there are only two studies included in this review that either found no relationship between formal education and moral reasoning development (Galotti, 1988) or failed to report differences in moral reasoning by formal education level (Mustapha & Seybert, 1989).

Longitudinal Studies

A series of longitudinal studies have been used to investigate the relationship between moral development and formal education by examining the effects of age and education on the development of moral reasoning. These studies suggest that collegiate experiences do promote moral development; more specifically, during college students tend to decrease their preference for conventional level reasoning and increase their preference for post-conventional moral reasoning (Rest, 1979b; Whiteley, 1982; Mentkowski & Strait, 1983; King et al., 1985; Shaver, 1985; Shaver, 1987; Burwell et al., 1992; King & Kitchener, 1994). Rest et al. (1999) argued for the use of the label "post-conventional" to replace "principled" moral reasoning; we have done so here as well.)

Several longitudinal studies have attempted to track the development of moral reasoning by testing students at two times during their collegiate experience, at the beginning of the freshman year and at the end of their senior year (Shaver, 1985, 1987; Burwell et al., 1992; Foster & LaForce, 1999). Other longitudinal studies have charted this development by testing students at multiple times during their college years (Rest, 1979b; Whiteley, 1982; Mentkowski & Strait, 1983; King & Kitchener, 1994). Rest (1979b) and Rest and Thoma (1985) also used longitudinal data to examine the relationship of moral judgement development to formal education. They tracked the course of moral judgement development of participants from the end of high school to 6 years beyond high school; some attended college and others did not. At the third time of testing, Rest (1979a) found that the course of development for the 38 college students was different from the 18 participants not in college: for those attending college, DIT scores continued to increase; for those not in college, scores were stable. At the fourth time of testing, Rest and Thoma (1985) regrouped the population into low education (less than two years of college) and high-education (more than two years of college) categories. While both groups showed increases in P scores 2 years after leaving high school, four years later the 23 students with two or more years in college were still showing gains while

the 13 less-educated subjects were not (Rest & Thoma, 1985). Because age and education are often confounded in student populations, especially among traditional age college students, it is important to control for age to test for the impact of college. The design of this study (use of a same-age non-college comparison group and a longitudinal design) provides a model research design for researchers interested in untangling the influence of education from that of maturation on moral development. From this study we can conclude that participation in higher education makes a substantial contribution to development in moral judgement beyond that attributable to age alone.

Other studies have also documented the effect on moral judgement of participation in higher education after controlling for age (Rest, 1979a, 1987, 1988; Kitchener et al., 1984; King et al., 1985; Rest & Thoma, 1985; Gfellner, 1986; Paradice & Dejoie, 1991; Cummings et al., 2001). From these studies, we can conclude that formal education makes a unique contribution to moral reasoning in that during college, students are more likely than nonstudents to use post-conventional moral reasoning.

Pascarella and Terenzini (in preparation) came to a similar conclusion, that the observed increase in post-conventional moral reasoning in college "appears to be substantially greater in magnitude than that due merely to maturation and cannot be attributed solely to initial differences in moral reasoning, intelligence, or social status between those who attend and those who do not attend college" (p. 5). This collection of studies provides strong evidence that student participation in higher education is associated with gains in moral development during the college years.

Moral Judgement Development by Ethnicity

There has been considerable interest among scholars and educators about the applicability of theories of college student development that were normed on white samples to students of other racial/ethnic backgrounds (e.g. McEwen et al., 1990; Evans et al., 1998), yet few studies have used the DIT to explore whether moral judgement differs by race or ethnicity among US college students (Gongre, 1981; Locke & Tucker, 1988; Murk & Addleman, 1992; Johnson et al., 1993; Loviscky, 2000).

We identified only two studies for which the primary purpose was to investigate differences in moral judgement by race or ethnicity (Gongre, 1981; Locke & Tucker, 1988). The others reported differences in moral judgement by race or ethnicity as they related to other research questions. Gongre (1981) examined the differences between moral judgement of 15 black American, 46 Native American and 53 white students at Bacone College, and found no differences between the three groups on the DIT. This study may be unique in the composition of its sample, as it is the only one in this review that explicitly sampled Native Americans. Although differences were reported among the tribes sampled, information is not provided regarding the sample sizes for the tribes, subgroup means, nor the direction of the difference.

Locke and Tucker (1988) tested black and white students to determine their reactions to moral dilemmas when the race of the central character in the dilemma was changed. They assigned 232 graduate and undergraduate students to one of two groups: the first group received the standard form of the DIT and the second group received a "revised DIT" in which the protagonists in the stories were identified as black. The post-conventional moral reasoning scores between the 109 white students taking the standard version of the DIT and those of the 103 white students taking the revised version were not significantly different. However, the 12 black students taking the revised version of the DIT scored significantly lower than the eight black students taking the standard version. This finding is provocative, and merits further exploration. Unfortunately, the small size of the black sample precludes making a strong conclusion about the research question asked, or whether, as the authors suggested, the racial manipulation triggered an emotional reaction among the black students that affected their DIT scores.

The remaining studies that address differences in moral judgement by race or ethnicity do so as supplementary rather than primary questions under investigation (Murk & Addleman, 1992; Johnson *et al.*, 1993; Loviscky, 2000). For example, in his examination of the construct validity of moral judgement as an alternative predictor of job performance, Loviscky (2000) tested 238 undergraduate and graduate students. In a *post hoc* analysis of DIT scores by ethnicity, he found that students who indicated their eth-

nicity was other or white had significantly higher DIT scores than black, Hispanic or Asian students, and that the P-scores for Black students were significantly higher than those for Hispanic or Asian students. Unfortunately, sample sizes were not reported by subgroup for this study; however, based on sample percentages reported, we calculated his sample sizes as follows: white ($n = 192$); Asian ($n = 22$); black ($n = 11$); Hispanic ($n = 7$); other ($n = 6$).

Research investigating the relationship between race and ethnicity and moral judgement development measured by the DIT is underdeveloped, and no clear pattern of results is yet available. That few studies have examined the relationship between race and ethnicity and the development of moral judgement is surprising given the racial and ethnic composition of US colleges and universities and the strong interest in diversity-related issues in higher education. Perhaps researchers and educators have a priori knowledge that the DIT was normed using white samples as norms, and for this reason have avoided its use as a metric of differentiation between ethnic groups when investigating moral judgement development. Or perhaps educators fear that the potential for misusing the DIT could lead to results that may further marginalise under-represented ethnic groups within higher education. Whatever the reason, the dearth of studies makes it impossible to determine whether there are differences by ethnicity on the DIT.

Collegiate Contexts that are Conducive to Moral Development

What types of educational experiences stimulate moral development among college students? What are the characteristics of collegiate learning environments that promote development in moral judgement? We turn next to these questions.

As shown above, significant growth in the use of post-conventional moral reasoning does occur in college, and this growth is not attributable to general maturation. There are many possible reasons why this might occur: the general intellectual milieu of colleges and universities that fosters the exchange of ideas, exposure to multiple perspectives regarding social issues, academic values of truth-seeking and careful reasoning, or institutional values of academic integrity and personal responsibility. It is also reasonable to assume that some contexts are more effective than others in promoting moral development. For example, those in which the moral dimensions of community life are explicit, where students are encouraged to wrestle with moral dilemmas, and where they are exposed to and encouraged to practise post-conventional moral reasoning would be expected to be more effective in promoting post-conventional moral reasoning than those without such opportunities and those in contexts that are not known for prosocial behaviours and attitudes. In the next section, we review studies that reflect four types of collegiate contexts and their relationship to moral reasoning. We start at a general level by looking at moral judgement development across institutional types, then consider how the development of moral judgement might differ by academic discipline. Next, we examine interventions that are explicitly designed to promote moral development, and conclude this section with a summary of particular collegiate experiences and their relationship to moral judgement.

Distinctive Institutional Contexts

Higher education in the United States is distinguished by the wide variety of types of collegiate institutions, which vary widely across a range of factors, including size, public or private control and mission. Major institutional types range from large public universities with multiple constituencies and missions to small private colleges serving distinctive student subgroups with distinctive missions. Accordingly, institutional type is a common research variable in higher education research, including research on moral judgement (Shaver, 1985, 1987; McNeel, 1991, 1994; Burwell et al., 1992; Good & Cartwright, 1998; Pascarella & Terenzini, 1991, in preparation). Based on these studies, it appears that the environment of liberal arts colleges tends to be more conducive to fostering the development of moral reasoning than that of other types of colleges and universities (Pascarella & Terenzini, 1991, McNeel, 1994; Good & Cartwright, 1998, in preparation). For example, Good and Cartwright (1998) compared levels of moral judgement development among undergraduate university students attending a state university, a Christian liberal arts university and a Bible university. They found no significant differences in post-conventional moral reasoning among the fresh-man students across institutions; however, senior students at state universities and at Christian liberal arts colleges showed higher levels of post-conventional moral reasoning than senior students at Bible colleges.

Shaver (1987) also compared the DIT scores of students attending a Christian liberal arts college and a Bible college, and did so using a longitudinal study. He found that at the time of entry and at the time of exit, post-conventional moral reasoning scores for Christian liberal arts students were significantly higher than those for Bible college students. Similarly, in their secondary analysis of data reported by Rest (1979a) on the DIT P-scores of college students, Pascarella and Terenzini (1991) found that moral reasoning differed significantly by institutional type, with students from church-affiliated liberal arts colleges scoring the highest, followed by those at public research universities, two-year colleges, private liberal arts colleges, private universities and public comprehensive universities, respectively. McNeel (1994) also conducted a meta-analysis of college effects on post-conventional moral reasoning by college type. Using 22 samples made up of students from seven liberal arts colleges, three universities and two Bible colleges; he reported large effect sizes for liberal arts colleges, large or moderate average effect sizes for universities, and no effect or a moderate effect size for the two Bible colleges. In other words, the only consistently large effect size was found among samples of students attending liberal arts colleges. This is consistent with other studies reporting that liberal arts colleges are more effective than their counterparts in promoting development in moral judgement.

These studies suggest that the development of moral reasoning is affected by the collegiate context. This is a very gross indicator, as "context" is a very general factor that might include a wide variety of more specific factors that are more directly related to change in moral reasoning. Further, there is great variability among institutions that share a similar "type". For example, some public universities work from an explicit value framework and encourage and expect students to discus s their values and ground their decisions in a value-based framework; others discourage initiatives that suggest religious values, holding separation of church and state as the higher value. Students attending these similar type institutions would probably have very different collegiate experiences. Nevertheless, findings of institutional differences do provide the impetus to look more closely at more specific features of the collegiate environment. Some of these are discussed below in the section on enriching experiences.

Disciplinary Contexts

The DIT has been used to measure differences in the moral reasoning of college students across academic disciplines (Zeidler & Schafer, 1984; St Pierre *et al.*, 1990; Icerman *et al.*, 1991; Paradice & Dejoie, 1991; Jeffrey, 1993; Ponemon & Gabhart, 1994; Snodgrass & Behling, 1996; Cummings *et al.*, 2001). Variability of moral reasoning scores within certain disciplines has also been observed (Icerman *et al.*, 1991; Paradice & Dejoie, 1991; Jeffrey, 1993).

Several studies have attempted to measure differences in moral reasoning between academic disciplines (St Pierre *et al.*, 1990; Snodgrass & Behling, 1996), yielding inconclusive results. For example, St Pierre *et al.*, (1990) found that accounting majors and students majoring in other business disciplines (i.e. finance, information systems, hotel/restaurant management, management, marketing and international business) showed lower levels of post-conventional moral reasoning than did students in psychology, maths and social work. Snodgrass and Behling (1996), by contrast, found no significant differences in the moral reasoning levels between business and non-business majors (i.e. arts and humanities, social sciences, natural sciences and undeclared).

Other studies have examined the development of moral reasoning of students majoring in disciplines that vary in their social orientation (St Pierre *et al.*, 1990; Paradice & Dejoie, 1991). For example, Paradice and Dejoie (1991) found that management information system (MIS) majors generally used higher levels of post-conventional reasoning than did non-MIS business majors. They found higher DIT scores among MIS majors, and concluded that these students were more socially orientated than students enrolled in other business majors.

Societal concern with unethical business practices (e.g. insider-trading, deceptive advertising, tax fraud, tax evasion) led researchers to investigate the development of post-conventional moral reasoning across a series of studies within the business community (St Pierre *et al.*, 1990; Icerman *et al.*, 1991; Paradice & Dejoie, 1991; Jeffrey, 1993; Ponemon & Gabhart, 1994; Snodgrass

& Behling, 1996). For example, Jeffrey (1993) examined differences in level of moral development among lower division business students, and found that accounting students had higher postconventional moral reasoning scores than non-accounting business students. Moreover, findings from this study show that senior students in each business major showed higher levels of moral reasoning development than entering students in each major, and the size of the differences was constant across business majors—indicating that the finding of differences in moral reasoning between business majors is not a result of self-selection into a given major. Similarly, Paradice and Dejoie (1991) found that MIS majors (juniors and seniors) used higher levels of post-conventional reasoning than did non-MIS business majors. They do not, however, identify specific factors that might contribute to these differences, one of which may be self-selection into specific majors.

Several researchers have proposed disciplinary-specific adaptations of the DIT by grounding the content of the dilemmas in discipline-specific contexts or issues. Specifically, Westbrook (1994) developed a DIT-like test for journalism students and professionals (called the "Journalist's Instrument"); Loviscky (2000) developed a "Managerial DIT"(MDIT) to measure the development of moral reasoning for management students and professionals; Lampe (Lampe & Walsh, 1992; Lampe, 1994) developed the "Survey of Educator Ethics Opinions" to measure the moral development for preservice and practicing teachers; and Zeidler and Schafer (1984) used the "Environmental Issues Test", developed by Iozzi (1978), to measure moral reasoning related to environmental issues. A detailed review of these instruments is beyond the scope of this article. However, they are mentioned here because they highlight the importance of issues of context when making educational decisions about students' moral reasoning. Some educators find it unwise to extrapolate from dilemmas of a general moral nature to those that are in the context of their field of study, and are less persuaded by psychometric data on national samples of students than by data from specific disciplinary contexts. The researchers who developed these new instruments have attempted to address this issue by retaining the structural format of the DIT, but by using discipline-specific moral dilemmas and items. Whether these adapted instruments will prove to be valid measures of moral judgement will depend on the results of future research.

To date, research on the development of moral judgement within academic disciplines has yielded results that are inconclusive and therefore provide little insight into the nature of the specific characteristics within disciplines that are the most conducive to growth in moral judgement. Although it is understandable that educators and researchers alike are curious about differences by academic discipline, it may be that this by itself serves as only a very preliminary unit of analysis. With that said, understanding the specific content and curricular approaches that make up any given academic discipline is useful for conducting interventions that promote growth in moral reasoning. We turn next to specific kinds of certain collegiate experiences (e.g. ethics courses, community service projects, pedagogies that invite the consideration of moral controversies) that may be more directly related to moral judgement development, and that thus provide more fruitful avenues for research on pedagogies that foster moral judgement.

Intervention Studies

The DIT has been used in a number of studies that investigated the effects of participation in educational experiences that were designed intentionally to promote the development of moral reasoning among college students. These vary widely in content and focus, including general education courses (Mustapha & Seybert, 1989, 1990), ethics courses or courses with an ethics component (Armstrong, 1993; Ponemon, 1993; Boss, 1994), social diversity courses (Adams & Zhou-McGovern, 1990, 1994), a freshman colloquium on psychosocial issues (Tennant , 1991), participation in service learning or community service programmes (Boss, 1994; Gorman et al., 1994) and an outdoor education programme (Smith & Bunting, 1999). A much more ambitious approach was the Sierra Project (Whiteley, 1982), an intervention designed to promote character development in students, combining residential, academic and personal elements, and testing students several times a year over several cohorts.

Given this remarkable variety of approaches, it is especially noteworthy that virtually all these approaches were effective in promoting moral judgement; exceptions were reported by Ponemon (1993) and Tennant (1991). Another distinctive feature of this group of interventions is that most took place in the context of one-term courses, including three that included direct instruction in ethics. However, the results are mixed for effectiveness of the ethics courses: significantly higher moral judgement scores were reported for the intervention samples by Armstrong (1993) using a sample of accounting students, and by Boss (1994; described below), but not by Ponemon (1993), who also studied accounting students.

Boss's (1994) study is noteworthy in that it controlled for class size, instructor, class exercises and text used across two sections of an ethics class. Boss found that the ethics curriculum and discussion of moral dilemmas and moral development was effective only for the ethics class, whose members also were also required to complete 20 hours of community service work "that involved working directly with people in need" (p. 187) and to keep a journal of their experiences. DIT scores for these students increased, while those of the control group remained stable. Further, 51% of the experimental group and only 13% of the control group used primarily postconventional moral reasoning at the post-test. A similar design (but with fewer controls) was used by Gorman et al. (1994), who tested students enrolled in two courses, "Perspectives on Western Culture", and "Person and Social Responsibility". The latter included field projects that "put the students into direct contact with examples of social injustice"(p. 426) and opportunities to reflect upon and discuss their field experiences. Post-test DIT scores were higher for students in the section with the service component.

Adams and Zhou-McGovern (1994) found that courses on social diversity and social justice could also be effective in promoting moral judgement. The course they studied focused on racism, anti-Semitism, sexism, homophobia and disability oppression. By the end of the course, DIT scores had increased significantly.

It appears that courses on topics with a less obvious link to moral education can also provide effective venues for promoting moral judgement. Other effective courses emphasised decision-making and active learning; these components were central to the structure of both the integrated general education curricula tested by Mustapha and Seybert (1989, 1990), the outdoor education course studied by Smith and Bunting (1999) and Tennant's (1991) psychosocial course for entering freshmen.

Abdolmohammadi *et al.*'s (1997) study was not an intervention *per se*, but employed a strategy that those designing interventions might find informative. They administered the DIT to 301 students near the end of a business ethics course; they then randomly assigned these students to three-member groups and asked them to come to a consensus response for each of the questions on the DIT. In the individual administration, P-scores of female students were significantly higher on the DIT ($M = 49$) than were the scores of the male students ($M = 38$). However, in the group administration, the scores of the women declined ($M = 44$) while the scores of the men increased significantly ($M = 43$). These results reveal differences in individual versus group decision-making and gender-related effects of group interactions on reasoning.

Two major institutionwide studies that include measures of character development have also employed the DIT and inform our understanding of the development of moral judgement in the college years. The first of these was the Sierra Project study conducted at the University of California-Irvine in the early 1980s, providing one of the most comprehensive longitudinal studies of character development available at that time. Successive cohorts of freshmen were tested on an array of instruments, including the DIT. Their DIT scores increased significantly over time, and were not attributable to growth in other dimensions of development (Whiteley, 1982).

Secondly, the faculty and staff at Alverno College have been engaged in a massive research effort to evaluate adaptable elements of their ability-based curriculum for deep and durable learning in college and beyond; a major volume summarising this effort has been published recently (Mentkowski *et al.*, 2000). They found that students' growth in moral judgement on the DIT (Rogers, 2002 this issue)was related to progress through Alverno's developmentally sequenced curriculum, which includes but is not limited to participation in the Valuing in Decision-Making ability area taught within the disciplines. Analysis of student interviews showed which elements of the curriculum and of the campus culture helped broaden their moral perspective. Further, the authors found that students "came to appreciate and understand differing values because they were repeatedly asked to examine and discuss them"(p. 130).

In summary, the majority of studies in this section did report significant increases in moral judgement after the intervention. However, several employed research designs that do not allow the reader to confidently attribute the increases to the intervention *per se*. Specifically, intervention studies designed to promote moral development would be strengthened by meeting experimental research design criteria: carefully selecting control or comparison groups, following strategies that allow for the control of selection effects, providing detailed descriptions of the major features of the intervention to readers, designing conceptually grounded interventions, and testing for stability in change scores after the posttests.

Effects of Other Collegiate Contexts on Moral Development

Several studies have examined aspects of specific collegiate experiences and their relationship to DIT score. Rest (1979a,b , 1986, 1987, 1988) initiated this line of study with data from his (Rest, 1979b) longitudinal sample of 59 students who were re-tested twice in two-year intervals. Of these 38 had attended college, 18 had not and three reported ambiguous information. DIT scores increased for both college and non-college students for the first two years out of high school, but at the third testing the DIT scores of the students still in college were still increasing, while those for the non-college cohort had decreased. Further, when asked to identify experiences they thought had influenced their moral thinking, a wide range of experiences was cited. One of the few that was cited by those who showed a greater rate of increase than those not citing it was "spending more time contemplating issues", suggesting that refection rather than instruction or other specific experiences is a key factor in promoting moral thinking. These preliminary results were examined and explored in more depth in Rest and Deemer (1986).

More recently, Thoma and Ladewig (1993) conducted a study that examined a particular aspect of students' experiences: they hypothesised that the quality of students' peer relationships would affect their moral judgement development during college. Using a sample of 156 college students, they found that both DIT scores and the number of close college friends increased for each class level from freshman to senior years. Students with close friendships who had multiple independent friendship groups (that is, those whose friends were not necessarily friends with one another) had higher DIT scores than other students. These findings suggest that diverse friendships may provide a context for challenging students to consider issues of fairness from different perspectives. Alternatively, it may be that those who seek multiple friendships are more open to developmental challenges. Although the links between types of friendships and development of moral judgement have not yet been explicated, this line of research bears much promise. (For a review of the literature on friendship and moral judgement, see Derryberry & Thoma, 2000.)

Two studies have examined the influence of membership in Greek organisations on moral development. Sanders (1990) administered the DIT to male freshmen at the beginning of the autumn term (n = 195) and nine weeks later at end of the term (n = 101). Independents scored significantly higher than fraternity members on both the pre- and post-test; P-scores for both groups are remarkably low, M = 10.0 and 8.6, respectively [1]. Cohen (1982) tested fraternity and sorority members in various leadership positions (23 executive committee members and 111 presidents)and 141 other individual members. She found no differences by membership category, gender or year in school; all had mean P-scores in the high 30s. Cohen interpreted these findings by suggesting that these students "do not seem to be having the upending experiences necessary to make the transition from conventional to post-conventional thinking" (p. 328). These two studies substantiate Derryberry and Theme's (2000) observation that "although the college data are supportive of Kohlberg's theory and suggest an influence of the college environment on moral thinking, it is surprising how little we know about exactly what contributes to this shift"(p. 14). Clearly, this is an area that merits more attention.

Last, an experiment by Real *et al.* (1998) compared the moral reasoning of 118 upper division business students in a non-competitive situation (using the DIT) and in a competitive game (using a Reasoning List based on the DIT that yields the 'moral reasoning during competition' [MRC] score). The average P-Score was low for college students, 37 (see [1]). The level of moral reasoning exhibited during competition was signifi-

cantly lower during the competitive game in this study, with the modal level of reasoning being at the pre conventional level. The authors concluded that the acceptance of business norms that reflect lower stage reasoning, e.g. 'that's the way it works so I'll do it that way too'(p. 1209) contributed to the lower scores in a competitive context. However, the comparability between the MRC scores and the DIT has not been established sufficiently to say whether this discrepancy is the result of the context or the measurement tool. Nevertheless, this study raises provocative questions regarding the effects of collegiate contexts that are competitive, especially among subgroups with P-scores that are below average among college samples.

These studies capture a few of the wide variety of contexts in which college students have experiences that may affect their moral development. Some collegiate environments may foster close friendships with diverse others and therefore foster moral perspective-taking, while others may foster close friendships that reinforce stereotyping or perpetuate non-moral values and behaviours; each in turn can lead to higher or lower moral judgement scores. The next section looks specifically at the links between moral judgement and moral behaviour.

The Relationship between Moral Judgement and Moral Behaviour in College Students

Many collegiate institutions purport to teach their students to be good citizens, provide moral leadership and teach democratic values and decision-making skills that students can use in their professions and in their communities after graduation. As a result, many who study institutional impact and effectiveness are keenly interested in the link between moral judgement and moral behaviour. The link between moral judgement and moral behaviour is critical because, as Thoma (1994) pointed out, understanding moral action may be seen as the "acid test" (p. 199) of the usefulness of research on morality. Fortunately, several studies have been done that examine this relationship. Comprehensive reviews of this literature that include detailed conceptual analysis are available elsewhere (see especially Blasi, 1980; Thoma & Rest, 1986; Rest *et al.*, 1986; Thoma, 1994). The current review is limited to DIT studies conducted with college student samples. It also excludes those studies examining factors that might affect moral judgement (e.g. comprehension, situational characteristics), but for which the observed behaviour (and dependent variable) was only a change in DIT scores. These studies are included in the final section.

We identified 10 studies that fit these criteria. Of these, two used creative experimental designs. Noting that "it is often easier to tell the truth when it is obvious what the truth is"(p. 41), Brabeck (1984) examined the act of whistleblowing under conditions that made it more difficult to ascertain the truth. She administered the DIT to a sample of 32 juniors and seniors in an introductory counselling class; this yielded a post-conventional group (those whose P-scores were above 50) and a conventional group (with scores 50 and below). Half of each group was then assigned randomly to one of two treatments. All were asked to help pilot test questions ostensibly written for a text by the investigator; the chapter contained two factual errors. In Treatment I ($n = 13$), the errors were pointed out by a peer-confederate from an article in the *American Psychologist*; in Treatment II ($n = 12$), the source of the contradictory evidence was ambiguous. No confederate was present for the control group ($n = 7$). Participants who brought either error to the investigator's attention were scored as whistle-blowing. Of those in the conventional group only 8% ($n = 1$) blew the whistle, while 54% ($n = 7$) of those in the post-conventional group did so; none in the control group blew the whistle. Although this sample was small, the trend was clear: students in the post-conventional group were significantly more likely to call a potential error to the attention of the investigator than were those in the conventional group.

The second innovative design was used by Ponemon (1993). The purpose of this study was to evaluate the effectiveness of a one-term case-orientated ethics intervention within an auditing course taken by 126 seniors and graduate students in accounting using a pretest–post-test, experimental–comparison group design; the comparison group received several weeks of instruction on the AICPA Code of Professional Conduct. No significant increases in DIT scores were found for either group of students or either treatment; Pscores remained low for college samples ($M = 38$; $SD = 12$; see [1]). An additional

measure of moral behaviour was used, as follows. Students were asked on the syllabus and at the beginning of the class to help pay for copies of the course lecture notes (114 pages; $11.40) due to financial constraints on the department copying budget. Payment was optional, and this served as the dependent behavioural variable; not paying was known as "free-riding". Median payments were between $4.50 (ethics class) and $5.00 (comparison class). Dividing the obtained DIT scores into quartiles, significant differences in payment amount were observed: average payments received from students in the first, second and third quartiles were $2.08, $5.92 and $8.52, respectively. However, the average payment by those in the fourth quartile (i.e. those with the highest DIT scores) was $2.95. Thus, fee payment was found to be related systematically to DIT score, but not in a linear fashion. The pattern of increasing payments from the first to third quartile is consistent with prior research on the judgement/behaviour relationship. However, both the overall low level of paying the fee and the break in the pattern by those with the highest scores raises further questions about the nature of this relationship.

In a debriefing survey, 43% reported that free-riding was unethical. Only 19% indicated they would free-ride, but actually over 67% did not pay the fee at all or in full. In a series of items related to the fee-paying decision, items corresponding to early stages of moral reasoning (preconventional or early conventional) were prevalent. These findings show that many factors affect moral behaviour, and that even reporting an act to be unethical is not a good predictor of acting in morally consistent ways. Whether this is related to the fact that this sample had relatively low P-scores remains to be seen.

Another study of academic responsibilities was conducted by Cummings *et al.* (2001); they examined self-reported propensity to engage in academic misconduct among teacher education students enrolled in an educational technology course. The average P-scores were also low (36.6) and they also used a quartile split (a high P-score was defined as 47 or above) to analyse the data. Students with higher P-scores reported that they engaged less frequently in academically dishonest behaviours. Whether they actually had done so is not known, a question that is made more salient in light of the discrepancies found in the Ponemon (1993) study between self-reported and actual behaviours. This suggests that the use of indirect measures such as used in this study are less reliable as indicators of moral behaviour.

Malinowski and Smith (1985) conducted an experiment with 53 male college students to examine the relation to cheating of moral judgement and other variables thought to affect cheating behaviour. The DIT was administered in a class, and students' participation in an seemingly unrelated laboratory study of attention–concentration was used to assess cheating behaviour. They found that although most (77%) cheated on at least one trial, the higher the DIT scores, the less cheating occurred. The higher the P-score, the fewer the number of trials on which students cheated, the fewer the number of seconds by which they inflated their scores, and the later in the process cheating began (if at all). DIT scores were also used to group the students into Stage 4 and Stage 3 groups. Stage 3 subjects cheated more and began cheating sooner. Of the 12 men who did not cheat, 11 were in the Stage 4 group. This study was conceptually grounded in Kohlberg's theory and in Rest's emerging research on the DIT, was carefully designed to take a variety of potentially confounding variables into account, and helps explicate the role of moral judgement as well as situational variables in determining moral behaviour.

Four studies (Taylor *et al.*, 1985; Cartwright & Simpson, 1990; Johnson *et al.*, 1993; Duckett & Ryden, 1994) examined the performance of students in professional programmes, nursing , business and education, respectively. Duckett and Ryden (1994) noted that nursing practice includes an important moral dimension, so evaluated the relationship between DIT score and clinical performance. However, they did not did not describe a moral component within either the curriculum or the clinical performance measure used. They reported a significant correlation between DIT score and a measure of clinical performance ($r = 0.58$, $P = 0.001$) among a group of 48 nursing students in their junior and senior years; DIT score accounted for 34% of the variance in the clinical performance of these students. This provides indirect evidence that the use of post-conventional moral reasoning contributes to clinical performance, but the nature of the link is not yet clear. Johnson *et al.* investigated the relationship between students' facility with business writing and moral judgement. Using a sample of 72 juniors and seniors, they found that GPA was the best predictor of DIT

score, accounting for 70% of the variance. Similarly, they also found a significant relationship between students' grades on a series of writing assignments that were scored for writing mechanics, completeness, tone and design. Whether earning high scores on these aspects of good writing constitutes moral behaviour is arguable. The noteworthy similarity between these two studies is that moral judgement was significantly related to performance variables within their respective disciplines.

Two studies examined performance of preservice teachers. Taylor *et al.* (1985) also investigated the general relationship between maturity in intellectual, moral and social domains and the quality of preservice teachers' interpretations of child behaviours. They found no significant relationships between DIT scores and the quality of students' interpretations. Similarly, Cartwright and Simpson (1990)found no significant relationship between DIT scores ($M = 36$) and teaching effectiveness of 53 student teachers.

Bredemeier and Shields (1984) examined the moral dimension of students' behaviours in the context of collegiate basketball games. They studied athletic aggression among 46 collegiate basketball players. Based on Bredemeier's (1975) article, they defined aggression as "the initiation of an attack with the intent to injure within a sport context" (Bredemeier & Shields, 1984, p. 141). The behavioural-dependent variables they used were the average number of fouls committed per minute per season game for each player, coaches' ratings of players' aggressiveness (extremely low to extremely high aggression level) and their rankings of the aggressiveness of all players in relation to their teammates. They found a significant inverse relationship between P-score and athletic aggression on all three measures and several variations by gender (the correlation for number of fouls was significant only for the males, and the correlation with the ratings was much higher for women; women had significantly higher P-scores than their male counterparts). The definition of aggressiveness used in this study makes clear the link to moral development; this study shows that for both genders, moral judgement is related inversely to sports aggression.

Hubbs-Tait and Garmon (1995) noted that decisions regarding whether to engage in sexual activity are often included in the domain of moral dilemmas, and that the moral dimensions of these decisions have been heightened since the spread of the AIDS virus. They hypothesised that level of moral reasoning would mediate the relationship between AIDS knowledge and sexual behaviour. Using a sample of 103 single college students, they found a non-significant relationship between AIDS knowledge and sexual behaviours, but a significant negative correlation between DIT score and condom use. Next, they performed a median split on the DIT scores, creating a "high" group ($n = 45$; DIT scores >26.7) and a low group ($n = 58$; scores <26.7). Among those in the high group, a significant negative correlation was found between knowledge and degree of risk: as knowledge of AIDS increased, risky sexual behaviours decreased. This pattern was not found among the low group, where risky sexual behaviours did not decrease as AIDS knowledge increased. Given the overall low DIT scores for this sample, these relationships are especially provocative, suggesting that moral judgement does mediate behaviour even among college students with relatively low DIT scores (see [1]).

Hay (1983) explored becoming a conscientious objector (CO) as an act that is experienced by some as a response to a moral dilemma (whether to serve in the military). He administered the DIT to a sample of young adults who had responded to compulsory draft registration by registering as COs in order to determine whether their scores were comparable to those of non-COs. He found that at each educational level (high school, college, and graduate school), COs scored about 10 points higher than Rest's norms (see [1]); the mean DIT score for the college students ($n = 101$) in his sample was 53. Hay also found that those who based their objections on a personal moral code (as opposed to religious training or belief, a criterion used by draft boards evaluating these appeals) had higher moral reasoning scores.

Lupfer *et al.* (1987) reported the results of four experiments examining student decision-making. Two of these took place in the context of a simulated trial in which the students (volunteers from an introductory psychology class) served as jurors. The dependent behavioural variable was the number of guilty votes cast in the simulation. After taking the DIT, three types of sixperson juries were formed: those with "high" P-scores (>29), (those with low P-scores (<21) and those with a mixture of scores. (The median score was low 25; see [1]) High-P juries cast significantly fewer guilty votes than low-P or mixed juries. In the mixed juries, those with higher leadership scores tended to have higher P scores ($r = 0.47$, $P<0.001$), and these leaders successfully promoted their preference for acquittal; this phenomenon was not observed in the other jury types. Two problems make it difficult to interpret these findings: first, the DIT scores were quite low, even among the "high" group; second, the authors do not explain why acquittal is morally preferable. If it is, then the findings strongly suggest that higher moral reasoning is associated with moral behaviour; if not, then other explanations should be offered to explain this observed relationship.

This section has summarised studies that link collegiate contexts to moral judgement development. Based on these studies, it is clear that a wide variety of factors can foster moral development, which is important as there are few distinct experiences that are shared by most college students. As Pascarella and Terenzini (in preparation) concluded, "The key role of college in fostering post-conventional moral reasoning may therefore lie in providing a range of intellectual, cultural, and social experiences from which a range of different students might potentially benefit" (p. 15). What is noteworthy is that most studies here examined the effects of students' experiences in classroom contexts, and that comparable attention has not been given to structured cocurricular experiences (e.g. participation on disciplinary boards or in other student leadership positions) that have potential to affect moral development.

The Relationship between Moral Judgement and Other Domains of Development

This review has included only attributes that are particularly germane to college students or the college experience. As a result, we did not include attributes that simply reported relationships with other variables from, for example, a personality perspective instead of a college student or college outcomes perspective. Even with these parameters in place, a full analysis of the shared relationships between moral judgement and other college-related domains of development is beyond the scope of this paper. However, we have compiled a list of studies that shows the breadth of topics that have been researched comparing DIT scores with those from other domains.

These studies address the following relationships: political orientation (n = 12); ego/identity development (n = 11), religious identification/religious attitude/spirituality (n = 12); social attitude/issues (n = 9); cognitive development (n = 8), academic achievement (n = 8), locus of control (n = 7); aptitude/intelligence (n = 6); values/ethics (n = 5); perspectivetaking (n = 4); emotion (n = 2); tolerance/diversity (n = 2), learning/analytical style (n = 2); and conflict resolution (n = 1). (This list is available upon request from the authors.)

Suggestions for Future Research

These findings not only provide a summary of past research, but insights that can be used to inform and direct future research. One important conclusion is that dramatic gains in moral judgement are associated with collegiate participation, even after controlling for age and entering level of moral judgement. This provides an important springboard for future research; we next suggest the types of studies that will further our understanding of moral judgement development in the college years.

First, what accounts for differences in gains by institutional type? Most of the studies noted here only alert us to the existence of these differences, not to their causes ; the Whiteley (1982) and Mentkowski *et al.* (2000) studies offer important exceptions, in that each of these documented the effects of specific, intentional educational activities. In the other studies, it is not clear whether obtained institutional differences are a result of other factors, such as: student self-selection (are those more open to thinking about moral dilemmas inclined to select a liberal arts college?); size (e.g. access to opportunities for direct involvement, smaller classes with more discussion); clarity of expectations regarding the role of values in students' lives; opportunities to practice reasoning about moral issues; or a liberal arts curriculum that stresses examining many issues from multiple perspectives. Discerning these influences not only across but within types of institutions is an important topic for future research.

Secondly, how can the finding that a remarkably diverse set of interventions appears to promote moral judgement development be ex-plained? What characteristics do these have in common? Is it making the moral dimension explicit? Using experiential learning strategies? Grounding discussions in personally meaning-

ful topics? We urge researchers interested in the question of what makes a moral intervention effective to consult the extensive literature on this topic that has used schoolaged samples, and (as discussed above) to employ rigorous research designs. Insights might also be gleaned from carefully examining those collegiate contexts that do *not* appear to promote moral development (e.g. fraternities and accounting courses). What are the characteristics of those collegiate subcultures? Are findings that students in these settings score lower than average an artefact of self-selection? A culture that gives higher value to non-moral attributes? Other factors? Investigating questions such as these could also contribute to our understanding of how collegiate contexts can support the development of moral judgement.

Thirdly, research in other domains has documented the powerful effects of student involvement in co-curricular activities (Kuh *et al.*, 1991; Pascarella & Terenzini, 1991), yet this context is minimally reflected in this review. The effects on moral judgement of student involvement in community-outreach activities, campus judicial systems, leadership positions, peer-conflict mediation programmes and intergroup dialogue programmes remains largely unexplored.

Fourthly, how do educators (faculty, student organisation advisers, housing professionals, etc.) envision their responsibility for promoting moral judgement development? How do they enact this vision in their interactions with students?

Fifthly, there is a great deal of variability among college students, including but not limited to race and ethnicity. A clearer understanding of student characteristics and student subcultures would inform our understanding of the kinds of experiences that enhance or inhibit moral development, and whether these reflect subgroup differences. Further, recent research on the power of campus climate variables (Hurtado *et al.*, 1999) offers some rich concepts and examples to guide other research.

Sixthly, given the complexity of both the construct and of institutional contexts, larger-scale studies utilising more sophisticated statistical techniques are needed to untangle factors that lead to the development of moral judgement. Few of the studies reviewed here partialled out the effects of covariates (such as SES, which is correlated strongly with ethnicity and educational level); none used causal modelling or hierarchical linear modeling to discern and weigh effects on moral development.

In addition to identifying these broad topics for future research, we now offer a few suggestions for researchers interested in conducting research using the DIT. First, the domain of morality is much broader than the moral judgement component that the DIT is designed to measure, and we urge researchers to be cognisant of its purpose and intended use. For example, some researchers described it as a measure of "morality", "ethics", "values " or "social reasoning". Although these are related domains, they are conceptually distinct from moral judgement and arguably inconsistent with the purpose of the DIT. Others used DIT scores to yield a single stage score as a proxy measure for Kohlberg's moral interview; for a review of the conceptual and methodological problems with this approach, see Thoma (1994).

Secondly, we urge researchers who are interested in the development of moral judgement to clarify their rationale and underlying assumptions regarding their selection of variables to investigate. Showing the conceptual linkages they are testing offers much more fertile ground for theory-building than do studies that leave the reader guessing about these proposed relationships.

Thirdly, well-designed intervention studies are very helpful in identifying useful ways to promote moral judgement development. We urge researchers to carefully evaluate their proposed studies against established criteria for intervention studies, along the lines suggested above.

Finally, several of the studies reported here failed to report relevant data (e.g. P-scores for subgroups, sample sizes and mean scores) that were essential for meaningful interpretation. Others mislabelled groups after breaking down the data (e.g. labelling as "principled moral reasoners" those with DIT scores that were above the median for the sample, but still low compared to college students in general). These practices are fraught with potential for misunderstanding. We also urge researchers to carefully report their findings so that readers can arrive independently at their own conclusions about the appropriateness of the conclusions drawn. We believe that if more researchers follow these basic guidelines, then the next generation of DIT research will provide a clearer picture and better inform our understanding of the moral development of college students.

Conclusion

The DIT has been used in an impressive array of studies to examine various aspects of the lives and experiences of college students. Educators concerned with broad issues of character development in college students will be reassured to learn that development in moral reasoning does tend to improve during the college years. Further, specific collegiate contexts (liberal arts colleges, certain types of educational experiences) are also associated with growth in moral judgement, and with the production of moral behaviour. These findings offer a significant foundation for the future work of both researchers and educators.

This array of studies demonstrates that college students' ability to base their moral judgements in postconventional moral reasoning does not simply unfold onto genetically by chronological maturation alone. Rather, it is important to remember that development occurs in context, and that colleges offer excellent contexts to stimulate moral reasoning. (Whether educators take full advantage of these contexts is another matter.) Even a gross indicator of context such as institutional type suggest s that students at some types of liberal arts colleges have higher potential to develop moral reasoning than they do at other types of colleges or universities.

This review has focused only on the DIT as a measure of moral judgement. The availability and demonstrated validity of this measure has clearly enabled the production of the plethora of studies summarised here. In the same spirit in which Jim Rest designed the DIT, we also urge researchers to continue to address theoretical questions, offer conceptual refinements, suggest alternative ways to measure both moral judgement and moral development and subject them to the scrutiny of sustained scholarly inquiry. Doing so would be a testament to the scholarly values that Rest inspired in the next generation of scholars whose own work is so richly represented in this volume.

Notes

[1] According to Rest (1994), the mean DIT P-scores by educational levels are as follows: junior high students = 21.9; senior high students = 31.8; college students = 42.3; moral philosophy and political science graduate students = 65.2.

References

Abdolmohammadi, M.J., Gabhart, D.R.L. & Reeves, M.F. (1997) Ethical cognition of business student individually and in groups, *Journal of Business Ethics*, 16, pp. 1717–1725.

Adams, M. & Zhou-McGovern, Y. (1990) Some cognitive developmental characteristics of social diversity education, paper presented at the Annual Meeting of the American Educational Research Association, Boston, MA, April 16, 1990. *ERIC Digest*, ED380344.

Adams, M. & Zhou-McGovern, Y. (1994) The socio-moral development of undergraduates in a "social diversity" course: developmental theory, research, and instructional applications, paper presented at the Annual Meeting of the American Educational Research Association, New Orleans, LA, April 4–8, 1994. *ERIC Digest*, ED380345.

Armstrong, M.B. (1993). Ethics and professionalism in accounting education: a sample course, *Journal of Accounting Education*, 11, pp. 77–92.

Bebeau, M. (2002). The Defining Issues Test and the Four Component Model: contributions to professional education, *Journal of Moral Education*, 31, pp. 271–295.

Blasi, A. (1980) Bridging moral cognition and moral action: a critical review of the literature, *Psychological Bulletin*, 88, pp. 1–45.

Boss, J.A. (1994)The effect of community service work on the moral development of college ethics students, *Journal of Moral Education*, 23, pp. 183–198.

Bouhmama, D. (1988) Relationship of moral education to moral judgement development, *Journal of Psychology*, 122, pp. 155–158.

Brabeck, M. (1984)Ethical characteristics of whistle blowers, *Journal of Research in Personality*, 18, pp. 41–53.

Bredemeier, B.J. (1975) The assessment of reaction and instrumental athletic aggression, in: D. Landers (Ed.). *Psychology of Sport and Motor Behaviour*, pp. 71–84. (State College, PA, The Pennsylvania State University).

Bredemeier, B.J. & Shields, D.L. (1984) The utility of moral stage analysis in the investigation of athletic aggression, *Sociology of Sport Journal*, 1, pp. 138–149.

Buier, R.M., Butman, R.E., Burwell, R. & Van Wicklin, J. (1989) The critical years: changes in moral and ethical decision-making in young adults at three Christian liberal arts colleges, *Journal of Psychology and Christianity*, 8, pp. 69–78.

Burwell, R.M., Butman, R.E. & Van Wicklin, J. (1992) Values assessment at three consortium colleges: a longitudinal followup study (Houston, TX, Houghton College). *ERIC Document Reproduction Service*, ED 345 635.

Cartwright, C.C. & Simpson, T.L. (1990) The relationship of moral judgement development and teaching effectiveness of students teachers, *Education*, 111, pp. 130–144.

Cohen, E. (1982) Using the Defining Issues Test to assess stage of moral development among sorority and fraternity members, *Journal of College Student Personnel*, 23, pp. 324–328.

Cummings, R., Dyas, L. & Maddux, C.D. (2001) Principled moral reasoning and behavior of preservice teacher education students, *American Educational Research Journal*, 38, pp. 143–158.

Derryberry, W.P. & Thoma, S.J. (2000) The friendship effect: its role in the development of moral thinking in students, *About Campus*, 5, pp. 13–18.

Duckett, L. & Ryden, M. (1994) Education for ethical nursing practice, in: J. Rest & D. Narvaez (Eds). *Moral Development in the Professions: psychology and applied ethics*, pp. 48–66 (Hillsdale, NJ, Lawrence Erlbaum Associates).

Evans, N.J., Forney, D.S. & Guido-DiBrito, F. (1998) *Student Development in College: theory, research, and practice* (San Francisco, CA, JosseyBass).

Foster, J.D. & LaForce, B. (1999) A longitudinal study of moral, religious, and identity development in a Christian liberal arts environment, *Journal of Psychology and Theology*, 27, pp. 52–68.

Galotti, K.M. (1988) Gender difference in self-reported moral reasoning: a review and new evidence, *Journal of Youth and Adolescence*, 18, pp. 475–488.

Gaurasci, R. (2001) Developing the democratic arts, *About Campus*, 5, pp. 9–15.

Gfellner, B.M. (1986) Ego development and moral development in relation to age and grade level during adolescence, *Journal of Youth and Adolescence*, 15, pp. 147–163.

Gongre, W.M. (1981) *A study of moral judgement, using the Defining Issues Test, for three ethnic groups at Bacone College*, unpublished doctoral dissertation, Oklahoma State University, OK.

Good, J.L. & Cartwright, C. (1998) Development of moral judgement among undergraduate university students, *College Student Journal*, 32, pp. 270–276.

Gorman, M., Duffy, J. & Heffernan, M. (1994) Service experience and the moral development of college students, *Religious Education*, 89, pp. 422–431.

Hay, J. (1983) A study of principled moral reasoning within a sample of conscientious objectors, *Moral Education Forum*, 7, pp. 1–8.

Hood, A. (1984) Student development: does participation affect growth?, *Bulletin of the Association of College UnionsInternational*, 54, pp. 16–19.

Hubb-Staitt, L. & Garmon, L.C. (1995) The relationship of moral reasoning and AIDS knowledge to risky sexual behavior, *Adolescence*, 30, pp. 549–564.

Hurtado, S., Milem, J., Clayton-Pederson, A. & Allen, W. (1999) *Enacting Diverse Learning Environments: improving the climate for racial/ethnic diversity in higher education*, ASHEERI C Higher Education Report, 26(8), Washington, DC.

Icerman, R., Karcher, J. & Kennelley, M. (1991) A baseline assessment of moral development: accounting, other business and nonbusiness students, *Accounting Educator's Journal*, 3, pp. 46–62.

Iozzi, L. (1978) The environmental issues test (EIT): a new assessment instrument for environmental education, in: C. Davis & A. Sacks (Eds). *Current Issues in Environmental Education—IV*, pp. 200–206 (Columbus, OH, ERIC Clearinghouse for Science, Mathematics, and Environmental Education).

Jeffrey, C. (1993) Ethical development of accounting students, non-accounting business students, and liberal arts students, *Issues in Accounting Education*, 8, pp. 86–96.

Johnson, J.L., Insley, R., Motwani, J. & Zbib, I. (1993) Writing performance and moral reasoning in business education, *Journal of Business Ethics*, 12, pp. 397–406.

King, P.M. & Kitchener, K.S. (1994) *Developing Reflective Judgement: understanding and promoting intellectual growth and critical thinking in adolescents and adults* (San Francisco, CA, JosseyBass).

King, P.M. & Kitchener, K.S. & Wood, P.K. (1985) The development of intellect and character: a longitudinal–sequential study of intellectual and moral development in young adults, *Moral Education Forum*, 10, pp. 1–13.

Kitchener, K.S., King, P.M., Davison, M.L., Parker, C.A. & Wood, P.K. (1984) A longitudinal study of moral and ego development in young adults, *Journal of Youth and Adolescence* 13, pp. 197–211.

Kuh, G.D., Schuh, J.H., Whitt, E.J., Andreas, R., Lyons, J., Strange, C., Krehbbiel, L. & MacKay, K. (1991) *Involving Colleges: successful approaches to fostering student learning and development outside the classrooms* (San Fransisco, CA, JosseyBass).

Lampe, J. (1994) *Teacher education students' moral development and ethical reasoning processes*, paper presented at the Annual Meeting of the American Educational Research Association, New Orleans, LA, April 4–8, 1994. *ERIC Digest*, ED375129.

Lampe, J. & Walsh, K. (1992) *Reflective teachers' ethical decision-making processes*, paper presented at the Annual Meeting of the American Educational Research Association, San Francisco, CA, April 20–24, 1992. *ERIC Digest*, ED346048.

Locke, D.C. & Tucker, D.O. (1988) Race and moral judgement development scores, *Counseling and Values*, 32, pp. 232–235.

Loviscky, G.E. (2000) *Construct validity of a managerial defining issues test*, unpublished doctoral dissertation, The Pennsylvania State University, PA.

Lupfer, M.B., Cohen, R., Bernard, J.L., & Brown, C.M. (1987) The influence of moral reasoning on the decisions of jurors, *Journal of Social Psychology*, 127, pp. 653–667.

Malinowski, C.I. & Smith, C.P. (1985) Moral reasoning and moral conduct: an investigation prompted by Kohlberg's theory, *Journal of Personality & Social Psychology*, 49, pp. 1016–1027.

McEwen, M.K., Roper, L., Bryant, D. & Langa, M. (1990) Incorporating the development of African-American students into psychosocial theories of student development, *Journal of College Student Development*, 31, pp. 429–436.

McNeel, S. (1991) Christian liberal arts education and growth in moral judgement, *Journal of Psychology and Christianity*, 10, pp. 311–322.

McNeel, S. (1994) College teaching and student moral development, in: J. Rest & D. Narvaez (Eds) *Moral Development in the Professions: psychology and applied ethics*, pp. 26–47 (Hillsdale, NJ, Lawrence Erlbaum Associates).

Mentkowski, M., Rogers, G., Doherty, A. *et al.* (2000). *Learning that Lasts: integrating learning, development, and performance in college and beyond* (San Francisco, CA, JosseyBass).

Mentkowski, M. & Strait, M.J. (1983) A longitudinal study of student change in cognitive development, learning styles, and generic abilities in an outcome-centered liberal arts curriculum, *Final Report to the National Institute of Education. Research Report Number Six*. (Milwaukee, WI, Alverno College Office of Research and Evaluation).

Murk, D.A. & Addleman, J.A. (1992) Relations among moral reasoning, locus of control, and demographic variables among college students, *Psychological Reports*, 70, pp. 467–476.

Mustapha, S.L. & Seybert, J.A. (1989) Moral reasoning in college students implications for nursing education, *Journal of Nursing Education*, 28, pp. 107–111.

Mustapha, S.L. & Seybert, J.A. (1990) Moral reasoning in college students: effects of two general education curricula, *Educational Research Quarterly*, 14, pp. 32–40.

Paradice, D.B. & Dejoie, R.M. (1991) The ethical decision-making processes of information systems workers, *Journal of Business Ethics*, 10, pp. 1–21.

Pascarella, E.T. & Terenzini, P.T. (1991) *How College Affects Students: findings and insights from twenty years of research* (San Francisco, CA, JosseyBass).

Pascarella, E.T. & Terenzini, P.T. (in preparation) Moral development, in E.T. Pascarella & P.T. Terenzini, *How College Affects Students Revisited: research from the 1990s* (San Francisco, CA, JosseyBass).

Ponemon, L. (1993) Can ethics be taught in accounting, *Journal of Accounting Education*, 11, pp. 185–209.

Ponemon, L.A. & Gabhart, D.R. (1994) Ethical reasoning in the accounting and auditing professions, in: J. Rest & D. Narvaez (Eds) *Moral Development in the Professions: psychology and applied ethics*, pp. 101–119 (Hillsdale, NJ, Lawrence Erlbaum Associates).

Quarry, E.B. (1997) *The Defining Issues Test as a measure of moral reasoning of undergraduate students at a Christian liberal arts institution in southern California*, unpublished doctoral dissertation, Talbot School of Theology, Biola University.

Reall, M.J., Baily, J.J. & Stoll, S.K. (1998) Moral reasoning "on hold" during a competitive game, *Journal of Business Ethics*, 17, pp. 1205–1210.

Rest, J. (1979a) The impact of higher education on moral judgement development (Technical report no. 5) (Minneapolis, MN, Moral Research Projects). *ERIC Digest*, ED196763.

Rest, J.R. (1979b) *Development in Judging Moral Issues* (Minneapolis, MN, University of Minnesota).

Rest, J.R. (1984) The major components of morality, in: W. Kurtines & J. Gewirtz (Eds), *Morality, Moral Development and Moral Behavior*, pp. 24–38 (New York, Wiley).

Rest, J.R. (1986) *Moral Development: advances in research and theory* (New York, Praeger Press).

Rest, J.R. (1987) *Moral judgement: an interesting variable for higher education research*, ASHE Annual Meeting Paper, paper presented at the Annual Meeting of the Association for the Study of Higher Education, Baltimore, MD, November, 21–24, 1987. *ERIC Digest*, ED292414.

Rest, J.R. (1988) Why does college promote development in moral judgement? *Journal of Moral Education*, 17, pp. 183–194.

Rest, J.R., Barnett, R., Bebeau M. *et al.* (1986) *Moral Development: advances in research and theory*, pp. 28–58 (New York, Praeger Press).

Rest, J., Cooper, D., Coder, R., Masanz, J. & Anderson, D. (1974) Judging the important issues in moral dilemmas—an objective measure of development, *Developmental Psychology*, 10, pp. 491–501.

Rest, J.R. & Deemer, D. (1986) Life experiences and developmental pathways, in: J.R. Rest (Ed.) *Moral Development: advances in research and theory*, pp. 28–58 (New York, Praeger Press).

Rest, J.R., Narvaez, D., Bebeau, M.J. & Thoma, S. (1999) *Postconventional Moral Thinking: a neoKohlbergian approach* (Mahwah, NJ, Lawrence Erlbaum Associates).

Rest, J. & Thoma, S. (1985) Relationship of moral judgment development to formal education, *Developmental Psychology*, 21, pp. 709–714.

Rogers, G. (2002) Rethinking moral growth in college and beyond, *Journal of Moral Education*, 31, p. 3.

Sanders, C.E. (1990) Moral reasoning of male freshmen, *Journal of College Student Development*, 31, pp. 5–8.

Shaver, D.G. (1985) A longitudinal study of moral development at a conservative, religious, liberal arts college, *Journal of College Student Personnel*, 26, pp. 400–404.

Shaver, D.G. (1987) Moral development of students attending a Christian liberal arts college and a Bible college, *Journal of College Student Personnel*, 28, pp. 211–218.

Smith, C.A. & Bunting, C.J. (1999) The moral reasoning of two groups of college students, *Research in Education*, 62, pp. 72–74.

Snodgrass, J. & Behling, R. (1996) Differences in moral reasoning between college and university business majors and non-business majors, *Business and Professional Ethics Journal*, 15, pp. 79–84.

St. Pierre, K.E., Nelson, E.S. & Gabbin, A.L. (1990) A study of ethical development of accounting majors in relation to other business and non-business disciplines, *Accounting Educators' Journal*, 3, pp. 23–35.

Stroud, S. (2000) *Universal elements in human nature: the putative connection between moral development and formal-pragmatic presupposition awareness*, paper presented at the 71st Annual Meeting of Western States Communication Association, Sacramento, CA, February 25–29, 2000. *ERIC Digest*, ED445381.

Taylor, J.B., Waters, B. & Surbeck, E. (1985) Cognitive, psychosocial, and moral development as predictors of preservice teachers' ability to analyze child behavior, *College Student Journal*, 19, pp. 65–72.

Tennant, S. (1991) Personal and moral development: a developmental curriculum intervention for liberal arts freshman, *Dissertation Abstracts International*, 51, p. 2657A.

Thoma, S.J. (1994) Trends and issues in moral judgment research using the Defining Issues Test, *Moral Education Forum*, 19, pp. 1–17.

Thoma, S. (2002) An overview of the Minnesota approach to research in moral development, *Journal of Moral Education*, 31, p. 3.

Thoma, S.J. & Ladewig, B.H. (1993) Close friendships, friendship networks, and moral judgment development during the college years, paper presented to the Society of Research in Child Development, New Orleans, LA, March 1993.

Thoma, S.J. & Rest, J.R. (1986) Moral judgment, behavior, decision making, and attitudes, in: J.R. Rest

(Ed.) *Moral Development: advances in research and theory*, pp. 133–175 (New York, Praeger Press).

Westbrook, T. (1994) Tracking the moral development of journalists: a look at them and their work, in: J. Rest & D. Narvaez (Eds) *Moral Development in the Professions: psychology and applied ethics*, pp. 189–197 (Hillsdale, NJ, Lawrence Erlbaum Associates).

Whiteley, J.M. (1982) Approaches to the evaluation of character development, in: J.M. Whiteley (Ed.) *Character Development in College Students*, pp. 111–172 (New York, Character Research Press).

Zeidler, D.L. & Schafer, L.E. (1984) Identifying mediating factors moral reasoning in science education, *Journal of Research in Science Teaching*, 21, pp. 1–15.

UNIT V

THEORY TO PRACTICE

Section 11

UTILIZING THEORY

CHAPTER 44

LEARNING PARTNERSHIPS MODEL: A FRAMEWORK FOR PROMOTING SELF-AUTHORSHIP

MARCIA B. BAXTER MAGOLDA

He takes the approach that he wants you to do it on your own. He will help you plot through your ideas and he will help you sort out what you are thinking and help direct you and he still encourages you to work independently. He just makes his office setting very comfortable. He'll ask "What are you confused about?" and he will your opinion on the matter rather than telling you what you should do. He will ask you exactly what is happening and what you need help with and try to direct you from there rather than presenting himself in a way that is kind of intimidating. . . . I think the way I see it is that he wants you to feel that you are at the same level as him, not in as far as the same knowledge, he wants the atmosphere to be such that you feel comfortable asking him or talking to him in any way. (Erica, in Baxter Magolda, 1999, pp. 133-134)

Erica's comments reflect the learning partnership she experienced with Professor Snowden, the instructor of her zoology course. The course introduced scientific complexity by virtue of Professor Snowden's statement on the syllabus that he wanted students to understand the tentative nature of scientific facts, and he wanted them to learn to think like scientists. Erica's description of Professor Snowden's approach to helping students meet these goals conveys the integration of challenge and support and the blend of connection and autonomy that characterize learning partnerships. Professor Snowden challenged Erica to work through her ideas to construct her own perspective yet supported her by helping her sort through her thinking. By respecting Erica as a capable learner, Professor Snowden offered connection and support that made her comfortable exploring her thinking with him. Refraining from telling her what to do in favor of helping her figure it out through accessing her thinking conveyed to Erica that Professor Snowden wanted her to think autonomously. This chapter describes the Learning Partnerships Model conceptualized from the characteristics Erica and other learners portrayed as central to their journeys toward self-authorship.

Origins of the Learning Partnership Model

The Learning Partnerships Model emerged from a 17-year longitudinal study of young adults' learning and development (Baxter Magolda, 1992, 2001). Grounded in the constructivist-development tradition of Perry's (1970) and Belenky, Clinchy, Goldberger, and Tarule's (1986) work, the college phase of the study traced epistemological development during college. Using an inductive approach consistent with this tradition (Piager, 1950) yielded dialogue during the college interviews about classroom and campus conditions that promoted or hindered developmental growth. Extensive data emerged from the 432 interviews conducted during the first 5 years of the study. Of 101 students interviewed in their first year of college, 95 returned for the sophomore-year interview, 86 for the junior-year interview, 80 for the senior-year interview, and 70 for the fifth-year interview. The participants were all students at Miami University, a public liberal arts institution with an enrollment of 16,000. Two students who transferred to other institutions their junior year remained in the study. The group was balanced by gender during the first year (51 women and 50 men) and remained reasonably so throughout the study. Only three participants were members of underrepresented populations.

Because I intended the longitudinal study to explore possibilities for development, the stories and my interpretations of them offer one possible portrayal of development during college and the conditions that promote it. I provide in-depth narratives elsewhere (Baxter Magolda, 1992, 2001) to help readers judge the degree to which this portrayal is applicable to other contexts. Miami attracts primarily traditional age students who have high entrance test scores and high school grades, are highly involved, and are highly motivated to succeed. The campus culture reinforces academic success and campus involvement. The participants were enrolled in all six divisions of the University (Applied Sciences, Arts and Science, Business Administration, Education and Allied Professions, Interdisciplinary Studies, and Fine Arts), involved in various campus activities (e.g., organizations related to academic majors, service organizations, Greek life, and leadership positions), and employed in diverse settings (e.g., computer labs, recreation centers, residence life, dining halls, and local businesses). Nine studied abroad while in college.

Continuing the constructivist approach to the study in the postcollege phase broadened the contexts in which to explore conditions to promote self-authorship. Study participants moved to diverse geographic locations, enrolled in various graduate and professional schools, accepted employment in multiple fields, and engaged in the diverse complexities of young adult life. Interviews reflected the participants' intrapersonal and interpersonal growth as well as their epistemological growth due in part to their shift from college to multiple contexts and due in part to my realization that their development could be best understood by integrating the multiple dimensions of development. Thirty-five participants have remained in the study for 17 years, yielding approximately 450 interviews from the 6th to the 17th year. These postcollege interviews, taking place in the participants' 20s and early 30s, reveal a more comprehensive understanding of the Learning Partnerships Model than was evident in the college years and show that it is applicable beyond the college years.

Participants' graduate or professional educational opportunities were another major source of data to identify the conditions that promoted self-authorship. Of the 35 longitudinal participants who currently remain in the study, 24 pursued some form of graduate or professional education. Seven others who are no longer in the study but participated in the early years after college also pursued graduate or professional study. The participants collectively attended a wide range of institutions, from small, private colleges to major research universities for their graduate/professional studies. Twelve participants completed their degrees part time while working full time. The majority worked for 1 to 3 years prior to pursuing graduate degrees, whereas those going into law, medicine, and the seminary generally began immediately after college graduation. The pursuit of advanced education was equally prevalent among women (16) and men (15). Eight participants pursued master's degrees in business in either business administration (6), economics (1), or international affairs (1). Six pursued master's degrees in education: 4 in teaching, 1 in supervision, and 1 in educational technology. Five studied social sciences, resulting in 2 master's degrees in psychology, 2 in social work, and 1 PhD in organizational behavior. Eight participants studied in professional schools: 2 in medicine, 3 in law, 2 in seminary, and 1 in culinary arts. Four participants pursued continuing education in teacher licensure, computer technology, mathematics education, and art history.

Postcollege employment provided another major source of experiences that promoted self-authorship. Participants entered the workforce in numerous occupations in diverse settings. Some followed the same career path from college graduation to their 30s, whereas others frequently changed paths. Although some stayed with the same institution or company for this span of time, most moved to new institutions or companies at least once or twice over these years. The two most prevalent work settings for the 35 participants remaining in the study were business and education. Fifteen participants, 8 women and 7 men, work in the business arena. One is an accountant. The majority work in sales and services, including insurance, computers, pharmaceutical or medical equipment, advertising, marketing, real estate, and chemical sales. A few work in retail sales, primarily in clothing and furniture. One participant owns a retail business. Ten participants are educators—9 in K–12 settings and 1 in higher education. Two of these participants are men, both of whom work in K–12 where 1 is a principal. The federal government employed 1 participant (a male) as an economist. Five (3 men and 2 women) work in human services in counseling, social work, services for the blind, and the Christian ministry. The group includes 2 practicing attorneys (1 female and 1 male), 1 physician (a male), and 2 restaurant professionals.

Finally, community and personal life contexts offered insights into the conditions that promote self-authorship. Many participants pursued leadership positions and volunteer work in their communities. These experiences often involved using their business or human relations skills to help others whose lives differed significantly from those of the participants. Interaction with diverse others contributed to the conditions for self-authorship to emerge. Participants' personal lives entailed intense relationship development, such as finding life partners, having children, and coping with parental or their own divorces. Thirty-three of the participants married after college; three of those divorced and two remarried. Twenty-five had children during their twenties or early thirties. In addition, six participants encountered major health problems. Responding to and managing these life experiences yielded important insights into the conditions that promote self-authorship.

An observational study provided one more source for exploring conditions that promote self-authorship (Baxter Magolda, 1999). In the interest of directly observing the optimal learning conditions described by longitudinal participants, I observed three semester-length college courses. I chose a large education course for first- and second-year students to observe how self-authorship might be prompted in younger students and two upper-division courses (i.e., zoology and mathematics) to observe how it might be promoted for more advanced students. Attending the course sessions, interviewing the instructors, and interviewing students in the courses confirmed the insights the longitudinal participants shared and yielded more tangible

possibilities for translating their insights to educational practice.

All four contexts—college education, graduate or professional education, employment, and community and personal life—not only revealed the conditions that promote self-authorship but also demonstrated how critical achieving self-authorship in one's early to mid-20s is for success in adult life. Minimal self-authorship was often the source of struggle in all these contexts. The stories in this chapter illustrate how educators can help learners successfully resolve these struggles to internally define their belief systems, identities, and relations with others in adult life.

The Learning Partnerships Model

I identified conditions that promote self-authorship from analyzing these multiple contexts and their influence on participants' journeys toward self-authorship (Baxter Magolda, 2001). Despite diversity across contexts, environments that promoted self-authorship consistently operated on *three key assumptions* and *three key principles*. The assumptions modeled the expectation for self-authorship in each developmental dimension, challenging learners to move toward self-authorship. The principles offered the support necessary to do so. The combination of these assumptions and principles forms the Learning Partnerships Model shown in Figure 1.

Learners were exposed to epistemological, intrapersonal, and interpersonal complexity via the three assumptions. First, these environments conveyed *knowledge as complex and socially constructed*. Whether engaged in a course assignment, job responsibility, or volunteer role, participants encountered challenges through multiple interpretations, ambiguity, and the need to negotiate what to believe with others. This complexity modeled the epistemological growth—the capacity to wisely choose from among multiple alternatives—needed for self-authorship. Framing knowledge as complex and socially constructed gave rise to the second assumption—that *self is central to knowledge construction*. Encouragement to define themselves and bring this to their way of learning, work, and relationships emphasized the intrapersonal growth, the internal sense of self, needed for self-authorship. The third assumption evident in these environments was that *authority and expertise were shared in the mutual construction of*

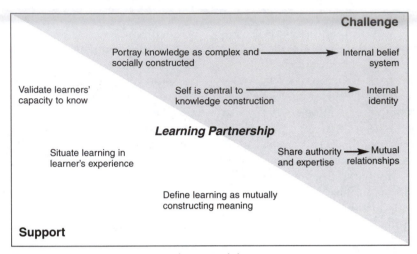

Figure 1 The Learning Partnerships Model

knowledge among peers. The invitation and necessity to participate as equal partners in this mutual construction modeled the interpersonal growth, or the ability to function interdependently with others, needed for self-authorship. These three assumptions were tightly linked in environments that were most effective in promoting self-authorship.

These three assumptions were usually not explicitly stated, however. They were, instead, enacted through the approach educators, employers, or other adults used when interacting with the longitudinal participants. These assumptions complemented *three principles for educational practice* initially identified from the college phase of the study (Baxter Magolda, 1992). These principles were derived from college experiences that longitudinal participants reported as aiding intellectual development and were further supported by the observation study in which the principles' use in college courses promoted students' intellectual development (Baxter Magolda, 1999). Participants' stories in their 20s provide further evidence that these three principles help educators join learners at their current developmental place in the journey and support movement toward self-authorship. These were powerful supports because they modeled and encouraged a blend of connection and autonomy. Thus, the three assumptions challenge learners to journey toward self-authorship, while the three principles bridge the gap between their current developmental place and authoring their own beliefs, identities, and relationships.

The first principle, *validating learners' capacity to know*, was evident in employers' soliciting employees' perspectives and trusting their judgments as well as in educators' interest in learners' experiences and respect for their beliefs. This validation invited participants into the knowledge construction process, conveyed that their ideas were welcome, and offered respect that boosted their confidence in themselves. Soliciting their perspectives reinforced the importance of connection with others' perspectives yet blended it with the autonomy implied in constructing one's own ideas. The second principle, *situating learning in learners' experience,* was evident in educational and employment settings that used participants' existing knowledge and experience as the basis for continued learning and decision making. Participants perceived the use of their current knowledge and experience as a sign of respect (emphasizing connection); it simultaneously gave them a foundation for enhancing their learning or work (the potential for autonomy). The third principle, *mutually constructing meaning*, involved educators or employers connecting their knowledge to that of the participants to arrive at more complex understandings and decisions. This welcomed participants as equal partners in knowledge construction, helped them clarify their own perspectives (emphasizing autonomy), and helped them learn how to negotiate with others (emphasizing connection). The blend of connection and autonomy inherent in mutually constructing meaning supported learners in moving toward the mutuality characteristic of self-authorship.

These three principles promoted self-authorship by modeling it and providing participants the kind of support they needed to shift from external to internal self-definition. Because participants were at varying places along the journey, the company they needed varied accordingly. Situating learning in learners' experience and mutual construction of meaning helped educators and employers connect to and stay in tune with participants' development. Mutual construction helped educators and employers understand participants' journeys. This connection aided but did not overshadow learners taking initiative, learning by doing, and experiencing consequences of their choices to grow toward self-authorship.[1]

The data from which the Learning Partnerships Model were constructed suggest that it is most effective when the assumptions and principles are used intentionally to create learning partnerships. As will be evident in the exemplars that follow, however, the assumptions and principles sometimes occurred naturally. For example, situating learning in learners' experience can be done intentionally, or it can occur by virtue of being directly immersed in what one is learning, as was the case in many employment settings. Similarly the complexity and social construction of knowledge was evident in some contexts regardless of whether educators or employers explicitly emphasized it. Thus, using the Learning Partnership Model intentionally is a matter of capitalizing on the assumptions and principles naturally occurring in a context and building in the others to achieve the combination of challenge and support that the collective set of assumptions and principles provide.

Exemplars: The Learning Partnerships Model in Action

Participants' narratives reveal the nuances of the Learning Partnerships Model in educational, employment, and community life settings. The variations of the model within and across these contexts illustrates that the model's basic assumptions and principles can be used flexibly and creatively rather than prescriptively. Exemplars from the longitudinal participants' graduate education illustrate the nature of learning partnerships in multiple academic disciplines. Undergraduate exemplars reveal that traditional age students are capable of and appreciate participating in learn-ing partnerships. Employment exemplars demonstrate the Learning Partnerships Model in diverse employment contexts and model types of learning partnerships that could be adopted by college educators in both academic and campus employment contexts. Community life exemplars show various forms the Learning Partnerships Model can take in everyday interactions with others and model learning partnerships college educators could translate to college community life, service learning, cultural immersion programs, and study abroad.

Graduate Education Exemplars

After working in business for a year after college, Andrew pursued his MBA. His story recounts numerous aspects of his graduate program that model learning partnerships and how this experience affected him. The three core assumptions are evident in this story about one of his courses:

> In graduate school there was a lot more taking a position and defending it. There were a lot of things where there wasn't exactly a right answer. But you could come up with better answers and explain why you got to them. I had a management class where we were in essence running a business. We ran a simulated airline. There was no one right answer because we had nine groups and nine airlines in the class and all of them chose different philosophies in how they wanted to run their business. And three completely different airlines finished up at the top. In fact, the way our airline did it was different, the teacher said, than any other class had ever done. We just took a completely different approach, yet it was still successful. He even said in the grading of our report that he completely disagreed with it, but it was well argued and reasoned out, and he still gave us an A. I guess I kind of respected that aspect of —you know, "We agree to disagree." I like not always thinking there was one right answer because when you go our and try to deal with a lot of things, there isn't always one right answer. I think too much as an undergraduate we're taught to believe in black and white and there is no gray. And I think there's a lot more gray than there is black and white. (Baxter Magolda, 2001, p. 197)

Rewarding multiple philosophies and approaches to running a successful business conveyed knowledge as complex and socially constructed. Students were encouraged to bring themselves into knowledge construction because the members of the group had to develop and support their approach. Taking and defending a position in the face of no right answer modeled the complexity of knowledge construction. The instructor's respect for Andrew's team, despite his disagreement with their approach, reflected sharing expertise and authority among knowledgeable peers. The instructor validated Andrew and his classmates as knowers by giving them responsibility to seek better answers and support them as well as affirming them for providing reasonable arguments for their stance. Running the simulated airline situated learning in their experience. Doing so as a team reinforced the definition of learning as mutually constructing meaning. Because Andrew had already discovered that gray prevailed over black and white in the business world, he appreciated the opportunity to explore it further in his studies. His economics course provided a similar opportunity:

> We had to pick a topic and kind of take a position—we had to use economic tools, supply and demand charts, and explain why we thought it was correct or incorrect. Which was something I had never done in economics. Someone had to explain why supply side economics would reduce the federal deficit or would not. You had to argue it. And we weren't told what topic to choose—it was our own decision. . . . Defending your point and getting your point across is important. You are presented with a lot—you have to defend your position and why you chose something . . . people asking questions "why?" You have to reason why did something. Every time I do something I think through it a little more. Asking that why question a lot more. (Baxter Magolda, 2001, pp. 197-198)

Again, the complexity and social construction of knowledge was evident in using economic tools to defend multiple positions. Andrew had to bring himself to the task to choose his topic, choose his position, determine how to support it, and ask himself why he believed a particular perspective. This sharing of expertise and authority helped Andrew establish the habit of reasoning in defining his beliefs. He had to make his beliefs his own and defend them with his peers. He was supported in doing so by being validated as a learner and having learning situated in his own experiences.

Sharing expertise and authority among diverse peers added another dimension to Andrew's graduate experience and modeled another component of the Learning Partnerships Model:

> For graduate school, something that added a lot was dealing with the different cultures and the people from different countries and backgrounds. Graduate school was very heterogeneous, very mixed, very unlike my undergraduate. And I think it was much better just because of that. You had people who came from different backgrounds with different opinions. And I think when you're put in a class where too many are exactly the same, a lot of things are not brought out just because you don't have anybody that's being a devil's advocate. I think a little bit of antagonism is good for learning because it forces you to think why you believe what believe and all that. It's not just a bunch of robots taking stuff in. (Baxter Magolda, 2001, p. 200)

This mutual construction of knowledge, even if it seemed somewhat antagonistic, forced Andrew to clarify why he held his beliefs. It also caused him to question perspectives he had accepted earlier without exploration:

> I mean, just a lot of things we're taught in business are from an American perspective and American approach. Well, that's not necessarily the best and most correct way. In fact, at least in the manufacturing environment, we're getting our rear ends kicked. The Japanese have a much better approach that seems to be working. They challenged a lot of what we took as standard. They even argued with some of the financial theories, which supposedly aren't one of the things that you debate. But it was really good. We had people from communist countries that just had a very different perspective. And a lot of what they said made sense from the type of situations they were dealing with. (Baxter Magolda, 2001, p. 200)

Andrew's openness to questioning the "standard" approach reflected growth on all three dimensions of development. As he gained experience in constructing and defending his own beliefs, he gained epistemological complexity. Learning to value diverse perspective, whether from classmates taking a different approach to business or from classmates from different cultural contexts, helped Andrew achieve interpersonal complexity, or the ability to meaningfully consider and appreciate others' perspectives.

Being consistently asked to decide for himself and learning to connect to others and to his own internal belief system also led to intrapersonal complexity. Although it is certainly possible that Andrew's year of work experience contributed to this growth, he linked specific aspects of his graduate program to his growth toward self-authorship.

Alice pursued a master's in counseling immediately following her college graduation. Although her program differed greatly from Andrew's, it offered another examplar of the Learning Partnerships Model. She described it like this:

> We did a lot of videotaping and audio taping that were reviewed with the professor and kind of critiqued with different counseling styles. And I thought that was real helpful. I guess just memorizing the concepts and writing them down is one thing, but then practicing them is a whole different ball game. And it helped me to find our which styles felt more natural for me, and it has kind of helped me evolve into what theoretical background that I adhere most strongly to. By doing it some of them really feel better, seem to fit better than others. And the actual doing them on tape really helped in that process, I think. (Baxter Magolda, 2001, p. 208)

Being new at counseling, Alice found learning situated in her own experience very helpful. Practicing counseling styles helped her meet the challenge her professors presented to construct her own theoretical framework. She explained this further:

> We, you read all these hundreds of different counseling theories and it's just real overwhelming and confusing. They tell you that they want you to work with it and develop your own—not that you have to pick one theory and say, "I'm this," and never do anything else. But they kind of want you to have in the back of your mind that you should be trying to evolve and select one that you feel is going to work best for your. You know, just try them on and see which ones fit your own personal philosophy and things like that. And by actually doing them and seeing them on tape, that helped me to do that process. (Baxter Magolda, 2001, pp. 208–209)

The challenge to develop her own theoretical foundation, one that is consistent with her own personal philosophy, was a more difficult task than Alice had been accustomed to as an undergraduate. Professors in her counseling program portrayed knowledge as complex and socially constructed. Further, it was clear that she was responsible for constructing her counseling knowledge in a way that fit her as a person. She learned more about the challenge of self as central to knowledge construction, as she reported here:

> The hands-on experience through my practicum and internship has made me realize nobody else is in this room with me when I'm doing this counseling session. And so, for me to be clear on these issues, I need to figure them out for myself. Not to say that I'm ever going to figure them out, but to know where I stand on them and to think them through. And I think that's kind of encouraged that process. It's you and your client sitting there. I feel like if I'm not sure where I stand or I'm not clear on what the issues are and what the arguments are both ways and process that myself, then I don't see how I can be of any help at all to this client. So I think that's really encouraged me to do that. (Baxter Magolda, 2001, p. 209)

Learning situated in her experience brought home the realization that it was just she and her client in the counseling relationship. She realized the necessity to work out her own stance, tentative as it must be because of the multitude of counseling theories and clients' diverse therapeutic needs. The process of practicing and mutually constructing knowledge with her instructors and supervisors supported her meeting this challenge. Validation as a learner led her to see herself as capable of constructing her own counseling style. She shared her sense of the outcome:

> I think that I'm more independent. I'm more of a self-thinker, if that makes sense. I'm questioning things more, and I'm not taking—just because I take notes and then that's the way it is and that's all that's been written and that's law. I'm finding that I'm really questioning things and issues. Like with the dual diagnosis. I'm really sorting stuff out for myself instead of just taking notes about everybody else's opinion. In what way I think I'm a lot different. (Baxter, Magolda, 2001, p. 210)

As a self-thinker, Alice established her own beliefs internally in the context of others' opinions and available knowledge, blending autonomy and connection. She had gained the intrapersonal confidence through establishing her own internal identity as a counselor to sort perspectives out for herself. Although she did not speak directly to interpersonal complexity, her growth on the epistemological and intrapersonal dimensions suggests that she could maintain her own identity and beliefs in mutual relations with others.

Undergraduate Education Exemplars

A few longitudinal participants described conditions that promoted self-authorship during their undergraduate experience. More substantive examples, however, are available from the course observation study with its combination of observational and interview data (Baxter Magolda, 1999). The zoology course Erica spoke of at the outset of this chapter modeled learning partnerships because of Professor Snowden's emphasis on integrating multiple disciplinary perspectives, recognizing that facts are tentative and subject to revision, and engaging students in thinking like scientists. This emphasis on the complexity and social construction of knowledge was apparent to Rich, a student in the course:

> The whole focus of most of my classes in college have been just regurgitating the facts, with the exception of a few like Winter Biology where the base facts were given to you on the ground level and where the actual learning was coming in above and beyond that. The learning was coming in where he would ask, "What do you think about this?" and you couldn't just look on your notes, you couldn't just remember what he said. It is not just blatant memorization; learning comes into it when you are utilizing the ideas towards something new that hasn't been done. That kind of set-up seems to stimulate me more than just being like a computer and storing this information to really do nothing with. This class gave more interest into the applications, what is going on right now, ideas of it, theories on what they don't know. The other classes it was "here is what we know and you have to know it too." There wasn't any fairly mutual exchange between the instructor and the class, no formulations of ideas beyond. (Baxter Magolda, 1999, p. 122)

Rich had lost interest in storing facts like a computer and regurgitating them on command. He preferred to use the facts as a foundation for exploring and constructing new knowledge. He elaborated on the mutual exchange between the instructor and the class that was absent in his other classes:

> [The lecture] has got to have structure because everybody is not on the same level. And it's got to have a mediator that can guide the group idea in the right direction and that lets certain instances of false knowledge kind of seep into the fact and encourage the idea to come out—but if it is wrong, fine, subtlety set is aside so it doesn't get into the collective. It takes some serious skills dealing with people, their collective knowledge. It is the best way to utilize other students' knowledge at least for me. There is a fine line—if I say something that is fundamentally wrong, you have to isolate that response as an instructor and figure out why that student came to that conclusion instead of being like, "No that is the wrong answer." Chris [Professor Snowden] would find out why that came about and steer it over to the rest of the idea; "Okay that is not quite right, but how did you get there? Is this how you got there?" That is what I mean by subtly bringing it back or saying that I would not be wrong if I came out and said something. (Baxter Magolda, 1999, p. 126)

These comments are Rich's interpretation of the class interactions that took place. Professor Snowden routinely engaged students in thinking with him about data and possible interpretations. As Rich reported, Professor Snowden respectfully pursued the source of students' contributions and mutually constructed meaning with them in ways that helped them correct faulty assumptions. Professor Snowden modeled epistemological complexity by noting that scientific knowledge construction is fraught with assumptions that must be pursued to determine the most reasonable interpretation. Inviting students into this process of analysis situated learning in their experience, validated them as capable of constructing knowledge, and taught them how to mutually construct meaning with others. Professor Snowden also modeled the core assumption that one brings oneself to the process of deciding what to believe.

In addition to modeling the core assumptions and principles through lecture and classroom interaction, Professor Snowden did so through the assignments. Students read primary literature on a topic of their choice and presented their findings to the class to simulate scientific conference presentations. They were also asked to write a grant proposal to seek funding for the research questions they had generated. Jill shared thoughts regarding the overall nature of the course and these assignments:

> There are some things that are left in the air but I think that is in a good sense. There are things that we don't quite understand yet, that would lend to grant proposals that would lend to further research. I think that is the key in science; you have to have questions to move further in science. It is the whole idea that science is futuristic, you are coming up with new ideas, you want to invent new things, you need to utilize other research to come up with your own. I think he sparks questions and I think that is what science is about—questioning things, pulling things together from different sources (that is what research is), everything that has been done in science, you take something that someone else has learned and you say I have an idea, this work proves this side of my project. I just did a report on cancer and cancer of the kidney. First someone develops an idea that it is the cortex and then someone realizes that it is in the tubules that run through the cortex, and even portions outside of the cortex, and then someone takes the ideas of these portions and say I discovered it looks like these type of cells, so that limits it to just the tubules that run in the tubules. I think you have to learn from what other people have done and apply it and ask questions and that is how you move forward and make discoveries. I think by asking questions constantly you come up with ideas for research and new discoveries. (Baxter Magolda, 1999, p. 120)

Jill, too, recognized the complexity and social construction of knowledge in the constant use of questions to lead to new discoveries. She accepted that some things are always uncertain in scientific work. She also recognized how various discoveries are coordinated to lead to future questions, an example of sharing expertise and authority among members of the scientific community in knowledge construction. The assumption of self as central was evident to her as well, as revealed in these comments:

> His point was he wanted us to learn how to be scientists. I just realized that by making us write this grant proposal, we have to put what we have learned—our topic, our seminar—into a question and be a scientist about

it and make a revelation. I have been sitting here talking about how science is moving forward and asking questions and that is exactly what we are doing by writing the grant proposal. That is why it is so scary, that is what science is about and if you can't do it and you can't write a proposal than maybe you shouldn't be in science. But I think the key to really being a scientist is to not just follow what other people are saying about their discoveries but to go out on your own. I think he is doing that. (Baxter Magolda, 1999, p. 130)

Although Jill was not totally confident going out on her own with discoveries, she recognized the challenge of acknowledging her own central role in constructing scientific knowledge. She felt validated by Professor Snowden's trusting that students could generate their own questions and write grant proposals. Having these experiences situated learning in her own experience and engaged her in mutually constructing knowledge with others.

In an end-of-semester interview, Professor Snowden shared his sense of the grant proposal assignment:

> The purpose of the proposal was accomplished in the sense that they [students] have a better idea now what it means to do primary research and how it is reported. Some of the things one has to think about if you are going to continue work—what it would take to write a proposal, how hard it is to define a question. Maybe a lot of what they got out of this isn't going to show up as a high quality proposal on a piece of paper and that's okay. Because in some ways they weren't ever in a position to do this and of course they found it extremely difficult, because it is extremely difficult. (Baxter Magolda, 1999, p. 133)

Professor Snowden's reflection revealed that he used the grant proposal as a process for exposing students to the nature of scientific research. Despite the fact that they had insufficient time and experience to produce a high-quality proposal, his goal of having students understand the complexity of defining questions was met. In the process, the three core assumptions and three principles were clearly evident.

This zoology course helped students learn to think scientists. They learned how to critique primary scientific literature, identify the next step in research, prepare a professional presentation, and write a grant proposal (the learning goals specified on the syllabus). More important, they learned how to think about and interpret scientific data and construct new knowledge. Thus, the learning goals of the course were met simultaneously with promoting self-authorship. Most students in the class reported that they were actively involved in the course and were able to envision their future role in science. The course promoted their ability to internally define scientific beliefs and themselves as scientists. Students in this course were generally open to the challenge for self-authorship because they used ways of knowing at the outset of the class that were not completely dependent on authority for knowledge (Baxter Magolda, 1999).

Similar outcomes occurred in the mathematics course, where students initially used authority-dependent ways of knowing. Melissa's report of her reaction to the course shows that the Learning Partnerships Model is useful for those who have further to travel toward self-authorship:

> With Math, up until now for me, in my own personal experience, there has always been one answer and how you arrive at it. [Sam's] trying to [help us] see that there is more than one possible answer or one possible solution. It gives you an opportunity to be creative and to try things. Sure you may be discouraged at times but I think it is very rewarding when you do come up with something and get excited and a lot of times the ideas just start flowing and you don't want to stop or put it down so it's kind of exciting. (Baxter Magolda, 1999, p. 160)

Although Melissa did not achieve self-authorship at the end of the semester, she was moving in that direction and excited about trying new things in math. Most students reported increased confidence in their ability to understand mathematical structure and generate mathematical ideas. They also succeeded in achieving one of the course goals: developing their personal (as opposed to memorized) understanding of the structure and functioning of mathematics. Most held more complex perspectives about knowledge construction at the end of the course than they did at the beginning (Baxter Magolda, 1999).

The Learning Partnerships Model promoted the journey toward self-authorship in a large education class as well. At the outset of this course, the majority of students used transitional knowing—the belief that while some knowledge

is certain, other knowledge is not yet known (Baxter Magolda, 1992). The goals of the course included learning to interpret, critique, and judge educational practices. The objectives of *recognizing* positions in educational discourse and *interpreting* educational practices as they related to the purpose of schooling required that students value their own perspectives or have a "mind of their own." Cheryl described coming to value her perspective in the course:

> I feel more like a part of this class. I feel less than the professor in a lecture where he is telling you his knowledge. I feel equal in this class because it is based on my experience. The students and teacher share experiences. I have something to contribute. I am usually quiet and don't speak in class. I feel like I can in here. (Baxter Magolda, 1999, p. 196)

Cheryl also reported that sharing her perspective prompted more internal self-evaluation and questioning. She noted that her family offered what she called a "one-way" background and that the class introduced her to alternative ways to think.

Critiquing positions in educational discourse and *evaluating* educational practices required going beyond an awareness of new perspectives. Elaine, who on a questionnaire at the outset of the course expressed interest only in students explaining material to each other, said in her interview at the end of the course that she was learning to critique:

> Hearing opinions is important to deciding my own. I read, take my opinions, ideas that have been put forth, look further into it, compare to my ideas, and think about what we should do. I combine different things, get the main idea, compare it to my idea. I became a better person by changing my views as I learn about others' experiences. (Baxter Magolda, 1999, p. 197)

Elaine's more recent view assigned greater value to what her peers think, and their views sometimes affected hers in a positive way. Elaine said that she had learned to critically analyze through the assignments and felt that the course offered a chance to evaluate her opinions.

Judging educational practice and *defending* positions in educational discourse required taking a stance on what information and beliefs to endorse. Hugh was confident that he could judge educational practices on the basis of the course, saying.

I think I can make judgments about educational practice. I will be able to make judgments in the classroom setting. This class has helped me by giving me different ways of seeing things and thinking about things. My judgments will be my own; not other people who told you you should think or do this. I appreciate this. I try to make decisions that say I've examined this situation and from past experience and what I've learned—what is the best way to handle this? (Baxter Magolda, 1999, p. 198)

These comments are an indication of contextual knowing in which one decides on the basis of appropriate evidence that particular approaches are better than others, thus representing a shift from Hugh's valuing all opinions equally at the outset of the course to deciding what he believed at the end of the course. Hugh thought that his classmates had helped him decide on a viewpoint and that the instructor had allowed him to make his own judgments. These stories reinforce the value of learning partnerships for helping students move toward self-authorship.

The next story illustrates that the Learning Partnerships Model can be effectively implemented early in college. A college sophomore participating in a panel on productive learning experiences shared this story about her first year in college:

Good Evening, My name is Erin and I am a sophomore at IUPUI. I am majoring in Social Studies Secondary Education. It was my first day in college, my first course, I was terrified. I was in a room full of people I did not know. The professor walks in wearing a sweater that says "Question Authority." I was somewhat shocked; coming from a small private school I was not expecting that to be the teacher's first statement. I was overwhelmed as he began to go over the syllabus. I just knew that I was doomed. Would college really kill me? I can remember asking myself that question as I slouched into my couch that night at home; little did I know that the next semester would hold the answer to my question. This particular professor's course would change my outlook on college and learning in general. Presenting new and thought-provoking information, creating an understanding atmosphere, and by altering the class routine this professor gave me the opportunity to gain a new perspective on learning and interpreting information.

The professor would present thought-provoking information, most of which was new to me. He went about telling the story or giving the facts without drawing conclusions. This gave me the opportunity to come to my own conclusions about the situations that he presented. My entire educational background to that point told me exactly what to think but now I had the opportunity to decide for myself. At first I looked for clues from the professor so I would know the "right" way to think, but he was very good at hiding and disguising his personal beliefs. Because I was not directed by the professor I became eager to find information on my own. I wanted to read the class text and even searched for articles that addressed our topics outside of the classroom.

The atmosphere created inside his classroom was one of understanding. Dividing the class into small groups the professor would initiate discussions. The small groups helped break down some of the barriers such as not knowing others in the class and allowed everyone to participate without feeling threatened. I was timid at first and I remember being reluctant to talk about my ideas and interpretations, but I quickly warmed up to group discussions. I found myself openly expressing my opinions. I always felt that my opinions were respected, not only by my classmates but also the professor. The lines of communication were always open between students and the professor. He seemed to enjoy our input and when we had error in our line of thought he never talked down to us. Through the discussions I gained new ideas and perspectives from other students. I began to have the ability to see issues from all sides of the argument. This not only helped in the classroom setting but in all other aspects of my life.

The class structure would vary. There were times when the professor would lecture and on other days our group discussions filled the entire class session. This continual change kept my interest. I looked forward to going to his class. I wanted to know what type of new and controversial information he would present and what my classmates and I would discuss.

I am thankful that I enrolled in this class my first semester even though it was not recommended. It didn't kill me but much rather made me a more responsible student. I walked away at the end of the semester with a new attitude toward learning. I no longer take things as I hear them but I compile information from many sources to evaluate them in order to apply them to my life. Because of the thoughtful information, the open atmosphere, and stylistic changes in the class structure I was able to gain a new perspective on learning. I learned to question authority. (Hillenburg, 2002)

Erin encountered knowledge as complex and socially constructed through her instructor's approach to teaching. She was invited to bring her own mind and opinions to the class and felt respected as thinker even when she and her peers had error in their thinking. The instructor organized the course in ways that invited Erin and her peers to mutually construct knowledge. Because the instructor invited and supported her in exploring ideas, learning excited Erin. Connection with her instructor and peers made questioning authority possible and educational. Her ability to question authority at the end of her first year suggests that the Learning Partnerships Model can be useful early in college with students who have not previously experienced questioning authority as a component of learning.

Employment Setting Exemplars

The components of the Learning Partnerships Model were evident, although not usually an explicit part of the culture, in employment settings. Employers were most likely interested in maximizing employee performance to achieve success relevant to the work setting. However, in their desire to maximize employee performance or perhaps in conveying the nature of their work settings, many employers provided the conditions to promote self-authorship.

Even in highly technical fields, ambiguity, complexity, and social construction of knowledge were common. Ned accepted a position selling paper chemicals on completing his paper science degree. His job involved analyzing extensive technical data to make decisions to address complex problems occurring at the paper mill that had contracted for his services. He explained,

> There are probably several hundred people working at a mill, making thousands of tons of paper a day using millions of gallons of water. So within that system there are many things that can go wrong on a day-to-day basis. So when I go into a mill, I never know what to expect. I start with a process engineer, and say, "What are the problems that you're encountering? Then the problem-solv-

ing process starts really by asking lots of questions and just getting the feel for what their process is like. A lot of it is by drawing simple diagrams at first and just getting comfortable with "What are they doing from start to finish there?" From that point I have to, on a rough scale, judge whether we can make a change or not with my chemicals. (Baxter Magolda, 2001, p. 246)

Ned had to understand the complexity of the mill operations before he could even offer a preliminary judgment about whether his chemicals would benefit the mill. This preliminary judgment was made in the context of his experience learning that particular mill's operation. If he judged that his chemicals might help, he then conducted laboratory tests in the mill to help determine the necessary changes. But the testing did not resolve the complexity. As Ned explained, "This test by itself might be extremely complex and require a lot of interpretation because they're not always exact science." The interpretation led to physically testing potential changes by using the new chemicals in the papermaking system and gathering data about the process for a week. This data served as the foundation for Ned's recommendations to the mill:

> I am responsible for deciphering—based on everything I know about the mill, all our tests that we did in the lab, based on the objections or problems the mill might have or the mill's limitations—take the data that we recorded as assimilate all that to say, "Did it work or not?" And it's not always easy to say that it did work. A lot of it is textbook kind of work—there's a certain way of running laboratory tests. But there's also a knowledge base back-ground for knowing "How do these classes of chemicals fit into this kind of paper making and how are they going to affect what happens at the end of the machine?" You read a couple of lines in a book saying this class of polymers should do this, but it never happens that way and there's always some good reasons why it doesn't. If you've seen the reasons enough times in different applications or different situations, you're going to be alerted or aware of the potential problems before they occur or look for those opportunities when they're there. (Baxter Magolda, 2001, pp. 246–247)

Conducting laboratory tests and then physically inserting the chemicals into the paper machine further situated learning in Ned's experience. He used previous experience o analyze and interpret the tests and outcomes. His experiences, framed in a context where knowledge was complex and socially constructed, enhanced his judgment. He was responsible for conducting the tests, interpreting them, and making his own judgment, illustrating the challenge of making self central to knowledge construction. Ned also mutually constructed these interpretations with others, including his supervisor and employees at the mill. Ned's experience eventually led him to develop what he called a framework for problem solving and decision making. Developing this framework was part of the self-authorship required of employees to effectively deal with the complexity of their work. Ned found the framework useful in the challenge of bringing self to knowledge construction. He shared,

> I'm acting more like myself. The more I like the job, the more my customers like me and want to do business with me. I'm developing my own style. You might have the title of whatever—there's this preconceived image of what that person should do. After a few years doing it, you realize you aren't that stereotype and are more successful if you don't act that way. Self-actualization, self-confidence—maybe that's it. Coming out of school I was worried about what people thought of me, how would I make the best impression. In retrospect, you say be yourself, you can be more motivated and do the best job. People judging you hopefully aren't so self absorbed that if you aren't identical to them its okay; hopefully they judge you on results. You figure out the stereotype is wrong but play that role until you change it. (Baxter Magolda, 2001, p. 257)

Ned's story illustrates movement toward self-authorship on all three dimensions. He became increasingly comfortable with the complexity of knowledge construction and adept at bringing his own experience to bear on decisions. His success led him to value his own style (i.e., intrapersonal complexity) and to be less concerned over what others thought of him (i.e., interpersonal complexity).

Complexity and social construction of knowledge were also prevalent in fields that combined artistic and technical skills. Dawn's experience in the restaurant business exemplified the Learning Partnerships Model in action. She reported,

> I'm one of the line cooks. I'm working with a certified chef—a brilliant woman—food is

second nature to her. When you are cooking food, it's easiest to just watch. I've learned so much in five months that I never knew before. I pick up things in conversation, but the easiest way to pick up this skills is to watch someone who knows how to do it. Also experimentation—make this, taste it, have chef taste it, and she knows what to do with it. I thought of myself as one who learns by doing or watching rather than actively pursuing knowledge by questioning. I notice now that I ask questions. There is wealth of information at my fingertips and I want to learn as much as I can while I have this opportunity. I never had a job like this—outside of theater—where I can actively pursue an art or craft. Acting is more of an exploratory thing—no right and wrong. That is true to some extent of culinary arts. But there are rights and wrongs—4 tablespoons rather than 2. But you taste, create, explore putting flavors together to come up with a final product that you present. It is experimentation like in theater. It is set up very much like theater is set up—work with a group of people, creating a product, give it out to the masses. Every night we look at elements we have, and we have to make something. The job appeals to my frame of mind. (Baxter Magolda, 2001, pp. 244-245)

Cooking in this setting centered on a combination of knowledge and experimentation to create flavorful foods, reflecting the social construction of knowledge. Engaging in this experimentation situated learning in Dawn's experience. Sharing expertise and authority were evidence in the openness to questions and she and the chef tasting food to determine the next step. The chef validated Dawn as a contributor rather than asking her to follow a recipe. Dawn's experience of creating something with her colleagues in the theater made her appreciate the mutual construction taking place in the kitchen. Her acting experience clearly reflected the notion of self as central to constructing characters, as she reported:

> I have had opportunities to play more than one type of character. The thing that's involved in that is exploring different parts of yourself, learning about how many different types of people you are within yourself and being take to apply that to a script that someone has written. And along with your imagination, you create these different personas. As far as the character aspect—I think there's a lot of self-learning

that goes on continually. And that's one of the things that I think that always fascinates me about this business is you never stand still. You're always progressing; you're always moving forward, learning new things about yourself, learning new ways to present you ideas to a group of people. Then that kind of melts into your technique. Oftentimes you have to get to a certain emotional level that you can't just create. So there's a process that you have to go through, self-disclosure, to some extent. You combine yourself with what you're given, what you interpret about a character. The technique comes in as transferring all that is within you to this character, your abilities to speak the character's truth from probably, your truth. There are a lot of techniques in acting that not everybody an use. You pick and choose the ones that are right for you. (Baxter Magolda, 2001, p. 151)

Dawn's description of creating the truth of a character revolves around making herself central to the task of knowledge construction. The multitude of techniques available reflected the complexity and social construction of knowledge; actors and directors shared authority and expertise. Thus, Dawn encountered conditions to promote self-authorship in both her acting and her cooking contexts, contributing to her self-authorship.

Barb, a new attorney, encountered learning partnerships in her law practice. She described translating her law school education into practice:

People are understanding. They know we are just starting out. They give samples and point you in the right direction to get started. With corporate work, I like it because it is new. You are drafting things you have no idea how to do, so you use samples. A lot of times, I'll be confident enough to know it is common sense. If there is no sample, I have friends that have worked on it so I ask them. Or look it up in reference books. Confidence is key. There is no right answer; with law you can argue both sides. You have to state your position with authority so people perceive you as knowing what you are talking about, to put clients at ease. Sometimes I tell clients both sides, but then you say which way we should go. This is all new; you don't learn everything in law school. Practicing law is doing it off-the cuff; I have no idea how to wing it. (Baxter Magolda, 2001, p. 245).

Complexity and social construction of knowledge permeated Barb's work, as is evident in her statement that no right answer exists. She was responsible for using her resources, both written and human, to craft arguments for both sides and choose one to recommend to her clients. She relied in part on her own training and common sense and in part on mutual construction with her colleagues. Practicing law was clearly situated in her experience, and her colleagues were willing to construct arguments with her knowing she was new at corporate law.

These stories, and many others like them, demonstrate that diverse employment setting required self-authored employees. Regardless of context, these work settings required employees to be able to analyze situations, use appropriate data, interpret it effectively, develop solutions to problems, and produce some type of product. Employers required employees to use the expertise of those around them yet also required them to develop and use their own expertise. Although degrees of support varied widely, very few of the longitudinal participants found themselves in work settings that did not demand self-authorship.

Community Life Exemplars

Similar to employment contexts, longitudinal participants' community life experiences were not intentionally structured to promote self-authorship. The conditions for promoting self-authorship were present, however, in many contexts in which participants chose to engage. One such context was Lydia's choice to live abroad for 2 years. She reported,

It has made me more independent of what I know—more willing to try new experiences and not be so hesitant about it. I was so shy when I started college; not anymore! Because if there is one thing that living in an area that is not yours teaches you, it is that you have to get out there and speak up for what you believe in and what is right. To not let others roll you over to their ideas and roll you over to their ways. (Baxter Magolda, 2001, pp. 289–290)

Living in another country challenged Lydia to express herself and her beliefs. Although she expressed not letting others "roll her over," her openness to new experience led to reinventing who she was:

It was a fabulous experience. I did things I never would have thought I would do. It makes you feel small; there are so many other people out there! If you have experienced this much, how much more is out there? I have a thirst for more. If you stay in the same place, you get in a rut. It is so exciting! You don't know what you are capable of; you reinvent yourself as you gain new experiences. We had earthquakes; we got used to it. We had [electrical] power-sharing there. There were 6 months when between two and four hours a day you had no power. It is fun to teach when the power goes out; 85 degrees—it gets overwhelming. It got to be a joke. Everybody accepted it. Here, the power goes out and people are beside themselves. I learned to be more flexible. When you experience other things and see other people deal with things, it puts your life into perspective. The more people you know and more experiences you hear about, you get stronger. I am a strong person now; we move and redo everything. I'm fortunate; I've stumbled onto things. I'm like a cat; land on my feet. Life is too short to be bothered by little things like moving and being uprooted from job and friends. There are other jobs and friends. (Baxter Magolda, 2001, p. 290)

New experiences to use to put her life into perspective introduced Lydia to multiple ways of living. Interacting with people who responded to life differently than she had been accustomed to doing helped Lydia reinvent herself. Her story reveals that she realized that she played a central role in constructing her view of life yet openly entertained others' ideas through mutual construction of knowledge. She reported gaining strength, flexibility, and security through this process. Regarding being uprooted from a job and friends as "little things" suggests that Lydia internally defines her beliefs, identity, and relations with others such that external changes do not shake her foundation.

Anita chose to volunteer after college in both a Big Sister program and a switchboard for runaways. Her story illustrates that learning partnerships were present in both these contexts:

The little girl I have is 9. She has very difficult problems. She was taken away from her mother, who has AIDs. The chances of her going home are nil, but she doesn't know it. We went out for her birthday and she picked out some clothes. When I took them over, she didn't want to see me, she just wanted the gift.

Her therapist said I should tell her how I felt, so I did. It went over poorly, she got angry, and now she doesn't want to see me. I also work for the national runaway switchboard. On the switchboard, you have to let them figure things out for themselves; try to turn the conversation around to steer them in a direction without giving them an answer. I'm getting used to not knowing at the switchboard. Nothing you can say is wrong, as long as you are trying to help. The same call could be handled differently by different people. Like with my little sis, I feel like I shouldn't have brought it up, but others said I had to do it. I'm learning to let things go. I'm better at realizing and admitting when I've made mistakes. I'm more humble. Sometimes I hear other calls and I wouldn't have done something that way. I'm trying to figure out for myself if I have the right to an opinion. Like if someone hits them, I have a hard time saying it is wrong. It can lead to an arrest, and make a bigger mess. I have a hard time being as directive as I should. I have to figure out for myself what my own beliefs are. I do have the right to an opinion. I know molestation is wrong, but what will life be like if I make the call? (Baxter Magolda, 2001, p. 298)

Anita's struggles with her little sister and the callers to the switchboard stemmed from the complexity of making sense out of the events that were reported and deciding how to respond. There were no sure answers or no proven solutions to these complex situations. Anita mutually constructed knowledge with others in these settings yet worked hard at defining her own beliefs. Mutual construction was also expected in how she dealt with callers: she was to guide them yet let them figure things out for themselves. Learning was clearly situated in Anita's experience, and others validated her as capable in these contexts. Anita was still struggling at the time of this story to sort out her own beliefs in the face of the serious consequences of her actions for others.

The Learning Partnerships Model's Potential for Transforming Higher Education

Following learners longitudinally from their college entrance to their mid-30s provided extensive interview data from which to conceptualize the Learning Partnerships Model. The observation study contributed to conceptualizing the model through observing learning partnerships in action in various disciplines. Interviewing learners about how these learning partnerships affected them augmented the outcome data emerging from the longitudinal study. The assumptions and principles that constitute the Learning Partnerships Model are consistent with scholarship on how to promote student development and learning. They are also inherent in scholars' descriptions of culturally inclusive pedagogy. As a result, the model holds substantial promise for transforming higher education to promote self-authorship during college.

The chapters in part 2 of this book reveal that potential by reporting specific uses of the Learning Partnerships Model in multiple contexts. Each chapter describes the implementation of the model in detail and the particular goals it is designed to achieve. Use of the model in these diverse contexts illustrates its flexibility to blend with other models and particular practice goals. Because the Learning Partnerships Model consists of a set of assumptions and principles to shape practice, it is intended to be used creatively rather than prescriptively. The authors report assessment data to indicate the model's effectiveness in promoting self-authorship in their particular contexts, adding to the growing data

that support the model. We invite you to reflect on your own educational practice as you explore these exemplars.

References

Baxter Magolda, M. B. (1992). *Knowing and reasoning in college: Gender-related patterns in students' intellectual development*. San Francisco: Jossey-Bass.

Baxter Magolda, M. B. (1999). *Creating contexts for learning and self-authorship: Constructive-developmental pedagogy*. Nashville: Vanderbilt University Press.

Baxter Magolda, M. B. (2001). *Making their own way: Narratives for transforming higher education to promote self-development*. Sterling, VA: Stylus.

Belenky, M., Clinchy, B. M., Goldberger, N., & Tarule, J. (1986). *Women's ways of knowing: The development of self, voice, and mind*. New York: Basic Books.

Hillenburg, E. (2002, November). *Response to transforming pedagogy to transform learning*. Paper presented at the Association of American Colleges and Universities Faculty Work and Student Learning Conference, Indianapolis.

Perry, W. G. (1970). *Forms of intellectual and ethical development in the college years: A scheme*. Troy, MO: Holt, Rinehart and Winston.

Piaget, J. (1950). *The psychology of intelligence* (M. Piercy and D. Berlyne, Trans.). London: Routledge & Kegan Paul.

CHAPTER 45

A DEVELOPMENTAL PERSPECTIVE ON LEARNING

PATRICIA M. KING AND MARCIA B. BAXTER MAGOLDA

Viewing the cognitive and affective dimensions of development as related parts of one process, we advance an integrated perspective on learning and personal development. From this integrated perspective, a successful educational experience simultaneously increases cognitive understanding and sense of self, personal maturity, and interpersonal effectiveness.

The Student Learning Imperative (SLI) (American College Personnel Association [ACPA], 1994) was written to spark discussion of "how student affairs professionals can intentionally create the conditions that enhance student learning and personal development" (p. 1); it is a call to transform student affairs practice to promote student learning and personal development. Although the terms *student learning* and *personal development* have different historical roots and focus on different aspects of the educational process, they are described in the *SLI* as "inextricably intertwined and inseparable" (p. 1). In this paper, we elaborate on this assertion and argue for an integrated view of learning and personal development. From this integrated perspective, the cognitive and affective dimensions are seen as parts of one process; dimensions as seemingly distinct as knowledge construction, meaning making, and awareness of self are presumed to be integrated within the developing human being.

The *SLI* argued that the educational experiences offered to college students—including those sponsored by student affairs—should be intentionally grounded in the educational missions of colleges and universities. This grounding requires a clear understanding of these missions and the educational goals they embody, as these are the goals toward which educational efforts should be directed. These efforts include the creation of "educationally purposeful" (Boyer, 1990, p. 9) experiences that should enable students to learn, practice, and develop the attributes of a college-educated person. As listed in the *SLI*, the hallmarks of a collegeeducated person include:

> (a) complex cognitive skills such as reflection and critical thinking; (b) an ability to apply knowledge to practical problems encountered in one's vocation, family, or other areas of life; (c) an understanding and appreciation of human differences; (d) practical competence skills (e.g., decision making, conflict resolution); and (e) a coherent integrated sense of identity, self-esteem, confidence, integrity, aesthetic sensibilities, and civic responsibility. (ACPA, 1994, p. 1)

Although it is helpful to list particular aspects of development for purposes of clarity and specificity, it is important to note that these aspects, too, are inextricably intertwined. For example, a broad understanding and deep appreciation of human differences require a developed sense of empathy and reflective thinking skills. Effective conflict resolution presupposes a degree of self-esteem and, perhaps, civic responsibility that enable the individual to rise to the challenge of a situation in which fair treatment is at issue. The qualities associated with a college-educated person include more than the cognitive ability to engage in critical thinking; they also include such affective attributes as an eagerness to continue to learn, an appreciation of the value of working with diverse others on problems of mutual interest, the will to take personal responsibility for one's views and actions, and the desire to make a positive contribution. From this integrated perspective, a successful educational experience simultaneously increases cognitive understanding and sense of self, personal maturity, and interpersonal effectiveness.

The interrelatedness of different aspects of development has often been observed by those who work closely with children, adolescents, or adults (parents, educators, counselors, social workers) and by those who study developmental phenomena (Belenky, Clinchy, Goldberger, & Tarule, 1986; Fischer, 1980; Kegan, 1994; Kitchener, 1982; Rest, 1986). Nevertheless, whether by language, organizational structure, or just habit, many in higher education continue to separate aspects of development into independent domains without considering the effects of one aspect on the others. For example, effective conflict mediation can require not only a complex understanding of the underlying issues (cognitive complexity), but also the ability to open and continue a dialogue between disputing parties (interpersonal skills) and an understanding of the limits of one's role (personal maturity). The "independent domains" approach ignores the experience of both students and educators who daily witness the overlap between students' ways of thinking about their courses, their personal lives, their career options, and their work settings, and who also witness how the relationships between and across domains change over time. This integration is evident in students' own descriptions of their experiences.

For example, as Dawn reflected on her own growth 4 years after her college graduation (Baxter Magolda, 1994, pp. 15–16), she explained:

> The more you discover about yourself, the more you can become secure with it. And that obviously leads to greater self-confidence because you become comfortable with who you really are. It's just [that] my confidence level is so much better than it ever has been. I'm more willing to express my ideas and take chances expressing my ideas. When you're not as self-confident, you're afraid that people are going to laugh at what you think or you're afraid that they're going to think you're stupid. . . . And I think self-awareness too, because you realize that it doesn't really matter if other people agree with you or not. You can think and formulate ideas for yourself and ultimately that's what's important. You have a mind and you can use it. That's probably the most impor-

tant thing, regardless of the content of what your thoughts and opinions are. It's the fact that you can form an opinion that's more important than the opinion itself. So it's kind of a self-confidence and self-awareness thing.

Dawn's integration of who she is with how she knows is clear in her comments. By contrast, talking about herself during her first year in college (Baxter Magolda, 1987), Dawn offered:

> I prefer to kind of sit back and take everything else in. And if I have questions, I'll ask them. If I have something to say, I'll usually say it, but I like to get an idea of what everybody else is thinking and what's going on. Take everything in, other than just listening to the teacher, taking down what they have to say. Taking in other students' ideas. Just taking it all in as a whole.

Dawn's development is evident in the lack of identity and voice in her first year versus their ascendance and integration 8 years later.

Another student, Ned, described the relationship of self and knowing in the context of his work four years after his college graduation (Baxter Magolda, 1994, pp. 18–19). Describing his job selling chemicals to paper mills, Ned said:

> The thing about paper mills is that they're extremely diverse and complex and unique. There's no one paper mill like the next one. So when I go into a mill I've got a basic set of textbook-type learning situations that I draw from and apply in a specific instance to each day, each application, each paper mill. In 65 or 85 percent of the cases, going into it I don't know what the end result is going to be. And I don't know how to get to the end result. I figure things out as I go along and adapt, change, redefine, until you get to the final conclusion. And you can be smart about it. I can cut down the amount of rework time by approaching it based on other past histories or other experiences that I've had that lead me or lend me a more accurate picture or more accurate hypothesis of what's going to happen. You read a couple of lines in a book saying this class of polymers should do this, but it never happens that way and there's always some good reasons why it doesn't. If you've seen the reasons enough times in different applications or different situations, you're going to be alerted or aware of the potential problems before they occur or look for those opportunities when they're there.

It is clear here that Ned used his own experience and his own sense of authority to make work decisions. This contrasts with his view of how he could know as a sophomore in college (Baxter Magolda, 1987), when he said:

> I find discrepancy between the professor's explanation and the book's description. You have to have an open enough mind to take it in at first and believe it, and then when you get the pieces of information that come in later that you can analyze it in an analytical way without discriminating. And then weigh A, B from what you know. It might not necessarily be the overall best choice, but from what you know you're going to have to decide. Sometimes that can be really confusing, too, because especially at a freshman-sophomore level as I am, I don't know enough about these things I'm reading to really have a masterful view of the big picture. That's why you're going to have to trust the author or whatever, and the inevitable conclusion is that they're going to be close, I think. You're just going to have to live with not knowing until it can be proved one way or the other.

Ned could not see himself as a knowledge constructor here because he lacked the sense of self needed to make his own judgments.

An Integrated View of Learning

This section outlines 4 key elements of an integrated view of learning that we believe can help educators, especially student affairs practitioners, promote student learning and personal development. Each of these is discussed below.

1. *What individuals learn and claim to know is grounded in how they construct their knowledge.*

Learning is defined in many different ways (King, in press), such as the accumulation of facts or the ability to recognize the underlying assumptions, to engage in scientific reasoning, or to invoke different problem-solving strategies for different problems. Each definition reflects a way of organizing what and how people come to know. In this article, we argue for a definition of learning that is broad enough to encompass many aspects of the learning process. Our argument is based on a key insight from the developmental perspective—that people not only *organize* but *reorganize* what and how they know, and that the process of reorganizing affects what and how they learn.

From a developmental perspective, it is assumed that learners actively attempt to interpret or make sense of their experiences. The process whereby people construct their understanding of their experiences (known as "knowledge construction") is challenging and complicated. It involves sorting through some fundamental issues about the nature of knowledge (epistemology): What can I know? How can I know? How should I decide what I believe? How certain can I be about what I claim to know? Just as the dance is inseparable from the dancer, so the known is inextricably connected to the knower—through his or her process of and assumptions about knowing. This is not a new idea: it is a long-established tenet of the constructivist developmental tradition (discussed in print as early as 1897 by Baldwin, 1902) that people actively interpret their life experiences, to make sense of them in an attempt to learn from them. In the preceding example, Ned was using his experience in different situations to determine what he could know and how he could approach a problem at the mill. Further, the way he knew at the mill was very different from the way he knew as a sophomore, reflecting a more complex way of knowing.

2. *How individuals construct knowledge and use their knowledge is closely tied to their sense of self.*

For example, a student who fails to participate in a class discussions or committee meetings may do so for a variety of reasons. She may simply dislike being in the spotlight, but she may also be struggling to define herself as a person with something to contribute. Further, she may also be trying to figure out how her peers, who appear to be no smarter than she is, think they have as much to contribute as the professor or staff member. After all, she reasons, aren't we here to learn from them? Shouldn't we listen more and discuss less? Dawn's earlier comments illustrate this relationship. As a freshman, Dawn described how she would sit back and take in other students' ideas, without a clear sense of her own ideas and her own voice. In the later quote, by contrast, she noted, "You can think and formulate ideas for yourself and ultimately that's what's important. You have a mind and you can use it." This insight represents what Kegan (1994) called an internal identity, which he defined as

> a *self-authorship* that can coordinate, integrate, act upon, or invent values, beliefs, convictions, generalizations, ideals, abstractions, interpersonal loyalties, and intrapersonal states. It is no longer *authored* by them, it *authors them* and thereby achieves a personal authority. (p. 185 [italics in original])

The achievement of self-authorship and personal authority should be heralded as a central purpose of higher education. Both aspects require an informed and refined sense of self.

Another example stems from educators' attempts to give students helpful feedback about their performance. Astute educators vary their feedback, depending not only on the student's cognitive complexity but also on his or her emotional maturity. To learn from this feedback, students need to be able to hear others' suggestions and criticisms from an open, nondefensive posture. This often takes a large measure of personal security and inner strength (and presupposes a willingness to engage in learning). Because a student's sense of self affects all teacher-student interactions, educators must understand the role of support in the developmental process.

3. *The process by which individuals attempt to make meaning of their experiences improves in a developmentally related fashion over time.*

As individuals mature, they become more skilled at completing the various tasks that help them interpret events in their lives, moving from simpler to more complex ways of making meaning. For example, older students with more education are better able to gather information, weigh its relevance, consider competing options with an open mind, come to a personal decision about the question, explain their decision to others, and be willing to reconsider their decision in light of new evidence or means for interpreting the evidence (for a summary of research, see King & Kitchener, 1994). They also become better able to observe and assess their own behavior in different contexts, and identify the factors that led to their competencies, patterns of personal needs, and areas of weakness. The ability to use both relational and impersonal modes of knowing also develops over time. Baxter Magolda (1995) discovered that gender-related patterns evident in the college phase of her (1992) study (knowing through connection or separa-

tion of the knower and the known—relational and impersonal knowing, respectively) converged in the students' postcollege experience as they adopted more complex epistemological assumptions.

It is important to remember that the emergence of these abilities involves a series of incremental and qualitative changes that may at first be irregular, unreliable and unpredictable. Students come to understand the role of evidence in decisionmaking, modes of knowing, and the dynamics of social relations in increasingly complex and comprehensive ways, and changes in students' ways of thinking about these topics often reflect observable developmental patterns. More developmentally advanced organizations reflect an approach to constructing knowledge that encompasses increasingly complex sets of ideas and perspectives (even those once seen as contradictory or incompatible); this approach is necessary for making appropriate decisions about complex issues. For example, members of campus judicial boards must not only consider the facts of each case but also weigh plausible (and sometimes contradictory) explanations, and in making a judgment, concurrently weigh the educational, legal, ethical, and sometimes political considerations. It is important to recognize that these skills are not typical of firstyear college students; rather, they emerge incrementally during the college years, with practice, feedback, and exposure to good role models.

4. *Educators who endorse these principles will use a broad definition of learning that encompasses both cognitive and personal development and that is sensitive to the developmental issues underlying the process of education.*

Developing thinking skills is only one aspect of achieving educational success in college. Although this is a key component in attaining the skills associated with having a college education, it is nevertheless only one part of the picture. For example, effective problem solving requires such attributes as awareness of the problem, the ability to gather and interpret relevant information, a willingness to try overcoming obstacles by making the best decision, and the personal "wherewithall" to implement the desired solution. Skills such as these have been found to influence whether and how people behave morally. For example, in his Four-Component Model of

Morality, Rest (1986, 1994) emphasized that the development of complexity in reasoning about moral issues was only one part of the psychology of morality. The four components (Rest, 1986; 1994) that affect moral behavior are as follows. Component I, *Moral Sensitivity*, refers to an individual's awareness of how his or her actions affect other people; without this awareness, people do not recognize the moral dimension of events. Component II, *Moral Judgment*, refers to the formulation of a plan by which an individual applies a moral standard (e.g., fairness to all parties). Component III, *Moral Motivation*, acknowledges that moral values are often in competition with other values (such as loyalty to friends, need for employment, political sensitivity, professional aspirations, and public relations impact); to behave morally, the individual must give a priority to moral over nonmoral values, to intend to do what is morally right. Component IV, *Moral Character*, refers to factors such as ego strength, perseverance, resoluteness, strength of conviction, and ability to resist distractions and overcome frustrations; to behave morally, the individual must be able to follow through with a moral plan of action. Rest (1986) notes that the psychological processes associated with the components interact and affect each other, and that failure to act morally can result from a deficiency in any one component:

> A person who demonstrates great facility at one process is not necessarily adequate in another. We all know people who can render very sophisticated judgments but who never follow through on any course of action; we know people who have tremendous follow-through and tenacity but whose judgment is simple-minded. In short, the psychology of morality cannot be represented as a single variable or process. (p. 4)

Similarly, the psychology (and sociology) of learning should not be viewed as a single variable or process. Applying the major features of Rest's (1986) model of morality to learning, we note that just as the domain of morality includes more than how one reasons about moral issues, so the domain of learning includes more than critical thinking skills or cognitive complexity (Component II). Although development in complexity of reasoning is an important part of the process of learning, it is not the only part. A broader, more holistic definition of learning would attend to the equivalent of the other three

components as well. For example, do students recognize class assignments or committee tasks as opportunities to learn new skills, to gain valuable experience, or to broaden their understanding? That is, are students sensitive to the educational (learning) purposes inherent within these activities (Component I)? What motivates students to learn? McMillan and Forsyth (1991, p. 50) found that "students are more likely to be motivated if their needs are being met, if they see value in what they are learning, and if they believe that they are able to succeed with reasonable effort." Educators who presume that these factors are in place are disappointed when students appears "unmotivated" or when they do not "live up to their potential" due to the distraction of competing events in their lives (Component III). Do students have the self-discipline to exert the appropriate amount of "time on task," the perseverance to see a problem or project through to completion, and the personal maturity to take responsibility for completing projects in a timely fashion (Component IV)? The affective or personal development dimensions that affect student learning are painfully clear when the answer to questions like these is "no." Using this integrated view of learning in responding to the *SLI*'s call for transformed practice in student affairs involves: heightening students' awareness of the learning dimension of the cocurriculum (Component I); improving their understanding of the skills, strategies, and assumptions underlying the learning process (Component II); developing student affairs practice to match student development needs (Component III); and helping students achieve the maturity necessary for active, life-long learning (Component IV).

Student Affairs Educational Agenda

One of student affairs' strengths is sensitivity to the developmental issues that underlie the process of education. In light of this strength, we advocate that student affairs' primary contribution to the integrated view of learning is to promote the developmental progression described here across both cognitive and affective dimensions within student affairs contexts. Just as our faculty colleagues offer an intentional curriculum, student affairs needs to intentionally identify learning goals, assess students' capabilities related to the goals, offer a developmentally oriented process through which to meet them, provide support to students to meet the goals, and evaluate students' progress on the plan.

Although educators already know a great deal about students' development and how to promote various aspects of it, the task of enhancing development remains a daunting one because students' starting points often differ so sharply from the developmental goals that educators envision. Kegan (1994) addressed this issue in his discussion of the mental demands of modern life. Viewing contemporary culture as a "school" with its own "curriculum," he suggested that the curriculum makes demands on its students that are "over their heads." That is to say, the expectations of contemporary culture require ways of making meaning that are more complex than the meaning-making structures that most young adults hold. A similar situation exists in higher education and student affairs. Educators want students to be reflective thinkers and self-authors of their beliefs, to appreciate human differences, and to act responsibly, based on their construction of their experience. Without sufficient support to meet these demands, however, students can find themselves overwhelmed, or in Kegan's terms, "in over their heads."

King and Kitchener (1994) reported that first-year college students generally were prereflective thinkers who recognized knowledge as uncertain, albeit temporarily. These students were confused about having to make decisions without absolute knowledge as Ned's comments quoted earlier convey. Similarly, Baxter Magolda (1992) noted that most of the first- and second-year students in her study assumed that knowledge is certain (absolute knowing), or realized that some knowledge is uncertain (transitional knowing). Eighty percent of those students as seniors still used transitional knowing, by relying on authorities for knowledge in certain areas and on their own opinions in uncertain areas. Comparably, King and Kitchener (1994) reported that seniors generally exhibited quasi-reflective thinking, a way of making meaning that assumes "many possible answers to every question and no absolutely certain way to adjudicate between competing answers. Individuals with this assumption will therefore argue that knowledge claims are simply idiosyncratic to the individual" (p. 225). These students do not demonstrate reflective thinking in which they can critique their own judgments in relation to alternative judgments. These works suggest that college students are just beginning to construct knowledge for

themselves and express their voices when they graduate. Kegan (1994) estimated that half of the adult population has yet to achieve an internally generated sense of self. In the comments cited earlier, Dawn and Ned indicated that as entering college students, they did not have this internal sense of self or belief in themselves as knowers.

The current challenge, then, is to help students develop ways of making meaning that enable them to meet the expectations necessary to function as effective citizens in today's complex culture and society. Kegan (1994) argued that contemporary culture is good at providing challenge but less effective at providing the necessary support for students who are in over their heads. Kitchener, Lynch, Fischer and Wood (1993) noted that students can use more complex forms of reflective judgment than they typically use when sufficient support is available to help them with the task. Perhaps this explains educators' mixed success in higher education in helping students rebuild their worlds from the initial versions to more complex ones. The challenges are clear, but the intentional support systems to meet the challenges are less clear. Support, according to Kegan, creates

> a holding environment that provides both welcoming acknowledgment to exactly who the person is right now as he or she is, and fosters the person's psychological evolution. As such, a holding environment is a tricky transitional culture, an evolutionary bridge, a context for crossing over. (p. 43)

This evolutionary bridge must be both *meaningful* to the students' current way of making meaning and *facilitative* of a more complex way of making meaning. As Kegan noted, "We cannot simply stand on our favored side of the bridge and worry or fume about the many who have not yet passed over. A bridge must be well anchored on both sides, with as much respect for where it begins as for where it ends" (p. 62). Student affairs educators need to help create these bridges.

Inviting Students to Cross New Bridges

How can student affairs professionals create and sustain support systems—bridges—for students that foster their learning and development? That is, how can students be encouraged to pay closer attention to the ways they make meaning, and to do so in ways that are increasingly comprehensive in scope, depth, and understanding? Kegan (1982) suggested that meaning is made in the space between an event and the person's reaction to it, the space in which the person privately composes and makes sense of the event. This active, individual construction of meaning is affected by individual's epistemic assumptions, previous life experience, and interaction with the environment surrounding the event. Thus, the side of the student's bridge that educators wish to respect and connect to initially is a complex human entity with multiple characteristics. As educators invite students onto and across the bridge, both the invitation and the journey itself will take multiple forms. That is, the dynamic nature of students' meaning making will necessitate a constant dialogue with them so that educators can, first, better understand how students are making meaning in a particular time and context and, second, make better-informed choices about the appropriate forms of invitation. Bridge-building requires mutual reinforcements and a dynamic relationship: students' current meaning making shapes the supports that educators erect, and those supports in turn shape how students continue the process of making meaning in their lives. (For a detailed discussion of ways to foster student learning and development see Baxter Magolda [1992] and King and Kitchener [1994]).

This dynamic relationship makes *assessment and evaluation* a constant feature of the bridge-building process. Student affairs professionals enter the assessment process from an informed vantage point, based on the extensive literature base on student development theory and on their experience working with successive cohorts of students. Educators must also build what Kuh, Whitt, and Shedd (1987, p. 47) have called "minitheories" to understand the development of particular students in particular contexts. The theoretical base offers possibilities for interpreting students' meaning making and provides insights for choosing appropriate questions during interactions with students. Continued dialogue during the bridge-building process provides educators with feedback on the progress, information on what supports are working, and insights into needed adjustments.

Developmental goals grow out of this ongoing, mutual dialogue with students. Student affairs educators enter the dialogue aware of their developmental goals, the anchor for the far side

of the bridge. Their initial assessment identifies the anchor for the beginning side of the bridge, or students' current ways of making meaning. By understanding how development occurs, educators can better identify the nature of the transformations necessary for students to move across the bridge. Then the educators are in a position to talk meaningfully with students about developmental goals that they see as within range of their current perspectives. Developmental goals emerge from mutual identification of reasonable expectations for students given their current ways of making meaning.

Plans to achieve these goals also emerge from the dialogue. Educators who know what students have experienced and how they make sense of events can offer experiences that create reasonable amounts of dissonance. Many of these experiences are a natural part of the college environment, thereby requiring only that educators help students reflect on them. By understanding students' context-specific development, educators can select more effective support systems to use to help students work through the dissonance to make meaning in more complex ways.

The *mutual exchange* inherent in this ongoing dialogue is an evolutionary bridge in and of itself. Students are validated as people who have something valuable to share, thereby supporting their ability to know and express their thoughts. Development is situated in their own experience as goals and plans for achieving them are created in contexts students view as meaningful. The mutual construction of meaning that underlies the dialogue encourages students to view themselves as knowledge constructors and people capable of creating their own values and beliefs. The increasing ability to view oneself in this manner is what eventually leads to an internally defined self that can construct knowledge reflectively.

Bridges to Appreciating Diversity

The particular learning goals of a student affairs division should reflect society's vision of the educated person and the institution's mission. Despite differences across divisions, one common learning goal is developing respect for human diversity. Using this goal, we will demonstrate how an integrated vision of learning affects students' abilities to meet this expectation and will illustrate the process of bridge-building described thus far. (In an actual case, of course, ongoing dialogue with students would be an integral part of the process; the dialogue is missing from this example.)

The educational goal in this example is to replace racism, sexism, and ethnocentrism with an appreciation for racial, gender, and cultural differences. What way of making meaning is required for this learning goal? Kegan (1994) described lack of respect for human diversity in terms of the construction of values and ideals. People construct values and beliefs within the context of their culture and use those constructions to make meaning of others' behavior. When others' behavior violates a person's values or beliefs, the individual tends initially to judge others to be wrong, rather than entertaining the notion that the others have different values and beliefs. To do the latter, Kegan argued that one needs

> a mind that can stand enough apart from its own opinions, values, rules, and definitions to avoid being completely identified with them. It is able to keep from feeling that the whole self has been violated when its opinions, values, rules, or definitions are challenged. (p. 231)

When people are captive to those values and beliefs, as is the case before an internally generated self exists and they believe that knowledge is certain, they cannot reflect such values and beliefs or see them in another way.

Two students' stories illustrate the support systems needed to move toward appreciating diversity. Candace, coming to a 16,000-student institution from her hometown of 200 people, reported being surprised at other students' values. She was surprised that most students she encountered had not even entertained the idea of marriage, whereas most of her high school classmates were already married (Baxter Magolda, 1992). Christine, also from a rural community, expressed surprise upon coming to the same school that other students were not Catholic (Schilling, Schilling, Baxter Magolda, & Morenburg, 1993). Both women noted that they had never met an African American person before coming to college. Like many students who are busy constructing a sense of self early in college (Chickering and Reisser, 1994; Josselson, 1987), Candace and Christine do not yet have the security to avoid feeling violated when their values are threatened. Although

both are interested in others' perspectives, Candace and Christine cannot take internal responsibility for their respective values because they, as Kegan suggested, "construct [their] sense of self in the relationship between [their] own point of view and the other's" (p. 126). Thus, they do not have a way of making meaning to stand apart from their values. They are made up of these values, rather than being generators of their own values. Adding the dimension of young college students' tendency to believing that knowledge is certain (Baxter Magolda, 1992; King and Kitchener, 1994) yields a developmental picture that makes appreciation of diversity difficult.

Although Candace and Christine had a similar lack of exposure to diversity as well as a similar interest in learning more about it, they experienced learning about diversity differently. Candace found herself living with three room-mates who had grown up in cities. She was as shocked at hearing their experiences as they were at hearing hers. Eager to learn more about each other, the room-mates went home with each other early in the first semester. Candace showed her room-mates her small town; her room-mates showed Candace the city. In talking about their experiences, they explored how each had grown up, what the advantages and disadvantages were, and how they felt about all they had seen. Candace found support among her room-mates to explore alternative ways of thinking about herself and relationships with others. Although her parents inquired about her plans for marriage at the end of her first year in college, Candace was able to share her evolving thinking with her parents and gain their support for her new perspectives.

Christine, on the other hand, found herself in a different holding environment. After meeting an African American man at a local bar and having an interesting conversation with him, she gave him her telephone number. Upon sharing the story with her room-mate, the room-mate said, "You wouldn't go out with him, would you?" Christine reported: "I felt I had to say no, because she would think I was stupid. Then my sister (who is an upper-class student here) said you can't; that surprised me too. I felt like I must be prejudiced because I couldn't stick up for dating a black man but I couldn't do it because my family and friends would think badly of me." Unlike Candace, Christine was not supported in exploring her interest in diversity. She reported that her father was very racist, so she just did not talk about the issue at home. Her family's and friends' disapproval reinforced her endorsement of her original cultural values, even though she felt some discomfort with them.

What would an intentional support system—bridge—look like to help these women move toward the goal of respecting diversity? Engaging Candace and Christine in dialogue would reveal all of the information shared here (indeed, both women freely volunteered this information to an unfamiliar interviewer who simply asked them to talk about their experience upon coming to college). The dialogue would also reveal the resources each woman has in her holding environment and the dilemmas each faces in exploring values that differ from family values. One could surmise from Candace's story that she already has support for exploring diversity regarding sex roles and the roles of young adults. Reasonable developmental goals might include helping her extend this exploration to increasing levels of intensity (e.g., race, ethnic diversity) and helping her reflect on her discoveries to determine how she might begin to define internally what she believes. Christine's story reveals a lack of support for exploring diversity, at least at the emotionally charged level of race, indicating that reasonable developmental goals that might emerge from dialogue with Christine would look different. Perhaps they would include creating opportunities for Christine to encounter less threatening levels of diversity (e.g., city lifestyle, personality differences), supporting her in developing an understanding of difference as positive, and helping her work toward relationships that could be sustained despite value differences.

The plans to achieve these respective sets of goals would develop out of the two women's interests and the student affairs educator's resources. Much as an academic advisor steers students toward courses that might further their educational agenda, the student affairs educator would intentionally steer Candace and Christine toward student groups, leadership opportunities, and activities that would promote the developmental goals established with the students. The mutual exchange occurring during this process would contribute to the goals as well. Validating their experiences would increase the probability that Candace and Christine would be willing to examine and then evaluate their perspectives. Consciously reflecting on their experiences would support their efforts at identity development. Mutual construction of meaning with the student affairs educator or others would offer these students experience in sustaining relationships despite value differences.

Conclusion

Students' stories recounted here and elsewhere in the literature support an integrated view of learning in which knowledge construction, meaning making, and awareness of self are intertwined. The developmental dimension of all of these learning components has been articulated in the human development research literature. Student affairs educators have traditionally concentrated their efforts on the identity dimension of students' learning. Less attention has been given to the knowledge construction dimension—or to promoting higher-order reasoning—by faculty or student affairs educators. This disjointed approach has not yielded the results educators, legislators, students and parents hope will prepare young adults for effective citizenship in today' complex culture. Student affairs educators have the expertise, both from a knowledge base on multiple dimensions of student development and interpersonal skills in maintaining productive relationships with diverse students, to approach student learning from the integrated view espoused here. Mutual dialogue with students reflecting on various dimensions of their learning will create educationally purposeful experiences for students and help educators better understand diverse students' experience. By creating intentional support systems to bridge gaps between students' current experience and the meaning making needed for effective citizenship, student affairs educators can make a substantive contribution to student learning.

References

American College Personnel Association. (1994). *The student learning imperative: Implications for student affairs*. Washington, DC: Author.

Baldwin, J. M. (1902). *Social and ethical interpretations in mental development*. New York: Macmillan. (Original work published 1897)

Baxter Magolda, M. B. (1987). [A longitudinal study of epistemological development]. Unpublished raw data.

Baxter Magolda, M. B. (1992). *Knowing and reasoning in college: Gender-related patterns in students' intellectual development*. San Francisco: Jossey-Bass.

Baxter Magolda, M. B. (1994). *Integrating self into epistemology: Young adults' experiences as contextual knowers*. Paper presented at the annual meeting of the American Educational Research Association, New Orleans, LA.

Baxter Magolda, M. B. (1995). The integration of relational and impersonal knowing in young adults' epistemological development. *Journal of College Student Development, 36* (3), 205–216.

Belenky, M. F., Clinchy, B. M., Goldberger, N. R., & Tarule, J. M. (1986). *Women's ways of knowing*. New York: Basic Books.

Boyer, E. (1990). *Campus life: In search of community*. Princeton, NJ: Carnegie Foundation for the Advancement of Teaching.

Chickering, A. W., & Reisser. L. (1994). *Education and identity (2nd ed.)*. San Francisco, CA: Jossey-Bass.

Fischer, K. (1980). A theory of cognitive development: The control and construction of hierarchies of skills. *Psychological Review, 87*, 477–531.

Josselson, R. (1987). *Finding herself: Pathways to identity development in women*. San Francisco: Jossey-Bass.

Kegan, R. (1982). *The evolving self: Problem and process in human development*. Cambridge, MA: Harvard University Press.

Kegan, R. (1994). *In over our heads: The mental demands of modern life*. Cambridge, MA: Harvard University Press.

King, P. M. (in press). Student learning. In S. R Komives & D. B. Woodard (Eds.), *Student services: A handbook for the profession*, (3rd ed.). San Francisco: Jossey-Bass.

King, P. M., & Kitchener, K. S. (1994). *Developing reflective judgment: Understanding and promoting intellectual growth and critical thinking in adolescents and adults*. San Francisco: Jossey-Bass.

Kitchener, K. S. (1982). Human development and the college campus: Sequences and tasks. In G. R. Hanson (Ed.), *Measuring student development*. New Directions for Student Services, No. 20, pp. 17–45. San Francisco: Jossey-Bass.

Kitchener, K. S., Lynch, C. L., Fischer, K. W., & Wood, P. K. (1993). Developmental range of reflective judgment: The effects of contextual support and practice on developmental stage. *Developmental Psychology, 29* (5), 893–906.

Kuh, G., Whitt E., & Shedd, J. (1987). *Student affairs 2001: A paradigmatic odyssey*. Alexandria, VA: American College Personnel Association.

McMillan, J. H., & Forsyth, D. R. (1991). What theories of motivation say about why learners learn. In R. F. Menges & M. D. Svinicki (Eds.), *College teaching: From theory to practice*. New Directions for Teaching and Learning, No. 45, pp. 39–52. San Francisco: Jossey-Bass.

Rest, J. R. (1986). *Moral development: Advances in research and theory*. New York: Praeger.

Rest, J. R. (1994). Background: Theory and research. In J. R. Rest & D. Narvaez (Eds.), *Moral development in the professions: Psychology and applied ethics* (pp. 1–26). Hillsdale, NJ: Erlbaum.

Schilling, K., Maitland Schilling, K., Baxter Magolda, M. B., & Morenburg, M. (1993, June). *Assessing general/ liberal education programs: A multi-faceted qualitative approach*. Presentation at the American Association of Higher Education Assessment Forum, Chicago.

CHAPTER 46

USING STUDENT DEVELOPMENT TO GUIDE INSTITUTIONAL POLICY

MICHAEL D. COOMES

This article draws a link between student development concepts and the institutional policies colleges formulate and implement. This article offers seven observations intended to guide institutional policy makers in light of the propositions about development identified by Strange (1994).

Consider the following illustrative statements of actual policies currently in effect at a variety of American colleges and universities:

> Once a grade is recorded it can be changed only through a request of grade change form, which should be completed by the instructor and countersigned by the department chairperson and dean of the school. Errors in grades must be reported within six months of date of issue of grade reports. *(Seattle University 1991–1992 Undergraduate Bulletin, 1991, p. 27)*

> All Owens Community College Buildings on the Toledo Campus and Findlay Campus are designated as **'Smoke Free Buildings.'** Eating and drinking of any beverage is not permitted in any classroom, laboratory, or the library. Please help us keep our buildings clean by supporting these policies. *(Owens Community College 94-95 Catalog, 1994, p. 66)*

> No person or group shall have the right to place political signs, posters, banners, or similar materials on University property, except for recognized student organizations, which may post signs announcing meetings of the organization which are in accordance with other provisions of University policy. *(1992–1994 Student Handbook: The University of Toledo, 1992, p. 31)*

> The policy of Bowling Green State University is that racial and ethnic harassment will not be condoned. Moreover, the University will use its influence to encourage the community at large to treat its students, faculty and staff and affiliated visitors in a manner consistent with the principles of this policy. The policy is in keeping with the spirit and intent of federal, state, municipal, and University guidelines governing racial discrimination. *(1993–1994 Student Code, 1993, p. 26)*

A cursory examination of student handbooks and college catalogs would yield numerous other policies intended to direct the academic and cocurricular life of students (e.g., admissions criteria, course attendance requirements, roommate assignment procedures, grade appeal policy, parking regulations). Institutional policy is frequently a missing aspect in discussions of linking theory to informed student affairs practice. Practice models like those advocated by Strange and Ring (1990) acknowledge that institutional values are frequently articulated through policy. Although the importance of values in shaping practice is acknowledged, the link between policy and practice is tenuous and only presented in the most cursory fashion. Individual practice models such as the Grounded

Formal Theory model (Rodgers & Widick, 1980) and the Practice-to-Theory-to-Practice model (Knefelkamp, 1984; Rodgers, 1985) outline a set of explicit steps for connecting theory to practice but do not devote extensive discussion to the policy implications of guiding practice from a theoretical perspective. This article will address the need to examine more closely the policy implications of theory directed practice through a discussion of how the 14 propositions about student development identified by Strange in this issue of the *Journal of College Student Development* can be useful in guiding the development of institutional policy. To realize this goal, I will: (a) examine the purpose of institutional policy and its relationship to institutional mission and educational practice, (b) present a set of observations about institutional policy grounded in propositions presented by Strange, and (c) discuss the value of shaping institutional policy from a developmental perspective.

Mission, Policy, and Practice

Prior to offering observations about the nature of campus policy, this section offers a brief discussion of the role policy plays in linking institutional mission, practice, and insights on the nature of the policy process.

Although much of the subsequent discussion will focus on ways campus policy makers can shape institutional policy, it should be noted that student development theory, and the 14 propositions articulated by Strange (1994), serve as only one source of direction and insight for institutional policy makers. Many student affairs administrators may have as their fundamental goal the formulation and implementation of policy that fosters individual growth and development. However, their actions must also be shaped by other considerations. These considerations may be within their control, such as the sound fiscal policies they formulate to direct the operation of their administrative units, or they may be beyond their control, such as changing student demographics or newly enacted state or federal legislation. Regardless of the genesis of the policy, this article advocates utilizing the 14 propositions presented by Strange as a guide for policy development.

The relationship of the mission of a college to the effective education of its students has been well established (Boyer, 1987; Carnegie Foundation, 1977; Chickering, 1969; Chickering &

Reisser 1993; Kuh, 1991; Kuh et al., 1991; Lyons, 1993). As Boyer (1987) noted:

> A quality college is guided by a clear and vital mission. The institution cannot be all things to all people. Choices must be made and priorities assigned. And there is, we believe, in the tradition of the undergraduate college, sufficient common ground on which shared goals can be established and a vital academic program built. (p. 288)

The institutional mission fulfills multiple purposes. Mission serves as a guide to academic decision makers in determining which programs and courses of study are appropriate for inclusion in the curriculum; it aids students in their efforts to determine if the institution meets their needs; and it provides evaluative criteria for trustees, legislators, accrediting agencies and other policy makers (Carnegie Foundation, 1977). First and foremost, however, the mission should be the embodiment of the basic values and assumptions of the institution. The basic beliefs and values of individual colleges will differ; but these values frequently focus on the purposes of undergraduate education, the nature of reality and truth (Schein, 1992), what it means to be an educated person, the relationship of the college to society, and the role of the individual in the learning process. The mission then becomes the overarching statement of institutional purpose, a definition of "what a college is or aspires to be" (Kuh, 1991, p. 12).

As Boyer (1987) implied, the mission serves as a guide for institutional choices and priorities which, in turn, become translated into policy. The term policy is frequently misunderstood and misused on college campuses. It has been equated with practice, procedures, regulations, standards, and criteria. For purposes of this discussion, the definition offered by Baldridge, Curtis, Ecker, and Riley (1978) is useful:

> Policy decisions are critical decisions, those that have a major impact on the organization's future. In any particular situation it may be difficult to separate the routine from the critical, for issues that seem minor at one point may later be of considerable importance, or vice versa. In general, however, policy decisions are those that bind the organization to important courses of action. (p. 34)

Policy is the link between mission and practice; the mission of the college shapes institutional policy and institutional policy guides practice. Policy should represent the prioritization and selection for action of important values and beliefs contained in the institution's mission. Institutional policies can be avowed or enacted, written or unwritten, proactive or reactive, consistently or inconsistently applied. It is not uncommon for colleges to state a policy but behave in a completely different manner. Administrators may state, for example: "It is our belief that all students matter and as such we have implemented policies to treat all students equitably and with respect." However, at the same time, commuter students may be required to park miles from classroom buildings; campus child care may not be available to students who are parents, and residential students may be given little, if any, control over the decoration and structure of their living space. Clearly such an institution's avowed policy does not match its practice.

The symbiotic relationship between policy and practice is an interesting one. Policy is frequently an outgrowth of practice. Campus administrators are often required to respond to new problems or issues (e.g., campus security personnel observe a handgun on the seat of a car in a campus parking lot). After dealing with the immediate issue, it is not uncommon for administrators to standardize the response in the form of a policy (e.g., a policy is developed banning guns from campus property). Although policies are frequently developed in response to unanticipated problems, they are also the articulation of institutional values and beliefs and, as such, are proactive rather than reactive in nature. Campuses committed to multiculturalism may utilize this commitment to shape curricular policy. As a result of this commitment, general education requirements may be expanded to include courses in non-Western cultures. Both proactive and reactive responses are appropriate methods for establishing policy as long as there is coherence between institutional mission, policy, and practice. Institutions that have a consistent set of objectives and a clear and consistent institutional philosophy create "a distinctive image of the institution in the minds of its constituents and others knowledgeable about higher education" (Kuh, 1991, p. 12).

Numerous models have been developed explaining the policy process (Brewer & deLeon, 1983; Jones, 1977; Jones & Matthes, 1983; Kelman, 1987; Lindbloom, 1968; Ripley & Franklin, 1986). Ripley and Franklin (1986) have suggested that, at its simplest level, policy making is envisioned as a two-step process of: (a) formulation and legitimation (i.e., the developmentand acceptance of policy), and (b) implementation. More extensive models have added other steps to the process. These models bear a striking resemblance to models that have been developed to guide the professional practice of student affairs work (e.g., Barr & Cuyjet, 1991; Rodgers, 1983, 1991; Strange & King, 1990). Common steps in the policy process include problem identification, the generation of alternative solutions, the selection of an appropriate solution, policy implementation, and finally, evaluation (and if appropriate, termination) of the policy. The first step, problem identification, includes not only the identification of problems to be addressed by institutional policy makers, but the articulation of the nature and scope of the problem. As such, a key task in the problem identification process is creative thinking about the problem (Brewer & deLeon, 1983). Questions to be considered during this phase of the process include: What is the nature of the problem? Who does the problem affect? Is this a problem the institution or student affairs division is compelled to address? Who should be involved in the generation of alternatives for addressing the problem (e.g., student affairs staff, students, faculty, community representatives)?

Once problems have been identified, the next step in the process is the generation of alternative solutions. Most problems can be addressed in multiple ways. Like problem identification, this step requires the use of insight and creativity and should result in the development of a number of possible solutions for the identified problem. It is important to remember in this step that "doing nothing should not be excluded from the list of alternative policies" (Brewer & deLeon, 1983, p. 64).

After the development of a number of possible alternative solutions for addressing the identified problem, the next step requires the selection of the "best" alternative from the available solutions. Selection of a single solution from a group of policy alternatives involves a wide range of political decisions including bargaining, compromise, and accommodation (Brewer & deLeon, 1983). As Strange and King (1990) have noted, it is during the selection process that the policy maker must consider the unique values of the policy making context. The selection of the most appropriate policy should be driven by the values (i.e., mission) of the college or university.

Once a policy has been selected, implementation of the policy becomes the next step. Implementation is a field of study unto itself (see Barr & Cuyjet, 1991; Lipsky, 1980; Pressman & Wildavsky, 1973; Ripley & Franklin, 1986). Through the implementation process, policy is translated into practice. Implementation includes the development of rules, regulations, and programs to realize the goals of the selected policy (Brewer & deLeon, 1983) and the assignment of appropriate staff to carry out the program. It is through the implementation process that policies become real. Policies may exist on paper (avowed policy); but the true policy does not exist until implemented by a staff member, the person Lipsky (1980) has called the "street-level bureaucrat." Most campuses have policies prohibiting the use of alcohol by underaged drinkers or by any member of the campus community in public spaces. However, unless these policies are enforced by residence hall staff (who serve as street-level bureaucrats) and campus security personnel, the policies are meaningless.

As noted above, the final step in the policy process is program evaluation and, when appropriate, termination. Readers are directed to Brown and Podolske (1993), Guba and Lincoln (1989), Kuh (1979), Lenning (1989), Madaus, Scriven, and Stufflebeam (1983), and Patton (1990) for extensive guidance on the process of evaluating policies and programs.

Observations about Campus Policy

Having briefly discussed the nature of policy, its relationship to institutional mission, and the process that results in the formulation and implementation of policy, it is helpful to examine the relationship of policy to the propositions offered by Strange (1994). The following observations about institutional policy will be grounded in the 14 propositions Strange has articulated to explain the nature of student development, the process that fosters development, the environmental factors that influence the developmental process, and the goals of education. No attempt will be made to examine the nature of institutional policy using the lenses of all 14 propositions. Rather, general observations about policy will be offered with connection to appropriate propositional statements. In addition, each of the following observa-tions will be supported with examples of relevant institutional policies.

Observation 1: Institutional policy must be general and flexible. The central concept of the first four propositions offered by Strange (1994) is respect for individual differences. Developmentally, students differ in the tasks they undertake during their lives (and their collegiate careers); in the way they interpret and make meaning of their experiences and the world; in the stylistic approaches they utilize for resolving the "challenges of learning, growth and development" (Strange, 1994, p. 403); and by their gender, race, ethnicity, and sexual orientation. The realization that students are inherently different makes the job of the institutional policy maker much more difficult. If all students were the same, one policy would be appropriate for all students in similar situations. However, students differ, and one-size-fits-all policies are seldom educationally or developmentally sound. Therefore, institutional policy should be general in its scope and flexible in its application. For example, many colleges require all first-year students (with the exception of students from the immediately surrounding communities or students with family responsibilities) to reside in on-campus housing. Although such a policy makes sound fiscal sense, and although the value of residential living has been well documented (Astin, 1993; Pascarella & Terenzini, 1991), a rigid adherence to such a policy may not be in the best interest of all students. Many current students come from situations in which they have had considerable autonomy (e.g., as latch-key children, as financially independent adults) and have developed many of the traits of interdependence and the interpersonal skills that group residential living hopes to foster. Such students may not benefit from being required to live on-campus during their first year and may view such a policy as requiring them to assume a more dependent, and therefore less adult, role on campus.

Policies that are general in nature (i.e., allowing for considerable opportunity for interpretation and exception) and that are flexibly applied (thus granting streetlevel bureaucrats considerable discretion in implementation) are most appropriate for responding to the multitude of differences that make up the student body. However, campus administrators too often choose to write policy that is narrow in its scope and inflexible in its application. Such policy is frequently the result of the desire on the part of campus administrators to "close up loop-holes" in existing policy to ensure that students conform to institutional needs and expectations. Institutional policy makers should carefully consider the value of narrowly defined and explicitly codified policies. Frequently, when such policies exist, exceptions become rules, rules spawn new exceptions, and the process devolves into a series of more and more narrow policies. The result is the development of a bureaucracy that has as its fundamental purpose not the education and development of students, but the maintenance of organizational directives, In such a highly routinized, centralized and formalized environment (Hage & Aiken, 1970), innovation is stifled, morale is depressed, and staff spend more time reading the policy manual than meeting the needs of students.

As Astin (1993) has commented many of the policies that drive higher education are based on economic rather than educational considerations. "Large institutions are presumably more economical because they allow us to capitalize on economies of scale" (Astin, 1993, p. 435). The value of "the bottom line" results in numerous policies that treat students similarly and serve as a deterrent to effective education. Economic considerations drive policies about residence hall living—large residence halls are preferable to small, staff size (and thus the staff-student ratio) is limited, and students are restrained from taking control of their own living space. Economic considerations drive policies about academics— graduate education thrives off of an increase in the undergraduate population, but undergraduate students rarely reap attendant benefits; large classes utilizing lectures as the primary pedagogical method become the norm for general education courses on many campuses; and faculty utilize multiple choice and other objective assessments that emphasize memorization and rote response because they are easier to grade and are more time efficient than are essay exams, term papers, oral presentations, or group projects. When college educators fail to offer multiple assessment options in their courses, they fail to recognize the different learning styles of students and thus fail to assist them in realizing their full potential and the full potential of the college experience.

Observation 2: Institutional policy must treat students as adults by emphasizing student responsibility. The first four propositions about

development also imply that students are adults and should be treated as such. At the heart of such an assumption is the belief that students should be empowered to take responsibility for their own education and development. Since the publication of the revised version of the Student Personnel Point of View (American Council on Education, 1949), the student as a responsible partner in the developmental process has been a major philosophical premise of the student affairs profession. With that premise as a guide, institutional policies should be developed that foster student responsibility. Similarly, institutional policy makers should critically examine all policies that place limits on the ability of students to take responsibility for their own actions. Too often, campus administrators implement policies that are grounded in the now-discredited philosophy of in loco parentis, making decisions "in the best interest" of students without first checking with students. This nouveau-paternalism displays itself in policies that limit the free expression of ideas, that mandate student class attendance, and that restrain students from developing new student organizations without expressed institutional approval.

Kuh et al. (1991) have pointed out that colleges must be encouraged to foster student responsibility and freedom of choice. Instead of distrusting students, colleges must trust them and expect them "to be responsible for their own learning and development, as well as for handling violations of community norms" (p. 137). Campus administrators are encouraged to consider whether their policies are designed to foster independence, freedom of choice, and student responsibility, or simply to make staff members' lives easier. Does the institution mandate a number of required courses in an effort to fill class seats under the guise of an ill-constructed general education program, or are students allowed to build academic programs that best meet their educational needs and fit their curricular interests? Are student committee meetings organized and run by full-time "advisors" who are primarily interested in ensuring that the latest program is successful, or are students empowered to develop and implement programs even when those programs may fail? Do parietal rules still function in the campus residence halls or are students charged with developing community standards to govern visitation policies, quiet hours, and the expenditure of hall funds? At the heart of the answers to these and numerous other policy concerns is the question, "Do campus administrators treat students as adults?" Campus administrators working from the developmental propositions outlined by Strange (1994) are encouraged to develop policies that demonstrate that they trust students to function as adults and that foster a sense of student responsibility. There is no guarantee that empowering students as adults will result in adult behavior, but it seems unlikely that treating students as children will foster such responsibility.

Observation 3: Institutional policy must be inclusive of differences. Propositions 4 and 14 offered by Strange (1994) serve as the foundation for this observation. Students come from diverse racial, ethnic, and cultural backgrounds; and these backgrounds shape how they see the world, interact with others, learn, study, and live. Institutional policy makers must be cognizant of these differences and refrain from developing policies that support only the values and norms of the dominant culture (Manning & Coleman-Boatwright, 1991). Furthermore, institutional policy makers should develop policies that lead to the development and support of multiple subcommunities (Kuh et al., 1991). An example would be general education policies that expose students to non-Western historical and cultural traditions like the Global Perspectives ability of Alverno College (Alverno College Faculty, 1992). As Boyer (1990) has noted:

> Higher learning builds community out of the rich resources of its members. It rejects prejudicial judgments, celebrates diversity, and seeks to serve the full range of citizens in our society effectively. In strengthening campus life, colleges and universities must commit themselves to building a just community, one that is both equitable and fair. (p. 25)

Building a campus community founded on the principles of equity and fairness presents a formidable task for campus administrators. Manning and Coleman-Boatwright (1991) have noted that the most difficult task for a university steeped in the traditions of White culture is to move from a period characterized by the height of conflict over core institutional values to an institutional rebirth reflecting multicultural goals. Such a change represents:

> a turning point or quantum leap of sorts after which organizational structures are transformed. A critical mass of understanding and

awareness precludes participants from settling for anything less than fully inclusive practices. Social justice and egalitarianism are institutionalized and systemic. (Manning & Coleman-Boatwright, 1991, p. 371)

To realize this goal requires developing policies that, for example, distribute power equitably, blur gender role boundaries, lead to the development and inclusion in the curriculum of course work that critically explores the contributions of multiple cultures to the history and development of our national culture, stress consensus and collaboration, and foster the development of nonbureaucratic organizational forms (Manning & Coleman-Boatwright, 1991). Pope (1993) has suggested that the concept of Multicultural-Organizational Development (MCOD) may be a useful tool for transforming colleges into "efficient, effective, socially diverse, and socially just work environments" (p. 203). Policy makers should look to models like MCOD and the Cultural Environment Transitions Model (Manning, 1994; Manning & Coleman-Boatwright, 1991) as guides for decision making to ensure that institutional policy is inclusive, responsive, and just. The development of inclusive, responsive, and just policies that recognize and celebrate diversity may be the most difficult task facing administrators today However, the cost of failing to enact policies that engender respect and embrace all members of the campus community are too great to bear. The outcome of the implementation of such policies will greatly benefit colleges that demonstrate the determination to change.

Observation 4: Institutional policy must encourage involvement across a range of activities that encompasses both the in-class and out-of-class lives of students. As Strange (1994) noted in the propositions on the nature of development (Propositions 5–9), growth occurs when students are ready to face challenges, are provided with adequate (but not stifling) support to meet those challenges, and are forced to interact with their environment. It is incumbent on colleges to offer students opportunities to stretch beyond their current level of development while providing adequate support structures to assist students as they strive to accomplish new and difficult tasks. In many ways, such a responsibility is not difficult for many colleges to accomplish. Colleges often provide ample opportunities for student involvement and challenge through their curriculum, administrative structure and procedures, physical environment, and the constitution of student peer groups. However, if they are not currently doing so, institutions should develop opportunities for students to become involved and experience challenges that will force them to move beyond their current level of development.

The positive impact of student involvement in the educational process has been well documented (Astin, 1984, 1985, 1993; Kuh et al., 1991). Encouraging students to be involved in a wide range of experiences in multiple institutional settings will expose them to the conditions that will move students to greater cognitive complexity and "qualitatively different assumptions about how the world functions with respect to a particular domain" (Strange, 1994, p. 402). For example, developing curricular or cocurricular policies that require students to participate in community service activities will pay multiple developmental dividends. Serving as a tutor in an adult literacy program, working with persons who are homeless, becoming a Big Sister or Brother, or renovating a house with Habitat for Humanity are important "teachable moments" (Havinghurst, 1972) that foster development across a wide range of psychosocial tasks and cognitive structures. Such activities force students to "respond to novel situations and tasks that challenge their current level or capacity" (Strange, 1994, p. 405). Required community service is just one example of the type of institutional policy that can foster involvement and thus bring students in contact with new and developmentally powerful experiences. Other examples are policies that support cooperative education experiences, study abroad programs, campus work programs like those at Berea College (Kuh et al., 1991), collaborative group-course work, and faculty mentorship programs.

Students do not compartmentalize their lives into the arbitrary distinctions of the academic and the cocurricular; they go to college and view the college experience holistically. The classroom teacher, the campus security officer, the custodian, the librarian, and the career counselor all provide different services to the student but are likely to be viewed similarly by most students as agents of the institution. What is important to students is not the role these individuals play or where their job falls on the college's organization chart, but rather, whether these individuals have enhanced or hindered the student's overall experience. Effective institutions understand that students do not differentiate between the in-class and the out-of-class experience and develop policies and practices to reflect that holism (Kuh et al., 1991). The student development propositions outlined by Strange (1994) serve as a guide for good educational practice, for educators in both the academic and student affairs realms. Academic policy makers would be well served to consider the propositions articulate by Strange as they design academic policies. Curricular content, teaching methods, grading schemes, and degree program composition should be developed with content goals in mind and also with an eye toward how course work can foster development. Faculty members who have utilized developmental constructs to guide the transmission of content and the fostering of critical thinking skills have been successful in a number of disciplines including English (Kroll, 1992a, 1992b; Widick & Simpson, 1978), chemistry (Finster, 1992), and honors programs (Haas, 1992).

Chickering (1969) has stated, "colleges and universities will be educationally effective only if they reach students where they live, only if they connect significantly with those concerns of central importance to their students" (p. 3). Similarly, Baxter Magolda (1992) identified the following three principles of effective educational practice: "validating the student as a knower, situating learning in the students' own experience, and defining learning as jointly constructing meaning" (p. 270). Both Chickering and Baxter Magolda's observations capture the essence of the link between theory and classroom practice and the relationship of course content to student experience. Classroom teachers who consider such principles will not only assist students in thinking more critically, but will probably do a more effective job of teaching curricular content.

In considering policies that provide opportunities for students to integrate their in-class and out-of-class lives, institutional policy makers should be mindful of the power of the student peer group. Whether the research is an ethnographic study of a single residence hall (Moffat, 1989), the examination of select number of involving colleges (Kuh et al., 1991), a comprehensive quantitative analysis of the outcomes of the college experience (Astin, 1993), or a meta-analysis of over 20 years of research on how college affects students (Pascarella & Terenzini, 1991), one conclusion is unmistakably clear: The primary influence on student development and on satisfaction with the college experience is the student's peer group. As Astin (1993) has concluded, "the student's peer group is the single most potent source of influence on growth and development during the undergraduate years" (p. 398). Strange (1994) would categorize many of the effects of the peer group under Proposition 11, which focuses on the conforming effects of human aggregates. Campus administrators may have little control over the interactions of students with the most influential members of the student's peer group (e.g., close friends), but policies can be developed to encourage students to expand their referent groups and, thus, become exposed to increased diversity. Such policies might include ones that consider how roommates living in campus residence halls are matched, how campus clubs and organizations are constituted, and how the needs of commuter and non-traditional students are met. For example, is there a viable commuter center maintained on campus? Are students encouraged to participate in organizations centered around academic disciplines and vocational interests? Do parents have administrative responsibility for the operation of campus child-care facilities? The student's peer group is a powerful force for shaping development, and institutional policymakers need to examine carefully their policies to determine if they capitalize on the impact of that group.

Observation 5: Institutional policy must be proactive and based on sound theoretical and ethical foundations. As noted previously, institutional policy can be developed in response to events, or proactively in anticipation of a situation or desired outcome. As should be apparent from the previous observations, the use of the theoretical propositions articulated by Strange (1994) can provide student affairs administrators with a more intentional guide to policy development. This does not imply that institutional policy makers should not be directed by other considerations (e.g., financial, legal) nor does it imply that they should not develop new policies when existing policies are inadequate. Furthermore, the above observation does not intend to imply that student development theories, with their strong foundation in psychology, should be the only guide to policies and practices. As others (e.g., Kuh, Whitt, & Shedd, 1987) have pointed out, a number of other disciplinary traditions (e.g., sociology, anthropology) can provide

additional perspectives that can usefully inform the development of policy. What is suggested is an echo of Strange's closing comments that professional practice should be driven by the application of "reasoned explanations" for the implementation of action.

To this point, this discussion has focused on the application of theory to the development of institutional policy intended to meet the educational needs of students. Institutional policy makers must also ensure that their policies are ethically as well as theoretically sound. The ACPA Statement of Ethical Principles and Standards (Standing Committee on Ethics of the American College Personnel Association, 1993) is predicated on a set of ethical principles that include: act to benefit others; promote justice; respect autonomy; be faithful; and do no harm. Much of what student affairs practitioners do is grounded in the first three of these principles, and these principles are supported by the previously described observations about policy. The previous observations suggest that policies should be established to facilitate development. Conversely, the injunction contained in the Statement of Ethical Principles and Standards to do no harm compels administrators to examine the deleterious effects of institutional policies. Are campus administrators formulating and implementing policies that can lead to either bodily or psychological harm? For example, consider an institution's policy relative to the cancellation of classes for severe inclement weather. Are students put at risk by asking them to travel to classes in the snow, ice, and frigid temperatures because "classes must go on?" Or is a more humane approach taken to cancel classes when there is a risk to student health? Such decisions are rather commonplace, and campus administrators may not critically examine the impact of these policies on student health and welfare. Although it is important that institutional policy makers develop policies that foster student growth and development, it is equally important that they examine all institutional policies to ensure that these policies do no harm to the students they are charged to serve.

Observation 6: Institutional policy must be open to periodic review. Although not based directly on the propositions offered by Strange (1994), this observation is rather a logical outgrowth of the preceding observations and an understanding of the factors that con-stitute effective professional practice (e.g., Strange & King, 1990). Most models of professional practice contain an evaluative step. Campus administrators must, on a regular basis, critically examine all the policies that serve to guide students' relationships with the institution. If nothing else, the propositions that Strange offers may provide a useful framework for conducting such a review, considering how such policies enhance or inhibit students' development. Students change, campus issues change, and occasionally educational missions change. It is important that institutional policy makers examine all campus policies in light of these changes. For example, as the lives of graduate students have become more complex, and as more graduate students are continuing to work full-time while completing a master's or doctoral degree on a part-time basis; traditional graduate programs need to reexamine carefully the purpose of residency requirements. Requiring graduate students to maintain full-time enrollment for a period of one or two academic terms may be an antiquated concept that does more harm than good to many students attempting to earn an advanced degree. Academic administrators should examine carefully the goals of such a policy (e.g., economic outcomes, educational outcomes) and determine if these goals truly warrant the continuation of such a policy. Institutional policy ought to be viewed pragmatically. If a policy supports or enhances the viability of the institution, it should be maintained; if it serves no valuable purpose, it should be eliminated. Most extensive models of the policy process include a policy termination step. Institutional policy makers are admonished to not be too wedded to their policies. Policies that have outlived their usefulness should be eliminated.

Observation 7: Institutional policy must be tied to the contextual dynamics of the particular institutional setting.

This final observation emanates from the proposition that "Educational systems are embedded in various contexts of select values and assumptions that shape their expectations, processes, and outcomes" (Strange, 1994, p. 409). The great beauty of American higher education is its diversity: 3,500 colleges and universities offer 3,500 different versions of the educational experience (Brubacher & Rudy, 1976). The relationship of institutional mission to institutional policy has already been discussed, but what is important to remember relative to this observation is that institutions must find their own ways of addressing the educational process and fostering development in students.

One of the most widely cited studies of institutional effectiveness is the College Experiences Study (Kuh et al., 1991; Kuh & Lyons, 1990; Kuh & Schuh, 1991; Whitt, 1994). The study identified common characteristics of "involving colleges" (e.g., mission and philosophy, campus environments, campus culture), but each of the colleges included in the study was unique; few would confuse The Evergreen State College with Miami University in Ohio, or the University of Louisville with Earlham College. By maintaining their own distinctiveness, these campuses have established themselves as places where students matter and where involvement is supported. Administrators must be careful (and the researchers involved in the College Experiences Study are quick to point this out) that while one can learn valuable lessons from "involving colleges," one cannot simply import policies from these campuses to other institutional contexts:

> The factors and conditions common to individual Involving Colleges are context bound and are, therefore, not generalizable. Because something— a program or policy—works (or seems to work) in one setting does not mean it will be effective in another. However, the principles on which the factors and conditions are based are transportable because institutional agents in other settings can reflect on how these ideas can be adapted to, and make the best use of, the learning opportunities present in their institution's context. (Kuh et al., 1991, p. 261)

For many years there has been an increase in the level of intervention in campus life by state legislatures, state governing boards, regional accrediting agencies, and the federal government (Buchanan, 1993; Coomes, in press; Gehring, in press). Institutional policy makers must comply with external policy mandates like the directives of the Americans with Disabilities Act (1990) or requirements to enhance multicultural course offerings mandated by a regional accrediting agency. However, institutional policy makers are cautioned not to see those mandates as stifling requirements for uniformity, but rather as opportunities for enhancing institutional distinctiveness. Legislation like the Student Right-to-Know and Campus Security Act (1990) necessitates a response; campuses must provide consumer information to students and other constituents. However, the form in which that information is provided to students is left to the institution. Most institutions present the information in a straightforward manner through existing campus publications (e.g., catalogs, financial aid brochures, direct mailings). Creative institutions will utilize that process not only to communicate the required information to students, but will do so in a manner that is easy for students to comprehend (Coomes, 1991) and that captures the essence of the unique characteristics of the institution.

Summary

The above observations about institutional policy stem from one basic assumption: "human development should be the organizing purpose for education" (Chickering & Reisser, 1993, p. 265). This assumption provides the fundamental rationale for using the propositions offered by Strange (1994) to guide institutional policy and practice. In this article, I have attempted to link Strange's propositions on student development to the policy process and to the policies colleges develop and implement. Like Strange, my observations about policy are general statements that serve more as points of reference than dictums requiring rigid adherence (after all, Observation 1 suggests just the opposite). I encourage readers to develop their own set of observations about institutional policy. Furthermore, I encourage readers to consider other implications of the propositions offered by Strange for the formulation and implementation of policy.

In the attempt to provide a theoretical justification for the development of institutional policy, I may have given the impression that theory should be the only guide to practice. However, institutional policy makers are guided by both pragmatic and philosophical concerns, and institutional policy must serve multiple goals. Colleges must remain financially viable if they hope to fulfill their educational and developmental missions. Policies that serve economic goals (e.g., late-fee policies, facilities usage policies, student-fee allocation policies) must be developed and maintained. Colleges are increasingly required to respond to legal and administrative mandates established by external agencies (Coomes & Gehring, in press). Colleges would be remiss and it would be unlawful if they failed to address legal and legislative mandates. Campus administrators must comply with the conditions of the Americans with Disabilities Act (1990) or the Student Right-to-Know and Campus Security Act (1990) whether or not the campus policies fostered by legal and legislative mandates are developmental. The previous seven observations on campus policy are not intended to encourage institutional policy makers to forego responsibilities to other mandates, rather they are intended to provide policy makers with another set of lenses for viewing institutional policy. Student affairs administrators will need to draw increasingly upon multiple perspectives for directing student affairs practice (Kuh, Whit, & Shedd, 1987). The use of the core concepts of student development can provide a useful guide for the formulation, implementation, and analysis of campus policy.

Fundamentally, the choice of using student development theory to guide the development of institutional policy is a value judgment. Astin (1993) concluded that "the problems of strengthening and reforming American higher education are fundamentally problems of *values*. Policy makers can justify . . . more economical approaches to undergraduate education as long as they value the 'bottom line' more than they do the quality of education offered" (p. 435). The use of student development to guide policy represents a value that encourages policy makers to look beyond the bottom line to the quality of the educational experience.

References

Alverno College Faculty. (1992). *Liberal learning at Alverno College* (5th ed.). Milwaukee, WI: Alverno Productions.

American College Personnel Association, Standing Committee on Ethics. (1993). Statement of ethical principles and standards. *Journal of College Student Development, 34,* 89–92.

American Council on Education, Committee on Student Personnel Work. (E. G. Williamson, Chair). (1949). *The student personnel point of view* (rev. ed.). (American Council on Education Studies, Series 6, No. 13.) Washington, DC: American Council on Education.

Americans with Disabilities Act, 42 U.S.C. § 12 101 et seq (1990).

Astin, A W. (1984). Student involvement: A developmental theory for higher education. *Journal of College Student Personnel, 25,* 297–308.

Astin, A. W. (1985). *Achieving educational excellence.* San Francisco: Jossey-Bass. Astin, A. W. (1993). *What matters in college: Four critical years revisited.* San Francisco: Jossey-Bass. Baldridge, J. V., Curtis, D. V., Ecker, G., & Riley, G. L. (1978). *Policy making and effective leadership.* San Francisco: Jossey-Bass.

Barr, M. J., & Cuyjet, M. J. (1991). Program development and implementation. In T. K. Miller & R. B. Winston, Jr. (Eds.), *Administration and leadership in student affairs: Actualizing student development in higher education* (2nd ed., pp. 707–739). Muncie, IN: Accelerated Development.

Baxter Magolda, M. B. (1992). *Knowing and reasoning in college: Gender-related patterns in students' intellectual development.* San Francisco: Jossey-Bass.

Boyer, E. L. (1987). *College: The undergraduate experience in America.* Princeton, NJ: Carnegie Foundation for the Advancement of Teaching. Boyer, E. L. (1990). *Campus life: In search of community.* Princeton, NJ: Carnegie Foundation for the Advancement of Teaching. Brewer, G., & deLeon, P. (1983). The foundations of policy analysis. Homewood, IL: Dorsey Press.

Brown, R. D., & Podolske, D. L. (1993). A political model for program evaluation. In M. J. Barr & Associates, *The handbook of student affairs administration* (pp. 216–229). San Francisco: Jossey-Bass.

Brubacher, J. S., & Rudy, W. (1976). *Higher education in transition: A history of American colleges and universities.* New York: Harper Row.

Buchanan, E. T. (1993). The changing role of government in higher education. In M. J. Barr &Associates, *The handbook of student affairs administration* (pp. 493–508). San Francisco: Jossey-Bass.

Carnegie Foundation for the Advancement of Teaching. (1977). *Mission of the college curriculum.* San Francisco: Jossey-Bass. Chickering, A. W. (1969). *Education and identity.* San Francisco: Jossey-Bass. Chickering, A. W., & Reisser, L. (1993). *Education and identity* (2nd ed.). San Francisco: Jossey-Bass. Coomes, M. D. (1991). Understanding students: A developmental approach to financial aid services. *NASFAA Journal, 22* (2), 23–31.

Coomes, M. D. (in press). A history of federal involvement in the lives of students. In M. D. Coomes & D. D. Gehring, (Eds.), *Student services in a changing federal climate* (New directions for student services, no. 68) San Francisco: Jossey-Bass.

Coomes, M. D., & Gehring, D. D. (Eds.). (in press). *Student services in a changing federal climate* (New directions for student services, no. 68). San Francisco, CA: Jossey-Bass.

Finster, D. C. (1992). New pathways for teaching chemistry: Reflective judgment in science. *Liberal Education, 78* (1), 14–19.

Gehring, D. D. (in press). The federal university. In M. D. Coomes & D. D. Gehring, (Eds.), *Student services in a changing federal climate (New* directions for student services, no. 68). San Francisco: Jossey-Bass.

Guba, E., & Lincoln, Y. (1989). *Fourth generation evaluation.* Newbury Park, CA: Sage. Haas, P. F. (1992). Honors programs: Applying the reflective judgment model. *Liberal Education, 78* (1), 20–27.

Hage, J., & Aiken, M. (1970). *Social change in complex organizations.* New York: Random House. Havinghurst, R. J. (1972). *Developmental tasks and education* (3rd ed.). New York: McKay. Jones, C. O. (1977). *An introduction to the study of public policy* (2nd ed.). Belmont, CA: Duxbury.

Jones, C. O., & Matthes, D. (1983). Policy formulation. In S. S. Nagel. (Ed.), *Encyclopedia of policy studies* (pp. 117–141). New York: Marcel Dekker.

Kelman, S. (1987). *Making public policy: A hopeful view of American government.* New York: Basic Books.

Knefelkamp, L. (1984). *Practice-to-theory-to-practice: Models and families of theory.* (Videotape, 2 volumes). Generativity project. Washington, DC: American College Personnel Association.

Kroll, B. M. (1992a). Reflective inquiry in a college English class. *Liberal Education, 78* (1), 10–13.

Kroll, B. M. (1992b). *Teaching hearts and mind: College students reflect on the Vietnam War in literature.* Carbondale, IL: Southern Illinois University Press.

Kuh, G. D. (Ed.). (1979). *Evaluation in student affairs.* Washington, DC: American College Personnel Association. Kuh, G. D. (1991). Characteristics of involving colleges. In G. D. Kuh & J. H. Schuh (Eds.),*The role and contribution of student affairs in involving colleges* (pp. 11–29). Washington, DC: National Association of Student Personnel Administrators.

Kuh, G. D., & Lyons, J. W. (1990). Fraternities and sororities: Lesson from the College Experiences Study. *NASPA Journal, 28,* 20–29.

Kuh, G. D., & Schuh, J. H. (Eds.). (1991). *The role and contribution of student affairs in involving colleges.* Washington, DC: National Association of Student Personnel Administrators.

Kuh, G. D., Schuh, J. H., Whitt, E. J., Andreas, R. E., Lyons, J. W., Strange, C. C., Krehbiel, L. E., & MacKay, K. A. (1991).*Involving colleges: Encouraging student learning and personal development through out-of-class experiences.* San Francisco: Jossey-Bass.

Kuh, G. D., Whitt, E. J., & Shedd, J. D. (1987). *Student affairs work, 2001: A paradigmatic odyssey* (ACPA Media Publication No. 24). Alexandria, VA: American College Personnel Association.

Lenning, O. T. (1989). Assessment and evaluation. In U. Delworth, G. R. Hanson, & Associates, *Student services: A handbook for the profession* (2nd ed., pp. 327–352). San Francisco: Jossey-Bass.

Lindbloom, C. E. (1968). *The policy making process.* Englewood Cliffs, NJ: Prentice Hall. Lipsky, M. (1980). *Street-level bureaucracy: Dilemmas of the individual in public sectors.* New York: Sage.

Lyons, J. W. (1993). The importance of institutional mission. In M. J. Barr & Associates, *The handbook of student affairs administration* (pp. 3–15). San Francisco: Jossey-Bass.

Madaus, G. F., Striven, M., & Stufflebeam, D. L. (1983). *Evaluation models: Viewpoints on educational and human services evaluation.* Boston, MA: Kluwer-Nijhoff.

Manning, K. (1994). Multicultural theories for multicultural practice. *NASPA Journal, 31,* 176–185.

Manning, K., & Coleman-Boatwright, P. (1991). Student affairs initiatives toward a multicultural university. *Journal of College Student Development, 32,* 367–374.

Moffatt, M. (1989). *Coming of age in New Jersey* New Brunswick, NJ: Rutgers University Press.

1992-1994 Student handbook: The University of Toledo. (1992). Toledo, OH: University of Toledo.

1993-1994 student code: Bowling Green State University. (1993). Bowling Green, OH: Bowling Green State University.

Owens Community College 94–95 Catalog. (1994). Toledo, OH; Owens Community College.

Pascarella, E. T., & Terenzini, P. T. (1991). *How college affects students.* San Francisco: Jossey-Bass.

Patton, M. Q. (1990). *Qualitative evaluation and research methods* (2nd ed.). Newbury Park, CA: Sage.

Pope, R. L. (1993). Multicultural-organization development in student affairs: An introduction. *Journal of College Student Development, 34,* 201–205.

Pressman, J. L., & Wildavsky, A. (1973). *Implementation.* Berkeley: University of California Press. Ripley, R. B., & Franklin, G. A. (1986). *Policy implementation and bureaucracy* (2nd ed.). Chicago: Dorsey Press.

Rodgers, R. F. (1983). Using theory in practice. In T. K. Miller, R. B. Winston, Jr., & W. R. Mendenhall (Eds.), *Administration and leadership in student affairs: Actualizing student development in higher education* (pp. 111–144). Muncie, IN: Accelerated Development.

Rodgers, R. F. (1985). *Practice-to-theory-to-practice: Using theories of Lee Knefelkamp and Arthur Chickering to create developmental programs.* (Videotape, 2 volumes). Generativity project. Washington, DC: American College Personnel Association.

Rodgers, R. F. (1991). Using theory in practice in student affairs. In T. K. Miller & R. B. Winston, Jr. (Eds.), *Administration and leadership in student affairs: Actualizing student development in higher education* (2nd ed., pp. 203–251). Muncie, IN: Accelerated Development.

Rodgers, R. F., & Widick, C. (1980). Theory to practice: Uniting concepts, logic and creativity. In F. B. Newton & K. L. Ender (Eds.), *Student development practices: Strategies for making a difference* (pp. 3–25). Springfield, IL: Thomas.

Schein, E. H. (1992). *Organizational culture and leadership* (2nd ed.). San Francisco: Jossey-Bass.

Seattle University 1991-1992 undergraduate bulletin of information. (1991). Seattle, WA: Seattle University.

Strange, C. C. (1994). Student development: The evolution and status of an essential idea. *Journal of College Student Development, 35,* 399–412.

Strange, C. C., & King, P. M. (1990). The professional practice of student development. In D. G. Creamer & Associates, *College student development: Theory and practice for the 1990s* (American College Personnel Association Media Publication No. 49, pp. 9–24). Alexandria, VA: American College Personnel Association.

Student Right-to-Know and Campus Security Act, 20 U.S.C. § 1092 (1990). Whitt, E. J. (1994). Encouraging adult learner involvement. *NASPA Journal, 31,* 309–318.

Widick, C., & Simpson, D. (1978). Developmental concepts in college instruction. In C. A. Parker (Ed.), *Encouraging development in college students* (pp. 27–59). Minneapolis: University of Minnesota Press.

CHAPTER 47

THE DILEMMAS OF TRANSLATING THEORY TO PRACTICE

M. LEE UPCRAFT

This paper addresses the challenges student affairs professionals encounter in translating student devel-opment theory in to practice, concluding with recommendations for maintaining a successful dialogue between theoreticians and practitioners.

Strange (1994) has performed an almost impossible task. Within an historical context, he has attempted, and for the most part succeeded, in distilling what is theorized and what is known about students and their development into 14 propositions. This is no small feat. He has borrowed and adapted from several academic disciplines and drawn heavily from the literature and research about college stu-dents to devise a very useful model for practitioners. This model can become the basis for rethink-ing a rationale for the student affairs profession, refocusing student affairs services and programs, and providing a stronger theoretical basis for the student affairs profession. It could and should trans-late quite easily into student affairs practice.

But, will it have the intended impact? Not if things go the way they have in the past. Upcraft (1993) stated

> there is an underlying suspicion, usually felt by the researchers and theoreticians in our field, that our theories are not used enough by practitioners as they develop policy, make decision, solve problems, deliver services and programs, manage budgets, and in general, do their jobs. (p. 260)

I was reminded of this suspicion recently when an administrative colleague of mine, who, when I asked if he had read a recent and very influential book in student affairs replied, "1 don't have the time to read anything. How about an hour when you tell me all about it." In defense of my very com-petent but beleaguered colleague, he's not a mindless practitioner with no interest in the theoreti-cal. He is just a very busy person who is trying to get his job done.

On the other hand, as Upcraft (1993) has pointed out, "Researchers, academicians, and theo-reticians are frequently guilty of writing in ways that, while contributing to the scholarly literature, do little to help the practitioner" (p. 265). It is almost as if true scholars disdain the practical, and real scholarship is in part defined by how specialized, esoteric, complex, and nontranslatable to prac-tice it is. Scholars developing theory are often so estranged from campus life, buried in a world of research and graduate students, that their theories many times have little relevance to campus prob-lems and issues, and even less relevance to practitioners.

The reality is that research and theories have far outstripped practice. In fact, since the early Sixties when Sanford (1962) published *The American College,* the research, theory, and literature about students has been prolific, remarkably current, and responsive to the changing needs and demo-graphics of students. As Strange (1994) correctly pointed out, "Although . . . the history of student development . . . has been a relatively brief one, it has posited a body of literature that is both complex and rich in ideas about college students and their educational environments" (p. 401).

But, in spite of the scholarly efforts by theoreticians, theory is often not known by practitioners, and when it is known, seldom integrated into practice. So, what must be done if a very viable theory, such as the one developed by Strange (1994), is to have an impact on student affairs practice? I believe it will require a change in attitude and behavior on the part of both theoreticians and practitioners if theory and practice are to be melded for the benefit of institutions of higher education, student affairs services and programs, and most of all, students.

What Theoreticians Can Do to Translate Theory Into Practice

First and foremost, theoreticians must be grounded in the realities of today's campus life. "If theory is to be applied, it must be relevant to the issues faced on a day to day basis by the practitioner" (Upcraft, 1993, p. 267). Among the many issues practitioners in the 1990s worry about are human and fiscal resources, racial tensions, sexual assault, AIDS, campus violence, alcohol abuse, students from dysfunctional families, drop out rates (particularly for racial/ethnic minorities), moral and ethical issues, diversity, older and part time students, and many others. So the first question that must be asked of Strange's theory is, does it apply to today's campus issues?

One of the campus realities frequently overlooked by current theoreticians is the diversity of today's students. Wright (1987) argued that theories specific to students from underrepresented racial and ethnic groups are based on the assumption that being raised in a minority culture in the middle of a majority society creates different outcomes for the persons of that culture. There has been significant progress in developing theories that fit individual underrepresented groups, including African Americans, Hispanics, Asian Americans, and American Indians. Likewise, theories have been postulated that help in understanding older students; women; gay, lesbian, and bisexual students; disabled students; and others.

Unfortunately, many "mainstream" developmental theories (those more global intended to fit all students regardless of race, ethnicity, age, sexual orientation, gender, disability, etc.) often apply most successfully to White males between the ages of 18 and 22. For example, the term "college age

student" is still sometimes used, even though that term now applies to almost anyone at almost any age. Nothing is more frustrating to a practitioner than to read and try to apply a theory that doesn't fit the demography of today's students.

One of the positive elements of Strange's (1994) model is that it does, in fact, seem well grounded in campus realities, while at the same time focusing on more universal developmental and environmental principles. For example, his first cluster of propositions focuses on how students differ in age-related tasks; how they interpret and construct their experiences; how they approach and resolve challenges of learning, growth, and development; and how they differ by gender, culture-ethnicity, and sexual orientation. This emphasis will be especially impressive to practitioners on campuses where diversity is the norm, not the exception. It will also help practitioners on campuses with little diversity by providing a strong theoretical basis for campus services and programs that meet the needs of all students.

Another important campus reality is the increased pressure on student affairs practitioners to justify programs and services in the light of declining resources. At first glance, Strange's (1994) model seems somewhat estranged from this reality. However, his propositions concerning educational environments do, in fact, provide a strong theoretical basis for justifying continued support of student services and programs. His 10th proposition asserts that "Educational environments restrict and enable individuals by the form and function of their natural and synthetic physical characteristics" (p. 407).

As the guardians of the out-of-class environment, student affairs practitioners must be familiar with the important elements of a constructive educational environment. Without this grounding, it is far more difficult to convince a faculty dominated budget committee that resources for student affairs should be maintained, or even enhanced. As Strange (1994) pointed out,

> this proposition gives rise to issues of facilities usage and control, human interaction, territoriality, privacy and personal space, community, isolation, noise, access, identity, and comfort. These issues, in turn, depending upon how they may or may not, be resolved, are important for the quality of students' campus experiences and can serve as prohibitive or positive forces for development, in students' lives. (p. 407)

The same connections can be made for the other environmentally focused propositions.

A second way in which theoreticians can help translate theory into practice is to provide direct assistance to the practitioner. Undoubtedly the most cogent, but largely ignored effort to translate theory into practice was Wells and Knefelkamp's (1982) "theory to practice to theory" model. They developed an 11 step process in which suggested educational goals are examined in the light of appropriate theory before interventions are designed and implemented:

Step 1: Identify pragmatic concerns

Define student, faculty, and staff concerns about something that is a problem or issue or that needs to be enhanced or initiated.

Step 2: Determine educational goals and outcomes

Specify the educational goals and outcomes that would be desirable for students to acquire, including information, concepts, and intellectual and auxiliary skills.

Step 3: Examine which theories may be helpful

Evaluate clusters of theories and specific ones to determine those related to goals and outcomes. From each theory or cluster chosen, identify those concepts that illuminate their developmental content and process, including psychosocial, cognitive development, maturity, and typology models.

Step 4: Analyze student characteristics from the perspective of each theoretical cluster

Select those theories that are most helpful in understanding the students involved. Use each of the clusters selected as a filter for viewing students, and assess their characteristics both informally and formally.

Step 5: Analyze environmental characteristics from the perspective of each theoretical cluster

Choose those characteristics that are most useful in understanding the students involved. Use each of the characteristics selected to assess environmental characteristics both informally and formally.

Step 6: Analyze the source of developmental challenge and support in the context of both student and environmental characteristics

Translate descriptive characteristics into prescriptive educational designs. Review the theoretical descriptions of both student and environmental characteristics. Identify specific sources of supports and challenges, and ensure a proper balance between the two.

Step 7: Reanalyze educational goals and outcomes

Determine whether students are ready for the intended learning goals. Determine if these objectives should be modified as a result of applying the first six steps. Design the learning process in such a way as to facilitate learning.

Step 8: Design the learning process using methods that will facilitate mastery of educational goals

Develop sequence and structure for teaching, content, process, and evaluation consistent with learning goals.

Step 9: Implement the educational experience

Step 10: Evaluate the educational experience

Assess learning outcomes, student satisfaction, and educator satisfaction. Develop suggestions for the future.

Step 11: Redesign the educational experience if necessary

Unfortunately, this model failed to catch on with either theoreticians or practitioners. I believe it failed for two reasons. First, it is a model that takes time and effort to implement, neither of which is a readily available commodity among practitioners or theoreticians. But second, and perhaps more importantly, this model neglects the essential step of reconsidering theory in the light of practice. Perhaps a "practice to theory to practice to theory" cycle is more appropriate, where the final step is to revise or confirm a theory on the basis of its practical application. Strange should recruit practitioners to use the Wells and Knefelkamp model to refine and test his theory in the light of practice.

A third and somewhat related way in which the theoretician can help translate theory into practice is to collaborate with practitioners in conducting research that tests the viability of the theory. For example, much research has been done in testing the application of Kohlberg's (1971) theory of moral and intellectual development to college students. The same is true of Perry's (1970) theory of intellectual and ethical development. Chickering's vectors have been operationalized in part through the creation and use of the Student Development Task And Lifestyle Inventory by Winston, Miller, and Prince (1987). Programs and services based on Hettler's (1980) wellness model have been developed and marketed. Strange's (1994) model must also be operationalized, perhaps in the form of an instrument and or an interview protocol, and tested with a wide variety of students at several different types of institutions in several different geographic locations, in collaboration with seasoned practitioners.

In summary, if theoretical models are to be successfully translated into practice, they must be grounded in current campus realities, translated into practice in somewhat formal and structured ways, and tested with a wide variety of students at several institutions. Strange's (1994) model seems to meet each of these criteria and, therefore, has the potential of providing a vehicle for tying theory to practice.

What Practitioners Can Do to Translate Theory into Practice

On the other side of the coin, what can practitioners do to better translate theory to practice? How can practitioners use Strange's theory to develop, enhance and improve student services and programs? First and foremost, practitioners must stay current with the theory that guides the student affairs profession, even if it means time away from the job. This is easier said than done. Practitioners are often caught in the crossfire between reading and digesting theory on the one hand and providing direct services to students and responding to bureaucratic demands on the other. Practitioners are paid to deliver services and

programs, whereas keeping current in the field is expected to be done on their own time. But just how does the practitioner keep current with theories such as the one postulated by Strange?

After 30 odd years as a student affairs practitioner, I have reluctantly concluded that going home after a long day at the office and settling into Astin, Pascarella and Terenzini, Chickering, or Strange just "doesn't cut it". On the other hand, the periods in my career when I made the most progress in keeping current with the research, literature, and theory was when I had sustained periods of time to focus on them.

For example, attending summer institutes and professional conferences away from the campus was especially important to keeping up with the theory in my field. Presenting at conferences and workshops was even more important, because the time spent in preparation increased my knowledge, which was then applied to my daily duties. Along these same lines, teaching courses in student affairs graduate preparation programs or freshman seminars forced me to read and think about the research, literature; and theory in my field in ways that were much more productive than simply reading the latest book or two on students.

Strange (1994) has taken the first important step by exposing his theory to the rigors of writers and readers of this journal, many of whom are practitioners. Other strategies that might be considered include presentations and discussions of this theory at regional and national conferences and workshops and the inclusion of this theory and reactions to it in courses in student affairs graduate programs.

A second way in which practitioners can help translate theory into practice is to take the time to keep theoreticians informed about contemporary campus issues and collaborate with theoreticians in the development of theory. Recently, a colleague of mine and I worked together on the development of an approach to administrative ethics. I was confronted with several ethical issues that I felt current professional ethics models did not address. My colleague, an ethicist by training, lacked the administrative experience to develop a useable model. After several long discussions/arguments, we devised a model that we presented at a national conference, revised, and later published (Upcraft & Poole, 1991). Interested and qualified practitioners need to take the initiative as Strange has done to open dialogues about his model and better connect it to the realities of today's campus life.

A third way in which practitioners can help translate theory into practice is to direct resources toward the promotion of professional development of staff, particularly the mastery of theory. Too often, professional development is practical, not theoretical, but this must change if theory and practice are to be integrated. As Upcraft (1993) pointed out,

> Practitioners should not dismiss theory as irrelevant or impractical because it does not fit into some idea of reality or because of an aversion to any theoretician who has never practiced. A conscious effort must be made to develop theory-based programs and to assess them in ways that confirm, revise, or refute the theory. (p. 268)

It is incumbent upon practitioners to include Strange's (1994) model in professional development, perhaps alongside other viable models, in an effort to encourage practitioners to make better use of theory.

Perhaps one of the ways to resolve this theoretician/practitioner dilemma would be to develop more scholarpractitioners and practitioner-scholars whose identities are rooted in both theory and practice. Individuals who earn a living by postulating theory should enter or reenter the world of the practitioner, whereas those who earn a living by providing services and programs for students should be encouraged to postulate and apply theory.

A Minor Reservation About Strange's Model

It should be obvious to the reader by now that I believe the dialogue between those who develop theory and those who practice must be expanded. Strange's (1994) model provides such an opportunity because it appears to be both theoretically sound, rooted in the realities of practice, and applicable to most, if not all students. It does, however, have a major flaw that will stand as a possible impediment to the successful translation into practice: The model does not make a strong enough connection between student development and student learning, thus not a strong enough connection to the academic mission of higher education. I will elaborate on this point.

As stated earlier, one of the campus realities practitioners must deal with is the pressure to maintain student services and programs and prevent their demise in an era of declining fiscal and human resources. I stated earlier that Strange's (1994) four propositions on educational environments provide a solid theoretical grounding for promoting and defending the role of student affairs in constructing and supporting strong educational environments. But, the tone of these propositions is clearly in support of students' development as psychosocial beings. It is here, I believe, that Strange does not make the next, and perhaps most important, connection between student development on the one hand and student learning and academic success on the other.

Unfortunately, the student affairs profession is somewhat divided on this point. The first point of view, and the one that appears to be neglected by Strange (1994), is probably best represented by NASPA's *A Perspective on Student Affairs* (1987) in which the first assumption and belief identified is that the academic mission of the institution is preeminent.

> Colleges and universities organize their primary activities around the academic experience: the curriculum, the library, the classroom, and the laboratory. The work of student affairs should not compete with and cannot substitute for that academic enterprise. As a partner in the educational enterprise, student affairs enhances and supports the academic mission. (pp. 9–10)

In other words, everything done in student affairs must somehow contribute to the academic mission of the institution, most often defined exclusively as students' academic development and retention, rather than their psychosocial development (Upcraft & Schuh, in press).

A second perspective, more compatible with Strange's (1994) model, is best described as promoting student development. That is, there are certain developmental goals (like those described in Strange's first four propositions), which are related to, but somewhat apart from students' academic goals, such as verbal, quantitative, and subject matter competence. In this view, student affairs assumes the primary responsibility for the achievement of developmental goals, whereas faculty assume the primary responsibility for the achievement of academic goals. Thus, everything done by student affairs must somehow contribute to students' development (Upcraft & Schuh, in press).

A third perspective is that although academic and developmental outcomes are important, other equally important institutional and societal expectations must be addressed. Providing basic services such as housing and financial aid is vital to the institution, somewhat independent of any educational or developmental outcomes. For example, students need a place to live, and colleges and universities assume varying degrees of responsibility in helping them find a place, not necessarily because of students' educational or developmental interests, but because if students do not have affordable, accessible, and livable housing, they will not be able to attend the institution.

In reality, of course, the practitioner does all three: services and programs contribute both the academic and developmental goals of students, as well as provide basic services to students and other clientele. But, it is also a reality in an era of declining resources, that defending what student affairs does on the basis of its contributions to the academic mission of an institution, or to students' and others' basic physical and financial needs is much easier than justifying student affairs strictly on the basis of its contribution to students' developmental goals. Put another way, faculty and upper level management are more likely to support student affairs on the basis of a model that makes the connection between students' development and their academic success.

The bad news is that Strange's (1994) model will not make a successful translation into practice if this connection is not made. The good news is that there is substantial evidence that there is such a connection. Students' experiences outside the classroom, and their subsequent development is essential to their learning and academic success. With this enhancement, Strange's model can and will become a viable model for practitioners.

Summary

Strange (1994) has provided us a very useful model with which to view students' development. It is well supported by the literature and research about students and is applicable to many of the issues facing practitioners. It is especially sensitive to today's increasingly diverse student populations and the effects of educational environments on students' development. It will also be useful in helping practitioners meet the challenges of justifying student services and programs in an era of declining fiscal and human resources. It does, however, fail to make the important connection between student development and the academic mission and goals of both institutions and students. Without this connection, the model will have considerably less influence and credibility with practitioners.

But, perhaps more importantly, the hard reality is that the successful translation of this model to practice will probably depend less upon its viability and more upon whether or not there is active and successful dialogue, cooperation, and collaboration between theoreticians and practitioners. Theoreticians must do a better job of grounding their theories in the realities of campus life and helping practitioners use and test theory. Practitioners must allow time to become more familiar with theory and translate theory into practice, along the lines suggested by Wells and Knefelkamp (1982). In short, individuals who earn a living by postulating theory should enter or reenter the world of the practitioner, whereas those who earn a living by providing student services and programs should be encouraged to read, assimilate, and translate theory to practice with the help of the theoreticians. Perhaps, only then will be gap between theory and practice be bridged.

Note

This article is in part based on a chapter by the author entitled "Translating Theory to Practice," from Margaret Barr and Associates' The Handbook of Student Affairs Administration, San Francisco: Jossey-Bass, Inc., 1993.

References

Hettler, W. (1980). Wellness promotion on a university campus. *Family and Community Health Promotion and Maintenance, 3* (l), 77–95.

Kohlberg, L. (1971). Stages of moral development. In C. M. Beck, B. S. Critenden, & E. V. Sullivan (Eds.), *Moral education.* Toronto, Canada: University of Toronto Press.

National Association of Student Personnel Administrators. (1987). *A perspective on student affairs.* Washington, DC: Author.

Perry, W. G. (1970). *Forms of intellectual and ethical development.* Troy, MO: Holt, Rinehart & Winston.

Sanford, N. (1962). *The American college.* New York: Wiley.

Strange, C. (1994). Student development: The evolution and status of an essential idea. *Journal of College Student Development, 35,* 399–412.

Upcraft, M. L. (1993). Translating theory into practice. In M. J. Barr and Associates, *The handbook of student affairs administration* (pp. 260–273). San Francisco: Jossey-Bass.

Upcraft, M. L., & Poole, T. G. (1991). Ethical issues and administrative politics. In P. L. Moore, (Ed.), *Managing the political dimension of student affairs* (pp. 81–94; New Directions for Student Services, No. 55). San Francisco: Jossey-Bass.

Upcraft, M. L., & Schuh, J. (in press). *Program assessment for student affairs practitioners.* San Francisco: Jossey-Bass.

Wells, E. A., & Knefelkamp, L. L. (1982). *A process model of practice to theory to practice.* Unpublished manuscript.

Winston, R. B., Jr., Miller, T. K., & Prince, J. S. (1987). *Student Development Task and Lifestyle Inventory.* Athens, GA: Student Development Associates.

Wright, D. (Ed.). (1987). *Responding to the needs of today's minority students.* San Francisco: Jossey-Bass.

Chapter 48

Meaning-Making in the Learning and Teaching Process

Michael Ignelzi

Meaning-making, the process of how individuals make sense of knowledge, experience, relationships, and the self, must be considered in designing college curricular environments supportive of learning and development.

Robert Kegan, whose theory of meaning-making is the focus of this chapter, relates a story told to him by a mother about her preschool-age son. The son, named Johnny, comes to his mother one day and tells her he needs some cow toenails. Living in the suburbs, the mother's first thought is how in the world she will obtain cow toenails, but she is even more intrigued by why her son needs these items. When she asks, Johnny informs her that he is starting a farm and wants to plant the cow toenails to grow some cows. Mom's initial thought is the confirming sense of how inventive and cute her son is. Upon reflection, however, she decides that since Johnny raised the issue, it might be a good time to teach him a little about "the birds and the bees" (or in this case, "the cows"). After telling him a few basic facts about reproduction, she says, "So you see, Johnny, *that* is where baby cows really come from." Johnny, who had been listening intently, pauses for a few moments and then replies, "Not on my farm!"

Children, who tend to be very honest about what they are thinking and feeling as well as what they do and don't understand, often provide clear insights into truisms about how human beings function. Although this volume is dedicated to developmental considerations in the learning and teaching of college students, the story about Johnny illustrates some key developmental principles that are useful in considering how all humans experience and learn:

1. *Humans actively construct their own reality.* William Perry (1970) states that what an organism does is organize and what a human organism organizes is meaning. Kegan (1982, 1994) calls this process *meaning-making*. Clearly, Johnny and his mother are making meaning in qualitatively different ways. In a sense, their understanding of reality resides on different "farms." We seem intuitively to understand that children and adults construct reality somewhat differently; however, we may not fully appreciate the extent to which adults can also make meaning in qualitatively different ways from each other.

2. *Meaning-making develops over time and experience.* Much of the reason Johnny and his mother construct their understanding of reality in different ways is due to their being at different points in their individual meaning-making development. Kegan views meaning-making as a process that continues to develop throughout one's life span. As Johnny grows and develops, he will move from his current "farm" (way of making-meaning) to new "farms," as may his mother as she continues to gain experience in her adult life.

3. *The process of learning and teaching is strongly influenced by the ways participants make meaning.* New experience and learning are interpreted through our current constructions of reality. When we are presented with information that doesn't fit our meaning-making, as Johnny did, we may discount or ignore it. Continuing to live on our "own farm" where we are comfortable and reasonably secure may at a given time look more desirable than moving to or even visiting that "new farm" down the road. Education isn't simply presenting more adequate information in an effective manner; it is a process that must incorporate the developmental readiness of the student (Johnson and Hooper, 1982) and must construct a developmental "bridge" between the student's current way of understanding and the new way, thus providing a path on which to cross over (Kegan, 1994).

This chapter provides an overview of Robert Kegan's theory of meaning-making development. It describes how individuals' understanding of their experience, of themselves, and of their interpersonal relationships evolves. The focus is on the portion of Kegan's model of self-evolution that describes the developmental transitions individuals face from adolescence through adulthood. Interview data are used to illustrate the theory and how it applies to the college learning and teaching process. Examples are given on how to assess students' developmental levels, along with suggestions on how faculty can support meaning-making development as a means of enhancing student learning.

Robert Kegan's Theory of Meaning-Making

Robert Kegan's theory of meaning-making development is a conceptualization of how human beings make meaning of themselves, of others, and of their experiences throughout the life span. Kegan (1982, 1994), along with other constructive developmental theorists (including Piaget, 1967; Kohlberg, 1984; Baxter Magolda, 1992; and King and Kitchener, 1994), contends that individuals actively construct their own sense of reality. An event does not have a particular solitary meaning attached that simply gets transferred to the individual. Instead, meaning is created between the event and the individual's reaction to it. Kegan (1982) refers to this as "the zone of mediation"—"the place where the event is privately composed, made sense of, the place where it actually *becomes* an event for that person" (p. 2). This zone where meaning gets made is also referred to by personality psychologists as the self, the ego, or the person. Kegan states: "The activity of being a person is the activity of meaning-making. There is no feeling, no experience, no thought, no perception, independent of a meaning-making context in which it *becomes* a feeling, an experience, a thought, a perception, because we *are* the meaning-making context" (p. 11).

Kegan's theory examines how meaning-making evolves throughout the life span. His developmental approach suggests that the internal structure individuals use to organize meaning-making, and therefore the self, change and evolve in regular and systematic ways. The general course and direction of these changes are predictable over time and experience. Kegan's theory is ambitious in that he proposes that one developmental process (meaning-making) encompasses or accounts for the variety of changes humans go through over the course of their lives pertaining to how they make sense of experience, knowledge, each other, and themselves. Furthermore, he contends that there is consistency in an individual's meaning-making at any particular point in time, such that how one understands knowledge or experience is directly related to how one understands others and the self.

Orders of Consciousness. Kegan proposes a series of six holistic (each with its own internal logic) and qualitatively different forms of meaningmaking that individuals may evolve through during their lifetime. He calls these major places along the path of self-evolution "orders of consciousness" and numbers them from 0 to 5 (Kegan, 1994). As a person's development proceeds between and through these orders, meaning-making undergoes changes that affect the person's view of the self, relations to others, and understanding of experience.

Kegan (1994) contends and research on his theory supports that the majority of the adult population (from late adolescence through adulthood) makes meaning at or between order 3 and order 4. The story of adult-meaning-making development seems to be largely described by the slow evolution of the self from order 3 to order 4. As such, it is useful in considering how meaning-making development affects learning and teaching in higher education, to examine the psychological characteristics of these two orders.

Order 3. Order 3 meaning-makers co-construct their sense of meaning with other persons and sources (books, ideas) in their environment. They are not psychologically differentiated from these "co-constructions." That is, the individual's sense of self is based on a *fusion* of others' expectations, theories, and ideas, and those expectations become integrated into how one thinks about oneself. The individual's sense of meaning-making resides partly in other people and sources and partly within the self, so there is no coherent sense of meaning-making or self apart from those other people and sources. An order 3 meaning-maker is masterful at coordinating others' points of view and can create a shared reality with others but is limited in the ability to reflect on that shared reality and how it is influencing or determining the person's own view (Kegan, Noam, and Rogers, 1982). When an order 3 meaning-maker shares what she or he thinks, believes, or feels, another (person or source) is always implicated.

An example of order 3 meaning-making is illustrated by Mike, a graduate student, who discusses the influence of a particular counseling theory on his thinking when working with others (Ignelzi, 1994, p. 133):

> I'm a Rogerian . . . like the Carl Rogers theory, you know. Client-centered theory and things like that. I believe in the empowerment of students and I believe . . . that it's important not to solve student problems but to help them solve problems for themselves. And that deals a lot with some of the theories that we learn in class and, of course, Rogers. So I think about that when dealing with students. I don't really think about it, but I think that those theories have become so much a part of me that they're almost innate, natural. . . . I think that's the framework that I'm in when I deal with students, and whatever style I'm developing, I think it is right off the heels of Rogers.

Mike's meaning-making is reflective of order 3 in that he uncritically adopts a particular theory that has come to guide his thinking and approach in his attempts to help other students. His philosophy, as he describes it, is co-constructed with an external source he accepts wholly without reflection or modification. He defines himself, at least in the counseling context, as fully identified with the Rogerian approach such that his view of himself as a counselor is indistinguishable from that approach.

Order 4. Order 4 meaning-makers construct their sense of meaning and the self such that self-authorship is the key feature. The order 4 individual transcends the co-constructed self of order 3 by developing the ability to differentiate a self-standard apart from, but in relation to, other people and sources. That is, the self can internalize multiple points of view, reflect on them, and construct them into one's own theory about oneself and one's experience. Thus the individual's meaning-making is influenced by but not determined by external sources. The self becomes identified through these self-authored conceptualizations, giving the self an enduring identity that remains fairly stable across contexts and interpersonal relationships.

An example of order 4 meaning-making is illustrated by Amanda, a recent M.A. graduate, who discusses how she is developing her own personal theory about how to make sense and use of theories and concepts she has studied (Ignelzi, 1994, pp. 218–219):

> I like to think that there's a framework of some sort, that there are obviously principles and values and different ideas which are part of a lot of different theories that help shape the way I do things and the way I interact with people. I've certainly never been able, you know, not been a person who could even subscribe to one particular theory or theorist and say, "This is it." Because they are all far too limiting, and there are so many that I'm attracted to, and different facets and different things click with me. . . . I think what I liked so much about theory was the process of applying theory, was the whole process of self-discovery with each new theory, that made me, as we talked about a theory, where I had to think about my own life and my own experiences and see, you know, Does this fit? Does this not fit? And I think that it's a process for me, with all the theoretical experiences and like who I've become as a result of that and the different things that I've thought

about. That's what I use the most. . . . So I think it's sort of an internalized, you know, inside there's your little self theory.

Amanda's meaning-making is reflective of order 4 in that she is self-authoring her own theory about how to interact with and help others in a counseling context. Though certain formal theories resonate with her more than others do, she reports being attracted to many or parts of many theories. The way she thinks about and uses these theories is highly personalized, based largely on her own values and experiences. Even if many of her ideas are influenced by various theoretical approaches, her understanding, organization, and use of them are determined by her own evolving theory about her work and herself.

"In over Our Heads" in the Learning and Teaching Environment

Given the two different forms of meaning-making (orders 3 and 4) illustrated by Mike and Amanda, it can be postulated that they experience and respond to college learning environments in contrasting ways. While Mike depends on his instructors, course concepts, and peers to co-construct and largely determine what he thinks and believes, Amanda internalizes these same sources to inform and influence (but not determine) her self-authored view. Mike has difficulty with and may not fully understand class assignments that require him to critique or evaluate conflicting perspectives on his own, while Amanda thrives on such learning opportunities. Amanda largely takes responsibility for her own learning, using available resources (professor, reading, peer discussion) in service of her own learning goals. Mike is likely to rely solely on learning goals and standards set by the professor and may hold the professor and others responsible for whether those goals are met. Amanda tends to view criticism of her ideas or work in relation to her own standards, and she ultimately decides their value to her selfauthored views of knowledge and self; Mike is much more sensitive to and affected by such constructive criticism because he co-constructs his ideas and sense of self with the same external sources from which the criticism may originate.

It is for these reasons, among others, that Kegan (1994) suggests that many college students may find themselves "in over their heads"

in their learning environments. Kegan contends that there is a developmental mismatch between the meaning-making order of most college students—predominantly order 3—and the mental demands of contemporary learning culture—predominantly order 4. Consequently, students like Mike, similar to our preschooler Johnny, are residing on one "farm" while the learning and teaching life of the college are occurring on another.

Kegan reviewed much of the contemporary literature on adult education and found that what is being demanded of students' minds by most education specialists and college faculty requires order 4 meaning-making. Kegan summarized these demands on the mind, which he referred to as the "hidden curriculum," as follows:

- Exercise critical thinking.
- Be a self-directed learner (take initiative; set our own goals and standards; use experts, institutions, and other resources to pursue these goals; take responsibility for our direction and productivity in learning).
- See ourselves as the co-creators of the culture (rather than only shaped by culture).
- Read actively (rather than only receptively) with our own purpose in mind.
- Write to ourselves, and bring our teachers into our self-reflection (rather than write mainly to our teachers and for our teachers).
- Take charge of the concepts and theories of a course or discipline, marshaling on behalf of our independently chosen topic its internal procedures for formulating and validating knowledge [Kegan, 1994, p. 303].

Kegan contends that as curricular aspirations for students to work toward, these goals are important and developmentally sound. In fact, as King and Baxter Magolda (1996) suggest, "The achievement of self-authorship and personal authority should be heralded as a central purpose of higher education" (p. 166). However, when faculty come to expect that all students have order 4 abilities, many students find themselves in a learning environment where they are "in over their heads." Being in over one's head is not a pleasant experience; it is often accompanied by feelings of anxiety, frustration, doubt, and helplessness. These feelings are not conducive to learning.

It is important to note that meaning-making level is not the same as intellectual potential or ability. Meaning-making level is a developmental measure of how individuals organize their experience, which evolves over time. Students at order 3 are not less intellectually capable than students at order 4. Learning difficulties experienced by order 3 meaning-makers in order 4 environments are not due to learning deficits; they are due to being at a different point in their meaning-making evolution than the environment demands.

Assessing Meaning-Making Order

Recall that Mike, the order 3 meaning-maker, was a graduate student and that Amanda, the order 4 meaning-maker, had recently graduated from a master's degree program. These individual case examples are representative of what Kegan (1994) found in his longitudinal research where he and his colleagues annually interviewed a sample of graduate students for four years. The research participants were interviewed and assessed using the Subject-Object Interview (Lahey and others, 1988), which is a measure of meaning-making development based on Kegan's model. The results showed that most students' meaning-making was predominantly at order 3 or in transition between orders 3 and 4 at the beginning of the four-year period and either in transition between orders 3 and 4 or predominantly at order 4 at the end of the four years. Kegan (1994) reviews the findings of several other studies measuring his developmental model, which also indicate that the story of adult development is the gradual transition from order 3 to order 4 meaning-making. These data also suggest that "at any given moment, around one-half to two-thirds of the adult population appears not to have fully reached the fourth order of consciousness" (p. 188).

Given these data, we can project that most traditional-aged undergraduate students and many non-traditional-aged undergraduates are either predominantly making meaning at order 3 or in transition from order 3 to order 4. Of course, this is not reflective of the meaning-making of any particular individual. To assess individual meaning-making, faculty must listen carefully to what students say about their understanding of their experiences, including how they make sense of learning experiences, their relationships with others, and themselves. In par-

ticular, faculty should listen to what individual students describe as needed support from faculty. This provides one avenue for assessing meaning-making order and, simultaneously, considering what a particular student expects from faculty.

I interviewed student affairs interns and professionals about what they thought they needed from their supervisors to feel supported in their work (Ignelzi, 1994). Though the relationship between supervisors and supervisees is somewhat different from those between faculty and students, there are some commonalties regarding the basic learning and teaching process evident in both types of relationships.

Stephanie, an order 3 meaning-maker, stated that she needed her supervisor to validate that she was doing things right and in a way that her supervisor liked:

> There are some times I just need to go in and just have her validate that what I'm doing is OK or I'm on the right track. It's just nice to run by what I'm doing and know that there's support there. That she, you know, that she's agreeing, that what I'm doing is good. . . . I feel comfortable knowing that there's, that she's supporting what I'm doing and that she's listening and that she seems excited about what I'm doing, that she likes my answers or my directions, what I'm coming up with [p. 130].

Sam, a transitional order 3–4 meaning-maker, appreciated that his supervisor allowed him the freedom to do things differently but still relied on his supervisor's feedback to evaluate himself:

> Aside from him being available and interested, the part that's nicest is that he'll allow you to try something different. . . . He comes from the frame of mind that, you know, if you can find a better way to do it, then do it your way. . . . I think as long as the end result is the same, he'll let you take whatever path you feel most comfortable with to get there. . . . And he gives me ongoing feedback. . . . I haven't had any surprises from him really in terms of how I've been performing. . . . That's important to me [p. 158].

Sarah, an order 4 meaning-maker, discussed how her view of her supervisor had changed to a collegial one:

I guess I've come to see that I do the work I do; I take feedback from her, and some of the feedback she's given me has been very helpful. At the same time, I know that we're all working in this together, and she's had some more experience . . . but what I have to say is also very important and has worth. . . . Isee us as very much like equals, in that we're dealing with the same situations. . . . She has some different responsibilities than I do, but it still comes back to we're all colleagues [p. 205].

As these three interview excerpts demonstrate, the way individuals view their relationship with their supervisors and what they want from their supervisors can be quite different and is influenced by meaning-making order. Translating this material to the learning and teaching context, it can be projected that these individuals would view the role of faculty differently as well. Stephanie would want a great deal of feedback and validation from her professor as she relies on external sources in helping her co-construct her views of knowledge and herself as learner. Sam wants to have some limited autonomy to try new approaches to learning as his own internal self-standards are developing, but he would still need instructor feedback to help him monitor and evaluate his performance. Sarah has reconstructed her view of the teacher-learner relationship to fit her sense of self-authorship, viewing the professor as peer and colleague in the learning endeavor.

Supporting Development Toward Self-Authorship

If, as suggested earlier, a central goal of higher education should be the achievement of self-authorship, how can faculty encourage its development while not contributing to students' experience of being "in over their heads"? In other words, how can faculty provide appropriate support and challenge that will facilitate the developmental transition from order 3 to order 4 meaning-making? Returning to the earlier "farm" metaphor may provide some guidance.

1. *Visit and appreciate the other people's farm before trying to get them to consider moving to that new farm up the road.* Supporting someone's development first requires comprehending and valuing how the other person currently understands his or her experience. Kegan (1982) suggests that to be of effective help to another, we need to be able to communicate that we

understand how it is for them. This act creates the interpersonal connection that is so important to order 3 meaning-makers: to feel supported by the external sources with whom they currently co-construct their meaning.

2. *Give the students good directions on how to get to the new farm or, better still, accompany them on the trip.* Giving students tasks that require order 4 meaning-making while providing them with little structure, guidance, or support does not facilitate becoming self-authored. A professor cannot tell students how to become self-authored in their learning but can provide learning experiences that provide incrementally-structured supervised practice in moving toward generating one's own ideas and theories about course material. Critical thinking exercises, ethical dilemma discussions, and journal writing are all valuable teaching methods in this process.

3. *Encourage students to travel together to visit the new farm.* Group work is a powerful developmental tool in facilitating movement from order 3 to order 4 meaning-making. The process of the developmental transition between order 3 and 4 is one of slowly creating and distinguishing one's own view from the view that is co-constructed with others. Students placed in learning groups will likely be at different points in this developmental process. As they work on tasks together, those closer to order 4 meaning-making will assert their more self-authored views and encourage their peers to articulate and assume responsibility for their own.

4. *Provide opportunities for celebrating the move to the new farm and reminiscing about leaving the old one.* The move toward self-authorship should be reinforced and celebrated as it progresses, through appropriate feedback, evaluation, and congratulatory acknowledgments. Likewise, students should be given opportunities to reflect on their thoughts and feelings about leaving the comfort of co-constructing the self to the somewhat frightening order 4 recognition that one is in charge of and responsible for one's own experience and self-construction. The

transition to self-authorship involves reconstruction not only of how the self makes meaning of knowledge but also of how the self makes meaning of relationships with others and the self. Fears about losing one's relational and psychological connection with others are perceived as real and need to be contradicted by important others (faculty, peers, family) standing by and with the student through this developmental transition.

The collegiate environment provides more developmental challenge (and demands) than support for students navigating the transition to selfauthorship. Therefore, it is important for faculty to ensure that adequate support is also provided. Kegan (1994) asserts that educators must be about building developmental bridges that are *meaningful* to the students' current meaning-making and *facilitative* of a more complex way. He states, "We cannot simply stand on our favored side of the bridge and worry or fume about the many who have not yet passed over. A bridge must be well anchored on both sides, with as much respect for where it begins as for where it ends" (p. 62).

References

Baxter Magolda, M. B. *Knowing and Reasoning in College: Gender-Related Patterns in Students' Intellectual Development.* San Francisco: Jossey-Bass, 1992.

Ignelzi, M. G. "A Description of Student Affairs Professional Development in the Supervisory Context and an Analysis of Its Relation to Constructive Development." Unpublished doctoral dissertation, Harvard University, 1994.

Johnson, J. E., and Hooper, F. E. "Piagetian Structuralism and Learning: Two Decades of Educational Application." *Contemporary Educational Psychology,* 1982, 7, 217–237.

Kegan, R. *The Evolving Self: Problem and Process in Human Development.* Cambridge, Mass.: Harvard University Press, 1982.

Kegan, R. *In over Our Heads: The Mental Demands of Modern Life.* Cambridge, Mass.: Harvard University Press, 1994.

Kegan, R., Noam, G. G., and Rogers, L. "The Psychologic of Emotion: A Neo-Piagetian View." In D. Chichetti and P. Pogge-Hesse (eds.), *Emotional Development.* San Francisco: Jossey-Bass, 1982.

King, P. M., and Baxter Magolda, M. B. "A Developmental Perspective on Learning." *Journal of College Student Development,* 1996, 37, 163–173.

King, P. M., and Kitchener, K. S. *Developing Reflective Judgment: Understanding and Promoting Intellectual Growth and Critical Thinking in Adolescents and Adults.* San Francisco: Jossey-Bass, 1994.

Kohlberg, L. *The Psychology of Moral Development.* San Francisco: HarperSanFrancisco, 1984.

Lahey, L., and others. "A Guide to the Subject-Object Interview: Its Administration and Interpretation." Unpublished manuscript, Harvard University, 1988.

Perry, W. G., Jr. *Forms of Intellectual and Ethical Development in the College Years: A Scheme.* Austin, Tex.: Holt, Rinehart and Winston, 1970.

Piaget, J. *Six Psychological Studies.* New York: Vintage, 1967.

CHAPTER 49

DECONSTRUCTING WHITENESS AS PART OF A MULTICULTURAL EDUCATIONAL FRAMEWORK: FROM THEORY TO PRACTICE

ANNA M. ORTIZ AND ROBERT A. RHOADS

Based on emerging theoretical work on White racial identity, the authors argue that a central problem of multicultural education involves challenging the universalization of Whiteness. The authors propose a theoretical framework to advance a multicultural perspective in which the exploration and deconstruction of Whiteness is key.

Over the past 20 years a host of educational researchers have explored the intersections of race and schooling as part of the larger project to achieve racial equality in the United States. Such efforts have focused both on K through 12 settings as well as postsecondary educational contexts (Altbach & Lomotey, 1991; Apple, 1982; Kozol, 1991; McCarthy & Crichlow, 1993; Ogbu, 1978). More recently, and most pertinent to this article, theory and practice has focused on multicultural education and the goal of building culturally inclusive schools, colleges, and universities (Astin, 1993a; Banks, 1988; Delpit, 1995; Giroux, 1992; hooks, 1994; Rhoads & Valadez, 1996; Sleeter & Grant, 1994; Tierney, 1993). This movement is also evident in the field of student affairs where a variety of researchers have explored multiculturalism in relation to out-of-class learning as well as the preparation of student affairs practitioners (Manning & Coleman-Boatwright, 1991; McEwen & Roper, 1994; Pope, 1993; Rhoads & Black, 1995; Strange & Alston, 1998). The vast majority of multicultural research and theorizing has focused on the problems and complexities faced by students of color as members of diverse minority cultures in the United States. Although many of these findings are helpful in advancing multiculturalism, a major gap exists in this body of literature.

The gap in higher education's knowledge base relates to the limited exploration of White racial identity, or what may be termed "Whiteness." By ignoring the cultural complexities associated with White racial identity, practitioners and scholars may unwittingly contribute to the universalization of Whiteness, and consequently, the marginalization of non-White racial identities. Fusco (1988) addresses this very issue: "Racial identities are not only black, Latino, Asian, native American, and so on; they are also White. To ignore White ethnicity is to redouble its hegemony by naturalizing it. Without specifically addressing White ethnicity, there can be no critical evaluation of the construction of the other" (p. 9). And Roediger explained,

> When residents of the US talk about race, they too often talk only about African Americans, Native Americans, Hispanic Americans, and Asian Americans. If whites come into the discussion, it is only because they have "attitudes" towards nonwhites. Whites are assumed not to "have race," though they might be racists. Many of the most critical advances of recent scholarship on the social construction of race have come precisely because writers have challenged the assumption that we only need to

explain why people come to be considered Black, Asian, Native American or Hispanic and not attend to . . . the "invention of the white race." (1994, p. 12)

We, along with others, concur with Roediger in seeing race largely as a social construction—meaning that little biological basis exists for grouping people by racial categories (Frankenberg, 1993, 1994, 1997; Giroux, 1997; hooks, 1992). However, we do not deny that as a social construction race has significant effects in terms of defining privilege and nonprivilege. As Roediger paradoxically notes, "Race is thus both unreal and a seeming reality" (1994, p. 6). For some, race is a very harsh reality, and this, ideologically and pragmatically, is what multiculturalism seeks to address.

Our goal in this article is to review recent scholarship on White racial identity and to suggest a theoretical framework for advancing multiculturalism in which the exploration and deconstruction of Whiteness is pivotal. Our fundamental assumption is this: If educators want to advance students' understanding of White privilege, and relatedly, racial inequality, they need to help students explore and deconstruct White racial identity, both among Whites and non-Whites. This is a pivotal step in promoting a multicultural perspective. However, placing Whiteness under the microscope is problematic; for example, significant resistance derives from the lack of consciousness among Whites about their own racial identity, and consequently, resentment is often directed at other racial groups who connect with their cultural heritage. Ultimately, our goal is to displace White racial identity as the universal norm by challenging ourselves and our students to name it. When students begin to see Whiteness as a visible aspect of society and culture, they are then in a better position to raise questions about its inequitable universalization.

Research on White Racial Identity

Research on White racial identity tends to be rooted in one of three general areas of inquiry: psychological, cultural, and educational. Psychological research on White identity development primarily revolves around Helms' work (1984, 1990). By focusing on the racial attitudes of Whites toward self and others, Helms identified six stages that Whites may pass through on the way to a more complex and integrated view of race. More recently, Helms and Piper (1994) have suggested that the stages may be best understood as statuses that do not necessarily follow a linear trajectory. The six statuses are: contact, disintegration, reintegration, pseudo-independent, immersion/emersion, autonomy.

Movement between these statuses generally flows from "a superficial and inconsistent awareness of being White" (Helms, 1990, p. 55) to high levels of consciousness characterized by a realization of White privilege and a commitment to pursuing social change.

Rowe, Bennett, and Atkinson (1994) developed a similar conception of White racial consciousness and suggested seven types reflective of one's attitudes toward racial identity; avoidant, dissonant, dependent, dominative, conflictive, reactive, and integrative. As with later explanations of the Helms model, the White racial consciousness model is not to be treated as a linear stage theory. Also, like the Helms model, the White racial consciousness model suggests that attitudinal differences among Whites range from a lack of "consideration of one's own White identity" (p. 136) to those reflecting a "pragmatic view of ethnic/minority issues" (p. 141). Block and Carter (1996) criticized the final location in the White racial consciousness model because it implies, in their words, "that an individual characterized by a healthy White identity could be seen as being passive and free of guilt with regard to racial/ethnic issues and simply be content with the status quo in this country, suggesting that he or she would be a supporter of a racist society" (p. 329). We also assert that any developmental model of Whiteness must include a commitment to social action as a central facet of a vital identity.

A serious problem with the preceding psychological theories is that they only address a portion of what it means to be White: a sole focus on racial attitudes toward oneself and others does not constitute a holistic view of White identity. This, as Roediger (1994) has pointed out, is problematic given the fact that one's sense of White racial identity involves much more than simply how one views Whites and non-Whites. Just as ethnic identity for culturally different people includes aspects of culture (language, customs, religion, food), identifying elements of White culture is necessary for a wholistic view. For example, specific aspects of U.S. culture predominantly reflect the White experience; the racial segregation of sports and genres of music offer some examples. Equally assured is the fact that if particular aspects of culture are part of the White experience, then they also contribute to White identity. After all, as Hall (1990) has pointed out, "Cultural identities are the points of identification . . . which are made within the discourses of history and culture" (p. 226). Similarly, Rhoads (1997) has argued, "Identities are constituted within the parameters of culture" (p. 95). The classic statement from Geertz (1973) alludes to the power of culture in shaping identity as well: "Man is an animal suspended in webs of significance he himself has spun" (p. 5). Let us turn then to cultural analyses of the construction of White racial identity.

In cultural studies, incorporating mostly feminist, historical, anthropological, and sociological frameworks, researchers also have uncovered understandings linked to the construction of White racial identity which more directly illustrate the connection between White racial identity and the supremcy of Whiteness in U.S. society. For example, Winant (1997) has argued that White identity has been reinterpreted and rearticulated "in a dualistic fashion: on the one hand egalitarian, on the other privileged; on the one hand individualistic and 'color blind,' on the other hand 'normalized' and White" (p. 42). Nowhere is this dualistic framework more evident than in the 1990s debate about affirmative action. Whereas one group of Whites has supported affirmative action as part of an egalitarian measure, the other, as Winant argued, has situated Whiteness as disadvantage. Despite the lack of empirical support for claims of reverse discrimination, a deeply resistant form of White identity emerged after the dramatic social and cultural upheaval of the 1960s, and, as Winant has maintained, "Provides the cultural and political 'glue' that holds together a wide variety of reactionary racial politics" (p. 42). Particular constructions of Whiteness, for Winant, have tended to fall into one of five categories ranging from a belief in the biological superiority of Whites (the far right racial project) to a belief in the need to abolish Whiteness altogether (the new abolitionist racial project).

The abolitionist project is most notable in the work of Roediger (1991, 1994), who has argued that "the idea of race is given meaning through the agency of human beings in concrete historical and social contexts, and is not a biological or natural category" (1994, p. 2). This supports our contention that race is largely socially constructed; and because race is a social construction it offers the possibility of being deconstructed and reconstructed. Intellectual efforts aimed at making Whiteness visible is for Roediger part of the political and cultural project of abolishing Whiteness altogether (something that remains largely invisible and often is deeply entrenched within the subconscious realm is hard to critique). And, of course, because Whiteness is the universal standard by which diverse others are measured, and, in turn, delimited and devalued, its abolition has the potential to be emancipatory for non-Whites.

Intellectually and pragmatically, we have concerns about the goal of abolishing Whiteness as a cultural construction and source of identity, as well as the logical conclusion of ultimately eliminating the entire category of race. The presumption underlying such a strategy suggests to us that equality cannot be achieved without complete elimination of racial identity differences and the related identity politics. We believe an alternative vision does in fact exist and is rooted in the ideals of multiculturalism and the valuing of difference. Briefly, multiculturalism advances the ideal of communities of difference in which concerns for dialogue and learning about one another's lives becomes a source of community building (Burbules & Rice, 1990; Rhoads, 1997; Rhoads & Valadez, 1996; Tierney, 1993). Hence, in terms of Whiteness, its elimination is not the only solution: Displacing Whiteness as the universal standard by which all other races are gauged is also a step toward racial and cultural equity. Frankenberg (1997) has spoken to this position when she argued for the need to "resituate Whiteness from its unspoken (perhaps unspeakable?) status; to displace and then reemplace it" (p. 3). Realistically, any movement toward denormalizing Whiteness is a positive step to be taken.

From the intellectual advances associated with the recent exploration of White racial identity have come educational research and theory aimed at exposing the underlying influences of Whiteness in teaching and learning contexts. Maher and Tetreault (1997), for example, sought to reexamine their study of college classrooms conducted from a feminist perspective. "We considered ourselves feminist researchers sharing a common perspective with the women of color that we studied," they explained, only later to discover that "as White researchers, we did not fully interrogate our social position of privilege, which made us vis à vis our subjects, oppressors as well as feminist allies" (p. 322). In the reexamination of the data that previously had formed the basis for *The Feminist Classroom* (1994), Maher and Tetreault sought to unearth racial privilege through the "excavation of Whiteness in its many dimensions and complexities" (p. 322). A key strategy they have recommended is the use of literature aimed in part at unearthing the effects of the cultural networks related to Whiteness. Examples of the literature they have recommended include Morrison's *The Bluest Eye* (1970) and *Playing in the Dark* (1993), McIntosh's (1992) work on White and male privilege, Ellsworth's (1997) pedagogical exploration of the effects of Whiteness, and Hacker's (1995) analysis of Black and White racial divisions and related discrimination.

Giroux (1997) also explored the educational implications of Whiteness and suggested that educators need to create learning opportunities that enable students to connect White ideology and identity with progressive social reform. "Central to such a task is the political and pedagogical challenge of refashioning an antiracist politics that informs a broader, radical, democratic project" (1997, p. 315). The deconstruction of Whiteness, especially its advantages and privileges, helps students to discover the direct impact of living in a society where being White is favored in the distribution of social capital and opportunity. Concerned with advancing antiracist politics, Fine (1997) offered insight into the potential of examining institutionalized discrimination in schools (e.g., tracking) "that renders Whiteness meritocratic and other colors deficient" (p. 64). Instead of focusing on students who continue to endure discrimination, Fine has suggested that institutional analyses may be better suited for exposing the ways that Whiteness is situated as advantage. Also concerned with unearthing advantage, Rosenberg (1997) found student autobiographies to be helpful tools in promoting understandings of privilege among White college students.

The preceding works reflect a belief in the political and cultural potential of educational interventions. In this regard, we agree with King and Shuford (1996), who have argued that a multicultural perspective actually depicts a cognitively more advanced view about cultural diversity. Ultimately, educational theory and practice concerned with unearthing Whiteness and advancing a more democratic, multicultural society needs to explore specific pedagogical strategies.

A Theoretical Framework

Theoretical and empirical evidence supports the development of educational strategies that challenge students to give serious consideration to the construction of Whiteness. Educational strategies that assist students in exploring White racial identity are likely to promote higher levels of White racial consciousness and at the same time offer the potential to deepen student understanding of culture and privilege. The problem, as most college and university educators are well aware, is that students, especially White students, tend to shut down when issues of race and privilege are introduced to classroom and cocurricular contexts. Students often fear that they may unintentionally make ignorant or racist statements, or that they may indeed expose prejudice and stereotypes they have. Therefore, multicultural education theories and strategies are needed for addressing this problem.

The following four assumptions undergird our theoretical approach:

1. Culture is a misunderstood construct, but one that is key for helping students understand diversity and confront their own racism.

2. Students in general and White students in particular have a difficult time identifying their own cultural connections.

3. Cultural diversity is a fact of life and efforts to build a common culture inevitably privilege the dominant culture.

4. Multiculturalism is a valued and desired view for students to develop.

Our framework follows five steps which are informed by the assumptions listed above: (a) understanding culture, (b) learning about other cultures, (c) recognizing and deconstructing White culture, (d) recognizing the legitimacy of other cultures, and (e) developing a multicultural outlook (see Figure 1). Our thinking reflects not only the work on Whiteness and White privilege by Roediger (1991, 1994), Frankenberg (1994, 1997), McIntosh (1992) and others, but also the work of Sleeter and Grant (1994) on multicultural educational strategies and Garcia's (1995) work on culture as a key con-

	Step 1: Understanding Culture	Step 2: Learning About Other Cultures	Step 3: Recognizing and Deconstructing White Culture	Step 4: Recognizing the Legitimacy of Other Cultures	Step 5: Developing a Multicultural Outlook
Cognitive Goal	To develop a complex understanding of culture (culture shapes people's lives and people shape culture).	To develop a more advanced understanding of diverse cultures.	To develop an understanding of how White culture has been universalized as the norm and to begin to question its privileged position.	To recognize that culture other than one's own is just as valued to another individual.	To recognize that all cultures within a given society shape each other and that the inclusion of all cultures requires the reconstruction of U.S. society.
Beginning Problem Statement	I see culture as something a society creates.	I know that differences between cultural groups exist, but the differences are only superficial.	I see culture as something that some have, but others do not.	I understand that there are many cultures, but we should agree on a common culture.	I value living in a society that is multicultural.
Ending Problem Statement	Culture is something I create, but that also creates me.	I understand that many cultural groups exist within the U.S. and each reflects deeply held norms, values, beliefs, and traditions.	I see culture as something that all people have.	I see that many diverse cultures can coexist including my own and that this is a good thing.	I can work to make society an equitable place for people of all cultural backgrounds because our vitality is intricately tied to one another's.
Activity	Understanding Culture —Observing and critically analyzing everyday events.	Exploring Cultures —Attending cultural events and reflecting on their meaning as well as dialoguing with culturally diverse others.	Analyzing White Culture —Learning to recognize White culture and to begin to challenge its normalization.	The Impact of Culture —Students identifying aspects of own cultures that play important roles in their lives and sharing these with other students.	Multiculturalism leads to Action —Discovering how institutions shape the ways in which culture is expressed.

Figure 1 Framework of multicultural education (Ortiz & Rhoads)

struct in multicultural training. The framework is not meant to be considered as an invariant linear model, but one in which each of the five steps contributes to an overall educational goal of enhancing multicultural education. Elements of each step may be incorporated in one educational intervention, used separately in individually designed educational programs, or the framework as a whole may be used to guide the development of curricula addressing multicultural issues.

Following the discussion of each step in the framework, we briefly discuss educational strategies that we have used to meet the cognitive goal of the step. We wish we could include student outcomes research verifying the effectiveness of

the framework and thus demonstrating that we have helped students to progress toward multicultural understanding, but this is not the case, nor is such data likely to become available anytime soon. The fact is that altering attitudes involves much more than simply exposing students to alternative forms of thought through a 1- or 2-hour exercise. The pedagogical strategies suggested should be viewed as part of a long-term process through which increased exposure to alternative ways of viewing race, culture, and identity eventually challenge students to rethink their own views. As student outcomes research has clearly shown, oftentimes the effects of college are long term (Astin, 1993b; Pascarella & Terenzini, 1991). In the end then, the development of meaningful pedagogical strategies must rest a great deal on the logical extensions drawn from sound theories.

Step 1: Understanding Culture

In Step 1, the overarching cognitive goal is for students to fully understand how culture shapes their lives and how they shape culture through their interactions. This is the more complex notion of culture, in which culture is much more than simply the artifacts that a society creates. Geertz's (1973) dynamic notion of culture as "webs of significance" that are in part created through human interaction and at the same time guide human interaction is the depth of understanding sought here. The beginning problem statement reads: "I see culture as something a society creates." However, the ending problem statement reads: "Culture is something I create, but that also creates me." An activity designed to promote a more advanced understanding of culture involves some type of exercise that gets at how culture shapes the human condition, but at the same time highlights the ability people have to alter culture. An advanced understanding of culture also should incorporate knowledge about how culture shapes one's worldview and hence, how one perceives others and their cultures.

For Step 1 a myriad of activities can be used to achieve the cognitive goal. Many of these come from the work of intercultural communication practitioners and scholars who train students and business personnel to sojourn abroad (Bennett, 1986; Gudyknust & Kim, 1984; Hess, 1997; Paige, 1993; Sorti, 1990; Stewart & Bennett, 1991). In Step 1 the bulk of learning comes from critical reflection and analysis of everyday events. From this examination comes the realization that culture indeed affects individuals and that individuals through social interaction also affect culture.

Because of the cognitive complexity of this stage we recommend two activities that have been particularly effective in helping students to understand culture as a dynamic and dialectical phenomenon. In the first activity, students observe a setting on campus where their attention is focused on one particular behavior or attribute. For example, a student may choose to study how students greet each other on the central quad area of campus. Before the observation, students, guided by the facilitator, generate a list of questions about the behavior and setting they are about to observe. Sample questions might be: Were the greetings loud and boisterous or more subdued? Did students use physical contact in some way? Were students walking alone or in groups? Did they stay or move on? What were the students wearing? Once the observations are complete, students are given quiet time to write down their reflections and discoveries from the exercise (this could be done as a homework assignment as well). The group then comes together and compares notes. Attention must be paid to the many "teachable moments" as students are often drawn to different attributes in the setting and will have divergent interpretations of the same setting. At this point students begin to see how culture shapes human behavior and perception. Facilitators can encourage this process by asking questions such as: What norms did you observe and did anyone violate those norms? From where do such norms come? These questions should help students to see how social lives are indeed shaped by culture, but also they come to understand how people shape cultural norms.

A more advanced activity for Step 1 is to conduct an analysis of a "critical incident." Kappler (1998) used the following critical incident in her study of intercultural perspectivetaking among U.S. students:

> Mariko is a student from Japan. Although when she first arrived she was a little uneasy, she is now used to the different routines and lifestyle and is doing quite well in school and is fluent in English. She has become good friends with one of her classmates, Linda. One afternoon, their professor asked for two volunteers to come in early the next class to help with a special project. Linda raised her hand and volunteered herself and suggested Mariko might also be willing. Mariko replied hesitantly that she did not think she could do it and that it would be better to ask someone else. Linda said that Mariko would be quite good and told the professor they would do it. The next day, Mariko did not turn up and Linda did all the work herself. The next time Linda saw Mariko she asked her rather coldly what had happened to her. Mariko apologized and said that she had to study for an exam that day and she didn't really feel capable of doing the work. Linda was frustrated and asked her why she had not said so clearly in the class at the time. Mariko looked down and said nothing.

Analysis of this critical incident challenges students to develop an explanation of what happened from Linda's point of view, from Mariko's point of view, and from the students' own points of view. The comparative analysis of the differing points of view helps to demonstrate how culture shapes our behavior and our perspectives. Additionally, the facilitator also needs to raise questions about how cultural norms might be altered by various actors in a critical incident. Of course, facilitators should be encouraged to write critical incidents that are highly relevant to the specific contexts of the students with whom they are working.

Step 2: Learning About Other Cultures

Step 2 provides the laboratory for Step 1. Much of the multicultural education that took place on college campuses in the 1980s focused on "cultural awareness." Programs and events were designed to expose students to the traditions, food, and music of distinct cultural groups. Although such programs are important in helping students experience aspects of diverse cultures, we contend that without serious reflection about culture as a construct, the potential for a deeper understanding of cultural diversity is likely to be lost. With the orientation to understanding culture that is offered in Step 1, the cultural exploration of others' lives becomes grounded in a theoretical understanding of culture. We have found through our own pedagogical efforts that students develop an enthusiasm for cultural exploration when it is enhanced by theoretical insights about culture. They begin to make connections between cultural artifacts such as food, clothing, and music, and the complex norms, values, and beliefs associated with various cultural groups. Hence, the beginning problem statement in Step 2 reads: "I know that differences between cultural groups exist, but the differences are only superficial." The ending problem statement is: "I understand that many cultural groups exist within the US and each reflects deeply held norms, values, beliefs, and traditions."

Step 2 activities should be designed to build energy and enthusiasm for learning about other cultures. Activities like this are probably a staple of multicultural education at most colleges and universities. The educational activity for this step involves motivating students to attend cultural events and programs already planned by groups on campus. Of course, an easy way to help students take the risk to attend such events is to go as a group. Although we tend to think that attending cultural events is a low-risk way to educate oneself, "I don't have anyone to go with" is a common refrain we hear from our students (and sometimes ourselves). Such outings should be accompanied by a reflection component as this will help to facilitate a more meaningful learning experience much in the way reflection adds to the community service experience.

In groups where participation is ongoing (i.e., an orientation course or student staff training), we also recommend an activity in which students engage in an ongoing dialogue with a culturally different person. We have used this strategy in courses by asking students to meet with their dialogue partner at least once a week for about 6 weeks. We do not encourage students to enter each encounter with a set of interview questions; rather, our preference is the student or facilitator determine a general topic for each meeting. We also stress that the dialogues are meant to be an exchange and not a one-way conversation in which the primary contributor is the cultural other. We have found that students learn a great deal about another culture and person through this exercise, and that their confidence level in having significant interactions with diverse others increases. The extent of this process can be quite basic or rather extensive, as in the "voice project" described by Strange and Alston (1998).

Step 3: Recognizing and Deconstructing White Culture

In Step 3, the overarching cognitive goal is helping students to see that Whites have culture, and that White culture has become in many ways the unchallenged, universal basis for racial identity. Experience tells us that in the preceding step students primarily will focus on aspects of culture typically derived from non-Whites (both White and non-White students when asked to explore a culture different from their own will rarely select White cultural groups). Because of a general lack of recognition of White culture, students are ill-equipped for deconstructing Whiteness. Recognizing and deconstructing Whiteness is particularly challenging to White students, because of White culture being so universalized. When White students begin to recognize that they in fact are culturally positioned, they are more likely to understand that others have culture too. Thus, White students begin to see the essence of racial differences. The beginning problem statement for Step 3 is: "I see culture as something that some have, but others do not." The ending problem statement reads: "I see culture as something that all people have." We call the pedagogical exercise for Step 3, "Analyzing White Culture," and we focus on getting students to reflect on aspects of White culture as a source of identity.

Step 3 is the key contribution we offer to a comprehensive multicultural educational intervention. We need to be clear here. We are not saying that White culture is in any way more significant or of greater value than any of the many other cultural identities. However, a lack of understanding of Whiteness is a major barrier to achieving a multicultural society. Therefore, we contend that the deconstruction of Whiteness must be central to educational interventions designed to challenge White privilege and advance a multicultural perspective.

The exercise we have used for Step 3 is called Analyzing White Culture and is quite simple to implement. However, although the exercise may be simple, the complications and discomforts associated with students' explorations of race need to be thought about in advance. Because the discussion has the potential to be animated and conflictual, the facilitator should establish some communicative guidelines before beginning the activity. Guidelines might include the following: only one person speaks at a time, no heckling, participants must agree to keep an open mind, and participants must agree to stay through the debriefing phase of the program. Analyzing White Culture involves asking students to list on a sheet of paper the 10 most significant characteristics, adjectives, or statements that come to mind when asked to describe White racial identity or White culture. We use the terms "White racial identity" and "White culture" interchangeably in this exercise because some students find it easier to describe one and not the other, and both capture various characteristics associated with the diversity of White experience in the U.S.

We use two basic permutations of this exercise. One strategy is to collect the lists and then pass them back to students randomly so that each student gets someone else's. Of course, to ensure anonymity, the same kind of paper should be

used by all students and they should not write their names on the paper. Another option, but one that only should be used with a diverse group of students, is to ask the students to indicate whether they are White or a person of color (specific racial or ethnic categories may compromise student anonymity, depending of course on the size and diversity of the group). This adds another dimension to the discussion in that theoretically one might expect to see some differences in the lists depending on the status of the student as White or as a person of color. For example, White students often ask, "What do you mean by White culture? There isn't one." Meanwhile, students of color may already be on item five or six. This is to be expected given the fact that the universalization of Whiteness is experienced most pointedly by people of color, while its normative status may be taken for granted by Whites. The fact that students of color may have an easier time completing their lists is an important outcome of the exercise and should be a key concern in the subsequent discussion. Again, attempting this exercise without adequate representation of both students of color and White students is not advisable because a degree of discomfort related to racial exploration is a likely result and small numbers of students from one group should not be forced to confront such psychological and emotionally challenging activities.

Once the responses have been collected and then randomly distributed, the facilitator will ask for volunteers to read their lists (and to identify the race of the person who completed the list, but only if the group is diverse!). Once several lists have been read the facilitator should solicit reactions from students. Debriefing involves the facilitator reconnecting the purpose of the Exploring White Culture exercise with the larger goal of advancing racial and multicultural understanding.

Step 4: Recognizing the Legitimacy of Other Cultures

The cognitive goal of Step 4 is recognizing that culture other than one's own is just as valuable and meaningful to another individual. This involves getting students to see that many cultures exist at the same time and that such multiplicity is not a bad thing. The beginning problem statement reads: "I understand that there are many cultures, but we should agree on a common culture." The ending problem statement is: "I see that many diverse cultures can co-exist including my own and that this is a good thing."

In Step 4 students move from general and specific understandings of culture and cultures to the realization that multiple cultures have a legitimate place in U.S. society. The activity recommended for this step helps students to recognize the impact of culture on individuals by identifying which aspects of their individual cultures play important roles in their lives. The worksheet for this exercise has three columns. In the first column (titled Cultural Attribute) students list important aspects of their culture. In the second column (titled Contribution to Sense of Self) students explain what each attribute contributes to their identity, how they feel about and perceive themselves in reference to others. Finally, in the last column (titled Affects How I See the World by . . .) students record the ways in which each attribute might shape their perceptions of themselves, other individuals, cultures, and societies.

After students have completed the grid they should be placed in small groups that are as diverse as possible (up to four). They are instructed to notice what attributes they have in common and those that are different. Those with common attributes are likely to have different responses for the last two columns. Students need to pay close attention to these as they are the prime examples of the ways in which culture affects individuals.

Step 5: Developing a Multicultural Outlook.

The cognitive goal for Step 5 is helping students to recognize that all cultures within a given society shape each other and that the inclusion of all cultures requires the reconstruction of U.S. society. The previous steps help students to learn more about other cultures and begin to incorporate multicultural perspectives into their own identities. Step 5 offers the potential to motivate students to take action to assist creating multicultural society. The beginning problem statement reads: "I value living in a society that is multicultural." The ending problem statement reveals a more complex understanding of the interface between culture, society, and its members: "I can work to make society an equitable place for people of all cultural backgrounds because our vitality is intricately tied to one

another's." Students need to focus on embracing multiculturalism and discover how societal institutions embrace or deny cultural difference and how the status of one's culture in a society affects individuals. Educational strategies used in this step help students move away from xenophobia and toward celebrating difference in such a way that they see taking social action toward the inclusion of diverse cultural perspectives as the logical next step in their own education and liberation. In this regard, we agree with Sleeter and Grant's (1994) view: The most valuable form of multicultural education is both multicultural and social reconstructionist.

In Step 5 students are encouraged to integrate a multicultural perspective that helps them to become critical consumers of culture. At this point students should be able to recognize that their culture changes over time (and their "selves" change as well) as they and their society embrace diverse cultural perspectives. In their quest to learn about other cultures, they may find that they incorporate aspects of other cultures into their own behavior and cognitive structures. They also begin to see societal consequences for the continuing marginality of diverse cultures in the U.S. Their multicultural outlook calls for them to take action on both internal and external levels.

The activity that helps students become more multiculturally oriented is an institutional analysis of how their colleges or universities support or do not support the expression of diverse cultures. This activity may be implemented two different ways. With an ongoing group such as a staff or a class, small groups of three students are given a unit or activity at the particular institution to analyze. They visit the space or context, speak with staff and students, examine the publications related to the unit or activity, and explore the connections the particular unit or activity has with other areas of campus life. Their charge is to unearth the ways in which diverse cultural expressions are present or absent from the particular environment and what might be done to enhance cultural inclusiveness.

With a group that meets only one time (i.e., a training session or one-shot educational program), the facilitator uses the same small group method, but instead of extended study of a particular unit or activity, the facilitator collects artifacts from various units or activities around campus. The artifacts may include publications, job descriptions, applications, photos, or newspaper clippings. Small groups then have the same charge as the more permanent groups: to unearth ways in which diverse cultural expressions are present or absent from the particular environment and what might be done to enhance cultural inclusiveness.

Conclusion

We believe that this framework helps to increase the multicultural understanding of all students, but especially White students. We see multicultural understanding as a developmental journey where a multicultural outlook is created by guiding students through a process where they are confronted with more difficult challenges as they accomplish those which are less challenging. This framework also promotes attitudes that encourage cultural learning and intercultural competence as Hess (1997) outlined by. These attitudes include: a high regard for culture, an eagerness to learn, a desire to make connections, and a readiness to give as well as receive.

One of the major limitations of this framework and of other frameworks or models of multicultural education or prejudice reduction is the paucity of research and evaluative findings. Although some specific interventions have been tested in small studies (Greenman & Kimmel, 1995; Suarez-Balcazar, Drulak, & Smith, 1995), we did not find widespread research on the effects of multicultural education and prejudice reduction models. We have begun to collect data for the activity described in Step 3 (Analyzing White Culture), and we will seek to examine the effectiveness of the framework and its activities in the future. We encourage other researchers and educators to collect evaluative data and share such findings through publication and conference presentations. Evaluative data need not be limited to the study of outcomes, but may also include qualitiative explorations of the dynamics of facilitating such activities and reports of student reactions to them. Obviously, all theoretical frameworks should be continually refined, and we expect no less for the framework proposed here. We also encourage educators to experiment with the kinds of activities suggested for each of the theoretical steps of our framework. We have described some that have worked for us, but at the same time improvements can be made here as well. The usefulness and success of some of the activities we list will vary depending on the contexts and the students involved.

We in no way expect that this framework completes a student's multicultural journey. We see students moving from this framework to others that focus on prejudice reduction (Helms's White Racial Identity Model), ally development (Washington & Evans, 1991), and more social-action-oriented goals (Sleeter & Grant, 1994).

One lesson that we have learned in the course of our work with students in multicultural education is that if more resistant White students are to be affected by multicultural education, the intervention and facilitators must be willing to meet the students at their respective level of development. For most college-aged White students, beginning the dialogue with discussions of White privilege or White racism provide too great a challenge. We assert that our framework of multicultural understanding begins at a less threatening point (but no less important) that teaches students basics about the importance of culture. As with other forms of learning, the goal of the educator is to foster students' enthusiasm for learning in a way that motivates them to take on greater challenges. Indeed, enthusiasm for cultural learning is at the heart of building a multicultural society and is key to the success of the framework we have proposed in this article.

References

Altbach, P. G., & Lomotey, K. (Eds.). (1991). *The racial crisis in American higher education*. Albany: State University of New York Press.

Apple, M. W. (1982). *Education and power*. Boston: Routledge and Kegan Paul.

Astin, A. W. (1993a). Diversity and multiculturalism on the campus: How are students affected? *Change, 25*(1), 44–49.

Astin, A. W. (1993b). *What matters in college: Four critical years revisited*. San Francisco: Jossey-Bass.

Banks, J. (1988). *Multicultural education: Theory and practice*. Boston: Allyn and Bacon.

Bennett, M. J. (1986). A developmental approach to training for intercultural sensitivity. *International Journal of Intercultural Relations, 2*, 179–96.

Block, C. J., & Carter, R. T. (1996). White racial identity attitude theories: A rose by any other name is still a rose. *The Counseling Psychologist, 24*(2), 326–334.

Burbules, N., & Rice, S. (1991). Dialogue across differences: Continuing the conversation. *Harvard Educational Review, 61*(4), 393–416.

Delpit, L. (1995). *Other people's children: Cultural conflict in the classroom*. New York: New Press.

Ellsworth, E. (1997). Double binds of Whiteness. In M. Fine, L. Weis, L. C. Powell, & L. M. Won (Eds.), *Off-White: Readings on society, race, and culture* (pp. 259–269). New York: Routledge.

Fine, M. (1997). Witnessing Whiteness. In M. Fine, L. Weis, L. C. Powell, & L. M. Won (Eds.), *Off-White: Readings on society, race, and culture* (pp. 57–65). New York: Routledge.

Frankenberg, R. (1993). *White women, race matters: The social construction of Whiteness*. Minneapolis: University of Minnesota Press.

Frankenberg, R. (1994). Whiteness and Americanness: Examining constructions of race, culture and nation in White women's life narratives. In S. Gregory & R. Sanjek (Eds.), *Race* (pp. 62–77). New Brunswick, NJ: Rutgers University Press.

Frankenberg, R. (1997). Introduction: Local Whitenesses, localizing Whiteness. In R. Frankenberg (Ed.), *Displacing Whiteness: Essays in social and cultural criticism* (pp. 1–33). Durham, NC: Duke University Press.

Fusco, C. (1988). Fantasies of oppositionality. *Afterimage, 16* (December), 6–9.

Garcia, M. H. (1995). An anthropological approach to multicultural diversity training. *Journal of Applied Behavioral Science, 31*(4), 490–504.

Geertz, C. (1973). *The interpretation of cultures.* New York: Basic Books.

Giroux, H. A. (1992). *Border crossings: Cultural workers and the politics of education.* New York: Routledge.

Giroux, H. A. (1997). Rewriting the discourse of racial identity: Towards a pedagogy and politics of Whiteness. *Harvard Educational Review, 67*(2), 285–320.

Greenman, N. P., & Kimmel, E. B. (1995). The road to multicultural education: Potholes to resistance. *Journal of Teacher Education, 46*, 360–368.

Gudyknust, W. B., & Kim, Y. Y. (1984). *Communicating with strangers: An approach to intercultural communication.* Reading, MA: Addison-Wesley.

Hacker, A. (1995). *Two nations: Black and White, separate, hostile, unequal.* New York: Ballantine Books.

Hall, S. (1990). Cultural identity and diaspora. In J. Rutherford (Ed.), *Identity: Community, culture, difference* (pp. 222–237). London: Lawrence & Wishart.

Helms, J. E. (1984). Toward a theoretical explanation of the effects of race on counseling: A Black and White model. *The Counseling Psychologist, 12*(4), 153–165.

Helms, J. E. (1990). *Black and White racial identity attitudes: Theory, research, and practice.* Westport, CT: Greenwood.

Helms, J. E., & Piper, R. E. (1994). Implications of racial identity theory for vocational psychology. *Journal of Vocational Behavior, 44*, 124–138.

Hess, J. D. (1997). *Studying abroad/learning abroad: An abridged edition of the whole world guide to culture learning.* Yarmouth, ME: Intercultural Press.

hooks, b. (1992). *Black looks: Race and representation.* Boston: South End Press.

hooks, b. (1994). *Teaching to transgress: Education as the practice of freedom* . New York: Routledge.

Kappler, B. J. (1998). *Refining intercultural perspective-taking.* Unpublished doctoral dissertation, University of Minnesota, Minneapolis.

King, P. M., & Shuford, B. C. (1996). A multicultural view is a more cognitively complex view: Cognitive development and multicultural education. *American Behavioral Scientist, 40*(2), 153–164.

Kozol, J. (1991). *Savage inequalities: Children in America's schools.* New York: Harper Perennial.

Maher, F. A., & Tetreault, M. K. T. (1994). *The feminist classroom: An inside look at how professors and students are transforming higher education for a diverse society.* New York: Basic Books.

Maher, F. A., & Tetreault, M. K. T. (1997). Learning in the dark: How assumptions of Whiteness shape classroom knowledge. *Harvard Educational Review, 67* (2), 321–349.

Manning, K., & Coleman-Boatwright, P. (1991). Student affairs initiatives toward a multicultural university. *Journal of College Student Development, 32*, 367–374.

McCarthy, C., & Crichlow, W. (Eds.). (1993). *Race, identity, and representation in education.* New York: Routledge.

McEwen, M. K., & Roper, L. D. (1994). Incorporating multiculturalism into student affairs preparation programs: Suggestions from the literature. *Journal of College Student Development, 35*, 46–53.

McIntosh, P. (1992). White privilege and male privilege: A personal account of coming to see correspondence through work in women's studies. In M. L. Anderson & P. Hill Collins (Eds.), *Race, class, and gender: An anthology* (pp. 70–81). Belmont, CA: Wadsworth.

Morrison, T. (1970). *The bluest eye.* New York: Holt, Rinehart & Winston.

Morrison, T. (1993). *Playing in the dark: Whiteness and the literary imagination.* New York: Vintage.

Ogbu, J. U. (1978). *Minority education and caste: The American system in cross cultural-perspective.* New York: Academic.

Paige, R. M. (Ed.) (1993). *Education for the intercultural experience.* Yarmouth, ME: Intercultural Press.

Pascarella, E. T., & Terenzini, P. T. (1991). *How college affects students.* San Francisco: Jossey-Bass.

Pope, R. L. (1993). Multicultural-organization development in student affairs: An introduction. *Journal of College Student Development, 34*, 201–205.

Rhoads, R. A. (1997). *Community service and higher learning: Explorations of the caring self.* Albany: State University of New York.

Rhoads, R. A., & Black, M. A. (1995). Student affairs practitioners as transformative educators: Advancing a critical cultural perspective. *Journal of College Student Development, 36,* 413–421.

Rhoads, R. A., & Valadez, J. R. (1996). *Democracy, multiculturalism, and the community college: A critical perspective.* New York: Garland.

Roediger, D. (1991). *The wages of Whiteness: Race and the making of the American working class.* New York: Verso.

Roediger, D. (1994). *Towards the abolition of Whiteness: Essays of race, politics, and working class history.* New York: Verso.

Rosenberg, P. M. (1997). Underground discourses: Exploring Whiteness in teacher education. In M. Fine, L. Weis, L. C. Powell, & L. M. Won (Eds.), *Off-White: Readings on society, race, and culture* (pp. 79–89). New York: Routledge.

Rowe, W., Bennett, S. K., & Atkinson, D. R. (1994). White racial identity models: A critique and alternative proposal. *The Counseling Psychologist, 22,* 129–146.

Saurez-Balcazar, J., Drulack, J. A., & Smith, C. (1995). Multicultural training practices in community psychology programs. *American Journal of Community Psychology, 22,* 785–798.

Sleeter, C. E., & Grant, C. A. (1994). *Making choices for multicultural education: Five approaches to race, class and gender* (2nd edition). New York: Macmillan.

Sorti, C. (1990). *The art of crossing cultures.* Yarmouth, ME: Intercultural Press.

Stewart, E. C., & Bennett, M. J. (1991) (2nd ed.). *American cultural patterns: A cross-cultural perspective.* Yarmouth, ME: Intercultural Press.

Strange, C., & Alston, L. (1998). Voicing differences: Encouraging multicultural learning. *Journal of College Student Development, 39,* 87–99.

Tierney, W. G. (1993). *Building communities of difference: Higher education in the 21st century.* Westport, CT: Bergin & Garvey.

Washington, J., & Evans, N. J. (1991). Becoming an ally. In N. J. Evans & V. A. Wall (Eds.), *Beyond tolerance: Gays, lesbians, and bisexuals on campus.* Alexandria, VA: American Association of Counseling and Development.

Winant, H. (1997). Behind blue eyes: Whiteness and contemporary U.S. racial politics. In M. Fine, L. Weis, L. C. Powell, & L. M. Wong (Eds.), *Off-White: Readings on race, power, and society* (pp. 40–53). New York: Routledge.

UNIT VI

ADDITIONAL READINGS LIST

ADDITIONAL READINGS

Unit 1:

Section 1: Student Development Theory: An Overview

Evans, N. J., Forney, D. S., & Guido-DiBrito, F. (1998). Using student development theory. In *Student development in college: Theory, research and practice* (pp. 15–30). San Francisco: Jossey-Bass.

Parker, C. A. (1974). Student development: What does it mean? *Journal of College Student Personnel, 15,* 248–256.

Stage, F. K. (1991). Common elements of theory: A framework for college student development. *Journal of College Student Development, 32,* 56–61.

Unit 2:

Section 2: Integrated Developmental Models

Pizzolato, J. E. (2003). Developing self-authorship: Exploring the experiences of high-risk college students. *Journal of College Student Development, 44,* 797–812.

Section 3: Spiritual and Faith Development

Constantine, M. G., Wilton, L., Gainor, K.A., & Lewis, E. L. (2002). Religious participation, spirituality, and coping among African American college students. *Journal of College Student Development, 43, 605–613.*

Dantley, M. E., & Rogers, J. L. (2001). Invoking the spiritual in campus life and leadership. *Journal of College Student Development, 42,* 589–603.

Fowler, J. W. (1981). *Stages of faith: The psychology of human development.* San Francisco: Harper Press.

Holmes, S. L., Roedder, B. S., & Flowers, L. A. (2004). Applying development theory to college students' spiritual beliefs. *College Student Affairs Journal, 23,* 130–145.

Love, P. G. (2002). Comparing spiritual development and cognitive development. *Journal of College Student Development, 43,* 357–373.

Nash, R. J. (2001). Constructing a spirituality of teaching: A personal perspective. *Religion and Spirituality, 28,* 1–20.

Unit 3:

Section 4: Psychosocial Development

Fries-Britt, S. (2000). Identity development of high-ability Black collegians. In M. B. Baxter Magolda (Ed.), *Teaching to promote intellectual and personal maturity: Incorporating students' worldviews and identities into the learning process* (pp. 55–65). New Directions for Teaching and Learning, No. 82. San Francisco: Jossey-Bass.

Josselson, R. (2000). Relationship and connection in women's identity from college to midlife. In M. E. Miller & A.N. West (Eds.), *Spirituality, ethics and relationship in adulthood: Clinical and theoretical explorations* (pp. 113–146). Madison, CT: Psychosocial Press.

Levinson, D. J., & Levinson, J. D. (1996). The human life cycle: Eras and developmental periods. In *The seasons of a woman's life* (pp. 13–37). New York: Ballantine Books.

Loevinger, J. (1976). Stages of ego development. In *Ego development.* (pp. 13–28). San Francisco: Jossey-Bass.

Maier, E. (1998). Do psychosocial development theories do justice to the traditional college women of today? *Initiatives, 58*(4), 19–35.

Marcia, J. E. (1966). Development and validation of ego-identity status. *Journal of Personality and Social Psychology, 3*, 551–558.

Martin, L. (2000). The relationship of college experiences to psychosocial outcomes in students. *Journal of College Student Development, 41*, 294–303.

Reisser, L. (1995). Revisiting the vectors. *Journal of College Student Development, 36*, 505–511.

Schlossberg, N. K. (1990). Training counselors to work with older adults. *Generations, 14*(1), 7–10.

Straub, C. A. (1987). Women's development of autonomy and Chickering's theory. *Journal of College Student Personnel, 28*, 198–205.

Taub, D. J., & McEwen, M. K. (1991). Patterns of autonomy and mature interpersonal relationships in Black and White undergraduate women. *Journal of College Student Development, 32*, 502–508.

Taub, D. J. & McEwen, M. K. (1992). The relationship of racial identity attitudes to autonomy and mature interpersonal relationships in Black and White undergraduate women. *Journal of College Student Development, 33*, 439–446.

Weathersby, R. P. (1981). Ego development. In A. W. Chickering and Associates, *The modern American college* (pp. 51–75). San Francisco: Jossey-Bass.

Section 5: Dynamics of Race and Ethnicity in Development

Adams, M. (2001). Core processes of racial identity development. In Wijeyesinghe, C. L. & Jackson, III, B. W. *New perspectives on racial identity development: A theoretical and practical anthology.* New York: New York University Press.

Alvarez, A. N. (2002). Racial identity and Asian Americans: Supports and challenges. In M. K. McEwen, C. M. Kodama, A. N. Alvarez, S. Lee, & C. T. H. Liang (Eds.), *Working with Asian American college students* (pp. 33–43). New Directions for Student Services, No. 97. San Francisco: Jossey-Bass.

Ferdman, B. M., & Gallegos, P. I. (2001). Racial identity development and Latinos in the United States. In C. L. Wijeyesinghe & B. W. Jackson III (Eds.), *New perspectives on racial identity development: A theoretical and practical anthology* (pp. 91–107). New York: New York University Press.

Hardiman, R. (2001). Reflections on White identity development theory. In C. L. Wijeyesinghe & Bailey W. Jackson (Eds.), *New perspectives on racial identity development: A theoretical and practical anthology (pp. 108–128).* New York: New York Press.

Helms, J. E. (1990). Toward a model of white racial identity development. In *Black and White racial identity: Theory, research and practice.* (pp. 207–225). New York: Greenwood Press.

Helms, J. E. (1994). The conceptualization of racial identity and other "racial" constructs. In E. J. Trickett, R. J. Watts, & D. Birman (Eds.), *Human diversity* (pp. 285–311). San Francisco: Jossey-Bass.

Helms, J. E. (1995). An update of Helms's White and people of color racial identity models. In J. G. Ponterotto, J. M. Casas, L. A. Suzuki, & C. M. Alexander (Eds.), *Handbook of multicultural counseling* (pp. 181–198). Thousand Oaks, CA: Sage.

Leach, M. M., Behrens, J. T., & LaFleur, N. K. (2002). White racial identity and White racial consciousness: Similarities, differences, and recommendations. *Journal of Multicultural Counseling and Development, 30*, 66–80.

Parham, T. A. (1989). Cycles of psychological Nigrescence. *Counseling Psychologist, 17*, 187–226.

Pope, R. L. (1998). The relationship between psychosocial development and racial identity of Black college students. *Journal of College Student Development, 39*, 273–282.

Renn, K. A. (2003). Understanding the identities of mixed-race college students through a developmental ecology lens. *Journal of College Student Development, 44*, 383–403.

Sue, D. W., & Sue, D. (2003). *Counseling the culturally diverse: Theory and practice* (4th ed.). New York: Wiley.

Tatum, B. D. (1997). Racial identity development and relational theory: The case of Black women in White communities. In J. V. Jordan (Ed.), *Women's growth in diversity* (pp. 91–106). New York: Guilford.

Vandiver, B. J. (2001). Psychological Nigresence revisited: Introduction and overview. *Journal of Multicultural Counseling and Development, 29*, 165–173.

Vandiver, B. J., Fhagen-Smith, P. E., Cokley, K. O., Cross, W. E., Jr., & Worrell, F. C. (2001). Cross's Nigresence model: From theory to scale to theory. *Journal of Multicultural Counseling and Development, 29*, 174–200.

Wijeyesinghe, C. L. (2001). Racial identity in multiracial people: An alternative paradigm. In C. L. Wijeyesinghe & B. W. Jackson III (Eds.), *New perspectives on racial identity development: A theoretical and practical anthology* (pp. 129–152). New York: New York University Press.

Section 6: Dynamics of Gender in Development

Ossana, S. M. Helms, J. E., & Leonard, M. M. (1992). Do "womanist" identity attitudes influence college women's self-esteem and perceptions of environmental bias? *Journal of Counseling and Development, 70*, 402–408.

Section 7: Dynamics of Sexual Orientation in Development

Bieschke, K. J. Eberz, A. B., Wilson, D. (2000). Empirical investigations of lesbian, gay, and bisexual college students. In V. A. Wall & N. J. Evans (Eds.), *Toward acceptance: sexual orientation issues on campus* (pp. 29–58). Lanham, Md. : University Press of America.

Cass, V. C. (1984). Homosexual identity formation: Testing a theoretical model. *The Journal of Sex Research, 20*(2), 143–167.

Dilley, P. (2002). Queer theory, identity development theories, and non-heterosexual students. In *Queer man on campus: A history of non-heterosexual college men, 1945–2000* (pp. 15–52). New York: Routledge Falmer.

Evans, N. J., & Broido, E. M. (1999). Coming out in college residence halls: Negotiation, meaning making, challenges, supports. *Journal of College Student Development, 40*, 658–668.

Fassinger, R. E., & Miller, B. A. (1997). Validation of an inclusive model of sexual minority identity formation on a sample of gay men. *Journal of Homosexuality, 32*, 53–78

Fox, R. C. (1996). Bisexuality in perspective: A review of theory and research. In B. A. Firestein (Ed.), *Bisexuality: The psychology and politics of an invisible minority* (pp. 3–50). Thousand Oaks, CA: Sage.

Klein, F., Sepekoff, B., & Wolf, T. J. (1990). Sexual orientation: A multi-variable dynamic process. In T. Geller (Ed.), *Bisexuality: A reader and sourcebook* (pp. 64–81). Ojai, CA: Times Change Press.

Levine, H., & Evans, N. J. (1991). The development of gay, lesbian, and bisexual identities. In *Beyond tolerance: Gays, lesbians and bisexuals on campus.* (pp. 1–24). Washington D. C. : American College Personnel Association.

Worthington, R. L., Savoy, H. B., Dillon, F. R., & Vernaglia, E. R. (2002). Heterosexual identity development: A multidimensional model of individual and social identity. *The Counseling Psychologist, 30*, 496–531.

Section 8: Multiple Dimensions of Development

Myers, L. J., Speight, S. L., Highlen, P. S., Cox, C. I., Reynolds, A. L., Adams, E. M., & Hanley, C. P. (1991). Identity development and worldview: Toward an optimal conceptualization. *Journal of Counseling & Development, 70*, 54–63.

Rust, P. C. (1996). Managing multiple identities: Diversity among bisexual women and men. In B. A. Firestein (Ed.), *Bisexuality: The psychology and politics of an invisible minority* (pp. 53–83). Thousand Oaks, CA: Sage.

Unit 4:

Section 9: Intellectual Development

Baxter Magolda, M. B. (2001). A constructivist revision of the measure of epistemological reflection. *Journal of College Student Development, 42*, 520–534.

Baxter Magolda, M. B. (2002). Epistemological reflection: The evolution of epistemological assumptions from age 18 to 30. In B. K. Hofer & P. R. Pintrich (Eds.), *Personal epistemology: The psychology of beliefs about knowledge and knowing* (pp. 89–102). Mahwah NJ: Lawrence Erlbaum Associates.

Baxter Magolda, M. B. (2004). Evolution of a constructivist conceptualization of epistemological reflection. *Educational Psychologist, 39*, 31–42.

Belenky, M. F., Clinchy, B. M., Goldberger, N. R., & Tarule, J. M. (1986). Toward an education for women. In *Women's ways of knowing* (pp. 190–229). New York: Basic Books.

Durham, R. L., Hays, J., & Martinez, R. (1994). Socio-cognitive development among Chicano and Anglo American college students. *Journal of College Student Development, 35*, 178–182.

Gallos, J. V. (1995). Gender and silence: Implications of women's ways of knowing. *College Teaching, 43*(3), 101–05.

Goldberger, N. R. (1996). Cultural imperatives and diversity in ways of knowing. In N. Goldberger, J. Tarule, B. Clinchy, & M. Belenky, Eds.), *Knowledge, difference, and power: Essays inspired by women's ways of knowing* (pp. 335–371). New York: Basic Books.

Goldberger, N. R. (1996). Looking back, looking forward. In N. Goldberger, J. Tarule, B. Clinchy, & M. Belenky (Eds.), *Knowledge, difference, power: Essays inspired by women's ways of knowing* (p. 1–21). NY: Basic Books.

Goldberger, N. R., Clinchy, B. M., Belenky, M. F., & Tarule, J. M. (1987). Women's ways of knowing: On gaining a voice. In P. Shaver, & C. Hendrick (Eds.), *Sex and gender* (pp. 201–228). Newbury Park, CA: Sage.

Hurtado, A. (1996). Strategic suspensions: Feminists of color theorize the production of knowledge. In N. Goldberger, J. Tarule, B. Clinchy, & M. Belenky (Eds.), *Knowledge, difference, and power: Essays inspired by women's ways of knowing* (pp. 372–392). New York: Basic Books.

King, P. M., & Kitchener, K. S. (1994). The seven stages of reflective judgment. In *Developing reflective judgment* (pp. 44–74). San Francisco: Jossey-Bass.

King, P. M. & Kitchener, K. S. (2002). The reflective judgment model: Twenty years of research on epistemic cognition. In B. K. Hofer and P. R. Pintrich (Eds.), *Personal epistemology: The psychology of beliefs about knowledge and knowing* (pp. 37–61). Mahwah, New Jersey: Lawrence Erlbaum.

Kronholm, M. M. (1996). The impact of developmental instruction on reflective judgment. *Review of Higher Education, 19*, 199–225.

Mines, R., King, P., Hood, A, & Wood, P. (1990). Stages of intellectual development and associated critical thinking skills in college students. *Journal of College Student Development, 31*, 538–547.

Moore, W. S. (1994). Student and faculty epistemology in the college classroom: The Perry scheme of intellectual and ethical development. In K. Pritchard & R. M. Sawyer (Eds.), *Handbook of college teaching* (pp. 45–67). Westport, CT: Greenwood Press.

Moore, W. S. (2002). Understanding learning in a postmodern world: Reconsidering the Perry scheme of ethical and intellectual development. In B. K. Hofer & P. R. Pintrich (Eds.), *Personal epistemology: The psychology of beliefs about knowledge and knowing* (pp. 17–36). Mahwah NJ: Lawrence Erlbaum Associates.

Scheurman, G. (1997). Using principles of constructivism to promote reflective judgment: A model lesson. *Journal of Excellence in College Teaching, 8*(2), 63–86.

Zhang, L. (2004). The Perry scheme: Across cultures, across approaches to the study human psychology. *Journal of Adult Development, 11*, 123–138.

Section 10: Moral Development

Bebeau, M. J., Rest, J. R., & Narvaez, D. (1999). Beyond the promise: A perspective on research in moral education. *Educational Researcher, 28*(4), 18–26.

Berkowitz, M. W., & Fekula, M. J. (1999). Educating for character. *About Campus, 4*(5), 17–22.

Brabeck, M. (1983) Moral judgment: Theory and research on differences between males and females. *Developmental Review, 3*, 274–291.

Bruess, B. J., & Pearson, F. C. (2002). The debate continues: Are there gender differences in moral reasoning as defined by Kohlberg? *College Student Affairs Journal, 21*(2), 38–52.

Derryberry, W. P., & Thoma, S. J. (2000). The friendship effect: Its role in the development of moral thinking in students. *About Campus, 5*(2), 13–18.

Giesbrecht, N., & Walker, L. J. (2000). Ego development and the construction of a moral self. *Journal of College Student Development, 41*, 157–171.

Jones, C. E., & Watt, J. D. (1999). Psychosocial development and moral orientation among traditional-aged college students. *Journal of College Student Development, 40*, 125–131.

King, P. M. & Mayhew, M. J. (2004). Theory and research on the development of moral reasoning among college students. In J. C. Smart (Ed.) *Higher education; Handbook of theory and research, Vol. XIX*, 375–440.

McCarthy, M. A., Phillips, B. A., Mills, J., & Horn, M. E. (2002). Moral reasoning: Does the college experience make a difference? *College Student Affairs Journal, 21*(2), 3–8.

Moreland, C., & Leach, M. M. (2001). The relationship between Black racial identity and moral development. *Journal of Black Psychology, 27*, 255–71.

Rest, J. R. (1993). Research on moral judgment in college students. In A. Garrod, *Approaches to moral development: New research and emerging themes* (pp. 201–213). New York: Teachers College Press.

Rest, J. R., Narvaez, D., Thoma, S. J., & Bebeau, M. J. (1999). DIT2: Devising and testing a revised instrument of moral judgment. *Journal of Educational Psychology, 91,* 644–659.

Rest, J. R., Narvaez, D., Thoma, S. J., & Bebeau, M. J. (2000). A neo-Kohlbergian approach to morality research. *Journal of Moral Education, 29,* 381–395.

Unit 5:

Section 11: Utilizing Theory

Baxter Magolda, M. B. (2000). Teaching to promote holistic learning and development. In M. B. Baxter Magolda (Ed.), *Teaching to promote intellectual and personal maturity: Incorporating students' worldviews and identities into the learning process* (pp. 88–98). New Directions for Teaching and Learning, no. 82. San Francisco: Jossey-Bass.

Jones, S. R., & Abes, E. S. (2004). Enduring influences of service learning on college students' identity development. *Journal of College Student Development, 45,* 149–165.

Parker, C. A. (1977). On modeling reality. *Journal of College Student Personnel, 19,* 419–425.

Pope, R. L., Reynolds, A. L., & Mueller, J. A. (2004). Multicultural competence in theory and translation. In R. Pope, A. L., Reynolds, & J. A., Mueller. *Multicultural competence in student affairs* (pp. 29–45). San Francisco: Jossey-Bass.

Strange, C. C. & King, P. M. (1990). The professional practice of student development. In D. Creamer & Associates, *College student development: Theory and practice for the 1990s* (p. 9–24). Alexandria, VA: ACPA Media.